Handbook of Latinos and Education

Theory, Research, and Practice

Edited by

Enrique G. Murillo, Jr.
Sofia A. Villenas
Ruth Trinidad Galván
Juan Sánchez Muñoz
Corinne Martínez
Margarita Machado-Casas

Routledge
Taylor & Francis Group

NEW YORK AND LONDON

First published 2010
by Routledge
270 Madison Avenue, New York, NY 10016

Simultaneously published in the UK
by Routledge
2 Park Square, Milton Park, Abingdon, Oxon OX14 4RN

Routledge is an imprint of the Taylor & Francis Group, an informa business

© 2010 Taylor & Francis

Typeset in Minion by EvS Communication Networx, Inc.
Printed and bound in the United States of America on acid-free paper by Sheridan Books, Inc.

Library of Congress Cataloging in Publication Data
Handbook of Latinos and education : theory, research and practice / edited by Enrique G. Murillo, Jr.... [et al.].
p. cm.
1. Hispanic Americans—Education—Handbooks, manuals, etc. I. Murillo, Enrique G.
LC2669.H36 2009
371.829'68073—dc22
2009019791

ISBN 10: (hbk) 0-8058-5839-3
ISBN 10: (pbk) 0-8058-5840-7
ISBN 10: (ebk) 0-203-86607-X

ISBN 13: (hbk) 978-0-8058-5839-6
ISBN 13: (pbk) 978-0-8058-5840-2
ISBN 13: (ebk) 978-0-203-86607-8

*"Se llevaron nuestros frutos, cortaron nuestras ramas,
quemaron nuestro tronco, pero no pudieron arrancar nuestras raices"*
Popol Vuh

To the ancients, memory, vision, spirit, and legacy.
To the unborn, the next seven generations, and imagination.

To the roll call of those who made and defied history, and those who lived it.
To the colonized masses of our *gente*; from the fields and factories, to the classrooms;
from the prisons and institutions, to the boardrooms; from the neighborhoods and *barrios*, to
the campuses of higher learning.

To our mentors *con puro respeto*, and those who have served as our personal and academic
sources of inspiration, *cariño* and nurturance.

To our *abuelas y abuelos*, *padres y madres*, siblings, spouses and extended *familias*, who represent the best of who and why we are.

To those who have struggled, fought, and died to make our lives better.

To those who have brought humor and joy in our lives.

Para nuestros hijos y la divina juventud. Shall your dreams know no bounds.

To researchers, teaching professionals and educators, academics, scholars, administrators, independent writers and artists, policy and program specialists, students, parents, families, civic
leaders, activists, and advocates who have made Education your life's work.

To our readers, in short, those sharing a common interest and commitment to the educational
issues that impact Latinos.

Last but not least, to all border-crossers. For when in the course of human history and events, it
becomes necessary to cross borders of political, social, linguistic, cultural, economic, and technological construction … we will cross. For long before there were borders, there was us. We are
the children of crossers. *¡Somos un chingo y seremos mas!*

HLE *Grupito*

Enrique G. Murillo, Jr.
Sofia A. Villenas
Ruth Trinidad Galván
Juan Sánchez Muñoz
Corinne Martínez
Margarita Machado-Casas

Contents

PART II
Policies and Politics

PART II EDITORS: RUTH TRINIDAD GALVÁN AND NORMA GONZÁLEZ

x *Contents*

Foreword

José Salvador Hernández
California State University, San Bernardino

As a young elementary school teacher in the early 1970s, I was always searching for knowledge that could help me better understand the problems, issues, and practices that would guide my teaching. In particular I was trying to understand why Mexican American children performed so poorly in our schools and what could be done to change that situation. The difficulty was that there were very few resources in our local schools, colleges and universities had very few if any Latino faculty, and there were no bilingual education credentials available at the time. The one possible exception where general knowledge might be organized was in the emerging ethnic studies programs being developed on some campuses. Nationally, what materials were being developed were coming out from the federal agencies spearheading the War on Poverty programs and the internet was decades away. What always perturbed me was that much of what was written always blamed poor school performance on the negative attributes of Latino students and their families. Latinos were seen as non-future time-oriented, did not have internal locus of control or were simply not motivated. It seemed as if the experts were describing people I did not know.

So, now when I look at what the authors, editors, consultants, advisory board, and staff of the *Handbook of Latinos and Education* have accomplished it is truly evolutionary and transformative. By this I mean the gradual process by which the human consciousness of the Latino educational community has been transformed into a more complex and focused form. I see this process of change and development as having three major mileposts:

1. the legitimization of Latino education as a valued field of study,
2. the emergence of a new generation of scholars that exemplify not only the multi-disciplinary scope of the field but the diversity of the Latino community, and
3. the continuing evolution of how the Latino community thinks, feels, and sees itself.

The legitimization of Latino education as a field worthy of study and investigation that informs discussion, analysis, policy and practice has been long overdue. For too long the study of Latino education has been relegated to the status of something spurious, non disciplined and of special interest to only a few, something not off the mainstream. As a child born out of wedlock, how can it expect the true rights and privileges of a legitimate academic area of study? The topics of interest to the Latino community are too narrow, their methodology unsophisticated and theoretically weak. What can possibly be of interest to the broader educational or academic community? Of what value is there in studying a minority group in the context of American scholarship? Is there any value in studying the needs or conditions in the Latino community for guiding teachers in classrooms?

If such questions are still being posed or discussed, then let them look at the last 100 years and more of Latino writers, artists, activists, educators, and academicians to answer the questions. If these questions are still being asked, look at the demographic shifts within the Latino communities and across the country. If yet the questions are still being asked, let them look at this handbook.

The second milestone that the handbook symbolizes is the fostering and emergence of a new generation of scholars with roots in the historical contexts and diversity of the Latino communities. Metaphorically speaking it is a "phylogeny," the evolutionary and historical development of a community of scholars. I believe that this handbook symbolizes an important transition in Latino education with its roots in the 20th century focusing its development into the 21. The new scholars who have contributed to this volume can certainly be counted as part of this new generation of Latino educators who will participate in the educational dialogue and practice that confronts our communities and the nation today. The struggle for educational equality and quality can no longer be seen simply from a nationalist perspective as a Mexicano, Puerto Riqueño, or Cubano concern. The diversity of the Latino communities demands that we speak with a strong, clear common voice, as illustrated in this volume.

Finally, what emerges from the following pages is the continuing evolution of consciousness within the Latino community. We exist in a certain time and space so we are very capable of thinking about ourselves and our place in the world. As Edelman (1992) cites de Unamuno's (1921, p. 34) observation in response to Decartes' famous maxim, "Cogito, ergo sum / I think, therefore I am," "The truth is sum, ergo cogito/I am, therefore I think…. Is not conscious thinking above all consciousness of being? Is pure thought possible, without consciousness of self, without personality?" This handbook project represents and presents the continuing development of the Latino community as a community that continues to exist and think. The Latino consciousness manifests itself through the thoughts and perceptions we have about ourselves and our place in American society and in the world. The handbook represents a continuation of the emotions that we feel and the will of a people who continue to struggle for their own rights and those of their children. Further, I believe the handbook represents a collective memory of the struggles and conflicts Latinos face, but it also represents a glimpse into the imagination and creativity of the Latino communities we inhabit.

References

de Unamuno, M. (1921). *Tragic sense of life* (C. J. Flitch, Trans.). New York: Macmillan.

Descartea, R. (2008). *Discourse on the method and meditations on first philosophy.* Miami, FL: BN Publishing. (Originally published 1637)

Edelman, G. M. (1992). *Bright air, brilliant fire: On the matter of the mind.* New York: Basic Books.

Preface

Enrique G. Murillo, Jr.

¡Bienvenidos!—Welcome to the *Handbook of Latinos and Education* (HLE) and our collective journey, vision, and voice.

Latin@s and Education[1]: Setting the Stage

Long before Europeans "founded" and colonized what is now the United States, with their own languages, traditions, and ideologies, this land was a rich seedbed of indigenous languages, cultures, and life patterns. Then, considering the rest of the American continent (North, Central, South, and the Caribbean), one can appreciate the vastness and complexity of this historical reality. Despite this diversity, the founders of the United States strived to create a nation with a unified history, traditions, culture, myths, and language. Nevertheless, since 1492 to the historical present, the changing political, social, and economic forces, rather than any consistent policy, practice, or ideology, are what have mostly shaped Latin@s in the United States.

Because of the varying contexts and broad forces that have functioned in the shaping of Latinos and Latinas in the United States, and because U.S. Latin@s are a uniquely diverse social category and a particularly complex subject of sociological analysis, it is near to impossible to provide a synthetic treatment of the significance of education.

Hispanicization, Anglicization, Americanization, nationalism, schooling practices, curricular issues and pedagogical effectiveness, prominent leaders, major institutions, struggles for self-determination, symbolic racism, the courts and the legal system, efforts at social control, exclusion and repression, professional organizations, cultural and linguistic practices, U.S. social systems, electoral politics, spirituality and rituals, economic access and opportunities, struggles for identity and rights, inter-ethnic competition, the role of higher education, the pursuit of equity and social justice, a commitment to the centrality of education, and the competing visions of the meanings and purposes of education have all been factors.

One can even go as far back as reviewing the formal educational systems of our pre-Columbian ancestors, for present-day influences. Factors like the non-rigid tracked curricula and the academic advancement of children based on aptitudes and abilities, could both be considered. Further, the early colonial periods along this continent provide additional various models and patterns that have also influenced present-day Latinos. For example, during the period of European invasion, issues of language were clearly and directly tied to expansion and the conquest of the "New World." It is a sound conclusion therefore that language ideology has been a highly prevalent issue for the *Latinidad*[2] from the end of the 15th century to the present.

Given all this, there should be no doubt that education for Latinos and Latinas has been formed, contested and reformulated within and among these varying historical, political, social, and economic contexts. But very importantly, across these contexts, education has been notably highly significant and valued among Latin@s in the United States.

Currently, education repeatedly has been an overriding concern for Latin@s, as documented by numerous research studies, polls, and surveys. In general, Latinos and Latinas offer positive views of their local schools, teachers and educational institutions, hold high expectations, and Latin@ parents say they are active in their child's school and involved in their education. The profound commitment to education among Latin@ families, the importance of the mother tongue, and the prominent position of women in Latin@ households all emphasize the significance of deeply ingrained family values and the strength of women as main reasons for resiliency.

This positive appraisal persists despite the perpetuation and permeation of power asymmetries in the educational system. Historically, Latin@ representation in the education system, at all its levels, remains low, while attrition rates are among the highest. Many Latinos and Latinas experience poor schooling conditions, and schools often fail to engage students, and push difficult and problematic students out. In fact, currently, Latin@s hold the highest high school dropout ("pushout") rates in the United States, almost 4 times higher than the rate of Whites, and have lower high school completion rates than White and Black students. At the same time, Latin@s are less likely than non-Latin@s to be enrolled in or graduate from colleges/universities, and receive less financial aid than other undergraduates.

Inequality due to differences has been an overarching issue. The reason for this has been the vehement and unrelenting discrimination that Latin@s and other groups in the United States have experienced at the hands of the dominant majority group. In its essence, the historical view held by the majority group about minorities is that they (we) are not worthy to have access to the benefits of society by virtue of differences, which makes them (us) inherently deficient and thus not only unworthy but also unable to benefit from Education, even if one should have access to it. This view has been prevalent since the arrival of the pilgrims and persists in a variety of mutated forms to this day. The most highly marked "differences" such as language culture, religious beliefs, etc., which are associated with us, have been readily taken up by the dominant group as justifiable reasons for educational and other discriminations.

Latinos and Latinas have always had to struggle to obtain an education. Despite intense and often violent efforts and societal attitudes aimed at denying most minority groups access to education (and other civil rights), these groups have undertaken extensive efforts to secure these rights. We have struggled for education for the same reasons that all groups struggle. First and foremost, all societies want to prepare their children to benefit from and be a benefit to their communities, for the future and for what they see is the purpose of education.

In fact, since its inception, the United States has embodied this fundamental contradiction. It has purported basic rights of inclusion, equal opportunity and justice for all, yet simultaneously has systematically excluded certain groups and individuals perceived to be different from the dominant Anglo American population. Currently, unparalleled change in economic and political structures have exacerbated these patterns of exclusion, be it on racial, cultural, or political terms. As such, there is a value to examining the political economy of racism, and analyzing racism as a central aspect of the economic system.

Having entered the 21st century, we are experiencing massive reconfigurations in the structure of the economy, a devolution and disintegration of social programs, an expansive retreat from Civil Rights, new political realignments, and a dissolution of the meaning of cultural democracy. Too, racialized inequalities have shifted, if not worsened for Latin@s.

Class and economic shifts have both exacerbated the racial and social divisions in the United States Moreover, economic restructuring has been accompanied by cultural and demographic shifts, including the knowledge that in many cities and states throughout the country, Latin@s have, or will soon become majority populations numerically. These have brought about and fed the newly fashioned discourses and practices. Despite the mentioned public rhetoric of equality and inclusion, Latinos and Latinas continually are often regarded as "problems" in the dominant discourse and remain liabilities in the public sphere.

The important structural transformations in the recent era to the economy have had a most significant impact on the labor force. A shift from manufacturing to services and knowledge industries, together with a labor force that is more contingent, flexible, and vulnerable, and the unstable, segregated, and unequal nature of the economy itself, have had their disproportionate affect on Latin@s. This is especially true of those who enter the new global economy already insecure and marginalized. Workplace segmentation and segregation extend beyond the work site to include the community social spaces as well.

Race, one can claim, is a one key intersection and practice of social life that is closely associated with severe social and economic injustices. Certain economic patterns encourage disparity and reinforce structures of exclusion and displacement. Race often organizes not only local labor, but local politics as well, and the process of uneven development has contributed to making these differences a durable diversity. Scapegoating too continues to increase through "racialized" fallacies of welfare parasitism, affirmative action as reverse discrimination, immigrant encroachment, and intelligence as a fixed genetic reality. All are part of a larger rhetoric of exclusion of anti-immigrant, reversal of civil rights' gains, attacks on affirmative action, bilingual education, ethnic studies, and promotion of English as the official language.

Even as the legal barriers of segregation have been torn down, the underclass of Latino/a and immigrant workers, and poor people at the margins of society have grown. These changes have their impacts on such things as infant mortality rates and life expectancies, the unemployment and poverty rates and incomes, areas such as the law and criminal justice, social needs such as housing and environment, and political participation. Education and schooling too are impacted, and contribute to the enduring and intensified inequality themselves, as a cycle. Current policies and practices have set the stage for detrimental effects on Latin@ academic achievement for decades to come.

An educational system that disenfranchises and fails many Latin@ children, links directly to the discrimination against Latin@ youth by the criminal justice system and courts, job discrimination, and at the same time, contributes to undermine their (our) political participation. Poverty continues to pose a serious challenge to learning opportunities and outcomes. Children of Latin@ poor, who are disproportionately tracked into an impoverished educational system, often then face unequal opportunities when they enter the labor force, or when they do enter are forced to occupy the most dangerous and tiresome occupations. Although there is a positive relationship between education and salary, across all ethnic/racial groups, Latino males still make less money than do White males across most of the educational levels. Dropouts are more likely to be unemployed, and earn less than high school completers, when they are employed. Despite the significant gains by Latin@ students and adults, made in educational attainment and achievement over the last few decades, the gaps between Latino and White students remain.

Handbook: Aims, Scope, Organization, and Audience

This *Handbook of Latinos and Education* (HLE) has the unique purpose and function of profiling the scope and terrain of this particular domain of academic inquiry. It presents the most significant and potentially influential work in the field of Latin@s and education, in terms of its contributions to research, to professional practice, and to the emergence of related interdisciplinary studies and theory. This volume captures the field at this point in time.

The chapters of the handbook, as a whole, offer a comprehensive review of theory, research, and practice on the topics of inquiry, as a focus, not a research report of a single study, per se. Providing rigorous, innovative, and critical scholarship, the volume is organized around five major themes:

- Part I: History, Theory, and Methodology
- Part II: Policies and Politics
- Part III: Language and Culture
- Part IV: Teaching and Learning
- Part V: Resources and Information

The increasing numbers and diversity of Latin@s creates a need to look at issues through and across the lens of multiple disciplines. The editors and authors of the *HLE* believe this volume will encourage novel ways of thinking about the ongoing and emerging questions around the unifying thread of Latin@s and education. The handbook will support dialogical exchange for researchers, practitioners, authors, and other stakeholders who are working to advance understanding at all levels and aspects, be it theoretical, conceptual, empirical, clinical, historical, methodological, and/or other in scope.

We expect that this handbook will serve as an impetus to raise the consciousness of other publication venues. The handbook is cross-, multi- and interdisciplinary, and reviews the varied research methodologies and narrative models that serve the field. Additionally, the chapters cover education in the broad cultural sense and, are not limited to just formal schooling.

The various manifestations of the diverse frameworks and topical areas range from, but aren't limited to, theoretical and empirical analyses, policy discussions, research reports, program recommendations, evaluation studies, finding and improving practical applications, carefully documenting the transition of theory into real-world practice, linking theory and research, new dissertation research, literature reviews, reflective discussions, cultural studies, and literary works.

The *Handbook of Latinos and Education* is a must-have resource for educational researchers, graduate students, and teacher educators. The broader audience is the spectrum of teaching professionals, administrators, policy and program specialists, civic leaders, activists, and advocates. In short, the volume can be drawn upon by individuals, groups, agencies, organizations, and institutions sharing a common interest and commitment to the educational issues which impact Latinos.

Collaboration and Mentoring: Our Definitive Source

This handbook was indeed a labor of love, taking us more than five years to plan and compile. This volume first began as an off-shot of the *Journal of Latinos and Education* (*JLE*). Close to a decade ago we inaugurated the new millennium with the journal project, and the major critical factor we considered, then as in now, is the ongoing demographic increase in Latin@s throughout the United States. As the numbers of Latin@s in education increase, there tends to be a concomitant increase in articles on research, policy and status related to us. The demographics augur for both an increase in publications on Latin@s and education and for an increase in consumers of those publications.

Our consideration for a handbook came when we realized that there were few to no comprehensive published reviews of theory, research and practice on the topic of Latin@s and education overall. There are research reports on Latin@s and education currently published all over the place or in highly specialized books and journals. The *JLE*, for example, has helped provide an important publication avenue for writers who seek to address Latin@ educational issues. However, our intent with this handbook project has been to provide chapters that serve as comprehensive reviews on the particular topics, and not a research report of a single study, as is commonplace for a journal such as the *JLE*.

Despite many groundbreaking publications[3] (and, of course, demographic benchmarks), Latin@ educational issues often still remain seen as limited in focus in the larger context (academic colonialism). One reason may be that established venues publish research oriented around a primary perspective, e.g., reading, and treat Latin@s and education as secondary categories. Reading publications, for example, may only be marginally concerned with Latin@ issues (if at all), or may consider it of limited interest. Mainstream or Whitestream publications tend to consider Latin@ issues as peripheral to the broader issues in the discipline or field. These publication venues also may tend to focus on nationally known "Latino" authors and look only to the work of a few to publish.

As the principal editor, I was first involved and responsible for the day-to-day management and oversight of the project, taking advantage of the *JLE*'s infrastructure and audience, working persistently with our editors, advisory board, office staff, and, of course, the acquisitions and production staff at first Lawrence Erlbaum Associates and then Routledge publishers. The editors of each of the volume's themes, in turn, worked with their respective section editor, chapter consultants, and lastly the chapter authors themselves. In all, this volume was only made possible through much collaboration, with even more persistence and patience.

We believed that we could set our project apart from others by following a deliberate organizational and collaborative model, with clearly articulated processual steps, with a timeline, employing a strategy that involved multi-stake holders and a collaborative team. It first began by articulating and textualizing a handbook prospectus and mock table of contents, that was revised repeatedly as more and more scholars became involved. The advisory board was first recruited from colleagues throughout the United Stats and beyond. Particular care was taken to ensure representation of all regions and Latin@ groups within the United States.[4] All members of the board have strong backgrounds in their areas of expertise and many served as the chapter draft reviewers or consultants. The editorial team (which we dubbed the *grupito*[5]) held regular teleconferences over a matter of years, working through all the issues and logistics over the phone, and then meeting face-to face while at professional conferences. Each theme editor worked with their respective section teams, which most hold leadership in a wide variety of professional groups, so as to hold the sections together conceptually and address any gaps in the knowledge base. Consultants worked with specific authors and chapters to comprehensively review key scholars, the array of conceptual, philosophical and methodological approaches, and the main programs of research and lines of thinking.

Through this method we were able to draft the contents map, and in our view, a mapping of the academic terrain. In all, several hundred scholars were recruited to this handbook project, and were involved in one capacity or other, be it as an advisor, member of a section team, or as a member of the National Latino Education Network (NLEN).[6]

Last but not least, we believe that one key dimension of this handbook project sets it apart from others, and that is the mentorship.[7] From the beginning, one of the established goals of the handbook was to actively mentor the next generation of educational researchers, Latin@ or otherwise, working with our populations. To integrate this into the pre-production processes of this handbook for Parts I–IV, each was overseen two Part Editors—one early career editor paired off with a veteran scholar whose reputation holds standing in the field. Both served in each respective theme section, but the weight of the management or oversight relied mostly with the junior scholars of early career, while the veteran or mentor scholars offered their experience and knowledge to better charter the terrain or mapping of the section's focus.

Additionally, each integrated a similar mentorship process with the respective chapter contributors of their section. That is, for as many chapters as possible, contributors paired themselves in the similar early career/veteran scholar dyads or teams. If an early career scholar was first recruited as a chapter contributor, he or she was asked to identify a veteran scholar for which to collaborate with. Similarly, as prominent scholars were invited to contribute, they were asked to identify an early career scholar for which to collaborate with. This collaboration among chapter contributors, working together with the editors, section editors, consultants, advisory board, and finally with me as the principal editor, served to triangulate the content, validity, reliability, and quality of the scholarship.

¡La Lucha Continua![8]

To this end, we return to where we started. The challenge of educational success is everyone's responsibility, and the economic and social conditions of the *Latinidad* is unlikely to improve until the educational status improves. Although graduating from high school in and of itself will not guarantee social and economic success, failure to complete high school and graduate most likely will deny it. Latinos and Latinas must address in themselves (ourselves), the role of multiple identities in developing resiliency, and a value for education. As parents, offering our children encouragement and praise makes them more responsible for their own behavior and attitudes, and helps develop their intrinsic motivation which improves academic performance. Staying involved in schools and maintaining ongoing communication with teachers and administrators is important for stronger home-school relationships and developing a more inclusive educational system. We must characterize resiliency as spiritual in nature, which allows them (us) to set up the support systems and networks necessary to survive emotionally and cognitively, as well as physically. That is precisely what (we) Latin@s want from education, an education that offers our children the same opportunities and pathways to benefit from school as other children.

Clearly, the plight of keeping Latino and Latina students in school is one of our major educational challenges of the time. Dwelling on the negative helps no one, but being oblivious to the actual conditions of the community doesn't either. The singular accomplishable solution to this educational dilemma lies in community activism and democratic participation. History shows that Latin@s don't dwell on the negative. Rather, we are willing to fight fiercely for the rights of our children.

Please invite this volume into your gatherings, classrooms, meetings, and organizations; this is our call to action!

In tlacahueyac cocheua—El gigante despierta—The giant awakens!

Notes

1. Latin@s is utilized as a gender neutral substitute for the terms Latinos and/or Latino/Latina.
2. Expansively defined here to include anyone of historical origin from the neocolonial territories under the yoke of the Monroe Doctrine.
3. Some of these groundbreaking publications share like-elements to the intent of this handbook without making the exact claims. They offer excellent reviews of Latino Educational issues. Some of these include:

   Darder, A., Torres, R. D., & Gutiérrez, H. (Eds.). (1997). *Latinos and education: A critical reader*. New York: Routledge.

   Delgado Bernal, D., Elenes, C. A., Godínez, F. E., & Villenas, S. (Eds.). (2006). *Chicana/Latina education in everyday life: Feminista perspectives on pedagogy and epistemology*. Albany, NY: SUNY Press.

   Díaz Soto, L. (Ed.). (2007). *The Praeger handbook of latino education in the U.S.* Westport, CT: Praegers.

   García, E. (2001). *Hispanic education in the United States: Raíces y alas*. Lanham, MD: Roman & Littlefield.

   MacDonald, V-M. (Ed.). (2004). *Latino education in the United States: A narrated history from 1513–2000*. New York: Palgrave Macmillan.

   Pedraza, P., & Rivera, M. (Eds.). (2005). *Latino education: An agenda for community action research*. Mahwah, NJ: Erlbaum.

Tejeda, C., Martínez, C., & Leonardo, Z. (2000). *Charting new terrains of Chicana(o)/Latina(o) education*. Cresskill, NJ: Hampton Press.

Valencia, R. R. (Ed.). (2002). *Chicano school failure and success: Past, present, and future*. New York: Routledge Falmer.

Wortham, S., Hamann, E., & Murillo Jr., E. G. (Eds.). (2001). *Education in the new Latino diaspora: Policy and the politics of identity*. Westport, CT: Ablex.

4. We believe that comparative group studies of region and areas are helpful to the understanding of education among Latinos and Latinas and speak to the range of Latino communities, contexts, and generations.

5. Translated as "small group," or in our case meant to denote "working group" or "steering committee."

6. The NLEN is a members-based electronic community made up of researchers, teaching professionals and educators, academics, scholars, administrators, independent writers and artists, policy and program specialists, students, parents, families, civic leaders, activists, and advocates. The website (http://nlen.csusb.edu/) provides numerous online features, among others a Resource Guide/Clearinghouse that allows members to search and browse for resources, opportunities and activities in the Latino Educational community (serving as an information source for this volume's section V).

7. In the unwritten history of Latino educational advocates and activists, we have organized ourselves into a "theory, research, and practice" movement, in which mentoring and collaboration have played key.

8. The struggle continues!

Acknowledgments

This handbook is the product of a collaborative effort among many individuals, too numerous to name. The editors are thankful principally to the veteran scholars, the architects, and pioneers of our field. We acknowledge your writing and thinking, for having inspired us. Among these, we are particularly grateful to the section editors who mentored and assisted us in elaborating the various themes. We would also like to thank the consultants who worked closely with the section teams to hold the themes together conceptually, and reading chapters in draft form. Thank you as well to our advisory board, who lent us their expertise and experience and shared valuable comments. Thank you to our colleagues, students, family, and friends who supported our efforts and nurtured our ideas. We are indebted to the contributing authors who worked so diligently in the creation and production of this volume. We are grateful to you for collaborating enthusiastically by pairing yourselves in the early career/veteran scholar dyads or teams, as was the collective vision for this handbook. We also thank Naomi Silverman, our acquisitions editor at, first, Lawrence Erlbaum Associates, and then together with the production team at Routledge. We know we extended beyond our time and deadlines in the preparation and compilation of this volume, but your patience has paid off for this is truly our individual and collective talents, insights, voice, and efforts. Last but not least, special thanks are due to our various assistants, administrative managers, and support personnel at all our institutions, but particularly the *Journal of Latinos and Education* staff at CSU San Bernardino.

Consultants and Administrative Management

Part I: History, Theory, and Methodology

María de la Luz Reyes *University of Colorado, Boulder*
Bernardo Gallegos *National University*
Bradley A. U. Levinson *Indiana University at Bloomington*
Gilberto González *University of California, Irvine*
Concha Delgado Gaitan *University of Texas, El Paso*
Hector Vélez *Cornell University*

Part II: Policies and Politics

Ricky Lee Allen *University of New Mexico*
Rebecca Blum-Martinez *University of New Mexico*
Edward Buendia *University of Utah*
James Crawford *Institute for Language and Education Policy*
Raymond V. Padilla *University of Texas, San Antonio*
Juan de Dios Piñeda *University of New Mexico*
David Quijada *University of Utah*
Ann-Marie Wiese *WestEd*
Stanton Wortham *University of Pennsylvania*
Tara Yosso *University of California, Santa Barbara*

Part III: Language and Culture

Carlos Ovando *Arizona State University*
Elena Izquierdo *University of Texas, El Paso*
Carolina Serna *California State University, Monterey Bay*
Robert Rueda *University of Southern California*
Ann-Marie Wiese *WestEd*

Part IV: Teaching and Learning

Marcos Pizarro *San Jose State University*
Virginia González *University of Cincinnati*
Robert Rueda *University of Southern California*
Tara Yosso *University of California, Santa Barbara*
Jamal Abedi *University of California, Davis*

Advisory Board

Alma Flor Ada   *University of San Francisco*
René Antrop-González   *University of Wisconsin, Milwaukee*
Gilberto Arriaza   *California State University, East Bay*
Alfredo Artiles   *Arizona State University*
María V. Balderrama   *California State University, San Bernardino*
Marta P. Baltodano   *Loyola Marymount University*
Patricia Baquedano-López   *University of California, Berkeley*
Lilia Bartolomé   *University of Massachusetts, Boston*
Scott A.L. Beck   *Georgia Southern University*
Ruth Behar   *University of Michigan, Ann Arbor*
Ursula Casanova   *Arizona State University*
Rudolfo Chávez Chávez   *New Mexico State University*
Antonia Darder   *University of Illinois, Urbana Champaign*
Dolores Delgado Bernal   *University of Utah*
Rubén Donato   *University of Colorado, Boulder*
Richard P. Durán   *University of California, Santa Barbara*
Barbara Flores   *California State University, San Bernardino*
René Galindo   *University of Colorado at Denver*
Margaret A. Gibson   *University of California at Santa Cruz*
Francisco Guajardo   *University of Texas, Pan American*
Juan Gutiérrez   *California State University, San Bernardino*
Kris Gutiérrez   *University of California at Los Angeles*
Edmund Hamann   *University of Nebraska, Lincoln*
José Salvador Hernández   *California State University, San Bernardino*
Janice Hurtig   *University of Illinois, Chicago*
Pablo Jasis   *California State University, Fullerton*
Jill Kerper Mora   *San Diego State University*
Bradley A. U. Levinson   *Indiana University at Bloomington*
Carmen I. Mercado   *City University of New York, Hunter College*
Liliana Minaya-Rowe   *Johns Hopkins University*
Luis Mirón   *Loyola University New Orleans*
Luis Moll   *University of Arizona, Tucson*
Martha Montero-Sieburth   *University of Amsterdam*
Sonia Nieto   *University of Massachusetts, Amherst*
Pedro A. Noguera   *New York University*
Carlos Ovando   *Arizona State University*
Raymond V. Padilla   *University of Texas, San Antonio*
Raymund A. Paredes   *Texas Higher Education Coordinating Board*
Pedro Pedraza   *City University of New York, Hunter College*
Laura Rendón   *Iowa State University*
María de la Luz Reyes   *University of Colorado, Boulder*
Robert Rueda   *University of Southern California*
Guadalupe San Miguel, Jr.   *University of Houston*
Armando Sánchez   *Latino Scholastic Achievement Corporation*
Sheryl Santos   *Texas Tech-Lubbock*
Daniel Solórzano   *University of California at Los Angeles*
Ricardo D. Stanton-Salazar   *University of Southern California*
Carlos Tejeda   *California State University, Los Angeles*
Josefina V. Tinajero   *University of Texas, El Paso*

Luis Urrieta, Jr.   *University of Texas, Austin*
Stephanie Urso Spina   *State University New York, Cortland*
Guadalupe Valdés   *Stanford University*
Richard Valencia   *University of Texas, Austin*
Angela Valenzuela   *University of Texas, Austin*
Olga Vásquez   *University of California, San Diego*
James Diego Vigil   *University of California, Irvine*
Stanton Wortham   *University of Pennsylvania*
Ana Celia Zentella   *University of California, San Diego*

Administrative Management

Department of Language, Literacy and Culture, College of Education
California State University, San Bernardino
Mario Valenzuela   Assistant to the Editor
Erika Bugarín   Information and Resource Manager
Karlo Ludwig   Office Manager
Esmeralda Sandoval   Pre-Production Liaison
María Titus   Fiscal Coordinator
Patricia Aguilera   Events Planner

Part I

History, Theory, and Methodology

Part Editors: Sofia A. Villenas and Douglas E. Foley

1 History, Theory, and Methodology

An Introduction

Sofia A. Villenas
Cornell University, Ithaca

Douglas E. Foley
University of Texas at Austin

Latina/o youths along with their families, communities, and advocate scholars have long experienced and tried to explain the challenges of education and schooling in the United States. They have told stories, created songs, provided *consejos* (advice), and conducted research with narratives and numbers to explain how they have succeeded and how schools have failed them. Recently, the field of Latino education emerged from an impressive accumulation of over half a century of research addressing Latinos/as' diverse histories and experiences of education and schooling (San Miguel & Donato, this section). Researchers, scholars, and practitioners have addressed and continue to address with great urgency what has become a crisis in Latino educational attainment and achievement (Gándara & Contreras, 2009). They have worked to interrogate educational inequities, to challenge deficit-oriented perspectives about language and culture, and to propose new ways for thinking about school reform and pedagogical practices. For such a task, researchers have contributed to and made great use of all the theoretical and methodological tools at their disposal including developments in critical and cultural studies, Mexican American studies, Puerto Rican and Latino/a studies, women of color and Chicana/Latina feminisms, linguistics and second language acquisition, critical race theory, ethnography, and narrative methodologies to name a few. The chapters in this section demonstrate how the field has merged these tools in unique ways to develop new understandings of Latino educational history and produce innovative conceptual frameworks and methodologies for naming and addressing the critical state of Latino education (Zarate & Conchas, this section; Elenes & Delgado Bernal, this section; Irizarry & Nieto, this section).

The chapters in this section collectively tell a story about research in Latino education. In a broader sense, it is a story about a community of scholars, Latino/a and non-Latino/a, who reflect on the questions we have pursued as a field of study, the body of knowledge we have created and the racially volatile contexts in which we have worked. This collective story concerns how we have come to explain educational inequities and school persistence and attainment in great part through a vision of hope for a more just world. Certainly, this community of scholars has believed in educational praxis as part and parcel of a process of community uplift. Finally, this collective story addresses how the field of Latino education has developed its hybrid concepts, theories and methodologies to produce what might now constitute a wealth of knowledge to influence educational practice and policy.

We refer to a "community" of scholars/educators because it is remarkable how the field's scholars/educators have engaged and built on each others' research findings and new explorations in theory. Due in large part to the urgency of the crisis in Latino educational achievement and the shared goals for collective community empowerment, the field is marked by productive and critical engagement rather than conflict or non-engagement. For example, both qualitative and quantitative research has been central in documenting the strengths of bilingualism and language socialization in order to make the case for bilingual education (Zarate & Conchas, this section). The same is true for mixed methods research documenting the Latino educational pipeline and Latinos/as' college attainment and persistence, among other very important research concerns. However, the chapters in this handbook do lean towards qualitative methodologies. This is reflective of the co-editors' and chapter authors' selective rather than exhaustive interpretations. It is also true that as qualitative research has moved from out of the shadows in the last decades towards more prominence in educational research, scholars in Latino education have taken advantage of research methodologies such as narrative and participant observation to center youth, parent, and teacher voices and perspectives, and to describe the complex forms of Latino cultural, literacy, and language practices (Zarate & Conchas, this section). Indeed, an important thread running through the five chapters in this section is how we go about *construyendo puentes* or building bridges (Irizarry & Nieto, this section), and creating affinities between qualitative and quantitative methodologies, theory and practice, community activism and scholarship, and between disciplines, ethnic studies, and subalternized knowledge (Elenes & Delgado Bernal, this section).

A second important theme that marks this "community" of scholars/educators is the refusal to treat Latinos/as as non-agents and victims of their lives. Rather, the field marks Latinos/as as creative actors in their families and communities and as producers of knowledge. The chapter authors in this section describe the resilience and activism of a people who creatively survive, respond, and thrive in the face of racialized and gendered practices and policies of labor, immigration, and education. This thrust is evident in MacDonald and Carrillo's historical overview of Latinos in the United States, "The United Status of Latinos." Their purpose is to convey a nuanced portrait of Latinos/as as agents of their destinies in the United States and to illustrate how distinct histories and different factors shape their new identities on U.S. soil. San Miguel and Donato in their chapter "Latino Education in Twentieth-Century America: A Brief History" also argue that during the 20th century, education was both an instrument of reproduction and an important site of *contestation* [our emphasis]. For Elenes and Delgado Bernal in their chapter, "Latina/o Education and the Reciprocal Relationship between Theory and Practice: Four Theories Informed by the Experiential Knowledge of Marginalized Communities," these forms of contestation and accommodation make up a community's experiential knowledge. They argue for the centrality of Latinos/as' knowledge production and its importance to theory-making, not only for addressing Latinos/as' educational experiences but also as a contribution to educational thought in its own right. Similarly, Zarate and Conchas in their chapter, "Contemporary and Critical Methodological Shifts in Latino Educational Research," focus on a community of scholars/educators who conduct research from a sense of commitment to the well-being and empowerment of Latino communities. In this way, the field of research in Latino education is marked by respectful treatment for the complexity of Latinos/as' actions and responses to histories of inequality. Finally, Irizarry and Nieto's chapter, "Latino/a Theoretical Contributions to Educational Praxis: Abriendo Caminos, Construyendo Puentes," paints a vibrant picture of a dynamic community of scholars/educators who are actively working to document how education must build from Latinos/as' strengths, knowledge, values, epistemologies and modes of resilience. As Maria de la Luz Reyes (2008) argues, we have a community of scholars and educators who are asserting their expertise and unapologetically continuing their advocacy as a way to build bridges between home and school.

Though collaboration and engagement mark the field in important ways, there are also critical differences and challenges. Latino diversity (MacDonald & Carrillo, this section), interethnic relations, and continued theorizing on the intersections of race, class, sexuality, gender, ethnicity, and citizenship are all held in tension in this section's chapters. For example, with respect to the question of Latino diversity, it is important to ask about the possibilities and limits of Southwest and Mexican American-oriented perspectives on the field of Latino education. This is especially important for understanding and documenting the educational experiences of indigenous Mexican, Guatemalan, Salvadorian, Puerto Rican, Cuban, Ecuadorian, and Dominican heritage youths, parents, and adult learners in different parts of the United States (see MacDonald & Carrillo, this section). We might ask how research in distinct communities might contribute new understandings and conceptual frameworks to the overall field of Latino education and for studying education in diverse Latino communities. For example, how might we address the different and similar ways in which Latinos/as are racialized in the United States, specifically in schools, and how might we look at these processes from hemispheric and transnational perspectives? Grosfoguel, Maldonado-Torres, and Saldívar (2005) urge attention to how "colonial immigrants," or those migrants coming from peripheral neocolonial locations in the capitalist world-economy, are "racialized" at the time of arrival in similar ways to the "colonial/racial subjects of empire"—Puerto Ricans, African Americans and Chicanas/os—who have been in the United States for a significant amount of time (2005, p. 9). They refer here to the "Puertoricanization" of Dominicans in New York City, the "Chicanoization" of Salvadoreans in Los Angeles, and the "Africanamericanization" of Haitians and Afro-Cuban marielitos in Miami (Grosfoguel et al., 2005). Divergent and convergent processes of racialization certainly have great consequences for addressing differential school achievement, Latino identities and identifications, and for Latino interethnic relationships along the axis of class, gender, nationality, sexuality and citizenship (see Elenes & Delgado Bernal, this section; Lopez, 2005; Bejarano, 2005; Bettie, 2003; Valero, personal communication). Likewise, the authors here allude to a Latino pan-ethnicity with consequences and possibilities for education that have yet to be fully explored.

In what follows, we offer an introduction to each of the chapters and how they individually contribute to history, theory, and methodology in the field of Latino education. Together, the chapters in this section constitute the field as an exploration of how scholars/educators, teachers, community leaders, youths and parents have currently and historically addressed the challenges of education for Latinos/as. This knowledge production and body of scholarship are not merely footprints in the sand, but rather an active presence of a people asserting their educational and human rights.

This section begins appropriately with Victoria-María MacDonald and Juan F. Carrillo's chapter, "The United Status of Latinos." They ask important questions central to the field of Latino education—mainly, who are Latinos and what are our distinct histories in the United States? Their play on words in their chapter title signals how Latinos/as have shaped the United States and their home countries, and how they have been shaped by the United States and the processes of transnationalism and globalization. As stated above, their purpose is to highlight Latinos as "agents of their destinies" and to illustrate how initial historical contact with the U.S., immigration patterns and policies, generational status, country of origin, political and legal status, language, geographical location, social class, gender, culture, and religion, among other factors, shape their new identities on U.S. soil. They go on to argue that Latinos/as have been dehistoricized. In bringing Latinos/as back into history, they point out how legacies of the Spanish colonial and nationalist eras, and how patterns of immigration and labor policies have shaped Latino populations in the United States. The authors also discuss the distinct histories of the newer Central American, South American, and Dominican diaspora, and the new and changing geographic destinations of Latino migration. In addition, the authors take up the question of culture, language, family and gender roles. They note continuity, change, and hybridity, even as the U.S. context has demanded assimilation through English-only legislation and educational policies. The authors end with a call for utilizing pan ethnicity and cross-generational alliances to protect language, employment, education, and citizenship rights.

From the larger history of Latinos/as in the United States, we move to a history of Latino education as interpreted by historians Guadalupe San Miguel and Rubén Donato in their chapter, "Latino Education in Twentieth-Century America: A Brief History." As stated earlier, their thesis concerns first how education served to reproduce a highly stratified society aimed at ensuring the political and cultural hegemony of the dominant Anglo group and the socioeconomic subordination of Latinos. The second part of their thesis is how education was also a site of contestation as reflected in the actions taken by Latinos/as. The authors point out that individuals did not passively accept their educational fates and either resisted, subverted, or accommodated the marginalization and conformist intentions of this education. In broad strokes, San Miguel and Donato go on to document the specific events, legislation, policies, and practices that shaped the educational experiences of Latinos/as in the United States. They describe patterns of exclusion including inequitable student access to education, separate and unequal education, institutional treatment and bias including biased testing practices, and curricular exclusion. The chapter then describes the different strategies promoted by Latinos/as and their allies for student access, quality, culturally relevant instruction, bilingual education, and student achievement at all levels. The authors describe a general struggle for community power, leadership, and self-determination. They conclude by reflecting how, despite the immense obstacles facing Latinos/as, these will not halt the tremendous will of the population to excel in this country.

The section continues with an exploration of some of the theoretical perspectives important in Latino education scholarship currently. C. Alejandra Elenes and Dolores Delgado Bernal in their chapter, "Latina/o Education and the Reciprocal Relationship between Theory and Practice: Four Theories Informed by the Experiential Knowledge of Marginalized Communities," show how theories informed by the experiential knowledge of non-dominant communities have been instrumental to the development of Latina/o education scholarship. The authors focus on four traditions—critical race theory, Latino critical race theory, borderland/border theories, and Chicana feminist theory. Across these traditions, the authors tease out their historical roots, their interdisciplinary nature, and how each tradition addresses the intersections of race, class, gender, sexuality, language, ethnicity, and citizenship. Importantly, the authors provide an overview of an extensive number of writings and studies in education informed by these traditions. This scholarship in Latino education contributes to thinking anew about school inequality, pedagogy, identity, curriculum, and, in general, a liberatory praxis of education for a more just society.

Next, Maria Estela Zarate and Gilberto Conchas follow with their chapter, "Contemporary and Critical Methodological Shifts in Research on Latino Education." Their aim is to articulate a specific Latino orientation to critical research and the political and social realities that inform it. They discuss "methodology" as the intertwining of theory, epistemology, and method. They begin by situating the "critical" in Latino education with a discussion of the historical drivers of methodology. These include a challenge to cultural deficit paradigms, anti-bilingualism and the backlash against affirmative action in higher education. They follow with a discussion of critical methodologies in three areas of research in Latino education. First, they explore diverse methodologies centering race and racism, including research from the lens of critical race theory. Second, they explore methodologies documenting Latino family cultural resources and strengths. They emphasize here interpretive and descriptive qualitative and ethnographic work as well as the methodological tools of socio-linguistics and linguistic anthropology. Third, they address methodologies exploring Latino ethnic/racial and cultural identities with an emphasis on the wide range of theoretical orientations from social psychology, cultural studies, borderlands theories, and postcolonial perspectives. Zarate and Conchas end their chapter with a discussion of researcher positionality and future directions for Latino research methodologies in education.

This section of the handbook comes full circle with Irizarry and Nieto's chapter, "Latino/a Theoretical Contributions to Educational Praxis: Abriendo Caminos, Construyendo Puentes." The authors bring together a discussion of history, theory, method, and praxis to provide an interpretation of the large and robust body of research that now constitutes the field of Latino education. Like the chapter authors before them, they too take the position that despite the grim picture that is well-documented in the pages of this handbook, there is also an outlook for the future that is hopeful. The authors begin by historically situating research about Latinos/

as and education. They document the cultural bias of much of this research that purported to explain Latino students' academic failure as rooted in a deficit perspective of Latino family life. They discuss IQ and testing practices that supported and followed from the deficit perspective. Next, Irizarry and Nieto outline research that has served to counter the deficit perspective. This literature highlights the distinct forms of Latino parental involvement and the role of families in fostering school success. They also explore research about language socialization and bilingual/multilingual language and literacy practices. In doing so, they outline Latinas/os' unique and creative theoretical contributions to "culture" and educational praxis such as "funds of knowledge" (González, Moll, & Amanti, 2005), "community cultural wealth" (Yosso, 2005), and linguistic and cultural borderlands (Anzaldúa, 1987). Finally, like Elenes and Delgado Bernal (this section) and Zarate and Conchas (this section), Irizarry and Nieto note how much of the theoretical contributions to educational praxis included in their chapter have been in some way informed by the values and epistemologies that have emerged from Latino communities. Some of these distinct values and ways of knowing such as *cariño* (caring), *consejos* (advice), and *respeto* (respect) serve as important conceptual tools for understanding education in families and classrooms. Irizarry and Nieto conclude with one of the themes of this introduction—that of a community of scholars who are building upon the foundation established for them by previous generations while simultaneously extending the body of knowledge related to Latino/a education.

Like the authors of this section, we too want to end this introduction of history, theory, and methodology with a sense of hopefulness. The challenges ahead are great and the consequences of inaction are dire. Yet, as these chapters show again and again, the wealth of knowledge and research is there to effect change for Latinos/as in education. Not only have we developed the tools of theory and methods, but we also have a history and tradition of enormous political will and advocacy to guide our present and future actions.

References

Anzaldúa, G. (1987). *Borderlands/La Frontera*. San Francisco: Aunt Lute Books.

Bejarano, C. L. (2005). *¿Que honda? Urban youth culture and border identity*. Tucson: University of Arizona Press.

Bettie, J. (2003). *Women without class: Girls, race, and identity*. Berkeley: University of California Press.

Gándara, P. & Contreras, F. (2009). *The Latino education crisis: The consequences of failed social policies*. Cambridge, MA: Harvard University Press.

González, N., Moll, L. & Amanti, C. (Eds.). (2005). *Funds of knowledge: Theorizing practices in households and classrooms*. Mahwah, NJ: Erlbaum.

Grosfoguel, R., Maldonado-Torres, N., & Saldivar, J. D. (2005). Latin@s and the Euro-American menace: The decolonization of the U.S. empire in the twenty-first century. In R. Grosfoguel, N. Maldonado-Torres, & J. D. Saldivar (Eds.), *Latino/as in the world-system: Decolonization struggles in the 21st century U.S. empire* (pp. 3–27). Boulder, CO: Paradigm.

Lopez, N. (2005). *Hopeful girls, troubled boys: Race and gender disparity in urban education*. New York: Routledge.

Reyes, M. L. (2008). Review for "Latino theoretical contributions to educational praxis: Abriendo cammos, construyendo puento" (Irizarry and Nieto, this volume).

Yosso, T. J. (2005). Whose culture has capital? A critical race theory discussion of community cultural wealth. *Race, Ethnicity and Education, 8*(1), 69–91.

2   The United Status of Latinos

Victoria-María MacDonald
University of Maryland, College Park

Juan F. Carrillo
University of Texas, Austin

Nuestra Tierra
   [To the tune of Woody Guthrie's (1997) *This Land is Your Land*]
Chorus:
Deeeez land eeezzz jour laaaannd
Deeeez land eeezzz mi tierra
From the California barrio, to la isla Nuyoricua
Del Redwood forest a las aguas marinas,
Deeez laaaannnd fue hecha por tu y yo

As I was caminando the highways and railroads of brown backed-braceros
I felt above me el sol tan fuerte
I saw below me the huertas picked by niños
Deeez laaaannnd fue hecha por tu y yo
Chorus
I've roamed and rambled and I've followed my hermanos, footsteps past la migra
In the sparkling sands of her desiertos sedientos y peligrosas
Chorus
He was born in the melting pot that became menudo
Of the tanned American Dream we speak
With the melodies of the tierra del ayer
In el corazón
Colorado Rocky Mountain sueños
Chorus
Disregarding the meteorologist's intuition
The sun was able to shine on the Spanish surname
It is the suburb of Latinidad
On Pacific blvd in LA.
On Dyckman street in NYC
On Riverside St. in Austin
Chorus
From state to state
Even with the hateful reply
Life is full of wonder
As buildings go up
And when your fruit got shipped on time
Nobody said *gracias*
Chorus

When Woody Guthrie penned the original version of *This Land is Your Land* in the 1940s, he did not have in mind a nation peopled with Latinos, nor probably with any other group of color. Utilizing the ideology of Manifest Destiny, the mythical Anglo Saxon Protestant pioneers claimed lands from East to West, regardless of any historic claims held by indigenous, formerly enslaved, colonized or otherwise conquered peoples present since the first explorers touched land in the 1500s. The relationship of the United States of the 21st century to Latinos is one that can no longer ignore history. The centuries-old mestizo population refreshed with recent immigration has proven resilient despite a pendulum swing between welcome and rejection from the formal government authorities and informal voice of the White majority. Suro (2006) captures it well, "the true character of the Hispanic people can only become clear if you hold these two ideas in focus at the same time: a population of newcomers and a population with a long history in this country" (p. xi). Attempts over the last 200 years to exterminate, push back (over the Rio Grande), disenfranchise, dispossess, and dehumanize Latinos has proven futile. The United States has not been able to hold back the swelling of the Brown tide (Rodriguez, 2001). The present discourse on illegal immigration often is laced with sociocultural prejudices that taint the prospects for a formal and lucid policy covenant that works with the ideas coming from those across multiple sites of the ideological axis. And yet, despite these histrionic, extralegal, and legal efforts to rid the country of immigrants, work ethic, resilience, robust fertility rates, and the strong cultural strength of *la familia* sustains their presence and continued arrival. They work amidst the pulling back of resources and the racialized critique of their right to self authoring. There is still an omnipresent dedication to a pluralistic vision of the American tomorrow. From the northwest tip of Oregon, to the red clay hamlets of Georgia and the rocky hills of New England, Latinos are present both geographically and historically as a force to be reckoned with.

The impact of the Latino presence is two way. It is an iterative process; Latinos shape and reshape this so-called "America" of the north and it, in turn, shapes a heterogeneous population originating from over 20 countries into one homogenous panethnic Latino group. Old and new immigration waves are politically juxtaposed amidst a familiar and repetitive narrative. This is woven with the role of social class. As in the case of Cuban immigration, initial middle-class and highly educated groups were welcomed, but as poverty stricken and darker-colored Cubans started to arrive in large numbers later, political barriers were put in place. Whether it is an historic African American urban area undergoing the browning of its population, the predominantly White and increasingly Asian suburbs of Maryland and Virginia reliant upon a Latino labor force to build the housing and road infrastructure of the DC megalopolis, or midwestern rural areas accustomed to the seasonal appearance of Latinos/as workers but not as permanent residents, the United States, with over 45million Latinos reported by the U.S. Census in 2007, has permanently changed (U.S. Bureau of the Census, 2008).

In this chapter we provide a broad introduction to the multi-colored palette of the 21st century Latino, situated within the critical historical legacies shaping the present. The purpose of this chapter is to convey a nuanced portrait of Latinos as agents of their destinies in the United States and to illustrate how initial historical contact with the United States, immigration patterns and policies, generational status, country of origin, political and legal status, language, geographical location, social class, gender, culture, and religion, among other factors, shape their new identities on U.S. soil, whether third generation Mexican American, undocumented El Salvadoreño, or Argentinean diplomat on assignment. The educational questions and issues raised in this volume are situated in this larger social, economic, political, and cultural context. Although cultural influences such as the media can exert an enormous influence on Latinos through advertisements and select images of what an Hispanic in the United States should look like and act (Dávila, 2001), it is education, particularly in the state-sanctioned public schools that is perhaps the single most influential acculturating societal institution for children and youth in the United States of America. As Carola and Marcelo Suárez-Orozco (2001) explain, schools are the places "where immigrant children first come into systematic contact with the new culture ... adaptation into school is a significant predictor of a child's future well-being and contributions to society" (p. 3). As such, education's critical role in Latinos' lives must intersect with an understanding of the larger contextual forces that have shaped and continue to shape Latinos not only within institutional settings such as schools, but the larger society.

Historical Context

Latinos have been dehistoricized in American history. Courses on Latino/Chicano history reached some of our colleges and universities after the Latino Civil Rights Movement of the 1970s, but have barely trickled into the mainstream history/social studies curriculum of our mandatory and politically shaped public schools. Teaching courses on Latino educational history at the university, both undergraduate and graduate students have expressed dismay that they have never been taught even basic information on Mexican American, Puerto Rican, or other Hispanic descent peoples (Ruíz, 2006). Re-inscribing Latinos into the historical memory of the United States will be a long process, and one that requires the initiative of scholars, the public will and the polity. In this brief overview, we provide a contextual framework from which to understand contemporary experiences of Hispanic peoples in schools today.

Today's Latinos are the descendents of peoples who evolved as the result of hundreds of years of mixing between the indigenous people of the Americas, European settlers and Africans brought involuntarily to work as enslaved laborers. Indeed, one hallmark of Latino peoples is their *mestizaje*—a term which can invoke numerous meanings but which in this essay denotes the celebration and ideological stance of embracing the multiple races/languages/cultures which comprise the Latino people. From the early 1500s when Spanish missionaries, soldiers, and settlers spread into the areas now recognized as U.S. land, Spanish culture, religion, and language were imposed upon Native Americans. Today's Latinos thus underwent successive waves of racialization, colonization, nationhood, and recolonization, as first the Spanish and then the Anglo American governments imposed their will on what Kelvin Santiago-Valles (1994) has called "subject peoples." However, as suggested in the title of Suárez-Orozco & Páez's edited collection, *Latinos Remaking America* (2002), Hispanic peoples have influenced, reshaped, and redefined the colonizers as well. The practice of Santería in Miami, for example, is a continuing reminder of the syncretized African and Catholic heritages brought from Cuba. Overall, Latinos have not been passive recipients of dominating cultures, but rather have found ways to retain elements of their culture, heritage, and language when possible. The resulting hybridity of the last five centuries is reflected in the diversity of Latino peoples today.

Four historical legacies from the Spanish colonial era (roughly 1500–1848 for most of Central and South America, 1500–1898 for Cuba and Puerto Rico) and the nationalist era (1810–present for most countries, except those sections of Mexico acquired during the Mexican American War of 1848) provide insight into Latinos populating the U.S. today, whether they are newcomers or choose to date their genealogy back to the 16th and 17th century elite *Hispanos* of Colorado and New Mexico.

The first legacy is that of the Roman Catholic religion. Spaniards arrived to the New World not only to conquer lands and acquire gold, but also convert natives to Christianity, specifically the Roman Catholic religion of the King and Queen of Spain. According to Spanish colonial law, by 1526, each exploratory party was required to have two priests accompany them. Although certainly well-meaning priests existed among them, numbers of priests utilized coercive means of torture, imprisonment, and death if Native Americans did not give up their polytheistic religions (MacDonald, 2004). Furthermore, European contact with Native Americans resulted in the decimation of indigenous tribes, some almost to the point of extinction (such as the Taino in Puerto Rico), others fared better but were nevertheless exposed to contagious diseases which spread rapidly among weakened tribes.

Catholicism also brought formal education to the Native peoples. In the famed missions of the colonial era, Native Americans, particularly boys, were schooled in the Spanish language and/or work skills and the Catholic religion. The Roman Catholic religion, both under Spanish colonial rule and under the independent Central and South American countries which followed, was almost always adopted as the government religion, reinforcing nationality and religion as one and the same. As such, schooling was conducted under the auspices of the Catholic Church in both the colonial and nationalist eras, a mix that Anglo Americans would later reject as an inappropriate and unenlightened mixture of religion, particularly "papism" and state (Mac-Donald, 2004). Although initially an institution imposed harshly upon the Hispanic peoples of the Americas, Catholicism over the years evolved into an institution with varying roles among Latinos, both positive and negative. For instance, missionary orders ranked education as a priority in their goals, resulting in the education of numerous sectors of Native Americans who would not have otherwise received formal education. Furthermore, Catholic schools and colleges provided bilingual Spanish/English instruction to Hispanic children under U.S. rule when Anglo American public schools rejected their language. Many priests and nuns in both formal and informal ways have worked hard for social justice. For instance, priests in Philadelphia assisted the Young Lords during the civil rights era with political strategies (Stevens-Arroyo, 2004). Although today's Latinos are more diverse in their religious affiliations, an estimated one-third have joined Pentecostal churches, the Mormon religion and other faiths, the unique historical rituals of Spanish Catholicism including its processionals, devotions, and reverence of the Virgin Mary, bind Latinos together in a panethnic identity that bridges loyalties to national homelands. Whether it is Mexico's Virgin of Guadalupe or my own *abuelita's* Virgen de Perpetuo Socorro (Virgin of Perpetual Help), Latinos recognize and respect the reverence due to *la virgencita* in ways foreign to most Protestant Anglo Americans (Bender, 2003).

The second historical legacy from the colonial and nationalist eras that has particular bearing on contemporary Latinos in the United States is the hierarchical racialization process created by the Spaniards in the 16th century. The caste system based upon percentage of Spanish, indigenous, or African blood, and Catholic baptism, which prized *limpieza de sangre* (blood purity) while degrading indigenous and African heritages has continued down to the present day through policies and practices. The highest tier in the complex Spanish caste system (which could include over 40 categories) was the *peninsulares*, individuals born in Spain (Weber, 1992). Next in line were the *criollos*, children born in the colonies to Spanish-born parents. *Mestizos*, were the unions of Native Americans and Spaniards, if the parents had been formally united under the Catholic Church and the child baptized, or the result of a "legitimate union." The multiplicity of categories which then extended to African and Native American mixing reflected the Spanish need to differentiate themselves from their colonists which would privilege those closest to Spanish purity (Nieto-Phillips, 2004). Bias towards European blood and appearances and its connections to high status, economic and political privileges, has remained as an important historical legacy among Latin American peoples, despite the indigenous rights movements of the late 20th century. Interestingly, Spaniards' willingness to enter unions with Native peoples was seen among 19th century Anglo Americans as a sign of Spanish backwardness and propensity for promiscuity (Horsman, 1981; De León, 1983). Previously, historians pointed to the Spanish experience of intermixture with Moors and Jews during the centuries-long Moorish occupation of Spain as explanation for the relative lack of disapprobation towards unions between Spanish conquistadores and Indian women (Crow, 1985, pp. 61–62). However, more recently, historians discuss the military and political strategy of marrying Spanish soldiers and officers with the daughters of Indian tribal leaders as reasons for the initial general acceptance of Spanish/ Native/ and African racial and ethnic mixture. The Spanish Crown furthered this practice through official sanction of inter-ethnic marriages between Spaniards and Indians in 1514 (Elliott, 2006, p. 81). A shortage of Spanish women, and tribal customs, which included giving daughters to the conquering party, further contributed to the selection of native women as wives and mistresses (Rodriguez, 2007). The hierarchical colonial racial categories experienced liberalization under the Mexican revolutionary period (1821–1848) and in its new constitution which eliminated racial and ethnic categories. In the rapidly racializing social order of the mid-19th-century United States, however, the racial hybridity of Mexican Americans was further justification of Anglo territorial aggression and superiority. Although legally White after 1848, Mexican Americans were viewed *socially* as "off-White," and, as a result of the historical ambiguity between their legal and social status, Mexican Americans in the past and tangentially Latinos today embrace "both a white and non-white racial identity, both collectively and individually" (Gómez, 2007, p.150).

The third legacy from the colonial and nationalist eras is the enduring notion of the Spanish Black Legend (*la leyenda negra*). During the height of Spanish power, Protestant European countries, particularly England, created and perpetuated the Black Legend which portrayed Spaniards and their descendents as superstitious, cruel, barbaric (e.g. the Spanish Inquisition), ignorant and anti-intellectual. The notorious pamphlet authored by Roman Catholic priest Bartolomé de las Casas in 1542, *A Brief Account of the Devastation of the Indies*, was a protest of the abuse and exploitation targeted at the Native Americans and was also used by critics of Spain as more evidence of the cruel nature of Spanish peoples. The Roman Catholicism of Spaniards was also critiqued as part of the Black Legend, indicating a slavish loyalty to the pope which could undermine nation states (Weber, 1979; Powell, 1971). The Black Legend carried down through the nationalist era and played a part in the formation of anti-Hispanic attitudes of Anglo Americans as they encountered Mexicans in the late 18th and early 19th centuries, justifying both the Mexican American War of 1846–48 and Spanish American War of 1898 (Horsman, 1981). Invidious comparisons between the enterprising British colonists and then new "Americans" were also made with the Latin American colonists and their fledgling republics who were reputedly held back by the "backwardness, superstition, and sloth" of the Spanish culture (Elliott, 2006, pp. 404–405). In an overwhelming European Pan Protestant U.S. culture, the Spanish and Catholic roots of Latinos remain suspect, fitting neither into the Black-White binary nor into the more easily assimilable White ethnic immigrant groups of the early 20th century.

The Spanish language is the fourth legacy which Spain gave to the Americas (except for Brazil and other minor exceptions). Spanish became the language of the conqueror and colonizer, the language of power required in schools and government laws and policies. Indigenous languages, however, existed side by side with the Spanish language, and although many have been extinguished, indigenous rights movements of the late 20th century and into the 21st century have pushed for the preservation of indigenous languages and their utilization as part of the public domain (May, 2001). Although as a historical legacy, the Spanish language serves as a "cultural mortar" (Tienda & Mitchell, 2006b) bringing together Latinos from all nationalities, it becomes a point of contention on U.S. soil from those constituents who insist upon the English language for all public discourse and schooling.

The context in which Anglo Americans and Latinos formally came together in the mid-19th century Mexican American War (1846–48) was that of conqueror and the conquered. Anglo Americans justified their acquisition of Mexican lands, partly on the concept of Manifest Destiny, an ideology based on the belief that Providence granted the United States a divine mandate to spread from coast to coast. Inherent in Manifest Destiny was also a belief in Anglo-Saxon Protestant superiority in which American rule was a beneficent act leading to the improvement of life for the purportedly uneducated, ignorant, and backwards Mexican peoples (Gonzales, 1999). The dehumanizing of Mexicans began in the 19th century, evolving from previous anti-Hispanic prejudices. Many Anglo settlers brought American notions of miscegenation (Black-White) with them and viewed the *mestizo* Mexicans as products of the mixing of two or more inferior races (Horsman, 1981). Bender (2003) points out that derogatory terms such as "wetbacks," "greasers," and "dogs" were also used to justify the Mexican American War, eventually spreading as terms utilized to describe other Latinos including Puerto Ricans and Cubans. The Treaty of Guadalupe Hidalgo of 1848, which concluded the Mexican American War, ceded to the United States 500,000 square miles—including the contemporary states of California, New Mexico, Arizona, Utah, Nevada, and parts of Colorado and Wyoming—for only $15 million. Terms of the 1848 treaty included the rights and responsibilities for Mexicans on the land that had been conquered. As Menchaca (2001) points out, however, suffrage guarantees for those Mexicans remaining on the new U.S. soil increasingly narrowed in the new state and territorial constitutions. Blacks and Native Americans who had been protected under the treaty were quickly disenfranchised as only Mexicans considered to be part of the "White" race were permitted citizenship. Mestizos, African Americans, and Afromestizos were denied political rights, such as practicing law, marrying Whites, and other discriminatory measures. For instance, by the early 1860s, California's school code stipulated that "Negroes, Mongolians and Indians" be segregated from Whites in the public schools (MacDonald, 2004, p. 56). The impact of the war and subsequent stripping of rights, particularly regarding land grants protected under the treaty, resulted in the social, political, and economic decline of Mexicans in the southwestern United States by the 1880s and 1890s (Pitt, 1999).

Many of the same themes of Anglo Saxon superiority and Hispanophobia emerged during the U.S. imperialist era of the late 19th century culminating in the brief Spanish American War (1898–99). Puerto Rico and Cuba were both acquired during this time, but experienced differential colonial status. The United States became involved to assist Cuba liberate itself from Spanish colonialism. In the brief war culminating in the Treaty of Paris in 1899, the United States acquired the Philippine Islands, Guam, Puerto Rico, and Guantánamo Bay, Cuba. Cuba was protected from outright acquisition in the 1898 Teller Amendment which had authorized President William McKinley to intervene in Cuba but not establish rule. The United States did, however, maintain the power to determine the "legal, civil and political status of the newly acquired peoples" (MacDonald, 2004, p. 93). Cuba was governed from 1901 to 1934, and afterwards the Platt Amendment established Cuba as an American protectorate.

In contrast, Puerto Rico was declared a U.S. territory, and, under the 1900 Foraker Act, the U.S. president, not Puerto Ricans, was given authority to appoint the governor and heads of all administrative departments. In 1917 the U.S. Congress passed the Jones Act which, according to many contemporary Puerto Ricans and current scholars, "imposed" U.S. citizenship upon Puerto Ricans. Despite objections to components of the Jones Act from Puerto Rican leaders, collective naturalization was imposed upon Puerto Rican citizens and those declining U.S. citizenship were required to individually appear in a court of law (Rivera Ramos, 2005). Among the objections to this act was the accompanying eligibility for military conscription. In 1952 Puerto Rico was established as a commonwealth with the ability to elect its own governor, but the U.S. Congress struck essential components of the Puerto-Rican authored Bill of Rights, including universal public education and health service (Santiago-Irizarry & Cabán, 2005). Over a century of colonized status and second-class citizenship with little prospect for either independence nor statehood has produced a series of nationalist and independence movements among Puerto Ricans, often ruthlessly crushed by U.S. governmental agencies. Both Cuba and Puerto Rico, hoping to escape Spanish colonial power, were not freed but initially placed under the power of a second colonizer. The differing treatment accorded Cuba and Puerto Rico during the post-Spanish American War era has had long-term implications for current relationships between Cubans and Puerto Ricans. The U.S. Supreme Court has consistently ruled that Puerto Rico is still "an unincorporated territory." Although U.S. citizens, Puerto Ricans have the advantage of not paying federal income taxes but neither can they vote in presidential or congressional elections (Acosta-Belén & Santiago, 2006). Beginning in the 1940s, with inexpensive airplane flights and labor needs on the mainland, Puerto Ricans began moving back and forth between the island and the continental U.S. with such regularity and consistency that the metaphor of a "commuter nation" was invoked to describe the populace (Torre, Vencchini, & Burgos, 1994; Duaney, 2002). The island's population of 3.8 million in the 2000 census is predicted to equal that of the number of Puerto Ricans residing on the mainland by 2010, but close familial and cultural ties endure between homeland and the mainland.

During the 20th century, Mexican Americans and Puerto Ricans utilized community and then regional and national organizations to push back the historic marginalization that resulted from political, linguistic, and social othering (Gonzalez, 2000). The Chicano Movement of the 1970s provided a bourgeoning of new awareness, much vested in pride in *mestizaje* and spiritual connection to *Aztlan* (the mythical homeland of the Aztecs; Rosales, 1996). Likewise, Puerto Ricans identified with their Native American *Boricua* roots during the civil rights era of the late 1960s and 1970s to inspire pride, and create an educational system responsive to their children's linguistic needs (Acosta-Belén & Santiago, 2006). The deep historical Spanish/Native American/African roots of the Latino relationship to the United States continues to be layered and contoured by the new Latinos themselves, despite arriving during an era in which institutional, political, and legal systems to protect the rights of Latinos permit at least a modicum of protection unavailable to earlier waves of immigrants and/or colonized peoples.

Immigration, Labor, and Latinos in the 20th Century

> When we need cheap labor our borders open up; when jobs are in short supply, we not only shut them closed, we want to ship the "others" home. (Hernandez-Truyol, 1998, p. 130)

The Case of Mexico

From the moment the ink was dry on the Treaty of Guadalupe Hidalgo in 1848, the thousands of Mexicans who had previously moved fluidly across the Rio Grande into Northern Mexico were now immigrants, not citizens of their own country. Under the terms of the treaty, Mexicans could elect to become U.S. citizens or move back over the border, approximately 100,000 chose that option, moving from being subjected peoples of Spain, to a brief period of independence (1821–848) before being incorporated into the U.S. population (Del Castillo, 1990). The 2,000 mile border between the United States and Mexico contributes to that nation's current status as the number one immigrant-sending (documented or undocumented) country to the United States. Mexican immigrants currently comprise almost one-third of the U.S. foreign-born population (Katz, Stern, & Fader, 2007). Immigration policy between Mexico and the United States is considered separately here first because of its unique political and economic relationship that distinguishes it from other Central and South American sending countries and from the other major border of the United States, Canada, which has a distinct immigration pattern from Mexico.

The decision to immigrate to the United States is contingent upon a semiotic relationship between the country of origin and the United States. As Portes (1997) expressed so well, Latino immigrant sending countries are maintained in a subordinate position to the United States, a factor that dominates the relationship; "migration control and the perpetuation of social and economic inequalities between advanced countries and the Third World are closely intertwined. The extent to which states succeed in maintaining such controls or are derailed in their enforcement efforts represents a central policy concern as well as a topic of considerable theoretical import" (p. 818). The discussion of immigration from Mexico is thus considered as one of imbalance within this relationship and distinct from refugee situations such as those relating to Cubans and some other Central American arrivers.

The enormous wave of the turn of the 20th century immigration (roughly 1880 to World War I) brought 25 million immigrants to the United States, mostly from Europe (Ngai, 2004). At the height of this wave of immigration, foreign-born immigrants represented 15% of the population, still less than the contemporary level of 10% of Americans born abroad (Foner, 2005). With the anti-German sentiments of World War I and subsequent anti-foreign climate of the 1920s, the borders of the once open United States of Ellis Island fame closed. Although immigrant restrictions begun in the late 19th century targeted mostly Asians, the 20th-century legislation was broadened, culminating in the Immigration Act of 1921, followed by the more famous Johnson Reed Act of 1924. The Immigration Act of 1924 as the Reed Act is also called, established quotas for the number of people arriving from European and Asian countries. However, of specific interest to this chapter is the exemption of Mexico and other Western Hemisphere countries from the numerical quotas. As established under the Treaty of Guadalupe Hidalgo, Mexicans were racially White, and thus exempt from the 1924 act's exclusion of immigrant arrivers racially ineligible for citizenship. The 1910 Mexican Revolution triggered migration to the United States, and over 600,000 Mexicans were enumerated by the 1920 U.S. Census, almost tripling the previous decades' number (651,596 vs. 224,275; Ngai, 2004).

The legal protections within the 1924 Act for Mexican immigrants and agricultural demands from U.S. farmers maintained the border legally open between the United States and Mexico until the late 1920s when the U.S. State Department decided to use administrative tactics to restrict immigration. The 1924 Immigration Act had also instituted deportation as a measure that could be utilized without a waiting period and created the Border Patrol to monitor the long Canadian and Mexican borders. During the Great Depression of the 1930s, Mexicans, whether citizens or legal residents, were harassed and sent back over the border in ruthless Border Patrol raids of housing *colonias* and places of employment (Meier & Ribera, 1972/1993). Over 400,000 were repatriated to Mexico, an estimated 20% of the entire Mexican U.S. population. According to immigration historian Ngai (2004), "the repatriation of Mexicans was a racial expulsion program exceeded in scale only by the Native American Indian removals of the nineteenth century" (p. 75).

By the 1940s the pendulum of rejection of Latinos had swung again and workers were again welcome, either from Puerto Rico (although U.S. citizens) and Mexico. The World War II domestic labor shortage led the U.S. Congress to pass the Migrant Labor agreement, more commonly known as the *bracero program.* Under the program (1942–1964), 4.6 million male contract workers from Mexico were permitted to enter the United States as agricultural workers only, guaranteed transportation, housing, food, and repatriation to work for employers at a set wage. In reality, conditions were often squalid, wage contracts violated, and many braceros returned or deserted their contracts, entering the United States as undocumented migrants. Ngai (2004) argues that the bracero program contributed to marginalizing Mexicans as a "migratory agricultural proletariat, a racialized, transnational workforce" excluded by immigration policies from entering mainstream American society (p. 128). The unintended consequences of the bracero program included the rise of illegal immigration from Mexico. Called the "wetback invasion" of the 1940s and 1950s, thousands of Mexicans came to the United States illegally during the years of the bracero program as a result of more demand for spots than the program offered (Gonzales, 1999). Furthermore, the exclusion of Texas, Arkansas, or Missouri in the initial agreement with the Mexican government because of their discriminatory and segregated "Jim Crow" practices against Mexicans, and the need of employers in the southwest to hire workers, legal or illegal, resulted in thousands of *mojados* (wetbacks), who could be paid minimal wages and possessed no rights because they were undocumented (Ngai, 2004), entering the United States.

By the 1950s, alarm over the number of illegal migrants from Mexico led to the creation of "Operation Wetback," in 1954, which returned hundreds of thousands of undocumented workers. By 1964, technological changes in agriculture (e.g., mechanization of cotton and sugar beet harvesting) contributed to a decreased demand for Mexican workers and the bracero program was officially closed just as the Civil Rights era ushered in a political and legal context in which new Mexican residents or Mexican American citizens were no longer willing to tolerate unjust and discriminatory labor practices.

Policies and Patterns of the Late 20th Century

The Cuban Revolution of 1959 resulted in a new form of arrival for Latinos to the United States: refugee status. The Cold War politics of the 1950s and 1960s contributed to the creation of a welcome mat unprecedented in American history. Cubans have arrived in roughly four waves, each possessing a distinct character, defying stereotypes that Cuban Americans are homogenously well-off and members of the elite class. The initial pattern of immigration, however, set the stage for the successful economic, social, and political integration of Cubans to the United States. The first wave (1959–1964) of Cuban refugees, dubbed the "Golden Exiles" because of their higher educational and social levels, received economic assistance and open arms from the U.S. government, religious agencies such as the Catholic Church, and private organizations. Adding to the original 200,000 Cuban refugees was a similarly-sized second wave, from 1965 to 1973. Furthermore, the 1966 Cuban Refugee Adjustment Act permitted any Cubans who were already on U.S. land to remain, regardless of how they entered. The third wave, the Mariel boatlift of 1980, was the most controversial as Fidel Castro declared he would empty his jails and mental institutions to fill boats leaving from Mariel harbor. In the end, less than 2,500 of the 125,000 Marielitos were found to be criminals by the U.S. government (Pérez, 2007). Between 1980 and the mid-1990s, small numbers of Cubans were admitted each year through a visa process. The fourth wave, called the "Rafter Crisis of 1994" was precipitated by the Cuban government's announcement that it would not stop individuals leaving on rafts or other vessels. To stop another wave, the Clinton administration ended the 1966 policy and created in 1995 what is called the "wet-foot, dry-foot" policy. Still in effect in 2008, if the Coast Guard or other authority intercepts a vessel before arriving to U.S. soil, they are returned to Cuba. Overall, Cubans are 4% of the total number of Latinos in the United States. However, the 1.3 million Cuban Americans are nonetheless a very visible Latino group because of their atypical integration into U.S. society and domination of the political, economic, and social institutions of Miami, Florida, where the majority (60%) currently reside, in addition to national political importance in the Republican Party (Pérez, 2007; Portes & Stepick, 1993).

When the long shadow that the 1924 Johnson Reed Act had cast across 20th-century immigration was lifted in 1965, the United States was a different country. The expanding industrial economy in which Italian, Polish, Russian Jewish, and other European immigrants had been able to find jobs was transformed. In the post-industrial economy of the late 20th century, Latinos from Central and South America encountered an hourglass shaped economic structure. Low skill, low paying jobs at one end and highly skilled professional jobs often requiring degrees at the other end, resulted in larger inequalities between wages among American employees. Low skill jobs in the service sectors of the restaurant and hotel industries; janitorial services; construction; agriculture; and the demographic movement of individuals and industries to the Sunbelt from the Midwest and Northeast provided jobs for Hispanic arrivers. The aging transportation and communications infrastructure provided jobs requiring road repair, expansion and upgrading of power and communication lines. Those Latino immigrants who had few educational opportunities in their native lands and spoke little English moved into these difficult and demanding jobs. Pay rates were low, but still represented a significant increase from their native countries. The trilateral passage of the North American Free Trade Agreement (NAFTA) between Mexico, Canada, and the United States in 1994 aimed to limit movement over the border and to strengthen the Mexican economy, but ultimately resulted in more Mexicans seeking jobs northward (Morín, 2005). In addition to the decrease in U.S. manufacturing jobs (from over one-fourth of the working population in 1970 to 15% by 2000), increased globalization and overseas outsourcing, economists also view the decline of labor unions as another transformation in the U.S. economy greeting recent immigrants (Kaushal, Reimers, & Reimers, 2007). By 2000 only 13% of the nonagricultural workforce was unionized. Agricultural laborers were successfully organized in the 1960s and 1970s, but unions suffered at the turn of the 21st century by trying to include undocumented workers (Kaushal, Reimers, & Reimers, 2007). In contrast, Latino immigrants arriving in the United States with higher-education degrees and English skills in areas of high demand—health care, engineering, science, and computer science—stepped into the higher wage and salary economy. Latin American immigrants from the higher social classes are more commonly representative of this sector of Latino immigrants.

When the Hart-Celler/Immigration Act of 1965 was passed, it was hailed as nondiscriminatory because it finally abolished national origins quotas. Furthermore, family reunification constituted one of its priorities, permitting large numbers of extended family members to migrate to the United States. In 1968, in a significant move for Hispanics in the Western Hemisphere, a numerical quota was placed on immigrants arriving from Central and South America, the unintended effect was to increase undocumented arrivals. In fact, Massey, Duran, and Malone (2002) label the period from 1965 to 1985 as "an era of undocumented migration" and a "de facto guest worker program" which brought young undocumented males from Mexico to work in the U.S. (quoted in Tienda & Mitchell, 2006a, p. 29). The 1986 IRCA (Immigration Reform and Control Act) was an attempt to stem the tide of undocumented workers and permitted Mexico to send more migrants, granted amnesty citizenship eligibility to undocumented workers who had lived in the United States since 1982, and other measures, resulting in 2.4 million undocumented individuals applying for and receiving citizenship. As a means of limiting illegal entry to the United States however, IRCA was seen as a failure because sanctions against employers were never sufficiently harsh (Gonzales, 1999).

The final significant federal policy in the 20th century to impact Latinos was the 1996 Illegal Immigration Reform and Immigrant Responsibility Act (IIRAIRA). Under this more stringent act, carried out during an era of anti-immigrant bashing which had produced measures such as Proposition 187 in California barring undocumented children from K-12 education and emergency services (later ruled unconstitutional), criminal penalties were increased for immigration violations and undocumented peoples were barred from other non-emergency publicly funded support programs and services (Tienda & Mitchell, 2006a). IIRAIRA had unintended effects of increasing naturalization rates among immigrants from Latin America, as many sought empowerment through voting and dual citizenship was also newly permitted between the United States and several Latin American countries such as Peru, Argentina, Mexico, and Costa Rica.

The "New Latinos"[1] in the U.S. Diaspora: Central, South American, and Dominican Immigrants

Prior to 1965, the majority of Latinos was of Puerto Rican, Cuban, or Mexican descent and concentrated in the Southwest, Northeast, Miami, and select urban areas in the Midwest such as Chicago. Since 1980, however, two major shifts have occurred, geographically and demographically. States such as California, Texas, New York, and Florida are still the largest recipients of newcomers and Mexicans are still the most numerous among undocumented (54%) and documented arrivers (Kaushal, Reimers, & Reimers, 2007). However, growth and industries in the Sunbelt have pulled Latinos into areas traditionally foreign to immigrants (Zuñiga & Hernández-León, 2005; Wortham, Murillo, & Hamman, 2002). Within more traditionally Southern states, e.g., local populations have begun to deconstruct what it means to move beyond the traditional Black-White duality that has characterized American race and ethnic relations. Cultures have come into contact with a speed that has fostered xenophobia and discrimination between the now dethroned African American "majority minority" and Latinos (MacDonald & Zoppi, 2007;

Straus, 2006). In this section we look at how Central and South American immigration (and also from the Dominican Republic) during the 1990s and early 2000s has drawn attention to both the dilemma of undocumented workers as well as the ambivalence of host municipalities and states. These newcomers, whose numbers grew rapidly from 3 million in the 1990 census to 6.1 million in 2000, present a new face to the mosaic of U.S. Latinos. The greater diversity of national origins and social and economic classes stretch the stereotypical view of migrant laborers and domestic workers. From Dominican Americans with low educational skills in their impoverished homeland who are then racialized in the United States as African Americans to highly skilled Colombians, the New Latinos are changing what it means to be Hispanic (Morawska, 2007; Guarnizo & Espitia, 2007). Central American immigrants are not just faceless automatons working in U.S. households. In chronicles such as *Enrique's Journey* (Nazario, 2006), the lives of Central American single mothers working as housekeepers and the children they left behind in desperation are personalized. For each gardener, dishwasher, technician, or construction worker we see, a story, often of hardship, courage, and determination, exists.

Central America is a diverse region comprising the nations of El Salvador, Guatemala, Honduras, Costa Rica, Panama, and Belize. Scholars of Central American history typically view Panama (formerly part of Colombia) and Belize (a former British colony and English-speaking nation with a large Afro-Caribbean population) as having distinct characteristics from the other five countries (Chinchilla & Hamilton, 2004). The push and pull factors accompanying migration included the civil war, unrest, and violence caused in part by United States government intervention in the Dominican Republic, Guatemala, Nicaragua, and El Salvador. Economic instability, continued political persecution, and natural catastrophes such as Hurricane Mitch in 1998, which severely impacted Honduras and Nicaragua, continued to encourage exodus well after civil wars had subsided (Chinchilla & Hamilton, 2004). As partial acknowledgement of the U.S. role in forcing thousands of Central Americans to flee their homelands, the United States took several policy and legal steps to ease the naturalization process for undocumented immigrants. The Refugee Act of 1980 defined a refugee as one unable to return to their homeland "because of persecution or a well-founded fear of persecution on account of race, religion, nationality, membership in a particular social group, or political opinion" (Soltero, 2006, pp. 142–143). It was soon found, however, that refugees were being granted asylum disproportionately from countries other than Central America. As a result, in 1990 the U.S. Congress granted Temporary Protected Status (TPS) to Salvadorans, Guatemalans, and Nicaraguans who could argue that they would be killed if returned to their homeland (LaRosa & Ingwersen, 2007). In two federal court cases, *American Baptist Churches et al. v. Richard Thornburgh et al.* (1991; Soltero, 2006, p. 143) and *Immigration and Naturalization Service v. Cardoza-Fonseca* (480 U.S. 421, 1987; Soltero, 2006, pp. 135–144), the U.S. government's limited protection for Central American refugees was brought to attention. Furthermore, the cases contributed to the passage of the 1997 Nicaraguan Adjustment and Central American Relief Act easing the procedures for application to legal permanent residency among the many undocumented Central Americans who had to flee their war-torn countries at moment's notice.

South American immigration has also reshaped the Hispanic dynamic, although certainly in smaller numbers. The total number of South Americans in the United States, documented and undocumented, is estimated at over 2 million and that number is considered an undercount (Marrow, 2007). With the exception of Colombia, which has recently produced the largest number of South American immigrants to the United States because of political instability, drug wars, and economic destabilization, South American countries have sent fewer documented or undocumented individuals to the United States, and the labor migration streams typical of Central American and Mexican workers are largely absent (Guarnizo & Espitia, 2007; Marrow, 2007). Scholars have concluded that this difference can be attributed to less U.S. colonialist and neocolonialist involvement than in the Caribbean and Central America. While not diminishing the complexity of the impact of globalization and economic restructuring on Latin American economies, in general it can be said that South American immigrants, including Colombians, tend to be better educated, more concentrated in white-collar managerial and technical occupations and possess lower poverty rates than their Central American and Mexican compatriots (Marrow, 2007). Overall, South American immigrants tend to enter the United States more as voluntary economic migrants than political refugees. Interactions between Argentineans and other long-established Latino groups in the United States, such as Puerto Ricans or Mexicans, is often initially rocky as South Americans, like many Central Americans, initially view themselves in nationalist terms rather than part of a larger Latino panethnic identity through which the U.S. majority views them. Panethnicity of Latinos serves as both an advantage and disadvantage. New immigrant arrivers, some with high social status, are disturbed with being connected to what is seen as an American-born lower class Latino. Eventually, the advantages of panethnicity become transparent either for political or economic reasons, or often after their first experiences of linguistic or racial/ethnic discrimination (Foner, 2005).

An additional characteristic of the New Latinos is their geographic destinations—from urban to suburban—and from Northeast and Southwest to mid-Atlantic and South. The traditional immigrant gateways to the United States—Los Angeles, San Francisco, New York—have not disappeared. But, beginning with the Cuban arrival to Miami in the early 1960s, Latin Americans have spread to other areas of the country, in some cases building upon social, political, and economic transnational networks established by earlier waves of Latinos or into completely new rural areas such as Arkansas or Mississippi. The Pew Hispanic Center found an increase of over half a million New Latinos in the greater South Florida area, including Fort Lauderdale, between the 1990 and 2000 censuses (Suro, 2002). Furthermore, besides the dramatic growth of Latinos into the former Confederate States (increases of 300–400% from 1990 to 2000, especially in North Carolina and Georgia), 16 states had more than 100,000 New Latinos among their ranks by 2000. In addition to Texas, particularly Houston, where many Central Americans have settled, areas such as metropolitan Washington, DC, have witnessed an increase of over 100% growth (300,000 New Latinos), mostly Salvadorans, Guatemalans, and Nicaraguans between 1990 and 2000. Pupusa trucks and "pupuserias" in Langley Park, Maryland, peddle the delicious Salvadoran staple, and restaurants in Alexandria, Virginia, offer Latin-Nicaraguan-Mexican plates to satisfy the increasingly diverse Latino palates (MacDonald & Zoppi, 2007). In suburban Long Island, New York, where Italians were banned from many neighborhoods in the 1940s and 1950s, Latinos are moving to the suburbs where lower costs and pooled family incomes permit home ownership outside of traditional urban immigrant enclaves (Logan, 2007; Tienda & Mitchell, 2006a).

Cultural Constructs

Language

Language has been described as the "blood of the soul into which thoughts run and out of which they grow" (Holmes, 1894, March 3). Language is indeed a primitive component of one's individual identity and a vital component of cultural identity. The Spanish language binds the panethnic Latino community with each other and the mother country. The monolingual heritage of the original British settlers and their persistent Anglophone domination has maintained an atmosphere in which English language proficiency is one of the major tenets of Americanization and citizenship, while many Latinos believe that "integration into a single linguistic community is a product of political domination" (Macedo, Bessie, & Panayota, 2003, p. 36). Despite grudging accommodations for English Language Learners in the public schools (described in more detail later in this volume), U.S. courts and policies have been historically consistent in depriving Latinos of native language use in sectors outside of the home. A general trend seems to encompass the notion that individual language proficiency has immense value, whereas group bilingualism is seen as a threat to the dominant society's notion of national (and homogenous) identity. The melting pot framework still drives much of the English Only debate.

During times of anti-immigrant xenophobia, such as the current climate in place since the 1990s, Spanish-speaking children have been stripped of the right to learn English through their native language, despite empirical research demonstrating that bilingual education is an effective means of acquiring a second language. Ironically, European children, who routinely learn two and three languages, are often held up as exemplars in international test comparisons. Yet, the U.S. Department of Education has moved away from bilingualism as a policy (August & Hakuta, 1998). In a telling political shift, the office created by the 1968 Bilingual Education Act and fortified by the U.S. Supreme Court case, *Lau v. Nichols,* 414 U.S 563 (1974), the Office of Bilingual Education & Minority Languages Affairs (OBEMLA) from 1974–2001, was changed in 2001 under the George W. Bush administration to the Office of English Language Acquisition, Language Enhancement, and Academic Achievement for Limited English Proficient Students (OELA), sanitizing from its title in symbolic and profound ways the word "bilingual." California's Proposition 227 (1998) required teachers to only use English in classes for Limited English Proficient students and states such as Arizona (2000) and Massachusetts (2002) followed suit in shifting bilingual education policies to Structured English Immersion programs. The deficit views towards Spanish speaking students have resulted in dire prospects in the eventual development of strong bilingual-bicultural education programs.

Outside of the school arena, language and accent discrimination plays a critical role in the acquisition of political and labor rights. In the 21st century of globalization and transnationalism, Spanish speakers are still considered in deficit terms, "in the American case, the ability to speak two or more languages would be viewed as advantageous unless the person who speaks the languages is a subordinate speaker (usually an immigrant), in which case it would be considered a handicap to the learning of English" (Macedo, Bessie, & Panayota, 2003, p. 9). The marginalization and linguicism that has been directed at Spanish speakers has received minimal protection in the U.S. court system. Puerto Rican voters on the mainland finally received the right to have Spanish ballots in *Katzenbach v. Morgan,* 384 U.S. 641 (1966), and a 1992 amendment requires states with more than 5% or 10,000 people with a similar language to provide bilingual voting information (Soltero, 2006).

In the employment arena, employers have generally won cases in which employees were forbidden to speak Spanish during work hours. Typically, defendants of Spanish language employment cases have cited Title VI of the Civil Rights Act of 1964 prohibiting discrimination on the basis of race, color, or national origin as a rationale for protecting language rights. However, in the most recent case, *Alexander v. Sandoval,* 532 U.S. 275 (2001), the Supreme Court did not rule specifically on the constitutionality of English-only laws, leaving it within the state's prerogative (Soltero, 2006).

Germane to the language debate is the idea of Spanish being a static and neutral corpus of sounds and linguistic modalities. What often happens is that Latinos in places such as Miami, New York, Los Angeles, and south Texas, take cues from peers, school, media, and family to develop variations of Spanish. Additional influences come from interactions with hip hop, salsa music, *corridos,* and the constant linguistic border crossing that is the norm in many spaces. Rural and urban conversation zones differentiate the idioms and rhythms and many become skilled code switchers. As Bakhtin (1981) contends, the "dialogization" process encompasses a competition for meaning, inference, and structure. This eclectic interaction has even lead to the "official" conceptualization of *Spanglish* (Stavans, 2004), language that is part English, part Spanish. Stavans (2004) and the Chicana feminist writer Gloria Anzaldua (1999) embrace these types of interchanges, while Spanish language purists like the Nobel Prize winning Mexican writer, Octavio Paz (1985), reject them.

The sociocultural contact zone between Spanish-speaking and monolingual Whites has resulted in immigrant waves becoming Anglicized at fast rates "with substantial attrition of the heritage languages by the second generation in this country" (Crawford, 2004, p. 12). Indeed, demographers have concluded that by the third generation, only one-quarter of Hispanic-descent peoples can speak Spanish. Unfortunately, anti-immigrant xenophobic sentiments have closed the eyes and ears of otherwise thoughtful policymakers and politicians, and public opinion fueled by right-wing organizations such as The Minutemen forcefully argue that "illegal aliens" are threatening the very fabric of the nation, rhetoric which has been used against immigrants since the 19th century. "Language vigilantes," is a term that Steven Bender coined to describe non-government individuals seeking to maintain English as the dominant U.S. language (Soltero, 2006, p. 193). In this author's (MacDonald) personal experience, language vigilantes have spit, screamed, and used other humiliating tactics against her and family members to attempt to maintain control over a changing world. In terms of language, the battle between assimilation and cultural plurality is likely to continue.

Family and Gender

The concept of familism, a "defining feature" (Baca Zinn & Kelly, 2005) of Latino communities is one that is best captured visually. Imagine watching a Cuban family on the beach near Hialeah, Florida, roasting *un lechón* (suckling pig) during the winter holidays. The *abuelitas* and *abuelitos* (grandmothers and grandfathers) sit in the shade of the palm trees watching their grandchildren. Their grandsons lugged heavy pots of black beans and rice from the car to the picnic site, after the beans were soaked overnight and cooked appropriately slowly. Cuban-born abuelitas scold their granddaughters for darkening themselves in the sun *casi desnudas* (almost naked) in their string bikinis and not subscribing to notions of Whiteness. The daughters born in Cuba but brought over as young children are caught between generations of *costumbres* (customs) frozen in time from 1950s Havana, which their mothers maintain, and that of their American-born daughters who are accused of permitting their daughters to mix too freely with the *Americano* boys. As cultural guardians of *la familia*, the mothers are expected to maintain traditions, particularly the purity of their daughters (Suárez-Orozco & Suárez-Orozco, 2001, p. 78). Gender-segregated, fathers sit with their brothers, uncles, and *compadres* (coparents) swapping stories of local successes and politics. Names of friends or other relatives who can find their *hijos* (sons) summer jobs are exchanged, reinforcing kin and social networks. In this portrait, aspects of Latino familism are captured. Familism is defined as the subordination of individual interests and needs to the family. Sociologist Maxine Baca Zinn has identified at least four major characteristics of Latino familism, while also pointing out how transnationalism, undocumented status, economic status, and immigration have reshaped traditional stereotypes of patriarchal "macho" Latino families. In particular, the employment of Latinas outside of the home in the United States and the increase of single-headed female households in the United States have lessened traditional patriarchal gender relations (Hondagneu-Sotela, 2004). Large family size is a primary characteristic of Latino familism. Among immigrant and second generation Latino households, average family size and fertility rates are higher than both Whites and African Americans (Tienda & Mitchell, 2006b). Multigenerational or extended households are a second characteristic of Latino familism. As illustrated in the above sketch and confirmed by demographers and economists, Latinos often live with extended family members, a feature that both reinforces family networks and also contributes to economic strength of the family through pooled incomes (Pessar, 2007; Tienda & Mitchell, 2006b). Third, family solidarity and loyalty to *la familia* is an ethic that is passed down from generation to generation, often through well-respected *dichos* (sayings) and *consejos* (advice). Kin networks are not only a source of economic utility, as seen in migration streams, with family members arriving first establishing a base for later family members to find housing and employment, but also they "operate as systems of cultural, emotional, and mental support" (Baca Zinn & Kelly, 2005, p. 94). Fourth, the system of *compadrazgo* (godparenting and coparenting) is a central feature of many Latino families. Godparents, often appointed at the time of baptism, are "fictive kin" with serious roles in guiding the child to adulthood and creating larger and intertwined networks between families with and without blood ties (Baca Zinn & Kelly, 2005, p. 94). Latino *familias* are a source of strength and pride to the Latino community and have cushioned the often difficult transitions from either another culture or from the home culture to that of the dominant Anglo world.

Contemporary Status of Latinos in the United States

During the Cold War 1960s, film director Norman Jewison won several awards for his comedic farce *The Russians are Coming! The Russians are Coming!* In this 1966 film, a small New England town is thrown into panic by the arrival of crew members from a Russian submarine which has accidentally run aground. I (MacDonald) am often reminded of this film, but with a new twist, "The Latinos Are Coming! The Latinos Are Coming!" The U.S. census predictions for Latino growth during the last two censuses of 1990 and 2000 actually underestimated Latino growth which had doubled between 1970 and 1990 and again between 1990 and 2000, largely fueled by high fertility rates among the second generation and continuing immigration. Current U.S. Census projections for 2050 continue to place the Hispanic population (not including Puerto Rico) at one-quarter of the U.S. population or nearly 103 million, an increase from the current (2007) enumeration of 45 million (U.S. Census Bureau, 2008). The fears over Latino population growth and so-called "illegal aliens"—similar to the alarmist fears over Russians invading during the Cold War—has operated in historical amnesia. As historians Joel Perlmann (2005) and Nancy Foner (2005) point out, during previous cycles of immigration to the United States, similar unfounded concerns over a lack of assimilation, connection to the homeland, and, in the post 9/11 world, terrorism and national security threats have resulted. Some Latino groups continue to learn English, access educational and economic resources, and generational mobility continues to be evident for most Latino populations, despite fears that a Latino "underclass" is being created as second generation Latinos assimilate into a segmented societal structure (Portes & Rumbaut, 2001). Transnationalism, technology, and the media have changed much of the contexts for current Latinos, permitting economic and social exchange between the homeland and the United States, impermissible to previous generations. Hundreds of Spanish-language newspapers, programs, and even favorite homeland *telenovelas* can still be enjoyed through the extensive provision of Spanish-language media. The 2008 Fox Searchlight/ Weinstein film *La Misma Luna* (*Under the Same Moon*) surprised its producers as mostly Hispanic audiences filled cineplexes for its opening weekend, netting the film the most money for any Spanish-language film in the United States. Films depicting the Hispanic immigrant experience are ripe for an audience that seeks affirmation of their stories and experiences (Keegan, 2008). Latinos continue to examine and suggest the role of the United States in a global society within and outside of its borders. Furthermore, mass media highlights the diversity amongst Latinos and their creative role in defining "Americaness." Drawing from Flores & Benmayor (1997), "Latino cultural citizenship" rearranges and extends the real and symbolic borders of the dominant portrait of "America." Situated within the culture wars, the fear of losing one type of exclusionary America is replaced by celebrating the historical corpus which is: the many faces and experiences of nationhood.

The natural desire to seek a better life will likely not stop the influx of Latino peoples. In fact, the *United States of the Americas* will develop naturally, even when the power-based oratory attempts to define another story. History tells us that regardless of the posture in the immigration debate, the cultural mosaic of communities on both sides of the conversation will continue to be impacted. Latinos continue to develop shifting identities as American society evolves over time. A panethnic Latino identity is constructed from Hispanics descended from Spanish explorers of the sixteenth and seventeenth centuries in New Mexico, with urban Dominican newcomers to New York City. Today, even the relatively recent dominance of Puerto Ricans in New York City is being replaced by rural Mexican immigrant newcomers (Bergad, 2005; Zuñiga & Hernández-León, 2005). Utilizing panethnicity and cross-generational alliances to protect language, employment, and citizenship rights will be the challenge and requisite of Latino integration. Tapping into the large numbers of Latinos will likely create more political clout at the local, state, and national levels. Presently, prominent figures such as Governor Bill Richardson of New Mexico and Senator Mel Martinez of Florida are among the most notable Latino politicians. Today, total assimilation is no longer a practical necessity. Many Latinos are in ideological alignment with the claim of cultural theorist, Homi K. Bhabha (1993), that "the time for 'assimilating' minorities to holistic and organic notions of cultural value has dramatically passed" (p. 193). A drive through certain sections of New York City, Los Angeles, and Miami illustrates the point quite well as Latino-centered businesses, the predominance of the public use of Spanish, and other Latino cultural forces are immersed within a vibrant and somewhat postmodern extension of what it means to participate in the mainstream society. In this way, intra-group negotiations interact with tradition and modernity, simultaneously, influencing the dynamic ontological center of the Latino experience in the United States. Still though, public officials like Sheriff Joe Arapaio in Phoenix, Arizona, terrorize Latino communities with a racialized tone that resembles the discourse of fascist governments of years past. His relentless pursuit of undocumented immigrants spills over to large questions about how Latinos are imagined in U.S. society. There are many struggles and battles to be fought and many historical lessons to learn from. The future is at once promising and layered with challenges that require a pooling of the immense resources that are available to the omnipresent Latino community.

Note

1. We are utilizing the definition of "New Latinos" adopted by the Pew Hispanic Center (Kochhar, Suro, & Tafoya, 2005) which include Dominicans, Central Americans, and South Americans.

References

Acosta-Belén, E., & Santiago, C. E. (2006). *Puerto Ricans in the United States: A contemporary portrait.* Boulder, CO: Lynne Rienner.

Anzaldua, G. (1999). *Borderlands, La Frontera: The new Mestiza.* San Francisco: Aunt Lute.

August, D., & Hakuta, K. (1998). *Educating language-minority children.* Commission on Behavioral and Social Sciences and Education. National Research Council. Institute of Medicine. Washington, DC: National Academy Press.

Baca Zinn, M., & Kelly, E. B. (2005). Familia. In S. Obeler & D. J. González (Eds.), *The Oxford Encyclopedia of Latinos and Latinas in the United States* (pp. 87–95). New York: Oxford University Press.

Bakhtin, M. M. (1981).*The dialogic imagination: Four essays* (M. Holquist, Ed., C. Emerson & M. Holquist, Trans.). Austin: University of Texas Press.

Bhabha, H. K. (1993). The postcolonial and the postmodern: The question of agency. In S. During (Ed.), *The cultural studies reader* (5th ed., pp. 189–208). London: Routledge.

Bender, S. W. (2003). *Greasers and gringos: Latinos, law, and the American imagination.* New York: New York University Press.

Bergad, L. W. (2005). Mexicans in New York City, 1990–2005. Center for Latin American, Caribbean, and Latino Studies, The Graduate Center, The City University of New York. Retrieved on July 23, 2008, from http://web.gc.cuny.edu/lastudies

Chinchilla, N. S., & Hamilton, N. (2004). Central American immigrants: Diverse populations, changing communities. In D. G. Gutierrez (Ed.), *The Columbia history of Latinos in the United States since 1960* (pp. 187–228). New York: Columbia University Press.

Crawford, J. (2004). *Educating English learners: Language diversity in the classroom.* Los Angeles: Bilingual Educational Services, Inc.

Crow, J. A. (1985). *Spain, the root and the flower: An interpretation of Spain and the Spanish people.* Berkeley: University of California Press.

Dávila, A. M. (2001). *Latinos, inc.: The marketing and making of a people.* Berkeley: University of California Press.

De las Casas, B. (1552/1992). *A short account of the destruction of the Indies.* Harmondsworth, UK: Penguin.

De León, A. (1983). *They called them greasers: Anglo attitudes toward Mexicans in Texas, 1821–1900.* Austin: University of Texas Press.

Del Castillo, R. G. (1990). *The Treaty of Guadalupe Hidalgo: A legacy of conflict.* Norman: University of Oklahoma Press.

Duaney, J. (2002). *The Puerto Rican nation on the move: Identities on the island and in the United States.* Chapel Hill: University of North Carolina Press.

Elliott, J. (2006). *Empires of the Atlantic world: Britain and Spain in America 1492–1830.* New Haven, CT: Yale University Press.

Flores, W. V., & Benmayor, R. (1997). Latino cultural citizenship: Claiming identity, space, and rights. Boston: Beacon Press.

Foner, N. (2005). *In a new land: A comparative view of immigration.* New York: New York University Press.

Gómez, L. (2007). *Manifest destinies: The making of the Mexican American race.* New York: New York University Press.

Gonzales, M. G. (1999). *Mexicanos: A history of Mexicans in the United States.* Bloomington: Indiana University Press.

Gonzalez, J. (2000). *Harvest of empire: A History of Latinos in America.* New York: Viking Press.

Guarnizo, L. E., & Espitia, M. (2007). Colombia. In M. C. Waters & R. Ueda (Eds.), *The new Americans: A guide to immigration since 1965* (pp. 371–385). Cambridge, MA: Harvard University Press.

Guthrie, W. (1997). This land is your land. On This Land is Your Land – Asch Recordings, Vol. 1 [CD]. Washington, DC: Smithsonian/Folkways.

Hernandez-Truyol, B. E. (1998). Natives and newcomers. In R. Delgado & J. Stefancic (Eds.), *The Latino condition: A critical reader* (pp. 125–132). New York: New York University Press.

Holmes, O. W. (1894). *The Oliver Wendell Holmes Year Book.* Cambridge, UK: The Riverside Press.

Hondagneu-Sotela, P. (2004). Gender and the Latino experience in late-twentieth century America. In D. G. Gutiérrez (Ed.), *The Columbia history of Latinos in the United States since 1960* (pp. 281–302). New York: Columbia University Press.

Horsman, R. (1981). *Race and manifest destiny: The origins of American racial Anglo-Saxonism.* Cambridge, MA: Harvard University Press.

Katz, M. B., Stern, M. J., & Fader, J. J. (2007). The Mexican immigration debate: The view from history. *Social Science History, 31,* 57–189.

Kaushal, N., Reimers, C. W., & Reimers, D. M. (2007). Immigrants and the economy. In M. C. Waters & R. Ueda (Eds.), *The new Americans: A guide to immigration since 1965* (pp. 176–188). Cambridge, MA: Harvard University Press.

Keegan, R. W. (2008, March 28). A Hispanic hit at the cineplex. *Time.* Retrieved on July 23, 2008, from http://www.com/time/printout/o,8816,1726377,00.html

Kochhar, R., Suro, R., & Tafoya, S. (2005). The New Latino south: The Context and consequences of rapid population growth. *Pew Hispanic Center.* Retrieved January 5, 2008, from http://pewhispanic.org/files/reports/50.pdf

LaRosa, M., & Ingwersen, L.R. (2007). U.S. immigration policies in historic context: A Latin American case study. In M. LaRosa & F. O. Mora (Eds.), *Neighborly adversaries: Readings in U.S.-Latin American relations* (2nd ed., pp. 249–269). Lanham, MD: Rowman & Littlefield.

Logan, J. R. (2007). Settlement patterns in metropolitan America. In M. C. Waters & R. Ueda (Eds.), *The new Americans: A guide to immigration since 1965* (pp. 83–97). Cambridge, MA: Harvard University Press.

MacDonald, V. M. (2004). *Latino education in the United States: A narrated history, 1513–2000.* New York: Palgrave/Macmillan.

MacDonald, V. M., & Zoppi, I. (2007). *When the minority is the majority: First generation Latino immi-*

grant parents and youth in African American schools. Paper presented at the meeting of the American Educational Research, San Francisco, CA.

Macedo, D, Bessie, D., & Panayota, G. (2003). *The hegemony of English*. Boulder, CO: Paradigm.

Marrow, H. B. (2007). South America: Ecuador, Peru, Brazil, Argentina, Venezuela. In M. C. Waters & R. Ueda (Eds.), *The new Americans: A guide to immigration since 1965* (pp. 593–611). Cambridge, MA: Harvard University Press.

Massey, D. S., Duran, J., & Malone, N. (2002). *Beyond smoke and mirrors: Mexican immigration in an era of economic integration*. New York: Russell Sage Foundation.

May, S. (2001). *Language and minority rights: Ethnicity, nationalism and the politics of language*. Harlow, UK: Pearson Education.

Meier, M. S., & Ribera, F. (1972/1993). *Mexican Americans/American Mexicans: From Conquistadors to Chicanos* (rev. ed.). New York: Hill & Wang.

Menchaca, M. (2001). *Recovering history, constructing race: The Indian, Black, and White roots of Mexican Americans*. Austin: University of Texas Press.

Morawska, E. (2007). Transnationalism. In M. C. Waters & R. Ueda (Eds.), *The new Americans: A guide to immigration since 1965* (pp.149–163). Cambridge, MA: Harvard University Press.

Morín, J. L. (2005). *Latino/a rights and justice in the United States: Perspectives and approaches*. Durham, NC: Carolina Academic Press.

Nazario, S. (2006). *Enrique's Journey: The story of a boy's dangerous odyssey to reunite with his mother*. New York: Random House.

Ngai, J. J. (2004). *Impossible subjects: Illegal aliens and the making of modern America*. Princeton, NJ: Princeton University Press.

Nieto-Phillips, J. M. (2004).*The language of blood: The making of Spanish American identity in New Mexico, 1850–1940*. Albuquerque: University of New Mexico Press.

Paz, O. (1985). *The labyrinth of solitude and other writings*. New York: Grove Press.

Pérez, L. (2007). Cuba. In M. C. Waters & R. Ueda (Eds.), *The new Americans: A guide to immigration since 1965* (pp. 386–98). Cambridge, MA: Harvard University Press.

Perlmann, J. (2005). *Italians then, Mexicans now: Immigrant origins and second-generation progress, 1890–2000*. New York and Annandale-on-Hudson, NY: Russell Sage Foundation/Levy Economics Institute of Bard College.

Pessar, P. R . (2007). Gender and family. In M. C. Waters & R. Ueda (Eds.), *The new Americans: A guide to immigration since 1965* (pp. 258–269). Cambridge, MA: Harvard University Press.

Pitt, L. (1999). *Decline of the Californios: A social history of the Spanish-speaking Californians, 1846–1890*. Berkeley: University of California Press.

Pitti, S. J. (2003). *The devil in Silicon Valley: Northern California, race, and Mexican Americans*. Princeton, NJ: Princeton University Press.

Portes, A. (1997). Immigration theory for a new century: Some problems and opportunities. *International Migration Review, 31*(4), 799–825.

Portes, A., & Rumbaut, R. G. (2001). *Legacies: The story of the immigrant second generation*. Berkeley and New York: University of California Press and Russell Sage Foundation.

Portes, A., & Stepick, S. (1993). *City on the Edge: The Transformation of Miami*. Berkeley: University of California Press.

Powell, P. W. (1971). *Tree of hate: Propaganda and prejudices affecting United States relations with the Hispanic world*. New York: Basic Books.

Riggen, P. (Director & Producer). (2007). *Under the Same Moon (La Misma Luna)* [Motion picture]. United States: Fox Searchlight.

Rivera Ramos, E. (2005). Jones Act. In S. Oboler & D. González (Eds.), *The Oxford encyclopedia of Latinos & Latinas in the United States. Vol. 2* (pp. 425–427). New York: Oxford University Press.

Rodriguez, G. (2007). *Mongrels, bastards, orphans, and vagabonds: Mexican immigration and the future of race in America*. New York: Pantheon Books.

Rodriguez, R. (2001). *Brown: The last discovery of America*. New York: Viking Penguin.

Rosales, F. A. 1996. *Chicano! The history of the Mexican American civil rights movement*. Houston, TX: Arte Público Press.

Ruíz, V. (2006). Nuestra America: Latino history in the United States. *Journal of American History, 93*(3), 1–18.

Santiago-Irizarry, V., & Cabán, P. (2005). Puerto Ricans. In S. Oboler & D. González (Eds.), *The Oxford Encyclopedia of Latinos & Latinas in the United States* (Vol. 2, pp. 506–515). New York: Oxford University Press.

Santiago-Valles, K. A. (1994). *"Subject people" and colonial discourses: Economic transformation and social disorder in Puerto Rico, 1898–1947.* Albany: State University of New York Press.

Santiago-Valles, K. A., & Jiménez-Muñoz, G. M. (2004). Social polarization and colonized labor: Puerto Ricans in the United Status, 1945–2000. In D. G. Gutiérrez (Ed.), *The Columbia history of Latinos in the United States since 1960* (pp. 87–145). New York: Columbia University Press.

Soltero, C. R. (2006). *Latinos and American law: Landmark Supreme Court cases.* Austin: University of Texas Press.

Stavans, I. (2004). *Spanglish: The making of a new American language.* New York: HarperCollins.

Stevens-Arroyo, A. M. (2004). From barrios to barricades: Religion and religiosity in Latino life. In D. G. Gutiérrez (Ed.), *The Columbia history of Latinos in the United States since 1960* (pp. 303–354). New York: Columbia University Press.

Straus, E. (2006). *The making of an American school crisis: Compton, CA and the death of the suburban dream* (Doctoral dissertation, Brandeis University, 2006). *Dissertation Abstracts International* (AAT 3232880).

Suárez-Orozco, M., & Suárez-Orozco, C. (2001). *Children of immigration.* Cambridge: Harvard University Press.

Suárez-Orozco, M., & Páez, M. M. (Eds.). (2002). *Latinos remaking America.* Berkeley: University of California Press and the David Rockefeller Center for Latin American Studies, Harvard University.

Suro, R. (2002). Counting the 'Other Hispanics': How many Colombians, Dominicans, Ecuadorians, Guatemalans, & Salvadorans are there in the U.S.? *Pew Hispanic Center Report.* May 9, 2002. Retrieved January 7, 2008, from http://pewhispanic.org/files/reports/8.pdf

Suro, R. (2006). Foreword. In M. Rivas-Rodriguez, J. Torres, M. Dipiero-D'sa, & L. Fitzpatrick (Eds.), *A legacy greater than words: Stories of U.S. Latinos & Latinas of the World War II generation* (pp. xi–xii). The Latino & Latina Oral History Project Group. Austin: University of Texas Press.

Tienda, M., & Mitchell, F. (2006a). *Hispanics and the future of America.* Committee on Population. Division of Behavioral and Social Sciences and Education. National Research Council. Washington, DC: The National Academies Press.

Tienda, M., & Mitchell, F. (2006b). *Multiple origins, uncertain destinies: Hispanics and the American future.* Committee on Population Division of Behavioral and Social Sciences and Education. National Research Council. Washington, DC: The National Academies Press.

Torre, C. A., Vencchini, H. R., & Burgos, W. (Eds.). (1994). *The commuter nation: Perspectives on Puerto Rican migration.* Rio Piedras, Puerto Rico: Editorial de la Universidad de Puerto Rico.

United States Bureau of the Census. (2008). Table 3 – Annual estimates of the population by sex, race, and Hispanic origin for the United States: April 1, 2000 to July 1, 2007 (Report No. NC-EST2007-03). Washington, DC: United States Bureau of the Census, Population Division.

Valdes, G. (1998). The world outside and inside schools: Language and immigrant children. *Educational Researcher, 27*(6), 4–18.

Valenzuela, A. (1999). *Subtractive schooling: U.S. Mexican youth and the politics of caring.* Albany: State University of New York Press.

Weber, D. (1979). Scarce more than apes: Historical roots of Anglo American stereotypes of Mexicans in the border region. In D. Weber (Ed.), *New Spain's far northern frontier: Essays on Spain in the American west, 1540–1821* (pp. 295–307). Albuquerque: University of New Mexico Press.

Weber, D. (1992). *The Spanish frontier in northern New Spain.* New Haven, CT: Yale University Press.

Wortham, S., Murillo, E. G., & Hamman, T. E. (2002). Education and policy in the New Latino diaspora. In S. Wortham, E. G. Murillo, & T. E. Hamman (Eds.), *Education in the New Latino diaspora: Policy and the politics of identity* (pp. 1–16). Westport, CT: Ablex.

Zuñiga, V., & Hernández-León (Eds.). (2005). *New destinations: Mexican immigration in the United States.* New York: Russell Sage Foundation.

3 Latino Education in Twentieth-Century America

A Brief History

Guadalupe San Miguel, Jr.
University of Houston

Rubén Donato
University of Colorado at Boulder

Introduction

This chapter discusses and explains the evolution of Latino education in the United States from the 1890s to the present. It examines, in broad strokes, the growth of Latinos over the twentieth century and the ways in which they have impacted and been impacted by education.

Although we use the term "Latino" as an umbrella group for several nationality groups whose country of origin is in the Spanish-speaking countries of Mexico, Central America, the Caribbean, and South America, the literature generally refers to the history and educational experiences of mostly Mexicans and, to some extent, Puerto Ricans. Occasionally, the literature describes the educational experiences of Cubans, especially those residing in Miami-Dade County, Florida, after 1959. The experiences of Central and South Americans, the most recent Latino groups to come to the United States, have not yet been written. Within this context then much of our historical analysis of Latino education will focus on Mexican Americans, Puerto Ricans and, to some extent, Cuban Americans.

The term "ethnic Mexicans" will be used to refer to all individuals of Mexican origin, whether they were citizens or not. Other terms such as "Mexicans" and "Mexican Americans" will also be used interchangeably with ethnic Mexicans. In a few cases, special terms such as "Hispano" or "Spanish American," labels utilized by Mexican origin individuals in New Mexico and Colorado, will be used, especially if we make reference to their history and to their educational experiences. The term "Anglo" will be used to refer to white Americans of European descent.

We argue that during the twentieth century education was both an instrument of reproduction and an important site of contestation.[1] With respect to the former, education, in all of its forms, served to reproduce a highly stratified society aimed at ensuring the political and cultural hegemony of the dominant Anglo group in the society and the socioeconomic subordination of Latinos. Education also was a site of contestation as reflected in the actions taken by Latinos. These individuals did not passively accept their educational fates and either resisted, subverted, or accommodated the marginalization and conformist intentions of this education. Latinos, likewise, sought to use education to promote their own identities and to improve their socioeconomic status in American society. The result has been many decades of conflict and tensions in the educational arena.

Latinos and the Expansion of Public Education, 1898–1960: Changes in the Latino Population

The Latino population increased and became more diverse during the twentieth century. Prior to 1890, three groups of Latinos, for the most part, resided in the United States—Mexicans,

Cubans, and Puerto Ricans. The largest of these groups were the Mexicans and most of them lived in the American Southwest. Over 100,000 Mexicans lived in the United States by the turn of the twentieth century.[2] Next in importance with respect to size of population were the Cubans, then the Puerto Ricans. Cubans comprised a small but significant group of political exiles, entrepreneurs, and tobacco workers. By 1900, approximately 20,000 had immigrated to the United States. The majority lived in Florida. Puerto Ricans, although extremely few—less than 500—were comprised of political exiles, enterprising entrepreneurs, a handful of students and both field hands and factory workers who migrated from the *campos* and *pueblos* of Puerto Rico to northern U.S. cities and other parts of the United States.[3]

The size of these three groups grew during the twentieth century but at varying rates and at different points in time. Cuban migration fluctuated and trickled in between 1899 and 1958.[4] Cuban immigrants came to the United States before 1960 because of employment opportunities. Many of them left after several years, but a significant number settled in the United States, mostly in south Florida.[5]

Puerto Rican migration also increased during these years. It began as a trickle in the early part of the twentieth century and soon grew into a large wave after the Second World War. American citizenship was granted to Puerto Ricans in 1917; in later years, cheap airfares and aggressive recruitment by agribusiness and industrial interests contributed to their emigration to the United States.[6] Puerto Ricans settled on the East Coast, the Midwest, and Hawaii.[7] Most of them, however, chose New York City.[8]

The number of Mexicans, unlike Puerto Ricans and Cubans, increased dramatically during the twentieth century. They came in waves. Over one million Mexicans came to the United States during the first major wave from the 1890s to 1930. This wave was temporarily halted during the Great Depression and for a brief period a reverse migration occurred because of repatriation. Approximately 460,000 Mexicans were repatriated and sent to Mexico from 1929 to 1937.[9] The next wave came from 1941 to 1964. Prompted by the labor shortage during the Second World War, Mexicans came with papers (legally), without papers (undocumented), and as *braceros* or temporary contract/guest workers. Over six million immigrants with documents and an unknown number without documents came during this period.[10]

Mexicans came for many reasons—to work in the developing industries of the United States, to escape the ravages of the Mexican Revolution from 1910 to 1920, and to search for better lives. Moreover, aggressive recruitment efforts by American agricultural and industrial interests, rapid economic development in the country, and changes in immigration policy also encouraged transnational migration of Mexican workers.[11]

Mexicans historically had settled in the border areas of the Southwest, but during the twentieth century they moved out of these traditional areas to other parts of the Southwest, the Midwest, and the Pacific Northwest.[12]

Latinos in the United States were diverse in many ways and, among other things, had distinct histories of race, class, and culture. Prior to 1900, the Cuban population were larger than the Puerto Rican population. Between 1900 and 1960, the Puerto Rican population exploded. Thus, by 1960, while there were three Latino groups in the United States, the two largest were Mexicans and Puerto Ricans. These groups tended to share certain social, economic, political, and cultural characteristics. They were politically powerless, economically impoverished, occupationally concentrated in unskilled and semi-skilled jobs, and socially alienated and discriminated by the dominant society.[13]

Cubans shared many cultural and linguistic similarities with Mexicans and Puerto Ricans, but they were socially and economically distinct and numerically small during this period. Their numbers did not increase significantly until after 1959.[14]

Patterns of Latino Education in the United States

The subordinate and culturally distinct positions of Mexicans and Puerto Ricans posed significant challenges for public schools over the decades. Schools, for the most part, were unable and unwilling to meet these challenges. They ignored their multiple needs or else, because of assimilationist ideology and deficit perspectives, interpreted them in such a way that the differences brought by these children had to be eliminated.[15] In many cases, the schools responded not to the genuine needs of this diverse group of children but to those of other stronger political and economic interests who sought to use schools as instruments of cultural conformity and of social and economic subordination.[16]

The history of these two groups indicates that schools served a reproductive function and sought to ensure that they remained a subordinate group by providing them with only limited access to separate, inferior, subtractive and non-academic instruction. The patterns of Mexican American and Puerto Rican public education reflected these marginalization and conformist intentions.

Community Exclusion from Power

One of the most important patterns of Latino education to emerge during this period was that of community exclusion from power. When public education originated in the second half of the nineteenth century, Latinos were provided with varying degrees of inclusion in important decision-making positions in teaching and in the governance and administration of the schools. For example, in the 1873–1874 school year, Hispanos comprised 77 percent of the total number of county superintendents in the New Mexico territory. Two decades later they comprised less than 33 percent of the county superintendents. By 1930, their numbers became insignificant. One of the last superintendents was Nina Otero Warren, who administered the Santa Fe County Schools from 1919 to 1929.[17] By the second quarter of the 1900s, for all intents and purposes, Latinos were absent from important positions of power in education.[18]

The pattern of structural exclusion continued in the post-World War II era as a growing number of Latinos asserted themselves and fought for increased access to these types of positions. Greater representation of Latinos in education did not increase appreciably until after the 1960s.

A few exceptions to the general pattern of community exclusion from the structures of power in education existed in the twentieth century, e.g., there were the instances of community control of the schools in several small communities in southern Colorado and in at least one rural district in West Texas.[19]

Inequitable Student Access

Latino students, unlike community members, were not excluded from the education process. Most pre-college age students were provided with access to pubic education, but two major groups of students continued to be out of school during the first half of the twentieth century—the children of agricultural workers and secondary school age youth.[20]

College age students, on the other hand, were only provided limited and inequitable access to institutions of higher learning, although there were no laws that prevented Latinos from attending them. Less than 5 percent of Latino students were enrolled in higher education during these years.[21]

In a few cases, political and school leaders took affirmative steps to increase Latino access to higher education. In the Southwest, for instance, political leaders and community activists established a university aimed at attracting Latino students from the rural parts of the state or else encouraged members from the community to attend a few select institutions in their local areas.[22] Among the institutions encouraging and allowing large numbers of Hispano students to enroll were New Mexico Highlands University, Western New Mexico University, Northern New Mexico Normal, New Mexico State University, and Adams State College in Southern Colorado. Significant numbers of Hispanos also were encouraged and did attend religious institutions such as St Josephs College and St Michaels College in New Mexico.[23]

On the East Coast, a few universities recruited Cuban teachers and college age youth in the years from 1899 to 1901.[24] American universities also actively recruited students from the island of Puerto Rico during the years from 1903 to 1907. Several thousand Cubans and over 500 Puerto Rican students successfully enrolled in these institutions during these years.[25]

These efforts were relatively successful in increasing Cuban and Puerto Rican access to higher education in these years, but the mixed-race population posed dilemmas for host U.S. institutions during an era of racial segregation. Afro-Cubans and dark-skinned Puerto Ricans were not allowed to enroll in white institutions but were welcomed by historically Black Colleges such as Hampton and Tuskegee.[26]

Separate and Unequal Education

Although some Latino students attended integrated schools, the majority enrolled in separate classrooms or separate school facilities. The phenomenon of Latino school segregation, mostly confined to Mexican Americans, originated in the middle part of the nineteenth century, but, between 1890 and 1960, it expanded significantly to other parts of the country. Segregation was confined to the elementary grades from 1890 to the 1920s.[27] It expanded to the secondary grades as early as the mid-1920s largely due to the growth in the Mexican school-age population.

State officials played an important role in the expansion of school segregation by sanctioning its presence and by funding local requests for increased segregation. Residential segregation, demographic shifts in the population, and economic conditions likewise greatly impacted the expansion of segregation in the twentieth century.[28]

School segregation increased, although no legal statutes mandated such isolation, as was the case with African Americans and other racial minority groups.[29] Local authorities used a variety of administrative means to establish these schools and developed several reasons for segregating Mexican children. Some argued that these children had lice, were dirty, or were irregular in attendance because of migration. Others noted that segregation was necessary because they were racially and culturally inferior to white children. Others still argued that Mexican children slowed instruction of English speakers and had a language handicap.[30]

Segregated schools were in many respects unequal to those provided for Anglo children. These schools generally were older than those for Anglos, their school equipment was generally less adequate, and per pupil expenditures extremely low.[31]

The unequal nature of public education for Latinos also was reflected in other measures, especially teacher standards. For the most part, the staff of these schools was less appropriately trained, qualified, and experienced than that of Anglo schools. In many cases, the teachers were sent to the segregated schools as a form of punishment or to introduce them to the teaching profession. Once their punishment was over or once they became expert teachers, they tended to leave these segregated schools.[32]

Not all schools were inferior and substandard. A few of them were equal in many respects to those found in Anglo communities. In 1946, however, the federal courts in the *Mendez vs. Westminster School District* case found that separate but equal facilities were inherently unequal because they denied these children social equality and because segregation fostered antagonisms and inferiority where none existed.[33]

Institutional Treatment: The Advent of Administrative Bias

Another pattern of Latino education dealt with institutional treatment in general and with administrative bias in particular. Mexican and Puerto Rican children were institutionally mistreated in these schools.

In the early part of the twentieth century, Latino children were classified as intellectually inferior on the basis of biased intelligence tests scores. In most cases, Latinos, like other racial and ethnic immigrant children, scored relatively low on intelligence tests and lower than Anglo students. Scholars interpreted these test scores as indicative of their innate abilities.[34] After the Second World War, testing expanded to include not only intelligence but language and aptitude. Latinos continued to score low on standardized tests. In this period, however, scholars abandoned the genetic interpretation of test scores and replaced it with one based on cultural attributes and behaviors.[35]

Educators used these biased test score results to classify Latino children, mostly Mexican and Puerto Rican, into one of at least four categories—educationally mentally retarded (EMR), slow, regular, or gifted. Because of their low test scores, Latino children, for the most part, were classified as either EMR or slow.[36]

Once Latino children were classified in this manner, they were systematically placed in so-called "developmentally-appropriate" instructional groups, classes or curricular tracks. These curricular tracks were comprised of all other children with similar abilities. At the elementary level, Latino children were assigned to mostly slow-learning or non-academic classes. At the secondary level (junior and high schools), administrators assigned them to non-academic classes, most of which were either vocational or general education courses. Once placed in a curricular track, students generally remained there until they graduated from high school or until they dropped out.[37]

Mexican and Puerto Rican students also were mistreated by teachers and other students. Teachers, for the most part, were insensitive or oblivious to the cultural and special educational needs of Latinos. Although some of these teachers were caring instructors, the majority had low expectations for them and, at times unwittingly, ridiculed them for their culturally distinctive traits. Many Latino children were punished simply for speaking Spanish at school or in the classroom. In some integrated classes, teachers interacted with Anglo students more and had less praise for Latino children.[38]

The peers of Latino students likewise mistreated and ostracized them over time. A quote from one of Paul Taylor's many studies of Mexicans in the 1920s illustrates what he called the severe "hazing" Anglo children subjected these students. "Some Americans don't like to talk to me," said one Latino youth in 1929. "I sat by one in high school auditorium and he moved away. Oh my God, it made me feel ashamed. I felt like walking out of school."[39]

The policies, procedures, and practices utilized by school administrators, teachers, and students served to stratify the student population according to various categories and to reproduce the existing relations of domination in the classroom. They also served to deprive Latinos of opportunities for success.

Curriculum

Another pattern of Latino education dealt with the curriculum and with both the lack of academic rigor and its subtractive character. Simply stated, this pattern indicated that during the twentieth century the curriculum for Latino children became increasingly imbalanced, that is, it began to emphasize non-academic instruction at the expense of academic learning. The academic curriculum either was diluted in an effort to make it more practical and utilitarian or else it decreased as a result of the introduction of more practical courses, especially vocational and general education classes.[40]

In a few cases, vocational education served as a means of upward mobility for Latino students but this was rare. The majority of secondary school students were provided more non-academic instruction and trained for low or semi-skilled jobs and minimal participation in American society.[41]

The curriculum also became linguistically and culturally subtractive. By subtractive we mean that the curriculum constantly devalued, demeaned, and distorted the children's linguistic and cultural heritage and systematically sought to eradicate it from the content and instruction of public education.[42] The latter was reflected in the campaign against diversity that emerged in the late nineteenth and early twentieth centuries. This campaign, in part, led to the establishment of English only policies throughout the nation and to the development of no Spanish-speaking practices found in most public school systems with significant numbers of Latino students.[43]

The campaign against diversity also led to the devaluation of the Mexican cultural and historical heritage in the schools and to its exclusion.[44] The devaluation of the cultural heritage was apparent in Americanization programs established for these children and in the attitudes of public school teachers, administrators, and staff towards Mexican culture in the schools. The exclusion and distortion of the Mexican heritage was apparent in the schools curricular textbooks and instructional materials.[45]

In sum, curricular, instructional, and language policies were aimed at meeting the subtractive, i.e., assimilationist and cultural conformist intentions of the public schools.

Performance

Except for Cuban Americans, the historiography of education suggests that the history of Latino academic performance has been solely one of unprecedented underachievement. We refute this myth and suggest a more diverse pattern of school performance for Mexicans and Puerto Ricans. These children had a checkered pattern of academic performance, not merely one of underachievement. This pattern was characterized by a dominant tradition of underachievement and a minor one of school success.

Contrary to popular opinion, then, a small but increasing number of Mexicans, Hispanos, and Puerto Ricans experienced school success. These experiences complemented the historic pattern of academic success common among Cubans in the United States.[46] Two distinct groups comprised the achievers in the Latino community during these years—those who completed secondary school and those who got a college education.[47] These students experienced a pattern of school success, not academic failure. They were the unsung heroines and heroes of their respective Latino communities.[48]

Despite this pattern of success, most scholars have only focused on documenting and explaining the tradition of underachievement, probably because it was the dominant trend in the Latino school population.[49]

The consequences of this dominant tradition in school performance led to limited economic mobility, stunted political participation, and restricted social development. In other words, it led to the continued marginalization and subordination of the growing Latino population.

Emerging Forms of Latino Responses

The use of schools for cultural conformity and for social and economic subordination by dominant groups led to the emergence of a complex pattern of contestation and adaptation within the Latino community. We want to underscore that ethnic Mexicans and Puerto Ricans did not passively accept these policies and practices. Before the civil rights era of the 1960s and 1970s, Latinos responded in number of ways. Their responses were reflected in five major strategies.

Encourage Non-Public School Attendance

One of these strategies focused on supporting and encouraging their children to enroll in Catholic, Protestant, and community-based schools. In many cases, they encouraged attendance in Catholic or Protestant schools to challenge conformist intentions and inferior or exclusionary educational opportunities. They also established community-based schools to challenge cultural conformity, to undermine/subvert exclusionary mechanisms, and to improve academic achievement.[50]

In the late 1890s, for instance, ethnic Mexicans opened a community school, El Colegio Altamirano, in Hebronville, Texas, a small rural community in the southern part of the state. Its purpose was to help the community maintain its cultural identity during the era of Americanization. This school, in existence until the early 1930s, opened with an enrollment of over one hundred children and was maintained by the Mexican community of Jim Hogg County. "The Mexican colony at Hebronville," noted Jovita Gonzalez, a well-known scholar and resident of that area, "is making superhuman efforts to maintain a school, not only for its own welfare but primarily to honor the land which was given to us by the noble, liberty loving Mexican insurgents"[51]

The Mexican community founded other schools aimed at promoting ethnic identity and at challenging cultural conformity during the early twentieth century. Community activists established the Colegio Preparatorio in Laredo, Texas, in 1906 and the Escuela Particular in 1909 in Zapata County also in south Texas. In July 1910, the latter community school held a public examination and a "fiesta escolar" (school festival) for the community. An additional private school taught by Maria Renteria was opened in Laredo, Texas in 1911.[52]

Other examples of schools for cultural maintenance were the Mexican Consul-sponsored schools found in several states of the Southwest during the second half of the 1920s. The primary purposes of these schools were to oppose Americanization of Mexican children in the public schools in general and to promote their Mexicanization in particular.[53]

Promote Community Access to Power

The second major strategy focused on promoting the structural inclusion of Latinos in school governance, administration, and instruction. Although more historical research needs to be done on power and politics in the Latino community, the little we have indicates that few were elected or appointed to these positions.

One important exception to this general pattern of exclusion occurred in the San Felipe barrio of Del Rio, a small border town in West Texas. In this community, Mexican Americans established their own school district in order to ensure that they would be elected to policy-making positions and hired in the schools as administrators and teachers. Between 1929 and 1972, they had significant control of all their public schools.[54]

What occurred in Del Rio is uniquely important for two major reasons. First, it is an example of Mexican American agency in education. Second, it shows the diversity of approaches to educational equality. Instead of integration, the traditional strategy utilized by community activists to achieve equality, the residents of Del Rio pursued a strategy of self-determination

Mexican Americans and Puerto Ricans also supported the hiring of public school teachers.[55] Legislators, educators, and community activists either developed policies or pressured local school districts to recruit Latinos as teachers in the public schools and enacted legislation to increase the supply of Latino teachers.[56]

The most well-known piece of legislation was passed in New Mexico legislature in 1909. This law called for the establishment of the Spanish American Normal School in El Rito, New Mexico. This school emphasized the training of Hispano teachers for Spanish-speaking children.[57]

Promote Student Access to Education

The third strategy focused on promoting the equitable access of students to the elementary, secondary, and post-secondary grades. Latinos developed organizations and initiatives aimed at increasing enrollment in both public education and in public higher education. Promotional activities can be readily seen in the years after the Second World War. In these years, especially the 1950s, both LULAC (League of United Latin American Citizens) and American G. I. Forum engaged in back-to-school rallies, lobbied local educators to open schools for migrant and non-migrant children, supported the enrollment of Latino children in high school, and established college scholarships for older students.[58] Individuals in the Mexican American Movement (MAM) organization in California during the 1930s and 1940s also avidly promoted cultural pride, self-improvement, and a college education.[59] Government officials in Cuba and Puerto Rico, as well as community organizations on the mainland, likewise promoted the education of Cuban and Puerto Rican children in U.S. schools. This is especially the case between 1900 and 1910.[60]

Promotion of Quality Academic Instruction

Another strategy focused on the promotion of quality academic instruction. In this historical period, most of the information we have is on Anglo educators. These individuals, for the most part, rejected inferior instructional practices and promoted innovative programs or policies aimed at improving the instruction and academic achievement of Latino children. The promotion of reading reforms in the 1920s, project-based teaching in the 1940s, and pre-school English-language instruction in the 1950s, were some of the specific innovations proposed during these decades.[61]

A few educators also occasionally promoted school-wide reforms aimed at improving Latino school achievement. One of these was Lloyd Tireman. He established several community schools for Hispano children in the 1930s and early 1940s aimed at accomplishing such a goal. Despite his commitment to improving the academic achievement of Hispano children through comprehensive school reforms, several scholars have noted that he was well-intentioned but misguided in his efforts.[62]

Promotion of Pluralism

Latinos also promoted pluralist policies and practices and in doing so indirectly challenged the cultural conformity intent of public education. They promoted a linguistically inclusive curriculum. This meant that they promoted the inclusion of non-English languages, especially Spanish, in the schools. Two distinct strategies were used. One of these was legislative and aimed at challenging English only policies for the public schools and allowing the use of non-English languages as languages of instruction in them.[63] The other strategy focused on pedagogy and encouraged the use of non-English languages as either subject matter or specific methods for teaching in the schools.[64]

Latinos, particularly Mexicans, likewise promoted a more positive and dynamic view of their community's history and heritage in education than did mainstream scholars. The dominant interpretation of history in the early part of the twentieth century either omitted the presence of Latinos or portrayed them in a negative light. Some Mexican Americans did not accept these views and provided what Garza-Falcón called "counter-narratives," i.e., interpretations that countered or corrected the omissions and dominant negative images Anglos had created of Latinos as culturally monolithic, socially unstratified, and racially deficient.[65] These counternarratives indicated that ethnic Mexicans were culturally diverse, internally divided by class, religion, customs, and language, and economically and politically deprived.[66] In other words, the works mentioned by Garza-Falcón showed that Mexicans were *gente decente*, i.e., people of worth, not merely some demeaning stereotype.[67]

Contest Discrimination

A final response to education was contestation. Latino parents and community people directly confronted the issues of school discrimination and took steps to eliminate it. This led to the emergence of a concerted campaign against discrimination in public education. Scholars have referred to this as the quest for educational equality.[68]

This quest for educational equality focused on contesting at least four specific policies. First, through a variety of mediums such as community newspapers, *juntas de indignación* (indignation meetings), and conferences, Mexican Americans protested a host of discriminatory and exclusionary policies and practices.[69]

Mexican Americans also challenged the testing of Spanish-speaking children. George I. Sanchez was one of the most important scholars to lead this challenge. Sanchez provided a critique of the intelligence testing of Mexican American children and questioned the validity, results, and explanations of I.Q. tests.[70] He refuted the innate capacity or racial basis of intelligence and argued for a serious consideration of environmental and linguistic factors in interpreting test scores.[71]

The third form of discrimination they contested was unequal funding of public education. Indicative of these types of struggles were those waged by George I. Sanchez at the state level in New Mexico during the 1930s and Eleuterio Escobar in San Antonio, Texas, from the 1930s to the 1950s.[72]

Finally, Latinos, especially Mexican Americans, directly challenged school segregation. For most of the twentieth century, Latinos in the community identified school segregation as the most despicable form of discrimination practiced against Spanish-speaking children and as the major factor impeding the educational, social, and economic mobility of the community.[73]

Prior to the 1920s, the struggle against segregation was highly localized and quite sporadic. For instance, Mexican Americans conducted a few boycotts or voiced their opposition to segregation in the local Spanish-speaking media or at community-sponsored conferences.[74] In the 1930s, the struggle against segregation assumed a more systemic character as Mexican American organizations began to file lawsuits against this school practice. This movement increased after the Second World War as a growing number of ethnic Mexican organizations diversified their attack against segregation. Spurred in large part by returning veterans, these organizations filed a variety of lawsuits against segregation in different states and lobbied state authorities to issue policy statements against this practice and pressured them to investigate pervasive forms of school segregation.[75]

Although Mexican Americans won most of these lawsuits, segregation practices continued because of widespread opposition from local school officials and white communities.[76]

The 1960s and Beyond: Latino Education in the Contemporary Period: Introduction

In the contemporary period, from 1960 to the present, the Latino community experienced dramatic changes. Despite these changes, education continued to be both an instrument of reproduction and a site of contestation.

Changes in the Latino Population

The Mexican origin population in the United States increased from 3.4 million in 1960 to over 21 million in 2000. These figures do not take into consideration the millions of undocumented persons who are living and working in the United States.[77]

For most of the twentieth century Mexicans were concentrated in three major areas of the country: the Southwest, the Midwest and the Northwest. During the latter part of this century, they also began to settle in significant numbers in the southern and eastern parts of the country.[78]

The Puerto Rican population, in turn, jumped from less than 1million in 1960 to over 3.4 million four decades later. Most of the Puerto Ricans settled in the eastern and midwestern part of the United States although some were found in Hawaii.[79]

The Cuban population jumped from around 79,000 in 1960 to slightly over 1.2 million in 2000. Cubans came to the United States in four different waves. Cubans were distinct from all other Latino groups in that a significant proportion came to the United States as exiles, not as immigrants.[80] The vast majority settled in Florida, especially in Dade County.[81]

The first wave, prompted by the Cuban revolution, brought about 200,000 to the United States between 1959–1962. The second wave started in 1965 and ended around 1973. This wave took place because Fidel Castro allowed individuals already in the United States to bring those relatives who wanted to leave Cuba back with them. During 1965–1973, two out-going flights per day from Cuba to Miami brought 260,500 persons into the United States. According to Grenir and Perez, this was the largest of all the waves, but was less politically intense. The third wave occurred in 1980, and those that came are known as Marielitos because they left Cuba from the Port of Mariel. The final wave occurred in the mid-1990s. Those who came during these years were the balseros, individuals who left Cuba in home-made rafts. For some unknown reason, less attention has been given to this wave by historians.[82] Social, class, and racial differences distinguished the different waves of Cuban immigration and the various responses by government officials to their arrival, including school officials.[83]

In addition to these three groups, this United States also experienced a significant growth of Spanish-speaking immigrants from South America, Central America, and the Dominican Republic. Dominican and South American immigration increased in the 1960s. Central American immigration also began in the 1960s but experienced significant increases in the following decades.

Dominicans came to the United States in relatively small numbers. In most cases, they fled political violence instigated by the United States.[84]

South American immigration especially from Colombia also increased appreciably during the 1960s. Most of these immigrants settled in New York City.[85] Included in the group of Centarl Americans were Salvadoreños, Guatemaltecos, Nicaraguenses, and Panameños. Their total number increased from less than one half million in 1960 to several million four decades later. Political conflict, poverty, and social unrest in the home countries, as well as global economic fluctuations, and changes in U.S. immigration policies contributed to their increase.[86]

By 2000, Latinos became the largest minority group in the country. They totaled well over 35 million and comprised close to 13 percent of the total population.[87]

Despite the diversity of race, national origins, and class, the majority of Latinos were Spanish speakers, culturally distinct, and economically poor, i.e., they were a subordinate population.[88] They lived in overcrowded, substandard homes and in poor residential neighborhoods throughout the country. Many of them, especially children and women, were traumatized by political violence in their home countries and various forms of state and personal violence against them on the trip to the United States and while in the country itself. Although there has been an improvement in their social, economic, and political status over time, Latinos are and continue to be a subordinate and marginalized population in the United States and are treated as such by mainstream institutions, including public schools.

Continuities and Discontinuities in the Patterns of Latino Education

During the latter part of the twentieth and early part of the twenty-first centuries, the patterns of Latino education changed as a result of new social, economic, and political factors. These factors differentially impacted them and led to some discontinuities or slight modifications of existing patterns and to the continued or strengthening of others.

Discontinuities in Patterns

During this period, two distinct patterns were significantly changed-the pattern of structural exclusion and one aspect of the subtractive curriculum. The pattern of structural exclusion from governance, administration, and teaching was disrupted and replaced with one of token inclusion during this period. In the post-1960 years, Latinos gained increased access to important positions in all of these areas. More particularly, they were elected to the state legislatures, to state, county, and local boards of education, and to state and private university board of regents. They also were hired in increasing numbers as superintendents, principals, teachers, counselors, and faculty members. A new development in this period was their appointment or election to federal policy-making positions in Congress and in the Department of Education. Despite their increased access, Latinos continued to be severely underrepresented in all of these positions. Their inclusion, in other words, was not significant but token in nature.[89]

The token inclusion of Latinos can be observed in local school board representation, especially in major urban areas where Latinos comprise a significant proportion of the school age population. In places such as Houston, Chicago, and Los Angeles, for instance, Latino representation went from zero percent in 1960 to 22, 17, and 14 percent, respectively, in 2006. Despite this increase, Latino representation failed to keep pace with their overall percentage in the school age population. Latinos, in other words, continued to be severely underrepresented in these school districts.[90]

However, not all communities experienced token representation. Some districts saw rapid and significant change in school board representation. In some cities, such as McAllen, Laredo, Mission and Edinburg, Texas, Mexican American school board representation increased from less than 10 percent to over 80 percent between 1960 and 2000. Significant representation however was concentrated in small or rural areas containing few numbers of Spanish-speaking children.[91]

In the final analysis, however, Latino school board representation remained extremely low. National data for 2004, for instance, shows that Latinos in the early twenty-first century only comprised 3.8 percent of local school board members throughout the country. Whites and African Americans, on the other hand, represented 85.5 percent and 7.8 percent, respectively.[92]

Another pattern that underwent significant modification was the linguistically subtractive curriculum. Prior to the 1960s, Spanish and other non-English languages were excluded from the public school and constantly repressed, discouraged or devalued. This changed after the passage of the federal bilingual education act of 1968. This bill led to several important developments including the elimination of no-Spanish-speaking rules at the local school level, the repeal of English only laws throughout the country, and the passage of state bilingual education policies throughout the country. Between 1968 and 1978, for instance, over thirty-four states both repealed their English only laws and enacted bilingual education policies.[93]

The successful repeal of restrictive language policies and practices in the schools, as well as the continued growth of bilingualism in the society, led to a backlash in the 1980s and 1990s.

In this period, repressive language legislation resurfaced and became increasingly widespread. This was reflected in policies aimed at undermining, dismantling, or repealing bilingual education legislation at the national and state levels and at formulating and enacting English only policies. In states such as California, Arizona, and Massachusetts it became illegal to use Spanish and other non-English languages for the instruction of all children in the public school during the mid- and late 1990s.[94] Between 1984 and 2004, over twenty-five states enacted English-only laws.[95] Bilingual education policies also came under attack in countless cities such as Houston, El Paso, New York, Chicago, and Miami. Educators responded in many cases by curtailing the use of these languages as mediums of instruction and implementing English only classes.[96]

Modification in Patterns

Several patterns of Latino education—student access to education, administrative bias (testing), the imbalanced curriculum, and the culturally subtractive curriculum—were slightly modified but not significantly changed during the post-1960 years. Because of limited space, we will only briefly discuss one of these-student access to the pre-school, elementary, secondary, and post-secondary grades.

By the 1960s, the vast majority of Latinos, for the most part, had gained parity in access to the elementary and secondary grades but they had not gained equitable access to the pre-school grades or to post-secondary education. Access to both the pre-school and the post-secondary grades increased gradually but inconsistently during the post-1960 years. By the early twenty-first century, however, Latino children were among those least likely to attend preschool. In 2001, for instance, approximately 36 percent of Latino preschool-aged children participated in a preschool program. In comparison, 64 percent of black and 46 percent of white children attended preschool that year.[97] No significant change had been made by early 2007.[98]

A similar development occurred in higher education. As we noted earlier, less than 5 percent of Latinos were enrolled in institutions of higher education in the United States before 1960.[99] Although their enrollments steadily increased over the years, they continue to be underrepresented in most colleges and universities. Latino undergraduate enrollments grew from 3.8 percent in 1976 to 4.2 percent in 1980, and from 4.4 percent in 1984 to 6.5 percent in 1991.[100] By 1997 the percentage of Latinos in degree granting institutions increased to 8.6 percent.[101]

It is important to note, however, that while the percentage of Latino enrollments steadily increased, most *were* enrolled in community colleges. In 1999–2000, for instance, 60 percent of Latinos attending post-secondary institutions were enrolled in two-year colleges, the largest percentage of any other racial and ethnic group.[102] This is problematic, noted Patricia Gandara, because "no more than 5% of these students will actually go on to complete a B.A."[103] Indeed, the number of Latinos attending four-year colleges and universities out of high school was very small. A 1998 survey, for example, found that of all the first full-time students attending public universities in the United States, 82.6 percent of freshman were white, 7.2 percent African American, and 1.4 percent Latino.[104] As Michal Kurlaender and Stella Flores note, Latinos showed the lowest rate of entry into four-year institutions and had the highest participation rates at two-year colleges.[105] Although community colleges have benefited many groups over time, critics note that they "can actually exacerbate race and class inequalities in educational attainment."[106]

Continuity and Strengthening of Patterns

Although most aspects of Latino education were modified or reformed, three patterns continued to be immune to change and actually strengthened during the post-1960s: segregation, unequal schools, and uneven school performance.

Despite federal court rulings, legislation, and community protests, Latino children continued to attend separate school facilities. Data suggests that their segregation increased significantly between 1968 and 1998. In the former year, more than half (54.8 percent) of Latino students attended predominantly minority schools across the nation. (Predominantly = a school with over 50 percent of Latino students.) Three decades later, three-fourths or 75.6 percent of these students were enrolled in such schools. In this year, 70.2 percent of African American children were attending predominantly African American schools. Thus by 1998, Latinos were more segregated than even African American students.[107] These children were not only segregated in their own schools, they also experienced resegregation in desegregated schools. This type of "academic" segregation, noted Richard Valencia, was as invidious as segregation on racial grounds.[108]

The pattern of unequal education, similar to school segregation, continued and strengthened during the post-1960 years. Latinos not only attended segregated schools, they attended unequal ones. During the past four decades, additional resources were provided for these schools because of federal legislation and litigation. Despite these additional resources, these schools continued to be unequal in many respects. Many of these schools were understaffed, inadequately funded, overcrowded, and substandard.[109]

The final pattern experiencing little change during the post-1960 years was that of uneven school performance. Latinos continued to have a major tradition of poor school performance and a minor one of school success but most scholars continued to focus on the former, not the latter.[110] Despite this emphasis, scholars in this period offered more complex and nuanced explanations for the underachievement than in previous decades.[111]

Intensification of Latino Responses

During these years, Latino responses to education intensified. Their diverse responses in many ways expanded and increased the historic quest for educational equality initiated in the early part of the twentieth century.

Contestation

During these years, Latinos pursued several major strategies. The most well-known was that of contestation. Several different types of educational policies and practices were contested during the decades under consideration.

In the late 1960s and early 1970s, for instance, youth, community, and parent activists as well as community-based organizations challenged a host of exclusionary and discriminatory school practices at the local level. Some of the most important were inequitable and unequal treatment of Latino children in the public schools, Anglo control of schools, an Anglo-centric curriculum, the suppression of their language and culture, and the exclusion of their community from the schools. In both Mexican American and Puerto Rican communities, a variety of tactics were used, including walkouts, boycotts, protests, and litigation to challenge school discrimination at the local level in this period.[112]

Most activists however generally tackled specific forms of discrimination in education. Three particular types of policies were targeted—school segregation, unequal schooling, and testing.

The struggle against school segregation originated in the early twentieth century but it was renewed in the late 1960s. Activists took local school districts to court, applied pressure on federal agencies to investigate and eliminate segregation against Latinos in the public schools, and supported pieces of legislation encouraging integration and opposing those that undermined it.[113] Towards the latter part of the 1970s, activists abandoned this strategy because opposition to integration by whites, the increasing burden of desegregation on minority communities, including Latinos, and the increased dependence on bilingual education as a more effective strategy of reform encouraged this action. In the meantime, segregation increased, and, by the early twenty-first century, Latinos were the most segregated group in the country.[114]

Unequal funding of schools was another form of discrimination contested by Latinos. For decades, schools serving these children had been underfunded, overcrowded, and inferior. During the 1960s, some of these inequalities were remedied as a result of demands from community groups and an influx of federal funds. The buildings, in many cases, were replaced with more modern facilities, qualifications of teachers increased, and per pupil expenditures improved. Despite the increased funding and channeling of resources to Latino schools the source of inequality—the state funding of public education—remained in place. In the late 1960s, Mexican American activists targeted state financing of public education and challenged it in the courts.

The two most important cases filed by these activists in the late 1960s were in California and Texas—the *Serrano vs. Priest* and the *Rodriguez vs. San Antonio ISD*, respectively.[115] These cases exemplified the two major approaches taken by activists set on challenging inequities in school finance. Those in California pursued their strategy in the state courts; activists in Texas took their case to the federal courts. During the 1970s, the California Supreme Court ruled on behalf of Mexican American plaintiffs in the California case. The U.S. Supreme Court, in contrast, ruled against them in Texas.

The struggle against unequal schools did not end in the 1970s. It slowed down but then picked up steam in the 1980s as activists pursued new litigation and political tactics with renewed vigor.[116]

A final form of discrimination challenged by activists and educators during this period was administrative bias in the schools, especially the use of testing and its impact on the classification, placement, and promotion of Latino children in public education. Two forms of contestation emerged during these decades—legal and scholarly. The legal challenge against testing in the schools began in the late 1960s and 1970s. The cumulative effect of litigation led to changes in the testing and placement of students in these types of classes during the 1970s and 1980s.[117]

Scholarly contestation of testing emerged during the 1960s and continued throughout the next several decades. Towards the latter part of the 1990s and into the early twenty-first century, many of these scholars extended their critiques to high stakes testing and its adverse impact on Latinos in the public schools.[118]

High stakes testing was also challenged legally and politically in the late 1990s, especially in Texas, the state leading this effort.[119] In the early twenty-first century, the struggle against high stakes testing became national in scope because of the passage of the No Child Left Behind Act of 2001. Since its enactment, an increasing number of organizations, professionals, and community activists have publicly opposed high stakes testing and supported the introduction of legislation allowing for multiple assessment criteria for students.[120]

More Than Contestation

The quest for equality was not only about eliminating various forms of discrimination in education, it was also a struggle for power, inclusion, quality education, and pluralism. Latino activists and educators wanted schools that were free from discrimination as well as schools that reflected their community and its cultural and linguistic heritage. They also wanted schools that met their academic needs as well as their social, economic, political and cultural interests. Let us elaborate briefly on each of these new thrusts in activism.

First, let's look at the quest for power. In addition to struggles against discrimination, for the past four decades Latino activists and educators have sought power to make decisions about education impacting their own children. The quest for power has been reflected in the struggles aimed at promoting community access to important decision making positions in three major areas of public education: school governance, educational administration, and teaching.[121]

The struggle for power in New York City during the 1960s and 1970s underscores this new thrust in Latino responses to education and how difficult it has been to gain and maintain power.[122] Puerto Ricans, in conjunction with African American activists, conducted boycotts, pickets, and mass mobilization struggles in an effort to gain community control of the local school boards in the late 1960s and early 1970s. Their efforts led to temporary control of three local school districts in that city (I.S. 201, Two Bridges, and Ocean-Hill Brownsville), to the increased hiring of Latino administrators and teachers, and to the establishment of bilingual education programs. This access to power however was short-lived and by the mid-1970s, established school elites regained control of the schools.[123]

The struggle for power was not only limited to the local boards of education. It also applied to the superintendency, to the principalship, to teachers, and to all other types of professional positions in the local schools. In a few cases, the struggle for access to these positions stirred up unfortunate tensions between Latinos and African Americans.[124]

Activists also struggled against exclusionary measures and for inclusion or full access of Latino students to public education. In the 1970s, for instance, activists struggled against the exclusion of undocumented immigrant children from the public schools. In later decades, they focused on gaining Latino student access to full day kindergarten classes and pre-kindergarten classes.[125]

At the post-secondary level, community activists protested the lack of access to higher education and supported the recruitment of Latino students to the undergraduate, graduate, and professional schools.[126] In the late 1960s and early 1970s, college students engaged in radical action such as taking over buildings or demonstrating on behalf of increased recruitment of Latino students to the universities. In later years, they turned to institutional mechanisms such as Educational Opportunity Programs (EOP) and Chicano Studies or Mexican American studies programs, to increase Latino student access to higher education and to improve their retention in these institutions.[127] Towards the latter part of the twentieth century and into the early twenty-first century, community activists struggled for the establishment of higher education facilities in their own communities.[128]

Another major strategy utilized by Latinos focused on promoting or improving quality academic instruction. Unlike the decades before the 1960s when the majority of reformers were Anglos, in this period an increasing number of educators, scholars, and community groups were Latino.[129]

Activists utilized two major approaches to promote quality instruction. One of these focused on developing or gaining access to innovative curricular programs aimed at improving the academic achievement of Latino students; the other focused on promoting comprehensive school changes to ensure the same goal.[130]

The former approach originated in the early twentieth century but expanded after the 1960s. A variety of specific innovations such as compensatory, adult, bilingual and migrant educational programs were promoted as a way of improving the academic achievement of Latino children in the 1960s. Most, however, began to concentrate on bilingual education. Bilingual education was viewed as the best means for bringing about significant changes in the way the schools educated these children and in addressing the linguistic, cultural, and academic concerns raised by these children.[131]

Latino educators and activists did more than simply promote specific reforms or innovations. During the 1990s, a select group of superintendents, principals, and teachers began to promote comprehensive changes in schools educating Latino students. Many of these individuals had bold visions of school change and were successfully initiating curricular, instructional, and administrative changes from within the schools aimed at transforming underachieving schools and districts into high achieving ones. Among the new visionaries during the 1990s and early twenty-first century were Joseph Fernandez and Ramon C. Cortines, both school chancellors of

New York City during the 1990s, and Dr. Abe Saveedra, superintendent of Houston Independent School District, Michael Hinojosa, superintendent of Dallas ISD, and Hector Montenegro, superintendent of Ysleta ISD.[132]

Community organizations also proposed comprehensive school reform plans. One of these was the Inter-cultural Development Research Association (IDRA). For over four decades, this organization has been in the forefront of school reform and has consistently fought for quality education in American life.[133] Recently, it developed the Quality Schools Action Framework (QSAF). This school reform plan, developed in collaboration with schools and communities in Texas and other parts of the country, offers a model for assessing school outcomes, identifying leverage points for improvement, and focusing and effecting change.[134]

The model is based on three premises. The first is that if the problem is systemic, the solutions must address schools as systems. The second is that if we support student success, then we have to develop a vision, and that vision for children has to seek outcomes for every child. School success, IDRA notes, is for all children "no matter where they come from, no matter the color of their skin, no matter the side of town they come from, no matter the language they speak." And the third premise of this framework is that schools are not poor because children in them are poor or black or brown. Schools are poor because we have poor policies, poor practices and inadequate investments.[135]

A final strategy used by activists during these years focused on struggling for a pluralistic curriculum, i.e., for the valuing and utilization of non-English languages and cultures in the schools. Since we have already covered their efforts to promote language in the schools, this section will focus on promoting Latino culture in education. Two major reforms were promoted: the revision of school textbooks to include Latino heritage and the incorporation of Latino culture in the schools.[136]

During the 1960s and 1970s, activists protested the culturally exclusive policies and practices of local schools and demanded the inclusion of their heritage in the textbooks and in the schools.[137] Most of the textbooks in these decades said little if anything about the role and contributions of Mexican origin individuals or about any other Latinos. Moreover, if any comments were made it was only about Mexican Americans and, as the U.S. Commission on Civil Rights noted in the early 1970s, they usually tended to be "negative or distorted in nature."[138]

By the 1980s, school textbooks gradually and grudgingly acknowledged Latino contributions to the building of the United States but in very stereotypical ways.[139] All Latinos, not simply Mexican Americans, were viewed negatively in these textbooks.

Textbooks continued to portray Latinos in stereotypical ways into the 1990s. Barbara Cruz, for instance, noted that secondary history textbooks in the early part of this decade still viewed Latinos (Mexican Americans, Puerto Ricans, and Cubans) as "lazy, passive, irresponsible, lustful, animalistic, and violent."[140] Two well-known historians noted that not much had changed by the late 1990s. History textbooks had more information on Latinos but they continued to have incomplete or stereotypic coverage of them and of their contributions to the larger society.[141]

The struggles to include the Latino cultural heritage in the schools were more successful than the textbook revision efforts. During the 1980s, the federal recognition of Hispanic heritage month encouraged the partial institutionalization of Latino culture in the schools. The rapid growth of immigration from Mexico and Central and South America during the latter decades of the twentieth century spurred and expanded the inclusion of Latino culture in the schools. By the end of the century, hundreds of thousands of schools throughout the country celebrated the cultural traditions of Latinos and Latinas in the public schools. In fact, the U.S. Senate and House of Representatives authorized and requested to issue annually a "proclamation designating the week including September 15 and 16 as 'National Hispanic Heritage week.'"[142] Educators from across the nation are encouraged to celebrate Latino contributions in America. Numerous web sites have been created to "help teachers focus attention on the contributions of people of Hispanic heritage to the history of the United States."[143]

Beyond Public Schools

One final observation. Most people assume that the quest for equality focused solely on public education but this is historically incorrect. It also included efforts aimed at supporting or establishing private schools.

This long-standing tradition of non-public education continued in the post-1960 years. During these years, Latino students attended Catholic schools, Protestant institutions, and private secular schools established and staffed by members of the community. These latter institutions for the most part were quite diverse and included after-school programs as well as elementary, secondary, or post-secondary institutions. Most of these programs and schools were established primarily with private funds and tended to supplement public education. They peacefully coexisted with public school systems.

During the protest era of the 1970s and 1980s, community-based schools were aimed at promoting ethnic pride, Spanish-language maintenance, and academic achievement in a "culturally relevant" context.[144] In many cases, Latino activists established these schools because the public schools were either unresponsive to their academic needs or hostile towards their cultural heritage.[145]

Towards the latter part of the 1990s, Latinos, especially Mexican Americans, continued this private school tradition, but they moved away from nationalist schools and towards charter institutions. These institutions, unlike those in the 1970s, were not aimed at promoting cultural and linguistic maintenance nor at providing "culturally-based" academic achievement of Latino students. They were simply aimed at improving academic achievement in the barrio. Examples of charter schools include the Raul Izaguirre School, the George I. Sanchez School, the Yes Prep School, all located in Houston, Texas, and the Cesear Chavez Academy and the Dolores Huerta Preparatory High School in Pueblo, Colorado.[146]

Although some Latinos have supported charter schools, the reform continues to be controversial. Critics argue that they are not genuine efforts aimed at improving public schools or that they take public funds away from public education and weaken rather than strengthen the primary means for instructing these children. Recent studies suggest that charter schools have not improved the educational achievement of minority youth, including Latinos.[147]

Conclusion

We have shown that the history of Latino education is intricately linked to the nation's social, political, and economic structures and is directly impacted by a variety of factors, especially immigration and migration from Spanish-speaking countries in the Western Hemisphere. Within this larger context, we have documented and explained the rapid growth of the Latino population in the United States and its relationship to education over a 100-year period. We argued that education was both an instrument of reproduction and a site of contestation.

With respect to the first argument, we noted that education was socially reproductive, that is, it was an instrument for reproducing a stratified social order whereby the dominant groups in the society maintained social, economic, and political hegemony or control over subordinate, racial, ethnic, and working-class groups. For Latinos, education became a means for maintaining the relations of domination that formed in the nineteenth century, and for delegitimizing and devaluing their cultural and linguistic identity. The schools, as we have shown, have not neglected or ignored Latinos. They have acknowledged them and taken concrete actions to ensure that Latinos remained a marginal population in the larger society.

Educators, policy makers, and school officials, for the most part, viewed Latinos as a subordinate and inferior group and treated them as such. Latino parents, especially Mexicans and Puerto Ricans, were viewed as racially and culturally unfit to assume important positions of power in the schools and excluded from the structures of governance, administration, and teaching. Although there were some exceptions—especially in northern New Mexico—it was rare to find Latino teachers, principals, central administrators employed in public schools prior to the 1960s.

Latino children also were viewed as intellectually and culturally inferior and treated as members of a subordinate population. They were denied equitable access to elementary, secondary and post-secondary educational opportunities, placed in separate and unequal facilities, grudgingly offered a subtractive curriculum, and tracked into low ability and vocational classes. The ultimate consequences of these actions were patterns of mostly underachievement as indicated by high drop out rates, low test scores, and limited enrollment in universities.

Likewise, we argued that education was more than simply one of reproduction. It was a site of contestation, i.e., a public space where statuses and identities were negotiated, contested, and constructed amid significant social change. While those in control of education used the schools or tried to use them for eliminating cultural differences and for promoting the subordination of ethnic and racial minority groups, Latinos, for the most part, have actively challenged, subverted, adapted, rejected, reinterpreted, co-opted, or contested these efforts. Not only have they resisted the conformist and marginalizing intentions of the schools, Latinos have also fought for an education that was reflective of their own cultural and linguistic heritage and in concert with their social and political interests.

Current conditions for Latinos indicate that their struggles for pluralism and social acceptance and against cultural conformity and social and economic subordination are far from over. The obstacles they face in the present are formidable and the future looks bleak, given that there is an educational trajectory of continued unequal education, high dropout rates, increasing segregation, campaigns to eliminate bilingual education, and a historic backlash against Latino immigrants in the United States. These obstacles, however, will not halt the tremendous will of the Latino population to excel. This brief history suggests that the community's determination to preserve its language and culture and to obtain an equitable and quality education will continue, and even escalate, in the years to come.

Notes

1. The notion of reproduction and contestation is similar to the methodology used by Guadalupe San Miguel, Jr. and Richard Valencia to study the history of Latino education. See San Miguel Jr. and Richard Valencia, "From the Treaty of Guadalupe Hidalgo to Hopwood: The Educational Plight and Struggle of Mexican Americans in the Southwest," *Harvard Educational Review* 68, 3 (Fall 1998): 363–377, and Guadalupe San Miguel, Jr., "Status of the historiography of Mexican American education: A Preliminary Analysis," *History of Education Quarterly* 26 (1986): 523–536. These scholars use two approaches to analyze this history. The first approach-the plight of Latino education, or what we call reproduction, focuses on the development of education, on how it responded to Latino students, and on how these students fared in it. The second approach—the struggle aspect of Latino education or contestation—explores the manner in which Latinos responded to the types of education offered them.
2. Manuel Gamio, *Mexican Immigration to the United States* (New York: Dover, 1971), 2. Gamio notes that the official census estimated 103,393 Mexican immigrants in the United States in 1900.
3. Victoria-Maria MacDonald, *Latino Education in the United States: A Narrated History from 1513–2000* (New York: Palgrave, 2004), 183; Louis A. Pérez, Jr., *On Becoming Cuban: Identity, Nationality, and Culture* (Chapel Hill: University of North Carolina Press, 1999); Guillermo Grenier and Lisandro Perez, *The Legacy of Exile: Cubans in the United States* (Boston: Allyn and Bacon, 2003), 17–20; Thomas Boswell and James Curtis, *The Cuban-American Experience: Culture, Images, and Perspectives* (Totowa, NJ: Rowman and Allanheld, 1983); Miguel Gonzalez-Pando, *The Cuban Americans* (Westport, CT: Greenwood Press, 1998); James Olson and Judith Olson, *Cuban Americans: From Trauma to Triumph* (New York: Twyne Publishers, 1995); Robert Levine and Moises Asis, *Cuban Miami* (New Brunswick, NJ: Rutgers University Press, 2000); Clara Rodríguez, Virginia

Sánchez Korrol, and José Oscar Alers, "The Puerto Rican Struggle to Survive in the United States," in *Historical Perspectives on Puerto Rican Survival in the United States,* ed. Clara E. Rodríguez and Virginia Sánchez Korrol (Princeton, NJ: Markus Wiener Publishers, 1996), 1; Jaime R. Vidal, "The Great Migration," *Puerto Rican and Cuban Catholics in the U.S., 1900–1965,* ed. Jay P. Dolan and Jaime R. Vidal (Notre Dame, IN: University of Notre Dame Press, 1994), 54–55.

4. The annual average number of Cuban immigrants admitted into the U.S. was 2,024 in 1899, 427 in 1931, and 3,366 in 1951. In 1955 it jumped to 12,390. For further information see table 4 in Lisandro Pérez, "Cuban Catholics in the United States," in *Puerto Rican and Cuban Catholics in the U.S., 1900–1965,* ed. Jay P. Dolan and Jaime R. Vidal (Notre Dame, IN: University of Notre Dame Press, 1994), 175.

5. Lisandro Perez, "Cuban Catholics in the United States," in *Puerto Rican and Cuban Catholics in the U.S.,* ed. Jay P. Dolan and Jaime R. Vidal, 174. See also Juan Gonzalez, *Harvest of Empire* (New York: Penquin, 2000) and Levine and Asis, *Cuban Miami.*

6. Jaime R. Vidal, "Citizens Yet Strangers: The Puerto Rican Experience," in *Puerto Rican and Cuban Catholics in the U.S.,* ed. Jay P. Dolan and Jaime R. Vidal, 56. Slightly over 1,500 Puerto Ricans were residing in the mainland in 1910. This number increased to over 52,000 by 1930 and to 887,000 two decades later. *U.S. Bureau of the Census, U.S. Census of Pop, 1960, Subject Reports. Puerto Ricans in the United States. Final Report.* PC(2)-ID (Washington, D.C.: U.S. Government Printing Office, 1963), table A, viii. For Puerto Rican U.S. citizenship, see *Puerto Rican Students in U.S. Schools,* ed. Sonia Nieto (Mahwah, NJ: Erlbaum, 2000), 9.

7. Puerto Ricans went to Hawaii to work on sugarcane plantations at the turn of the twentieth century. Between 1900 and 1901, 5,000 Puerto Ricans immigrate to Hawaii. See Iris Lopez, "Borinkis and Chop Suey: Puerto Rican Identity in Hawai'i, 1900–2000," in *The Puerto Rican Diaspora: Historical Perspectives,* ed. Carmen Teresa Whalen and Victor Vazquez-Hernandez (Philadelphia: Temple University Press, 2005), 43–67; Puerto Ricans were also recruited to nearby islands to work in the sugarcane plantations. After the United States purchased the Virgin Islands from Denmark in 1917, Puerto Ricans were hired to work in agriculture and stock farms. After 1927, Puerto Ricans migrated to Vieques and St. Croix. See Edna Acosta-Belén and Carlos E. Santiago, *Puerto Ricans in the United States: A Contemporary Portrait* (Boulder, CO: Lynne Rienner, 2006), 53, 55.

8. In the early 1900s close to 90 percent settled in New York. By 1960, approximately 69 percent of all Puerto Ricans in the U.S. resided in New York City. U.S. Bureau of the Census, *U.S. Census of Pop, 1960, Subject Reports. Puerto Ricans in the United States. Final Report.* PC(2)-ID (Washington, D.C.: U.S. Government Printing Office, 1963), table A, viii.

9. Abraham Hoffman, *Unwanted Mexican Americans in the Great Depression, 1929–1939* (Tucson, University of Arizona Press, 1974). See also Joan W. Moore and Harry Pachon, *Mexican Americans* (Englewood Cliffs, NJ: Prentice Hall, 1976), 42.

10. For data on immigration from 1890 to 1930 see Ricardo Romo, "Responses to Mexican Immigration, 1910–1930," *Aztlan* 6, no. 2 (1975): 173–194; for data on the number of braceros imported into the United States from 1942 to 1962 see Julian Samora, "Mexican Immigration" in *Mexican Americans Tomorrow: Educational and Economic Perspectives.* ed. Gus Tyler (Albuquerque: University of New Mexico Press, 1975), 72.

11. Ricardo Romo, "Responses to Mexican Immigration, 1910–1930," *Aztlan* 6, no. 2 (1975): 173–194; Samora, "Mexican Immigration," 1975, 72.

12. Rodolfo F. Acuña, *Occupied America* (New York: Pearson Longman, 2007); *The Chicano Experience in the Northwest,* ed. Carlos S. Maldonado & Gilberto Garcia (Dubuque, IA: Kendall/Hunt, 1995).

13. Kenneth J. Meier and Joseph Stewart, *The politics of Hispanic education: un paso pa'lante y dos pa'tras* (Albany: State University of New York Press, 1991).

14. Felix Roberto Masud-Piloto, *From Welcomed Exiles to Illegal Immigrants: Cuban Migration to the U.S., 1959–1995* (Lanham, MD: Rowman, 1996); Gonzalez, *Harvest of Empire.*

15. San Miguel, Jr. and Valencia, "From the Treaty of Guadalupe Hidalgo to Hopwood," 363–377, *The Evolution of Deficit Thinking: Educational Thought and Practice,* ed. Richard Valencia(Washington, D.C.: Falmer Press, 1997); Nick Vaca, "The Mexican American in the Social Sciences, 1912–1970," Parts I (1912–1935) and 2 (1936–1970), *El Grito* 3 (Spring 1970): 3–24; 16 (Fall 1971): 17–51.

16. Gilbert G. Gonzalez, *Chicano Education in the Era of Segregation* (Philadelphia: Balch Institute Press, l990); Nieto, *Puerto Ricans in U.S. Schools.*

17. William Ritch, Education in New Mexico (Santa Fe: Manderfield and Tucker, 1874), 14; Superintendent Annual Report, 1892 (Santa Fe: New Mexican Printing Company, 1892); Lynne Marie Getz, *Schools of their Own: The Education of Hispanos in New Mexico, 1850–1940* (Albuquerque: University of New Mexico Press, 1997), 41–45.

18. Guadalupe San Miguel, Jr, "The Schooling of Mexicanos in the Southwest, 1848–1891," In José F. Moreno, ed., *The Elusive Quest for Equality* (Cambridge, MA: Harvard Educational Review, 1999): 40–46.

19. For Colorado, see Rubén Donato, *Mexicans and Hispanos in Colorado Schools and Communities, 1920–1960* (Albany: State University of New York Press, 2007); and for Texas see Steven W. Prewitt, "We Didn't Ask to Come to This Party": Self Determination Collides with the Federal Government in the Public Schools of Del Rio, Texas, 1890–1971" (PhD diss., University of Houston, May 2000).

20. Meyer Weinberg, *A Chance to Learn: The History of Race and Education in the United States* (Cambridge: Cambridge University Press, l977), 140–152; Gonzalez, *Chicano Education in the Era of Segregation;* Guadalupe San Miguel, Jr., "Inside the Public Schools: A History of the Chicano Educational Experience," *Atisbos: Journal of Chicano Research* (Summer-Fall 1978): 86–100.

21. For an overview of the status and reasons for limited enrollment in higher education, see Meyer Weinberg, *A Chance to Learn,* l977, 140–152 and Victoria-María MacDonald and Teresa García, "Historical Perspectives on Latino Access to Higher Education, 1848–1990," in *The Majority in the Minority: Expanding the Representation of Latina/o Faculty, Administrators and Students in Higher Education,* ed. Jeanett Castellanos and Lee Jones (Sterling, VA: Stylus, 2003): 15–43.

22. In 1910 political leaders established the Spanish-American Normal School in El Rito, a community in northern New Mexico, for Latino students. On this school see Lynne Getz, *Schools of their Own,* 22–23; see also Guillermo Lux, *Politics and Education in Hispanic New Mexico: From the Spanish American Normal School to the Northern New Mexico Community College* (El Rito: Northern New Mexico Community College, 1984). In Southern Colorado two institutions served Latinos-the Adams State College and, for a short period, the San Luis Institute in the town of San Luis. For further information on these schools see Donato, *Mexicans and Hispanos in Colorado Schools and Communities, 1920–1960.*

23. Bernardo Gallegos. "Review of Latino Education in The United States: A Brief History," Feb., 19, 2008 (in authors' possession).

24. Over 5,500 Cuban teachers and college age youth enrolled in several universities in the U.S. during these years, in *Latino Education in the United States,* ed. Victoria-María McDonald (New York: Palgrave Macmillan, 2004), 95.

25. The recruitment of Puerto Rican students to the mainland ended in 1907 as more funds were channeled into developing normal schools and a university in Puerto Rico. MacDonald, *Latinos in the United States,* 98.

26. MacDonald, *Latinos in the United States,* 95.

27. San Miguel, Jr. "The Origins, Development, and Consequences of the Educational Segregation of Mexicans in the Southwest," in *Contemporary Issues in Chicano Studies: A Multidisciplinary Approach,* ed. G. Garcia, I. Ortiz, and F. Lomeli (New York: Teachers College Press, 1984, 195–208).

28. Gonzalez, *Chicano Education in the Era of Segregation.*

29. Gonzalez, *Chicano Education in the Era of Segregation;* Guadalupe San Miguel, Jr. *"Let all of them take heed": Mexican Americans and the campaign for educational equality in Texas, 1910–1981* (Austin: University of Texas Press, 1987).

30. These initial reasons for segregation were developed in a 1930 desegregation case. See *Independent School District v. Salvatierra, 33 SW.2d 790* (Tex. Civ. Appl-San Antonio, 1930).

31. San Miguel, Jr., "Let all of them Take Heed," 53–54; Everett Ross Clinchy, Jr., "Equality of Opportunity for Latin Americans in Texas" (doc. diss., Columbia University, 1954).

32. George I. Sanchez, "The Education of Bilinguals in a State School System," (PhD diss., University of California, Berkeley, 1934).

33. *Mendez v. Westminster School District,* 64 F. Supp. 544 (S.D. Cal. 1946), 161 F.2d 774 (9th Cir. 1947). See also Richard R. Valencia, "The Mexican American Struggle for Equal Educational Opportunity

in Mendez v. Westminster: Helping to Pave the Way for Brown v. Board of Education." *Teachers College Record* 107, no.3 (March 2005): 389–423.

34. Gilbert G. Gonzalez, "Racial Intelligence Testing and the Mexican People," *Explorations in Ethnic Studies* 5, no. 2 (July 1982): 36–49; A. M. Padilla, "Early Psychological Assessments of Mexican American Children," *Journal of the History of the Behavioral Sciences* (1988): 111–116; E. C. Condon, J. Y. Peters, and C. Suiero-Ross, "Educational Testing and Spanish-speaking Exceptional Children," in *Special Education and the Hispanic Child: Cultural Perspectives (Reston, V: Council for Exceptional Children,* 1979): 16–32.

35. These "new" deficit theorists frequently turned to the works of anthropologist Oscar Lewis who popularized the "culture of poverty" theory. The literature of the 1960s is replete with the new social constructions of the "culturally deprived" or "culturally disadvantaged" family, home, and child. For a review of these studies see *The Evolution of Deficit Thinking: Educational Thought and Practice,* ed. Richard R. Valencia (Washington, D. C.: Falmer Press, 1997).

36. Valencia, *Evolution of Deficit Thinking.*

37. Gonzalez, *Chicano Education in the Era of Segregation.*

38. U.S. Commission on Civil Rights, *Report 1: Ethnic Isolation of Mexican Americans in the Public Schools of the Southwest. Mexican American Education Study,* 1971. Nieto, *Puerto Ricans in U.S. Schools,* 2004.

39. Paul Schuster Taylor, *An American-Mexican Frontier: Nueces County, Texas* (New York: Russell & Russell, 1934), 210.

40. Thomas P. Carter, *Mexican Americans in Schools: A History of Educational Neglect* (New York: College Entrance Examination Board, 1970).

41. Gonzalez, *Chicano Education in the Era of Segregation.* See chapter Four, "Training for Occupational Efficiency: Vocational Education," 77–93.

42. In many ways it also sought to de-ethnicize or de-culturalize Latina/o children. See Joel Spring, *Deculturalization and the Struggle for Equality: A Brief History of the Education of Dominated Cultures in the United States* (New York: McGraw-Hill, 1997).

43. Arnold Leibowitz, *Educational Policy and Political Acceptance: The Imposition of English as the Language of Instruction in American Schools* (Washington, D.C.: Center for Applied Linguistics, 1971); Erlinda Gonzales-Berry, "Which language Will Our Children Speak? The Spanish language and Public Education Policy in New Mexico, 1890–1930," in *The Contested Homeland: A Chicano History of New Mexico,* ed. Erlinda Gonzales-Berry and David R. Maciel (Albuquerque, NM: University of New Mexico Press, 2000: 169–190).

44. Joel H. Spring, *Deculturalization and the Struggle for Equality.*

45. For a critique of Anglo views of Mexicans in American and Texas history see Carlos E. Castañeda, "The Broadening Concept of History Teaching in Texas," *Inter-American Intellectual Interchange,* Institute of Latin American Studies of the University of Texas, 1943.

46. Perez, for instance, points to the high enrollment of Cuban students in the secondary grades and in institutions of higher learning in the U.S. starting as early as 1916. He also notes that between 1923 and 1958, several thousand Cubans enrolled in U.S institutions of higher education. This data suggests that Cubans in the U.S. have been relatively successful in American schools during the twentieth century. Louis A. Pérez, *On Becoming Cuban: Identity, Nationality, and Culture* (Chapel Hill: University of North Carolina Press, 1999), 406–412.

47. It cannot be ignored that some Latino war veterans benefited from the G.I Bill during the 1940s. Some received vocational training; others earned college degrees. See Donato, *Mexicans and Hispanos in Colorado Schools and Communities,* 1920–1960.

48. San Miguel and Valencia, "From the Treaty of Guadalupe Hidalgo."

49. Sociological, cultural, and structural reasons have been given for the pattern of poor academic performance. During the years from 1938 to 1965, these three frameworks competed for ascendancy in the literature. By the early 1960s, the cultural determinist perspective became the dominant paradigm for explaining underachievement. The reason for this dominance was ideological—it absolved American society from placing blame for this social problem and placed it on the victims themselves. See Nick Vaca, "The Mexican American in the Social Sciences, 1912–1970," Parts 1 (1912–1935) and 2 (1936–1970), *El Grito,* 3 (Spring 1970): 3–24; 16 (Fall 1971): 17–51.

50. San Miguel, "Let All of Them Take Heed." James William Cameron, "The History of Mexican Public Education in Los Angeles, 1910–1930" (PhD diss., University of Southern California, 1976).

51. Jovita Gonzalez, Social Life in Cameron, Starr, and Zapata Counties, M.A. thesis, University of Texas, Austin, 1930, 75.

52. Francisco Hernandez, "Mexican Schools in the Southwest," Unpublished paper, n.d. (In author's possession).

53. James Cameron, "Schools for Mexicans." In James William Cameron, "The History of Mexican Public Education in Los Angeles, 1910–1930" (PhD. diss., University of Southern California, 1976, 169—183).

54. Prewitt, "We Didn't Ask to Come to This Party," 33–44.

55. In some cases, Latinos themselves sought positions as teachers. The most well known was George I. Sanchez. For a brief overview of this aspect of his life see Getz, *Schools of their Own*.

56. On the establishment and evolution of a teacher-training institute for Latino teachers in the early 1900s see Getz, *Schools of their Own*, pp. 22–23 and Guillermo Lux, *Politics and Education in Hispanic New Mexico*. Religious schools also encouraged teacher training for Latinos. For information on Catholic and Protestant efforts to promote teacher training see F. Campbell, "Missiology in New Mexico, 1850–1900: The success and failure of Catholic education," in *Religion and Society in the American West*, ed. C. Guerneri & D. Alvarez (Lantham, MD: University Press of America, 1987): 59–78. For information on the role played by Nina Otero Warren, the first female superintendent of Santa Fe County to encouraged the hiring of bilingual teachers for the Spanish-speaking children in her county from 1918 to 1929 see Charlette Whaley, *Nina Otero-Warren in Santa Fe* (Albuquerque: University of New Mexico Press, 1994): 42–44. On the role of Puerto Rican community activists in the hiring of Puerto Rican teachers in New York City especially in the post-WWII era see C. E. Rodriguez & V. Sanchez Korrol, *Historical perspectives on Puerto Rican survival in the United States* (Princeton, NJ: Markus Weiner, 1996).

57. See Lynne Marie Getz. *Schools of their Own*, 22–23; see also Guillermo Lux, *Politics and Education in Hispanic New Mexico: From the Spanish American Normal School to the Northern New Mexico Community College* (El Rito: Northern New Mexico Community College, 1984).

58. Carl Allsup, *The American G.I. Forum: Origins and Evolution* (Austin: Center for Mexican American Studies, 1982).

59. Carlos Muñoz, Jr., *Youth, Identity, Power: The Chicano Movement* (New York: Verso, 1990).

60. MacDonald, *Latino Education in the United States*. See chapter 4, "Education and Imperialism at the turn of the Century; Puerto Rico and Cuba, 1898–1930," 93–100.

61. Elma A. Neal, "Adapting the Curriculum to Non-English-speaking Children," *Elementary English Review*, 6–7 (September 1929): 183–185; Clara Peterson Ebel, "Developing an Experience Curriculum in a Mexican First Grade" (M.A. Thesis, Arizona State Teachers College, Tempe, 1940); David Bachelor, *Educational Reform in New Mexico: Tireman, San José, and Nambé* (Albuquerque: University of New Mexico Press, 1991); Getz, *Schools of their own*, 66–103; Gonzalez, *Chicano Education in the Era of Segregation*, 1990, 113–135; Mathew D. Davis, *Exposing a culture of neglect: Herschel T. Manuel and Mexican American Schooling* (Greenwich, CT: Information Age, 2005); Rodríguez, Clara, Virginia Sánchez Korrol, and José Oscar Alers, "The Puerto Rican Struggle to Survive in the United States," in *Historical Perspectives on Puerto Rican Survival in the United States* ed. Clara E. Rodríguez and Virginia Sánchez Korro (Princeton, NJ: Markus Wiener, 1996); San Miguel, Jr., "Let All of them Take Heed," 114–145.

62. In addition to San Jose and Nambe, Tireman also worked in two other New Mexico communities-Cedro in 1932 and Taos in 1939. See Getz, *Schools of Their Own*, 92–95.

63. Leibowitz, *Educational Policy and Political Acceptance*, 1971; Getz, *Schools of their Own*, 35; Erlinda Gonzales-Berry, "Which language Will Our Children Speak? The Spanish Language and Public Education Policy in New Mexico, 1890–1930," in *The Contested Homeland: A Chicano History of New Mexico*, ed. Erlinda Gonzales-Berry and David R. Maciel (Albuquerque: University of New Mexico Press, 2000).

64. Theodore Andersson, *Foreign languages in the elementary school; a struggle against mediocrity* (Austin: University of Texas Press, 1969).

65. For a critical view of dominant interpretations of Mexican Americans in American history text-

books during the first half of the twentieth century see Carlos E. Castaneda, "The Broadening Concept of History Teaching in Texas," *Inter-American Intellectual Interchange*, Institute of Latin American Studies of the University of Texas, 1943.

66. Leticia Garza-Falcón, *Gente decente: a borderlands response to the rhetoric of dominance* (Austin: University of Texas, 1998). For examples of this more complex views see Jovita González and Eve Raleigh, *Caballero: A Historical Novel* (College Station: Texas A&M University Press, 1996); Americo Paredes, *George Washington Goméz: A Mexicotexan Novel* (Houston: Arte Publico Press, 1990); George I. Sanchez, *Forgotten People* (Albuquerque: University of New Mexico Press, 1940): 3–42.; Carey McWilliams, *North from Mexico* (Philadelphia: J.B. Lippincott Company, 1948); Americo Paredes, *With a Pistol in His Hands* (Austin: University of Texas Press, 1957).

67. See Garza-Falcón, *Gente Decente*, 1998.

68. San Miguel, *"Let All of Them Take Heed;"* Gonzalez, *Chicano Education in the Era of Segregation*; Donato, *The Other Struggle for Equal Schools.*

69. See, for instance, Phillip B. Gonzales, *Forced sacrifice as ethnic protest: the Hispano cause in New Mexico & the racial attitude confrontation of 1933* (New York: Peter Lang, 2001); Weinberg, *A Chance to Learn*, 164; José E. Limón, "EL Primer Congreso Mexicanista de 1911: A Precursor to Contemporary Chicanismo," *Aztlán* 5, nos. 1 & 2 (Spring-Fall, 1974): 85–117.

70. George I. Sánchez, "Group Differences and Spanish-Speaking Children — A Critical Review," *The Journal of Applied Psychology* (1932):550.

71. Sanchez, *Group Differences*, 1932. See also George I. Sanchez, "The Education of Bilinguals in a State School System" (PhD diss., University of California, Berkeley, 1934).

72. On Sanchez see Getz, *Schools of their Own*, ch. III; On Escobar see Mario T. García, *Mexican Americans: Leadership, Ideology, and Identity, 1930–1960* (New Haven, CT: Yale University Press, 1989), 62–83.

73. San Miguel, *"Let All of Them Take Heed,"* 117.

74. One of the earliest struggles occurred in 1910. See Arnoldo de Leon, "Blowout 1910 Style: A Chicano School Boycott in West Texas," *Texana* 12(1974): 124–140. Jose E. Limon, "EL Primer Congreso Mexicanista de 1911: A Precursor to Contemporary Chicanism," *Aztlán* 5, nos. 1 & 2 (Spring-Fall, 1974): 85–117.

75. For an overview of these struggles see San Miguel, *"Let All of Them Take Heed"*; Mary Melcher, "'This is not right': Rural Arizona Women Challenge Segregation and Ethnic Division, 1925–1950," *Frontiers* 20, no. 2 (1999):190–214; L. K. Munoz, "Separate but Equal? A Case Study of Romo v. Laird and Mexican American Education," *Organization of American Historians Magazine of History* 15, no. 2 (2001): 28–35; Guadalupe San Miguel, Jr., "The Struggle Against Separate and Unequal Schools," *History of Education Quarterly* 23 (Fall 1983): 343–359; Richard R. Valencia, "The Mexican American Struggle for Equal Educational Opportunity in Mendez v. Westminster: Helping to Pave the Way for Brown v. Board of Education," *Teachers College Record* 107, no. 3 (March 2005): 389–423.

76. San Miguel, *"Let All of them Take Heed,"* 134.

77. The total number of undocumented immigrants, most of whom were Mexicans, was estimated to be 5.8 million in 1996, 7 million in 2001, and 11 million in 2005. See "INS: Illegal immigrant totals show sharp rise," *Houston Chronicle*, February 1, 2003, 19A; "U.S. Undocumented Population Nears 11 million," March 21, 2005. *HispanicBusiness.com*, http://www.hispanicbusiness.com/news/news_print.asp?i (accessed March 22, 2005).

78. For information on these new settlement patterns and their impact on education in the South see Stanton Wortham, Enrique G. Murillo, and Hamann, eds., *Education in the New Latino Diaspora: Policy and the Politics of Identity* (Westport, CT: Ablex, 2002).

79. Carmen Teresa Whalen, "Colonialism, Citizenship, and the Making of the Puerto Rican Diaspora," in *The Puerto Rican Diaspora: Historical Perspectives*, ed. Carmen Teresa Whalen and Victor Vazquez-Hernandez (Philadelphia: Temple University Press, 2005), 3.

80. Guillermo Grenier and Lisandro Perez underscore the distinct status of Cubans in the United States. They note that "[A]ny overview of U.S. immigration or of the Latino population is likely to note that the Cuban experience has been different, that Cubans represent a distinct group that should be viewed separately." Grenier and Perez, *The Legacy of Exile*, 34.

81. In 1980 just under 60 percent of Cubans lived in Florida, about 20 percent in New Jersey and New York, and the remaining 20 percent was dispersed across the nation. Moreover, 87 percent of the Cuban population in Florida settled in Dade County, the greater area of Miami (Boswell and Curtis, *The Cuban-American Experience*, 108).

82. For a pictorial view of the "balsero phenomenon" of the 1990s see http://www.cuba-junky.com/cuba/blaseros.htm.

83. For the various ways in which government and school officials responded to the different waves of Cuban exiles/immigrants see Granier and Perez, *The Legacy of Exile*, 23–24, 52; MacDonald, *Latino Education in the United States*, 186–187. See also Boswell and Curtis, *The Cuban–American Experience*, 107, 127; on the treatment of Marielitos see Lavine and Asis, *Cuban Miami*, 51–52.

84. Gonzalez, *Forced Sacrifice as Ethnic Protest*.

85. Marcelo Suarez-Orozco, *Central American Refugees and U.S. High Schools: A Psychosocial Study of Motivation and Achievement* (Stanford, CA: Stanford University Press, 1989).

86. Marcelo Suarez-Orozco, *Central American Refugees and U.S. High Schools*.

87. "Population of the United States by Race and Hispanic/Latino Origin, Census 2000 and July 1, 2005" available from http://www.infoplease.com/ipa/A0762156.html. The article compares Latino census data for 2000 and for 2005. In 2000, there were 35,305,818 Latinos. By July 1, 2005, this figure had jumped to 42,687,224.

88. The only major exception to this generalization is the first and second wave of Cuban immigrants.

89. Fredrick M. Hess, *School Boards at the Dawn of the 21st Century* (Alexandria, VA: National School Boards Association, 2004), 25. Cited in Joel Spring, *American Education* 158; Roberto Haro "The Dearth of Latinos in Campus Administration," in *The Status of Hispanics in Higher Education*, Tuesday, reported in *The Chronicle of Higher Education*, December 11, 2001. Report sent by email to author by Baltazar A. Acevedo, Jr. (December 12, 2001); *Crisis in the Ranks: The Underrepresentation of Hispanic Faculty and Administrators in Texas Public Institutions of Higher Education*, report prepared by Ed. C. Apodaca to the Texas Association of Chicanos in higher Education, 1974 (report in author's possession); Antonia Darder, Rodolfo Torres, & Henry Gutierrez. *Latinos and Education*. (New York: Routledge, 1997).

90. Contemporary data notes the percentage of Latino school board members in the following urban areas.

L.A.	7	1	14%
Chicago	6	1	17%
Houston	9	2	22%

91. Examples of a few local school districts in rural areas of south Texas that had significant representation by 2003 were the following: McAllen, 57 percent (4 of 7 board members were Latinos); Laredo, 86 percent (6 of 7); Mission, 86 percent (6 of 7); and Edinburg 100 percent (7 of 7).

92. Fredrick M. Hess, *School Boards*, 25. Cited in Joel Spring, *American Education*, 158.

93. Guadalupe San Miguel, Jr., *Contested Policy: The Rise and Fall of Federal Bilingual education in the United States, 1960–2001* (Denton: University of North Texas Press, 2002).

94. See, for instance, Susana Flores and Enrigue G. Murillo, Jr., "Power, Language, and Ideology: Historical and Contemporary notes on the Dismantling of Bilingual Education," *Urban Review* 33, no. 3 (Sept 2001): 183–206.

95. San Miguel, Jr., *Contested Policy* and "Language Legislation in the USA," *James Crawford Website and Emporium,* http://ourworld.compuserve.com/homepages/JWCrawford/langleg.htm.

96. For an example of how one local community responded see Lourdes Diaz Soto, *Language, Culture, and Power: Bilingual Families and the Struggle for Quality Education* (Albany: State University of New York Press, 1997).

97. "News Release: NCLR Applauds Introduction of Congresswoman Solis' Preschool bill," Sept. 16, 2004. Email sent to one of the authors by the National Council de La Raza (NCLR), Sept. 17, 2004.

98. In early May 2007, Congress passed federal legislation to expand access to early childhood and education programs for Latino children. See "News Release: NCLR Applauds Passage of the Improving Head Start Act of 2007," May 3, 2007. Email sent to one of the authors on May 3, 2007.

99. Meyer Weinberg, *A Chance to Learn*, 1977, 140–152 and Victoria-María MacDonald and Teresa García, "Historical Perspectives on Latino Access to Higher Education, 1848–1990," in *The Majority*

in the Minority: Expanding the Representation of Latina/o Faculty, Administrators and Students in Higher Education, ed. Jeanett Castellanos and Lee Jones, 15–43.

100. Christine I. Bennett, "Research on Racial Issues in American Higher Education," in *Handbook of Research on Multicultural Education,* ed. James Banks and Cherry McGee Banks (San Francisco: Jossey-Bass, 2004), 852.

101. Harriett Romo and Joanne Salas, "Successful Transition of Latino Students from High School to College," in *Latinos in Higher Education,* ed. David J. Leon (Boston, MA: Elsevier Science, 2003), 108.

102. David Leon, *Latinos in Higher Education,* 3; Also see William B. Harvey and Eugene L. Anderson, *Minorities in Higher Education: Twenty-First Annual Status Report* (Washington, D.C: American Council on Education, 2005), 11.

103. Patricia Gandara, "Forward," in David Leon, *Latinos in Higher Education,* xi.

104. Romo and Salas, "Successful Transition of Latino Students from High School to College," 108.

105. Michal Kurlaender and Stella M. Flores, "The Racial Transformation of Higher Education," in *Higher Education and the Color Line: College Access, Racial Equity, and Social Change,* ed. Gary Orfield, Patricia Marin, and Catherine L. Horn (Cambridge, MA: Harvard Education Press), 21.

106. Kurlaender and Flores, "The Racial Transformation of Higher Education," 24.

107. Gary Orfield, "Schools More Separate: Consequences of a decade of Resegregation." Harvard Civil Rights Project, Cambridge, MA, 2001, 33, Table 9; See also, Gary Orfield, "The Growth of Segregation: African Americans, Latinos, and Unequal Education," in *Dismantling Desegregation: The Quiet Reversal of Brown v. Board of Education,* Gary Orfield, ed. Susan E. Eaton, and the Harvard Project on School Desegregation (New York: The New Press, 1996), 53–72; Richard R. Valencia, Martha Menchaca, and Rubén Donato, "Segregation, desegregation, and integration of Chicano students: Old and New Realities," in *Chicano School Failure and Success,* ed. Richard R. Valencia, 2002, 73.

108. Valencia, *Chicano School Failure and Success,* 2002, 95.

109. For examples of unequal education and the efforts made to reform the school finance system in one state see Gregory C. Rocha and Robert H. Webking, *Politics and Public Education: Edgewood v. Kirby and the Reform of Public School Financing in Texas* (Minneapolis: West Publishers, l992).

110. Nieto, for instance, underscores the pervasive and deplorable pattern of underachievement in New York City. She notes that in 1963 a "minuscule number of Puerto Ricans graduated from New York City high schools with academic diplomas." Out of the 21,000 academic diplomas granted, 331 or 1.6 were awarded to Puerto Rican students. This was a stark contrast, she said, to the 150,000 Puerto Ricans living in New York at the time. Moreover, of the 331 Puerto Ricans that earned academic high school diplomas, only 28 went to college. Sonia Nieto, "Puerto Rican Students in U.S. Schools: A Troubled Past and the Search for a Hopeful Future," in *Handbook on the Research on Multicultural Education,* ed. James Banks and Cherry Banks, 526.

111. See for instance, Angela Valenzuela, Subtractive schooling: *U.S.-Mexican Youth and the Politics of Caring.* (Albany: State University of New York Press, 1999); also see Michelle Fine, *Framing Dropouts: Notes on the Politics of an Urban High School* (Albany: State University of New York Press, 1991).

112. Dennis Shirley, *Valley Interfaith and School Reform: Organizing for Power in South Texas* (Austin: University of Texas Press, 2002); Armando Navarro, *Mexican American Youth Organization: Avantgarde of the Chicano Movement in Texas* (Austin: University of Texas Press, 1995); Guadalupe San Miguel, Jr. Brown, *Not White: School Integration and the Chicano Movement* (College Station: Texas A&M University Press, 2001); Sonia Nieto, "Puerto Rican Students in U.S. Schools: A Troubled Past and the Search for a Hopeful Future," 515–541; Luis Fuentes, "Community control did not fail in New York: It Wasn't Tried," Phi Delta Kappan 57,10 (1976): 692–695; Rodriguez & Sánchez Korrol, *Historical perspectives on Puerto Rican Survival in the United States,* 1996. For the Puerto Rican experience, see MacDonald, *Latino Education in the United States,* 221–229.

113. George A. Martinez, "Legal Indeterminacy, Judicial Discretion and the Mexican American Litigation Experience: 1930–1980," *University of California at Davis Law Review* 27(1994): 557–618; Rangel, Jorge C. and Carlos M. Alcala, "Project Report: De Jure Segregation of Chicanos in Texas Schools," *Harvard Civil Rights-Civil Liberties Law Review* 7(1972): 331–349; Steven H. Wilson, "Brown over

'Other White': Mexican Americans' Legal Arguments and Litigation Strategy in School Desegregation Lawsuits," *Law and History Review* 21, no. 1(Spring 2003): 145–194; Guadalupe San Miguel, Jr. "The Impact of Brown on Mexican American Litigation Strategies, 1950s to 1980s," *Journal of Latinos and Education* 4, no. 4 (2005): 221–236.

114. San Miguel, *"Let All of Them Take Heed,"*; Gary Orfield, Susan E. Eaton and the Harvard Project on School Desegregation, *Dismantling Segregation: The Quiet Reversal of Brown v. board of Education* (New York: New York Press, 1996), 53–56.

115. *Serrano v Priest*, 5 Cal.3d 584, 96 Cal. Reptr. 601, 487 Pac.2d 1241 (1971); Serrano v. Priest, Civil No. 938,254 (Cal. Super. Ct., April 10, 1974), 102–103; *Rodriguez v. San Antonio Independent School District*, C.A. No. 68-175-5A (W.D. Tex 1971). For a detailed discussion of these and other school finance cases as well as the issues raised by school finance reform in general see *School Finance: The Economic and Politics of Public Education*, ed. Walter I. Garms, James W. Guthrie, and Lawrence C. Pierce (Englewood Cliffs, NJ: Prentice-Hall, Inc., 1978) and *Inequality in School Financing: The Role of the Law* (U.S Commission on Civil Rights, 1973).

116. For an overview of the developments in Texas from the 1980s to the present see the following: "Note: After Rodriguez: Recent developments in School finance Reform," *Tax Lawyer* 44, no. 1(1990–91): 313–340; Lt. Gov. Bill Ratliff, "Finding a way to equitably fund Texas schools hasn't been easy," *Houston Chronicle*, sun October 28, 2001, editorial; and Connie Mabin, "Property-rich districts claim funding system is illegal tax," *Houston Chronicle*, Fri, March 28, 2003, 1A, 43A. See also Gregory C. Rocha and Robert H. Webking, *Politics and Public Education: Edgewood v. Kirby and the Reform of Public School Financing in Texas* (Minneapolis: West Publishers, 1992).

117. Blandina Cárdenas, "Defining Equal Access to Educational Opportunity for Mexican American Children: A Study of three Civil rights Actions Affecting Mexican American Students and the Development of a Conceptual Framework for Effecting institutional Responsiveness to the Educational Needs of Mexican American Children" (PhD diss., University of Massachusetts, 1974).

118. See, for instance, Richard R. Valencia, "Educational Testing and Mexican American Students: Problems and Prospects," in *The Elusive Quest for Equality: 150 Years of Chicano/Chicana Education*, ed. J. F. Moreno (Cambridge, MA: Harvard Educational Review, 1999), 123–140; and Richard R. Valencia, Bruno J. Villarreal, and Moises F. Salinas, "Educational Testing and Chicano Students: Issues, Consequences, and Prospects for Reform," (289–292), in *Chicano School Failure and Success: Past, Present, and Future, ed.* Richard R. Valencia (London: Routledge Falmer, 2002), 253–309.

119. For the ruling of a challenge to high stakes testing in Texas see *GI Forum et al v. Texas Education Agency et al*, 87 F. Supp.2d 667 (W.D. Tex. 2000). Phillips, S. E., (Ed.), "Defending a High School Graduation Test: GI Forum v. Texas Education Agency [Special issue]," *Applied Measurement in Education*, 13,4(2000); Richard R. Valencia and E. M. Bernal (Eds.), "The Texas Assessment of Academic Skills (TAAS) Case: Perspectives of Plaintiffs' Experts [Special issue.]," *Hispanic Journal of Behavioral Sciences* 22, no. 4 (2000). For information on opposition to Senate Bill 4, an anti-social promotion bill incorporating high stakes testing and passed by the Texas state legislature with the support of then Governor George W. Bush in 1999 see Richard R. Valencia, Bruno J. Villarreal, and Moises F. Salinas, "Educational Testing and Chicano Students: Issues, Consequences, and Prospects for Reform" (289–292), in Valencia, *Chicano School Failure and Success*, 2002, 253–309.

120. For information on one Texas organization's position see http://www.texastesting.org/TQABrief.htm. For its legislative agenda see http://www.texastesting.org/LegislativeSummary.htm.

121. Prior to the 1960s, this strategy was aimed primarily at the K-12 public school system. Afterwards, efforts were expanded to the post-secondary level. For an overview of the politics of appointing Latinos to federal office see Julie Leininger Pycior, *LBJ & Mexican Americans: The Paradox of Power* (Austin: University of Texas Press, 1997), 185, 199–201; see also Donato, *The Other Struggle for Equal Schools* (Albany: State University of New York Press, 1997), 61; Clayton Brace, *Federal Programs to Improve Mexican-American Education* (Washington, D.C.: U.S. Office of Education, Mexican-American Affairs Unit, 1967), ERIC Document no. ED014338; Report by the National Advisory Committee on Mexican American Education, *The Mexican American: Quest for Equality* (Washington, D.C.: U.S. Department of Health, Education and Welfare, 1968). ERIC no. ED049841.

122. These types of struggles occurred throughout the country. For studies aimed at gaining power in the Southwest see Navarro, Armando, *The Cristal Experiment: A Chicano Struggle for Community Con-

trol. (Madison: University of Wisconsin Press, 1998); Dennis Shirley, *Valley Interfaith and School Reform*; Armando Navarro, *Mexican American Youth Organization: Avant-garde of the Chicano Movement in Texas* (Austin: University of Texas Press, 1995); Guadalupe San Miguel, Jr. *Brown, Not White: School Integration and the Chicano Movement* (College Station: Texas A&M University Press, 2001).

123. Nieto, *Puerto Ricans in U.S. Schools*, 18–19. See also Nieto, "Puerto Rican Students in U.S. Schools: A Troubled Past and the Search for a Hopeful Future," 515–541; See also Luis Fuentes, "Community control did not fail in New York: It Wasn't Tried," 692–695; Luis Fuentes, "The Struggle for local Political control," in *The Puerto Rican Struggle: Essays on Survival in the U.S.,* ed. C. E. Rodriguez, V. Sánchez Korrol, and I. O. Alers (New York: Puerto Rican Migration Research Consortium, Inc., 1980: 111–120); Rodriguez & Sanchez Korrol, *Historical Perspectives on Puerto Rican Survival in the United States.*

124. On the clash between Latinos and blacks in search of a superintendent for the Houston schools see Donald R. McAdams, *Fighting to Save Our Urban Schools-And Winning, Lessons from Houston* (New York: Teachers College Press, 2000). For information on Chicago see Jorge Oclander, "Hispanics condemn Lack of School Jobs," *Chicago Sun-Times*, Dec. 12, 1994, 6. For a recent view of the struggle for Latino power in education and the impact it has had on race relations in one Chicago community see Abdon M.Pallasch, "Curie principal still out: Hispanic majority on LSC refuses to reverse vote," March 11, 2007, *Chicago Sun-Times*, http://www.suntimes.com/news/education/292313,CST-NWS-curie11.article (accessed March 11, 2007).

125. The struggle for Latino access to the early grades continues into the present as illustrated by the support of the National Council de La Raza (NCLR), the largest national Latino civil rights and advocacy organization in the United States, for passage of the Improving Head Start Act of 2007. This bill, NCLR notes, "will significantly expand access to the nation's premier early childhood and education program for Hispanic children, who represent the fastest-growing segment of the Head Start eligible child population." See "News release: NCLR Applauds Passage of the Improving head Start Act of 2007," May 3, 2007. Email sent to Dr. San Miguel by NCLR, May 3, 2007.

126. Antonia Darder, Rodolfo Torres, and Henry Gutierrez, *Latinos and Education* (New York: Routledge, 1997); Carlos Muñoz, "From Segregation to Melting Pot Democracy: The Mexican American Generation," (19–46), in *Youth, Identity, Power: The Chicano Movement* (New York: Verso, 1989).

127. Dolores Delgado Bernal, "Chicana/o Education from the Civil Rights Era to the Present." In José F. Moreno, ed., *The Elusive Quest for Equality: 150 Years of Chicana/o Education* (Cambridge, MA: Harvard Educational Review, 1999): 77–110.

128. For an example of a community struggle to establish a university that would benefit Latino students living in the inner city see *Bringing the University Home: The San Antonio community's Struggle for Educational Access*, ed. Louis Mendoza and Rodolfo Rosales (San Antonio, TX: Hispanic Research Center, 1999).

129. Among some of the better known activist scholars of the 1960s and 1970s were Jose Cardenas, Tom Carter, Alfredo Castaneda, and Josue Gonzalez. These scholars and others played leading roles in promoting school change in general, in supporting the enactment of culturally relevant educational policies such as bilingual education, and in the development of compensatory, migrant and bilingual educational programs in the schools. Prominent scholar Gary Orfield acknowledged the impact of the new Latino voices in educational research in the 1980s. See Gary Orfield, "Hispanic Education: Challenges, Research, and Policies," *American Journal of Education* 95, no. 1 (Nov. 1986): 1–25.

130. Guadalupe San Miguel, Jr., "Actors Not Victims: Chicanas/os and the Struggle for Educational Equality," in *Chicanas/Chicanos at the Crossroads: Social, Economic, and Political Change*, ed. David R. Maciel and Isidro Ortiz (Tucson: University of Arizona Press, 1996): 159–180; San Miguel, *Contested Policy.*

131. San Miguel, *Contested Policy*; Lourdes Diaz Soto, *Language, Culture, and Power: Bilingual Families and the Struggle for Quality Education* (New York: State University of New York Press, 1997); Isaura Santiago Santiago, "ASPIRA v. the Board of Education of the City of New York: A History and Policy Analysis" (PhD diss., Fordham University, 1987); Isaura Santiago, *A Community's Struggle for Equal Education Opportunity: ASPIRA vs. the Board of Education* (Princeton, NJ: Educational

Testing Service, 1987), Sandra Del Valle, "Bilingual Education for Puerto Ricans in New York City: From Hope to Compromise," *Harvard Educational Review* 68, no. 2 (Summer 1998): 193–217.

132. San Miguel, 1996. For Fernandez's autobiography see Joseph A. Fernandez and John Underwood, *Tales Out of School* (Boston: Little, Brown, 1993). For further information on Fernandez see the following: http://biography.jrank.org/pages/3354/Fernandez-Joseph-1921-Chancellor-Educator.html. On Cortines see http://www.ed.gov/offices/OS/cortines.html.

133. Another well-known community-based organizations supportive of comprehensive school reform was ASPIRA.

134. María "Cuca" Montecel, "A Quality Schools Action Framework: Framing Systems Change for Student Success," http://www.idra.org/IDRA_Newsletters/November_-_December_2005_Access_and_Success (accessed January 10, 2007).

135. For more information on IDRA's comprehensive school reform plan see María "Cuca" Montecel, "A Quality Schools Action Framework: Framing Systems Change for Student Success," http://www.idra.org/IDRA_Newsletters/November_-_December_2005_Access_and_Success (accessed January 10, 2007).

136. In some cases, they also demanded the development of Latino history classes. The number of courses focusing on the Latino community briefly increased during the 1970s but only in a few schools. These types of courses, for the most part, were non-existent by the 1980s and 1990s. For efforts in Houston, see De Leon, *Ethnicity in the Sunbelt*.

137. Unlike activists in public education, those in higher education were highly dissatisfied with the pace of change in the history textbooks. Beginning in the late 1960s, they developed their own histories and their own courses. The new histories, for the most part, rejected the master narrative developed my mainstream historians and social scientists and created an alternative view of American development in general and Latina/o participation in that development. These scholars also established and taught Latino history and studies classes at the universities and pressured universities to develop courses dealing with Latina/o experiences in the United States. Well over 100 programs and a lesser number of academic departments and centers in Latina/o Studies were teaching Latino courses by the late 1980s. Most of these programs had anywhere between 3 and 30 courses specifically on the Latina/o experience. See Alan Edward Schorr, *Hispanic Resource Directory* (Juneau, AK: Denali press, 1988), pp. 327–330; Ramon A. Gutierrez, "Ethnic Studies: Its Evolution in American Colleges and Universities," (157–167), in *Multiculturalism: A Critical Reader,* ed. David Theo Goldberg (Cambridge, MA: Blackwell, 1994).

138. *Toward Quality Education for Mexican Americans* (1974). Report VI: Mexican American Education Study. U.S. Commission on Civil Rights, 8. In another study, John S. Gains noted that the "treatment of Mexican Americans in American history textbooks has been grossly inaccurate, subjective, and marred by the omission of important facts, the use of stereotypes, and elements of latent nativism." See John S. Gains, "Treatment of Mexican American History in High School Textbooks." *Civil Rights Digest*, (October 1972): 35–40.

139. Linda K Salvucci, "Mexico, Mexicans and Mexican Americans in Secondary-School United States History Textbooks," *The History Teacher* 24, no. 2, (February 1991): 203–222; Johnathan Arries, Decoding the Social Studies Production of Chicano History," *Equity and Excellence in Education* 27, no. 1 (2007): 37–44; Vicki Ruiz, "Teaching Chicano/American History: Goals and Methods," *The History Teacher* 20, no. 2 (February 1987): 167–177.

140. Barbara Cruz, "Stereotypes of Latin Americans Perpetuated in Secondary School History Textbooks," *Latino Studies Journal* 1, no. 1 (1994): 51.

141. Joseph A. Rodríguez and Vicki L. Ruiz, "At Loose Ends: Twentieth-Century Latinos in Current United States History Textbooks, *The Journal of American History* 86, no. 4 (March 2000): 1689–1700.

142. "Legislative History of Hispanic Heritage Month: Public Law 90–498, Approved September 17, 1968, 90th Congress." http://www.clnet.ucla.edu/heritage/hhhispan.htm.

143. See also the following websites on Hispanic Heritage month: http://www.educationworld.com/a_lesson/lesson/lesson023.shtml http://www.factmonster.com/spot/hhm1.html http://teacher.scholastic.com/activities/hispanic/ http://www.mcps.k12.md.us/curriculum/socialStd/Hispanic.html http://www.history.com/classroom/hhm/

144. See Clementina Almaguer, Francisco Hernandez, and Anais Mock, "Casa de la Raza," (69–77), Mario Barrera, "The Struggle for third College at UC San Diego," (62–68), Eliezer Risco, "Before universidad de Aztlan: Ethnic Studies at Fresno State College," (41–47). All of these are found in *Parameters of Institutional Change: Chicano Experiences in Education* (Hayward, CA: Southwest Network of the Study Commission on Undergraduate Education, 1974). See also Joan Kalvelage, "Cinco Exemplos," *Edcentric*, October-November, n.d.): 5–7, 28–42; Juan Jose Sanchez, "A Study of Chicano alternative Grade schools in the SW, 1978–1980" (PhD diss., Harvard University, 1982); Carlos S. Maldonado, *Colegio Cesar Chavez, 1973–1983: A Chicano Struggle for Educational Self-Determination* (Garland, 2000); Arnoldo De Leon, *Ethnicity in the Sunbelt*, p. 227. For a brief history of private schools found in the Mexican community in the Southwest during the nineteenth and twentieth centuries see Francisco Hernandez, "Mexican Schools in the southwest," Unpublished paper, n.d., 1–25, (in author's possession); Luis Rey Cano, "A Case Study of a Private Community Based Alternative School Program for Dropouts and Potential Dropouts" (PhD diss., University of Houston, 1981); Marjorie Evans, "From success comes growth at Sanchez," *Houston Chronicle*, September 20, 2001, 1A. On Puerto Rican schools see Ana Y. Ramos-Zayas, "Nationalist Ideologies, Neighborhood-Based Activism, and Educational Spaces in Puerto Rican Chicago," *Harvard Educational Review* 68, no. 2 (Summer 1998): 164–192.

145. Elena Aragon de McKissack, *Chicano Educational Achievement: Comparing Escuela Tlatelolco, a Chicanocentric School, and a Public High School.* (New York: Garland, 1999). Ana Y. Ramos-Zayas, "Nationalist Ideologies, Neighborhood-Based Activism, and Educational Spaces in Puerto Rican Chicago," *Harvard Educational Review* 68, no. 2 (Summer 1998): 164–192.

146. For supporting charter schools as a response to the neglect of Latinos in the public schools see Richard Farias, "Charter schools triumphing as public ones fail," *Houston Chronicle* (March 20, 2000), 23A. For the charter schools serving Latinos in Pueblo, Colorado, see "CDE Charter Search Results," http://www.cde.state.co.us/scripts/chartersearchresults.asp

147. "Charter School Achievement on the 2003 National Assessment of Educational Progress. Executive Summary." http://www.ncspe.org/publications_files/OP111.pdf.

Bibliography

Acosta-Belén, Edna, and Carlos E. Santiago. *Puerto Ricans in the United States: A Contemporary Portrait.* Boulder, CO: Lynne Rienner, 2006.

Acuña, Rodolfo F. *Occupied America: The Chicano's Struggle Toward Liberation.* New York: Pearson Longman, 2007.

Allsup, Carl. *The American G.I. Forum: Origins and Evolution.* Austin, TX: Center for Mexican American Studies, 1982.

Almaguer, Clementina, Francisco Hernandez, and Anais Mock. "Casa de la Raza" (69–77). In *Parameters of Institutional Change: Chicano Experiences in Education.* Hayward, CA: Southwest Network of the Study Commission on Undergraduate Education, 1974.

Anderson, Theodore. *Foreign Languages in the Elementary School; A Struggle Against Mediocrity.* Austin: University of Texas Press, 1969.

Aragon de McKissack, Elena. *Chicano Educational Achievement: Comparing Escuela Tlatelolco, a Chicanocentric School, and a Public High School.* New York: Garland, 1999.

Arries, Johnathan. "Decoding the Social Studies Production of Chicano History," *Equity and Excellence in Education* 27, no. 1 (2007): 37–44.

Bachelor, David L. *Educational Reform in New Mexico: Tireman, San José, and Nambé.* Albuquerque: University of New Mexico Press, 1991.

Baltazar A. Acevedo, Jr. *The Status of Hispanics in Higher Education*, Tuesday, Reported in *The Chronicle of Higher Education*, December 11, 2001. Report sent by email to author by Baltazar A. Acevedo, Jr. (December 12, 2001).

Barrera, Mario. "The Struggle for third College at UC San Diego," (62–68). In *Parameters of Institutional Change: Chicano Experiences in Education* (Hayward, CA: Southwest Network of the Study Commission on Undergraduate Education, 1974).

Bennett, Christine I. "Research on racial Issues in American Higher Education." In *Handbook of Research on Multicultural Education*, edited by James Banks and Cherry McGee Banks, 847–868. San Francisco: Jossey-Bass, 2004.

Boswell, Thomas D., and James R. Curtis. *The Cuban–American Experience: Culture, Images, and Perspectives*. Totowa, NJ: Rowman and Allenheld, 1984.

Brace, Clayton.*Federal Programs to Improve Mexican-American Education*. Washington, D.C.: U.S. Office of Education, Mexican-American Affairs Unit, 1967. ERIC Document no. ED014338.

Brazier, Arthur M. *Black Self-Determination: The Story of the Woodlawn Organization*. Grand Rapids, MI: William B. Eerdmans, 1969.

Bureau of the Census. *U.S. Census of Pop, 1960, Subject Reports. Puerto Ricans in the United States*. Final Report. PC (2)-ID (Washington, D.C.: U.S. Government Printing Office, 1963).

Cameron, James William. "The History of Mexican Public Education in Los Angeles, 1910–1930." PhD diss., University of Southern California, 1976.

Campbell, F. "Missiology in New Mexico, 1850–1900: The Success and Failure of Catholic Education." In *Religion and Society in the American West*, edited by C. Guerneri and D. Alvarez, 59–78. Lanham, MD: University Press of America, 1987.

Cano, Luis Rey. "A Case Study of a Private Community Based Alternative School Program for Dropouts and Potential Dropouts." PhD diss., University of Houston, 1981.

Cárdenas, Blandina. "Defining Equal Access to Educational Opportunity for Mexican American Children: A Study of three Civil rights Actions Affecting Mexican American Students and the Development of a Conceptual Framework for Effecting Institutional Responsiveness to the Educational Needs of Mexican American Children." PhD diss., University of Massachusetts, 1974.

Carter, Thomas P. *Mexican Americans in Schools: A History of Educational Neglect*. New York: College Entrance Examination Board, 1970.

Castaneda, Carlos E. "The Broadening Concept of History Teaching in Texas," *Inter-American Intellectual Interchange*. Institute of Latin American Studies of the University of Texas, 1943.

Clinchy, Everett Ross Jr. "Equality of Opportunity for Latin Americans in Texas." PhD diss., Columbia University, 1954.

Condon, E.C., J. Y. Peters, and C. Suiero-Ross. "Educational Testing and Spanish-speaking Exceptional Children." In *Special Education and the Hispanic Child: Cultural Perspectives*. Reston, VA: Council for Exceptional Children, 1979: 16–32.

"Charter School Achievement on the 2003 National Assessment of Educational Progress. Executive Summary." F. Howard Nelson, Bella Rosenberg, and Nancy Van Meter, eds. (n.d.). http://www.aft.org/pubs-reports/downloads/teachers/NAEPCharter Schools Report.pdf (accessed July 24, 2009).

"Charter Search Results." Colorado Department of Education. (n.d.). http://www.cde.state.co.us/scripts/chartersearchresults.aspCDE (accessed July 24, 2009).

"Celebrate Hispanic Heritage Month!" Education world. (n.d). http://www.factmonster.com/spot/hhm1.html (accessed July 24, 2009).

Crisis in the Ranks: The Underrepresentation of Hispanic Faculty and Administrators in Texas Public Institutions of Higher Education. Report prepared by Ed. C. Apodaca to the Texas Association of Chicanos in higher Education, 1974 (report in author's possession).

Cruz, Barbara. "Stereotypes of Latin Americans Perpetuated in Secondary School History Textbooks." *Latino Studies Journal* 1, no. 1 (1994): 51–66.

Darder, Antonia, Rodolfo Torres, and Henry Gutierrez. *Latinos and Education*. New York: Routledge, 1997.

Davis, Matthew. *Exposing a Culture of Neglect: Herschel T. Manuel and Mexican American Schooling*. Greenwich, CT: Information Age, 2005.

De Leon, Arnoldo. *Ethnicity in the Sunbelt: A History of Mexican Americans in Houston*. Houston, TX: Center for Mexican American Studies, 1989.

De Leon, Arnoldo. "Blowout 1910 Style: A Chicano School Boycott in West Texas." *Texana* 12 (1974): 124–140.

Delgado Bernal, Dolores. "Chicana/o Education from the Civil Rights Era to the Present." In *The Elusive Quest for Equality: 150 Years of Chicano/Chicana Education*, edited by Jose F. Moreno, 77–108. Cambridge: MA: Harvard University Press, 1999.

Del Valle, Sandra. "Bilingual Education for Puerto Ricans in New York City: From Hope to Compromise." *Harvard Educational Review* 68, no. 2 (Summer 1998): 193–217.

Diaz Soto, Lourdes. *Language, Culture, and Power: Bilingual Families and the Struggle for Quality Education*. Albany: State University of New York Press, 1997.

Donato, Ruben. *Mexicans and Hispanos in Colorado Schools and Communities, 1920–1960*. Albany: State University of New York Press, 2007.

Donato, Ruben. *The Other Struggle for Equal Schools: Mexican Americans during the Civil Rights Era*. Albany: State University of New York Press, 1997.

Ebel, Clara Peterson. "Developing an Experience Curriculum in a Mexican First Grade." MA thesis, Arizona State Teachers College, Tempe, 1940.

Evans, Margorie. "From Success Comes Growth at Sanchez." *Houston Chronicle*, September 20, 2001, 1A.

Farias, Richard. "Charter Schools Triumphing as Public Ones Fail." *Houston Chronicle*, March 20, 2000, 23A.

Fish, John Hall. *Black Power/White Control*. Princeton. NJ: Princeton University Press, 1973.

Flores, Susana, and Enrigue G. Murillo, Jr. "Power, Language, and Ideology: Historical and Contemporary notes on the Dismantling of Bilingual Education." *Urban Review* 33, no. 3 (Sept 2001): 183–206.

Fraga, Kenneth Leo Meier, and R. England. "Hispanic Americans and the Educational Policy: Limits to Equal Access." In *Latinos and the Political System*, edited by D. F. Garcia, 385–410. Notre Dame, IN: Notre Dame University Press, 1988.

Fuentes, Luis. "Community Control Did Not Fail in New York: It Wasn't Tried." *Phi Deta Kappan* 57, no. 10 (1976): 692–695.

Fuentes, Luis. "The Struggle for Local Political Control." In *The Puerto Rican Struggle: Essays on Survival in the U.S.*, edited by C. E. Rodriguez, V. Sánchez Korrol, and I. O. Alers, 111–120.New York: Puerto Rican Migration Research Consortium, Inc., 1980.

Fuentes, Luis. "Puerto Ricans and New York City School Board Elections: Apathy or Obstructionism?" In *Puerto Rican Politics in Urban American*, edited by James Jennings and Monte Rivera, 127–137. Westport, CT: Greenwood Press, 1984:

Gains, John S. "Treatment of Mexican American History in High School Textbooks." *Civil Rights Digest*,(October 1972): 35–40.

Gamio, Manuel. *Mexican Immigration to the United States*. New York: Dover, 1971.

Gandara, Patricia. "Forward." In *Latinos in Higher Education*, edited by David J. Leon, ix–xii. Boston: Elsevier Science, 2003.

Gann, L. H., and Peter J. Duignan. *The Hispanics in the United States*. Boulder, CO: Westview Press, 1986.

García, Mario T. *Mexican Americans: Leadership, Ideology, and Identity, 1930–1960*. New Haven, CT: Yale University Press, 1989.

Garms, Walter I., James W. Guthrie, and Lawrence C. Pierce, eds. *School Finance: The Economic and Politics of Public Education*. Englewood Cliffs, NJ: Prentice-Hall, Inc., 1978.

Garza-Falcón, Leticia. *Gente decente: A Borderlands Response to the Rhetoric of Dominance*. Austin: University of Texas, 1998.

Getz, Lynne, *Schools of their Own: The Education of Hispanos in New Mexico, 1850–1940*. Albuquerque: University of New Mexico Press, 1997.

GI Forum et al v. Texas Education Agency et al, 87 F. Supp.2d 667 (W.D. Tex. 2000); Phillips, S. E., (Ed.) "Defending a High School Graduation Test: GI Forum v. Texas Education Agency [Special issue]," *Applied Measurement in Education*, 13, 4 (2000).

Gonzales-Berry, Erlinda. "Which language Will Our Children Speak? The Spanish language and Public Education Policy in New Mexico, 1890–1930." In *The Contested Homeland: A Chicano History of New Mexico*, edited by Erlinda Gonzales-Berry and David R. Maciel, 169–190. Albuquerque: University of New Mexico Press, 2000.

Gonzalez, Gilbert G. *Chicano Education in the Era of Segregation*. Philadelphia: Balch Institute Press, 1990.

Gonzalez, Jovita, and Eve Raleigh. *Caballero: A Historical Novel*. College Station: Texas A&M University Press, 1996.

Gonzalez, Juan. *Harvest of Empire*. New York: Penquin, 2000.

Gonzalez, Phillip B. *Forced Sacrifice as Ethnic Protest: The Hispano Cause in New Mexico & the Racial Attitude Confrontation of 1933*. New York: Peter Lang, 2001.

Gonzalez-Pando, Miguel. *The Cuban Americans.* Westport, CT: Greenwood Press, 1998.

Gonzalez, Gilbert G. "Racial Intelligence Testing and the Mexican People." *Explorations in Ethnic Studies* 5, no. 2 (July 1982): 36–49.

Grenier, Guillermo, and Lisandro Perez. *The Legacy of Exile: Cubans in the United States.* Boston: Allyn and Bacon, 2003.

Gutierrez, Ramon A. "Ethnic Studies: Its Evolution in American Colleges and Universities." In *Multiculturalism: A Critical Reader,* edited by David Theo Goldberg, 157–167. Cambridge, MA: Blackwell, 1994.

Haro, Roberto. "The Dearth of Latinos in Campus Administration." *The Chronicle of Higher Education,* December 11, 2001.

Harvey, William B., and Eugene L. Anderson., *Minorities in Higher Education: Twenty-First Annual Status Report.* Washington, D.C: American Council on Education, 2005.

Hernandez, Francisco. "Mexican Schools in the southwest" (unpublished paper, n. d., 1–25; in author's possession.)

Hess, Fredrick. *School Boards at the Dawn of the 21st Century.* Alexandria, VA: National School Boards Association, 2004.

History Channel, (n.d.), http://www.history.com/classroom/hhm/(accessed July 24, 2009).

Hoffman, Abraham. *Unwanted Mexican Americans in the Great Depression, 1929–1939.* Tucson: University of Arizona Press, 1974.

Houston Chronicle, February 1, 2003, "U.S. Undocumented Population Nears 11 million," p. 19A.

Independent School District v. Salvatierra, 33 SW.2d 790 (Tex. Civ. Appl-San Antonio, 1930).

Kalvelage, Joan. "Cinco Ejemplos." *Edcentric,* October-November, n.d.: 5–7, 28–42.

Kurlaender, Michal, and Stella M. Flores. "The Racial Transformation of Higher Education." In *Higher Education and the Color Line: College Access, Racial Equity, and Social Change,* edited by Gary Orfield, Patricia Marin, and Catherine L. Horn, 11–32. Cambridge, MA: Harvard Education Press.

Leibowitz, Arnold. *Educational Policy and Political Acceptance: The Imposition of English as the Language of Instruction in American Schools.* Washington, D.C.: Center for Applied Linguistics, 1971.

Leininger Pycior, Julie, *LBJ & Mexican Americans: The Paradox of Power.* Austin: University of Texas Press, 1997.

Leon, David J., ed. *Latinos in Higher Education.* Boston, MA: Elsevier, 2003.

Levine, Robert, and Asis, Moises. *Cuban Miami.* New Brunswick, NJ: Rutgers University Press, 2000.

Limon, José E. "EL Primer Congreso Mexicanista de 1911: A Precursor to Contemporary Chicanismo." *Aztlán* 5, Nos. 1 & 2 (Spring-Fall, 1974): 85–117.

Lopez, Iris. "Borinkis and Chop Suey: Puerto Rican Identity in Hawai'i, 1900–2000." In *The Puerto Rican Diaspora: Historical Perspectives,* edited by Carmen Teresa Whalen and Victor Vazquez-Hernandez, 43–67. Philadelphia: Temple University Press, 2005.

Lucas, Tamara, Rosemary Henze, & Ruben Donato. "Promoting the Success of Latino Language-Minority Students: An Exploratory Study of Six High Schools." *Harvard Educational Review* 60, no. 3 (1990): 315–340.

Lux, Guillermo. *Politics and Education in Hispanic New Mexico: From the Spanish American Normal School to the Northern New Mexico Community College.* El Rito: Northern New Mexico Community College, 1984.

MacDonald, Victoria-María, ed. *Latino Education in the United States.* New York: Palgrave Macmillan, 2004.

MacDonald, Victoria-María, and Teresa García. "Historical Perspectives on Latino Access to Higher Education, 1848–1990." In *The Majority in the Minority: Expanding the Representation of Latina/o Faculty, Administrators and Students in Higher Education,* edited by Jeanett Castellanos and Lee Jones, 15–43. Sterling, VA: Stylus, 2003.

Maldonado, Carlos, and Gilberto Garcia, eds. *The Chicano Experience in the Northwest.* Dubuque, IA: Kendall/Hunt, 1995.

Maldonado, Carlos S. *Colegio Cesar Chavez, 1973–1983: A Chicano Struggle for Educational Self-Determination.* New York: Garland, 2000.

Martinez, George A. "Legal Indeterminacy, Judicial Discretion and the Mexican American Litigation Experience: 1930–1980." *University of California at Davis Law Review* 27(1994): 557–618.

Masud-Piloto, Felix Roberto. *From Welcomed Exiles to Illegal Immigrants: Cuban Migration to the U.S., 1959–1995.* Lanham, MD: Rowman & Littlefield, 1996.

McAdams, Donald R. *Fighting to Save Our Urban Schools-And Winning, Lessons from Houston.* New York: Teachers College Press, 2000.

McWilliams, Carey. *North from Mexico.* Philadelphia: J.B. Lippincott, 1948.

Meier, Kenneth J., and Joseph Stewart. *The Politics of Hispanic Education: Un Paso Pa'lante y Dos Pa'tras.* Albany: State University of New York Press, 1991.

Melcher, Mary. "'This is not right': Rural Arizona Women Challenge Segregation and Ethnic Division, 1925–1950." *Frontiers* 20, no. 2 (1999): 190–214.

Montecel, Maria "cuca." "A Quality Schools Action Framework: Framing Systems Change for Student Success." http://www.idra.org/IDRA_Newsletters/November_-_December_2005_Access_and_Success (accessed January 10, 2007).

Mongomery County Public Schools. "Bookmarks to Celebrate and Research our Hispanic Heritage." (n.d.). http://www.montgomeryschoolsmd.org/curriculum/socialStd/Hispanic.html (accessed July 24, 2009).

Moore, Joan W., and Harry Pachon. *Mexican Americans.* Englewood Cliffs, NJ: Prentice Hall, 1976.

Munoz, Carlos. "From Segregation to Melting Pot Democracy: The Mexican American Generation." In *Youth, Identity, Power: The Chicano Movement,* edited by Carlos Munoz, 19–46. New York: Verso, 1989.

Munoz, Carlos. *Youth, Identity, Power: The Chicano Movement.* New York: Verso, 1990.

Munoz, L. K. "Separate but Equal? A Case Study of Romo v. Laird and Mexican American Education." *Organization of American Historians Magazine of History,* 15, no. 2 (2001): 28–35.

Navarro, Armando. *Mexican American Youth Organization: Avant-Garde of the Chicano Movement in Texas.* Austin: University of Texas Press, 1995.

Navarro, Armando. *The Cristal Experiment: A Chicano Struggle for Community Control.* Madison: University of Wisconsin Press, 1998.

Neal, Elma A. "Adapting the Curriculum to Non-English-Speaking Children." *Elementary English Review,* 6-7 (Sept., 1929): 183–185.

Nieto, Sonia. "Puerto Rican Students in U.S. Schools: A Troubled Past and the Search for a Hopeful Future." In *Handbook on the Research on Multicultural Education,* edited by James Banks and Cherry Banks, 515–541. San Francisco: Jossey-Bass, 2004.

Nieto, Sonia, ed. *Puerto Rican students in U.S. schools.* Mahwah, NJ: Erlbaum, 2000.

Oakes, Jennie. *Keeping Track: How Schools Structure Inequality.* New Haven: CT: Yale University Press, 1985).

Oclander, Jorge. "Hispanics Condemn Lack of School Jobs." *Chicago Sun-Times,* Monday, Dec. 12, 1994, p. 6.

Olson, James, and Judith Olson. *Cuban Americans: From Trauma to Triumph.* New York: Twyne, 1995.

Olsen, Lorrie, and Marcia Chen. *Crossing the Schoolhouse Border: A California Tomorrow Policy Research Report.* San Francisco: California Tomorrow, 1988).

Orfield, Gary. "Schools More Separate: Consequences of a Decade of Resegregation." Harvard Civil Rights Project, Cambridge, MA, 2001.

Padilla, A. M. "Early Psychological Assessments of Mexican American Children." *Journal of the History of the Behavioral Sciences* (1988): 111–116.

Paredes, Americo. *George Washington Goméz: A Mexicotexan Novel.*Houston, TX: Arte Publico Press, 1990.

Paredes, Americo. *With a Pistol in His Hands.* Austin: University of Texas Press, 1957.

Perez, Lisandro. "Cuban Catholics in the United States." In *Puerto Rican and Cuban Catholics in the U.S., 1900–1965,* edited by Jay P. Dolan and Jaime R. Vidal. Notre Dame, IN: University of Notre Dame Press, 1994.

Pérez, Louis A. Jr. *On Becoming Cuban: Identity, Nationality, and Culture.* Chapel Hill: University of North Carolina Press, 1999.

Prewitt, Steven W. "We Didn't Ask to Come to This Party": Self Determination Collides with the Federal Government in the Public Schools of Del Rio, Texas, 1890–1971." PhD diss.,University of Houston, May 2000.

Ramos-Zayas, Ana Y. "Nationalist Ideologies, Neighborhood-Based Activism, and Educational Spaces in Puerto Rican Chicago." *Harvard Educational Review* 68, no. 2 (Summer 1998): 164–192.

Rangel, Jorge C., and Carlos M. Alcala. "Project Report: De Jure Segregation of Chicanos in Texas Schools." *Harvard Civil Rights-Civil Liberties Law Review* 7(1972): 331–349.

Risco, Eliezer. "Before Universidad de Aztlan: Ethnic Studies at Fresno State College" (41–47). In *Parameters of Institutional Change: Chicano Experiences in Education*. Hayward, CA: Southwest Network of the Study Commission on Undergraduate Education, 1974.

Report by the National Advisory Committee on Mexican American Education. *The Mexican American: Quest for Equality*. Washington, D.C.: U.S. Department of Health, Education and Welfare, 1968. ERIC no. ED049841.

Reyes, Luis O. "The Aspira Consent Decree: A Thirtieth-Anniversary Retrospective of Bilingual Education in New York City." *Harvard Educational Review* 76, no. 3 (2006): 369–400.

Rocha, Gregory C., and Robert H. Webking. *Politics and Public Education: Edgewood v. Kirby and the Reform of Public School Financing in Texas*. Minneapolis, MN: West Publishers, 1992.

Rodriguez, C. E., and V. Sanchez Korrol. *Historical Perspectives on Puerto Rican Survival in the United States*. Princeton, NJ: Markus Weiner, 1996.

Rodriguez v. San Antonio Independent School District, C.A. No. 68-175-5A (W.D. Tex 1971).

Rodriguez, Clara, Virginia Sánchez Korrol, and José Oscar Alers. "The Puerto Rican Struggle to Survive in the United States." In *Historical Perspectives on Puerto Rican Survival in the United States*, edited by Clara E. Rodriguez and Virginia Sánchez Korrol, 1–10. Princeton, NJ: Markus Wiener, 1996:

Rodríguez, Joseph, A., and Vicki L. Ruiz. "At Loose Ends: Twentieth-Century Latinos in Current United States History Textbooks. *The Journal of American History* 86, no. 4 (March 2000): 1689–1700.

Romo, Harriett, and Joanne Salas. "Successful Transition of Latino Students from High School to College." In *Latinos in Higher Education*, edited by David J. Leon, 107–130. Boston: Elsevier Science, 2003.

Romo, Ricardo. "Responses to Mexican Immigration, 1910–1930." *Aztlan* 6, no. 2 (1975): 173–194.

Ruiz, Vicki. Teaching Chicano/American History: Goals and Methods. *The History Teacher* 20, no. 2, (Feb 1987): 167–177.

Salvucci, Linda K. "Mexico, Mexicans and Mexican Americans in Secondary-School United States History Textbooks." *The History Teacher* 24, no. 2, (Feb 1991): 203–222.

Samora, Julian. "Mexican Immigration." In *Mexican Americans Tomorrow: Educational and Economic Perspectives*, edited by Gus Tyler. Albuquerque: University of New Mexico Press, 1975.

San Miguel, Guadalupe Jr. "The Schooling of Mexicanos in the Southwest, 1848–1891." In *The Elusive Quest for Equality*, edited by José F. Moreno, 31–52. Cambridge, MA: *Harvard Educational Review*, 1999.

San Miguel, Guadalupe Jr. *Contested Policy: The Rise and Fall of Federal Bilingual Education in the United States, 1960–2001*. Denton: University of North Texas Press, 2002.

San Miguel, Guadalupe Jr. *Brown, Not White: School Integration and the Chicano Movement*. College Station: Texas A&M University Press, 200.

San Miguel, Guadalupe Jr. "The Origins, Development, and Consequences of the Educational Segregation of Mexicans in the Southwest." In *Contemporary Issues in Chicano Studies: A Multidisciplinary Approach*, edited by G. Garcia, I. Ortiz, and F. Lomeli, 195–208. New York: Teachers College Press, 1984.

San Miguel, Guadalupe, Jr. "The Impact of Brown on Mexican American Litigation Strategies, 1950s to 1980s." *Journal of Latinos and Education* 4, no. 4 (2005): 221–236.

San Miguel, Guadalupe, Jr., and Richard R. Valencia. "From the Treaty of Guadalupe Hidalgo to Hopwood: The Educational Plight and Struggle of Mexican Americans in the Southwest." *Harvard Educational Review* 68, no. 3 (Fall 1998): 363–377.

San Miguel, Guadalupe, Jr. "Inside the Public Schools: A History of the Chicano Educational Experience." *Atisbos: Journal of Chicano Research* (Summer-Fall 1978): 86–100.

San Miguel, Guadalupe, Jr. *"Let All of Them Take Heed": Mexican Americans and the Campaign for Educational Equality in Texas, 1910–1981*. Austin: University of Texas Press, 1987.

San Miguel, Guadalupe, Jr. "Social and Educational Influences Shaping the Mexican American Mind: Some Tentative thoughts." *Journal of the Mid-West History of Education Society* 14 (1986): 99–118.

San Miguel, Guadalupe Jr. "Actors Not Victims: Chicanas/os and the Struggle for Educational Equality."

In *Chicanas/Chicanos at the Crossroads: Social, Economic, and Political Change,* edited by David R. Maciel and Isidro Ortiz, 159–180. Tucson: University of Arizona Press, 1996.

San Miguel, Jr., Guadalupe. "The Struggle Against Separate and Unequal Schools." *History of Education Quarterly* 23 (Fall 1983): 343–359.

Sánchez Korrol, Virginia. "Towards Bilingual Education: Puerto Rican Women Teachers in New York City Schools, 1947–1967." In *Puerto Rican Women and Work: Bridges in Transnational Labor,* edited by Altagracia Ortiz, 82–104. Philadelphia: Temple University Press, 1996.

Sanchez, George I. "The Education of Bilinguals in a State School System." PhDl diss., University of California, Berkeley, 1934.

Sánchez, George I. "Group Differences and Spanish-Speaking Children — A Critical Review." *The Journal of Applied Psychology,* 1932: 549–558.

Sanchez, George I. *Forgotten People.* Albuquerque: University of New Mexico Press, 1940.

Sanchez, Juan Jose. "A Study of Chicano alternative Grade schools in the SW, 1978–1980." PhD diss., Harvard University, 1982.

Schorr, Alan Edward. *Hispanic Resource Directory.* Juneau, AK: Denali Press, 1988: 327–330.

Serrano v Priest, 5 Cal.3d 584, 96 Cal. Reptr. 601, 487 Pac.2d 1241 (l971); Serrano v. Priest, Civil No. 938,254 (Cal. Super. Ct., April 10, 1974), 102–103.

Shirley, Dennis. *Valley Interfaith and School Reform: Organizing for Power in South Texas.* Austin: University of Texas Press, 2002.

Shirley, Dennis, *Community Organizing for Urban School Reform.* Austin: University of Texas Press, 1997.

Spring, Joel. *American Education,* 12th ed. Boston, MA: McGraw Hill, 2006.

Spring, Joel. *Deculturalization and the Struggle for Equality: A Brief History of the Education of Dominated Cultures in the United States.* New York: McGraw-Hill, 1997.

Suárez-Orozco, Marcelo M. *Central American Refugees and U.S. High Schools: A Psychosocial Study of Motivation and Achievement.* Stanford, CA: Stanford University Press, 1989.

Taylor, Paul Schuster. *An American-Mexican Frontier: Nueces County, Texas.* New York: Russell & Russell, 1934.

U.S. Bureau of the Census, *U.S. Census of Pop, 1960, Subject Reports. Puerto Ricans in the United States.* Final Report. PC(2)-ID. Washington, D.C.: U.S. Government Printing Office, 1963.

U.S. Commission on Civil Rights, Report 1: *Ethnic Isolation of Mexican Americans in the Publish Schools of the Southwest.* Mexican American Education Study, April, l971.

U.S. Commission on Civil Rights, Report V: *Teachers and Students, Differences in Teacher Interaction with Mexican American and Anglo Students.* Mexican American Education Study, 1973.

U. S Commission on Civil Rights, Report VI: *Toward Quality Education for Mexican Americans.* Mexican American Education Study, 1974.

Vaca, Nick. "The Mexican American in the Social Sciences, 1912–1970," Parts 1 (1912–1935) and 2 (1936–1970). *El Grito,* 3 (Spring 1970): 3–24; 16 (Fall 1971): 17–51.

Valencia, Richard R. "The Mexican American Struggle for Equal Educational Opportunity in Mendez v. Westminster: Helping to Pave the Way for Brown v. Board of Education." *Teachers College Record* 107, no. 3 (March 2005): 389–423.

Valencia, Richard R., ed. *The Evolution of Deficit Thinking: Educational Thought and Practice.* Washington, D. C.: Falmer Press, 1997.

Valencia, Richard R. "The Mexican American Struggle for Equal Educational Opportunity in Mendez v. Westminster: Helping to Pave the Way for Brown v. Board of Education." *Teachers College Record* 107, no. 3 (March 2005): 389–423.

Valencia, Richard R., and E. M. Bernal. "The Texas Assessment of Academic Skills (TAAS) Case: Perspectives of Plaintiffs' Experts" [Special issue]. *Hispanic Journal of Behavioral Sciences* 22, no. 4(2000).

Valencia, Richard R., ed. *Chicano School Failure and Success: Past, Present, and Future.* London: Routledge Falmer, 2002: 253–309.

Valencia, Richard R. "Educational Testing and Mexican American Students: Problems and Prospects." In *The Elusive Quest for Equality: 150 Years of Chicano/Chicana Education,* edited by J. F. Moreno), 123–140. Cambridge, MA: Harvard Educational Review, 1999.

Valencia, Richard, Bruno J. Villarreal, and Moises F. Salinas. "Educational Testing and Chicano Students:

Issues, Consequences, and Prospects for Reform." In *Chicano School Failure and Success: Past, Present, and Future,* edited by Richard R. Valencia, 253–309. London: Routledge Falmer, 2002.

Valencia, Richard R., Martha Menchaca, and Rubén Donato. "Segregation, Desegregation, and Integration of Chicano Students: Old and New Realities." In *Chicano School Failure and Success: Past, Present, and Future,* edited by Richard R. Valencia, 2nd ed., 70–113. New York: Routledge/Falmer, 2002.

Valenzuela, Angela. *Subtractive Schooling: U.S.-Mexican Youth and the Politics of Caring.* Albany: State University of New York Press, 1999.

Vidal, Jaime R. "The Great Migration." In *Puerto Rican and Cuban Catholics in the U.S., 1900–1965,* edited by Jay P. Dolan and Jaime R. Vidal, 54–69. South Bend, IN: University of Notre Dame Press, 1994.

Weinberg, Meyer. *A Chance to Learn: The History of Race and Education in the United States.* Cambridge: Cambridge University Press, 1977.

Whalen, Carmen Teresa. "Colonialism, Citizenship, and the Making of the Puerto Rican Diaspora." In *The Puerto Rican Diaspora: Historical Perspectives,* edited by Carmen Teresa Whalen and Victor Vazquez-Hernandez, 1–42. Philadelphia: Temple University Press, 2005.

Whalen, Carmen Teresa, and Victor Vazquez-Hernandez. *The Puerto Rican Diaspora: Historical Perspectives.* Philadelphia: Temple University Press, 2005.

Whaley, Charlotte. *Nina Otero-Warren of Santa Fe.* Albuquerque: University of New Mexico Press, 1994.

Wilson, Steven H. "Brown over 'Other White': Mexican Americans' Legal Arguments and Litigation Strategy in School Desegregation Lawsuits." *Law and History Review* 21, no. 1(Spring 2003): 145–194.

Wortham, Stanton, Enrique G. Murillo, Jr., and Edmund Hamann, eds., *Education in the New Latino Diaspora: Policy and the Politics of Identity.* Westport, CT: Ablex, 2002.

4 Latina/o Education and the Reciprocal Relationship between Theory and Practice

Four Theories Informed by the Experiential Knowledge of Marginalized Communities

C. Alejandra Elenes
Arizona State University

Dolores Delgado Bernal
University of Utah

Since many of us come from disenfranchised communities of color, we feel compelled to "look to the bottom," to involve ourselves in the development of solutions to our people's problems. A number of us feel that that we cannot afford to adopt the classic detached, ivory tower model of scholarship when so many are suffering, sometimes in our own extended families. We do not believe in praxis instead of theory but that both are essential to our people's literal and figurative future.

(Wing, 2003, p. 6)

What is considered theory in the dominant academic community is not necessarily what counts as theory for women-of-color.... *Necesitamos teorías* that will rewrite history using race, class, gender and ethnicity as categories of analysis, theories that cross borders, that blur boundaries— new kinds of theories with new theorizing methods.... And we need to find practical applications for those theories. We need to de-academize theory and to connect the community to the academy.

(Anzaldúa, 1990, pp. xxv–xxvi)

The discourses of knowledge represent a hierarchy that classifies theory as legitimate knowledge based on the sacred canons of objective truth, while lived experiences and everyday practices are supposedly devoid of theory. The narrow expectations and assumptions of neutrality and objectivity within academia have often pushed scholars to divide, order, and disconnect theory from praxis. Most often, scholars feel confined to teach and conduct research as if there is no meeting place between what we know and learn from our life experiences and what we know and learn from our formal education within the academy. Rather than detach and compartmentalize theory and praxis, many scholars of color and feminist scholars of color have called for theory to be informed by the lives of those it presumes to explain and understand. They have insisted on "new kinds of theories" (Anzaldúa, 1990, p. xxv) that are not formed on "the classic detached, ivory tower model of scholarship..." (Wing, 2003, p. 6), but instead recognize the reciprocal relationship between theory and praxis.

This reciprocal relationship has been instrumental to the development of Latina/o education scholarship as scholars have looked to the lives of Latina/o students, parents, educators, and communities to critically explore, better understand, and begin to transform the education of Latinas/os. In highlighting the affinities of theory and praxis in Latina/o education, we focus on four theoretical traditions including critical race theory, Latina/o critical race theory, borderland/border theories, and Chicana feminist theory. We have chosen these perspectives because they each (in their own way) emphasize the importance of the experiential knowledge of marginalized peoples and how this knowledge links the interdependent relationship between theory and praxis. In other words, collectively these bodies of scholarship demonstrate the ways in which theory informs practice at the same time practice informs theory. Importantly, these theoretical traditions also primarily emerge from and are developed by scholars of color who critically utilized the lessons learned from their lived practices and that of their families and communities. These four traditions represent innovative interdisciplinary scholarship that draws from other intellectual traditions to move us beyond binaries and deficit understandings of Latina/o students and communities, while also actively connecting scholarship with different forms of social justice activism.

For this chapter, we have grouped these four traditions into two sections because of the natural connections between them. The first section addresses critical race theory and Latina/o critical race theory while the second section addresses both borderland/border theories and Chicana feminist theory. Each section provides a brief genealogy, a discussion of key theoretical concepts and ideas, and a review of empirical scholarship that draws from and contributes to the theory. In each section, we demonstrate the implications of these theoretical traditions as they relate to pedagogy, methodology, epistemology, educational policy, and the making of multiple subjectivities. We end the chapter by sketching out a synthesis of our analysis. In the process, we argue not that these theories are the only theoretical perspectives or the best perspectives for addressing Latina/o education. Rather, we propose that education scholars, researchers and practitioners should be aware of the conceptual tools each of these frameworks provide, how these tools have been employed in education scholarship, and how they might be helpful in transforming the education of Latina/os.

Critical Race Theory and Latina/o Critical Race Theory

Critical race theory is a framework that was first developed primarily, though not exclusively, by legal scholars of color to address social justice and racial oppression in U.S. society. According to Richard Delgado and Jean Stefancic (2001), "The critical race theory (CRT) movement is a collection of activists and scholars interested in studying and transforming the relationship among race, racism, and power" (p. 2). The genealogy of CRT reveals a contextual and historical relationship to critical legal studies, ethnic social movements, U.S. third world feminisms, ethnic studies, and other theoretical traditions from which it borrows (Matsuda, Lawrence, Delgado, & Crenshaw, 1993). Some argue that the genealogy of CRT goes back as far as W.E.B. Dubois, Sojourner Truth, Frederick Douglas, Cesar Chavez, and the Black Power and Chicano movements of the 1960s and 1970s (Delgado & Stefancic, 2001). Looking forward, CRT in legal studies has branched into related frameworks such as Latina/o Critical Race Theory (LatCrit), Critical Race Feminism (FemCrits), Asian Critical Race Theory (AsianCrit), and Queer Critical Race Theory (QueerRaceCrit). The affinities among and between these frameworks and transnational scholarship, Black feminist thought, borderland/border theory, queer theory, Chicana feminist theories and other critical scholarship are immense. Since 1994 numerous scholars of color in the field of education have employed and further developed critical race theories with a particular emphasis on CRT and LatCrit in their research and practice (i.e., DeCuir & Dixson, 2004; González, 1998; Ladson-Billings & Tate, 1995; Lopez, 2003; Lynn, 1999, 2006; Lynn & Parker, 2006; Parker, 1998, 2003; Parker, Deyhle, & Villenas, 1999; Rolon-Dow, 2005; Solórzano, 1997, 1998; Solórzano & Yosso, 2000, 2001, 2002; Stovall, 2005, 2006: Tate, 1994, 1997; Vann Lynch, 2006; Villalpando, 2003).

As theoretical frameworks in the field of law, CRT and LatCrit theories share some basic assumptions. Both frameworks view racism as endemic to U.S. society and explore the ways that so called race-neutral laws and policies perpetuate racial subordination. They also emphasize the importance of viewing laws and lawmaking within a historical and cultural context in order to deconstruct their racialized content (Crenshaw, Gotanda, Peller, & Thomas, 1995). Racism, White privilege, and the myths of meritocracy,[1] neutrality, and objectivity are understood to dominate institutions, social norms, and daily practice. CRT and LatCrit scholars also argue that providing a space for and utilizing the knowledge of marginalized people is vital for theory, practice, and social transformation. We will elaborate on some of the conceptual contributions of these frameworks later, but here it is important to note that concepts such as interest convergence (Bell, 1987), Whiteness as property (Harris, 1993), and the methodology of counterstorytelling (Delgado, 1989, 1995; Bell, 1985, 1987) are important tools developed and utilized by CRT and LatCrit scholars.

LatCrit (like FemCrit and the other CRT-related frameworks) emerged partially as a result of what some scholars felt was a CRT Black/White binary that did not allow the intersections of race, class, gender, sexuality, language, immigration status, and other important issues related to Latinas/os to be sufficiently addressed. It developed out of the CRT movement as a project to highlight the "racing" of Latinas/os in legal discourse and to provide an intersectional analysis of issues related specifically to Latinas/os (Trucious-Haynes, 2001; Valdes, 1996). It is concerned with a progressive sense of a coalitional Latina/o pan-ethnicity (Valdes, 1996), yet scholars argue that LatCrit scholarship should not eliminate race discourse or substitute ethnicity-centered explanations as a way to understand Latina/o identity and marginalization (Haney-López, 1998; Trucious-Haynes, 2001). LatCrit theory is usually viewed as compatible, supplementary, and complementary to CRT and not as something to replace CRT (Valdes, 1996). Although the basic tenets of CRT and LatCrit are similar, LatCrit in legal studies clearly focuses on the unique experiences, identities, and oppressions of Latinas/os while CRT does not.

In education, CRT has been defined as a "discourse of liberation" that "can be used as a methodological tool as well as a greater ontological and epistemological understanding of how race and racism affect education and lives of racially disenfranchised" (Parker & Lynn, 2002, pp. 7–8). It has also been defined as "a framework that can be used in theorizing about the ways in which educational structures, processes and discourses support and promote racial subordination" (Solórzano & Delgado Bernal, 2001, pp. 314–315). However, the distinction between CRT and LatCrit in education is sometimes less clear than in legal studies. Some Latina/o education scholars (Alemán 2006, 2007a; Delgado Bernal, 2002; Covarrubias, 2005; Marrun, 2007; Rolon-Dow, 2005; Villalpando, 2003) utilize both CRT and LatCrit together to form a theoretical lens that addresses issues such as immigration, language, culture, gender, and sexuality with a focus on the education of Latinas/os. Others, like Daniel Solórzano and Tara Yosso (2002) have argued for a reconceptualization of CRT in education to include a more intersectional analysis that encompasses issues specifically related to Latinas/os. They state that their understanding of CRT is informed by a "LatCrit consciousness." However, to re-center CRT and avoid the Black/White binary that plagued the CRT movement in legal studies, their scholarship on Chicana/o education names only CRT as their guiding theoretical framework. For the purposes of this chapter and in order to highlight how these frameworks have collectively contributed to Latina/o education scholarship, we will use "CRT/LatCrit" except when making a clear distinction between the two. The remainder of this section will discuss the following three conceptual contributions of CRT/LatCrit to Latina/o education: (a) CRT/LatCrit theorize about race while also addressing the intersectionality of racism, classism, sexism, heterosexism, and other forms of oppression; (b) CRT/LatCrit propose raced-gendered epistemologies that challenge Eurocentric epistemologies and dominant ideologies such as meritocracy, objectivity, and neutrality; and (c) CRT/LatCrit utilize counterstorytelling as a methodological and pedagogical tool.[2] CRT/LatCrit are not the only theoretical frameworks that offer these contributions, but collectively they do represent a challenge to the existing hierarchy of knowledge that disconnects theory and praxis and important ways to conceptualize Latina/o education.

Race and Intersectionality as Analytical Tools

Education scholars using CRT/LatCrit theorize about "raced" education and combat racism as part of a larger goal of ending all forms of subordination. What Gloria Ladson-Billings and William Tate (1995) pointed out nearly 15 years ago remains true today; there is a need to do this because race remains untheorized as a topic of scholarly inquiry in education. Although scholars have examined race as a tool for understanding social inequities, "the intellectual salience of this theorizing has not been systematically employed in the analysis of educational inequality" (p. 50). CRT/LatCrit scholars believe that race as an analytical tool, rather than a biological or socially constructed category used to compare and contrast social conditions, can deepen the analysis of educational barriers for people of color, as well as illuminate how they resist and overcome these barriers.

Whiteness as property is an example of how race (and its intersection with class) as an analytical tool can offer a more complete understanding of the current inequities in schools and districts where a growing majority of students are poor and Latina/o. Critical race legal scholars introduced the property issue by examining the historical construction of Whiteness as the ultimate property and how the concept of individual rights has been linked to property rights in the United States since the writing of the Constitution (Bell, 1987; Harris, 1993). Ladson-Billings and Tate (1995) extended legal scholarship to demonstrate how property relates to education in explicit and implicit ways. One of the more obvious examples is how property owners largely reap the highest educational benefits—those with the best property are entitled to the best schools. "Recurring discussions about property tax relief indicate that more affluent communities (which have higher property values, hence higher tax assessments) resent paying for a public school system whose clientele is largely non-white and poor" (p. 53).

Applying the property issue to the education of Mexican Americans, Enrique Alemán (2006, 2007a) uses CRT/LatCrit to analyze the inherent institutional racism of Texas school finance policy. After demonstrating how race and property rights formed the foundation for the history of Texas school funding, he then examines three chapters of the Texas education code and identifies the racial effects that the current school funding system has on seven majority-Mexican American school districts (Alemán, 2007a). He argues that while the overtly racist finance policy prior to the *Edgewood ISD v. Kirby* (1987) is gone, today the "…Texas school finance policy [has] evolved into a more subtle brand of institutional racism and inequity" (p. 12). Alemán provides a critical race policy analysis that is often absent in educational policy studies. He utilizes a CRT/LatCrit framework that brings theory and praxis together and traces the historical origins and racialized effects of policy decisions (Parker, 2003).

In addition to using race as an analytical tool, many CRT/LatCrit theorists have challenged the separate discourses on race, class, and gender and focused on the intersectionality of identities and subordination. Kimberlé Crenshaw (1993) saw intersectionality as a concept that links various forms of oppression (racism, classism, sexism) with their political consequences (e.g., global capitalism, growing poverty, and large numbers of incarcerated youth of color). Global capitalism and labor exploitation have had a profound impact on Latina/o populations not only in the United States but in Mexico and other Latin American countries. In legal studies, the LatCrit movement in particular has added layers of complexity to the concept of intersectionality by analyzing Latinas/os' subjectivities and positionalities in relation to race, class, and gender, as well as language (Romany, 1996), immigration (Garcia, 1995; Johnson, 1996–97), culture (Montoya, 1994, 1997), religion/spirituality (Iglesias & Valdes, 1998; Sanchez, 1998), and sexuality (Iglesias & Valdes, 1998; Valdes, Culp, & Harris, 2002). Some scholars have explored the transnational effects of domestic subordination and the racial impact of U.S. immigration law (Iglesias, 1998; Johnson, 2002). In doing so, their analyses are often congruent with those found in the border scholarship that we discuss later in this chapter. This is because they too address how the geopolitical border is related to socio-economic and political relations, as well as (immigration) policy. Kevin Johnson (2002) provides a legal and historical analysis and argues that immigration law has been central to Asian and Latina/o subordination in the United States. He also demonstrates how race, in combination with economic and other social forces, is crucial to understanding the United States' response to immigration flows from developing nations and the ways in which immigration from "non-White" countries or regions has and continues to be restricted. Within LatCrit scholarship, ideas of citizenship are also expanding and evolving in ways that do not center on one nation-state, such as the increase in dual or multiple citizenship, the development of a formal European Union citizenship, the push for a globalized citizenship grounded in human rights, and the call to focus on Latina/o cultural citizenship (Delgado Bernal, Alemán, & Flores, 2008; Hernández-Truyol & Hawk, 2005; Hernández-Truyol, 2005).

At the same time, LatCrit scholars have an affinity to the borderland theories that we address in more detail in the latter half of this chapter. Borderland theories capture the complex ways in which Latinas/os negotiate and make sense of their position in society, and also highlight the significance of Latina/o subjectivity and hybrid identities. Johnson's (1999) *How Did You Get to Be Mexican* and Margaret Montoya's (1994) classic "Máscaras, Trenzas, y Greñas: Un/masking the Self While Un/braiding Latina Stories of Legal Discourse" are but two examples of how legal scholars have theorized the ways in which Latinas/os negotiate living in the metaphorical borderlands. Montoya addresses the linguistic and sociocultural conditions of living between two worlds by highlighting the hierarchical physical and symbolic boundaries she moved between and among from second grade to her post graduate work at Harvard Law School. As a hybrid Chicana she notes that she is a product of "Mexican-Indian-Irish-French relations...English-speaking schools and a Spanish-speaking community." Using a counterstory methodology, her personal narrative speaks of the masks or cultural disguises we often put on, take off, or hide behind in schools.

In the educational research community, scholars have examined how the intersection of racism with other forms of oppression impacts the education of Latinas/os. Drawing on race and/or intersectionality as analytical tools and arguing for social change, they have examined the leadership of Mexican American superintendents (Alemán, 2006), the experiences of Chicana/o graduate students (Solórzano & Yosso, 2001), how Chicana/o undergraduate students draw from their language, religion/spirituality, and culture as tools for success in higher education (Delgado Bernal, 2002; Villalpando, 2003), how student services staff can better serve Latina/o college students (Villalpando, 2004), what we can learn from the counterstories of Chicanas/os along the entire educational pipeline (Yosso, 2006), how caring counternarratives can be used to create connections between teachers and middle school Puerto Rican girls (Rolon-Dow, 2005), and how Latina student activists combat racism, sexism, classism, and heterosexism via social justice education (Revilla, 2004).

Anita Tijerina Revilla's (2003, 2004) interdisciplinary scholarship is an example of an intersectional analysis that engages both theory and praxis around four fundamental axes of identity and discrimination—race, class, gender, and sexuality. Her five-year study that focused on members of an undergraduate student organization called Raza Womyn explicitly draws upon three of the frameworks we write about in this chapter CRT, LatCrit, and Chicana feminist theories. The students in her study employ a distinct kind of education Revilla calls *muxerista* pedagogy. This pedagogy understands that there are different positions of truth as it values dialogue, questioning, dialectical exchanges, lived experiences, a commitment to social justice, and recognition of multiple identities among Latinas. One of the most powerful illustrations of *muxerista* pedagogy "includes the production of knowledge that leads to such things as new redefined, reclaimed, and or reconstructed terminology used for self-identification" (2004, p. 87). The members of Raza Womyn continuously (re)think and (re)create terms to express their identities—strategically mobile and contingent—based on their social justice agenda and desire to disrupt dominant power relations. For example, the term "Queer," often used in a derogatory way, is commonly used in an empowering way by Raza Womyn to self-identify as gay, lesbian, bisexual, and/or transgender members. They have claimed and redefined the word Queer in their concerted effort to carve alliances in spite of differences between straight and Queer members. The term *muxerista* is another (re)created term that literally translates to womanist, the concept coined by Alice Walker (1983) that refers to a certain kind of black feminist who engages in outrageous, audacious, courageous, or willful behavior. Revilla points out that the members of Raza Womyn make it their own by changing the spelling and replacing the "j" with an "x" to signify a connection to the ancestry and languages of Mexico and Latin America. Similarly, responding to the Latina diaspora the founding members of the student organization engaged in dialogue about their diverse and multiple identities based on sexuality, nationality, ethnicity, and immigration status to decide on the term "Raza" as an umbrella for all Latinas. Their group included Central Americans (Salvadorena and Guatemalteca) South Americans, Latinas from the Caribbean, and mixed-ethnicity Latinas. Revilla's study demonstrates how these diverse Latinas negotiated different forms of knowledge, engaged in different social justice struggles, built political alliances around multiple subjectivities, and reshaped how they identify themselves through their affinities and differences.

Revilla and other Latina/o education scholars who draw from CRT/LatCrit have utilized race as a conceptual tool to look at educational policies, practices, and experiences, while they have also looked at how the intersection of race, class, gender, sexuality, immigration, language, and/or other identities shape the education of Latinas/os. The work of many of these scholars specifically illustrates the clear affinities CRT/LatCrit theories have with border/borderland theories, transnational scholarship, and Chicana feminist theories. In the next section, we address another conceptual contribution of CRT/LatCrit theories and continue to note the connections to other intellectual traditions.

Raced-Gendered Epistemologies

A second potential contribution of CRT/LatCrit is the articulation of raced-gendered epistemologies that challenge a Eurocentric epistemology and question dominant discursive notions of meritocracy, objectivity, knowledge, and individualism. Ladson-Billings (2000) argues that "there are well-developed systems of knowledge, or epistemologies, that stand in contrast to the dominant Euro-American epistemology" (p. 258) and that these systems of knowledge have long been recognized by communities of color and scholars of color such as W.E.B. Dubois (1903/ 1953), Gloria Anzaldúa (1987), and R. A. Warrior (1995). CRT/LatCrit theorists ground their research in these systems of knowledge and "...integrate their experiential knowledge, drawn from a shared history as 'other' with their ongoing struggles to transform..." (Barnes, 1990, pp. 1864–1865). CRT/LatCrit in education attempts to connect with the collective experiences, ways of thinking, believing, and knowing in racial communities especially in relation to the struggle for equity in schools and self-determination (Parker & Stovall, 2004). Indeed, a number of education scholars have employed CRT/LatCrit as a framework for discussing and conceptualizing Chicana/o, Latina/o, and Chicana feminist epistemologies (Delgado Bernal, 2002; Gonzalez, 1998; Pizarro, 1998; Hidalgo, 1998; Revilla, 2004).

Yosso's (2005a) scholarship draws on the epistemologies of communities of color, especially Latina/o communities to conceptualize community cultural wealth "...as the array of cultural knowledge, skills, abilities and contacts possessed by socially marginalized groups that often go unrecognized and unacknowledged" (p. 69). Understanding that culture is evidenced in material and nonmaterial productions of people and that it is neither fixed nor static, she outlines six forms of capital (e.g., aspirational, linguistic, familial, social, navigational, and resistant) that are interrelated and based upon the systems of knowledge students of color bring to schools from their everyday practices in homes and communities. For instance, she argues that aspirational capital is the ability to hold onto hopes and dreams in the face of structured inequality. Yet, the different forms of capital overlap since "aspirations are developed within social and familial contexts, often through linguistic storytelling and advice (*consejos*) that offer specific navigational goals to challenge (resist) oppressive conditions" (p. 77). Her conceptualization of community cultural wealth demonstrates the deep reciprocal relationship between theory and praxis. It also resonates with earlier ethnographic research that documents Mexicana/o/Latina/o teaching and learning as cultural strengths and demonstrates how students draw on their diverse linguistic and cultural resources to function in schools and society (Trueba 1988, 1991). Similarly, it connects to the anthropology of education research that defines "funds of knowledge" as those historically developed and accumulated strategies or bodies of knowledge that are vital to Latina/o family survival (González et al., 1995; Vélez-Ibánez & Greenberg, 1992).

By grounding itself in systems of knowledge that counter a dominant Eurocentric epistemology, CRT/LatCrit in education offer a tool for dismantling prevailing notions of fairness, meritocracy, colorblindness, and neutrality (Parker, Deyhle, & Villenas, 1999). Raced-gendered epistemologies allow CRT/LatCrit scholars to deconstruct master narratives and illustrate the way in which discursive and cultural sites "may be a form of colonialism, a way of imparting white, Westernized conceptions of enlightened thinking" (Roithmayr, 1999, p. 5). For example, Gutiérrez (2000) examined Walt Disney's ideological shift from conservatism (1930s-1970s) to present-day liberal multiculturalism particularly within its Spanish-speaking market. He argued that Disney continues to discursively promote Eurocentric ideologies that maintain a form of cultural hegemony. He offered critical race theory as one of several ways to examine the master narratives that Latino children are exposed to (i.e., global capitalism as benefiting all, the dominance of English monolingualism at the expense of other languages, and heteronormativity to name a few). At the same time, Disney movies may also be used as a pedagogical tool. Gutierrez believed Disney movies provide "numerous opportunities for children and adults to engage in critical discussions regarding power, domination, and repression" (p. 31). These types of critical discussions that challenge the insidious nature of a Eurocentric epistemological perspective and dismantle master narratives can and should take place more frequently in K-12 and postsecondary classrooms. As this example shows, by engaging teachers, parents, and students in a critical analysis of epistemological underpinnings of curriculum and other school processes, CRT/LatCrit offer tools that can impact the practice of Latina/o education.

The epistemological challenge offered by CRT/LatCrit is not solely about race, but about the nature of truth, production of knowledge, and the power to name one's reality. CRT/LatCrit provide examples of scholars who have developed specific epistemological stances informed by their own cultural identity, yet should not be interpreted as an attempt to essentialize Black, Latina/o, American Indian, or Asian American ways of knowing. Out of these epistemological stances emerge particular methodologies that can challenge the dominant perception of truth and reality. The next section addresses a counterstory methodology that is grounded in experiential knowledge and systems of knowledge that stand in contrast to the dominant Euro-American epistemology.

Counterstory Methodology

A third and potentially the greatest contribution of CRT/LatCrit is its development and use of storytelling in legal analysis and educational scholarship. CRT/LatCrit work in storytelling provides a rich way of conceptualizing methodology, pedagogy, and curriculum. Because critical race scholars view experiential knowledge as a strength, they draw explicitly on the lived experiences of people of color by including such methods as storytelling, family history, biographies, parables, *testimonios, cuentos, consejos*, chronicles, and narratives. Storytelling has a rich legacy and continuing tradition in communities of color. Indeed, legal scholar, Delgado (1995) asserted that many of the "early tellers of tales used stories to test and challenge reality, to construct a counter-reality, to hearten and support each other and to probe, mock, displace, jar, or reconstruct the dominant tale or narrative…" (p. xviii).

Counterstorytelling is a methodological tool that allows one to tell the story of those experiences that are not often told (i.e., those on the margins of society) and to analyze and challenge the stories of those in power (Delgado, 1989). The stories Latinas/os tell related to education often counter the majoritarian or stock story that is a natural part of the dominant discourse. Building on the work of Delgado (1989), some education scholars argue that these counterstories serve multiple methodological and pedagogical functions such as building community among those at the margins of society, putting a human and familiar face to educational theory and practice, challenging perceived wisdom about the schooling of students of color, and telling the story behind the story (Lopez, 2003; Solórzano & Delgado Bernal, 2001; Solórzano & Yosso, 2001).

Solórzano and Yosso (2002) arrange counterstories into three categories: personal narratives, other people's narratives, and composite narratives. First, personal stories or narratives are those that describe an individual's experience with racism, sexism, heterosexism, and other forms of oppression. While there might be themes that many people of color can identify with, it is a nuanced, unique, and individualized story. We posit that these autobiographical counterstories are sometimes similar to the personal narratives and *testimonios* often found in borderland and Chicana feminist scholarship. The work of Tate (1994) and Parker (1998) provide examples of personal counterstories in education scholarship. Second, other people's stories or narratives recount and analyze a person of color's experiences and responses to various forms of oppression. These stories are usually based on personal interviews, *platicas*, or observation and can be told in third person voice or using direct quotes from another person's narrative. Fernández (2002), Lynn (2006), and Rolon-Dow (2005) illustrate this type of counterstory. Fernández (2002) explores how Pablo, a "successful" Latino student, reflected on his educational experiences in a public high school in Chicago as part of a larger study on Latina/o youth culture. Her counterstory is based on the in-depth interviews she conducted with Pablo and provides insight into how he understood his and his Latina/o classmates' educational experiences and how he and his classmates resisted inadequate schooling. While Fernández reminds education scholars that counterstories based on someone else's narrative are mediated communicative events, her counterstory demonstrates that using Latina/o students' stories as the centerpiece of qualitative research can provide nuanced understandings of how Latina/o students experience and respond to their educational experiences.

The third category of counterstories outlined by Solórzano and Yosso (2002) are composite stories or narratives that draw on various forms of "data" to recount the racialized, gendered, sexualized, and classed experiences of people of color. Composite characters are based on the (quantitative and qualitative) data gathered during the research process, the existing literature on the topic, professional experience, and personal experience. Composite stories in education build on the legal scholarship of Bell (1985, 1987), who tells stories of society's treatment of race through his protagonist and alter ego Geneva Crenshaw, and Delgado (1995, 1999) who addresses race, class, and gender issues through Rodrigo Crenshaw, the half-brother of Geneva. The web of composite characters that have appeared in Latina/o education represent very real life experiences and are created to illuminate the educational system's role in racial, gender, and class oppression, as well as the myriad of responses by Latinas/os (Alemán & Alemán, 2006; Delgado Bernal, 1999; Delgado Bernal & Villalpando, 2002; Smith, Yosso, & Solórzano, 2006;

Solórzano & Delgado Bernal, 2001; Solórzano & Villalpando, 1998; Solórzano & Yosso, 2000; Solórzano & Yosso, 2001; Villalpando, 2003; Yosso, 2006).

Counterstories can serve as an important curricular tool in Latina/o education. They have the potential to move a watered-down "diversity" or multicultural curriculum away from simply celebrating difference and food, fun, and fiestas to a curriculum that actively names and challenges racism and other forms of injustice. For example, Yosso (2002) examined how a critical race media literacy curriculum influenced Chicana/o community college students. She proposed a critical race curriculum that is based on the counterstories of "others," thereby providing "students with an oppositional language to challenge the deficit societal discourses with which they are daily bombarded" (p. 15). Rather than adding on the experiences of "Others" or pushing students toward "discovering" a monolithic people of color, her understanding of a critical race curriculum "explores and utilizes shared and individual experiences of race, class, gender, immigration status, language, and sexuality in education" (p. 16).

Counterstories as pedagogical and methodological tools provide us with an opportunity to stand in a different relationship to the research and researched; an opportunity to draw upon the knowledge of and by people of color that has been distorted or excluded by Euro-American cultural logic (Ladson-Billings, 2000). Yet, counterstorytelling also generates another set of methodological and ethical questions about who can tell counterstories and for what purposes counterstories are written or told? Does it matter how and under what circumstances educators or researchers make use of counterstories? How do the issues here differ—if they do at all—for educators of color and White educators writing, reading, or teaching counterstories? We need ways to approach thinking about these questions (and others) without giving prescriptions and issuing policies or rules related to who can engage counterstory methodology. We propose that we move from prescriptions and policies to guiding principles and a deeper understanding of the different investments in writing or reading counterstories.[3] Finally, there are numerous critiques of critical race scholars' use of stories and narratives in legal scholarship (e.g., Farber & Sherry, 1993, 1997; Posner, 1997). The critiques are grounded in a debate over alternative ways of knowing and understanding, subjectivity versus objectivity, and different conceptions of truth. Some critics also argue that just because counterstories draw explicitly on the lived experiences of people of color does not prove the existence of a new perspective based on "a voice of color."

Future Directions for CRT/LatCrit

CRT/LatCrit in education are liberatory discourses that center the experiences of people of color and value those experiences as sources of knowledge and as the basis of theory. We have demonstrated that this has direct implications for methodologies, pedagogies, epistemologies, educational policy, and the linguistic and sociocultural conditions of living between multiple worlds. CRT/LatCrit offer a theoretical perspective that centers race/ethnicity as endemic to U.S. society and its effects on educational (in)equity. Education scholars using CRT/LatCrit perspectives have examined educational structures and policies, as well as the agency enacted by students, educators, and parents of color in relation to these structures and policies. Indeed, legal scholars such as Margaret Montoya, Kevin Johnson, and Richard Delgado have pointed out that the active engagement, intellectual growth, and future development of both CRT and LatCrit are most visible within the field of education.[4]

While education scholars are reshaping and extending critical race theory in ways very different from legal scholars, CRT/LatCrit in education has for the most part not made its way into K-12 educational practice, in much the same way that CRT has virtually not made its way into courtrooms. Perhaps the challenge for CRT/LatCrit (and for all the frameworks we address in this chapter) is that they are counter-hegemonic and as such they are in constant battle with conservative forces. For example, at the time of this writing, the Arizona legislature is currently debating a bill that would prohibit teaching material that challenges Western values and history in K-12 schools.[5] This kind of a law or curriculum surveillance is in direct conflict with a CRT/LatCrit perspective which contests a Western Eurocentric epistemology that is grounded in one Truth. We do not believe that being counter-hegemonic is a limitation of CRT, but rather we point out the challenge of CRT/LatCrit in regards to practice and its impact in K-12 education.

CRT/LatCrit need to continue to address current limitations within the frameworks and in the way these frameworks are utilized and taken up. For example, LatCrit specifically provides an intersectional lens that addresses how Latinas/os' unique experiences, identities, circumstances and issues such as immigration, citizenship, and language are necessary categories of analysis to understand educational inequality. Yet, most of the education scholarship still is missing a strong intersectional analysis that includes gender, sexuality, and or the body in the way that Revilla does (2003, 2004). Analyses that address transnationalism for Latinas/os are also limited. In addition, while a LatCrit intersectional analysis lends itself to studying Latina/o pan-ethnicity most of the scholarship that focuses on Latinas/os really addresses the education of Chicanas/os and often does not address the nuances related to the experiences of other Latinas/os. Finally, while CRT/LatCrit opens up a space for alternative epistemologies and the examination of physical places (i.e., schools, courtrooms) and social spaces (i.e., positions people occupy), it does not specifically theorize space and place in the way that borderland theory does. To continue to move CRT/LatCrit forward and address the educational inequity that the majority of Latinas/os in this country experience, limitations of the two frameworks need to be engaged. In the next section, we look at borderland/border theories and Chicana feminist theories in their own right, but we also encourage readers to think about how all of these theoretical perspectives complement each other and at times address one another's limitations.

Borderland/Border Theories and Chicana Feminist Theories

Borderland/border and Chicana feminist theories offer different, but equally important conceptual tools to account for the complexities of Latinas/os' positions in society and in systems of U.S. education. Borderland/border theories were primarily developed by Mexican American scholars who turned to the history of the México-U.S. border region as a point of departure to explain the historical, social, political, economic, and cultural position of people of Mexican descent in the United States (e.g., Paredes, 1958; J. D. Saldívar, 1997; Calderón & Saldívar, 1991; Gutiérrez-Jones, 1995; R. Saldívar, 1990).[6] One of the goals of borderland scholars is to explain the condition of Chicanas/os/Latinas/os living between worlds, cultures, and languages. As C. Alejandra Elenes (1997) asserted, "the *Borderlands* is the discourse [language, modes of knowing and living] of people who live between different worlds" (p. 359). Additionally, Gloria Anzaldúa's conceptualization of borderland theories, published in her book, *Borderlands/La Frontera* in 1987, inspired a variety of scholars in various fields—from literature to education—to adopt her conceptualizations of *mestiza* consciousness, *facultad*, and *nepantla* to explore alternative ways of knowing and experiencing the world (e.g., Burciaga, 2007; Saldívar-Hull, 2000; Martínez, 2002; Delgado Bernal, 1998, 2006). *Mestiza* consciousness refers to the process of developing a Chicana consciousness that recognizes the struggle and need to straddle cultures, languages, spirituality, and sexuality. *La facultad* is the ability to see beyond surface phenomena. And *Nepantla* is the Nahuatl word for the land in the middle, which is also considered a space of transformation. Other Latino scholars such as Frank Bonilla, Edwin Meléndez, Rebecca Morales, and María de los Angeles Torres (1998) in their edited text *Borderless Borders: U.S. Latinos, Latin Americans, and the Paradox of Interdependence* adopted the notions of the borderland and the border because it also helps explain their position and relations with the United States.

In this section, we examine Latina/o educational scholarship that draws from borderland, border, and Chicana feminist theories to show their contribution to educational research and praxis. We start by explaining the theoretical foundations of borderland and border theorizing adopted from the field of cultural studies and show their influence on Latina/o education scholarship. It is important to note that there are overlaps between these conceptualizations. While both refer to boundaries, the former more specifically recognizes the metaphorical borders that can exist among social groups. In this chapter, we highlight the specific concepts of borderland and border theories that are important to the field of education and that have helped advance the field. These include: (a) the importance of place and space, (b) the formation of hybrid identities, and (c) border pedagogy. We end the section with an examination of Chicana feminist theory. We explore how it is being developed in the field of Latino education to interpret Latinas' diverse ways of knowing and creating spaces of teaching and learning. We find that there is a reciprocal relationship between borderland theories and Chicana feminism in that they have both influenced each other. That is, borderland theorists often include Chicana feminist theory, and Chicana feminists often incorporate borderland theories.

We have chosen to highlight scholarship that demonstrates applications of borderland/border and Chicana feminist scholarship to Latina/o education. While they operate in different educational contexts and in some cases their conceptualizations might seem too abstract for the practitioner, these studies offer applicable approaches to education—approaches that promote a humane praxis committed to social justice. Moreover, proponents of borderland theorizing have an affinity with other fields such as cultural studies, Chicana/o/Latina/o studies, and women of color feminist theories.

Cultural Studies and Borderland Theories

Chicana/o cultural studies scholars adopted the concept of borderlands and the border in the late 20th and early 21st centuries as a critical language capable of explaining Mexican American's socio-political conditions in the United States, and as forms of cultural expressions (Anzaldúa 1987/2007; Chabram-Dernesesian, 1992, 2007; Gaspar de Alba, 1998; Pérez, 1999; J. D. Saldívar, 1997; R. Saldívar, 1990; Saldívar-Hull, 2000). Chicana feminist historian Emma Pérez (1999) proposes that for many Chicana/o cultural studies scholars, the border is used as a "cohesive metaphorical linchpin" (p. 25; see also Villenas & Foley, 2002), and through this imagery and history they offer a decolonizing paradigm. A decolonizing paradigm is a mode of thinking that emanates from indigenous and Latinas/os multiple viewpoints. This paradigm, instead of accepting mainstream educational theories as the only acceptable mode of theorizing and producing scholarship, proposes to develop theories that honor and recognize the diversity and richness of the knowledge produced by Latinas/os and other people of color from their perspectives and lived experiences. Borderland theories also speak of the experience of ethnoracial discrimination suffered by people of Mexican descent in the Southwest.

The imagery of crossing borders that is quite present in Chicana/o cultural theory, aesthetics, and popular culture does not only speak of the México-U.S. border, but of crossing borders along institutional (schools, the media, government), racial, gender, class, and sexual orientation lines. As members of groups that simultaneously are located inside and outside social structures, including educational institutions, and historically marked by way of race, ethnicity, socioeconomic status, language, and oftentimes citizenship, Chicanas/os and Latinas/os must navigate the contradictions of living between two or more worlds. These worlds mark inter- and intra-group political, socioeconomic, and cultural differences among Latinos/as, and between Latinos/as and White Americans and other people of color. While Latinos/as are also in the ranks of the middle class, race/class-based structural inequalities in particular contribute to Latinas/os' differing experiences and material conditions. In terms of education, the contradictions of living between multiple worlds is magnified when Latinos/as' cultural practices, heritages, languages (including indigenous languages), and socioeconomic position are devalued. At the same time, Latinos/as' cultural productions reflect how they straddle these multiple worlds.

In returning to both the distinctions and interrelatedness of the borderland and the border, scholars differentiate between the concrete and the symbolic border. While the borderlands refer to geo-political regions along a borderline, they also speak of boundaries along multiple identity markers such as race, class, gender, and sexuality. A border, especially among nation-states, implies an area that is clearly marked, concrete and static. Its function is to demarcate the outer limits among peoples, nations, and property. The purpose of borders is to designate who can and cannot legitimately enter and occupy such spaces. The México-U.S. border region is quite unique because it is a very large border (1950 miles long) and is perhaps the only one in the world where a first and third world country converge. In her aforementioned text *Borderlands/La Frontera*, Gloria Anzaldúa (1987/2007) described the México-U.S. border as "una herida abierta" (an open wound; p. 25). Anzaldúa contributed to borderland/border scholarship by emphasizing the physical and symbolic characteristics of the borderlands. Therefore, she added a new dimension in the conceptualization of the borderlands in that she deals with the specific México-U.S. border, as well as with psychological, sexual, and spiritual borderlands that are not specific to any geopolitical region. Anzaldúa's theorizations served as foundation for the development of Chicana feminist theory, inspiring the work of Chela Sandoval (1998, 2000), Emma Pérez (1999), and Sonia Saldívar-Hull (2000).

The metaphorical meanings of the borderlands, or borderland theories, when applied to education permit us to study the various aspects within formal and informal educational settings. Such aspects include educational policy, curriculum, school practices, language and culture, as well as the importance of identity, subjectivity, and struggle. The individuals involved in education (teachers/professors, administrators, elected officials, students, parents, community members, and cultural workers) are affected by and can affect such structures. A key feature of borderland/border theories is that they take into account how individuals will their agency in response to changing social conditions. Borderland theories seek to explain how the aforementioned different elements interact often times in contradictory ways, and how individuals negotiate the different forces that inform educational practices. An underlining goal of borderland/border scholars, similar to the CRT/LatCrit scholars we reviewed earlier, is to transform practices and policies that reproduce racist, sexist, and homophobic forms of oppression to ones that are more egalitarian.

Proponents of borderland theories privilege an examination of how educational institutions can structure both inequality and liberation at the same time. They advocate not limiting the analysis of education to dominant views and how those who are negatively affected by these views resist them. Rather, they suggest seeing how individuals in their everyday practices navigate between dominant and resisting practices. Its proponents emphasize a double move that critiques dominant cultural (and educational) practices which subordinate Latinas/os at the same time that that they offer a new language of possibility to counter the aforementioned dominant forms of thinking (Bejarano, 2005; Cruz, 2006; Darder, 1998; Elenes 1997, 2006; McKenna, 2003; Vera & de los Santos, 2005; Villenas & Foley, 2002; Villenas, 2006a). Borderland theorizing offers a theoretical lens that "valorize the lived realities of Latinas/os in the face of insidious new forms of racist and deficit thinking" (Villenas & Foley, 2002, p. 218). Through the combination of new methodologies and ways of thinking about identity, these scholars offer a framework to analyze education and schooling outside traditional Western-based and positivist approaches such as the cultural deficit models still prevalent in educational research. Moreover, scholars who advocate borderland theorizing take into account the interrelationship between educational institutions and outside forces such as the land, identity, and cultural practices.

The Borderlands as Educational Places and Spaces

Because borderland theories are anchored on the relationship between land and identity, we argue that its proponents situate their scholarship by looking at place and space. Place refers to the physical location where groups are located, for example the border region or a classroom. Space refers to the position groups or individuals occupy in a society as a result of their race, class, gender, and sexuality; as well as the roles people might play in a society or location such as students, teachers, mothers, or cultural workers. To illustrate how the relationship between place and space is operationalized in Chicana/Latina critical education scholarship, we turn first to the work of Karleen Pendleton Jiménez (2006) and her examination of the relationship between land, identity, colonialism, and sexuality. In articulating what she calls Chicana peda-gogies of the land, she situates Chicana bodies at the center of colonial relations. She proposes that women's bodies, as the land, have been devalued in Western thought, a process that began during the era of European expansionism. The association between place and space is exempli-fied when Pendleton Jiménez links her embodiment with colonialism and hybridity not only as a Chicana with British blood, but also in her identification as butch lesbian. She writes, "Because my very body is a product of these multiple ancestries, because my very body, as a butch lesbian, is the image of both genders, because my sexual desire and love are for feminine women, my relation as a Chicana dyke to this land is a mess" (p. 223). This discussion makes it clear that colonialism and identity are interrelated and affect us all in that we can simultaneously accept and reject mainstream ideas about race, gender, and identity. That is, we can struggle against these ideas and we can unwittingly reproduce them. Thus, progressive educational practices can help transform education by including an examination of colonialism in the curriculum.

Given that debates over land are usually associated with histories of colonization, Cindy Cruz (2006) claims that making Chicana voices and history visible is part of the "struggle to develop a critical practice that can propel the brown body from a neocolonial past into the embodiments of radical subjectivities" (p. 60). That is, educators, students, and community members or activists can take into account these complicated and often painful histories and use this knowledge as a strategy to construct an educational practice committed to social justice.

Such critical educational practices are not easy as they require bringing together disparate issues. One could easily ask how critical educational practices can indeed "start with the land" (Pendleton Jiménez, 2006). Perlita Dicochea (2006), for example, explains how she bridged the disciplinary differences between ethnic studies and environmental economic and policy to study water pollution in the New River in the border between Calexico, California and Mexi-cali, Baja California. The interrelationship between place (the river) and spaces (ethnic studies and environmental economics and policy) link disciplines that tend not to speak to each other. In doing so, she bridged the differences in methodological approaches by applying a border methodology that permitted the "inclusion of traditional social sciences and cultural studies methods and tools" (p. 239). The goal was to be able to influence public policy by providing rich data that would be beneficial for policymakers and to value people and their sense-making as much as the numerical data.

Jennifer Ayala, Patricia Herrera, Laura Jiménez, and Irene Lara (2006) also connect place and space in their application of borderland theories to their analysis of their collaboration in the development and implementation of the Intergenerational Latina Health Leadership Project via bi-costal *pláticas* through courses offered at Hunter College (New York) and the University of California, Berkeley. The courses brought together the separate places of the university and the community, as well as distinct forms of knowledge, by discussing the "self-help process" to address health issues. Ayala and her co-authors explained this process as a "spiritual, intellec-tual and emotional process, [that] brings people together for support with the goal of healing wounds inflicted by oppression, and facilitating social change" (p. 262). This bicoastal long-distance class was also located in the borderlands, because it brought together experiences between different worlds of students, women, Latinas, and multiple communities associating mind, body and spirit or "mindbodyspirit." The mindbodyspirit usually is invisible in institutions of higher education, where rationality is more legitimate than the body and the spirit. Graduate student participants are also in a borderland space because they are between faculty and undergraduate students, and making contributions in both directions of the hierarchy. The work of Dicochea (2006) and Ayala et al. (2006) opens up a space for innovative dialogues about the places where education can take place; the borderlands are a site for often unrecognized, yet essential epistemologies, methodologies, and pedagogies.

Other examples of the classroom as borderland places and spaces are provided by Elenes (2006) and Teresa McKenna (2003). They each offer instructive discussions of how borderland theories are applied in classroom practices. Elenes applies borderland theories in an effort to avoid dualistic thinking between professors and students about each other, especially when there are many different ideological positions present in the university classroom. She argues that using relational theories of difference as part of border/transformative pedagogies offer the possibility to engage with multiple differences in the classroom beyond the duality of liberatory and oppressive forms of teaching and learning. For instance, she tries to move classroom discussions away from ideological positions in favor of philosophical ones. That is, instead of arguing positions from an individualistic "commonsensical" position, she encourages students to articulate the principles from which a particular point of view emerges. She seeks to open a third space where all the untidy and painful dynamics that can be encountered in a classroom can be recognized and used as pedagogical strategies rather than be avoided. Likewise, McKenna (2003) proposes that the classroom should be a fluid, transitory place. For her, pedagogies are a "conversation in which questions are asked, contradictions are exposed, and no solutions are reached" (p. 347). McKenna contributes to borderland scholarship by endorsing a practice where classroom participants get to "feel what it might be like to cross into the borderlands" (p. 437). Elenes and McKenna's borderland pedagogies demonstrate the relationship between hybridity and embodiment in progressive educational praxis.

In as much as place and space are central to borderland discussion, the bodies of the inhabitants of the borderlands cannot be ignored. This is why Cruz (2006) proposes that educators can enact a Chicana critical practice of education by incorporating the body. For example, in her ethnography of Latina/o lesbian and gay youths in alternative schools, Cruz found that it was precisely through their embodiment that the emerging identity of Latina and lesbian youth contested dominant ideas of race, class, gender, and sexuality. Queer youth made sense of their social position and "used" their brown bodies to contest mainstream definitions and surveillance practices aimed at enacting "appropriate" sexual and gender roles For example, some students wrote powerful poems about their "inappropriate" bodies (too large or too brown), while others used their bodies to challenge patriarchal conventions. Cruz (2006) concludes, "For the educational researcher, the inclusion of the body holds the beginning of charting new territories in epistemic approaches, where we can begin to develop strategies to rethink our work in education to reflect the multiplicities of language and history in less partial and less distorted ways" (p. 72). That is, the inclusion of the body allows for example, Latinas, queer youth, and brown men to become the subjects and not objects of knowledge. The places and spaces exemplified in the borderlands, signal to the need to recognize that progressive educational practices should not ignore the significance of the body; as it is also linked to the formation of hybrid cultural identities.

Hybrid Identities and Methodologies

Latina/o scholars construct hybrid identities within particular and diverse social spaces and places they occupy. In turn, hybridity is also manifested in the development of innovative

Chicana/o/Latina/o methodologies. Hybrid identifications refer to the process by which marginalized groups construct alternative identities in order to negotiate distinct cultural milieus, including dominant mainstream cultural practices such as English monolingualism. As Antonia Darder (1998) explains, people of color in general, including Latinas/os, live in a hybrid condition because their histories and cultural practices have been created and re-created within a context of both forced assimilation and segregation. This compulsory interrelation has resulted in forms of adaptation which, in Darder's words, have "in many instances, eroded, restructured, and reconstructed the language system, cultural beliefs, and social traditions of these groups" (p. 130). Education borderland scholars have applied a variety of methodologies that highlight the significance of Latina/o subjectivity and hybrid identities to educational scholarship. The purpose for these modes of thinking is to work toward the development of alternative and critical educational practices. Some examples of the different methodologies Latina/o scholars have applied include *testimonio*, critical ethnography, reflection on pedagogical practices, and *pláticas*. These methodologies, like the counterstory methodology of CRT/LatCrit, draw upon the experiential knowledge of both the researcher and the participants.

Sofia Villenas (2006b), for example, uses her personal *testimonio* based on her mother's, and her own mothering practices as a backdrop to her study of Latina mothers in North Carolina. Villenas questions dominant views of motherhood that tend to follow a middle class model that devalues working class and Latina mothering practices. Instead of following definitions of motherhood that either position one type of mothering as "good" (e.g., Anglo American middle class) or "bad" (working-class Latinas), Villenas shows that the Latinas in her study enacted hybrid practices and identities that "encompass … racialized, ethnicized, Chicanized, 'Americanized', hyphenated lives in the borderlands" (p. 149). In showing how Latina mothers will their agency, she demonstrates that their mothering practices are based on the implementation of different perspectives that create a third space between what often times seem to be polar opposites. In particular, she looks at the borderlands between "cultural sensibilities and ethnicities, between citizen and 'alien', between generations, between diverse mothering practices, and between meanings of womanhood" (p. 147). Villenas' analysis provides an important tool for an educational praxis that offers an alternative to the tendency of accepting middle class standards as the norm without question. If educators have an understanding of and respect for different family organization without creating hierarchies, the arguments on cultural deficit can be put into question.

Similarly, Pendleton Jiménez (2006) in addressing her hybrid identity as a butch lesbian, and her identification with masculinity, is able to offer a critical view of a masculinity that is defined in terms of power, oppression and the devaluation of what is deemed to be feminine. From a borderland perspective, Pendleton Jiménez puts into question the rigid boundaries between masculinity and femininity, and offers a critical space to create a new definition of masculinity that does not have to be overpowering. The combination of personal narrative, curriculum theory, and borderland pedagogies of the land show how hybridity can be used as innovative methodology. These strategies can be helpful for educators who are working with students struggling with constructing their sexual identity under the stress created by homophobia. Pendleton Jiménez (2006) and Cruz's (2006) aforementioned work presents a radical move in educational research and practice because they center the butch lesbian body and the formation of alternative subjectivities.

Borderland scholarship developed from Chicana/o/Latina/o unique conditions and histories. The primary theoretical perspective for explaining how physical and symbolic boundaries among groups, especially between groups that are hierarchically organized, affect the material conditions of those on the bottom of the hierarchies; and how subordinate groups negotiate these boundaries can help explain and offer models to groups and institutions beyond the Latina/o context. To a certain extent there are boundaries between many different social groups that interact in vertical and horizontal ways; and these differences affect relationships along different dimensions of race, gender, class, and sexual orientation. For example, race relations in the United States cannot be explained only in binary terms between Whites and people of color. Race relations need to be understood in how a multiracial society operates, including the inter-relationships and tensions that can exist among different groups of color. Borderland theorizing, then, can be extremely important in developing multicultural education programs (see Butler, 2001). At the same time, borderland theories can also provide a useful perspective from which to develop social service programs such as assistance for women on welfare or victims of domestic violence. For example, current policy makes it very difficult, if not impossible, for welfare recipients to attend college due to the work requirements. A borderland sensibility would help recognize that a narrow definition of work only helps to keep women in poverty. Redefining college attendance as part of the work requirement would be beneficial for the women and society as a whole. Similarly, a domestic violence shelter can be understood as borderland place and space aimed at keeping women safe, while they work at re-crafting their lives.

One of the limitations of borderland theories is that, like CRT/LatCrit theories, they have not been able to impact K-12 education. There are few teacher education programs that systematically include borderland theories in their curriculum. To date, borderland theories have contributed more to higher education curriculum in ethnic studies, women's studies, and graduate education programs. The limitations are due, in part, to the abstract nature of the theoretical constructions which are not often accessible to a larger audience. However, borderland theories have not been appropriated by mainstream education, we argue, because they offer a radical alternative to contemporary educational practices. Mainstream education models are somewhat antithetical to the modes of thinking offered by borderland theories. For example, at this juncture, teacher preparation programs and practicing teachers are obligated to respond to educational policy based on positivistic approaches. Legislation such as No Child Left Behind requires that schools prove learning *only* through scores on standardized tests. The complex understandings of how teaching and learning can occur in an environment where there are multiple identities, languages, and modes of thinking that borderland theories call for cannot be reduced to scores on a test. By no means are we arguing that borderland theorists and practitioners should alter their perspectives; what we would like to see are more possibilities for utilizing these perspectives to improve education. Moreover, as we shall see in the following section, we can learn from scholars who have implemented border pedagogies in teacher preparation and in-service training for teachers on the México-U.S. border region (Cline & Necochea, 2006; Romo & Chavez, 2006).

Border Theory, Identity, and Politics

As we have examined the relationship between place and space, we can also look at the relationship between border and borderland theories. They both recognize that the border and the borderlands are literal and metaphorical; however, border theory privileges the literal meaning. They both offer new ways of thinking in relation to the México-U.S. border and of the borderlands region and the relationships existing among peoples and institutions. This is particularly so with respect to immigration issues, culture, economics, and identity on the borderlands. Border theory as applied by Latina/o and education scholars speaks specifically and concretely on how the border affects policy, identity, and pedagogy. For example, Jaime Romo and Claudia Chavez (2006) proclaim that "the geopolitical border between Mexico and the United States represents the beginnings, endings, and blending of languages, cultures, communities, and countries" (p. 142). That is, border theory offers an explanation of the different cultural, linguistic, socio-economic, and political dynamics of the borderlands and its inhabitants (Bejarano, 2005). In this sense, border theory, while it addresses metaphorical conceptualizations similar to borderland theories, also looks at the physical dimension of the border. For Latina/o education, border theory is concerned with how the literal border affects educational policy and pedagogy (Bejarano, 2005).

Specifically, border theory provides an analytical axis to understand what happens to communities on both sides of the México-U.S. border due to immigration and its consequences on transnational communities. For educators, the effects on youth should be of paramount importance. From a human rights perspective, children and youth must receive an education regardless of citizenship status and immigration policy debates. To offer the best education possible, teachers must be well prepared to work within this transnational context. Border theory highlights the hybrid nature of the border experience and its fluidity. Cynthia Bejarano (2005) writes, "[the border] represents a living, breathing experience that penetrates the very being of people of Mexican descent living in the United States, including youth" (p. 28). Border theory, then, cannot ignore the consequences of identity politics and how they affect students, teachers, administrators, and policy makers.

Latina/o education scholars who have applied border theory offer concrete examples of how to enact border pedagogies in the K-12 system offering a praxis that is missing from borderland scholars. Border pedagogies refer to the multifaceted and complex educational factors and knowledge, such as policies, curriculum, and institutional practices, that teachers and students need in order to enhance the academic attainment of students in the borderlands (Cline, Reyes & Necochea, 2005). For example, Zulmara Cline and Juan Necochea (2006) offer strategies on how to implement border pedagogies for teachers and future teachers on the borderlands. Cline and Necochea (2006) advance educational praxis by looking into the Mexican educational system, something that is missing even in teacher in-service training near the México-U.S. border. They propose that "for schools to successfully educate transnational children, teachers must possess certain dispositions that allow them to incorporate students' needs into the educational setting, thus enabling learners to negotiate both cultures academically and socially" (p. 269). Through dialogues with teachers from Tijuana and San Diego who participated in a Border Pedagogy Biliteracy Institute, Cline and Necochea identified five teacher dispositions that enable teacher effectiveness on the borderlands: (a) open-mindedness and flexibility, (b) passion for borderland education, (c) ongoing professional development, (d) cultural sensitiveness, and (e) pluralistic language orientation. They propose to include these five themes in teacher preparation because current programs are "not designed to help teachers develop the instructional programs needed when students' language and cultural needs are the nucleus of effective educational practices" (p. 280).

Concordantly, Romo and Chavez (2006) offer a practical approach to border pedagogy for teacher preparation based on a study of 48 undergraduate and graduate students, mostly European-American female pre-service teachers, enrolled in a course titled "Philosophical and Multicultural Foundations of Education" (p. 145). Their data showed that students were unprepared to deal with the complexities of the border region and that in order to be effective teachers on the borderlands they "must be fluent in the hidden dynamics that affect schools: immigration, poverty, race, culture, and language" (p. 146). Romo and Chavez (2006) conclude that students and teachers must be "skilled in negotiation, language, immigration, race, culture, and class issues" (p. 152). In order for teachers to become skilled in these issues, pre-service education programs must not ignore the cultural, social, political and economic conditions that affect the inhabitants of the borderlands.

Bejarano (2005, 2006) advanced border pedagogical praxis (the enactment of teaching and learning practices with a border sensitivity) through a complicated analysis of how youth of Mexican descent construct different notions of identity through a continuum of Mexicanness. These youths' construction of identity was not isolated from the larger societal racial, gender, and immigration politics. Bejarano (2005) studied how Latina/o youth, specifically Mexican and Chicana/o, "navigated their ethnic self-identities, their relationships with one another via youth cultures, and how and why this process explodes into conflict between Latinas/os" (p. 57). She found that there are significant differences in how Mexican and Chicana/o students constructed their identities. This point, while it is well known to Latina/o scholars and teachers, is missed by the larger public, teachers and administrators who tend to view Latinas/os as a homogenous group. Bejarano also shows the serious tensions between Mexican and Chicana/o students and how larger racial, gender, and immigration politics can be reproduced by young people. Students developed different modes of identification and affinity that signaled their survival strategies, some were able to adapt to U.S. mainstream cultural practices, while others maintained a sense of Mexican pride and language. Yet, these processes of identification did not always or necessarily fall into binary categories. Rather, Bejarano found that there was a continuum or a mosaic of Mexicanness among the students' forms of identification. Indeed, there were students who identified with both groups and were able to construct their Mexican/Chicana/o identity in a third or middle space that included both identities. She concludes that "Mexicana/o and Chicana/o identities are defined according to the physical boundaries of the international border where people's racial and/or ethnic status is politically, socially, culturally, and legally magnified" (2006, p. 60).

These applications of border theory provide clear examples of the affinities of theory and praxis in educational research. This praxis responds to, but also informs larger social structural racial and ethnic politics; mostly informed by discussion about immigration in the United States. Their weakness, with the exception of Bejarano, is that they do not take into account the importance of gender in such debates. An inclusion of feminist theorizing will make border theory praxis more substantial. We now turn to Chicana feminist theorizing.

Chicana Feminist Theorizing and Latina Education

Similar to Critical Race Theory/Lat Crit and borderlands/border theory, Chicana feminism also breaks with Western binary systems. However, Chicana feminism focuses its analyses from critical, social, economic, political, and cultural perspectives specifically on Chicanas' material conditions in the United States and in a global context due to race, class, gender, sexuality, and linguistic inequalities. Chicana feminists highlight how Chicanas struggle against these forms of oppression. From a theoretical perspective, it provides a theory of agency (how women act upon their world) showing how Chicanas have not passively accepted racist, sexist, classist, and homophobic institutional and cultural practices. Therefore, Chicana feminist theory has much to offer Chicana/Latina progressive education. Chicana feminist theorist Chela Sandoval suggests that a Chicana feminist analysis should begin from a starting point that is uniquely Chicana, rather than trying to adapt or respond to mainstream modes of thinking. Feminist theories as those developed by Sonia Saldívar-Hull's (2000) feminism on the border, Chela Sandoval's (1998, 2000) differential consciousness, and Emma Pérez's (1999) decolonial imaginary have served as theoretical foundations for feminist educational scholarship. Following we illustrate Chicana feminism's contribution to Chicana/Latina feminist education scholarship.

The anthology *Chicana/Latina Education in Everyday Life: Feminista Perspectives on Pedagogy and Epistemology* (2006), co-edited by Dolores Delgado Bernal, C. Alejandra Elenes, Francisca Godinez, and Sofia Villenas, illustrate how Chicana feminist theories and practices can be incorporated in education. The anthology centers on the educational experiences of Chicanas and Latinas, and their survival strategies and resiliency in high school, college, graduate education, as teachers/professors, and in community settings. A significant contribution of this anthology is the inclusion of Chicana/Latina everyday experiences of teaching, learning, and communal knowing as forms of education. By embracing educational theories and methods, they offer "women-centered definitions of teaching, learning and ways of knowing rooted in Chicana/Latina theories and visions of life, family, community, and [the] world" (Villenas,

Godinez, Delgado Bernal, & Elenes, 2006, p. 2). The book is organized in four sections following the life span of youth, college-age students, mature women and motherhood. The final section makes use of borderland theories from feminists' perspectives. Many of the contributors make use of the theories developed by Anzaldúa, Saldívar-Hull, Sandoval, and Pérez.

Saldívar-Hull's (2000) feminism on the border acknowledges the urgency of acting on political issues that exploit and oppress Chicanas (and, we argue, Latinas) globally, nationally, and within Chicana/o communities and cultures. These include reducing sexism and homophobia in Chicana/o communities, confronting institutional racism, fighting against economic exploitation, and grappling with the demands from traditional patriarchal Chicano and Mexican cultures. The border feminism that Saldívar-Hull proposes deals with "material geopolitical issues" (p. 34) that redirect feminist theory to address the "multiplicity of experiences" of Chicanas in solidarity with third world feminists. As we elaborated in the previous section, feminism on the border can enhance border pedagogy by adding a needed feminist analysis. In an era of heightened globalization, transnational communities and families are becoming a norm. Educational practices centered on the relationship between globalization, transationalism, and feminism can offer woman-centric curricular practices that can bring awareness of how global capitalism oppresses women, and show how women world-wide have organized against such practices. Moreover, globalization and transnationalism have transformed communities across the United States expanding the definition of the borderlands, where border and feminist pedagogies can assist in developing transformational educational practices that take these conditions into account.

Chela Sandoval (2000) proposes that by developing what she calls "differential consciousness" we can create a new way of thinking and praxis. Sandoval defines differential consciousness as a "kinetic motion" (p. 44) that functions within, yet beyond the demand of dominant ideology. What she means is that differential consciousness develops its own mode of thinking that takes into consideration disparate viewpoints rather than working on binary oppositional contestations. In other words, Sandoval proposes that to provide a new form of thinking it is necessary to incorporate different and sometimes contradictory discourses simultaneously. Sandoval's approach recognizes that there is a multiplicity of standpoints with contradictory meanings, which we can simultaneously evoke and reject. Oppositional consciousness tactically recognizes multiple perspectives and operates among them, accepting and rejecting them at the same time. One example of what differential consciousness looks like in practice can be found in Anita Tijerina Revilla's aforementioned study of the Raza Womyn (2003, 2004) student organization. Her research and, as she argues, the actual practice of Raza Womyn reflects a pedagogy that is grounded in Chicana/Latina feminist theory and activism that engages social justice from multiple and intersecting axis of discrimination and identity, namely race, class, gender, and sexuality. While Revilla specifically grounds her scholarship in Chicana/Latina feminist theory, she does not directly link her work to the idea of differential consciousness. Yet, we believe the theoretical connection is implicitly present as her research demonstrates the ways in which Chicana/Latina college students engage a differential consciousness that allows them to move within and between different oppositional ideologies in their struggles against racism, classism, sexism, and heterosexism. The Chicana and Latina student activists involved in Raza Womyn consciously articulated their activism within a new language, which is an enactment of differential consciousness that bridged "new and long time activists" (p. 81).

Following Sandoval's differential consciousness, Pérez emphasizes the decolonial imaginary, which is akin to a third space, in which we can recognize the mobility of identities between and among varying power bases. The decolonial process offers a theory of agency where Chicanas self-consciously negotiate opposing stances. The decolonial imaginary is a theoretical tool for uncovering hidden voices of Chicanas that have been relegated by colonial categories as silent and passive. For example, deficit theories of education tend to render Chicanas and Latinas as passive and victims of Latino patriarchal cultures. The decolonial imaginary permits us to see how everyday women can contest these practices that seemingly portray them as invisible and silent, by showing the complex process of negotiation and incorporation of contradictory viewpoints and agency. For example, the struggle to carve spaces of belonging in higher education by Chicana graduate students is theorized in Esthela Bañuelos (2006) ethnographic study of Chicanas in graduate education. Bañuelos illustrates how oppositional consciousness and the decolonial imaginary emerges when enacted by Chicana graduate students. She applies third space feminism, and decolonial imaginary to explain how Chicana graduate students negotiate spaces of belonging in academia. This oppositional consciousness situates Chicana graduate students in a paradoxical position of rejecting the dominant culture and practices of higher education at the same time that they were inscribed within academia. Yet, Bañuelos concludes that "these challenges to exclusion represent important counterdiscourses with the potential to transform higher education" (p. 108).

Whether it is through the enactment of oppositional consciousness, the decolonial imaginary, or mestiza consciousness, some of the data produced by Chicana feminist education scholars demonstrate that feminism offers an important strategy for Chicana progressive education. For example, Delgado Bernal's (2006) ethnographic study of how Chicana undergraduate students enacted pedagogies of the home illustrates this point. Delgado Bernal shows students use of bilingualism, bicultural identities, sense of community and service, and spiritualities as examples of *mestiza* consciousness. She concludes by proposing that educators could "reconceptualize what are often thought of as cultural deficits and turn them into cultural resources, thus allowing them to understand the lives of Chicana/*Mexicana* students in ways that are often overlooked in the field of education" (p. 127). Chicana feminist praxis has the potential to enact educational practices committed to gender justice. Yet, its impact (as with all the theories highlighted in this chapter) in the K-12 system is also limited. This is so because feminism is a contested social movement that many individuals (including women) continue to view suspiciously. Popular culture and mass media tend to present feminism in a negative light and as a political movement that is no longer necessary. Women's material conditions globally are a manifestation that feminism is much needed. We maintain our commitment to CRT/LatCrit, borderland/border theory, and Chicana feminist theories and praxis as they can transform Latina/o education.

Conclusion

In this chapter we have illustrated how four different theoretical domains—critical race theory, Latina/o critical race theory, borderland/border theories, and Chicana feminist theory can contribute to the advancement of a progressive and transformative vision for Latina/o educational theory and praxis. These four conceptualizations, while different in some respects, each share a reciprocal relationship between theory and practice. This reciprocal relationship has been crucial to the development of Latina/o education scholarship as scholars have drawn upon the lives of Latina/o students, parents, educators, and communities to critically explore, better understand, and begin to transform the education of Latinas/os. In doing so, they have advanced Chicana/o/Latina/o methodologies, pedagogies, and epistemologies, which, in turn, can intervene in re-thinking educational policy and practice. Some of the areas where these frameworks can intervene, for example, include curricular practices centered on the multiplicity of Latina/o cultural practices and languages. The four theoretical domains also share certain affinities with each other. Primarily they are concerned with gender, race, sexuality, and class and how these intersect in people's lived experiences, particularly Latinas/os educational experiences. They emphasize the relevance of taking into account Latinas/os' history in the United States in relation to transnational and global contexts, and its relevance to the field of education. In addition, these theories are articulated and operationalized with a commitment to social justice.

Another significant aspect of these theories is that they have been, for the most part, developed by scholars of color who draw upon long intellectual traditions such as critical legal studies, ethnic studies, U.S. third world feminisms, and queer theories to mention but a few. In doing so, these scholars relied on culturally-situated knowledge and continue with a trajectory of always rethinking identity, agency, and the praxis of teaching and learning. For scholars committed to developing innovative practices in educational institutions, the characteristics of the theories and praxis outlined in this chapter are empowering. We have shown their potential for a kind of education that acknowledges students' and family's everyday knowledge. We would like to see more programs at the K-12 levels draw from these theories so that classrooms can be reconfigured as borderlands spaces where the hybrid identities of students and teachers are seen as a benefit and not a deficiency. As we have highlighted in this chapter, these four theoretical perspectives can also offer strategies to struggle against multiple forms of oppression. For example, they can offer approaches of how to examine the ways racism manifests in disciplinary policy, respond to racialized or gendered kinds of bullying, or recognize and utilize children's hybrid language practices.

We believe that one of the strengths of the theoretical frameworks we illustrate in this chapter is their critique of forms of domination and power, but they also show the power of the subordinate to use the margin to resist and to move beyond such forms of domination. CRT, LatCrit, borderland/border theories and Chicana feminist theories all propose, in their own way, complicated and nuanced analyses of education; and they all insist in avoiding and going beyond binary forms of thinking. Therefore, they are able to articulate their concerns from their own perspectives and in their own terms, and not by reacting and responding to dominant discourses (even though they must also respond to those forms of domination in order to develop critical language and praxis).

We believe that these four theoretical perspectives offer important tools for the advancement of Latina/o education, yet we do not propose that these are the only or the best perspectives. Based on the belief that there are multiple ways of creating effective educational praxis, we are not suggesting that all educators employ these perspectives. Rather, we are proposing that education scholars be aware of the conceptual tools each framework offers and how these tools might allow us to interpret and transform the education of Latinas/os in different ways.

Notes

1. Meritocracy is a system of rewards presumably based solely on ability and talent, so that rewards go to those who "perform the best." Meritocratic values drive a wide range of educational practices that have marginalized students of color such as testing, grading, admissions, and ability tracking, all in the spirit of "equality." The notion of meritocracy allows people to believe that all people—no matter what race, class, gender, or sexual orientation—get what they deserve based solely on their individual efforts. Those who believe that our society is truly a meritocratic one, find it difficult to believe that men gain advantage from women's subordination or that whites have any advantage over people of color.
2. While developed and discussed differently, these three contributions were also outlined as having implications for multicultural education in C. Sleeter & D. Delgado Bernal (2004). Critical pedagogy, critical race theory, and antiracist education: Implications for multicultural education. In J. A. Banks & C. M. Banks (Eds.), *The handbook of research on multicultural education* (pp. 240–258). New York: Macmillan.
3. We thank the students in Dolores Delgado Bernal's Critical Race Theories courses since fall 2000, Audrey Thompson and Octavio Villalpando for this insight, and the thoughtful discussions around the many concerns regarding White educators taking up CRT/LatCrit and how educators of color can be responsible and accountable in their CRT/LatCrit scholarship and praxis.
4. In personal conversations at professional conferences (American Educational Research Association, National Association for Chicana and Chicano Studies, and LatCrit Annual Conference) each of

these scholars has noted the important contributions currently being made by education scholars utilizing CRT/LatCrit.

5. SB1108 states that "A public school in this state shall not include within the program of instruction any courses, classes or school sponsored activities that promote, assert as truth or feature as an exclusive focus any political, religious, ideological or cultural beliefs or values that denigrate, disparage or overtly ENCOURAGE dissent from the values of American democracy and western civilization, including democracy, capitalism, pluralism and religious toleration." SB 1108 will also prohibit student groups in colleges and universities that are based on racial identity such as MEChA, Black Student Union, etc.

6. The concept of the borderlands dates back to the early 20th century and was primarily developed by historians referring to the territory in the Continental U.S. that was part of the Spanish colonies (most of the current Southwest and parts of the West, Louisiana, and Florida; see De León, 1989). In education fields, scholars in critical pedagogy, particularly Henry Giroux and Peter McLaren in the early 1990s, also advocated for border pedagogy. Given that the purpose of this chapter is to examine how Latina/o scholars have developed the concept, it is beyond our scope to examine this literature here.

References

Alemán, E., Jr. (2006). Is Robin Hood the "Prince of Thieves" or a pathway to equity? Applying Critical Race Theory to school finance political discourse. *Educational Policy, 20*(1), 113–142.

Alemán, E., Jr. (2007a). Situating Texas school finance policy in a CRT framework: How "substantially equal" yields racial inequity. *Educational Administration Quarterly, 43*(5), 525–558.

Alemán, E., Jr. (2007b). Critical race theory and human capital theory: Framing the discourse on the nexus between social justice and education finance. In G. M. Rodriguez & R. A. Rolle (Eds.), *To what ends and by what means: The social justice implications of contemporary school finance theory and policy* (pp. 35–57). New York: Routledge.

Alemán, E., Jr. (2009). LatCrit educational leadership and advocacy: Struggling over whiteness as property in Texas school finance. *Equity & Excellence in Education, 42*(2), 183-201.

Alemán, E., Jr. (in press). Through the prism of CRT and LatCrit: Niceness and coalition building in the politics of education. Originally submitted to *Journal of Latinos and Education* in October 2007.

Alemán, E., Jr. & Alemán, S. M. (2006). Highlighting Latina/o interests with racial realism: Interest convergence, identity politics, and the permanence of racism. Paper presented at the LatCrit XI Conference, October 5–8 in Las Vegas, NV.

Anzaldúa, G. (1987). *Borderlands/La frontera: The new mestiza*. San Francisco: Aunt Lute Books.

Anzaldúa, G. (1990). *Making face, making soul/haciendo caras: Creative and critical perspectives of feminists of color*. San Francisco: Aunt Lute.

Anzaldúa, G. (2007). *Borderlands/La frontera* (3rd ed.). San Francisco: Aunt Lute. (Original work published 1987)

Ayala, J., Herrera, P., Jiménez, L. & Lara, I. (2006). *Fiera, Guambra, Y Karichina!* Transgressing the borders of community and academy. In D. Delgado Bernal, C. A. Elenes, F. Godinez, & S. Villenas (Eds.), *Chicana/Latina education in everyday life: Feminista perspectives on pedagogy and epistemology* (pp. 261–280). Albany: SUNY Press.

Bañuelos, L. E. (2006). "Here They Go again with the Race stuff": Chicana negotiations of the graduate experience. In D. Delgado Bernal, C. A. Elenes, F. Godinez & S. Villenas (Eds.), *Chicana/Latina education in everyday life: Feminista perspectives on pedagogy and epistemology* (pp. 95–112). Albany: SUNY Press.

Barnes, R. (1990). Race consciousness: The thematic content of racial distinctiveness in critical race scholarship. *Harvard Law Review, 103*, 1864–1871.

Bejarano, C. (2005). *¿Qué onda? Urban youth cultures and border identity*. Tucson: University of Arizona Press.

Bejarano, C. (2006). Latino youths at the crossroads of sameness and difference: Engaging border theory to create critical epistemologies on border identities. In C. A. Rossatto, R. Lee Allen, & M. Pruyn (Eds.), *Reinventing critical pedagogy: Widening the circle of anti-oppression education* (pp. 49–62). Lanham, MD: Rowman & Littlefied.

Bell, D. (1985). The civil rights chronicles. *Harvard Law Review, 99*, 4–83.

Bell, D. (1987). *And we are not saved: The elusive quest for racial justice*. New York: Basic Books.

Bonilla, F., Meléndez, E., Morales, R., & Torres, M. (Eds.). (1998). *Borderless borders: U.S. Latinos, Latin Americans, and the paradox of interdependence*. Philadelphia: Temple University Press.

Burciaga, R. (2007). *Chicana Ph.D. students living nepantla: Educación and aspirations beyond the doctorate*. Unpublished doctoral dissertation, University of California, Los Angeles.

Butler, J. (Ed.). (2001). *Color-line to borderlands: The matrix of American ethnic studies*. Seattle: University of Washington Press.

Calderón, H., & Saldívar, J. D. (1991). Editor's Introduction: Criticism in the borderlands. In H. Calderón & J. D. Saldívar (Eds.), *Criticism in the borderlands: Studies in Chicano literature, culture, and ideology* (pp. 1–7). Durham: Duke University Press.

Chabram-Dernersesian, A. (1992). I throw punches for my race, but I don't want to be a man: Writing Us—Chica-nos (Girl, Us)/Chicanas—into the movement script. In L. Grossberg, C. Nelson, & P. A. Treichler (Eds.), *Cultural Studies* (pp. 81–95). New York: Routledge.

Chabram-Dernersesian, A. (Ed.). (2007). *The Chicana/o cultural studies forum: Critical and ethnographic practices*. New York: New York University Press.

Cline, Z, Reyes, M. L., & Necochea, J. (2005). Introduction to the special issue: Educational lives on the border. *Journal of Latinos and Education, 4*(3), 149–152.

Cline, Z., & Necochea, J. (2006). Teacher dispositions for effective education in the borderlands. *The Educational Forum, 70*, 268–282.

Covarrubias, A. (2005). *Agencies of transformational resistance: Transforming the intersection of race, class, gender, and sexuality oppression through Latino critical race theory (LatCrit) and praxis*. Unpublished doctoral dissertation, University of California, Los Angeles, Los Angeles, CA.

Crenshaw, K. (1993). Beyond racism and misogyny: Black feminism and 2 Live Crew. In M. J. Matsuda, C. R. Lawrence, R. Delgado, & K. W. Crenshaw (Eds.), *Words that wound: Critical race theory, assaultive speech, and the first amendment* (pp. 111–132). Boulder, CO: Westview Press.

Crenshaw, K., Gotanda, N., Peller, G., & Thomas, K. (Eds.). (1995). *Critical race theory: The key writings that formed the movement*. New York: The New Press.

Cruz, C. (2006). Toward an epistemology of a brown body. In D. Delgado Bernal, C. A. Elenes, F. Godinez, & S. Villenas (Eds.), *Chicana/Latina education in everyday life: Feminista perspectives on pedagogy and epistemology* (pp. 59–75). Albany: SUNY Press.

Darder, A. (1998). The politics of biculturalism: Culture and difference in the formation of *Warrior from Gringostroika* and the new mestizas. In A. Darder & R.D. Torres (Eds.), *The Latino studies reader: Culture, economy & society* (pp. 129–142). Malden, MA: Blackwell.

DeCuir, J. T., & Dixson, A. D. (2004). "So when it comes out, they aren't that surprised that it is there": Using critical race theory as a tool of analysis of race and racism in education. *Educational Researcher, 33*(5), 26–31.

Delgado, R. (1989). Storytelling for oppositionists and others: A plea for narrative. *Michigan Law Review, 87*, 2411–2441.

Delgado, R. (1995). *The Rodrigo chronicles: Conversations about America and race*. New York: New York University Press.

Delgado, R. (1999). *When equality ends: Stories about race and resistance*. Boulder, CO: Westview Press.

Delgado, R. & Stefancic, J. (2001). *Critical race theory: An introduction*. New York: New York University Press.

Delgado Bernal, D. (1998). Using a Chicana feminist epistemology in educational research. *Harvard Educational Review, 68*(4), 555–582.

Delgado Bernal, D. (1999). Chicana/o education from the civil rights era to the present. In J.F. Moreno, (Ed.), *The elusive quest for equality: 150 Years of Chicano/Chicana education* (pp. 77–108). Cambridge, MA: Harvard Educational Review.

Delgado Bernal, D. (2002). Critical race theory, Latino critical theory, and critical raced-gendered epistemologies: Recognizing students of color as holders and creators of knowledge. *Qualitative Inquiry, 8*(1): 105–126.

Delgado Bernal, D. (2006). Learning and living pedagogies of the home: The mestiza consciousness of Chicana studies. In D. Delgado Bernal, C. A. Elenes, F. Godinez, & S. Villenas (Eds.), *Chicana/Latina education in everyday life: Feminista perspective on pedagogy and epistemology* (pp. 113–132). Albany: SUNY Press.

Delgado Bernal, D., Alemán, E. Jr., & Flores, J. (2008). Transgenerational and transnational Latina/o cultural citizenship among kindergarteners, their parents, and university students in Utah. *Social Justice, 35*(1), 28–49.

Delgado Bernal, D., Elenes, C.A., Godinez, F. & Villenas, S. (Eds.). (2006). *Chicana/Latina education in everyday life: Feminista perspectives on pedagogy and epistemology.* Albany: SUNY Press.

Delgado Bernal, D. & Villalpando, O. (2002). An apartheid of knowledge in the academy: The struggle over "legitimate" knowledge for faculty of color. *Equity and Excellence in Education, 35*(2), 169–180.

De Leon, A. (1989). Whither Borderlands history? A review essay. *New Mexico Historical Review, 64,* 349–360.

Dicochea, P. (2006). Environmental justice on the Mexico-U.S. Border: Toward a borderlands methodology. In D. Delgado Bernal, C. A. Elenes, F. Godinez, & S. Villenas (Eds.), *Chicana/Latina education in everyday life: Feminista perspectives on pedagogy and epistemology* (pp. 231–243). Albany: SUNY Press.

DuBois, W.E.B. (1953). *The souls of Black folk.* New York: Fawcett. (Original work published 1903)

Elenes, C. A. (1997). Reclaiming the borderlands: Chicana/o identity, difference, and critical pedagogy. *Educational Theory, 47,* 359–375.

Elenes, C. A. (2006). *Transformando fronteras*: Chicana feminist transformative pedagogies. In D. Delgado Bernal, C. A. Elenes, F. Godinez, & S. Villenas (Eds.), *Chicana/Latina education in everyday life: Feminista perspectives on pedagogy and epistemology* (pp. 245–259). Albany: SUNY Press.

Farber, D., & Sherry, S. (1993). Telling stories out of school: An essay on legal narratives. *Stanford Law Review, 45,* 807–855.

Farber, D. & Sherry, S. (1997). *Beyond all reason: The radical assault on truth in American law.* New York: Oxford University Press.

Fernández, L. (2002). Telling stories about school: Using critical race and Latino critical theories to document Latina/Latino education and resistance. *Qualitative Inquiry, 8*(1), 45–65.

Garcia, R. (1995). Critical race theory and Proposition 187: The racial politics of immigration law. *Chicano-Latino Law Review, 17,* 118–148.

Gaspar de Alba, A. (1998). *Chicano Art inside/outside the master's house: Cultural politics and the CARA exhibition.* Austin: University of Texas Press.

Gonzalez, F. (1998). The formations of Mexicananess: Trenzas de identidades multiples. Growing Up Mexicana: Braids of multiple identities. *International Journal of Qualitative Studies in Education, 11*(1), 81–102.

González, N., Moll, L. C., Tenery, M. F., Rivera, A., Rendón, P., Gonzáles, R., & Amanti, C. (1995). Funds of knowledge for teaching Latino households. *Urban Education, 29*(4), 443–470.

Gutiérrez, G. (2000). Deconstructing Disney: Chicano/a children and critical race theory. *Aztlán 25*(1), 7–46.

Gutiérrez-Jones, C. (1995). *Rethinking the borderlands: Between Chicano culture and legal discourse.* Berkeley: University of California Press.

Haney-López, I. (1998). *White by law: The legal construction of race.* New York: New York University Press.

Harris, A. P. (1993). Whiteness as property. *Harvard Law Review, 106,* 1707–1791.

Hernández-Truyol, B. E. (2005). Globalized citizenship: Sovereignty, security and soul. *Villanova Law Review, 50,* 1009–1061.

Hernández-Truyol, B. E., & Hawk, M. (2005). Traveling the boundaries of statelessness: Global passports and citizenship. *Cleveland State Law Review, 52,* 97–120.

Hidalgo, N. M. (1998). Toward a definition of a Latino family research paradigm. *International Journal of Qualitative Studies in Education, 11*(1), 103–120.

Iglesias E. M., & Valdes F. (1998). Religion, gender, sexuality, race, and class in coalitional theory: A critical & self critical analysis of LatCrit. *Chicano-Latino Law Review, 19,* 503–588.

Johnson, K. R. (1996/97). The social and legal construction of nonpersons. *Inter-American Law Review, 28*(2), 263–292.

Johnson, K. R. (1999). *How did you get to be a Mexican?: A white/brown man's search for identity.* Philadelphia: Temple University Press.

Johnson, K. R. (2002). Race and the immigration laws: The need for critical inquiry. In F. Valdes, J. M. Culp, & A. P. Harris (Eds.), *Crossroads, directions, and a new critical race theory* (pp. 187–198). Philadelphia: Temple University Press.

Ladson-Billings, G. (2000). Racialized discourses and ethnic epistemologies. In N. K. Denzin & Y. S. Lincoln (Eds.), *Handbook of qualitative research* (2nd ed., pp. 257–277). Thousand Oaks, CA: Sage.

Ladson-Billings, G.. & Tate, W. (1995). Toward a critical race theory of education. *Teachers College Record, 97,* 47–68.

Lopez, G. R. (2003). The (racially neutral) politics of *education*: A *critical race theory* perspective. *Educational Administration Quarterly, 39*(1), 68–94.

Lynn, M. (1999). Toward a critical race pedagogy: A research note. *Urban Education, 33*(5), 606–626.

Lynn, M. (2006). Dancing between two worlds: A portrait of the life of a black male teacher in South Central LA. *International Journal of Qualitative Studies in Education, 19*(2), 221–242.

Lynn, M., & Parker, L. (2006). Critical race studies in education: Examining a decade of research on U.S. schools. *The Urban Review, 38*(4), 257–290.

Marrun, N. A. (2007). *Understanding informal mentoring in the big house through a critical race and Latina/o critical race theory framework.* Unpublished master's thesis, University of Utah, Salt Lake City.

Martínez, T. A. (2002). The double-consciousness of Du Bois & the "mestiza consciousness" of Anzaldúa. *Race, Gender & Class, 9*(4), 158–170.

Matsuda, M., Lawrence, C., Delgado, R., & Crenshaw, K. (Eds.). (1993). *Words that wound: Critical race theory, assaultive speech, and the first amendment.* Boulder, CO: Westview Press.

McKenna, T. (2003). Borderness and pedagogy: Exposing culture in the classroom. In A. Darder, M. Baltodano, & R. D. Torres (Eds.), *The critical pedagogy reader* (pp. 430–439). New York: RoutledgeFalmer.

Montoya, M. (1994). Mascaras, trenzas, y greñas: Un/masking the self while un/braiding Latina stories and legal discourse. *Chicano-Latino Law Review, 15,* 1–37.

Montoya, M. E. (1997). Academic mestizaje: Re/Producing clinical teaching and re/framing wills as Latina praxis. *Harvard Latino Law Review, 2,* 349–373.

Paredes, A. (1958). *With his pistol in his hand: A border ballad & its hero.* Austin: University of Texas Press.

Parker, L. (1998). Race is...race ain't": An exploration of the utility of critical race theory in qualitative research in education. *International Journal of Qualitative Studies in Education, 11*(1), 7–24.

Parker, L. (2003). Critical race theory and its implications for methodology and policy analysis in higher education desegregation. In G. R. López & L. Parker (Eds), *Interrogating Racism in Qualitative Research Methodology* (pp. 145–180). New York: Peter Lang.

Parker, L., Deyhle, D., & Villenas, S. (Eds.). (1999). *Race is...race isn't: critical race theory and qualitative studies in education.* Boulder, CO: Westview Press. This edited book is a version of a special issue on "Critical Race Theory and Qualitative Studies in Education" in the *International Journal of Qualitative Studies in Education 11,* (1998).

Parker, L., & Lynn, M. (2002). What's race got to do with it? Critical race theory's conflicts with and connections to qualitative research methodology and epistemology. *Qualitative Inquiry, 8*(1), 7–22.

Parker, L., & Stovall, D. O. (2004). Actions following words: *Critical race theory* connects to *critical* pedagogy. *Educational Philosophy and Theory, 36*(2), 167–182.

Pendleton Jiménez, K. (2006). "Start with the land": Groundwork for Chicana Pedagogy. In D. Delgado Bernal, C. A. Elenes, F. Godinez, & S. Villenas (Eds.), *Chicana/Latina education in everyday life: Feminista perspectives on pedagogy and epistemology* (pp. 219–230). Albany: SUNY Press.

Pérez, E. (1999). *The decolonial imaginary: Writing Chicanas into history.* Bloomington: Indiana University Press.

Pizarro, M. (1998). "Chicana/o power!" Epistemology and methodology for social justice and empowerment in Chicana/o communities. *Qualitative Studies in Education, 11,* 57–80.

Posner, R. A. (1997). Narrative and narratology in classroom and courtroom. *Philosophy and Literature, 21*(2), 292–305.

Revilla, A. T. (2003). *Raza womyn re-constructing revolution: Exploring the intersections of race, class, gender and sexuality in the lives of Chicana/Latina student activists.* Unpublished doctoral dissertation, University of California, Los Angeles.

Revilla, A. T. (2004). Muxerista pedagogy: Raza womyn teaching social justice through student activism. *The High School Journal, 87*(4), 80–94.

Roithmayr, D. (1999). Introduction to critical race thoery in educational research and praxis. In L. Parker, D. Deyhle, & S. Villenas (Eds.), *Race is...race isn't: Critical race theory and qualitative studies in education* (pp. 118–127). Boulder, CO: Westview Press.

Rolon-Dow, R. (2005). Critical care: A color(full) analysis of care narratives in the schooling experiences of Puerto Rican girls. *American Educational Research Journal, 42*(1), 77–111.

Romo, J. J., & Chavez, C. (2006). Border pedagogy: A study of preservice teacher transformation. *The Educational Forum, 70*, 142–153.

Romany, C. (1996). Gender, race/ethnicity and language. *La Raza Law Journal, 9*(1), 49–53.

Sandoval, C. (1998). Mestizaje as method: Feminists-of-color challenge the canon. In C. Trujillo (Ed.), *Living Chicana theory* (pp. 352–370). Berkeley, CA: Third Woman Press.

Sandoval, C. (2000). *Methodology of the oppressed.* Minneapolis: University of Minnesota Press.

Saldívar, J. D. (1997). *Border matters: Remapping American cultural studies.* Berkeley & Los Angeles: University of California Press.

Saldívar, R. (1990). *Chicano narrative: The dialectics of difference.* Madison: University of Wisconsin Press.

Saldívar-Hull, S. (2000). *Feminism on the border: Chicana gender politics and literature.* Berkeley & Los Angeles: University of California Press.

Sanchez, V. (1998). Looking upward and inward: Religion and critical theory. *Chicano-Latino Law Review, 19*, 531–435.

Smith, W. A., Yosso, T. J., & Solórzano, D. G. (2006). Challenging racial battle fatigue on historically white campuses: A critical race examination of race-related stress. In C. A. Stanley (Ed.), *Faculty of Color Teaching in Predominantly White Colleges and Universities* (pp. 299–327). Bolton, MA: Anker.

Solórzano, D. G. (1997). Images and words that wound: Critical race theory, racial stereotyping and teacher education. *Teacher Education Quarterly, 24*, 5–19.

Solórzano, D. G. (1998). Critical race theory, race and gender microaggressions, and the experience of Chicana and Chicano scholars. *International Journal of Qualitative Studies in Education, 11*(1), 121–136.

Solórzano, D. G., & Delgado Bernal, D. (2001). Examining transformational resistance through a critical race and LatCrit theory framework: Chicana and Chicano students in an urban context. *Urban Education, 36*(3), 308–342.

Solórzano, D. G., & Villalpando, O. (1998). Critical race theory, marginality, and the experiences of students of color in higher education. In Torres, C. A. & Mitchell, T. R. (Eds.), *Sociology of education: Emerging perspectives* (pp. 211–224). New York: SUNY Press.

Solórzano, D., & Yosso, T. (2000). Toward a critical race theory of Chicana and Chicano education. In C. Tejeda, C. Martinez, & Z. Leonardo (Eds.), *Charting new terrains of Chicana(o)/Latina(o) education* (pp. 35–65). Cresskill, NJ: Hampton Press.

Solórzano, D., & Yosso, T. (2001). Critical race and LatCrit theory and method: Counter-storytelling, Chicana and Chicano graduate school experiences. *International Journal of Qualitative Studies in Education, 14*(4), 471–495.

Solórzano, D., & Yosso, T. (2002). Critical race methodology: Counter-storytelling as an analytical framework for education research. *Qualitative Inquiry, 8*(1), 23–44.

Stovall, D. (2004). School leader as negotiator: Critical race theory, praxis, and the creation of productive space. *Multicultural Education, 12*(2), 8–12.

Stovall, D. (2005). A challenge to traditional theory: Critical race theory, African-American community organizers, and education. *Discourse: Studies in the Cultural Politic of Education, 26*(1), 95–108.

Stovall, D. (2006). Forging community in *race* and class: *Critical race theory* and the quest for social justice in *education. Race, Ethnicity and Education, 9*(3), 243–259.

Tate, W. (1994). From inner city to ivory tower: Does my voice matter in the academy? *Urban Education 29*, 245–269.

Tate, W. F. (1997). Critical race theory and education: History, theory, and implications. *Review of Research in Education, 22*, 195–247.

Trucios-Haynes, E. (2001). Why "race matters:" LatCrit theory and Latina/o Racial identity. *Berkeley La Raza Law Journal, 11/12*(2/1), 1–42.

Trueba, H. T. (1988). Culturally based explanations of minority students' academic achievement. *Anthropology and Education Quarterly, 19,* 270–287.

Trueba, H. T. (1991). From failure to success: The roles of culture and cultural conflict in the academic achievement of Chicano students. In R. Valencia (Ed.), *Chicano school failure and success: Research and policy agendas for the 1990s* (pp. 73–87). London: The Falmer Press.

Valdes, F. (1996). Forward: Latina/o ethnicities, critical race theory and post-identity politics in postmodern legal culture: From practices to possibilities. *Berkeley La Raza Law Journal,* 9(1), 1–31.

Valdes, F., Culp, J. M., & Harris, A. P. (2002). *Crossroads, directions, and a new critical race theory.* Temple University Press.

Vann Lynch, R. (2006). Critical-race educational foundations: Toward democratic practices in teaching "other people's children" and teacher education. *Action in Teacher Education, 28*(2), 53–65.

Vélez-Ibáñez, C., & Greenberg, J. (1992). Formation and transformation of funds of knowledge among U.S. Mexican households. *Anthropology and Education Quarterly, 23,* 313–335.

Vera, H., & de los Santos, E. (2005). Chicana identity construction: Pushing the boundaries. *Journal of Hispanic Higher Education, 4,* 102–113.

Villalpando, O. (2003). Self-segregation or self-preservation? A critical race theory and Latina/o critical theory analysis of a study of a Chicana/o college students. *International Journal of Qualitative Studies in Education, 16*(5), 619–646.

Villalpando, O. (2004). Practical considerations of critical race theory and Latino critical theory for Latino college students. *New Directions for Student Services, 105,* 41–50.

Villenas, S. (2006a). Latina/Chicana feminist postcolonialities: un/tracking educational actors' interventions. *Qualitative Studies in Education, 19,* 659–672.

Villenas, S. (2006b). Mature Latina adults and mothers: Pedagogies of wholeness and resistance. In D. Delgado Bernal, C. A. Elenes, F. Godinez, & S. Villenas (Eds.), *Chicana/Latina education in everyday life: Feminista perspectives on pedagogy and epistemology* (pp. 147–159). Albany: SUNY Press.

Villenas, S., & Foley, D. E. (2002). Chicano/Latino critical ethnography of education: Cultural productions from *la frontera.* In R. R. Valencia (Ed.), *Chicano school failure and success: Past, present and future* (pp. 195–226). New York: RoutledgeFalmer.

Villenas, S., Godinez, F., Delgado Bernal, D., & Elenes, C.A. (2006). Chicanas/Latinas building bridges: An introduction. In D. Delgado Bernal, C. A. Elenes, F. Godinez, & S. Villenas (Eds.), *Chicana/Latina education in everyday life: Feminista perspectives on pedagogy and epistemology* (pp. 1–9). Albany: SUNY Press.

Walker, A. (1983). *In search of our mothers gardens: Womanist prose.* New York: Harcourt, Brace, and Company.

Warrior, R. A. (1995). *Tribal secrets: Recovering American Indian intellectual traditions.* Minneapolis: University of Minnesota Press.

Wing, A. K. (Ed.). (1997). *Critical race feminism: A reader.* New York: New York University Press.

Wing, A. K. (Ed.). (2003). *Critical race feminism: A reader* (2nd ed.). New York: New York University Press.

Yosso, T. J. (2002). Critical race media literacy: Challenging deficit discourses about Chicanos/as. *Journal of Popular Film and Television, 30,* 52–62.

Yosso, T. J. (2005a). Whose culture has capital? A critical race theory discussion of community cultural wealth. *Race Ethnicity and Education, 8*(1), 69–91.

Yosso, T. J. (2005b). Toward a critical race curriculum. *Equity and Excellence in Education, 35*(1), 93–107.

Yosso, T. J. (2006). *Critical race counterstories along the Chicana/Chicano educational pipeline.* New York: Routledge.

5 Contemporary and Critical Methodological Shifts in Research on Latino Education

María Estela Zarate and Gilberto Q. Conchas
University of California, Irvine

Overview

Educational research is one lens that can be used to understand current events, public discourse, and existing political climates. Latino education research is especially political and frequently has the objective of illuminating the schooling conditions and challenges that Latino students face in U.S. schools. To address these challenges, Latino education research draws on and creates critical methodologies that give agency to students' lived experiences. This chapter examines three methodological trends in Latino education research: (a) methodologies centering race and racism, (b) methodologies documenting family cultural resources and strengths, and (c) methodologies exploring ethnic identity. We argue that these methodologies have been instrumental in shaping emancipatory and critical research.

Contemporary and Critical Methodological Shifts in Research on Latino[1] Education

This chapter addresses critical methodologies in contemporary Latino education research and discusses possible future directions. Given the large numbers of Latino student enrollment in the schools of major metropolitan areas, research on the educational experiences of Latinos in the United States has grown considerably in the past two decades. The development of research on Latino education can be measured not only in volume, but also in scope and in the advancement of novel paradigms, theories, and methodologies. This chapter seeks to capture such critical methodological developments in educational research.

In this chapter critical methodologies are defined as methodologies that have moved our understanding of the experiences of Latino students forward in new and fruitful directions. A critical methodology involves a de-emphasis on method per se, the need for methodological innovation and the continual critical examination of the assumptions that undergird methods and other research resources, especially as they pertain to how Latinos experience American schooling. We posit that under a critical methodology, the processes of theory construction and research would be essentially processes of argument construction, where arguments can be supported with many types of robust evidence that advance a holistic portrait of Latinos' educational experiences. Although there is no final certainty through method under this framework, progress can result from the tension between various perspectives and power relations that are context dependent. In some cases, this involves research that has used innovative methods, theories, and methodologies. In other cases, established methods viewed through a different conceptual lens have yielded findings that produce new knowledge about Latinos and their oppressive and emancipatory relations in K-12 and postsecondary institutions. This chapter does not provide a wide-angle view of all existing methodologies in educational research of Latinos. Rather, we aim to present how pivotal developments in the methodological evolution of educational research have amplified our grasp of the conditions of Latinos in U.S. schools.

An initial challenge that we faced was to distinguish methodology from methods and theory—and a definition for each concept is offered in this chapter. However, in engaging in discussions about methodologies, it is much more difficult to separate theories from methodologies. After all, theoretical frameworks give shape to methodology and methods, and the findings yielded through this methodology in turn sometimes result in new theoretical frameworks. In this chapter, we accept the perspective that methodology captures both method and theory and therefore cannot be discussed without reference to its theoretical underpinnings. As a result, this chapter discusses pivotal methodological turns in actual *research* about Latinos and education. We have identified three themes or strands of methodologies that we feel have introduced critical perspectives on Latino education: (a) methodologies centering race and racism, (b) methodologies documenting family cultural resources and strengths, and (c) methodologies exploring ethnic identity.

We posit that education research and its methodologies are politically situated because they intentionally confront contemporary public discussions and debates about Latinos, immigration, language policy, and education policy. We also glance at some of the political movements and popular ideology that have stimulated new paradigms and frameworks from which to examine Latinos' educational experiences. The persistent presence of cultural deficit explanations to describe Latino families, a backlash against affirmative action, and nativist assimilation policies, has motivated most of the educational research in recent decades. Research on Latino education has responded to these public policy discussions by challenging dominant frameworks and presenting methodological approaches that reveal previously overlooked experiences of not only Latinos, but students of color more generally. Methodologies that center race and racism have been useful in addressing affirmative action backlash. Methods examining the family in Latino education have taken on cultural deficit arguments explaining low Latino education attainment, and methodologies that allow us to explore ethnic identities have helped researchers to humanize and contextualize anti-immigrant nativist arguments.

Finally, we present a discussion of possible directions for research methodologies in Latino education. We also discuss other methodological approaches that have sought to address the educational conditions of Latinos. Traditional methods, such as experimental designs and quantitative analysis, have made significant contributions in disclosing the schooling conditions of Latinos. Research in Latino education still has many areas of inquiry left unexplored, and we propose several considerations for scholars to engage in ongoing discussion. After all, as the Latino population continues to expand and gain traction in political, social, and economic spheres, educational researchers will need to consistently devise new approaches to their research.

Historical Drivers of Methodology: Situating the "Critical" in Latino Education

Throughout U.S. history, inequitable policies or practices have inspired research concerning Latinos' educational experiences conducted by Latino scholars and non-Latino scholars (see San Miguel Jr. and Donato, this volume; Irizarry and Nieto, this volume). Although research concerning Latinos' school achievement has sometimes served to disparage Latinos, it has also served to contest dominant racist or discriminatory paradigms about Latinos. In examining contemporary education research, it is apparent that three events or movements have motivated novel methodological approaches to research on Latino education: (a) continued use of cultural deficit paradigms to explain persistent low academic achievement among Latinos, (b) attacks against Spanish-language accommodation in schools, and (c) backlash against affirmative action in higher education. These historical movements or practices have prompted some researchers to challenge mainstream perceptions and give voice to the educational experiences of Latinos in the United States.

Challenging Cultural Deficit Paradigms

The use of cultural deficit paradigms to examine learning and explain educational achievement among Latinos is not a recent development. Valencia (1997) and Gándara (1995) comprehensively reported on this topic over 10 years ago and discussed its eugenics roots and its application in explaining low academic achievement among Latinos. While it is not as common to hear blatant denigration of a racial group in public discourse, it remains acceptable to insidiously blame "Latino culture" for their low academic achievement (Conchas, 2006; Rowland, 2007; Volkmann, 2007; Llorente, 2007). Pearl (1997) argues that some federal programs, such as Head Start, are based on the premise that Latino families are not raising their children with the "correct" family values. Similarly, we argue that the emergence of outreach programs aimed at "increasing" parental involvement are based on the assumption that Latino parents do not know how to be involved in their child's education. Some college outreach programs sometimes similarly have the operating assumption that Latino students don't want to be educated and need to be convinced of the merits of education. These assumptions exist despite the abundance of evidence that Latino parents and students value and aspire to higher education but do not know how to navigate the process of getting to college (Conchas, 2001; Goldenberg, Gallimore, Reese, & Garnier, 2001; Tornatsky, Cutler, & Lee, 2002; Zarate, 2006). Educational research continues to challenge the cultural blame paradigm for low academic achievement among Latinos and to present evidence that structural and institutional inequities remain a significant barrier to their educational success.

Challenging Anti-Bilingualism

Most recently, official-English movements have targeted bilingual education and limited primary-language instruction in schools. Historically, support or tolerance for non-English language use in official and school settings in the United States has ebbed and flowed, depending on popular opinion towards the non-English speaking group (Dicker, 1996; Krashen, 1996; Kloss, 1998). Despite federal rulings and policy dictating language accommodation in schools, state-based movements, such as Proposition 227 in California and Proposition 203 in Arizona, have successfully restricted native-language instruction and accommodation in the classroom. These types of movements have used language policy to force adherence to specific mainstream notions of language and cultural assimilation. By outlawing Spanish in schooling practices, an important dimension of immigrants' cultural identity is denied in schools. Restrictive language policy is misguided given empirical evidence supporting the use of primary-language instruction in the early years to advance content learning and facilitate English-language acquisition in the latter years (see chapters in this volume). In attempts to inform public discussions that both prefaced and followed these statewide movements, educational research has produced volumes about how Spanish-speaking children acquire English, cultural literacy practices, and language identity.

Challenging the Backlash Against Affirmative Action in Higher Education

At the other end of the educational pipeline, Latinos have been persistently underrepresented in colleges and universities. For several decades, affirmative action programs were instrumental in increasing the enrollment of racial minorities and women in colleges and universities (Conchas, 2001; Anderson, 2002). However, relying on false claims of fair opportunity and claims of "reverse discrimination," affirmative action has periodically been contested in state law and federal courts. Such claims assume that social and economic progress is the result of individual effort alone and do not take into account the inherent privilege benefiting certain social groups and classes. In the 1990s several states passed statutes successfully banning the consideration of race in college and university admissions, and this has resulted in a decline in the concentration of Latinos and Latinas at some colleges and universities (Saenz, Oseguera, & Hurtado, 2007; Tienda, Leicht, Sullivan, Maltese, & Lloyd, 2003). Much educational research about Latinos in higher education has focused on the detrimental effects of banning affirmative action and the ongoing inequitable college access practices. College admissions practices that inadvertently privilege access to students with college-educated parents often deem policies like affirmative action and proactive outreach to students of color a necessary route to increasing the enrollment of students of color in college. Moreover, the success in restricting affirmative action has also compelled educational researchers to investigate campus racial climate and retention issues as the enrollment of Black and Latino students plateaus or diminishes at flagship campuses (Barreto & Pachon, 2003; Hurtado, 1992).

Because education is a public good, a basic right, and contested in public space, education research more often than not has political implications. Given that women and people of color have historically been denied access to equitable education, educational research on Latinas reasonably involves and engages the political origins of Latinas' educational experiences. Moreover, the backlash against affirmative action and the limitations imposed on bilingual education has involved electoral decisions and state legislation, thus prompting forceful public debates on how best to educate Latinos. Unfortunately, public debates often oversimplify or rely on simplistic cultural deficit explanations to understand the educational status of Latinos. Topics in public discourse inevitably beckons social researchers and we suspect that increasingly restrictive immigration legislation and the immigrant rights movements that took demonstrations to the streets in 2006 will inform future educational research. Educational research about movements and immigration will be able to addresses how these significant social experiences influence young adults. In the following section, we outline how different methodologies can be useful to participate in public debates about Latino education.

Defining Methodology

Education research has been instrumental in uncovering Latinas' previously unheard and non-mainstream educational experiences. Using innovative research methodologies, educational researchers have been able to challenge educational practices that otherwise assume "neutral" schooling and learning conditions. Diverse theoretical frameworks, and methodologies have been instrumental to researchers seeking to understand from a variety of perspectives the educational conditions faced by Latinos in various educational contexts.

To capture the broad spectrum of approaches to research on Latino education, it is important to understand the differences and relationships between methodology, method, epistemology, and theory. Harding (1987) distinguishes method from methodology by defining method as the "technique" used to gather evidence or data, such as interviews or records. Methodology, on the other hand, is the theory and analysis of how research is carried out; it is the way in which a specific theory is applied to a particular research objective (Harding, 1987). For example, grounded theory is an analytical approach that uses a comparative, inductive, and iterative analytical process and that works well with theoretical frameworks that privilege the standpoint of the research subjects, e.g., feminist theory. Solorzano and Yosso (2002) define methodology as the place where theory meets method. In the context of this chapter, we further define theory as a conceptual framework that attempts to explain educational experiences, outcomes, and processes, based on certain "untested" assumptions. Epistemology, meanwhile, may be understood as the theory of knowledge, and for the purpose of this discussion, we use this term to examine who can claim the origins of knowledge or knowledge production. Epistemological questions can challenge macro theories as well as universalistic approaches and assumptions that do not capture nuances in the educational experiences of Latinos.

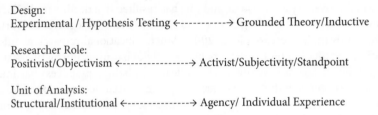

Design:
Experimental / Hypothesis Testing ←-----------→ Grounded Theory/Inductive

Researcher Role:
Positivist/Objectivism ←----------------→ Activist/Subjectivity/Standpoint

Unit of Analysis:
Structural/Institutional ←---------------→ Agency/ Individual Experience

Figure 5.1 Three dimensions of methodological approaches.

Using these definitions, we argue that placing research methodologies along a qualitative-quantitative spectrum limits how we can examine the rich methodologies used in educational research about Latinos. In Figure 5.1 we present a mapping to organize research methodologies that have been used in Latino education research.

These different dimensions of methodologies do not exhaust all of the different approaches to education research but present several dimensions from which to examine research methodologies. We also chose to present these categories in a range because education research methodology is often driven by mixed approaches and frequently introduces variations of established theories and methodologies. By presenting methodologies in a range format, we also purposefully move away from further placing methodologies in binary positions and instead argue for exploration of hybrids of these dimensions of methodology.

The first dimension captures the range of research designs. It captures methodologies that on one end determine the scope of a research question a priori and, on the other end, methodologies that are driven by inductive inquiry, the scope of which emanates from the data itself. The second dimension captures the standpoint of the researchers and the role of the researchers throughout the research. As we will discuss below, the researchers' and participants' standpoint is a central theme of research in Latino education, with research increasingly engaging the researcher as an element of the discussion. This dimension also engages questions about privileged or subjugated epistemologies in existing research in Latino education.

The third dimension addresses the unit of analysis, or the subject of the research, that the researcher is attempting to understand. This methodological dimension describes the nature of the subject that is targeted by the research, e.g., family, schools, student, community, or policy. In naming the unit of analysis and research subject, the purpose or aim of the research is also implied. For example, if a study examines school practices versus individual students' drop out decisions, then the research is poised to present evidence about institutional culture, policy, etc. In contrast, where the unit of analysis is a student's lived experience, we would argue those studies are in a position to examine a student's agency in the educational process. This is not to say that research on individual students is not capable of offering observations about institutional practices. It can offer observations and recommendations for change, but not an understanding of *why* institutions behave the way they do.

Existing theoretical frameworks inform these different dimensions of educational research methodologies; depending on the research design, some theoretical discussions and modifications may also emanate in the course of the research. Methodologies and theories, in turn, implicitly privilege certain epistemological sources over others, even when this is not discussed explicitly in the research. This dialogical relationship between theory, epistemology, and methodology will be explored in our overview of methodological advances in education research about Latinos.

It is difficult to separate methodologies from their theoretical underpinnings; thus in discussing methodological developments, the underlying theory and methods are also presented. Our aim is to present pivotal methodological developments that capture Latinas' educational experiences. The methodological developments considered here have served to reveal previously overlooked Latinos' educational experiences, perspectives, and struggles. The methodologies highlighted do not represent any one theoretical paradigm. Instead, we argue that methodologies with various origins and diverse applications have the potential to depict and contest the structural oppression often faced by Latinos in schools. In what follows, we discuss how three methodological themes have addresses deficits in Latino education research.

Methodologies Centering Race and Racism

Frequently, race or ethnicity in education research is a variable or factor to be considered alongside other factors relevant to the education experience (Portes & Rumbaut, 2001; Hurtado, Kurotsuchi Inkelas, Briggs, & Rhee, 1997; Perna, 2000). For example, in addressing racial differences in access to college, Perna (2000) and Hurtado et al. (1997) use race or ethnicity as a category for which to compare outcomes across racial and ethnic groups. In our mapping of methodologies (Figure 5.1), such an approach focuses on capturing individual-level experiences and "testing" existing theories of access to higher education. Similarly, Portes and Rumbaut (2001) and Conchas (2006) also employ racial and ethnic categories to compare immigrant youth experiences. In their work, the unit of analysis is also the student and both use research designs driven by established theoretical frameworks. For Conchas (2006) and Portes and Rumbaut (2001), the theoretical frameworks guiding their work allows them to frame their research within the political landscape of immigration and school hierarchies, respectively. Conchas (2006) uses an inductive analytical method combined with social capital theory that lends to a discussion of structural and institutional dimensions of students' racialized experiences. On the other hand, Portes and Rumbaut's (2001) segmented assimilation framework combined with quantitative analysis leads to a discussion of how different immigrant groups socially and psychologically adapt to their immigrant status.

In the examples above, comparing outcomes and experiences across immigrant groups captures how Latino students' learning and schooling experiences differ from other groups. After establishing statistical or empirical differences in outcomes across groups, such differences are then explained as cultural phenomena or the results of policy (Hurtado et al., 1997; Portes & Rumbaut, 2001; Perna, 2000). The authors also provide many references and evidence to suggest that the national status of race relations has a lot to do with the predicament of students of color. Although racial differences are remarkable in the studies, the impact of racism as a political or institutional condition is not discussed due to the parameters of a methodology that focuses on documenting individual-level outcomes. Racism, per se, is difficult to capture unless the theoretical framework directly addresses race issues.

It is not necessary to undertake a comparative approach to capture the racial dimension of learning experiences and social interactions. For example, Valenzuela (1999) examines the role of race in student-teacher interactions and school culture without including a comparison group. Rather, she explores racial tensions from the standpoint of the students departing from positivist approaches that seek validity inspection. This approach yielded insight into the educational experiences of Latinas and offered an analysis of how racism permeates the structure and culture of student-teacher relationships.

Methodologically speaking, most analyses of race and ethnicity do not necessarily invoke discussions about racism prevalent in educational institutions. Without dismissing other forms of oppression, Critical Race Theory (CRT) has emerged as a theoretical and methodological instrument that has been useful to centering education research on race and racism (see also Elenes and Delgado Bernal, this volume). Briefly, proponents of CRT challenge dominant notions of racial progress and color-blind institutions in a commitment toward bringing about a more just society. CRT scholars center the experiential knowledge of peoples of color to expose everyday forms of racial violence, placing these experiences within a collective historical context. Most recently, Latino Critical Race Theory (LatCrit) has emerged to complement CRT by including other forms of oppression unique to Latinos' experiences in its analysis of racism in schools and education. For example, immigration and language policies are practices that have deeply influenced the educational experiences of Latinos (Montoya, 2000).

In part because of its origins in the legal discipline, CRT is often used in discussions of affirmative action (Aguirre, 2000; Solórzano & Villalpando, 1998; Solórzano, 1998; Solórzano & Yosso, 2001; Taylor, 2000; Solórzano & Ornelas, 2004). The threat of bans on affirmative action practices in college selection processes has preoccupied education researchers interested in exposing existing inequalities in schooling opportunities. The reasoning is that unequal schooling opportunities between racial groups warrant affirmative action to correct greater racial inequalities. Although other research that highlights differences in academic achievement and schooling conditions across racial groups has also bolstered the argument in favor of affirmative action policies, CRT is particularly useful in this debate because it has guided researchers to focus on the importance of race in determining schooling conditions and experiences.

Methodologies informed by CRT delve head on into issues of race and racism in schools, families, and communities. This perspective has helped shed light on the educational experiences of Latino students in higher education (Solórzano & Villalpando, 1998), scholars of color in the academy (Solórzano, 1998; Solórzano & Yosso, 2001; Aguirre, 2000), and student teachers aiming to teach in underrepresented communities (Smith-Maddox & Solórzano, 2002). Critical race theory has also been used alongside concepts such as racial micro aggression (Solórzano, 1998; Solórzano, Ceja, & Yosso, 2000), marginality (Solórzano & Villalpando, 1998), transformational resistance (Solórzano & Delgado Bernal, 2001); and Freire's problem-posing methodology (Smith-Maddox & Solórzano, 2002; Solórzano & Yosso, 2001) to further understand the impact of overt and subtle forms of racism on Latino students and scholars. A specific methodology that is closely aligned with CRT is counterstorytelling (Solórzano & Delgado Bernal, 2001; Aguirre, 2000; Delgado, 2000; Solórzano & Yosso, 2002), and is true to the theme of experiential knowledge in CRT. Counterstories are narratives that can be either autobiographical or composite sketches emanating from research participants' experiences and autobiographical accounts. There is no one single method associated with counterstorytelling. The counterstories can draw on interviews, observations, historical records, or the researchers' experiences (Solórzano & Delgado Bernal, 2001; Aguirre, 2000; Solórzano & Yosso, 2001). Counterstorytelling is an important methodological contribution to education research because it gives voice to previously suppressed stories or narratives of oppression not captured in educational research. It emphasizes the subjects' standpoint when existing theoretical frameworks do not shed light on racist school culture. Counterstories with a CRT framework are able to explicitly place these alternative narratives within the context of racist educational practices and institutions.

Much of the educational research using CRT has focused on exposing the unique and racialized educational experiences of students of color. To a lesser extent, CRT has also been employed to explore macro-policy issues, such as anti-affirmative action voter initiatives and the relative unavailability of AP classes in high schools with large populations of Latino and African American students (Taylor, 2000; Solórzano & Ornelas, 2004). Research designs that compare racial and ethnic groups on a variety of measurements are valuable to illustrate inequitable access to quality education. However, CRT is a methodological contribution because it moves discourse on racial differences to discussions about racism in institutional practices.

Methodologies Excavating the Cultural Resources and Strengths of Latino Families

Historically, the educational attainment levels of Latinos and other people of color have been explained by cultural deficit frameworks (Conchas, 2006; Valencia, 1997; Valencia & Solórzano,

1997). Latino families are often blamed for the academic failures of their children. Latino families are said to have tight kin networks. These close bonds between nuclear and extended family members are perceived to limit the child's school success by placing obligations to the family unit above personal achievement. When conflicts arise between family responsibilities, such as providing income or childcare for other members, and school commitments, schoolwork suffers (Heller, 1966; Kuvelesky & Patella, 1971; Sanchez-Jankowski, 1991; Vigil, 1997). This has been injurious to Latino students as schools and educators are then absolved of their role in shaping the educational outcomes for Latinos; instead, the family and the culture are blamed for low educational outcomes of Latinos (Goyette & Conchas, 2001).

Hidalgo (1999) has proposed a shift in research paradigms for studying Latino families, where "families, not individuals are placed at the center of the analysis" (p. 108). The family, as the unit of analysis, is then examined within the social context of the family's experiences, including "ethnic, race, class, and gender systems of power" (p.109). According to Hidalgo (1999), the research then yields an "understanding and interpretation of forms of Latino family cultural knowledge grounded in the experiences and adaptations they make" (p.117). Similarly, "funds of knowledge" is conceptualized by researchers Moll, Amanti, Neff, and Gonzalez (2001) to "refer to the historically accumulated and culturally developed bodies of knowledge and skills essential for household or individual functioning and well-being" (p. 133). In their work, the Latino household, therefore, is proposed as a fundamental and necessary source of cultural knowledge. These important works speak more broadly about the critical methodologies that have been used to counter deficit thinking by excavating Latino families' cultural knowledge and cultural/linguistic and literacy practices and highlighting these as strengths.

Some methodologies address the cultural pathological perception of Latino families by presenting counter-evidence illustrating inadequate schooling conditions faced by Latinos. There is also another approach that addresses the question of familial cultural knowledge directly, demonstrating the various dimensions of Latinos' cultural schemas and values about education. Specifically, in the past two decades ethnographic studies of Latino families have yielded the concept of *educación* to explain how Latino parents interface with formal education. Methodologies that have allowed the researcher to depict how Latino families view schooling, education, and *educación* have been a critical development in educational research of Latinos because it has highlighted the many ways that Latino families support formal education, albeit in ways that vary from mainstream expectations of parental support (Lopez, 2001; Zarate, 2007). Ethnographies, and interpretive work in general, have been essential in documenting positive cultural/linguistic/literacy practices in contrast with quantitative and experimental studies that depict deficient Latino cultural practices.

To be sure, ethnographies and open-ended interviews alone do not contest dominant and simplistic representations of Latino families (Paredes, 1984). Rather, it is a combination of centering Latino families in the design of the study, systematically observing the family in various dimensions of school and family life, and intentionally giving agency to families' struggles for education that allows for unique constructs and concepts to emerge. Without the constraints of predefined measurements of family involvement, Delgado-Gaitan (1994), Reese, Balzano, Gallimore, and Goldberg (1995), and Valdés (1996), for instance, help us understand how Latino families experience schooling institutions. The analytical contribution of these studies has been to move away from a dominant interpretive lens of school involvement and allow for new paradigms of family-education connections to emerge.

Delgado-Gaitan (1994) first discussed *consejos* (cultural narratives providing guidance and direction) as practices that often capture the importance of schooling and education. Delgado-Gaitan (1994) presents this cultural practice as a problem-solving strategy used by parents to support their children's education, advocate for their children, and instill a sense of independence and self-determination in their children. Perhaps not openly visible to schools or outside observers of Latino students, *consejos* are one such example of discursive practices that demonstrate how some Latino families are involved in their child's education. Delgado-Gaitan (1994) deliberately examines her observations and interviews with Latino families from a perspective that acknowledges power hierarchies in schools. By not neutralizing school sites, Delgado-Gaitan (1994) can examine parent-school relationships critically and give voice to families' strategies for underscoring the importance of education in the household.

Like Delgado-Gaitan (1994), Valdés (1996), and Reese et al. (1995) introduce new concepts that challenge cultural deficit perspectives of Latino families. Valdés (1996) introduced one of the most extensive ethnographic studies that sought to document how a group of Latino immigrant parents, as the central unit of analysis, participated in their child's education while struggling to survive in a hostile new setting. However, unlike middle-class parents who may engage in academic tasks with their children to advance educational outcomes, the parents in the study used moral teachings, such as *consejos* (advice catered to a specific behavioral objective) and *respeto* (respect) for others, to prepare their children to be worthy individuals in society. In this ethnography, Valdés (1996) deliberately sets out to illustrate how Latino families participate in education outside the dominant norms of parental involvement and in the context of unfavorable schooling conditions.

Also employing ethnography as a research method, Reese et al. (1995) explored the concept of *educación* in their study of over 100 Latino immigrant families. But rather than compartmentalize *educación* as the moral counterpart to formal education, Reese et al. (1995) describe it as an essential aspect of formal education: "a part of the larger whole." In dissecting how *educación* is evidenced in the parents' upbringing of their children, the authors find that *educación* permeates every aspect of raising children, including how parents shape their educational aspirations for their children. Unlike, Valdés (1996), Reese et al. (1995) do not engage or examine the structural constraints faced by Latino families in their interactions with schools. Nonetheless, their ethnographic approach allowed the subjects to challenge mainstream definitions of familial participation in education and weaken prevailing assumptions about Latino families' "values."

Both Reese et al. (1995) and Valdés (1996) emphasize that schools should not perceive Latino families' values about education and *educación* as necessarily problematic for American schooling practices. Rather, the conflict arises when school policy or practices are ignorant of parenting practices and may design interventions that inadvertently seek to change the families' commitment to moral upbringing. Reese et al. (1995), Reese (2001), and Valdés (1996) all document the way Latino immigrant families actually seek to adapt familial practices to incorporate American ideas of prosperity, opportunity, and economic demand. Reese (2001) and Valdés (1996) both question why schools and U.S. educational practices do not do more to recognize and make use of the value that parents place on *educación* and moral identity. These how and why questions that directly speak to processes are precisely what mainstream quantitative studies are not able to capture, thus rendering a culturally deficient understanding of Latino families and educational achievement while ignoring the structural factors that promote inequality.

The results of Delgado-Gaitan's (1994), Reese et al.'s (1995), and Valdés' (1996) studies have illustrated how some Latino cultural practices related to education are undervalued in mainstream educational institutions. This is an important methodological contribution because it shifts blame for deficit educational practices to the institutions and reaffirms Latino families' commitment to education. They situate the family as the unit of analysis to debunk cultural deficit models that assume Latino parents do not care about their children's educational mobility. These studies, in turn, place importance to the agency of Latino parents despite structural constraints. This is done despite the studies' use of a wide range of theoretical underpinnings.

All the studies used ethnographic methods for data collection and all drew from diverse methodological approaches and theoretical frameworks, such as cognitive anthropology, sociocultural reproduction, cultural and social capital, and assimilation theories. Yet, it is clear that none of the existing theoretical questions the authors used to structure their research projects begin to name the specific cultural practices found in the study. Rather, the themes of *educación*, *consejos*, and *respeto* emerge from the researchers' conversations with the participants. As our aforementioned figure suggests (Figure 5.1), experimental designs do not allow for the collection of such rich and theoretically grounded information. These studies move away from the extremely limited positivist research that dominates the field of education in favor of grounded analytic designs. This is an important methodological contribution: to define Latino parents' cultural assets organically and not "operationalize" them externally or "test" them for presence or frequency. The aim is to emphasize Latino families' agency and to overcome the structural and cultural forces that too often promote inequity instead of social mobility.

Methodologies Exploring Latina Ethnic and Racial Identities

In recent decades, the backlash against increased immigration from Latin America and Mexico has led to a public discourse reflecting fear of a "cultural invasion" from south of the border. Public debate for and against immigration control has inspired historical and massive public demonstration supporting immigrants and their economic contribution to the nation. Although we have yet to document the impact of this discourse and movements on Latino adolescents, we can guess that Latino youth will incorporate these public events in the formation of their ethnic identity. For many Latino students, their race and ethnic identity has emerged from their own or their parents' immigrant status, public opinions on ethnic minorities, current immigration policy, peer group associations, and many other factors that color students' daily experiences. Ethnic identity has been a particularly useful analytical construct for scholars seeking to map the adaptation of immigrant Latina/o youth in the United States and to investigate if acculturation or assimilation is indeed related to the educational attainment of Latina youths in the United States (Conchas, 2006; Hurtado, Gonzales, & Vega, 1996; Niemann, Romero, & Arbona, 2000; Matute-Bianchi, 1986; Lopez & Stanton-Salazar, 2001; Portes & Rumbaut, 2001; Vigil, 1997; Zarate, Bhmji, & Reese, 2005).

Studies examining Latino student identities have relied on a variety of methods and research designs to understand how Latino students negotiate their status as immigrants or racial minorities (Hurtado et al., 1996; Neumann et al., 2000; Matute-Bianchi, 1986; Lopez & Stanton-Salazar, 2001; Portes & Rumbaut, 2001; Vigil, 1997; Zarate et al., 2005; Zentella, 1997). Methods used to understand ethnic identity have included statistical correlations (Portes & Rumbaut, 2001), surveys (Zarate et al., 2005) and interviews (Zentella, 1997). In our mapping of methodologies (Figure 5.1), research on Latino ethnic identity spans the spectrum in the at least two of the dimensions of methodology. Research on ethnic identity has included both research designs that seek to "test" associations between ethnic identity and educational outcomes (Niemann et al., 2000) as well as research designs that rely on a grounded approach to understanding the dynamic nature of ethnic identity (Vila, 2000; Vigil, 1997). A grounded analytical process allows for understanding how ethnic identity is a nuanced and a political reflection of adolescents' lived experiences. Such an approach has also moved us to capture even more labels articuluated by adolescents. Instead of researchers defining labels *a priori*, researchers have incorporated the participants' standpoints and subjectivities to acknowledge their characterization of various ethnic labels (Zarate et al., 2005). We argue that both a grounded analysis and incorporation of participants' standpoints have moved the discussion of ethnic identity forward by pointing out how assimilation or acculturation is not a linear and stepwise process.

Ethnic identity is undoubtedly difficult to capture since it encapsulates a constellation of experiences. Many theoretical frameworks have been used to interpret the implications of adolescents' ethnic identity on education. Ethnic identity among Latinos has been interpreted by socio-psychology and post-modern theory, and even by literary perspectives. A socio-psychological interpretation of Latino adolescents' ethnic identity has been used most consistently over the years to understand how immigrant and minority youth adapt to their marginal status in schools or communities (Hurtado, 2003; Lopez & Stanton-Salazar, 2001; Portes & Rumbaut, 2001; Suárez-Orozco & Suárez-Orozco, 1995). Such a perspective has been useful to generalize how individual students negotiate different influences in their identity formation (e.g., family, school culture, community), and how this can influence their academic success. On the other hand, such an approach limits researcher claims of *how* macro policy, institutions, and school practices influence students' ethnic identity formation. It is our opinion that post-modern concepts of identity formation have best been able to document how institutions influence the ethnic identity of Latinos (Torres & Valle, 2000; Vila, 2000). This perspective has been important because it moves the discussion of ethnic identity away from individual interactions to the broader political and cultural climate and captures how public discourse can influence Latino students' engagement in schools.

A critical and pivotal methodological and epistemological development that has influenced research on Latino identity is Anzaldúa's (1999) eloquent description of borderlands, *mestiza* consciousness, and *fronteras*. Anzaldúa's discussion of Chicano identities resembles Du Bois's (1995) use of "double consciousness" to describe black identity in a predominantly white nation, and post-modernists' (Kellner, 1995) discussions of hybrid identities. However, Anzaldúa (1999) places her discussion of Chicano identity within a historical and geographical context that captures Mexico's and Mexicans' relation(s) to the United States. The *mestiza* consciousness, as Anzaldúa (1999) presents it, is the result of living in between and within plural cultures with sometimes contradictory Mexican, indigenous, and U.S. influences. As a result of these experiences, a *mestiza* consciousness allows for greater skill at negotiating boundaries, deconstructing rigid frameworks, and building new paradigms: "She copes by developing a tolerance for contradictions, a tolerance for ambiguity" (p. 79). According to Anzaldúa (1999), a Chicana with a *mestiza* consciousness can critically examine inherited, imposed, and acquired cultures to develop a theoretical framework that captures her experiences as a border crosser. Anzaldua's (1999) hybrid identities, *mestiza* consciousness, and plural feminisms have been useful to educational research because it has (a) moved forward the exploration of hybrid/bicultural/bilingual identity among Latino students and beyond assimilationist paradigms of immigrant adaptation, and (b) it has provided a stepping stone for addressing methodological concerns regarding the role of the researcher's ethnic identity in education research.

Despite the different methodological approaches used by scholars to look at ethnic identity among Latina/o immigrants, most agree on the dynamic nature of ethnic identities. Studies on Latino identities have thus far confirmed that Latino students must negotiate different worlds and identities in institutions that have historically marginalized their experiences (Conchas, 2001; Hurtado, 2003; Matute-Bianchi, 1986; Portes & Rumbaut, 2001; Vigil, 1997; Valenzuela, 1999). Studies confirm Anzaldua's argument that a Latino identity cannot be captured by rigid categories or spectrums. Ethnic identity is situational, constantly malleable, historically produced and politically positioned (Anzaldúa, 1999; Gonzales, 1999; Hurtado & Gurin, 1987; Hurtado, 2003; Oboler, 1995; Valenzuela, 1999; Zarate et al., 2005).

Positionality and Reflexivity in Research on Latino Education

In our discussion of the different dimensions of methodology (Figure 5.1), we present a spectrum to depict the range of positionality claims by researchers. We have also discussed how Latino education research has taken advantage of methods and research designs that privilege the voice of students and their families. This is in part due to scholars' own exploration of their insider knowledge, subjectivities, and standpoints to formulate new research queries, provide new frameworks for examining the educational experiences of Latino students, and reexamine previous assumptions dominant in education research methodologies. Some scholars understand their research as a critical venue for voicing the experiences of Latino and Latina students and changing mainstream consciousness (Conchas, 2006; Pizarro, 1999; Hidalgo 1999; Cordova, 1998). As illustrated in this chapter, several Latino scholars and scholars of Latina educational issues have relied on ethnographic methods to develop theories that reflect the experiences of Latino students. Many scholars use critical ethnographies precisely because they intend to transform the institutions that have marginalized and continue to marginalize Latino students. This type of voice in research also reflects a subjective positionality where the scholar's role is explicitly discussed.

One example of this type of research is Villenas and Foley's (2002) review of critical ethnography where they argue that in order to "reveal oppressive relations of power" researchers must sometimes collaborate with research gatekeepers while simultaneously moving away from scientific notions of detached objectivity in research. Echoing Anzaldúa's (1999) call for a *mestiza* consciousness that skillfully negotiates multiple borders, Villenas and Foley (2002) described a critical ethnographer's journey as one that straddles academic and working-class-Chicano identities. This often means addressing the limitations of being both the colonized and the colonizer (Cordova, 1998; Villenas, 1996). Such tensions are not uncommon in Latino education research.

Incorporation or acknowledgement of a researcher's subjectivities and experiences is not limited to ethnographic or qualitative research. In fact, we propose that all methods of research would benefit from an examination of the scholar's standpoint. One such example is illustrated by Zarate (2005) where her own familial experiences informed the strategy for statistical comparisons. Specifically, initial analysis in the study confirmed a deterministic portrait of Latino immigrant families where early academic achievement determined college enrollment twelve years later with no mediating factors. After documenting her own family's educational trajectory for a non-related manuscript, she recognized that the educational trajectory for women in her family contrasted with the educational trajectories of the men. This observation led her to reconsider the analysis and reorganize the comparative groups to discover that Latinas and Latinos have different predictors of college enrollment. Indeed, scholars' personal experiences provide a very valuable source for methodological developments.

In challenging objectivist and detached approaches to the study of Latinos' educational experiences, Latino scholars have argued that they are in unique positions to understand the lived experiences of Latino students because their own lived experiences have involved negotiating different voices, strategies, and identities for survival in educational institutions (Anzaldúa, 1999; Gonzales, 1999; Villenas & Foley, 2002; Delgado Bernal, 1998). Delgado Bernal (1998, p. 562) argues that Chicanas have "unique viewpoints that can provide 'cultural intuition'." This cultural intuition derives from personal and professional experiences, existing literature, and the analytical process. For Delgado Bernal (1998), cultural intuition allows Chicanas to draw on their own experiences to form the basis of an epistemology that "allows Chicano and Chicana scholars to uncover and reclaim their own subjugated knowledge." In his book, *The Color of Success*, Conchas (2006) similarly discloses his "subjugated knowledge" (p. 574) when referring to research subjectivity. The following excerpt from his book clearly speaks to his stance as a Chicano social scientist:

> Another issue with which I dealt related to my politics. I chose to concentrate more on programs that best represented the racial and ethnic composition of the school and that made strong steps toward dismantling inequality. I firmly believe that racial inequality must be addressed. Thus, my sympathies lie with the teachers who held similar views ... I cannot hide the fact that I was less sympathetic to individuals that maintained the status quo. As a racial minority researcher, I strongly believe that schools should be places of fairness and

equal participation. My critical stance, I hope, has allowed me to illuminate agents, those individual and group behaviors, involved in seeking to improve the quality of schooling for urban youth. (pp. 125–127)

Delgado Bernal's (1998) and Conchas' (2006) arguments are pivotal methodological turns because they grant legitimacy to the experiential knowledge of the researcher in developing the research objective, theoretical framework, and methodology of a study when existing paradigms do not capture the nuances of Latinos' educational experiences.

Insider status based on ethnic membership alone is not a clearance to make unchecked assumptions about research subjects. Zavella (1996) cautions against assuming that insider status diminishes class, education, or identity differences that may permeate the researchers' interactions with the subjects. Maxwell (1996) and Hammersley and Atkinson (1983) argue that researchers' background and cultural identity offer an acceptable source of theoretical insights and valid interpretations to findings. However, Peshkin (1988) offers that it is not sufficient to simply acknowledge researcher subjectivity; it is also important to "systematically identify" subjectivities so that researchers can critically and methodically "attend to it" throughout the research process.

In our perusal of the recent research on Latinos and education, it was apparent that many Latino scholars discussed their ethnic and language background to explain some of the methodological decisions of their research on Latinos (Conchas, 2006; Delgado-Gaitan, 1994; Valdes, 1996; Stanton-Salazar, 2001; Hurtado, 2003; Valenzuela, 1999; Hidalgo, 1999; Delgado Bernal, 1998; Gonzales, 1999). For example, Stanton-Salazar (2001) describes his status as an alum of the high school that served as a research site and the impact this had on access to research subjects and his analytical lens. We propose that Latino scholars are especially cognizant of the impact of researcher subjectivities in research because past research on Latinos has sometimes misrepresented the group as homogenously and inaccurately frozen-in-time (Paredes, 1984). It is also the case that the role of the researcher in research has historically been considered a topic aligned with research in anthropology or feminist methodology. We argue instead that all research is equally susceptible to researcher subjectivities, regardless of methods utilized, identity of the researcher, or the discipline informing the study. As we will discuss below, the audience or purpose of the research may determine when researcher subjectivities are a relevant aspect of a methodological discussion.

Discussion and Future Directions

Transformational education research need not be associated with one method of research only, or a finite set of theoretical frameworks. Referring to our mapping of the methodological categories (Figure 5.1), it would appear that our selection of themes to discuss in this chapter highlights research with characteristics on the right side of the spectrums only. This is not to say that studies and research with methodological characteristics on the other end of the spectrum do not have the potential to transform the educational realities of Latinos. We have not discussed this category of research in this chapter because despite adding to the theoretical understanding of Latino education, the methods used in this category have not necessarily been transformative. That is, the findings of experimental and positivist research design have been important to Latino education research but the research designs are not necessarily transformational to social science research.

Research using experimental designs or institutional-level analysis are equally important for Latino education advocacy. For example, experimental designs may be important in determining and advocating for the optimal language accommodation or reading instruction program (Greene, 1997; Valdes, 2005). Ramirez (1991) and Thomas and Collier (2002) provide pivotal longitudinal evidence supporting bilingual education. Zarate (2006) finds that schools with large concentrations of students of color offer less college preparatory courses. Oakes et al. (2007) find that schooling conditions facing Latinos are substandard. These studies provide important evidence of the unfavorable conditions facing Latinos and the effectiveness of some programs over others. Although critical methodologies have been instrumental in providing new perspectives of Latinos/as' educational experiences, methodologies using traditional methods have the potential to also describe the educational conditions that Latinos face.

Considerations for Future Research

Some of the methodologies that we reviewed have the objective of challenging others to "examine their existing assumptions about Mexican families" (Valdés, 1996). This objective is both important in the academy and in policy. However, beyond informing perceptions of Latinos, research can also be an important instrument to inform and shape education policy on, namely, the factors and influences that promote success instead of failure (Conchas, 2006). Moreover, one of the ways that research on Latinos and education can have the most impact is to affect policy and schools that serve the greater Latino communities directly. We believe most scholars of education seek to have such an impact. Unfortunately, the dissemination format for which the academy rewards merit, i.e., peer-reviewed journals, is not accessible or widely available to practitioners, community organizers, and policy makers.

If the objective of research on Latino education is in large part to effect change on what works, then what is recognized as valid research in the academy is sometimes at odds with researchers seeking to disseminate their research to lay audiences or engage in action-research methodologies (Ginwright, Noguera, & Cammarota, 2006). Indeed, research can be disseminated to both academic audiences and practitioners simultaneously, but given the reward structure in the academe, this is not always practical. Without a doubt, peer-reviewed research gains integrity in the review process that is lacking in non-peer-reviewed research, so it would be dangerous to rid educational research of some sort of rigorous standards. On the other hand, the research using critical methodologies precisely critiques the epistemological origins of current academic standards for what constitutes valid research and dissemination practices. Many of the scholars explicitly seek to have broader impact with their research and in the research process. The field of education research merits examination in how the purpose of research is defined, how it is rewarded, and who is the audience.

Much of the research on Latinos and education that we have discussed is viewed from the historical perspective of immigration, racist policies, or colonial experiences. For the most part, scholars also currently agree that most Latinos can be characterized as working class and marginalized from mainstream institutions in the United States. As Latinos continue to become a greater proportion of the population, one would expect that the economic and social status of Latinos would become increasingly variable as some Latinos accomplish economic stability. We acknowledge that there is no consistent or reliable forecast on the economic and social status of Latinos in the future. But in the event that increasing numbers of Latinos gain access to middle-class status or economic and political leadership positions, social science research will have to gain new methodologies and theories to understand the divergent experiences of Latinos. Currently, traces of colonialism, economic exploitation, racist public discourse and discriminatory policy inform the methodologies and theoretical lenses used in education research. These conditions may well persist in the future, but it is likely that new demographic shifts and conditions will require new paradigms to explain the conditions of Latinos left behind. For example, in the past decade the academic achievement gap between Latinos and Latinas has increased dramatically (Peter & Horn, 2005). In such a case, a methodological framework grounded in gendered standpoints, in addition to a race-conscious approach, is needed (Villenas & Moreno, 2001; Zarate & Gallimore, 2005).

New angles and perspectives on Latinos' educational experiences can emerge from research using critical methodologies incorporating grounded analysis, and attentive to the perspectives and voices of the community. Scholars will want to continuously examine assumptions rooted in their cultural intuition, privileged subjectivities, and insider status, as Latinos' status in the United States changes or increasingly varies. For example, will class standpoints gain importance when discussing Latinos' educational experience, or will racial experiences dominate discussions on Latinos' trajectory? It is important that education scholars' assumptions about Latinos' identity and cultural practices continuously evolve alongside changing political, social, and demographic realities.

Note

1. The terms *Latino* and *Latina* are used interchangeably in this chapter.

References

Aguirre, A. (2000). Academic storytelling: A critical race theory story of affirmative action. *Sociological Perspectives, 43*(2), 319–339.

Anderson, J. D. (2002). Race in American higher education: Historical perspectives in current conditions. In W. A. Smith, P. G. Altbach, & K. Lomotey (Eds.), *The racial crisis in American higher education: Continuing challenges for the twenty-first century* (pp. 3–21). Albany: State University of New York Press.

Anzaldua, G. (1999). *Borderlands/La Frontera: The new mestiza* (2nd ed.). San Francisco: Ann Lute Books.

Barreto, M. A., & Pachon, H. P. (2003). *The reality of race neutral admissions for minority students at the University of California: Turning the tide or turning them away?* Los Angeles: Tomas Rivera Policy Institute.

Conchas, G. (2001). Structuring failure and success: Understanding the variability in Latino school engagement. *Harvard Educational Review, 70*(3), 475–504.

Conchas, G. Q. (2006). *The color of success: Race and high-achieving urban youth.* New York: Teachers College Press.

Cordova, T. (1998). Power and knowledge: Colonialism in the academy. In C. Trujillo (Ed.), *Living Chicana theory* (pp. 17–44). Berkeley, CA: Third Woman Press.

Delgado Bernal, D. (1998). Using Chicana feminist epistemology in educational research. *Harvard Educational Review, 68*, 555–581.

Delgado, R. (2000). Storytelling for oppositionists and others: A plea for narrative. In R. Delgado & J. Stefancic (Eds.), *Critical race theory: The cutting edge* (pp. 60–70). Philadelphia: Temple University Press.

Delgado-Gaitan, C. (1994). Consejos: The power of cultural narratives. *Anthropology and Education Quaterly, 25*(3), 298–316.

Dicker, S. J. (1996). *Languages in America: A pluralist view.* Philadelphia: Multilingual Matters Ltd.

Du Bois, W. E. B., (1995). *The souls of Black folk / W.E.B. DuBois; With a new introduction by Randall Kenan.* New York: Signet/Penguin Books.

Fry, R. (2005). *The high school Hispanics attend: Size and other key characteristics.* Washington, DC: Pew Hispanic Center.

Gándara, P. (1995). *Over the ivy walls: The educational mobility of low-income Chicanos.* Albany: State University of New York Press.

Ginwright, S., Noguera, P, & Cammarota, J. (2006). *Beyond resistance! Youth activism and community change: New democratic policies for practice and policy for America's youth.* New York: Routledge.

Goldenberg, C., Gallimore, R., Reese, L., & Garnier, H. (2001). Cause or effect? A longitudinal study of immigrant Latino parents' aspirations and expectations, and their children's school performance. *American Educational Research Journal, 38*(3), 547–582.

Gonzalez, D. J. (1997). Chicana identity matters. *Aztlán, 22*(2), 124–138.

Gonzales, F. E. (1999). Formations of Mexicananess: Trenzas de identidades multiples (Growing up Mexicana: Braids of multiple identities). In L. Parker, D. Deyhle, & S. Villenas (Eds.), *Race is ... race isn't: Critical race theory and qualitative studies in education* (pp. 125–154). Boulder, CO: Westview Press.

Goyette, K. A., & Conchas, G. (2001). The race is not even: Minority education in a post-affirmative action era. *Harvard Journal of Hispanic Policy, 13*, 87–102.

Greene, J. (1997). A meta-analysis of the Rossell and Baker review of bilingual education research. *Bilingual Research Journal, 21*(2/3), 1523–5882.

Hammersley, M., & Atkinson, P. (1983). *Ethnography: Principles in practice*. New York: Routledge.

Harding, S. (1987). Introduction: Is there feminist method? In S. Harding (Ed.), *Feminism and methodology: Social science issues* (pp. 1–14). Bloomington: Indiana University Press.

Heller, C. (1966). *Mexican American youth: Forgotten youth at the crossroads*. New York: Random House.

Hidalgo, N. M. (1999). Toward a definition of Latino family research paradigm. In S. Villenas, D. Deyhle, & L. Parker (Eds.), *Race is...race isn't: Critical race theory and qualitative studies in education* (pp. 101–124). Boulder, CO: Westview Press.

Hurtado, A. (2003). *Voicing Chicana feminisms: Young women speak out on sexuality and identity*. Albany: New York University Press.

Hurtado, A., Gonzales, R., & Vega, L. (1996). Social identification and the academic achievement of Chicano students. In R. Figueroa, E. Garcia, & A. Hurtado (Eds.), *Latino eligibility study* (pp. 57–73). Santa Cruz: University of California.

Hurtado, A., & Gurin, P. (1987). Ethnic identity and bilingual standards. *Hispanic Journal of Behavioral Sciences, 9*(1), 1–18.

Hurtado, S. (1992). The campus racial climate: Contexts of conflict. *Journal of Higher Education, 63*(5), 539–569.

Hurtado, S., Kurotsuchi Inkelas, K., Briggs, C., & Rhee, B. (1997). Differences in college access and choice among racial/ethnic groups: Identifying continuing barriers. *Research in Higher Education, 38*(1), 43–75.

Kellner, D. (1995). *Media culture, cultural studies, identity and politics between the modern and the postmodern*. London: Routledge.

Kloss, H. (1998). *The American bilingual tradition*. McHenry, IL: Center for Applied Linguistics and Delta Systems.

Krashen, S. D. (1996). *Under attack: The case against bilingual education*. Culver City, CA: Language Education Associates.

Kuvelesky, W. P., & Patella, V. M. (1971). Degree of ethnicity and aspirations for upward social mobility among Mexican American youth. *Journal of Vocational Behavior, 1*(3), 231–244.

Llorente, E. (2007, August 29). Empowering Hispanic youth. *The Record*, retrieved September 7, 2007, from http://www.northjersey.com/page.php?qstr=eXJpcnk3ZjcxN2Y3dnFlZUVFeXkzJmZnYmVsN2Y3dnFlZUVFeXk3MTg3Nzgz

Lopez, D. E., & Stanton-Salazar, R. D. (2001). Mexican Americans: A second generation at risk. In R. G. Rumbaut & A. Portes (Eds.), *Ethnicities: Children of immigrants in America* (pp. 57–90). Berkeley: University of California Press.

Lopez, G. (2001). The value of hardwork: Lessons on parental involvement from an (im)migrant household. *Harvard Educational Review, 71*(3), 416–437.

Matute-Bianchi, M. E. (1986). Ethnic identities and patterns of school success and failure among Mexican-descent and Japanese-American students in a California high school: An ethnographic analysis *American Journal of Education, 95*(1), 233–255.

Maxwell, J. A. (1996). *Qualitative research design: An interpretive approach*. Thousand Oaks, CA: Sage.

Moll, L., Amanti, C., Neff, D., & Gonzalez, N. (2001). Funds of knowledge for teaching: Using a qualitative approach to connect homes and classrooms. *Theory Into Practice, XXXI*, 2, 132–141.

Montoya, M.E. (2000). Mascaras, trenzas, y grenas: Un/masking the self while un/braiding Latina stories and legal discourse. In R. Delgado & J. Stefancic (Eds.), *Critical race theory: The cutting edge* (pp. 514–524). Philadelphia: Temple University Press.

Niemann, Y. F., Romero, A., & Arbona, C. (2000). Effects of cultural orientation on the perception and education goals for Mexican American college students. *Hispanic Journal of Behavioral Sciences, 22*(1), 46–63.

Oakes, J., Valladares, S., Renee, M., Fanelli, S., Medina, D., & Rogers, J. (2007). *Latino Educational Opportunity Report*. Los Angeles, CA: UCLA IDEA and UC/ACCORD.

Oboler. (1995). *Ethnic labels, Latino lives: Identity and the politics of (re)presentation in the United States.* Minneapolis: University of Minnesota Press.

Paredes, A. (1984). On ethnographic work among minority groups: A folklorists perspective. In R. Romo & R. Paredes (Eds.), *New directions in Chicano scholarship* (pp. 1–31). Santa Barbara, CA: Center for Chicano Studies.

Pearl, A. (1997). Cultural and accumulated environmental deficit models. In R. R. Valencia (Ed.), *The evolution of deficit thinking: Educational thought and practice* (pp. 211–240). London: The Falmer Press.

Perna, L. W. (2000). Differences in the decision to attend college among African Americans, Hispanics, and Whites. *The Journal of Higher Education, 71*(2), 117–141.

Peshkin, A. (1988). In search of subjectivity - one's own. *Educational Researcher, 17*(7), 17–21.

Peter, K., & Horn, L. (2005). *Gender differences in participation and completion of undergraduate education and how they have changed over time*, NCES 2005-169, U.S. Department of Education National Center for Education Statistics Washington, DC: Government Printing Office.

Pizarro, M. (1999). "¡Adelante!": Toward a social justice and empowerment in Chicana/o communities and Chicana/o studies. In L. Parker, D. Deyhle, & S. Villenas (Eds.), *Race is ... Race isn't: Critical race theory and qualitative studies in education* (pp. 53–82). Boulder, CO: Westview Press.

Portes, A., & Rumbaut, R. G. (2001). *Legacies: The story of the immigrant second generation*. Berkeley: University of California Press.

Ramirez, J. D. (1991). *Longitudinal study of structured English immersion strategy, early-exit and late-exit transitional bilingual education programs for language-minority children*. Washington DC: Department of Education.

Reese, L. (2001). Morality and identity in Mexican immigrant parents' visions of the future. *Journal of Ethnic and Migration Studies, 27*(3), 455–472.

Reese, L., Balzano, S., Gallimore, R., & Goldberg, C. (1995). The concept of educación: Latino family values and American schooling. *International Journal of Educational Research, 23*(1), 57–61.

Rowland, K. (2007, August 18). Successful on the field, not so in the classroom. *News Register*, retrieved September 7, 2007, from http://www.newsregister.com/news/results.cfm?story_no=225178

Saenz, V. B., Oseguera, L., & Hurtado, S. (2007). Losing ground? Exploring racial/ethnic enrollment shifts in freshman access to selective institutions. In G. Orfield, P. Marin, S. M. Flores, & L. M. Garces (Eds.), *Charting the future of college affirmative action: Legal victories, continuing attacks, and new research* (pp. 79–104). Los Angeles: University of California, Los Angeles, The Civil Rights Project.

Sanchez-Jankowski, M. (1991). *Islands in the street: Gangs and American urban society*. Berkeley: University of California Press.

Smith-Maddox, R., & Solorzano, D. G. (2002). Using critical rate theory, Paulo Freire's problem-posing method, and case study research to confront race and racism in education. *Qualitative Inquiry, 8*(1), 66–83.

Solórzano, D. G. (1998). Critical race theory, race, and gender microaggressions, and the experience of Chicana and Chicano scholars. *Qualitative Studies in Education, 11*(1), 121–136.

Solórzano, D. G., Ceja, M., & Yosso, T. (2000). Critical race theory, racial microaggressions, and campus racial climate: The experiences of African American college students. *The Journal of Negro Education, 69*(1/2), 60–73.

Solórzano, D. G., & Delgado Bernal, D. (2001). Examining transformational resistance through a critical race theory and LatCrit theory and framework: Chicano and Chicana students in urban context. *Urban Education, 36*(3), 308–342.

Solórzano, D. G., & Ornelas, A. (2004). A critical race analysis of Latino/a and African American advanced placement enrollment in public high schools. *High School Journal, 87*, 15–26.

Solórzano, D. G., & Villalpando, O. (1998). Critical race theory: Marginality and the experience of students of color in higher education. In *Sociology of Education: Emerging perspectives* (pp. 211–224). Albany: State University of New York Press.

Solórzano, D. G., & Yosso, T. (2001). Maintaining social justice hopes within academic realities: A Freirean approach to critical race/Latcrit pedagogy. *Denver University Law Review, 78*(4), 595–621.

Solórzano, D. G., & Yosso, T. (2002). Critical race methodology: Counter-storytelling as an analytical framework for education research. *Qualitative Inquiry, 8*(1), 23–44.

Stanton-Salazar, R. D. (2001). *Manufacturing hope and despair: The school and kin networks of U.S. Mexican youth.* New York: Teachers College Press.

Suárez-Orozco, C., & Suárez-Orozco, M. M. (1995). *Transformations: Immigration, family life, and achievement motivation among Latinoadolescents.* Stanford, CA: Stanford University Press.

Taylor, E. (2000). Critical race theory and interest convergence in the backlash against affirmative action: Washington state and Initiative 200. *Teachers College Records, 102*(3), 539–560.

Thomas, W. P., & Collier, V. P. (2002). *A national study of effective of effectiveness for language minority students' long term academic achievement.* Santa Cruz, CA: Center for Research on Education, Diversity, and Excellence.

Tienda, M., Leicht, K. T., Sullivan, T., Maltese, M., & Lloyd, K. (2003). *Closing the gap?: Admissions and enrollments at the Texas public flagships before and after affirmative action.* Unpublished manuscript, Princeton University.

Tornatsky, L. G., Cutler, R., & Lee, J. (2002). *College knowledge: What Latino parents need to know and why they don't know it.* Los Angeles: Tomas Rivera Policy Institute.

Torres, R. D., & Valle, V. M., (2000). *Latino metropolis.* Minneapolis: University of Minnesota Press.

Valdes, G. (1996). *Con respeto: Bridging the distances between culturally diverse families and schools.* New York: Teachers College Press.

Valdes, R. M. (2005). *Second literacy plan evaluation: 2003–04 (Second Year) Report.* Los Angeles: Los Angeles Unified School District.

Valencia, R. R. (Ed.). (1997). *The evolution of deficit thinking: Educational thought and practice.* London: The Falmer Press.

Valencia, R. R., & Solorzano, D. G. (1997). Contemporary deficit thinking. In R. R. Valencia (Ed.), *The evolution of deficit thinking: Educational thought and practice* (pp. 160–210). London: The Falmer Press.

Valenzuela, A. (1999). *Subtractive schooling: U.S.–Mexican youth and the politics of caring.* Albany: State University of New York Press.

Vigil, D. (1997). *Personas Mexicanas: Chicano high schoolers in a changing Los Angeles.* Orlando, FL: Harcourt Brace and Company.

Vila, P. (2000). *Crossing borders, reinforcing borders: Social categories, metaphors, and narrative identities on the U.S.-Mexico frontier.* Austin: University of Texas Press.

Villenas, S. (1996). The colonizer/colonized Chicana ethnographer: Identity, marginalization, and co-optation in the field. *Harvard Educational Review, 66*(4), 711–731.

Villenas, S., & Foley, D. E. (2002). Chicano/Latino critical ethnography of education: Cultural productions from la frontera. In *Chicano school failure and success: past, present, and future* (2nd ed., pp. 195–225). London: Routledge/Falmer.

Villenas, S., & Moreno, M. (2001). To valerse por si misma between race, capitalism, and patriarchy: Latina mother daughter pedagogies in North Carolina. *Qualitative Studies in Education, 14,* 671–687.

Volkmann, K. (2007, August 28). Nonprofit teaches Hispanic students, parents about the road to college. *Examiner.com*, retrieved September 7, 2007, from http://www.examiner.com/a903173~Nonprofit_teaches_Hispanic_students__parents_about_the_road_to_college.html.

Zarate, M. E. (2005). *When grades don't matter: Schooling and family experiences of college bound and non-college-bound Latinas.* Unpublished doctoral dissertation, University of California, Los Angeles.

Zarate, M. E. (2006). *Equity in offering Advanced Placement courses in California high schools, 1997–2003.* Los Angeles: Tomas Rivera Policy Institute.

Zarate, M. E. (2007). *Understanding Latino parental involvement in education.* Los Angeles: Tomas Rivera Policy Institute.

Zarate, M. E., Bhmji, F., & Reese, L. (2005). Ethnic identity and academic achievement among Latino/a adolescents. *Journal of Latinos and Education, 4*(2), 95–114.

Zarate, M. E., & Gallimore, R. (2005). Gender differences in factors leading to college enrollment: A longitudinal analysis of Latino and Latino students. *Harvard Educational Review, 75*(4), 383–407.

Zavella, P. (1996). Feminist insider dilemmas: Constructing identity with "Chicana" informants. In D. L. Wolf (Ed.), *Feminist dilemmas in fieldwork.* Boulder, CO: Westview Press.

Zentella, A. C. (1997). *Growing up bilingual: Puerto Rican children in New York.* Malden, MA: Blackwell.

6 Latino/a Theoretical Contributions to Educational Praxis

Abriendo Caminos, Construyendo Puentes

Jason G. Irizarry
University of Connecticut

Sonia Nieto
University of Massachusetts, Amherst

Although Latinos/as have had a long-standing presence in the United States and despite their pioneering efforts in addressing issues of educational equity, educational outcomes for Latino/a students have been largely problematic. For instance, dropout rates, an often disputed yet widely popular indicator of academic failure, reflect an alarming state of affairs for Latino/a youth (Orfield, 2004). Census Bureau estimates suggest that almost one-quarter of all Latinos/as in the United States between the ages of 16 and 19 have not completed and are not currently enrolled in high school (U.S. Census Bureau, 2003). Statistics for older Latinos/as are similarly bleak. Educational research and personal narratives emerging from the Latino/a community suggest that dropout rates may in fact be underreported (Conchas & Rodríguez, 2003; Noguera, 2003). This lack of academic success presents serious implications that reverberate within and well beyond the Latino/a population.

In spite of the grim picture of the history of education among Latinos/as in the United States—a picture that is well documented in the chapters in this handbook—the outlook for the future is not without hope. On the contrary, given the growing number of Latino/a students in U.S. schools, and the growing number of scholars (particularly Latino/a scholars) whose research and practice focuses on the education of Latinos, there is good reason to believe that more attention and interest will be given to this topic in the coming years. As Latinos/as have struggled to navigate an educational system that many scholars would argue is constructed to impede their progress and limit their access to quality educational opportunities, progressive educational researchers, including a growing number of Latino/as, have worked to generate and disseminate research to help explain and ultimately ameliorate these conditions. They have engaged in *educational praxis*—a process of "reflection and action upon the world in order to transform it" (Freire, 1970, p. 36). Building on Paulo Freire's (1970) definition, we assert that engaged action is at the heart of educational praxis. Scholarship with a praxis orientation reflects a commitment to traditionally marginalized communities and the development of a "theoretical understanding and critique of society and action that seeks to transform individuals and their environment" (Leistyna, 1999, p. 224).

Much of the scholarship aimed at improving the education of Latino/a students in U.S. schools is rooted in this notion of praxis. The contributors to this emerging body of literature are diverse and their contributions unique and invaluable. Most are Latinos/as, while others represent other backgrounds. Regardless of their ethnic or racial identities, they share a commitment to using scholarship as a means of forging new pathways—*abriendo caminos*—for Latino/a students that can lead to increased and enhanced opportunities for school success. Their work also serves as a *puente,* or bridge, between theory and practice or, more specifically, as a bridge between educational research and the sociocultural realities of Latino/a communities. Departing from an academic tradition that rarely addresses the material conditions of marginalized peoples, the contributions to educational praxis discussed here have redefined the role of the academic and transformed the landscape of educational research, offering new ideas, language and methodologies to better serve Latino/a students and families. The result has been a wealth of scholarship rooted in, and emerging from, Latino/a communities. Hoping to continue in this tradition, in this chapter we synthesize research that has made meaningful contributions to the field of Latino/a education, unpacking some of the commonalities as well as distinct features of this body of scholarship and discussing the implications of this research to positively transforming the educational trajectories of Latino/a students.

Research on Latino/a Students: A Sociohistorical Perspective

The traditional educational research literature on the experiences of Latinos/as in U.S. schools has been rooted in a deficit perspective, attributing Latinos/as' lack of educational success to cultural, linguistic and even genetic deficiencies, and some scholars have been challenging this deficit perspective for years (Valencia, 1997; Valenzuela, 1999; Nieto, 1998). Deficit-centered research about Latino/a students has generally been done by "outsiders," individuals who are not Latino/a or meaningfully connected to Latino/a communities. This body of research explicitly demonstrates a lack of value placed on Latino/a students' cultural, linguistic, and experiential resources, a stance clearly reflected in the low quality of education provided for Latinos/as throughout history. For example, Mexican Americans in the Southwest, the largest group of Latinos/as in the United States, have endured sustained efforts to significantly compromise their access to quality education. Such acts of violence, both physical and symbolic (Bourdieu and Wacquant, 1992), range from limiting access to school facilities and qualified teachers to corporal punishment and sink or swim approaches to language learning. Similarly, during the U.S. colonization of Puerto Rico beginning at the turn of the 20th century, all schools on the island were forced to operate in English, a language spoken by few of the students or teachers. The schools were renamed after famous figures in U.S. history, and the school curriculum was changed to introduce Puerto Ricans to the espoused benefits of American culture (Negrón de Montilla, 1971).

Culture and Cultural Bias

Much of the educational research emanating from the context described above was characterized by a blatant disregard for the cultures of Latino/a students and a paternalistic approach to their education. The tone and content of much of the research reified the notion that Latinos/as were culturally deprived individuals and it was their supposed "cultural deficiencies" that were to blame for their lack of academic success in U.S. schools. Beginning with the educational reform movement of the 1920s, standardized tests purporting to measure intelligence were used to support the notion of intellectual inferiority among Latinos/as (García, 2001; Nieto, 2000). A 1936 U.S. chamber of commerce report based on IQ test administered in English to 240 Puerto Rican school children claimed that Puerto Rican students were "mentally deficient" and "intellectually immature" (Cockcroft, 1995, p. 59). It is clear that the researchers in this case failed to consider the issues of language and content bias, among other factors, that may have impacted their results. Nevertheless, these wide-ranging conclusions are representative of popular sentiment regarding Latino/a students and families during this time.

The body of research purporting to explain the failure of many Latino/a students to excel in school served to justify their segregation and exclusion from equitable educational opportunities and a lack of financial investment in schools and districts that serve them. Segregation based on race/ethnicity and language has been a salient characteristic of Latino/a education in the United States for the past century (Spring, 2006). As early as 1921 Mexican Americans and Puerto Ricans were active and successful in winning school desegregation lawsuits against school districts limiting access and opportunity for Latino/a students (Ruiz, 2001; Nieto, 2004; San Miguel Jr., 2005).

The sociopolitical factors that impacted Latino/a students beginning in the 1920s and 30s continue to have deleterious effects on the educational aspirations and outcomes of this group. Drawing largely from standardized test score data, popular texts such as the *Bell Curve* (Herrnstein & Murray, 1994) and research articles in reputable journals with mass appeal (Jensen, 1969) have been used to locate the "problem" of Latino/a educational underachievement as an intractable phenomenon and unavoidable consequence of genetic inferiority.

Practices based on IQ scores and other standardized tests are not a thing of the past. They continue to be used by many school districts serving Latinos/as to determine student placement in various tracks, or academic paths, within the school. Important research by Oakes (2005), Romo and Falbo (1996), and Fernández (2002) among others (Durán, 1988; Coutinho & Oswald, 2000; Noguera, 2001, 2003; Conchas, 2006) suggests that Latinos/as continue to be overrepresented in special education and in the less academically rigorous, non college-prep tracks of their schools. Consequently, Latinos/as are often less prepared to meet the requirements for college admission and less likely to have the skills necessary to complete a college degree. Standardized exams such as the Scholastic Aptitude Test (SAT), often used as part of the college admissions process, have also served as a barrier for many Latino/a students. Although SAT scores have been found to be weak predictors of Latino/a students' likelihood to complete a college degree, their college GPA, or their likelihood of applying to graduate school, they still serve to limit access to higher education for otherwise high achieving Latino/a students (Gándara & Lopez, 1998).

A more current popular trend in research regarding Latino/a students focuses on the achievement gap—the discrepancy between the test scores and academic performance of Latinos/as (and other students of color) and White students. Although not directly referring to Latino/a students as "culturally deprived" or "deficient," much of this more recent work focuses on student performance as measured by outcomes on a single measure, with little to no emphasis on the needs of the learner, quality of instruction, language spoken in class, cultural bias of tests, and a plethora of other confounding variables that should be considered. Focusing solely on student performance continues to locate the problem of underachievement on Latino/a students and families with little to no emphasis on the sociopolitical factors that impact their access to quality education. Certainly, individuals have some agency and responsibility for their actions. However, overemphasizing performance in lieu of the factors that influence these outcomes—many of which are beyond the control of Latino/a students and families—presents a fundamental flaw in much of the literature.

Many studies and other reports make claims about groups of students that are often disconnected from the context in which they occur, presenting another significant flaw within the deficit-centered literature. It is important to consistently locate Latinos/as' struggles for equal education within larger sociohistorical and sociopolitical contexts. Examining student achievement without taking these contexts into account suggests that the achievement gap has not been a widespread reality over time. Focusing on the outcomes of individual participants to the exclusion of influential institutional structures can imply that institutions are absolved of responsibility from their responsibility to address this issue.

Promoting a Paradigm Shift

The history of Latino/a education has been one of struggle with a long legacy of community activism aimed at combating egregious learning conditions and poor educational quality. As many Latinos/as and allies took to the streets and courtrooms in protest, speaking out against injustice and attempting to influence policy makers, educational research also became a vehicle for activism and a site through which to combat educational, cultural, and social oppression. The important body of research that has emerged from this struggle represents a shift from purportedly objective accounts of Latino/a student performance that fail to acknowledge and remain distant from the sociocultural contexts in which Latino/a students are embedded to more culturally connected approaches that value the cultural wealth (Yosso, 2005) and funds of knowledge (Moll, Amanti, Neff, & González, 2005) present in these communities.

Notably, George I. Sanchez's groundbreaking text, *Forgotten People* (1940), examined the experiences of Mexicans and Mexican Americans in New Mexico during the 1930s. He found that despite the fact that the districts in the county explored in his study were grossly under-funded, receiving on average approximately half of the financial support of districts serving White students, students in these schools were able to make remarkable progress. He focused not on school failure but rather emphasized the fact that despite being embedded in an oppres-sive system, students were able to achieve at high levels. His work departs from other research on Latino/as during this time by emphasizing that the problem was not the students but rather the system in which they were being educated. Sanchez's research offered a sharp critique of the school funding system of the time and of the state's allocation of resources, noting "There is no reason why such facilities as adequate high schools, transportation, school sup-plies, supervision and administration, and teachers should not be as available to Taos as they are elsewhere in the state" (p. 73). In addition, he called upon teacher education programs to do a better job of preparing teachers to work with students for whom English is a second language. His critique of school funding systems and teacher education continues to be valid almost 70 years later.

One of the most significant works addressing the needs of Puerto Rican school children in New York City (where the great majority of Puerto Ricans lived until the 1970s) was *The Puerto Rican Study 1953–1957* (Morrison, 1958). The primary goal of this project was to examine the educational experiences of Puerto Rican students and to utilize the findings to inform a city-wide initiative to improve the educational experiences of Spanish-speaking students. Although there was a gaping lack of representation of Puerto Ricans among the advisory panel members, which undoubtedly influenced the process and the outcome of the report, it still made impor-tant recommendations including placing an emphasis on improving ESL (English as a Second Language) instruction and the need to increase the number of Puerto Rican faculty, staff, and administrators in schools.

Historically, much of the research on the education of Latino/a students had been done by non-Latinos/as and those disconnected from the Latino/a community, with a particular focus on the cultural differences between Latino/a and White students, often privileging the cultures of the latter and portraying the former as "deficient." The portrayal of Latinos/as as empty ves-sels lacking the prerequisite knowledge and experience necessary to be successful in school and locating the problem of Latino/a underachievement within families, communities, cultures and language is, unfortunately, characteristic of much of the literature regarding the education of Latinos/as—particularly, although not confined to the early- to mid-20th century. Unpacking this research and briefly exploring alternative research that has challenged these characteriza-tions and promoted alternative explanations provides a backdrop for understanding more cur-rent scholarship regarding the education of Latino/a students in U.S. schools.

In what follows, we explore three themes that characterize much of the more recent Latino/a contributions to theoretical praxis. They include: *research as a vehicle to challenge deficit per-spectives; culturally responsive research and practice; and research grounded in, and informed by, Latino/a communities.*

Research as a Vehicle to Challenge a Deficit Perspective

As Latino/a researchers have made clear in the past several decades, much of the discourse regarding Latino/a students has been grounded in deficit perspectives, and these perspectives continue to be proliferated through educational research and within teacher training programs (Trueba, 1988; Valencia, 1997; González, 2005). There is a growing body of literature that aims to shift this discourse to a more accurate and robust view of Latino/a students and their efforts to attain an equal education. A significant feature of this work is highlighting success stories —examples where Latino/as have succeeded in spite of the institutional barriers that serve to replicate unequal social relations in school and within the broader society (see, for example, Gándara, 1995; Reyes, Scribner, & Scribner, 1999; Tinajero & Spencer, 1999; Espinoza-Herold, 2002; Antróp-González, Vélez, & Garrett, 2005; Conchas 2006). This research often takes an emic perspective to highlight the voices of Latino/as to demonstrate how they use their agency to contest, resist, redefine, and negotiate the way Latino/as are positioned in school and within the broader society.

Latinos/as have consistently challenged their depiction within society and much of this resistance has been manifested through language. The work of Raul Ybarra (2004) is a clear illustration of a call for alternative discourses to examine and explain the experiences of Latino/a students. These alternative discourses on research concerning the education of Latinos/as suggest that a shift is needed away from a focus on changing Latino/a culture and family structure to conform to Anglo norms, to instead build on the cultural and intellectual richness that exists within Latino/a communities. Ybarra (2004) convincingly argues that "what is missing from this basic educational discourse is the demand to discuss Latino education that explores and acknowledges the complex structural and cultural forces that play a major role in influencing Latino/a students to either stay in school or leave" (p. 2). Recent research has directly sought to "RicanStruct" the discourse regarding Latino/a student achievement to include models that reflect success and hope rather than failure and despair (Irizarry & Antróp-González, 2007).

Much of the deficit-centered literature suggests that a lack of involvement among families living in poverty, including Latino/a families, is in part responsible for the educational outcomes of this community (see, for example, Payne, 2003). However, much of this work fails to consider the fact that traditional avenues for parent participation in schools are closed off to Latino/a families (Delgado-Gaitán, 1991). In an ethnographic study of Latino/a families, Concha Delgado-Gaitán (2001) found that almost all the teachers in her study believed parental involvement was extremely important, yet they also asserted that the majority of Latino/a parents were not sufficiently involved in their children's education. In another example, Nitza Hidalgo (1997, 2000) explored the contributions Latino/a parents make to the educational experiences of their children. The findings from her study of four Puerto Rican families in Boston, Massachusetts, suggest that Latino/a parents, and the extended familial social networks that they develop, contribute to the educational experiences of their children in meaningful ways that often remain unrecognized by schools. Similarly, in Carmen Rolón's (2000) study of the narratives of 10 Puerto Rican female students, the participants cite their mothers as the most important individuals supporting their educational goals.

Exploring the role of the Latino/a family in fostering school success has been a focal point for other researchers as well. In their study of academically successful Puerto Rican students in the midwestern United States, René Antróp-Gonzalez, William Vélez, and Tomás Garrett (2005) found that students' families, and particularly their mothers, played a large role in fostering academic success. More specifically, the mothers of the students in the study assisted their children with schoolwork, helped locate resources to help support their learning, and served as friends and mentors, guiding them through the learning process.

Also contributing to debunking the myth that Latino/a families are apathetic about education, Gerardo Lopez's (2001) study of a migrant family in Texas challenges rigid definitions of parental involvement that typically involve parental participation in school-sanctioned events such as Parent Teacher Organizations and fundraising. He cogently argues that the family in his study was highly involved in what he refers to as the "transmission of sociocultural values" (p. 430). That is, the family taught their children the value of hard work and underscored the importance of getting an education in part by taking their children with them to do physically demanding agricultural work, explicitly "giving their children the 'choice' to work hard at school or work hard in the fields" (p. 420).

While this is not an exhaustive account of research that challenges the positioning of Latino/a families as an impediment to the academic success of their children, the research and findings discussed here suggest that, contrary to what is purported in much of the deficit-centered literature, education is, in fact, highly valued among Latino/a families. Recent research also points to the need to reconceptualize parental involvement based on the various practices taking place in the home and communities of Latinos/as. More specifically, researchers are calling for a shift within research to focus on how parents and community members define involvement rather than on static definitions created by school personnel and others who may be less connected to the Latino/a community. Recent literature also represents a change from comparing Latino/a families to established norms—which usually reflect White middle-class values—to learning from Latino/a families how to better support the educational and personal development of their children. Finally, a growing body of research advocates that schools acknowledge the social and cultural capital present in Latino/a communities (Moll & Greenberg, 1990; Darder, 1991; Stanton-Salazar, 1997; González et al., 2005; Yosso, 2005) and provides alternatives to assimilationist notions evident in school policies and practices.

Research Critiquing Language as a Deficit among Latino/a Students and Families

Beginning in the 1920s in the southwest, Mexican and Mexican American students were segregated in part because school agents and others believed that integrating Spanish-speaking students in class with their monolingual English-speaking peers would hinder the academic progress of White students. This view of language as a deficit has persisted over time. During the 1930s, Spanish-speaking students were often positioned within educational research as slow learners as a result of their performance on standardized tests given in English (Nieto, 2000). During the 1940s and 50s, the perception of bilingualism shifted slightly as educational research began portraying speaking a language other than English as a hindrance to assimilation and becoming fully American (Flores, 2005). Research in the following two decades described Latinos/as as culturally and linguistically deprived, and more recently, in the 1980s and 90s, as being at risk of failing because they spoke a language other than English as their native language (Flores, Tefft-Cousin, & Díaz, 1991; Flores, 2005). Such deficit approaches assume that schools function well and are effective, and that if students are not achieving the desired outcomes, schools are not at fault. Instead, the thinking goes, it is the students, their families, and communities that must change to fit into the existing mold.

Important theoretical contributions to educational praxis have challenged such deficit perspectives regarding language use and language learning among Latinos/as, positioning bilingualism and multilingualism as strengths upon which to build rather than as problems that need correcting. Ana Celia Zentella (2005), a language socialization researcher, asserts that "researchers [need to] go beyond 'the problem is they don't speak English' to investigate which immigrant traditions are functional or dysfunctional in mainstream schools and other institutions that determine whether children flourish or fail" (p. 13). Her work exploring language and literacy practices within Latino/a families and communities debunks widely held assumptions about literacy development among Latino/a children. More specifically, she urges teachers and researchers not to view all Latino/a English Language Learners (ELLs) as if they were identical, stressing that umbrella terms such as Latino/a, Hispanic, and ELL tend to homogenize individuals within groups without acknowledging their diversity. A common perception in much of the literature regarding literacy development among Latino/a children is that students' academic performance is a direct result of their parents not reading to them in English at home. Zentella challenges this perception, accurately noting that there are children who have made great academic gains in spite of not having early exposure to such experiences. While acknowledging the benefits of early exposure to literacy practices, she simultaneously reminds us that there are many students who struggle in school even though they had access to a wealth of educational resources and experiences.

Using an autoethnographic approach, Mariana Souto-Manning (2006) has reflected on how as a Latina immigrant, teacher and faculty researcher, she is consistently bombarded with deficit discourse regarding bilingualism in her personal and professional life. Despite more than three decades of research that suggests that bilingualism is an asset for children, enhancing their problem-solving ability and language processing, her personal account of everyday interactions with individuals and institutional structures, particularly schools, demonstrates that the deficit view of language learners is still pervasive. She uses the findings in her research to critique common misconceptions about bilingual learners including the notion that bilingual children struggle with learning new concepts as a result of their brains using two linguistic systems (Lambert, 1990).

Drawing from five years of data collection related to their research exploring the potential to enhance teachers' ability to work with culturally and linguistically diverse students, Shernaz García and Patricia Guerra (2004) present a conceptual framework aimed at deconstructing deficit teaching among educators. Drawing from their research and experiences in presenting professional development workshops, they suggest that many teachers and administrators assume students are "at risk" of failure because of sociocultural variables such as poverty and speaking English as a second language. As a result, teachers may overgeneralize the impact of these factors and widely apply this lens within their classrooms. García and Guerra (2004) argue that staff development needs to deconstruct these beliefs because they serve as impediments to culturally responsive curriculum and instruction.

Researchers challenging deficit explanations of Latino/a underachievement have not limited their study of language acquisition and use to the English-Spanish binary. Rather, several have looked at language and culture more broadly to include language variations and multidialectalism (González, 2005; Schecter & Bayley, 2002; Zentella, 2005) as well as cultural and linguistic hybridity (Gutiérrez, Baquedano-Lopez, & Tejeda, 1999; Irizarry, 2007). Important research by Ernest Morrell and Jeffrey Duncan-Andrade (2002) examines the potential influence of urban youth culture on the literacy development of youth in urban communities. While urban youth language and culture are acknowledged as powerful influences on the lives of Latino/a as well as other youth, they tend to be examined through a deficit lens. To the contrary, Morrell and Duncan-Andrade (2002) highlight the potential of building upon urban youth language and culture and using them as a bridge to more standard academic literacies. Unfortunately, teachers and other school agents tend to view culture as static so that subtle variations within language and culture remain unrecognized, resulting in discontinuities between teachers and students (Darder 1991; Nieto & Bode, 2008).

Whose Story Gets Told? Who is the Storyteller?

As scholarship has continued to emerge from Latino/a communities, new voices and perspectives have been introduced into the discourse regarding the education of Latinos/as. Whereas Latino/as were typically solely positioned as subjects to be studied, they have increasingly assumed roles as researchers. Another important, yet often unrecognized, part of what these researchers do is give voice to members of a community whose voices are often suppressed (Cammarota & Romero, 2006; Diaz-Greenberg, 2003). The shift from being the studied to doing the studying has not come without a perception that researchers studying communities with which they are connected often lack the objectivity necessary for quality scientific research. We assert, to the contrary, that Latino/a researchers offer unique and invaluable contributions to the field, amplifying voices that have consistently been excluded from the research. Research emerging from this community has continuously sought to reconcile emic and etic perspectives, drawing from multiple sites to inform their analysis of schooling for Latinos/as, including Latino researchers' own lived experiences with oppressive education institutions as well as the skills developed through their professional preparation. Thus, many Latino/a scholars have used their scholarship as a way to build bridges between home and school (see, for example, Reyes & Halcón, 2001; Vásquez, 2003). Their work has contributed new and significant insights that impact Latino/a communities in the United States.

Pamela Anne Quiroz's (2001) study of the narratives of 27 Puerto Rican and Mexican students is a prime example of the potential of using research as a vehicle to challenge hegemonic practices in schools that serve to subordinate Latino/a students. Quiroz critically examined essays constructed by students in 8th and 11th grade and found that their high school narratives were less hopeful than those constructed by the same students three years earlier. In addition, she found that in the later essays the students took a more critical stance, implicating schools as contributing to their failure to achieve academic success. She contends that as a result of neglect and "school sponsored silencing," Latino/a students' voices and aspirations become suppressed (Quiroz, 2001, p. 328).

Issues of voice are also central to the work of Tara Yosso (2005, 2006) who uses counterstories—narratives that reflect the lived experiences of people of color—to highlight how Latino/as are responding to and challenging forces of assimilation and social reproduction. For example, Yosso (2005, 2006) contests Pierre Bourdieu's (Bourdieu & Passeron, 1977) notion of cultural capital which asserts that the cultural knowledge and norms of middle and upper class individuals are essential for upward social mobility. Many educators, drawing from Bourdieu's theory, consequently believe that Latino/a students enter school without the prerequisite knowledge and skills to be successful. Instead, she asserts that the existing cultural capital model centers the cultural knowledge and experiences of the dominant group, thereby positioning Latino/as and their cultures as deficient and less valuable. She proposes a community cultural wealth framework which underscores the valuable capital (i.e., resiliency) that many Latino/a students bring to school that, if valued by teachers, has the potential to contribute to their academic success.

While early research about Latino/a children typically generated data by relying on their parents and/or teachers, more recent scholarship has placed special emphasis on collecting data from, and telling the stories of, young people themselves. Catherine Walsh (1991), for example, interviewed Puerto Rican children about language, culture, and school and demonstrated how power relations in school and society influence the perceptions and experiences of children who speak a marginalized language. The work of María Torres-Guzmán and Yvonne Martínez-Thorne (2000) highlights the potential of researchers, practitioners and policy makers to learn from Latino students, asserting that student perspectives are central to "understand[ing] the schooling experiences of American youth or fully understand[ing] the process of educational change embodied in school restructuring" (p. 269). They argue that in educational reform efforts the perspectives of individuals positioned as external experts are all too often privileged over student voices.

Another significant feature of research that presents a more authentic and accurate portrayal of Latinos/as is that it also privileges the knowledge of Latinos/as working in K-12 schools and institutions of higher education and views their contributions as adding unique perspectives to research on teaching and learning. For example, Robert Rueda, Lilia D. Monzó, and Ignacio Higareda (2004) highlight how teachers can learn to be more effective with their Latino/a students by modeling the sociocultural scaffolding practices of 24 Latino/a paraeducators (see also Monzó & Rueda, 2003). Similarly, Xaé Alicia Reyes and Diana Rios (2005) draw from their own experiences to shape a dialogue that unpacks issues facing women of color within the academy and use this information to propose strategies for increasing pathways into higher education for underrepresented populations. Research by Sonia Nieto and Carmen Rolón (1997) presents the perspectives of Latinas on the professional development of teachers informed by research and personal experiences as Latina educators. Such perspectives are also evident in a published conversation among Latino/a literacy researchers (Jiménez, Moll, Rodríguez-Brown, & Barrera, 1999). This creative publication combines excerpts from a plethora of conversations among leading literacy researchers to explore important themes related to literacy development among Latino/a students. Using both English and Spanish in the text and drawing from empirical research as well as personal narratives, the authors include emic perspectives that powerfully illuminate not only the problems that exist in the field but also the possibilities for improving literacy learning among Latinos/as.

Latino/a theoretical contributions to educational praxis have played a pivotal role in deconstructing deficit notions and constructing new paradigms through which to examine teaching and learning (Solórzano, 2001). This body of research serves as a response to problematic positioning of Latino/as within educational research This body of literature functions as a counterhegemonic force, working to deconstruct and challenge inaccurate and harmful characterizations of Latinos/as within educational research. Scholarship that challenges deficit-centered educational research, we contend, serves a revolutionary function as it attempts to help liberate Latino/a students and families from the detrimental policies and practices rooted in problematic notions of Latino/a culture.

Reconceptualizing Culture in Culturally Responsive Research and Practice

Schools as they are currently constructed do not work for many students. As documented in the previous section, this may be partially as a result of school agents taking a deficit view of Latino/a culture, that is, viewing it as a hindrance rather than an asset. As researchers have sought to develop remedies for ameliorating the experiences of Latino/a students, one potential remedy to combat the cycle of academic underachievement can be the implementation of culturally responsive curriculum and instruction (Ladson-Billings, 1994; Gay, 2000). However, as this body of research has evolved, many scholars have called for more fluid understandings of culture. Some scholars, although supportive of culturally responsive pedagogy, have explicitly addressed the pitfalls associated with essentializing culture. Instead, they propose that culture be viewed as ever-changing and dynamic. This work has informed research and practice in the area of culturally responsive teaching, providing valuable resources for teachers of culturally and linguistically diverse students.

Addressing the challenges associated with attributing patterns in behavior to an individual's cultural background, Kris Gutiérrez and Barbara Rogoff (2003) warn against treating regularities of cultural practices as static. They draw from a cultural-historical approach to suggest that researchers and practitioners be attentive to the variations that exist among group members. As a result, they propose that educators and researchers consider not individual traits per se, but rather the contexts in which people with distinct histories engage in fluid cultural practices. In their framework, individual and group experiences rather than individual traits are foregrounded. Along those lines, the work of Norma González (2005) challenges the notion that "all members of a particular group share a normative, bounded, and integrated view of their own culture" (p. 35), asserting instead a view of culture and cultural practices as hybrid funds of knowledge. That is, while Latinos/as may indeed share some commonalities, they also differ in many ways. Even within a particular Latino/a ethnic group, individuals have different histories and experiences that shape their perspectives and cultural identities. Consequently, like other groups, they draw from varied, intercultural knowledge bases and therefore create and enact unique hybrid identities. This heterogeneity among Latinos/as, and even more specifically within all the ethnic groups that fall under that umbrella term, is rarely acknowledged by schools, yet is important to consider.

The research included here approaches culture not only as a construct consumed by individuals but rather as one created by individuals in specific contexts. If this is the case, cultural expressions will most certainly be varied. These conceptualizations of culture have informed approaches to teaching and learning that have far-reaching implications for schools serving Latino/a students. Carmen Rolón, for example, has developed the notion of "centering pedagogies"—approaches to teaching and learning that allow students' identities and the various sociocultural factors that influence the creation of those identities to be examined and affirmed—as a framework for teachers to consider when working with culturally and linguistically diverse students (Nieto & Rolón, 1997).

Another powerful example can be found in youth popular culture. Whereas culture is typically defined in terms of race or ethnicity, other sites and manifestations of cultural production also need to be considered. Given their contributions to and engagement with popular culture, many urban youth are heavily influenced by music, television, movies, sports, language practices, and other modes of popular culture (Duncan-Andrade, 2004). Given the complex nature of culture and the importance of individual histories, Jeffrey Duncan-Andrade (2004) argues that overcoming "oppressive conditions requires context-specific solutions" (p. 315). He advocates for fluid approaches to culturally responsive teaching that take into account the variety of cultural activities with which students are involved, urging teachers to engage in what he refers to as "youth popular culture pedagogy and curriculum" (p. 331).

Another approach that centers culture was developed by Julio Cammarota and Augustine Romero (2006) who call for a critically compassionate pedagogy when working with Latino/a youth. They assert that Latino/a academic development would be significantly enhanced by educational praxis that draws from the tenets of critical pedagogy (Freire, 1970), authentic caring (Valenzuela, 1999), and social justice curriculum (Ginwright & Cammarota, 2002). In a similar vein, research by Anthony De Jesús (2005) calls for an culturally additive approach to schooling which values students' cultural identities, gives them access to the codes of power (Delpit, 1995), and frames education as a vehicle for community uplift.

Additional pedagogical innovations that center students' cultures and experiences are described by Carlos Tejeda, Manuel Espinoza, and Kris Gutiérrez (2003) who offer a response to "backlash pedagogies" (Gutiérrez et al., 2002, p. 337) aimed at continuing the subordination of marginalized peoples. They propose instead what they call "decolonizing pedagogies," that is, approaches aimed at contesting the continued legacy of colonization and subordination endured by indigenous peoples and other colonized groups.

The culture-specific educational accommodations described here all aim to make instruction more culturally responsive to the educational and personal needs of Latino/a students. Each provides positive illustrations of the potential of culturally responsive teaching to improve academic achievement among Latino/as and other students who are traditionally underserved by schools.

Research Grounded in and Informed by Latino/a Communities

Much of the research explored within this chapter has emerged from scholars who were born and/or raised in Latino/a communities in the United States. However, it is important to note that all of the theoretical contributions to educational praxis included here have been in some way informed by values and epistemologies that have emerged from Latino/a communities. An illustration of research informed by Latino/a communities is found in scholarship that addresses the concept of caring, or *cariño*—as it is more commonly known within Latino/a communities. Caring, or the supposed lack of caring, have been at the center of the discourse regarding the education of Latinos/as. A long-standing and almost intractable myth regarding Latino/a students and families is that they don't care about education. At the same time, many Latino/a students have consistently proclaimed that teachers and other school agents don't care about them. As such, *cariño* has been a central theme in research emanating from and informed by Latino/a communities. Care, in this sense, is conceptualized as much more than simple displays of affection or taking pity on students, also known to Mexican Americans as the "Pobrecito syndrome" (García, 2001) or to Puerto Ricans and other Spanish-speaking Caribbeans as the "Ay Bendito syndrome" (De Jesús & Antróp-González, 2006), the Spanish language phraseology for pity. Rather, *cariño* is an unwavering belief in students' ability to learn and perform at the highest levels, reflective of mutually enriching relationships that are forged between school agents and communities (Nieto, 2003). How Latino/a students experience care has been at the forefront of important recent contributions to educational praxis.

For example, Angela Valenzuela's (1999) research with Mexican American students in the southwest United States critiques oversimplified explanations of Latino/a student disengagement and the racist undertones often evident in claims that Latino/a students don't care about school. She notes, "The overt request [that students 'care' about school] overlies an overt demand that students embrace a curriculum that either dismisses or derogates their ethnicity and that they respond caringly to school officials who often hold their culture and community in contempt" (pp. 24–25). Based on her findings, she calls for schools to implement curricula and pedagogical strategies that are sensitive to the needs of Latino/a students.

Research by Rosalie Rolón-Dow (2005) explores the relationship between race/ethnicity and caring in the educational experiences of a group of middle school Puerto Rican girls. While she builds on the work of Nel Noddings (1984, 1992) and other theorists whose work centers on caring, she also challenges some of the more formulaic aspects of caring theory, pointing out that the construction of caring among theorists and practitioners is often rooted in a color-blind perspective, dismissing the impact of race/ethnicity on caring relationships. Conversely, Rolón-Dow contends that caring relationships must consider race/ethnicity and the personal histories of individuals and their relationship to institutional structures. She calls for school agents to adopt a color(full) critical care praxis that is rooted in a historical understanding of students' lives, is culturally responsive for Latino/a students, and uses caring counternarratives to help facilitate the development of more caring relationships between teachers and Latino/a students.

Similar work by Anthony De Jesús and René Antróp-González (2006) forwards the notion of critical care, characterized by high-quality authentic relationships and high academic expectations, as a factor contributing to the academic and social success of Latino/a students within two small community-based high schools. Like De Jesús and Antróp-González (2006), Nilda Flores-González (2002) suggests that students' academic success is inextricably linked to the relationships that they develop with school personnel and peers. Flores-González (2002) suggests that contributing to the discrepancy in high school completion among Latinos, African Americans, and White students are the identities students adopt and the influence of school practices on their identity development. Using role identity theory as a framework, Flores-González describes how early in the education process, Latino students develop either "School Kid" or "Street Kid" identities. "School kids" are those students who identify with the culture of the school, participate in a variety of school activities, and receive praise for doing well academically. Overall, their relationship with the school is positive. Conversely, "street kids" have few if any meaningful connections with school culture, and they develop negative school identities as a result of being judged harshly by their teachers. Her work suggests that schools can better support Latino/a students in the development of identities that are more congruent with school success. The voices of the students and families in this research demonstrate that *cariño*, as well as other values and concepts rooted in Latino communities such as *respeto* (Valdés, 1996) and *consejos* (Delgado Gaitan, 1994) are, in fact, an important aspects of the schooling experiences of Latino/a students that needs to be further explored.

New Voices, New Insights, New Possibilities

While each of the theoretical contributions presented in this chapter is on its own unique and provides important insights into the educational experiences and outcomes of Latino/a students, collectively they constitute the development and dissemination of new voices, new insights, and new possibilities for Latinos/as navigating the educational system. The voices of Latino/a scholars, students, and communities have often been excluded or marginalized within educational research and practice. The research discussed here represents the insertion of Latino scholars and others invested in improving educational outcomes and opportunities for Latino/a students into the broader educational discourse. Moreover, this evolving body of scholarship also amplifies the voices of Latino communities, more accurately describing their experiences and strategies for improvement, resulting in a transformation within the discourse of educational research.

Latino/a theoretical contributions to educational praxis have been enormously significant. Among these are creative contributions to language that have been made to the field, including but not limited to funds of knowledge (Moll et al., 2005), community cultural wealth (Yosso, 2005), cultural and linguistic borderlands (Anzaldúa, 1999), third space (Gutiérrez, Baquedano-Lopez, & Tejeda 1999), critical care (Rolón-Dow, 2005), and affirming diversity (Nieto & Bode, 2008), changing not only the way we speak about these issues, but actually helping to transform policies and practices within K-12 schools and higher education. These changes in language, and approaches to research, policy and practice have enhanced opportunities for Latino/a researchers to practice engaged scholarship (Pedraza & Rivera, 2005) and have had an increasing influence on the educational experiences and outcomes within Latino/a communities.

As we look toward the future, a time when the Latino/a population in the United States is expected to grow significantly despite the federal government's efforts to curb immigration from Latin America, we remain hopeful. Our hope is grounded in our experiences living and working in Latino/a communities and seeing first-hand how many students and families have drawn upon their community's cultural resources to challenge, transform, and successfully navigate oppressive school systems and other institutional structures. Many of those who have achieved academic success, as is clear from much of the research reviewed here, have used their platforms to conduct research that aims to improve the educational experiences and outcomes of Latino/a students. This talented group of individuals is multigenerational, ranging from senior scholars with decades of experience to more novice researchers looking to build upon the foundation established for them by previous generations while simultaneously extending the body of knowledge related to Latino/a education. It is our hope that these efforts to open pathways of possibility and build bridges of hope will continue to positively influence the life trajectories of Latino/a students and other marginalized peoples.

References

Antróp-González, R., Vélez, W., & Garrett, T. (2005). ¿Donde están los estudiantes puertorriqueños/os exitosos? [Where are the academically successful Puerto Rican students?]: Success factors of high-achieving Puerto Rican high school students. *Journal of Latino/as and Education, 4*(2), 77–94.

Anzaldua, G. (1999). (Eds.). *Borderlands: La frontera* (2nd ed.). San Francisco: Aunt Lute Books.

Bourdieu, P., & Passeron, J. C. (1977). *Reproduction in education, society and culture.* Beverly Hills, CA: Sage.

Bourdieu, P., & Wacquant, L. J. D. (1992). *An invitation to reflexive sociology.* Chicago: University of Chicago Press.

Cammarota, J., & Romero, A. (2006). A critically compassionate pedagogy for Latino/a youth. *Latino/a Studies, 4*(3), 305–312.

Cockcroft, J. D. (1995). *Latino/as in the struggle for equal education.* New York: Franklin Watts.

Conchas, G. Q. (2006). *The color of school success: Race and high-achieving urban youth.* New York: Teachers College Press.

Conchas, G. Q. & Rodríguez, L. F. (2003). *Engaging urban youth through community-based action: How the 'School Success' Truancy Prevention Program motivates middle graders.* Boston, MA: Boston Urban Youth Foundation.

Coutinho, M. J., & Oswald, D. P. (2000). Disproportionate representation in special education: A synthesis and recommendations. *Journal of Child and Family Studies, 9*(2), 135–156.

Darder, A. (1991). *Culture and power in the classroom: A critical foundation for bicultural education.* New York: Bergin and Garvey.

Delgado-Gaitán, C. (1991). Involving parents in the schools: A process of empowerment. *American Journal of Education, 100*(1), 20–46.

Delgado-Gaitán, C. (1994). Consejos: The power of cultural narratives. *Anthropology and Education Quarterly, 25*(3), 298–316.

Delgado-Gaitán, C. (2001). *The power of community: Mobilizing for family and schooling.* Lanham, MD: Rowan and Littlefield.

De Jesús, A. (2005). Theoretical perspectives on the underachievement of Latino/a students in U.S. schools: Toward a framework for culturally additive schooling. In P. Pedraza & M. Rivera (Eds.), *Latino/a education: An agenda for community action research* (pp. 343–371). Mahwah, NJ: Erlbaum.

De Jesús, A., & Antróp-González, R. (2006). Instrumental relationships and high expectations: Exploring critical care in two Latino/a community-based schools. *Intercultural Education, 17*(3), 281–299.

Delpit, L. (1995). *Other people's children: Cultural conflict in the classroom.* New York: New Press.

Diaz-Greenberg, R. (2003). *The emergence of voice in Latino/a/a high school students.* New York: Peter Lang.

Duncan-Andrade, J. M. R. (2004). Your best friend or your worst enemy: Youth popular culture, pedagogy, and curriculum in urban schools. *The Review of Education, Pedagogy, and Cultural Studies, 26,* 313–337.

Durán, R. (1988). Testing of linguistic minorities. In R. Linn (Ed.), *Educational measurement 3rd ed.* (pp. 573–587). New York: MacMillan.

Espinoza-Herold. M. (2002). *Issues in Latino/a education: Race, school culture, and the politics of academic success.* Boston: Allyn and Bacon.

Fernández, L. (2002). Telling stories about school: Using critical race and Latino/a critical theories to document Latina/Latino/a education and resistance. *Qualitative Inquiry, 8*(1), 45–65.

Flores, B. (2005). The intellectual presence of the deficit view of Spanish-speaking children in the educational literature during the 20th century. In P. Pedraza & M. Rivera (Eds.), *Latino/a education: An agenda for community action research* (pp. 75–98). Mahwah, NJ: Erlbaum.

Flores, B., Tefft-Cousin, P., & Díaz, E. (1991). Transforming deficit myths about learning, language, and culture. *Language Arts, 68*(5), 369–379.

Flores-González, N. (2002). *School kids/street kids: Identity development in Latino students.* New York: Teachers College Press.

Freire, P. (1970). *Pedagogy of the oppressed.* New York: Continuum.

Gándara, P. (1995). *Over the ivy walls: The educational mobility of low-income Chicanos.* Albany: State University of New York Press.

Gándara, P., & Lopez, E. (1998). Latino/a students and college entrance exams: How much do they really matter? *Hispanic Journal of Behavioral Sciences, 20*(1), 17–39.

García, E. E. (2001). *Hispanic education in the United States: Raíces y alas.* Lanham, MD: Rowman & Littlefield.

García, S. B., & Guerra, P. L. (2004). Deconstructing deficit thinking: Working with educators to create more equitable learning environments. *Education and Urban Society, 36*(2), 150–168.

Gay, G. (2000). *Culturally responsive teaching: Theory, research, and practice.* New York: Teachers College Press.

Ginwright, S., & Cammarota, J. (2002). New terrain in youth development: The promise of a social justice approach. *Social Justice, 29*(4), 82–96.

González, N. (2005). Beyond culture: The hybridity of funds of knowledge. In N. Gonzalez, L. C. Moll, & C. Amanti (Eds.), *Funds of knowledge* (pp. 29–46). Mahwah, NJ:, Erlbaum.

González, N., Moll, L., Tenery, M. F., Rivera, A., Rendón, P., Gonzales, R., & Amanti, C. (2005). Funds of knowledge for teaching in Latino/a households. In N. Gonzalez, L. C. Moll, & C. Amanti (Eds.), *Funds of knowledge* (pp. 89–118). Mahwah, NJ: Erlbaum.

Gutiérrez, K. D., Baquedano-Lopez, P., & Tejeda, C. (1999). Rethinking diversity: Hybridity and hybrid language practices in the third space. *Mind, Culture and Activity, 6*(4), 286–303.

Gutiérrez, K., Asato, J., Santos, M., & Gotanda, N. (2002). Backlash pedagogy: Language and culture and the politics of reform. *The Review of Education, Pedagogy, and Cultural Studies, 24*(4), 335–351.

Gutiérrez, K. D., & Rogoff, B. (2003). Cultural ways of learning: Individual traits or repertoires of practice. *Educational Researcher, 32*(5), 19–25.

Herrnstein, R. J., & Murray, C. (1994). *The bell curve: Intelligence and class structure in American life.* New York: Free Press Paperbacks.

Hidalgo, N. M. (1997). A layering of family and friends: Four Puerto Rican families' meaning of community. *Education and Urban Society, 30*(1), 20–40.

Hidalgo, N. M. (2000). Puerto Rican mothering strategies: The role of mothers and grandmothers in promoting school success. In S. Nieto (Ed.), *Puerto Rican students in U.S. schools* (pp. 167–196). Mahwah, NJ: Erlbaum.

Irizarry, J. G. (2007). "Ethnic and Urban Intersections in the Classroom: Latino/a Students, Hybrid Identities, and Culturally Responsive Pedagogy." *Multicultural Perspectives, 9*(3), 1–7.

Irizarry, J. G., & Antróp-González, R. (2007). RicanStructing the discourse and promoting school success: Extending a theory of culturally responsive pedagogy for DiaspoRicans. *Centro Journal of Puerto Rican Studies, 19*(2), 36–59.

Jensen, A. R. (1969). How much can we boost IQ and scholastic achievement? *Harvard Educational Review, 39*, 1–123.

Jiménez, R. T., Moll, L. C., Rodríguez-Brown, F. V., & Barrera, R. B. (1999). Latina and Latino/a researchers interact on issues related to literacy learning. *Reading Research Quarterly, 34*(2), 217–230.

Ladson-Billings, G. (1994). *The dreamkeepers: Successful teachers of African American children.* San Francisco: Jossey-Bass.

Lambert, W. E. (1990). Persistent issues in bilingualism. In B. Harley, P. Allen, J. Cummins, & M. Swain (Eds.), *The development of second language proficiency* (pp. 201–220). Cambridge, England: Cambridge University Press.

Leistyna, P. (1999). *Presence of mind: Education and the politics of deception.* Boulder, CO: Westview Press.

Lopez, G. R. (2001). The value of hard work: Lessons on parent involvement from an (im)migrant household. *Harvard Educational Review, 71*(3), 416–437.

Moll, L. C., Amanti, C., Neff, D., & González, N. (2005). Funds of knowledge for teaching: Using a qualitative approach to connect homes and classrooms. In N. Gonzalez, L. C. Moll, & C. Amanti (Eds.), *Funds of knowledge* (pp. 71–87). Mahwah, NJ: Erlbaum.

Moll, L. C., & Greenberg, J. B. (1990). Creating zones of possibilities: Combining social contexts for instruction. In L. C. Moll (Ed.), *Vygotsky and education: Instructional implications and applications of sociohistorical psychology* (pp. 319–348). New York: Cambridge University Press.

Monzó, L. D., & Rueda, R. (2003). Shaping education through diverse funds of knowledge: A look at one Latino/a paraeducator's lived experiences, beliefs, and teaching practice. *Anthropology and Education Quarterly, 34*(1), 72–95.

Morrell, E., & Duncan-Andrade, J. M. R. (2002). Promoting academic literacy with urban youth through engaging hip-hop culture. *The English Journal, 91*(6), 88–92.

Morrison, J. C. (1958). *The Puerto Rican study, 1953–1957.* Brooklyn: New York City Board of Education.

Negrón de Montilla, A. (1971). *Americanization in Puerto Rico and the public-school system 1900/1930.* Puerto Rico: Editorial Universitaria.

Nieto, S. (1998). Fact and fiction: Stories of Puerto Ricans in U.S. schools. *Harvard Educational Review, 68*(2), 133–163.

Nieto, S. (2000). Puerto Rican students in U.S. schools: A brief history. In S. Nieto (Ed.), *Puerto Rican students in U.S. schools* (pp. 5–39). Mahwah, NJ: Erlbaum.

Nieto, S. (2003). *What keeps teachers going?* New York: Teachers College Press.

Nieto, S. (2004). Black, White and us: The meaning of Brown v. Board of Education for Latino/as. *Multicultural Perspectives, 5*(4), 22–25.

Nieto, S. & Bode, P. (2008). *Affirming diversity: The sociopolitical context of multicultural education.* Boston: Pearson.

Nieto, S., & Rolón, C. (1997). Preparation and professional development of teachers: A perspective from two Latinas. In J. Irvine (Ed.), *Critical knowledge for diverse teachers and learners* (pp. 99–133). New York: AACTE.

Noddings, N. (1984). Caring: *A feminine approach to ethics and moral education.* Berkeley: University of California Press.

Noddings, N. (1992). *The challenge to care in schools: An alternative approach to education.* New York: Teachers College Press.

Noguera, P. (2001). Racial politics and the elusive quest for excellence and equity in education. *Education and Urban Society, 34*(1), 18–41.

Noguera, P. (2003). *City schools and the American dream: Reclaiming the promise of public education.* New York: Teachers College Press.

Oakes, J. (2005). *Keeping track: How schools structure inequality,* 2nd ed. New Haven, CT: Yale University Press.

Orfield, G. (Ed.). (2004). *Dropouts in America: Confronting the graduate rate crisis.* Cambridge, MA: Harvard Education Press.

Payne, R. K. (2003). *A framework for understanding poverty.* Highlands, TX: RFT.

Pedraza, P., & Rivera, M. (Eds.). (2005). *Latino/a education: An agenda for community action research.* Mahwah, NJ: Erlbaum.

Quiroz, P. A. (2001). The silencing of Latino/a student "voice": Puerto Rican and Mexican narratives in eighth grade and high school. *Anthropology and Education Quarterly, 32*(2), 326–349.

Reyes, M., & Halcón, J. J. (Eds.). (2001). *The best for our children: Critical perspectives On literacy for Latino students.* New York: Teachers College Press.

Reyes, P., Scribner, J., & Scribner, A. P. (Eds.). (1999). *Lessons from high-performing Hispanic schools: Creating learning communities.* New York: Teachers College Press.

Reyes, X. A., & Rios, D. (2005). Dialoguing the Latina experience in higher education. *Journal of Hispanic Higher Education, 4*(4), 377–391.

Rolón, C. (2000). Puerto Rican female narratives about self, school and success. In S. Nieto (Ed), *Puerto Rican students in U.S. schools* (pp. 141–165). Mahwah, NJ: Erlbaum.

Rolón-Dow, R. (2005). Critical care: A color(ful) analysis of care narratives in the schooling experiences of Puerto Rican girls. *American Educational Research Journal, 42*(1), 77–111.

Romo, H. D., & Falbo, T. (1996). *Latino/a high school graduation: Defying the odds.* Austin: University of Texas Press.

Rueda, R., Monzó, L., & Higareda, I. (2004). Appropriating the sociocultural resources of Latino/a para-educators for effective instruction with Latino/as students. *Urban Education, 39*(1), 52–90.

Ruiz, V. L. (2001). South by southwest: Mexican Americans and segregated schooling, 1900–1950. *Organization of American Historians Magazine of History, 15*(2), 23–27.

Sanchez, G. I. (1940). *Forgotten people.* Albuquerque: University of New Mexico Press.

San Miguel, Jr., G. (2005). The impact of *Brown* on Mexican American desegregation litigation, 1950s to 1980s. *Journal of Latino/as and Education, 4*(4), 221–236.

Schecter, S. R., Bayley, R. (2002). *Language as cultural practice: Mexicanos en el Norte.* Mahwah, NJ: Erlbaum.

Solórzano, D. G. (2001). From racial stereotyping and deficit discourse toward a critical race theory in teacher education. *Multicultural Education, 9*(1), 2–8.

Souto-Manning, M. (2006). A critical look at bilingualism discourse in public schools: Autoethnographic reflections of a vulnerable observer. *Bilingual Research Journal, 30*(2), 559–577.

Spring, J. (2006). *Deculturalization and the struggle for equality,* 5th ed. New York: McGraw-Hill.

Stanton-Salazar, R. D. (1997). A social capital framework for understanding the socialization of minority children and youths. *Harvard Educational Review, 67,* 1–40.

Tejeda, C., Espinoza, M., & Gutiérrez, K. (2003). Toward a decolonizing pedagogy: Social justice reconsidered. In P. Trifonas (Ed.), *Pedagogy of difference: Rethinking education for social change* (pp. 10–40). New York: Routledge.

Tinajero, J. V., & Spencer, D. A. (1999). Creating hope and a future for Hispanic mothers and daughters in the boderlands. In M. O. Loustanau & M. Sanchez-Bane (Eds.), *Life, death, and in between on the U.S. Mexico Border: Asi es la vida.* Greenwich, CT: Greenwood Publishing.

Torres-Guzmán, M. E., & Martinez-Thorne, Y. M. (2000). Puerto Rican/Latino/a student voices: Stand and deliver. In S. Nieto (Ed.), *Puerto Rican students in U.S. schools* (pp. 269–292). Mahwah, NJ: Erlbaum.

Trueba, E. H. T. (1988). Culturally based explanations of minority students' academic achievement. *Anthropology & Education Quarterly, 19*(3), 270–287.

U.S. Census Bureau. (2003). *School enrollment: 2000* (C2KBR-26). Washington, DC: Author.

Valdés, G. (1996). *Con respeto: Bridging the distances between culturally diverse families and schools: An ethnographic portrait.* New York: Teachers College Press.

Valencia, R. (Ed.). (1997). *The evolution of deficit thinking: Educational thought and practice.* Washington, DC: Falmer Press.

Valenzuela, A. (1999). *Subtractive schooling: U.S.-Mexican youth and the politics of caring.* Albany: State University of New York Press.

Vásquez, O. A. (2003). *La clase mágica: Imagining optimal posibilities.* Mahwah, NJ: Erlbaum.

Walsh, C. E. (1991). *Pedagogy and the struggle for voice: Issues of language, power and schooling for Puerto Ricans.* Boston, MA: Bergin & Garvey.

Ybarra, R. (2004). Creating alternative discourses in the education of Latinos and Latinas: Introduction. In R. Ybarra & N. Lopez (Eds.), *Creating alternative discourses in the education of Latinos and Latinas: A reader* (pp. 1–8). New York: Peter Lang.

Yosso, T. (2005). Whose culture has capital? A critical race theory discussion of community cultural wealth. *Race, Ethnicity, and Education, 8*(1), 69–91.

Yosso, T. (2006). *Critical race counterstories along the Chicana/Chicano educational pipeline.* New York: Routledge.

Zentella, A. C. (2005). Premises, promises, and pitfalls of language socialization research in Latino/a families and communities. In A. C. Zentella (Ed.), *Building on strength: Language and literacy in Latino/a families and communities* (pp. 13–30). New York: Teachers College Press.

Part II

Policies and Politics

Part Editors: Ruth Trinidad Galván and Norma González

7 Policies and Politics

An Introduction

Ruth Trinidad Galván
University of New Mexico

Norma González
University of Arizona

> Today, wherever we turn, we witness a nasty wrestling match between a global consumer transculture and the resurgence of virulent ultranationalism.
>
> (Gomez-Peña, 1996, p. 11)

At the crux of our current Latin@ educational discussion is the current global state and the manner it impacts the movement of people across the globe, citizenship rights across borders, redefines racial and ethnic belonging, and influences educational policies and politics at home. As Gomez-Peña (1996) suggests, although we find ourselves in the midst of transcultural consumerism and global economics, ultranationalism and ideological borders still prevail. While the United States' history of slavery, imperialism, and colonization has defined its transcultural contacts, relationship to the "other," and threats to its hegemonic power (Acuña, 2006), the time-space compression of the era introduces new understandings, problems, and solutions to historically constituted legacies. Contemporary legislative policies have mirrored the xenophobic upheaval of the times in border-state operations (border enforcement such as Gatekeeper in San Diego, Operation Hold-the-Line in El Paso, and Operation Rio Grande in McAllen; Cornelius, 1998) and in the passing of several propositions attempting to deny Latinos and other marginalized pockets of the population their civil rights (Proposition 187, 227, 209 in California and the English-Only movement).

Some argue that legislation such as Proposition 187 in California and other nativist backlash around the country represent social discontent and not, as some politicians argue, the economic disadvantaging of U.S. citizens due to the purported benefits that undocumented people reap (see Chavez, 1997; Muller, 1997; Tatalovich, 1997). This social discontent has roots in ultranationalist sentiments that have little to do with economic globalization and more to do with responses to the perceived threats to the nation and a fear of challenging the status quo. As Chavez explains, "new immigrants pose a transnationalist challenge to a narrow nationalist construction of the nation. In this sense, the current wave of immigration reform proposals reflect a nationalist response to this transnational challenge" (1997, p. 73). For instance, the legalization of English-only initiatives have heightened the animosity of some groups against anyone who looks like they may speak another language without concern for their actual citizenship status. In the anti-terrorist discourse of the Bush administration as well as the introduction of such initiatives as the HR 4437,[1] which provides stricter punitive measures for aiding immigrants, enforces stricter and lengthier jail sentences for illegal immigration, as well as the proposed border wall, we can observe a narrowing of the discourses surrounding nation-state formations.

The counterdiscourse to the antagonism and ultranationalism that prevails in this global context is a claim to civil rights unconditionally granted to most other groups and currently still absent for Latin@s (Flores, 1997). While expanding global relations have forced individuals to uproot themselves in the hopes of better opportunities elsewhere, these processes have also increased the degree to which we discuss issues of citizenship that go beyond the political and legal rights of citizens around the world. It requires, as Flores suggests, a view of cultural citizenship

> that can be thought of as a broad range of activities of everyday life through which Latinos and other groups claim space in society, define their communities, and claim rights. It involves the right to retain difference, while also attaining membership in society. It also involves self-definition, affirmation and empowerment. (1997, p. 262)

Redefining citizenship beyond a nation-state affiliation centers the role of community in redefining membership, belonging, and national identities (Moreno, 2008). These redefinitions do more than replace old ones, but rather heighten our awareness of its meaning and give us an understanding and language for re-imagining and refashioning social and civil policies. Indeed, what educational implications do these globalized issues have for Latin@s, and how are they operationalized in everyday school pedagogies? The chapters in this section provide a comprehensive snapshot of the current policies, politics and trends framing Latin@ education.

The current movement and migration of Latin@s beyond the traditional Southwest United States, for instance, push the boundaries of belonging, home, and bordercrossing. Referred to as the New Latino Diaspora, these movements consist of younger immigrant families with children, who are predominantly Spanish speaking and are confronting the intricacies of communities with no history of Latino immigration (Hamann & Harklau, this volume). Emma Pérez (1999) loosely defines diaspora as a "history of dispersal coupled with myths and memories of a homeland," where "alienation in the host country often fosters a desire for eventual return while collective memory reconstructs the alienated group's history whether real or imagined" (p. 78). She further expands the notion of diaspora by utilizing Stuart Hall's definition of diaspora identities as "those which are constantly producing and reproducing themselves anew, through transformation and difference" (cited in Pérez, 1999, p. 79). Although, it cannot be assumed that "new" communities, such as Georgia, Arkansas, and North Carolina, are not impacted by the country's anti-immigrant sentiment of the last decade, it is also true that they have encouraging and detrimental social and educational models to learn from (Hamann & Harklau, this volume).

The movement of people, ideas, and commodities affects not simply definitions of nation-state, citizenship and diasporic identities it is also reflected in the role education and schooling has in shaping and addressing these issues. Latin@ students face an ambivalent atmosphere that negates their linguistic and cultural contributions, expects full assimilation even when they are not fully adopted into the cultural fabric of the country, and sorts them into the demands of the global market (Montero, Cabrera, & Espinola, this volume). Montero and colleagues suggest that a truly global focus in education would consider students as historical agents, with a past that is alive and well and that constitutes them within everyday practices. Their cultural background is, consequently, understood as dynamic and changing, and their linguistic knowledge valued and an asset. Moreover, Latin@ students' transnational identities pioneer new forms of citizenship as bordercrossers, cultural and linguistic brokers, and contributors to more than one nation-state. These are certainly qualities and knowledge rarely tapped into or valued in the manner they would be for whitestream student populations. The lack of epistemic acknowledgment is especially evident when we consider the role language has historically played in U.S. ideologies and policies with regard to Latin@s.

Language Policies English-Only: Hegemonic Ideals

> So, if you want to really hurt me, talk badly about my language. Ethnic identity is twin skin to linguistic identity—I am my language. (Anzaldúa, 1987, p. 59)

For the last half a century a monolingual ideology has driven U.S. language policies towards the 30 million Spanish-speaking Latinos in this country (Garcia & Torres-Guevara, this volume; Valencia, 2002). The controversial debates surrounding the education of English Language Learners or the inclusion of students' native languages in the curriculum have been an uphill battle for educators concerned with maintaining students' native language and culture. Add to this the repercussions that a hegemonic ideal grounded on fear of the "other"—"their" language, culture and sheer presence—and this has an impressive social impact on whole communities across the nation.

Landmark U.S. Supreme Court decisions and federal mandates, such as *Brown v. Board of Education* (1954) and *Title VI Civil Rights Act of 1964,* paved the way for more equitable school practices, while the *Bilingual Education Acts of 1968 and 1974, Equal Educational Opportunity Act of 1974,* and *Lau vs. Nichols* (1974) addressed the special needs of English Language Learners (García & Torres-Guevara, this volume; García & Wiese, 2002). Interestingly enough, while the world market opened up and these mandates and court decisions moved to create linguistic and cultural recognition in the 1960s and 70s, the United States closed itself (ideologically), and an English-only standard emerged in the 1990s.

As partially discussed above, while the current global state attempts to stay open (to the world market) the nation wants to remain closed (to different ideologies). Appadurai (1990), for instance, argues fears of homogenization "can also be exploited by nation-states in relation to their own minorities, by posing global commoditization … as more real than the threat of its own hegemonic strategies" (p. 6). This was certainly the case as bilingual education came under attack with *Proposition 227* in California in 1998[2] and the subsequent English-only movement across the nation. These attacks not only attempted to dismantle bilingual education across the country, but like Proposition 187, gave people the right and language to exploit the fissures between language groups.

As Anzaldúa intimates, the complex relationship between language and a sense of peoplehood is indexed in large part by language (Anzaldúa, 1987; Delgado Bernal, 2003; González, 2005). Since the number of children who speak a language other than English at home rose from 3.8 to 9.9 million between 1979 and 2004, this is one of many issues that the education system cannot ignore (Contreras, this volume). García and Weise (2002) remind us that "educating students from immigrant families, particularly Hispanic immigrant families, may seem like an entirely new challenge, but it is not; such students have always been in American schools in large numbers. Throughout most of U.S. history, one in four or five White Americans grew up in an immigrant family" (p. 150). The encoding of language can simply not be disconnected from the manner in which the discourse around propositions, such as 187 and 227, has been racially driven.

Fergus, Noguera, and Martin (this volume) argue that the social construction of race and Latinos ambiguous positioning within the White-Black paradigm will need to move beyond skin color when determining racial markers and the manner Latinos are "othered" in the United States. Reexamining the social construction of race will also require questioning the panethnic identity that is assumed with such nation-state imposed labels as Hispanic (see also Gomez, 2008; Menchaca, 2003). Since Latinos fall easily within the entire gamut of the Black and White continuum, Fergus and colleagues press us to consider how this paradigm falls short of describing the racial category of Latinos.

> Theories of race as a social construct need to involve more integration that argues the positionality of power and privilege as also bound to experiences of language, immigrant/non-immigrant, and skin color variation labels. (i.e., White, Black, brown, mestizo, indio, güero, negro, Moreno, etc., p. 179)

Clearly the language and immigration debate have been racially driven, but the racial markers that drive society's discussion of race also ignore how language and citizenship rights determine how race is socially constructed. No educational topic marks most the racial stratification of Latin@s than does the achievement gap.

The Achievement Gap and Education Pipeline

Important pieces of legislature and national reports leading to educational policy initiatives like No Child Left Behind (NCLB) exist to the detriment of all students, but certainly did not begin with NCLB. "School segregation of Chicanos throughout the Southwest became the crucible in which Chicano school failure originated and festered" and continues in the era of de facto segregation (Valencia, 2002, p. 6). The Elementary and Secondary Education Act (ESEA) of 1965 aimed to address the educational needs of low-income students.[3] As Contreras (this volume) describes, such reports as *A Nation at Risk* (1983), bills like *Goals 2000, Improving America's Schools Act* (IASA, 1994) and our current NCLB have progressively moved towards greater accountability and standards based assessment. What this has meant for Latin@ students has gone contrary to what ESEA aimed to do—to equalize the playing field between well-prepared affluent students and disadvantaged poor students. Rather than close the education gap, these policies have emphasized testing outcomes and so created greater roadblocks for students from minoritized communities.

While standardized testing, including exit exams, certainly impact the motivation of high school Latin@ students, the quality of teachers, teacher certification, differential access to curriculum, grade retention, segregation, and lack of resources[4] amongst others continually influence the overall educational achievement of Latin@ students not only to graduate from high school but in their hopes to eventually attend an institution of higher learning (Contreras, this volume; Valencia, 2002). Indeed, "school holding power"[5] has been a perpetual concern (Valencia, 2002).

Villalpando (this volume)[6] explains that "out of 100 Latinos who begin elementary school, only 50 are likely to eventually graduate from high school, compared with 84 white males. And of these original 100 Latinos, only about nine will complete a college degree and less than one is likely to complete a doctoral degree" (p. 234). Latin@s predominantly low-income status, state and federal financial aid policies, society's meritocratic values, and the added stress that high school exit exams have imposed influence in significant ways the 50 or so students who never finish school (Contreras, this volume; Delgado Bernal, 2003; Flores, this volume; Gándara, 2003; Villalpando, this volume). Moreover, the probability of attending a four-year institution straight out of high school or while initially attending a two-year/community college are low and transfer data rarely reported or collected (Flores; Villalpando, this volume). Hispanic Serving Institutions (HSI) may play a significant role since a majority of Latin@s attend a HSI, and, although they do not have the historical and cultural groundings of historically Black colleges and universities, the additional resources that Title V funds provides should require that these institutions demonstrate a commitment to Latin@ students, faculty, and communities (Flores, this volume). Race-conscious policies have had a mixed effect in determining, refashioning, or reinscribing the status quo. According to Flores,

> Race-conscious policies and programming have experienced a volatile era of retraction, reinstatement, and readjustment since the 1996 *Hopwood* decision regarding the use of race in college admissions at the University of Texas at Austin. Although the use of race as a factor in college admissions was formally reinstated via the *Grutter* decision in 2003, not all eligible institutions complied and a number of questions were left unanswered. (p. 214)

According to Flores, issues of citizenship and immigration law complicate the college-attainment possibilities of Latin@s over any other racial group. What continues to pervade, according to Villalpando (this volume), are "objective," "merit-based," and "race-neutral" policies and practices that have not succeeded in providing Latin@s true educational opportunities.

While some of us might push through the cracks or miraculously "make-it" into the system, the struggle in our respective institutions and in academia does not falter. Considered by some as key to Latin@ student access and recruitment to an institution of higher education, Latin@s in the professoriate continue to be at a 3.38% low in 2005 while less that 1% of full-time faculty are Latina (Urrieta & Chavez Chavez, this volume). Latin@ faculty describe feeling isolated, victims of microaggressions, miniassaults, and discrimination, the token-hire or representative of their race, and unrecognized for the service they provide to their communities (Urrieta Jr. & Chavez Chavez, this volume). Although work in academia may seem like an upward battle, Urrieta and Chavez Chavez also underscore Latin@ faculty *supervivencia* (survival) and the many contributions they make to their respective institutions. Latin@ faculty, as agentive individuals, transform physical and cultural spaces with their brown bodies and sheer presence, challenge and introduce community-based epistemic, pedagogical, and conceptual frames, and redefine what counts as scholarship, service, mentorship, and teaching (Murillo Jr., 1999; Solórzano, 1998; Urrieta & Chavez Chavez, this volume; Villenas & Foley, 2002).

"Globalizing from Below"

Appadurai's (2000) discussion of "grassroots globalization" brings us back to our initial discussion of our current global state and to the role that communities and grassroots organizations hold by introducing these new social forms to the overall Latin@ educational spectrum. He argues for the importance of new social forms that "globalize from below" and combat the negative effects of globalization. He describes grassroots organizations and their work as:

> A series of social forms [that] emerged to contest, interrogate, and reverse these developments and to create forms of knowledge transfer and social mobilization that proceed independently of the actions of corporate capital and the nation-state system (and its international affiliates and guarantors). These social forms rely on strategies, visions and horizons for globalization on behalf of the poor that can be characterized as "grassroots globalization." (Appadurai, 2000, p. 3)

In a similar light Montero, Cabrera, and Espinola (this volume) discuss "transnationalism from below" as grassroots activities that move beyond borders and strict cultural definitions. Grassroots organizing and collective endeavors have consistently been part of the history of Latin@s in the United States and Latin America (Mercado & Reyes, this volume; Torres & Katsiaficas, 1999; Urrieta Jr., 2004), and are now becoming more global and transnational in their vision and work (Trinidad Galván, 2005). This type of activism and civic engagement, according to Mercado and Reyes (this volume), needs much more attention in the United States at both the collective and individual level. Collective endeavors as those led by Puerto Rican organizations, such as *Aspira*, the *Puerto Rican Legal Defense and Education Fund* (PRLDEF), the *Puerto Rican Association for Community Actions* (PRACA), and the *Puerto Rican Educators Association* (PREA), "were founded in the 1960s and 1970s as a programmatic response to the educational needs of its children and to the lack of inclusion of Puerto Ricans in the educational establishment" (Mercado & Reyes, this volume, p. 255). They also suggest that Latin@ activism must learn from past struggles and new visions of "globalizing from below" so as to create new collective endeavors that establish alliances across groups, arenas, and borders within that tradition of positive resistance that framed many student movements.

For instance, during the 1960s and in the midst of the civil rights movement, more than 10,000 Chicano students in the Los Angeles Unified School District held mass movement protests for an equitable education better known as the East Los Angeles Blowouts (Delgado Bernal, 1998). After going through the necessary channels without an adequate response, students from six high schools took to the streets. Thirty-six demands were presented to the school board that included general demands, such as: bilingual personnel and instruction, improved installations, the dismissal of racially-intolerant personnel, culturally-relevant curriculum, the elimination of the tracking system, and the hiring of teachers and administrators of Mexican heritage (Delgado Bernal, 1998). Essentially, students participating in the East LA Blowouts wanted to raise the quality of public education in their communities.

Clearly, youth have the potential of organizing, conceptualizing a collective agenda, and of executing their dissatisfaction with the current system. The type of grassroots and community work they have the potential of achieving require that schools become community-building sites with emancipatory purposes (Hidalgo & Duncan-Andrade, this volume). Considering the level of "push-out" our Latin@ youth experience, Hidalgo and Duncan-Andrade's discussion of the use of a critical pedagogical approach and the transformational potential of youth resistance becomes crucial in connecting students and communities in a manner that re-envisions youth potential, self-determination, and community work and activism. In essence it requires, as Duncan-Andrade and Morrell suggest, an education model that fosters critical and engaged citizenry that oppose all forms of injustices and aim to create a more democratic society (2008, p. 11).

All of this brings us to the function of schooling to either contest or reinforce the agenda of the last century. Our hopes for this millennium and the new administration remain that education may become the driving force for future generations' membership into the political process and struggle for human rights, of which schooling is simply one. Considering that our new president, Barack Obama, has been dedicated to grassroots and community organizing, we may be optimistic that the future, although not without struggle, may indeed bring us closer to a more equitable educational experience for all students. As President Obama suggested in his November 4th election victory speech:

> What began twenty-one months ago in the depths of winter must not end on this autumn night. This victory alone is not the change we seek—it is only the chance for us to make that change. And that cannot happen if we go back to the way things were.[7]

Notes

1. HR 4437 – *The Border Protection, Antiterrorism, and Illegal Immigration Control Act of 2005*. Also known as "Sensenbrenner Bill" after its creator Congressman James Sensenbrenner.
2. The California ballot designated "English For All Children" mandated (a) students receive "Structured English Immersion" in English classrooms, (b) provide a transition period of no more than one year, (c) provide native language instruction only when waived, and (d) no native language instruction beyond the age of 10 and once the student has mastered the English language (García & Wiese, 2002).
3. Head Start, Follow-Through (support for those who participated in Head Start), Bilingual Education, and counseling programs were a result of the Elementary and Secondary Education Act.
4. Valencia (2002) draws attention to two well-known lawsuits that focused on education financial equity in *Serrano v. Priest* (1969) in California and *Rodriquez v. San Antonio Independent School District* (1971) in Texas.
5. The capacity of schools to maintain students through the 12th grade as defined by the U.S. Commission on Civil Rights. See Valencia (2002).

6. Villalpando (this volume) also provides an ethnic (Chican@s; Puerto Ricans; Cubans; Dominicans; Salvadorans) breakdown of Latin@ educational attainment.
7. President Elect Barack Obama Election Night Victory Speech, Grant Park, llinois. November 4, 2008. Retrieved from http://obamaspeeches.com/

References

A Nation at Risk: The Imperative for Educational Reform. (1983). The National Commission on Excellence in Education. Retrieved from http://www.ed.gov/pubs/NatAtRisk/title.html

Acuña, R. (2006). *Occupied America: A history of Chicanos* (6th ed.). New York: Longman.

Anzaldúa, G. (1987). *Borderlands/La Frontera: The new Mestiza.* San Francisco: Aunt Lute Books.

Appadurai, A. (1990). Disjuncture and difference in the global cultural economy. *Public Culture, 2*(2), 1–24.

Appadurai, A. (2000). Grassroots globalization and the research imagination. *Public Culture, 12*(1), 1–19.

Chavez, L. (1997). Immigration reform and nativism: The nationalist response to the transnationalist challenge. In J. Perea (Ed.), *Immigrants out! The new nativism and the anti-immigrant impulse in the United States* (pp. 61–77). New York: New York University Press.

Cornelius, W. (1998). The structural embeddedness of demand for Mexican immigrant labor: New evidence from California. In M. Suarez-Orozco (Ed.), *Crossings: Mexican immigration in interdisciplinary perspectives* (pp. 113–155). Cambridge, MA: Harvard University Press.

Delgado Bernal, D. (1998). Grassroots leadership reconceptualized: Chicana oral histories and the 1968 East Los Angeles school blowouts. *Frontier: A Journal of Women Studies, 19*(2), 113–142.

Delgado Bernal, D. (2003). Chicana/o education: From the civil rights era to the present. In J. F. Moreno (Ed.), *The elusive quest for equality: 150 years of Chicano/Chicana education* (pp. 77–108). Cambridge, MA: Harvard Educational Review.

Duncan-Andrade, J., & Morrell, E. (2008). *The art of critical pedagogy: Possibilities for moving from theory to practice in urban schools.* New York: Peter Lang.

Flores, W. (1997). Citizens vs. citizenry: Undocumented immigrants and Latino cultural citizenship. In W. Flores & R. Benmayor (Eds.), *Latino cultural citizenship: Claiming identity, space, and rights* (pp. 255–278). Boston: Beacon Press.

Gándara, P. (2003). Staying in the race: The challenge for Chicanos/as in higher education. In J. F. Moreno (Ed.), *The elusive quest for equality: 150 years of Chicano/Chicana education* (pp. 169–196). Cambridge: MA: Harvard Educational Review.

García, E., & Wiese, A-M. (2002). Language, public policy, and schooling: A focus on Chicano English language learners. In R. Valencia (Ed.), *Chicano school failure and success: Past, present and future* (pp. 149–169). New York: Routledge.

Goals 2000: Educate America Act. (1994). Retrieved from http://www.ed.gov/legislation/GOALS2000/TheAct/index.html

Gomez, L. (2008). *Manifest destinies: The making of the Mexican-American race.* New York: New York University Press.

Gomez-Peña, G. (1996). *The new world border: Prophecies, poems, and loqueras for the end of the century.* San Francisco: City Lights Books.

González, N. (2001). *I am my language: Discourses of women and children in the borderlands.* Tucson: University of Arizona Press.

Menchaca, M. (2003). The Treaty of Guadalupe Hidalgo and the racialization of the Mexican population. In J. Moreno (Ed.), *The elusive quest for equality: 150 years of Chicano/Chicana education* (pp. 3–30). Cambridge, MA: Harvard Educational Review.

Moreno, M. (2008). Lessons of belonging and citizenship among hijas/os de inmigrantes Mexicanos. *Social Justice, 35*(1), 50–75.

Muller, T. (1997). Nativism in the mid-1990's: Why now? In J. Perea (Ed.), *Immigrants out! The new nativism and the anti-immigrant impulse in the United States.* New York: New York University Press.

Murillo Jr., E. (1999). Mojado crossings along neoliberal borderlands. *Educational Foundations, 13*, 7–30.

Pérez, E. (1999). *Decolonial imaginary: Writing Chicanas into history.* Indianapolis: Indiana University Press.

Solórzano, D. (1998). Critical race theory, racial and gender microaggressions, and the experiences of Chicana and Chicano scholars. *International Journal of Qualitative Studies in Education, 11*(1), 121–136.

Tatalovich, R. (1997). Official English as nativist backlash. In J. Perea (Ed.), *Immigrants out! The new nativism and the anti-immigrant impulse in the United States.* New York: New York University Press.

Torres, R., & Katsiaficas, G. (1999). *Latino social movements.* New York: Routledge.

Trinidad Galván, R. (2005). Transnational communities *en la Lucha: Campesinas* and grassroots organizations "Globalizing from below." *Journal of Latinos and Education, 4*(1), 3–20.

Urrieta Jr., L. (2004). Chicana/o activism and education: An introduction to the special issue. *The High School Journal, 87*(4), 1–9.

Valencia, R. (2002). The plight of Chicano students: An overview of schooling conditions and outcomes. In R. Valencia (Ed.), *Chicano school failure and success: Past, present and future* (pp. 3–51). New York: Routledge.

Villenas, S., & Foley, D. (2002). Chicano/Latino critical ethnography of education: Cultural productions from *la frontera.* In R. Valencia (Ed.), *Chicano school failure and success: Past, present and future* (pp. 195–226). New York: Routledge.

8 The Effects of Globalization and Transnationalism on Policies and Practices in the Education of Latinos in the U.S. and Latin Americans in Spain

Martha Montero-Sieburth
University of Amsterdam

Lidia Cabrera Pérez
University of La Laguna, Canary Islands, Spain

Celoni Espínola Mesa
University of Massachusetts, Boston

Purpose and Rationale[1]

Globalization and transnationalism are without doubt, two of the most contemporary topics in the social sciences and studies of migration. Globalization is what happens as economic exchanges and goods intersect with worldwide migration, and ideas, communication, political, economic, and social activities unfold (Held, Mc Grew, Goldblatt, Perraton, 1999). These processes tend to become intensified at global levels of interaction, interconnectedness across regions and continents, and between societies and states. Transnationalism according to Bauböck (2008, p. 2) "refers to the processes and activities that transcend international borders" and which have to do with phenomena that takes place within limited social and geographic spaces, non-state actors, and the unfolding of migrant associations as well. However, transnationalism involves multiple definitions. Basch, Glick-Schiller, and Blanc-Szanton's seminal definition focuses on "the process by which transmigrants, through their daily activities, forge and sustain multi-stranded social, economic, and political relations that link together their societies of origin and settlement, and through which they create transnational social fields that cross national borders" (1994, p. 6). Morawska (2003) stresses the structure and agency of transnationalism as critical, Guarnizo (1997) focuses on the transnational social formations, and Sorensen and Fog Olwig (2002) define the ways that transnationalism produces social spaces and practices that unfold from such migration as transnational livelihoods. While globalization and transnationalism may become "de-linked from specific national territories," Levitt, in agreeing with Kearney, stipulates they remain "anchored in and transcend one or more nation-states" (2001, p. 14).

Globalization and transnationalism are recognized processes within the disciplines of sociology, anthropology, education, and international development (Appadurai, 1990; Appadurai, 1996; Castles, 2005; Sassen, 1996; Glick-Schiller, 2003; Glick Schiller & Basch, 1995; Glick-Schiller, Basch, & Blanc-Szanton, 1992) and have become major research foci. Institutes,[2] academic institutions,[3] and international organizations are engaged in studying how the migration of people affects the development of socioeconomic infrastructures, ethnic enterprises, cultural productions, and transnational development. Hence mapping these two fields within the confines of this chapter, does not do justice to the exhaustive research that has proliferated in the past three decades.

Instead, we propose to focus on the effects that globalization and transnationalism have had on the educational policies and practices of immigrant Latinos in the United States and of Latin Americans in Spain through reviews of secondary research and recent research on Latin Americans in Spain as a means to lay out how these two fields influence education.[4] The research on Latinos in the United States is derived from multiple sources including a dissertation by Espínola Mesa.[5] The research representing the perspectives of Latin Americans is taken from studies of immigrants in Spain and the collaborative work of Cabrera Pérez and a team of transcontinental researchers who completed a first-of-its-kind study on the social and cultural integration of Latin American immigrants to Spain during 2004–2007, making the perspectives of Latin Americans in Spain known[6] (Cabrera & Montero-Sieburth, 2007; Cabrera Pérez, 2008).

Even though the experiences of Latinos in the United States and Latin Americans in Spain may be differentiated by historical, sociocultural, schooling policy, and language incorporation contexts, in this age of globalization and transnational optics, they are confronting similar educational concerns. First, Latinos now attending U.S. schools in greater numbers are in need of quality, non-segregated schools that offer them opportunities for their future. Arriving immigrants with children to Spain seek schools that will transition their children into the Spanish system with the educational backgrounds they have from their native countries and will work with parents in making such transitions possible even in those schools where immigrants are now burgeoning.[7] Second, Latinos seek equitable schooling in the United States that provides services that help their children academically progress, and immigrants in Spain seek educational services mandated through governmental policies and practices that meet the needs of immigrant and human rights. Third, Latinos in the United States expect their children to be placed in educational programs that respond to district and state mandates, while in Spain it is the autonomous communities and in this case, the Canary Islands, which concretely meets the educational needs and integration of immigrants.

Highlighted in this chapter is how comparative migration and transnationalism research helps to identify some of the educational obstacles, challenges, policy, and institutional structures that either facilitate or hinder academic achievement and learning. In speaking about Latinos in the United States, we focus primarily on immigrants and the children of immigrants studied through U.S.-based and English-speaking research, since immigrants constitute much of the growing schooling-age population. Latin Americans in Spain were identified as Venezuelans, Colombians, Ecuadorians, Cubans, Bolivians, and Dominicans.[8] Although the number of Latin Americans varies, the population is concentrated in Madrid, Barcelona, Valencia, and other major cities and autonomous communities. Many of the Latin American immigrants of the Canary Islands and Granada were of three types: (a) returnees, the children or grandchildren of Spaniards who left for Latin America, (b) temporary, or (c) permanent settlers.

While this chapter does not pretend to be exhaustive nor comprehensive, it does target specific issues outlined in the following sections: (a) Section 1 discusses *the relationship of education to citizenship discourses* that prevail for Latinos and Latin Americans, the formation of citizens in relation to immigrants, and their inclusion or exclusion in schooling; (b) Section 2 identifies the *contemporary discourses of citizenship* of the past decade and a half and refers to the existence of *cultural citizenship and transnational citizenship* as Latino and Latin American discourses; (c) Section 3 addresses *how citizenry is highly influenced by some of the realities and paradoxes of globalization* and shows *how schooling policies have responded to such economic and social demands* with certain practices. Outlined are the implementation of reform initiatives and their effect on Latinos, and the use of explanatory academic achievement models in the education of Latinos in the United States in relation to different modes of incorporation (assimilation, accommodation, cultural pluralism, segmented downward and upward assimilation, and transnationalism) (Alba & Nee, 2007). Also identified are the effects that globalization and transnationlism has had on Latin American immigrants in Spain, as it has evolved from being a country of emigrants to becoming a country of immigrants. Discussed are the implementation of policies for the regularization of undocumented immigrants and the emergence of education laws that focus on the diversity of students. (d) Section 4 presents some of the *current trends in transnationalism* and introduces the concept of *mestizaje,* not in its biological meaning, but in relation to the blending and cultural fusion described by Trueba (2004) for Latinos in the United States and their participation as "New Americans," and can be used for forging new identities in the Canary Islands, Spain. The re*conceptualization of culture and cultural diversity* is discussed from fixed, static, and essentialized interpretations to more permeable and flexible conceptualizations. The ways these concepts are being currently reframed by social scientists and educators in relation to globalization, social mobility factors, learning and development, research, the creation of transnational social spaces and identities in relation to Latinos and Latin Americans is also discussed.

In addition, multiculturalism as depicted in U.S. schooling and policies and interculturalism as proposed by the Spanish government in fulfilling the European Union's goals, and carried out by regional educational programs for integrating newcomers in schools is discussed (Consejo de Europa, 1984; Sabariego, 2005). These growing differences of students, national identities, cultural affinities, and complexity created by demographic changes are crucial in comprehending globalization according to Suárez-Orozco (2004). The last section *synthesizes the discussion on globalization and transnationalism and outlines future trends* in the education of Latino transnational immigrants and Latin Americans as global citizens. Such synthesis is particularly significant in representing much of the growing modalities that will be evident as future transculturalism mediates the influences of globalization, transforms social identities, and eventually becomes legitimated as a research field.

I. The Relationship of Education to Citizenship Formation

As one of the primary institutions of socialization next to family influences, education: (a) identifies the normative values, behaviors, and beliefs that are constituted by the majority and dominant culture of any society, and ensures that these will be transmitted to future generations; (b) enculturates future citizens through membership into the civic curriculum, providing knowledge and skills so that they may dutifully serve the nation and state; and (c) reinforces the adoption of the majority language and culture as a means to affirm and maintain the continuity and uniformity of the nation among diverse ethnic groups. Education also ensures that future citizens gain membership within a political unit, have values directed to a common good, are conferred an identity, have knowledge of the political process, and are able to participate (Eslin, 2000).

Yet, all formal education depends upon the prevailing policies that emanate at a national or federal level and are implemented institutionally at the state, province, local district, school, or autonomous community level. Such policies are usually created in times of change, whether through colonization,[9] expansionism, political turmoil,[10] international trade, technology, and massive migrations,[11] or to rectify a historical wrongdoing.[12]

According to Coatsworth (2004), there have been four major globalization cycles: (a) The first, which began in 1492 and lasted until 1600, was the colonization of the Americas by Spain and Portugal and the development of transatlantic and transpacific trades; (b) The second from the 1700s led to the establishment of European colonies in North America and resulted in European trade and conquest in the Indian Ocean as well as the French Revolution and the Haitian Revolution; (c) The third, which began in the late 1900s and lasted until the Great Depression of the 1930s, saw increases in international trade, migration, capital, and technology from Asia and Europe to the Americas; and (d) the most recent, which began after World War II with the liberalization of international trade, saw the intensification of such after 1967, but East Asian and Latin American countries continued to have protectionist policies until the 1980s, at which time Latin America experienced a financial crisis. For each of these cycles, different educational policies have been enacted and, while their intent is to meet educational needs, other competing interests are also highly influential. In fact, Torres advances the idea that "education within the nation-state…has been shaped by the demands…to prepare labor for participation in the economy and to prepare citizens to participate in the polity" (2002, p. 363).

While foreigners and migrants may be economic labor participants, some argue that their ability to become citizens is determined by how well they can be responsive and knowledgeable actors, capable of demonstrating engagement as well as human agency in the social, cultural, political, and educational outcomes of a country. Laguerre (as cited in Sagas & Molina, 2004, p. 67) asserts that: "Citizenship was once defined to meet the needs of the residents of Athens, then to meet the needs of the nationals in the era of the bound nation-state; now it needs to be redefined to take stock of globalization, transnational processes, and the porous nature of the modern nation-state." Acquiring citizenship is not a given and requires meeting not only the conditions set forth by the nation-state for participation, but also fulfilling the social and political conditions that define: *Who is regarded as a citizen? What rights does that citizenship confer? How is such citizenship determined, and on what basis? And how are citizens incorporated for future generations?*

Meeting these conditions of incorporation falls squarely on the shoulders of legal and undocumented immigrants—whether they be newcomers or established members of the adopted country. For them, the *before and after migration* factors such as (a) country and context of departure and entry, (b) immigrant characteristics, (c) types of social and organizational enclaves, and (d) social, cultural, and economic contexts of both the receiving and sending countries identified by Waters and Jiménez (2005) are crucial. But they also have to confront the (e) *the receiving country's acceptance or rejection of them* and (f) *the conditions they are willing to accept to become incorporated.*

Because their entry into a receiving community is precarious and fraught with many obstacles, the manner in which they are received and accepted sets the stage for their future integration. Immigrants may be perceived as providing needed services, but they can also be considered security threats, people who create problems or may become problems and who erode the host country's dominant culture (Murillo, Jr., 2002). Labor demands may support salutary and benign policies towards immigrants, but, under fears of economic misuse or oversaturation of needed services, these can quickly become harsh and punitive. Taken to an extreme, the reactions may lead to the elimination of a group's mother tongue, the imposition of heavier restrictions, or the erection of walls as is now the case between the U. S. and Mexican border.

In fulfilling the "American Dream," or finding a better quality of life, immigrants are required to voluntarily become part of the majority, through displays of belonging and accommodation, learning the social capital, and the language of the country. Many may be invisible as they pass unperceived, without needing to speak English or Spanish, working in isolation as they take care of elderly and young children, clean offices, work in factories, and move into "jobs that no one else wants to do."[13] They can also be targets of overt apprehension and rejection by others, feelings that are fueled by fears and distrust growing out of the media's sensationalization of immigrants taking jobs away from citizens, taking advantage of social and medical services available, and the educational system. Growing xenophobic and racist sensitivities often describe their migration as an invasion or as a tsunami. Accused of oversaturating the available host countries' social, health, and economic services, without contributing any resources, immigrants can be seen as opportunists, and the reason for an increase in crime. Thus, how they are regarded matters in the types of economic, immigration, and educational responses and policies that governments enact.

Immigration policies are established to include or exclude immigrants, manifested in overt or covert actions with some immigrants being favored for their economic viability, expertise, and contributions while others are rejected because of their race, socioeconomic status, gender, language, culture, and religion. Proponents of immigration sustain social and economic reasons based on liberal market and capitalist arguments for not erecting walls and maintaining borders open, while opponents demand greater law enforcement, immigration control policies and militarization to curtail the flow of immigrants. Not understood is the fact that immigration policies are not the result of individual actions or decisions made by immigrants based on seeking better economic opportunities, as Sassen (1996) points out, but are connected to the international activities of governments and firms that have formed powerful economic linkages that serve to bridge capital and migration. Sassen argues that "Economics in the 21st century is about an economy which is itself global, and about governments which further globalization rather than contain economic activities within their national territories" (p. 12).

Such economic interplay in its global dimensions implies that educational policies respond to the political milieu in which they are enacted. Torres (2002) explains that the reproductionist argument that economic demands are inextricably tied to educational policies makes sense. Most of these policies while country specific, tend to be vaguely defined, and are often influenced by more global scale issues as for example, the immigration debates that are taking place on both sides of the Atlantic and in the rest of the world. What is happening in the Canary Islands[14] with the entry of many Sub-Saharan immigrants is not simply a Spanish issue, but an issue that affects Europe as well as other countries. Mexican immigration to the United States is not simply a Mexico/U.S. issue, but one that affects North American, South American, Caribbean, and other countries' immigration policies as well. The furthering of globalization plays a significant role in influencing educational policies, but how these are institutionalized and implemented at the national, regional, and local levels,[14] and actualized at the school and classroom levels for newcomers and immigrants, determines whether a quality education is being provided that allows immigrants and newcomers to achieve socioeconomic and cultural parity with their native counterparts.

Furthermore, how immigrants are *included or excluded* in the educational process, how their *mother tongue* is considered and supported, and how they are *able to gain the social and cultural capital* that affords them a stake in the receiving country's citizenry and how the *educational institutions respond to supporting and meeting their needs* become not only important markers of educational access, but also of educational success or failure in schools. The next section although attending to ideological discourses and values, continues the discussion on immigrant incorporation, but shifts now to how schools using specific ideological discourses, also influences the kinds of subjectivities that are developed in children.

II. Citizenship Discourses and Values

Knight Abowitz and Harnish's (2006) identification of citizenship discourses found in U.S. textbooks from 1990 to 2003, in which they asked *How citizenship is conceptualized? and How it is represented and by whom?* is useful to the discussion of citizenship incorporation and socialization issues, with particular reference to ideology. The discourses they identify, ranging from civic republic to liberal, to neoliberal, critical to the more recent transnational discourses, the values, knowledge, and practices these discourses ascribe meaning to, as well as the embedded thoughts, cultural struggles, and identity issues these discourses shape, persist in schools today. Liberal citizenship, for example, "prioritizes the rights of individuals to form, revise, and pursue their own definition of the good life, within certain constraints that are imposed to promote respect for and consideration of the rights of others" (Knight Abowitz & Harnish, 2006, p. 661), while the neoliberal discourse for citizenship, an offshoot of the latter, and a cornerstone since the 1980s of U.S. educational reforms so heavily entrenched in U.S. schools, combines market liberal ideology and individualism. The political liberal discourse of Feinberg (1998) (as cited by

Knight Abowitz & Harnish, 2006) values learning skills that enable citizens to live in a culturally diverse society, but requires schools to have dual roles in providing culturally different opportunities and learning to students, while also maintaining a national core and focus. Furthermore, Knight Abowitz and Harnish (2006), identify "…cultural respect and cultural engagement as required skills and understandings for a 'multicultural citizen,' and cultural competence and cultural understanding as required cognitive skills for such a citizen" (p. 664). Such bifurcated learning appears to obliterate the underlying Western and capitalistic nature of schooling and its basic preparation of future workers and managers addressed in Bowles and Gintis' (1976) correspondence theory analogy. Caught in this ambivalence between having to conform to citizenship as defined by the nation-state while needing to be recognized and respected for multicultural differences are Latinos who fall through the cracks. Not only are they marginalized, but they have limited participation.

Counteracting these entrenched traditional discourses, are the critical and cosmopolitan discourses of citizenship which address feminist, cultural, queer, and reconstructionist discourses and the transnational discourse. Knight Abowitz and Harnish (2006) argue that these new discourses not only question the meaning of identity, citizenship, and belonging and identify boundary locations, agency, and the enactment of citizenship, but they heighten our awareness, and help determine issues of equity and human rights. The transnationalism that Knight Abowitz and Harnish (2006) identify focuses on local, national, and international communities as another promising discourse and one that needs to be more widely adopted and implemented in U. S. public schools. They argue that through transnationalism, "A citizen…is one who identifies not primarily or solely with her own nation but also with communities of people and nations beyond the nation-state boundaries" (2006, p. 275). Such a citizen expresses agency across various strata and fosters his/her participation in local, national, global organizations and social spaces. By developing transnational citizens, not only will students learn to become consciously aware of their critical thinking and the political and social decisions they make, but also to call into question exclusionary practices that exist within the boundaries of the nation-state. More importantly, such transnational learning will bring human rights and social justice issues to the forefront. Unlike the U.S. public school curriculum and dominant discourse of American schools, in Europe transnationalism has been more widely been integrated, forming part of the International Baccalaureate Organizations and human rights thinking.

The discourse of cultural citizenship, introduced by Rosaldo and Flores, "names a range of social practices which taken together, claim and establish a distinct social space for Latinos in this country" (1997, p. 1). Cultural citizenship not only serves to confront the normative influence of the society, the nation-state and its assimilative processes, but it claims membership to one's identity while contributing through that membership to the larger society. Such citizenship is about the right to be racially, ethnically, and linguistically different from the norms of the dominant national society and to recognize such differences as resources to be respected and not threats (Flores & Benmayor, 1997).

According to Rosaldo (1997), Latino identity, referred to by Trueba under the concept of *mestizaje*, is the co-mingling of cultures, which in its actions invites both the confrontation of discrimination and the development of collective efforts that socially interjects Latino culture within American society. The contradictions and ambivalences faced by Latino students in regard to schooling become strikingly evident when: (a) they are expected to have a democratic commitment, yet are not regarded as part of the state and national culture; (b) the validity of their language and the legitimacy of their discourses are not accepted, even though Latinos contest the entrenchment of "English only" thinking and the denial of their mother tongue in schools; and (c) as poor and underrepresented students, who often experience devaluing of their home culture and have limited or no access to mainstream social capital, are denied participation in the state and national culture yet are expected to assimilate and fully participate in a democracy.

Applied to Latin Americans in the Canary Islands, Spain, cultural citizenship is about using Spanish as a means of communication, but also contributing to Canarian identity through the maintenance of cultural roots and nuances. For the Canary Islanders this extends to retaining their historically, socially, and culturally derived identity linked to Africa and Latin American, while also being Spaniards. Yet for such a discourse to be fully understood, the historical legacies of Spain's past, as a colonial power, post-colonial nation-state, under Franco's rule, and into its present democratic social state need to be examined. Thus, even though citizenship in Spain has become more restrictive, the linguistic and cultural convergence and the ability to maintain identity make access to such democratic citizenry possible for Latin Americans.

Clearly, transnationalism and cultural citizenship have not been embraced within the entrenched traditional citizenship discourses in U. S. education and curriculum. Knight Abowitz, and Harnish (2006) assert that future citizens will continue to be shaped by what they call bounded membership that remains fixed at the national borders but cultural citizenship and transnationalism discourses will also continue to push through these borders. They will create what Bauböck calls the "emergence of an interstate citizenship," where the formation of alliances transcend national boundaries and membership (1994, pp. 20–21). Without doubt, cultural citizenship and transnationalism discourses will continue to reclaim space, demand active participation, voice, and agency—processes and practices that have been historically, educationally, and socially denied to Latinos in the United States and that are gradually being gained by Latin Americans in other transnational spaces.

III. Globalization in Relation to Schooling Policies and Practices, Reforms, and Educational Achievement Explanatory Models

Globalization is a product and a process of the emergence of a global economy linked to a set of social, economic, and overlapping networks, spatial organization of social relations and transactions that become closely linked to the immigrant and transnational experience (Held et al., 1999). Suárez-Orozco considers globalization "…as processes of change simultaneously generating centrifugal (as the territory of the nation-state) and centripetal (as supra-national nodes) forces that result in the deterritorialization of basic economic, social and cultural practices from their traditional moorings in the nation-state" (2003, p. 50).

Yet even though it is often considered a new phenomenon, its newness is derived from the emerging technologies, enhanced economic interdependence, increased cultural influences, rapid communication technology and transformations it creates. Moreover, according to Suárez-Orozco (2003), globalization has lead to increased migration as a consequence of: (a) transnational capital flows; (b) new information, communication, and media technologies; (c) increase need for foreign workers; (d) affordability of mass transportation; and (e) stimulation of new migration.

While, on the one hand, it contributes to an increase in the homogeneity of societies and the exercise of power by multinational corporations, Torres (2002) considers that it also increases heterogeneity, diversity, environmental action, and democratization. Globalization creates a bipolar existence, but as Torres states, "[it]…cannot be analyzed only in terms of polar discrete opposites, but should be seen as a borderline situation between two historical epochs." (2002, p. 365).

Similarly, the incorporation of immigrants in globalization processes, argue Khagram and Levitt (2005, p. 26), need not be considered as binary because immigrants can be located within what they call a "host-land-incorporation and enduring transnational attachments" that are highly contextualized and combine assimilation and transnational connections at the same time. They stipulate that, in fact, "It is no longer enough, if it ever was, to only examine and analyze experiences within or across presumably bounded or closed societies or cultures whether they are categorized as localities, regions, nations, states, nation-states, nation-state systems, empires or world systems, etc." (2005, p. 4).

Globalization can be a powerful economic process in influencing positive and negative market investment, outcomes, and responses. It can be productive and beneficial, creating foreign investment and innovations and developing people skills and building industrial capacity, but it can also have dire consequences for individuals, such as when the local farmer or worker loses his/her job or livelihood as a multinational corporation takes over massive production in their countries, or when local traditions and customs of folk cultures become eroded and suppressed by dominant cultures. Globalization and its concomitant ideology of neoliberalism can also favor richer countries in relation to the poorer, contributing to greater inequality (Bloom, 2004), particularly as "…a diminishing and one-dimensional model of development (and therefore demeaning) rather than an enhancing and equity-oriented model" with subsequent negative effects on women and girls, and indigenous populations (Robertson et al., 2007, p. 207).

Globalization can also, according to Lam, create social spaces and communicative linkages for youth, who can "play the role of active cultural workers, reshaping and recontextualizing global materials in their particular communities and local settings" (2006, p. 223). For example, Dominican women raised in Spain as second generation have, upon their return to Santo Domingo, different expectations about bearing children and place prime importance on education of those children, as compared to Dominicans who never left their home country (Carro, Montero-Sieburth, Cabrera, 2009). These social spaces and communicative linkages affect the identity formation of youth as they interact with media and popular cultures, and develop social affinities through such interactions with social affiliations and cultural materials. Moreover, as Suárez-Orozco (2004) points out, immigrant:

> Youth are challenged to navigate between achieved identities and ascribed or imposed identities…with achieved identity [being] the extent to which an individual achieves a sense of belonging—"I am a member of this group." An ascribed identity is imposed either by coethnics—"You are a member of our group"–or by members of the dominant culture—"You are a member of that group." (p. 177)

This process argues Lam (2006) engenders a "hybrid" or "multicultural" rather than bicultural identity, a notion that Arnett (2002) considered inappropriate, since the identity of immigrants is not only formed by their native or local culture, but also by a global culture.

As migrations and diasporas[15] continue to grow and cultural, capital, media, and technology exchanges take place, questions about the need to go beyond the bounded traditional framework of the nation-state are being raised. In this respect, Gilroy's analysis in *Black Atlantic* (1992) is a case in point in raising the theme of Double Consciousness to a level of hybridity in that diasporic people strive to be both European and Black to their land of origin but also to the transformation they face in a new environment. Considerations of the overlap of social and cultural spaces (e.g., the development of affinity groups), and the intercultural transactions that are being created as means to interpret issues of diversity (race, ethnicity, class, gender, ability) within more global frameworks, are being made (Lam, 2006). Thus the language introduced by Appadurai of ethnoscapes, for peoples' movement, financescapes for money and trade, mediacapes for images and ideas in popular culture, and ideoscapes for ideas and practices has, according to Joel Spring, become commonplace (Appadurai, 1996, cited by Spring 2008). For some scholars, globalization is contributing to the blurring of national borders, eroding the demarcations of the nation-state, and deconstructing and transforming the state (Lam, 2006; Knight Abowitz & Harnish, 2006), while for others, the national may actually be strengthened (Levitt & Jaworsky, 2007). Globalization can best be thought of as Levitt and Jaworksy (2007) propose—a stage in an ongoing historical process—but as Lam (2006) stipulates, a stage that is actively being reshaped.

Along with its reflected political uncertainties, globalization affects not only the role of citizenship, but, according to Torres (2002), also shapes education and schooling outcomes in the direction of a marketplace ideology or an ideology of human rights. Today's schooling, he contends, is about making labor highly skilled and competitive and about educating people in problem-solving, issues that reverberate throughout the national standards for curriculum, teacher professionalization, certification, and educational reform in the United States. In a market oriented education, democratic citizenship falls by the wayside as tolerance, conviviality, and the respect for human rights become secondary.

Explanations on the second generation of Latino students, the effects of transnationalism and global perspectives present a picture of Latinos that challenges explanations of the past and presents their adaptation and difficulties amidst complexity (Montero-Sieburth, 2006; Montero-Sieburth & Batt, 2001; Montero-Sieburth & Villarruel, 2000). Research shows that their educational profile is improving (Lowell & Suro, 2002), resilience is evident in their adaptability in schools; different motivation and achievement strategies using their culture of origin and acquired culture are used (Suárez-Orozco & Suárez-Orozco, 2001, 1995; De Vos, 1980; De Vos, & Suárez-Orozco, 1990), multiple identities are being developed, peer and youth culture can be viewed for its complexity and counter-cultural manifestations (Gándara & Gibson, 2004; Gibson, Gándara, & Koyama, 2004; Mehan, Villanueva, & Hubbard, 1996; Olsen, 1997), and social and cultural capital influences are becoming highly significant access issues (Noguera, 1999, 2001). Furthermore, this research has also begun to identify the educational institutional structures that often deter the educational advancement of Latinos, namely segregated schools, tracking, poor teacher preparation, low level curriculum, low expectations, and underdeveloped support mechanisms and limited resources.

Educators contribute to the educational attainment of Latinos as they perpetuate a symptomatic spiral that attributes differences in learning and achievement to the ethnicity of the students as normal and predictable, given the persistence of high rates of low achievement and failure among underrepresented groups. Normalization theory, advanced by Noguera (2001), tends to obscure the vision of teachers, administrators, and support staff as they try to make sense of the contradictory context of schools, and excuses them and the institution from having any responsibility for the achievement gap. Instead of accepting a shared responsibility for the underachievement of these students, these educators rely on the "blaming the victim paradigm," use the research literature to support their claims, and justify failure as a means to save face for themselves and the school. They view failure as the result of a negative family situation, of deeper societal problems, or of a students' lack of effort and motivation in school. As Noguera (1999) suggests, the "failure of urban schools and the children they serve" "...is not problematized, but rather is expected" (p. 3) and therefore normalized. Left alone to deal with normalization beyond their control, urban educators fail to see that access to caring, equitable, and competent schools is a resource inequitably distributed among disadvantaged students and their more privileged counterparts. In mediating among extreme contradictions, these educators are ill-equipped to deal with the impossible demands of bridging the academic gap and the disproportionate academic failure of Latinos.

The research on the second generation, transnationalism, global perspectives, and the challenges presented by situating immigrants and their learning has lead to the development of a cultural-historical approach[15] and a closer examination of contextual effects. Lam (2006; citing Faist, 2000) states that such an approach has created a "new pluralism of space" through population movements, media flows, and communication technologies. These explanations now focus on "...ways of acting and participating in diverse social groups and the heterogenous sets of cultural knowledge, skills, and competence that are acquired in the process" (Lam, 2006, p. 17) and are a shift from acculturation to a more multidimensional view of transculturation. Portes and Lingxin Hao (2004) analyze school contextual effects on the basis of data from Children of Immigrants Longitudinal Study, and they show that longer periods of U.S. residence actually lowers the academic performance of underrepresented students, irrespective of school context, and that class and ethnic composition of schools make a difference. Chinese, Korean, and Vietnamese immigrants fare better than Mexican-origin students who have lower achievement levels and higher drop out rates, particularly in schools predominated by students with high socioeconomic status (SES). Dropping out becomes their only solution given the competitive and discriminatory nature of the schools they attend. Portes and Lingxin Hao conclude that, as Mexican youth bring their experiences of poverty to school, yet do not have the knowledge to succeed, schools respond by upholding stereotypic views of these students, reproducing a vicious cycle that, in their opinion, can only be broken by strong family and community constellations, and not by schools.

On the other side of the Atlantic, globalization has also affected Spain's educational policies and practices and the integration of immigrants. Until the 1990s, Spain's educational policies were primarily monocultural, undifferentiated, and undiversified, especially in regard to immigrants. However, with Spain's entry into the European Union, the growing economic boom of the 1990s, and Spain's shift from becoming a country of emigrants to becoming a country of immigrants (Agrela, 2002), the focus on the economy, as well as on education, changed. With the infusion of European Union funds and a liberalized market economy, Spain emerged during the 1990s as one the fastest growing economies in Europe after having had 30 years of a residual closed economy. Globalization in Spain became a "dynamic process of greater freedom and world wide integration of markets, goods, services, technology and capitals" (De la Dehesa, 2007, p. 19). In this respect, immigrants are favored because they contributed to the country's economic growth and development.

Spain has institutionalized several policies and practices in response to its foreign and immigrant populations: (a) institutionalized several regularization processes to incorporate undocumented immigrants, and (b) introduced intercultural education as part of a European Council initiative and as an integration strategy for its immigrant populations.

While Spain's immigration policies during the past 10 years have become more restrictive for "irregular or undocumented" immigrants who seek work without permits, the government passed several "regularization" measures granting amnesty to undocumented immigrants with residence and work contracts. In 2005, over 600,000 such requests were conceded to Ecuadorians, Rumanians, Moroccans, Colombians, Bolivians, and Argentineans and thereby made it possible for many Latin American immigrants to become integrated through this process of inclusion. Spain also has implemented several education policies and practices of quality directed at the well-being and integration of incoming newcomers and native citizens.[16] Among these are the Ley Orgánica (1990) de Ordenación General del Sístema Educativo (LOGSE) (The Organic Law and General Organization of the Educational System), the Ley Orgánica 4/2000 sobre Derechos y Libertades de los Extranjeros en España y su Integración Social (The Organic Law on the Rights and Liberties of Foreigners and their Social Integration in Spain), and its subsequent reform in 2003 (14/2003), the Ley Orgánica (2002) de Calidad de la Educación (LOCE) (Organic Law on the Quality of Education), and the Ley Orgánica de la Educación (LOE) of 2006 (The Organic Law of Education), the goals of which are: (a) to provide students with social, personal, economic, cultural differences, and/or disadvantages to an education that is compensatory; (b) to teach foreigners or immigrants, and (c) to respect their cultural identity while integrating them into Spanish society.

Each autonomous community government plans and implements its programs of education. In some communities, intercultural education is identified as the means to deal with such differences at a social and community level. In these cases, the regional governments develop social integration plans and programs that focus on: (a) the integration of cultural elements into the curriculum; (b) the professionalization and assessment of teachers; and (c) the expansion of human and material resources (CIDE, 2005). In some schools, reception programs with sociolinguistic support, the use of interpreters, and cultural mediators for immigrant families and students, are put into practice (CIDE, 2005). In almost all schools, orientation and guidance/psycho-pedagogical teams identify the needs of each student and teacher, offer individualized plans and assessments, and coordinate ways to help students advance. These teams develop educationally appropriate curricular adaptations with teachers for their special needs students. Of particular significance is the role of *orientadores* or guidance personnel, who are university graduates and whose jobs are similar to guidance counselors in U.S. schools but more expansive. They not only do the intake of students and offer psychological counseling, but also provide curricular support, instructional adaptation, outreach to teachers and families, and offer higher education counseling for graduating students.

Rather than addressing the regional government's lack of planning in light of the changing demographics, the public at large has tended to use the "blame the immigrants" paradigm, making the immigrants the "problem." This situation parallels some of the issues that have been raised in the education of Latinos in the United States. For Spanish citizens to not blame immigrants and to view them as contributors and resources will require that Spain's intercultural educational policies and practices become a fundamental reality of all its citizens, across all of the autonomous communities, and not specifically targeted at immigrants.

Depending on how globalization is considered, through prevalent market economic ideology, which leads to commodification, neoliberal ideology, which rigidifies education, or through the human rights ideology, which permeates social relationships, creates fluid social spaces, and filters through in the formation of multiple social identities, institutionalized policies and practices of schooling directly affect learning. Lam (2006) argues that learners in this situation are not passive agents who simply fit the influences of globalization as an objective reality, but are active learners who are also shaping and reshaping the influences of communication networks and technological advances of globalization. Globalization, as Lam (2006) comments, "…is creating greater fluidity and multiplicity in the identity formation of young people" (2006, p. 218). In this respect the earlier explanations about the academic achievement of Latino students can be contested and refocused toward some the cultural transformations that mestizaje, interculturalism, multiculturalism, culture in its new conception, and transnationalism are creating, and which contribute to the education of Latinos and Latin Americans.

IV. Transnationalism in Relation to Mestizaje, Culture, Interculturalism, and Multiculturalism

Transnational activities as Morawska (2007) points out are a product of and contributor to the processes of globalization. She distinguishes between two interpretations. Transnationalism is "…a shift beyond… membership in a territorial state or nation and its accompanying civic and political claims, toward more encompassing definitions such as universal humanism, membership in a supra-state and pan-religious solidarity." It is also "…some combination of plural civic and political memberships, economic involvements, social networks, and cultural identities that reach across and link people and institutions in two or more nation states" (p. 149).

However, since Bourne's 1916 essay, "Transactional America,"[17] about the immigrant assimilation process, transnationalism has been criticized for its ambiguousness, inclusiveness, and lack of delineations between what is international versus what is global, and what is accepted as transnational (Khagram & Levitt, 2005). Waldinger and Fitzgerald (2004) view transnationalism as not being any different than assimilation. However Glick-Schiller and Levitt (2006) counteract by stating that the transnationalism's novelty is its analytic framework which is due to the restructuring of capital and financial and political power under globalization. Levitt and Jaworsky (2007) also point out that new terminology has emerged as a consequence of transnationalism, and terms such as *translocalism* (Barkan, 2006), *bilocalism*, and *trans-state activity*

(Waldinger & Fiztgerald, 2004) are now common. Glick-Schiller differentiates transnationalism from the global by referring to the former as "the ongoing interconnection or flow of people ideas, object and capital across borders of nation states, in which the state shapes but does not contain such linkages and movements" and the latter as "…phenomena that affect the planet's inhabitants irrespective of borders and local." Thus transnationalism is viewed as both mitigating and mediating the effects of globalization (2003, p. 104).

Transnationalism, according to Levitt and Jaworksy (2007), grew out of the global activities of large economic enterprises and language of transnational corporations, and, by the 1980s, it began to be refined towards identifying the embeddedness of immigrants in more than one single nation-state. While the lead came from postmodern discourse and cultural studies scholars interested in transnational processes and practices (Appadurai 1990) to identify just a few, this was followed by the studies in communication (Castles, 2005; Castles & Davidson, 2000) and migration networks (Massey, 1994; Basch, Glick-Schiller, & Blanc-Szanton, 1994).

Steven Vertovec (2004) has characterized transnational migration in terms of its modes of transformation, identifying: (a) *the perceptual*, which deals with migrants bi-focal orientation in the social cultural domain; (b) *the conceptual*, which deals with the meanings attributed to identities, orders and borders in the political domain; and (c) *the institutional*, which has to do with financial transfer and the development of public private relationships in the economic domain. In addition, Smith and Guarnizo (1998) contributed the notion of *transnationalism from above*, referring to global capital, media and political institutions and *transnationalism from below*, which refers to local, grassroots activity that exists through multi-positionality, cultural hybridity, and border crossings. In discussing transnationalism from below, Guarnizo and Smith (1998) point out that while grassroots activities are often viewed in relation to power, economic interplay, cultural constructions, and social organizations and as subversive popular resistance in which people can escape the control and domination by capital and the state from above, they are not inherently subversive or counter-hegemonic. Rather, they assert "…they are different… and are interstitial,…[that is]…they open up between such dominant discursive venues as the 'the nation-state', the 'local community' and the 'ethno-racial community'" (1998, p. 23). Smith also addresses the notion of *transnationalism from the middle* in its two distinct ways: (a) as the mediation of "…social relations of power-domination-accommodation-resistance between national actors from 'above' and from 'below'" (2005, p. 241) or (b) as "…the transnational practices of social actors occupying more or less middle class or status positions in the national class structure of their countries of origin…" (2005, p. 242).

Also advanced has been the notion of the *transnational optic* as a way to study both the historical similarities and differences between immigrants of the past and the present (Morawska, 2003) and as a way to analyze the replenishment factors of immigrants and their generations (Waters & Jimenez, 2005). Smith further expands this notion to the *transnational urbanism optic*: "The study of transnational urbanism thus underlines the socio-spatial processes by which social actors and their networks forge the translocal connections and create the translocalities that increasingly sustain new modes of being-in-the-world" (2005, p. 237). Fouron and Glick-Schiller (2002) identify as "the new world order," the promotion, reproduction, and reinvention taking place of nationals residing abroad by their sending states, which leads to what Glick-Schiller and Basch (1995) label as a "deterriotorialized" nation-state formation. A case in point is Mexico's expansion of its influence through the Institute of Mexicans Abroad in the United States, the use of an identification card issued by Mexican consulates, the recognition of dual citizenship for Mexicans, and the spread of social hometown civic organizations in the United States. Through these, Mexicans are able to maintain political, social, and cultural allegiances to Mexico, inhibit to some degree cultural assimilation while accommodating to the receiving community (Montero-Sieburth, 2007). This notion of a deterritorialized state that feeds into trasnationalism as "boundless" and as a liberatory process has nevertheless been questioned by Smith and Guarnizo, who stipulate that:

> ...transnational practices cannot be construed as if they were free from the constraints and opportunities that contextuality imposes. Transnational practices, while connecting collectivities located in more than one national territory, are embodied in specific social relations established between specific people, situated in unequivocal localities, at historically determine times. The "locality" thus needs to be further conceptualized. (1998, p. 11)

Presently transnationalism has come to be the realm of anthropologists, sociologists, political scientists, geographers, educators, and other scholars interested in understanding the overlapping "...transnational social field of variable character, scale and intensity that shape ostensibly bordered and bounded structures, actors, and processes" (Khagram & Levitt, 2005, p. 14). According to Levitt and Jaworksy (2007, p. 131) the concept and its research has subsequently been clarified and now refers to: 1) "...the social spaces in which transnational migration takes occurs, 2) the social structures it generates, 3) the variations in dimensions and forms, 4) the relationship between processes of incorporation and enduring transnational involvements, 5) the ways in which contemporary iterations of cross-border memberships compare to earlier incarnations, and their durability."

Through their given situations, the history of human contacts, of movements and interactions in multiple contexts, and the confluence of cultures and relationships of power and conflicts being produced, Latinos in the United States and Spain are linked to worldwide transnationalism.[18] Human movements take place for a variety of social, cultural, economic, and religious reasons, and are expressed through voluntary or forced migrations (Ogbu, 1987) or as desperate escapes from unsafe conditions. This pattern is not always peaceful and easy, and, in most cases, has generated resistance from majority groups asserting predominant sociocultural control.

For Trueba (2004), this human contact has come with a price. Improvements in transportation, communication, and open markets have created opportunities for interactions, but such interactions can also generate gains or losses. In this confluence of human contact, which is the blood line of new immigration, mestizaje is taking place. Mestizaje is not the result of cross-racial breeding and segregation based on principles of Eurocentric superiority, but rather the consequence of cross-cultural, linguistic blending and about being transnational. As transnationals, immigrants engage in this mestizaje beyond ethnic boundaries as they attempt to become aware of and have control over their new reality. "Becoming a transnational is often living in perpetual conflict between two cultures, in two languages, with divided loyalties and opposite constituencies [...] and it might become the most predominant way for many new Americans" (Trueba, 2004, p. 75).

Trueba acknowledges that transnationalism, is the "capacity to handle different cultures and lifestyles, different social status, different roles and relationships and to function effectively in different social, political, and economic systems" (2004, p. 39). The main challenge for educators is precisely to be able to facilitate the way that biology gives way to history. This process is particularly challenging in a context of globalization and transnationalism.

Rather than ignoring and preventing the advancement of racially, linguistically, and culturally diverse students, Trueba (2004) urges urban schools need to be open to the new racial, cultural, and linguistic mestizaje growing within their schools. Such "new Americans," contends Trueba (2004), are the result of that new mestizaje, which gives a different meaning to the old concept of mestizo. The new Amerizan mestizaje is happening everyday in the corridors of urban public schools in the United States, and is shaping a new identity, a new way of relating to and of perceiving the world. Consequently, there is an urgent need for schools and educators to pay attention to the voices of those who are hardly listened to and to sail on their side when they embark on a journey toward a promising bicultural and bilingual identity (Suárez-Orozco & Suárez-Orozco, 2001). True for any child will be the statement by Brittain (2005, p. 13) that, "immigrant students will thrive in environments where they feel accepted, validated, and valued as important participants and contributors."

In the same way that mestizaje becomes a conceptual framework advocating for the education of Latinos in the United States, it also has a place in the lives of Latin Americans in the Canary Islands. The notion of mestizaje has been historically and culturally experienced as the islands have been conduits for passage and for movements between Europe, Africa, and the Americas, and Latin Americans today are part of that cultural blending, demanding that their unique identities also be recognized.[21]

Throughout Europe, the Council of Europe and other international organizations have adopted the use of *intercultural education* as a model of integration for countries and regions to consider and implement in order to counteract racism and discrimination leading to xenophobic attitudes. Under such a model, culture is considered a phenomenon that is in constant interaction with other cultures and where barriers cannot be erected. *Interculturalism* demands that human rights and opportunities be available to all and that the beneficiaries of this process be not only immigrants who are being integrated but the society-at-large (Aguado, 2003; Sabariego, 2005). The goals of interculturalism as defined by the Council of Europe (1984) and interpreted in Spain are: (a) to create a cultural synthesis of the diverse cultures of immigrants inserted into the native Spanish culture; (b) to sensitize people to acknowledge differences as assets and unique characteristics which inevitably contribute to the society at large; (c) to create bridges for marginalized groups such as the Roma, known as gypsies in Spain; (d) to foster the respect for human rights and recognize the privileges accorded to all; and (e) to integrate those who need to participate in a democratic society. In this process, educational policies and practices are directed at changing attitudes that reflect an intercultural way of life. How this is carried out is reflected in the case of Latin Americans in the Canary Islands.

Another critical concept that is useful in understanding transnationalism and globalization in education is the concept of culture. Culture has traditionally been considered an ideation, or a set of fixed set of attributes that include values, behaviors, and attitudes characterizing a group within a society. Those attributes are often viewed in deference to other groups often presenting differentiating opportunities for success and failure in schools. As inherent factors to be identified in students, students lacking majority culture, need to be modified and re-socialized towards the dominant institutional expectations and practices (Lam, 2006). Obviously through this characterization of culture, students are not only stereotyped and evaluated but as Lam indicates, are "minoritized"—"explained only in terms of their minority" vis à vis dominant mainstream status, characterized as distinctively defined or categorized by certain values, beliefs, attitudes and behaviors, and they set up in a "majority-minority binary opposition within the boundaries of a multicultural nation-state" (2006, p. 216). This culturalistic fallacy states Vermeulen, presents culture as "sharply bounded, homogeneous and relatively unchanging entities, transmitted from one generation to generation," but it does little to elucidate issues that relate more to social mobility factors (2000, p. 2). More significantly, as Flip Lindo (2000) points out, culture used in this manner, glosses over any of the variations and behavioral patterns that may exist in a group and by identifying and labeling these patterns, culture is not explained but reified. Rather he insists, "It is best to view culture as a concept that makes us aware of the historical singularity of the interaction patterns we observe within the direct social environments of individuals" (2000, p. 221).

The new reconceptualization of culture based on cultural-historical approach, advocated by Erickson (2002); Gutierrez and Rogoff (2003); Moll and Gonzales (2004); Orellana and Bowman (2003); Orellana, Thorne, Chee, and Lam (2001); and others, addresses how individuals develop, participate, engage in, and create affiliations and cultural practices in multiple, overlapping, and, at times, conflictive communities. The focus is on ways of acting and participating in diverse social groups, and the types of cultural knowledge, skills, and competences that are acquired through such engagement (Lam, 2006). Furthermore, as Orellana and Bowman (2003) point out, research should treat culture as dynamic toolkits that can be used for obtaining studies of group practices and individual outcomes that are also contextually understood. While we may acknowledge internal differences amongst groups when we study culture, we fall into the use of static labels for identifying such dimensions, which only reifies the labels. Instead, Orellana and Bowman suggest that "We need to know more about how these different aspects of identities work, separately and together as well as in relation to particular contexts, rather than search only for average differences between groups" (2003, p. 26). Otherwise, the differences that are emphasized may be interpreted as deficits. Certainly it is this conceptualization of culture that links up clearly to the types of transnational transformations that are taking place for Latinos and Latin Americans.

V. Synthesis of Globalization and Transnationalism: Future Trends for Global Citizens

As the discussion on globalization and transnationalism has indicated, the reality of immigrants, transnationals, or transmigrants is not fixed, but is in constant flux, socially and contextually embedded, requiring ever changing adaptation. As such the social spaces, contexts, and multiple identities that transnational Latinos and Latin Americans are creating from such experiences need to be at the center of any future educational plans, programs, policies, and practices.

These trends toward reinvention need to be considered in education by schools, administrators, teachers, parents, and communities. Such an education will need to consider Latinos/Latin Americans in terms of their (a) *historical agency*, how their past has been shaped and defined, and how they through mestizaje are now contesting, questioning, and reinventing themselves in the present; (b) *cultural heritage*, not in the static or reified fixed meaning, but in the sense of culture as evolving and re-adaptive, in different contexts and with varied meanings and constituting blended identities; (c) *language diversity* as a strength and not as a barrier to learning, recognizing the crossover of language and skills, ability to communicate, and express *cariño* (endearment) and well-being; (d) *social organizing and community development*, including the type of social, cybernetic, and cultural networks being developed and their effect on creating community; (e) their assets as *contributing citizens in society*, and not simply for their "immigrant worker role," but for their social, cultural, economic, and public contributions to multiple countries; (f) their *transnational lives in global systems* that go beyond disciplinary boundaries; and (g) their *generational learning*, particularly in terms of the second generation, and the roles that children play in migration (Orellana, Thorne, Chee, & Lam, 2001). Moreover, each of these domains will need to be understood as functioning on local, regional, national, and global terrains, as technological connectivity and cultural and social influences replenish these exchanges. Interacting across and within cultural spaces will require knowledge and respect of not only one's cultural traditions but that of others and willingness to forge equality of opportunities that speak to human rights.

Schools will need to restructure themselves around creating such transnational knowledge, skills, and competencies in all areas and should consider that in teaching transnational Latino/Latin American students they will need to understand: (a) the similarities and differences between systems of education between the home and host country; (b) the parity that exists/or does not exist in educational systems; (c) preparation that students bring with them, and the transitions that are put into place by the receiving school to accommodate such students, including transitions from mother tongue to second language; (d) the ways that schools, teachers, and the curriculum address issues of race, gender, culture, and language considered from one context to the other, and the types of intercultural, multicultural, global education that will be espoused; (e) the adaptation mechanisms that schools and teachers put into place to help transnational students belong in the host society, whether through intercultural, multicultural education, or diversity focused activities and interventions; (f) the preparation of teachers in working with diverse immigrant and non-immigrant students, and the need for them to participate in the cultural production and renewal of information with students; (g) the assessment measures used and their adaptability for transnational students; (h) the types of citizen discourses taught, and the messages and meanings transmitted about transnational students, immigrants, and the like; (i) the curriculum, instructional programs, and actual teaching of transnational students; and (j) finally, the role that parents and community play within the walls of the schools.

Notes

1. This chapter grew out of the collaboration among the authors, and it includes sections of each other's work on Latinos in the United States and Latin Americans in Spain. The sections written by Lidia Cabrera Perez have been translated from Spanish to English by Martha Montero-Sieburth.
2. See, for example, the following web sites:
   Centre for the Study of Global Governance http://www.lse.ac.uk/Depts/global/
   Global Policy Forum http://www.globalpolicy.org/ngos/role/campaign/ciccindex.htm
   Centre for the Study of Globalisation and Regionalisation http://www.warwick.ac.uk/csgr
   Center for the Study of Contentious Politics at Cornell University [see also Workshop on Transnational Contention]. Civil Society International http://www.civilsoc.org
   Transnational Institute http://www.tni.org
   Indymedia http://www.indymedia.org
   Transnational Communities Programme http://www.transcomm.ox.ac.uk
   Global Policy Forum http://www.globalpolicy.org
   One world www.oneworld.net
3. Among some of the authors who have written on the convergence between Latin Americans and the Canary Islands are the following: J. C. Lorenzo Diaz (1992). *Los transatlánticos de la emigración (1947–1974)* [The Trans Atlantics of Immigratione]. Sta. Cruz de Tenerife: Viceconsejeria de cultura y deportes del Gobierno de Canarias; A. López Cantos (1999). *El tráfico comercial entre Canarias y América durante el siglo XVII.* [The commercial traffic between the Canary Islands and America during the 17th century]. Cabildo Insular de las Palmas de Gran Canaria; A. Macías Hernández (1994). *La emigración canaria a América: estado de la cuestión.* [The Canary Islands emigration to America: The state of the issue]. Cabildo Insular de las Las Palmas de Gran Canaria. N. Naranjo Santana (1991). Lo lejano y lo cercano. Reflexiones antropológicas sobre las relaciones entre América y Canarias, [The faraway and near. Anthropological reflections about the relationships between America and the Canary Islands]. In J. R. Santana Godoy (1991). (Comp.), *Canarias entre Europa y América.* [Canary Islands between Europe and America]. Las Palmas de Gran Canaria: Edirca. A. Pérez Voituriez y O. Brito González (1982). *Canarias: encrucijada internacional.* [Canary Islands: International crossroads]. Sta. Cruz de Tenerife: Círculo de estudios culturales de Canarias.
4. There are extensive micro, meso, and macro networks of institutes throughout the world, dedicated to the study of migration with some in the process of being developed. Given their numbers it is not possible to provide for a comprehensive and updated list. However, to name just a few, some of the institutes and centers in the U. S. are the Center for Migration and Development at Princeton University; the Center for Comparative Immigration Studies at the University of California, San Diego; and the Center for the Study of Contentious Politics at Cornell University. Among those found in Europe are: the Institute for Migration and Ethnic Studies at the University of Amsterdam, ERCOMER at the University of Utrecht, Center for the Study of Globalization and Regionalization in the United Kingdom, and COMPAS.

5. See "Shared Perspectives between Experts and Immigrants: A Study of Social and Cultural Integration," presented by Lidia Cabrera Perez and Martha Montero-Sieburth at the V Congress on Immigration to Spain, in Valencia, Spain, 2007.

6. Celoni Espínola Mesa (2007). The Kids on the Other Side of the Hallway: Teachers Perspectives of the Academic Achievement of Latino English Language Learners." Unpublished Doctoral Dissertation, University of Massachusetts-Boston.

7. Lidia Cabrera Pérez (Ed.). (2008). La Integración Cultural y Social de Inmigrantes Latinoamericanos: Inquietudes y Sugerencias para Políticas de Cambio [The social and cultural integration of Latin Americans: Concerns and implications for the politics of change]. Madrid id: Universitas.

8. See Mark Thomson and Maurice Crul's discussion on The Second Generation in Europe and the United States: How is the Transatlantic Debate relevant for further research on the European Second Generation? *Journal of Ethnic and Migration Studies, 33*(7), Sept. 2007, pp. 1015–1041, as an example of an embryonic transatlantic dialogue about different patterns of second generation integration in different countries.

9. These groups were the most salient in the study of Latin Americans in Spain for the Canary Islands and Granada, yet, in this chapter, the discussion is on the Latin Americans of the Canary Islanders.

10. During the 15th and 16th century expansion of Spain, the types of policy changes that determined the type of educational and religious practices that the new hybrid mestizos were to receive after their "conquest"were put into practice.

11. Spain lost many of its intellectuals as refugees during the 1930s under Franco's rule. Many of these went to teach at Latin American educational institutions, contributing to one of the largest intellectual brain drains of the social and cultural capital of Spain.

12. The need for guest workers throughout Europe during the 1970s unto the 1990s saw the exodus of Spaniards for other parts of Europe, but, at the same time, the sons of Spaniards, now Latin Americans or the retornados (returnees), began to appear in Spain. Close to 2 million Spaniards and Portuguese emigrated as guest workers to other European countries during the 1970s to 1990s according to Adela Pellegrino (2000) in her report on *Migration from Latin America to Europe: Trends and Policy Challenges*, published by the International Organization for Migration. However, later in the 1990s, Spain began to experience a shift from being a country of emigrants to becoming one receiving increasing numbers of foreign populations, which now account for close to 10% of the total; close to 45 million inhabitants. This has set into motion new educational laws and policies for educating immigrant students.

13. An example of this was the denial of equal education during the period of U.S. slavery, from colonial times to the reconstruction of the South.

14. A case in point is the New Bedford, Massachusetts, federal agents' raid of 2007 in which close to 300 undocumented workers, many of whom were mothers and fathers, were arrested and detained while their children were left behind. Although the Department of Social Services stepped in, many of the children were not reunited with their families for some time. The case brought to light how hiring undocumented workers was profitable for the company at the risk of the unsafe and unhealthy conditions for the workers.

15. To date, well over 16,000 adults and children have entered the Canary Islands without legal documentation during 2006–2007, making this a crisis that involves not only Spain and western Africa, but also other European nations.

16. Article 26 of the Universal Declaration of Human Rights of 1948 states that: (1) Everyone has the right to education. Education shall be free, at least in the elementary and fundamental stages. Elementary education shall be compulsory. Technical and professional education shall be made generally available and higher education shall be equally accessible to all on the basis of merit. (2) Education shall be directed to the full development of the human personality and to the strengthening of respect for human rights and fundamental freedoms. It shall promote understanding, tolerance and friendship among all nations, racial or religious groups, and shall further the activities of the United Nations for the maintenance of peace. (3) Parents have a prior right to choose the kind of education that shall be given to their children.

17. Bauböck (2008) contends that diasporas originally referred to the historic experiences of specific

groups such as Jews, Armenians, Greeks, and Chinese. But four elements describe the present definition: (a) traumatic dispersal from homeland, (b) resistance against assimilation and retention of group identify across multiple generations, (c) adopting horizontal ties of solidarity between groups of same origin in different places, and (d) homeland-oriented projects that shape country's future.

18. The term *foreigner* is generically used throughout Spain to refer to entrants into Spain from another country. However, this same term in Canary Islands is most often used to designate northern Europeans while the term "immigrants" is used more widely to designate those who are socioeconomically different and come from Latin America and Africa.

19. Compulsory schooling in Spain covers: (a) Pre-Primary (3–5 years of age); Primary (6–11 years of age); and Secondary levels (12–15 years of age).

20. Randolph Bourne. Transnational America, *Atlantic Monthly, 118*, July 1916, pp. 86–97.

21. See Wortham, Murrillo, Jr., and Hamann, *Education in the New Latino Diaspora* (2002), Westport, CT: Ablex Publishing, as evidence of the growing significance of this topic for Latinos and education in the United States; the research of Gitlin, Buendia, Crosland, and Doumbia in The Production of Margin and Center: Welcoming-Unwelcoming of Immigrant Students, *American Education Research Journal* (2003), *40*(1) pp. 91–122; and Buendia, Gitlin (with Fode Doubmia), Working the Pedagogical Borderlands: An African Critical Demagogue Teaching within an ESL Context, *Curriculum Inquiry*, (2003), *33*(3), pp. 291–320 on the hybridity that is being created as immigrant students become part of the pedagogical borderlands.

References

Aguado, T. (2003). *Pedagogía intercultural*. Madrid: McGraw-Hill.

Agrela, B. (2002). *Spain as a recent country of immigration: How immigration became a symbolic, political, and cultural problem in the "new Spain."* Working Paper 57: The Center for Comparative Immigration Studies, University of California, San Diego.

Alba, R., & Nee, V. (2007). Assimilation. In M. C. Waters & R. Ueda with H. B. Marrow (Eds.), *The new Americans: A guide to immigration since 1965* (pp. 124–136). Cambridge, MA. Harvard University Press.

Appadurai, A. (1990). Disjuncture and difference in the global culture economy. *Theory, Culture, and Society, 7*, 295–310.

Appadurai, A. (1996). *Modernity at large: Cultural dimensions of globalization*. Minneapolis: University of Minnesota Press.

Arnett, J. J. (2002). The psychology of globalization. *American Psychologist, 57*, 774–783.

Barkan, E. R. (2006). Introduction: Immigration, incorporation, assimilation and the limits of transnationalism. *Journal of American Ethnic History, 25*, 7–32.

Basch, L., Glick-Schiller, N., & Blanc-Szanton, C. (Eds.). (1994). *Nations unbound: Transnational projects, postcolonial predicaments, and deterriorialized nation-states*. Basel, Switzerland: Gordon and Breach.

Bauböck, R. (1994). *Transnational citizenship: Membership and rights in international migration*. Brookfield, VT: Edward Elgar.

Bauböck, R. (2008, October, 1–8). *Ties across borders: The growing salience of transnationalism and diaspora politics*. IMISCOE [database] Policy Brief, No. 13.

Bloom, D. E. (2004). Globalization and education: An economic perspective. In M. Suárez-Orozco & D. B. Qin-Hilliard (Eds.), *Globalization: Culture and education in the new millennium* (pp. 56–77). Berkeley: University of California Press and the Ross Institute.

Bowles, S., & Gintis, H. (1976). *Schooling in capitalist America: Educational reform and contradictions of economic life*. New York: Basic Books.

Brittain, C. (2005). On learning English: The importance of school context, immigrant communities, and the racial symbolism of the English language in understanding the challenge for immigrant adolescents. *Working Paper 125*. Center for Comparative Immigration Studies, University of California San Diego. Retrieved December 10, 2006, from http://www.ccis-ucsd.org/publications/wrug125.pdf

Cabrera, L., & Montero-Sieburth, M. (2007, March). Perspectivas compartidas entre expertos e inmigrantes: un estudio de integración cultural y social. En *Actas del V Congreso sobre la Inmigración en España. Migraciones y Desarrollo Humano* [Shared perspectives between experts and immigrants: A study of social and cultural Integration]. In the Conference Proceedings of the V Congress on Immigration in Valencia, Spain.

Cabrera Pérez, L. (2008). *La Integración Cultural y Social de Inmigrantes Latinoamericanos: Inquietudes y Sugerencias para Políticas de Cambio.* Madrid: Universitas.

Carro, L., Montero-Sieburth, M., & Cabrera, L. (2009, April). *Identifying the familia, social, educational and personal implications of "Staying Behind and Reuniting" in the lives of children of transnational Dominican immigrants: Educational, Sociological and Anthropological Implications.* Paper presented at the American Educational Research Association Annual Meeting, San Diego, California.

Castles, S. (2005). Migration and community formation under conditions of globalization. In P. Kivisto (Ed.), *Incorporating diversity: Rethinking assimilation in a multicultural age* (pp. 277–298). Boulder, CO: Paradigm.

Castles, S., & Davidson, A. (2000). *Citizenship and migration: Globalization and the politics of belonging.* New York: Routledge.

CIDE. Centro de Investigación y Documentación Educativa (Research Center and Educational Documentation), (2005). *La atención al alumnado inmigrante en el sistema educativo español.* [Attention to the immigrant student in the Spanish educational system]. Madrid: Secretaría General Técnica. Ministerio de Educación y Ciencia.

Coatsworth, J. (2004). Globalization, growth and welfare in history. In M. Suárez-Orozco & D. B. Qin-Hilliard (Eds.), *Globalization: Culture and education in the new millennium* (pp. 38–55). Berkeley: University of California Press and the Ross Institute.

Consejo de Europa (Council of Europe). (1984). *Recomendación del Comité de Ministros del Consejo de Europa a los Estados Miembros sobre el componente intercultural en la formación del profesorado* [Recommendations of the Committee of Ministers of the Council of Europe to its member states on the Intercultural component in the formation of Teachers]. Stausborg, France: Consejo de Europa.

De la Dehesa, G. (2007). *Comprender la globalización* [Understanding globalization]. Madrid: Alianza Editorial.

DeVos, G. (1980). Ethnic adaptation and minority status. *Journal of Cross-Cultural Psychology, II*(i), 101–125.

De Vos, G., & Suárez-Orozco, M. (1990). *Status inequality: The self in culture.* Newbury Park, CA: Sage.

Eslin, P. (2000). Education and democratic citizenship: In defense of cosmopolitanism. In M. Leicester, C. Modgil, & S. Modgil (Eds.), *Politics, education and citizenship* (pp. 115–130). New York: Falmer Press.

Espínola Mesa, C. (2007). *The kids on the other side of the hallway: Teachers' perspectives of the academic achievement of Latino English language learners.* Unpublished Doctoral Dissertation, University of Massachusetts-Boston.

Erickson, F. (2002). Culture and human development. *Human Development, 45,* 299–306.

Feinberg, W. (1998). *Common schools/uncommon identities: National university and cultural difference.* New Haven, CT: Yale University Press.

Flores, W. V., & Benmayor, R. (1997). Introduction: Constructing cultural citizenship. In W. V. Flores & R. Benmayor (Eds.), *Latino cultural citizenship: Claiming identity, space and rights* (pp. 1–26). Boston: Beacon Press.

Fouron, G., & Glick Schiller, N. (2002). The generation of identity: redefining the second generation within a transnational social field. In P. Levitt & M. Waters (Eds.), *The changing face of home: The transnational lives of the second generation* (pp. 168–208). New York: Russell Sage Foundation .

Gándara, P., Gibson, M. A., & Koyoma, J. P. (Eds.). (2004). *School connections: U.S. Mexican youth, peers, and school achievement.* New York: Teachers College Press.

Gilroy, P. (1992).*The black Atlantic: Modernity and double consciousness.* Cambridge, MA: Harvard University Press.

Glick-Schiller, N. (2003). The centrality of ethnography in the study of transnational migration. In N. Foner (Ed.), *American arrivals: Anthropology engages the new immigration* (pp. 99–128). Santa Fe, NM: School American Research Press.

Glick-Schiller, N., & Levitt, P. (2006). *Haven't we heard this somewhere before? A substantive review of transnational migration studies by way of a reply to Waldinger and Fitzgerald.* Working Paper, 06-01. Princeton, NJ: Center for Migration Development, Princeton University.

Glick-Schiller, N., & Basch, L. (1995). From immigrant to transmigrant: Theorizing transnational migration. *Anthropological Quarterly, 68*(1), 48–63.

Glick-Schiller, N., Basch, L., & Blanc-Szanton, C. (1992). *Towards a transnational perspective on migration: Race, class, ethnicity, and nationalism reconsidered.* New York: New York Academy of Sciences.

Guarnizo, L. (1997). The emergence of a transnational social formation and the mirage of return migration among Dominican transmigrants. *Identities, 4,* 281–322.

Guarnizo, L., & Smith, M. (1998). The location of transnationalism. In M. P. Smith & L. E. Guarnizo (Eds.), *Transnationalism from below. Comparative urban and community research* (Vol. 6, pp. 3–34). Davis: University of California.

Gutiérrez, K., & Rogoff, B. (2003). Cultural ways of learning: Individual traits or repertoires of practice. *Educational Researcher, 32*(5), 19–25.

Held, D., Mc Grew, A., Goldblatt, D., & Perraton, J. (1999). *Global transformations: Politics, economics, and culture.* Stanford, CA: Stanford University Press.

Khagram, S., & Levitt, P. (2005). *Towards a field of transnational studies and a sociological transnationalism research program.* Cambridge, MA: John F. Kennedy School of Government.

Knight Abowitz, K., & Harnish, J. (2006). Contemporary discourses of citizenship. *Review of Educational Research, 76*(4), 653–690.

Lam, W. S. E. (2006). Culture and Learning in the Context of Globalization: Research Directions. *Review of Research in Education, 30,* 213–237.

Ley Orgánica 14/2003 (The Organic Law 14/2003). (2003). de 20 de noviembre, de Reforma de la *Ley Orgánica 4/2000,* de 11 de Enero, sobre derechos y libertades de los extranjeros en España y su integración social. [of the 20 of November of the Reform of the Organic Law of 4/2000 of the 11th of January over the rights, liberties, and social integration of foreigners in Spain]. Madrid: Spanish government.

Ley Orgánica 4/2000 (The Organic Law 4/2000). (2000). de 11 de Enero sobre derechos y libertades de los extranjeros en España y su integración social [of thd llth of January on the Rights, liberties, and social integration of foreigners in Spain]. Madrid: Spanish government.

Ley Organica. (1990). de Ordenación General del Sistema Educativo. (Boletín Oficial del Estado de 4 de Octubre de 1990) [Organic Law of 1990 of the General Coordination of the Educational System, Official Bulletin of the State on the 4th of October of 1990]. Madrid: Spanish government.

Ley Orgánica. (2002). de Calidad de la Educación, Boletín Oficial del Estado de 24 de Diciembre de 2002. [The Organic Law on the Quality of Education, Official Bulletin of the State on the 24th of December of 2002]. Madrid: Spanish government.

Ley Orgánica. (2006). de Educación (Boletín Oficial del Estado de 4 de Mayo de 2006). The Organic Law 2/2006 of the 3rd of May in Education, Official Bulletin of the State for the 4th of May 2006]. Madrid: Spanish government.

Levitt, P. (2001). *The transnational villagers.* Berkeley: University of California Press.

Levitt, P., & Jaworsky, B. (2007) Transnational migration studies: Past developments and future trends. *Annual Review of Sociology, 33,* 129–156.

Lindo, F. (2000). Does culture explain? Understanding differences in school attainment between Iberian and Turkish youth in the Netherlands. In H. Vermeulen & J. Perlmann (Eds.), *Immigrants, schooling and social mobility. Does culture make a difference?* (pp. 206–224). New York: St. Martin's Press.

Lowell, B., & Suro, R. (2002). *The improving educational profile of Latino immigrants. A project of the Pew Charitable Trust and USC Annenberg School for Communication.* Washington, DC: Pew Hispanic Center.

Massey, D. (1994). The new immigration and ethnicity in the United States. *Population and Development Review, 21*(3), 631–652.

Mehan, H., Villanueva, I., & Hubbard, L. (1996). *Constructing school success, the consequences of untracking low achieving students.* Cambridge, UK: Cambridge University Press.

Moll, L., & González, N. (2004). Engaging life: A funds of knowledge approach to multicultural education. In J. Banks & C. McGee Banks (Eds.), *Handbook of research on multicultural education* (2nd ed., pp. 699–715). New York: Jossey-Bass.

Montero-Sieburth, M. (2006). An overview and critique of the educational models used to explain the academic achievement of Latino students in elementary and secondary schooling in the United States. In L. Diaz Soto (Ed.), *Praeger handbook of Latino education in the United States* (pp. 8–23). Santa Barbara, CA: Greenwood Press.

Montero-Sieburth, M. (2007). The "Si Se Puede" Newcomers: Mexicans in New England. In M. Montero-Sieburth & E. Melendez (Eds.), *Latinos in a changing society* (pp. 58–91). Westport, CT: Praeger Press.

Montero-Sieburth, M., & Batt, M. (2001). An overview of educational models used to explain the academic achievement of Latino students: Implications for policy and research into the new millennium. In R. Slavin & M. Calderón (Eds.), *Effective programs for Latino students* (pp. 331–368). Hillsdale, NJ: Erlbaum.

Montero-Sieburth, M., & Villarruel, F. A. (Eds.). (2000). *Making invisible Latino adolescents visible. A critical approach to Latino diversity.* New York: Falmer Press.

Morawska, E. (2003). Immigrant transnationalism and Assimilation: A variety of combinations and the analytic strategy it suggests. In C. Joppke & E. T. Morawska (Eds.), *Towards assimilation and citizenship: Immigrants in liberal nation-states* (pp. 133–176). Basingstroke, UK: Palgrave MacMillan.

Morawska, E. (2007). Transnationalism. In M. C. Waters & R. Ueda (Eds.), *Harvard encyclopedia of the new Americans* (pp. 149–163). Cambridge, MA: Harvard University Press

Murillo Jr., E. G. (2002). How does it feel to be a problem? "Disciplining" the transnational subject in the American south. In S. Wortham, E. G. Murillo, Jr., & E. T. Hamann (Eds.), *Education in the new Latino diaspora. Policy and politics of identity* (pp. 215–241). Westport, CT: Ablex.

Noguera, P. A. (1999). Transforming urban schools through investments in social capital. [Electronic version]. *In Motion Magazine.* Retrieved June 24, 2002, from http//www.inmotionmagazine.com/pncapl.html

Noguera, P. A. (2001). Racial politics and the elusive quest for excellence and equity in education. [Electronic version]. *In Motion Magazine.* Retrieved September 9, 2002, from http//www.inmotionmagazine.com/er/pnrp1.html

Ogbu, J. U. (1987). Variability in minority school performance: A problem in search of an explanation. *Anthropology and Education Quarterly,* 18(4), 312–334.

Olsen, L. (1997). *Made in America: Immigrant students in our public schools.* New York: New Press.

Orellana, M. F., & Bowman, P. (2003). Cultural diversity research on learning and development. *Educational Researcher,* 32(5), 26–32.

Orellana, M. F., Thorne, B., Chee, A. E., & Lam, W. S. E. (2001). Transnational childhoods: The participation of children in the processes of family migration. *Social Problems,* 48, 572–591.

Portes, A., & Lingxin Hao (2004, August). The schooling of children in immigrants: Contextual effects on the educational attainment of the second generation. *National Academy of Sciences, PNAS 10*(33). Retrieved January 15, 2008, from www.pnas.org/cgi/doe/10.1073/pnas0403418101

Robertson, S., Novelli, M., Dale, R., Tikly, L., Dachi, H., & Ndibelema, A. (2007). *Globalization, education and development: Ideas, actors and dynamics.* Bristol, UK: University of Bristol, Department of International Development, Educational Papers, Centre for Globalisation.

Rosaldo, R. (1997). Cultural citizenship, inequality, and multiculturalism. In W. V. Flores & R. Benmayor (Eds.), *Latino cultural citizenship: Claiming identify, space and rights* (pp. 27–38). Boston: Beacon Press.

Rosaldo, R., & Flores, W. V. (1997). Identity, conflict, and evolving Latino communities. Cultural citizenship in San Jose, California. In W. V. Flores & R. Benmayor (Eds.), *Latino cultural citizenship: Claiming identify, space and rights* (pp. 57–96). Boston: Beacon Press.

Sabariego, M. (2005). *La educación intercultural ante los retos del Siglo XXI* [Intercultural education as a challenge in the 21st century]. Bilbao, Spain: Desclée del Brouwer.

Sassen, S. (1996). *Transnational economies and national migration policies.* Amsterdam, the Netherlands: Institute for Migration and Ethnic Studies, University of Amsterdam.

Smith, M. (2005, March). Transational urbanism revisited. *Journal of Ethnic and Migration Studies,* 31(2), 235–244.

Smith, M., & Guarnizo, L. (1998). *Transnationalism from below. Comparative urban and community research* (vol. 6). Davis: University of California, Davis.

Sorensen, N. N., & Fog Olwig, K. (2002). *Work and migration: Life and livelihoods in a globalizing world.* London: Routledge.

Spring, J. (2008). Research on globalization and education. *Review of Educational Research,* 78(2), 330–363.

Suárez-Orozco, C. (2004). Formulating identity in a globalized world. In M. Suárez-Orozco & D. B.

Qin-Hilliard (Eds.), *Globalization: Culture and education in the new millennium* (pp. 173–202). Berkeley: University of California Pres and the Ross Institute.

Suárez-Orozco C., & Suárez-Orozco, M. (1995). *Transformation: Migration, family life, and achievement motivation among Latinos adolescents.* Stanford, CA: Stanford University Press.

Suárez-Orozco C., & Suárez-Orozco, M. (2001). *Children of immigration.* Cambridge, MA: Harvard University Press.

Suárez-Orozco, M. (2003). Right moves? Immigration, globalization, utopia and dystopia. In N. Foner (Ed.), *American arrivals: Anthropology engages the new immigration* (pp. 45–74). Santa Fe, NM: School of American Research Press and Oxford, UK: James Currey.

Torres, C. (2002). Globalization, education and citizenship: Solidarity versus Markets? *American Educational Research Journal, 39*(2), 363–378.

Trueba, E. T. (2004). *The new Americans: Immigrants and transnationals at work.* New York: Rowman & Littlefield.

Universal Declaration of Human Rights. (1948). General Assembly, res. 217A (III), U.N. Doc A/810 at 71. New York: United Nations.

Vermeulen, H. (2000). Introduction: The role of culture in explanations of social mobility. In H. Vermeulen & J. Perlmann (Eds.), *Immigrants, schooling and social mobility. Does culture make a difference?* (pp. 1–21). New York: St. Martin's Press.

Vertovec, S. (2004). Migrant transnationalism and modes of transformation. *International Migration Review, 38,* 970–1001.

Waldinger, R., & Fitzgerald D. (2004). Transnationalism in question. *American Journal of Sociology, 109,* 1177–1195.

Waters, M., & Jiménez, T. (2005). Assessing immigrant assimilation: New empirical and theoretical challenges. *Annual Review Sociology, 31,* 105–125.

9   Education in the New Latino Diaspora

Edmund T. Hamann
University of Nebraska-Lincoln

Linda Harklau
University of Georgia

In 2002 Hamann, Wortham, and Murillo noted that many U.S. states were hosting significant and often rapidly growing Latino populations for the first time and that these changes had multiple implications for formal schooling as well as out-of-school learning processes. They speculated about whether Latinos were encountering the same, often disappointing, educational fates in communities where their presence was unprecedented as in areas with a longstanding Latino presence. Only tentative conclusions could be provided at that time since the dynamics referenced were frequently novel and in flux.

In this chapter we revisit their inquiry in light of 6 subsequent years of research and outcome data. We begin by defining and elaborating on the concept of "new Latino diaspora," tracing its origins, and noting the diverse populations and contexts it represents. Next, we turn to an analysis of educational outcomes in new Latino diaspora communities in light of two competing hypotheses. The first would suggest that in areas where there has been little history of anti-Latino institutionalized racism and little record of Latino school success or failure, educational improvisation might lead to better outcomes than in areas with long established racialized patterns of weak Latino educational outcomes. Alternatively, the second would suggest that racialized patterns of interaction with and schooling for Latino communities in California, Texas, or Chicago are carried into and recreated in new settings, leading to similar or even poorer educational outcomes. We conclude with a review of emergent scholarship and suggestions for further work that might shed light on education in the new Latino diaspora and, in some instances, on Latino education more generally.

Revisiting the Concept of a New Latino Diaspora

The term *diaspora* refers to "people settled far from their homeland" (Merriam-Webster, 2003) with the connotation of being forcibly expelled by religious, political, or economic forces (Brettell, 2006). It has become a key, if somewhat imprecise, construct in recent anthropological and sociological scholarship on global migration, transnationalism, and ethnicity (Brettell, 2006; Lukose, 2007). The term *new Latino diaspora* was first used in the late 1990s (see Murillo & Villenas, 1997). As Hamann and colleagues (2002) explain, the term denotes the fact that "Increasing numbers of Latinos (many immigrant and some from elsewhere in the United States) are settling both temporarily and permanently in areas of the United States that have not traditionally been home to Latinos—for example, North Carolina, Maine, Georgia, Indiana, Arkansas, rural Illinois, and near resort communities in Colorado" (p. 1). These locales mostly contrast with the nine states of the traditional Latino diaspora—Arizona, California, Colorado, Florida, Illinois, New Jersey, New Mexico, New York, and Texas (National Taskforce on Early Childhood Education for Hispanics, 2007)—that have longstanding Latino populations as well as many newcomers, although the mentioning of Colorado and Illinois on both lists highlights some of the limitations of defining *new* and *traditional* using state borders.

The rise of the new Latino diaspora in the United States can be attributed to changing patterns of U.S. labor markets where several industries in particular are driving Latino immigration and in-migration to new, often rural areas, including agriculture, construction and landscaping, assembly and manufacturing, and poultry and meat processing (Kandel & Cromartie, 2004; Schmid, 2003; Zuñiga & Hernández-Leon, 2005). No matter what the draw, these newcomers are more likely to be young and more likely to have children than existing residents (Schmid, 2003); hence, the character and quality of their educational experiences in the new diaspora become especially significant. Compared to more established Latino communities, current 'new' Latino diaspora locations tend to be characterized by higher proportions of Latinos who speak Spanish as a first language and struggle with English (Singer, 2004). They also have substantial numbers of undocumented parents (Pew Hispanic Center, 2006), although most children of undocumented parents are themselves documented (National Task Force on Early Childhood Education for Hispanics, 2007; Passel, 2006).

Hamann et al. (2002) suggested that in the new Latino diaspora, newcomer Latinos were confronted with "novel challenges to their senses of identity, status, and community" (p. 1) and that responses by non-Latino established residents were improvisational, as local norms of inclusion/ exclusion and assimilation/accommodation were lacking. In short, the new Latino diaspora was defined by *who* (Latinos), *where* (places were Latinos have not previously lived in significant number), and *encountering what* (improvised inter-ethnic interaction). Each of these can be further considered.

While *who* gets counted as Latino (or Hispanic) is mainly a topic for other entries in this handbook, it is worth mentioning four dynamics here. First, as Oboler (1995) noted in her study of Peruvian newcomers to the United States, newcomers from Latin America who come to the United States often arrive thinking of their ethnic identity in nationalistic terms (e.g., Peruvian) and are surprised by the racialized nature of the Latino/Hispanic identity in the country. The relatively small initial number of Latinos in new diaspora communities tends to facilitate the formation of a pan-ethnic Latino identity. Nevertheless, although members of the new Latino diaspora may embrace a pan-Latino identity, it is not automatic that they will, nor that, if they do, they will continue to feel a pan-Latino solidarity. Referencing a *new Latino diaspora* in some ways measures the semiotic taxonomies of the host society as much as the self-identity of the diaspora's ostensible members.

Comparatively, in most sites in the new Latino diaspora, those of Mexican descent form the majority of Latinos, and *Latino* verges on becoming a short-hand for *Mexican* (Wortham et al., 2002). Yet as large Dominican and Guatemalan populations in Rhode Island (Portes, Guarnizo, & Haller, 2002), large Salvadoran populations in metropolitan Washington, DC (Portes et al., 2002), and Central American populations in post-Katrina New Orleans (Campbell, 2005; Lovato, 2005) make clear, Mexicans are not always the dominant Latino group in new Latino diaspora settings. Moreover, who is *Mexican* can be a complicated question as non-Spanish-speaking or limited-Spanish-speaking indigenous Mexicans from Oaxaca, Chiapas, and elsewhere make up a new portion of the transnational migration stream, including into new Latino diaspora locations like Hillsboro, Oregon (Zehr, 2002). (See also Villenas, 2007, p. 421, for a discussion of nation-state identities, like Mexican and American, that obscure indigenous identities.)

Third, with relocation across the United States in connection with jobs becoming the norm for all, but particularly for educated professionals and the military, third and fourth generation Chicanos are now living in places that historically have had few Latinos. In 2001, for example, the U.S. military was 15.3% Hispanic and made up more than one fifth of all Marines (Pew Hispanic Center, 2003), so it follows that in communities with large military facilities a military-related Latino population exists. Counting Latino U.S. Marines' training in North Carolina as participants of an education in the new Latino diaspora seems to make sense. More generally, it makes sense to count established Latinos (e.g., Tejanos) as part of the new Latino diaspora when they are located away from the nine traditional Latino gateway states. At the same time, however, this discussion highlights the fact that up to this point new Latino diaspora locales have been of interest primarily because of their new immigrant populations whose linguistic and ethnic outsider status is clear. In a country with a powerful drive towards assimilation, the perceived linguistic, ethnic, and racial distinctiveness and thus diasporic status of third or fourth or fifth generation Latinos in their adopted communities is a much more open question.

Fourth, all the original cases in *Education in the New Latino Diaspora* (Wortham et al., 2002) reference emergent Latino communities and presume that Latino children are growing up in Latino families. While this assumption is often safe, it is not always so. Transracial and transnational adoptions often locate Latino children away from Latino communities and reference points. According to a November 5, 2006, the *New York Times* story (Lacey, 2006), Americans adopted 18,298 Guatemalan babies in 2005. When these babies end up with Anglo parents in Vermont, Kentucky, or Maryland, should they be counted as part of the new Latino diaspora? Are these children treated as Latinos by their adoptive parents or siblings? By their larger communities? Villenas (2002) notes of Latina parenting in North Carolina, that Latina mothers raise them using *dichos* (aphorisms/stories), tell them to be *al pendiente*, (on guard), and hope *se comporten bien* (that they comport themselves well). If adoptive parents do not do that, should we talk about adoptive parent practices as part of education in the new Latino diaspora?

Writing about Latinos in the southeastern United States, Villenas and Murillo noted that in that part of the new Latino diaspora, "There is no Alamo to remember, nor occupied territories to claim, nor a legendary Aztlán to recreate" (cited in Villenas, 2002, p. 30). As we consider *where* to locate the new Latino diaspora, is this paucity of a history and related claims to place and precedent important? Answering "yes" would obviate at least some of the need for explaining the improvisation of inter-ethnic interaction and the intermittent resistance of the established non-Latino community. But if we want to also locate the new Latino diaspora in the Midwest, Great Plains, Northwest, and non-Mid-Atlantic Northeast where there are some Latino memories and histories, do we risk being complicit in established communities' erasure of Latino histories (an erasure that explains the surprised and improvised reaction to the newcomers) if we call these places new?

In her compilation of historic *corridos* (folksongs) created by Mexican migrants and immigrants in the 19th and early 20th centuries, folklorist Herrera-Sobek (1993) notes references in song to steel work in Pennsylvania and work with sugar beets in Kansas and Michigan. Likewise, McConnell (2004) traces the beginnings of recruitment of Mexican labor in the rural upper Midwest to the 1917 Immigrant Act that curtailed supplies of European-origin labor. While resulting Latino communities were disrupted by the depressions of 1920–21 and 1929 when many of those of Mexican origin left or were forcibly repatriated, recruitment and migration flows renewed during labor shortages in World War II and subsequent years.

Gouviea, Carranza, and Cogua (2005) propose the phrase re-emerging Latino communities. Acknowledging that Nebraska's Latino population was estimated at 125,000 in 2005, they also point out that Nebraska's 1980 Census Count tallied 28,000 Latinos (many were third and fourth generation with ties to the railroad and/or sugar beet industries). Describing Nebraska's new demographic reality and the fact that in many communities Latino newcomer/established resident interaction has been improvised and tentative should not obscure the long-time presence of Latinos in that state. Does our desire to call these sites "new" obscure these histories? Yet would excluding them from our list, mean we overlook locations where there is now much improvised interaction (despite modest-sized antecedent populations)?

Conversely, in the original crafting of the concept of new Latino diaspora, it was not made clear whether the arrival of new Latino nationalities to a setting that has hosted other Latino groups should be included. Put tangibly, should the new arrival of a large Mexican-origin population in New York City be counted as part of the new Latino diaspora? There is not much of a history of a Mexican presence there, although there is long history of Puerto Ricans, Cubans, and other immigrant groups (from Latin America and the rest of the world). Clearly, Mexican newcomers are now an important population there, and the scholarship on their negotiation of this new setting includes the negotiation of schooling (e.g., Cortina & Gendreau, 2003). Does our desire to exclude New York because it is a traditional diaspora site limit a substantial piece of the *new* story?

Defining such a wide portion of the country as the new Latino diaspora may also obscure important regional differences in Latino educational enrollment patterns and their impact. In much of the new Latino diaspora, notably the South and Pacific Northwest, the growth in Latino populations is occurring concurrently with growth in the population generally, although not necessarily growth in student populations. In 1995–96 Virginia counted 1,079,854 students, of whom 34,597 were Hispanic. Washington state counted 956,572 students, of whom 74,871 were Hispanic (National Center for Education Statistics, 1998). A decade later in 2005–06, Virginia enrolled 1,193,378 students (+113,524), of whom 91,557 were Hispanic (+55,960). Washington's student population grew to 1,020,311 (+63,739) and its Hispanic population to 139,005 (+65,134; National Center for Education Statistics, 2007). In other words, while increased Hispanic enrollment accounted for half the growth in Virginia's student population, it accounted for *all* of the increase in school enrollment in Washington. This in spite of the fact that Washington's non-Hispanic total population grew in that period from 5.13 million (Campbell, 1996) to 5.73 million (U.S. Census Bureau, 2007). These demographics also bring into relief another trend: Latino and non-Latino households increasingly differ in terms of the likelihood of including school-age children. Part of the educational reception of Latinos in the new Latino diaspora is likely shaped by many non-Latino established residents not having children and a racialized aversion to paying taxes or otherwise supporting other people's children. In contrast, in Iowa recently, immigration is credited for being the reason that the state's total population is not declining even as non-Latino school enrollments fall substantively (Grey, 2006).

Thus the context for inter-ethnic interaction in the new Latino diaspora varies. In some places, growth of the new Latino diaspora helps explain the proliferation of classroom trailers (as existing facilities are inadequate for the growing enrollment) and the shortage of teachers, particularly those trained in TESOL (Teachers of English to Speakers of Other Languages). In other places, the growth of the new Latino diaspora is the reason that schools have not closed and that teaching lines have not been discontinued; they are the reason for the stability of the school (although they are not necessarily viewed as such).

Rural and metropolitan areas also vary in terms of how they have become part of the new Latino Diaspora. In many Southern and Midwestern small towns, the new Latino diaspora is characterized by very sudden and rapid increases in Latino school age students (Kochhar et al., 2005). Often these rural areas have not experienced such dramatic demographic changes since White settlers first entered the area (Hamann, 2003; Kochhar et al., 2005). In these settings, Latino immigration to the region has consisted primarily of first generation immigrants who are more likely to be novice speakers of English (Kochhar et al., 2005).

In many cases, Latino students in new diaspora communities are encountering improvisational educational responses, particularly in regard to language issues. Many teachers in new diaspora communities are untrained in TESOL and home-school communication is hampered in many cases by a lack of bilingual educators or translators (Bohon, Macpherson, & Atiles, 2005). Dalla, Gupta, López, and Jones (2006) report, for example, that in 2004 of Nebraska's 22,000 educators, fewer than 200 were trained in TESOL. Even when TESOL programs and other pedagogical responses to newcomers exist, they may be thought of as "elaborate experiments" (Grey, 1993)—albeit experiments that suffer from a lack of a "control" population. In other words, the improvisation of programs and teaching methods is applied to all. Grey (1993) also notes that these experiments are led or managed—particularly at the school and district administration level—by those untrained and unfamiliar with newcomers (i.e., educational leaders who do not know what they do not know). Some new Latino diaspora locations serve as reluctant experiments, resulting in inadvertent or even intentional flouting of educational laws set in place to protect the rights of language minority students (see Beck & Allexsaht-Snider, 2002) and halfhearted teacher professional development efforts (Zehr, 2005).

Finally, we again face complications revisiting the *encountering what* dimension of defining the new Latino diaspora. While the notion of a new Latino diaspora might imply a blank slate for the local negotiation of inter-ethnic relationships and educational policies and practices, local interaction can never be entirely free of outside influence. Indeed, the general mobility of the U.S. population as well as a common pattern of secondary migration of Latino immigrants from established to new diaspora areas make it all but inevitable that some individuals will carry with them thoughts, scripts, and experiences that have been extant nationwide or in the traditional Latino diaspora. Moreover, even in the absence of inter-ethnic contact, local communities are immersed in nationally circulating images of Latinos in mass media (Berg, 2002; Mastro, 2003; Mastro & Behm-Morawitz, 2005) as well as ideologies concerning linguistic and cultural diversity and educational policy (see Ricento, 2000). For example, national media coverage of California's Proposition 227 seems to explain why some educators in northern Georgia turned away from bilingual education although they had initially embraced it (Hamann, 2003).

More optimistically, traditional Latino diaspora locations have also exported more promising educational innovations. With support of the Bill and Melinda Gates Foundation, the Cassin Educational Initiative Foundation, and several other philanthropies, the Cristo Rey High School model from Chicago has been or will be replicated in Baltimore, Birmingham, Indianapolis, Omaha, and Portland, among other cities. The original Cristo Rey is a bilingual Catholic high school in Chicago's Pilsen and Little Village neighborhood with dramatically reduced tuition that makes ends meet by having students work one-day a week as temp workers through a complex and highly successful internship program. Cristo Rey takes only low-income students. In Chicago this has consisted of 99% Latino enrollment. In the new sites—where the internship model is being replicated but not necessarily the bilingual component—Latino and African American students are expected to be the main enrollees (Zehr, 2006).

Even with all these caveats, we hold on to all three words: *new*, *Latino*, and *diaspora*. It is still true that in large swaths of the United States inter-ethnic interaction related to the education of Latinos is primarily a new phenomenon and the habits and expectations that will steer that interaction are still far from set. In these settings, people with ancestries tracing from Mexico, Central America, Puerto Rico, Ecuador, and the Dominican Republic, view themselves and/or are being viewed as belonging to a singular, inclusive pan-ethnic identity: i.e., Latino.

Capps et al. (2005, p. 8) noted that 55% of elementary school students with immigrant parents have parents who were born in Mexico (38%) or elsewhere in Latin America (17%). They then remark (p. 13) that the states with the fastest growth between 1990 and 2000 in children of immigrant elementary students include:

1st Nevada (+206%)
2nd North Carolina (+153%)
3rd Georgia (+148%)
4th Nebraska (+125%)
5th Arkansas (+109%)
6th Arizona (+103%)
7th South Dakota (+101%)
8th Oregon (+96%)
9th Colorado (+94%)
9th Iowa (+94%)

Eight of these states (all but Colorado and Arizona) have not historically hosted a substantial Latino population. What else should they be called if not *new Latino diaspora*?

Finally, we hold on to the concept of a new Latino Diaspora mostly because it has unfortunate predictive power. Hispanic (the term of most government datasets) appears to be a predictor in new Latino diaspora states of lesser academic success, as the next section traces.

Educational Outcomes in the New Latino Diaspora

Are Latinos in the new Latino diaspora subject to the equivalent obstacles and hazards as those that have hindered Latino achievement in traditional Latino locations? One way to answer that question would be to ask the families themselves whether they believe they are better off in new diaspora schools. Wortham and Contreras (2002), for example, report that Latino families in one rural New England community found the quality of schools to be higher than those they had previously attended in Texas border communities. Parents also found the area and schools to be freer of dangers for their children, such as drugs and gang violence. Thus Latino families may be judging the quality of schooling their children receive more by comparison to previous educational experiences in established Latino communities or in Mexico (Zúñiga & Hamann, 2006) than by comparison to the educational experiences of other ethnic and racial groups at the same school.

Another potential source for optimism is provided by Stamps and Bohon (2006), who found that Latinos living in new gateway (Suro & Singer, 2002) metropolitan areas in the United States tend overall to have higher educational levels than counterparts in established areas. However, they caution that this result may be because of in-migration to new gateway areas by more highly educated Latinos in search of economic opportunities.

In spite of these encouraging signs, large education achievement datasets such as high school graduation statistics tell a different story. Table 9.1 (next page) allows us to see how well Latino students were doing in a number of new Latino diaspora locations in 2005–2006. The third column shows the percentage of these state's public (pre)K-12 enrollment that is Latino. Comparing column 3 to column 5, in none of the states listed is the Latino high school graduation rate close to what one would predict based on total Latino enrollment.

As Table 9.1 illustrates, none of the states in this cross-section of the new Latino diaspora have Latino high school graduation rates that come close to the proportion of their Latino enrollments, and the Deep South seems to be the weakest. This can be partially explained and predicted by the national age distribution of the Latino population. For instance, according to the April 2006 U.S. Census population estimates, the number of Hispanic 5- to 9-year-olds was 4,090,814. The population of 10- to 14-year-olds was 3,942,042 (96.4% of the 5- to 9-year-old range) and of 15- to 19-year-olds was 3,622,784 (88.6% of the 15- to 9-year-old range). However, the steeply pyramidal ratios of Latino graduates to total Latino enrollments in the states named here range from just 39% in Alabama (the lowest) to only 67% in Rhode Island (the highest). These ratios are more disappointing when one notes that new Latino diaspora parents tend to have higher education achievement levels than Latino parents in the traditional diaspora (National Task Force on Early Childhood Education for Hispanics, 2007) and that parent education levels are generally a strong predictor of parent involvement and student academic achievement (although working class minority parents can participate effectively in their children's schooling, e.g., Dauber & Epstein, 1993).

Moreover, Table 9.1 obscures some of the negative story because it compares how Latinos fare only to students who graduate from other groups within the same state. Students, for instance, in southeastern states with some of the lowest high school graduation rates in the country (Editorial Projects in Education, 2007), have a worse chance overall of finishing high school than counterparts in midwestern states such as Iowa that rank high nationally in school completion.

Table 9.1   Hispanic Enrollment and High School Graduation Rates as Percentage of Total

State	Hispanic enrollment (2005–06)	Percentage of all enrollment	Hispanic high school graduates (2005–06)	Percentage of all HS grads
Alabama	20,479	2.8	404	1.1
Arkansas	32,132	6.8	998	3.7
Delaware	11,100	9.2	322	4.6
Georgia	135,010	8.7	2,590	3.7
Idaho	33,599	12.8	1,260	8.0
Indiana	59,387	5.7	1,636	3.0
Iowa	28,145	5.8	999	3.0
Kansas	55,117	12.1	2,019	6.7
Nebraska	32,887	11.5	1,194	6.0
North Carolina	118,505	8.4	2,864	3.8
Oregon	85, 461	15.9	2,717	8.3
Rhode Island	26,559	17.3	1,153	11.7
Virginia	91,557	7.7	3,556	4.8
Washington	139,005	13.6	4,893	8.0

Source: Data are derived from Sable & Garafono, 2007

But in these low graduation states (i.e., with lower White and African American graduation rates), Latinos proportional success is not better. If anything, it seems worse.

Another troubling indication from schooling in the new Latino diaspora comes from the Southern Regional Education Board (SREB, 2007), which found that between 1997 and 2006 Hispanic scores on the SAT or ACT had declined in 8 of the 14 new Latino diaspora SREB member states and that test score gaps between Hispanics and Whites had widened in all 14 of those states.[1] Recently, the Tomás Rivera Policy Institute (2004) sharply criticized the educational treatment of Latinos in Georgia, North Carolina, and Arkansas. It noted, for example, that in Northwest Arkansas, "Hispanics have experienced difficulty making their way to local universities. While they now make up almost one-third of the K-12 student population in the public school system, the University of Arkansas in nearby Fayetteville has a 1 percent Latino student population" (p. 18). In aggregate, Latinos in the new Latino diaspora do not fare as well in school as their non-Latino peers.

Emerging New Latino Diaspora Education Research

As this review suggests, the state of research on education in the new Latino diaspora is still in its formative stages, and at present we have more questions than answers. One question that remains to be explored, for example, is how the more limited political power of new diasporic Latino communities affects educational experiences and opportunities (see Bullock & Hood, 2006). (As evidence that Latinos in the new Latino diaspora have less political power, consider that none of the 21 members of the 110th Congress's [2007–08] Congressional Hispanic Caucus come from non-traditional, i.e., new, Latino diaspora states.)

One might hypothesize that a lack of obvious political power would manifest itself in lower educational achievement, but that does not seem to describe the new Latino diaspora in comparison to traditional settlement areas. According to the National Task Force on Early Childhood Education for Hispanics (2007) in the Northeast, Midwest, and South, both U.S.-born and immigrant Latino parents are more likely to have earned a college degree than the national average for Latinos. Also in the South and Midwest, Latino children of both immigrant parents and native-born parents are also more likely to have parents who have finished high school than the national average for Latinos (National Task Force on Early Childhood Education for Hispanics, 2007). If there is a link between accrued political power and group educational achievement, the nature of that link is not yet satisfactorily depicted.

Another issue to be addressed in future research is: How does the particular lack of Latino educators in new diaspora communities matter? Meier and Stewart (1991) long ago identified a correlation between the proportion of Latino educators, administrators, and board members, on the one hand, and how Latino students fared, on the other. They did not claim that Latino children need Latino teachers to learn well (although they did not argue against there being value to this match either). Rather they claimed that employment of Latino educators was a good proxy for measuring the available upward mobility for local Latinos.

Using Meier and Stewart's lens, there is reason for pessimism. For example, four of Nebraska's five majority Latino school districts employed no Latino teachers in 2005–06 (of 402 teachers) (Nebraska Department of Education, 2006) and only 1% of Georgia's teachers and administrators were Latino in 2005–06 (Georgia Department of Education, 2006). One proposed remedy to the lack of Latino educators has been to provide paraprofessionals from the local community with training and support to earn teacher certification (see Dalla et al., 2006), but thus far such programs have generated only a very finite supply of Latino teachers.

Another area that remains to be addressed more thoroughly is the role of race and racialized identities in Latino students' school experiences in the new diaspora. As we have noted throughout this chapter, Latinos are entering communities with historically very different racial dynamics; e.g., the Southeast with a history of experiencing race as a Black and White dichotomy (see Gilpin & Beck, 2006), and the rural Midwest dominated by non-Hispanic White descendents of European settlers, with American Indians as the "other" population (Kandel & Cromartie, 2004). As a result, established, historicized, and racialized Chicano or Latino communities or identities may not yet exist in the new diaspora in the same way they do in the Southwest, for example (Bohon et al., 2005). However, work in new Latino diaspora communities thus far already shows considerable ambivalence, paternalism (Richardson Bruna & Vann, 2007; Richardson Bruna, Vann, & Perales Escudero, 2007), xenophobia (Rich & Miranda, 2004), and some troubling processes of racialization and subordination underway (Millard, Chapa, & McConnell, 2004). We have yet to fully reckon with how Latino students entering new diaspora communities are positioned and position themselves racially, and how such positioning might affect their socialization into particular life and career pathways in and out of school.

We might also want to investigate the potential role of civic and religious organizations in Latino communities and youth adaptation and education. Such organizations have historically played a vital role in the educations of immigrant youth in new communities (Berrol, 1995). We might ask if and how such organizations are being formed and how they contribute to the educations of Latino youth in new diaspora communities. Arbelaez (2000), for example, provides an example of how civic life in one Omaha Latino community centers around church activities and is coordinated with parish legal, educational, health, and counseling services. Such work could also show how education and *educación* (Villenas, 2002) are interwoven to symbolic processes used by Latinos in new and perhaps tenuous diasporic communities to maintain a collective memory about another time and place or to reattach successive generations to the culture and traditions of homelands (see Brettell, 2006).

In the new Latino diaspora and the traditional one, a comparatively small number of schools absorb most of the growth in Latino enrollment (Fry, 2006). Sometimes, as in Lexington, Nebraska, Anglo enrollment declines (from 1,591 to 664 between 1989 and 2005) as Hispanic enrollment grows (in this case from 75 to 1,988; Nebraska Department of Education, 2006). Gouveia and Stull (1997) reported that the influx of new families to Lexington in the late 1990s was also accompanied by a significant increase in student turnover. One particularly urgent issue is to find ways for these small town and rural schools, accustomed to highly stable populations and strong informal social networks, to adapt school-home communication and record keeping for a new student population that is more mobile and largely unconnected to existing informal networks.

In her blog for *Education Week*, Mary Ann Zehr (2007) noted that there was little research on how immigrant students and ELLs were faring in the Great Plains and then pointed to Lourdes Gouviea's work at the University of Nebraska-Omaha's Office of Latino and Latin American Studies (OLLAS) as an important exception (citing Gouviea, 2006, and Gouviea & Powell, 2007). Zehr seemed unaware of pioneering older work from Mark Grey in Garden City, Kansas in the early 1990s and current work by Richardson Bruna in a meatpacking town in Iowa (e.g., Richardson Bruna & Vann, 2007; Richardson Bruna, Vann, & Perales Escudero, 2007). Conceding that there are exceptions to Zehr's claim, that she makes such a claim was hardly surprising. Media accounts of newcomers and schooling, precipitated in some instances by ICE raids and the recent nationwide debate about an overhaul of immigration laws, clearly are more numerous and visible than scholarly works. Moreover, the scholarly works that do exist are not necessarily easily found, not least because of the abundance of research on the four fifths of Latino children who do not reside in the new Latino diaspora.[2] Zehr's claims are also unsurprising given the relative neglect of homegrown scholarship on diaspora communities. The preponderance of media attention and funding in recent years for work on the new Latino diaspora has gone to agencies and scholars from outside the affected communities, and this work may not always reflect a full understanding of the history or social contexts of new diaspora areas. We are also lacking in work that is explicitly comparative in nature (although see Stamps & Bohon, 2006). In preparing this review, for example, we encountered several studies that, while conducted in new diaspora areas, were nonetheless of limited value in elucidating how educational experiences might be similar to or different from the abundant existing research from established Latino settlement areas.

Finally, while the role of schools in producing low levels of Latino educational achievement elsewhere in the United States has been underscored, we have yet to explore the place of schools as potential sites for community support and advocacy for Latino families in new diaspora communities. Sink, Parkhill, Marshall, and Norwood (2005), for example, describe how a partnership was established between a community college and school district to provide literacy and academic instruction for Latino families and concurrent Spanish instruction for educators in one North Carolina community. More dramatically, in 2006 when six concurrent U.S. Immigration and Customs Enforcement (ICE) raids at Swift Company meatpacking plants in Minnesota, Iowa, Nebraska, Utah, Colorado, and northern Texas led to the deportation of thousands and the division of undocumented parents from their U.S. citizen children, newspapers chronicled how schools became places of refuge for children whose home life had just been turned upside down (e.g., Jacobs, 2006; Lucin, 2006).

Conclusion

Almost by definition, the concept of a "new" Latino diaspora will continue to change and evolve. The phenomenon presents educational researchers with a tremendous opportunity to trace the evolution of new communities as they become established and enter the second and third generations. Whether new diaspora communities thrive will depend on the evolution of U.S. immigration policy. The signs here are ominous. In 2007 an anti-immigration tide brought down the U.S. Senate's attempt to forge a bill on comprehensive immigration reform. Much of the opposition to the bill came from the South and Midwest, two regions of the country with unprecedented recent Latino immigration and in-migration. In 2008, nativism appears ascendant, or at least powerful, and the prospects that Latino children—immigrant or fourth generation—will be viewed without the paternalism, fear, intolerance, or subordination seems less sure than when these new patterns of migration began.

Yet there remains some promising and innovative educational news coming from the new Latino diaspora as well. Several new Latino diaspora states have crafted "Dream Act" state laws permitting undocumented high school graduates to pay in-state tuition for college (Herrera, Morales, & Murry, 2007). Jacobson (2003) reports that a school readiness pre-K program in Tulsa, Oklahoma, targeting African American and Latino children had particularly favorable effects on Latino youngsters' test scores. In Siler City, North Carolina, *Time* magazine reporter Paul Cuadros (2006) wrote an inspirational story about a state championship soccer team made up predominantly of Latino newcomers. Hamann and colleagues (2002) once raised the prospect that maybe, away from Florida, California, New York, Texas, Arizona, New Mexico, Illinois, New Jersey, and Colorado—with their entrenched habits of Latino under-education—just maybe, in the new Latino diaspora things would be better. So far that prospect seems too often unrealized. There are success stories, but not yet any large-scale success systems.

Notes

1. The SREB states where the ACT is the dominant college entrance test include: Alabama, Arkansas, Kentucky, Louisiana, Mississippi, Oklahoma, Tennessee, and West Virginia. The SREB states where the SAT predominates include: Delaware, Florida, Georgia, Maryland, North Carolina, South Carolina, Texas, and Virginia. Texas and Florida are excluded from this calculation (as both are traditional Latino diaspora locations) although the White/Hispanic test score gap widened in both of those states too.
2. According to the National Task Force on Early Childhood Education for Hispanics, 2007, one fifth of the 6,797,303 Hispanic 0- to 8-year-olds counted by the 2000 Census lived in the 41 states of the new Latino diaspora.

References

Arbelaez, M. S. (2000). Good Friday in Omaha, Nebraska: A Mexican celebration. Paper presented at the National Association of African American Studies & National Association of Hispanic and Latino Studies 2000 Literature Monograph Series. Proceedings (Culture Section), Houston, TX.

Beck, S. A. L., & Allexsaht-Snider, M. (2002). Recent language minority education policy in Georgia: Appropriation, assimilation, and Americanization. In S. Wortham, E. G. Murillo, & E. T. Hamann (Eds.), *Education in the new Latino diaspora: Policy and the politics of identity* (pp. 37–66). Westport, CT: Ablex.

Berg, C. R. (2002). *Latino images in film: Stereotypes, subversion, & resistance.* Austin: University of Texas Press.

Berrol, S. C. (1995). *Growing up American: Immigrant children in America, then and now.* New York: Twayne Publishers.

Bohon, S. A., Macpherson, H., & Atiles, J. H. (2005). Educational barriers for new Latinos in Georgia. *Journal of Latinos and Education, 41,* 43–58.

Bullock, C. S., & Hood, M. V. (2006). A mile-wide gap: The evolution of Hispanic political emergence in the deep South. *Social Science Quarterly, 87,* 1117–1135.

Brettell, C. B. (2006). Introduction: Global spaces/local places: Transnationalism, diaspora, and the meaning of home. *Identities: Global Studies in Culture and Power, 13,* 327–334.

Campbell, M. (2005, October 4). Post-Katrina easing of labor laws stirs debate: Foreign workers may form a big part of Gulf Coast reconstruction effort. *Christian Science Monitor.* Retrieved July 16, 2009, from http://www.csmonitor.com

Campbell, P. R. (1996). *Population Projections for States, by Age, Sex, Race and Hispanic Origin: 1995 to 2025, Report PPL-47.* Washington, DC: U.S. Bureau of the Census, Population Division.

Capps, R., Fix, M., Murray, J., Ost, J., Passel, J. S., & Herwantoro Hernandez, S. (2005). *The New demography of America's Schools: Immigration and the No Child Left Behind Act.* Washington, DC: Urban Institute. Retrieved June 14, 2007, from http://www.urban.org/publications/311230.html

Cortina, R., & Gendreau, M. (Eds.). (2003). *Immigrants and schooling: Mexicans in New York.* New York: Center for Migration Studies.

Cuadros, P. (2006). *A home on the field: How one championship team inspires hope for the revival of small town America.* New York: Rayo.

Dalla, R. L., Gupta, P. M., Lopez, W. E., & Jones, V. (2006). "It's a balancing act!": Exploring school/work/family interface issues among bilingual, rural Nebraska, paraprofessional educators. *Family Relations, 55,* 390–402.

Dauber, S. L., & Epstein, J. L. (1993). Parent attitudes and practices of involvement in inner-city elementary and middles schools. In N. F. Chauvkin (Ed.), *Families and schools in a pluralistic society* (pp. 53–71). Albany: State University of New York Press.

Editorial Projects in Education Research Center. Education Week. (2007). *Ready for what? Preparing students for college, careers, and life after high school.* Washington, DC: Education Week Research Center. Retrieved July 16, 2007, from http://www.edweek.org/ew/articles/2007/06/12/40sgb.h26.html

Fry, R. (2006). *The changing landscape of American public education: New students, new schools.* Washington, DC: Pew Hispanic Center.

Georgia Department of Education. (2006). *2005–2006 K-12 Public Schools Annual Report Card.* Atlanta, GA: Author. Retrieved June 19, 2007, from http://reportcard2006.gaosa.org/k12/persfiscal.aspx?TestType=pers&ID=ALL:ALL

Gilpin, L., & Beck, S. A. L. (2006). Voices from the margins: Black Caribbean and Mexican heritage women and educators in the rural South. *Journal of Praxis in Multicultural Education 1,* 29–44.

Gouviea, L. (2006). Nebraska's responses to immigration: Nebraska's context of reception, the role of policy and community responses. In G. Anrig & T. A. Wang (Eds.), *Immigration's new frontiers: Experiences for the emerging gateway states* (pp. 143–227). New York: The New Century Press.

Gouviea, L., Carranza, M., & Cogua, J. (2005). The Great Plains migration: Mexicanos and Latinos in Nebraska. In V. Zúñiga & R. Hernández-León (Eds.), *New destinations: Mexican immigration in the United States* (pp. 23–49). New York: Russell Sage.

Gouviea, L., & Powell, M.A. (2007). *Second generation Latinos in Nebraska: A first look.* Washington, DC: Migration Policy Institute.

Gouveia, L., & Stull, D. D. (1997). *Latino immigrants, meatpacking, and rural communities: A case study of Lexington, Nebraska.* East Lansing, MI: Julian Samora Research Institute.

Grey, M. A. (1993). Applying concepts of marginality to secondary ESL programs: Challenges for practitioners and researchers. In *Proceeding of the third national research symposium on limited English proficient student issues: Focus on middle and high school issues, Washington DC, August 1992* (pp. 831–850). Washington, DC: U.S. Department of Education, Office of Bilingual Education and Minority Language Affairs.

Grey, M. A. (2006). State and local immigration policy in Iowa. In G. Anrig & T. A. Wang (Eds.), *Immigration's new frontiers: Experiences for the emerging gateway states* (pp. 33–66). New York: The New Century Press.

Hamann, E. T. (2003). *The educational welcome of Latinos in the New South.* Westport, CT: Praeger.

Hamann, E. T., Wortham, S., & Murillo, E. G. (2002). Education and policy in the new Latino diaspora. In S. Wortham, E. G. Murillo, & E. T. Hamann (Eds.), *Education in the new Latino diaspora* (pp. 1–16). Westport, CT: Ablex.

Herrera, S., Morales, A., & Murry, K. (2007). *Navigating the tides of social and political capriciousness: Potential CLD student beneficiaries of the DREAM Act in the Midwest.* Paper presented April 10 at the American Educational Research Association annual meeting. Chicago, IL.

Herrera-Sobek, M. (1993). *Northward bound: The Mexican immigrant experience in ballad and song.* Bloomington: Indiana University Press.

Jacobs, J. (2006, December 17). Mom, kids spend 3 days in agony. *Des Moines Register.* Retrieved Dec. 21, 2006, from: http://www.desmoinesregister.com/apps/pbcs.dll/article?AID=2006612170327

Jacobson, L. (2003, October 29). Oklahoma Pre-K program found effective. *Education Week.* Retrieved June 30, 2007, from http://www.edweek.org/ew/articles/2003/10/29/09okla.h23.html?qs=@0+Hispanic+Latino

Kandel, W., & Cromartie, J. (2004). *New patterns of Hispanic settlement in rural America.* Washington, DC: United State Department of Agriculture. Economic Research Service.

Kochhar, R., Suro, R., & Tafoya, S. (2005). *The new Latino South: The context and consequences of rapid population growth.* Washington, DC: Pew Hispanic Center. Retrieved June 19, 2007, from http://pewhispanic.org/reports/report.php?ReportID=50

Lacey, M. (2006, November 5). Guatemala system is scrutinized as Americans rush in to adopt. *New York Times*, Section 1, pp. 1, 6.

Lovato, R. (2005, November 15). Gulf Coast slaves. Salon.com. Retrieved June 28, 2007, from http://dir.salon.com/story/news/feature/2005/11/15/halliburton_katrina/index.html

Lucin, K. (2006, December 14). Community prepares to help displaced children. *Worthington Daily Globe*. Retrieved Dec. 17, 2006, from http://www.dglobe.com/articles/index.cfm?id=3239&section=collections

Lukose, R. (2007). Reflections from the field: The difference that diaspora makes: Thinking through the anthropology of immigrant education in the United States. *Anthropology & Education Quarterly, 38*(4), 405–418.

Mastro, D. E. (2003). A social identity approach to understanding the impact of television messages. *Communication Monographs, 70*(2), 98–113.

Mastro, D. E., & Behm-Morawitz, E. (2005). A social identity approach to understanding the impact of television messages. *Journalism and Mass Communication Quarterly, 82*(1), 110–130.

McConnell, E. D. (2004). Latinos in the rural Midwest: The twentieth-century historical context leading to contemporary challenges. In A. V. Millard & J. Chapa (Eds.), *Apple pie & enchiladas: Latino newcomers in the rural midwest* (pp. 26–40). Austin: University of Texas Press.

Meier, K., & Stewart, J. (1991). *The Politics of Hispanic Education: Un paso pa'lante y dos pa'tras.* Albany: State University of New York Press.

Merriam-Webster Inc. (2003). *Merriam-Webster's collegiate dictionary* (11th ed.). Springfield, MA: Merriam-Webster Inc.

Millard, A. V., Chapa, J., & McConnell, E. D. (2004). 'Not racist like our parents': Anti-Latino prejudice and institutional discrimination. In A. V. Millard & J. Chapa (Eds.), *Apple pie & enchiladas: Latino newcomers in the rural midwest* (pp. 102–124). Austin: University of Texas Press.

Murillo, E., & Villenas, S. (1997). East of Aztlán: Typologies of resistance in North Carolina communities. Paper presented at *Reclaiming Voices: Ethnographic inquiry and qualitative research in a postmodern age,* Los Angeles.

National Center for Educational Statistics. (1998). *Downloadable Tables from the compendium: State Comparisons of Education Statistics: 1969–70 to 1996–97.* Washington, DC: U.S. Department of Education. Retrieved January 29, 2008, from: http://nces.ed.gov/pubs98/98018/#chap2a

National Center for Educational Statistics. (2007). *Public Elementary and Secondary School Student Enrollment, High School Completions, and Staff from the Common Core of Data: School Year 2005–06: Table 2.* Washington, DC: U.S. Department of Education. Retrieved January 29, 2008, from http://nces.ed.gov/pubs2007/pesenroll06/tables.asp

National Task Force on Early Childhood Education for Hispanics. (2007). *Para nuestros niños: A demographic portrait of young Hispanic children in the United States.* Tempe, AZ: Mary Lou Fulton College of Education, Arizona State University.

Nebraska Department of Education. (2006). *2005–2006 State of the Schools Report A Report on Nebraska Public Schools.* Lincoln, NE: Author. Retrieved January 27, 2008, from http://reportcard.nde.state.ne.us/20052006/Main/Home.aspx

Oboler, S. (1995). *Ethnic labels, Latino lives: Identity and the politics of (re)presentation in the United States.* Minneapolis: University of Minnesota Press.

Passel, J. S. (2006). *The size and characteristics of the unauthorized migrant population in the U.S.* Washington, DC: Pew Hispanic Center. Retrieved June 19, 2007, from http://pewhispanic.org/reports/report.php?ReportID=61

Pew Hispanic Center. (2003). *Pew Hispanic Center fact sheet: Hispanics in the military.* Retrieved July 30, 2007, from pewhispanic.org/files/factsheets/6.pdf

Pew Hispanic Center. (2006). *Estimates of the unauthorized migrant population for states based on the March 2005 CPS.* Washington, DC: Author. Retrieved June 19, 2007, from http://pewhispanic.org/factsheets/factsheet.php?FactsheetID=17

Portes, A., Guarnizo, L. E., & Haller, W.J (2002). Transnational entrepreneurs: An alternative form of immigrant economic adaptation. *American Sociological Review, 67*(2), 278–298.

Ricento, T. (2000). *Ideology, politics, and language policies: Focus on English.* Philadelphia: John Benjamins.

Rich, B. L., & Miranda, M. (2004). The sociopolitical dynamics of Mexican immgration in Lexington, Kentucky, 1997 to 2002: An ambivalent community responds. In V. Zúniga & R. Hernández-León (Eds.), *New destinations: Mexican immigration in the United States* (pp. 187–219). New York: Russell Sage Foundation.

Richardson Bruna, K. (2007). Traveling tags: The informal literacies of Mexican newcomers in and out of the classroom. *Linguistics and Education, 18*, 232–257.

Richardson Bruna, K., & Vann, R. (2007). On pigs & packers: Radically contextualizing a practice of science with Mexican immigrant students. *Cultural Studies of Science Education, 2*, 19–59.

Richardson Bruna, K., Vann, R., & Perales Escudero, M. (2007). What's language got to do with it?: A case study of academic language instruction in a high school 'English Learner Science' classroom. *Journal of English for Academic Purposes, 6*(1), 36–54.

Schmid, C. (2003). Immigration and Asian and Hispanic minorities in the New South: An exploration of the history, attitudes, and demographic trends. *Sociological Spectrum, 23*, 129–157.

Singer, A. (2004, February). The rise of new immigrant gateways. *Living Cities Census Series.* Washington, DC: Brookings Institution: Center on Urban and Metropolitan Policy.

Sink, D. W., Parkhill, M. A., Marshall, R., & Norwood, S. (2005). Learning together: A family-centered literacy program. *Community College Journal of Research and Practice, 29*, 583–590.

Southern Regional Education Board. (2007). *Improving SAT and ACT scores: Making progress, facing challenges.* Atlanta, GA: Author.

Stamps, K., & Bohon, S. A. (2006). Educational attainment in new and established Latino metropolitan destinations. *Social Science Quarterly, 87*, 1225–1240.

Suro, R., & Singer, A. (2002). *Latino growth in metropolitan America: Changing patterns, new locations.* Washington, DC: Brookings Institution.

Tomás Rivera Policy Institute. (2004). *The new Latino South and the challenge to public education: Strategies for educators and policymakers in emerging immigrant communities.* Los Angeles: Author.

U.S. Census Bureau. (2007). Table 3: Annual Estimates of the Population by Sex, Race, and Hispanic or Latino Origin for Washington: April 1, 2000 to July 1, 2006 (SC-EST2006-03-53). Washington, DC: Author.

Villenas, S. (2002). Reinventing *educación* in new Latino communities: Pedagogies of change and continuity in North Carolina. In S. Wortham, E. G. Murillo, & E. T. Hamann (Eds.), *Education in the new Latino diaspora* (pp. 17–36). Westport, CT: Ablex.

Villenas, S. (2007). Diaspora and the anthropology of Latino education: Challenges, affinities, and intersections. *Anthropology & Education Quarterly, 38*(4), 419–425.

Wortham, S., & Contreras, M. (2002). Struggling towards culturally relevant pedagogy in the Latino Diaspora. *Journal of Latinos and Education, 1*(2), 133–144.

Wortham, S., Murillo, E. G., & Hamann, E. T. (Eds.). (2002). *Education in the new Latino diaspora: Policy and the politics of identity.* Westport, CT: Ablex.

Zehr, M. A. (2002, March 27). Ore. School district reaches out to new arrivals from Mexico. *Education Week.* Retrieved June 29, 2007, from http://www.edweek.org/ew/articles/2002/03/27/28hillsboro.h21.html?qs=@0+Hispanic+Latino

Zehr, M.A. (2005, May 11). Influx of new students can outpace teacher preparation: But training programs don't always find a receptive audience. *Education Week.* Retrieved June 29, 2007, from http://www.edweek.org/ew/ articles/2005/05/11/36teachers.h24.html

Zehr, M. A. (2006, November 8). Cristo Rey schools receive $6 million to expand network. *Education Week.* Retrieved July 30, 2007, from http://www.edweek.org/ew/articles/2006/11/08/11briefs-2.h26.html?qs=cristo+rey

Zehr, M. A. (2007, March 19). Immigrants and ELLs on the Great Plains. *Learning the Language Blog at Education Week.* Retrieved June 28, 2007, from http://blogs.edweek.org/edweek/learning-the-language/2007/03/immigrants_and_ells_on_the_gre_1.html?qs=Latino

Zúñiga, V., & Hamann, E. T. (2006). Going home? Schooling in Mexico of transnational children. *CONfines de relaciones internacionales y ciencia política, 2*(4), 41–57.

Zúñiga, V., & Hernández-León, R. (Eds.). (2005). *New destinations: Mexican immigration in the United States.* New York: Russell Sage.

10 Construction of Race and Ethnicity for and by Latinos

Edward Fergus, Pedro Noguera, and Margary Martin
New York University

Since the 1990s, the national discourse on Latinos has focused on the growing presence of America's new largest minority group—who are they, where are they coming from, are they legal, and will they assimilate. Even though many scholars have documented the extraordinary diversity of the Latino population with respect to national origin, ethnic and phenotypic diversity, the face of Latinos on CNN, Fox News, and MSNBC is, more often than not, White or at best bronze (Candelario, 2007; Rivera, 2007).

According to the 2000 Census, over 35 million Latinos were living in the United States By mid-decade, this number rose to 42 million, and the 2007 American Community Survey estimates Latino groups at 45 million. The rapid and dramatic growth of the Latino population represented 51% of the change in racial/ethnic groups between 2000 and 2005 (Pew Hispanic, 2006). Given our shared border, the majority of the 42 million (64%) are Mexican, followed by Puerto Ricans (9.1%), Cubans (3.5%), Salvadorans (3.0%), and Dominicans (1.7%). In the 2000 Census, over 900,000 (2.7%) self-identified as Black Hispanic and 17.6 million (47.9%) as White Hispanic, and yet another 15 million (42.2%) identified as "some other race" (Logan, 2003). The Black Hispanic as an identification was most prominent among Dominicans (12.7%) followed by Puerto Ricans (8.2%), Cubans (4.7%), and finally Central Americans (4.1%) (Logan, 2003). On the other hand, White Hispanic identification is most prevalent among Cubans (85.4%) followed by South Americans (61.1%); Mexicans (49.3%); and then Puerto Ricans (49%). In 2007, these identification patterns changed; ACS estimates 677,000 (1.5%) self-identify as Black Hispanic and 24 million (54.3%) self-identify as White Hispanic and another 18 million (40%) self-identify as "other race." This difference in race and ethnic identification between 2000 and 2007 could either signal a particular migration pattern among Latino groups entering the United States or a shift in the identification patterns of Latino groups. Whatever the specific explanation for this shift, Latino groups still need to situate their identification as both a race and ethnicity.

Over the last three decades the US Census has situated Hispanics as a distinct ethnic group (Rodriguez, 2000). Since the enactment of Public Law 94-311, "Economic and Social Statistics for Americans of Spanish Origin." on June 16, 1976, Hispanic origin and race have been included jointly in the decennial census. Anyone familiar with the diversity among those who identify (and are identified as) Latinos will recognize the irony of this designation because Hispanics can come from any racial group. Still, the creation of the Hispanic category can be seen as somewhat of an accomplishment given that prior to 1980 Hispanics were identified as Hispanics, even though the rights and privileges accorded to Hispanics in terms of public education, housing, and even voting rights, were often not the same as those held by Whites (Ruiz, 2007).

In the 2000 Census, Latinos were required to answer both race and ethnicity questions: Question #7: Is Person 1 Spanish/Hispanic/Latino? And Question #8: What is Person's 1 race? (See Figure 10.1.)

These questions from the US Census continued maintained the distinction between race and ethnicity. That is, while race has historically been used in reference to essential biological group

➔ **NOTE: Please answer BOTH Questions 7 and 8.**

7. Is Person 1 Spanish/Hispanic/Latino? *Mark* ☒ *the* **"No"** *box if* ***not*** *Spanish/Hispanic/Latino.*

☐ **No,** not Spanish/Hispanic/Latino   ☐ Yes, Puerto Rican
☐ Yes, Mexican, Mexican Am., Chicano   ☐ Yes, Cuban
☐ Yes, other Spanish/Hispanic/Latino — *Print group.* ↘

| | | | | | | | | | | | | | | | | | | | | | |

8. What is Person 1's race? *Mark* ☒ *one or more races* to *indicate what this person considers himself/herself to be.*

☐ White
☐ Black, African Am., or Negro
☐ American Indian or Alaska Native — *Print name of enrolled or principal tribe.* ↘

| | | | | | | | | | | | | | | | | | | | | | |

☐ Asian Indian   ☐ Japanese   ☐ Native Hawaiian
☐ Chinese   ☐ Korean   ☐ Guamanian or Chamorro
☐ Filipino   ☐ Vietnamese ☐ Samoan
☐ Other Asian — *Print race.* ↘   ☐ Other Pacific Islander — *Print race.* ↘

| | | | | | | | | | | | | | | | | | | | | | |

☐ Some other race — *Print race.* ↘

| | | | | | | | | | | | | | | | | | | | | | |

Figure 10.1 United States Census Form 2000.

differences, ethnicity has primarily been used to draw distinctions between groups based upon religion, culture, language, and even nationality. Given the confusion surrounding these categories, it is not surprising that the operation of these policy definitions utilized by the federal government do not serve as a basis for everyday race-making (Lewis, 2003) for those who identify as Latino.

For many Latinos, the meaning making of what is race and ethnicity is a complex process. For many, it can involve an ongoing tension between the subjective (who I think I am) and objective (who others think I am) dimensions about race that may not be easily resolved (Fergus, 2004). For others, especially recent immigrants, there is the additional confusion that arises from the fact that the categories operative in Latin America are not operative in the U.S. context. For example, whereas phenotype figures prominently in the racial categories utilized in most Latin American countries, the United States has historically treated racial categories as immutable, rooted in biology, and tied to the Black-White binary (Almaguer, 1994). And yet for other Latinos, the use and non-use of racial categories is tied to perceived social meanings of self-identifying as White, Black, or Asian. And these social meanings have significance in everyday mobility. For example, the educational attainment of those who identify as Black Hispanic is higher than White Hispanic (a mean 11.7 years vs. 10.5 years), however Black Hispanics have a lower median income, higher unemployment, and higher poverty rates than White Hispanics (Logan, 2003). Such discrepancies in the relationship between income and educational attainment are highly significant because for most groups in American society there is a high degree of correspondence between these patterns. Similar differences between Black and White Latinos have also been noted in studies on skin color and labor market participation (Espino & Franz, 2002), and political activities and attitudes (Hochschild, et. al., 2006). Such complexities and ambiguities necessitate the exploration of the following question: how should Latinos fit into the

U.S. social landscape with respect to the well established race and ethnicity constructs? More importantly, should Latinos utilize current race constructs that are based on a Black-White paradigm to explain the "otherizing" of Latinos, or is a tri-fold racial hierarchy as articulated by Bonilla-Silva (2004) necessary? Or should Latinos solely be constructed as an ethnicity with differing racial categories? Also, given the subjective nature of these racial designations one question that emerges is just how "White" and/or "Black" are Latinos? That is, even though they may lay claim to Whiteness or Blackness to what degree are they accepted and treated as White or Black in the communities where they reside?

The purpose of this chapter is to provide a historical outline of the predominant theories on race and ethnicity and what they have meant for those who identify as Latino. We also examine the ways in which the concept of race does and does not consider the interaction of markers such as language, skin color, and culture found among Latino national groups. Drawing upon Cornell and Hartmann's (1998) construct of race as external and ascribed, and ethnicity as an internally constructed concept, we extrapolate on the applicability of race and ethnicity and its utility to the experiences of Latinos. Our particular focus is in the theoretical expansion of the discourse on race and ethnicity, and its potential in interpreting disparate social mobility and educational outcomes within Latino groups, such as the high drop-out rate among Mexicans, Puerto Ricans, and Dominicans and the low drop out rate among White Cubans.

Theoretical Conversations of Race/Ethnicity

The Meaning of Race as Social Construct

Numerous social scientists have pointed out that U.S. notions of race and ethnicity have been premised on a Black-White dichotomy or continuum. This dual framework of race and ethnic construction subjugates all groups to define themselves within this dichotomy or continuum (Bashi & McDaniel, 1997; Bonilla-Silva, 2004). As Andrew Hacker (1992) suggests, "[i]n many respects, others groups find themselves sitting as spectators, while the two prominent players try to work out how or whether they can co-exist with one another" (p. 38). The dominant paradigm of race, which positions Whites as the superior group and Blacks as the inferior (the ultimate "other"), has shaped the ways in which Americans have thought about race and racial disparities. Throughout much of the 19th century, race was used as the primary basis for determining rights and status in American society, and those regarded as non-Whites—Asians, Native Americans, Latinos, and even some Eastern Europeans—were generally denied privileges held by Whites (Fredrickson, 2002). For example, prior to a Supreme Court ruling early in the 20th century that Armenians were in fact Whites (this was a reversal of an earlier ruling), they experienced many of the same forms of discrimination that non-Whites were subjected to—segregated housing and education, limited rights in the courts, etc. (Takaki, 1987). After World War II and especially after the passage of civil rights legislation and changes in immigration policy in the mid-1960s, the system of racial hierarchy became complex even as the Black-White paradigm remained intact. Increasingly, groups were assigned status by virtue of their proximity to either Blacks or Whites. The relative success of Asians in education and employment led to an "upgrading" of Asians such that they were increasingly regarded as "honorary Whites" (Lee, 1994). Meanwhile, Latinos were more often than not lumped together with Blacks and Native Americans as disadvantaged minorities.

Regardless of the time period, Latinos have posed a quandary for those who sought to situate them within the American racial hierarchy. This is because diversity related to region, nationality, socioeconomic status and, most importantly, phenotype, has played an important role in determining how Latinos have been treated. Several scholarly analyses of the discrimination experienced by Latinos in the United States have consciously or unconsciously ignored this diversity as they have applied the dominant Black-White racial paradigm to an examination of the Latino experience. For example, although Carnoy's *Faded Dreams* (1998) provides a well-documented historical analysis of the ways in which changes in federal policies related to civil rights have affected opportunities for African Americans, his treatment of Latinos is at best superficial. Rather than taking the time to carefully interrogate the variegated experience of Latinos, Carnoy simply throws in "and Latinos," as though the Latino experience could be assumed to be equivalent to that of Blacks (Carnoy, 1998). A similar approach has been taken in several other important scholarly treatments of race in recent years (Massey, 1998; Omi & Winant, 1989). While such an approach may have been useful in cases where Latinos have been subject to blatant forms of discrimination on the basis of race, this paradigm has not been as useful for understanding the nuanced social histories of Latinos when other factors, namely, immigration status, nationality or phenotype, may have been more important in understanding the experience of particular groups. For example, long before the ban on inclusion was lifted for Blacks, there are several examples where Latinos played professional baseball, served in the military, attended White segregated schools, and held public office in states that practiced blatant racial discrimination (Almaguer, 1994). Such examples should not be taken as proof that Latinos were treated as Whites because they co-exist with other examples of blatant discrimination directed specifically at Latinos (e.g., racial segregation in schools). However, the historic contradictions and inconsistencies in the treatment of Latinos should force us to rethink the narrow restrictions created by the Black-White paradigm of race.

Biology Confuses Us

Throughout most of the 20th century, the social construction and social discourse on race treated group differences as though they were rooted in innate biological distinctions (Lipsitz, 1998). Within this framework, racial differences were regarded as conferring certain biologically determined advantages on Whites—superior intellect, and disadvantages on Blacks—a proclivity for criminal and licentious behavior. With Blacks serving as the negative reference point, membership in the White racial category was used as the basis for extending important rights and privileges to some, and denying these to others (Omi & Winant, 1989). By essentializing race in this way, and supporting these racist notions with numerous pseudo-scientific studies that argued physical differences existed (i.e., neurological, IQ, cranial, etc.; Jensen, 1979; Morton, 1849), "Whiteness" and "Blackness" could be used as the basis for constructing a racial hierarchy. Latinos, like Asians, people of mixed racial heritage, middle easterners, and others, were in turn placed along the Black-White racial hierarchy, never as equal to Whites, but above Blacks. While such a position of limited privilege contained its own hardships and indignities, Latinos could find solace in the fact that at least they were better off than Blacks.

This biological-based race definition began formally with the development of the Eugenics Education Society in 1907 (later Eugenics Society). As a term, "eugenics" involves the scientific marking of hereditary traits. "Scientists" associated with eugenics were preoccupied with finding ways to promote genetic traits associated with superior intellect and physical ability, and discouraging and even eliminating those associated with inferiority. One part of the agenda of the Eugenics Education Society was to utilize the information of hereditary traits in the explanation of "poverty and pauperism" (Kenny, 2004). Prominent researchers, Charles Galton Darwin, Leonard Darwin, Robert Baker, and others argued the inequalities experienced by Blacks, Latinos, and Native Americans were due to genetic deficiencies that were reflected in cultural attributes. Long after the Society lost its influence and credibility (due in part to its similarity with Nazism), this line of research assisted in the development of terms such as "culture of poverty" and "cultural deficiency." The publication of *The Bell Curve* (1996) by Hernstein and Murray and recent comments by Nobel Laureate Charles Watson, serve as a potent reminder that the idea of innate racial superiority of Whites over Blacks is still very much alive in this country.

With few exceptions, for much of the 20th century sociologists moved away from the notion of race as a biological concept (i.e., skin color, hair texture, and other features). With the emergence of the Chicago School of sociology social scientists began treating race as a social construct (e.g., DuBois, 1899; Drake & Cayton, 1945; Myrdal, 1944) that had to be understood as a by-product of the particular historical experience of the United States. In what is widely regarded as one of the most important theoretical treatments on race in the last twenty years, Omi and Winant (1994) argue that even though early efforts to use race as a demarcation of social status and privilege attempted to use physical variations among humans as the basis for their system of classification, they were forced to recognize that such distinctions were arbitrary and fraught with ambiguity. Given America's long history of race mixing, there is a high degree of variability with respect to phenotype within group. Therefore, it is the social meanings that humans place upon physical markers such as hair texture and skin color that matter far more than any "objective" or "scientific" distinctions. Winant defines race as "a concept that signifies and symbolizes sociopolitical conflicts and interests in reference to different human bodies" (2000, p. 172), and he adds that there is a contextualization that assigns meaning to biological or physical features. That is, even though the darkness of Black skin color has been used to justify discrimination against them, some Blacks are light enough to "pass" and as light as individuals classified as White. For this reason, several scholars have treated the American concept of race as a social construct that can only be understood within the context of America's sordid history of race relations (Cornell & Hartmann, 1998).

Other research on race as a social construct and the perpetuation of racial inequities also illuminated the presence of racial hierarchies with an awareness that they operate differently in relation to multiple groups (Bashi & McDaniel, 1997). The construct of racial hierarchy is loosely defined as the stratification of racial categorization with Whites at the top and Blacks at the bottom (Song, 2004). The stratification of Whites on top comes from social and economic-based privileges in the form of institutionalized racism that has allowed for wealth accumulation and other forms of social mobility (Bobo, Keugel, & Smith, 1997; Hacker, 1992). The stratification of Blacks at the bottom is determined by a socio-history of negative social and economic policies based on the privileging of Whites and subjugating of Blacks. Much of this racial hierarchy construct is situated on a history of discrimination and systematic exclusion, which few groups have experienced similar to Native Americans and Black Americans. Although there is much agreement in the presence of a racial hierarchy, there is less agreement as to what groups are experiencing it the worst and more importantly whether it is a static hierarchy. Proponents of the Black-White binary model of racial hierarchy (e.g., Feagin, 2000; Hacker, 1992) posit this framework is the basis of oppression for other non-White groups. Feagin argues that the oppression other groups experience (i.e., Arabs, Latinos, Asians) experience is based on an anti-Black framework; "white elites and the white public have long evaluated, reacted to, and dominated later non-European entrants coming into the nation from within a previously established and highly imbedded system of antiblack racism" (pp. 204–205). This argument is exemplified in the experiences of non-U.S. native Blacks also experiencing racial discrimination, even though they assert a Black immigrant identity (Kasinitz, 1992; Waters, 1994). In addition, proponents of the Black-White model also look to the dominant narrative of assimilation (i.e., gaining English language proficiency, attainment of U.S. citizenship, etc.) as having occurred among Black Americans but not resulting in the social mobility found among European immigrants.

On the other side of this conversation are the proponents of the racial hierarchy who consider the racialization experiences of other groups beyond Blacks and Whites as expanding our notions of the racial hierarchy (Almaguer, 1994; Bashi & McDaniel, 1997; Bonilla-Silva, 2004). This line of research posits a need for expanding racial hierarchy beyond Black-White and to consider other factors beyond skin color, such as religion (Arab-Americans), citizenship (Latinos), culture (Indians), and language. Several researchers note the experiences of race riots (Yoon, 1997), and the racial tensions between Black Americans and Asians, and Mexicans (Murguia & Foreman, 2003) as representing some of the inapplicability of the Black-White model. More specifically, the Black-White model of racial hierarchy centers racial discrimination and oppression as solely skin-color bound, however the discrimination research on new immigrants, particularly Asians and Latinos exemplify oppression as multimodal.

The construction of race and its racial hierarchy matters significantly for Latinos because the daily operation of these hierarchies primarily relies on skin color. The skin color variation among Latinos highlighted earlier and the differential outcomes along these variations makes the application of racial hierarchy a very pertinent construct in defining who is allowed to be Latino and what are the social mobility consequences. Numerous studies of Latinos and these variations illuminate the slippery operation of this racial hierarchy because it presents that some Latinos are not able to exist as Latino but rather solely Black or White. For instance, in a study of Puerto Ricans in New York City, Rodriguez and Cordero-Guzman (1992) noted that among 240 randomly selected Puerto Ricans, 40% of the sample saw themselves differently from the way in which they perceived that Americans (Whites) viewed them. Additionally, the participant's ethnic/racial identification was strongly influenced by their perceptions of how Americans identify them. For example, participants that believed North Americans viewed them as White were more inclined to identify themselves as White. Such findings were also apparent in a study of Mexican Americans in which the 546 respondents used various ethnic identities depending on context in order to minimize their social distance from those with whom they interacted (Saenz & Aguirre, 1991). In another study of high school Mexican and Puerto Rican students of varying skin color (i.e., White-looking, Hispanic/Mexican-looking, and Black/Biracial-looking), there was a continuing vacillating of race and ethnicity identification (Fergus, 2004). More specifically, the darker skin Latinos primarily situated a Black identity within their interactions with African Americans, while the lighter skin Latinos went back and forth between a White and/ or an ethnic identity. Such differences also moderated their perceptions of opportunity and engagement in school. Other studies of skin color variation among Chicanos in the southwestern United States also noted differences in educational attainment between dark and light skin Chicanos (Murguia & Telles, 1996), as well as Dominicans and Cubans (Aguirre & Bonilla-Silva, 2002). In these studies, we are able to understand that multiple Latino groups are cognizant of how skin color signifies a racial and ethnic identification, as well as in aggregate analyses of social, economic, and educational outcomes a racial hierarchy is present along the color line. And, in the everyday race-making of Latinos, this racial hierarchy based on skin color has substantive consequences for life chances. However, the question that remains of race and racial hierarchy is what are the markers that allow for Latinos to make movement up and down this hierarchy? And since language and other cultural attributes are described as pertinent in the self-identification of Latinos, what do those markers mean in the operation of Latinos within the racial hierarchy? Some of the literature on ethnicity and its construction focuses on the self-ascription of ethnic labels due to structural forces faced by specific groups, some of which includes conversations on race but it has been limited in regards to Latinos. The following discussion is to unpack what this self-ascription notion of ethnicity has constructed about Latinos, particularly in understanding various social outcomes.

Latino as an Ethnic Label

The ethnicity or ethnic label research on Latinos has explored what undergirds the selection of specific ethnic tags, and, as a result of this research, we understand ethnicity as a complex construct among Latino groups. During the 20th century, the research on ethnicity[i] attended to the ways in which ethnicity was formed, maintained, and, in some instances, diminished by language, culture, immigrant status, identity labels, occupational status, and other factors (e.g., Barth, 1969; Gordon, 1975; Greeley, 1971; Handlin, 1951; Lieberson, 1980; Novak, 1973; Park, 1914). The propensity in early ethnicity research, which focused on extrapolating the assimilation process of European immigrants, described ethnicity or ethnic labels as fading overtime and resulting in a homogenous "American identity." This research, known as assimilation and pluralism (e.g., Glazer & Moynihan, 1963; Handlin, 1951), examined ethnicity as a diminishing factor among immigrant groups and situated the absorption of an American identity as an inevitable product. Park (1914, p. 615) defined assimilation as "a process of inter-penetration and fusion in which persons and groups acquire the memories, sentiments, and attitudes of other persons and groups, and by sharing their experience and history, are incorporated with them in a common cultural life." Such an explanation of did not explain the persistence of non-American ethnic labels found among Latino groups, especially the emergence of a Chicano and Puerto Rican identity during the 1960s civil rights movements. Various researchers began refuting the inevitability of an American ethnic label and offered a differing rendering in which attention was given to the presence of ethnicity as a matter of "interest" and "context" in which the individual has a choice of identifying or not (Espiritu, 1992).

Early discussions of ethnicity as "communities of interests" involved Glazer and Moynihan's (1963) research on Blacks, Puerto Ricans, Jews, Italians, and Irish in New York City. Glazer and Moynihan assert this group of ethnic immigrants' retention of their ethnic identification is because of common interests and in major cities religion and race are the two areas of interests that defined ethnic groups. Unlike Germans who come from differing religious backgrounds, Jews, Italians, and Irish maintained their respective religious institutions (i.e., Judaism and Catholicism) that exist for the specific purpose of serving ethnic interests. However, Glazer and Moynihan consider ethnic identification amongst Italians and Irish as declining from one generation to another and a new Catholic identification as emerging. Subsequently, even though they note racial discrimination and culture as significant factors in the ethnic identification among Blacks, Chicanos, and Puerto Ricans, Glazer and Moynihan are unable to articulate how interests are structured by race and racial identifications. Despite this theoretical shortcoming, this instrumentalist perspective introduced the notion that Latinos developed an ethnicity that was tied to contextual interests.

Barth (1969) introduced a major shift in this instrumentalist discourse on ethnic labels by suggesting that ethnicity is about boundaries—who is in and who is out. Barth's focus was primarily on the self-ascription and the ascription of others that create an ethnic or cultural boundary. Those boundaries of ethnicity involve structural and agency conditions. On the structural side, Yancey, Erickson, and Julian (1976) suggest that "the development and persistence of ethnicity is dependent upon structural conditions characterizing American cities and position of groups in American social structure" (p. 391). Yancey et al. suggest that ethnic identity is not a discrete variable but rather a continuous identification; "ethnicity may have relatively little to do with Europe, Asia or Africa, but much more to do with the exigencies of survival and the structure of opportunity in this country" (p. 400). In addition, they site changes in ecological and structural conditions, such as labor market opportunity and housing environment, as assisting in the maintenance and development of ethnic associations and affiliation. Unfortunately, Yancey et al. do not develop the persistence of ethnic identity among contemporary ethnic groups (e.g., Puerto Ricans, Mexicans, Africans, Black Americans, Asians, and West Indians) but they note a difference in ecological and structural conditions from European immigrants. These differences are identified in some of the status attainment research which outlined Blacks and Latinos experiencing ecological factors in distinct ways that moderate and mediate their social mobility (Portes & Wilson, 1976). Therefore, such researchers have conveyed ethnic identification can be both a function of how they enter the economic structure, such as laborers or professionals, and the structural conditions they endure (e.g., residential segregation and employment discrimination); for instance the entrée of Cubans during the 1960s versus the Marielitos in the 1980s.

Although, discourse on ethnicity has continued to develop this notion of situational or structural construction of ethnic identification, there has been little attention to how these structural conditions facilitate ethnic cohesion, particularly given its importance in the development of a Latino and Hispanic identification also known as panethnicity. Espiritu (1992) operationalizes panethnicity as a politico-cultural collectivity made up of peoples of several, hitherto distinct, tribal or national origins. Among Latinos, the construction of a collective panethnicity emerged in the 1970s with the use of "Hispanic" to ascribe various groups with an overarching label for political mobility. The resulting effect of an official use of Hispanic was the treating of Latinos as if they represent a real cultural and historical group (Portes & MacLeod, 1996). The use of a Hispanic label not only lumped together subgroup boundaries between Puerto Ricans, Dominicans, Panamanians, and other Latin American countries but also "encourage[d] individuals to broaden their identity to conform to the more inclusive ethnic designation" (Espiritu, 1992, p. 6). In some regions of the United States, use of the word Hispanic did not erase cultural distinctions among ethnic groups but rather was used to designate a particular political and economic orientation. Massey (1993) contends that the term "Hispanic" does not have any real existence beyond its original use as a statistical device:

> There is not a "Hispanic" population in the sense that there is a Black population. Hispanics share no common historical memory and do not compromise a single, coherent, community... Saying that someone is Hispanic or Latino reveals little or nothing about likely attitudes, behaviors, beliefs, race, religion, class, or legal situation in the United States. The only thing reasonably certain is that either the person in question or some progenitor once lived in an originally colonized by Spain. (pp. 453–454)

These labels imposed by nation-states upon immigrant groups from Latin America do not illustrate the heterogeneity of these immigrant groups:

> Procrustean, one size fits-all pan-ethnic labels such as Asian, Hispanic, Black are imposed willy-nilly by the society at large to lump ethnic groups together who may hail variously from Vietnam or Korea, India or China, Guatemala or Cuba, Haiti or Jamaica, and who differ widely in national and class origins, phenotypes, languages, cultures, generations, migration histories, and modes of incorporation in the United States. Their children, especially adolescents in the process of constructing and crystallizing a social identity, are challenged to incorporate what is "out there" into what is "in here," often in dissonant social contexts. (Rumbaut, 1994, p. 749)

Although these labels have been constructed by nation-states, their usage has allotted Latinos political and economic leverage. For instance, Padilla (1985) notes that in Chicago during the early 1970s, Mexicans and Puerto Ricans adopted a collective Latino or Hispanic identity for a common struggle. The two groups united as a "Hispanic" collective in order to acquire Hispanic representation by voting for a Hispanic political candidate making Latino/Hispanic a situational ethnic identity that is

> fabricated and becomes most appropriate or salient for social action during those particular situations or moments when two or more Spanish-speaking ethnic groups are affected by structural forces [e.g., discrimination in housing, education, and employment] and mobilize themselves as one to overcome this impact. (p. 4)

Also pertinent to understand within this conversation of ethnic cohesion is the decision-making processes by which individuals elect to use particular ethnic labels. Nagel (1994) asserts "ethnic identity...is the result of a dialectical process involving internal and external opinions and processes, as well as the individual's self-identification and outsider's ethnic designations—i.e., what you think your ethnicity is, versus what they think your ethnicity is" (p. 154). Self-identification involves a "layering" effect that sustains various meaning for the individual and group. For example, Padilla (1985) and Pedraza (1992) note that amongst Latinos that self-identifying as Mexican, Cuban, Puerto Rican, Dominican, Latino, or Hispanic serves various purposes and functions with the different groups. As Nagel (1994) illustrates,

> an individual of Cuban ancestry may be a Latino vis-a-vis non-Spanish-speaking ethnic groups, a Cuban-American vis-a-vis other Spanish-speaking groups, a Marielito vis-a-vis other Cubans, and white vis-a-vis African Americans. The chosen ethnic identity is determined by the individual's perception of its meaning to different audiences, its salience in different social contexts, and its utility in different settings. (p. 155)

The shift in boundary making conversation opens the door to the question of how these boundary making activities occur and who dictates the perimeters. This is where the self-ascription process of ethnicity meets the external ascription process of race, how does race and ethnicity interact when it comes to those that self-ascribe as Latino? A myriad of research demonstrates that this interaction functions differently among various Latino populations and has implications for mobility (e.g., Fergus, 2004; Gomez, 2000; Murguia & Telles, 1996; Rodriguez, 1992, 2000). And in some ways this research has also suggested the possibility of self-ascribed ethnicity as dominant in intra-group situations and race as dominant in inter-group situations. In other words, "while an individual can choose from among a set of ethnic identities, that set is generally limited to socially and politically defined ethnic categories with varying degrees of stigma or advantage attached to them" (Nagel, 1994, p. 156). For instance, ethnic identity functions differently among White Americans and Americans of African ancestry; "white Americans have considerable latitude in choosing ethnic identities...Americans of African ancestry, on the other hand, are confronted with essentially one ethnic option Black" (Nagel, 1994, p. 156). This difference in latitude is noted in a study of Mexican and Puerto Rican high school students of different skin color, in which the lighter-skin students were allowed to be White and Latino, but the darker-skin students were limited to solely a Latino identity (Fergus, 2004). Such differences in the latitude of ethnic options demonstrates the boundary of individual ethnic options and the significant role outside agents play in restricting available ethnic identities. Even though, dark-skin Latinos may distinguish themselves in intra-racial settings, such distinctions are unimportant in inter-racial settings because of the power of race as a socially defining mechanism of U.S. society. However, race is interpreted in such contexts as biological, i.e., there is something physical that makes someone Black or Latino. Therefore, in discussing the self-ascription of individuals and groups, it is critical to note that there are limits to individual choice and external ascription plays an important role in restricting available ethnic labels. And much of this external ascription is the moment in which race as a biological construct takes center stage as demonstrated in the popular identification of individuals like Tiger Woods as Black, George Lopez as Mexican, Zoe Saldana as Black, Cameron Diaz as White, and Jimmy Smits as Latino.

Discussion

The presence of Latinos in the United States, unlike any other group, in some ways challenges and in other ways disrupts the manner in which race and ethnicity has been constructed. Both constructs are developed from the social experiences of Blacks and Whites; however the emergence of Latinos who can be easily situated in both categories and along the continuum, raises questions as to the breadth and depth of these categories. As we've outlined, neither category has sufficiently accounted for the dynamism of Latino groups, which, in turn, has limited our theoretical and empirical conversations of what is occurring with the Latinos in the United States.

The consideration of Latinos into the racial hierarchy discourse has been at best a sideline approach or afterthought (Bonilla-Silva, 2004). Even though, the social construct conversation continues to situate the meaning of race as continuously shifting, it is premised on the Black-White experience of race as a social construct. This is also apparent in some of the racial hierarchy literature on other racialization markers (Bashi, 1998; Bonilla-Silva, 2004); the meaning of power and privilege of self-identification in relation to external identification is premised on skin color power and privilege of Blacks and Whites. Such bifurcation continues to locate the notion of race as a social construct of skin color and facial/hair features of Blacks and Whites. Theories of race as a social construct need to involve more integration that argues the positionality of power and privilege as also bound to experiences of language, immigrant/non-immigrant, and skin color variation labels (i.e., White, Black, Brown, *mestizo, indio, guero*, negro, Moreno, etc.).

The shifts in ethnicity conversation from assimilation to pluralism to primordialism attend to the significance of language, immigrant status, and other markers as relevant in the self-ascription of ethnic identification. However, this research has not systematically considered individual and group consequences of this dialectical process of ethnic identity in relation to labor market opportunity, educational opportunity and resilience, and perceptions of individual opportunity. Particularly when juxtaposing to notions of power and privilege in positionality, which racial hierarchy conversations illuminate as directing social and economic mobility. For instance, do dark-skin Latinos experience labor market employment opportunities and participation in similar ways as light-skin Latinos? How would these dark-skin Latinos fair if they exhibited a Spanish accent? Or Spanish surname? The conversation of Latinos as solely a self-ascription prevents us from understanding the realities and tensions that exist when Asians from Venezuela speak Spanish and identify as Chino-Latinos.

As we continue to explore the empirical realities of Latinos in the United States, it will necessitate a theoretical expansion of race and its racial hierarchies as it pertains to other markers beyond skin color. Such expansion can allow for understanding the realities of how Spanish language (e.g., "Yo quiero Taco Bell," "Living la vida loca") and accents, undocumented immigrant status, and the Latinization of food (e.g., "Mexican" cheese) serve to position the role of Latino group culture as subordinate to dominant White culture. And such positionality illustrates the power of Whiteness in otherizing Latinos as a cultural phenomenon. Also, by limiting the conversation of Latinidad to an ethnic label dialogue, our research has only centered its theoretical and empirical exploration as to what it means for Latinos to call themselves Hispanic, Mexican, Puerto Rican, Dominican, etc. As we establish the new frontiers of research regarding Latinos, positionality, power, and self-ascription need to be critical elements of theoretical and empirical exploration when looking at language, skin color, immigrant status, and culture of Latino groups in the United States.

Note

1. Throughout this review we will use ethnicity and ethnic identity interchangeably.

References

Aguirre, B. E., & Bonilla-Silva, E. (2002). Does race matter among Cuban immigrants? An analysis of the racial characteristics of recent Cuban Immigrants. *Journal of Latin American Studies, 34*(2), 311–324.

Almaguer, T. (1994). *Racial fault lines*. Berkeley: University of California Press.

Barth, F. (1969). *Ethnic groups and boundaries: The social organization of culture difference*. Boston: Little, Brown.

Bashi, V. (1998). Racial categories matter because racial hierarchies matter: A commentary. *Ethnic and Racial Studies, 21*, 959–968.

Bashi, V., & McDaniel, A. (1997). A theory of immigration and racial stratification. *Journal of Black Studies, 27*, 668–682.

Bobo, L., Kluegel, J. R., & Smith, R. A. (1997). Laissez faire racism: The crystallization of a 'kinder, gentler' anti-black ideology. In S. A. Tuch & J. Martin (Eds.), *Racial attitudes in the 1990s: Continuity and change* (pp. 15–44). Greenwood, CT: Praeger.

Bonilla-Silva, E. (2004, November). From bi-racial to tri-racial: Towards a new system of racial stratification in the USA. *Ethnic and Racial Studies, 17*, 931–950.

Candelario, G. (2007). Color matters: Latina/o racial identities and life chances. In J. Flores & R. Rosaldo (Eds.), *A companion to Latina/o studies* (pp. 337–350). New York: Blackwell.

Carnoy, M. (1998). *Faded dreams: The politics and economics of race in America*. New York: Cambridge University Press.

Cornell, S., & Hartmann, D. (1998). *Ethnicity and race: Identities in a changing world*. Thousand Oaks, CA: Pine Forge Press.

Drake, S., & Cayton, H. (1945). *Black metropolis*. Chicago: The University of Chicago Press.

DuBois, W. (1899). *The Philadelphia negro: A social study*. Philadelphia: The University Pennsylvania Press.

Espino, R., & Franz, M. (2002). Latino phenotypic discrimination revisited: The impact of skin color on occupational status. *Social Science Quarterly, 83*, 612–623.

Espiritu, Y. (1992). *Asian American panethnicity: Bridging institutions and identities*. Philadelphia: Temple University Press.

Feagin, M. (2000). *Racist America*. New York: Routledge.

Fergus, E. (2004). *Skin color and identity formation: Perceptions of opportunity and academic orientation among Puerto Rican and Mexican youth*. New York: Routledge.

Fredrickson, G. M. (2002). *Racism: A short history*. Princeton, NJ: Princeton University Press.

Glazer, N., & Moynihan, D. P. (1963). *Beyond the melting pot: The Negroes, Puerto Ricans, Jews, Italians and Irish of New York City*. Cambridge, MA: MIT Press.

Gomez, C. (2000). The continual significance of skin color: An exploratory study of Latinos in the Northeast. *Hispanic Journal of Behavioral Sciences, 22*, 94–103.

Gordon, M. (1975). Toward a general theory of racial and ethnic group relations. In N. Glazer & D. P. Moynihan (Eds.), *Ethnicity: Theory and experience* (pp. 84–110). Cambridge, MA: Harvard University Press.

Greeley, A. M. (1971). *Why can't they be like us? America's white ethnic groups*. New York: E.P. Dutton.

Hacker, A. (1992). *Two nations: Black and white, separate, hostile, unequal*. New York: Scribner.

Handlin, O. (1951). *The uprooted*. Boston: Little Bay Books.

Hernstein, R., & Murray, A. (1996). *The bell curve: Intelligence and class structure in American life*. New York: Free Press.

Jensen, A. R. (1979). *Bias in mental testing*. New York: Free Press.

Kasinitz, P. (1992). *Caribbean New York*. Ithaca: Cornell University Press.

Kenny, M. (2004). Racial science on social context. *Isis, 95*, 394–419

Lee, S. J. (1994). Behind the model-minority stereotype: Voices of high- and low-achieving Asian American students. *Anthropology and Education Quarterly, 25*, 413–429.

Lewis, A. (2003). *Race in the schoolyard*. New Brunswick, NJ: Rutgers University Press.

Lieberson, S. (1980). *A piece of the pie: Blacks and white immigrants since 1880*. Berkeley: University of California Press.

Lipsitz, G. (1998). *The possessive investment in whiteness*. Philadelphia: Temple University Press.

Logan, J. (2003). *How race counts for Hispanic Americans*. Unpublished manuscript. University at Albany, NY: Mumford Center.

Massey, D. (1993). Latinos, poverty, and the underclass: A new agenda for research. *Hispanic Journal of Behavioral Sciences, 15*, 449–475.

Massey, D. (1998). *Worlds in motion: International migration at the end of the millenium.* Oxford, UK: Oxford University Press.

Morton, G. (1849). *An illustrated system of human anatomy.* Philadelphia: Grigg, Elliott and Co.

Murguia, E., & Foreman, T. (2003). Shades of whiteness: The Mexican American experience in relation to Anglos and Blacks. In A. W. Doane & E. Bonilla Silva (Eds.), *White out: The continuing significance of racism* (pp. 63–79). London: Routledge.

Murguia, E., & Telles, E. (1996). Phenotype and schooling among Mexican Americans. *Sociology of Education, 69,* 276–289.

Myrdal, G. (1944). *An American dilemma.* New York: Harper Press.

Nagel, J. (1994). Constructing ethnicity: Creating and recreating ethnic identity and culture. *Social Problems, 41,* 152–176.

Novak, M. (1973). *The rise of the unmeltable ethnics: Politics and culture in the seventies.* New York: Macmillian.

Omi, M., & Winant, H. (1989). *Racial formation in the United States: From the 1960s to the 1990s.* New York: Routledge.

Padilla, F. (1985). *Latino ethnic consciousness.* Notre Dame, IN: University of Notre Dame Press.

Park, R. E. (1914). Racial assimilation in secondary groups. *American Journal of Sociology, 19,* 606–623.

Pedraza, S. (1992). *Ethnic identity: Developing a Hispanic-American identity.* Paper presented at the 5th Congreso Internacional sobre las Culturas Hispanas de los Estados Unidos, Madrid, Spain.

Pew Hispanic Center. (2006). *Pew Hispanic Center tabulations of 2005 American community survey.* Washington, DC: Pew Hispanic Center.

Portes, A. (1996). *The new second generation.* New York: Russell Sage Foundation.

Portes, A., & Bach, R. L. (1985). *Latin journey: Cuban and Mexican immigrants in the United States.* Berkeley: University of California Press.

Portes, A., & MacLeod, D. (1996). What Shall I Call Myself? Hispanic identity formation in the second generation. *Ethnic and Racial Studies, 19*(3), 523–547.

Portes, A., & Wilson, K. L. (1976). Black-white differences in educational attainment. *American Sociological Review, 41,* 414–431.

Rivera, R. (2007). Between blackness and Latinidad in the hip hop zone. In J. Flores & R. Rosaldo (Eds.), *A companion to Latina/o studies* (pp. 351–362). New York: Blackwell.

Rodriguez, C. (1992). Race, culture, and Latino "Otherness" in the 1980 census. *Social Science Quarterly, 73,* 930–937.

Rodriguez, C. (2000). *Changing race: Latinos, the census, and the history of ethnicity in the United States.* New York: New York University Press.

Rodriguez, C., & Cordero-Guzman, H. (1992). Placing race in context. *Ethnic and Racial Studies, 15,* 523–542.

Ruiz, V. (2007). Coloring class: Racial constructions in twentieth-century Chicana/o historiography. In J. Flores & R. Rosaldo (Eds.), *A companion to Latina/o studies* (pp. 169–179). New York: Blackwell.

Rumbaut, R. G. (1994, Winter). The crucible within: Ethnic identity, self-esteem, and segmented assimilation among children of immigrants. *International Migration Review, 28*(4), 748–794.

Saenz, R., & B. Aguirre. (1991). The dynamics of Mexican ethnic identity. *Ethnic Groups, 9,* 17–32.

Song, M. (2004). Who's at the bottom? Examining claims about racial hierarchy. *Ethnic and Racial Studies, 27,* 859–877.

Takaki, R. (1987). *From different shores: Perspectives on race and ethnicity in America.* New York: Oxford University Press.

Waters, M. (1994, Winter). Ethnic and racial identities of second-generation black immigrants in New York City. *International Migration Review, 28*(4), 795–821.

Yancey, W., Erickson, E., & Julian, R. (1976). Emergent ethnicity: A review and reformulation. *American Sociological Review, 41*(3), 391–403.

Yoon, In-Jin. (1997). *On my own.* Chicago: The University of Chicago Press.

11 Monoglossic Ideologies and Language Policies in the Education of U.S. Latinas/os

Ofelia García
The City University of New York

Rosario Torres-Guevara
Borough of Manhattan Community College, CUNY

Introduction

Language is perhaps the most important tool in education because language is needed to communicate ideas and negotiate understandings. When we narrowly consider only the education that takes place in school, then language becomes paramount for three reasons: (a) schooling often takes place in the language of power in a nation-state—different, at times, from that used by students; (b) language is the medium through which instruction takes places; and (c) it is an important school subject.

The United States is a highly multilingual country. Notwithstanding its multilingualism, the country has constructed for itself an identity as an English-only[1] speaking country. Despite the presence and advances of bilingual education in the United States,[2] the language of schooling is, and has been, English. Spanish, the language used by approximately 30 million Latinas/os in the United States,[3] is only considered a "foreign" language, and taught as such.[4] It is English that is used as the medium of instruction, and it is English literacy and language arts that are emphasized and assessed. Thus, when addressing the education of Latinas/os in the United States, much emphasis is placed on two issues that U.S. mainstream discourse perceives as Latinas/os' problems: (a) their English language proficiency, sometimes not considered appropriate; and (b) their use of Spanish, a "foreign" language, and yet spoken by Latinas/os in the United States.

As we will see, U.S. Latino students have different linguistic profiles—some use Spanish all the time, some may not use and/or know Spanish at all; some are quite fluent in English, some may not need to use English at all; and some may engage in a combination of English and Spanish as it may represent a sort of language "currency" in their respective communities.[5] This chapter will start out by reviewing the linguistic profile of U.S. Latinas/os, thereby demonstrating the complexity of their language use.

U.S. Latinas/os are expected to fit within schools that value English only, and where Spanish is appreciated only as a foreign language subject. Thus, language policies in education (LPiE) for the education of Latinas/os in the United States have focused on trying to make their *English fit "native" standards*, and their *Spanish fit "foreign" standards*. It is precisely because the education of U.S. Latinas/os is framed within a *monoglossic ideology,* which values only monolingualism and ignores bilingualism, that much Latino educational failure occurs. A monoglossic language ideology sees language as an autonomous skill that functions independently from the context in which it is used.[6] U.S. schools ignore how English and Spanish are used by U.S. Latinos. Thus, the academic failure rate of U.S. Latinas/os is high, regardless of whether instruction is in English only or with some use of Spanish.

This chapter reviews the language policies that have been used in the education of U.S. Latinas/os. It then analyzes the construction of monoglossic language ideology and debunks the notion of English as a native language and Spanish as a foreign language in educating U.S. Latinas/os. This chapter also reconstitutes the notion of bilingualism for U.S. Latinas/os in the 21st century, and discusses the current "miseducation" of many Latino students today as a result of a monoglossic language ideology and limited understandings of the complexity of bilingualism.

This chapter is divided into three sections:

- The varying linguistic profiles of U.S. Latinas/os;
- The Language Policies in Education (LPiE) that have impacted the education of U.S. Latinas/os; and
- A U.S. monoglossic language ideology and its impact on the education of Latinas/os.

The Varying Linguistic Profiles of U.S Latinas/os: The Entire Linguistic Elephant

The literature on the education of Latinas/os most often focuses on those who are "Limited English Proficient," or "English Language Learners."[7] As García, Kleifgen, and Falchi (2008) have pointed out, it is the reluctance to recognize these students as "Emergent Bilinguals" who are developing English proficiency and thus becoming bilingual that results in much of their miseducation.

But as García (2006) has also indicated, this emphasis on "English Language Learners" ignores "the elephant in the room"—the fact that most U.S. Latinas/os have good English language proficiency. Thus, much attention is being paid to the tail of the animal while ignoring the elephant—those who are fluent in English and bilingual, and yet, continue to fail in the nation's schools.

The U.S. Census asks whether respondents speak English or Spanish at home. In 2005, 22% of those who identified themselves as "Hispanics"[8] and who were over 5 years of age spoke English at home (see Table 11.1, next to last column).[9] The U.S. Census also asks those who speak Spanish at home about their English Language proficiency.[10] Statistics show that more than two thirds of these Hispanics (69%) speak English very well or well, with only a third (31%) speaking English less than well or not well. In fact, only 12% of Hispanics who speak Spanish at home do so because they do not speak English well (see Table 11.1, last column).

If we then consider Latinas/os who speak English Only at home, and those who speak Spanish at home but who also speak English Very Well and Well, the percentage of U.S. Latinas/os who are English proficient is around 75%. That is, unlike the portrayal of U.S. Latinas/os as lacking English proficiency, three fourths of them speak English more than well (See Table 11.2, last column).[11] Even for immigrants, learning English is a necessity, not a luxury, so there is high motivation to learn English and they learn it well, despite the high academic failure (Valdés, 1997; Tse, 2001). It might help readers who are not familiar with the literature on bilingualism to have a quick overview in this section on bilingualism, especially as it functions in real life.

Table 11.1 Language Choice of U.S. Latinas/os Over 5 Years of Age

Eng. or Spa. at home	Eng. Ability Spa. Spkrs.	Totals	% Eng. or Spa. at home	% Eng. Ability Spa. Spkrs.
Speak Eng. Only		8,131,764	22%	
Speak Spanish		29,073,428	78%	
	Spk. Eng. Very Well	14,417,687		50%
	Spk. Eng. Well	5,559,872		19%
	Spk. Eng. Less th. Well	5,616,346		19%
	Spk. Eng. Not Well	3,479,526		12%
TOTAL Latinas/os		**37,346,131**		

Source: U.S. Census, 2005 American Community Survey, Table B16006.

Table 11.2 English Proficiency of U.S. Latinas/os Over 5 Years of Age

Lang. Spkn. at Home & Eng. Proficiency	Totals	%	% Eng. Proficiency
Speak Eng. Only	8,131,764	22%	
Spk. Spa., Eng. Very Well	14,417,687	39%	
Spk. Spa., Eng. Well	5,559,872	15%	
English Proficiency More than Well	28,109,323		75%
Spk. Spa., Eng. Less thanWell	5,616,346	15%	
Spk. Spa., Eng. Not Well	3,479,526	9%	
English Proficiency Less than Well	9,095,872		25%
TOTAL Latinas/os	**37,346,131**	**100%**	**100%**

Source: U.S. Census, 2005 American Community Survey, Table B16006.

Underscoring its multifunctions establishes that bilinguals use both languages in their lives in different ways and equally underscores that it does *not* (for the most part) constitute the reason for low test scores.

U.S. Latinas/os are also categorized as Spanish speakers, but not all Latinas/os speak Spanish. Almost one fourth of U.S. Latinas/os are not using Spanish even in the privacy of their home (see Table 11.1, next to the last column). However, we cannot be sure of their Spanish language proficiency since the U.S. Census does not pose that question. The fact that three fourths of U.S. Latinas/os speak Spanish in their homes, even when they are fully bilingual, is most important, for it makes clear that the language situation of U.S. Latinas/os cannot be understood as one of English on the one hand, and Spanish on the other. The language situation of Latinas/os must be understood in terms of the complex interactions of their bilingualism.

Bilingual Latinos in the United States are often perceived as being two monolinguals in one, capable of using English or Spanish interchangeably. But the use of two languages by bilinguals is not simply like having two balanced wheels in a bicycle. Instead, bilinguals use their two languages as an all-terrain-vehicle, adjusting the unbalanced wheels to the ridges and craters of the communicative act. Their complex bilingual interactions, what García (2009) has called their "translanguaging," characterize their language practices in bilingual communities, as they interact with others and make sense of the linguistic and cultural context. These complex language practices are important resources for bilingual communities and for bilingual children, regardless of the inability of schools to acknowledge them.

Language Policies in Educating U.S. Latinas/os

Although the United States, as a nation of immigrants, has always been multilingual, English monolingualism has been constructed as the only acceptable language use of loyal and true United States citizens. Almost a century ago, Theodore Roosevelt said, "it would not be merely a misfortune but a crime to perpetuate differences of language in this country" (Castellanos, 1983, p. 40). In 1915, he declared:

> [t]here is no room in this country for hyphenated Americanism…. [the foreign born] must talk the language of its native-born fellow-citizens…we have room for but one language here, and that is the English language, for we intend to see that the crucible turns our people out as Americans, of American nationality, and not as dwellers in a polyglot boarding house. (cited in Edwards, 1994, p. 166)

And in 1917, Theodore Roosevelt added:

> We must have but one flag. We must also have but one language. That language must be the language of the Declaration of Independence, of Washington's Farewell address, of Lincoln's Gettysburg speech and second inaugural.... We call upon all loyal and unadulterated Americans to man the trenches against the enemy within our gates. (cited in Crawford, 1992, p. 19)

Throughout the first half of the 20th century, this monolingual ideology predominated in schools—English Only was the language of loyal and unadulterated Americans and U.S. Latinas/os who spoke Spanish were enemies within our gates.

Despite the fact that the Spanish language could be considered to have special rights because it was spoken by original settlers (Kloss, 1977) and is not only a language of immigrants, its presence in U.S. schools to educate U.S. Latinas/os has always been short-lived and controversial (for more on this, see Castellanos, 1983; Del Valle, 2003; García, 2009). There is, however, an elite tradition of teaching Spanish as a foreign language in the United States, focusing on the reading of the literature of Spain, a tradition that was initiated at Harvard in 1813[12] (for more on this, see García, 1997, 2003). During World War I, the teaching of German at the secondary level was substituted by Spanish. But it was Castilian Spanish, meaning the language of Spain,[13] that became the preferred variety to be taught to Anglos, while the Spanish of the new U.S. territories was relegated to an inferior position and restricted in *all* educational enterprises. Only Spanish as a foreign language was accepted, and U.S. Latinas/os were excluded from this educational opportunity also.

In 1954, the U.S. Supreme Court ruled in *Brown v. Board of Education* that segregated schools were unconstitutional, ushering in a new era in U.S. Civil Rights that has had a profound impact in the education of U.S. Latinas/os. (For more on this entire history, see Crawford, 2004; E. Garcia, 2005; and http://www.ncela.gwu.edu/policy/1_history.htm.) In 1964, *Title VI of the Civil Rights Act* was passed by Congress, prohibiting discrimination on the basis of race, color or national origin.

The educational situation of U.S. Latinas/os around this time was dire. In 1960 of all Puerto Ricans 25 years of age and older in the United States, 87% had dropped out without graduating from high school, and the dropout rate in Grade 8 was 53% (Castellanos, 1983). In the Southwest, the average Chicano child had only a seventh grade education. In Texas, the high school dropout rate for Chicanos was 89%. And in California, less than a half of 1% of college students at the University of California campuses were Chicanos (Mackey & Beebe, 1977).

In the words of Senator Ralph Yarborough of Texas who sponsored *Title VII of the Elementary and Secondary Education Act—the Bilingual Education Act*—bilingual education was a way of making U.S. Latino children fully literate in English (Crawford, 2004). But when the Bilingual Education Act was first reauthorized in 1974, its limitation as a transitional temporary measure to educate only those who did not speak English fluently was codified. The law stated:

> It [bilingual education] is instruction given in, and study of, English and (to the extent necessary to allow a child to progress effectively through the education system) the native language of the children of limited English speaking ability. (cited in Castellanos, 1983, p. 120)

The use of transitional bilingual education in educating those with limited English proficiency was also supported in the *Lau v. Nichols* U.S. Supreme Court decision in 1974. In providing relief to the Chinese plaintiffs, the court ruled that "There is no equality of treatment merely by providing students with the same facilities, textbooks, teachers and curriculum; for students who do not understand English are effectively foreclosed from any meaningful education."

In an important judicial case (*Castañeda v. Pickard*, 1981), the Fifth Circuit Court of Appeals for the Southern District of Texas substantiated the holding of Lau that schools must take "appropriate action" when educating emergent bilinguals and that such action must be based on sound educational theory, produce results, and provide adequate resources, including qualified teachers, and appropriate materials, equipment and facilities. The case, however, did not mandate a specific program such as bilingual education or ESL support.

Despite the very limited use of Spanish in the nation's schools, sporadically utilized to teach those U.S. Latinas/os who were yet to develop English proficiency, bilingual education has always been contested. In 1980 then President Ronald Reagan echoed Theodore Roosevelt's English Only ideology when, opposing bilingual education, he said:

> [I]t is absolutely wrong and against American concepts to have a bilingual education program that is now openly, admittedly dedicated to preserving their native language and never getting them adequate in English so they can go out into the job market and participate. (cited in Crawford, 2004, p. 120)

This English Only ideology has persisted even after the world has been enmeshed in the movements of peoples, products, and communication that characterize globalization in the 21st century. Wright (2004, pp. 163, 165) warns that despite the fact that the United States has been the promoter of globalization in the world,

> [s]ome of the most robust resistance to globalization comes from within the United States itself.... The US government is able to guard its sovereignty and autonomy in the classic manner of the nation states.... [W]e appear to be witnessing asymmetric developments within globalization: loss of economic autonomy and political sovereignty for many states; continuing economic autonomy and political sovereignty together with the survival of some elements of traditional '*one nation, one territory, one language*' nationalism for the United States. [italics added]

In the 1990s, the use of Spanish to support learning came under siege. The most effective attack against bilingual education was spearheaded by Ron Unz, a Silicon Valley software millionaire. In 1998, Proposition 227 (California Education Code, Section 305-306) prohibited the use of Spanish in teaching U.S Latinas/os. It mandated the use of Sheltered English Immersion programs (also known as Structured English Immersion) for a period not to exceed 1 year.

In 2000, Arizona voters approved Proposition 203 (Arizona Revised Statutes 15-751-755) which banned bilingual education and limited school services for those who were yet to become bilingual to a 1-year English-Only structured immersion program. In 2002, the proposition in Massachusetts (Question 2, G.L. c. 71A) did the same.

As many have remarked, the word "bilingual" (what Crawford has called "the B-Word") has been progressively silenced (Crawford, 2005; García, 2003; García, 2006; Hornberger, 2006; Wiley & Wright, 2004). García (2009) portrays this silencing of the word bilingual in the change of names of official bureaus and laws, as in Table 11.3.

The use of Spanish as a medium in the bilingual schooling of U.S. Latinos in elementary and secondary schools has had a different trajectory from that of the teaching of the Spanish language in secondary schools and universities to U.S. Latinos. In the early 1980s, Spanish-language educators had started clamoring for the recognition that Spanish was much more than a foreign language. Pioneer scholars, especially Guadalupe Valdés, called attention to the inadequacies of teaching Spanish as a foreign language to the growing number of U.S. bilinguals.

Table 11.3   Silencing of Bilingualism

Office of Bilingual Education and Minority Languages Affairs (OBEMLA) →	Office of English Language Acquisition, Language Enhancement and Academic Achievement for LEP students (OELA)
National Clearinghouse for Bilingual Education (NCBE) →	National Clearinghouse for English Language Acquisition and Language Instruction Educational Programs (NCELA)
Title VII of Elementary and Secondary Education Act: The Bilingual Education Act →	Title III of No Child Left Behind, Public Law 107-110: Language Instruction for Limited English Proficient and Immigrant Students

Spanish language educators focusing on what was then known as "Spanish for Spanish speakers" joined rank with bilingual educators to improve the Spanish-language education of U.S. Latinos, recognizing their bilingualism.

Recently, and in the wake of the bilingual education controversy, some Spanish language professionals have taken refuge in a monoglossic vision of the Spanish of U.S. Latinas/os, claiming Spanish as a "heritage" language, and distancing themselves from bilingual education. Although the use of heritage language has been used in Canada since 1977, the term was not embraced in the United States until the First Heritage Languages in America conference was held at the University of California at Los Angeles in 1999 (Cummins, 2005). Cummins suggests some reasons for the change:

> [R]ecent academic initiatives in relation to heritage languages can be seen as an attempt to establish an independent sphere of discourse where heritage language support can be debated on its own merits rather than viewed through the lens of preexisting polarized attitudes towards bilingual education and immigration. (p. 586)

García (2005) has suggested that this shift in naming Spanish a heritage language points to an unfortunate silencing of U.S. Spanish itself. Spanish has been relegated to a position of heritage, something not relevant, something of the past. And in so doing, bilingualism in education as a viable and equitable approach to teach U.S. Latinas/os is dismissed. Valdés, Fishman, Chávez, and Pérez (2006) claim that theories concerning the teaching of Spanish to U.S. bilinguals remain underdeveloped, while teaching programs themselves, especially at the secondary level, are too few.

In 2002, the Bilingual Education Act (Title VII) was repealed. The new legislation, known as No Child Left Behind (NCLB) contains Title III (Public Law 107-110)—"Language Instruction for Limited English Proficient and Immigrant Students." NCLB expects that by the 2013–2014 school year, all students achieve the level of "proficient" in state assessment systems (U.S. Department of Education, 2001). NCLB has forced schools to pay attention to ensuring that all U.S. Latinas/os meet educational standards. But as many have remarked (Crawford, 2004; García, Kleifgen & Falchi, 2008; Hornberger, 2006; Wiley and Wright, 2004), the present emphasis on assessment strictly in English denies the bilingual condition of U.S. Latinas/os. Without recognition of the bilingualism of U.S. Latinas/os both in teaching and in assessment, there is little hope that the educational playing field will ever become equal. Indeed, the teaching of Spanish to U.S. Latinos continues to suffer losses, as English Only is emphasized.

Monoglossic Language Ideologies and Practices: Bilingualism Misunderstood

In U.S. education, and especially in assessment, the notion of a "native" speaker of English is reified. But in the context of globalization, and as bilingualism has become commonplace around the world, the notion of a native speaker of English has become highly contested.

English has been increasingly appropriated by speakers all over the world, especially in Asia and Africa. Brutt-Griffler (2004) refers to this process as "macroaquisition," that is, second language acquisition as a social process involving an entire speech community. Canagarajah (1999), Mazrui (2004), Pennycook (1994), Phillipson (1992), and others have made us well aware that the teaching and learning of English has to take into account the sociolinguistic and sociohistorical context of the language community involved and to resist, in Canagarajah's (1999) words, the linguistic imperialism in English teaching. García and Bartlett (2007), in their study of a successful bilingual high school, also allude to the relevance of envisioning language acquisition as a social process of the speech community, not only as an individual psycholinguistic process.

The traditional individual models of second language acquisition have ignored three factors that have been shown to be most important in learning and using an additional language:

1. the role that *communities of practice* (Lave & Wenger, 1991)[14] play in providing positions for participants' second language practices;
2. the complex ways in which learning and speaking a second language engages speakers' *social identities* (Norton, 2000; Norton Peirce, 1995); and
3. the way *power relations* influence linguistic interaction (Bourdieu, 1991).

English language education in the United States is categorized as "English as a second language" or "native," leaving little room for the English of Latinas/os, fluent and yet rich in Spanish language influences. Little room is made for acknowledging the fact that in the segregated residential communities in which U.S. Latinas/os often live, English is often the language of choice, especially for young people, but is practiced in bilingual communities which show distinct sociolinguistic characteristics from monolingual communities. The different power relationship of English and Spanish in U.S. society also impacts the sociolinguistic identities of U.S. Latinas/os. Thus, English-speaking Latinas/os often mark English as their own—with phonological characteristics, loanwords, and code-switching (García & Menken, 2006). Although most accepted in the community and perfect for communication, this Latino English is often stigmatized in school where teachers demand that U.S. Latinas/os shed all traces of their bilingualism in speaking English.

The tradition of teaching Spanish in the United States has become more inclusive in the last 20 years as more U.S. Latinas/os have become students of Spanish. Yet, Spanish teaching at the secondary and tertiary level continues to uphold a "monolingual" standard which often does not take into consideration the bilingualism of U.S. Latino Spanish speakers, their practices within a bilingual community, and their social identities as Spanish speakers. As with English, although most accepted in the community and perfect for communication, U.S. Latino Spanish is often stigmatized in schools and society where it is labeled as "Spanglish," a debased and mixed contact variety (Stavans, 2003). The words of Dame Edna, in an advice column, reflect this linguistic prejudice or what Skutnabb-Kangas (2000) terms "linguicism":

> Forget Spanish. There's nothing in that language worth reading except Don Quixote.... There was a poet named García Lorca, but I'd leave him on the intellectual back burner if I were you. As for everyone's speaking it, what twaddle! Who speaks it that you are really desperate to talk to? The help? Your leaf blower? (p. 116)

Thus, in schools Spanish-language teachers demand that U.S. Latinas/os shed all traces of their bilingualism in speaking Spanish.

Even when bilingualism has been accepted in U.S. education, schools have continued to exert their monoglossic ideologies, insisting that bilingualism is about one language and then the other. For example, transitional bilingual education uses Spanish until academic English profi-

$$L1 \rightarrow + L2 - L1 \rightarrow L2$$

Figure 11.1   Subtractive bilingualism.

$$L1 + L2 = L1 + L2$$

Figure 11.2   Additive bilingualism.

ciency is developed. But each language is seen as separate and following each other. The so called "dual language education" programs use the two languages throughout the child's education. But one of its principles is that the two languages be strictly separated and that the two languages not be used in the same context.[15]

The model of bilingualism that is followed in transitional bilingual education programs is subtractive as shown in Figure 11.1.

In this model, the student speaks Spanish at home, English is added in school, while Spanish is subtracted. The result is a Latino child who speaks English only.

The model of bilingualism that is followed in *dual language education* is additive as in Figure 11.2, with both English added and Spanish maintained.

Despite the benefits of additive bilingualism, bilingualism here is still seen from the perspective of monolingualism as the norm; that is, it reveals a monoglossic ideology. Bilingualism in this view is simply double monolingualism, a category different from monolingualism, but with bilingual individuals expected to be and do with each of their languages the same thing as monolinguals. Therefore, one can assess each of these languages separately and students are expected to achieve as monolinguals in each of their languages.

But bilingualism in the 21st century must reflect a language competence that shifts and bounces, that is not linear but dynamic, drawing from the different contexts in which bilingualism develops and functions. In the linguistic complexity of the 21st century, bilingualism for U.S. Latinas/os involves a much more dynamic cycle where language use is multiple, recursive, coming and going without end poles, but rather adjusting to the multilingual multimodal terrain of the communicative act, as shown in Figure 11.3.

With language interaction taking place in different planes that include multimodalities, that is, different modes of language (visuals as well as print, sound as well as text, etc.) as well as multilingualism, it is possible for individuals to engage in multiple complex communicative acts that do not in any way respond to the linear models of bilingualism proposed earlier (for more on this, see García, 2009).

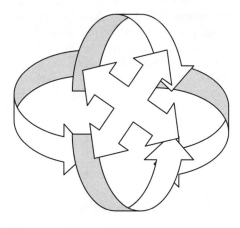

Figure 11.3   Dynamic bilingualism in the 21st century.

Dynamic bilingualism has much to do with how the Language Policy Division of the Council of Europe (2000) has defined the concept of plurilingualism as "the ability to use several languages to varying degrees and for distinct purposes," as well as "an educational value that is the basis of linguistic tolerance." And schools throughout the European Union are working on making their children fluent in "Mother Tongue + 2." In the 21st century, we need to reconstitute our concept of bilingualism and bilingual individuals in order to fit the communicative exigencies of "languaging," that is, the language as action needed in today's interdependent and technologically-enriched world (for more on languaging, see Swain, 2006). We need to shed our concept of balanced bilingualism adopting instead a contextualized sense that values bilinguals' use of languages to varying degrees, as in the definition of plurilingualism given by the Council of Europe.

It turns out that in the United States, a country with a monoglossic ideology, even the bilingual profession has sold itself short—settling for the use of two languages sequentially (as in transitional bilingual education) or separately (as in the "so called" dual language education programs), without acknowledging the dynamic plurilingualism of U.S. Latinos. As a result, U.S. Latinos' use of their two languages and literacies are always assessed separately, without regard to how their complex and rich sociolinguistic context impacts on their ability to "language."

It is this focus on monolingual assessment, important more than ever today in the era of No Child Left Behind, that creates the inequities in the education of U.S. Latinos. It is difficult for bilingual Latinos to compete with monolinguals in assessments that ignore linguistic diversity. This poor performance of bilingual Latinos on monolingual assessments in turn leads to remediation and placement in compensatory programs. The cycle never ends. Poor performance on monolingual assessments by bilingual Latinos leads to placement in English Only remedial programs where their bilingualism is made to go underground. But being made invisible in school is not the same as not existing. Ignoring the bilingualism of U.S. Latinos is costing all of us dearly. It is the cause for educational failure, which could be avoided with deeper understandings of how bilingualism works.

Conclusion

As long as the United States does not recognize the potential of bilingualism that U.S. Latinos hold for the future of our country, schools will continue to demand rigid monolingual standards that do not acknowledge languaging skills that will be needed in the future. It is clear, for example, that to continue to compete in a world of multilingual and multimodal communication systems, workers will have to be able to work across languages, with translanguaging[16] and translating as most important abilities. It is also evident that linguistic tolerance will be increasingly important and that schools play an important role in developing this value.

U.S. Latino students are often seen as a linguistic "problem." Thus, their defining characteristic—the complex way in which they use their bilingualism—is seldom tapped as a cognitive and educational resource. And because U.S. schools do not teach the value of linguistic tolerance, U.S. Latinos are made to feel that the bilingual ways in which they speak at home are not appropriate or "standard." Educational failure is sure to follow. It will take breaking the monoglossic ideology that permeates U.S. schools to develop educational ways of building on the strength of U.S. Latinos—their dynamic bilingualism. But even more important would be to design ways of assessing their academic progress, including that in academic English, in ways that tap their bilingual abilities. Ensuring this would go a long way towards solving the present inequities in the education of U.S. Latinos and improving their academic achievement, as well as developing their academic use of language—both in English and Spanish.

Notes

1. "English only," with a small "o," will be used here to denote a broader understanding of English as *the only* language for all communicative exchange, whereas "English-Only" with a capital "O" will be used to denote language policy campaigns and/or movements, which aim at making English the official U.S. national language.
2. As we will outline below, bilingual education has waxed and waned. For a more complete history of the presence of languages other than English in U.S. education, see Castellanos 1983; Crawford, 2004; García, 2009, chapter 8; Wiley & Wright, 2004.
3. This is according to the 2005 American Community Survey (U.S. Census). Readers are reminded that it is estimated there are approximately 10 million undocumented Latinas/os and that the actual figure is probably much higher.
4. There are some exceptions to this. See, for example, the work of Valdés et al., 2006.
5. We use "currency" here in the Bourdieunian sense of seeing language as capital, an asset of quantifiable value (for more on this, see Bourdieu, 1991).
6. For more on this, see Del Valle, 2006.
7. Limited English Proficient (LEP) is the term used by the U.S. Department of Education and other official government documents. Most of the literature refers to English Language Learners.
8. The U.S. census uses the term "Hispanics" instead of "Latinas/os."
9. We cannot presume that these Latinas/os are English monolinguals, for the census only asks what language they speak at home.
10. The U.S. Census does not ask about the level of Spanish proficiency.
11. We use as a cut-off point of fluent English proficiency the Speak English Well category. We note that this differs from the way in which the U.S. Department of Education calculates the number of English Language Learners for they also include the Well category. We have made this decision based on our understandings of bilingualism, much of which will be discussed in the section below.
12. George Ticknor was the first professor at Harvard, and this chair was occupied by well-known American literati such as Henry Wadsworth Longfellow, James Russell Lowell, and Washington Irving.
13. We're reporting here what was meant in the context as Castilian Spanish and not what it is.
14. According to Lave and Wenger (1991), communities of practice are groups who interact and communicate regularly and have shared ways of communicating, including the use of two languages.
15. Much confusion exists regarding this label. Most of the time the label is used in conjunction with two-way bilingual programs in which two linguistic groups participate but in which instruction in one language and the other is strictly separated. Other times the label is used to refer to what are otherwise known as "developmental" bilingual education program. The choice of the term "dual language" is a way of avoiding the term "bilingual," which has become controversial in the United States. But it is also a way of signaling that both languages are developed separately at all times.
16. The term "translanguaging" is used in Wales by Cen Williams to refer to a bilingual teaching methodology that changes the languages of input and output. Baker (2003) clarifies that translanguaging is not about code-switching, but rather about an arrangement that normalizes bilingualism without functional separation. García (2009) uses the term translanguaging to refer to the dynamic plurilingual practices of bilingual communities and their children.

References

Baker, C. (2003). *Foundations of bilingual education.* Clevedon, UK: Multilingual Matters.

Bourdieu, P. (1991). *Language and symbolic power.* Cambridge, MA: Harvard University Press.

Brutt-Griffler, J. (2004). *World English: A study of its development.* Clevedon, UK: Multilingual Matters.

Campaign for Educational Equity. Retrieved from http://www.tcequity.org/i/a/document/6468_Ofelia_ELL_Final.pdf

Canagarajah, S. (1999). *Resisting linguistic imperialism in English teaching.* Oxford, UK: Oxford University Press.

Castellanos, D. (1983). *The best of two worlds. Bilingual-bicultural education in the U.S.* Trenton: New Jersey State Department of Education.

Council of Europe. (2000). Common European Framework of referencer for Languages: Learning, teaching, assessment. Language Policy Division, Strasbourg. Retrieved from http://www.coe.int/t/dg4/linguistic/CADRE_EN.asp.4

Crawford, J. (Ed.). (1992). *Language loyalties: A source book on the official English controversy.* Chicago: University of Chicago Press.

Crawford, J. (2004). *Educating English learners: Language diversity in the classroom* (5th ed.). Los Angeles: Bilingual Educational Services.

Crawford, J. (2005). Hard sell: Why is bilingual education so unpopular with the American public? *Language Policy Website and Emporium.* [Online]. Available at: http://ourworld.compuserve.com/homepages/JWCrawford/

Cummins, J. (2005). A proposal for action: Strategies for recognizing heritage language competence as a learning resource within the mainstream classroom. *Modern Language Journal, 89*(4), 585–591.

Dame Edna. (2003, February). Ask Dame Edna. *Vanity Fair,* 116.

Del Valle, S. (2003). *Language rights and the law in the United States.* Clevedon, UK: Multilingual Matters.

Edwards, J. (1994). *Multilingualism.* New York: Routledge.

Garcia, E. (2005). *Teaching and learning in two languages. Bilingualism and schooling in the United States.* New York: Teachers College Press.

García, O. (1997). From Goya portraits to Goya beans: Elite traditions and popular streams in U.S. Spanish language policy. *Southwest Journal of Linguistics, 12,* 69–86.

García, O. (2003, July/August). La enseñanza del español a los latinas/os de los EEUU. Contra el viento del olvido y la marea del inglés [The teaching of Spanish to Latinas/os in the United States. Against the wind of the forgotten and the English tide]. *Ínsula,* 679–680.

García, O. (2005). Positioning heritage languages in the United States. *Modern Language Journal, 89*(4), 601–605.

García, O. (2006). Equity's elephant in the room. Multilingual children in the U.S. are being penalized by current education policies. *TC Today, 31*(1), 40.

García, O. (2009). *Bilingual education in the 21st century: A global perspective.* Malden, MA: Wiley Blackwell.

García, O., & Bartlett, L. (2007). A speech community model of bilingual education: Educating Latino newcomers in the U.S. *International Journal of Bilingual Education and Bilingualism, 10,* 1–25.

García, O., Kleifgen, J. A., & Falchi, L. (2008). *Equity in the education of emergent bilinguals. The case of English language learners.* New York: Teachers College.

García, O., & Menken, K. (2006). The English of Latinos from a plurilingual transcultural angle: Implications for assessment and schools. In S. Nero (Ed.), *Dialects, other Englishes, and education* (pp. 167–184). Mahwah, NJ: Erlbaum.

Hornberger, N. H. (2006). Nichols to NCLB: Local and global perspectives on US language education policy. In O. García, T. Skutnabb-Kangas, & M. E. Torres-Guzmán (Eds.), *Imagining multilingual schools: Languages in education and glocalization* (pp. 223–237). Clevedon, UK: Multilingual Matters.

Kloss, H. (1977). *The American bilingual tradition.* Rowley, MA: Newbury House.

Lau v. Nichols (1974), 414 U.S. 563

Lave, J., & Wenger, E. (1991). *Situated learning: Legitimate peripheral participation.* Cambridge, UK: Cambridge University Press.

Mackey, W. F., & Beebe, V. N. (1977). *Bilingual schools for a bicultural community. Miami's adaptation to the Cuban refugees.* Rowley, MA: Newbury House.

Mazrui, A. (2004). *English in Africa after the Cold War.* Clevedon, UK: Multilingual Matters.

Norton, B. (2000). *Identity and language learning: Gender, ethnicity and educational change.* London: Longman/Pearson Education.

Norton Peirce, B. (1995). Social identity, investment, and language learning. *TESOL Quarterly, 29,* 9–31.

Pennycook, A. (1994). *The cultural politics of English as an international language.* New York: Longman.

Phillipson, R. (1992). *Linguistic imperialism.* Oxford, UK: Oxford University Press.

Skutnabb-Kangas, T. (2000). *Linguistic genocide in education — or worldwide diversity and human rights?* Mahwah, NJ: Erlbaum.

Stavans, I. (2003). *Spanglish: The making of a new American language.* New York: Rayo.

Swain, M. (2006). Languaging, agency and collaboration in advanced second language learning. In H. Byrnes (Ed.), *Advanced language learning: The contributions of Halliday and Vygotsky* (pp. 95–108). London: Continuum.

Tse, L. (2001). *Why don't they learn English? Separating fact from fallacy in the U.S. language debate.* New York: Teachers College Press.

U.S. Census. (2005). *2005 American Community Survey* [Data file]. Retrieved from http://www.census.gov/acs/

Valdés, G. (1997). The teaching of Spanish to bilingual Spanish-speaking students: Outstanding issues and unanswered questions. In M. C. Colombi & F. X. Alarcón (Eds.), *La enseñanza del español a hispanohablantes: Praxis y teoria* (pp. 263–282). Boston: Houghton Mifflin.

Valdés, G., Fishman, J. A., Chávez, R., & Pérez, W. (2006). *Developing minority language resources. The case of Spanish in California.* Clevedon, UK: Multilingual Matters.

Wiley, T. G., & Wright, W. E. (2004). Against the undertow: Language minority education policy and politics in the 'Age of Accountability.' *Educational Policy, 18*(1), 142–168.

Wright, S. (2004). *Language policy and language planning. From nationalism to globalisation.* New York: Palgrave Macmillan

12 The Role of High-Stakes Testing and Accountability in Educating Latinos

Frances E. Contreras
University of Washington

High-stakes testing and accountability mechanisms are fast becoming the primary tool for education reform in the United States. Many states are grappling with low passing rates on statewide assessments and constrained resources to compensate for these gaps in achievement, particularly among Latino and African American students. Thus, a paradigm shift in education service delivery has occurred throughout the P-16 continuum, with an emphasis on outcomes and standardized exams, and punitive consequences for all stakeholders involved. The biggest losers in this "high stakes" framework however are the students, as the myriad of achievement and exit exams are being utilized to withhold high school diplomas as well as make grade promotion decisions. While the content that Latinos are learning in schools is necessary and important to assess, it is equally important to consistently evaluate *how* these assessment and accountability mechanisms are being utilized and where the onus for the achievement gap is being placed.

Given the current accountability framework for education, with over twenty-five states requiring exit exams,[1] the emphasis on learner outcomes for schools is clear. A multitude of state level assessments like the WASL in Washington, the CAT6 in California, TAKS in Texas, and AIMS in Arizona to name a few, illustrate the continued if not increasing emphasis on accountability mechanisms for students and schools. And since close to half of Latinos in public schools attend high poverty schools, Latino students are more likely to attend schools in states that have exit exams (Zabala et al., 2007). Thus, high-stakes testing is a prevalent feature directly tied to education service delivery for Latino students in the United States. The growing concern with the current policy framework is the trend among schools and districts to "teach to the test" to improve exam scores to acceptable levels and raises the following set of questions: What challenges do high-stakes tests create for educating Latino students? What challenges are embedded in the current policy framework and is it fostering an increase in the number of Latinos being left behind in schools? Do high-stakes tests address the issue of resource inequities? And finally, what approaches to assessment may be more beneficial to meeting the needs of Latino students?

While this chapter cites several critiques of the high-stakes nature to the current accountability framework, it acknowledges the important role of assessing student learning and progress as a means of *improving* the opportunities that Latino students have to learn in the education system in the United States. Some of the well-documented critics of high-stakes exams (Nichols & Berliner, 2007; Valenzuela, 2005) also value the role that assessment plays as a measure of understanding the gaps in education that Latinos and other minority students are exposed to in this country.

This chapter is intended to provide an overview of the current context of accountability in the United States and the role that high-stakes testing plays in the education of Latino students. The chapter concludes by providing policy considerations, as educators and policy makers alike continue to grapple with low Latino student performance on state and federal exams and their implications for Latino student success along the P-16 continuum of education.

Context for Accountability

The issue of assessment and evaluation of student learning has historically been based on the premise that the function of testing is to improve student learning and ultimately raise achievement levels. Measuring student progress has been a prevalent feature of the American public education landscape with respect to policy and practice.

However, the increased role of the federal government in public education service delivery is a relatively recent phenomenon, as states have primarily controlled approaches to schooling in the United States (McGuinn, 2006). The Smith Hughes Act of 1917 was among the first pieces of legislation by the federal government to allocate funding to K-12 schools to teach agriculture. And the 1954 Supreme Court decision in *Brown v. Board of Education* represents the first federal attempt to desegregate schools in America. *Brown* found segregated schools to be a violation of the 14th Amendment and was one of the early attempts to provide all students with access to an equitable education, and the foundation for academic achievement.

The concern for student achievement is evident throughout history, as the United States has attempted to remain competitive if not ahead of other developed nations. The launching of the Sputnik Space Shuttle in 1957, for example, initiated an era of science education reform, as political leaders in the United States worried about losing ground in the field of science and being second to the Soviet Union in space exploration. The successful launching of the Soviet Spacecraft led to nationwide efforts and federal investment through the office of Education's National Defense Education program[2] in the late 1950s and 1960s, supporting collaboration between notable science professors and classroom teachers on curriculum development and revision, science standards, and fostering the development of science labs in schools (Rutherford, 1998). Sputnik also led to greater attention to science with over 15 years of investment by the federal government, and largely placed the responsibility of raising the nation's level of competitiveness in science on schools. However individual schools were not singled out nor penalized for the lack of student knowledge of science concepts. Rather, this encouraged greater attention to the field of science in K-12 schools.

Several pieces of legislation followed Sputnik in part to pressures emerging from the Civil Rights movement and served to complement the Civil Rights Act of 1964 established by the Johnson Administration. The Elementary and Secondary Education Act (ESEA) of 1965 served as the foundation for a more direct relationship between the federal government and state education systems. ESEA in particular, was a key element of the "War on Poverty" under the Johnson Administration, and sought to address school inequalities in the United States by creating a special funding allocation, Title I, for schools to better meet the needs of low-income children in the United States. ESEA also marked the beginning of Head Start. ESEA was amended in 1968 to establish Title VII and The Bilingual Education Act to address the needs of bilingual and multicultural children in schools with limited English speaking skills. One important result of these federal policy approaches was the creation of categorical aid programs that directly relate to the national policy arena (e.g., poverty, economic competitiveness), features that remain prevalent in current educational policy initiatives like No Child Left Behind.

The National Assessment of Educational Progress (NAEP) dates back to 1969 are among the early attempts to measure student achievement in grades 4, 8, and 12. Otherwise known as "The Nation's Report Card," NAEP assesses student knowledge in reading, mathematics, science, writing, U.S. history, civics, geography, and the arts from a subsample of the school-age population. NAEP expanded to provide state level assessment in 1990, to assess how states are performing among student subpopulations.

The passage of the report *A Nation at Risk* in 1983 by the National Commission on Excellence in Education spawned an even greater emphasis on accountability and raised concern that the students attending U.S. schools were not prepared to meet the demands of the workforce nor to be leaders in key industries that fuel the American economy. The report reflects the framework for education reform today, one rooted in fear of falling behind as a world leader and the need for greater accountability among schools and colleges. The report uses the term "mediocrity" to describe the students that we are preparing: "the educational foundations of our society are presently being eroded by a rising tide of mediocrity that threatens our very future as a Nation and as a people" (p. 5). The report goes on to make strong statements that compare the education delivered to an "act of war," as evident in the following excerpt:

> If an unfriendly foreign power had attempted to impose on America the mediocre educational performance that exists today, we might well have viewed it as an act of war. As it stands, we have allowed this to happen to ourselves. We have even squandered the gains in student achievement made in the wake of the Sputnik challenge. Moreover, we have dismantled essential support systems which helped make those gains possible. We have, in effect, been committing an act of unthinking, unilateral educational disarmament. (p. 5)

A Nation at Risk was in large part a direct response to the Cold War era under the Reagan administration and led to increased federal investments in public education. The broad areas of reform outlined in the report include: (a) Content of the curriculum to include emphasis on the core subjects, (b) Standard and Expectations, (c) Time on task learning the New Basics, (d) Teaching, and (e) Teaching Leadership and Fiscal Support. The "content" area includes five "New Basics" that essentially outlines "the following curriculum during their 4 years of high school: (a) 4 years of English; (b) 3 years of mathematics; (c) 3 years of science; (d) 3 years of social studies; and (e) one-half year of computer science. For the college-bound, 2 years of foreign language in high school are strongly recommended in addition to those taken earlier" (p. 5). *A Nation at Risk* led to a greater emphasis on standards as well as attention to high school graduation requirements and reinforced students learning what the report coined as "the new basics."

Following *A Nation at Risk,* a shift also occurred from an emphasis on content of the curriculum as seen in the case of Sputnik to greater importance placed on the outcomes of student learning. This paradigm shift can be seen through Goals 2000 in 1993, a bill that sought to increase the federal level of influence over states and local reform efforts by providing incentives to states to implement standards-based reforms (McGuinn, 2006).

Following Goals 2000, the Elementary and Secondary Schools Act of 1965 was up for reauthorization, and led to the Improving America's Schools Act (IASA) in 1994. IASA became part of the Clinton administration's effort to reform schools in the United States and built on the efforts of Goals 2000 to align existing federally funded education programs with state standards. IASA required annual student assessment and encouraged a single state accountability system, but did not penalize states for not having a single statewide accountability system as seen in the case of No Child Left Behind. IASA placed increased emphasis on state standards, the alignment of assessments with standards, the option for Title I schools and districts to establish charter schools, and introduced the notion of adequate yearly progress (AYP) that states were to define based on performance on state assessments (McGuinn, 2006, p. 96). The Improving America's Schools Act and efforts under the Clinton Administration to move schools closer to creating state and federal standards can be described as providing a narrower framework for federal intervention in K-12 education to raise achievement in poor schools.

No Child Left Behind

The alarmist language of "falling behind" presented in *A Nation at Risk* and IASA of 1994 together served as a foundation for the political discourse for education reform in the present, namely the No Child Left Behind Act of 2001, which became law in 2002. No Child Left

Behind, a product of the Bush Administration, has expanded the themes and concerns raised in *A Nation at Risk* and IASA, and further expands the federal role in education reform and applies an accountability framework for all states. No Child Left Behind outlined the following priorities to be funded under Titles I-VII federal funding programs:

1. Improving the academic performance of disadvantaged students
2. Boosting teacher quality
3. Moving limited English proficient students to English fluency
4. Promoting informed parental choice and innovative programs
5. Encouraging safe schools for the 21st century
6. Increasing funding for Impact Aid
7. Encouraging freedom and accountability (NCLB, 2002)

No Child Left Behind represents a top down approach to education, with the federal government mandating reform and placing emphasis on testing and outcomes, while teachers and school staff are left with how to develop approaches to raise student scores without overshadowing daily instruction (Moran, 2000, p. 8). Many researchers and practitioners are claiming that the policy has not held up to its promise of "leaving no child behind" and that it has fostered a greater number of students that are being left behind under the current accountability framework.[3] Under NCLB, states must develop a statewide accountability system to measure AYP. And by 2014, all students are supposed to test at the "proficient level" in reading and math.

NCLB is part of the accountability movement that has led to the development of ongoing measures that are designed to create statewide assessment systems to measure student performance and address areas for improvement among students not performing at passable rates. This approach to assessment has adversely impacted Latino students in the K-12 schools as it has led to statewide and local approaches that focus on outcomes (test performance) rather than the inputs necessary for optimal learning and achievement. The underlying assumption of the present accountability framework is that attaching consequences to education reform will raise student achievement. The approach does not solve the *education gap* that exists for Latino students.

The use of assessments to retain or promote students and withholding a student's diploma for not passing an exit-level examination is an example of how the current NCLB accountability framework emphasizes outcomes rather than the inputs (curricular resources, teacher professional development, physical resources) that students are exposed to in school (see Valencia, Villareal, & Salinas, 2002). This approach also serves as an example of how assessment, as it is currently being used, is perhaps doing more harm than good for students and education stakeholders alike (see Nichols & Berliner, 2007). Valencia et al. (2002) discuss how Senate Bill 4 in Texas[4] went into effect in 2002 as an extension of the NCLB accountability framework and requires third graders to pass a reading exam (in English or Spanish) to be promoted to the fourth grade. SB4 raises concern over the detrimental impact of this high-stakes educational statute for Latino students, as many Latino students are likely to represent the largest portion of students retained.

A great deal of research confirms that students who are retained are more likely to have lower achievement levels (Valencia et al., 2002; Holmes, 1989) and are more likely to drop out of high school (Rumberger, 1995; Brooks-Gunn, Guo, & Furstenberg, 1993; Valencia et al., 2002; Warren, Jenkins, & Kulick, 2006). For example, Warren et al. (2006) explored the role of high school exit exams on completion rates and found that the more difficult state exit exams did in fact lead to lower high school completion rates and higher rates of GED test taking (p. 146).

As a result of NCLB, states continue to create statewide assessment mechanisms as well as exit exams for high school graduation but have not adequately addressed the root causes of lower passing rates among students of color, including Latinos. In many states it has led to high failure rates among Latino and African American students from high poverty areas, leaving students that are from the most disenfranchised communities without a high school diploma upon exiting high school, and raises concerns about their life options beyond secondary education. The intent of the ESEA and subsequent acts that started with ESEA have fallen short of their goal of addressing the needs of poor and minority children in school via categorical aid such as Title I.

The inequitable practices in the K-12 system have led to landmark cases on behalf of students that have been subject to unjust practices in school through the use of testing. In the case of *Debra P. v. Turlington* (1984) in Florida, African American students questioned the high school graduation test required for a diploma on the basis that the exam was being administered without notice to students and used to segregate African American students into remedial courses. The court ruled on behalf of the students, requiring schools to provide adequate notice regarding both the test administration schedule as well as exposure to the curriculum that reflects the content of the exam.

The state of Texas, perhaps one of the leading states in this high-stakes accountability framework for education, is also the furthest along in legal action against high-stakes tests. The Mexican American Legal Defense and Educational Fund (MALDEF) filed a class action suit against the state, in *American GI Forum v. Texas Education Agency* (2000), citing that the TAAS (Texas Academic Assessment System) graduation requirement discriminates against Latino and African American students and violates their due process, as they have unequal access to resources in schools. The court ruled that while the exams do appear to negatively affect Latinos and African American students, this was not the "intent" of the TAAS exam. Rather it was designed to motivate students to learn and perform on such exams (Moran, 2000; Valencia et al., 2002). While this case was largely a defeat in Texas, it raises the important issue of whether the legal system in other states may be a venue for such action. In *American GI Forum v. Texas Education Agency* (2000), one important acknowledgement the courts made was the fact that the TAAS exam did, in fact, have a disparate impact on Latinos and African Americans, as they encountered far lower passing rates than their White peers.

In *Valenzuela v. O'Connell* (2007), the court first ruled against maintaining the California High School Exit Exam as a condition of graduation for the class of 2006 by an Alameda County Superior Court judge. The ruling suspended the California High School Exit Exam (CAHSEE) as a requirement for graduation. State Superintendent of Public Instruction Jack O'Connell, however, asked the California Supreme Court to appeal the Alameda County court decision and uphold the exit exam. The California Supreme Court ruled in favor of O'Connell in 2007, mandating the implementation of the CAHSEE required by all schools and districts in the state of California. While the arguments included a discussion of the differential passing rates for low-income and minority populations, the trend in placing the onus of an inequitable education and preparation is placed on the student in states where exit exams are in place.

This trend is likely to exacerbate higher drop out rates and a greater level of disengagement with school among students failing such exams after repeated attempts. The underlying question we should be asking is: Why are these students failing and what can we do to improve this situation? NCLB and subsequent statewide exit exams that have evolved as a result of meeting the requirements of this legislation move away from the initial intent of ESEA. NCLB calls for accountability without the emphasis on collective responsibility to raise achievement and provide greater levels of investment for Title I schools and populations in greatest need of academic supports.

The Achievement Gap as a Reflection of the Education Gap

Differential achievement levels are largely a result of the differential inputs in education services that Latinos receive as they progress through the public school system. A myriad of factors play a role in the educational status of Latino youth, ranging from an uneven distribution of school resources, inequitable access to curriculum, lack of intervention and services for English Learners, coming from low-income households, and limited access to highly trained teachers. A student's experience in school plays a vital role in how a student navigates the preK-12 system and beyond, providing (or not) youth with the tools to acquire academic, life, and social skills to navigate through life.

The majority of Latino students in the United States attend urban schools and close to half of the Latino students have parents with less than a high school education (U.S. Census Bureau, 2004). According to the National Center for Education Statistics (NCES), 49% of Latino fourth-grade students were enrolled in schools with the highest measure of poverty (schools with greater than 75% of students eligible for free or reduced-price lunch), compared to 5% of White and 16% of Asian/Pacific Islander students (NCES, 2006). The low-income levels of Latino students also translate into limited (if any) access to health care and lower levels of pre-school enrollment. Thus, Latino students are more likely to enter school with greater needs and less preparation (Gándara & Contreras, 2009).

In addition, Latinos are more likely to attend segregated schools in the United States, segregated by race and poverty, language, and now represent the group with the highest high school dropout rates (Frankenberg, Lee, & Orfield, 2003; Gándura & Contreras, 2009). The context of education for Latino students explains, in part, the patterns of low achievement in schools, as Latino students are more likely to have differential inputs both within the school and in their communities to support their educational development. Table 12.1 presents the NAEP scores for math for fourth graders in the United States in 2005. The data illustrates 33% of Latinos below basic compared to 11% of Whites and Asians Americans in the fourth grade.

The data further illustrates 48% scoring at the "At Basic" level, for a total of 81% of the Latino test takers "At Basic" or "Below Basic" in the scores. If this pattern continues for these Latino students as they progress through their primary and secondary grades, then they are also likely to score low on state-level assessments including high school exit exams. The NAEP data shows that gaps in achievement, particularly among Latinos and Whites, and Latinos and Asian Americans begins very early.

Statewide Standardized Exams

All states have some form of standardized exams to measure student performance in content areas. As a requirement under NCLB, states are required to measure AYP on statewide assessments. Thus, greater emphasis continues to be placed on statewide assessment mechanisms to meet NCLB requirements for student learning in the content areas of reading and math. In 2005, approximately half of all Latino students attended public schools that required exit exams, and by 2012, this number is expected to increase to 87% (Center on Education Policy, 2006).

Table 12.1 NAEP Scores for 4th Graders in Math, 2005 (Percent)

Race/ethnicity	Below Basic	At Basic	At Proficient	At Advanced
White	11	42	40	7
Black	40	47	12	1
Latino	33	48	18	1
Asian American	11	35	40	14
American Indian	31	47	20	2

Source: U.S. Department of Education, Institute of Education Sciences, National Center for Education Statistics, National Assessment of Educational Progress (NAEP), 2005 Mathematics Assessment.

Table 12.2   AIMS Test Results, All Districts, All Grades, by Ethnicity (2005–2006)

			White	African American	Latino	Native American	Asian American	Total
READ	%	04–05	74.9	52.6	52.3	44.0	78.0	60.7
	Meeting		(11231)	(2128)	(15783)	(1398)	(830)	(31370)
	Standard	05–06	75.4	55.2	53.9	45.3	80.4	61.6
			(10367)	(2108)	(16035)	(1329)	(813)	(30652)
	Change		0.5	2.6	1.6	1.3	2.5	0.9
MATH	%	04–05	74.2	50.4	51.8	38.9	80.6	59.9
	Meeting		(11312)	(2148)	(15963)	(1394)	(825)	(31642)
	Standard	05–06	74	52.2.6	53.7	41.6	83.2	60.9
			(10159)	(2069)	(15849)	(1321)	(790)	(30188)
	Change		0.4	1.8	1.9	2.8	2.6	1.0

Source: www.ade.state.az.us, 2006.

In Arizona, 40% of the student population is Latino (Arizona Department of Education, 2007). The AIMS exam in Arizona is administered for grades 3–12 in the academic areas of reading writing and math. The scores for reading and math for the 2005–2006 testing cycle below illustrate lower levels of performance among all underrepresented groups, with very minimal gains from the previous year.

The AIMS data illustrates a recurring issue for students of color—lower performance on standardized achievement exams, and raises a serious concern over the "exit exam" feature of these assessments.

In California, the same pattern emerges on the CAT 6 exam. Close to half of the students at the K-12 level in the state of California are Latino (48%, with 21.3% English Learners) compared to 30.3% Whites, the second largest ethnic group in the state (California Department of Education, 2006). However, achievement patterns differ significantly, with Latino students scoring far below their White peers as seen in Table 12.3.

Table 12.3   California Standards Test Results in English Language Arts & Math Percentage of Students Scoring at Proficient and Above by Subgroup (All Students) 2003–2006

Subgroup	2003		2004		2005		2006	
	English	Math	English	Math	English	Math	English	Math
African American	22	19	23	19	27	23	29	24
American Indian	31	29	31	28	36	32	37	35
Asian	55	60	56	60	62	65	64	67
Filipino	48	44	50	45	55	50	58	54
Latino	20	23	21	23	25	27	27	30
Pacific Islander	31	31	31	31	36	35	39	38
White	53	47	54	46	58	51	60	53
English Learners	10	20	10	20	12	24	14	25
Economically Disadvantaged	20	24	21	25	25	29	27	30

Note: These are aggregate data for students in Grades 2–11 and represent the state totals.
Source: California Department of Education, 2006.

Table 12.4 California High School Exit Exam (CAHSEE) Results for Mathematics and English Language Arts (ELA) by Ethnicity, 2006 (Percent)

Subject		All Students	African American	American Indian	Asian	Hispanic or Latino	White
# Tested	Math	795,243	85,298	7,586	54,812	391,090	221,611
Passing		59	40	56	83	49	77
# Tested	ELA	777,702	75,376	7,145	62,782	383,506	214,999
Passing		61	50	63	70	50	81

Note: The data for all grades represents grades 10–12.
Source: California Department of Education.

The California data mirrors Arizona's pattern with Latino students scoring far below their White counterparts on the CAT 6 exams. As for exit exam performance among Latino students, close to half of the Latinos passed the exam in 2006 (see Table 12.4). Like many other states with exit exams, the data is alarming with Latino and African American students in particular having the lowest passing rates. These data illustrate a failure to educate students of color at levels comparable to their White and Asian peers. In fact, this achievement gap is but a reflection of the gap in education provided to these students.

English Learners in the Accountability Framework

English learners in this country are largely underserved in the K-12 system. Between 1979 and 2004, the number of children (ages 5–17) who spoke a language other than English at home increased from 3.8 to 9.9 million, or from 9 to 19% of all children (NCES, 2006). Of the students designated as EL students, 80% are Latino (U.S. Department of Education, 2006). The disparate achievement levels of English learners compared to their peers has been well documented, and illustrates the largest gaps in achievement on statewide assessments (Gándara, Rumberger, Maxwell-Jolly, Callahan, 2003; Fry, 2007). In the wake of English Only policies and efforts, such as Proposition 227 in California, schools are left with few options and minimal resources to adequately address the needs of English Learners in this country. While this student population requires the greatest investment to minimize test score gaps and raise levels of linguistic development, funding for English Learner (EL) programs is tenuous at best, and varies widely across state and district contexts.

Gándara et al. (2003) attribute a set of unequal resources that lead to the unequal outcomes that we witness in student achievement among EL students in California. Gándara et al. (2003) present a range of inequitable conditions that EL students experience in California's schools, including: inequitable access to highly trained teachers, limited professional development opportunities for teachers of English learners, lack of appropriate assessments to measure EL achievement, lack of access to materials and curriculum resulting in a weak curriculum, and inequitable access to adequate facilities. This context for EL education they contend is an unequal foundation for learning and explains the low-achievement among this growing segment of the K-12 population (Gándara et al., 2003).

For English learners in this country, having to pass exit exams is likely to be an even greater obstacle as the programs for youth who need to learn English are underfunded, poorly staffed, and lack the appropriate resources within schools (Rumberger & Gándara, 2000). Given this grossly deficient context for educating Latino EL students, we can only assume that exit exams are likely to further demonstrate gaps in achievement. The passing rates for English learners are therefore even lower for this group, as seen in the achievement levels on exit exams for select states in Table 12.5.

Table 12.5   Passing Rates on Exit Exams Among English Learners on the First Attempt, Select States 2003–2004 (Percent)

State	All Students Math	ELLs Math	All Students Reading Language Arts English	ELLs Reading Language Arts English
Arizona	39	10	59	12
California	74	49	75	39
Florida	76	48	54	13
Washington	44	10	65	17

Source: Center on Education Policy, February 2006 (based on state department of education data collected by the Center July 2005).

According to the Center on Education Policy, less than half of the English Learners in the states they assessed passed the exit exams in their respective states on the first attempt. And in states like Arizona and Washington, a mere 10% of ELs passed the math exit exam on the first try. This has serious implications for graduation with a diploma, but more importantly causes us to question the curricular offerings and additional academic support services English Learners are receiving in their school context to raise achievement levels.

Plausible explanations for Gaps in Achievement

Researchers have attributed these differential achievement levels to the uneven inputs within schools, student curricular choices that mirrors tracking, and limited social capital within the home and community (Nettles, Millett, & Ready, 2003; Jencks & Phillips, 1998; Zwick, 2004; Gándura & Contreras, 2009). While others have attributed differential performance on standardized exams, like state exams, to testing biases that adversely affect communities of color (see Gould, 1995). This section presents the challenges that high-stakes tests create for educating Latino students as well as the challenges embedded in the current policy framework, including a discussion of resource inequities.

Fulfilling the Stereotype

Steele (1997) has developed the theory of "stereotype threat" to explain why many African Americans, as well as other students of color, may perform poorly or become disengaged with school. Steele explains that African Americans are more likely to worry about their academic performance, particularly the risk of confirming the stereotype that they are intellectually inferior. Steele found that African American students scored lower on tests after being told that other ethnic groups regularly performed better on the exam than African Americans. He asserted that as a result of this pre-exam information, these students experienced a level of performance anxiety, or pressure that they might fulfill the previous patterns of low performance associated with their ethnic group. African Americans internalize these stereotypes in testing situations, often paralyzing their optimal performance on exams. Steele also suggests that this belief of inferiority can lead to greater disengagement with school in general out of fear of living up to the stereotypes that exist regarding their ethnic group.

Given comparable educational experiences for African American and Latino youth, similar patterns have emerged for Latino students with respect to performance on standardized exams and disengagement in school. While the psychological impact of exit exams has yet to be revealed for Latino students, informal accounts from parents suggest that exit exams are adversely affecting Latino student motivation to graduate from high school due to a sense of hopelessness that they experience after failing initial attempts (Contreras et al., 2008). Fear that they can not pass the exit exam the state requires may contribute to higher levels of disengagement with school.

In the state of Washington for example, according to parent feedback given at a statewide LEAP conference in March 2005, parents expressed that the exit exam "was affecting the self-esteem of their child"—to the point that their student asked, "what is the point if I am going to fail the exam anyway?" (LEAP parent participant, 2005). As a result of exit exams, a common fear of educators across the country is the degree to which the policy will contribute to already differential levels of engagement among students of color.

In addition to the issue of stereotype threat on exams, even Latino high achievers are more likely to have a lower self-perception of their ability in the content areas of reading, writing, and science. For example, in a study conducted on the SAT test taking pool of high school students, Latinos were less likely than their peers to rate themselves in the Highest 10th percentile in comparison to their peers across all areas, particularly in math (Gándara & Contreras, 2009). These Latino students, while a self-selected sample, represent the likely college-going pool of students. Yet these high achievers, regardless of the fact that many had GPAs exceeding a 3.6, were more likely to rate themselves in the "Above Average" or "Average" categories when asked to compare their ability to their peers on given subjects, rather than in the Highest 10th percentile category. These findings suggest that perhaps Latino students do not receive adult affirmation with respect to their ability in schools nor among their peers (see, for example, Valenzuela, 1999).

Quality of Teachers

One of the key issues regarding the high-stakes nature of education service delivery for Latinos is teacher quality and experience. I have already noted earlier that Latino students are more likely to attend urban schools in high poverty neighborhoods. Latinos are also more likely to attend schools with less qualified teachers. According to the Urban Institute, teachers in schools with high concentrations of English learners are more likely to have "provisional, emergency, or temporary certification than are those in other schools" (Cosentino De Cohen, & Clewell, 2007, p. 4).

Not only are schools in more affluent areas better organized to provide more rigorous curricula, they also tend to have stronger teachers (Haycock, 1998; Ferguson, 1998). However, Haycock (1998) reviews research that show children of color, regardless of their socioeconomic level, are more likely to be taught by teachers with lower test scores and less academic preparation than those that teach predominantly White children. The quality of the teacher, measured by certification, quality of institution from which the teacher received his or her degree, and test scores, has been shown in a number of studies to have a significant impact on student performance. Ferguson (1998) found that teachers with higher scores on the exams for teachers were more likely to produce significant gains in student achievement than their lower scoring counterparts. Goldhaber and Brewer (1997), in an analysis of the National Educational Longitudinal Survey (NELS 88), also found a positive relationship between postsecondary degrees held by teachers in technical areas (math and science) and student achievement levels.

A study by the Education Trust (Peske & Haycock, 2006) examined teaching inequality for poor and minority students in Cleveland, Chicago, and Milwaukee schools. Similar to previous research on teacher quality, they found large differences between the qualifications of teachers in high minority, high poverty schools among their key findings. In particular, they found that more classes in high poverty, high minority schools are more likely to be taught by out of field teachers. This finding reinforces the already apparent fact that Latino, poor and underrepresented students are less likely to attend schools with highly qualified teachers in comparison to more affluent, non-minority concentration schools. Peske and Haycock (2006) also call for addressing teacher equity more directly by investigating the allocation and uneven usage of Title I money (p. 10) among districts. They claim that some districts may be using funds that should be used toward professional development and salaries for teachers in Title I schools, that tend to be new to the field, to fund teacher salaries and professional development efforts (Peske & Haycock, 2006, p. 10).

Darling-Hammond (2000) also describes how teachers at successful schools tend to have strong academic credentials and have been prepared to teach students with special needs, and, consequently, this enhances the success of the students in their classroom. Teachers with high levels of education and certification are more likely to also create a strong coherent curriculum through the processes of planning and their own professional development and individual efforts to learn more about pedagogical approaches to best serve their students. They are also more likely to collaborate with their peers and develop a peer mentoring network, which allows them to share information and approaches to teaching. Conversely, in poor urban schools, there is a high teacher turnover and limited resources for teachers to be supported professionally (e.g., professional development opportunities). With the uneven access to qualified teachers and issues of high turnover in poor urban schools and the fact that Latino students are less likely to be exposed to a coherent curriculum, reducing gaps in achievement represents a challenge and multi-faceted dilemma.

School Inequity: Access to Curriculum and Quality of Instructional Offerings

Differential access to curriculum and knowledge begins early. In a study primarily focusing on Mexican immigrant children, Crosnoe (2006) discusses how the children from Mexican immigrant families had lower rates of learning in the subject of math compared to their native peers across races/ethnicities, which represented a long-term risk for learning and achievement in school. Crosnoe, using the ECLS-K, which essentially assesses what children know before entering school, showed differences in pre-K knowledge (p. 37). He also describes how these initial differences become compounded or magnified in the process of formal schooling. While Crosnoe's findings were specific to Mexican immigrant children, he also found similar patterns of socioeconomic inputs across native Latino groups and comparable predicted achievement in math, although they were slightly higher than the Mexican immigrant children. His findings therefore are applicable to the umbrella Latino student group. His study conveys that attention in the earlier grades, particularly in math, is one effort worth investing in as a solution to reducing gaps in student achievement.

The particular school that a student attends can also have a significant impact on his or her academic achievement. Schools in more affluent neighborhoods have been shown to provide more rigorous college preparatory and honors courses than schools in lower income communities that largely serve populations of underrepresented students. For example, in a recent study of California schools, Betts, Rueben, and Danenberg (2000) found that the lowest income schools offered only 52% of their classes as meeting college preparatory requirements, while this figure rose to 63% in the highest income schools. Similar patterns held up when the analysis was done by percent of non-White students enrolled in the school. Likewise, Betts et al. (2000) found that "the median high [socioeconomic status] school has over 50 percent more AP courses than the median low-SES school" (2000, p. 72). Based on analyses of High School and Beyond data, Adelman (1999) concluded that the rigor of the curriculum to which students are exposed is more predictive of long-term academic outcomes than even the powerful variable of family socioeconomic status. That is, Adelman argues, that the greatest amount of the variance in long-term academic outcomes among ethnic groups can be attributed to the differences in the groups' exposure to high level curricula—particularly to advanced mathematics. Black and

Latino students are least likely to take advanced mathematics courses because they are not available in their schools and because they are less frequently counseled or "tracked" in to them.

The state of California, where nearly half of the K-12 population are Chicano/Latino, these curricular and school inequities are apparent, and, ultimately, affect student performance on statewide assessments and the high school exit exam. In an effort to directly address the school inequities that poor and minority students experience, *Williams v. State of California* (2002) sought to "ensure that every student in California is provided basic educational necessities, such as trained teachers, adequate textbooks, and minimally habitable facilities." The case argued that Latino and underrepresented students were grossly underserved in the California public education system. The case settled with the ACLU on behalf of low-income students of color in 2004 for the uneven resources that these youth are exposed to in California schools and has led to greater state oversight on educational services and inputs that poor students of color receive in public schools.

Financial Support for NCLB

The lack of resources and overall investment in schools, teachers, and students, in large part, explains the achievement gap between Latino students and their peers. Therefore we should not be surprised by the fact that under NCLB the gaps in overall achievement are not significantly improving among Latino, African American, and poor students.

The current accountability framework raises the overarching question, why do we continue to accept and endorse the high-stakes nature of testing, particularly if we are not providing youth from poorer schools and neighborhoods with the necessary resources to perform on these exams? The investment in schools that have pronounced achievement gaps have not received a level of funding that would help them to achieve NCLB goals.

While setting high standards and expectations for our students is essential, we also need to ensure that we provide schools with the resources to deliver the results we expect from them. According to the American Federation of Teachers, since the passage of No Child Left Behind, there has been a gap between the amount of funding has promised and the amount provided for NCLB programs (AFT, 2007). Critics of NCLB argue that the previous Bush Administration provided less funding than the education arena had expected to implement this policy change. Table 12.6 shows the trends in funding that Congress authorized versus the amount actually appropriated for NCLB efforts under federal government allocations.

The gap from 2002–2006 between the amount that Congress had committed and the actual funding allocated is $40 billion dollars according to the AFT's estimates. One would think that the gaps in achievement presented for the state level assessments as well as passing rates on exit exams would lead to greater levels of investment in Latino youth and English learners, the stu-

Table 12.6 NCLB Funding Allocations 2002–2007 (in Billions of Dollars)

Year	Funding Authorized	Actual Funding Appropriated	Gap
2002	26.4	22.2	4.2
2003	29.2	23.8	5.4
2004	32.0	24.5	7.5
2005	34.3	24.5	9.8
2006	36.9	23.5	13.4
2007	39.4	23.7	15.8

Source: U.S. Department of Education.

dents with the lowest passing rates on exit exams and lowest scores on state level exams. According to AFT, the opposite has happened and the gap in the amount promised versus allocated has increased. This suggests a shift in priorities on the part of Congress and diminishes the potential for schools and districts to achieve NCLB goals.

Conclusion

The differential achievement levels between Latinos and Whites illustrate serious implications for the successful progression of Latino students beyond high school. The high-stakes accountability framework, while designed to address the gaps in achievement, has served to exacerbate the problem of uneven access by creating an outcomes oriented model, one rooted in a deficit model paradigm (see for example, Valenzuela 1999). It is no wonder that by the time Latinos get to the point of high school graduation, if they make it, they have not received an education that prepares them for life beyond high school and higher education. The gaps in achievement discussed here clearly point to uneven "inputs" in education service delivery.

The growing importance placed on exit exams requires ongoing analysis and evaluation, particularly with respect to the detrimental impact of these assessments are having on the educational progression of Latino students. While assessment is necessary and may be extremely useful to educators as well as the policy arena in knowing the achievement levels of students, how we use these measures needs greater attention and thoughtful action. The following recommendations are designed to provide tangible approaches toward changing the current punitive accountability paradigm to one of investment and shared responsibility for our collective future.

Recommendations

1. *Provide schools with the resources to reduce the achievement gaps that exist among Latino students and their peers.*   Policy initiatives designed to invest, not punish are the first step towards changing the high-stakes nature of education. For example, the City of Seattle has passed a Families and Education Levy, the most recent totaling $120 million to invest in select schools to raise the achievement levels of students of color and low-income students not meeting the WASL standards. While test scores have not dramatically increased, it is too soon to judge the progress of the scores. The program has resulted in greater collaboration among teachers, administrators, service providers and families, and uses a holistic approach to education service delivery and drop out prevention.

2. *Provide teachers with the necessary support and resources to modify curriculum and adhere to state content standards.*   Resources for professional development among teachers are an important step towards validating and supporting their efforts to address the needs of Latino students.

3. *Provide English Learners with the resources and strong curricular offerings to raise achievement.*   Expecting EL students to pass an exit exam when in many cases they do not receive services or additional academic support is inefficient public policy and tells us very little more than what we already know—that EL students need additional investment in education and a meaningful curriculum designed to accelerate learning.

4. *Provide English Learners with assessments in Spanish until English literacy skills are adequately developed.*   For students that are classified as English Learners and have a better command of the Spanish Language, provide assessment for these youth in Spanish until they are competent in the English language for assessment. Many states have already taken these steps such as the Standards Based Tests in Spanish (STS) in California, where the purpose is to assess Reading/Language Arts and Mathematics performance in a student's

home language of Spanish for grades 2–4. For grades 5–11, students have the option of taking the Aprenda 3 exam which measures student knowledge of reading, mathematics, language, and spelling (for grades 5–8). Both the STS and Aprenda 3 exams are designed to measure student knowledge in content areas and take into account the fact that a student's best language may be Spanish, depending on where these students are with their English Language development.

5. *Develop exams that measure the content of what is taught in schools.* Continued efforts to align statewide assessments with state standards should remain a priority as this approach is likely to provide the best measure of student learning for teachers and provide a mechanism for intervention. Teachers should also play a role in providing direct feedback on these statewide assessments to ensure that they match the curriculum being taught in the classroom.

6. *Do away with exit exams as a requirement for high school graduation.* Ongoing assessment of student learning throughout grades K-12 is necessary to monitor student knowledge acquisition. However, withholding diplomas does more harm than good for Latino students and as discussed, may lead to greater levels of disengagement or higher drop out rates (Valencia et al., 2002) as seen in the high correlation between dropping out and failure on the TAAS examination (American GI Forum v. State of Texas, 2000).

7. *Place value on locally developed and implemented assessments of student Learning.* While emphasis in the high-stakes accountability framework is on statewide assessments, placing greater value on locally developed and implemented assessments of student learning is a stable measure of progress and a more applicable approach for intervention. This also moves states and local school districts away from the strong federal role in assessment and balances the "outcome" approach with one that can adapt and react to student needs.

Blanket accountability policies like NCLB need to be evaluated as to whether they are adversely affecting students, teachers, schools, and districts. Have we set up a culture of fear within our schools? Assessment should be used to better children, not point the finger at individuals that are falling behind. How do we shift the paradigm from a deficit model to one that focuses on the need for greater investment rather than punishment? We ask schools to make up for the socioeconomic differences, health disparities, and institutionalized barriers that exist in society without a fraction of the resources and level of investment necessary to accomplish the task. The gap in fiscal support from Congress authorized under NCLB tells a story of the failure to invest in Latino and underserved youth.

Greater attention must be placed on the serious crisis that exists in the education of Latino students—a 52% high school completion rate does a fairly good job of telling the current story— one of too little invested in a youthful and growing segment of the population. Indeed, assessments are one way that we can measure student progress. However, as seen with the data on passing rates for state level assessments, the current accountability framework under NCLB appears to be further exacerbating the problem rather than fostering solutions to raise Latino student achievement. And since 1 in 4 residents in the United States will be Latino by the year 2050 (U.S. Census, 2004), the need to invest in this growing majority is critical for the economic infrastructure of several agricultural, technological, and business industries in the U.S.

The current story of Latino underachievement must be rewritten. Testing and accountability measures only explain part of the current crisis, and as I have summarized, are contributing to the problem by using assessment to withhold diplomas and influence how education is delivered in schools. This story, while it is still in the process of being written for the growing numbers of Latinos in the K-12 system, has the potential to be altered rather than predetermined. And perhaps in this revised storyline, the Latino students that successfully persist in the pipeline might not be depicted as the anomalies, but represent the norm, where a standard of high expectations and access to academic resources applies to all students, regardless of their racial, linguistic, neighborhood, parental education, and economic backgrounds. We as a society should bear the "high stakes" for our collective failure to educate all children equitably and responsibly. The stakes are too high for us to sit back and allow a punitive approach to dominate the education of our children.

Notes

1. The State of Washington will phase in the math portion of the WASL as an exit measure in 2010.
2. The National Defense Education Act of 1958 (NDEA), led to the creation of the National Defense Education Program under the Department of Education, administered from 1949–66.
3. For a detailed discussion of NCLB and its impact in Texas, see Angela Valenzuela's edited volume, *Leaving Children Behind*.
4. For a detailed account and critique of SB 4, please see Valencia, R. R., & Villarreal, B. J. (2003). Improving students' reading performance via standards-based school reform: A critique. *The Reading Teacher, 56*(7), 612–621.

References

A Nation at Risk: The Imperative for Educational Reform. (1983). Washington, DC: United States Department of Education.

Adelman, C. (1999). *Answers in the Tool Box: Academic intensity, attendance patterns, and bachelor's degree attainment.* Washington, DC: U.S. Department of Education.

Betts, J., Rueben, K., & Danenberg, A. (2000). *Equal resources, equal outcomes? The distribution of school resources and student achievement in California.* San Francisco: Public Policy Institute of California.

Brooks-Gunn, J., Guo, G., & Furstenberg, F. (1993). Who drops out of and who continues beyond high school? A 20-year follow up of Black youth. *Journal of Adolescent Research, 3,* 271–294.

Contreras, F., & Stritikis, T. (2008). Understanding opportunities to learn for Lationos in Washington State. Report prepared for the Washington State Legislature and Commission on Hispanic Affairs.

Cosentino De Cohen, C., & Clewell, B. (2007). *Putting English language learners on the educational map.* Education in Focus Policy Brief. Washington, DC: Urban Institute Education Policy Center.

Crosnoe, R. (2006). *Mexican roots, American schools.* Stanford, CA: Stanford University Press.

Darling-Hammond, L. (2000). Teacher quality and student achievement. *Educational Policy Analysis Archives, 8*(1). Retrieved from http://epaa.asu.edu/epaa/v8n1

Debra P. v. Turlington, 474 F.Supp. 244 (M.D. FL 1979).

Debra P. v. Turlington, 730 F.2d 1405 (11th Cir. 1984).

Ferguson, R. (1998). Can schools narrow the Black-White test score gap? In C. Jencks & M. Phillips (Eds.), *The Black-White test score gap* (pp. 318–374). Washington, DC: The Brookings Institution.

Frankenberg, E., Lee, C., & Orfield, G. (2003). A multiracial society with segregated schools: Are we losing the dream? Report prepared for The Harvard Civil Rights Project.

Fry, R. (2007). *How far behind in math and reading are English Language learners?* Washington, DC: Pew Hispanic Center.

Gándara, P., & Contreras, F. (2009). *The Latino education crisis: The consequences of failed social bolicies.* Cambridge, MA: Harvard University Press.

Gándara, P., Rumberger, R., Maxwell-Jolly, J., & Callahan, R. (2003). English learners in California schools: Unequal resources, unequal outcomes. *Education Policy Analysis Archives, 11*(36), 1-54.

Goldhaber, D., & Brewer, D. (1997). Evaluating the effect of teacher degree level on educational performance. In W. Fowler (Ed.), *Developments in school finance, 1996* (pp. 197–210). Washington, DC: U.S. Department of Education, National Center for Education Statistics.

Gould, S. J. (1995). *The mismeasure of man.* New York: Norton.

Haycock, K. (1998). *Good teaching matters. A lot. Thinking K-16.* Washington, DC: The Education Trust.

Jencks, D., & Phillips, M. (1998). *The Black White test score gap.* Washington, DC: The Brookings Institution Press.

McGuinn, P. (2006). *No Child Left Behind and the transformation of federal education policy, 1965–2005.* Lawrence: University Press of Kansas.

Moran, R. (2000). Sorting and reforming: High-stakes testing in the public schools. *Akron Law Review, 107,* 34.

Nettles, M., Millett, C., & Ready, D., (2003). *Attacking the African American-White achievement gap on college admissions tests* (pp. 215–238). Brookings Papers on Education Policy. Washington, DC: Brookings.

Nichols, S., & Berliner, D. (2007). *Collateral damage how high-stakes testing corrupts America's schools.* Cambridge, MA: Harvard Education Press.

O'Connell v. Superior Court (Valenzuela). (2005), Cal.App.4th [No. A113933. First Dist., Div. Four. Aug. 11, 2006.]

Peske, H., & Haycock, K. (2006). *Teaching inequality. How poor and minority students are shortchanged in teacher quality.* Washington, DC: The Education Trust.

Rumberger, R. (1995). Dropping out of school. A multi-level analysis of students and schools. *American Education Research Journal, 32,* 583-625.

Rumberger, R., & Gandara, P. (2000). *The schooling of English learners.* Report prepared for the Linguistic Minority Research Institute, University of California, Santa Barbara, and PACE at the University of California, Davis.

Rutherford, F. (1998). Sputnik and Science Education. Paper posted online by the American Association for the Advancement of Science. Retrieved from http://www.nationalacademies.org/sputnik/ruther1.htm

Steele, C. (1997, June). A threat in the air: How stereotypes shape intellectual identity and performance. *American Psychologist, 52*(6), 613–629.

The American GI Forum v. Texas Education Agency, 87 F. Supp. 2d 667 (W.D. Tex. 2000).

The Nation's Report Card. (2005). *National assessment of educational progress.* Washington, DC: U.S. Department of Education Institute of Education Sciences, NCES 2006–453.

U.S. Census Bureau. (2004). American Community Survey. Washington, DC: U.S. Census Bureau Reports.

Valencia, R., Villareal, B., & Salinas, M. (2002). Educational testing and Chicano students: issues, consequences, and prospects for reform. In R. Valencia (Ed.), *Chicano school failure and success* (pp. 253–309). New York: Routledge/Falmer Press.

Valenzuela, A. (1999). *Subtractive schooling.* Albany: State University of New York Press.

Valenzuela, A. (2005). *Leaving children behind.* Albany: State University of New York Press.

Warren, J., Jenkins, K., & Kulick, R. (2006, Summer). High school exit examinations and state-level completion and GED rates, 1975 through 2002. *Educational Evaluation and Policy Analysis, 28*(2), 131–152.

Williams v. State of California, (2002) No. 312236.

Zabala, D., Minnici, A., McMurrer, J., A., Hill, D., Bartley, A., & Jennings, J. (2007). State high school exit exams: Working to raise test scores. Publication of the Center on Education Policy, retrieved from http://www.cep-dc.org.

Zwick, R. (2004). *Rethinking the SAT.* New York: Routledge/Falmer Press.

13 Assessing the Higher Education Opportunity Structure for Latino Students
Research and Policy Trends at the Turn of the Century

Stella M. Flores
Vanderbilt University

Introduction

Public policy has become a constant, even if not always welcome, companion of educational research. The relationship between public policy and educational outcomes has played a particularly prominent role in the higher educational opportunity structure of Latino students in the United States. From the lingering effects of the *Brown v. Board of Education* U.S. Supreme Court ruling on desegregation in 1954 to the *Gratz v. Bollinger* and *Grutter v. Bollinger* decisions on affirmative action in 2003, the implementation of educational law and policy at the local, institutional, state, and federal levels are often in direct response to (or in direct neglect of) major public policy institutions, such as U.S. courts. Latino students have been at the forefront of these events since before the *Brown* decision, as seen in the 1947 *Méndez v. Westminster School District* case, and in recent years as one of the primary groups affected by Supreme Court rulings on desegregation/resegregation cases regarding voluntary student assignment plans in Louisville and Seattle (Ancheta, 2007; *Parents Involved in Community Schools v. Seattle School Dist. No. 1, 2007; Meredith v. Jefferson County Bd. of Educ., 2007*; Valencia, 2005). Although the *Brown* and *Méndez* cases involved elementary and secondary school access, these decisions set the stage for college access in very tangible ways. Opportunities afforded at the elementary and secondary level create the foundation for the realization of college aspirations. Ironically, even when court decisions and other policy were passed to better the socioeconomic status of Latinos, tracking the effects of such rulings at the national level, particularly educational attainment outcomes, was often not possible until recent decades. In the 1970s, "Hispanic" finally became an official category on the U.S. Census, a policy decision that made it possible to better track this group's status in the nation's higher education enrollment and completion records (MacDonald, Botti, & Clark, 2007). The availability of more reliable and representative methods of counting Hispanic/ Latino individuals in the United States changed the nature of the research, policy decisions, and attention afforded this long-ignored constituency.

Recently, however, multiple public policy actors beyond the courts and the schools now play a powerful role in who is able to obtain a college degree. Some of the most important educational decisions affecting low-income and racial minority students, particularly Latinos, have taken place outside of state and federal courts and have been made instead through state legislatures, voter referenda, and leaders of postsecondary institutions. These situations are most prevalent in states that have instituted voter-mandated bans on affirmative action, including California, Washington, and Michigan. Similarly, Arizona has now voted in a ban barring specific college access opportunities and services to undocumented immigrants in the state's public colleges and universities. It appears that Latino students are once again one of the groups most affected by these policies, due to their youth, strong demographic presence, consistent low-income status, often a vulnerable immigration status, and the U.S. locations to which they migrate or choose to reside in.

The remainder of this chapter provides a snapshot of the relevant research and public policy that affect the current and future higher education opportunity structure for Latinos in the United States. I describe how select public policy trends have influenced Latino access to U.S. higher education. The opportunity structure of higher education for Latinos is a critical topic for analysis not only for the generations of Latinos that are affected, but also for the welfare of the economies and educational systems in which Latinos participate. In sum, the state of this population's educational attainment has reached a crossroads between a public education crisis, economic possibility, and substantial retreat from the equity laws that led to and resulted from the U.S. civil rights movement. In Section I, I provide a description of the growing prominence of Latinos in the higher education opportunity structure of the United States. In Section II, I offer a policy prognosis and an assessment of primary issues regarding the educational attainment of Latinos. Section III offers my concluding thoughts.

I. The Growing Prominence and State of Progress for Latinos in the Higher Education Opportunity Structure

Seven years into the new millennium, Latinos comprised the largest minority in the United States and the largest minority in 22 states (U.S. Census Bureau, 2007). In addition, the dispersion of Latino families into areas beyond traditional "gateway" cities and into the South and the Midwest call for more careful attention to state higher education policies in these regions (Massey & Capoferro, 2008; Waters & Jimenez, 2005). Historically, Latin American migration has not been equally dispersed across the United States. It has instead concentrated primarily in U.S.-Mexico border states such as California, Arizona, and Texas, and in particular states with a high labor demand, such as Illinois (Durand, Massey, & Capoferro, 2005). However, with the unprecedented dispersion of Latin American immigrants across the United States beginning in the 1990s, it is no longer accurate to consider these few states in the traditional Latino migration settlement regions if we are to consider the national welfare of all Latinos in the United States. It is now essential to consider the effects of higher education policies in many other states, including North Carolina, Georgia, and Tennessee. The higher education opportunities for Latinos in these states will be just as crucial as they have been in the Southwest. An evaluation of Latino postsecondary attainment over time and through various policy cycles offers insightful lessons as to where this community will go in the future under current educational conditions and policies.

Few will contest the value of a college degree in the current technological environment and global economy. Access to a college education has become the primary gateway to the middle class, a development that has implications for subsequent generations, given the role parental income and education play in the odds of enrolling in college (Ellwood & Kane, 2000; Long & Riley, 2007). As the largest minority in the nation and in nearly half of all U.S. states, Latinos' opportunities for college access go beyond an individual concern to one of state and national economic health. Figure 13.1 presents data from the U.S. Current Population Survey, across various decades, for Hispanic, White Non-Hispanic, and Black Non-Hispanic individuals. Educational progress for Latinos in terms of college enrollment can be seen over several decades from a low of approximately 26% in 1972 to 36% in 2000 (Kurlaender & Flores, 2005). However, this rise over time in Latino college enrollment cannot be described as consistent, linear progress. Instead, Latino enrollment shows sudden increases in 1976, 1983, and 1992, with dramatic drops in 1978, 1985, 1994, and 1999. College completion rates over time, as shown in Figure 13.2, indicate an even bleaker picture for Latino individuals age 25 to 29. College completion rates for this group are the lowest when compared to White, Black, and Asian individuals, and their rate of completion hovers at just below 10% from 1975 to 2000, except for a slight peak into double digits (approximately 11%) in 1984. Thus, while enrollment rates are increasing, completion rates have remained relatively stagnant for Latinos even as they have increased their share of the general college age and college enrolled population over time.

These statistics, which can best be described as lukewarm stability rather than a triumph, lead to the following questions. What is the Latino role in the U.S. higher education story? Do providing greater access opportunities to Latino students yield social and economic benefits for the nation as a whole? How will the next generation of Latinos in the U.S. experience having access to or being barred from higher education opportunity? Responsible public policy that addresses the effects of the educational status of the current generation of Latinos on the higher education opportunities of future generations will require a number of educational strategies from multiple policy actors and disciplinary perspectives.

II. Policy Prognosis: Research and Projected Issues of Concern

We have seen considerable development in research on Latino students since the 1980s. From research on bilingual and migrant education (San Miguel & Valencia, 1998; Salinas & Fránquiz, 2004) to the inclusion of Latino students in desegregation studies (Orfield & Lee, 2005) to the assessment of the impact of major federal education laws such as No Child Left Behind on the Latino population (Valenzuela, 2004), the status of the educational experience of Latino students has received increased attention from researchers and practitioners.

Previous research on postsecondary education issues, such as public funding for higher education, provided an analysis of how general higher education policies might affect Latino students even if such policies were not specifically targeted at this group (Olivas, 1997). However, the last two decades have seen an almost unprecedented surge of activity in the courts, state legislatures, and among voters regarding educational policies, including state financial aid and race-conscious programs, that inevitably affect Latino students. This policy activity, in conjunction with the undeniable demographic growth and dispersion of the Latino population since the 1990s, calls for another updated assessment of these policy decisions on the higher educational opportunities and outcomes of this population. That is, to examine the opportunity structure for this population more comprehensively, researchers and practitioners should expand their analyses to include various aspects of higher education policy. Not doing so will limit our knowledge of how all areas of higher education are relevant to the mobility of Latino students in the greater postsecondary structure.

Using a multidisciplinary framework, then, what are key issues currently affecting Latino students in the higher education opportunity structure? At the turn of this century primary issues include (a) college chances and college choice, including the role of the community college and Hispanic Serving Institutions (HSIs); (b) the unintended and unexpected effects of state and federal financial aid policies; and (c) the delicate future of race-conscious policies and their interconnection with citizenship issues.

College Chances and College Choice

The college access literature (Bowen & Bok, 1998; Dynarski, 2003; Kane, 1998; Long & Riley, 2007; McDonough, 1997; Terenzini, Cabrera, & Bernal, 2001) has offered a number of explanations as key factors in college entry. These factors fall into one of three categories: academic preparation, cost and financial aid, and information constraints (Pallais & Turner, 2007). However, with the exception of a few studies, a number of earlier analyses do not include Latinos in sufficient numbers, if at all, to appropriately diagnose what influences and/or barriers are most significant to this population (Olivas, 1986). What, then, are the odds of college enrollment and completion for Latinos? Burgeoning research on this population since the 1990s has added significantly to an understanding of this issue (Cabrera, Nora, & Castañeda, 1992; Chapa & De la Rosa, 2004; Gándara, 1995; Hurtado & Carter, 1997; Hurtado & Ponjuán, 2005; Niu, Tienda, & Cortés, 2006; Solórzano, 1994, 1995; Tienda & Niu, 2006). Part of the answer to this question can be found by looking at a student's parental income and education. Even among students with similar academic achievement records, those from more privileged backgrounds are significantly more likely to attend college (Ellwood & Kane, 2000). It has therefore become a notable fact that college attendance in the United States is associated with parental income and education, regardless of academic ability. As Latino students on average have lower incomes and educational attainment rates than majority students, addressing the educational opportunities of Latino families, rather than just the students, appears to be a logical and sustainable policy recommendation.

Of the Latino students who overcome dismal graduation rates well below the national average (Swanson, 2004), most will enter a community college as their first postsecondary institution (Adelman, 2005; Kurlaender, 2006). It is therefore also important to examine the quality and performance of community college systems as a predictor of educational attainment. If community colleges are as relevant to Latino students as are the public secondary schools, then what level of scholarly, programmatic, and governmental attention should these institutions receive? To what extent should institutional accountability processes be incorporated into the transfer process for students seeking a four-year degree? While not all Latinos entering community colleges ultimately seek a four-year degree, many do, and a sizeable majority of them never realize this goal (Leigh & Gill, 2003). The college choice literature has consistently suggested that starting a postsecondary degree at a community college decreases the odds of completing a four-year degree (Rouse, 1995). However, any gain in educational attainment affects the overall goal of increased economic and social welfare for a Latino family, which in turn will increase the educational prospects of successive generations.

Embedded in the generational issue of differential educational outcomes among racial and ethnic groups and which organizations are best suited to address these gaps is the question of institutional identity. The Hispanic Serving Institution (HSI), with its unique history in U.S. higher education, will be at the center of these debates. These institutions do not share the historical grounding of Historically Black Colleges and Universities (HBCUs), but they are nonetheless growing in number and evolving in character. If Latinos are significantly more likely to attend an HSI than a non-HSI, what are the appropriate expectations to have of and levels of support for these institutions in terms of quality and graduation outcomes, given the student population they are likely to educate? Recent work on HBCUs suggests that there is a wage penalty for having attended one of these schools in the 1990s, compared to those who attended in the 1970s (Fryer & Greenstone, 2007). Other research shows that the benefits of attending an HBCU extends beyond education by providing social, political, and religious leadership for the African American community that can not be quantified (Allen & Jewell, 2002). A logical question for the HSI, then, is how to measure the status and progress of these institutions in the future—by wages, leadership development, graduation outcomes, all of the above? What types of labor market and graduate school options will Latino HSI graduates have? Do particular economic and social benefits exist from attending an HSI versus a non-HSI? The HSI has had an understated yet important role in the development of Latino college graduates.

Research has documented that the Hispanic Serving Institution is a primary staple of Latino higher education (Benitéz & DeAro, 2004; Laden, 2004; Santiago, Andrade, & Brown, 2004). Only 12.9% of African Americans in the United States attend an HBCU, yet nearly a majority of Hispanic students attend an HSI (Benitéz & DeAro, 2004; Provasnik & Shafer, 2004). As a bedrock of educational access, the critical role the HSI, whether a two- or four-year institution, plays in producing a national population of college-educated Latinos cannot be ignored by public policy. Additional research that builds upon the pioneering research of previous examinations

(Laden, 1999, 2004) is a necessary academic and social contribution for future postsecondary studies. In addition, increasing their visibility in the policy world will be essential if the survival and rise in quality of HSIs are to be sufficiently sustained well into the future.

The Unexpected Beneficiaries of Financial Aid Policies from States and the Federal Government

Financial aid policies resulting from the authorization of the Higher Education Act of 1965 ushered in a new era of fiscal accessibility to low-income students (Fitzgerald & Delaney, 2002). In 1990, however, the proportion of need-based aid awarded by federal and state governments began to dramatically decrease, as the merit-based aid—financial aid based on academic achievement outcomes—offered by states increased (Doyle, 2006; Dynarski, 2004; Heller, 2005). While offering incentives to perform well in high school and therefore attend college appears to be a useful strategy to increase academic achievement, public aid distributed to students who are significantly more likely to go to college based on family income and education levels distorts the original intentions of U.S. financial aid programs (Doyle, 2006; Heller & Marin, 2004). Since Latino students are a group with high odds of not completing high school, overwhelmingly poorer than their peers, and have parents who do not have a college education, the implications of state aid programs that are likely to benefit the privileged are particularly grave for the Latino population. A relevant geographic consideration of these aid programs, then, is whether states with large Latino populations are merit-aid states. Of the 15 states that had merit-aid programs in 2006, most were in the South. New Mexico, Nevada, and Florida are the only states in this group that traditionally have had a large Latino population. However, the demographic growth of Latinos in the South foreshadows new challenges, as Latino school-age children begin to enter higher education in this region. In other words, if demographic trends continue, Latino students may comprise a high percentage of high school gradates in states that prioritize merit aid funding over need-based funding. Educational projections of Latino high school graduates indicate that this population will comprise the largest demographic growth in every state in the nation, except Hawaii (Western Interstate Commission for Higher Education, 2008).

The Delicate Future and Interconnection of Race-Conscious Policies and Citizenship Status in Colleges and Universities

Race-conscious policies and programming have experienced a volatile era of retraction, reinstatement, and readjustment since the 1996 *Hopwood* decision regarding the use of race in college admissions at the University of Texas at Austin. Although the use of race as a factor in college admissions was formally reinstated via the *Grutter* decision in 2003, not all eligible institutions complied and a number of questions were left unanswered. For example, race-based scholarships and what were formerly known as minority recruitment and retention programs remain unsettled educational policy issues (Ancheta, 2007). Such issues are particularly relevant for Latinos receiving scholarship aid from all levels of postsecondary institutions (two-year to professional schools), and for university-sponsored retention programs tailored to underrepresented students like Latinos. Adjusting institutional strategies to reflect legal developments is as critical for HSIs as it is for highly selective institutions if persistence and graduation rates are a goal.

Also embedded in race-conscious programs are issues of citizenship and immigration law. Latinos face citizenship complications in the college-attainment process overwhelmingly more than any other race or ethnic group, due to their immigration rates and history. While undocumented students gained the guarantee of a free public school education via the *Plyler v. Doe* decision, they are not guaranteed the opportunity to attend a postsecondary institution in the

United States. A number of states have extended the opportunity for talented high school graduates to enroll in college by passing in-state resident tuition policies, also known as state dream acts that significantly discount the cost of attending college, while other states, including Arizona, have restricted access for this population (Olivas, 2004; Redden, 2007). However, state legislation designed to create opportunity for the undocumented immigrant population, a majority of which is from Latin America, is limited in effectiveness because it does not supersede federal immigration law (Olivas, 2004; Passel, 2005). The result is a generation of students caught in a limbo of unclear race-conscious and citizenship-restricted laws that govern their higher education access. This "policy interaction" between institutions and state and federal governments will define the future of college access for this population. Furthermore, because Latino family members often have differing citizenship status, the issue does not affect the undocumented student alone. Family education policy targeted at the Latino population will have to take all of these factors into account. Understanding the direct role of citizenship in conjunction with and separate from ethnicity will require more detailed, better funded, and creative data-collection methods than are currently available in any public dataset.

III. Conclusion

As Latinos continue to participate in the U.S. education system in unprecedented numbers, the public policy and institutional issues that affect them will also continue to grow in number and evolve in character. College choice, financial aid, and race/citizenship policies are the higher education matters most significant to this population. However, as research and policy activity over the last decade has shown, the way to address each of these higher education issues may require a detailed state-by-state prognosis of opportunity before a national prognosis can be accurately assessed. Moreover, Latinos are no longer the domain of particular U.S. regions, in that the migration patterns and shifts in economic development of the last 20 years have modified the traditional Latino immigrant story.

Previous legal victories have presented expanded educational opportunity for Latino students. However, legal challenges to and the retraction of civil rights policies have also added new barriers. Nowhere are these barriers more evident than in California, where all race-conscious programming and employment programs are prohibited, including the provision of bilingual education in the public schools without a specific waiver. Despite these challenges, demographic

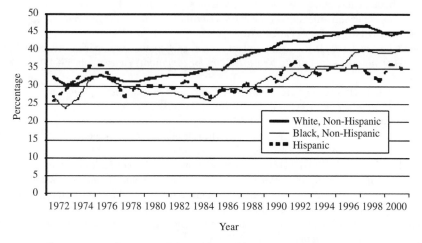

Figure 13.1 Enrollment rates of 18- to 24-year-olds in degree-granting institutions, by race/ethnicity: 1972–2000. Source: U.S. Department of Commerce, Bureau of the Census, Current Population Survey, unpublished data. Kurlaender & Flores, 2005.

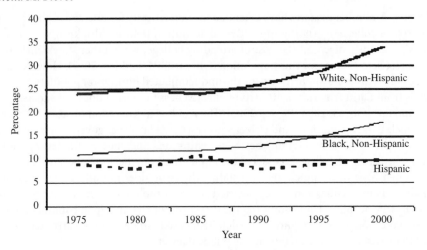

Figure 13.2 Percent of 25- to 29-year-olds who have completed college (Bachelor's Degree or higher), by race/ethnicity: Selected years, 1975–2000. Source: U.S. Department of Education, National Center for Education Statistics, Digest of Education Statistics (2001), based on U.S. Department of Commerce, Bureau of the Census, March Current Population Surveys. Kurlaender & Flores, 2005.

reports and substantiated projections have confirmed that the Latino influence on almost all public institutions in the country will be of the utmost significance. A continuous assessment of challenges, opportunities, and successes as a multidisciplinary community of researchers and practitioners will be essential to the progress of Latino students in the higher education opportunity structure of the United States well into the new millennium.

References

Adelman, C. (2005). *Moving into town—and moving on: The community college in the lives of traditional-age students.* Washington, DC: U.S. Department of Education.

Allen, W. R., & Jewell, J. O. (2002). A backward glance forward: past, present, and future perspectives on historically Black colleges and universities. *Review of Higher Education, 25,* 241–261.

Ancheta, A. (2007). Anti-discrimination law and race-conscious recruitment, retention, and financial aid policies in higher education. In G. Orfield, P. Marin, S. M. Flores, & L. M. Garcés (Eds.), *Charting the future of college affirmative action: Legal victories, continuing attacks, and new research* (pp. 15–34). Los Angeles: The Civil Rights Project at UCLA.

Benitéz, M., & DeAro, J. (2004). Realizing student success at Hispanic-serving institutions. In B. V. Laden (Ed.), *Serving minority populations: New directions for community colleges* (pp. 35–49). San Francisco: Jossey-Bass.

Bowen, W., & Bok, D. (1998). *The shape of the river: Long-term consequences of considering race in college and university admissions.* Princeton, NJ: Princeton University Press.

Brown v. Board of Education I. 347 U.S. 483 (1954).

Cabrera, A. F., Nora, A., & Castañeda, M. B. (1992). The role of finances in the persistence process: A structural model. *Research in Higher Education, 33*(5), 571–593.

Chapa, J., & De La Rosa, B. (2004). Latino population growth, socio economic and demographic characteristics, and implications for educational attainment. *Education and Urban Society, 36*(2), 130–149.

Doyle, W. R. (2006). Adoption of merit-based student grant programs: An event history analysis. *Educational Evaluation and Policy Analysis, 28,* 259–285.

Dynarski, S. M. (2003). Does aid matter? Measuring the effect of student aid on college attendance and completion. *American Economic Review, 93,* 279–288.

Dynarski, S. M. (2004). The new merit aid. In C. M. Hoxby (Ed.), *College choices: The economics of where to go, when to go, and how to pay for it* (pp. 63–97). Chicago: University of Chicago Press and the National Bureau of Economic Research.

Durand, J., Massey, D. S., & Capoferro, C. (2005). The new geography of Mexican immigration. In V. Zuniga & R. Hernández-León (Eds.), *New destinations: Mexican immigration in the United States* (pp. 1–20). New York: Russell Sage.

Ellwood, D. T., & Kane, T. J. (2000). Who is getting a college education? Family background and the growing gaps in enrollment. In S. Danziger & J. Waldfogel (Eds.), *Securing the future: Investigating in children from birth to college* (pp. 283–324). New York: Russell Sage.

Fitzgerald, B. K., & Delaney, J. A. (2002). Educational opportunity in America. In D. E. Heller (Ed.), *Condition of access: Higher education for lower income students* (ACE/Praeger Series on Higher Education; pp. 3–24). Westport: Praeger.

Fryer, R. G., & Greenstone, M. (2007, April). *The causes and consequences of attending historically black colleges and universities* (NBER Working Paper No. 13036). Cambridge, MA: National Bureau of Economic Research.

Gándara, P. C. (1995). *Over the ivy walls: The educational mobility of low-income Chicanos.* Albany: State University of New York Press.

Grutter v. Bollinger, 539 U.S. 306 (2003)

Heller, D. (2005). Can minority students afford college in an era of skyrocketing tuition? In G. Orfield, P. Marin, & C. Horn (Eds.), *Higher education and the color line: College access, racial equity, and social change* (pp. 83–106). Cambridge, MA: Harvard Education Press.

Heller, D. E., & Marin, P. (Eds.). (2004). *State merit scholarship programs and racial inequality.* Cambridge, MA: The Civil Rights Project at Harvard University.

Hopwood. v. Texas, 78 F. 3d 932 (5th Cir. 1996); cert denied, 518 U.S. 1033 (1996).

Hurtado, S., & Carter, D. F. (1997). Effects of college transition and perceptions of the campus racial climate on Latino college students' sense of belonging. *Sociology of Education, 70,* 324–345.

Hurtado, S., & Ponjuán, L. (2005). Latino educational outcomes and the campus climate. *Journal of Hispanic Higher Education, 4*(3), 235–251.

Kane, T. J. (1998). Racial and ethnic preferences in college admissions. In C. Jencks & M. Phillips (Eds.), *The Black-White test score gap* (pp. 431–456). Washington, DC: Brookings Institution.

Kurlaender, M. (2006). Choosing community college: Factors affecting Latino college choice. *New Directions for Community Colleges, 133,* 7–19.

Kurlaender, M., & Flores, S. M. (2005). The racial transformation of higher education. In G. Orfield, P. Marin, & C. Horn (Eds.), *Higher education and the color line: College access, racial equity, and social change* (pp. 11–32). Cambridge, MA: Harvard Education Press.

Laden, B. V. (1999). Two-year Hispanic-serving community colleges. In B. K. Townsend (Ed.), *Two-year colleges for women and minorities* (pp. 225–243). New York: Garland.

Laden, B. V. (2004). Hispanic-serving instituions: What are they? Where are they? In B. V. Laden (Ed.), Special Issue on Hispanic-serving community colleges. *Community College Journal of Research and Practice, 28*(3), 181–198.

Leigh, D. E., & Gill, A. M. (2003). Do community colleges really divert students from earning bachelor's degrees? *Economics of Education Review, 22,* 23–30.

Long, B., & Riley, E. (2007). Financial aid: A broken bridge to college access? *Harvard Educational Review, 77,* 39–63.

MacDonald, V. M., Botti, J. M., & Clark, L. H. (2007). From visibility to autonomy: Latinos and higher education in the U.S., 1965–2005. *Harvard Educational Review, 77,* 474–504.

Massey, D., & Capoferro, C. (2008). The geographic diversification of American immigration. In D. S. Massey (Ed.), *New faces in new places: The changing geography of American immigration* (pp. 25–50). New York: Russell Sage Foundation.

McDonough, P. (1997). *How social class and schools structure opportunity.* Albany: State University of New York Press.

Méndez v. Westminster School District, 64 F. Supp 544 (S.D. Cal 1946), affirmed 161 F.2d 774 (9th Cir 1947).

Niu, S., Tienda, M., & Cortés, K. (2006). College selectivity and the Texas top 10% law: How constrained are the options? *Economics of Education Review, 25,* 259–272.

Olivas, M. (Ed.). (1986). *Latino college students.* New York: Teachers College Press.

Olivas, M. (1997). Research on Latino college students: A theoretical framework and inquiry. In A. Darder,

R. D. Torres, & H. Gutierrez (Eds.), *Latinos and education: A critical reader* (pp. 468–486). New York: Routledge.

Olivas M. (2004). IIRIRA, the dream act, and undocumented college student residency. *Journal of College and University Law, 30,* 435.

Orfield, G., & Lee, C. (2005). *Why segregation matters: Poverty and educational inequality.* Cambridge, MA: The Civil Rights Project at Harvard University.

Pallais, A., & Turner, S. E. (2007). Access to elites. In S. Dickert-Conlin & R. Rubenstein (Eds.), *Economic inequality and higher education: Access, persistence and success* (pp. 128–156). New York: Russell Sage Foundation.

Parents Involved in Community Schools v. Seattle School Dist. No. 1 and Meredith v. Jefferson County Bd. of Educ., 2007 WL 1836531.

Passel, J. S. (2005) *Estimates of the size and characteristics of the undocumented population.* Washington, DC: Pew Hispanic Center.

Plyler v. Doe, 457 U.S. 202 (1982).

Provasnik, S., & Shafer, L. L. (2004). *Historically black colleges and universities, 1976 to 2001* (NCES 2004–062). Washington, DC: Government Printing Office.

Redden, E. (2007). An in-state tuition debate. *Inside Higher Education.* Retrieved March 1, 2007, from http://www.insidehighered.com/news/2007/02/28/immigration

Rouse, C. E. (1995). Democratization or diversion — the effect of community-colleges on educational-attainment. *Journal of Business and Economic Statistics, 13,* 217–224.

Salinas, C., & Fránquiz, M. (Eds.). (2004). *Scholars in the field: The challenges of migrant education.* Washington, DC: AEL

San Miguel, G., & Valencia, R. (1998). From the treaty of Guadalupe Hidalgo to *Hopwood:* The Educational plight and struggle of Mexican Americans in the Southwest. *Harvard Educational Review, 68,* 353–412.

Santiago, D. A., Andrade, S. J., & Brown, S. E. (2004). *Latino student success at Hispanic serving institutions.* Washington, DC: Excelencia in Education. Retrieved November 4, 2005, from http://www.cierp.utep.edu/projects/lss/pbrief.pdf

Solórzano, D. G. (1994). The baccalaureate origins of Chicana and Chicano doctorates in the physical, life, and engineering sciences: 1980–1990. *Journal of Women and Minorities in Science and Engineering, 1,* 253–272.

Solórzano, D. G. (1995). The baccalaureate origins of Chicana and Chicano doctorates in the social sciences. *Hispanic Journal of Behavioral Sciences, 17,* 3–32.

Swanson, C. B. (2004). Sketching a portrait of public high school graduation: Who graduates? Who doesn't? In G. Orfield (Ed.), *Dropouts in America: Confronting the graduation rate crisis* (pp. 13–40). Cambridge, MA: Harvard Education Press.

Terenzini, P., Cabrera, A. F., & Bernal, E. M. (2001). *Swimming Against the Tide: The Poor in American Higher Education.* College Board Research Report No. 2001–1. New York: The College Board.

Tienda, M., & Niu, S. (2006). Capitalizing on segregation, pretending neutrality: College Admissions and the Texas top 10% law. *American Law and Economics Review, 8,* 312–346.

U.S. Census Bureau. (2007, July 16). *Facts for features: Hispanic heritage month 2007.* Retrieved October 14, 2007, from http://www.census.gov/Press-Release/www/releases/archives/facts_for_features_special_editions/010327.html

Valencia, R. R. (2005). The Mexican American struggle for equal educational opportunity in *Mendez v. Westminster:* Helping pave the way for *Brown v. Board of Education. Teachers College Record, 107,* 389–423.

Valenzuela, A. (Ed.). (2004). *Leaving children behind: How "Texas-style" accountability fails Latino youth.* Albany: State University of New York Press.

Waters, M., & Jimenez, T. R. (2005). Assessing immigrant assimilation: New empirical and theoretical challenges. *Annual Review of Sociology, 31,* 105–25.

Western Interstate Commission for Higher Education. (2008). *Knocking at the college door: Projections of high school graduates by state and race/ethnicity, 1992–2002.* Boulder, CO: Author.

14 Latin@ Faculty in *Academelandia*

Luis Urrieta, Jr.
University of Texas, Austin

Rudolfo Chávez Chávez
New Mexico State University

Introduction

When Latin@ faculty come together, because we are indeed a small group of faculty stretched out across higher education institutions around the country, there are, in most cases, genuine happy greetings. We often exchange *abrazos* of solidarity, and smiles of affirmation. We ask each other how we are; how our respective families are doing; we ask about and brainstorm about our academic and personal projects; we talk about the travel we all love to hate; our health is many times a topic of interest and concern; and many times we ask the pervasive question, "how are things going for you?" At that point, the tone often shifts and we begin to use that space of comfort to express the issues that make our work as faculty both difficult and fulfilling. In this chapter we will address the broad topic of Latin@ faculty in the academy from a historical perspective to address the issues that most affect Latin@ faculty and to identify the creative ways we survive and often resist in *academelandia*.

A Backdrop to Latin@ Faculty[1] in *Academelandia*

Research supports and affirms that the story of Latin@ faculty in the academy is a story of struggle (Delgado Bernal & Villalpando, 2002). Academic life is full of unforeseen forces pulling in contradictory and cacophonic cadence in which Latin@ faculty, in general, feel isolated (Delgado Bernal, Elenes, Godínez, & Villenas, 2006; Gándara, 1995; Padilla & Chávez Chávez, 1995). Yet, it is in the academy that Latin@ faculty make their professional lives (Yosso, 2006).

We are not trying to essentialize a narrative about being a Latin@ faculty member because surely there are, we hope, Latin@ faculty within the academic world who have always been treated with a sense of fairness, dignity, and respect. Yet, keeping in mind the overall institutional and structural "chilly" and "alienating" tenor of academe (Aguirre, 2000, p. vi), faculty of color, Latin@ faculty included, have documented with *testimonios* the disrespect and oftentimes hardships of being one of the few faculty of color and moreover the only Latin@ faculty in their respective sites of struggle (Padilla & Chávez Chávez, 1995; The Latina Feminist Group, 2001). Disrespect against Latin@ faculty is often not blatant and seemingly oppressive; it is the subtle, cumulative miniassaults (Pierce, 1974, in Smith, Yosso, & Solórzano, 2006) and microaggressions (Solórzano, 1998) that make such revelations instructive.

While the culture of the academy can be alienating even to White males of humble origins, for faculty of color with further detachment from its normative indicators, alienation seems to happen with great consistency. For Latin@ faculty in general, and especially for Latinas, Latin@s of working-class origins, and queer Latin@s, the academy can be particularly an unwelcoming place socially, culturally, and economically (Baca, 1992; Cuádraz, 1992; Garza, 1992; Guerrero, 1998; Sandoval, 1998; Sotello Viernes Turner, Myers, & Creswell, 1999; Segura, 2003; Verdugo, 1992). Interestingly, it is this place of ambivalence and precariousness that places many faculty of color, including Latin@ faculty, as central players to the diversity drama that transpires within higher education institutions (Torres, 2006).

The dynamic of hostility experienced by Latin@ faculty in the academy, we believe, is "a struggle of borders" (Anzaldúa, 1987, p. 77) that results in a psychic restlessness. Anzaldúa (1987) describes this restlessness as the "constant state of mental *nepantilism,* an Aztec word meaning torn between…the cultural and spiritual values of one group to another" (p. 78). It is this complexity that makes Anzaldúa's ideological concept of *mestizaje* a state of beginning for many Latin@ faculty, who have, rightly so, decided to make teaching and learning within the many private and public institutions of higher education our spaces, our terrains of engagement. Anzaldúa provides for us a *rendija* into understanding and coming to terms with our own complexity as cultural entities that are raced, gendered, sexualized, classed, and always, so it seems, in perpetual transition because of the many, sometimes unforeseen, tensions that result from hegemonic cultural bias and prejudice in the academy.

In 2003, the U.S. Census Bureau officially declared the Hispanic population to be the largest minority group in the United States totaling 38.8 million (Census, 2004). When this population increase is compared with other racialized groups—Whites, Blacks, Asians, and other non-Hispanics—the share of the total change is a whopping 51.3% (Fry, 2006). The vivid presence of Latin@s is rooted within an array of cultural and linguistic desires that meld into a thick complexity of economic, cultural, and linguistic symbiosis. This includes the reality that nation-wide, enrollment at U.S. universities is growing in its diversity profiles and that great benefits are incurred when a diverse student body and faculty is present (Bennet, 2004; Sotello Viernes Turner et al., 1999; Wilds, 2000).

Yet, as the U.S. Census Bureau (2006) reports in the years surveyed (1992, 1998, and 2003) the rising percentage of Latin@s in the professorate can be deceiving, increasing from 13.9%, to 18.5%, and more recently to 23.8%, for the respective years. Promising it seems. However, the total of full-time and part-time instruction faculty and staff in degree-granting institutions, in "research," "doctoral," and "comprehensive," both "public" and "private" as well as "private liberal" and "public 2-year" is 3.5%. As of 2003, the White full-time and part-time instructional faculty and staff comprised 80.3% of those same degree-granting institutions, while African Americans were 5.6%; Asian/Pacific Islanders were 9.1% (a growth of 29.8%), and American Indian/Alaskan Native comprised 1.5% of the total.

The origins of academia, depending on the contexts and in degrees, function with tacitly understood social, cultural, and economic synchrony that promote well-to-do if not wealthy, White, male, and heterosexual cultural norms (Córdova, 1998; McLaren, 1997; Stanley, 2006a, 2006b). Yet, for many Latin@ faculty, academia is a chosen space, a place for struggle coupled with social and intellectual activism that demands political action (Delgado-Romero, Manlove, A. N., & Manlove, J. D., 2007; Ginsburg, 1995; Rosaldo, 1997). Although early prominent Latin@ faculty members from previous eras come to mind, such as Américo Paredes, George I. Sánchez, and Tomás Rivera (Saldívar, 1997), the academy has traditionally not been welcoming to Latinos and especially non-welcoming for Latinas (Pesquera & Segura, 1997; Segura, 2003).

Within this mélange, civil rights struggles in different eras were crucial for Latin@ groups in terms of access to higher education. Federal programs facilitated Latin@ and Chican@ participation in higher education through the G.I. Bill of Rights, the National Defense and Education Act of 1958, the Civil Rights Act of 1964, and the Higher education Act of 1965. Such legislation coupled with federal financial aid programs, grants, and affordable tuition initiatives allowed for more access for Latin@s to attend colleges and universities (Aguirre & Martínez, 1993; Orfield, Marin, & Horn, 2005); nevertheless, the number of Latin@ faculty has increased at an extremely slow rate since the late 1960s (Aguirre & Martínez, 1993).

In the 1970s, the number of Latin@ faculty was sparse at best. Aguirre and Martínez (1993) found that in 1976 Chican@ faculty numbered less than 1% of the total full-time faculty within higher education institutions. "Five years later," they reported, "Chicano [*sic*] faculty constituted 1.1 percent of the total full-time faculty in the United States" (p. 53). By 1985, Chican@ faculty were still less than 1%. By 1989, based on a trend analysis by Milem and Astin (1993), Aguirre and Martínez realized that the Chican@ professorate had not "increase[d] appreciably" since 1976.

In 1988 in a *Change* essay, Michael A. Olivas called the Carnegie Foundation readership for self-examination regarding Latin@ faculty recruitment. Olivas made his position clear:

> I could cite more subtle practices, such as the heightened reliance on standardized testing and the indifference of philanthropy to Hispanic communities. The laundry list could continue but advances no purpose. Instead, I choose one issue on which to focus my point: the need for more Latino [*sic*] professors. *I believe that this need is the single most important key to any hope for increasing Latino access* [italics added]. (1988, p. 6)

Olivas highlighted the importance of Latin@ faculty recruitment to increase access and educational attainment for future generations of Latin@ family members, students, and other faculty. The increased presence of Latin@ faculty would subsequently increase recruitment, retention, and thus increase diversity.

Similarly, in an explosive monograph titled *Women and Minority[2] Faculty in the Academic Workplace: Recruitment, Retention, and Academic Culture,* commissioned by the Association for the Study of Higher Education, using 1980 and 1993 data sets, Adalberto Aguirre, Jr. (2000) conducted a comprehensive investigation to understand the significance of rethinking the academic culture that has, per his analysis, kept many women and minority faculty in marginal status. In the past three decades, recruitment, retention and academic culture for women and minorities, Latin@ faculty notwithstanding, have been continuously at odds with the very nature of higher education institutions since little regard is given to how diverse faculty "fit" in institutions dominated by mostly White men (Aguirre, 2000). In the 1990s, Latin@ faculty continued to remain underrepresented despite appreciable gains in the earning of PhDs. Additionally, Latin@s and faculty of color in general were immersed in struggles that challenged and questioned the assumption that some knowledge is of more value than others (Acuña, 2000).

In this regard, Aguirre (2000) argued, "faculty members must align themselves with and participate in institutional networks that define one's position in a knowledge hierarchy" (p. iv). Aguirre's argument is then driven by the idea that workplaces can be described as "chilly" and "alienating" both for women and faculty of color who also have heavier teaching and service loads thereby reducing their opportunities for research and publications. The paradox is clear: Aguirre found that on one hand women and minority faculty assume institutional roles that place higher education institutions in favorable light when it comes to the surface structure ideology of diversity and pluralism; on the other hand, the deep ideological structures of tenure and promotion for women and minority faculty are ignored (Aguirre, 2000). Therefore, "[t]he academic workplace is thus chilly and alienating for women and minority faculty because they are ascribed a peripheral role in the academic workplace and are expected to perform roles that are in conflict with expectations" (Aguirre, 2000, p. v).

To many Latin@ faculty,[3] colleges and universities are often places where sustained epistemological racism and elitism limiting epistemic possibilities create an "apartheid of knowledge" (Delgado Bernal & Villalpando, 2002; Villalpando & Delgado Bernal, 2002); marginalizing structures that maintain an "academic apartheid" (Padilla & Chávez Chávez, 1995); racial stratification because of "ideological" and "structural" mechanisms (Verdugo, 1995, p. 670); and places where underrepresentation is the unspoken norm (Sotello Viernes Turner, Meyers, & Meyers, 2000; Stanley, 2006b). For Latinas and Chicanas in particular, the academy has been a closed institution where lack of representation, misrepresentation, alienation, and exploitation are common themes (Aguilar, MacGillivray, & Walker, 2002; Gloria, 1997; Ingle, 2000; Reyes & Ríos, 2005; The Latina Feminist Group, 2004; Sotello Viernes Turner, 2002; Walker, MacGillivaray, & Aguilar, 2001). Lack of representation and misrepresentation in the academy remains poignant.

Bittersweet Success

Access to the academy for Latin@ faculty has come with "bittersweet success" (Sotello Viernes Turner & Meyers, 2000). Despite Olivas's call for Latin@ faculty recruitment in the 1980s, based on Table 229 of the *Digest of Education 2006* (U.S. Census, 2007, p. 357) in Fall 2005, there were a total of 675,624 faculty members in the U.S.; only 22,818 identified as Hispanic. The specific breakdown of Hispanic Faculty is shown in Table 14.1.

In 2005, self-identified Hispanic faculty comprised a mere 3.38% of the total number of faculty members in the United States, and, although the number did increase from 2003 by 2,739, these numbers are disproportionately low given the population increase and do not reflect population parity. Additionally, Latin@ faculty enter the academy heavily coded with significations that are historical, economic, cultural, and linguistic—both conscious and unconscious, that often determine the types of positions they have access to and acquire in the academy (Fenelon, 2003; Flores & Benmayor, 1997; Trujillo, 1998; Sotello Viernes Turner, 2002; The Latina Feminist Group, 2004; Stanley, 2006a; 2006b). In terms of Latinas, Segura (2003) instructively illustrates that: "less than 1% of all full-time faculty teaching in institutions of higher education are Latina. Only 0.4% of full professors are Latina, 0.7% are associate professors, and 1.3% are assistant professors" (p. 28). Martínez Alemán (1995) captures this tension:

> Moving into my faculty office, taking my seat at the faculty meeting or at commencement, sampling the hors d'oeuvres at the president's holiday bash, I am struck by my lived contradictions: To be a professor is to be an anglo; to be a Latina is not to be an anglo. So how can I be both a Latina and a professor? To be a Latina professor, I conclude, means to be unlike and like me. ¡Qué locura! What madness! (cited in Padilla & Chávez Chávez, 1995, p. 74)

Differentiating between elite and less elite two-year institutions, Delgado Bernal and Villalpando's (2002) findings are instructive and riveting given the slow increase in Latin@ faculty members. Delgado Bernal and Villalpando (2002) found that small, more prestigious, private four-year institutions had the smallest percentage of faculty of color; "less than 8% of the faculty at private four-year institutions self-identified as members of an underrepresented ethnic/racial group in 1998" (2002, p. 170). Contrast this with "the larger and less elite two-year institutions… [with]…the highest percentage and growth of faculty of color during the same period. In 1998,

Table 14.1   Hispanic Faculty in the United States in Fall 2005

Rank	Total	Males	Females
	22,818	12,486	10,332
Professor	3,793	2,680	1,113
Associate Professor	4,319	2,551	1,768
Assistant Professor	5,728	3,003	2,725
Instructor	5,261	2,581	2,680
Lecturer	1,233	495	738
Other Faculty	2,484	1,176	1,308

Source: *Digest of Education 2006* (U.S. Census, 2007, p. 357)

approximately 12% of the faculty at these institutions self-identified as persons of color" (2002, p. 170). Overall, Latin@ faculty account for a small percentage of the faculty on most colleges and universities, but especially at the most prestigious of them.

Sardonically, the two populations most likely to establish diversity within the lecture halls and laboratories of higher education will be women and minorities (Aguirre, 2000). Yet, all this is occurring during a time when it appears that "faculty pools are shrinking as the demand for new faculty increase[s]" (Aguirre, 2000, p. ii). Since the 1970s, faculty of color, including Latin@ faculty representation, has increased by less than 6% (Aguirre, 2000; Astin & Villalpando, 1996; Sax, Astin, Korn, & Gilmartin, 1999). Aguirre (2000) further argues that institutions of higher education have been deliberately slow in creating substantive pathways that take into account the diverse cultural capital faculty of color bring to the workplace. Institutional contradictions in the academy often create barriers that make life in *academelandia* difficult for Latin@ faculty.

> On the one hand, women and minority[4] faculty find themselves burdened with heavy teaching and service responsibilities that constrain their opportunity to engage in research and publication. On the other hand, women and minority faculty are expected to assume and perform institutional roles that allow higher education institutions to pursue diversity on campus. *But those roles are ignored in the faculty reward system, especially the awarding of tenure* [italics added]. (Aguirre, 2000, pp. iv–v)

Thus, from a structural perspective Latin@ faculty are said to be held to the same standard as all faculty, namely through the tenure and promotion process within each respective academic unit at different institutions (Perna, 2001). The tenure and promotion process is usually divided into three areas of evaluation: research, teaching, and service. Different types of universities weigh each of the three areas differently (Holling & Rodríguez, 2006). In Research I universities, tenure is often awarded on high or almost exclusively on research and scholarly production, while at some teaching institutions teaching and service is said to matter more than research. How these three areas are evaluated is not transparent because each tenure and promotion case is evaluated differently, which often makes tenure a dubious and dangerous endeavor, idiosyncratic to the department, college, and institution.

For example, research and scholarly work translate into acquiring grant money to conduct investigations, presenting papers at national conferences, and publishing in academic journals (Holling & Rodríguez, 2006). Each field and discipline has its own organizations, grant sources, and academic journals and conferences that are accorded different and often hierarchical forms of whitestream[5] prestige. The most exclusive of these organizations, journals, and conferences become the most coveted and most rewarded in terms of tenure and promotion (Holling & Rodríguez, 2006). Teaching is also evaluated differently depending on each unit and institutions, but generally student end of course evaluations are the most common way of assessing teaching ability and effectiveness.

Bauman (2004) has argued that in the olden days Big Brother was preoccupied with *inclusion*—with integration that is, getting people into line and keeping them there. Presently, *ignited by fear*, the present-day Big Brother's concern is *exclusion*—spotting the people who 'do not fit' into the place they are in, banishing them from that place and deporting them 'where they belong', or better still never allowing them to come anywhere near in the first place (Bauman, 2004, p. 132). For Latin@ faculty in the academy, the parallel to deportation is a "no" for promotion or tenure (Bower, 2002; Fenelon, 2003; Flores, Merino, & Aguirre, 1992; Tierney & Rhoads, 1993, Stanley, 2006a,b), and/or negative teaching evaluations (Chesler, Lewis, & Crowfoot, 2005), as well as rejection of their research and writings via, so called "mainstream" journals (Felon, 2003; Stanley, 2006b). It is in these acts of exclusion that Latin@ faculty are concretely shown that, per Bauman's insights, Latin@s "do not fit" and "do not belong" (Padilla & Chávez Chávez, 1995).

Until census reports began to predict the rapid growth of the Hispanic population, research agendas focused on Latin@ issues had also traditionally limited access to the most prestigious publishing, presenting, and funding venues. In political science, for example, Avalos documents (1991) that between 1964 and 1988, top ranked political science journals were significantly less likely to publish articles on race, gender, and ethnicity compared to top ranked sociology journals. Avalos (1991) found that not a single article studying the intersection of race and gender had been published in the top political science journals during that period. While overall some fields and disciplines are better at epistemological diversity than others, publishing in perceived top ranked journals has been one of the biggest obstacles for Latin@ faculty, not necessarily because of lack of capability, but because of lack of interest in our work. Avalos concluded that the few Latin@ faculty in political science doing work on race and gender issues ended up seeking publishing outlets outside of the discipline which in turn decreased their chances for tenure and promotion.

Although the blind peer review process claims to be objective, publishing in academic journals is not a neutral activity (Holling & Rodríguez, 2006). Holling and Rodríguez illustrate, through their own experience, that much of what is published in academic journals depends on the editors of these journals, the people on the editorial board, how reviewers are chosen and for what manuscripts they will serve as reviewers. Editorships and being invited as board members and as a reviewer is also not an objective selection processes. These positions and service endeavors are offered to, and accessed through networks, alliances, loyalties, and prestige—social capital. Likewise, knowledge production is not a neutral enterprise (Fenelon, 2003) and lack of epistemological diversity in the academy has been a major problem and obstacle to Latin@ faculty success resulting in what Delgado Bernal and Villalpando (2002) call "apartheid knowledge."

The subtlety of racism and inequities within the workplace is indeed a significant overbearing impediment to women and minority faculty's advancement (Baez, 2000). Aguirre's (2000) findings, without frills, speak directly to salary inequities and biased reward systems within an academic workplace where women and minorities are perceived as less competent than White male faculty. Aguirre makes the argument that White males often discredit feminist and minority research and question their legitimacy as academics, thus limiting "their access to institutional resources and rewards that promote professional socialization" (p. v). All this is occurring during a time when minorities and women have become the symbols of diversity in shrinking faculty pools.

Latin@ faculty also often see the classroom as an opportunity to raise students' consciousness and critical thinking skills even when faced with resistance because we know that teaching is not a neutral activity, but a highly political act (Freire, 1970). Issues dealing with race, social inequality, rights, gender discrimination, sexuality, citizenship, immigration and language issues, to name a few, are often taught by Latin@ faculty in college courses. Latin@ faculty are often hired to teach required courses that address diversity or "multicultural" issues, or are expected to be the experts on such subjects (Brayboy, 2003). The problem is that Latin@ faculty often are met with verbal or physical hostility by students, often predominantly White students, who do not agree with the perspectives or are ill prepared for the challenge of seeing these issues through alternative paradigms (Chesler et al., 2005; Reyes & Halcón, 1991; Urrieta & Reidel, 2006; Torres, 2006).

The microaggressions and miniassaults here described, over time, create negative, hostile, and antagonistic learning environments that cause undue stress, anxiety, and even chronic illness for Latin@ faculty (Smith, Yosso, & Solórzano, 2006). In her recent extensive literature review about faculty of color experiences at predominantly White colleges and universities, Stanley (2006a) found a variety of terms and phrases used by faculty of color to describe the overall character of many institutions of higher education: "multiple marginality, otherness, living in two worlds, the academy's new cast, ivy halls and glass walls, individual survivor or institutional transformers, from border to center, visible and invisible barriers, the color of teaching, and, navigating between two worlds" (p. 3). Dey (1994) also found that the greatest differences in stress levels for minority faculty and White faculty came from subtle or covert discrimination. Women of color, in particular, experienced excessive stress due to a perception of subtle discrimination. Racial, gender, and sexual microaggressions added to the already politically charged social relations of department and university politics (Escobedo, 1980; Aguirre, 1987; Padilla & Chávez Chávez, 1995).

What constitutes service and how service is disproportionately distributed among faculty is also a problem faced by Latin@s in academia (Holling & Rodríguez, 2006). Latin@ faculty's sense of obligation to their respective communities has often come in conflict with what institutions define as service. Latin@ faculty find that their work in communities, on certain issues, or with particular groups of students often "does not count" as service and will not be recognized as such for tenure and promotion by the institution (Baez, 2000). On the other hand, Latin@ faculty are sometimes overburdened with exhaustive committee work and other duties that usually have to do with minority issues (Brayboy, 2003). Latin@ faculty are often positioned as the spokespeople for their racial group and for diversity issues and initiatives (Baez, 2000; Torres, 2006). Due to their sense of obligation, many Latin@ faculty usually take on the added responsibilities and sacrifice their own personal time to write and conduct research creating hectic schedules and stressful lives (Medina & Luna, 2000).

Although heavily burdened, Latin@ faculty traditionally have spent and continue to spend considerable amounts of time on minority-oriented, affirmative action, and ethnic topics as well as retention and recruitment activities (Aguirre, 1987). According to a recent analysis of the Faculty Survey of Student Engagement (Kuykendall, Johnson, Laird, Ingram, & Niskode, 2006), on average, Hispanic and Asian faculty spend more time per week on research and scholarly activity than White faculty across ranks. In addition, faculty of color also reported a higher proportion of administrative duties, consulting and volunteering than White faculty. Latin@ faculty often endure the stress of participating in committees as token representatives of diversity, where their voice is minimized or dismissed, shifting their presence from invisible to marginal (Medina & Luna, 2000). The outcome is physical and mental exhaustion, emotional drainage, and the channeling of Latin@ faculty into a "limited opportunity structure" in the "periphery of mainstream activities" (Aguirre, 1987, p. 78). Smith et al. (2006), adapting the work of Pierce (1970, 1974, 1980, 1989), studying the effect of this type of drainage in faculty of color has referred to this phenomenon as "racial battle fatigue."

The paradoxes of the academy create new dilemmas because the academy is not race-neutral, nor gender-neutral, nor class-neutral (Baez, 2003). The structures within the academy themselves unwittingly procure isolation and lack of mentoring opportunities for faculty of color, occupational stress, institutional racism, "token hire" misconceptions (Sotello Viernes Turner, García, Nora, & Rendón, 1996, p. xx), and racial battle fatigue (Smith et al., 2006) as we endure the bittersweet success of the academy. It is here that we begin to peek through Anzaldúa's *rendija* of *how* and maybe even *why* Latin@ professors would want to continue to participate in the academy that, to a great extent, excludes, isolates, and alienates (Padilla & Chávez Chávez, 1995; Sotello Viernes Turner, Myers, & Myers, 2000) our many raw and refined talents, our unique genius, our creative flair, our ability to read the world through different eyes. Working within and even having a semblance of professional accomplishment, bittersweet success is a euphemistic phrase that carefully captures the subtle yet substantive inequities of so many Latin@ faculty (Sotello Viernes Turner et al., 2000).

The Making of Cultural/Academic Citizenship

In his book *Culture and Truth: The Remaking of Social Analysis*, Rosaldo (1989) speaks to cultural workers not just in cultural studies (Saldívar, 1997), but to the many and diverse marginalized "us" in *academelandia*. Despite the problems traditionally faced by Latin@ faculty, a growing number of faculty survive in this system despite the drawbacks while staying whole and while trans/forming academia through cultural and academic citizenship. Latin@ faculty, like Latin@s in other cultural spaces, are not passive victims, but also survivors and trans/formers of the institution. González (2002) specifically writes about three areas where the Chicano students in his study became cultural workers and trans/formed the whitestream university: the physical, epistemic, and social spaces. We argue that Latin@ faculty do the same and are key to helping Latin@ students embark in cultural worker activist journeys.

It is evident that Latin@ faculty trans/form the physical space, if not only with our bodies—often not the bodies students expect to see when they enter our classrooms (Laden & Hagedorn, 2000)—but also with the ways we use physical space. This use of physical space ranges from the ways we decorate our offices, to the political messages we place on our office doors, to the ways we appropriate space physically when we speak languages other than standard English, including the languages we speak with our very bodies, our hands, our gestures, our ways of being. Physical use of space, in some ways, and the ways we trans/form the use of space is more profound than our very presence and requires a commitment to cultural dignity and integrity not willing to be compromised to whitestream norms and expectations.

Epistemological trans/formation, often for Latin@ faculty, becomes an issue of knowledge production that validates our communities' knowledges and experiences. In general, Latin@ faculty's survival is nourished by our felt commitment and responsibility to the various Latin@ communities we feel connected to (Urrieta & Méndez Benavídez, 2007). An example: this commitment and responsibility was evidenced at UCLA in 1993 during the student-led hunger strike for a Chicana/o Studies Department where Chican@ faculty, staff, and community members played key roles in supporting the student cause (Acuña, 2000). Dr. Jorge Mancillas, a faculty member in the UCLA Medical School, participated in the hunger strike along with the students. Numerous faculty members across campus (Acuña, 2000) rallied and demonstrated their sense of obligation and deeply affirmed what many Latin@ faculty share to resist and "fight back" the racist practices of everyday life in the academy (Reyes & Halcón, 1991).

Although the "bourgeois model of intellectual" work predominates as *the* epistemological model (West, 1993) in *academelandia*, Holling and Rodríguez (2006) argue that Latin@ faculty can, and often do, find ways to negotiate the dominant scholarship model of intellectual work in the academy. Often the culprit of academic deportation for Latin@ faculty, this bourgeois model of intellectual activity, according to Holling and Rodríguez (2006), can be negotiated by looking at service as scholarship, pedagogy as scholarship, and intellectual work as scholarship that remains truthful to our very being as Latin@s who remain connected and committed to the betterment of our communities. Many Latin@ faculty, especially those that identify as Chican@, generally do not see knowledge production simply as an expected, objective, and benign practice of their career, but as a form of activism—activist scholarship (Villenas, 1996; Urrieta & Méndez Benavídez, 2007).

The academy also must be held accountable for the emotional, cultural, and social support provided to Latin@ faculty. Laden and Hagedorn (2000) found that social isolation was one of the main sources of lack of job satisfaction for faculty of color. Latin@ faculty networks often become important for personal and professional well-being, mentoring, and support both on campus and nationally. The social trans/formation of the academy by our cultural and academic citizenship, however, does not free the institution of its obligation to accommodate to us as much as we accommodate to it. Institutional academic social trans/formation must go beyond mere diversity statements and vocal commitments, but to structural changes in the everyday interactions of academic life (Baez, 2000). According to Baez (2000), as a society, we have come to think of acts of racism as overt individual acts of violence and in the process have come to ignore the daily workings of racist ways in everyday life, in the very climate of academe that is often hostile to "strangers" (Aguirre, 1995). *Academelandia*, like Latin@ faculty, other faculty of color, and White faculty must commit to a continuous social justice struggle to undo the racism of daily activity in the academy, for in coming to feel too comfortable in the whitestream academy, in its current state, can be dangerous.

Conclusion: Upstream in the Whitestream

Latin@ faculty are often the harbingers that critique and push the boundaries of the mainstream prescription of what the whitestream defines as "good" research. Activist scholarship, however, is not unsound or unrigorous research, but rather scholarship about issues undervalued or dismissed in the whitestream academy and by whitestream researchers (Urrieta & Méndez Benavídez, 2007). Because activist scholarship challenges previously misguided and unchallenged research that supports White supremacy, or simply because it is about Latin@ communities, it is often perceived by the whitestream as controversial, biased, or subjective. Holling and Rodríguez (2006), however, have challenged the entire Latin@ academic community to continue the struggle for a liberatory authenticity beyond academic survival and into academic and community trans/formation.

Holling and Rodríguez (2006) highlight the importance of Latin@ faculty to denounce compartmentalized and fractured models of being in the academy. They advocate that Latin@ faculty "live our intellectual-scholarly work in localized communities, in classrooms, and professional settings, and in everyday interactions" (p. 62). A living tension must remain within us in the academy that embodies culture and truth (Rosaldo, 1989) and obligates each of us to promote and personify an inclusive, decolonized imaginary to our creation of scholarship (Sandoval, 2000). Latin@ academic citizenship should de-privilege privilege (Hurtado, 1996; Rosaldo, 1997) and, in the end, denounce articulations of power by the critical trans/formations (Holling & Rodríguez, 2006; San Juan, 1992) we live in everyday as Latin@ faculty members in *academelandia*.

Notes

1. Latin@ will be the nomenclature used to identify the array of ethnicities and nationalities that make the meta-group. The PEW Hispanic Center, however, uses the term "Hispanic," which includes 20 nationalities (e.g., Mexican, Peruvian, etc.) including the general categories of "Other South American countries," "Spaniard," plus an all-inclusive category of "All Other Spanish/Hispanic/Latino" (Pew Hispanic Center: Hispanics at Mid-Decade, http://pewhispanic.org/reports/middecade/). Within this review, however, Chicana/o were also identifiers as were Mexican and Mexican American, Puerto Rican, and Cuban. Leal and Monjivar (1993, in Aguirre & Martínez), found that there were ideological, cultural, and social differences among women from Latin American, and between Chicanas and Puerto Rican women. Simply put, the identifier of "Hispanic" does not necessarily imply that all groups will have similar ethnic identification. Moreover, depending on not only the geographic spaces but also on social class, identification will incur a heterogeneity that is not present in either the term Hispanic or Latin@.

2. Aguirre was specific with his use of the term "minority," which includes Asians, African Americans, Latin@s, and American Indians. He points out that the research literature primarily focuses on the African American and Latin@ faculty populations. Alas, the research literature does not omit Asians and Native American Indians but recognizes that limitations do exist in the relatively small numbers, even though the Asian faculty population grew dramatically within those same years.

3. Several accounts (Delgado Bernal & Villalpando 2002; Sotello Viernes Turner, García, Nora, & Rendón, 1996; Stanley, 2006a, 2006b; Sotello Viernes Turner, Meyers, & Myers, 2000; Villalpando & Delgado Bernal, 2002) speak to faculty of color or minority faculty or both and include Latin@ faculty.

4. Aguirre (2000) states that "minority faculty" are not a homogeneous population. Rather, the term "minority" is a descriptive category of non-White faculty that included Latin@s, African Americans, Asians, and Native American Indians.

5. Sandy Grande (2000) refers to "whitestream" as the cultural capital of Whites in almost every facet of U.S. society. Grande uses the term whitestream as opposed to mainstream in an effort to decenter Whiteness as dominant. Whitestream, according to Claude Denis (1997), is a term which plays on the feminist notion of "malestream." Denis defines whitestream as the idea that while (Canadian) society is not completely white in socio-demographic terms, it remains principally and fundamentally structured on the basis of the Anglo-European White experience. Urrieta (2004) also refers to the whitestream as the official and unofficial texts used in U.S. educational institutions that are founded on the practices, principles, morals, values, and history of White Anglo-American culture, i.e., White cultural capital. I must clarify that whitestream indoctrination and the promotion of whitestream practices is not exclusively the domain of Whites in U.S. society, but of any person, including people of color, actively promoting White models as "standard."

References

Acuña, R. (2000). *Anything but Mexican: Chicanos in contemporary Los Angeles.* London: Verso.

Aguilar, J. A., MacGillivray, L., & Walker, N. T. (2002). *Latina educators and school discourse: Dealing with tension on the path to success* (CIERA Report). Center for the Improvement of Early Reading Achievement, University of Michigan, Ann Arbor, MI.

Aguirre, A. (1995). A Chicano farmworker in academe. In R. Padilla & R. Chávez Chávez (Eds.), *The leaning ivory tower: Latino professors in American universities* (pp. 17–27). Albany, NY: SUNY Press.

Aguirre, A. (2000). Women and minority faculty in the academic workplace: Recruitment, retention, and academic culture. *ASHE-ERIC Higher Education,* No. 27(6).

Aguirre, A., & Martínez, R. O. (1993). Chicanos in higher education: Issues and dilemmas for the 21st century. *ASHE-ERIC Higher Education,* No. 3. (ERIC Document Reproduction Service No. ED365207)

Anzaldúa, G. (1987). *Borderlands/La Frontera: The new mestiza.* San Francisco. Aunt Lute Books.

Avalos, M. (1991). The status of Latinos in the profession: Problems of recruitment and retention. *PS: Political Science and Politics, 24*(2), 241–246.

Baca, M. L. M. (1992). Hispanic underrepresentation in higher education: A personal perspective. *The Journal of the Association of Mexican American Educators,* 44–51.

Baez, B. (2000). Agency, structure, and power: An inquiry into racism and resistance for education. *Studies in Philosophy and Education, 19,* 329–348.

Baez, B. (2003, July-August).Outsiders within? *Academe Online, 89*(4), http://www.aaup.org/AAUP/pubsres/academe/2003/JA/Feat/baez.htm?PF=1

Bauman, Z. (2004). *Wasted lives: Modernity and its outcasts.* Malden, MA: Polity Press.

Brayboy, B. M. J. (2003). The implementation of diversity in predominantly white colleges and universities. *Journal of Black Studies, 34*(1), 72–86.

Chesler, M., Lewis, A., & Crowfoot, J. (2005). *Challenging racism in higher education: Promoting justice.* Boulder, CO: Rowman & Littlefield.

Córdova, T. (1998). Power and knowledge: Colonialism in the academy. In C. M. Trujillo (Ed.), *Living Chicana theory* (pp. 17–45). Berkeley, CA: Third Woman Press.

Cuádraz, H. (1992). Experiences of multiple marginality: A case study of Chicana "scholarship women." *The Journal of the Association of Mexican American Educators,* 31–43.

Delgado Bernal, D., Elenes, C. A., Godinéz, F. E., & Villenas, S. (Eds.). (2006). *Chicana/Latina education in everyday life: Feminista perspectives on pedagogy and epistemology.* Albany, NY: SUNY Press.

Delgado Bernal, D., & Villalpando, O. (2002). An apartheid of knowledge in academia: The struggle over the "legitimate" knowledge of faculty of color. *Equity & Excellence in Education, 35*(2), 169–180.

Delgado-Romero, E. A., Manlove, A. N., & Manlove, J. D. (2007). Controversial issues in the recruitment and retention of Latino/faculty. *Journal of Hispanic Higher Education, 6*(1), 34–51.

Denis, J. C. (1997). *We are not you: First nations and Canadian modernity.* Peterborough, Ontario, Canada: Broadview Press, Collection Terra Incognita.

Dey, E. L. (1994). Dimensions of faculty stress: A recent survey. *Review of Higher Education, 17*(3), 305–22.

Escobedo, T. H. (1980). Are Hispanic women in higher education the nonexistent minority? *Educational Researcher, 9*(9), 7–12.

Fenelon, J. (2003, September). Race, research, and tenure: Institutional credibility and the incorporation of African, Latino, and American Indian faculty. *Journal of Black Studies, 34*(1), 87–100.

Flores, W. V., & Benmayor, R. (Eds.). (1997). *Latino cultural citizenship: Claiming identity, space, and rights.* Boston, MA: Beacon Press.

Flores, J., Merino, R., & Aguirre, A. (Eds.). (1992). *The Journal of the Association of Mexican American Educators, Collected Works.*

Freire, Paulo. (1970). *Pedagogy of the oppressed.* New York. Continuum.

Fry, R. (2006). The changing landscape of American public education: new students, new schools. Pew Hispanic Center Research Report. Washington DC, October 5, 2006

Gándara, P. (1995). *Over the ivy walls: the educational mobility of low-income chicanos.* Albany, NY: SUNY Press.

Garza, H. (1992). Dilemmas of Chicano and Latino professors in U. S. universities. *The Journal of the Association of Mexican American Educators,* 6–22.

Ginsburg, M. B. (Ed.). (1995). *The politics of educators' work and lives.* New York: Garland.

Gloria, A. M. (1997). Chicana academic persistence: Creating a university-based community. *Education and Urban Society, 30*(1), 107–121.

González, K. P. (2002). Campus culture and the experiences of Chicano students in a predominantly white university. *Urban Education, 37*(2), 193–218.

Grande, S. M. A. (2000). American Indian geographies of identity and power: At the crossroads of indígena and mestizaje. *Harvard Educational Review, 70*(4), 467–498.

Guerrero, J. K. (1998). *Latino faculty at research institutions in the southwestern United States.* Unpublished manuscript, Charles A. Dana Center, The University of Texas at Austin.

Hurtado, A. (1996). *The Color of Privilege: Three Blasphemies on Race and Feminism.* Ann Arbor, MI: University of Michigan Press.

Holling, M., & Rodríguez, A. (2006). Negotiating our way through the gates of academe. *Journal of Latinos and Education, 5*(1), 49–64.

Ingle, Y. R. (2000). *The chosen few: Latinas and the new technologies* (JSRI Occasional Paper, Latino Studies Series No. 65). East Lansing: Michigan State University, Julian Samora Research Institute.

Kuykendall, J., Johnson, S., Laird, T., Ingram, T. & Niskode, A. (2006). *Finding time: An Examination of faculty of color workload and non-instructional activities by rank.* Paper Presented at the Annual Meeting of the Association for the Study of Higher Education, Anaheim, CA.

Laden, B. V., & Hagedorn, L. S. (2000). Job satisfaction among faculty of color in academe: Individual survivors or institutional transformers? *New Directions for Institutional Research, 27*(1), 57–66.

Latina Feminist Group. (Ed.). (2004). *Telling to live: Latina feminist yestimonios.* Durham, NC: Duke University Press.

Martínez Alemán, A. M. (1995). Actuando. In R. Padilla & R. Chávez Chávez (Eds.), *The leaning ivory tower: Latino professors in American universities* (pp. 67–76). Albany, NY: SUNY Press.

McLaren, P. (1997). Liberatory politics and higher education: A Freirean perspective. In P. McLaren (Ed.), *Revolutionary multiculturalism: Pedagogies of dissent for the new millennium* (pp. 42–75). Boulder, CO: Westview Press.

Medina, C., & Luna, G. (2000). Narratives from Latina Professors in higher education. *Anthropology and Education Quarterly, 31*(1), 47–66.

Milem, J., & Astin, H. (1993). The changing composition of the faculty: What does it really mean for fiversity?. *Change, 25,* 21–27.

Olivas, M. (1988). Latino faculty at the border: Increasing numbers key to more Hispanic access. *Change, 20*(3), 6–9.

Orfield, G., Marin, P., & Horn, C. L. (Eds.). (2005). *Higher education and color line: College access, racial equity, and social change.* Cambridge, MA: Harvard Education Press.

Padilla, R., & Chávez Chávez, R. (1995). *The leaning ivory tower: Latino professors in American universities.* Albany: SUNY Press.

Perna, L. (2001). Sex and race differences in faculty tenure and promotion. *Research in Higher Education, 42*(5), 541–567.

Pesquera, B., & Segura, D. (1997). There is no going back: Chicanas and feminism. *Chicana feminist thought: The basic historical writings.* New York: Elsevier.

Pierce, C. (1970). Offensive mechanisms. In F. B. Barbour (Ed.), *The black seventies* (pp. 265–282). Boston, MA: Porter Sargent.

Pierce, C. (1974). Psychiatric problems of the black minority. In S. Arieti (Ed.), *American handbook of psychiatry* (pp. 512–523). New York: Basic Books.

Pierce, C. (1980). Social trace contaminants: Subtle indicator of racism in TV. In S. B. Withye & R. P. Abeles (Eds.), *Television and social behavior: Beyond violence and children* (pp. 249–257). Hillsdale, NJ: Erlbaum.

Pierce, C. (1989). Unity in diversity: Thirty-three years of stress. In G. L. Berry & J. K. Asamen (Eds.), *Black students: Psycholsocial issues and academic ahcievement* (pp. 296–312). Newbury Park, CA: Sage.

Reyes, M. L. & Halcón, J.J. (1991). Practices of the academy: Barriers to access for Chicano academics. In P. G. Altbach & K. Lomotey (Eds.), *The racial crisis in American higher education* (pp. 167–186). Albany: State University of New York Press

Reyes, X. A., & Ríos, D. I. (2005). Dialoging the Latina experience in higher education. *Journal of Higher Education, 4*(4), 377–391.

Rosaldo, R. (1989). *Culture and truth: The remaking of social analysis.* Boston, MA: Beacon Press.

Rosaldo, R. (1997). Cultural citizenship, inequality, and multiculturalism. In W. V. Flores & R. Benmayor (Eds.), *Latino cultural citizenship: Claiming identity, space, and rights* (pp. 27–38). Boston: Beacon Press.

San Juan, Jr., E. (1992). *Racial formations/critical transformations: Articulations of power in ethic and racial studies in the United States.* Atlantic Highlands, NJ: Humanities Press International.

Saldívar, J. D. (1997). *Border matters: Remapping American cultural studies.* Berkeley: University of California Press.

Sandoval, C. (1998). Mestizaje as method: Feminists-of-color challenge, the canon. In C. M. Trujillo (Ed.), *Living Chicana theory* (pp. 352–370). Berkeley: Third Woman Press.

Sandoval, C. (2000). *Methodology of the pppressed.* Minneapolis: University of Minnesota Press.

Sax, L. J., Astin, A. W., Korn, W. S., & Gilmartin, S. K. (1999). The American college teacher: National norms for the 1998–99 HERI faculty survey. (ERIC Document Reproduction Service No. ED435272)

Segura, D. A. (2003, September). Navigating between two Worlds: The labyrinth of Chicana intellectual production in the academy. *Journal of Black Studies, 34*(1), 28–51.

Smith, W. A., Yosso, T. J., & Solórzano, D. G. (2006). Challenging racial battle fatigue on historically white campuses: A critical race examination of race-related stress. In C. A. Stanley (Ed.), *Faculty of color: Teaching in predominantly white colleges and universities* (pp. 299–327). Bolton, MA: Anker.

Solórzano, D. G. (1998). Critical race theory, race and gender microaggressions, and the experience of Chicana and Chicano scholars. *Qualitative Studies in Education, 11*(1), 121–136.

Sotello Viernes Turner, C. (2002, January). Women of color in academe: Living with multiple marginality. *The Journal of Higher Education, 73*(1), 74–93.

Sotello Viernes Turner, C., García, M., Nora, A. & Rendón, L. I. (1996). *Race and ethnic diversity in higher education: ASHE reader series.* Boston, MA: Pearson Publishing

Sotello Viernes Turner, C., Myers, S. L., Jr., & Creswell, J. W. (1999). Exploring underrepresentation: The case of faculty of color in the midwest. *The Journal of Higher Education, 70*(1), 27–59.

Sotello Viernes Turner, C. Meyers, C., & Meyers, S. L. (2000). *Faculty of color in academe: Bittersweet success.* Needham Heights, MA: Allyn & Bacon.

Stanley, C. A. (Ed.). (2006a). *Faculty of color: teaching in predominantly white colleges and universities.* Bolton: Anker.

Stanley, C. A. (2006b, Winter). Coloring the academic landscape: Faculty of color breaking the silence in predominantly white colleges and universities. *American Educational Research Journal, 43*(4), 701–736.

A Statistical Portrait of Hispanics at Mid-Decade. [Data file]. (2006). Retrieved from PEW Hispanic Center Web site: http://pewhispanic.org/reports//

Tierney, W. G., & Rhoads, R. A. (1993). Enhancing promotion, tenure and beyond: Faculty socialization as a cultural process. *ASHE-ERIC Higher Education Report*, No. 6.

Torres, R. (2006). Being seen/being heard: Moving beyond visibility in the academy. *Journal of Latinos and Education*, 5(1), 65–69.

Trujillo, C. (Ed.). (1998). *Living Chicana theory*. Berkeley, CA: Third Woman Press.

Turner, C., García, M., Nora, A., & Rendón, L. I. (Eds.). (1996). *Racial and ethnic diversity in higher education*. ASHE Reader Series, B. Townsend, Series Editor. Boston, MA: Pearson.

Urrieta, L. Jr. (2004). Dis-connections in "American" citizenship and the post/neo-colonial; people of Mexican descent and whitestream pedagogy and curriculum. *Theory and Research in Social Education*, 32(4), 433–458.

Urrieta, L. Jr., & Reidel, M. (2006). Avoidance, anger, and convenient amnesia: White supremacy and self-reflection in social studies teacher education. In E. Wayne Ross (Ed.), *Race, ethnicity, and education*. (pp. 279–299). Praeger Press.

Urrieta, L. Jr., & Méndez Benavídez, L. (2007). Community commitment and activist scholarship: Chicana/o professors and the practice of consciousness. *Journal of Hispanic Higher Education*, 6(3), 222–236.

U.S. Census. (2004). The Hispanic population in the United States. In *Historic documents of 2003*. Washington, DC: CQ Press. Retrieved November 8, 2007, from CQ Electronic Library, CQ Public Affairs Collection, http://library.cqpress.com/cqpac/hsdcp03-229-9912-639168. Document ID: hsdcp03-229-9912-639168.

U.S. Census. (2007). *Digest of education statistics, 2006*. National Center for Educational Statistics. Institute of Education Sciences. Retrieved from http://nces.ed.gov/pubs2007/2007017.pdf

Verdugo, R. (1992). Analysis of tenure among Hispanic higher education faculty. *The Journal of the Association of Mexican American Educators*, 23–30.

Verdugo, R. R. (1995, November). Racial stratification and the use of Hispanic faculty as role models: Theory, policy, and practice. *The Journal of Higher Education*, 66(6), 669–685.

Villalpando, O., & Delgado Bernal, D. (2002). A critical race theory analysis of barriers that impede the success of faculty of color. In W. A. Smith, P. G. Altbach, & K. Lometey (Eds.), *The racial crisis in American higher education: Continuing challenges for the twenty-first century* (pp. 243–269). New York: SUNY Press.

Villenas, S. (1996). The colonizer/colonized Chicana ethnographer: Identity, marginalization, and co-optation in the field. *Harvard Educational Review*, 66(4), 711–731.

Walker, N. T., MacGillivray, L., & Aguilar, J. A. (2001). *Negotiating higher education: Latina teachers' memories of striving for success* (CIERA Report). Ann Arbor, MI Center for the Improvement of Early Reading Achievement, University of Michigan.

West, C. (1993). The dilemma of the black intellectual. *Journal of Blacks in Higher Education*, 2, 59–67.

Wilds, D. J. (2000). *Minorities in higher education, 1999–2000: Seventeenth annual status report*. Retrieved November 28, 2007, from ERIC Document Reproduction Service database. (ERIC Document Reproduction Service No. ED457768)

Yosso, T. (2006). *Critical race counterstories along the Chicana/Chicano educational pipeline*. New York: Routledge.

15 Latinas/os in Higher Education
Eligibility, Enrollment, and Educational Attainment

Octavio Villalpando
University of Utah

Introduction

The 2000 Census confirmed the demographic reality that Latinas/os[1] had become the largest ethnic/racial group in the United States, representing approximately 13% of the total population. During the 1990s, many had projected a steady growth in this population (Chapa, 1997), but few had anticipated the wide discrepancies that would emerge between their population increase and their levels of educational attainment (Ramirez & De la Cruz, 2003). Indeed, today, Latinas/os are not only the largest and fastest growing ethnic/racial group (Villalpando, 2004), they are also the least educated major population group in the country (Fry, 2002).

Higher education is perhaps most illustrative of the wide educational disparities. Only 11% of Latinas/os over the age of 25 hold a bachelor's degree, in contrast to over 30% of Whites (U.S. Census Bureau, 2004). Across almost every indicator of success in higher education, Latinas/os have lower achievement rates than White students (Miller, 2004). And, while the number of college-age 18- to 24-year-old Latinas/os continues to increase, their college enrollment and graduation rates are not increasing in similar proportions.

When we examine educational attainment by gender, we find even greater disparities. In comparison to White males and females, Latinos[2] (i.e., Latino males) have not performed as well and appear to be losing ground at a much faster pace. Between 1990 and 2000, Latinos enrolled in and graduated from college at lower rates than White men and women, while Latinas posted slight improvements (Gonzales, Jovel, & Stoner, 2004). In 1990, for example, while over 83% of all bachelor's degrees awarded to men went to White males, only about 3% of these degrees went to Latinos. A decade later, despite a large increase in the population of college-age Latinos, less than 6% of all bachelor's degrees awarded to men went to Latinos, in contrast to over 75% that went to White males.[3] During this same period, Latinas/os increased their presence in the United States by another 13 million people, representing almost 13% of the total population in the year 2000 (U.S. Census Bureau, 2001). Clearly, as a group, Latinos are not making gains in proportion to their growing representation in the population, and they continue to fall behind White males and females in attainment of advanced degrees.

If demographic patterns of the last decade continue to hold true, the population of Latino/a youth is expected to continue to increase, but the educational achievement levels among college-age Latinos/as will not increase at proportionate rates. Given this growing discrepancy, there is a compelling need for higher education to better understand the factors that influence the achievement of Latinos/as. To more fully understand the conditions that affect the participation and success of Latinas/os in postsecondary education, this analysis examines their enrollment status and changes in attainment rates. When possible, their status is disaggregated by Latina/o-origin, generation, immigration status, and gender in order to obtain a better understanding of the heterogeneity—and complexity—of their experiences.

Enrollment Status

An analysis of the enrollment status of Latinas/os in higher education must begin with an understanding of the pool of students who are eligible to enroll in postsecondary education. This section begins with a brief overview of the educational pipeline that leads to college admissions.

College Eligibility

In general, eligibility for admission to college depends on having completed high school, fulfilling a college preparation curriculum, achieving a competitive grade point average (GPA), and obtaining a competitive score on a national college entrance standardized exam (Pascarella & Terenzini, 2005). For example, in California, where the largest representation of Latina/o high school students reside, the University of California system and the California State University system both not only require the completion of a high school diploma or its equivalent, but also require students to have completed a rigorous college readiness curriculum (known as the A-G Requirements) during high school and to have achieved a competitive minimum GPA. These multiple eligibility requirements have become even more complex in recent years, as the more prestigious and elite public and private institutions increasingly expect applicants to have completed a larger number of honors and advanced placement courses as well (Solórzano & Ornelas, 2004). This last development has placed Latinas/os and other students of color at a further disadvantage. These students often attend poor, racially segregated urban schools, which tend not to offer advanced placement or honors courses as often as the more affluent schools in the largely White, suburban neighborhoods do (Solórzano & Ornelas, 2002).

Educational researchers and policy makers have concluded that the pool of college eligible Latinas/os is small because of the large proportion of Latinas/os students who do not transition from one K-12 educational level to the next. These leaks in the educational pipeline are illustrated in Figure 15.1, which draws from U.S. Census Bureau data for the year 2000 to compare

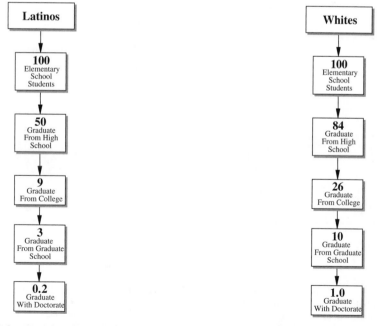

Figure 15.1 Educational transition points for Latinos. Sources: Adapted from T. Watford, M. Rivas, R. Burciaga, & D. Solórzano (2006); D. Solórzano, O. Villalpando, & L. Oseguera, (2005); and U.S. Census Bureau, (2001).

educational transition and completion rates between Latinos and White males from elementary school through the doctorate.

Figure 15.1 shows that, out of 100 Latinos who begin elementary school, only 50 are likely to eventually graduate from high school, compared with 84 White males. And, of these original 100 Latinos, only about nine will complete a college degree and less than one is likely to complete a doctoral degree.

Figure 15.1 also shows that, in contrast to White males, the college eligible pool of Latinos is clearly much smaller. Indeed, if we assume that high school completion is one of the most important benchmarks of eligibility for college admissions, then Latinos are at great risk of not meeting eligibility requirements. In fact, they are the major population group most at risk of being ineligible for college, since from 1980 to 2001 the high school dropout rate for Latinos was the highest among all racial/ethnic groups, regardless of gender.[4]

Despite this large high school dropout rate among Latinos, as Table 15.1 demonstrates, their sheer growth in the population has enabled them to more than double their high school graduation numbers between 1980 and 2000. Yet the tremendous disparity between their high school enrollment and their graduation is evidenced by their dismal completion rates during this same 20-year period, which have consistently remained between 51 and 54%. In other words, even

Table 15.1   High School Completion Rates and College Participation Rates for Latinos: Selected Years, 1980–2000

Year	18- to 24-Year Old High School Graduates		
	Number Completed	*Completion Rate*	*Enrolled-in-Post-Secondary Educ. Rate*
	(thousands)	*(percent)*	*(percent)*
Latino[b] Males			
1980	518	51.2	30.9
1984	549	57.4	28.1
1988	724	52.7	31.5
1992	720	52.0	34.3
1996	994	54.8	30.2
2000	1,173	54.0	34.2
White[a] Males			
1980	9,686	80.6	33.8
1984	9,348	81.1	36.4
1988	8,268	79.7	39.4
1992	7,911	81.2	41.6
1996	8,000	80.8	42.7
2000	7,494	86.4	41.9

[a]After 1997, the category White does not include Whites of Hispanic origin.

[b]Latinos may be of any race.

Note: College participation rates were calculated using the total population and high school graduates as the bases. High school graduates are persons who have completed four or more years of high school during the period 1977 to 1991. Beginning in 1992, they were persons whose highest degree was a high school diploma (including equivalency) or higher. Data for 1986 and later use a revised tabulation system. Improvements in edits and population estimation procedures caused slight changes in estimates for 1986. Data for 1980 through 1992 use 1980 Decennial Census-based estimates, and data for 1993 and later use 1990 Decennial Census-based estimates. The ever-enrolled-in-college rate column was removed from this year's version of this table.

Source: U.S. Census Bureau. Current Population Survey Reports, School Enrollment-Social and Economic Characteristics of Students, 1980-2000.

though a larger number of Latinos are attending high school, their likelihood of graduating has not changed during the last 20 years—only about half of all Latinos who enter high school can expect to graduate.

Moreover, despite the fact that more than twice as many Latinos graduated from high school in 2000 than in 1980, the rate at which Latino high school graduates enroll in postsecondary education has remained almost unchanged during this same period, ranging between 31 and 34%. Thus, in the last 20 years, neither the high school graduation rate nor the college enrollment rate of Latinos has increased substantially.

In contrast, while the absolute number of White males who have graduated from high school during this same 20-year period has decreased, their high school completion rates have actually increased by about 6%, as have their postsecondary enrollment rates, which posted a gain of over 8%.

Table 15.1 also shows that during those 20 years, between 66 and 72% of Latinos who graduated from high school did not enroll in any postsecondary institution. This means that the potential pool of Latino college students might have been at least 66% larger during that period.

Clearly, one of the ways to increase the enrollment and educational attainment of Latinos in college would appear to be increasing the number of Latino high school graduates and ensuring that they are meeting eligibility requirements for college admission, including the completion of an appropriate college preparation curriculum.

However, an increase in the eligible pool of students will not necessarily result in the instantaneous improvement of educational attainment rates for Latinos. As Figure 15.1 illustrates, the dismal educational transition and attainment rates of Latinos requires a deeper understanding of how their success is impeded as they move through every level of postsecondary education. An important place to begin, then, is by better understanding their enrollment status in higher education. The next section takes a closer look at the enrollment of Latinos in higher education.

Enrollment by Type of Institution

This section explores two guiding questions:

1. What have been the postsecondary enrollment patterns of Latinas/os?
2. What are noteworthy characteristics with respect to the types of postsecondary institutions in which they enroll?

Table 15.2 presents enrollment data for Latinas/os and White students for selected years between 1990 and 2002. The data clearly show that their absolute enrollment numbers (both in two- and four-year institutions) increased during this period. Yet, their overall enrollment growth appears to have been largely fueled by increases in two-year institutions, which posted larger proportional increases than the four-year campuses. For example, from 1990 to 2002, there was an enrollment increase of 3.5% among Latinas/os in all two-year institutions, yet the percentage of Latina/o enrollment in all four-year campuses actually declined by 3.5% during the same time period. Even though there was an increase in the absolute number of Latina/o high school graduates during the 1990s, Table 15.2 shows that their enrollment continued to be disproportionately overrepresented in the two-year institutions. In fact, this enrollment disparity appears to have widened even more during the 1990s, given that in 1990 only 8.4% more Latinas/os were enrolling in two-year campuses than in four-year campuses, but by 2002, 15.4% more Latinas/os were enrolling in two-year campuses. The implications of this enrollment disparity are noteworthy given the extent to which two-year institutions have been criticized for failing to help Latinas/os transfer to four-year campuses to complete a baccalaureate degree (De los Santos, Jr. & De los Santos, 2006; Solórzano, Villalpando, & Oseguera, 2005).

Table 15.2   College Enrollment for Latinas/os by Type of Institution: Selected Years, 1990–2002[1]

	Fall 1990	%	Fall 1995	%	Fall 2002	%
Latinas/os						
All Latinas/os	782,400	100.0	1,093,800	100.0	1,661,700	100.0
Men	353,900	45.0	480,200	44.0	699,000	42.0
Women	428,500	55.0	613,700	56.0	962,700	58.0
Institution Type						
Public 4-year	262,500	33.6	346,800	31.7	468,100	28.2
Public 2-year	408,900	52.3	590,300	54.0	920,500	55.4
Private 4-year	95,700	12.2	138,700	12.7	234,700	14.1
Private 2-year	15,300	1.9	18,100	1.7	38,300	2.3
Composition						
Undergraduate	724,600	93.0	1,012,000	92.5	1,533,300	92.3
Graduate	47,200	6.0	68,000	6.2	112,300	6.7
Professional	10,700	1.3	13,800	1.3	16,100	1.0
White, non-Latina/o						
All White Students	10,722,500	100.0	10,311,200	100.0	11,140,200	100.0
Men	4,861,000	45.0	4,594,100	45.0	4,897,900	44.0
Women	5,861,500	55.0	5,717,200	55.0	6,242,300	56.0
Institution Type						
Public 4-year	4,605,600	43.0	4,303,300	41.7	4,551,700	41.0
Public 2-year	3,779,800	35.3	3,642,100	35.3	3,938,800	35.4
Private 4-year	2,162,500	20.2	2,213,900	21.5	2,502,100	22.3
Private 2-year	174,500	1.6	152,000	1.5	147,700	1.3
Composition						
Undergraduate	9,272,600	86.5	8,805,600	85.4	9,564,900	85.9
Graduate	1,228,400	11.5	1,282,300	12.4	1,348,000	12.1
Professional	221,500	2.0	223,300	2.2	227,400	2.0

[1] Figures for 1999 and beyond are not directly comparable with those of previous years because of a change in the way the U.S. Department of Education categorizes colleges and universities. Until 1996, enrollment data covered institutions accredited at the postsecondary level by an agency recognized by the department. Starting in 1996, the data cover degree-granting institutions eligible to participate in federal Title IV programs. The two classification systems are similar; the new one includes some additional, primarily two-year colleges, and excludes a few colleges that did not award degrees. *Source:* Adapted from the U.S. Department of Education, *The 2005–6 Chronicle of Higher Education Almanac*, vol. 52, iss. 1 (2005): 13. Because of rounding, details may not add to totals.

In contrast, despite fluctuations in their high school graduation rates, White students have consistently maintained a much larger proportion of their enrollment in four-year institutions rather than in two-year campuses. Indeed, Table 15.2 shows that from 1990 to 2002, White students only increased their enrollment rate in two-year institutions by less than one fourth of 1%.

To compare differential enrollment rates by gender, Table 15.3 shows the percentage of Latinos and Latinas enrolled in two- and four-year degree-granting institutions from 1976 through 2002 and contrasts their enrollments with White males and females. According to these data, the late 1970s and early 1980s appear to mark the beginning of a reversal in the gender composition of college enrollments, as evidenced by the proportion of Latinas and White women who began to enroll in colleges in larger percentages than men of both races.

For example, in 1980, about 3% more White women than men were enrolled in two- and four-year institutions. Similarly, approximately 2% more Latinas than Latinos were enrolled in these same institutions. But, by 2002, there were 16% more Latinas than Latinos enrolled in two- and four-year postsecondary institutions. This increase in the proportion of Latina enrollment

Table 15.3   Percentage of Total Public and Private Degree-Granting Institutional
Enrollment for Latinos: Selected Years, 1976–2002[1]

Year	Percent White			Percent Latina/o		
	Male	Female	Difference	Male	Female	Difference
1976	53	47	-6	55	45	-9
1980	49	52	3	49	51	2
1990	45	55	9	45	55	10
2002	44	56	11	42	58	16

[1] Data from 1976 to 1990 are for institutions of higher education that were accredited by an agency or association that was recognized by the U.S. Department of Education or recognized directly by the Secretary of Education. Data after 1996 are for degree-granting institutions. The new degree-granting classification is very similar to the earlier higher education classification, except that it includes some additional institutions, primarily two-year colleges, and excludes a few higher education institutions that did not award associate or higher degrees. Detail may not sum to totals because of rounding.

Source: Adapted from U.S. Department of Education, National Center for Education Statistics, *Digest of Education Statistics, 2004,* based on Higher Education General Information Survey (HEGIS), "Fall Enrollment in Colleges and Universities" surveys, 1976 and 1980; and Integrated Postsecondary Education Data System (IPEDS), "Fall Enrollment" survey, 1990, and Spring 2001 through Spring 2003 surveys. Note: In this table, "Latino" refers to males and females.

was due to a combined increase of 7% in their enrollment and an equal decrease of about 7% in the proportion of Latino male enrollment. Thus, while the absolute number of Latina/o enrollment in two- and four-year institutions increased between 1980 and 2002, most of the growth came from a larger proportion of Latinas who enrolled in postsecondary education, given that the proportion of Latino male enrollment actually declined during this period.

In fact, as Table 15.3 shows, since 1976, the proportion of Latino males enrolled in higher education has actually declined by about 13%, from 55% to 42%. This decline appears to be the single largest decline among all major male population groups.

Analysis of Enrollment Status

In general, the data in this section show that despite a growth in the number of Latina/o high school graduates since the 1980s, their percentage of college enrollments has not increased proportionately. Indeed, their college enrollment rate has remained almost stagnant during the last 20 years. Evidence suggests that one of the reasons their enrollment has not increased is that they had the highest high school dropout rates of any racial/ethnic group during the last two decades. Another recent explanation suggests that the emerging practice of requiring college applicants to complete a college preparation curriculum with more advance placement and honors courses is further placing Latinos at a disadvantage for college admission (especially at the more competitive campuses) since a large proportion of their schools do not offer sufficiently adequate college preparation coursework. Even among the Latino students who do successfully complete high school with a competitive GPA and college preparation curriculum, many do not enter four-year colleges because they do not achieve competitive scores on the national college entrance exams that these colleges require. Thus, the complex issues related to eligibility requirements still remain important considerations when examining the factors that contribute to college access for Latinos since they clearly help explain part of the reason for their lack of increase in college enrollment rates.

With respect to actual enrollment in postsecondary institutions, the data reviewed in this section show that although Latinos have increased their absolute numbers in college during the last 20 years, in contrast to White students (especially males), they have not made similar proportional enrollment gains in four-year institutions. A substantial share of their enrollment gains occurred at the two-year campuses, in contrast to White students who posted proportionately higher enrollments at four-year campuses during the same time period. Thus, in comparison to White males, a smaller percentage of Latinos pursue a college education at four-year campuses, which clearly diminishes the possibility of completing a bachelor's degree.

A study by the Pew Hispanic Center discovered that 80% of Latinos are enrolled in colleges in just seven states (California, New York, Arizona, New Jersey, Florida, Texas, and Illinois; Fry, 2005). In over half of these states, the enrollment disparities reviewed in this section are actually more acute, with significantly greater numbers of Latinos than Whites enrolling in two-year campuses. Indeed, in California alone, it is estimated that approximately 80% of Latinas/os who enroll in postsecondary education immediately after high school graduation do so in two-year community colleges. The Pew report concludes that "in a relative sense, therefore, Latino youth are falling further behind their white counterparts" (Fry, 2005, p. i).

Clearly, the enrollment status of Latinos in higher education requires complex analysis. For example, if one simply reviews their enrollment data during the last 20 years, it would be misleading to conclude that given their overall numerical increases in postsecondary institutions, there should be little concern about their sustained educational attainment in the future. However, enrollment increases cannot guarantee sustained and proportionate improvements in their educational attainment levels. Indeed, even if we were to reach parity between their enrollments in higher education and their representation among the college-age population, as Turner and Myers (2000) remind us, "the concept of parity speaks to a statistical picture of numerical 'inclusion' but does not say anything about the quality of that inclusion" (p. 40).

Thus, to better understand the complex nature of the conditions that affect the participation and success of Latinos in postsecondary education, the next section analyzes the relationship between their enrollment status and educational attainment.

Educational Attainment

Two questions guide the analysis in this section, given the enrollment increases during the last decade:

1. What has been the educational attainment of Latinos?
2. What types of changes can we anticipate in their future attainment?

Differences by Latino-Origin

One of the most challenging tasks in analyzing the conditions that affect the participation and success of Latinos in postsecondary education is locating national-level data that disaggregates their experiences. Given the tremendous heterogeneity that exists within the Latina/o population, it is imperative to understand how each of the groups that make up the "Latina/o" U.S. population census category fares in our postsecondary education institutions.

However, this analysis did not discover much substantive, reliable, reported data drawn from national, large-scale databases that disaggregate Latinos by the important characteristics that have long been established as key to their identity and related educational and social experiences in the United States, including Latina/o ethnic-origin, immigration status, generation status, language, socioeconomic status, sexual orientation, and gender. The Pew Hispanic Center is to be commended for its attempts to include several of these important characteristics in analyses of Latinas/os by accessing raw data collected through the national Census Bureau's Current Population Surveys (CPS) and triangulating it with some of the U.S. Department of Education's

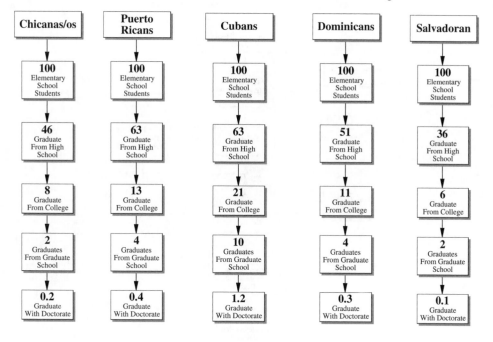

Figure 15.2 Latina/o educational attainment. Source: D. Solórzano, O. Villalpando, and L. Oseguera (2005).

data. However, the Pew Hispanic Center is in a very exclusive category in this regard. For example, despite the fact that Latinas/os constitute the largest ethnic/racial group in the country, the U.S. Department of Education still does not report any extensive data on these important characteristics of the Latina/o population. Thus, the educational policy arena is seldom able to draw from reliable, disaggregated data to inform analyses and related proposals.

Notwithstanding the lack of disaggregated data for Latinas/os, this analysis drew from previously reported work on the educational attainment of some of the larger Latina/o-origin groups in the United States to produce Figure 15.2, which illustrates their overall educational attainment. By disaggregating Latinos into ethnic-origin subgroups, Figure 15.2 demonstrates an even more marked discrepancy in their educational outcomes.

The largest Latina/o origin group is comprised of Chicanas/os[5] who represent over 65% of all Latinas/os in the United States. Yet, out of approximately 100 Chicanas/os who begin elementary school, over one-half will not finish high school, and among those who do, only about 8 will eventually graduate from college.

Disaggregating Latinas/os by group of origin clearly illustrates some of the differences that exist between some of the groups. Cuban Americans, for example, demonstrate greater levels of educational attainment than every other Latina/o group. If analyses of the educational attainment of the aggregated Latina/o ethnic/racial group were not to include data for Cuban Americans, it is very likely that we would observe even more modest levels of success for Latinas/os. This type of within-group heterogeneity illustrates why disaggregated data must be routinely collected and reported for individual Latina/o subgroups.

Pathways to a Four-Year College Degree

To further understand the specific pathways followed by Latinos on their educational attainment trajectory, Figure 15.3 illustrates how the community college or two-year college factors

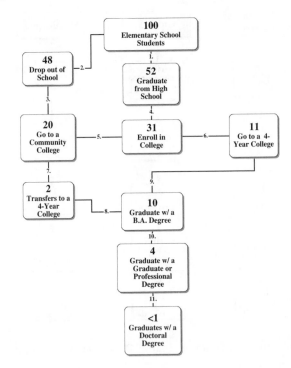

Figure 15.3 A profile of the educational attainment pathway of Latinos. Sources: Adapted from T. Watford, M. Rivas, R. Burciaga, & D. Solórzano (2006); D. Solórzano, O. Villalpando, & L. Oseguera, (2005); and U.S. Census Bureau (2001).

into their postsecondary educational attainment. If we begin with 100 Latino male students at the elementary level, we can anticipate that about 48 will drop out of high school and 52 will graduate. Of those 52 who graduate from high school, about 31, or 60%, will continue on to some form of postsecondary education. Of those 31, about 20, or 65%, are likely to go on to a community college and 11, or 35%, will go to a four-year institution. Of those 20 in a community college, only 2 will transfer to a four-year institution. Of the 11 students who attend a four-year college and the 2 who transferred, about 10 will graduate from college with a baccalaureate degree. Finally, 4 students will continue on and obtain a graduate or professional degree, and less than 1 will receive a doctorate.

In addition to illustrating the educational pathways that Latinos follow in their pursuit of a college degree, Figure 15.3 also points out the extent to which they succeed at each level. In particular, it shows the low probability of transferring to a four-year institution when students begin at a two-year/community college. Again, this is an important issue to consider given the increasingly large numbers of Latinos who appear to be on this community college track as a pathway toward a bachelor's degree.

Admittedly, the community college/two-year institution does not have as its only function to promote the transfer of students to four-year campuses. Some students enroll in two-year campuses specifically to obtain a terminal associate's degree. To further understand the extent to which Latinos succeed at obtaining a degree from two-year campuses, Table 15.4 presents the percentage of associate degrees conferred to Latino males and females for selected years, and compares them with White males and females.

Table 15.4 shows that the total percentage of associate's degrees earned by Latinos and Latinas nearly doubled for each gender from 1980 to 2001. In 1980, 6% of the degrees earned by males

Table 15.4 Associate's Ddegrees Conferred by Degree-Granting Institutions for Latinas/os: Selected Years, 1980, 1990, 2001

	Total	White, non-Hispanic	Latina/o	Others
Male				
1980–81	188,638	86 %	6 %	8 %
1990–91	198,634	82 %	5 %	13 %
2001–02	238,109	72 %	10 %	18 %
Female				
1980–81	227,739	83 %	4 %	13 %
1990–91	283,086	81 %	5 %	14 %
2001–02	357,024	69 %	10 %	21 %

Source: U.S. Department of Education, National Center for Education Statistics (NCES), *Digest of Education Statistics 2003*, NCES 2005-025 (2005), Table 261. Data from U.S. Department of Education, NCES, Higher Education General Information Survey (HEGIS), "Degrees and Other Formal Awards Conferred" and Integrated Postsecondary Education Data System, "Completions Survey" (IPEDS-C; 1990–91 and 2001–02).

went to Latinos, while 86% went to White males. Twenty years later, in 2001, among all males who earned an associate's degree, approximately 10% of the degrees were earned by Latinos, and the remaining 72% of degrees went to White males.

As the enrollment of Latinos increased in the two-year institutions, so too did their attainment of associate's degrees, which nearly doubled in proportion to about 10% of all degrees earned by males. This increase clearly stems from the fact that, as reviewed in the previous section, their enrollment in these institutions also doubled during this same time period. Conversely, White students earned less associate's degrees during this time period, even though their enrollment in two-year campuses remained relatively unchanged.

While Table 15.4 illustrates the increasing percent of Latinas/os who earned an associate's degree at two-year campuses, without additional data concerning the extent to which Latinas/os transfer to four-year campuses, or how long it takes them to transfer, it is not possible to reach a reliable conclusion about whether the institutions or students are genuinely making progress. Transfer rates or time-to-degree rates are not routinely collected or reported by two-year institutions and, when they are, the data are frequently not comparable across different districts given the decentralized nature of two-year institutions and their districts. In order to reach a more reliable assessment about whether Latinas/os are progressing in these campuses—or knowing whether a 10% degree conferral rate may be sufficient, outstanding, or poor—it will be necessary for basic transfer rate and time-to-degree/transfer data to be routinely and systematically collected and reported.

The next question with respect to educational attainment focuses on the bachelor's degree. Table 15.5 presents the percentage of degrees conferred to Latinos for selected years.

Table 15.5 clearly shows that Latinas/os increased their share of absolute numbers of bachelor's degrees from 1990 to 2000. The increase was more than double for Latinas, who went from earning approximately 27,700 of all bachelor's degrees conferred to women in 1990, up to nearly 46,400 in 2000, an absolute increase of over 25,600 degrees in 10 years. Similarly, even though Latinos started from a much smaller base, earning only about 16,600 of all degrees conferred to men in 1990, by the year 2000, they increased their total share of bachelor's degrees to approximately 31,400, an increase of about 14,800 degrees.

The data presented in Table 15.5 reflect the same type of trend presented in Table 15.2—namely, an absolute increase in the number enrolled in four-year institutions but a percentage growth

Table 15.5 Bachelor's Degrees Conferred by Degree-Granting Institutions to Latinas/os: Selected Years, 1990, 1995, 2000

		1990–2000		
	Total	*White, non-Hispanic*	*Latina/o*	*Latina/o Increase*
		Total		
1990	1,094,538	914,093	37,342	
		83.5 %	*3.4 %*	
1995	1,164,792	905,846	58,351	
		77.8 %	*5.0 %*	
2000	1,244,171	927,357	77,745	+ 40,403
		74.5 %	*6.2 %*	
		Male		
1990	504,045	421,290	16,598	
		83.6 %	*3.3 %*	
1995	522,454	409,565	25,029	
	531,840	*78.4 %*	*4.8 %*	
2000		401,780	31,368	+ 14,770
		75.5 %	*5.9 %*	
		Female		
1990	590,493	492,803	20,744	
		83.5 %	*3.5 %*	
1995	642,338	496,281	33,322	
		77.3 %	*5.2 %*	
2000	712,331	525,577	46,377	+ 25,633
		73.8 %	*6.5 %*	

Source: Adapted from U.S. Department of Education, Digest of Education Statistics (2002).

in bachelor's degrees conferred that has been dismal, at best. For example, Table 15.5 shows that during the decade of the 1990s, Latino men increased their share of bachelor's degrees by only 2.6%, earning only 5.9% of all bachelor's degrees conferred to men in the year 2000, in contrast to White men who earned 75.5% of all bachelor's degrees conferred that year. Latinas also increased their percentage share of bachelor's degrees during the 1990s by an additional 3%, earning 6.5% of all bachelor's degrees conferred to women in the year 2000, in contrast to White women who earned 73.8% of all bachelor's degrees conferred to women that year. Thus, despite a decade-long enrollment growth in four-year campuses of approximately 344,600 additional Latinas/os (see Table 15.2), by the year 2000, there were only an additional 40,403 bachelor's degrees earned by Latinas/os. This represents a decade-long increase in the yearly conferral of bachelor's degrees to Latinos of only 2.8%.

Another noteworthy point to consider about these increases in degree completion rates is that most of the increase for White students occurred in four-year institutions. There appears to have been a greater shift by White students toward enrolling in and completing degrees at four-year campuses. In contrast, much of the increase during this same time period in postsecondary enrollments and degree attainment for Latinas/os seems to have occurred at two-year campuses (Fry, 2005). Again, the implications of this divergence between White students and Latinos are significant in the context of overall educational attainment levels.

When we disaggregate the two- and four-year collegiate attainment of Latinos by generation, we find some significant changes in their attainment rates. Table 15.6 illustrates how much higher the collegiate attainment levels are for second- and third-generation Latinas/os, suggesting that the large pool of foreign-born, recently immigrated students will fare worse than other Latinas/os who have been here for one or two generations.

Table 15.6 Collegiate Attainment Among 25–29-Year-Old High School Completers, 2001

	Latina/o Generation			
	Foreign Born	*Second Generation*	*Third Generation*	*White non-Hispanic*
Associate's Degree	7.2 %	14.6 %	11.0 %	10.5 %
Bachelor's Degree	15.2 %	16.1 %	18.6 %	36.5 %

Note: The CPS reveals the highest degree attained. Persons attaining both a bachelor's and associate's degree report attaining a bachelor's degree.

Source: Current Population Survey; Fry (2002).

These data leave little doubt that, unlike previous generations of American immigrants, Latina/o immigrants may not be able to reap the same educational benefits until their descendants have been in the United States for one or two generations. This is sobering data given the large number of Latina/o youth who are currently enrolled in our nation's K-12 educational systems. The large and continuing increase in the presence of new immigrants clearly affects the overall levels of educational attainment for Latina/o college students. Clearly, the strategies that we employ to support their collegiate attainment will need to be different than what we do for second and third generation Latina/o students, and will likely rely more heavily on second language-based approaches (Santiago & Brown, 2004).

The final significant measure of educational attainment for Latinos focuses on their graduation rates. Again, along with increases in enrollment and attainment rates, it is important to understand how long Latinos are taking to graduate with a four-year degree and the factors that contribute to their graduation rates.

Table 15.7 presents six-year graduation rates of Latina/o freshmen at four-year campuses and contrasts them with White students. The data show that, as a group, Latinas/os have the lowest graduation rates overall. In every category shown in Table 15.7, Latinas/os have the lowest of all six-year graduation rates. It is especially striking that Latinas/os only have a 19.6% graduation

Table 15.7 Six-Year Graduation Rates of 1996–97 Latina/o Freshmen at Four-Year Institutions

	Total	*White, non-Hispanic*	*Latina/o*
Gender			
All	54.4 %	57.2 %	44.8 %
Men	51.0 %	53.9 %	40.6 %
Women	57.2 %	60.1 %	48.3 %
Baccalaureate Liberal Arts			
Public	41.7 %	42.7 %	30.9 %
Private non-profit	72.2 %	74.0 %	68.2 %
Baccalaureate General			
Public	31.1 %	33.7 %	19.6 %
Private non-profit	49.6 %	54.3 %	40.7 %

Note: The figures cover the population of first-time, full-time degree-seeking students who enrolled in college any time during 1996-97 and earned a degree within 150 percent of the normal time to program completion. Statistics for men, women, and all students include those enrolled at types of institutions not shown separately.

Source: Adapted from the U.S. Department of Education, *The 2005–6 Chronicle of Higher Education Almanac*, vol. 52, iss. 1 (2005), 12.

rate at the public general baccalaureate campuses—precisely the four-year institutions that have the highest number of Latina/o college students. Only 1 out of every 5 Latinas/os attending these public campuses can expect to graduate within six years.

With respect to gender, Latino men have the lowest graduation rate among all students, with a 40.6% overall six-year graduation rate, nearly 20% lower than White women. Indeed, both individually and collectively, White women and White men had the highest graduation rates among 1996 freshmen at four-year campuses.

The private baccalaureate campuses report the highest graduation rates for Latina/os, with private liberal arts institutions graduating about 68.2% of their 1996 Latina/o freshmen class within six years. Even though these types of campuses have historically enrolled the lowest proportion of Latinas/os in higher education, especially in contrast to the public two- and four-year campuses, they have consistently shown the greatest success in graduating a significant percentage of Latina/o students. In fact, private liberal arts campuses with a religious affiliation—especially Catholic-affiliated institutions—have among the highest graduating rates for Latinas/os. This suggests that they might offer an opportunity to learn about the types of strategies and approaches that can be adopted by other campuses to support Latina/o educational attainment.

Indeed, campuses with an explicit emphasis or mission to serve Latinas/os or other historically underrepresented students might hold some promise in helping inform policies and practices related to improving the educational attainment of Latinas/os. Hispanic Serving Institutions (HSI), discussed in the following section, are such campuses.

Hispanic Serving Institutions

In the early 1990s, the U.S. Congress created an opportunity for accredited, not-for-profit, two- and four-year institutions to qualify for Title V funds as "Hispanic Serving Institutions (HSI)." To earn an HSI designation, the campus had to enroll an undergraduate population of at least 25% Latina/o students, with at least 50% of these students qualifying as "low-income." By the year 2000, approximately 230 two- and four-year institutions had earned a designation as an HSI and qualified for Title V funding.[6]

The 25% Latina/o enrollment requirement to become an HSI has led to the belief that campuses earning this designation will or should offer an education to Latina/o students that produces a richer experience and more equitable outcomes for them. Presumably, when one-fourth of a campus's student body is Latina/o, the institution's response to these students' needs will be more culturally relevant and more focused on enhancing their overall success. However, as the private liberal arts campuses have proven over time, an institution's success at promoting the educational attainment of Latinas/os does not necessarily depend only on their total enrollment on the campus. With respect to HSIs, it is not entirely clear to what extent they are succeeding at converting the larger presence of Latina/o college students into equally impressive graduation rates. Unlike Historically Black Colleges and Universities or Women's Colleges which were generally founded upon an explicit mission to support and promote the educational and professional success of African Americans and White women, almost none of the campuses designated as an HSI follows an explicit or clear mission to serve the needs of Latina/o college students.

In fact, in their investigation of HSI institutional identity and educational outcomes for Latinas/os at HSIs, Contreras, Malcom, and Bensimon (2005) discovered that the 10 two- and four-year campuses they studied did not offer any public evidence of the implications of having an HSI designation, nor did they generally achieve equitable degree attainment outcomes. They did find that HSIs produced equitable access for Latinas/os, but underscored their concern that access is insufficient "to close the educational opportunity gaps that keep Latinas/os in the lower-power jobs, lower quality schools, and in segregated neighborhoods" (2005, p. 17).

The one place where Contreras and colleagues did appear to find references to a campus's HSI designation was in written material about initiatives associated with Title V funds they were seeking or receiving. However, once obtained, these Title V funds were managed at the institution's complete discretion and did not necessarily have to be earmarked for initiatives designed to enhance the success of Latinas/os. Thus, the institutions appeared to have selectively claimed an HSI designation only in relationship to Title V-related funding material and/or initiatives related to such funding.

Thus, unlike the private liberal arts colleges that report large levels of success in graduating Latina/o college students, it is not clear whether HSIs are adding any additional value to a Latina/o college students' attainment that can be directly associated with their HSI designation or a related Hispanic Serving Institutional identity.

Analysis of Educational Attainment

The above section addressed the importance of analyzing data on Latina/o college students that is disaggregated by Latino/ethnic-origin, immigration status, generation status, language, socioeconomic status, sexuality, and gender. Given the significant heterogeneity of Latina/o subgroups, it is imperative that a systematic approach be employed at the national level to collect more reliable data on these characteristics.

The second major point discussed above is the increasing presence of Latinos in our two-year community colleges. While proportionately much of the enrollment among Latinas/os during the 1990s occurred in these institutions and we have witnessed a doubling in the rate of associate's degrees conferred to Latinos, it is still unclear the extent to which they succeed in promoting the transfer of Latinas/os to four-year institutions. Indeed, fully understanding the role of community colleges in this regard will require deeper and more thoughtful analysis.

Similarly, while the absolute number of Latinas/os enrolled in four-year institutions increased substantially during the 1990s, the percentage of baccalaureate degrees they earned during this same period increased by less than 3%. To help explain this perniciously low attainment rate, some reports point to the growing presence of part-time versus full-time Latina/o students (Fry, 2002), as well as the increasing difficulty of obtaining Pell Grants, Supplemental Educational Opportunity Grants, College Work-Study, Perkins Loans, and other similar forms of financial aid (Santiago & Brown, 2004). Fry (2002) specifically points to the high labor force participation rate for school-age Latino youth as one of the reasons why they are not able to pursue a four-year degree as full-time students, while Santiago and Brown (2004) highlight recent policy shifts in financial aid programs that appear to place a higher debt burden on college students, which clearly place Latinas/os at a disadvantage.

A final significant area that surfaced in the preceding analysis was the immigration or generation status of Latina/o college students. There is a compelling need to address the educational attainment needs of the large and growing immigrant population, given the tremendous impact it will continue to have on the overall Latina/o attainment. During the last few years, the U.S. Congress has considered legislation, referred to as the Development, Relief, and Education for Alien Minors Act (DREAM Act), which proposes to enable undocumented immigrant students to attend public four-year campuses while paying in-state fees and tuition (which they otherwise cannot do because they cannot provide legal proof of U.S. residence or citizenship).[7] The DREAM Act, however, continues to stall in the U.S. Senate, prompting many states to independently address in-state-tuition issues for undocumented students. For example, in spring 2007 alone, 22 states introduced or debated legislation addressing the possibility that undocumented immigrant students who have resided continuously in the United States and have met all college eligibility requirements for their state-run postsecondary institutions might pay the in-state resident tuition rather than the out-of-state tuition. However, support for in-state tuition legislation has been mixed across the states, with a growing majority of states opposing this legislation as it is increasingly packaged with highly politicized xenophobic debates about immigration. The result is that, if not permitted to pay in-state resident tuition, undocumented immigrant students will be required to pay a tuition fee that could be as much as five times higher than what students who have proof of residence would pay.

If passed, the DREAM Act would enable public higher education institutions to follow a uniform policy concerning tuition fees for undocumented students and would formally establish the opportunity for them to attend college after successfully completing all educational requirements, including a college-prep curriculum, and achieving the minimum GPA and a competitive score on a standardized entrance exam.

Discussion

The analyses presented in this chapter explore the major conditions that affect the participation and success of Latino males in postsecondary education. The slow pace of success for Latino males is raising compelling questions about the reasons that affect their higher education enrollment and attainment rates.

During the last 25 years, we have witnessed a significant increase in the population of Latinas/os in the United States, particularly among college-age Latina/o youth. However, their progress and success across higher education has not kept pace with their overall population growth. Indeed, with respect to their educational attainment, their success has been dismal. The present seems more than appropriate timing to understand the conditions that affect their lack of success in order to propose policies that could reverse their persistently poor educational attainment rates.

Clearly, the educational attainment trend has not favored men of color during the last two decades. We lost important ground, time, and labor productivity and witnessed a terrible decline in the quality of life for several generations of African American men when higher education failed to respond to their educational needs (McCall, 1995). The hope is that we have learned important lessons about the social, psychological, and personal costs to our collective society when we fail to respond to the educational needs of such a large and important segment of our population.

Guiding Assumption

To consider more robust policies and practices that can improve the participation and success of Latino males in postsecondary education, the following discussion is framed by a critical assumption derived from the long historical exclusion of people of color from American higher education. The deliberate, legally sanctioned, and in many cases, centuries-long exclusion from U.S. higher education of African Americans, Asian Americans, and peoples indigenous to this continent has left a permanent imprint on the prevailing norms, beliefs, and values that inform current policies and practices in American postsecondary institutions. This historical legacy of exclusion permeates how we think about and respond to race and racism in higher education today (Hurtado, Milem, Clayton-Pedersen, & Allen, 1998).

Lest we be lulled into thinking that the quantitative data presented in this analysis provide us with a clear sense of the educational conditions experienced by Latinas/os in higher education, it is important to remember that they provide but one piece of the mosaic that makes up their complete experience in higher education. The numbers and percentages clearly do not tell their full stories. The remaining missing pieces are related to the centrality of their race and the effects that racism has on their educational participation and success. Thus, this present discussion is based on the assumption that these often overlooked dimensions of the educational experiences of Latinos are essential pieces to gaining a better understanding of their educational condition.

Race and Racism in Higher Education

Most of our higher education structures, policies, and practices that affect the participation and success of Latinas/os males are informed by how we understand and believe in the presence and salience of race and racism. Today, as perhaps never before in American higher education, we have a better understanding of how the concept of race exists as an historical, social, and variable concept that has consistently changed over time. The meaning of "race"—the way it is used in social discourse, by whom, and its role in educational policies and practices—very much depends on the socio-political context and on the classifier's own norms and values. While on the one hand higher education policy makers can be persuaded that the concept of race represents one of many characteristics (such as gender, class, culture, sexual orientation, language, etc.) that comprise a human identity, there still remains a strong resistance to accepting the legacy and presence of racism in our educational systems.

Education policy makers appear to be unwilling to accept the historical implications of how the concept and meaning of race has been manipulated for racist and xenophobic motives over time by all of our major political and social institutions. The idea that this key historical fact may play a role in how we respond to the needs of historically excluded populations of color today is seldom, if ever, considered in policy analysis or in the creation of racially conscious educational practices. Instead, there is a strong belief that since race is only one (and certainly not the most essential) of the many individual characteristics of human identity, and given that racism has been legally forbidden since the 1960s, neither of these two issues should constitute any significant consideration in current policy analysis or proposals.

Yet, when we consider that today racism no longer simply represents an individual act of "meanness," but is most often present on a broader macro-social level, we can begin to understand how people of color continue to experience racial inequality and subordination at multiple levels in our educational systems. The traditional way of understanding racism—mostly as an overt, public, or conscious act committed with the intent of harming a person(s) of another race because of her/his race—has been transformed in the present into a more covert form of racism. While this current, covert form of racism is seldom as explicit as in the past, and is no longer based on clearly distinguishable intentions to harm others because of their race, many argue that its effects are more pernicious and dangerous than overt racism.

For example, because covert racism appears as invisible and normal, educational institutions have succeeded in engaging in practices that are purported to be racially neutral, or color-blind, yet have clearly racist effects. Scheurich and Young (1997) refer to these types of practices as examples of institutional racism, which rely on intended or unintended "standard operating procedures" that benefit members of a dominant race at the expense of members of other races. Higher education institutions claim that these types of standard operating procedures are based on objective, merit-based, and color-blind purposes, yet at the same time these practices and procedures have a racially biased effect that clearly inhibits the success of students of color. An example of this type of practice in higher education is the insistence that standardized college entrance exams provide an accurate predictor of success for students of color. Despite decades of research that debunks the myth that these standardized exams have any predictive validity for students of color, beyond occasionally predicting first-year persistence rates (Pascarella & Terenzini, 2005), most four-year colleges continue to use them. Indeed, more recently, some have even established that there is a stronger relationship between socioeconomic class and standardized exam scores, meaning that the more affluent a student is the higher score he/she is likely to obtain on these exams. Clearly, both of these findings would suggest that the application of these exams have little to no value for students of color, yet four-year campuses insist that all students comply with this exam requirement as a prerequisite for college eligibility.

Clearly, any policy considerations that address the educational attainment of Latino males must draw from the effects of racism in higher education.

Race and "Merit" in Higher Education

Higher education has operated and continues to operate in contradictory ways. While colleges and universities clearly provide economic, social, political, and other benefits to the small trickle of Latina/o college graduates who can navigate them successfully, they also create significant barriers that inhibit the success of Latinas/os, often by sustaining a campus culture and climate that marginalizes and devalues these students.

The disparity in Latina/o student enrollments between two- and four-year institutions, their low transfer rates to four-year campuses, and their equally dismal graduation rates at public four-year campuses illustrate the chronically persistent racial stratification of higher education in the United States. The "overrepresentation" of Latina/o students in the two-year colleges, and their continuing underrepresentation in four-year colleges, represents the effects of continuing notions of racial neutrality and meritocracy by higher education institutions.

Despite an official end to de jure racial segregation, higher education continues to reflect a state of de facto racial segregation for Latina/o college students. Latina/o college students are not only concentrated in institutions considered to be of lesser prestige and to have fewer resources, such as the community colleges, but can expect to achieve lower levels of academic achievement—and social mobility—as a result of attending these types of institutions.

The "objective," "merit-based," and "race-neutral" policies and practices that higher education has adopted to better serve the needs of Latina/o college students clearly do not have the effect of promoting greater equitable outcomes.

Notes

1. *Latinas/os* include men and women of Mexican, Central American, South American, Cuban, and Puerto Rican origin, regardless of birthplace, immigration, or generation status.
2. Throughout this text, future references to Latino males will generally be identified with the gender-specific term *Latino*; conversely, any reference to Latina females will be identified as *Latina*.
3. NCES-Digest of Education Statistics, "Higher Education General Information Survey (HEGIS), Fall Enrollment in Colleges and Universities" (2002).
4. NCES-Digest of Education Statistics, "Higher Education General Information Survey (HEGIS)."
5. *Chicanas* and *Chicanos* are men and women of Mexican origin living in the United States, regardless of birthplace, immigration, or generation status. These terms are also used synonymously with Mexican American, though they carry a different socio-historical and geo-political dimension that this paper does not address.
6. Title V authorizes a HSI Program, designed to expand educational opportunities for, and improve the academic attainment of Hispanic students, as well as the academic offerings, program quality, and institutional stability HSI-designated campuses (Title V of the Higher Education Act, 2005).
7. As described on the Library of Congress Thomas.loc.gov website, the bill (S.1545) is intended to "amend the Illegal Immigration Reform and Immigrant Responsibility Act of 1996 to permit States to determine State residency for higher education purposes and to authorize the cancellation of removal and adjustment of status of certain alien students who are long-term United States residents." See http://thomas.loc.gov/cgibin/bdquery/z?d108:SN01545:@@@L&summ2=m&

References

Chapa, J. (1997). Special focus: Hispanic demographic and educational trends. In D. J. Carter & R. Wilson (Eds.), *Minorities in higher education* (Ninth Annual Status Report). Washington, DC: American Council on Education.

Contreras, F., Malcom, L., & Bensimon, E. (2005). *Hispanic-serving institutions: Closeted identity and the production of equitable outcome for Latino/a students.* Paper presented at the Annual Meeting of the Association for the Study of Higher Education (ASHE), Philadelphia, PA.

De los Santos, Jr., G., & De los Santos, A. (2006). Latinos and community colleges. In J. Castellanos, A. Gloria, & M. Kamimura (Eds.), *The Latina/o Pathway to the Ph.D* (pp. 37–54). Sterling, VA: Stylus.

Fry, R. (2002). *Latinos in higher education: Many enroll, too few graduate.* Washington, DC: The Pew Hispanic Center.

Fry, R. (2005). *Recent changes in the entry of Hispanic and white youth into college.* Washington, DC: The Pew Hispanic Center.

Gonzales, K., Jovel, J., & Stoner, C. (2004). Latinas: The new Latino majority in college. In A. Ortiz (Ed.), *Addressing the unique needs of Latino American students, new directions for higher education* (pp. 17–27). San Francisco: Jossey-Bass.

Hurtado, S., Milem, J., Clayton-Pedersen, A., & Allen, W. (1998). Enhancing campus climates for racial/ethnic diversity: Educational policy and practice. *The Review of Higher Education, 21*(3), 279–302.

McCall, N. (1995). *Makes me wanna holler: A young black man in America.* New York: First Vintage Books, Random House.

Miller, L. S. (2004). Exploring high academic: The case of Latinos in higher education. *Journal of Hispanic Higher Education, 4,* 252–271.

Pascarella, E., & Terenzini, P. (2005). *How college affects students: A third decade of research* (Vol. 2). San Francisco: Jossey-Bass.

Ramirez, R., & De la Cruz, P. (2003). "The Hispanic population in the United States: March 2002" *Current Population Reports.* Washington, DC: U.S. Census Bureau.

Santiago, D., & Brown, S. (2004). *Federal policy and Latinos in higher education.* Washington, DC: The Pew Hispanic Center.

Scheurich, J., & Young, M. (1997). Coloring epistemologies: Are our research epistemologies racially biased?" *Educational Researcher, 6*(4), 4–16.

Solórzano, D., & Ornelas, A. (2002). A critical race analysis of advance placement classes: A case of educational inequalities. *Journal of Latinos and Education, 1,* 215–229.

Solórzano, D., & Ornelas, A. (2004). A critical race analysis of advance placement classes and selective admissions. *High School Journal, 87,* 15–26.

Solórzano, D., Villalpando, O., & Oseguera, L. (2005). Educational inequities and Latina/o undergraduate students in the United States: A critical race analysis of their educational progress. *Journal of Hispanic Higher Education, 4,* 272–294.

Turner, C. S., & Myers, S. L. (2000). *Faculty of color in academe: Bittersweet success.* Boston: Allyn and Bacon.

U.S. Census Bureau, (2001). *Educational attainment in the U.S.: 2000.* Washington, DC: U.S. Census Bureau.

U.S. Census Bureau. (2004). *Educational attainment in the U.S.: 2003* (P20-550). Washington, DC: U.S. Census Bureau.

Villalpando, O. (2004). Practical considerations of critical race theory and Latino critical theory for Latino college students. In Ortiz (Ed.), *Addressing the unique needs of Latino American students, new directions for higher education* (pp. 40–50). San Francisco: Jossey-Bass.

Watford, T., Rivas, M., Burciaga, R., & Solórzano, D. (2006). Latinas and the doctorate: The "status" of attainment and experience from the margin. In J. Castelanos, A. Gloria, & M. Kamimura (Eds.), *The Latina/o pathway to the Ph.D.* Sterling, VA: Stylus.

16 Latino Community Activism in the Twenty-First Century

Confronting the Future, Learning from the Past

Carmen I. Mercado and Luis O. Reyes
Hunter College, CUNY

This chapter is about community activism that seeks to affect change in public school policy with the goal of improving the education of Latina and Latino students in U.S. schools. As Puerto Rican activist Antonia Pantoja (1989) reminds us, it is part of a broader struggle for a just and humane society. Activism in response to oppression, powerlessness, and invisibility has a long history in the Americas, as the historical record documents. However, the goals and purposes of Latino community activism have changed over time as U.S. communities grapple with dramatic demographic change as well as the changing dynamics of geographical, political, social, and economic forces that shape and influence all facets of life. Michael Apple illuminates the problem when he says that, "powerful movements and alliances can radically shift the relationship between educational policies and practices and the relation of dominance and subordination in the larger society, but not in a direction that any of us find ethically or politically justifiable" (2006, p. 203). Events during the last two decades of the 20th century, beginning with one of the legacies of the Reagan Administration, *A Nation at Risk*, are testimony to changing dynamics that have had an adverse impact on Latino communities.

Possibly as a response to educational changes produced by the Civil Rights Movement of the 1960s, we have seen extraordinary activism by coalitions of neoliberal, neoconservative and a professional class of parents in urban public school policy, with the human and material resources to shape the educational landscape to suit their individual, and often, contradictory interests (Apple, 1996, 2006). Neoliberals have sufficiently weakened the state's role in education to gain access to free markets, while neoconservatives have increased state control over what should be taught in the curriculum. Nowhere is this clearer than in the federal No Child Left Behind (NCLB) Act, successor to the Civil-Rights era Elementary and Secondary Education Act (ESEA) and offspring to *A Nation at Risk*. Since 2002, NCLB has served to advance the interests of both neoliberals and neoconservatives by promoting an educational agenda focused on increasing standards, high-stakes testing in reading and mathematics, and paving the way for free-market parental choice and privatization. The consequences of these movements for children in working class communities have been documented by many, but most recently by the Center on Education and Policy, which reports that since the passage of NCLB, subjects or activities such as science, social studies, art and music, gym, lunch, and recess are getting less attention, as schools increasingly focus on raising reading and mathematics scores on high-stakes standardized tests (McMurrer, 2007). At the same time that curriculum and standards narrow the content of instruction for some students, the children of the professional class gain a broader choice of programs for the gifted and advanced placement in pre-collegiate programs, the result of coalitions formed with neoliberal and neoconservative alliances. That this is happening in the midst of one of the most dramatic technological revolutions in history (Kellner, 2000) and about which little is mentioned in the public discourse on educational policy, should alert us to the gravity of the matter.

Some scholars (Anyon, 2005; Apple, 1996; Reyes, 2006) suggest that these changing conditions require that we find common ground to build coalitions across affinity groups to press for policy changes and to increase public understanding of social issues impacting our society, not just Latino communities and education. It has become apparent that we need to re-conceptualize Latino activism as a collective project that demands new alliances and the use of local resources and technological tools in new ways and in diverse social arenas. There is a broad body of practical knowledge that informs this new collective project; the problem is that that body of literature, including tools and resources, has yet to be organized and synthesized to make it useful.

How should Latino community activism be conceptualized for the world of the 21st century? What lessons have been learned from the past that may guide what we do in the future? How are local communities responding to state and national policies that do not serve them well? These are the questions we find compelling and that we address in this chapter. We will frame issues from the perspectives and experiences of two major Latino communities with historical connections to the United States: Mexicans/Chican@s and Puerto Ricans/Boricuas. The goal is to learn from the past and to understand the present in order to shape the future in the direction we value.

It is important to mention that we combine work from inside and outside the academy in the interest of presenting a more nuanced and representative description of community activism. Thus we reference books and articles by scholars from diverse disciplines and viewpoints, including feminist scholarship, LatCrit theory, critical educational studies—in general, "research and creative intellectual work that align with communities, organizations, movements, or networks working for social justice" (UTSA website, retrieved February 2005).

The authors of this chapter are hopeful that our voices will add to others in this volume in keeping the historical memory fresh, in illuminating the present, and, hopefully, in serving as a source of inspiration for teachers/educators and future generations of activist-scholars, no matter their location.

Reconceptualizing Community Activism

In social science literature by Latino academics and grassroots leaders as well as others, activism is a term that is synonymous with civil and human rights, human agency, self-determination, and voice. In fact, the history of educational activism among Latinos during the last 40 years is most often cast as a quotes struggle for equal educational opportunity (Santiago-Santiago, 1978; Valenzuela, 1999). However, in the public eye, the connotations of this community activism are more likely to be pejorative, as when activism is linked to "radicalism," "extremism," violence, and opposition/resistance as a negative force. Critical scholars such as Hill Collins and Macedo theorize that the use of words and images may be manipulated to produce these negative connotations—a form of symbolic oppression and control. This hegemonic control of public discourse is deliberately crafted to minimize sympathy and support for causes of concern to Latina/o communities in the court of public opinion. That community activism has received relatively little scholarly attention may be due to the limited number of engaged scholars for whom "community activism" matters a great deal but whose priorities are not those of writing and publishing in traditional scholarly venues.

During the last two decades, we have witnessed growing concern and interest in legitimizing the study of activism as a form of civic engagement, a connection that makes this specialization acceptable to a broader public and important in the process of movement building. Several colleges and universities now offer specializations in community activism and, the crown jewel of the City University of New York, the Graduate Center, offers a doctoral program in Urban Education that has attracted an unusual representation of Latina/o educational activists and community organizers, many of whom are women. These emerging scholars of color are engaging in rigorous, theoretically grounded scholarship that combines the passion of lived experiences with powerful theoretical lenses to theorize, understand and address social and educational inequalities in locally appropriate ways, having both practical and policy implications. In effect, these emerging scholars are transforming the genre of policy research into one that is driven by and responsive to what is valued and needed in local communities, certainly not the way educational policy is traditionally formulated.

Seen in this light, it is not surprising that *The High School Journal* devoted the entire April/May 2004 issue to Chican@ activism and education, with Luis Urrieta Jr. as editor. In his incisive and insightful introduction, Urrieta provides a succinct and comprehensive overview of the history of Chican@ activism in education and lays out critical issues of concern. Urrieta emphasizes the urgency of re/thinking activism given the lessons of history, for example, that power responds to resistance through surveillance, infiltration, and acts of violence. He joins a chorus of voices (Apple, 1996; Pantoja, 1989) that calls for an understanding of how power operates to shape and control policy (Reyes, 2006) and how policies, in turn, contribute to racial and socio-economic inequities in society, as is the case with "vouchers, charter schools, and accountability through high stakes testing" (p. 1). Although Urietta is primarily concerned with Chican@ activism, the conceptions of activism he presents have much in common with those presented by others working from different intellectual traditions and diverse social and geographic locations, as exemplified in the work of Puerto Rican Latin@ activist scholars such as Luisa Capetillo (1909/2004) in Puerto Rico and Tampa, Florida Antonia Darder (1995) in California, and Antonia Pantoja (1989), and Luis O. Reyes (2006) in New York.

Chican@ (Cordova, 1999), Puerto Rican (Darder, 1995), and Black (Hill Collins, 1992/2000) feminist scholars argue for a broader understanding of resistance to subordination and oppression that is anti-patriarchal and anti-colonial, and, as Darder states, anti all the –isms, especially class. Stated differently, these scholars conceptualize activism as the voice of positive resistance to all forms of powerlessness and invisibility, emphasizing those intersecting with gender, ethnicity, race and class. According to Cordova (1999), the very act of speaking in your own voice and renaming yourself in your own image, rather than that of the oppressor is an act of resistance.

Some scholars focus their analysis more narrowly on educational reforms that are intended to respond to the needs local communities, as Urietta's discussion on activism as a response to educational policies that affect non-English speaking and migrant students, in particular, bilingual education, and on the constant struggle against alienating schooling practices such as tracking, standardized testing, the "whitestream" curriculum, and access to higher education. Other scholars (Anyon, 2005; Cordero-Guzman, 1997; Torres & Katsiaficas, 1999) do not minimize the importance of school reform efforts at the local level, but theirs is an analysis that views educational problems more systemically, that is, in terms of social policy that impact the political economy. Scholars working from this intellectual tradition make the claim that community activism by people of color and other marginalized groups needs to link the conditions of these communities to the political economy and global economy, and place labor, class, patriarchy, and capital.

Addressing urban school reform specifically, Anyon (2005) makes a compelling argument when she says that no existing educational policy or urban school reform can transcend the conditions that macroeconomic policies regulating minimum wage, job availability, tax rates, federal transportation, and affordable housing, create in cities and that contribute to low-achieving, under-resourced schools. Among others, Anyon stresses that we must know where the problem lies in order to identify workable solutions and advocate for meaningful change. Consequently, community activism in education necessitates shifting major sites of struggle in order to address the root causes of our educational problems.

However, recent scholarship also suggests that progress made through Latino activism is possibly more profound at the level of the individual than we realize. In focusing on the conditions that are necessary to engage in activism, scholars hypothesize a reciprocal relationship between activism and individual/group consciousness. Accordingly, participating in different forms of activism requires a sense of community consciousness, that is, a sense of who we are as a people, and has the potential to change individuals in important ways, including contributing to identity formation, to strengthening the will to resist and subvert the control of our minds, and to remaining *en la lucha*. At the same time, activism has the potential to unite groups and communities from different sectors of society in a common cause and contribute to strengthening social ties with others who share fundamental affinities in the struggle for social and economic justice. In the next section, we look to the past as a way of illuminating the present.

Lessons from the Past

The history of Latinos in the United States is one of conquest, colonization, and marginalization, the result of economic exploitation. However, this history of oppression in the Americas since the time of colonization has a parallel history of activism gleaned from a historical record created by the great civilizations that existed on this hemisphere before the arrival of Columbus. For the Mayans, this history (dates and events) is inscribed in stellae that withstood the destruction of the Spaniards, as well as from accounts made by Spaniards who were sympathetic to the indigenous populations of the Americas at the time, as Cabeza de Vaca was. But, it is also rooted in Africa, as Simon Bolivar (1819) suggests when addressing the Congress of Angostura. Latin@s are "neither European nor North American; rather, they are a mixture of African and the Americans who originated in Europe.... It is impossible to determine with any degree of accuracy where we belong in the human family. The greater portion of the native Indians has been annihilated; Spaniards have mixed with Americans and Africans, and Africans with Indians and Spaniards. While we have all been born of the same mother, our fathers, different in origin and in blood, are foreigners, and all differ visibly as to the color of their skin..." Thus, despite ongoing controversies associated with the meaning and use of the term, *mestizaje* is also reality rooted in the economic exploitation of the Americas by Europeans.

There is now substantial documentation of violent resistance to enslavement that began in slave factories of West Africa, documented during Middle Passage and in American colonies soon after slave ships arrived on this hemisphere. Maroon communities of runaway slaves throughout the Americas, in places we now refer to as Colombia, Venezuela, and Ecuador, are proof of resistance to White authority, and evidence of the willful refusal to be defined and manipulated by White masters. In sum, under great odds, maroons, were among the first Americans in the wake of 1492 to resist colonial domination, striving for independence, forging new cultural identities, and developing solidarity out of diversity—processes which only later took place, on a much larger scale, in emerging nation states.

This legacy of activism is evident in the Chicano or Mexican American communities in the South/West and the Boricua or Puerto Rican communities in the Northeast. Both communities have a long history of activism that predates incorporation to US territories, what for Mexican Americans began with the signing of the Treaty of Guadalupe-Hidalgo in 1848 and for Puerto Ricans with the Treaty of Paris in 1898. However, Puerto Ricans have been migrating to large urban centers in the northeastern United States since the turn of the 20th century, and the emergence of group consciousness so essential to community activism is a relatively recent development. As some scholars explain, the 1960s and 1970s represent the emergence of a Puerto Rican consciousness or group solidarity in the diasporic community of the United States (Melendez, 2003; Pantoja, 1989). Given the longer history of relationship that Chicanos have in the United

States, this consciousness was forged early on, which is why the oldest Mexican-American community based organization (CBO), the League of United Latin American Citizens (LULAC), was founded in 1927, and Aspira of New York in 1961 (see summary Tables 16.1 and 16.2 in the Appendix for a summary of major CBOs).

Further, despite arguments to the contrary, and as evident from the work of major CBOs, Latino activism has not been exclusively focused on education because education forms a central part of a larger set of interrelated issues that are affected by the level of economic development of Latino communities. Latino activism has played out in different sites of struggle and has engaged different social actors—for example, community organizers and community activists (including many young high school and college students) in public spaces such as the streets of large urban centers; through study by activist scholars in the academy; through the day-to-day activities of ordinary people, especially women and mothers, in particular; and more recently, by community leaders who harness the considerable power of the Internet and public access TV to widely disseminate timely information to the general public and to special interest groups.

Hill Collins (2000), like Urietta (2004), argues forcefully that while the common perception of activism associates it with large-scale, organized initiatives intended to confront institutional power, struggles for group survival by individuals, especially women of color, have played a fundamental role in sustaining these very same large-scale, organized initiatives. Hill Collins is especially critical of social science research that typically focuses on public, official, visible political activity, such as the activism of CBOs or of individuals who identify themselves as and who are known to be community activists. While the importance of this form of community activism is indisputable, recent scholarship is also paying close attention to the range of actions, some less visible than others, through which activism is manifested, and, in particular, the relationship between activism and group consciousness and identity development among youth.

In sum, many valuable lessons have been learned from this history of activism that inform future actions. Some major insights are:

1. It is possible to push our political, economic, and cultural institutions in the direction we value through large-scale social movements.
2. We need to understand the problem to advocate for meaningful change.
3. It is possible to build powerful social movements through alliances that unite groups and communities from different sectors of society that share fundamental affinities despite other types of differences that ordinarily serve to separate individuals and groups.
4. Community activism is everyone's responsibility and therefore needs to play out in different social arenas.
5. We need to reconsider what counts as public policy in education.

A Local Case: Activism in New York City

In this section Luis O. Reyes combines multiple sources of data to present a synthesis of major moments in educational activism in the nation's largest and most diverse city, and one of three "global" cities in addition to London and Tokyo. New York City has a history of multiculturalism and multilingualism that dates from the beginning of the public school system more than a century ago, and has been predominantly African American and Latino for close to half a century.

Educational activism in New York City among Puerto Ricans can be conceptualized as a conscious movement to assert human agency and to be a voice for a people who have experienced powerlessness and invisibility within the city's educational and political institutions. This activism took many forms, combining community research, legal analysis and challenges in court, mass mobilization, community education, and subsequent negotiation between Puerto

Rican community leaders and educational officials. "Taking it to the streets" went hand-in-hand with going to court and negotiating compromises in boardrooms (Reyes, 2000). Puerto Rican educational activism also expressed itself in collective efforts to create alternative institutions like Aspira of New York, the Puerto Rican Community Development Project, the Puerto Rican Forum, and Universidad Boricua

Many Puerto Rican organizations, such as Aspira, the Puerto Rican Legal Defense and Education Fund (PRLDEF), the Puerto Rican Association for Community Actions (PRACA), and the Puerto Rican Educators Association (PREA), in fact, were founded in the 1960s and 1970s as a programmatic response to the educational needs of its children and to the lack of inclusion of Puerto Ricans in the educational establishment. The many "alternative institutions" created by the Puerto Rican community in those years, institutions as diverse as Aspira, the Young Lords Party, El Centro de Estudios Puertorriqueños at Hunter College of the City University of New York (CUNY) and PRACA, all shared a similar underlying ideology. They all envisioned the improvement of life conditions for Puerto Ricans as flowing from self-reliance, community development, and advocacy vis à vis the larger society and its formal institutions.

The mission and practice of these Puerto Rican community organizations also made explicit the commitment to the cultural self-affirmation of the Puerto Rican community, that is, a determined resistance to forced assimilation (Reyes, 2000). What others defined as the "Puerto Rican problem" (Association of Assistant Superintendents, 1948), namely, our collective refusal to melt linguistically and culturally into the modal Anglo-American "melting pot" (Glazer & Moynihan, 1963), our community leaders regarded as a means of survival. These leaders refused to acquiesce to the "blame the victim" ideology adopted by local officials and mainstream social scientists when addressing the educational experiences of Puerto Rican students. Instead, they rejected analyses that frame the question as "the Puerto Rican problem" and challenged the public school system and the society at large to adapt to the needs of our children and to reform structural arrangements, organizational culture, and funding policies (Reyes, 2000).

The ideology of resistance to forced assimilation led to many collective efforts to assert our right to be both bilingual and bicultural in our personal and public lives (Reyes, 2000). Aspira's mission of developing a new generation of Puerto Rican leaders successful in academics and committed to community service and community development was one of many examples of this marriage of ideology and praxis. In 1982, I (Luis Reyes) became intimately involved in one of these collective efforts of Puerto Rican activism, becoming the Co-Coordinator of the New York Coalition for Bilingual Education, an ad-hoc collection of mostly Puerto Rican educators, community activists, parents and students, that organized a demonstration of hundreds of Puerto Rican, Dominican, and other bilingual community advocates in downtown Brooklyn to protest then Schools Chancellor Frank Macchiarola's unilateral actions to cut back the numbers of New York City students served by bilingual education programs.

PRLDEF concurrently returned to the U.S. District Court that helped to force a settlement of the original 1972 lawsuit, *Aspira v. Board of Education,* resulting in the 1974 Aspira Consent Decree. The Consent Decree, issued by U.S. District Court Judge Marvin E. Frankel, ordered the New York City Board of Education to implement transitional bilingual programs for Spanish-surnamed students with limited English proficiency, in effect, establishing bilingual programs in New York City public schools as an educational entitlement for Puerto Rican students. In 1983, the U.S. district judge ordered the New York City Board of Education to desist from any action to implement Macchiarola's "opt-out memo" citing the board's callous disregard for the needs of language minority students. The coalition's deeper purpose and meaning was to rekindle the fires of the grass-roots campaign in the Puerto Rican communities of New York City for equal educational opportunity and community empowerment (Reyes, 2000).

As I wrote in 2000 (Reyes):

as a transplanted island people whose demographic dispersion precludes us from becoming a majority group dominating other groups, we have a particular imperative to work out a place in American society based on an ideology of cultural and structural pluralism. Acting locally and thinking globally leads many of us Puerto Ricans to fight police brutality, miseducation, and environmental racism in our neighborhoods, while calling on the U.S. Congress and the United Nations, no matter what our political persuasion, to grant us our rights to self-determination. These sociopolitical realities may be the last thing that a New York City teacher has in mind when she enters her classroom each September, but they are truly part and parcel of our educational vision for our Puerto Rican children to be educated for the world they will inhabit at the opening of the new millennium (p. 79).

Puerto Rican educational activists not only have attempted to change and transform policies and practices, but we also have tried to challenge the hegemonic discourse of the educational and political power elites regarding the purpose and goals of public education. All too often our recommendations to policy makers have been ignored or misunderstood because of the technocratic obsession of policy-makers and the mass media with reading and math scores as the only measurement of success in public schooling. This tendency has gained ascendancy under recent New York City mayors, including Rudolph Giuliani, who sought unsuccessfully to "sunset" the provisions of the Aspira Consent Decree in 2000–2001, and now Mayor Michael Bloomberg, who gained direct control over the public school system in 2003.

In both instances, Puerto Rican activists have mobilized, now, joined by other Latino groups and by newer immigrant-serving organizations like the New York Immigration Coalition and educational advocacy groups like Advocates for Children, on behalf of the rights of English Language Learners (ELLs). Over the last four decades, activists have engaged in efforts to gain Puerto Rican community control over neighborhood schools in the 1960s, to ensure bilingual instruction in the 1970s, to maintain Puerto Rican/Latino representation on the New York City Board of Education in the 1980s, and inclusion of our history and contributions in the multicultural education curriculum of the school system in the 1990s. Now, in the first decade of the 21st century, Puerto Ricans and other newer immigrant Latino communities, such as Dominicans, Mexicans, and other Central and South Americans, are focused more on issues of equal access of ELL/immigrant students to new small high schools and charter schools, translation and interpretation services for the parents of ELL/immigrant students, and closing the achievement gap.

I have argued elsewhere (Reyes, 2000) that the improvement of education for Puerto Rican students in U.S. public schools must be multifaceted, requiring Puerto Rican educational leaders to develop a comprehensive agenda for change and to play multiple roles. The New York City Board of Education's Latino Commission on Educational Reform, which I convened and chaired between 1991–1994, represented just such a change agenda and change process. Previous reports on the failure of Puerto Rican students to do well in New York City public schools had highlighted student and parental characteristics as causal factors. Puerto Rican researchers and advocates, in response, argued that school characteristics were more salient and had the advantage of being subject to change and improvement by public school officials.

Puerto Rican researchers and educational leaders who comprised the Latino Commission identified the problems to be addressed comprehensively, as follows: the continuing and disproportionately high dropout rate among Puerto Rican and Latino students, academic underachievement in core subject areas, the lack of guidance and support services, negligence in implementing quality bilingual education programs, the discouragement of Puerto Rican parent and community group participation, and the low representation of Puerto Ricans in the teaching and administrative ranks.

Many of these problems had been addressed in previous reports done by Aspira of New York's

Office of Research and Advocacy (A-ORA), which I established and headed between 1985 and 1990. For example, two A-ORA reports, *Su Nombre Es Hoy I* (Reyes, 1988) and *Su Nombre Es Hoy II* (Reyes, 1989), were prepared and delivered to Chancellors Richard Green and Joseph A. Fernández at the beginning of their respective administrations, each documenting a series of educational problems facing Puerto Rican/Latino students and presenting a plan of action for Green and Fernandez's consideration. In 1983, the Puerto Rican/Latino Education Roundtable had spearheaded a community teach-in on bilingual education (Caballero, 2000) flowing from the 1982 community mobilization efforts of the New York City Coalition for Bilingual Education discussed at the beginning.

The Latino Commission took the position, in its two reports (Latino Commission on Educational Reform, 1992, 1994) that piece-meal solutions focusing on add-ons to an unchanged school system were inadequate. Instead, we argued for a re-visioning of public education to incorporate the Puerto Rican/Latino communities' demands and goals. These demands included valuing bilingualism and multiculturalism (i.e., adding linguistic diversity and cultural diversity as goals of the board's non-discrimination policy and pedagogical instruction); empowering parents and community members to participate in all governance decisions, starting at the school level; providing students with a clear understanding of the link between school success and the world of work (career guidance, financial assistance, and employment internships); and engaging students in building community and exploring citizenship roles.

The Latino Commission had the political support of David M. Dinkins, the first African American New York City Mayor (who had been swept into office in 1989 with the support of a rainbow coalition made up of members of the Black and Puerto Rican communities). However, facing acute budget constraints, he was unable or unwilling to deliver any significant resources. The commission was able to garner support to implement only a handful of our almost 100 recommendations: helping to establish the Leadership Secondary School (a dual language, college-preparatory high school with a focus on leadership development and community service), obtaining state funding for the Bilingual/Multicultural Institute within the Board's Office of Bilingual Education, obtaining federal funding for the opening of a Migration/Immigration Resource Center for parents and children in District 10 in the Bronx (the Welcome Center), and advocating for the initiation of the Math and Science Institute that would provide Latino and African American middle school students with enriched instruction and test preparation to facilitate their admission to the city's specialized high schools such as Stuyvesant and Bronx Science.

The Latino Commission's final report (1994) focused attention on special education, college preparation, community collaborations, and fiscal and staffing equity. Having incorporated students, parents, teachers, researchers, and many other members of the Puerto Rican/Latino educational community into our work groups, we failed to produce systemic changes or to impel the board and chancellor to initiate strategic planning in response to our recommendations. We received much criticism as a commission, including the following: that the commission was all over the map; and that the recommendations were noteworthy but unrealistic. In fact, the recommendation for a salary differential for bilingual teachers has never succeeded in gaining political traction. However, the recommendation of an overhaul of the board's budget allocation to funnel more funding to poorer districts has finally been implemented under Mayor Michael Bloomberg and Chancellor Joel Klein.

In our three years of sustained work as a commission and in the subsequent efforts to hold subsequent Chancellors Ramón Cortines and Rudy Crew accountable for implementing our recommendations, Puerto Rican educators and advocates had penetrated the inner reaches of the central bureaucratic system. We had amassed a wealth of data and analyses that represented some of the most creative, collective work ever done by Puerto Rican educators and advocates. And, we had laid out a comprehensive reform agenda.

One of our weakest connections has been to the majority of our elected officials. Another is the traditional wariness and mistrust between Puerto Rican progressive educators and activists and Puerto Rican politicians. Many of the former, who have gone on to college and become professionals and academicians, can seem isolated and out of touch, while the latter, many of whom rose to power through anti-poverty and community control struggles, seem unwilling to study the larger picture and support systemic change. While Puerto Rican educators and activists often lack the patience and the foresight to build our agendas from the ground up, local politicians seem to be consumed with delivering needed services to their poor constituencies while protecting their political viability from election to election.

I have asserted elsewhere that Puerto Rican/Latino educators and activists have to play various interconnecting roles to be effective: teacher, researcher, advocate, administrator, litigant, policy-maker, role model, public spokesperson, group facilitator, problem-solver, politician, activist, bureaucrat, coalition-builder, fundraiser, keynote speaker, and public intellectual, not to mention family member and school parent (Reyes, 2000). I have argued that these different roles are indispensable to the change process and to advance the vision of quality education for Puerto Rican/Latino students in New York City and in the United States. It is not that each and every Puerto Rican/Latino educator and activist has to play *all* these roles; but, that we must be able to engage in these activities collectively if we are to realize the vision that we espouse. And, a value-neutral, unidimensional educational role is illusory and ultimately detrimental to our children's education.

What we present here is a gloss of events we viewed as important and illustrative of Latino activism in the post Civil Rights era.

Obviously, rendering an accurate portrayal of community activism requires attention to a range of strategies and activities that comprise activism. In this chapter, we have explored different conceptualizations of Latino community activism for the world of the 21st century; analyzed lessons learned from the past, and provided a case study of how one of the largest Latino communities in the United States (New York City) has (and continues to) respond to educational policies that do not serve Latin@ children and youth well. We have featured New York City because it is a place where Latinos from throughout the Americas have historically united forces in the struggle for self-determination, locally, nationally, and internationally. It is our hope that this information will guide and inspire future generations to understand some of the choices we have in responding to social and educational injustices. Conceptualizing activism as everyone's responsibility heightens our consciousness of the many moments in a day in which activism is as simple and as complex as a willful refusal to be complicit in policies and practices that affect in negative ways Latino children and youth, in and out of school. Conceptualizing activism as broad scale efforts to contest educational policy recognizes that these forms of activism are also needed to remind elected officials that we will remain vigilant and that we will hold them accountable for representing the interests of those who elected them. We will form coalitions to take the argument directly to the court of public opinion because in a democracy, it is ultimately informed taxpayers who shape social and educational policy.

References

Anyon, J. (2005). *Radical possibilities*. New York: Routledge.

Apple, M. (1996). *Cultural politics and education*. New York: Teachers College Press.

Apple, M. (2006). Critical education, politics and the real world. In L. Weis, C. McCarthy, G. Dimitriadis (Eds.), *Ideology, curriculum, and the new sociology of education: Revisiting the work of Michael Apple* (pp. 87–118). New York: CRC Press.

Association of Assistant Superintendents. (1948). *A program of education for Puerto Ricans in New York City*. Brooklyn, NY: New York City Board of Education.

Bolivar, S. (1819). Address delivered at the inauguration of the Second National Congress of Venezuela in Angostura. Retrieved, Dec. 1, 2008, from http://faculty.chass.ncsu.edu/slatta/hi216/documents/bolivar/sbagostura1819.htm

Caballero, D. (2000). The Puerto Rican/Latino Roundtable: Seeking unity in vision and organizing for educational change. In S. Nieto (Ed.), *Puerto Rican students in U.S. schools* (pp. 203–221). Mahwah, NJ: Erlbaum.

Capetillo, L. (2004). *A nation of women: An early feminist speaks out* (F. V. Matos Rodríguez, Ed., & A. West-Duran, Trans.). Houston, TX: Arte Publico Press. (Original work published 1909)

Cordero-Guzman, H. (1997). The structure of inequality and the status of Puerto Rican youth in the US. In A. Darder, R. D. Torres, & H. Gutiérrez (Eds.), *Latinos and education: A critical reader* (pp. 80–94). New York: Routledge.

Cordova, T. (1999). Anti-colonial Chicana feminism. In R. D. Torres & G. Katsiaficas (Eds.), *Latino social movements* (pp. 11–41). New York: Routledge.

Darder, A. (1995). Introduction. The politics of biculturalism: Culture and difference in the formation of warriors for gringostroika and the new mestizas. In A. Darder (Ed.), *Culture and difference* (pp. 1–20). Westport, CT: Bergin & Garvey.

Glazer, N., & Moynihan, D. P. (1963). *Beyond the melting pot.* Cambridge, MA: MIT Press.

Hill Collins, P. (2000). *Black feminist thought* (2nd ed.). New York: Routledge. (Original work published 1992)

Kellner, D. (2000). Globalization and new social movements. In N. C. Burbules & C. A. Torres (Eds.), *Globalization and education* (pp. 299–321). New York: Routledge.

Latino Commission on Educational Reform. (1992). *Towards a vision for the education of Latino students: Community voices, student voices* (Vol. 1 & 2). Brooklyn, NY: New York City Board of Education.

Latino Commission on Educational Reform. (1994). *Making the vision a reality: A Latino agenda for educational reform.* Brooklyn, NY: New York City Board of Education.

McMurrer, J. (2007, July). Choices, changes, and challenges: Curriculum and instruction in the NCLB era. Washington, DC: Center on Education and Policy. Retrieved from http://www.cepdc.org/index.cfm?fuseaction=document.showDocumentByID&nodeID=1&DocumentID=212

Melendez, E. (2003, Spring). Puerto Rican politics in the United States: Examination of major perspectives and theories. *CENTRO, XV*(1), 9–39.

Pantoja, A. (1989). Puerto Ricans in New York: A historical and community development perspective. *CENTRO, II*(5), 20-31.

Reyes, L. (1988). *Su nombre es hoy I: Aspira educational reform agenda.* Unpublished report submitted to Chancellor Richard R. Green, New York.

Reyes, L. (1989). *Su nombre es hoy II: Aspira educational reform agenda.* Unpublished report submitted to Chancellor Joseph A. Fernández, New York.

Reyes, L. O. (2000). Educational leadership, educational change: A Puerto Rican perspective. In S. Nieto (Ed.), *Puerto Rican students in U.S. schools* (pp. 73–89). Mahwah, NJ: Erlbaum.

Reyes, L .O. (2006, Fall). The Aspira Consent Decree: A thirtieth-anniversary retrospective of bilingual education in New York City. *Harvard Educational Review, 76*(3), 369–400.

Santiago-Santiago, I. (1978). *A community's struggle for equal educational opportunity: Aspira v. Board of Education.* Princeton, NJ: Office for Minority Education, Educational Testing Service.

Torres, R. D., & Katsiaficas, G. (1999). Introduction. In R. D. Torres & G. Katsiaficas (Eds.), *Latino social movements* (pp. 1–10). New York: Routledge.

Urrieta, L. Jr. (2004, April/May). Chican@ activism and education: An introduction to the special issue. *The High School Journal,* 1–9.

Valenzuela, A. (1999). *Subtractive schooling: U.S.-Mexican youth and the politics of caring.* Albany: State University of New York Press.

Table 16.1   Summaries of Representative West Coast Community-Based Organizations/Coalitions

	Date Founded	Mission	Reach	Singular Accomplishments
LULAC	1927	To advance the economic condition, educational attainment, political influence, health, and civil rights of the Hispanic population of the United States through community service and activism	National councils	Education, employment, housing, civil rights, economic development
NCLR	1972, when the Southwest Council of la Raza went national	Works to improve opportunities for Hispanic Americans through capacity building and applied research, policy analysis, and advocacy	A network of about 300 affiliated community-based organizations represents and serves Hispanic Americans in 41 states and Puerto Rico	National Policy efforts on the socioeconomic condition of US Hispanics, their views on public policy issues, and levels of services they receive
MEchA	1969 a student movement that grew from student strike/ walkout of 1968	Self-determination requires political involvement and is the only way for the Chicano/a community to gain socioeconomic justice; strategic use of education to study what the community values and resist European colonialism	Gaining access to postsecondary education that responds to who students are	Creation of Chicano/a (Ethnic) Studies Programs and courses, and on campus support services to build Latina/o self respect, self-confidence, and understanding through a study of their heritage

Table 16.2   Summaries of Representative East Coast Community-Based Organizations

	Date Founded	Mission/Purpose	Reach	Singular Accomplishments
ASPIRA	Founded in New York City by Antonia Pantoja and community leaders in 1961	To reduce the Hispanic drop-out rate and promote economic development through education	Now has over 200 partnerships with universities, government agencies, other Latino CBOs across the US	By 2003, over 200 ASPIRA Leadership Clubs primarily secondary schools in low-income communities. ASPIRANTES have a 95% graduate rate (90% attend college)
United Bronx Parents (UBA)	A community-grown organization founded by activist Dra. Evelina Lopez Antonetty in 1965 in partnership with parents and local businesses in the South Bronx	To provide basic human services necessary for families and individuals to obtain self-sufficiency through dignity in their struggle to participate as functioning and valuable citizens	UBA has broadened its reach locally and is now a multiple services agency (MSO) that addresses basic survival needs	Now has 8 facilities and a staff of over 200 offering ambulatory and multiple services, e.g., adult education; primary care clinics; treatment and housing to substance abusing women and their children; men and women with AIDS; senior centers
National Congress for Puerto Rican Rights (NCPRR)	A grassroots, voluntary organization founded in the South Bronx in 1981	Advocates for the human and civil rights of Puerto Ricans	NCPRR has chapters in NYC, Boston, San Francisco, and Philadelphia.	Local and national campaigns drawing public and political attention to police brutality, environmental racism, racially motivated violence in Puerto Rican and Latino communities. Education, leadership development, and coalition building to address conditions affecting PR and Latino communities

17 When Stepping to College is Stepping to Consciousness

Critical Pedagogy, Transformational Resistance, and Community Building with Urban Latin@ and African American Youth

Nicole D. Hidalgo
University of California, Santa Cruz

Jeffrey M. R. Duncan-Andrade
San Francisco State University

It helps us think in another way. Like before I just wanted to go to college and, I don't know, just get on with my life, but thanks to this program I now understand why it's important for me to go back to my community, or at least a place that's similar to my community... Because, I could come back and help others, and those others could go and then come back, and that's how we start rising.

(Lisette, third-year student in the Step to College program)

Introduction

In this chapter, we attempt to unite the conceptual frameworks of critical pedagogy (Darder, 1991; Duncan-Andrade & Morrell, 2008; Freire, 1970/2002) and transformational resistance (Solórzano & Delgado Bernal, 2001) to explore the ways teaching beliefs, practices, and curriculum can encourage transformational resistance among urban youth. The first section of the chapter discusses the educational theory that guided the pedagogical practices discussed in the second section.

The second portion of this chapter provides an on-the-ground look at how classroom curriculum and pedagogy can encourage young people to challenge, disrupt, and transform social inequities in their school and community by using the tools of literacy, research, and media production. It examines the process of cultivating transformational resistance within an educational intervention called Step to College (STC).

The STC program was designed by the current Dean of the College of Education at San Francisco State University as a response to the disturbingly low levels of academic engagement, achievement, graduation, and college eligibility among poor and working-class youth of color. The STC program partners a university professor with a local high school, allowing students to cross-enroll in a high school class and a university seminar class each semester. By taking these classes from a professor, students are exposed to the rigor and culture of university courses. Ultimately, the program aims to prepare underrepresented youth for college success and foster in them a sense of critical civic responsibility to create positive social change. The STC program currently operates in one East Oakland (California) public high school and one San Francisco public high school. Specifically, the second section discusses a 10th-grade urban sociology class in the East Oakland STC program.

Setting

The STC program in East Oakland takes place in an "intensely segregated"[1] high school. The class had 30 students—16 Latin@s (10 girls and 6 boys) and 14 African American students (8 girls and 6 boys). All the Latin@ student participants are first-generation immigrants whose primary home language is Spanish, and they all will be the first in their immediate family to attend college. The African American students will also be first-generation college students, with the exception of one young woman who will be second-generation. The class was untracked (Oakes, 1985), although the overwhelming majority of the students in the class would have been considered low achievers by traditional measures at the start of the program. Approximately half of the students were recruited by a school leader based on their reputation as some of the most challenging students to work with in the school. The other half of the students chose the course from a list of several elective classes offered at the school. The school was on a block schedule, which meant that our class met three times a week for ninety minutes.

Duncan-Andrade, who has been a teacher and teacher educator in urban schools for 15 years, volunteers as the lead instructor for the STC courses. He teaches the courses while also serving as a tenure track professor at San Francisco State University (SFSU) in Raza Studies and Education. Hidalgo volunteers as the teaching assistant in the course and is also the research coordinator for the project. She juggles her research responsibilities with individual student support responsibilities, particularly for students confronting major social, economic, and/or academic challenges.

Methods

Using critical ethnographic and action research methods, this study analyzes the STC program over a three-year period (August 2005 to June 2008). Data collection techniques in the class include daily videotaping, analyzing student work and achievement data, and interviewing the STC students, parents, and teachers. Critical ethnography aims to challenge power structures, engage in emancipatory practices, and understand how schools are contradictory sites that both "reproduce and transform power" (Collatos, 2005, p. 131; see also Denzin & Lincoln, 2005). In a critical paradigm, researchers "function as intellectual advocates and activists" and "use the tools of research to discover inequities and to find ways…to bring about change in inequitable distributions of power, cultural assets, and other resources" (LeCompte & Schensul, 1999, p. 45). Critical researchers "believe that institutions can be transformed, and they seek ways of using research to serve the transformation process" (p. 46). Critical ethnography utilizes traditional ethnographic data gathering techniques such as surveys, interviews, observations, and field notes, and adds the critical elements of subjectivity and intervention (Carspecken, 1996; Delgado-Gaitan, 2001).

The study also employs a form of action research methods (McNiff, Lomax, & Whitehead, 1996; Somekh, 2006) that we might call "insider research," because the practitioners are using the tools of research to analyze their own work. Some treat this as a limitation and question the ability of practitioners to make valid claims about their own teaching (Huberman, 1996). Yet, action research takes the stance that "only those close to a particular situation can truly understand it" (Morrell, 2004b, p. 154). This study uses data triangulation to ensure the validity of our claims by comparing and contrasting them across multiple data sources, such as participant observation, surveys, and interviews (Zeichner & Noffke, 2001). Ultimately, our model for educational research is grounded in *cariño* (care), or relationships based on reciprocal care, trust, respect, and love (Duncan-Andrade, 2006a; Valenzuela, 1999). These reciprocal relationships aim to produce "real change in the schools where the research is taking place" (Duncan-Andrade, 2006a, p. 454).

Youth and Community Building

As teachers are asked to focus more of their energy on test scores, they often de-prioritize curriculum and pedagogy that builds critical consciousness, solidarity, and a sense of community among Latin@ youth. However, the national emphasis on basic skills, standards, and tests under the guise of increasing accountability for public education has not produced more achievement for youth of color, nor has it improved accountability. Equally as troubling is the fact that this approach to improving education for youth of color all but ignores most of the research on effective teaching, which overwhelmingly suggests that performance tends to be highest in classrooms employing curriculum and pedagogy that foster a sense of community among the students. This chapter is further confirmation of that expanding body of research that continues to prove that accountability and achievement are possible when teachers treat the classroom as one of the most important and logical places to build community with youth. We do not treat the idea of classroom as community lightly. So, we will argue that the results produced by STC must be understood as the outcomes of an intense commitment to the development of pedagogy and curriculum that create meaningful relationships between teachers and students, while maintaining a high level of critical intellectual rigor.

We frame our discussion of this approach to the classroom as a central site for community building with Latin@ and African American urban youth by drawing from literature on resistance and critical pedagogy, such as the works mentioned in the introduction. Our framework recognizes that young people's opposition to inequities in their schools and communities takes many shapes and forms, including self-defeating, reactionary, conformist and transformative behaviors (Solórzano & Delgado Bernal, 2001). By recognizing the potential of youth resistance to foment social change, this approach to working with youth moves us beyond negative reactions to youth resistance, and toward a plan that embraces the potential of youth resistance to be directed toward liberating purposes for communities such as East Oakland. This approach complicates how we understand our responsibilities to urban youth, forcing us to consider the value of pedagogical strategies that develop transformational resistance rather than devising strategies for eliminating resistance in youth.

Transformational resistance refers to young people's behaviors that consciously oppose social oppression by engaging in actions that promote social justice (Delgado Bernal, 1997; Solórzano & Delgado Bernal, 2001). It is a form of resistance that responds to the structural mechanisms and cultural processes in schools that help reproduce social inequalities. Scholarship on socioeconomic and cultural reproduction contends that meritocratic ideologies and structural mechanisms in U.S. public schools such as academic tracking and ability grouping often work to maintain the social status quo (Althusser, 1971/1994; Bourdieu & Passeron, 1977; Bowles & Gintis, 1976; Carnoy, 1974; Oakes, 1985). Several studies have documented how young people resist these schooling conditions through counter-school cultures or oppositional frames of reference (Fine, 1991; MacLeod, 1987; Ogbu, 1978, 1995; Willis, 1977). These studies suggest that students tend to resist schooling if they feel it is unlikely to result in social mobility, or if it conflicts with the values and beliefs of their communities or cultural groups. Each of these studies has connected students' acts of resistance to detrimental consequences such as academic failure or dropping out of school, and these consequences have been connected to the process of social reproduction. However, by conceptualizing students as agents who actively resist structural constraints they recognize the possibility for young people to resist in ways that can disrupt the reproduction of inequalities and bring about positive social change.

Several scholars have reexamined the concept of resistance to account for the healthy and liberating ways that poor and working-class youth of color engage in actions that counter domination and exploitation (Ginwright, Noguera, & Cammarota, 2006; Robinson & Ward, 1991). Giroux (1983, 2001) characterizes resistance as behavior that critiques domination and struggles for individual and social emancipation. This conception of youth resistance requires an analysis of the "*range* of oppositional behaviors" and an examination of "how subordinate groups embody and express a combination of reactionary and progressive ideologies, ideologies that both underlie the structure of social domination and contain the logic necessary to overcome it" (Giroux, 2001, p. 103). This reexamination moves beyond a narrow analysis of resistance as merely self-defeating to a more nuanced understanding of the multiple and contradictory ways that young people resist, the motivations and social critiques that guide their actions, and the possibilities for breaking the cycle of social reproduction in schools and the larger society (Akom, 2003).

Critical theories such as women of color feminism (Hill Collins, 1989; hooks, 1989; Hurtado, 1989; Zavella, 1991), critical race theory (Crenshaw, Gotanda, Peller, & Thomas, 1995; Delgado & Stefancic, 2001), and Latin@ critical race theory (LatCrit; Hernandez-Truyol, 1997; Johnson, 2002; Valdes, 1996) also extend the analysis of resistance beyond oppositional behaviors that maintain current relations of power.[2] By situating people of color's experiential knowledge and historical struggles against social injustices, these theories reveal the abundance of "accumulated assets and resources" that low-income youth of color draw from their families and communities (Yosso, 2005, p. 77). These frameworks are mindful of the structural constraints under which poor people of color in the United States often live, and also highlight their strengths and daily acts of resistance against these oppressive conditions. They recognize structural commonalities, but emphasize the "intersectionality" or "simultaneity" (Hurtado, 1989) of multiple forms of oppression (e.g., race, class, gender, language, citizenship status, sexual orientation), which contribute to a *range* of social critiques, motivations, and resistant behaviors within cultural groups. In contrast to traditional conceptions of youth resistance, these theories contend that oppositional behaviors and worldviews can support rather than hinder social transformation.

The concept of transformational resistance was initially developed to describe Chicana students' participation in the 1968 East Los Angeles student walkouts and the 1993 UCLA Chicana and Chicano Studies protests (Delgado Bernal, 1997), which are historical moments that cannot be accounted for within traditional notions of youth resistance. The students who participated in these acts of transformational resistance against educational inequalities reported having access to *transformational role models*, or "visible members of one's own racial/ethnic and/or gender group who actively demonstrate a commitment to social justice" (Solórzano & Delgado Bernal, 2001, p. 322). They also attributed their critiques, motivations, and resistant behaviors to having relationships with *transformational mentors*, or those who "use…their own experiences and expertise to help guide the development of others" (p. 322). Educational research sometimes portrays family, peer, and community forces as hindering the academic success of low-income students of color (Phelan, Davidson, & Yu, 1998; see also Valencia & Solórzano, 1997). Yet, examining the influences of transformational mentors and role models reveals that family, peer, and community forces also serve as sources of strength and support for poor and working-class students of color, and nurture their critical sensibilities to fight for social justice.

Youth transformational resistance takes shape in both subtle and explicit ways. *External transformational resistance* is conspicuous, overt behavior that "does not conform to institutional or cultural norms and expectations" (Solórzano & Delgado Bernal, 2001, p. 325), such as participation in boycotts or protest marches. In contrast, *internal transformational resistance* refers to subtle or silent resistance in which students appear to conform, for instance, doing well in school in order to come back to their community (or a community like theirs) and use their knowledge of dominant institutions to implement social change. Solórzano and Delgado Bernal assert that educational researchers most often overlook forms of internal transformational resistance. They explain, "too often, external resistance is romanticized by liberal and progressive scholars while internal resistance is not identified, misidentified, or even ignored" (p. 326). To identify these internal forms and to avoid romantic notions of transformational resistance, we argue that it is necessary to understand not only the motivations behind youth resistance, but also the day-to-day, on the ground processes that lead up to more overt or public moments of resistance.

Transformational resistance is a mode of behavior that strives for social justice outcomes, but should be understood as a complex process rather than a final or unchanging product. One's consciousness of structural inequities and motivation toward social emancipation is not static and is often "uneven" (Solórzano & Yosso, 2005). For instance, one might resist in transformative ways against discrimination based on socioeconomic class or race, but not against inequities based on gender or sexual orientation. Moreover, people may engage in transformational resistance some of the time, and at other times behave in self-defeating, reactionary, or conformist ways. The goal, however, is a lifetime commitment to resisting all forms of social oppression; a journey none of us may ever complete, but one that we can all be committed to developing in ourselves and our young people.

The problem is that there is a dearth of educational research on how teachers actually go about cultivating transformational resistance within a K-12 classroom setting, or what types of support are required to develop and sustain this type of resistance within structural and political constraints (Solórzano & Yosso, 2005). Further research is needed to better understand the ways in which transformational resistance can be fostered through teaching and learning among adults and youth in a classroom community. In an effort to fill this gap in the literature, we have been investing our own practice as educators by asking: (a) What does transformational resistance look like when it is implemented in classroom practice, and (b) What outcomes emerge for teachers and students engaged in such a process?

Cultivating transformational resistance in the classroom involves a critical pedagogy, which does not seek "*to transfer knowledge* but to create the possibilities for the production or construction of knowledge" (Freire, 1998, p. 30; emphasis original). For critical pedagogues, knowledge is created in a process of co-participation, with the explicit aim of critiquing and responding to material and social conditions that are oppressive. Critical pedagogues act to create tangible change *with* rather than *for* students, and understand themselves to be servants of the people as opposed to leaders or missionaries whose goal is to "save" disenfranchised youth.

Critical pedagogy brings oppressed students' histories, biographies, and systems of meaning into the classroom so they can "name and authenticate their own experiences," which are often blatantly ignored by traditional curriculum and pedagogy (Darder, 1991, p. 80). This approach can help students to identify and analyze how oppression impacts their lives, and to understand themselves as agents with the ability to create positive social change. Thus, critical pedagogy is a *pedagogy of resistance* that aims to "construct different sets of lived experiences—experiences in which students can find a voice and maintain and extend the positive aspects of their own social and historical realities" (Darder, 1991, p. 90). This type of pedagogy helps to cultivate a "community of practice" (Wenger, 1998) in the classroom that engages in transformational resistance. Thus, the combination of the principles of transformative resistance and critical pedagogy aim to produce a critical transformative pedagogy. This pedagogy works to build a sense of community in the classroom and creates "a shared commitment and a common good," as well as "a climate of openness and intellectual rigor" (hooks, 1994, p. 40). The classroom community is joined in solidarity (Freire, 1970/2002), and relationships are grounded in *cariño* and love (Valenzuela, 1999). Ultimately, this pedagogical approach emphasizes a critique and resistance of social inequalities to foster student actions that fight for individual and collective empowerment.

Urban Sociology at an East Oakland High School

The remainder of this chapter will examine this critical and transformative pedagogical approach. We will present the "Doc Ur Block" project, the major class undertaking for the spring semester in the Step to College students' 10th-grade year. The project developed students as sociological researchers of their own communities taking them through the five stages of critical praxis: (a) identify a problem, (b) analyze the problem, (c) develop a plan to address the problem, (d) implement the plan, and (e) evaluate the impact of the plan (Duncan-Andrade & Morrell, 2008). The curriculum that was used to move through these stages with students will be discussed in three segments.

Segment 1: Identifying and Analyzing a Problem   The first two stages (identify and analyze a problem) took about eight weeks. The class was introduced to three key sociological terms using readings, lectures, films, and discussion. These terms were hegemony, introduced through excerpts from Gramsci (1971) and films such as *Bus 174* (Padilha & Lacerda, 2002) and *The Matrix* (Wachowski & Wachowski, 1999); counter-hegemony, through Freire (1970/2002), Solórzano and Delgado Bernal (2001), Malcolm X's speeches, Lolita Lebrón's life, and hip-hop artists such as Immortal Technique, GOODIE MOB, and Tupac; and habitus, through Bourdieu (1999) and *The Matrix* (Wachowski & Wachowski, 1999).

Next, the class developed a list of influential elements of youth popular culture that they believed promoted these three sociological concepts in their communities. Their list included television shows, movies, music, fast food, snack food, advertisements, videogames, fashion, and professional sports. Students were then placed in groups of five according to the neighborhoods where they lived. Each group chose a guiding sociological term to add to the above listed three core terms. These were sociological terms that we had discussed in class or that students had investigated on their own, such as "social degradation" or "social reproduction." In their groups, students used their selected term and the three core terms to conduct a sociological analysis of the various forms of popular culture that young people interact with on a regular basis. We did some initial modeling of this process with the class, after which the students spent a week doing their own research and analysis.

After their study, students used PowerPoint to develop 25-minute research presentations to explain the presence or absence of the four sociological terms in the popular culture they studied. Presentations were attended by members of the school community, including teachers, administrators, other students, community members, and parents. The presentations consisted of a literature review, in which they explained the terms they had learned to the audience. This forced them to rephrase much of the academic language traditionally used to explain sociological phenomena so that people without their level of training could understand their work. For instance, to describe the difference between "materialism" and "popular materiality" to the audience, Yamina explains, "Materialism is when you're greedy about your stuff. You want all the materials for you. But then *materiality* is when you want to get material things, but to bring them to your community. That's the difference."

Following the literature review, students presented examples from their research to reveal the existence of these sociological phenomena in popular culture and to explain their analysis of its impact on the community. Amadi exemplifies this in her analysis of popular songs:

> Examples of counter hegemony in popular culture include TLC's song "Unpretty," Tupac's song, "Keep Your Head Up," and India Arie's song, "Video." The song, "Video," by India Arie is important because she encourages young women to be themselves because that's where true beauty comes from, being yourself. As a young woman growing up in East Oakland there are not a lot of positive things I'm used to listening to, so that's why these songs are so important.

Amadi notes that although much of the popular music she listens to contains lyrics that promote the dominant hegemony, she also finds examples that counter negative stereotypes and provide positive inspiration. These types of investigations helped students become more critically aware of socially oppressive and socially transformative messages they encounter through popular culture on a daily basis.

Segment 2: Planning and Implementing through Street Sociology   In this segment we prepared students to move their research to the community. We spent a week-and-a-half giving students basic training in qualitative research methods. We began by introducing them to an adapted version of Burawoy's (1998) "extended case method." Burawoy's approach has the ethnographic researcher conduct the following four steps: examine existing theory, enter the field as a participant-observer, document counter-instances of the theory, and reconstruct theory on the basis of those observations. We adapted Burawoy's approach by putting the tools of study, research, and theory construction into the hands of the students themselves (Burawoy's "natives"), rather than keeping them in the hands of the university researcher.

Each research group used their lived experience and the aforementioned studies of social theory and popular culture to develop a hypothesis about what they would see when they researched their community. The idea here was that they would take the prevailing logic about their community (dysfunctional, pathological, resource poor, disenfranchised, hopeless, hostile), including their own notions, and investigate whether these assumptions were borne out in fact or whether there was significant evidence to counter these opinions.

To prepare the class to carry out the extended case method in the community, students received a week of training on basic ethnographic research tools: digital video and still photography, observational field notes, formal and informal interviews, basic surveys, and artifact collection. Students practiced these techniques with each other and around the school and then hit the streets of their community over the next three weeks to collect information. We took out two groups each day, one group during lunch and another group after school. Each group had at least one video camera and one still camera to gather visual evidence and to conduct interviews. Groups were largely self-directed during their field research. They told us where they wanted to go, and they decided how to split themselves up.

Segment 3: Evaluating—Data Analysis and Research Conference   After the field research, the next four weeks were spent analyzing the data and preparing for a research conference that would once again be attended by key stakeholders in the school community. The groups had to prepare three main products for the conference: a 20-minute PowerPoint presentation, an 8- to 10-minute "Blocumentary" (documentary) film, and a 12- to 15-page research report. The division of labor for these products was the decision of the research group. The minimum requirements for each of the assignments were as follows: (a) the PowerPoint presentation needed to have slides covering their literature review of social theoretical terms, research methods, hypothesis, findings, and reconstructed theory; (b) the research report needed to have sections covering the same topics as the PowerPoint; and (c) the "Blocumentary" film needed to have visual examples of the social theoretical terms, counter-instances, and reconstructed theory.

Implications of a Critical Transformative Pedagogy

Gramsci (1971) wrote that "all [people] are intellectuals, one could therefore say; but not all [people] have in the society the function of intellectuals" (p. 9). He went on to argue that schools are often the social institution used to validate this unnatural division in a society, one where an individual is cast as either homo sapien (one who thinks/works with his or her mind) or homo faber (one who labors/works with his or her hands). Education should deconstruct the division between thinker and worker and replace it with a paradigm that values the intellectual potential in all people.

The Doc Ur Block project was a commitment to those principles by providing young people an education that prepared them to critically analyze their world. It put tools of critical thinking, research, and intellectual production in their hands so that they could counter-narrate pathological stories of their families and communities. Along the way, many students discovered that they also had come to believe the dominant discourse about their community and had lost sight of the countless indicators of hope and strength that are present on their blocks everyday. Shakari notes,

> What we thought we would see was showoffs (people who are flashy and flaunt what they have) and wannabes (people who try to imitate the people who are flashy)…But what we saw on the block was counter hegemony, people wanting to help others instead of themselves. Most people in our community cared deeply about the neighborhood, wanted to contribute to the community, and were not overly concerned about material things.

This project did not attempt to shelter students from the harsh reality of urban life. In fact, while one group was conducting an interview on the block, they witnessed the shooting of a high school-aged student and chose to include the footage of the incident in their film. When they returned to the classroom to reconstruct their theory, they developed the term "habitus of hopelessness" to describe these types of self-defeating actions by community members. However, the project also allowed them to find counter-instances to negative responses to the conditions of oppression in the community. That same group called this the "agency of hope." Every group reconstructed social theory to capture the strength and self-determination that they witnessed. As one example, Alejandro and Isabel made the following comments while presenting their group's research at the American Educational Research Association's (AERA) national conference. After introducing the research methods his group used, Alejandro stated:

> Our findings were very polarized. Some people had hope that Oakland would change, some didn't have hope, and these were people living in the same community. Based on this, my research group decided to come up with some terms, which were "habitus of hopelessness," which is basically a pattern of behavior from lack of hope, and "agency of hope," which is when people decide to make a change in the community.
>
> To demonstrate the habitus of hopelessness, Alejandro played a clip from his group's video documentary where students interviewed community members on their block:

> [Alejandro]: Do you think Oakland will ever change/get better?
> [Community member 1]: I strongly disagree.
> [Community member 2]: Oh no, hell no, not in the Town.
> [Community member 3]: There are a lot of things going on out here like the Hyphy movement, everybody wants to have drugs, everybody wants to have this whole persona about themselves that they want to be thugs. That's what it is.

After this film clip, Isabel walked to the podium to continue discussing the group's research findings, and to explain their reconstructed theory and its implications for Oakland. In front of a standing-room-only audience of more than 150 graduate students and professors, Isabel said:

> This interview data reveals what we term the "habitus of hopelessness," which is a pattern of thinking, speaking, and behaving as if there is no hope. It gets reproduced within a social group, in this case, among our urban poor and working class communities…The implications of what you just saw in the video are incidences of violence, degradation of women, and a higher value placed on material things. This can help people feel hopeless, which

allows the problem to reproduce itself. But we also saw evidence of "agency of hope," such as we see in this video clip.

To demonstrate this agency of hope, Isabel played a brief video clip of a community member telling the youth researchers, "And I love you little ones trying so hard. Nobody else is trying." Then, Isabel turned back to the microphone and said:

> What this shows is that there is hope in our community, and we are the hope. Every member of our class of 2008 tutors at Howard Elementary. Several times a week we go to the mayor's office and to the Black Panther's *Commemorator* and work with our community members. But most important, to quote Huey P. Newton, "We view each other with a great love and understanding, and that's what sets us apart from other oppressed groups." Quoting Gandhi, "We have to be the change we wish to see in the world." And we saw multiple examples of people in our community doing similar things. What our research suggests is that as an individual in our community we have the choice to be hopeless, which will lead to social reproduction, or to be hopeful, which will make change. By our being here and continuing our work we choose the latter. We choose to take responsibility for ourselves and for the future of our community.

The students' analyses and constructions of social theories as they applied to their communities are indicators of the power of the critical transformative pedagogical approach discussed in this chapter. However, the real value of this project rests in the way it helped students re-envision themselves, their communities, and their roles in creating and contributing to counter-narratives that promote hope and self-determination. Since they presented their findings to their community, students have presented their work on this project more than a dozen times to youth, educators, and educational researchers from across the nation. Additionally, they have distributed more than 50 copies of their documentary films, many of which are being used by teachers and teacher educators to develop curriculum projects for other urban students.

Looking Forward

The Doc Ur Block project allowed this group of urban Latin@ and African American youth to critically examine the impact of media and popular culture on their community. It also positioned them to take media production into their own hands in order to "document and publicly voice their ideas and concerns regarding the most important issues in their lives" (Goodman, 2003, p. 3; see also Duncan-Andrade, 2006b; Morrell, 2004a, 2004b). This critical transformative pedagogy creates the opportunities for youth to use the tools of literacy, research, and media to gain deeper and more critical understandings of the forms of oppression and resiliency within their neighborhoods. These tools positioned them as public intellectuals during their research and when they disseminated their findings to the community and national audiences of educators and educational researchers.

Yet, Doc Ur Block was part of a process that goes beyond apprenticing youth in critical research methods. The broader vision of the pedagogy used in this project, and the STC program, is to foster youth transformational resistance through academic resilience and achievement. This includes an explicit commitment to cultivating Latin@ and African American youth who resist social and educational inequities. Nationwide, Latin@ and African American students graduate from high school prepared for college in disproportionately lower numbers when compared to their White and Asian[3] peers (Alliance for Excellent Education, 2006, 2007a, 2007b). East Oakland youth (predominantly low-income Latin@ and African American youth) are no exception. They graduate from high school and go to college in numbers disproportionately lower than their peers in the district, the county, and the state. Of all 9th graders entering East Oakland high schools in 2002, only 32% graduated four years later, and only 10% were eligible to apply to the California public university system (UC/CSU).[4] In contrast, all 26 students in this year's STC senior class have applied to one or more four-year universities.

STC is not perfect by any means, and has faced some notable barriers. There has been some ebb and flow in the student enrollment in the program, but patterns of school persistence in STC continue to surpass those of the Oakland Unified School District. In the second year of the program (2006–2007), 27 of the original 30 students re-enrolled in STC for their 11th grade year. This 90% persistence rate for STC compares favorably to the district's 75% persistence rate for Latin@ and African American 11th graders that year.[5]

We are not arguing that the Doc Ur Block project alone will result in youth transformational resistance, but that it is a piece of the larger curriculum, pedagogy, mentorship, and advocacy that works to cultivate public intellectuals and "insurgent scholars" (Ladson-Billings, 2007). Doc Ur Block is one of several projects that have apprenticed the STC youth in research methods, media production, academic writing, and public speaking to help them "step to college," as well as to "step to [a] consciousness"[6] that encourages them to take action against the inequities they witness and experience daily.[7] We describe their academic achievement and public intellectualism as transformational resistance because the STC youth are learning to use their academic skills and resources not to escape their community, but to foment social transformation and renewal in their community. Whether they plan to become doctors, lawyers, teachers, architects, interior decorators, or fashion designers, their aspirations for the future are linked to the well being of their community as a whole. This is captured in aspiring clothing designer Ismael's comments:

> I feel like I will contribute with my t-shirt design idea because I'm teaching somebody else and I'm not taking for granted everything I've learned in the STC program…For them to see a story in the t-shirt, that's my vision, so for a person to look at my design and see the struggle and see the suffering and be like, there's something we can do. They'll just glance at the image that's on my shirt, and I'll teach them a little bit of knowledge by them just glancing at me. I'm still trying to claim better schools, and better stuff for our community, but with a career that I would like to do. And I think that everybody in this program should find that connection, whatever they're going to major in.

In addition to nurturing a community-oriented sense of purpose for their lives, the STC community is also committed to building tight-knit family-like relationships, and providing the day-to-day support needed to attain college aspirations. In another interview, Marisol discussed the differences in the types of relationships, levels of support, and academic rigor she encounters in her STC class and her other classes:

> You hear teachers be like, "Yeah you need to go to college. Oh, college this, college that," but that's nothing. Stop saying, "You guys need to go to college," and *help* them go to college. We're getting the support because of the STC teachers but other teachers just be like, "You guys have to go to college." Okay. How?…You go to STC and you have this *family* thing right here, and we're thinking way beyond the lines we usually think of. And then we go to our other classes and it's like the level we have at STC just goes down…They make me feel like I'm *grown* [in STC]. They are talking to me like I'm not even a little kid no more. And then I go to my other classes and I'm over here like, okay I already know this…STC teachers make us *want* to come to the class…how you guys talk to us, what you guys make us do…And then just the fact that we have everybody and all the support there at STC…So you're like, "fuck that," you're not going to just let that go. You have to take advantage of all that support

and go there. And then you go to [the other classes] and you're like, "Whatever, I can't wait for lunch, or I can't wait to go home."...To me it's just about getting my credits. I just want to get it done...And at STC it's like I'm getting ready for other stuff, not just getting my credits. They're preparing us for *life*.

Marisol identifies several key aspects of the STC program that help prepare her for college and life in general: (a) rhetoric is accompanied by actual support, (b) it's a family-like community, (c) teachers have high expectations of students' intellectual capabilities, and (d) course work makes students feel more mature by engaging with issues that are relevant and meaningful to their lives.

A more comprehensive analysis of the extent to which the STC program is enhancing youth transformational resistance would require attention to the daily practices and struggles within the STC classroom and the students' social and personal lives within and beyond the school-house doors. It would also entail an examination of the range of "oppositional behaviors" these youth engage in (e.g., reactionary, self-defeating, conformist, transformational), and the various forces that influence those actions. We need to look beyond observable behaviors to gain a deeper understanding of the factors that lead to transformative resistance. That is, an in-depth comprehension of the critiques and motivations that inform their behaviors is also necessary (Giroux, 1983, 2001; Solórzano & Delgado Bernal, 2001). We contend that the ability to cultivate and understand resistance at this level is enhanced when relationships among participants, teachers, and researchers are based on *cariño* (Duncan-Andrade, 2006a). Such family-like relationships within a classroom community cannot be created through intent or rhetoric, but only through sustained actions over time.

As we pursue these deeper understandings about cultivating transformative resistance in our community, we can say with certainty that Latin@ and African American students participating in STC are achieving levels of social and academic success that are rarely found in Oakland public high schools. Their skills as critical thinkers, writers, researchers, and public speakers continue to show measurable improvement. They have found the motivation to persist and pursue college in a school district where less than 10% of their peers find similar results. As educators and educational researchers, we attribute the successes of STC to a number of factors that have been discussed in this chapter. However, perhaps the most significant of these factors is STC's commitment to using critical pedagogy to develop a classroom community focused on transforming the habitus of hopelessness.

We cannot argue that this program has fully met the challenge of cultivating classroom success for all of our students. But, we do believe that our work adds to the growing body of evidence that suggests there is a profound impact on the achievement of Latin@ and African American urban youth when classrooms are comprised of academically rigorous material, critical pedagogy, and committed and caring teachers. When these conditions are put into place in schools, they serve as key institutions for building transformative communities both in and out of the classroom. Such a pedagogical approach not only produces college bound students, but also prepares those college students to come back to serve the community. To truly build a transformative community with youth we must provide critical spaces that prepare young people to serve. These are the preconditions for transforming our communities.

Notes

1. An "intensely segregated minority school" is a school that enrolls more than 90% students of color (Orfield, 1996; Rogers, Terriquez, Valladares, & Oakes, 2006).
2. There are discontinuities and critiques between women of color feminism and critical race theories, but they share in common a complex analysis of the intersectionality of oppression, a focus on the

experiences and histories of communities of color, and an understanding of resistance that moves beyond self-defeating oppositional behaviors.

3. Data for Asian American students are not disaggregated. Current statistics "primarily reflect East Asians' overall academic successes and obscure the scholastic struggles of groups such as Southeast Asians and Pacific Islanders" (Alliance for Excellent Education, 2007).

4. District-wide, 46% of the original number of entering ninth graders in 2002 graduated from high school four years later, and 17% were UC/CSU eligible. Countywide, the rates increased even further to 70% high school graduation and 33% UC/CSU eligible, which surpassed the California's state-wide rates of 67% high school graduation and 24% UC/CSU eligible.

5. Data from http://dq.cde.ca.gov/dataquest/DstEnrAll.asp?cYear=2005-06&cChoice=DstEnrAll Select=0161259--OAKLANDUNIFIED&Level=District&myTimeFrame=S&cTopic=Enrollment&c Level=District&TheName=Oakland

6. This phrase came from an audience member's response to Hidalgo's presentation on Step to College at the 2007 American Anthropological Association conference.

7. In their 11th-grade year, STC students completed research on the quality of their school and created a viable plan for school improvement. During their 12th-grade year, they are researching the presence and/or absence of human rights in classic literature and popular films, as well as within their schools and the Oakland community. The youth analyze why these human rights are essential to a person's quality of life and how to fight to gain access for those who are denied their basic rights.

References

Akom, A. (2003, October). Reexamining resistance as oppositional behavior: The nation of Islam and the creation of a Black achievement ideology. *Sociology of Education, 76*, 305–325.

Alliance for Excellent Education. (2006). *Understanding high school graduation rates.* Retrieved September 14, 2007, from http://www.all4ed.org/files/National_wc.pdf

Alliance for Excellent Education. (2007a). *Fact sheet. Latino students and U.S. high schools.* Retrieved September 27, 2007, from http://www.all4ed.org/publications/FactSheets.html#HSDrop

Alliance for Excellent Education. (2007b). *Fact sheet. African-American students and U.S. high schools.* Retrieved September 27, 2007, from http://www.all4ed.org/publications/FactSheets.html#HSDrop

Althusser, L. (1994). Ideology and ideological state apparatuses (notes towards an investigation). In S. Zizek (Ed.), *Mapping ideology* (pp. 99–138). New York: Verson. (Original work published in 1971)

Bourdieu, P. (1999). Structures, *habitus*, practices. In C. Lemert (Ed.), *Social theory: The multicultural and classic readings* (pp. 441–446). Boulder, CO: Westview. (Reprinted from *The logic of practice*, pp. 52–58, by R. Nice (Trans.), 1990, Stanford: Stanford University Press)

Bourdieu, P., & Passeron, J.-C. (1977). *Reproduction in education, society and culture* (R. Nice, Trans., Vol. 5). Beverly Hills, CA: Sage.

Bowles, S., & Gintis, H. (1976). *Schooling in capitalist America: Educational reform and the contradictions of economic life.* New York: Basic Books.

Burawoy, M. (1998). The extended case method. *Sociological Theory, 16*(1), 4–33.

Carnoy, M. (1974). *Education as cultural imperialism.* New York: David McKay.

Carspecken, P. F. (1996). *Critical ethnography in educational research: A theoretical and practical guide.* New York: Routledge.

Collatos, A. (2005). *Critical college access: Reframing how we empower urban youth toward higher education and social change.* Unpublished doctoral dissertation, University of California, Los Angeles.

Crenshaw, K., Gotanda, N., Peller, G., & Thomas, K. (1995). *Critical race theory: The key writings that formed the movement.* New York: The New Press.

Darder, A. (1991). *Culture and power in the classroom: A critical foundation for bicultural education.* Westport, CT: Bergin & Garvey.

Delgado Bernal, D. (1997). *Chicana school resistance and grassroots leadership: Providing an alternative history of the 1968 East Los Angeles blowouts.* Unpublished doctoral dissertation, University of California, Los Angeles.

Delgado-Gaitan, C. (2001). *The power of community: Mobilizing for family and schooling.* Lanham, MD: Rowman & Littlefield.

Delgado, R., & Stefancic, J. (2001). *Critical race theory: An introduction.* New York: New York University Press.

Denzin, N. K., & Lincoln, Y. S. (2005). *The Sage handbook of qualitative research.* Thousand Oak, CA: Sage.

Duncan-Andrade, J. M. R. (2006a). Utilizing cariño in the development of research methodologies. In J. Kincheloe, P. Anderson, K. Rose, D. Griffith, & K. Hayes (Eds.), *Urban education: An encyclopedia* (pp. 451–486). Westport, CT: Greenwood.

Duncan-Andrade, J. M. R. (2006b). Urban youth, media literacy, and increased critical civic participation. In S. Ginwright, P. Noguera, & J. Cammarota (Eds.), *Beyond resistance! Youth activism and community change: New democratic possibilities for practice and policy for America's youth* (pp. 149–169). New York: Routledge.

Duncan-Andrade, J. M. R., & Morrell, E. (2008). *The art of critical pedagogy: Possibilities for moving from theory to practice in urban schools.* New York: Peter Lang.

Fine, M. (1991). *Framing dropouts: Notes on the politics of an urban public high school.* Albany: State University of New York Press.

Freire, P. (1998). *Pedagogy of freedom: Ethics, democracy, and civic courage* (P. Clarke, Trans.). Lanham, MD: Rowman & Littlefield.

Freire, P. (2002). *Pedagogy of the oppressed* (30th anniversary ed.). New York: Continuum. (Original work published 1970)

Ginwright, S., Noguera, P., & Cammarota, J. (2006). *Beyond resistance! Youth activism and community change: New democratic possibilities for practice and policy for America's youth.* New York: Routledge.

Giroux, H. A. (1983). Theories of reproduction and resistance in the new sociology of education: A critical analysis. *Harvard Educational Review, 53*(3), 257–293.

Giroux, H. A. (2001). *Theory and resistance in education: Towards a pedagogy for the opposition.* Westport, CT: Bergin & Garvey.

Goodman, S. (2003). *Teaching youth media: A critical guide to literacy, video production and social change.* New York: Teachers College Press.

Gramsci, A. (1971). *Prison notebooks.* New York: International Publishers.

Hernandez-Truyol, B. (1997). Borders (en)gendered: Normativities, Latinas and a LatCrit paradigm. *New York University Law Review, 72*, 882–927.

Hidalgo, N. (2007, December). *Stepping to college: Cultivating transformational resistance and critical college access in an urban high school classroom.* Paper presented at the meeting of the American Anthropological Association, Washington, DC.

Hill Collins, P. (1989). The social construction of Black feminist thought. *Signs: Journal of Women in Culture and Society, 14*(4), 745–773.

hooks, b. (1989). *Talking back.* Boston: South End Press.

hooks, b. (1994). *Teaching to transgress: Education as the practice of freedom.* New York: Routledge.

Huberman, M. (1996). Moving mainstream: Taking a closer look at teacher research. *Language Arts, 73*, 124–140.

Hurtado, A. (1989). Relating to privilege: Seduction and rejection in the subordination of white women and women of color. *Signs, 14*(4), 833–855.

Johnson, K. R. (2002). Race and the immigration laws: The need for critical inquiry. In F. Valdes, J. M. Culp, & A. P. Harris (Eds.), *Crossroads, directions, and a new critical race theory* (pp. 187–198). Philadelphia: Temple University Press.

Ladson-Billings, G. (2007, November). *Diaries of insurgent intellectuals: Research on race, merit, and the paradox of colorblindness in the post civil rights era.* Paper presented at the meeting of the American Anthropological Association, Washington, DC.

LeCompte, M. D., & Schensul, J. J. (1999). *Designing & conducting ethnographic research.* Walnut Creek, CA: AltaMira Press.

MacLeod, J. (1987). *Ain't no makin' it: Aspirations and attainment in a low-income neighborhood.* San Francisco: Westview Press.

McNiff, J., Lomax, P., & Whitehead, J. (1996). *You and your action research project.* New York: Routledge.

Morrell, E. (2004a). *Becoming critical researchers: Literacy and empowerment for urban youth.* New York: Peter Lang.

Morrell, E. (2004b). *Linking literacy and popular culture*. Norwood, MA: Christopher Gordon.

Oakes, J. (1985). *Keeping track: How schools structure inequality*. New Haven, CT: Yale University Press.

Ogbu, J. (1978). *Minority education and caste: The American system in cross-cultural perspective*. New York: Academic Press.

Ogbu, J. (1995). Cultural problems in minority education: Their interpretations and consequences—Part one: Theoretical background. *The Urban Review, 27*(3), 189–205.

Orfield, G. (1996). The growth of segregation: African Americans, Latinos, and unequal education. In G. Orfield & S. Eaton (Eds.), *Dismantling desegregation: The quiet reversal of Brown v. Board of Education* (pp. 53–72). New York: The New Press.

Padilha, J., & Lacerda, F. (Directors). (2002). *Bus 174* [Motion picture]. New York: ThinkFilm.

Phelan, P., Davidson, A. L., & Yu, H. C. (1998). *Adolescents' worlds: Negotiating family, peers, and school*. New York: Teachers College Press.

Robinson, T., & Ward, J. V. (1991). "A belief in self far greater than anyone's disbelief": Cultivating resistance among African American female adolescents. In C. Gilligan, A. G. Rogers, & D. L. Tolman (Eds.), *Women, girls & psychotherapy: Reframing resistance* (pp. 87–103). New York: Harrington Park Press.

Rogers, J., Terriquez, V., Valladares, S., & Oakes, J. (2006). California educational opportunity report 2006: Roadblocks to college. *UCLA Institute for Democracy, Education, and Access. UC All Campus Consortium on Research for Diversity*. Retrieved September 14, 2007, from http://www.edopp.org

Solórzano, D. G., & Delgado Bernal, D. (2001). Examining transformational resistance through a Critical Race and LatCrit theory framework: Chicana and Chicano students in an urban context. *Urban Education, 36*(3), 308–342.

Solórzano, D. G., & Yosso, T. J. (2005). Maintaining social justice hopes within academic realities: A Freirean approach to critical race/LatCrit pedagogy. In Z. Leonardo (Ed.), *Critical pedagogy and race* (pp. 69–91). Malden, MA: Blackwell.

Somekh, B. (2006). *Action research: A methodology for change and development*. New York: Open University Press.

Valdes, F. (1996). Forward: Latina/o ethnicities, critical race theory and post-identity politics in postmodern legal culture: From practices to possibilities. *La Raza Law Journal, 9*, 1–31.

Valencia, R., & Solórzano, D. (1997). Contemporary deficit thinking. In R. Valencia (Ed.), *The evolution of deficit thinking: Educational thought and practice* (pp. 160–210). London: The Falmer Press.

Valenzuela, A. (1999). *Subtractive schooling: U.S.-Mexican youth and the politics of caring*. Albany: State University of New York Press.

Wachowski, A., & Wachowski, L. (Writers/Directors). (1999). *The Matrix* [Motion picture]. Hollywood, CA: Warner Brothers.

Wenger, E. (1998). *Communities of practice: Learning, meaning and identity*. Cambridge, UK: Cambridge University Press.

Willis, P. (1977). *Learning to labor: How working class kids get working class jobs*. New York: Columbia University Press.

Yosso, T. (2005). Whose culture has capital? A critical race theory discussion of community cultural wealth. *Race, Ethnicity, and Education, 8*(1), 69–91.

Zavella, P. (1991). Reflections on diversity among Chicanas. *Frontiers: A Journal of Women Studies, 12*(2), 73–85.

Zeichner, K. M., & Noffke, S. E. (2001). Practitioner research. In V. Richardson (Ed.), *Handbook of research on education* (pp. 298–330). Washington, DC: American Educational Research Association.

Part III
Language and Culture

Part Editors: Juan Sánchez Muñoz and Eugene García

18 Language and Culture
An Introduction

Juan Sánchez Muñoz
Texas Tech University, Lubbock

Eugene García
Arizona State University at Tempe

The summons to change educational practices in the face of continued Latino student under achievement is not to be ignored. Collectively, this volume of leading edge research, that seeks to build upon decades of scholarship and practice, affirms a clarion call for a continuation of nuanced understandings which capture the unique personal sensibilities and academic approaches required to dislodge seemingly intractable obstacles to full Latino educational realization. In this section we have been called upon to translate such calls in ways that might be helpful in understanding the "education" issues regarding the language and culture of our Latino students, families and communities and the broader social context in which that language and culture reside. Indeed, as the following chapters will evidence, the imposition of social context presents an inescapable dynamic that frequently informs the educational circumstances in which Latinos learn...In so doing, we have provided in this section extensive educational overviews of these issues by a well regarded set of colleagues working in this area. In this introduction, we have called upon a summary of the following chapter contributions that use a particular mnemonic, "remember the five R's." For this section, we as editors, suggest that the scholarly contributions contained within this section conclude that educational programs, initiatives, strategies, and policies that assist Latino students and attend to their language and culture are: *Respectful, Responsive, Responsible, Resourceful*, and *Reasonable*.

Respectful

Everyone wants Respect. Throughout the corpus of qualitative and quantitative studies that have sought to authentically examine the circumstance of Latinos in the preceding 25 years, the notion of Respect, has been and remains a hallmark of Latino culture and value systems. Not surprisingly, Latino parents want to be respected and want their children respected as well. Both empirically and anecdotally, it is common to hear the refrain from Latino parents and their children that in schools they do not receive that respect. Scholars have posited, including some in this volume, that the curricular paradigms, organizational structures, and prevailing ideologies of schooling dramatically influence the circumstances in which students can be academically success. This assertion is particularly evident for students whose social, cultural, economic, and immigration backgrounds are constructed as inherently *deficient*. Specifically, Latino students across the country are too often seen as the foreigner, the immigrant, the non-English speaker, the disadvantaged, someone who does not belong, who is "less than," and the school's mission is to change them so that they can belong. This essentially assimilation is optic immediately positions students at a disadvantage to learn, insofar as curriculum, content, and academic skills become secondary to transforming the student into something other than who and what they already are. The most detrimental lack of respect for Latino language minorities might be identified as *el pobrecito* or *el benditio* syndrome—"Oh, you poor thing—unwashed, of and in poverty, immigrant, non-English speaking; we sympathize with your circumstances and lower our expectations for what you might be able to learn." A steady stream of educational researchers have debunked this *deficit learning model*, which has plagued the educational experience of Latino, and other minorities, in American schools. The expression of the deficit model appears when an educator or an educational system actually begins down the slippery slope of lowering expectations and academic standards, begins to devise selection devices that separate the deserving from the non-deserving, the smart from the dumb, those with and those without a future. Latino students find themselves at the bottom end of this continuum through no fault of their own. Moreover, individual efforts by Latino students and their families are often ineffective at destabilizing or disrupting the persistence and prevalence of this deficit outlook.

In the proceeding chapters, educational programs, classroom teachers, and school administrators are highlighted that serve these students well and that respect them for what they bring to the learning enterprise—their language, culture, world view—and do not see disadvantages that place students only "at risk" but see in these students resources that can be marshaled to meet learning goals, particularly high learning goals. This final point should not be understated, that is the notion of minority students as being *at-potential* rather than *at-risk*. Within this new paradigm of educational excellence and equity, educational programs, classroom teachers, and school administrators are required to extract from and cultivate the already existing intellectual attributes that Latino and other minority students introduce to the schooling context. Latino students, their families, culture, and language—indeed, those of other minorities as well— become additive and essential, rather than *deficit*. For schools that foster a culture of *potential*, there is an acceptance and a respect that is to be honored and displayed for all students and for the families and the communities from which they come. Within antiquated school context where the *"Pobrecitos"* syndrome pervades, Latino students and their families are not.

Angela Arzubiaga and Jennifer Adair as well as Aída Hurtado, Karen Cervantez, and Michael Eccelston address these issues in their contributions to this section. Latinos are continuously negotiating several conflicting and parallel social worlds as they navigate complex and interrelated structures endemic to educational institutions. They are often perceived as marginalized for suspected cultural attributes that are too often considered to be of limited educational value. At the same time, they are seeking to define themselves and others as their own self-definitions shift with new experiences, many in educational venues. As a whole, Latinos are highly resourceful and resilient in dealing with these challenges, optimistically seeking the minor fissures of educational opportunities that occasionally present themselves in the apparatus of schooling. These opportunities can be characterized by well-defined positive cultural attributes that to often are ignored by the custodians of learning, but quite effective in negotiating educational and social circumstances that shifts with each subsequent generation of classroom teacher and school administrator. Patricia Baquedano-López, Jorge Solís, and Gabino Arredondo more fully extend this analysis by incorporating language in this social/cultural milieu, reminding us that for Latino students and their families, language and culture are inextricable. Together, these contributions assist in more fully *respecting* who these families, children, and communities are, what they are facing as they strive for cultural, linguistic, and educational well-being and equity in the United States. The culture and language of Latinos are resources that cannot be ignored in the enterprises of their teaching and learning.

Responsive

Functionally speaking, for education it is not sufficient just to have respect. Educational programs and those individuals who serve in them must be directly responsive to the students and families they serve. They must further be reflective, fluid, and dynamic. This requires an active assessment of the learning assets that the student brings to the schooling process coupled with the utilization of those tools and assets that, when *responsively* conceptualized, can optimize student learning. This new approach requires shifting the emphasis from "needs assessments" to "asset inventories." In other related literature, this approach is also referred to as mining the existent funds of knowledge that students and their families introduce to the schooling process. However, it is not enough to just know your students well, but to take that knowledge and make it come alive in organizing and implementing teaching and learning environments in which all students may be equally successful. Borrowing from an unknown educational colleague, "the general can only be understood in its specifics." That is, we can come to know all our students in various intellectual ways, but until we can translate that knowledge into the very specific ways in which we teach them, maximum benefits of the intellectual knowledge they possess will go unrealized. This is the truest illustration of educational underachievement.

The major contribution of this section is the realization that "actionable" knowledge exists when it comes to serving Latino students. Several contributions to this section provide the research and analyses that allows such a conclusion. Virginia González provides an insightful articulation of the need to understand the intersections of language, culture, and cognition when it comes to the education of Latino students. Although too often portraying learning as primarily a cognitive undertaking, she offers an empirical narrative that encourages a much deeper appreciation of specific cognitive processes involved in this intersection which necessitate the further animation of other related student attributes so as to maximize learning. The contribution of Kellie Rolstad and Jeff MacSwan permit us to delve into both the simplicity and complexity of bilingualism, its basic developmental attributes, and its significance regarding the education of so many U.S. Latino and other multi-lingual children in American schools. Already mentioned earlier, Patricia Baquedano-López, Jorge Solís, and Gabino Arredondo also add a theme of *responsiveness*, by further evidencing how the integration of language and culture into the education of Latinos endeavors is theoretically and educational sound. Teresa M. Huerta and Carmina M. Brittain provide a robust review of teacher/teaching best practices that are directly *responsive* and effective for securing academic achievement in Latino students. Huerta and Brittain posit, as have others, that the key placement of *responsive* teachers who understand instructional challenges and can implement effective strategies for academic success can almost single handedly eliminate seemingly inescapable achievement gaps for Latinos. Acknowledging that Latino students, like all students, come to the classroom with various ability challenges, Alfredo J. Artiles, Amanda L. Sullivan, Federico R. Waitoller, and Rebecca A. Neal address the important issues of our Latino students with special educational needs. Arguably, one of the least examined areas of Latino educational experiences, too often these students are not matriculated well into mainstream or even special education classrooms. The misdiagnoses and over representation of Latinos in special education, and the pejorative stigma of special education make this chapter particularly critical in the evolution of new approaches, strategies, and practices to better serve the educational interests of existing and emerging Latino student populations. Cumulatively, these contributors offer us an opportunity to understand the assets Latino students bring to their own educational efforts and how educators can be most effective in generating positive academic outcomes.

Responsible

Federal legislation as well as state and district level policy making are continually confronted with the unequal achievement outcomes for Latino students in U.S. schools. As a nation we have not created a policy mechanism to assist the delivery of educational services specifically for Latinos, or for holding educational institutions accountable for these disparate educational results in a sustained manner that has lead to equally sustainable improvements. For Latinos, research that has failed to make distinctions between data for immigrants versus non-immigrants, Spanish-speakers versus English-speakers, the role of socioeconomics and previous educational backgrounds make interpreting this data confusing and unproductive. Most significantly, limited English-speaking students are often out of the bounds of accountability simply because they are not assessed at all or worse thrown recklessly into accountability processes that do not recognize their linguistic or cultural characteristics. Confusion across national, state, and local policy has resulted in the failure to develop clearly funded, implemented and measured mechanisms to determine the opportunities that are consistently provided for Latino students to achieve.

Tom Stritikus and Bonnie English provide a thorough policy perspective regarding the efforts to "accommodate" teaching and learning to Latino students. Realizing as others have that *tinkering* with incremental educational improvements has typically resulted in the conclusion that indeed one size does not fit all. Policy makers have for some time sought to sporadically modify various attributes of education policy and its attendant structures to address persistent under-realization of Latino students. This has occurred most notably at the federal level, but has received serious state and local attention as Strikus and English demonstrate. The reader will be invited to determine whether these policy interventions are appropriately aligned with current research and best practices available throughout this volume. We have concluded with the contributors to this section that most often they are not.

Resourceful

We often are encouraged, particularly in education, that less is more. However, the simply unnuanced investment of resources has been historically ineffective in proffering sustainable and measurable solutions to ameliorate the chronic underachievement of discernable student populations . Many of the present generation of educational professionals are aware of the mathematics teacher from East Los Angeles, Jaime Escalante, as portrayed in the popular movie, *Stand and Deliver,* who takes low-achieving Latino students and with little more than engendering *ganas* in these students, produces a cadre of mathematics success stories. While certainly the notion of *ganas* was modestly explicated in the film, it indeed charaterizes a variety of Latino cultural attributes already mentioned, such as resiliency, resourcefulness, tenacity, self awareness, and internal loci of control. For many students in circumstances similar to those depicted in the film, these adages sound hollow in the face of the challenges they confront in everyday educational settings. *Ganas* is good, but a systematic effort to improve education on a variety of fronts is also needed. In this later context, *ganas* is effectively appropriated by respectful and responsive teachers trained to cull from students their inherent resourcefulness and have it brought to bear in pursuit of their intellectual and educational benefit, and, ultimately, our larger benefit.

This section affirms the centrality of a rich and rigorous, culturally responsive curriculum, valid and reliable assessments, and the expertise of the instructor as a critical resources in need of greater attention if Latino students are to do well. Teachers with bilingual and English development instructional skills, reduction of class size and resources (time and money) for professional development combined with extended opportunities for student learning are further critical resources required in pre-schools and throughout the early grades. Within secondary schools, access to college bound activities, honors credit, magnet opportunities, dual enrollment, advanced placement courses and rigorous International Baccalaureate programs require the redeployment of new resources in schools that have been historically organized to respond to *probrecitos*, rather than a student and community demographic of *promise*. Of course, the greatest resource that can be mined for the advancement of all Latinos is *la familia*.

Flora V. Rodríguez-Brown helps us understand how parents and family members of Latino background can specifically be brought to engage in the educational enterprise. Understanding the concept of *educación—ser educado* from a parent's perspective as well and garnering *confianza* can maximize the positive educational attainment so much desired by our Latino parents.

The Latino family is too often perceived as uninterested or unable to support their children's education. We arrive at the most opposite conclusion in that they are a necessary resource for academic success.

Reasonable

Committed educational practitioners and scholars are right to pursue and insist on immediate solutions to the education circumstances of Latino, and other marginalized, students. The U.S. Department of Education concluded that U.S. education needed "No More Excuses." The University of California forcefully concluded, *Ya Basta* (Enough) with regard to university under-representation of Hispanics. Yet the urgency of such conclusions must be tempered and coupled with reasonable actions. This section hopes to offer a modern framework guided by the five R's with which to advance a new optic by which to conceptualize and examine the inextricable relationship between language and culture, with respect to the full realization of Latino educational efficacy and achievement.

In California some years ago, the anti-bilingual education movement led by California's Proposition 227, but with extensions into other states most recently Arizona and into proposed federal initiatives aimed at immigrant students, sought to unreasonably restrict the flexibility of states and local school districts to respond to the instructional needs, of Latino students and their families. These new assaults in the guise of policy mandate that prescriptive instructional treatments limit temporal access of programs to these students (from 1–3 years) and focus their efforts only on English-language development instead of high academic achievement. Additionally, these same policies that purport to be research based and politically unmotivated are without any accountability of the mandates they impose. As an example, consider the new proposed assessment practices in the U.S. Department of Education's Reading-by-Third-Grade initiative. This initiative would require all students to be assessed in English reading, although the Department of Education presently funds programs to teach children to read in their native language with English reading competencies expected after the third grade. Does this incongruence seem reasonable? In our urgency and good will, we need not act unreasonably or inconsistently.

The identification of "being unreasonable" as it directly relates to Latino education is provided explicitly. In this section, Tom Stritikus and Bonnie English address "unreasonable" education policy often aimed at Latinos—anti-bilingual education and English-only policies in particular; Virginia González looks at assessments that too often lack the required psychometric properties to adequately elevate educational accountability; and Alfredo J. Artiles, Amanda L. Sullivan, Federico R. Waitoller, and Rebecca A. Neal pinpoint issues of over-representation of Latino Students in special education venues due to ill-advised assessments and policies. Together, these contributions caution practitioners that a reasonable effort must be made not to impose practices that are injurious to Latino students and their families. It requires all of us to perform a more judicious evaluation of what we know and assure that what we do is appropriately aligned with a sound knowledge base.

We are optimistic that as readers of this section profit from the contributions of these distinguished authors, they too may come to embrace our focus on the five R's as our best way to summarize and organize their offerings. Of course, this mnemonic device does little justice to the comprehensiveness of the chapters in this section. However, if one only reads this short introduction, we hope it can do nothing more than to induce the reading of these important works and to make the suggestions here "actionable" for Latino students, families, and communities. Educational policies and practices that respect who Latino students are, respond directly to a sound knowledge base, hold themselves responsible for academic outcomes, and provide for and maximize new and existing resources organized in ways that are reasonable can make a huge difference. We need no more excuses and enough is enough.

19   Infinite Possibilities, Many Obstacles

Language, Culture, Identity, and Latino/a Educational Achievement

Aída Hurtado, Karina Cervantez, and Michael Eccleston
University of California, Santa Cruz

Overview

The educational achievements of Latino/as have historically lagged behind those of other ethnic and racial groups in the United States. In recent years, the Latino/a population within the United States has undergone dramatic changes: the substantial increase in number, nation-wide dispersion, and relatively young ages of the Latino/a population place the educational achievement of this group at the center of state, national, and international policy. This chapter examines the impact that Latino/a language use and maintenance, cultural practices, and identity formations have on their education. Although many obstacles persist in the pursuit of educational parity, there are also many opportunities and innovative programs contributing to Latino/as' educational success and the enrichment of the field of educational theory and practice to help all students succeed.

For Latino/as, as for many other groups of Color in the United States, educational achievement cannot be conceptualized as an individual process. Context, community, and family form a seamless network leading to educational progress. In the recent past, Latino/a educational trajectories were conceptualized as being determined largely by individual dispositional characteristics such as resilience, mettle, self-efficacy, and resistance to stigma (Close & Solberg, 2008; Phinney, Dennis, & Gutierrez, 2005). These characteristics may help to explain the achievement of extraordinary individuals, students who may be found in all groups in society; but there are always a few individuals who do not fit the norm and are considered outliers. However, the successes of individuals do not help move the average (nor the median) level of achievement for Latino/as forward. This is an essential component, especially as the group becomes the numerical majority in many states and school districts (U.S. Census Bureau, 2007; Fry, 2007; Gonzales, 2007). The question then becomes, what structural issues need to be addressed for large numbers of Latino/a students to succeed and substantially increase the overall level of achievement throughout the educational pipeline? In this chapter we examine three areas of research that may provide some guidance in answering the question of how to increase the educational achievement of Latinos: language, culture, and identity. By educational achievement, we specifically mean reducing the dropout rate and increasing the number of high school graduates and the number of Latino/as who attend college and graduate and professional schools.

A Brief Overview of the Educational Status of Latinos

The educational achievements of Latino/as have been steadily increasing since the 1970s, an era when the participation of Latino/as in higher education was an anomaly. The progress along the educational pathways, however, has not kept pace with the growing Latino/a population. As Latino/as have become the majority population in many K-12 school systems, most notably in Texas and California (the most populous states in the country), they still graduate from high school at much lower rates than do Whites, Asians, and African Americans. Figures 19.1 and 19.2 present a snapshot of the educational pipeline in the United States. As Figure 19.1 indicates, for every 100 school children that begin first grade, only 54 Latina women and 51 Latino men finish high school (in comparison to 84 White women and 83 White men, 78 Asian women and 83 Asian men, 73 African American women and 71 African American men, 72 Native American women and 70 Native American men). Not surprisingly, the low rates in high school graduation also affect the college graduation rates for Latino/as; only 11 Latina women and 10 Latino men graduate from college, the lowest rates of all ethnic and racial groups. The most dramatic under-representation for Latino/as is seen in the graduate school rates, with only 4.3 Latina women and 4.4 Latino men out of 100 first-graders obtaining graduate or doctoral degrees. The most likely group to obtain graduate and doctoral degrees are Asian men (26.4) and Asian women (14.4) followed by White men (12.4) and White women (8.6).

It is also important to note that the educational progress of Latino/as varies by national origin. The most educationally successful Latino/a group is the Cuban population (see Figure 19.2), followed by Puerto Ricans and Dominicans; these groups have greater high school and college graduation rates as well as higher rates of obtaining graduate and doctoral degrees. The least educationally successful are Salvadorians and Chicano/as.[1] The uneven distribution of educational achievement among different Latino/a groups is largely attributable to the different modes of immigration and incorporation into the United States. Puerto Ricans and Mexicans endured colonization of their homelands, which has been accompanied by cultural, linguistic, and socio-economic oppression. New arrivals in the United States from these groups inherit the disadvantaged status of long-time residents. Dominicans and Salvadorians are more recent immigrants to the United States, mostly arriving in the late 1970s and 80s and joining predominantly urban

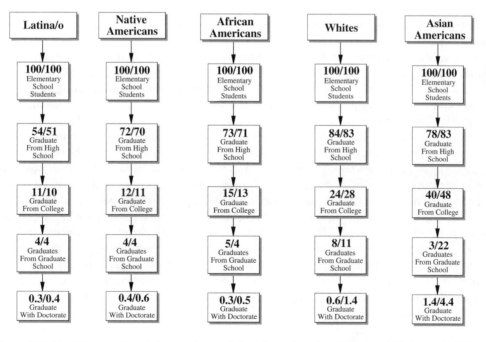

Figure 19.1 The U.S. educational pipeline, by race/ethnicity and gender, 2000. From: Huber, L. P., Huidor, O., Malagon, M. C., Sanchez, G., & Solorzano, D. G. (2006, March). Falling through the cracks: Critical transitions in the Latina/o educational pipeline. 2006 Latina/o Education Summit Report. CSRC Research Report. Number 7. Los Angeles: UCLA Chicano Studies Research Center.

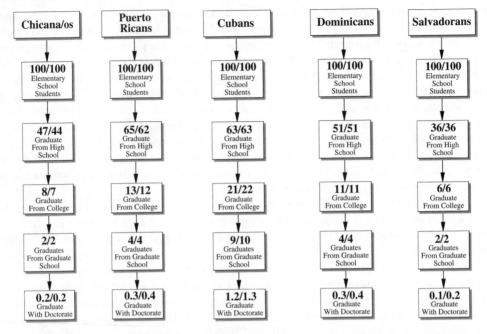

Figure 19.2 The U.S. educational pipeline, by subgroup and gender, 2000. From: Huber, L. P., Huidor, O., Malagon, M. C., Sanchez, G., & Solorzano, D. G. (2006, March). Falling through the cracks: Critical transitions in the Latina/o educational pipeline. 2006 Latina/o Education Summit Report. CSRC Research Report. Number 7. Los Angeles: UCLA Chicano Studies Research Center.

job markets, bypassing the traditional rural job markets that have been the starting point for many Mexican immigrants.

Conversely, the economic and educational trajectories of Cubans have been influenced by the initial experience of arriving in the United States as political refugees after the Marxist/socialist revolution led by Fidel Castro in the 1950s. The original cohort of political Cuban exiles was middle class, both in wealth and in education, and predominantly of White European ancestry. There have been subsequent, albeit smaller, waves of Cuban exiles, most notably in the 1980s with the arrival of the *Marielitos*, who were largely of African ancestry and not as prosperous as the initial cohort. The Cuban exiles also had the advantage of settling, for the most part, in Miami, Florida, a concentrated geographical area, which allowed them to form their own economic institutions, use their educational and social capital to form successful businesses, and eventually have a strong voice in local politics. Given the disparate economic and educational status among the Latino subgroups, an analysis of the educational trajectories of Latino/as must take into account the historical diversity of these national groups. For example, Cubans arriving to the United States as political refugees with educational, social, and cultural capital in contrast to the colonization experiences of Puerto Ricans and Mexican descendants, results in different educational trajectories and outcomes. The complexities of these different forms of incorporation into U.S. society must be an integral part of the analysis in understanding Latinos' educational trajectories.

The Cost of Not Educating Latino/as

The education of Latino/as is certainly a social justice issue; solving this issue would contribute to educational equity. However, also important are the economic consequences of not educating this population. Increasingly, a degree beyond high school has become necessary for gainful employment. According to the Bureau of Labor Statistics, 9 of the 15 occupations that will experience substantial growth between the years 2004 and 2014 (i.e., increases of at least twice that of the national average) will require an associate's degree or higher (Gonzales, 2007; Immigration Policy Center, 2007). As Figure 19.3 indicates, in the year 2000 only 4% of Latino/as 25 years of age and older had obtained a bachelor's degree although, as the most recent census figures indicate, they represent 15% of the population (Huber, Huidor, Malagon, Sanchez, & Solorzano, 2006). Obviously, Latinos' chances in the current and future job market will be affected by their lack of advanced degrees (Huber, Huidor, Malagon, Sanchez, & Solorzano, 2006).

At the opposite end of the spectrum from Latino/as are Asians and Whites; both of these groups are above population parity in their educational achievement. Whereas Whites represent 79% of the population, 84% of those 25 and older have obtained a bachelor's degree. Similarly, Asians in the same age group represent 4% of the population but 6% have received a college degree. These population comparisons are important. Thirty years ago, the educational progress of Latino/as, although of some concern, was not tied to the success or failure of the overall economy. Latino/as in the 1960s and 70s were primarily a numerical minority confined to low-wage and low-skill jobs. At that time, educating Latino/as was largely a social justice issue, not an economic imperative (Hurtado, Haney, & Garcia, 1998). The changing demographics have reframed the terms of the education debate. Latino/as are now the largest non-White group in the United States, having surpassed African Americans in number. Equally important is the fact that Latino/as are now the youngest population in the United States; they will be largely responsible for generating future taxes to support the social security of an aging White population (Hayes-Bautista, 2004). Furthermore, Latino/as have, on average, more children than do other ethnic and racial groups in the United States. As such, they stand to grow as a population, coupled with a steady flow of immigration from all of Latin America. As predicted by sociologist David Hayes-Bautista, in California, where the majority of Latino/as reside, it can be expected that

in the fall of 2013, the majority of children entering the state's high schools will be Latino. In the fall of 2016, the majority of new workers entering the labor force will be Latino. By 2019, the majority of young people who have turned 18 and are eligible to register and vote will be Latino. (Ferraez, 2003)

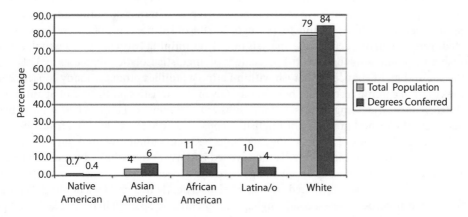

Figure 19.3 Percentage of students, aged twenty-five and older, attaining a bachelor's degree, by race/ethnicity, 2000. From: Huber, L. P., Huidor, O., Malagon, M. C., Sanchez, G., & Solorzano, D. G. (2006, March). Falling through the cracks: Critical transitions in the Latina/o educational pipeline. 2006 Latina/o Education Summit Report. CSRC Research Report. Number 7. Los Angeles: UCLA Chicano Studies Research Center.

Not educating Latino/as at a rate that reaches parity with their population places the U.S. economy, as well as other institutions, including education, at risk.

In drawing an accurate picture of Latino/as in the U.S. educational system, it is important to note the disparity in population sizes among different Latino/a groups. Of the 45.5 million Latino/as in the United States, 64% (29 million) of the Latino/a origin population is of Mexican descent, 9% (4 million) of Puerto Rican descent, 3.5% (1.5 million) of Cuban descent, 3% (1.3 million) of Salvadorian descent, and 2.7% (1.2 million) of Dominican descent. The remainder hail from other Central American, South American, or other Latino/a origins (U.S. Census Bureau, 2007, 2008). Equally important is each group's geographical location within the United States. Whereas roughly one half of the nation's Dominicans live in New York City, and about half of the nation's Cubans live in Miami-Dade County, Latino/as of Mexican descent are dispersed throughout the country. Although the majority of the Mexican descent population resides in the southwestern United States, there are sizeable segments of Mexican descendants in the Midwest and Southern United States, and, most recently, in the Northeast, including New York City (U.S. Census Bureau, 2006a). The sheer number of Mexican descendants and their geographical dispersion make them an essential part of the current and future work force. Consequently, their educational success will have a major impact on the economic and social future of this country.

We now turn to the three areas of research—language, culture, and identity—that have substantively impacted the educational trajectories of Latino/as in the United States. We review the research in each of these areas and analyze the effect these conditions have on Latino/as' educational achievement.

Language

In 2007, the United States joined China and India as countries with populations in excess of 300 million people (the U.S. population is 301,621,157). Latino/as represent 15% (45.5 million) of the total U.S. population (U.S. Census Bureau, 2006a, 2006b, 2008), making people of Latino/a descent the nation's largest ethnic and racial minority (this estimate does not include the 4 million residents of Puerto Rico [U.S. Census Bureau, 2008]). When applying the U.S. Census Bureau definition of linguistic isolation where "the dominant language at home is a non-English language, and that no one in the family speaks English at a fluency level greater than 'well'" (Verdugo, 2006, p. 7), 1 in 5 Latino/as in the United States report that they do not speak English or do not speak English "well." According to Verdugo, 26.28% of Latino/as in 2004 were linguistically isolated. Verdugo further refined the analysis by only examining Latino/as in households where Spanish is the dominant language; the percentage of linguistic isolation increases to 33.17%.

The use and maintenance of Spanish within Latino/a families produces many consequences for the children coming from these households. Given the statistics on the use of Spanish, limited English fluency, and linguistic isolation, a substantial number of Latino/a first-graders begin school with little or no knowledge of English (Capps, Fix, & Murray, 2005; Garcia, 1994). For many students, their lack of English language skills becomes cumulative, making it difficult for them to catch up on the academic skills they missed because of their limited fluency in English (Gándara, 2006). The academic disadvantage becomes especially pronounced in mathematics and the sciences where training needs to begin relatively early in a child's schooling (Gándara, 2006). Furthermore, because a second language in general, and Spanish in particular, is not perceived as an asset, even students who manage to acquire English quickly enough to succeed in school are never rewarded or acknowledged for having such a valuable language skill.

Beyond the individual consequences of not speaking English, there is also a serious gap between the home language and the language spoken in schools that permeates the entire context of schooling (Garcia, 1994, 2001). For instance, the lack of English fluency of many Latino/a parents limits their participation in their children's schooling. They often are unable to help students with homework, do not feel comfortable participating in school activities, and ultimately are unable to adequately advocate for their children in their schools (Zarate, 2007).

Many Latino/as come from families where Spanish is the primary language. The prevalence of Spanish in the home and community is likely to persist primarily for two reasons. First, Latino/as have a deep commitment to language maintenance, exemplified in the number that report preferring to speak Spanish at home, even when they are fluent in English. Currently there are 34 million U.S. residents 5 years and older who speak Spanish at home; of those, more than one half say they speak English very well (U.S. Census Bureau, 2008). Second, as stated earlier, Latino/as are a substantial segment of the U.S. population, making Spanish persistence even greater. Under these circumstances, it becomes incumbent on schools to restructure their activities and to be more responsive to the increasing number of Latino/a immigrants who are Spanish dominant.

There are many small-scale, inventive programs responding to these changing demographics. One example is the *Abriendo Puertas* (Opening Doors) program established in 2003 by Texas A&M University's College of Agriculture and Life Sciences. The program, developed by Dr. Ida Acuña-Garza, teaches parent volunteers the instrumental knowledge necessary for students to apply to and enter college. The structured curriculum is administered to an initial cohort of parents in middle and high schools. In turn, these parents visit other parents in their communities to spread the word about the requirements necessary to successfully finish high school and apply to college. The program has been very successful in San Antonio, Houston, and other communities in South Texas, as well as in the Tri-Cities Area in Washington State. The parent volunteers participating in *Abriendo Puertas* do not fit the profile of parent volunteers in mainstream educational intervention programs: their schools have 50% high school drop-out rates; they are predominantly Latinas (98% women); they are first-generation or undocumented U.S. immigrants; they live below the poverty level, with many having a household income of less than $10,000 a year; and they do not have a high school diploma (http://tamusystem.tamu.edu/systemwide/06/10/features/openingdoors.html). Nonetheless, the program in these sites has successfully recruited parent volunteers, as well as a cadre of parents in these communities, to contribute to their children's educational success.

A further development in this area is to redefine parental engagement in education beyond the usual measures of participation in parent-teacher conferences, attendance at PTA meetings, and volunteering in the classroom. More inclusive measures should include parent participation in cultural activities in which Latino parents may feel more comfortable (Zarate, 2007). For example, providing support for folkloric dance troupes and mariachi musical groups can be especially effective in increasing parent participation (Hurtado, 1997; Hurtado & Gurin, 2004). Such innovations promise to be more attractive to Spanish-speaking parents by increasing their comfort level in participating in their children's schooling.

In spite of the hurdles many Spanish-speaking children encounter in their schooling, eventually most Latino/a students do acquire English. It is also worthwhile to note that regardless of the high rates in Spanish prevalence, children born in the United States to immigrant parents and children brought to this country before the age of 12 experience high levels of English acquisition. However, because their native language is not supported within the education system, the transition to English is often traumatic and affects their academic achievement (Gándara, 2006).

Undocumented Students

Closely tied to language use is immigration status. First-generation immigrants are more likely to use Spanish as their primary language, as are their children, slowing down the children's educational progress. Furthermore, the educational level attained is closely tied to Spanish use and immigrant status such that lack of English skills results in limited employment opportunities for immigrants. The issue of language isolation is a primary concern among adult immigrants as most of their children acquire English. For younger immigrants, the acquisition of English happens rather rapidly although Spanish is not abandoned. For immigrants and their children to succeed educationally, they must have opportunities to acquire English quicker and integrate Spanish-dominant parents into their children's educational process. The quicker the linguistic integration of immigrant parents, the more their children are likely to benefit educationally.

Of special concern are the children of undocumented immigrants who may be undocumented themselves. According to a recent report, U.S. high schools graduate approximately 65,000 undocumented immigrant students every year. These students, for the most part, are brought to the United States as young children and have grown up attending K-12 schools in this country (Lazarin, 2007). They may achieve extraordinary educational heights but are often unable to pursue higher education because of restrictions placed on financial aid to attend colleges and universities. A major breakthrough to provide educational opportunities to undocumented students was the federal legislation commonly referred to as the DREAM Act (Development, Relief, and Education for Alien Minors), a bipartisan bill that would restore states' rights to offer in-state tuition to immigrant students residing in the state. The sticking point in this piece of legislation, which ultimately led to its defeat, was a provision that presented a pathway to citizenship. A substantial number of law makers felt the bill would reward undocumented students for "breaking the law," although, of course, the students had no control over their parents' decision to enter the country without documentation. With the defeat of this legislation, undocumented students are subjected to out-of-state tuitions and financial aid ineligibility. In 2007 the DREAM Act was reintroduced in Congress as part of the comprehensive immigration legislation; it failed once again to pass the U.S. Senate. Nevertheless, the DREAM Act remains viable because of bipartisan support and the backing of the House and Senate leadership. The failure of this piece of legislation to pass is yet another obstacle to many talented Latino/a youth on their path to higher education (National Immigration Law Center, 2007).[2]

Culture

Most educational researchers agree that Latino/as have both cultural similarities and differences based on their countries of origin and their histories in the United States (Trumbull, Rothstein-Fisch, Greenfield, & Quiroz, 2001). As stated earlier, of all the Latino/a nationalities, Latino/as of Mexican ancestry are the largest group and have had the longest presence in the United States, dating to even before this country became a nation. In particular, Mexican-ancestry Latino/as have a unique connection to the southwestern United States because of their history of colonization and strong cultural ties, evidenced in the names of the towns and cities located there (Verdugo, 2006). In addition, many cultural practices deriving from the Spanish and Mexican colonial past are still evident in many Western states such as Arizona, California, Colorado, New Mexico, and Texas.

Other Latino/a groups also have specific historical and political trajectories that result in unique relationships with U.S. mainstream culture. For example, Puerto Ricans are U.S. citizens who are allowed to vote in presidential primaries but not in presidential elections. Furthermore, Puerto Rico lacks official representation in the U.S. House of Representatives and Senate despite island residents' long history of migration to New York, which has consequences for cultural adaptation as Puerto Ricans experience increasing visibility in all areas of social life in the United States. Similarly, the historical uniqueness of Cuban immigration to this country as a result of the Cuban revolution positions Cubans in alliance with conservative political forces in the United States. The large numbers of Cubans in Florida, and their educational and social capital, have given rise to political and social power, which, in turn, has made their cultural adaptations different from that of other Latino/a immigrant groups who generally came to the United States seeking employment opportunities rather than as political refugees united against the communist take-over of their native homeland.

While this discussion of the intrinsic cultural, social, political, and economic diversity of different Latino/a groups represents a very cursory overview of the cultural complexity of the Latino/a population in the United States, it serves to highlight the broad spectrum of differences among the Latino/a populace. Such diversity must be addressed by the school system as a whole to insure Latino/a children do not fall behind as they progress through the educational system.

The Changing U.S. Cultural Landscape

With the advent of multicultural education in the 1990s and the continuing diversity move-ment in higher education, many educators are now convinced that the cultural and linguistic assimilation strategies proposed prior to this era are no longer viable, or even desirable (Banks, 1995; Giroux, 1983; hooks, 1994). Instead, the conversation has shifted to identify new strate-gies necessary to incorporate different cultures and languages throughout the schooling process (McLaren, 1997). This is obviously good news for the many Latino/a students and their parents who are dedicated to educational success but who may not have the knowledge or tools to suc-ceed in the education system. One point of entry for implementing this new point of view on cultural diversity is to increase the number of Latino/a teachers and, at the same time, finding strategies for transculturating non-Latino/a teachers to be more responsive to the increasing number of Latino/a students.

The diversification of the teaching work force is especially relevant. In California, where the greatest number of Latino/as reside, of the K-12 teachers in 2004–2005, 72.1% were White, 14.5% were Hispanic, 4.5% were African American, and 4.6% were Asian (the remaining teach-ers were of various ethnicities and races; California Department of Education, 2007). In fact, the California figures fare better in terms of percentage of Latino/a to non-Latino teachers than the national figures do. In 2004, there were a total of 6.2 million K-12 teachers in the United States; 83.2% were White, 8.4% were African American, 5.5% were Hispanic, and 2.9% were Asian (also, 71% were women; U.S. Census Bureau, 2004; California Department of Education, 2007). The less-experienced, non-credentialed teachers were the most likely educators to be found in the poor schools with large numbers of students of Color (Oakes et al., 2006). In urban areas, where most Latino/as reside, 80% of the 54 largest urban districts had non-credentialed teachers on their staff (Urban Teachers Collaborative, 2000). As Verdugo (2006) points out, "Hispanic students do not, generally, get qualified teachers" (p. 31). Specifically, non-credentialed teachers, who are not teaching within their areas of expertise and who lack extensive teaching experience, predominantly teach Latino/a students. To their credit, many teachers express their desire to have more diversity training to deal with the increasing number of Latino/a students and other students of Color. Unfortunately, there is no national policy, or even a state policy, that addresses increasing the cultural competencies of all teachers to deal with the changing demographics (Verdugo, 2006).

The lack of a diverse teaching force is also a concern because the Latino/a population is not only growing in the five southwestern states, it is also dispersing demographically in significant numbers throughout the country. Although 45% of Latino/as still reside in two regions of the United States—the West and the South—in 2004 the five states with the greatest number of Latino/as were California, Texas, Florida, New York, and Illinois (Verdugo, 2006). Latino/as have moved to regions of the country where they can find employment that does not require an educational degree (e.g., the service sector in Las Vegas, the meat and poultry industry in the Midwest, and the fish canning industry along the East Coast). Latino/as are usually con-centrated within defined communities in these regions (e.g., Dalton, Georgia, where there is a revitalized carpet industry). They also seek areas where they can find low-cost housing (Durand & Massey, 2003). Consequently, these small communities may rather suddenly receive a large number of Latino/a students, forcing school personnel to scurry and find solutions for the newly arrived students who do not fit their usual profile (Verdugo, 2006).

Cultural Diversity as an Asset

Many scholars have begun to outline the aspects of cultural diversity that are helpful for students of Color to navigate the systems of education (Gurin, Nagda, & Lopez, 2004; Saenz, Ngai, & Hurtado, 2007). For some, Latino/a students and other students of Color bring funds of knowledge that have not been recognized as valuable by schools or standardized forms of assessments (Gonzalez & Moll, 2002; Moll, Amanti, Neff, & Gonzalez, 1992; Vélez-Ibáñez & Greenberg, 1992). In addition to advocating rigorous training of Latino/a students from an early age (Gándara, 2006), some scholars also recognize that the skills provided by poor, Spanish-dominant, immigrant families are valuable and worth reinforcing in school curricula as well as in the reconceptualization of education in general (Carreón, Drake, & Barton, 2005; Lopez, Scribner, & Mahitivanichcha, 2001; Ramirez, 2003). For example, Tara Yosso (2005) argues that students of Color in general and Latino/a students in particular bring various forms of "community capital wealth" to their schooling that include "aspirational, navigational, social, linguistic, familial and resistant capital" (p. 69).

In her theoretical discussion, Yosso (2005) critiques scholars who apply Pierre Bourdieu's theories to propose that only the upper and middle classes can provide the kind of knowledge and skills that constitute valuable capital toward succeeding in school and in life in general. From this perspective, it would seem that Latino/as are lacking in the "social capital" necessary to succeed in school, and that all educational interventions should be directed at bringing these students up to par by instructing them in hegemonic knowledges, ignoring the assets they may bring to their schooling. Instead, Yosso (2005) proposes there are at least six areas or skills (as outlined below) that Latino/as and other students of Color (and we would add other non-traditional students, such as re-entry students and students from poor backgrounds) bring to bear on their education. *Aspirational capital* is the ability of a student to maintain hopes and dreams for the future even in the "face of real and perceived barriers" (p. 77). *Linguistic capital* includes a student's "intellectual and social skills attained through communication experiences in more than one language and/or style" (p. 78). This ability extends to communicating and navigating various social systems and class and social hierarchies. For example, linguistic capital includes the skill bilingual children use to translate for their parents when dealing with institutions such as the government and the medical establishment. *Familial capital* refers to the student's "cultural knowledges nurtured among *familia* (kin) that carry a sense of community history, memory and cultural intuition" (p. 79). Closely related to familial capital is *social capital*, which is a student's knowledge of the social networks of people and the community resources available to them given the embeddedness of their neighborhoods and their extended, many times, transnational families. Their existence in multiple worlds also facilitates the development of *navigational capital*, the student's ability to maneuver through social institutions (Padilla, 1999). Finally, many Latino/a students negotiate multiple social systems as they traverse from homes, to schools, neighborhoods, and, at times, different countries. Through this social knowledge, the arbitrary nature of social and political rules, as well as the unfair practices of many social institutions, is exposed. Yosso (2005) hypothesizes that these experiences lead to *resistant capital*—that is, a student's knowledges and skills fostered through "oppositional behavior that challenges inequality" (p. 80).

Obviously, the educational system would look dramatically different if these kinds of community cultural wealth were fully recognized and integrated into curricula, teaching practices, and pedagogies. Equally important, the students (i.e., the non-Latino students) who do not have such community cultural wealth would also benefit from being educated beyond the existing curricula and dominant knowledge, especially given our increasingly globalized world requiring skills to communicate and function across differences. Some institutions of higher education are recognizing the need to transculturate students to "dialogue across difference" by providing small spaces where they can learn to speak to others unlike them (Gurin & Nagda, 2006; Nagda & Gurin, 2007; Zuñiga, Nagda, Chesler, & Cytron-Walker, 2007). Other scholars advocate the integration of indigenous knowledges and spirituality into our existing pedagogies to deepen the transmission of knowledge (Rendón, 2008). This innovative integration of various cultural assets into the educational process promises to be the new frontier in teaching and education.

Identity

The heterogeneity of the Latino/a population based on their varied histories, national origins, and reasons for U.S. immigration, as well as the numerous modes of incorporation into the nation, are amply manifested in the diversity of their identifications. Most Latino/a groups have a deep attachment to the nation-specific label that denotes their origin: Mexican American, Puerto Rican, Cuban American, Salvadorian, Honduran. There is also internal diversity within each national group denoting different cultural and political adaptations to their subordinate status in the United States. For example, the terms *Chicana/o* and *Boricua* highlight the "in-between" status of ethnic and racial groups that endured colonization by the United States and incorporation of their native lands after wars and treaties; for Chicano/as, U.S. rule was imposed through political treaties in 1848 at the end of the Mexican American War, and for Boricuas, in 1898 at the end of the Spanish American War. Latino/as who use the ethnic labels Chicano/as and Boricuas are making the statement that they are neither fully accepted as members in the United States nor in their countries of ancestry. Instead, their identities, language, and culture are a hybrid of both the United States and their countries of origin. Furthermore, individuals who identify with these political terms reject cultural and linguistic assimilation into the U.S. mainstream and instead seek to create a third culture through the hybridization of their ancestries and their status as residents (and at times citizens) of the United States.

With the tremendous increase in immigration from Latin America, however, individual national groups have had to choose an ethnic label that will benefit them in their struggle to gain political, social, and economic recognition in the United States. The labels for Latino/a panethnic identity vary by region (Oboler, 1995). For example, on the East Coast, Hispanic is the preferred panethnic label of many Latino/a ancestry individuals, while on the West Coast Latino/a is the most widely used term. These panethnic labels, however, are not yet tied to a new ethnic group that has indeed emerged from the intermarriage and co-mingling of different Latino/a cultures and language. In many ways, Latino/a panethnicity is a meta-identity that is deployed for political, social, and economic recognition of a variety of Latino/a groups, with the largest group being of Mexican ancestry, followed by Puerto Ricans and Cuban Americans. Other Central American groups, like Guatemalans and Salvadorians, are smaller in number. Regardless of the internal diversity and lack of amalgamation of these different groups, the political, social, and especially educational realities they face have much in common, making the panethnic label of Latino/a real in its consequences. Also, the similarities in culture and language across Latin America are such that the panethnic label is based on commonalities sufficiently powerful to warrant its use.

Identity and Achievement

There is a long-standing debate in the social science literature on whether students of Color identifying with their ethnic and racial group leads to negative consequences for their educational engagement. Among the concerns documented in the literature is that strong ingroup identification with ethnicity and race leads students to disidentify with educational achievement (Ogbu, 1978, 1991, 1993); creates stereotype threat, impairing educational performance (Steele, 1997); and impairs the positive self-esteem necessary to succeed in school. There is also research documenting that adherence to particular ethnic identities does not have an effect on the educational success of Mexican-descent college students, as measured by their college grade point average (Hurtado, García, Vega, & Gonzalez, 2003). Instead, these students' identification with being a parent and a good student predicted their college grades. Other research has documented that the maintenance of culture (Pease-Alvarez, 2002), ethnic identity, and bilingual skills results in higher educational achievement than for Latino/as that lose their cultural distinctiveness. For example, Feliciano (2001) used U.S. Census data from 1990 to examine high school dropout rates among 18- to 21-year-old youth in Asian groups (Vietnamese, Koreans, Chinese, Filipinos, and Japanese) and Latino/a groups (Mexicans, Puerto Ricans, and Cubans). She concludes that:

> bilingual students are less likely to drop out than English-only speakers, students in bilingual households are less likely to drop out than those in English-dominant or English-limited households, and students in immigrant households are less likely to drop out than those in nonimmigrant households. These findings suggest that those who enjoy the greatest educational success are not those who have abandoned their ethnic cultures and are most acculturated. Rather, bicultural youths who can draw resources from both the immigrant community and mainstream society are best situated to enjoy educational success. (p. 856)

Feliciano's (2001) findings of the positive aspects of ethnic cultures (as measured by language use and the presence of immigrants in the household) may be explained by the increasing acceptance of cultural diversity in U.S. society in general and in schools in particular. There is still much to be done to fully implement multicultural education at every level of schooling but we cannot overlook the increasing cultural diversification that is now becoming commonplace in U.S. society and in the world.

New Directions for Improving Education for all Students

In the effort to expand the educational achievements of Latino/as, educational practices and educational institutions can also be analyzed to improve the general education of all students. Although improving educational achievement for Latino/as has predominantly been approached as solving a "social problem," many of the successful interventions and innovations in the K-12 system and in higher education can also be perceived as good educational practices for all students. Below we provide only two of many examples to illustrate how a paradigm shift may make these innovations worthwhile for *all* students although they were developed to help Latino/as succeed educationally.

The Use of Spanish as an Asset Rather than a Deficit

In the not too distant past, Spanish use by Latino/a (predominantly Mexican) students in schools was physically punished by school staff. Hurtado and Rodriguez (1989) report that schools in South Texas communities had various strategies to dissuade students from using Spanish on the school premises, including imposing fines, ordering lap runs, issuing after-school detention for repeat offenders, and, in some occasions even taping students' mouths closed. These actions took place in the early 1980s; although there have been no follow-up studies since then, it is highly unlikely that in this era of increasing multicultural education these actions would be perceived as desirable.

Ironically, at the same time that students were punished for speaking Spanish, enormous resources were invested in instructing students to learn a second language as part of the high school curriculum (a requirement that is still necessary for eligibility to attend college). Many Latino/a parents who feared for the educational success of their children stopped speaking Spanish in their children's presence, and many of these children grew up either not having language skills in Spanish or with receptive bilingualism—that is, the ability to understand but not speak Spanish.

Latino/as' linguistic adaptations are negotiated within this history of coercive language policies. As a result, many Latino/a students grow up in households with different "linguistic bands," which Hurtado & Vega (2004) define as the "different levels of language *use* and *exposure*" from "only Spanish to only English, and the continuum in between" (p. 140). For a linguistic band to exist, there must be at least two or more people in the household who speak the same language. The exposure to different languages can also take place through different language media, be it visual like television, books, newspapers, and magazines, or audio like radio and recorded music, as well as the World Wide Web. When parents speak Spanish to each other, children may learn to understand Spanish (receptive bilingualism) but not to speak it. However, when they enter college, many of these students learn to speak Spanish at a much faster rate than if they had never been exposed to the language. Educational institutions could take advantage of this overt and latent cultural and linguistic knowledge, cultivating it to blossom into full English/ Spanish bilingualism with equivalent skills in both languages (Garcia, 2001). Given the increasing Latino/a population, Spanish/English bilingualism will be desirable as well as necessary in many economic and social arenas of American life.

Increasing the Participation of Parents throughout the Educational Cycle

Educational achievement is usually conceptualized as occurring in a linear fashion from parents to their offspring; that is, parents are responsible for providing the educational opportunities and resources for children to succeed in school. Furthermore, the degree of direct parental involvement decreases as children begin pre-school, enter elementary school, go on to middle school, and graduate from high school. Usually at the high school level, many parents who can afford the costs enlist experts to tutor their children in difficult subjects like chemistry and advanced math courses. Once students are ready to apply for college, many families are willing to pay "coaches" to oversee the college application process. By the time students attend higher education, they are solely responsible for navigating their education, consulting parents only occasionally on crucial decisions like selecting a major or deciding on graduate or professional school.

The typical trajectory for Latino/a students is somewhat different. Many of the educational decisions made by Latino/a students are not based solely on their individual concerns. The family unit (with many variations as to whom is included in this constellation) becomes central in making educational decisions. Furthermore, the more involved and knowledgeable Latino/a families are about their children's schooling, the more supportive they tend to be (Hurtado, 2003). Several innovative programs have capitalized on this tendency. As mentioned earlier, the program *Abriendo Puertas* (Opening Doors) uses parent volunteers to spread the word about college requirements and involve parents in other ways as well. For example, the program facilitates parents' becoming an integral part of the milestones in their children's education, like graduation from middle school, potluck dinners for students' acceptance into college, and certificates to parents who complete the *Abriendo Puertas* training. These events create a sense of community and cohesion between parents, students, and schools.

Similarly, the Hispanic Mother-Daughter Program (HMDP) takes advantage of the natural alliance many Latina mothers have with their daughters, which has been documented in the research literature (Hurtado, 2003; Suárez-Orozco & Suárez-Orozco, 1995). HMDP is directed under the auspices of Student Affairs at Arizona State University. The stated mission of the program is to "increase the number of first generation Hispanic women who complete a bachelor's degree by directly involving the mothers in the educational process of their daughters" (www.asu.edu/studentaffairs/mss/msc/docs/WEB%20Parent%20Recruitment.pdf). The program begins when the students are in seventh grade and continues until the students graduate from college (most of the students attend Arizona State University). The mother-daughter teams attend nine workshops per year covering topics ranging from self-empowerment, to developing leadership skills, to instruction on the courses necessary to attend college. The mother-daughter teams make a 10-year commitment to see their daughters succeed in school and in higher education. The program is in its 20th year of existence and has persistence rates ranging from 74 to 90%. The success of this program has been replicated at the University of Texas, Austin, and University of Texas, El Paso. Often mothers with more than one daughter participate in the program, with each of their daughters entering as they reach the grade at which the program begins. For example, the program at UT Austin highlighted a "dream team" of three sisters (18, 15, and 11 years old) who wanted to pursue "becoming a lawyer, a psychologist and a veterinarian" with "a best friend—their mother" (www.utexas.edu/features/archive/2002/motherdaughter.html). The activities sponsored by the program create a bond between the mother and daughters but also among the daughters. The daughters, in turn, influence their friends who may not be participating in the program. This activity creates a "college-going culture" in the community, which is essential in encouraging large numbers of students within vulnerable high schools to begin thinking about attending college.

An important by-product of this program is that many mothers, inspired by their daughters' educational successes, have had their aspirations rekindled and have sought their GED (graduate equivalence degree) and enrolled in junior colleges, and some have even graduated from college. The knowledge mothers obtain about the logistics of college is used to explore their own academic dreams and to encourage other women in their communities to pursue education. This model of spreading educational success is not commonly supported in most educational institutions. It is an innovative intervention using naturally occurring networks and alliances to enhance educational achievement (Hurtado, 1997). Educational engagement is not a priori defined as occurring in a linear fashion from parent to child, rather it is a relational analysis of educational achievement that involves naturally occurring human relations and institutional resources and assets to enhance the probability that individuals will become interested in pursuing higher education (Hurtado, 1997).

Lessons Learned

These two examples provide inspiration for broadening our conceptualization of the function of education and its outcomes for individual well-being as well as overall societal health. If second language learning, especially Spanish, is conceptualized as an asset rather than as a barrier to educational achievement, how can these naturally occurring skills be cultivated not only for Latino/a students but for monolingual English-speaking students as well? Why are Spanish-speaking students not treated as experts who can share their skills with other students? When Spanish-speaking students experience limitations in English, pairing them with English-dominant students who want to learn Spanish may be an educational plus for all involved. Given that Spanish knowledge is likely to be desirable in many professions in the near future, Spanish-speaking students (and parents) should be better integrated into the educational process and training of monolinguals. There are many creative ways in which an important asset such as fluency in Spanish could be used in educational institutions at all levels.

The HMDP example also merits consideration for non-Latino/a interventions. For example, if the mother-daughter programs were integrated by ethnicity and race, what would non-Latino/a parents learn about raising children that are connected to families throughout the developmental cycle? What if the programs were integrated by gender so that fathers were also encouraged to become an active part of their daughters' education? What if there was a father-son program? Might such a program diminish the incidence of gang membership, truancy, and drop-out rates among boys of all races and ethnicities? The reconceptualization of the function and purpose of education can benefit from looking beyond Latino/as' lack of educational achievement as a "social problem" and, instead, conceptualize it as providing infinite possibilities for expanding educational theory and practice.

Conclusion

There is no doubt that many challenges remain for educating the majority of Latino/as. These challenges, however, should be viewed within the context of the enormous progress made within the last 30 years. The context should also include the diversity within the Latino/a population based on the national origin, size of the population, and geographical dispersion of each Latino/a group. These factors contribute to a powerful structural context that should be taken into account when developing local and national policy interventions (Oakes et al., 2006). A further consideration is the enormous growth of the Latino/a population. If current demographic projections are correct, educating Latino/as will become an economic and social imperative, as well as a social justice issue. The obstacles obstructing Latino/as' educational achievement also present infinite possibilities for improving education for all students.

Notes

1. We use the ethnic terms that appear in the sources cited. In this case, Chicano/as refers to Mexican ancestry Latino/as.
2. In 2008, California was once again considering reintroducing SB 1301, California's DREAM Act.

References

Banks, J. A. (1995). Multicultural education: Historical development, dimensions, and practice. In J. A. Banks & C. A. McGee Banks (Eds.), *Handbook of research on multicultural education* (pp. 3–24). New York: Macmillan.

California Department of Education. (2007). *Numbers of teachers by ethnicity 1981–2004.* Retrieved July 20, 2008, from http://www.cde.ca.gov/ds/ss/cb/ethteach.asp

Capps, R., Fix, M., & Murray, J. (2005). *The new demography of America's schools: Immigration and the No Child Left Behind Act.* Washington, DC: The Urban Institute.

Carreón, G. P., Drake, C., & Barton, A. C. (2005). The importance of presence: Immigrant parent's school engagement experiences. *American Educational Research Journal, 42*(3), 465–498.

Close, W., & Solberg, S. (2008). Predicting achievement, distress, and achievement among lower-income Latino youth. *Journal of Vocational Behavior, 72*(1), 31–42.

Durand, J., & Massey, D. S. (2003). *Clandestinos: Migracion Mexico Estados Unidos en los albores de siglo XXI* [Clandestine migrations Mexico-United States in the dawn of the 21st century]. Mexico, DF: Editorial Miguel Angel Porrua.

Feliciano, C. (2001). The benefits of biculturalism: Exposure to immigrant culture and dropping out of school among Asian and Latino youths. *Social Science Quarterly, 82*(4), 865–879.

Ferraez, J. (2003, April 1). David Hayes-Bautista: The end of California as we know it—*Q&A. Latino Leaders: The Magazine of the Successful American Latino, 8.* Retrieved July 16, 2008, from http://www.latinoleaders.com/buscar_ejemplar.php?id_ejemplar=6&method=view&ejemplares=2003

Fry, R. (2007). *The changing racial and ethnic composition of U.S. public schools.* Washington, DC: The Pew Hispanic Center.

Gándara, P. (2006). Strengthening the academic pipeline leading to careers in math, science, and technology for Latino students. *Journal of Hispanic Higher Education, 5*(3), 222–237.

Garcia, E. (1994). *Understanding and meeting the challenge of cultural diversity.* Boston, MA: Houghton Mifflin.

Garcia, E. (2001). *Hispanic education in the United States: Raíces y alas* [Roots and wings]. Lanham, MD: Rowman & Littlefield.

Giroux, H. J. (1983). *Theory and resistance in education: A pedagogy for the opposition.* South Hadley, MS: Bergin & Garvey.

Gonzales, R. (2007). Wasted talent and broken dreams: The lost potential of undocumented students. *Immigration Policy In Focus, 5*(13). Retrieved February 8, 2008, from http://www.immigrationpolicy.org/index.php?content=f071001

Gonzalez, N., & Moll, L. C. (2002). Cruzando el puente: Building bridges to funds of knowledge. *Educational Policy, 16*(4), 623–641.

Gurin, P., & Nagda, B. A. (2006). Getting to the "what," "how," and "why" of diversity on campus. *Educational Researcher, 35*(1), 20–24.

Gurin, P., Nagda, B. A., & Lopez, G. E. (2004). The benefits of diversity in education for democratic citizenship. *Journal of Social Issues, 60*(1), 17–34.

Hayes-Bautista, D. (2004). *La nueva California: Latinos in the Golden State.* Berkeley: University of California Press.

hooks, b. (1994). *Teaching to transgress. Education as the practice of freedom.* New York: Routledge.

Huber, L. P., Huidor, O., Malagon, M. C., Sanchez, G., & Solorzano, D. G. (2006). *Falling through the cracks: Critical transitions in the Latina/o educational pipeline. Latina/o Education Summit Report.* CSRC Research Report, no. 7. Los Angeles: UCLA Chicano Studies Research Center.

Hurtado, A. (1997). Understanding multiple group identities: Inserting women into cultural transformations. *Journal of Social Issues 53*(2), 299–238.

Hurtado, A. (2003). *Voicing Chicana feminisms: Young women speak out on sexuality and identity.* New York: New York University Press.

Hurtado, A., García, E., Vega, L. A., & Gonzalez, R. (2003). Beyond stigma: Social identities and the educational achievement of Chicanos. In D. J. León (Ed.), *Latinos in higher education* (pp. 73–84). Oxford, UK: Elsevier Science.

Hurtado, A., & Gurin, P. (2004). *Chicana/o identity in a changing U.S. Society. ¿Quién soy? ¿Quiénes somos?* [Who am I? Who are we?]. Tucson: University of Arizona Press.

Hurtado, A., Haney, C., & Garcia, E. (1998). Becoming the mainstream: Merit, changing demographics, and higher education in California. *La Raza Law Journal, 10*(2), 645–690.

Hurtado, A., & Rodriguez, R. (1989) Language as a social problem: The repression of Spanish in south Texas. *The Journal of Multilingual Multicultural Development, 10,* 401–419.

Hurtado, A., & Vega, L. A. (2004). Shift happens: Spanish and English transmission between parents and their children. *Journal of Social Issues, 60*(1), 137–155.

Immigration Policy Center. (2007). *Dreams deferred: The costs of ignoring undocumented students.* Washington, DC: Immigration Policy Center. Retrieved February 8, 2008, from http://www.immigrationpolicy.org/index.php?content=b070919

Lazarin, M. (2007). *The "Dream Act" and the "American Dream Act." Fact sheet.* Washington, DC: The National Council of La Raza.

Lopez, G. R., Scribner, J. D., & Mahitivanichcha, K. (2001). Redefining parent involvement: Lessons from high-performing migrant-impacted schools. *American Educational Research Journal, 38*(2), 253–288.

McLaren, P. (1997). Decentering whiteness: In search of a revolutionary multiculturalism. *Multicultural Education, 5*(1), 4–11.

Moll, L. C., Amanti, C., Neff, D., & Gonzalez, N. (1992). Funds of knowledge for teaching: Using a qualitative approach to connect homes and classrooms. *Theory into Practice, 31*(2), 132–141.

Nagda, B. A., & Gurin, P. (2007). Intergroup dialogue: A critical-dialogic approach to learning about difference, inequality, and social justice. *New Directions for Teaching and Learning,* (111), 35–45.

National Immigration Law Center. (2007, October). *Dream act: Basic information.* Retrieved February 9, 2008, from http://ww.nilc.org/immlawpolicy/dream/index.htm

Oakes, J., Rogers, J., Silver, D., Valladares, S., Terriquez, V., McDonough, P., et al. (2006). Removing the roadblocks: Fair college opportunities for all California students. Los Angeles: UC/ACCORD & UCLA/ IDEA. Retrieved November 2, 2006, from http://www.ucla-idea.org

Oboler, S. (1995). *Ethnic labels, Latino lives: Identity and politics of (re)presentation in the United States.* Minneapolis: University of Minnesota Press.

Ogbu, J. U. (1978). *Minority education and caste: The American system in cross-cultural perspective.* New York: Academic Press.

Ogbu, J. U. (1991). Minority coping responses and school experience. *The Journal of Psychohistory, 18*(4), 433–456.

Ogbu, J. U. (1993). Differences in cultural frame of reference. *International Journal of Behavioral Development, 16*(3), 483–506.

Padilla, R. (1999). College student retention: Focus on success. *Journal of College Student Retention, 1*(2), 131–145.

Pease-Alvarez, L. (2002). Moving beyond linear trajectories of language shift and bilingual language socialization. *Hispanic Journal of Behavioral Sciences, 24*(2), 114–137.

Phinney, J. S., Dennis, J. M., & Gutierrez, D. M. (2005). College orientation profiles of Latino students from low socioeconomic backgrounds: A cluster analytic approach. *Hispanic Journal of Behavioral Sciences, 27*(4), 387–408.

Ramirez, A. Y. F. (2003). Dismay and disappointment: Parental involvement of Latino immigrant parents. *The Urban Review, 35*(2), 93–110.

Rendón, L. I. (2008). *Sentipensante (sensing/ thinking) pedagogy. Educating for wholeness, social justice, and liberation.* Sterling, VA: Stylus.

Saenz, V. B., Ngai, H. N., & Hurtado, S. (2007). Factors influencing positive interactions across race for African American, Asian American, Latino, and white college students. *Research in Higher Education, 48*(1), 1–38.

Steele, C. M. (1997). A threat in the air: How stereotypes shape intellectual identity and performance. *American Psychologist, 52*(6), 613–629.

Suárez-Orozco, C., & Suárez-Orozco, C. (1995). *Trans-formations. Migration, family life, and achievement motivation among Latino adolescents.* Stanford, CA: Stanford University Press.

Trumbull, E., Rothstein-Fisch, C., Greenfield, P. M., & Quiroz, B. (2001). *Bridging cultures between home and school: A guide for teachers.* Mahwah, NJ: Erlbaum.

Urban Teachers Collaborative. (2000). *The urban teachers challenge: Teachers demand and supply in the great city schools.* Washington, DC: Council of the Great City.

U.S. Census Bureau. (2004). *Facts for features: Teacher appreciation week May 2–8.* Retrieved July 25, 2008, from http://www.census.gov/Press-Release/www/releases/archives/facts_for_features_special_editions/001737.html

U.S. Census Bureau. (2006a). *Louisiana loses population: Arizona edges Nevada as fastest-growing state.* Retrieved June 20, 2008, from http://www.census.gov/Press-Release/www/releases/archives/population/007910.html

U.S. Census Bureau. (2006b). *Minority population tops 100 million.* Retrieved from http://www.census.gov/Press-Release/www/releases/archives/population/010048.html

U.S. Census Bureau. (2007). *Facts for Features: Hispanic heritage month 2007: September 15–October 16.* Retrieved June 20, 2008, from: http://www.census.gov/Press-Release/www/releases/archives/facts_for_features_special_editions/010327.html

U.S. Census Bureau. (2007). *More than 300 counties now "majority-minority."* Retrieved July 28, 2008, from http://www.census.gov/Press-Release/www/releases/archives/population/010482.html

U.S. Census Bureau. (2008). *Facts for features: Hispanic heritage month 2008: September 15–October 16.* Retrieved July 28, 2008, from: http://www.census.gov/Press-Release/www/releases/archives/facts_for_features_special_editions/012245.html

Vélez-Ibáñez, C., & Greenberg, J. (1992). Formation and transformation of funds of knowledge among U.S.-Mexican households. *Anthropology and Education Quarterly, 23*(4), 313–335.

Verdugo, R. (2006). *A report on the status of Hispanics in education: Overcoming a history of neglect.* Washington, DC: National Education Association.

Yosso, T. J. (2005). Whose culture has capital? A Critical race theory discussion of community cultural wealth. *Race Ethnicity and Education, 8*(1), 69–91.

Zarate, M. E. (2007). *Understanding parental involvement in education. Perceptions, expectations, and recommendations.* Los Angeles: The Tomas Rivera Policy Institute.

Zuñiga, X., Nagda, B. A., Chesler, M., & Cytron-Walker, A. (2007). Intergroup dialogue in higher education: Meaningful learning about social justice. *ASHE Higher Educationt Report, 32*(4), 1–28. San Francisco: Jossey-Bass.

20 Misrepresentations of Language and Culture, Language and Culture as Proxies for Marginalization

Debunking the Arguments

Angela E. Arzubiaga and Jennifer Adair

Arizona State University

The term *Latino* refers to a group, which includes descendants of the inhabitants of territories incorporated by the United States, immigrants from several countries, and people of various educational levels, who speak different languages[1] and engage in multiple literacies and cultural practices. The panethnic conception of Latinos in the United States, however, carries the burden of representing a monocultural group that is often represented as the paragon of what is wrong with society. Balibar (1990) argues certain national/cultural groups are demonized, ascribed negative stereotypes, and marginalized to fulfill a scapegoat role. The confluence of sociopolitical, historical, and cultural legacies (e.g., Santa Ana, 2002) mark Latinos and the only language they are mistakenly associated with as the target of these negative projections.

Though the reasons underlying the marginalization of Latinos are complex, and, as previously stated, part of a legacy of sociocultural-historical-political influences, the educational achievement gap between Latinos and White students is often brought to bear as another argument that represents the burdens Latinos impose on U.S. society.[2] Such arguments fuel the discourses on the Latino population and the anti-immigrant rhetoric. In the United States, anti-immigrant discourses are anti-Latino because the majority of immigrants are from Mexico. While there is no denying that an abysmal achievement gap persists between Latina/os and White students,[3] the explanations for these differences in school achievement often rest on assumptions about Latina/os' language and culture.[4]

The achievement gap between Latinos and Whites is often attributed to the language spoken at home or the lack of English spoken in the home (Chapa & De la Rosa, 2004). At the same time, Latina/o students' failure is equated to the failings or the shortcomings of their home culture (Suàrez-Orozco & Suàrez-Orozco, 2001; Valdés, 1996). Though the arguments of attributing children's low achievement to the home culture and their use of Spanish have been refuted (e.g., Jimenez, 2000; Valdés, 2001) assumptions related to these beliefs continue to shape the approaches taken to study Latinos and education (Arzubiaga, 2007; Arzubiaga, Artiles, King, & Murri, 2008; Arzubiaga, Ceja, & Artiles; 2000; Delgado-Gaitán, 2001; Moll, Amanti, Neff, & Gonzalez, 1992).

This chapter draws examples from two major studies, *Proyecto Educando Niños* (*Raising Children Project*; PEN)[5] and *Children Crossing Borders*,[6] funded by the Spencer Foundation, to illustrate important notions related to studying the Latina/o population's language usage and cultural practices. The examples highlight Latina/os ecological pragmatism and their hybrid practices, as well as direct us to examine the multiple ways Latina/os forge cultural pathways for themselves and their children. These examples question the misguided explanations for the educational achievement gap (between Latinos and Whites). They question the explanations because they highlight how arguments about the language of instruction in school and arguments about the poverty of culture of non-dominant groups emerge from worn out fallacies for which we have no more room.

Why Target Spanish?

A prevalent myth about language is that certain groups, whose native language is other than the dominant one, do not want to learn or have their children learn the dominant language. Instead, the opposite is true; generally, language minority groups desire language fluency and proficiency in dominant languages (Cornfield & Arzubiaga, 2004). Concerns about language are rather in regard to the loss of the native language. However, as the following examples demonstrate, it is through language policies, and discourses about language that in the U.S. issues of belonging and entitlement or rights are argued and exercised. In other words, in the United States, the discourses about language and language policies serve the function of perpetuating the marginalization and domination of non-dominant groups including Latinos.

Children Crossing Borders is an ongoing, five country multisited ethnographic approach study. The five countries include France, Germany, Italy, United Kingdom, and the United States. These countries are post-industrial nations that have recently experienced a surge in their immigrant population. The purpose of the study is to bring together the voices of stakeholders, including parents and teachers, to the discourses on the early education of immigrant children.

The core method for data collection was the use of video to stimulate reflection and discussion. The method was developed by Tobin for *Preschool in Three Cultures: Japan, China, and the United States* (1989). The methodology is about the use of video as a cue to stimulate a polyvocal and polypositional conversation. We have adapted this method for the study of how preschool programs in Europe and the United States work with children of im/migrants. Each country made one short (15–20 minute) video of a typical preschool day. The editing was purposefully conducted so that all countries' videos included their routines and had comparable themes such as how discipline was handled by adults. The videos were then shown as an introduction to focus group discussions. Participants watched their country of residence's video and one or two of the other country's video.

Focus groups were conducted in urban, suburban, and semi-rural areas that were traditional and non-traditional immigrant settlement areas including enclave and diaspora communities. For the focus groups, parents of preschoolers met separately from teachers and school personnel. Groups were conducted in the language of participants whenever possible. In the United States, for example, participants included Chinese, Arabic, French, Somali, Spanish, Sudanese, and Taiwanese speakers. Sites included public and private preschools housed in elementary schools, refugee organizations and religious communities. In addition to a range of locations, we purposefully included participants that represented a mix of social class, regions, and national origins.

As mentioned previously, during the focus groups, we found that in the U.S. issues related to language were the most frequently debated. In line with Bakhtin (Bakhtin, Holquist, & Liapunov, 1990), we take the position that the meanings of what people say or their utterances reflect tensions in the larger society in which the speakers live. In Tennessee, for example, one teacher questioned "I know they speak a lot of Spanish, but we're in America. Why don't they speak a lot of American? The kids speak a lot of American. Don't they speak English?" For this teacher speaking English was part of being an American. In fact, the words reflect a conflation between the term American and English. They reveal the tension surrounding language and that English stands for belonging to the teachers' America

However, in the other countries issues about belonging and rights are also present within discussions about themes such as secularism. In France, in contrast to the United States,[7] the debates about belonging are about the expression of religion versus secularism in the context of republicanism. As a teacher in Mantes, France, explains "We are under the school of the Republic, *liberté, égalité, fraternité* [Liberty, equality, brotherhood],[8] or..., in other words, lay, (no) presence of religions.... We try to erase religion, as my colleague was saying." In this manner, contestations about belonging and rights are embedded in discourses about religion.

The national debate in France about diversity in schools emerges through discussions about peoples' rights to engage in the expression of religion within schools (Guenif-Souilamas, 2006).

Policies surrounding the use of the headscarf, for example, represent how who belongs and who is entitled is debated. In France, the contestation of the marginalized including immigrants is played out under the guise of religion.

Ecological Pragmatism

McDermott argues pragmatism is a consequence of culture; people make sense as they adapt within ecologies that classify and organize the tools available to them and the people that use them. In this sense, language as a tool is associated with certain groups and a hierarchy socially and politically constructed around its value. What we have found is that in accordance with what McDermott writes, people's "actions make sense" when we take into account how ecologies organize and stratify the use of English (McDermott, Goldman, & Varenne, 2006). The parents in our study adapted to the classification and organization of uses of language within their local or ecological realities. That is, they made sense of the resources and the constraints of where they lived and acted accordingly to adapt to the language hierarchy.

In response to the U.S. video, which shows a classroom where both Spanish and English were used, we found parents' comments reflected this ecological pragmatism. The video as a stimulus would evoke conversation about language of instruction and parents' preferences generally reflected support for both languages. However, parents' pragmatism was reflected in regard to the role of Spanish. In an extreme example, in Phoenix, Arizona, where the anti-immigrant rhetoric was on the rise a mother stated,

> I have learned English…and the rest of the family speak English at home. But when I came and when my son (came), I forced myself because also, *my children need it*. My children do not speak Spanish because we are in a country where we need this, to speak English. We are not in Mexico anymore. It is important because it is our roots, but we have to think that we are no longer in Mexico and that it is, it is the language here, it's the language here and we have to learn it. We have to make an effort, *not so much for ourselves but for our children*. (Emphasis added)

Ecological pragmatism argues people do not do what they wish they could do but rather they do their best within a set of resources and constraints. The mother believed that for her children to succeed in the United States it was necessary for them to speak only English. This approach to language, in our study, seems to also be linked to the challenges the parents themselves had when they came to the United States. Parents expressed a strong desire to prevent their children from encountering the obstacles they had when they migrated.

However, because parents were located in specific local contexts with diverse resources and constraints that situated English and Spanish in different ways, their concerns with learning English and maintaining Spanish varied and related to these differences. The Children Crossing Borders project held focus groups with over 200 immigrant parents of Latina/o descent. The focus groups took place in preschool classrooms and community centers in several locations in New York, Arizona, Iowa and Tennessee. Latina/o parents in the United States expressed their language preferences for the education of their children based on where they lived and the language resources available to them.

Parents' pragmatism became evident when what they stated is taken into account with information about where they live or where they are forming their positions about language preferences. San Luis, Arizona, is a town on the border with Mexico, which was incorporated to the United States. Its twin city San Luis, Mexico, is a stone's throw away on the other side of the border. Given the history of San Luis, Arizona, Spanish is the language that is spoken as people engage in their everyday activities. From the parents' perspective, English is the language that children will need to receive support for in the schools.

A parent in San Luis, for example, stated, "What they need the most here is English." Another mother agreed "They should focus more in English in the school, the teachers should do it (teaching) in English" because "they (children) practice Spanish with us, so they can speak more English here (preschool)." Parents appear ecologically pragmatic, aware of the resources and constraints of where they live; they balance these notions with the language needs they foresee their children will have later as adults.

In Columbus Junction, Iowa, parents had a different stance in regard to their language preferences for the education of their children. There, parents were more concerned about children losing their Spanish. One mother stated, "Well if we could choose we all would say to have Spanish." Another mother explained why parents would choose Spanish:

> Because there are some times when some parents don't speak English at all and sometimes the kids well, like in the school it's pure English, and at home too they (parents) tell them something and they (children) don't understand because they don't, don't practice much. Even though sometimes the mother tells them (to speak in Spanish) but they don't, sometimes they don't know what Spanish is.

Parents' concern about the loss of Spanish was also based on the language resources available to their children given where they lived. Columbus Junction was destined to be a ghost town until the people employed at a meatpacking plant revived it. The newcomers, mostly Mexicans, were aware that they were surrounded by predominantly English-speaking towns that are facing, for the first time, changes in their demographic landscape. Parents believed that children would learn English as part of their everyday activities, but Spanish would be harder to maintain.

Parents' pragmatism led them to make difficult choices. These choices, when examined out of context, can lead to mistaken assumptions about Latina/o parents. For example, at one of the elementary schools in Iowa, issues about a bilingual program that ended abruptly were discussed. On the one hand, the teachers and the principal explained that there was little interest in the bilingual program. They stated parents were supportive and satisfied with English-only instruction. The school personnel believed the assistance parents received from one family-resource staff, a native Spanish speaker, was sufficient to address parents' language needs. On the other hand, when we met separately with parents, they had a different perspective on the cancellation of the bilingual program. Parents explained that the meeting to discuss the bilingual program was in the evening and because they worked in the meat-packing plant they had been unable to attend. One parent stated that making the meeting mandatory would help parents to attend. "It's that here for us to be able to come to a meeting there has to be a mandatory note. Just like there in my village." Parents agreed with the suggestion of making the meeting mandatory and another parent reiterated that he could only miss work if it was made mandatory. "I work there in the factory and they only let you go if it's mandatory, and if not, they don't let you."

The difficult choices parents made were pragmatic because they chose not to miss work and not to endanger their employment over attending a meeting about language of instruction at school. When parents have to face being able to provide for their families or not, they make sensible or rational choices. The parents were torn, but chose the less risk to the maintenance of their household. A few parents chose to attend but most parents chose to go to work. Parents emphasized the strict leave policies of the factory.

Misconceptualizations of Culture Make Culture Become a Symbol of Shortcomings

Noted earlier, was the notion that Latina/o students' failure is often equated to the failings or the shortcomings of their home culture (García, 2001). These views on Latina/o culture stem from perspectives which equate poverty with poverty of culture.[9] Louie (2005) argues the culture of poverty arguments continue to shape the conceptualization of non-dominant groups. In the past decade, however, research on Latina/os (e.g., Gonzáles, Andrade, Civil, & Moll, 2001; Moll & González, 1996) has turned this argument around by interrogating rather the politics involved in what counts as knowledge in the schools and questioning who sets the norm.

Sedentarist assumptions about place (Malkki, 1992) lead to representations of Latina/o culture as driven by static cultural models disaffected by place or time. Sedentarist assumptions about place that root people, ethnic groups, communities to specific physical places contribute to the conceptualization of the displaced, disenfranchised, marginalized, as missing something, lacking, or in deficit. Misconceptualizations of culture or research approaches that study culture as static contribute to the perpetuation of myths about Latina/os. They lead to trait-based statements about Latina/os, which distract from understanding cultural practices.

The *Proyecto Educando Niños* (PEN) is a study on the socialization of preschoolers of Mexican descent. The study focused on 26 families living in the Phoenix metropolitan area or the Bay Area in California. Participants were either second or third generation Mexican descent with a child between 3 and 4 years of age. All 26 of the families asked to join the study, except one, and continued to participate throughout the study. The families included 18 second-generation (first generation mothers), and 8 third-generation families (second generation mothers). Second-generation families were defined as families with a U.S.-born child and Mexican born parents. Third-generation families had a U.S.-born child, U.S.-born parents, and at least one Mexican-born grandparent. All families had a child between 3 and 4 years old. Twelve of the 26 children were male, and 8 of the children did not go to preschool.

Data collection methods included participant observations, structured and semistructured interviews, and spot observations. Mothers were also individually interviewed during the course of three separate meetings about demographics, their immigration experience, and their experiences within institutions including schools. The interviews were audio recorded, transcribed, and translated.

Participant observations of families took place over the course of 9 months and included a minimum of 12 home visits. Field workers shadowed families as they engaged in their everyday practices at home and in their communities. The fieldworkers included native Spanish speakers who introduced themselves as either researchers or research assistants from their universities. Fieldworkers often engaged by helping mothers with household chores. The visits were approximately between one and five hours in length of time. The average time per visit was two hours. By examining the cultural practices families engaged in routinely with their children we were able to study the variety of practices which constituted children's cultural pathways. Cultural pathways are made up of everyday routines of life which in turn are made up of children's cultural activities (Weisner, 2002).

We found important cultural models embedded in families' practices. *Cultural models* are shared meanings and understandings about the way the world is organized and works (D'Andrade & Strauss, 1992). For example, the concept of *buena educación* represents an important cultural model for immigrants from Mexico (Valdés, 1996; Villenas, 2002; Villenas & Dehyle, 1999). Buena educación centers around *respeto* (respect), moral values, and loyalty to family. Or as one participant stated, "this is were you put it all together: respect, obedience, responsibility with your family. Being the best that you can be."

What needs to be emphasized, however, is that families' practices revealed the many different ways buena educación was exercised. In the pursuit of providing children a buena educación, parents engaged in practices with their children that looked like school practices and practices that were less formal. They engaged in practices, which involved explicit teaching and practices when teaching was implicit.

Parents' teachings related to buena educación included the construction of polite and appropriate interpersonal courtesies related to "being respectful" or "showing respect" and presenting oneself respectfully. These practices however were not limited to good manners but rather were part of how children were to understand their obligations to others. In some instances parents' teachings were clearly related to comportment or polite behavior, such as when one of the children, Titatalln wanted to use chopsticks to eat her food and asked her dad to teach her how to use them. He took a pair of chopsticks and showed her how to hold them, "hold them, like, just like a pencil," he said as Titatalln tried to imitate him. Later, Titatalln successfully picked up a piece of chicken and put it in her mouth.

In other instances the practices displayed several characteristics and goals of officially sanctioned knowledge. For example, when Titatalln put the chopsticks together to form a "T" and said, "Mommy, 'T' for Titatalln," her mother responded, "Yes, Titatalln, very good!" praising her. "Okay, can you make an 'I' now?" asked the mother displaying explicit academic sanctioned knowledge. The mother continued to direct Titatalln to use the two chopsticks to spell out the remaining letters of her name, "make a 'T,' now an 'A' and an 'L,' another 'L,' and an 'N.' You spelled your name! Very good!" Both parents praised the child for following their directions. Titatalln smiled and continued to eat with her chopsticks. Her parents had followed her lead and purposefully supported her learning of the officially sanctioned alphabet.

At other times the hybrid nature of parents' teaching practices was also evident. For example, during a dinner conversation a family recounted stories from their past in Mexico. The story was about how some boys in their community had been *groseros* (rude). Fabiola, the mother, asked her son, Alex, to explain the children's behavior to their guest. After Alex spoke, Fabiola made it clear that the rude boys' behavior was unacceptable and warned her son about the consequences of such behavior. In this example, the family's practice of storytelling became an opportunity for the preschooler to engage in narrative skills, but a lesson on buena educación was also embedded in the conversation. The practice involved both implicit and explicit instructions which exposed its hybrid characteristics. Both sanctioned knowledge and storytelling were goals of the practice, but, more to the point, the practice was held by a cultural model of buena educación. The buena educación model shaped the development of the practice because it was bound to different purposes. The purposes included socializing Alex into ways of entertaining guests, developing storytelling skills, and constructing his identity as a person who is *bien educado* or in other words worthy, valuable, and valued.

Conclusions

In the United States, issues of belonging and entitlement or rights are argued and exercised through language policies, and discourses about language. These discourses about language and language policies serve the function of perpetuating the marginalization and domination of non-dominant groups including Latina/os. Our Children Crossing Borders study revealed the place language has in parents' and teachers' discourses. We found that issues related to language are those most frequently debated. Utterances reflected the tensions in the larger society or communities where speakers lived. Parents' positions in regard to these tensions revealed their ecological pragmatism or their rational approach in response to the resources and constraints of their ecologies. In other words, they made sense of the resources and the constraints of where they lived and acted accordingly to adapt to the language hierarchy.

The maintenance of languages other than English will depend on the opportunities afforded people. Mexican descent parents appeared ecologically pragmatic, aware of the resources and constraints of where they lived; they balanced these notions with the language needs they foresaw their children would have later as adults. If current trends continue, the United States will continue to be the cemetery of languages due to nativist sentiments (Louie, 2005). In an increasingly globalized world, the United States may miss the opportunity to nurture the language skills its children could potentially develop.

Misconceptualizations of *culture* make culture a symbol of shortcomings. Sedentarist assumptions about place lead to representations of Latina/o culture as driven by static cultural models disaffected by place or time. The PEN study allowed us to identify a rich set of practices associated with the cultural model of buena educación. The practices exposed how cultural practices were dynamic adaptations that at times involved powerful lessons beyond those officially recognized in the classroom. There is a need for the continued interrogation of the politics involved in what counts as knowledge in the schools and who sets the norm. Questioning whose cultural practices and knowledge count will lead us to understand that there needs to be room for the cultural practices and languages of all. Studying the cultural practices of Mexican descent families revealed a rich set of practices bound by the resources and constraints of where they lived. More importantly, however, they were evidence of the adaptability of families. Such practices need to be nurtured and valued.

Notes

1. Latinos in the United States include people whose native languages include, for example, French, Mixtec, Portuguese, Spanish, and Quichua.
2. Murillo (2002) argues Latinos are represented as takers not givers.
3. The achievement gap is between Whites and other non-dominant groups.
4. Gloria Ladson Billings argues discussions about the achievement gap should rather be about the education debt. In other words, she directs us to focus on the production of the achievement gap and the failure of society and government in meeting the educational needs of all students.
5. *Proyecto Educando Niños*, is codirected by Angela E. Arzubiaga, Margaret Bridges, Bruce Fuller, and Eugene Garcia (alphabetical order), with generous funding from the Spencer Foundation.
6. The Spencer Foundation funds the United States portion of the international study. *Children Crossing Borders,* funded by the Bernard van Leer Foundation, includes five countries' study of immigrants and preschool.
7. People have migrated to the United States, in the past, seeking freedom of religion.
8. The slogan of the French revolution and the first French Republic.
9. Though there is a range of variation, Latina/os in the United States earn less money as a group than Whites, and children from immigrant families are more likely to be poor.

References

Arzubiaga, A. (2007). Transcending deficit thinking about Latina/o parents. In L. Diaz Soto (Ed.), *Latino education in the U.S.: An encyclopedia* (pp. 102–105). Westport, CT: Greenwood Press.

Arzubiaga, A., Artiles, A., King, K., & Murri, N. (2008). Beyond culturally responsive research: Challenges and implications of research as situated cultural practice. *Exceptional Children, 74,* 309–327.

Arzubiaga, A., Ceja, M., Artiles, A. J. (2000). Transcending deficit thinking about Latinos' parenting styles: Toward an ecocultural view of family life. In C. Tejada, C. Martinez, & Z. Leonardo (Eds.), *Charting new terrains of Chicana(o)/Latina(o) education* (pp. 93–106). Cresskill, NJ: Hampton Press.

Bakhtin, M. M., Holquist, M., & Liapunov, V. (1990). *Art and answerability: Early philosophical essays* (1st ed.). Austin: University of Texas Press.

Balibar, E. (1990). Paradoxes of universality. In D. T. Goldberg (Ed.), *Anatomy of racism* (pp. 283–294). Minneapolis: University of Minnesota Press.

Chapa, J., & De la Rosa, B. (2004). Latino population growth, socioeconomic and demographic characteristics, and implications for educational attainment. *Education and Urban Society, 36,* 130–149.

Cornfield, D. B., & Arzubiaga, A. (2004). Immigrants and education in the US interior: Integrating and segmenting tendencies in Nashville, Tennessee. *Peabody Journal of Education, 79,* 157–179.

D'Andrade, R., & Strauss, C. (Eds.). (1992). *Human motives and cultural models.* Cambridge, UK: Cambridge University Press.

Delgado-Gaitán, C. (2001). *The power of community: Mobilizing for family and schooling.* Lanham, MD: Rowman & Littlefield.

García, E. (2001). *Hispanic education in the United States: Raíces y Alas*. Boulder, CO: Rowman & Littlefield.

Gonzáles, N., Andrade, R., Civil, M., & Moll, L. (2001). Bridging funds of distributed knowledge: Creating zones of practices in mathematics. *Journal of Education for Students Placed At-Risk*, 6(1, 2), 115–132.

Guenif-Souilamas, N. (2006). The other French exception: Virtuous racism and the war of the sexes in postcolonial France. *French Politics, Culture and Society*, 24(3), 23–41.

Jimenez, R. (2000). Literacy and the identity development of Latina/o students. *American Educational Research Journal*, 37, 971–1000.

Louie, V. (2005). Immigrant newcomer populations, ESEA, and the pipeline to college: Current considerations and future lines of inquiry. *Review of Research in Education*, 29, 69–105.

Malkki, L. (1992). National geographic: The rooting of peoples and the territoralization of national identity among scholars and refugees. *Cultural Anthropology*, 7, 24–44.

McDermott, R., Goldman, S., & Varenne, H. (2006). The cultural work of Learning Disabilities. *Educational Researcher*, 35(6), 12–17.

Moll, L. C., Amanti, C., Neff, D., & Gonzalez, N. (1992). Funds of knowledge for teaching: Using a qualitative approach to connect homes and classrooms. *Theory into Practice*, 31, 132–141.

Moll, L., & González, N. (1996). Teachers as social scientists: learning about culture from household research. In P. M. Hall (Ed.), *Race, ethnicity and multiculturalism: Missouri Symposium on Research and Educational Policy* (Vol. 1, pp. 89–114). New York: Garland

Murillo, E. G., Jr. (2002). How does it feel to be a problem?: "Disciplining" the transnational subject in the American South. In S. Wortham, E. G. Murillo, Jr., & E. T. Hamann (Eds.), *Education in the new Latino diaspora* (pp. 215–240). Westport, CT: Greenwood.

Santa Ana, O. (2002). *Brown tide rising: Metaphors of Latinos in contemporary American public discourse*. Austin: University of Texas Press.

Suàrez-Orozco, C., & Suárez-Orozco, M. M. (2001). *Children of immigration*. Cambridge, MA: Harvard University Press.

Tobin, J. J. (1989). *Preschool in three cultures: Japan, China, and the United States*. New Haven, CT: Yale University Press.

Valdés, G. (1996). *Con respeto: Bridging the distances between culturally diverse families and schools*. New York: Teachers College Press.

Valdés, G. (2001). *Learning and not learning English: Latino students in American schools*. New York: Teachers College Press.

Villenas, S. (2002). Reinventing education in new Latino communities: Pedagogies of change and continuity in North Carolina. In S. Wortham, E. G. Murillo, Jr., & E. T. Hamann (Eds.), *Education in the new Latino diaspora* (pp. 215–240). Westport, CT: Greenwood.

Villenas, S., Dehyle, D. (1999). Critical race theory and ethnographies challenging the stereotypes: Latino families, schooling, resilience and resistance. *Curriculum Inquiry*, 29(4), 413–445.

Weisner, T. S. (2002). Ecocultural understanding of children's development pathways. *Human Development*, 45, 275–281.

21 Bilingualism

An Overview of the Linguistic Research

Kellie Rolstad and Jeff MacSwan

Arizona State University

Bilingualism refers to the ability to speak two (or more) languages, either at the individual level or within a community. Bilingualism is a large and vibrant field internationally; in the U.S. context, it has long centered on Spanish speakers in the Latino community. Bilingualism can develop simultaneously, as when two languages are acquired in infancy (*simultaneous bilingualism*), or sequentially (*sequential bilingualism*), as in the case of second language acquisition. In significant respects, the field of bilingualism emerged in response to the suggestion among researchers in related fields that bilingualism in and of itself is a source of difficulty for Latino children's cognitive and academic development, a notion now known to be false. (See Appel & Muysken, 1984; and Zentella, 1997, for additional general information.)

U.S. Bilingualism

In a famous and oft-quoted definition of bilingualism, Haugen (1956) said that bilingualism began at the point where the speaker of one language could produce complete meaningful utterances in another language. While others have insisted that "true bilinguals" are equally capable of discussing any topic in either language (*ambilingualism*), a more common view is that, because bilinguals typically use their languages in different domains of interaction, they should be expected to develop non-overlapping vocabularies. Indeed, Fishman, Cooper, and Ma (1971) have argued that this *diglossia*, or use of separate languages in distinct domains, has the effect of preserving bilingualism in communities where social and political forces may discourage it.

Although the United States is widely perceived internally and externally as a monolingual English-speaking society, there are, in fact, numerous bilingual communities with long histories throughout the country. The 2000 U.S. census determined that 18% of people aged 5 and over, or 47 million individuals, spoke a language other than English at home. Of these, 60% reported speaking Spanish as their heritage language. Nearly three quarters of Spanish speakers in the United States said that they speak English "well" or "very well," while 18% reported that they could not speak English well and 10% said they could not speak English at all. In all, 25.2 million surveyed indicated that they were bilingual in English and Spanish, with varying levels of English proficiency, constituting just about 10% of the total U.S. population aged 5 or older. Between 1990 and 2000, there was an overall increase of 62% in the number of Spanish speakers in the United States, and an increase of about 51% for speakers of other non-English languages in the same time period.

While Spanish speakers in the United States live predominantly in the West, they may be found in all regions of the country. The Northeast is home to 4.5 million Spanish speakers; 2.6 million live in the Midwest, 9.9 million in the South, and 11.1 million in the West. The concentration of Spanish speakers is especially high in areas which border Mexico. In seven counties in Texas, for instance, more than 80% of the population spoke a language other than English at home (see Shin & Brun, 2003, for more information).

Bilingual Language Acquisition

Researchers in bilingualism have long been concerned with the question of whether children who grow up with two languages initially develop a unified linguistic system which later separates, or begin with two separate linguistic systems from the earliest stages of acquisition. Early research on bilingual language acquisition proposed that children initially use both linguistic systems in an undifferentiated manner, and that a gradual process of separation begins with the lexicon (vocabulary), then moves on to morphology (rules or word formation), and finally to syntax (rules of word order). However, critics of this perspective charged that, on close analysis, there is no compelling evidence for the presence of an undifferentiated language system in early bilinguals. Indeed, nearly all of the evidence appears to have relied on the observation that infant bilinguals frequently do not have "translation equivalents" for items in their lexicon, an observation true of many adult bilinguals as well.

More recently, research has focused on grammatical (rather than lexical) aspects of bilingual language development, and it has been found that the two systems appear to be differentiated from the earliest stages. Although simultaneous bilinguals appear to have separate grammatical systems for their two languages from the earliest stages of development, they often mix their languages in a variety of ways—*codeswitching, borrowing,* and *calquing,* among them. We separately address each of these aspects of language contact directly.

Codeswitching

Codeswitching is a speech style in which fluent bilinguals switch languages between or within sentences. For instance, Spanish-English bilinguals might say, *This morning mi hermano y yo fuimos a comprar some milk* ("This morning my brother and I went to buy some milk"), where the sentence begins in English, switches to Spanish, and then moves back to English again. Codeswitching within a single sentence like this is called *intrasentential codeswitching*; codeswitching between sentences is known as *intersentential codeswitching*. In the past, educators and others often assumed that codeswitching was indicative of a language disability of some kind. It was often alleged that bilinguals used codeswitching as a "coping strategy" for incomplete mastery of both languages. However, recent research into the social and linguistic characteristics of codeswitching indicate that it is a marker of bilingual identity, and has its own internal grammatical structure just like monolingual language.

The term *codeswitching* itself emerged in the 1950s and 1960s, and became a well-established, independent field of research by the 1970s. At the Thirteenth Annual Round Table Meeting on Linguistics and Languages at Georgetown University, held in 1962, Haugen claimed origination of the term; however, the word first appeared in print in Vogt's (1954) review of Weinreich's (1953) *Languages in Contact* and two years later in Haugen (1956), according to Benson (2001). Despite these early interests, an actual codeswitching research literature did not emerge until the late 1960s and early 1970s, when work focusing on both social and grammatical aspects of language mixing began steadily appearing with scholarly engagement of previously published research.

Gumperz (1967, 1982), an early researcher in the field, identified six major functions of conversational codeswitching: (a) quotation, (b) addressee specification, (c) interjection, (d) reiteration, (e) message qualification, and (f) personification vs. objectification. Gumperz analyzed codeswitching as a discourse strategy, and found that participants in his study were able to use it effectively to convey meaning and build group identity. In related work, Wei, Milroy, and Ching (1992) have further developed a *social network theory* of bilingual codeswitching.

In addition to the social aspects of bilingual codeswitching, much attention has been given to the study of its linguistic structure. Like monolingual language, bilingual codeswitching is highly structured and rule-governed. Specifically, language mixture appears to be constrained by the interaction of subtle grammatical principles in bilingual speech. For instance, simultaneous bilinguals commonly codeswitch between subjects and verbs, as in *Mis amigos finished first* ("My friends finished first"), but would judge codeswitches between a subject pronoun and a verb (like *Ellos finished first*, "They finished first") to be ungrammatical. (By ungrammatical, we mean that simultaneous native bilinguals presented with this sentence have a negative psychological reaction similar to the reaction English speakers have to sentences like *Martin built a barn red*, in contrast to our positive reaction to *Martin painted a barn red*; our subconscious knowledge of grammar tells us that the first sentence is structurally flawed but the second is fine.)

A number of linguists have formulated theories about the underlying structure of codeswitching. Poplack's (1980) Equivalence Constraint and Free Morpheme Constraint are among the most widely known. Poplack's Equivalence Constraint postulated that codeswitches will tend to occur where word orders are similar in the two languages. For instance, in English, object pronouns follow the verb, whereas in Spanish they precede the verb. Thus, while bilingual codeswitchers regard *I saw la muchacha* ("I saw the girl") as well-formed, *Yo her ví* or *Yo ví her* ("I saw her") is judged to be ill-formed. In Poplack's view, the difference in psychological judgment is explained by the Equivalence Constraint: The first example (*I saw la muchacha*) is well-formed because the English and Spanish word orders are the same at the junction of the switch, but the second example (*Yo ví her*) is ill-formed because English and Spanish word orders differ in this instance. Poplack's Free Morpheme Constraint posits that codeswitches cannot occur between a free morpheme (a word that can stand alone, like *walk* or *eat* in English) and a bound morpheme (a meaningful part of a word that cannot stand alone, like *-ed* in the English word *walked*, or *-ó* in Spanish *habló*, "He spoke"). This constraint is intended to explain the ungrammaticality of examples like *He eat-ó* ("He ate"), where a Spanish bound morpheme (*-ó*, past tense marker) is attached to an English free morpheme (eat).

Although Poplack's work, carried out in the early 1980s, is illustrative and perhaps most accessible to non-specialists, considerable research has been done on the grammatical structure of codeswitching since her initial studies. As mainstream linguistic theory continued to develop, it led to new insights into our understanding of bilingual codeswitching in subsequent decades. For instance, a recently proposed theory of codeswitching applies current work in syntactic theory known as the Minimalist Program to the data of language mixture, arguing that the contemporary "lexicalist character" of syntax, in which hierarchical sentence structure is built from a small (and possibly bilingual) set of lexical items, is sufficient to account for the grammatical restrictions observed by earlier researchers (see MacSwan, 2000a, 2004, 2009).

Contrary to early impressions, the linguistic study of bilingual codeswitching has revealed that simultaneous bilinguals, just like monolinguals, are sensitive to extremely subtle requirements of their linguistic systems, and use their languages creatively to satisfy a variety of social purposes, and to achieve a sense of identity as part of a bilingual or multilingual community.

Borrowings and Calques

Words are often *borrowed* from one language by another in situations of language contact. Similarly, language contact often results in *calquing*, expressions which appear to use the grammar of one language but the vocabulary of another. Although borrowing is common in contact situations, the degree to which speakers are aware of the non-native character of borrowed words may differ with each borrowed item.

For instance, a monolingual English speaker might use the term *pork* without the slightest awareness that it was borrowed from French during the Norman Conquest. On the other hand, a speaker might use the expression *tour de force* fully aware that the expression is of French origin.

In this latter case, the English speaker may have some grasp of the grammatical structure of the phrase without having full knowledge of the grammar of French. An English speaker who encounters the French word *genre* may also have difficulty pronouncing the word (because the first sound of the word introduces a sequence which English phonology does not readily permit).

Borrowing should be carefully distinguished from codeswitching. Borrowed words are usually marked by what has been called *morphological nativization*. For instance, Nahuatl, an indigenous language in Mexico which has borrowed heavily from Spanish, marks Spanish verbs incorporated into the language with the thematic suffixes *-oa* (transitive), *-(i)hui* (intransitive), and *-lia* (applicative). Thus, a Nahuatl speaker might say *Costarihui in neca trabajo* ("That work is costly"), where the Nahuatl intransitive suffix has been affixed to the Spanish word *costar* ("cost"). So marked, these Spanish words have been morphologically nativized, and can no longer be regarded as Spanish words, except in an etymological sense (just as the English word *pork* is etymologically French, but an English speaker who uses it is not necessarily a French-English bilingual).

Another indication that a word has been borrowed is *phonological nativization*. Here, the *loan item* (or word borrowed from another language) is pronounced using the sound system of the language into which it has been borrowed, as when English speakers pronounce the Spanish-origin word *taco* with aspiration following the /t/ and a [w]-off glide following the /o/, among other features characteristic of English phonology. Most speakers of English who use the word *taco*, then, use it as an English word, and could not be said to be bilingual simply because they incorporated this word into their vocabulary. Such speakers are borrowing words from other languages, but they are not codeswitching. Codeswitching involves the use of more than one language in a single sentence or block of discourse, and can only be done by bilinguals.

It is also possible to borrow only pragmatic or morphosyntactic properties while using the phonetic material of the native language; this is the case of *calques*, also called "loan translations." These are special instances of borrowing in which the phonetic properties of words from one language are used in combination with pragmatic or morphological properties of words from another. For instance, Nahuatl speakers in the towns around the Malinche Volcano use *Nimayana* ("I am hungry"); however, while conducting research on Nahuatl in Mexico, Hill and Hill (1986) observed a Spanish-Nahuatl bilingual who used the expression *Nicpia apiztli*, which literally means "I have hunger," apparently modeled after the Spanish equivalent *Tengo hambre* ("I have hunger"). Thus, while *Nicpia apiztli* is well-formed from the point of view of grammar (just as English "I have hunger" is well-formed), we might think of this loan translation as pragmatically, or perhaps stylistically, disfavored.

Research on codeswitching, borrowing, and calques, among other aspects of language contact, provides evidence that bilinguals are exquisitely sensitive to extremely nuanced aspects of linguistic knowledge associated with both their languages. Prior to the emergence of an active field of research, instances of language contact were naively assumed to illustrate language confusion, and educational institutions might have imposed any number of "remedies" on bilingual children in school.

Bilingualism and the Education of Linguistic Minorities

School is a domain of language use, so it is expected that children will develop school vocabulary in whatever language or languages happen to be used at school. Research has shown that language minority children, who speak a non-majority language which is generally stigmatized in the larger community, benefit from instruction in their native language at school. Bilingual instruction allows these children to develop school-related vocabulary in their native language while learning English. More importantly, however, it allows them to keep up academically with other children because they are able to understand instruction during the years it takes to master English.

Rolstad, Mahoney, and Glass (2005), for instance, reviewed research on language programs for English learners conducted in the two decades prior to their work. Using meta-analysis, a research tool which summarizes the relative effectiveness of competing treatments, the researchers found that schools which provided home language support for the longest period of time were the most effective at helping children overcome language barriers. Children enrolled in Transitional Bilingual Education (TBE) programs, where Spanish-language support is phased out after the first two or three years, performed better on academic tests than did children enrolled in English-only programs. Moreover, children enrolled in Bilingual Maintenance Programs, in which students remain in bilingual classes for the duration of their educational experience, did even better than TBE students. Another popular program model, known as Dual Language Immersion, enrolls English- and Spanish-speaking children in roughly equal numbers with the goal of all students becoming bilingual. These programs function as Bilingual Maintenance Programs for the Spanish speakers in the class and as foreign language immersion programs for the English speaking children. Research on bilingual programs has led to a fairly clear understanding of the expected factual outcomes regarding language of instruction in the classroom: Children enrolled in bilingual programs will outperform children enrolled in English-only programs. An equally important research question that is more theoretical in nature asks why children do better under these conditions, and what role language plays.

Some researchers concerned with the education of linguistic minorities have characterized school-related language as a kind of special stage of linguistic development which evidences "complex syntax" and "expanded vocabulary." However, while there certainly are vocabulary, speech styles and other aspects of language which are peculiar to the school environment, there is no empirical or theoretical justification for the claim that these forms constitute a stage of greater linguistic sophistication. The language of school is domain-focused, like the language of farms or the language of fast-food restaurants, but the presumption that it is more sophisticated derives from social and political values, not empirically-grounded linguistic analysis.

Nonetheless, the view is widespread, and has been extremely influential in the scholarly literature on bilingual education. Cummins (1979), for instance, proposed the Threshold Hypothesis, in which he hypothesized that negative cognitive and academic effects result from low levels of competence in both languages. Following Scandinavian researchers, Cummins referred to this presumed "low ability" in both languages as *semilingualism*, but later changed the term to *limited bilingualism*.

Although the Threshold Hypothesis has been widely publicized, evidence presented in support of the associated idea of semilingualism has not been persuasive. Paulston (1983), for instance, reviewed numerous Scandinavian studies which sought linguistic evidence for the existence of semilingualism in Sweden, and found no empirical evidence to support that such a thing exists. MacSwan (2000b) reviewed reputed evidence from studies of language variation, linguistic structure, school performance, and language loss, and concluded that it was all either spurious or irrelevant to the basic proposal. A concept related to semilingualism in Cummins's framework is the distinction between BICS (Basic Interpersonal Communication Skills) and CALP (Cognitive Academic Language Proficiency). Again, critics have been uncomfortable with equating the language of school, and hence the language of the educated classes, with language that is said to be inherently more complex, richer, and which places greater demands on cognitive resources. See MacSwan and Rolstad (2003) for further discussion of Cummins' BICS/CALP dichotomy.

Conclusion

Although much has been learned, the study of bilingualism is still very much in its infancy. However, the field appears to be growing and to be attracting great interest throughout the world. The social and linguistic analysis of bilingual speech is an exciting field with implications for linguistics, psychology, education, and a host of other areas of inquiry. Latinos in the United States and other groups with large numbers of bilinguals stand to benefit from an improved understanding of bilingualism. The research illuminates our understanding of knowledge and use of language among bilinguals, and therefore informs all domains of human life where language is used—school, yes, and everywhere else.

References

Appel, R., & Muysken, P. (1984). *Language contact and bilingualism*. New York: Edward Arnold.

Benson, E. J. (2001). The neglected early history of codeswitching research in the United States. *Language & Communication, 21*(1), 23–36.

Cummins, J. (1979). Linguistic interdependence and the educational development of bilingual children. *Review of Educational Research, 49*, 221–251.

Fishman, J. A., Cooper, R. L., & Ma, R. (1971). *Bilingualism in the barrio*. Bloomington: Language Science Monographs, Indiana University.

Gumperz, J. (1967). On the linguistic markers of bilingual communication. *Journal of Social Issues, 28*(2), 48–57.

Gumperz, J. (1982). *Discourse strategies*. Cambridge, UK: Cambridge University Press.

Haugen, E. (1956). *The Norwegian language in America*. Philadelphia: University of Pennsylvania Press.

Hill, J. H., & Hill, K. C. (1986). *Speaking Mexicano: Dynamics of syncretic language in central Mexico*. Tucson: The University of Arizona Press.

MacSwan, J. (2000a). The architecture of the bilingual language faculty: Evidence from codeswitching. *Bilingualism: Language and Cognition, 3*(1), 37–54.

MacSwan, J. (2000b). The threshold hypothesis, semilingualism, and other contributions to a deficit view of linguistic minorities. *Hispanic Journal of Behavioral Sciences, 20*(1), 3–45.

MacSwan, J. (2004). Code switching and linguistic theory. In T. K. Bhatia & W. Ritchie (Eds.), *Handbook of bilingualism* (pp. 415–462). Oxford, UK: Blackwell.

MacSwan, J. (2009). Generative approaches to codeswitching. In A. J. Toribio & B. E. Bullock (Eds.), *Cambridge handbook of linguistic codeswitching* (pp. 309–335). Cambridge, UK: Cambridge University Press.

MacSwan, J., & Rolstad, K. (2003). Linguistic diversity, schooling, and social class: Rethinking our conception of language proficiency in language minority education. In C. B. Paulston & R. Tucker (Eds.), *Sociolinguistics: The essential readings* (pp. 329–340). Oxford, UK: Blackwell.

Paulston, C. B. (1983). *Swedish research and debate about bilingualism*. Stockholm: National Swedish Board of Education.

Poplack, S. (1980). Sometimes I'll start a sentence in Spanish y termino en Español: Toward a typology of code-switching. *Linguistics, 18*, 581–618.

Rolstad, K., Mahoney, K., & Glass, G. V. (2005). The big picture: A meta-analysis of program effectiveness research on English language learners. *Educational Policy, 19*, 572–594.

Shin, H. B., & Brun, R. (2003). *Language use and English-speaking ability: 2000*. Washington, DC: U.S. Department of Commerce.

Vogt, H. (1954). Review of languages in contact. *Word, 10*, 79–82.

Wei, L., Milroy, L., & Ching, P.-S. (1992). A two-step sociolinguistic analysis of code-switching and language choice. *International Journal of Applied Linguistics, 2*(1), 63–86.

Weinreich, U. (1953). *Languages in contact*. The Hague: Mouton.

Zentella, A. C. (1997). *Growing up bilingual: Puerto Rican children in New York*. Oxford, UK: Blackwell.

22 Language, Culture, and Cognition

From Research to Improving Educational Practice for Latino Students

Virginia González
University of Cincinnati

In this chapter, I attempt to review the state-of-the-art of research contributions aimed at improving educational practices with Latino students by focusing on the interface between language, cognition, and culture from an Ethnic Researcher approach. First, I will discuss this philosophical and theoretical framework, comparing its developmental characteristics and its continuities and discontinuities with traditional approaches to the study of the interaction of language, cognition, and culture. Second, I will present a Socio-Constructivistic approach to the study of cognitive development, taking into account socio-cultural factors such as language and culture in the case of Latino low socio-economic status (SES) students. Finally, I will close by discussing some educationally applied implications of research for improving the state-of-the-art of instructional and assessment practices with Latino low SES students in the U.S. public school system, and finally for teacher preparation programs. Throughout the sections, emphasis will be given to the discussion of socio-cultural factors, such as language, culture, and poverty, on cognitive and learning processes and academic achievement in Latino students.

An Ethnic Researcher Approach to the Study of Language, Cognition, and Culture

The Ethnic Researcher approach is a philosophical, theoretical, and methodological framework that is ecological and developmental. It studies the interface of cognition, culture, and language from a multidimensional perspective. With this approach, the interaction of cognition, culture, and language represents internal (i.e., biological, psychological cognitive, socio-emotional/affective) factors (e.g., individual differences and developmental continuities) and external mediating (i.e., socio-cultural and SES) factors (e.g., family structure and cultural factors, and school environments) that differently affect minority and mainstream children's developmental patterns, learning processes, and variations in academic achievement.

Presently, contemporary research literature that studies minority and mainstream low SES children, represents two contradictory paradigms: (a) the traditional methodological paradigm that endorses the medical model derived from research conducted with mainstream children (e.g., uses primarily standardized discrete-point tests and a prescriptive pedagogy); and (b) the minority perspective, that endorses alternative qualitative measures and instructional and research methodological procedures that tap the cultural and linguistic diversity of minority children. Thus, given the multidisciplinary backgrounds of researchers attempting to study minority children, the application of multiple theoretical paradigms and philosophies has resulted in a diverse set of measures and data analysis procedures and, in some instances, contradictory research findings.

The bottom line is that *all* poor children are at-risk for or vulnerable to actualizing, at some point in time, some developmental and achievement delays and difficulties. Research trends show that there is no full proof or super child, who *will not* be affected at all by poverty conditions.

Instead, contemporary research has uncovered that internal and external mediational factors can interact positively or negatively with at-risk internal (i.e., biological and psychological) and external (i.e., mentors and healthy family environments, high-quality instruction) conditions to help poor children to become resilient and overcome developmental delays, premature births, lack or poor quality early stimulation, low-quality or inappropriate schooling, etc. Then, minority children are *not* at-risk of underachievement and developmental delays because of cultural/linguistic differences, but primarily because they are *poor.*

In a similar manner, *mainstream poor* children (e.g., Appalachian White children) suffer from high underachievement and high school drop out rates. Thus, poverty has equal powerful negative effects across races, ethnicities, and monolingual or bilingual, monocultural mainstream or bicultural minority young children. In addition to poverty, minority children, have an additive effect of cultural/linguistic differences (i.e., English as a second language—ESL and lack of cultural adaptation to the mainstream school culture). However, in the same manner as minority children, mainstream poor children also lack proficiency in *academic* English (in comparison to middle- and upper-class peers), and they are not prepared at home to develop *socialization* skills that respond to the expectations of the mainstream school culture. As a result, both groups of minority and mainstream poor children become vulnerable or at-risk for developmental delays and underachievement, and they are in need of supporting external mediating factors at home and school to help them actualize their learning potential into skills and abilities at age level.

Because of their low SES, minority children are not exposed to rich, early stimulation that develops their learning potential into readiness for academic skills and social adaptation to the mainstream school environment. Instead, poor minority children come to school with learning potential that has not been actualized yet into skills and abilities or actual competence, or that has stagnated due to lack of stimulation and has resulted in developmental delays. That is why, it is important to focus on developmental *processes* and external factors when evaluating young Latino poor children. In this way we can make an accurate differential diagnosis between genuine learning disabilities and handicapping conditions and just normal second language (L2) learning processes, and externally driven developmental delays (see e.g., González, Brusca-Vega, & Yawkey, 1997, for further discussion of this topic).

Similar to the central role of poverty on minority students' academic achievement identified in the Ethnic Researcher approach, Gordon (1999) has discussed the relation between the affirmative development of intellective competence and students' SES. He endorses principles of social justice and democracy. That is, for minority poor students to have equal access to high-quality educational opportunities that implement research-based educational recommendations into praxis. His vision recognizes social dimensions of schooling, development, learning, and teaching including access to good mentors who support educational advocacy for affirming social policy programs of affirmative development. So, for Gordon, a democratic society should enforce social justice policy that provides access to equal educational opportunities to low-income minority students.

Thus, the Ethnic Researcher approach incorporates contemporary mainstream research within a broader ecological minority framework that represents external mediating factors such as the effect of low SES on developmental and learning potential, and its interaction with developmental universals and culturally and linguistically loaded developmental and learning processes in Latino students. The Ethnic Researcher approach has been coined, discussed (see e.g., González & Yawkey, 1993; González et al., 1997; González, Yawkey, & Minaya-Rowe, 2006), and implemented in research studies by González and colleagues since the middle 1990s (Gonzalez, 2006, 2007; Gonzalez, Bauerle, & Felix-Holt, 1994, 1996; González, Clark, & Bauerle, 2007).

Figure 22.1 illustrates the complexity of the interaction between language, cognition, and culture represented in the Ethnic Researcher approach. This prospective is ecological and multidimensional and can help study at deeper levels the particular ways in which socio-cultural fac-

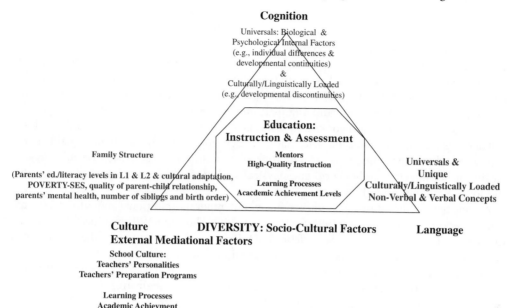

Cognition

Universals: Biological &
Psychological/Internal Factors
(e.g., individual differences &
developmental continuities)
&
Culturally/Linguistically Loaded
(e.g., developmental discontinuities)

**Education:
Instruction & Assessment**

Family Structure

Mentors
High-Quality Instruction

Universals &
Unique

(Parents' ed./literacy levels in L1 & L2 & cultural adaptation,
POVERTY-SES, quality of parent-child relationship,
parents' mental health, number of siblings and birth order)

Learning Processes
Academic Achievement Levels

Culturally/Linguistically Loaded
Non-Verbal & Verbal Concepts

**Culture
External Mediational Factors**

DIVERSITY: Socio-Cultural Factors

Language

School Culture:
Teachers' Personalities
Teachers' Preparation Programs

Learning Processes
Academic Achievment

Figure 22.1 An ecological and multidimensional perspective of the interaction of language, cognition, and culture.

tors (i.e., minority culture and language present in the family, as well as the mainstream school culture) act as external mediators for the qualitatively different effect of low SES on cognition, developmental and learning processes, and academic achievement levels attained by minority young children. This perspective also takes into account *universals or developmental continuities* present among minority as well as mainstream children across social classes (low, middle, middle upper, and high), such as individual differences (e.g., strengths and weaknesses across developmental areas-such as resilience level and maturation levels for reading readiness, individual differences in first language-L1 and L2 learning aptitudes, interests, personality traits, etc.).

Moreover, this perspective also takes into account specific *developmental discontinuities* brought by exposure to two languages and cultural settings, which creates *qualitatively different* developmental patterns and characteristics in Latino children. These developmental discontinuities bring for Latino children some developmental patterns that are *unique* to their bilingualism and biculturalism and present characteristics that are culturally and linguistically loaded. When the exposure to L1 and L2 is within an enrichment home and school setting, these bilingualism and biculturalism brings *advantages* to cognitive (and overall) development (see e.g., Garcia, 1999, 2001; Genesee, 1987; Hakuta, 2001; Ovando, Collier, & Combs, 2003), in the form of *additive bilingualism* (Cummins, 1991) and significant increase in academic achievement (Collier, 1992; Thomas & Collier, 2003). However, when there is *discontinuity* between the minority family and mainstream school language and culture (Delgado Gaitan, 1994; Wong Fillmore, 1991), Latino children suffer from low levels of L1 and L2 proficiency (or *substractive bilingualism*; Cummins, 1991) that negatively impacts their learning processes and academic achievement.

In addition, the Ethnic Researcher multidimensional perspective brings a deeper understanding of the *cumulative interacting patterns* among mediating external cultural factors when studying language, cognition, and culture (for a further discussion of this topic see González, 2001b). For instance, how poverty can be scaffold by the presence of positive family factors (e.g., quality of the parent-child relationship providing a stable emotional and nurturing family setting, see e.g., Garrett, Ng'andu, & Ferron, 1994; McLoyd, 1998; Walker, Greenwood, Hart, & Carta, 1994) or high-quality school environments resulting in minority children being able to develop resilience for at-risk external conditions (and even at-risk internal biological conditions, such as premature and low birth weight rather common among low SES children). High-quality school environments relate to teachers acting as committed mentors and providing high-quality instruction, and related factors such as teachers' personalities (i.e., teachers' attitudes, beliefs and cultural values, teacher's cultural and linguistic knowledge of the child's minority background; teachers' prior knowledge of theories and research about how minority low SES children learn and develop; see e.g., González, Bauerle, Black, & Felix-Holt, 1999). The particular quality of the family and school environment includes multiple socio-cultural characteristics resulting in supportive or detrimental psychological and physical settings for biological, cognitive, linguistic, and socio-emotional growth.

Among the significant variables uncovered by contemporary traditional and Ethnic Research studies (see e.g., Delgado Gaitan, 1994; Garrett et al., 1994; Harrison, Wilson, Pine, Chan, & Buriel, 1990; McLoyd, 1998; Ochs & Schieffelin, 1984; Ogbu, 1982; Shatz, 1991; Walker et al., 1994) impacting low SES minority and mainstream children's development and academic achievement are: (a) *degree of family cultural adaptation* such as value and belief systems, attitudes, socialization goals, patterns of cultural adaptive strategies to the mainstream American social and school cultures, and home language use; (b) *family structure characteristics* such as number of sibling, continuous presence of a paternal figure, presence of extended family members -such as supporting grandparents; (c) *parents' characteristics* such as degree of literacy and education, occupation, degree of acculturation, and physical and mental health; and (d) *quality of neighborhood and community resources* such as availability of mentors (e.g., teachers; extended family, community or church members; peers and siblings, etc.), social services available (e.g., federal/ state programs providing health care ands nutritious food).

The challenge of understanding the interaction of internal and external factors on poor minority children's cognitive development and learning processes is increased by scarcity of studies that control for confounding socio-cultural (i.e., cultural and linguistic) and low SES factors on these protective internal or external mechanisms. That is, there is need for conducting studies that broaden our understanding of the interacting effects of poverty with other internal and external mediating factors (i.e., biological, psychological, and family and community structure) on cognitive (as well as socio-emotional) *developmental processes* in minority and mainstream children.

Much mainstream research has been conducted on performances or actual levels of skills and abilities developed: that is, research with a focus on products (instead of on developmental *processes*). In contrast, studies following an Ethnic Researcher perspective focusing at the *process* level are still scarce. But nonetheless there is growing evidence of cognitive advantages of bilingualism and biculturalism in relation to high-level abilities such as problem-solving, giftedness, creativity, bilingualism, biculturalism, cultural identity, cultural thinking styles, academic achievement, and so forth (see e.g., Collier, 1992; Collier & Thomas, 2004; Cummins, 1991; Diaz, 1985; Diaz & Klingler, 1991; Diaz & Padilla, 1985; Garcia, 1994, 1999, 2001; Genesee, 1987; Hakuta, 1998; Ovando et al., 2003; Thomas & Collier, 2003; Wong Fillmore, 1991). Examples of more permanent child's characteristics that can be studied at the *process* level and that need to be further studied are temperament and personality traits, unique individual needs, and self-regulation of attention, emotion, and behaviors. Examples of changing child's characteristics at the *process* level that need to be studied are developmental stages, interests, attitudes, perceptions, and values and belief systems. Examples of ecological factors that need to be studied at the *process* level are quality of parent-child relationships, parental cultural values about education and child rearing practices, the effect of home language, and the effect of mentors and high-quality educational programs for academic success.

In summary, there is some degree of progress achieved by contemporary Ethnic Researchers uncovering new knowledge about the interaction between language, cognition, and culture. We have been able to uncover the presence of some mediating factors when studying the effect of low SES on the development and academic achievement of language-minority, and particularly Latino, children. However, still new lines of research need to be open in order to understand how these external mediating factors, stemming from socio-cultural and SES variables, interact with at-risk internal factors (i.e., biological and psychological) in Latino children. Finally, more research studies need to be conducted using new research methodologies, stemming from the Ethnic Researcher perspective, for measuring the effect of poverty and cultural and linguistic diversity on developmental processes and achievement levels attained by Latino children. With the new millennium, a bright and broad future opens up for the new generations of Ethnic Researchers who will pursue this challenging task.

A Socio-Constructivistic Perspective to the Study of Language, Cognition, and Culture

Piaget was the founder of cognitive psychology, generating a constructivistic approach for exploring cognitive development in young children as non-verbal abstract processes that precede language development. From the 1940s through the 1960s, Piaget and collaborators (Piaget, 1964, 1967, 1970) conducted series of qualitative studies to demonstrate that abstract operational (or conceptual non-verbal) thinking is deeper (and more mature) than semantic (or verbal) and semiotic (figurative or perceptual-non-verbal motor behaviors such as drawing, imitation, and play) functions.

A more contemporary Socio-Constructivistic approach adds a central component, *culture*, to the interaction between cognition and language. That is, the specific socio-cultural context influences how children construct concepts and map words into meanings (semantic development). As ESL children learn the similarities and differences of L1 and L2 concepts across abstract, symbolic, and verbal domains, they also gain awareness of how some concepts are culturally and linguistically bounded, and how other concepts are universal and can be transferred across languages (i.e., metalinguistic awareness; for further discussion of this topic see Gonzalez & Schallert, 1999).

Furthermore, within the school context language becomes the most important method for instruction. Schools use language as a tool for learning, it is a prerequisite for the study of all other subjects or content areas (i.e., math, science, social studies, etc.). Therefore, during the primary grades, language becomes a cognitive process when used for learning and thinking about concepts and content. Therefore, language becomes the foundation to thinking about learning (metalearning) because it is used as a metacognitive tool for learning. During the later early childhood years (5 to 8 years of age), language can help the young child to make cognitive connections at three levels: (a) *concrete* via recalling and transforming direct experiences with objects at a manipulative or motor level, (b) *perceptual or figurative* via recalling and transforming experiences with drawings and graphic representations, and (c) *conceptual or constructive* via recalling and transforming experiences at a more abstract non-verbal or verbal level.

Language also makes possible for the young child to establish relations to other cognitive processes such as attention, perception, problem-solving, creativity, symbolic representations, analogical reasoning, formation of verbal concepts and networks, verbal creativity, and cognitive operations (e.g., classification, conservation, seriation, number, space, etc.). That is why, as mentioned earlier, in cases of young children presenting additive bilingualism, having access to two languages enriches their cognitive developmental processes. Moreover, memory grows from a non-verbal stage in infants and young toddlers to incorporating a verbal encoding process in older toddlers and preschoolers. Then, language influences automatic memory cognitive processes such as storage, retrieval, and recalling (i.e., recognition, association) strategies. In addition, language influences constructive or semantic memory processes such as metacognition including monitoring and content knowledge (i.e., using prior knowledge as advance organizers to facilitate storage and recalling of information, helping in the recall of details and reconstruction of sequences of events experienced; organizing networks that integrate new information resulting in assimilation processes, and forming new concepts or categories resulting in accommodation processes). Some memory strategies using cognitive and metacognitive verbal labels and verbal conceptual processes include: rehearsal, organization, categorization (i.e., use of constructive semantic or verbal memory to link labels and verbal experiences with verbal and non-verbal new and prior concepts), and elaboration (i.e., using verbal and non-verbal images and mnemonics as a strategy for connecting information in a meaningful manner).

Then, language becomes a semantic tool for conveying meaning and for representing ideas and events through symbols that can be communicated. Language also provides flexibility and creativity for expressing unique ideas with a system that offers an infinite number of possible combinations. Thus, language stimulates problem-solving, concept formation, and active learning because children can create and recreate dynamically their ideas through a language system that can help them think via internal verbal thoughts or in a social context through group brainstorming, instructional conversations, inquire-based learning, and dialogue. That is why, bilingual children benefit from having a L2 acting as a second representational or symbolic tool for stimulating their cognitive, metacognitive, and metalearning developmental processes.

However, a higher difficulty level is imposed by school language in comparison to natural social contexts—like home settings. School language tends to be more abstract as it presents verbal content in a de-contextualized manner. School language uses logical and expository verbal communication for presenting subject areas and topics. That is why ESL children tend to have more learning difficulties when literacy skills in L2 are used for learning content areas. During the primary grades, reading and writing and oral language become more abstract and de-contextualized because logically organized linguistic input is mostly used for communicating content.

Thus, because of the emphasis of schools on using language as a method of instruction, teachers are practicing psycholinguists because they use language as a tool for developing thinking and for learning. For example, assessment of children's cognitive skills is done primarily through verbal stimuli, which present some methodological difficulties for assessing ESL students. Reading requires active processing of written language, and thus is a good example of the interaction between cognition and language. Teachers are good users of language learning strategies because they need to communicate with young children who are at various developmental levels of language competence and literacy skills.

In sum, a Socio-Constructivistic perspective takes into account social and cultural factors, such as culture and language and poverty, affecting learning and academic achievement in young children. For the case of poor Latino students, having access to two symbolic tools stimulating their cognitive developmental and learning processes can be an advantage for academic achievement, provided that they are proficient in at least one language (additive bilingualism). Language proficiency in L1, and even better also in L2, can provide access to abstract metacognitive and metalearning processes in a faster and higher level, than monolingual children. However, most poor Latino children do not have the opportunity to develop proficiency in L1 nor in L2 (a case of substractive bilingualism), becoming at-risk for developmental and learning difficulties due to low-quality and/or inappropriate educational monolingual English educational programs and inaccurate assessment practices, a problem that we will discuss in the section below.

From Research to Improving Educational Practice for Latino Students

We know that high-quality instruction, the presence of committed teachers and administrators acting as mentors, and the development of collaborative partnerships between minority families/communities and schools can make a significant difference in low SES Latino students' cognitive and learning processes and academic achievement levels. However, in spite of significant research knowledge gained in the area, culturally and linguistically diverse educational practices for poor Latino students still show their school drop-out rates have epidemic characteristics and point to a massive failure of the school system and call for systemic change and school reform (for a discussion of this topic based on US Census data, see González, 2001a, 2001b). An informed and socially responsible way to respond to this challenge is to apply state-of-the-art research knowledge into the educational practices with low SES Latino students and to infuse change in mainstream teacher preparation programs and school cultural settings.

Two bodies of contemporary research are interconnected as a philosophical and theoretical framework for the proposed educational implications offered, including: (a) mainstream studies in cognitive and developmental psychology and cognitive science, following a traditional paradigm, resulting in educationally applied recommendations made by the National Research Council (1999a, 1999b); and (b) studies in the area of bilingual and ESL education, following an Ethnic Researcher paradigm, resulting in instructional and assessment educationally applied recommendations derived from contemporary Socio-Constructivistic and developmental research.

Research-Based Implications for Teaching and Learning in Latino Students

Following a Socio-Constructivistic perspective, the role of language and culture on cognitive development and school learning can be better understood in relation to educational principles derived from research-based knowledge. Based on the National Research Council document on *How People Learn* (1999a), a core set of two major learning principles derived form contemporary research on learning and teaching are a powerful tool for understanding that the selection of teaching and learning strategies is mediated by subject matter, grade level, and purpose of education. A single panacea cannot solve every learning and teaching situation, especially in relation to the unique needs of diverse, low SES, Latino, ESL students. But a more "wholistic" perspective of using teaching and learning principles can help design and evaluate classroom environments that are optimal learning settings. The two major learning principles discussed below encompass: (a) the central role of *prior knowledge* for learning, (b) the development of a *metacognitive approach* to teaching and learning, with an analysis of the implications for teacher preparation programs.

Central Role of Prior Knowledge for Learning   Teachers need to tap into students' use of prior knowledge, skills, and attitudes for developing an understanding of concepts within specific topic and content knowledge (National Research Council, 1999a). This means that classrooms need to be more learner-centered, and aware of students' preconceptions, cultural differences, values and beliefs about educationally relevant concepts (e.g., how intelligence develops, the effect of teachers' expectations), their personal interests (to maintain their task engagement), individual progress, and developmental growth and maturation.

Extensive research evidence stemming from studies conducted during the 1980s and 1990s (e.g., Bruner, 1990; Cole, 1996; Tobin, Wu, & Davidson, 1989) showed that learning, both in terms of acquisition and use of knowledge, is the result of the interaction between internal variables such as individual cognitive processes and external factors such as the context of cultural and social norms and expectations. The implications of these research findings about the effect of culture and language on cognition and learning are many. Teachers need to infuse in their classroom environments a community-centered approach in which classroom norms and connections to the external real-world supports core learning values. Students can use collaboration to develop knowledge and help each other to solve problems. Through engaging in dialogue and inquiry, students and teachers can contribute to the creation of new knowledge, which can establish clear connections to their real-world experiences at home and in their family and communities.

Development of a Metacognitive Approach for Teaching and Learning   In order to learn at a conceptual level, students need to develop a deep foundation of factual knowledge and a strong conceptual framework for transforming information into meaningful knowledge. Conceptual knowledge is defined as a network of meaningful patterns that can be retrieved for problem-solving and transference of learning (National Research Council, 1999a). Students also need to learn how to organize knowledge into hierarchical conceptual networks though cognitive and metacognitive strategies, so that they can become experts and transform factual into conceptual knowledge. Thus, most effective teaching practices stimulate students to develop conceptual knowledge and metacognitive skills, such as learning, thinking, and problem-solving abilities, at an abstract level, and to apply them to well-selected topics or content across subject areas.

Most importantly, learning has a social dimension, so cognitive processes can be stimulated by a supportive social environment that provides intellectual tools, such as the transmission of language and other cultural representational symbolic systems. This recognition is also made by the National Research Council (1999a) in relation to the cultural and linguistic diverse characteristics of ESL students, "The social perspective of learning has also focused scholarly attention on understanding populations of learners and revealed learning differences among children of different social class and learning variations associated with race and ethnicity" (p. 28). Thus, language and culture become cognitive tools for learning factual knowledge and higher-level critical thinking skills (i.e., cognitive, metacognitive, and metalinguistic strategies). Taking into account the central role of language and culture for cognition and learning is even more important for the case of Latino students who may have an ESL and low-income situation.

Research-Based Implications for Linking Assessment to Instruction

Research-based and educationally applied knowledge provides principles, which can be connected to national and professional Standards (American Educational Research Association [AERA], American Psychological Association [APA], and National Council for Measurement and Statistics [NCME], 1999; Teaching English To Speakers of Other Languages-TESOL, 2005), to conduct classroom-based assessments of learning, development, and academic achievement in Latino students. These assessments need to be conducted in a systematic valid and reliable manner that fulfills both instructional (i.e., links assessment to instruction) and accountability purposes (i.e., program evaluation) of the *Standards* movement. This objective is achieved by integrating research-based knowledge with guidelines of best practices for educational and psychological testing of Latino students in two areas: (a) a contemporary view of the Psychometric paradigm, and (b) an alternative assessment model that is based on the Ethnic Researcher approach. This alternative assessment model endorses an ecological perspective, with its derived applications on developmental stages of L1 and L2 learning.

Alternative assessments used in research studies representing the Ethnic Researcher paradigm show construct and criterion validity, because they include: (a) different informants, (b) verbal and non-verbal tasks representing the children's minority culture, and (c) administrations in the dominant minority language of the children (allowing also for code switching and code mixing between L1 and L2). Furthermore, when alternative assessments methodologically control for cultural and linguistic factors, the significant relation of family structure factors (such as low SES) to Latino children's cognitive and linguistic development (and the advantages of bilingualism) can be shown.

In terms of practical educational implications, Ethnic Research studies present empirical evidence for the importance of involving parents in the referral process of potentially gifted, minority and mainstream children, who come from low SES backgrounds. Information provided by parents on family structure factors become of paramount importance for evaluators to understand how ecological variables are related to L1 and L2 learning processes, and to cognitive development in Latino low SES children. For instance, parents do have certain perceptions about their child's cognitive abilities and what constitutes giftedness even *before* their children are identified as gifted (see e.g., Clark & González, 1998; González & Clark, 1999; González, Clark, & Bauerle, 2007). More importantly, parents also have certain beliefs about what internal and/or external factors influence the cognitive development (and possible giftedness) of their child. In fact, parental perceptions and beliefs about cognitive development and giftedness also form part of the home environment.

Thus, the Ethnic Researcher paradigm has generated new research methodologies (i.e., research designs and assessment instruments) that are valid and reliable for exploring socio-cultural factors (including linguistic and cultural diversity, and low SES) acting as mediating external variables on cognitive developmental and learning processes in Latino students. These alternative measures represent accurately the social, cultural, and linguistic diverse characteristics of Latino low SES children (i.e., *developmental discontinuities* or qualitative developmental patterns unique to bilingual/bicultural children), while at the same time are sensitive to tap *universals or developmental continuities* (i.e., individual differences and developmental changes).

Research-Based Implications for Teacher Training

Given that a large proportion of poor Latino students have a L1 other than English, and qualify to receive ESL educational services, all cohorts of teacher preparation programs need to infuse diverse content. Some content areas that need to be included by effective teacher training models include, the development of: research-based knowledge about pedagogical approaches for meeting the educational needs of minority low SES children; teachers' metacognitive thinking and learning skills, and advocacy attitudes about learning potential in minority poor students.

Firstly, training programs need to infuse in all teachers' research-based knowledge about diverse pedagogical approaches, so that they can learn how to make informed decisions about the selection and use of instructional and assessment strategies for matching the educational needs of diverse students have (Ladson-Billings, 1999; Menken & Antunez, 1991; Minaya-Rowe, 2002). So, teacher training programs need to model Pluralism, and not eclecticism, because principles or methods and research-based theories are the basis for high-quality teaching.

Second, the same educational principles used by teachers stimulating their ESL students to develop conceptual competence and topic and content knowledge should be used in higher education teacher training and professional development programs. Relatedly, professors in teacher education programs also need to model and prepare teachers for designing and implementing curriculums that improve students' conceptual learning and critical-thinking skills. According to the National Research Council (1999a), teachers need to integrate three critical elements for deep understanding: (a) in-depth knowledge of content and topic knowledge (subject matter), (b) conceptual understanding in order to gain awareness of discipline knowledge structure, and (c) critical thinking skills (i.e., metacognitive strategies-metalearning). Thus, both ESL teachers and their ESL students need to develop and use conceptual competence in topic and content knowledge leading to become better instructors and learners at a metacognitive level as well as at a topic or content level for specific segments of information across subject areas.

That is, teachers need to be involved in sustained learning through professional development opportunities, that model for them translation of learning and teaching principles into as many inquiry-based strategies as possible (Ladson-Billings, 1999; Menken & Antunez, 1991; Minaya-Rowe, 2002). For instance, teacher preparation programs need to model for teachers: curriculum examples, real-life case studies, practice problem-solving within specific situations, self-study and reflection, cooperative learning involving practicing metacognitive strategies (such as thinking-aloud), simulations and role-playing, videos of their own teaching, formative assessment linked with instruction, diversity in learners, etc.

Moreover, teachers need to develop themselves strong metacognitive strategies, applied to specific subject matter, and then learn "how to model" and "how to teach" explicitly these strategies to their students. Teachers can act as role models for how to use metacognitive skills with specific topics across content areas, such as engaging in meaningful instructional conversations that teach students explicitly how to use strategies for problem solving (e.g., thinking-aloud for articulating observations, and making deductions and elaborations; engaging in alternative thinking; using active learning and discovery of concepts). Furthermore, teachers must be knowledgeable of subject matter as well as understand how children of different ages think about subject matter.

Third, sound minority research has generated high-quality educational programs, but we also have learned that teachers' moral reasoning development is necessary to facilitate their implementation as caring and committed mentors and advocates of Latino students and their families. Empathic mainstream and more specialized (e.g., ESL, bilingual) teachers can act as external socio-cultural mediators and can provide minority students with genuine opportunities to actualize their potential for development and achievement. Based on an Ethnic Researcher approach, teachers need to gain social and moral responsibility so that they can become committed mentors acting as role models and cultural bridges between the mainstream school culture and the minority language and culture experienced at home. Teachers who develop cultural and linguistic awareness of their minority students' family and community backgrounds are able to develop more positive attitudes towards valuing diversity as an asset and enrichment for developing their minority poor students' potential for learning English while still continuing to develop their bilingualism and biculturalism (resulting in transculturation instead of assimilation). Teachers who represent in their curriculums and assessment practices their minority students' cultural values and beliefs, and cultural and linguistic background knowledge, are able to support their minority cultural identities, more positive self-concepts and self-esteem, ad ultimately their learning and developmental processes. Diverse and inclusive curriculums and assessment practices provide equal educational opportunities for minority students to actualize their learning potential into meeting high-stakes standards of academic achievement.

In addition, teachers need to develop more sensitive and caring attitudes about minority low SES children "wholistic" development across cognitive, linguistic, social, and affective/emotional areas. That is, *for* all teachers to help minority children by becoming caring mentors, committed advocates, and trusted adults who assume moral responsibility to help them develop socio-cultural adaptation (i.e., integration of bicultural and bilingual cultural identities), reach their developmental potential, and become achievers within the mainstream American school culture and broader society. The goal is not to acculturate minority students to assimilate into the status quo of mainstream school culture. Instead the goal is for committed teachers to initiate a process of reciprocal adaptation across school, family, and community environments in order to facilitate for minority students the engagement in an accommodation process of integration of their bicultural and bilingual identities (i.e., transculturation). Both sides of the socio-cultural environments (i.e., home and school) need to adapt and learn about minority and mainstream cultures and languages. That is, all teachers need to become aware of the powerful effect of home minority culture and language on learning processes, and of the necessary integration with the curriculum content and instructional and assessment methodology across subject areas. Thus, teacher-training programs need to infuse understanding of other cultures and languages in order to graduate teachers who can establish rapport and empathy with minority children and their families.

The Ethnic Researcher approach advocates for pre-and-in-service educators to make a personal connection between their own family history and the role of ESL immigrants in the socio-historical context of U.S. education (see González et al., 2006). Out of the 270 million Americans today, about 100 million are descendents from at least one ancestor who had an ESL background and immigrated within the last 120 years (see González, 2001a). This factual statement describes the socio-cultural reality of America as a nation of immigrants and can be used for motivating educators to develop a personal connection or rapport with the ESL pedagogy. Building rapport with ESL students is key for educators to drop affective filters that prevent them from implementing high-quality and state-of-the-art, research-based pedagogy that fosters minority students' learning and academic achievement at excellence levels. Building rapport connotes infusing among educators cultural awareness of the effect of teachers' attitudes and motivation on their own and their minority students' instructional and learning processes.

In sum, teaching as a social and affective experience is emphasized in the Ethnic Researcher approach, with the endorsement of the education of the "whole" learner (i.e., academic, social, emotional developmental areas), as well as for teacher preparation programs to develop in teachers also a "wholistic" vision of education that aims to develop cognitive and ethical and moral abilities in minority students. The Ethnic Researcher approach to teacher training centers on the idea that schooling can be successful for Latino poor students if educators serve as a mediational social agents or cultural brokers to facilitate students' adaptation process to access and integrate into middle-class America. Endorsement of an Ethnic Researcher approach for teacher preparation leads to *integration* (leading to valuing multiple languages and cultural identities), and not assimilation (leading to enforcing mainstream culture and language only), as a cultural adaptation process for ESL students and their families.

Conclusions

Combining a minority or Ethnic Researcher approach with a Socio-Constructivistic framework provides a powerful research and educationally applied strategy. The philosophical and theoretical framework for understanding contemporary research on the interaction between language, cognition, and culture proposed here endorses an ecological and multidimensional view of developmental and learning processes, and academic achievement in low SES Latino students. From an Ethnic Researcher approach, teaching as a social and affective experience is emphasized in mainstream teacher preparation programs, so that educators develop advocacy, commitment, empathy, and rapport for assuming social and moral responsibility when serving Latino at-risk students. From a Socio-Constructivistic theoretical position, the interaction of internal and external factors in development and learning in Latino students is highlighted, with the need to stimulate universal and culturally/linguistically loaded verbal and non-verbal conceptual development as mental tools for thinking and learning. We endorse pedagogical theory, principles, and strategies that all teachers can use to develop high-level critical thinking skills and problem-solving strategies that can actualize Latino students' potential for learning into academic excellence.

Moreover, within an Ethnic Researcher approach, we celebrate cultural and linguistic diversity as assets that can enrich the developmental and learning potential of ESL students into brighter bi-lingual, bi-cultural, and bi-cognitive minds and spirits. We endorse *transculturation*, and not assimilation, in order to use education as an enrichment tool that nurtures Latino students' culturally and linguistically diverse identities. Transculturation allows Latino students to move freely between their minority and mainstream personalities or cultural identities, and thus enjoying the freedom provided by a truly democratic classroom and schooling process. Collaborative partnerships need to be established between schools and minority families and communities; for teachers and parents to act as mentors to support the academic excellence of Latino students. In this way, the American Dream pursued by Latino immigrant families will become a reality for their children.

We need to generate more studies from an Ethnic Researcher perspective on how to integrate national high-academic standards for *all* students with high-quality education for meeting the cultural and linguistic needs of Latino low SES students. We have learned from minority research that Latino students perform at higher academic achievement levels when their L1 and L2 are used as methods of instruction; and when parents and teachers develop partnerships to value cultural and linguistic diversity as an asset for increasing cognitive, academic, and socio-cultural adaptation and development. In sum, together and while mentoring the next generation of minority scholars, we need to continue advancing Ethnic Research studies to better understand the complex interaction of internal psychological processes and external mediating socio-cultural factors impacting cognitive development in culturally and linguistically diverse children, such as at-risk of underachievement Latino poor students. In addition, we need to apply this gained theoretical and methodological knowledge to systematically improving the effectiveness of pedagogical models for successfully integrating minority students' real-life cultural and linguistic experiences in their family and community environments with teacher training programs, curriculums, educational methodologies and strategies, and educational materials across content areas in the U.S. public school system.

References

American Educational Research Association (AERA), American Psychological Association (APA), and National Council on Measurement in Education (NCME). (1999). *Standards for educational and psychological testing.* Washington, DC: AERA.

Bruner, J. (1990). *Acts of meaning.* Cambridge, MA: Harvard University Press.

Clark, E. R., & González, V. (1998). *Voces* and voices: Cultural and linguistic giftedness. *Educational Horizons, 77*(1), 41–47.

Collier, V. P. (1992). A synthesis of studies examining long-term language minority student data on academic achievement. *Bilingual Research Journal, 16,* 1–2, 187–212.

Collier, V., & Thomas, W. (2004). The astounding effectiveness of dual language education for all. *NABE Journal of Research & Practice, 2*(1), 1–19.

Cole, M. (1996). *Cultural psychology: A once and future discipline.* Cambridge, MA: Harvard University Press.

Cummins, J. (1991). Interdependence of first- and second-language proficiency in bilingual children. In E. Bialystock (Ed.), *Language processing in bilingual children* (pp. 70–89). Cambridge, UK: Cambridge University Press.

Delgado Gaitan, C. (1994). Socializing young children in Mexican-American families: An intergenerational perspective. In P. M. Greenfield & R. R. Cocking (Eds.), *Cross-cultural roots of minority child development* (pp. 55–86). Hillsdale, NJ: Erlbaum.

Diaz, R. M. (1985). Bilingual cognitive development: Addressing three gaps in current research. *Child Development, 56,* 1376–1388.

Diaz, R. M., & Klingler, K. (1991). Towards an exploratory model of the interaction between bilingualism and cognitive development. In E. Bialystock (Ed.), *Language processing in bilingual children* (pp. 167–192). Cambridge, UK: Cambridge University Press.

Diaz, R. M., & Padilla, K. A. (1985). *The self-regulatory speech of bilingual preschoolers.* Paper presented at the April Meeting of the Society for Research in Child Development. Toronto, Canada.

Garcia, E. (1994). *Understanding and meeting the challenge of student cultural diversity.* Boston, MA: Houghton Mifflin.

Garcia, E. (1999). *Student cultural diversity: Understanding and meeting the challenge* (2nd ed.). Boston, MA: Houghton Mifflin.

Garcia, E. E. (2001). *Hispanic education in the United Stated: Raices y alas*. Lanham, MD: Rowan & Littlefield.

Garrett, P., Ng'andu, N., & Ferron, J, (1994). Poverty experiences of young children and their quality of their home environment. *Child Development, 65*, 331–345.

Genesee, F. (1987). *Learning through two languages: Studies of immersion and bilingual education*. Cambridge, MA: Newbury House.

González, V. (2001a). The role of socioeconomic and sociocultural factors in language-minority children's development: An ecological research view. *Bilingual Research Journal, 25*(1, 2), 1–30 (adapted and reprinted by the College Board, available at http://www.collegeboard.com/about/association/academic/2000_2001_scholars.html#gonzalez)

González, V. (2001b). Immigration: Education's story past, present, and future. *College Board Review, 193*, 24–31.

González, V. (2006). Profiles of cognitive developmental performance in gifted children: Effect of bilingualism, monolingualism, and SES factors. *Journal of Hispanic Higher Education, 5*(2), 142–170. Thousand Oaks, CA: Sage.

González, V. (2007). Relationship of family structure factors to gifted, Hispanic, poor children's cognitive and linguistic development. In V. González (Ed.), *Minority and majority children's development and achievement: An alternative research and educational view* (pp. 127–175). Bethesda, MD: University Press of America.

González, V., Bauerle, P., Black, W., & Felix-Holt, M. (1999). Influence of evaluators; beliefs and personal backgrounds on their diagnostic and placement decisions. In V. González (Ed.). *Language and cognitive development in second language learning: Educational implications for children and adults* (pp. 269–297). Needham Heights, MA: Allyn & Bacon.

González, V., Bauerle, P., & Felix-Holt, M. (1996). Theoretical and practical implications of assessing cognitive and language development in bilingual children with qualitative methods. *The Bilingual Research Journal, 20*(1), 93–131.

González, V., Bauerle, P., & Felix-Holt, M. (1994). A qualitative assessment method for accurately diagnosing bilingual gifted children. *NABE Annual Conference Journal, 92–93*, 37–52. Washington, DC: NABE.

González, V., Brusca-Vega, R., & Yawkey, T. (1997). *Assessment and instruction of culturally and linguistically diverse students with or at-risk of learning problems: From research to practice*. Needham Heights, MA: Allyn & Bacon.

González, V., & Clark, E. R. (1999). Folkloric and historic views of giftedness in language-minority children. In V. González (Ed.), *Language and cognitive development in second language learning: Educational implications for children and adults* (pp. 1–18). Needham Heights, MA: Allyn & Bacon.

González, V., Clark, E. R., & Bauerle, P. (2007). Cultural and linguistic giftedness in Hispanic Kindergartners: Analyzing the validity of alternative and standardized assessments. In V. González (Ed.), *Minority and majority children's development and achievement: An alternative research and educational view* (pp. 87–126). Bethesda, MD: University Press of America.

González, V., & Schallert, D. L. (1999). An integrative analysis of the cognitive development of bilingual and bicultural children and adults. In V. González (Ed.), *Language and cognitive development in second language learning: Educational implications for children and adults* (pp. 19–55). Needham Heights, MA: Allyn & Bacon.

González, V., & Yawkey, T. D. (1993). The assessment of culturally and linguistically diverse students: Celebrating change. *Educational Horizons, 72*(1), 41–49.

González, V., Yawkey, T. D., & Minaya-Rowe, L. (2006). *English-as-a-second-language (ESL) teaching and learning: Classroom applications for Pre-K-12th Grade students' academic achievement & development*. Needham Heights, MA: Allyn & Bacon.

Gordon, E. W. (1999). *Education and justice: A view from the back of the bus*. New York: Teachers College Press.

Hakuta, K. (1998). Improving education for all children: Meeting the needs of language minority children. In D. Clarke (Ed.), *Education and the development of American youth*. Washington, DC: The Aspen Institute.

Hakuta, K. (2001, April). *The education of language-minority students.* Testimony to the U.S. Commission of Civil Rights. Retrieved August 26, 2001, from http://www.stanford.edu/~hakuta/Docs/CivilRightsCommission.htm

Harrison, A. O., Wilson, M. N., Pine, C. J., Chan, S. Q., & Buriel, R. (1990). Family ecologies of ethnic minority children. *Child Development, 61,* 347–362.

Ladson-Billings, G. (1999). Preparing teachers for diverse student populations: A critical race theory perspective. In A. Iran-Nejad & D. P. Pearson (Eds.), *Review of Research in Education, 24* (pp. 211–247). Washington, DC: AERA.

McLoyd, V. C. (1998). Socioeconomic disadvantage and child development. *American Psychologist, 53*(2), 185–204.

Menken, K., & Antunez, B. (1991). *An overview of the preparation and certification of teachers working with low English proficiency students.* Washington, DC: National Clearinghouse for Bilingual Education.

Minaya-Rowe, L. (Ed.). (2002). *Teacher training and effective pedagogy in the context of student diversity.* Greenwich, CT: Information Age.

National Research Council. (1999a). *How people learn.* Washington, DC: National Academy Press.

National Research Council. (1999b). *Improving student learning.* Washington, DC: National Academy Press.

Ochs, E., & Schiefelin, B. B. (1984). Language acquisition and socialization: three developmental stories. In R. Shweder & R. LeVine (Eds.), *Culture theory: Essays on mind, self, and emotion* (pp. 276–320). Cambridge, UK: Cambridge University Press.

Ogbu, J. (1982). Cultural discontinuity and schooling. *Anthropology and Education Quarterly, 13*(4), 290–307.

Ovando, C. J., Collier, V. P., & Combs, M. C. (2003). *Bilingual and ESL classrooms. Teaching in multicultural contexts* (3rd ed.). Boston, MA: McGraw Hill.

Piaget, J. (1964). *The early growth of logic in the child, classification, and seriation.* New York: Columbia University Press.

Piaget, J. (1967). *Mental imagery in the child, a study of the development of imaginal representation.* New York: Oxford University Press.

Piaget, J. (1970). Piaget's theory. In P. Mussen (Ed.), *Carmichael's manual of child's psychology* (Vol. 1, pp. 703–732). New York: Wiley.

Shatz, M. (1991). Using cross-cultural research to inform us about the role f language in development: Comparisons of Japanese, Korean, and English, and of German, American English, and British English. In M. H. Bornstein (Ed.), *Cultural approaches to parenting* (pp. 139–153). Hillsdale, NJ: Erlbaum.

TESOL. (2005). *Pre-K-12 English language proficiency standards in the core content areas.* Retrieved March 14, 2008, from http://www.tesol.edu/assoc/k12standards/it/09.html

Tobin, J. J., Wu, D., & Davidson, D. (1989). *Preschool in three cultures: China, Japan, and the United States.* New Haven, CT: Yale University Press.

Thomas, W. P., & Collier, V. P. (2003). The multiple benefits of dual language. *Educational Leadership, 61*(2), 61–64.

Walker, D., Greenwood, C., Hart, B., & Carta, J. (1994). Prediction of school outcomes based on early language production and socioeconomic factors. *Child Development, 65,* 606–621.

Wong Fillmore, L. (1991). Second language learning in children: A model of language learning in social context. In E. Bialystok (Ed.), *Language processing in bilingual children* (pp. 49–69). Cambridge, UK: Cambridge University Press.

23 Language Socialization Among Latinos

Theory, Method, and Approaches

Patricia Baquedano-López and Gabino Arredondo

University of California, Berkeley

Jorge Solís

University of California, Santa Cruz

The education of Latinos continues to be a central topic of inquiry and concern in educational research. When young Latino students enter schools, they learn more than just subject matter, they must also learn to negotiate cultural expectations, languages, dialects, registers, and the often conflicting ideologies of what counts as knowledge and how to learn it. The increase in the number of Latinos in the overall U.S. population and their growing presence in public schools are making it imperative that researchers, administrators, and government agencies coalesce around an educational agenda that would maximize the educational attainment of Latino students. Earlier research on Latinos in schools aimed to solve the "Mexican problem" and attempted to provide explanations for their limited educational achievement. Latino cultural and linguistic practices and the lack of English language proficiency (often meaning the Standard English variant) were attributed to a lack of assimilation into the American mainstream (García, 2001; G. G. González, 1997; Trueba, 2002). Building on a legacy of work that has challenged a deficit approach to understanding Latino experience in schools (Durán, 1981; Valencia, 1997, 2002; Zentella, 1997), linguists, sociolinguists, and language development professionals are pushing educational and research agendas that invite us to reconsider the affordances of the language practices of many bilingual, bi-dialectical, and Spanish-speaking Latino students as resources for learning (K. D. Gutiérrez, Baquedano-López, & Alvarez, 2001; Moll, 1990; Valdés, 1996; Wong-Fillmore, 1992; Zentella, 1997). Among these efforts, researchers working within the language socialization paradigm have contributed a unique perspective on the role that language plays in the learning process, in particular, in the development of multiple competencies (linguistic and cultural) across a myriad of social institutions, but most particularly, in schools. Building on human developmentalist notions of learning, in particular social and cognitive competences that arise in interaction, language socialization research offers a complementary view to psychological approaches to learning. Thus language socialization research offers a linguistic anthropological perspective to address the complex questions of learning to participate in multiple communities and institutions. This chapter provides a review of this work with particular attention to Latino populations in the United States. In the next sections we review the goals and premises of language socialization research. We then discuss the influence of Latino experiences on language socialization research and related studies on language use and learning. We also review language socialization studies across different educational contexts. We conclude our chapter with a discussion on how language socialization research on Latinos can provide a window into understanding the role of language across contexts of learning.

Language Socialization Research

It has been more than 20 years since the first programmatic statement was published in which the language socialization paradigm emerged as a research perspective (Ochs & Schieffelin, 1979, 1984; Schieffelin & Ochs, 1986a, 1986b). Deeply influenced by theories on socialization

(Bernstein, 1971/1974) and acculturation (M. Mead, 1950), language socialization research emerged from a body of work studying child language and cognitive development in (social) context (Ervin-Tripp & Mitchell-Kernan, 1977). The influence of Basil Bernstein's theories reverberated across studies of family and school interactions examining the socialization of the child and the relationship between cognitive development, including language, and social stratification. Cook-Gumperz (1973) captured the significance of language as part of the process of socialization being studied at the time:

> [T]he study of socialization is the study of how the child learns to demonstrate his [sic] membership of the society, to recognize and practice the making of social events and structures in common with others. The key to this process which makes it *visible* for everyday members, and for members as researchers, is language, or rather *talk*. (p. 9)

Engaging in the study of this form of socialization required a view of the child as participating in interpretive social practices or in "the interpersonal activity of becoming," and not simply as a product of biology or a repository of social structure (Cook-Gumperz & Corsaro, 1986). Inspired by this perspective and the growing research on developmental and social approaches to child language acquisition of the time, a body of work firmly grounded in anthropological fieldwork began to focus on what was beginning to be called, *language socialization*.

Tenets of Language Socialization Research

The language socialization approach seeks to understand the ways in which individuals acquire the norms and competencies valued and expected by members of their social group. Branching out of the studies on the pragmatics of early child language acquisition (Ervin-Tripp & Mitchell-Kernan, 1977; Schieffelin & Ochs, 1986a, 1986b), language socialization research began to be identified as a unique research approach in the mid-eighties. In their 1986 essay in the *Annual Review of Anthropology*, the co-founders of the language socialization paradigm, Elinor Ochs and Bambi Schieffelin, proposed that the acquisition of language and socio-cultural dispositions was best understood through an integrated, means-ends theoretical and methodological approach. This approach, supported by longitudinal empirical research, captured the process of socialization *through the use of language* and *to the use language* (1986a). The study of socialization interactions, the authors indicated, was not to be limited to young children and their caregivers in everyday activity as was the focus of the early work in developmental pragmatics but rather, the focus was to be longitudinal, across developmental time, and across the lifespan. Through a focus on everyday routines embedded in social interaction, it was possible to capture how individuals acquired dispositions and behaviors, much of what Bourdieu (1977) has called *habitus*, and how individuals interacted with social structures and institutions (Giddens, 1977). In short, language socialization provided a way to empirically illustrate the patterns of social reproduction, transformation, and change.

 While the general criteria for what constitutes a language socialization study can be found in the earlier programmatic statements of the paradigm (Schieffelin & Ochs, 1986a, 1986b), these have been expanded to clarify its theoretical and methodological underpinnings. The criteria include an orientation towards socialization research that is (a) longitudinal and ethnographic with the aim of describing an individual's acquisition of socio-cultural knowledge across time and contexts (Garrett & Baquedano-López, 2002; Kulick & Schieffelin, 2004; Schieffelin & Ochs, 1986a); (b) analytical and descriptive of field-based data, with reliance on recorded data where possible (Garrett, 2006); and (c) concerned with studying the connection between micro and macro processes, that is, focusing analytical attention to the ways in which everyday, face-to-face interactions both construct and reflect the social order (Garrett & Baquedano-López, 2002;

Kulick & Schieffelin, 2004; Ochs, 2002). These criteria have made it possible to articulate an important distinction between language socialization studies and studies that look at language socialization interactions. The former adhere to the tenets outlined above, the latter vary in methodology and disciplinary orientation and follow a synchronic approach to socializing interactions.

The interest in language socialization as a viable method and theory for studying language development and cultural competence across the life span is evident in the fast growing number of recent anthologies, special journal issues, and reviews of research in psychology (Cervantes & Perez-Granados, 2002), education (Bayley & Schecter, 2003; Hornberger & Duff, 2008; Zentella, 2005), applied linguistics (Auer & Wei, 2007), and linguistic anthropology (Garrett & Baquedano-López, 2002; Kulick & Schieffelin, 2004). We also note the inclusion of a language socialization entry in the recently published *The Prager Handbook of Latino Education in the U.S.* (Bhimji, 2007; Soto, 2007). Across these studies, the questions guiding the work have been influenced by the learning experiences and linguistic practices of different cultural and linguistic groups, including Latinos in the United States.

The Latino Diacritic in Studies of Language Use and Language Socialization

The rich range of linguistic and cultural experiences among Latinos has been central to empirical research that has pushed the theoretical scope of language socialization research and related studies. While not necessarily a unique or explicit focus of the earlier studies, the experiences of Latinos[1] were documented as exemplars of the complexity of the acquisition of communicative competence and knowledge and especially in the context of multilingual contact. We call this significant imprint the "Latino diacritic" to capture the multilingual contact, semiotically and materially experienced, that was studied through the analysis of everyday language practices among Latinos. These experiences were foundational to the analysis of studies of speech communities, classroom studies, and studies of peer cultures. We review some of this work below.

Drawing from a longitudinal, linguistic acquisition corpus from Quiché-speaking Guatemalan toddlers, Pye's (1980, 1983) findings demonstrated how children's early higher cognitive and complex understandings of language were evidenced in their selective use of linguistic and cultural expectations. Pye's work became part of the empirical research that supported Schieffelin and Ochs' (1986a) distinction between major forms of communicative accommodations given to children in their description of child-centered versus situation-centered approaches to socialization (p. 175) (that is the idea that across cultural groups, there is variability among caregivers in the ways they produce "baby talk" or accommodate talk to infants and young children), and how much of this variability (never a dichotomous "either/or" approach) would depend on the context of interaction or learning situation. Thus, the cross-cultural comparison of children's language development, and among them Latinos, was used to develop a nascent field studying cognition in social context. We will return to this point, and, in particular, the researchers' focus on Latino language practices in a moment, but we first want to provide the scope of this work.

A brief overview of other research on Latinos that influenced early language socialization research include the study of code-switching practices among Puerto Rican speakers (Zentella, 1981), sayings and clichés in Puerto Rican (Lauria, 1964) and Mexican communities (Farr, 1994), and teasing routines among Mexican families (Eisenberg, 1986). Schieffelin and Ochs cite (1986b) Eisenberg's research as evidence of language socialization of children in multi-cultural, multilingual, and polyadic communities in contrast to dyadic turn-taking models in White middle-class family interactions. Eisenberg (1986) had examined the socializing routines of two Mexican immigrant families living in northern California. Her study of "teasing" as a speech form in Mexican families suggested that the activities in which it occurred were varied in range and form, these included: (a) forms of play, (b) part of social bonds and means of social control/

moralizing values, and (c) valued social skills in adult interaction (p. 182). This work illustrated the multifaceted nature of one speech event in its varied contexts of interaction. Other sociolinguistic work on transnational Mexican families engaged similar analytical attention to teasing, this time as verbal art among Mexican immigrant family members in Chicago (Farr, 2006; Farr & Domínguez Barajas, 2005). Spanish-English speaking Latino practices and settings thus provided a context for cross-cultural comparisons and challenged the dominant American White middle-class models of interaction, learning, and development that were predominant in earlier research on acquisition and competence. These and other language practices became central to discussions of speech community. Derived from earlier work on recognizable language patterns that identified a social group (Bloomfield, 1933/1984), the notion of speech community as a more dynamic, heterogeneous analytic concept did not emerge as such until the work of John Gumperz (1968) and Dell Hymes (1972). Instead of the traditional one to one correspondence between a language and their speakers/ethnic groups, a speech community began to be seen as a complex of multiple languages, codes, and registers not necessarily determined by locale (i.e., practices could be learned or shared across geographical and temporal boundaries, that is in a broader socio-historical context).

In addition to monographs describing the Latino speech community (Peñalosa, 1980), we mention two noteworthy volumes addressing the Spanish language context for Latinos in the U.S.—*Latino Language and Communicative Behavior* (Durán, 1981) and *Spanish in the United States: Sociolinguistic Issues* (Bergen, 1990). Many of the studies included in these two collections ranged from formal linguistic analysis of local varieties of Spanish (M. Gutiérrez, 1990; Jacobson, 1990) to pragmatic concerns including the usage of *tu* and *usted* (Jaramillo, 1990). In these early studies there is the recognition of the diversity *within* community rather than across community. A prime example of this work is Ana Celia Zentella's (1981) ethnographic study of a Puerto Rican neighborhood in New York City, mentioned at the outset of this section, a study documenting the cultural logic of code-switching strategies among Latino youth— work that would lead to her landmark monograph, *Growing Up Bilingual*, where she examined those code-switching socializing practices in their contexts of immigration and socio-political contact (Zentella, 1997). Similarly, Valdés' (1981) and Silva-Corvalán's (1991, 1994) studies on code-switching and language patterns also influenced the study of language development and practices of immigrant Latino groups in the United States, including important studies of language learning in school and of language contact and change in Los Angeles.

Drawing on research carried out in England and the United States, Gumperz (1982) became a leading figure in studying language competence in context, what we now know as sociolinguistics. The major premises for defining sociolinguistic competence were derived from analyses of audio-recorded talk of a range of bi-dialectical and bilingual speech communities including those of English, Slovenian-German speakers, and those of Spanish-English Chicano[2] interlocutors. Gumperz' early analyses of code-switching and language borrowing were laden with references to language attitudes and identity markers that reflected a variety of language repertoires and worldviews of Chicano Spanish and *Caló*[3] as were used by Mexican American speakers residing in the U.S. Southwest. In his collaborative work with noted Chicano sociolinguist Enrique Hernández-Chávez, both authors asserted, and in effect, advanced earlier work on language ideologies, now an area of central concern in language socialization research:

> [W]hen political ideology changes, attitudes to code switching may change also. In California and elsewhere in the South West *pocho* or *caló* served as a pejorative term for the Spanish of local Chicanos. But with the awakening of ethnic consciousness and the growing pride in local folk traditions, these speech styles and the code switching they imply have become symbolic of Chicano ethnic values…. In bilingual groups as in other human com-

munities the relationship of language usage to language ideology is a complex one which cannot be taken for granted. (Gumperz & Hernández-Chávez, 1972, p. 63)

It is important to recognize that Latino scholars at the time wrote theoretical and reflective pieces on the research that was being carried out among Latinos, or as they were increasingly being recognized, Chicanos. In a poignant critique of anthropological and linguistic research on Chicano[4] language practices, Américo Paredes (1977) reminded linguists and anthropologists that code-switching and word play expressed particular worldviews and histories beyond their denotational forms. He warned that a narrow understanding of distinct (and rich) language practices could lead to essentializing descriptions of their speakers and their practices and produce an early mapping of language practice with ethnic group. Regrettably, in spite of Paredes' call, essentializing analyses of Latinos and their practices remain a problem in the study of minority groups and their cultural and linguistic practices. Briggs (1984) has provided a methodological approach to Paredes' critique. Drawing on his experience conducting fieldwork among Mexicano[5] communities in New Mexico, Briggs wrote on the importance of conducting field interviews through the identification of what he called, metacommunicative actions, or actions that provide insight into cultural specific beliefs about language. In his words: "Native meta-communicative routines provide a rich source of sociolinguistic and social/cultural data and that awareness of theses repertoires can assist fieldworkers in using interviews more appropriately and effectively" (Briggs, 1984, p. 2). Thus, it is not just the linguistic data that matter in fieldwork situations, but developing the socio-cultural sensitivities through extended observation and participation in the activities being investigated.

The study of everyday language use and the language learning experiences of Latinos in the United States contributed to theoretical developments in the related field of second language acquisition (SLA). For example, Schumann's *Acculturation Model* (1978) was largely based on the communicative experiences of his Costa Rican informant, Alberto, who did not display language development beyond a certain measurable point. In the larger project from which Schumann's theory was developed, a study looking at discrete acquisition of English grammar among adults, there were four other Latino immigrant informants from Colombia and Puerto Rico (Cancino, Rosansky, & Schumann, 1975). The practices of these speakers crystallized into theories of language development, and while rigorously adhering to the methodology of the time, absent in this work is an examination of the socio-historical and economic factors that may have influenced these speakers' decisions to either integrate or distance themselves from the mainstream of U.S. society. Notwithstanding, these theories continue to be central to an understanding of SLA theoretical developments and principles.

Classroom Studies

Perhaps the most salient, yet unintended, contribution of Latinos to early language research in general was the description of Latino language practices and cultural worldviews that were captured in the classic classroom discourse studies of the 1970s and early 1980s (Cazden & Hymes, 1972; Mehan, 1979). Of significance, Mehan's (1979) study of interactional routines in the classrooms took place in a San Diego school located in a low-income Black and Mexican American neighborhood. Mehan's study provided foundational evidence for describing how social status and roles are structured through schooling. Mehan's Initiation-Response-Evaluation (I-R-E) model, which captured among other things, the control of knowledge by teachers, has become the cornerstone of classroom discourse analysis validating and inspiring interest in the use of naturalistic language analysis methodology for studying conditions of structure and achievement in schools (Macbeth, 2003).

The earlier focus on studying children and youth in educational contexts which had been led by Bernstein's (1971/1974) in his studies of social stratification and language code differences in London, led to a number of other studies focusing on language code. Most importantly, Bernstein's analysis of the educational opportunities that language code and class afforded made an important argument for looking at the integrated contexts of schooling. Thus, the importance of educational contexts as sites for testing out theories of language use, including code-switching, and for their potential for informing and shaping student achievement disparities was highlighted and was to form the core of new fields that were generated at the time, including sociolinguistic theory and language socialization. The experience of bilingual young Latino children, in particular the contexts for the development of code-switching skills, were also the subject of these earlier research efforts. Early language socialization research focused on the development of communicative competence of Spanish-English bilinguals (Genishi, 1976; Gumperz, 1982). This work represented a blend of approaches to describe the social aspects and parameters of language *in use* through the ethnography of communication framework (Hymes, 1972) and the then emergent language socialization paradigm. Genishi (1976) carried out one of the earliest exploratory studies investigating language socialization of bilingual children.

Predating the current language socialization framework, Genishi's (1976) study of code-switching among 6-year-old Latino Spanish-English bilinguals living in northern California drew on Hymes' ethnographies of communication model describing the "microparameters of language use" defined by four variables including contexts or situations, communicative acts, rules for communication, and the social meaning of talk. Genishi recorded naturally occurring talk among these children in a variety of settings and with different interlocutors. Her work aimed at challenging popular deficit notions of interlanguage interference[6] in the development of two languages. We note that Genishi's work appeared at a time when a number of significant studies were being carried out and when attention to the role of language in context in the learning process was given primary attention across child development studies (Ervin-Tripp & Mitchell-Kernan, 1977; Ochs & Schieffelin, 1979). Genishi's (1976) study thus set the stage for continued work on bilingual code-switching in practice.

Peer Cultures

William Corsaro's (1985) studies provided some of the earliest accounts of childhood socialization in peer cultures, in particular of friendship and social status, among pre-school age children. His studies extended notions of human development by drawing from symbolic interaction theory (Cicourel, 1973; G. H. Mead & Murphy, 1932), bringing a social perspective to the study of questions of growth and maturation. The children participating in Corsaro's studies were from White middle-class backgrounds and minority group populations including Mexican American, Black, and Asian families. His work influenced a number of current studies on peer culture, some of which have critiqued the earlier focus of many language socialization studies which tended to focus on only adult-child based models of socialization (Kyratzis, 2001a, 2004). Kyratzis' (2001b) recent study of male and female peer groups of pre-school age children (3- and 4-year-olds) in a university preschool classroom that included Anglo American and Mexican American students she examined "emotion talk" (p. 361) and peer socialization. Kyratzis has argued for the use of peer-based children's models of language socialization since children produce and organize themselves through a variety of stances and activities "that have not been previously modeled by adults" (Kyratzis, 2001b).

In the tradition of the ethnography of speaking, Goodwin (1995) examined the distinctions made between male and female peer group during play, where female gamesmanship had been seen as less complex and more conflict-free, through the observation of participant routines in the game of Hopscotch. Goodwin set out to understand this perception. The participants in Goodwin's studies were bilingual Spanish/English-speaking second- third-, and fifth-grade girls (mostly second generation Central Americans) residing in Los Angeles. Goodwin observed that girls actively co-constructed and negotiated the rules of their participation in the game. She has provided a nuanced typology of speech acts and pitch alternations through which girls refereed their own participation and stance taking that included calling out transgressors and the strict enforcement of rules. Her work has challenged deficit interpretations that girls' games were not intellectually complex—assertions that had ramifications for understanding the development of social skills socialization among girls. Research among older peer groups have included socio-linguistic studies of Latina gangs in Northern California (Mendoza-Denton, 1999a, 1999c) and of socialization of Latino male gang behavior and language in school (Rymes, 1996, 2001). We will review Rymes' language socialization study in later sections of this chapter.

In this section we have reviewed how the experiences of Latinos have been central to empirical research that pushed the theoretical scope of studies, and which in turn, led to a more defined articulation of the language socialization paradigm among other related disciplines. Yet we note that a notion of Latino as a cultural group remains unproblematized. While "culture" is often used as an identity marker, culture is not synonymous with a particular ethnic, linguistic, racial or national identities, and certainly not with an abstract, unified, or universal pattern of behavior. Cultural phenomena are never universal, they are always varied, local, and situated in a particular social context. Rosaldo (1989/1993) notes the limitations of early (and functionalist) interpretations of culture, which emphasized "shared patterns at the expense of processes of change and internal inconsistencies, conflicts, and contradictions. By defining culture as a set of shared meanings, classic norms of analysis make it difficult to study zones of difference within and between cultures" (pp. 27–28). Language socialization research can move us away from the unproblematic mappings of language onto culture and provide insights into how cultural knowledge is mediated and how membership to particular cultural identities is negotiated by examining both shared *and* varied cultural interactions. But this relationship requires explicit articulation otherwise we run the risk of continuing to work on an ascribed category of "Latino" as a cultural given and not as construct of social analysis.

The work described in this section also raises questions on the role of researchers engaged in studies of Latino populations. We argue that the analytical attention to the language practices of the everyday and routine as promoted in the past (and encouraged today), has the potential to exclude attention to the broader context. Aside from Paredes' and Briggs' critiques, attention to the socio-political context of Latino experience in the United States had been minimized, if not ignored. In the 1970s and 1980s, Latinos had taken significant political stances against poverty and had organized and contributed to the civil rights movement. We note too that by the time studies on the Chicano speech community were published, there were broader discourses on Latinos' organizing efforts around school desegregation and immigration laws (Rosales, 1997; Vigil, 1999). That is, the presence of Latinos in the United States was not simply that of an immigrant or cultural group, but of social actors in the making of a democratic nation.

The attention given to Latinos in early language socialization research and other related areas of inquiry offered at best a limited scope and view of the Latino experience. Perhaps more unsettling is to accept that the focus on collecting data at the local level reinforced the practices of anthropologists and other social scientists concerned with understanding human behavior and development that constructed a cultural "other," a static and invariant object of scrutiny and comparative analysis. The investigative lens hardly ever turned to the researcher engaged in the practice of ethnographic work or disciplinary field expansion (Fabian, 1983; Kulick, 2006). We are compelled to engage this discussion, for while attention to Latino experience provides a much-needed deviation from White middle-class norms and moved us towards a more dynamic understanding of learning, it does not escape the grip of the "otherizing" gaze without conscious investment. These points need to be engaged openly when conducting language socialization research since the paradigm has the potential to analytically tie the local and the global and as we seek to understand the processes of reproduction, transformation, and social change. The research enterprise is also part of these processes of transformation.

Language Socialization Practices of Latinos across Educational Contexts

Today, there is a growing body of language socialization studies examining a variety of educational settings and practices among Latinos. Challenged by the realities of a history of exclusion of Latinos in the academic pipeline, researchers whose work addresses the nexus between language, culture, and education are increasingly turning their attention to the language socialization paradigm to complicate one-to-one correspondences between variables such as low socio-economic status and low educational attainment and to explore the complexity of learning and becoming students in U.S. schools from a more integrated approach.

Language socialization research offers a framework for capturing learning processes in context and as a collaborative activity among experts and novices where language is the main tool for learning (Vygotsky, 1978). In addition to book-length monographs on Latino families and schooling practices (N. González, 2001; Vásquez, Pease-Alvarez, & Shannon, 1994; Zentella, 2005), research drawing on the language socialization research paradigm can now be found across a wide range of journals and disciplinary fields. We sound the same cautionary note stated at the start of this chapter, that is, that much work, and much of it good, has been done under the banner of language socialization research, but the studies, which are often identified as language socialization, are not always so in theoretical or methodological orientation; rather, they often examine instances of language socialization and do not emerge from description and analysis of long-term, ethnographic studies of socialization *to* language as well as socialization *through* language. The notion of "language" that language socialization research undertakes includes the symbolic systems used to encode socio-cultural models of learning and of competence. Ochs (1988) references this meaning of language as including both the grammatical sentence and other structures.[7] Language use encompasses "discourse" which includes sets of norms, preferences, and expectations related to linguistic structures including "speech acts, conversational sequences, episodes, rounds, speech activities, speech events, genres, and registers" (p. 8). The relevance of this notion of language to studies of Latinos and education can be appreciated at two levels. First, as the body of work across discourse-related activities illuminates, there are situated practices that shape a range of social identities. Second, and most importantly, the view of language and discourse afforded by the language socialization paradigm provides opportunities to examine the relationship between language structure and the social processes in which it is embedded.

Home and School Continuities

The investigation of language socialization practices in the home has provided a view into the relationship between home and school that has often highlighted the discontinuities across these two important socializing domains. This concern, first taken up by Heath's (1983) landmark study of Black and White working communities in the Piedmont Carolinas can be traced to Basil Bernstein's discussion of the relationship between restricted and elaborated codes and the opportunities that elaborated codes provided for some children's productive participation in school. Language socialization research began to address this relationship more formally in work carried in Northern California (Pease-Alvarez, 2002; Vásquez et al., 1994) and in New York (Zentella, 1981, 1997), indicating that the discontinuities for Latinos may not be as marked as those outlined in the Heath (1983) study.

The Vásquez et al. (1994) studies built on data they had collected in the late 1980s examining the differences between home and school contexts for language development. Through a comparison of scaffolding scripts between home and school, the authors sought to find discontinuities or mismatches across these settings, to understand school failure of minority students. Ethnographic studies at the time, and many of them language socialization studies (Boggs, 1985; Heath, 1983; Philips, 1983), had indicated that students from ethnic minority communities did not engage in speech with peers and adults in ways that were extended, structured, directive, or expanded as those that occurred among White, middle-class children and their interlocutors. Vásquez et al. (1994) focused on adult "contingent queries" as conversational supports to clarify and elaborate on requests. The authors noted that these conversational patterns functioned to clarify and elaborate on children's requests. This was an important finding that cautioned researchers and educators not to assume that the differences between home and school were neatly separated. The discourse patterns found in Latino homes were similar to discourse patterns of the school, and to those identified with White middle-class homes. The authors also noted the deliberate ways parents enforced maintenance of the home language and culture. This set of language socialization studies opened up opportunities to reframe attention to home-school connections. Farr's (1994) sociolinguistic study of literacy practices of Mexicanos[8] in Chicago supported the Vásquez et al. study. Farr described local literacy practices in public and private domains that overlapped with the contexts of school and home. Her ethnographic observations offered a detailed description of rich literacies outside school that included Catholic religious education using Spanish texts during church services on Sunday, prayer days during the week, and Saturday catechism classes in Spanish (*doctrina*). Farr explained that all oral and written language used by teachers in the religious classes promoted the unique use of Spanish language skills by integrating a range of texts almost exclusively in Spanish as well as other genres in Spanish (such as songs or prayers; p. 32). As with the Vásquez et al. study, the links to classroom practices were seen less discontinuous in these studies, providing an important view on the potential to tap on Latino language and literacy practices across home and school.

Perhaps the most comprehensive and in-depth analysis of language and literacy practices in Latino homes can be found in Norma González' (2001) study of families in Arizona. Designed as a language socialization study, González' research began to incorporate the larger dimensions of the socio-cultural context of the borderlands, including the interplay of political economies and social identities. Her study provided an illustration of the ways in which socialization does not necessarily mean that only one ideology (or cultural norm) is transmitted to young children. On the contrary, what Latino children learn is the unique way their immediate social context of interaction evokes and embodies their race and class minority status. A significant contribution to educational research is her critique of what we generally conceive as "culturally relevant" may actually be more indicative of a position that considers *all* Latinos to share the same socio-historical dispositions. The call here is for research and pedagogy that can consider that while there is a great deal that is shared in terms of linguistic and cultural practices, there are unique practices to households and local communities.

As our knowledge of Latino student experiences in schools increases through multiple methods and theoretical approaches, Rodríguez (2005) reminds us that there are significant numbers of Latino students with special needs in our schools. There is urgency to understand and promote home-school continuities for these students. While language socialization research in other settings has turned its attention to students with special needs (Ochs, 2002), we know relatively little of these language socialization practices among Latino students at home and at school. Rodríguez (2005) conducted observations of Dominican families in New York focusing on literacy practices at home and found that there were many rich literacy texts and activities that involved parents and children in productive and sustained interaction. Of interest, these activities were also related to the practical problems that families needed to solve, such as paying bills or writing money orders or checks. All of these are fundamentally problem-solving practices that invoke not just cognitive attention, but socio-economic dispositions as well. Similar to Rodríguez' study of home interactions, Mercado (2005) investigated the *funds of knowledge* (N. González, Moll, & Amanti, 2005) that underlie the communicative, emotional, and spiritual resources for learning in the homes and community of the Puerto Rican participants in her study. Her research, conducted with a team of teachers, revealed that families valued literacy practices at home which in addition to school subjects, also ran the gamut of family life and experience—legal matters, health concerns, and religious and spiritual activities. Of significance were the teachers' responses to the home visits and interviews they carried out as part of the design of the study. They reported that they had gained valuable perspectives on how important it was for them to become familiar with not just the socialization practices of the broader community, but also with the socialization practices of their particular students and their families of their classrooms. An important implication of Mercado's study, and indeed of all "funds of knowledge" research, is the assertion that that teacher contact with the home affords the possibility of *informed* curricular reform.

The Broader Context of School Reform

Rymes (2001) study examined the language socialization experiences of Black and Latino students and teachers at a continuation high school in Los Angeles, she focused on the narratives of "dropping out" and "dropping in" that Latino students told to frame the tensions they experienced between their peer activities, many gang-related, and their dis-engagement and participation in school practices. These students' narratives provided insight into the larger tensions that these students experienced as minority youth in Los Angeles (Rymes, 2001). Rymes' nine-month study was the first attempt to examine school reform through the language socialization paradigm. In her study, Rymes (2001) followed the discourses and practices of stakeholders in the creation, and the unfortunate closing, of the school.

The other significant contribution to the study of school reform is Yang's (2004) two-year ethnographic study of a largely Black and Latino school district in northern California. Yang studied more centrally the discourses of school reform at public meetings among parents, school administrators, and the staff of the main school reform office that led to the formation of a small schools movement in northern California, and the eventual autonomy from the school district. Yang contributes an important critique of the "complicitous researcher" who never plays a detached or distant role. In his case, he was a key player in the office for school reform in the district. These two studies provide a broad view of language socialization not appreciated before, that is, how schooling institutions are locally structured and in turn, how these structuring processes shape and influence the dispositions and actions of individuals participating in those institutions (Giddens, 1984). This area of research has the potential to expand into complex and integrative research, especially as education researchers incorporate language socialization approaches to the study of institutional and organizational structures.

Home and Community Contexts

Eisenberg's (2002) study addresses a different type of discontinuity, one previously identified between European and Mexican-descent socialization to cognitive development in children, and that is the quality of maternal teaching talk and register. Eisenberg observed interactions during tasks and activities at home that were coded for teaching and scaffolding registers and which included the use of positive-negative feedback, structuring, questioning, and degrees of demand and directiveness of attention (understood as supporting cognitive complexity). The study uncovered a range of responses across socio-economic statuses and tasks suggesting the importance of examining individual variation in the context of everyday activities (p. 222). While not strictly a language socialization study, Eisenberg's study draws on its distinctive methodology in that it included ethnographic observation and detailed analysis of language form. Bhimji's (2005) study provides a complementary example to Eisenberg's findings as she studied the use of directives, identified as a distinctive dis-preferred feature of American White middle-class maternal discourse in low-income Mexican families. Bhimji relied on longitudinal, ethnographic methodology to document how directives were not uniformly controlling processes or imperative in form, but rather they could include other types of directives (e.g., declaratives and interrogatives) to socialize young children to valued local socio-cultural practices and competencies (p. 75). We find it important to mention here the extraordinary body of work by de León (2000),[9] now spanning 15 years of fieldwork, studying language socialization practices of Tzotzil family interaction in the home in Chiapas, Mexico. Studies by de León have been contributing significantly to language socialization theory and method, particularly for her detailed study of the participatory linguistic and interactional patterns of infants' early communication with caregivers, expanding on the earlier distinction between child-oriented and situation-oriented interactions. Her studies provide a nuanced description of pointing, gaze direction, and directives ("say x") that socialize participatory competence prior to language development (2000, p. 138) beyond the mother-child dyad.

The findings in Schecter and Bayley's (2002) study of Mexican groups in Texas and California incorporate concepts and themes from language socialization research. The study draws on an initial corpus of interviews of forty Mexican-origin families that included both nested and purposeful sampling of parents and children within each family. These data included a smaller pool of interviews of families that ranged in their use of English and Spanish (p. 17). While there is attention to language form and expression, the focus in this study is on language as *habitual* rather than as a tool for learning. A critique advanced in this study is the need to deepen our understanding of how immigrant and language minority communities maintain and manage the use of English and Spanish at home, in school, and at work. This is an example of code persistence that has the potential to counter arguments of language loss, especially in the United States where English is the favored code.

Zentella's long-term ethnographic study (1997) of the language repertoires of *el bloque*, a working-class Puerto Rican community in New York City, demonstrated that bilingual development was a collaborative, multi-directional process that relied on the social interactions between caregivers-children, children-caregivers, children-children, and caregivers-caregivers. These social interactions were multi-layered in that they drew from existing social networks and resources in the community and were composed of a diversity of bi/multi-dialectal repertoires that were complex, dynamic, and strategic. Zentella offered important insight into strategic code-switching of bi/multi-dialectal speakers who through selective code alternation purposefully reconnected "with people, occasions, settings, and power configurations from their history of past interactions, and imprinting their own 'act of identity'" (p. 114). Zentella demonstrated that "language shift," or loss of Spanish and preference for English monolingualism, required a grounded analysis of how social networks and local resources are shaped in turn by macro-structurations that impinge on speech communities, for example, migrations out of the community due to economic flux.

Religious Contexts

A strand of language socialization studies has looked at religious institutions and their socializing force through language and literacy instruction. The analyses of the language socialization practices of the Christian church are not new, and they have also been explored in other cultural contexts by language socialization researchers (Duranti, Ochs, & Ta'ase, 1995; Schieffelin, 2002). More specific to Latino populations, the *doctrina* context for immigrant Mexican children's literacy development had already been identified (Farr, 1994) as a site of potential cultural continuity. Baquedano-López' (1997, 1998, 2001) studies of religious instruction in Spanish for children, *doctrina,* at two Catholic parishes in California have provided a window into understanding the processes of transnational identity formation and literacy. Through narrative tellings of the religious icon of *Nuestra Señora de Guadalupe* (Our Lady of Guadalupe) and other literacy practices such as saying prayers and telling Bible stories, the *doctrina* children were taught to adopt was a collective social identity as they learned to identify with Mexico in the context of Catholic instruction in the United States—even when children participating in these classes were not all of Mexican descent. These practices influenced linguistic and cultural continuity, including actual religious practice across space and time in spite of documented exclusionary debates against Mexican immigrants in the public discourse of the state of California and within one of the parishes where *doctrina* was offered (Baquedano-López, 2004; Baquedano-López, Leyva, & Baretto, 2005). Ek's study (2002, 2005) of a Los Angeles Pentecostal church's classes for adolescents illuminated different socialization dynamics that through the moral force to stay on the Christian path universalized and erased ethnic differences for the mostly Central American congregation. These studies invite an examination of the different political presence of Latino ethnic groups in the United States and of the history of the various religious traditions in the Americas as they illustrate how in one context, students identify ethnically with the majority group and in the other, those ethnicities are minimized.

The responses of Latinos to church discourses and practices are significant as Relaño-Pastor (2005) has illustrated. Drawing primarily from interview data in southern California, Relaño-Pastor explained how immigrants sometimes find themselves at odds with an institution that fails to recognize their cultural values. Relaño-Pastor described a mother's moralizing and socializing responses to what she perceived and evaluated as exclusionary (and insulting) practices during Catholic mass where English was used instead of Spanish for a largely Spanish-speaking audience.

In this section we have reviewed language socialization studies across educational contexts. Our survey of home and school research reveals a tendency in this work to focus on continuities rather than discontinuities. That is, the work we reviewed illustrates that the practices of the home are not always at odds with the practices of school. This might be indicative of the attention that language socialization researchers pay to the use of language in context. Thus attention to routine activities that involve parents, siblings, peers, and others, expand the participation framework in these activities and draw on a variety of resources. The result is a view of Latinos that is not rooted in "deficit" notions of educational attainment. Our review of research of Latino practices across the contexts of home, school, and community provides opportunities to understand the complexity of the social order(s) that Latinos in the United States negotiate in the day to day activities across these domains. There is the pull to assimilate into mainstream practices and schooling plays a significant role in this process, yet there are spaces and opportunities for resistance and change as captured in the studies of school reform movements of Rymes (2001) and Yang (2004). The contexts of religious instruction, for example, provide both the means to reproduce systems of ideology and practice but they also generate the tensions that lead to practices of cultural and linguistic resignification in the context of immigration to the United States. In the following section we review the influence of language socialization research on other disciplines, in particular in second language acquisition research and in behavioral studies.

Language Socialization Research across the Disciplines

While language socialization research is incorporated into other disciplines, the possibilities for change within the paradigm, or of its premises and tenets, are likely to occur. Language socialization research is a relatively new approach and although it has solidified its methodology and theoretical orientation in the last few years, it will be difficult to predict the direction that language socialization research might take as it is used to examine new topics and new questions, and as technology and methods are continually redefining qualitative inquiry. In this section we review two disciplinary fields that have begun to incorporate language socialization approaches to learning and development.

Second Language Socialization Studies and Second Language Acquisition

Language socialization theory and method have inspired new approaches to the study of second-language acquisition (SLA) in ways that are redefining dominant themes, including notions of language, learning, and identity in multilingual settings (Kramsch, 2002). There is however, a distinction here (and a comprehensive review is beyond the scope of this chapter) between language socialization studies carried out in bilingual and multilingual settings and those addressing SLA questions in those communities. SLA studies are characterized by their explicit attention to classic questions of language learning of *individuals* in mixed code settings such as the development of specific linguistic features, the preference for certain codes, or the acquisition of pragmatic competence in another language-culture system. Language socialization studies, on the other hand, give preference to an examination of broader social processes that shape individual and collective cultural identities (Garrett & Baquedano-López, 2002). SLA research has maintained a special position in the study of Latino education in the United States providing explanations and description of contexts of bilingual interaction in and out of school (Valdés, 1981; Zentella, 1997) and language maintenance and shift (Silva-Corvalán, 1991, 1994). Recent contributions drawn from language socialization research in education that examine SLA are proliferating and they are attending to the social contexts for learning in the study of language acquisition.

Rymes' proposal for a new approach to SLA as *second language socialization* (Rymes, 1997) is grounded in her ethnographic study of the linguistic practices of students in an alternative high school in Los Angeles where 50% of the student body was Spanish-speaking Latino. In her study she examined how Latino and African American students contested and engaged, and at times, reframed, the code-switching practices and ideologies about the value of English and Spanish in school and society at large. Rymes suggests that language socialization theory and methodology can contribute to a better understanding of how second-language status is used in daily interactional routines to enforce or resist stigmatized identities. For example, posing questions that are not readily observable in classic SLA research, such as how routines and habits involving second-language speakers or bilingual speakers reproduce languages and ideologies about languages, could provide a view into the socio-historical setting where language acquisition is taking place. Rymes and Pash (2001) expanded on this view. In their study of the classroom experiences of René, a second-grade boy from Costa Rica, Rymes and Pash examined the ways that he compromised his understanding of his social identity and language use. In school he was "passing" as competent in oral skills during classroom interaction, yet he was being designated for special education classes. The study's focus on classroom routines as preserving identity but perhaps standing in contrast with literacy routines is instructive for understanding the multiple meanings and outcomes of seemingly innocuous classroom practices. As René's case illustrates, the participation of a student in classroom routines is intertwined with the expression of other social identities, and in many instances, the conflict generated by participating in classroom routines is not always satisfactorily resolved.

Willet's (1995) study of interactional classroom routines in an ESL classroom was also carried out from a language socialization perspective. She described the socio-cultural dimensions, or what she calls the micro-politics of classroom interaction, to explain how ESL students in first grade become socialized to school routines, communicative competence, and academic identities. While located in a classroom where many languages were being spoken including Korean,

Hebrew, Arabic, and Spanish, Willet described the case of Xavier (a Latino Spanish-speaking student) whose classroom strategies were similar to those of René in the Rymes and Pash (2001) study. Willet described, using discourse-analytic methodology and sustained ethnographic observation, how Xavier was set-up to fail in this classroom through routines that positioned him in need of more guided adult support and away from the rich contexts of peer support. Thus, in comparison to two girls, the other focal students in Willet's study, Xavier learned to competently navigate the general social contours of classroom participation, but did not acquire the necessary collaborative strategies that could have helped him develop academic skills.

Relevant to the design and implementation of studies of second language socialization is Watson-Gegeo's (2004) review of the changing nature of second-language acquisition theory. She has called for an integration of socio-cultural "insights" of language socialization research into new developments of SLA theories and perspectives as a way to balance mentalistic learning theories. She proposes that reviewing the classic questions that inspired early language social- ization work, including questions about theory of mind and linguistic relativity can bolster and legitimize emerging language socialization research in SLA. According to Watson-Gegeo (2004), language socialization theory can offer six insights that SLA research could incorporate. First, language and culture are mutually constitutive and socially constructed. Second, all cultural activities across different contexts are socio-historically marked. Third, studies of language use offer rich ethnographic context. Fourth, child and adult interactions produce more than gram- matical units they generate culturally meaningful ways of thinking, feeling, and being in the world. Fifth, language socialization uses cultural anthropological concepts of development to describe community, cognition, and identity. In summary, she lays out requirements for the application of language socialization theory in SLA studies that must combine ethnographic, sociolinguistic and discourse analytic methods and that may include ecologically valid quan- titative methodology. Watson-Gegeo notes that this enterprise could represent the birth of a new paradigm, yet welcomes the idea that SLA research would move away from the study of learning in a context that "typically derives from a positivist, experimental model of research that attempts to control variables rather than account for the complexities of people's real lives situations" (p. 341).

Behavioral and Developmental Studies

In addition to integrating perspectives in the field of Second Language Acquisition, language socialization research has been taken up in the behavioral sciences. We highlight here a the- matic issue entitled "Language socialization and Learning in Mexican-Descent Families" where six studies were published in the *Hispanic Journal of Behavioral Sciences* (Cervantes & Perez-Granados, 2002). From the editors' perspective, the studies provide a more comprehen- sive view of Mexican family life and of children's and parents' attitudes and beliefs regarding language choice. Our review of this collection supports the editors' assertion and we further note that the work challenges deficit views of Mexican families' language practices, such as infrequent use of cognitively complex talk by mothers (Eisenberg, 2002; Moreno, 2002). The studies highlight the role of other conversational partners besides the mother (Perez-Grana- dos, 2002), expanding the documentation of the range of participation frameworks for the developing child, breaking away from dyadic interactions. The various articles address topics as diverse as emotion (Cervantes, 2002), the social context of home literacy (role of siblings in socialization) and the learning of normative scripts such as objective labeling and school- like scaffolding strategies (Perez-Granados, 2002). Except for the Pease-Alvarez study, these studies could not be characterized as language socialization studies in their design, but they do focus on many instances of socializing interactions using a variety of methods from quasi- experimental to ethnographic.

Future Trajectories

The review of the work presented in this chapter gives us a way to appraise the development and direction of language socialization research conducted among Latinos. Language socialization is a viable approach for understanding the complex of experience of Latinos in the United States. In this era of high-stakes accountability that drives educational policy, narrow notions of learning are being generated as benchmarks for achievement and competence. This current educational landscape fails to recognize the centrality of language and social interaction and the ways in which Latino students manage the multiple demands of the educational contexts they participate in. As the language socialization approach is taken up by education researchers and researchers in other disciplines, we can begin to move away from attention to the principles and premises of language socialization research (often focusing on both perceived and actual limitations) and move towards more theoretically nuanced and complex studies that could expand its conceptual domain. In her recent edited book, Zentella (2005) reminds us of the work that still needs to be done to counter the ways Latino children are misunderstood and understudied. Language socialization research offers a way to understand the lives of children and their families while attending to both their local and larger contexts of interaction.

Zentella has offered challenging critiques to researchers working among minority populations. She reminds us of the need to be accountable (other than the accountability created through peer-review) for the work that we do. Her call for a more "anthropolitical linguistics" is fitting and relevant to language socialization research as well. In our review of the early research on language use and classroom discourse, it was surprising to find research that did not identify student populations, yet pseudonyms with Spanish-sounding names were the only indicators that the English translated dialogue had taken place among Latinos. As we have indicated, much of the earlier research of Latinos tended to be carried outside of its socio-historical context. To paraphrase Hymes' (1972) call for a fuller description of speech in community—it matters who speaks, to whom, and under what conditions. To revoice Zentella's words—it matters who does the research and for what purposes. We conclude our chapter with two concrete and brief suggestions for language socialization research on Latinos and education.

Revisiting the Meaning of Competence

As research in language socialization proliferates, it is important to revisit the meaning behind the concept of "competence," which does not simply refer to the acquisition of language. Language socialization points to language as the primary tool for expressing socio-cultural and pragmatic meaning and as the focal means for competent socialization. Ochs (1986b) illustrates what it means for children to acquire pragmatic competence:

> One critical area of social competence a child must acquire is the ability to recognize/interpret what social activity/event is taking place and to speak and act in ways sensitive to the context. Children must also have the competence to define activities/events through their language and nonverbal actions...language is not simply responsive to the social activity/event; it is the social activity (Hymes 1974), as in teasing, negotiating, telling a story, tattletelling, explaining. (p. 3)

In this respect, competence is not simply a means toward a greater end but also an end onto itself. While the quote above references children, it is not difficult to extend this meaning to a variety of contexts and age groups. The core of socialization lies in the ability to display expected competencies, yet it does not always guarantee the display of such knowledge. The research we reviewed here illustrated many instances where norms of expected behavior were not displayed, for example the actions of René in the Rymes and Pash (2001) study. Investigating why competencies are displayed in some cases but not in others demands paying attention to both the local organizations of activities but also the broader socio-political and economic contexts. There is an urgent need to revisit what competence means for Latinos (in particular English-Language Learners) (Dúran, 2008; García, 2005). Language socialization research has the methodological and theoretical tools to help us examine these contexts.

A Move away from Comparisons to American White Middle-Class Norms

As language socialization research expands into other fields and domains, it would be important to see a shift away from the tendency of using AWMC cultural models as benchmarks for understanding Latino practices (and indeed of other minority group practices). After 20 years of language socialization research, we find that this approach still filters through the most recent language socialization studies among Latinos. An exhaustive examination of how home literacy activities in a variety of Latino homes (e.g., across socio-economic statuses, region, country of origin, or language registers) contrasted to those of Anglo families might not necessarily provide a fuller account of how language, culture, and learning are integrated in the context of Latino experience. Language socialization researchers can develop a different approach to conceptualizing socialization practices *within* a broader field of Latino/Chicano Education and culture. In this regard, language socialization with its core approach to understanding learning and development in social context has the potential to bring into focus internal variation, that is, the diversity that exists within Latino linguistic and cultural practices and worldviews. We add here a reference to Mendoza-Denton (1999b) who finds that the study of a "linguistics of contact" (citing Pratt, 1987), and what we capture in this chapter under the rubric *Latino diacritic*, provides a conceptual entry to examine how cultural borders and the practices within and across them are shared and enacted. Mendoza-Denton explains that through this type of analysis we can "find the articulation of different levels of semiotic systems, where subtle linguistic cues work in tandem with material culture to index history and ideology" (p. 388). This is precisely the area where studies of Latino language socialization can deepen our understanding of how macro-social processes shape educational practices and how cultural process become naturalized in face-to-face interaction and in everyday practice. Language socialization research can bridge this divide.

Acknowledgments

We express our appreciation and respect to all the scholars who have contributed to our current understanding of the role of language socialization in learning, in particular Elinor Ochs and Bambi Schieffelin. We thank Ana Celia Zentella for inspiring and challenging the way we frame research for and by Latinos. We are grateful to the members of the Laboratory for the Study of Interaction, Discourse, and Educational Research (L-SIDER) at UC Berkeley for providing us with a resourceful space to collaborate. We thank Sera Hernández, Shlomy Kattan, and Ariana Mangual for comments and suggestions on earlier drafts.

Notes

1. While many studies on Latinos assume that the majority of Latinos speak Spanish, we include here indigenous languages of the Americas and make reference to the research among indigenous groups that have influenced language socialization research.
2. Gumperz refers here to Mexican-Americans of the U.S. Southwest.
3. Spanish variant spoken by Chicanos.

4. We use here Paredes' meaning to indicate Mexican-descent populations in the United States. We acknowledge that the term "Chicano" and the recent variants "Chicana/o" and "Chican@" carry historical meanings and important socio-political connotations. Here we adhere to the use that the authors we review employed in their work.
5. Spanish speakers in northern New Mexico.
6. The idea that in the development of second language grammars learners encounter and work against dissimilar features of each source language.
7. See V. González (2001), however, for an alternative, perhaps less inclusive, interpretation of this definition.
8. Mexican immigrants in Chicago.
9. We direct the reader to de León's article for a complete list of references of this formidable work.

References

Auer, P., & Wei, L. (2007). *Handbook of multilingualism and multilingual communication*. New York: Mouton de Gruyter.

Baquedano-López, P. (1997). Creating social identity through doctrina narratives. *Issues in Applied Linguistics, 8*(1), 27–45.

Baquedano-López, P. (1998). *Language socialization of Mexican children in a Los Angeles Catholic parish*. Unpublished doctoral dissertation, University of California, Los Angeles.

Baquedano-López, P. (2001). Creating social identities through doctrina narratives. In A. Duranti (Ed.), *Linguistic anthropology: A reader* (pp. 343–358). Malden, MA: Blackwell.

Baquedano-López, P. (2004). Traversing the Center: The politics of language use in a Catholic religious education program for immigrant Mexican children. *Anthropology & Education Quarterly, 35*(2), 212–232.

Baquedano-López, P., Leyva, L. R., & Baretto, T. (2005). *Strategies for linguistic and cultural continuity in Spanish-based Catholic religious education programs (doctrina)*. Paper presented at the 4th International Symposium on Bilingualism, Tempe, AZ.

Bayley, R., & Schecter, S. R. (Eds.). (2003). *Language socialization in bilingual and multilingual societies*. Buffalo, NY: Multilingual Matters.

Bergen, J. J. (1990). *Spanish in the United States: Sociolinguistic issues*. Washington, DC: Georgetown University Press.

Bernstein, B. B. (1971/1974). *Class, codes and control*. London: Routledge and K. Paul.

Bhimji, F. (2005). Language socialization with directives in two Mexican immigrant families in South Central Los Angeles. In A. C. Zentella (Ed.), *Building on strength: Language and literacy in Latino families and communities* (pp. 60–76). New York: Teachers College Press.

Bhimji, F. (2007). Mexican American families: Socializing bilingualism/biculturalism in South Central Los Angeles. In L. D. Soto (Ed.), *The Praeger handbook of Latino education in the U.S.* (pp. 300–306) Westport, CT: Praeger.

Bloomfield, L. (1984). *Language*. Chicago: University of Chicago Press. (Original work published 1933)

Boggs, S. (1985). *Speaking, relating, and learning: A study of Hawaiian children at home and at school*. Norwood, NJ: Ablex.

Briggs, C. L. (1984). Learning how to ask: Native metacommunicative competence and the incompetence of fieldworkers. *Language in Society, 13*, 1–28.

Bourdieu, P. (1977). *Outline of a theory of practice*. New York: Cambridge University Press.

Cancino, H., Rosansky, E. J., & Schumann, J. H. (1975). The acquisition of the English auxiliary by native Spanish speakers. *TESOL Quarterly, 9*(4), 421–430.

Cazden, C. B., John, V. P., & Hymes, D. H. (1972). *Functions of language in the classroom*. New York: Teachers College Press.

Cervantes, C. A. (2002). Explanatory emotion talk in Mexican immigrant and Mexican American families. *Hispanic Journal of Behavioral Sciences, 24*(2), 138–163.

Cervantes, C. A., & Perez-Granados, D. R. (2002). Language socialization and learning in Mexican-descent families: An introduction. *Hispanic Journal of Behavioral Sciences, 24*(2), 107–113.

Cicourel, A. V. (1973). *Cognitive sociology: Language and meaning in social interaction*. Harmondsworth, UK: Penguin Education.

Cook-Gumperz, J. (1973). *Social control and socialization: A study of class differences in the language of maternal control*. London: Routledge & K. Paul.

Cook-Gumperz, J., & Corsaro, W. A. (1986). Introduction. In J. Cook-Gumperz, W. A. Corsaro, & J. Streeck (Eds.), *Children's worlds and children's language* (pp. 1–12). Berlin: M. de Gruyter.

Corsaro, W. A. (1985). *Friendship and peer culture in the early years*. Norwood, NJ: Ablex.

de León, L. (2000). The emergent participant: Interactive patterns in the socialization of Tzotzil (Mayan) infants. *Journal of Linguistic Anthropology, 8*(2), 131–161.

Durán, R. P. (1981). *Latino language and communicative behavior*. Norwood, NJ: Ablex.

Dúran, R. P. (2008). Assessing English-language learners' achievement. *Review in Research in Education, 32*, 292–327.

Duranti, A., Ochs, E., & Ta`ase, E. (1995). Change and tradition in literacy instruction in a Samoan American community. *Educational Researcher*, 57–74.

Eisenberg, A. R. (1986). Teasing: Verbal play in two Mexicano homes. In B. B. Schieffelin & E. Ochs (Eds.), *Language socialization across cultures* (pp. 182–198). New York: Cambridge University Press.

Eisenberg, A. R. (2002). Maternal teaching talk within families of Mexican descent: Influences of task and socioeconomic status. *Hispanic Journal of Behavioral Sciences, 24*(2), 206–224.

Ek, L. (2002). *Language, identity, and morality in an immigrant Latino Pentecostal church*. Unpublished doctoral dissertation, University of California, Los Angeles.

Ek, L. (2005). Staying on God's path: Socializing Latino immigrant youth to a Christian Pentecostal identity in Southern California. In A. C. Zentella (Ed.), *Building on strength: Language and literacy in Latino families and communities* (pp. 77–92). New York: Teachers College Press.

Ervin-Tripp, S. M., & Mitchell-Kernan, C. (1977). *Child discourse*. New York: Academic Press.

Fabian, J. (1983). *Time and the other: How anthropology makes its object*. New York: Columbia University Press.

Farr, M. (1994). En los dos idiomas: Literacy practices among Chicano Mexicanos. In B. J. Moss (Ed.), *Literacy across communities* (pp. 9–47). Cresskill, NJ: Hampton Press.

Farr, M. (2006). *Rancheros in Chicagoacán: Language and identity in a transnational community*. Austin: University of Texas Press.

Farr, M., & Barajas, E. D. (2005). Mexicanos in Chicago: Language ideology and identity. In A. C. Zentella (Ed.), *Building on strength: Language and literacy in Latino families and communities* (pp. 137–147). New York: Teachers College Press.

García, E. E. (2001). *Hispanic education in the United States: Raíces y alas*. Lanham, MD: Rowman & Littlefield.

García, E. E. (2005). *Teaching and learning in two languages: Bilingualism & schooling in the United States*. New York: Teachers College Press.

Garrett, P. B. (2006). Language socialization. *Elsevier Encyclopedia of Language and Linguistics, 6*, 604–613.

Garrett, P. B., & Baquedano-López, P. (2002). Language socialization: Reproduction and continuity, transformation and change. *Annual Review of Anthropology, 31*(1), 339–361.

Genishi, C. S. (1976). *Rules for code-switching in young Spanish-English-speakers: An exploratory study of language socialization*. Unpublished doctoral dissertation, University of California, Berkeley.

Giddens, A. (1977). *Studies in social and political theory*. London: Hutchinson.

González, G. G. (1997). Culture, language, and the Americanization of Mexican children. In A. Darder, R. D. Torres, & H. Gutiérrez (Eds.), *Latinos and education: A critical reader* (pp. xxii, 488). New York: Routledge.

González, N. (2001). *I am my language: Discourses of women & children in the borderlands*. Tucson: University of Arizona Press.

González, N., Moll, L. C., & Amanti, C. (2005). *Funds of knowledge: Theorizing practice in households, communities, and classrooms*. Mahwah, NJ: Erlbaum.

González, V. (2001). The role of socioeconomic and socio-cultural factors in language minority children's development: An ecological research view. *Bilingual Research Journal, 25*(1, 2), 1–30.

Goodwin, M. H. (1995). Co-constructing in girls' hopscotch. *Research on Language and Social Interaction, 28*(3), 261–281.

Gumperz, J. J. (1968). The speech community. *International Encyclopedia of the Social Sciences,* 381–386.

Gumperz, J. J. (1982). *Discourse strategies.* New York: Cambridge University Press.

Gumperz, J. J., & Hernandez-Chavez, E. (1972). Bilingualism, bidialectalism, and classroom interaction. In C. B. Cazden, V. P. John, & D. Hymes (Eds.), *Functions of language in the classroom* (pp. 84–108). New York: Teachers College Press.

Gutiérrez, K. D., Baquedano-López, P., & Alvarez, H. (2001). Literacy as hybridity: Moving beyond bilingualism in urban classrooms. In M. Luz-Reyes & J. Halcón (Eds.), *The best for our children: Critical perspectives on literacy for Latino students* (pp. 122–141). New York: Teachers College Press.

Gutiérrez, M. (1990). Sobre el mantenimiento de las cláusas subordinadas en el español de Los Angeles. In J. J. Bergen (Ed.), *Spanish in the United States: Sociolinguistic issues* (pp. 31–38). Washington, DC: Georgetown University Press.

Heath, S. B. (1983). *Ways with words: Language, life, and work in communities and classrooms.* New York: Cambridge University Press.

Hornberger, N. H., & Duff, P. A. (Eds.). (2008). *Encyclopedia of language in education* (2nd ed., Vol. 8: Language socialization). New York: Springer/Kluwer Academic Publishers.

Hymes, D. (1972). Introduction. In C. Cazden, V. P. John, & D. Hymes (Eds.), *Functions of language in the classroom* (pp. xi–lvii). New York: Teachers College Press.

Hymes, D. (1974). *Foundations in sociolinguistics: An ethnographic approach.* Philadelphia: University of Pennsylvania Press.

Jacobson, R. (1990). Intrasentential code-switching and the socioeconomic perspective. In J. J. Bergen (Ed.), *Spanish in the United States: Sociolinguistic issues* (pp. 59–66). Washington, DC: Georgetown University Press.

Jaramillo, J. A. (1990). Domain constraints on the use of *tú* and *usted.* In J. J. Bergen (Ed.), *Spanish in the United States: Sociolinguistic issues* (pp. 14–22). Washington, D.C: Georgetown University Press.

Kramsch, C. J. (2002). *Language acquisition and language socialization: Ecological perspectives.* London: Continuum.

Kulick D. (2006). Theory in furs: Masochist Anthropology. *Current Anthropology, 47,* 933–952.

Kulick, D., & Schieffelin, B.B. (2004). Language socialization. In A. Duranti (Ed.), *A companion to linguistic anthropology* (pp. 496–517). Oxford, UK: Blackwell.

Kyratzis, A. (2001a). Children's gender indexing in language: From the separate worlds hypothesis to considerations of culture, context, and power. *Research on Language and Social Interaction, 34*(1), 1–13.

Kyratzis, A. (2001b). Emotion talk in preschool same-sex friendship groups: Fluidity over time and context. *Early Education & Development, 12*(3), 359–390.

Kyratzis, A. (2004). Talk and interaction among children and the co-construction of peer groups and peer culture. *Annual Review of Anthropology, 33,* 625–649.

Lauria, A. (1964). "Respeto," "Relajo" and inter-personal relations in Puerto Rico. *Anthropological Quarterly, 37*(2), 53–67.

Macbeth, D. (2003). Hugh Mehan's Learning Lessons reconsidered: On the differences between the naturalistic and critical analysis of classroom discourse. *American Educational Research Journal, 40*(1), 239–280.

Mead, G. H., & Murphy, A. E. (1932). *The philosophy of the present.* Chicago: Open Court.

Mead, M. (1950). *Sex and temperament in three primitive societies.* New York: New American Library.

Mehan, H. (1979). *Learning lessons: Social organization in the classroom.* Cambridge, MA: Harvard University Press.

Mendoza-Denton, N. (1999a). Fighting words: Latina girls, gangs, and language attitudes. In D. L. Galindo & M. D. Gonzales (Eds.), *Speaking Chicana: Voice, power, and identity* (pp. 39–56). Tucson: University of Arizona Press.

Mendoza-Denton, N. (1999b). Sociolinguistics and linguistic anthropology of U.S. Latinos. *Annual Review of Anthropology, 28*(1), 375–395.

Mendoza-Denton, N. (1999c). Turn-initial no: Collaborative opposition among Latina adolescents. In M. Bucholtz, A. C. Liang, & L. A. Sutton (Eds.), *Reinventing identities: The gendered self in discourse* (Vol. 1, pp. 273–292). New York: Oxford University Press.

Mercado, C. I. (2005). Seeing what's there: Latino and literacy funds of knowledge in New York Puerto Rican homes. In A. C. Zentella (Ed.), *Building on strength: Language and literacy in Latino families and communities* (pp. 134–147). New York: Teachers College Press.

Moll, L. C. (Ed.). (1990). *Vygotsky and education: Instructional implications and applications of sociohistorical psychology.* Cambridge, UK: Cambridge University Press.

Moreno, R. P. (2002). Teaching the alphabet: An exploratory look at maternal instruction in Mexican American families. *Hispanic Journal of Behavioral Sciences, 24*(2), 191–205.

Ochs, E. (1988). *Culture and language development: Language acquisition and language socialization in a Samoan village.* New York: Cambridge University Press.

Ochs, E. (2002). Becoming a speaker of culture. In C. J. Kramsch (Ed.), *Language acquisition and language socialization: Ecological perspectives* (pp. 99–120). New York: Continuum.

Ochs, E., & Schieffelin, B. B. (1979). *Developmental pragmatics.* New York: Academic Press.

Ochs, E., & Schieffelin, B. B. (1984). Language acquisition and socialization: Three developmental stories and their implications. In R. A. Shweder & R. A. LeVine (Eds.), *Culture theory: Essays on mind, self, and emotion* (pp. 276–320). New York: Cambridge University Press.

Paredes, A. (1977). On the ethnographic work among minority groups: A folklorist's perspective, *New Scholar, 6,* 1–32.

Pease-Alvarez, L. (2002). Moving beyond linear trajectories of language shift and bilingual language socialization. *Hispanic Journal of Behavioral Sciences, 24*(2), 114–137.

Peñalosa, F. (1980). *Chicano sociolinguistics: A brief introduction.* Rowley, MA: Newbury House.

Perez-Granados, D. R. (2002). Normative scripts for object labeling during a play activity: Mother-child and sibling conversations in Mexican-descent families. *Hispanic Journal of Behavioral Sciences, 24*(2), 164–190.

Philips, S. U. (1983). *The invisible culture: Communication in classroom and community on the Warm Springs Indian Reservation.* New York: Longman.

Pratt, M. L. (1987). Linguistic utopias. In N. Fabb, D Attridge, A. Durant, & C. McCabe (Eds.), *The linguistics of writing: Arguments between language and literature* (pp. 48–66). Manchester, UK: Manchester University Press.

Pye, C. (1980). *The acquisition of grammatical morphemes in Quiché Mayan.* Unpublished doctoral dissertation, University of Pittsburgh, PA.

Pye, C. (1983). Mayan Telegraphese: Intonational determinants of inflectional development in Quiche Mayan. *Language, 59*(3), 583–604.

Relaño-Pastor, A. M. (2005). The language socialization experiences of Latina mothers in Southern California. In A. C. Zentella (Ed.), *Building on strength: Language and literacy in Latino families and communities* (pp. 148–161). New York: Teachers College Press.

Rodríguez, M. V. (2005). Dominican children with special needs in New York City: Language and literacy practices. In A. C. Zentella (Ed.), *Building on strength: Language and literacy in Latino families and communities* (pp. 119–133). New York: Teachers College Press.

Rosaldo, R. (1989/1993). *Culture and truth: The remaking of social analysis.* Boston: Beacon Press.

Rosales, A. (1997). *Chicano! The history of the Mexican-American civil rights movements.* Houston, TX: Arte Público Press/University of Houston.

Rymes, B. (1996). Naming as social practice: The case of Little Creeper from Diamond Street. *Language in Society, 25*(2), 237–260.

Rymes, B. (1997). Second language socialization: A+ new approach to second language acquisition research. *Journal of Intensive English studies, 11,* 143–155.

Rymes, B. (2001). *Conversational borderlands: Language and identity in an alternative urban high school.* New York: Teachers College Press.

Rymes, B., & Pash, D. (2001). Questioning identity: The case of one second-language learner. *Anthropology & Education Quarterly, 32*(3), 276–300.

Schecter, S. R., & Bayley, R. (2002). *Language as cultural practice: Mexicanos en el norte.* Mahwah, NJ: Erlbaum.

Schieffelin, B. B. (2002). Marking time: The dichotomizing discourse of multiple temporalities. *Current Anthropology, 43*(5–17).

Schieffelin, B. B., & Ochs, E. (1986a). Language Socialization. *Annual Review of Anthropology, 15,* 163–191.

Schieffelin, B. B., & Ochs, E. (1986b). *Language socialization across cultures.* New York: Cambridge University Press.

Schumann, J. H. (1978). The Acculturation model for second-language acquisition. In G. Gingras (Ed.), *Second language acquisition and foreign language teaching* (pp. 27–50). Washington DC: Center for Applied Linguistics.

Silva-Corvalán, C. (1991). Spanish language attrition in a contact situation with English. In H. W. Selinger & R. M. Vago (Eds.), *First language attrition* (pp. 151–174). New York: Cambridge University Press.

Silva-Corvalán, C. (1994). *Language contact and change: Spanish in Los Angeles.* Oxford, UK: Oxford University Press.

Soto, L. D. (2007). (Ed.). *The Praeger handbook of Latino education in the U.S.* Westport, CT: Praeger.

Trueba, H. T. (2002). Multiple ethnic, racial, and cultural identities in action: From marginality to a new cultural capital in modern society. *Journal of Latinos and Education, 1*(1), 7–28.

Valdés, G. (1981). Code switching as a deliberate verbal strategy: A microanalysis of direct and indirect requests among Chicano bilingual speakers. In R. P. Durán (Ed.), *Latino language and communicative behavior* (pp. 95–107). Norwood, NJ: Ablex.

Valdés, G. (1996). *Con respeto: Bridging the distances between culturally diverse families and schools: An ethnographic portrait.* New York: Teachers College Press.

Valencia, R. R. (1997). *The evolution of deficit thinking: Educational thought and practice.* Washington, DC: Falmer Press.

Valencia, R. R. (Ed.). (2002). *Chicano school failure and success: Past, present, and future* (2nd ed.). New York: Falmer Press.

Vásquez, O. A., Pease-Alvarez, L., & Shannon, S. M. (1994). *Pushing boundaries: Language and culture in a Mexicano community.* New York: Cambridge University Press.

Vigil, E. (1999). *The crusade for justice: Chicano militancy and the government's war on dissent.* Madison: The University of Wisconsin.

Vygotsky, L. S. (1978). *Mind in society.* Cambridge, MA: Harvard University Press.

Watson-Gegeo, K. A. (2004). Mind, language, and epistemology: Toward a language socialization paradigm for SLA. *The Modern Language Journal, 88*(3), 331–350.

Willet, J. (1995). Becoming first graders in an L2: An ethnographic study of L2 socialization. *TESOL Quarterly, 29*(3), 473–503.

Wong-Fillmore, L. (1992). Learning a language from learners. In C. J. Kramsch & S. McConnell-Ginet (Eds.), *Text and context: Cross-disciplinary perspectives on language study* (pp. 46–66). Lexington, MA: D.C. Heath.

Yang, W. (2004). *Taking over: The struggle to transform an urban school system.* Unpublished doctoral dissertation, University of California, Berkeley.

Zentella, A. C. (1981). *"Hablamos los dos. We speak both": Growing in el barrio.* Unpublished doctoral dissertation, University of Pennsylvania, Philadelphia.

Zentella, A. C. (1997). *Growing up bilingual: Puerto Rican children in New York.* Malden, MA: Blackwell.

Zentella, A. C. (Ed.). (2005). *Building on strength: Language and literacy in Latino families and communities.* New York: Teachers College Press.

24 Latino Families

Culture and Schooling

Flora V. Rodríguez-Brown
University of Illinois at Chicago

Introduction

According to Fry (2006), the enrollment in U.S. public schools has increased due mainly to the growth of the Hispanic population. Between Fiscal Year 1993–94 and Fiscal Year 2002–03, Hispanics have accounted for 64% of the increase in public school enrollment. In general, Latinos have positive attitudes toward their local schools and report that they are involved in their children's education (The Pew Hispanic Center & the Kaiser Family Foundation, 2004). The same report explains that Latino parents believe that their children do not do as well in school as other populations because of a disconnection between home and school, and the lack of a bridge between teachers and parents and community. In contrast to the White population, Latinos are in favor of improving the schools where they live, rather than moving their children to different schools. In relation to attitudes toward English, data from the Pew Hispanic Center (2006) show that Hispanics (both immigrant and natives) endorse the relevance of the English language "regardless of income, party affiliation, fluency in English or how long they have been living in the United States" (p. 1). As a result of immigration, the number of Spanish-speaking adult Latinos is greater than those who are bilingual or English dominant, but data show that second generation Latinos are more English than Spanish dominant (Pew Hispanic Center-Survey Brief, 2004).

A fact sheet from the Pew Hispanic Center (2002) shows that Latinos are diverse and there are within group differences. Current statistical data on Latinos show that they are the least educated population in the United States, due mostly to continuous immigration of adults with little education from Latin America. Comparisons between native born and immigrant Latinos show that 73% of native born Latinos finish high school in comparison to adult Whites (89%). When the Latino population data (native born and immigrant) are not desegregated, only 57% of Latinos finish high school. The data also show that 66% of Latino children attend predominantly minority schools in comparison to only 9% of White children. In California alone, 16% of the teachers in minority predominant school districts do not have the proper credentials, while only 9% do not have the proper credentials in schools attended by Whites. These data show differences in the quality of education received by Latino children when compared with Whites.

Data from the Condition of Education (U.S. Department of Education, 2007) indicate that the number of U.S. children who speak another language than English at home has more than doubled between 1979 and 2005 and the majority of those children spoke Spanish at home. These children attend schools all over the United States, but the largest concentration of children who speak Spanish at home live and attend school in New Mexico, Texas, California, Arizona, Nevada, Colorado, Florida, New York, New Jersey, and Illinois.

The demographic data describing the Spanish population in the United States are relevant to this chapter because it calls for attention to the cultural and linguistic differences within the Latino populations and also states a necessity for schools to address the needs of a more diverse group than previously described. According to Zentella (2005), "in addition to national origin and linguistic distinctions, class and race account for telling intragroup differences" (p. 21) among Latinos, which may show differences as to how some individuals accommodate well to new situations while others have more trouble adapting to new environments. It is important for schools districts and teachers to be aware of cultural and linguistic aspects of the Latino culture which influence values and beliefs, especially in relation to schooling. Information about Latino families could help teachers understand and accept the particularities of these families. This will allow them to see the relevance of the knowledge that these children bring from home to school, their cultural ways and discourses. In turn, teachers will be able to use this knowledge as a stepping-stone to new knowledge, and it also would enhance continuity between home and school in support of Latino children's learning and school success.

Latino Culture and Education

The concept of *familia* is central to life for Latinos (Abi-Nader, 1991). This term means that whatever is done in everyday life should benefit not only the individual but also the family. It provides the individual with a sense of belonging and interdependence, and it also requires loyalty and obligation. The concept of *familia* implies responsibility and collaboration. *Familia* includes not only parents and children, but the extended family and their networks. This family system provides support, resources, and information to families and individuals within those families. The *familia* shares responsibility for a child's success or failure. In relation to parent involvement in schooling, teachers have to understand that the extended family, rather than just the parents, may be partners in supporting children's learning. Supporting the child while in school is a "shared responsibility" among Latinos (De La Vega, 2007). For this reason alone, it is important for teachers to learn about culturally different parents' perspectives in getting involved in their children's education. Schools, and teachers in particular, need to realize that for immigrant parents of English language learners, schooling in the United States is new and complex, and they will need support from the school in understanding the school expectations as they become involved in their children's education in ways that are different from those already offered at home and through the *familia*.

Cultural Differences and the Home-school Connection

Many times, the expectations of the school, in relation to parent involvement in their children's education, may be in conflict with the parents' beliefs as to what their responsibility and role are in their children's education. Research (Goldenberg, 1989; Goldenberg & Gallimore, 1995; Reese, Gallimore, & Goldenberg, 1999; Rodriguez-Brown, 2004; Valdes, 1996) have found and discussed widely several salient concepts in relation to a definition of a Latino parent's role in their children's education. Goldenberg (1987), Reese, Balzano, Gallimore, & Goldenberg (1995), Rodriguez-Brown (2001), and Valdes (1996) have described a dichotomy in the way Latino parents, particularly new immigrants, perceive their role as teachers. These parents differentiate between *educar* (to educate) and *enseñar* (to teach) in their relationship with their children. They describe their role as teachers as one of helping their children become good people. They believe that their role and responsibility is the teaching of morals, manners and values. When one asks Latino parents what and how they support their children's learning at home, they explain that they teach their children to be *bien educados* (well educated). Delgado-Gaitán and Trueba (1991) also found the Latino parents' expectation that their children have *buena educación* (p. 35). When you ask Latino parents directly about whether they teach their children to read and write at home, they look at you with surprise. They believe that it is the role of the school to teach (*enseñar*) such things as reading, writing, and math. Carrasquillo and London (1993) describe how Latino parents in their study believed that the school had the responsibility for their children's academic development. Many Latino parents explain that they do not have the education to teach the children school related subjects. They also believe that their lack of English proficiency precludes them from supporting their children's learning at home. When one tries to explain to them that they can teach their children in Spanish, they are surprised. Latino parents always find it surprising when a teacher explains to them that it is the expectation of the school that they teach their children such things as the letters and numbers and that they read to their children a lot before they get to school.

It is not that Latino parents do not want to support their children's learning. Besides their described lack of schooling experiences and lack of English proficiency, they also believe that it is disrespectful to usurp the teachers' role. Latinos show great *respeto* for teachers and schools. The concept of *respeto* (respect) is discussed widely in Valdes (1996). Teachers are highly respected in the Latino culture. Latino parents believe that teachers know more than parents or others in the community. Latinos see the school and the teacher with *respeto* and feel they should not interfere with the teachers' role (Flores, Cousin, & Diaz, 1991). They believe that teachers know more about how to teach (*enseñar*), and they have special ways and knowledge to teach children because of their college training. In contrast, Latino parents believe that they do not have the knowledge, language, or education to take the role of teachers with their children. Findings from a longitudinal study by Reese and Gallimore (2000) show that a teacher's explicit demands for Latino parents to read to their children at home as part of the daily homework had a positive effect on the families' behaviors and on their view of their role as teachers in relation to literacy development. Although parents in the study showed specific cultural ways of learning and teaching which were different from the school, they were able to learn and use new strategies and activities as long as their values and morals were not compromised.

Latino Parents and School Involvement

Vásquez, Pease-Alvarez, and Shannon (1994, p. 43) found that current school structures that draw "mainstream" parents to the school (e.g., PTA) are not effective in attracting the participation of Latino families. Delgado-Gaitán (1991) and Valdes (1996) explain that parents lack cultural knowledge in relation to schools in the United States. This does not mean that parents are not interested in their children's education. Goldenberg (1987) found that that when Latino parents were told explicitly how to teach their children at home, and about school expectations, they reacted positively toward their role in supporting their children's learning. According to Alexsaht-Snider (1991), lack of communication between families and teachers results in teachers' low expectations for performance for children who are culturally and linguistically different, and this has an effect on the children's achievement.

Delgado-Gaitán (1987) and Shannon (1996), among others, argue that teachers and schools do not have accurate perceptions about Latino immigrant families in relation to schooling because of cultural differences. Valdes (1996) believes that the image of what it is to be a "good" parent is different for Latino immigrant parents and teachers, and schools do not understand the possibility of differences across diverse families. Many times schools expect that parents serve as an extension of the school in support of their children's learning, but according to Carrasquillo and London (1993), Latino parents believe it is the responsibility of the school to teach their children and support their academic development. Differing expectations between teachers and parents can produce misunderstandings that interfere with the development of relationships between Latino immigrant families and the schools. Moll (1992) and Valdes (1996) believe that Latino parents lack familiarity with the educational system in the United States. As a result, parents tend to participate in their children's education only on things that they can do at home, and according to their school experiences in their countries of origin which are often different from school expectations and experiences in the United States.

Trueba and Delgado-Gaitán (1991) believe the success or failure of a school intervention or program for Latino parents depends on whether there is collaboration with the parents and/or the community in the development of the program. Delgado-Gaitán found that when systematic linkages between teachers and Latino parents existed, the interventions or programs were co-constructed in a mutual and respectful manner. Programs created according to what the school thinks the parents need to know to support their children are not very successful. Rodriguez-Brown (2004, 2009) calls programs planned without parents and community input "functional" programs. Programs which take into account and respect parents' knowledge, cultural ways, and discourse differences are more relevant to culturally and linguistically different parents. These programs accept what parents bring to the learning situation and share with them new activities which add new repertoires that can be used within the parents' cultural ways as they share knowledge with their children. Delgado-Gaitán (1996) found that Mexican parents who participated in her project COPLA were very committed and interested in the literacy activities taught through the program because they participated in the creation of the program. Vasquez (1994) also found that parents were interested in supporting their children's literacy learning when the activities taught in the program were relevant to them.

School programs and activities that are relevant and support Latino parents' involvement in their children's learning as expected in U.S. schools need to be based on principles of *respeto* and *confianza* (mutual trust). *Confianza* is attained through the involvement of teachers and other school personnel in existing community networks. The community and the school should work together in creating participatory structures in schools that are relevant to different types of parents. Programs for Latino families should be directed to the development of knowledge that leads to self-efficacy for parents. To do so, they should be able to support their children's learning through new repertoires while using their cultural ways of sharing knowledge with their children at home. This way, Latino parents will become partners with the school in creating continuity in learning at home and school and thus support their children school success.

It is then important for teachers to get to know the parents of the children in their classroom and to develop relationships with those parents and the community. According to Zentella (2005), successful connections between "educators and Latino families must be based on mutual respect for our cultural differences, without exaggerating them to the point that they obscure our shared humanity and dreams" (p. 29). To develop relationships with parents and community, it is important to develop a sense of *confianza* with them. *Confianza* is developed by making connections with the existing social networks (Moll, 1992; De La Vega, 2007). It is through social networks that one develops trust with the parents. Trust then leads to a sense of *confianza,* which allows for better communication between parents and teachers. It is within these networks and in *confianza* that the teacher or school is more effective in conveying to the Latino parents the school's expectations in relation to parent's involvement in school learning. It is also necessary that the school offers parents opportunities to learn what goes on in classrooms in the United States. It is important that the schools and teachers learn about cultural ways and discourses used by the children at home, so that the school can create some continuity between learning at home and learning at school.

According to De La Vega (2007), *confianza* is central to working with the Latino community and particularly. She believes that understanding the concept of *confianza* is central for schools to develop relationships with Latino parents. De la Vega sees the taxonomy developed by Epstein (1995) in relation to parent involvement as problematic to explain Latino parents' participation in their children's education because it is based on what middle class parents do to get involved in their children's education. She believes that it is important to pay attention to what and how culturally and linguistically different parents use personal resources and knowledge to support their children's learning (Moll, 1992; Valdes, 1996) rather than categorize what they do within an existing taxonomy. To De La Vega, it is more relevant to find out the why and how parents get involved. Rodriguez-Brown (2004, 2009) believes that it is very important to find out how parents see their role as teachers through the awareness of cultural learning models used at home to support children's learning. She also believes that Epstein's taxonomy is general enough that it could be useful in categorizing what culturally and linguistically different parents do. Researchers and teachers should be able to modify or add new categories to the ones in the existing model (Epstein, 1995), if needed. More relevant to this issue is to find out what Latino parents do and how they support their children's learning, and whether there is congruency between ways of learning at home and at school. The issue of congruency or bridging home-school learning is critical to the education of culturally and linguistically different children, particularly Latino children. Teachers need to learn about the knowledge that exists in the community and the homes of the children in their classrooms. They also need to understand the relevance of knowing and accepting the kinds of knowledge that Latino children bring from home in order to create continuity between home and school in support of young Latino children's transition between home and school. This will also allow the teachers and the school to become partners with the families in their children's education.

Research on Schooling and Latino Families

Research on schooling with Latino families has shown that parents have high expectations for their children, but they are not sure how they can help or foster school success (Delgado-Gaitán, 1992; Goldenberg & Gallimore, 1991). Goldenberg, Gallimore, Reese, and Garnier (2001) found that although educational aspirations of Latino parents are high through their children's elementary education years, their expectations fluctuate in relation to their children's school performance. Reese and Gallimore (2000) found that Latino families are willing to learn and use new ways to share literacy with their children. Goldenberg (1987) and Goldenberg and Gallimore (1991) found that teachers who gave specific instructions on ways parents could help children with their homework were more effective in involving parents in their children's school learning. Because of their view about family, Latino parents prefer to participate in school related activities and/or interventions that benefit not only the parents, but also the whole family (Rodriguez-Brown & Meehan, 1998). To this effect, parents would be more inclined to participate in school activities that benefit not only themselves, but also have a direct effect in their children's schooling.

The issue of discontinuity between home and school has been widely discussed in the research literature in relation to the schooling of Latino and other linguistically and culturally different children (Gallimore, Boggs, & Jordan, 1974; Moll, 1994; Reese & Gallimore, 2000; Trueba, Jacobs, & Kirton, 1990; Valdes, 1996), but not everyone shares the discontinuity perspective. Weisner, Gallimore, and Jordan (1988) criticize discontinuity explanations in relation to why linguistically and culturally different children do not perform well in U.S. schools. They raise the issue of within group variability among people from the same ethnic group. Other critics (Chandler, Argiris, Barnes, Goodman, & Snow, 1985) have found variability among people in different cultural groups in the ways they adapt to change and new circumstances. Issues of discontinuity are further clouded by a contrasting and deficit perspective, in which cultural ways of non-mainstream groups are seen as inadequate. Other researchers, such as Weisner (1997) and Gutierrez and Rogoff (2003) believe that there is a problem with studying issues of discontinuity between home and school under the presumptions that culture is static and categorical, and that differences can be defined as traits. The issues of discontinuity, individual variability, group traits, and cultural ways of learning have been studied from a variety of perspectives and with various approaches or models. Each perspective colors the analysis of the data and thus the results and interpretation of the researchers.

From a sociohistorical perspective, Gutierrez and Rogoff (2003) believe that when culture is defined as static and categorical, it is difficult to study the relationship of individual learning to the practices of cultural communities. They call for an approach to the study of home-school discontinuities that takes into account the histories and valued practices of cultural groups—a cultural-historical approach to the study of learning at home versus learning at school. Within a cultural-historical approach, learning is studied as "a process occurring within activity" (p. 20), where there is not a separation between individual characteristics and the context where the activity takes place. Gutierrez and Rogoff differentiate between identifying characteristics of individuals or groups and understanding the processes in the study of cultural ways of learning.

Cultural models is another perspective used to study and explain the effect of discontinuities between home and school. A cultural models perspective includes the cultural and social resources that individuals or groups of individuals bring to their understanding of social situations (Rogers, 2001). Gee (1999) describes cultural models as "storylines" or scripts that people have in their mind when they engage in meaning-making activities. When literacy is involved in the meaning-making, the term can refer to resources that people have to interpret or produce texts (Fairclough, 1992). In regard to families and their participation in their children's schooling, cultural models influence not only what parents teach their children at home but also how they do it.

Reese and Gallimore (2000) studied changes in beliefs and literacy practices at home with immigrant Mexican families. They considered culture as a flexible and dynamic construct rather than an unchanging and external force. In their study, they used a cultural model approach to studying learning at home, specifically early literacy development in children. This approach has been used previously by other researchers, such as LeVine (1977), Weisner (1997), and D'Andrade (1995), in studying issues related to socialization and child development.

Reese and Gallimore (2000) describe the effect that Mexican and Mexican American parents' views and beliefs about literacy have on the way they structure activities that support literacy learning at home. One belief that families have is that children learn to read through repeated practice when they start school. Reese and Gallimore feel that this belief, or cultural model, is derived from the experiences of previous generations in rural ranchos where there was little formal schooling. This Latino cultural model, brought by Latino immigrants to the United States, guides what they do with their children in support of their literacy learning here. Reese and Gallimore (2000) found variability and flexibility within the Latino cultural model used to teach literacy at home. They reported that Mexican and Mexican American parents in their study were willing to modify or adapt their cultural ways to support their children's learning according to expectations from U.S. schools, so long as the adaptations did not compromise their morals and values. The Latino parents in their study saw their beliefs as flexible and adaptable to new circumstances, and the researchers viewed these parents as "powerful agents of adaptation." According to Reese and Gallimore (2000), changes in the Mexican parents' cultural model for literacy development recommended by the school teachers were not seen as threats to their traditional values. For example, although the parents in the study did not see themselves as teachers, once they learned that reading to children at home supported literacy learning at school, they complied with teachers' assignments and suggestions.

Because of the flexible nature of the Mexican parents' cultural model, Reese and Gallimore (2000) found that continuities and discontinuities co-exist in home-school literacy interactions. This finding contrasts with discontinuity explanations from previous research (Goldenberg & Gallimore, 1995), which describe discontinuities and no commonalities between learning at home and school, as Latino immigrant parents adapt to their new context. Reese and Gallimore (2000) conclude that while parents did not initially share the teacher's view that reading aloud to young children was helpful in terms of their subsequent literacy development, they did follow through on teacher suggestions and requirements to read at home and appreciated the effects that this newly appropriated activity had produced. (pp. 130–131)

In this situation, continuity between home and school was created in response to teachers' requests and not just from parents' observations in the new environment. Perhaps the viewpoint that cultural models are flexible helps to explain why new immigrant parents are willing to modify and adapt their cultural ways in a new context in response to teachers' requests.

This case is an example of what can be accomplished with Latino families through parents' training, particularly in situations where parents' cultural ways are accepted and new practices are taught and discussed with them as they become more involved with their children's education and as they learn more about school expectations for parents in U.S. schools. According to Rodriguez-Brown (2004, 2009), this kind of acceptance and training are required for the process of adaptation to be effective with Latino families.

Another theoretical construct used to explain mismatches and discontinuities between home and school are the discourse differences between the home and the community and the schools and other social institutions (Gee, 1996). Differences in discourse are described by Gee (1999), who makes a distinction between d (discourse), which relates to linguistic aspects of language defined as "language-in-use or stretches of language (like conversations or stories)" (p. 17), and D (Discourse), which includes linguistic aspects of language and also beliefs, sociocultural issues, and political issues related to language. Gee calls D "language plus 'other stuff'" (p. 17). The "other stuff" includes beliefs, symbols, objects, tools, and places related to a particular identity. Gee believes that discourses do not have discrete borders (p. 19). They can split into one or more discourses, or several discourses can meld together. New Discourses can appear and old Discourses can disappear.

According to Gee (1996), children acquire their primary discourse at home and in the community by exposure, immersion, and practice. As children learn their primary discourse, they also learn ways of believing, practicing, and performing literacy. Children must learn a secondary discourse when they come in contact with social institutions such as schools. This is the situation for Latino children, particularly those from immigrant families.

The discourse construct has been used to explain the mismatch or the discontinuity that exists between home and school for Latino and other culturally and/or linguistically different children (Moll, Amanti, Neff, & Gonzalez, 1992; Purcell-Gates, 1995). Purcell-Gates (1995) and Teale (1986), among others, believe that children whose primary discourse is similar to the school discourse are able to adjust to school easier and faster and can be more successful than children whose primary discourse is very different from the discourse of school. Usually mainstream children's primary discourse closely resembles school discourse.

However, children from culturally and linguistically diverse families, many of them Latino, bring to the school setting primary discourses that are different from the mainstream. Learning the secondary discourse of school is more tenuous for those children. Children who come from homes and communities where the discourse and cultural ways of learning are different from those used in school settings have the most trouble in the transition between home and school.

Rogers (2003) describes a case study of literacy practices in an African American family. Building on the work of others (i.e., Delpit, 1995; Erickson, 1993; Gee, 1996; Heath, 1983; Mercado & Moll, 1997), Rogers situates her research on family literacy practices "within the cultural discursive mismatch social debate" (p. 4). She describes the discourse mismatch as a "lack of alignment between the culture, language and knowledge of working-class students and dominant institutions such as schools" (p. 5). Rogers uses the discourse construct because she felt that none of the typical responses reported by other researchers explain the mismatch.

Rogers (2003) recognizes that in culturally different families differences might occur in literacy learning at home because of an intergenerational transfer of ideologies about schooling and parents' work, rather than from a difference between primary and secondary discourses. In her case study, Rogers found that a conflict existed between discourse communities for her subjects due more to "fragmented subjectivities" (p. 154) in the family literacy practices of the mother as she worked with her children at home. Although the values, beliefs, and actions of the schools were represented in the home practices, reading and writing were seen as individual endeavors that were judged, measured, and valued by someone other than the individual. Rogers believes that more equitable schooling would make space for the literacy that is learned and used at home and in the classroom.

Most recently, the New London Group (1996) has been developing a theoretical framework to deal with diverse classrooms where teachers have to negotiate a multiplicity of primary and secondary discourses, as well as the multiple subjectivities (interests, intentions, and purposes) that students bring to the learning situation. The theoretical framework tries to connect the "what" and "how" of literacy pedagogy within the changing social environments of classrooms. From the New London Group perspective, when students face a learning situation, they have to design new meanings and remake themselves within historical and cultural patterns of meaning.

From this perspective it is important, then, that teachers accept what students bring to the learning situation and provide them with multiple pedagogical perspectives to learn. The New London Group discusses the limitations of using, for example, only situated practice as a classroom methodology. They explain the need to include overt (direct) instruction, and critical framing, which requires students to think and make connections between what they know and what they have learned. These multiple ways to learn lead to transformed practice and new learning.

From the previous discussion on issues that can impact the schooling and learning possibilities for children who are culturally different from the "mainstream," Latinos included, there are several points that teachers, school personnel, and program directors and developers should keep in mind when working with diverse parents and communities, and specifically in Latino communities.

First of all, it is necessary to accept and respect the language and knowledge that children bring to school. Teachers should learn not only about the knowledge existent in the community, but cultural models and literacy practices used at home. In Latino communities, it is necessary for teachers to gain *confianza* with the parents by participating in existent networks.

In terms of school structures that support Latino parents learning about schools in the United States, interventions or programs can be created in consultation with parents in order to explain to parents the expectations of the schools in the United States. in relation to the education of their children. These programs should recognize and accept the linguistic characteristics, cultural practices, and knowledge that families bring to the learning situation and add new repertoires which would enhance the connection between learning at home and at school.

In working with Latino families, it is important for schools and teachers to let parents know that their contributions to their children's learning are important and wanted. Encourage them to use the language they know better to support their children's learning. Connect with the knowledge that participants bring to a learning situation in order to make new knowledge more relevant for participants. Funds of knowledge, discourses, and cultural ways existing in the community should be recognized in the development of school programs and activities in order to develop some congruency as Latino children transition between home and school, and to facilitate children's learning and school success.

Conclusion

In this the chapter, we have described issues related to diversity and variability within the Latino community, which should be taken into account when planning educational programs for this population. Several cultural concepts *familia, confianza, respeto,* and a dichotomy between the meanings of *educar* and *enseñar* have impacted Latino parents' beliefs as they describe their role in their children's education. This view contrasts with the expectations of schools that are developed to reflect mainstream values and beliefs. The differences in expectations, values, and beliefs have created some discontinuities between home and school for Latino families, which have been researched from different perspectives, namely, sociohistorical, cultural ways, and discourse. Research discussed shows that Latino parents are willing to learn new ways to support their children's learning, provided that new teaching repertoires do not compromise their values and morals. They also are very curious about schools in the United States and need explicit instruction on ways to support their children's learning and facilitate an easier transition between home and school for their children.

Research shows that programs and interventions in support of Latino families are more successful when parents participate actively in the planning of program activities; and when the knowledge, discourses, cultural ways, and languages that exist among families and the community are used as a stepping-stone to new learning.

References

Abi-Nader, J. (1991, April). *Family values and the motivation of Hispanic youth.* Paper presented at the annual meeting of the American Educational Research Association, Chicago.

Alexsaht-Snider, M. (1991). *When schools go home and families come to school.* Unpublished dissertation, University of California Santa Barbara.

Carrasquillo, A. L., & London, C. B. G. (1993). *Parents and schools: A source book.* New York: Garland.

Chandler, J., Argyris, D., Barnes, W., Goodman, I., & Snow, C. (1985). Parents as teachers: Observations of low-income parents and children in a homework-like task. In B. Schieffelin & P. Gilmore (Eds.), *The acquisition of literacy: Ethnographic perspectives* (pp. 171–187). Norwood, NJ: Ablex.

D'Andrade, R. (1995). *The development of cognitive anthropology.* Cambridge, UK: Cambridge University Press.

De La Vega, E. (2007, April). *Culture, confianza, and caring: A key to connections between Mexicana/Latina mothers and schools.* Paper presented at the Annual Meeting of the American Educational Research Association in Chicago.

Delgado-Gaitán, C. (1987). Mexican adult literacy: New directions for immigrants. In S. R. Goldman & H. Trueba (Eds.), *Becoming literate in English as a second language* (pp. 9–32). Norwood, NJ: Ablex.

Delgado-Gaitán, C. (1992). School matters in the Mexican-American home: Socializing children to education. *American Educational Research Journal, 29,* 495–513.

Delgado-Gaitán, C. (1993). Research and policy in reconceptualizing family-schools relationships. In P. Phelan & A. Locke-Davidson (Eds.), *Renegotiating cultural diversity in American schools* (pp. 139–158). New York: Teachers College Press.

Delgado-Gaitán, C. (1996). *Protean literacy: Extending the discourse on empowerment.* Washington, DC: Farmer Press.

Delgado-Gaitán, C. (2001). *The power of community: Mobilizing for family and schooling.* Lanham, MD: Rowman and Littlefield.

Delgado-Gaitán, C., & Trueba, H. (1991). *Crossing cultural borders.* London: Farmer.

Delpit, L. (1995). *Other people's children: Cultural conflict in the classroom.* New York: New Press.

Epstein, J. L. (1995). School-family-community partnerships: Caring for the children we share. *Phi Delta Kappan, 76,* 701–712.

Erickson, F. (1993). Transformation and school success: The politics and culture of educational achievement. In E. Jacob & C. Jordan (Eds.), *Minority education: Anthropological perspectives* (pp. 27–52). Westport, CT: Greenwood.

Fairclough, N. (1992). *Discourses and social change.* Cambridge, UK: Polity Press.

Flores, B., Cousin, P. T., & Diaz, E. (1991). Transforming the deficit myths about learning, language and culture. *Language Arts, 68,* 369–379.

Fry, R. (2006). *The changing landscape of American public education: New students, new schools.* Washington, DC: The Pew Hispanic Center.

Gallimore, R., Boggs, J. W., & Jordan, C. (1974). *Culture, behavior and education: A study of Hawaiian-Americans.* Beverly Hills, CA: Sage.

Gallimore, R., & Goldenberg, C. (2001). Analyzing cultural models and settings to connect minority achievement and school improvement research. *Educational Psychologist, 36*, 1, 45–56.

Gallimore, R., & Reese, L. J. (1999). Mexican immigrants in urban California: Forging adaptations from familiar and new cultural resources. In M. C. Foblets & C. I. Pang (Eds.), *Culture, ethnicity and immigration* (pp. 245–263). Leuven, Belgium: ACCO.

Gee, J. P. (1996). *Social linguistics and literacies: Ideologies in discourses.* London: Farmer Press.

Gee, J. P. (1999). *An introduction to discourse analysis: Theory and method.* New York: Routledge.

Goldenberg, C. N. (1987). Low-income Hispanic parents' contributions to their first grade-children's word recognition skills. *Anthropology of Education Quarterly, 18*, 149–179.

Goldenberg, C. N. (1989). Parents' effects on academic grouping for reading: Three case studies. *American Educational Research Journal, 26*, 329–352.

Goldenberg, C. (2006, May). Involving parents of English language learners in their children's schooling. *Instructional Leader,* 1–3. (Texas Elementary Principal and Supervisors Association).

Goldenberg, C. N., & Gallimore, R. (1991). Local knowledge, research knowledge, and educational change: A case study of early reading improvement. *Educational Researcher, 20*, 2–14.

Goldenberg, C. N., & Gallimore, R. (1995). Immigrant Latino parents' values and beliefs about their children's education: Continuities and discontinuities across cultures and generations. In P. Pintrich & M. Maehr (Eds.), *Advances in motivation and achievement* (Vol. 9, pp. 183–228). Greenwich, CN: Ablex.

Goldenberg, C. N., Reese, L., & Gallimore, R. (1992). Effects of literacy materials from school on Latino children's home experiences and early reading achievement. *American Journal of Education, 100*, 497–536.

Goldenberg, C, Gallimore, R., Reese, L., & Garnier, H. (2001). Cause or effect? A longitudinal study of immigrant Latino parents' aspirations and expectations, and their children's school performance. *American Educational Research Journal, 38*, 3, 547–582.

Gutierrez, K. D., & Rogoff, B. (2003). Cultural ways of learning: Individual traits or repertoires of practice. *Educational Researcher, 32*(5), 15–25.

Heath, S. B. (1983). *Ways with words: Language, life and work in community and classrooms.* Cambridge, UK: Cambridge University Press.

LeVine, R. (1977). Child rearing as cultural adaptation. In P. Leiderman, S. Tulkin, & A. Rosenfeld (Eds.), *Culture and infancy* (pp. 15–27). New York: Academic Press.

Mercado, C. I., & Moll, L. C. (1997). The study of funds of knowledge: Collaborative research in Latino homes. *CENTRO, The Journal of the Center for Puerto Rican Studies, IX* (9), 26–42.

Moll, L. C. (1992). Bilingual classroom studies and community analysis: Some recent trends. *Educational Researcher, 21*(3), 20–24.

Moll, L. C. (1994). Literacy research in community and classrooms: A sociocultural approach. In R. B. Ruddell, M. R. Ruddell, & H. Singer (Eds.), *Theoretical models and processes of reading* (pp. 179–207). Newark, DE: International Reading Association.

Moll, L. C., & Greenberg, J. B. (1990). Creating zones of possibilities: Combining social contexts for instruction. In L. C. Moll (Ed.), *Vygotsky and education* (pp. 319–348). New York: Cambridge University Press.

Moll, L. C., Amanti, C., Neff, D., & Gonzalez, N. (1992). Funds of knowledge for teaching: Using a qualitative approach to connect homes and classrooms. *Theory Into Practice, 31*, 132–141.

Purcell-Gates, V. (1995). *Other people's words: The cycle of illiteracy.* Cambridge, MA: Harvard University Press.

Reese, L., & Gallimore, R. (2000). Immigrant Latinos' cultural models of literacy development: An alternative perspective on home-school discontinuities. *American Journal of Education, 108*, 103–134.

Reese, L., Gallimore, R., & Goldenberg, C. N. (1999). Job-required literacy, home literacy environments, and school reading: Early literacy experiences of immigrant Latino children. In J. G. Lipson & L. A. McSpadden (Eds.), *Negotiating power and place at the margins: Selected papers on refugees and immigrants* (Vol. VII, pp. 232–269). Washington, DC: American Anthropological Association.

Reese, L., Balzano, S., Gallimore, R., & Goldenberg, C. (1995). The concept of "educación": Latino family values and American schooling. *International Journal of Educational Research, 23*(1), 57–81.

Rodriguez-Brown, F. V. (2001). Home-school connections in a community where English is the second language. In V. Risko & K. Bromley (Eds.), *Collaboration for diverse learners: Viewpoints and practices* (pp. 273–288). Newark, DE: International Reading Association.

Rodriguez-Brown, F. V. (2004). Project FLAME: A parent support family literacy model. In B. Wasik (Ed.), *Handbook of family literacy* (pp. 213–229). Mahwah, NJ: Erlbaum.

Rodriguez-Brown, F. V. (2009). *The home-school connection: Lessons learned in a culturally and linguistically diverse community.* New York: Routledge.

Rodriguez-Brown, F. V., & Meehan, M. A. (1998). Family literacy and adult education: Project FLAME. In C. Smith (Ed.), *Literacy for the twentieth-first century* (pp. 176–193). Westport, CT: Praeger.

Rogers, R. (2001). Family literacy and cultural models. *National Reading Conference Yearbook, 50,* 96–114.

Rogers, R. (2003). *A critical discourse analysis of family literacy practices: Power in and out of print.* Mahwah, NJ: Erlbaum.

Shannon, S. M. (1996). Minority Parent Involvement: A Mexican's mother's experience and a teachers interpretation. *Education and Urban Society, 29,* 1, 71–84.

Teale, W. H. (1986). Home background and young children's literacy development. In W. H. Teale & E. Sulsby (Eds.), *Emergent literacy: Writing and reading* (pp. 173–206). Norwood, NJ: Ablex.

The New London Group. (1996). A pedagogy of multiliteracies: Designing social futures. *Harvard Educational Review, 66*(1), 60–62.

The Pew Hispanic Center (2006, June). *Hispanics attitudes toward learning English: Fact sheet.* Washington, DC: The Pew Hispanic Center.

The Pew Hispanic Center and the Kaiser Family Foundation. (2004). National Survey of Latinos. Washington, DC: Pew Hispanic Center. Retrieved June 24, 2007, from http://pewhispanic.org/reports/report.php?ReportID=25

Trueba, H., & Delgado-Gaitan, C. (Eds.). (1988). *School and society: Learning content through culture.* New York: Praeger.

Trueba, H., Jacobs, L., & Kirton, E. (1990). *Cultural conflict and adaptation: The case of Hmong children in American society.* New York: Farmer Press.

U.S. Department of Education. (2007). *The Condition of Education, 2007* (NCES 2007-064). Washington, DC: U.S. Government Printing Office.

Valdes, G. (1996). *Con respeto: Bridging the differences between culturally diverse families and schools.* New York: Teachers College Press.

Vásquez, O. A., Pease-Alvarez, L., & Shannon, S. M. (1994). *Pushing boundaries: Language and culture in a Mexicano community.* New York: Cambridge University Press.

Weisner, T. (1997). The ecocultural project of human development: Why ethnography and its findings matter. *Ethos, 25,* 1977–1990.

Weisner, T., Gallimore, R., & Jordan, C. (1988). Unpackaging cultural effects on classroom learning: Native Hawaiian peer assistance and child-generated activity. *Anthropology and Education Quarterly, 19,* 327–353.

Zentella, A. C. (Ed.). (2005). *Building on Strength: Language and literacy in Latino families and communities.* New York: Teachers College Press.

25 Latinos in Special Education

Equity Issues at the Intersection of Language, Culture, and Ability Differences

Alfredo J. Artiles, Amanda L. Sullivan,
Federico R. Waitoller, and Rebecca A. Neal
Arizona State University

The purpose of this chapter is to synthesize the scholarship on Latino students placed in special education and to discuss equity questions that are raised in this literature. Because Latino students constitute a minority[1] group that has occupied a lower position in society, it is important to examine equity issues in the provision of educational services for this population. Our analysis is complicated by the fact that special education was created in response to civil rights concerns for students with disabilities. Thus, the question is often raised as to why placement in special education is deemed an equity concern for Latino students. Equity issues have been debated in this context for at least 40 years due to the disproportionate representation of racial minority students in special education (Donovan & Cross, 2002). Equity issues include questions about student misidentification (i.e., over- or underrepresentation), and equally important, concerns about the long-term consequences of special education placement (e.g., persistent low achievement, high drop out rate, reduced access to higher education, lower occupational outcomes; Artiles, Trent, & Palmer, 2004).

It is important to define several key terms before we address the chapter purpose. First, we prefer to use the term "Latino," though we use it interchangeably with "Hispanic," since this is the term used in federal policies. Latino/Hispanic is defined as "a person of Mexican, Puerto Rican, Cuban, South or Central America, or other Spanish culture or origin regardless of race" (U. S. Census Bureau, 2004, p. 1). Latinos constitute a heterogeneous population that varies substantially across generations, national origins, ethnic identities, racial ancestries, and socioeconomic strata (SES). Latinos are also identified as members of language minority groups as well as in terms of their level of English proficiency.

A language minority student "comes from a home where a language other than English is spoken" (Ovando, Collier, & Combs, 2003, p. 10), and whose language has a subordinate position in U.S society. Latinos whose English proficiency is limited are given the label Limited English Proficient (LEP) or English Language Learner (ELL). LEP is defined as "students who are either monolingual in the home language, or have some English proficiency but are still fluent in the home language" (Ovando et al., 2003, p. 10).[2] ELL has been favored in the literature over LEP,

> for it conveys that the student is in the process of learning English, without having the connotation that the student is in some way defective until full English Proficiency is attained. Like the term LEP, however, the ELL designation is still somewhat problematic because it focuses on the need to learn English without acknowledging the value of the child's proficiency in L1. The term is superficially less offensive, but also less precise. It conveys single-minded focus on learning English that tends to restrict discussion about the students' pedagogical needs. (Ovando et al., 2003, p. 445)

Latinos in Special Education:[3] A Sociocultural View of Difference and Inequality

We approach the analysis of Latino students in special education with a conceptual framework that has informed our scholarship for several years (Artiles & Trent, 1994). We have used a culturally responsive lens to examine equity concerns in the education of minority students, as well as to design and implement alternative educational options for these students. We assume that educational systems are built on a set of assumptions that define *competence* and *difference*. These notions frame how students are classified, how programs are organized and personnel are prepared, the strategies used to promote learning, and the resources allocated. Historically, the notion of *difference* has not been seen on a positive light, and those individuals considered *different* are often regarded as deviant, which has long-term consequences (Minow, 1990).

Assumptions about *difference* have been applied to minority students, including Latinos, for many generations (Valencia, 1997). This logic is also used in the case of minority students in special education (Artiles, 1998). To analyze assumptions about *difference* and create culturally responsive educational options, it is necessary to understand the interplay of three domains, namely people, policies, and practices (Klingner et al., 2005). It is critical to understand the *people* targeted in analyses—in this case Latinos—to gain an in-depth perspective on their historical trajectories, their characteristics, and other relevant sociocultural aspects. People's actions, in turn, are shaped by *policies* that configure educational systems' structures and processes. Hence, it is necessary to examine the intended and enacted policies that shape the experiences of Latinos in special education. Policies typically have historical sediments that are ideologically charged with assumptions about the people that they intend to serve or the institutions that they aim to regulate. Attention to how assumptions about *difference* underlie policies, therefore, is critical. Finally, policies are enacted through *practices*, which we define as "actions that are repeated, shared with others in a social group, and invested with normative expectations and with meanings or significances that go beyond the immediate goals of the action" (Miller & Goodnow, 1995, p. 7). Thus, *practices* include what Latino families and students do in everyday life as well as what educators do to administer schools, promote student and teacher learning, communicate with families, and so forth. We use this framework that accounts for the interrelated configuration of people, policies, and practices to examine the topic of Latinos in special education.

People

To understand the richness and heterogeneity of the Latino population and to do justice to the complexity of the topic of Latinos in special education, we must alert readers to the role of globalization in the experiences of Latinos as well as their unique demographic and educational profiles. Exhaustive discussions of these topics have been published elsewhere (see Garcia & Cuellar, 2006, this volume).

Suárez-Orozco (2001) defined globalization as a "process of change, generating at once centrifugal (qua the borders of nation state) and centripetal (qua the post-national) forces that result in the de-territorialization of important economic, social, and cultural practices from their traditional moorings in the nation state" (p. 347). Globalization plays a crucial role in creating socioeconomic conditions that increase the number of Latino families entering the U. S. Globalization also shapes Latino experiences and opportunities in this country. This includes segregation, as Latino immigrant settlements are increasingly segregated from White communities, which, in turn, has contributed to similar racial segregation in schools (Orfield & Yun, 1999).

While the overall public school enrollment has decreased since 1976, the population of Latino students has increased more than 300% to nearly 10 million (Garcia & Cuellar, 2006), with the largest concentrations of these students in California, Texas, Florida, New York, and Arizona (National Center for Education Statistics [NCES], n.d.a), and more than 1 million Latino students placed in special education (Donovan & Cross, 2002). Bilingual students, the majority of whom are Latino, constitute approximately 11% of all school enrollment, or 3.8 million students (NCES, 2006). Most of these students (70%) attend schools in urban areas (Garcia & Cuellar, 2006) and many are in schools that are considered linguistically segregated; that is, more than 30% of their peers are also bilingual (Kohler & Lazarin, 2007).

In general, research on the educational outcomes for this population raises concerns, as Latino students are more likely to dropout of high school than their White peers, are less likely to enroll in AP courses, are less likely to receive diplomas or college degrees, and score lower on measures of math, reading, writing, and science (Garcia, 2004; NCES, n.d.d). Outcomes are even poorer for Latino bilingual students versus their Latino monolingual peers (Kohler & Lazarin, 2007).

It is important to consider the role of globalization and the unique sociodemographic and linguistic characteristics of Latinos in analyses of their placement in special education. Consideration of these aspects raises questions such as: Which Latino subgroups tend to be placed more frequently in special education? What do we know about the academic performance of Latino students placed in special education? How does school segregation affect Latino placement in special education? What is the role of globalization forces in urban school special education placement practices with Latinos? To what extent does Latino educational attainment level relate to special education placement? Does ELL status increase the special education placement odds of Latino students? Although the existing research does not answer all of these questions, we offer some responses in a subsequent section. The point we emphasize here is that Latino population characteristics and experiences should be examined and interpreted as interacting within the enabling and constraining contexts created by national, state and local policies. We outline policies germane to the education of Latino students in special education in the next section.

Policies

We include in this arena legislation, regulations, case law, and other mandates at the federal, state education agency (SEA), local education agency (LEA), and school levels that shape key aspects of schooling, such as governance and organization, curriculum and instruction, assessment and accountability, service provision, and funding or resource allocation (Klingner et al., 2005). National and local policies have important implications for equity, access, and opportunities to learn. Federal legislation (e.g., the No Child Left Behind Act [NCLB] of 2001, the Individuals with Disabilities Education Act [IDEA]) is particularly important because it affects policy and practice at all subsequent levels of the educational system. In this section, we discuss briefly general education, special education, and bilingual education policy germane to the educational experiences of Latinos.

General Education

No Child Left Behind Act   NCLB is a comprehensive reform of the Education and Secondary Education Act of 1965 that redefines the federal role in elementary and secondary education via the stated goals of improving the achievement of all students and closing the achievement gaps among subgroups of students. NCLB is grounded in four domains: (a) accountability for educational outcomes, (b) emphasis on evidence-based practices, (c) parent options, and (d) local control and flexibility. Under NCLB, states must assess student achievement in the areas of reading, math, and science through tests aligned with state curriculum and standards. The data obtained from these assessments must be provided to parents, with detailed school reports cards for LEAs and schools made publicly available. Within these report cards, district and school-level results are disaggregated by race/ethnicity, language status, SES, and disability status. Based on the results of student assessments, states must identify schools that fail to meet adequate yearly progress (AYP), apply sanctions and interventions to improve outcomes, and allow students and families in poorly performing schools the option of transferring to schools that have made AYP. While the legislation requires states to establish these accountability systems and procedures, states have autonomy in defining their particular criteria for academic proficiency and AYP.

Despite the intense focus NCLB places on outcomes, the achievement gap between Latino students and their White peers remains largely unchanged. Unfortunately, minority students (including Latinos) are more likely to attend low-performing schools that receive significantly less resources. The focus on the performance of particular student subgroups is potentially positive since it forces schools and districts to be accountable for the education of students who have been historically neglected. On the other hand, the accountability focus is potentially stigmatizing, as differences in performance may be attributed to within-group characteristics, rather than to contextual factors such as the quality of instruction, particularly when there is a gap between the achievement of Latino and White students, and when educators fail to account for structural inequities and systemic bias that influence the educational outcomes of Latino students. An unfortunate consequence of the accountability movement is the potential manipulation of data to obscure continued disparities (Rodriguez, 2007). As a result of such practices, the educational needs of Latino students risk going unmet. Still others note the possibility that pressure to demonstrate improved outcomes will encourage educators to funnel low-performing students into special education to avoid being held accountable for those students' progress or lack thereof (Paul, 2004).

NCLB is also controversial because it sets forth the expectation that all students can achieve at an equal standard, including those with disabilities, which many people view as unreasonable and unrealistic. This has created tensions within the special education system, as NCLB appears to treat all students uniformly and place uniform expectations regardless of individual differences. This practice is in direct conflict with the tenets of federal special education policy, which instead focuses on individualized educational programs and goals for students with disabilities (McLaughlin, 2008). On the other hand, one benefit of this policy is that it has placed an emphasis on students with disabilities' access to the general education curriculum.

Special Education

The Individuals with Disabilities Education Act   IDEA, originally the Education for All Handicapped Children Act of 1975 (PL 94-142), protects the right of students with disabilities to free and appropriate public education. IDEA requires states to seek out and identify all children who may have disabilities, to provide individualized educational programs for all identified students, and to provide services in the least restrictive environment to the maximum extent possible. The law also sets forth standards for confidentiality, parent involvement, multidisciplinary evaluations, and due process. All state educational agencies accepting federal funds for special education must comply with the law, even though the level of funding received tends to be low.

IDEA mandates multifaceted, nondiscriminatory assessment, and includes limited English proficiency and ethnic and cultural difference factors in exclusionary considerations in order to ensure that children are not misidentified. Moreover, the law also stipulates that assessments must be "provided and administered in the language…most likely to yield accurate information," used only for the purposes for which they are valid and reliable, and administered by "trained and knowledgeable personnel" [P.L. 108-446 §614(b)(3)(A)(ii–iv)].

State Efforts to Reduce Disproportionality The disproportionate representation of minority students, including Latinos, has been addressed in federal legislation due to concerns for the appropriate treatment of students of all cultural and linguistic backgrounds. The 2004 reauthorization of IDEA also requires that states collect and examine data on rates of special education identification, placement, and discipline for minority students, and that they establish policies and practices to prevent the inappropriate identification of minority students for special education.

These data are reported to the U.S. Department of Education Office of Special Education Programs as part of each state's Annual Performance Reports documenting their efforts to improve outcomes for students with disabilities. IDEA does not specify criteria for determining the extent of disproportionality, so there is substantial variation in reported levels of disproportionate representation and in state practices correcting disparities. While this aspect of the legislation does pertain to the representation of Latino students in special education, it does not hold states accountable for the treatment of language minority students to the same degree, so the possible disproportionate representation of students identified as ELLs is not examined by many states.

Disproportionality Case Law The overrepresentation of minority students in special education has resulted in several well-known cases challenging practices around identification and treatment (e.g., *Larry P. v. Riles*, 1984; *PASE v. Hannon*, 1980). Cases before the passage of P.L. 94-142 generally challenged assessment and identification practices while later cases pertained to equity in treatment (Artiles & Trent, 1994). The outcomes of these cases have been mixed, ranging from judicial degrees barring the use of IQ tests to findings that disproportionality is not discriminatory.

The issue of Latino disproportionality gained national prominence with California's 1970 case of *Diana v. State Board of Education*, a class-action suit in which the families of nine Mexican American students alleged that their children had been inappropriately identified as mentally retarded after being assessed with English IQ tests. In a groundbreaking consent decree, the court required that students be tested in their primary language or through nonverbal means, with instruments that reflected Mexican American culture. In addition, LEAs were to monitor the potential overrepresentation of Mexican American students in programs for children with mental retardation (Rueda, Artiles, Salazar, & Higareda, 2002). In 1992, a similar Arizona case, *Guadalupe Organization v. Tempe Elementary School District No. 3*, resulted in a consent decree requiring that examiners establish students' primary language for testing and to use culturally relevant IQ tests when mental retardation is suspected (MacAvoy & Sidles, 1991).

Response to Intervention The 2004 reauthorization of IDEA also includes powerful changes to the requirements for the identification of learning disabilities (LDs). The legislation now allows for the use of scientifically based interventions, commonly organized around the notion of Response to Intervention (RTI), when determining students' special education eligibility. As a result, LEAs throughout the nation are now implementing RTI as a means for providing early intervening services and identifying students with LDs. This approach is based on the notion that instruction should be research-based, featuring a three-tiered system of universal preventative strategies, group interventions, and intensive individualized supports. The progression to increasingly intensive interventions is predicated upon the implementation of effective, appropriate curriculum and instruction in general education.

RTI has been debated recently and a number of concerns have been raised; however, RTI has also been recognized for its potential to improve students' educational opportunities and reduce disproportionality in special education *if* the model is used to ensure that all students have adequate culturally responsive opportunities to learn (NCCRESt, 2005). Moreover, it could improve the education of ELLs by ensuring the implementation of research-based practices. The success of the implementation of RTI with diverse populations will depend on the use of culturally responsive, ecologically valid pedagogical approaches and interventions.

Bilingual Education

Federal Bilingual Education Policy   The minimum standard for the education of students from cultural and linguistically diverse backgrounds is set by Title IV of the Civil Rights Act of 1964, which prohibits discrimination on the basis of race, color, or national origin in programs or agencies receiving federal funds. The breadth of the act was further extended by the Equal Educational Opportunities Act of 1974, which holds that LEAs must afford students education access via evidence-based strategies to reduce language barriers (Garcia & Wiese, 2002).

The Bilingual Education Act of 1968 was passed as Title VII of the Elementary and Secondary Education Act, and was grounded on the assumption that sink-or-swim approaches violated language minority students' civil rights, though the actual stipulations of the policy were vague and produced programs with lackluster results (Ovando et al., 2003). Amid fears of separatism, the act was amended in 1978 so that it was limited to transitional programs that only used native language to the extent necessary to support the development of English proficiency. Although financial assistance was provided on a competitive basis to support bilingual programs, the legislation limited student participation to a maximum of three years. Moreover, the law did not include any mandates, but rather allowed for voluntary LEA participation, so its impact has been limited. Under NCLB, the law was renamed the English Language Acquisition, Language Enhancement, and Academic Achievement Act, and included repeals of the funding for native language programs, instead placing emphasis on English acquisition and achievement (Ovando et al., 2003).

Case Law   The civil rights issues involved in the education of bilingual learners were brought to the forefront in the 1974 case of Lau v. Nichols, in which Chinese students in San Francisco alleged that their LEA denied their rights by failing to provide special instruction in their native language. The court found that ELLs must be provided with language support in order to make instruction accessible and to be in compliance with the Civil Rights Act (Garcia & Wiese, 2002). In 1981, in *Castañeda v. Pickard*, the Fifth Circuit Court ruled that LEAs must make available appropriate resources, including trained personnel and materials, to ensure effective implementation of language supports (Garcia & Wiese, 2002). The court ruled that LEAs would be evaluated to determine whether a pedagogically sound approach was selected and implemented with appropriate assessment procedures to address the needs of students identified as ELLs and determine their success under the program, which has set precedence for later cases (Suárez-Orozco, Roos, & Suárez-Orozco, 2000).

State Policies Regarding the Education of ELLs   Latino students and families are also confronted with a political landscape that increasingly emphasizes English as the official and only language for use in a variety of public institutions, including schools. Nearly half of all states have passed legislation establishing English as the official language for all state affairs despite strong opposition in states such as Arizona, California, Colorado, and Florida (Ovando et al., 2003).

Given the persistence of assimilationist ideology, increasing pressure for English-only education of bilinguals is not surprising. Three states, Arizona, California, and Massachusetts, have passed English-only educational policies that require ELL to be educated solely in English. The legislation is predicated on the faulty assumption that students can achieve proficiency in only one year of English immersion, and as a result, such approaches lack evidence-base and restrict the right of parents to choose programs for their children. The notion of the 1-year transition period is incongruous with the literature on second language acquisition, which indicates that it takes as many as 4 to 7 years to develop full academic English proficiency (Hakuta, Butler, & Witt, 2000). English-only supporters have asserted that bilingual education impedes the academic and social development of students identified as ELLs as it impairs English language acquisition (Johnson, 2005), yet the research literature has failed to support such claims while substantiating the benefits of bilingualism and bilingual education (August & Shanahan, 2006; Rolstad, Mahoney, & Glass, 2005).

In each state, the number of students educated through primary language instruction has decreased drastically. For instance, in Arizona, the proportion of ELLs served in bilingual programs has dropped by nearly 70% (Cashman, 2006). The legislation has met with much opposition, with critics pegging such policies "anti-bilingual ideology," arguing that it restricts students' linguistic rights and positions the language of minority groups as problematic (Cashman, 2006). Others suggest that such policies represent racism by proxy as it primarily affects individuals from Latino and Asian backgrounds (Johnson & Martinez, 2000).

The policies' disregard for the language acquisition process, paired with unrealistic expectations for academic progress in English-based instruction, is posited to exacerbate the chances for the misidentification of Latino ELLs as disabled, especially as learning disabled (Case & Taylor, 2005). Researchers have called attention to the fact that ELL Latino student special education referrals and potential misdiagnoses are influenced by the availability of instructional services that promote English proficiency and acquisition of academic content simultaneously, and premature exiting from language support programs (Ochoa, Robles-Piña, Garcia, & Breunig, 1999).

In summary, NCLB, special education law, and bilingual education policy have important implications for the education of Latinos. Issues of accountability, disproportionality, appropriate intervention, and language of instruction are points of continued controversy. The policies here demonstrate the potential for such regulations to both improve outcomes for Latino students and to continue patterns of marginalization.

Practices

Educational policies shape working conditions in schools and LEAs and interact with the characteristics and experiences of the Latino students, but it is in the practice realm that we see how such interactions ultimately define the nature of educational experiences and their consequences for these students. As we explained above, we focus on equity issues related to a critical set of practices in special education, namely the disproportionate placement of Latinos in these programs.

The disproportionate representation of minority students has been a persistent and controversial issue in the special education literature for 40 years. Disproportionality is defined as "the extent to which membership in a given…group affects the probability of being placed in a specific disability category" (Oswald, Coutinho, Best, & Singh, 1999, p. 198). The definition includes over- and underrepresentation. The persistence of this problem is evident in the fact that it has twice been studied by the National Research Council (NRC; Donovan & Cross, 2002; Heller, Holtzman, & Messick. 1982) and has been the subject of decades of litigation, advocacy efforts, and actions by professional organizations and the scholarly community.

As we explained above, IDEA includes mandates and safeguards to prevent and address this problem for minority and low-income students. Nevertheless, individuals who are culturally and linguistically diverse continue to be disproportionately represented in special education, particularly in the high incidence categories of LD, mental retardation (MR), and emotional/behavioral disturbances (E/BD), and in some cases, speech and language impairments (SLI). These categories are described as subjective or judgmental (Donovan & Cross, 2002). Federal definitions of these categories are broad and state definitions, identification practices, and placement patterns vary considerably (Coutinho & Oswald, 1998). Students with high incidence disabilities constitute the overwhelming majority of the special education population.

Students identified as Black or Latino are more likely to receive more restrictive placements (Parrish, 2002) and are subject to disciplinary consequences at higher rates than their White counterparts (Skiba, Michael, Nardo, & Peterson, 2002), which further limits their access to the educational and social curricula of the general education environment (Ferguson, Kozleski, & Smith, 2003). Disproportionality is a problem of equity and access as these students are often subjected to reduced opportunities to learn (de Valenzuela, Copeland, Qi, & Park, 2006), and the stigma that accompanies the labels (Losen & Welner, 2002). Just as concerning is the evidence that indicates that minority students who receive special education services have less positive long-term outcomes in the domains of post-secondary education, employment, and independent living than their similarly labeled White peers (Losen & Orfield, 2002).

Measuring the Problem

Neither the research community nor state departments of education have reached a consensus as to the most appropriate method for measuring and determining the extent of disproportionality. Several indices have been used including the composition index, risk index, relative risk ratio, and other statistical approaches. Each method addresses a different aspect of the enrollment data, and therefore only provides partial information about a group's representation. It is suggested that multiple indicators be used to gain a thorough understanding of patterns for a particular data set (Artiles, Rueda, Salazar, & Higareda, 2005).

Composition Index   The composition index was a method preferred by early disproportionality researchers (Chinn & Hughes, 1987). It provides the percentage of students from a particular group in a given disability, and is calculated by dividing the number of students from the group in the disability category by the total number in the disability category. The obtained value is then compared to the group's representation in the general population to determine whether they are over- or underrepresented. Chinn and Hughes (1987) defined the acceptable range of the composition index as +/–10% of the value expected given a group's total enrollment; anything outside the range was considered disproportionate.

Risk Index   The risk index provides the percentage of individuals from a group that is identified in a particular disability. It is calculated by dividing the number of group members in the disability category by the total number of those individuals in the population. The main difference with the composition index is the denominator used to make the calculations. For instance, the *composition index* enables us to make statements such as "20% of students with LD in the district are Latinos," whereas the *risk index* would allow us to state that "4% of all Latino students in the district have LDs" (these percentages are fictitious for illustrative purposes).

Relative Risk Ratio   This index provides a group's relative likelihood of identification or placement in comparison to some other group. It is represented by a ratio of the risk indices for two groups (i.e., risk index of group A ÷ risk index of group B). A ratio of 1 indicates that the groups are equally likely to be identified, while a ratio greater than 1 indicates that the focal group is more likely to be identified than the referent. A ratio less than 1 indicates that the focal group is less likely to be identified. While Westat (2003) suggests using *all other groups* as the reference group, other scholars prefer to use White students. However, there are districts or schools in which White students are not enrolled or have a small representation, thus making it impossible to use this group as a reference. Similarly, there are districts with substantial variability in demographic distributions that affect the comparisons of risk ratios across districts. There are also districts with small numbers of students from particular ethnic groups, which complicates the calculation and interpretation of risk ratios. Several measurement guidelines have been offered recently for such cases that include the use of weighted risk ratios and an alternate risk ratio which "uses district-level data to calculate the risk for the racial/ethnic group and state-level data to calculate the risk for the comparison group" (Bollmer, Bethel, Garrison-Mogren, & Brauen, 2007, p. 193).

There is no agreement as to what values are to be considered disproportionate under the relative risk ratio. As with the composition index, the criteria are fairly arbitrary. One study set the criteria at 1.5 for overrepresentation and 0.75 for underrepresentation (Skiba et al., 2004). Others have used 2 and 0.5 as the values for disproportionate representation (Parrish, 2002). A recent analysis of states' practices (Sullivan, Kozleski, & Smith, 2008) indicated significant variability in how the problem is measured and the cut off point used to trigger actions from SEAs or LEAs (see also Burdette, 2007). For instance, some states defined the criteria for overrepresentation as risk ratios greater than 1, while other selected values greater than 3 or higher. Nonetheless, the relative risk ratio continues to be the preferred measure of disproportionality and provides information that is more accessible than other indices.

Statistical Approaches   Statistical approaches have also been used to evaluate the extent of disproportionality in order to reach conclusions about the statistical significance of placement pattern differences. These approaches include z-tests, chi-square, and the E-formula (Figueroa & Artiles, 1999). In general, these methods indicate the probability that the difference between the enrollment in general education and a specific disability category could occur by chance when there is no true difference in the population, with an error level typically set at .05 (Skiba et al., 2000).

Placement Patterns for Latinos in Special Education

Early research showed that Latinos were underrepresented in most special education categories at the national level (Chinn & Hughes, 1987). The Handicapped Minority Research Institutes found in the 1980s that Latino students were more likely to be placed in special education if their parents were foreign-born or they were tested in English (Rueda et al., 2002). In an analysis of the 1998 Office for Civil Rights (OCR) national data, Donovan and Cross (2002) found that Latinos were proportionally represented in most of the high-incidence categories, and were 25–30% less likely to be identified in E/BD and SLI than their White peers. These patterns were also common in the low-incidence categories.

While Latinos tend to have placement rates equal to Whites at the national level, this is the result of complex patterns of under- and overrepresentation in states and districts in different areas of the country, especially those with large Latino populations, such as Arizona, Colorado, New Mexico, and Texas (Finn, 1982). For instance, Latino students were not overrepresented at the national level between 1974 and 1998 in the high incidence categories of MR, LD, and E/BD (see Table 25.1). However, they were overrepresented in the 1980s in the categories of MR, SLI, and SLD in California's school districts (Wright & Santa Cruz, 1983).

The poverty rate is disproportionately high among Latinos (Skiba et al., 2005). Thus, it has been suggested that poverty's effects might exacerbate the disability identification rates for Latinos, particularly in the low incidence disability categories that often have a clear organic cause. Nevertheless, the data do not seem to support this hypothesis. The latest NRC report indicated Latino students were not overrepresented in any of the disability categories at the national level, including the low incidence groups (Donovan & Cross, 2002). In fact, they were underrepresented in Other Health Impairments (OHI) and Developmental Delay (DD).[4] These

Table 25.1   Latino Risk Ratios for Identification in the High Incidence
Disability Categories: 1976–1998, OCR Data

Year	MR	LD	EB/D
1974	1.26	1.04	n/a
1976	1.04	1.13	0.97
1978	0.96	1.12	1.00
1980	0.81	1.01	0.89
1984	1.17	1.07	0.64
1986	0.73	1.00	0.79
1988	1.41	0.98	0.57
1990	1.21	0.94	0.48
1992	0.71	1.23	0.59
1994	0.74	1.00	0.62
1997	0.65	1.08	0.66
1998	0.78	1.07	0.60

Source: Office of Civil Rights, 1974–1998. Adapted from Donovan and Cross (2002).

patterns are consistent with state-level data such as Arizona. Sullivan, Artiles, Caterino, and Moore (under review) reported that the highest risk indices for Latinos in this state were in mental retardation categories. However, Latinos were not overrepresented in any of the disabilities, including low incidence categories (see Table 25.2). Latino student underrepresentation was observed in E/BD, Autism, and OHI. On the other hand, poverty has been linked to greater LD identification rates among Latinos and African Americans; it is interesting however, that the link between poverty and LD is counterintuitive for White and Native American students since the association is negative (i.e., LD identification rate decreases as poverty level increases; Oswald, Coutinho, & Best, 2002).

There are several additional considerations in the analysis of placement patterns. For example, it is necessary to analyze relative risk ratio evidence alongside risk indices because their relationship is not always straightforward. This is particularly important to do across states and categories due to the variability in identification rates reported across regions and states. To illustrate this point, consider the data reported in Table 25.3 for the states with the highest risk indices for Latinos in MR, LD, and E/BD. Latino students have considerable overrepresentation

Table 25.2   Risk Index and Risk Ratio for Latino Students in Arizona

Ethnicity	# of Students	Risk Index	Risk Ratio
All disabilities	43,996	11.03	.96
ED	1,525	.38	.37
Mild MR	2,457	.62	1.38
SLD	23,895	5.99	1.19
Autism	637	.16	.42
Deaf-Blindness	30	.00	1.00
Hearing Impairment	792	.19	1.12
Multiple disabilities	743	.19	.95
Moderate MR	922	.23	1.35
Orthopedic Impairment	217	.05	.71
Other health impairment	952	.24	.40
Speech/language impairment	7,855	1.97	.86
Severe MR	355	.08	1.33
Traumatic Brain Injury	134	.03	.75
Visual Impairment	221	.05	.71

Source: Arizona Department of Education, 2004. Adapted from Sullivan, Artiles, Caterino, and Moore (under review).

Table 25.3   Comparison of Risk Ratios in States with the Highest Risk Indices for Latino Students in the High Incidence Disability Categories

	Risk Ratio	Risk Index
Mental Retardation		
Massachusetts	3.39	4.48%
Nebraska	1.35	2.68%
Hawaii	2.51	2.41%
Indiana	1.21	2.23%
Learning Disability		
Delaware	1.25	8.93%
New York	1.20	8.42%
New Mexico	1.20	8.21%
Emotional Disability		
Hawaii	1.12	2.68%
Vermont	1.20	2.16%
Maine	1.15	1.99%
Minnesota	1.36	1.61%

Note: The risk index provides the likelihood of identification in a given category, while the risk ratio provides an index of likelihood relative to White students.

Source: Office of Civil Rights, 1998. Adapted from Donovan and Cross (2002).

in the MR category in Hawaii and Massachusetts, but they are not overrepresented in MR, LD, and E/BD in any of the remaining states on this list (see risk ratio column in Table 25.3). In contrast, the overrepresentation patterns are not clearly associated with the risk index evidence. That is, the states with the highest Latino student risk indices do not exhibit overrepresentation patterns (i.e., Delaware, New York, and New Mexico).

Moreover, the proportion of the minority student population in a state or district has been proposed as a mediating factor in disproportionality patterns. The evidence reported on this issue supports such link (e.g., Parrish, 2002). Table 25.4 describes the MR placement risk ratios for four ethnic minority student groups (including Latinos) in the 10 highest and 10 lowest minority enrollment states in the nation. All four ethnic groups exhibit an increment in the MR placement odds in the states with higher minority enrollment. Latinos are underrepresented in the low enrollment states and are clearly overrepresented in the high enrollment states. The most affected, however, was the African American group (see Table 25.4).

The relationship between minority enrollment and disproportionate representation, nonetheless, might vary depending on the target disability category, student, gender, and other sociodemographic factors. Coutinho and her colleagues (2002), for instance, found that Latino student

Table 25.4   Mental Retardation Risk Ratios in High- and Low-Minority States by Race

	10 Lowest States		10 Highest States	
	Risk Ratio	Percentage of Total Enrollment	Risk Ratio	Percentage of Total Enrollment
Latino	0.42	1.2	1.55	25.6
American Indian	1.07	0.2	1.75	8.4
Asian	0.66	0.7	1.14	10.8
Black	1.77	0.8	3.59	31.6

Source: U.S. Department of Education's National Center for Education Statistics, 1997. Adapted from Parrish (2002).

Table 25.5   Predictors of Latino Disproportionality in Arizona

	Percentage of students on free lunch	District size	Student-teacher ratio	Percentage of minority teachers	Percentage of minority students	ΔR^2
All disabilities	.20	-.09	.22**	-.43***	-.65***	.19
MIMR	-.04	.06	-.24*	.35*	-.51**	.14
LD	.17	-.08	.30***	.22*	-.54***	.17

Note: *$p<.05$; **$p<.01$; ***$p<.001$.
Source: Arizona Department of Education, 2004. Adapted from Sullivan, Artiles, Caterino, and Moore (under review).

LD identification rates decreased substantially as the percentage of minority student enrollment increased. In addition, Coutinho and her colleagues examined the role of gender and ethnicity in LD placement. They reported the risk of Latino male and female students increased after taking into account sociodemographic factors[5] (beyond gender and ethnicity). Latino male students were over twice as likely to be placed in LD than the comparison group (White females). Latina female students were not disproportionately represented though their placement risk increased.

Other studies support the need to examine sociodemographic factors at the local level (i.e., LEA or school levels) to understand the complexity of this problem. In Arizona, Latino student placement in special education (across all categories) was predicted by factors like teacher student-ratio, the percentage of minority teachers, and the percentage of minority students in the district (Sullivan et al., under review). Latino student disproportionate representation in special education increased as the student-teacher ratio increased. In contrast, special education disproportionality increased as the percentage of minority students and minority teachers *decreased* in the district (see Table 25.5). These patterns varied, however, when the data were disaggregated by disability category. In the case of mild MR, Latino student disproportionality *decreased* as the student-teacher ratio and the percentage of minority students in the district *increased*. Disproportionate patterns were also positively correlated with the percentage of minority teachers in the districts (see Table 25.5). Finally, Latino student disproportionate representation in LD increased as the student-teacher ratio and the percentage of minority teachers in the districts increased. However, LD disproportionality decreased as the proportion of minority students in LEAs increased (see Table 25.5).

Other studies have assessed the predictive value of academic factors. For instance, Hosp and Reschly (2004) tested the contributions of economic, demographic, and academic factors in the prediction of disproportionality across various ethnic groups. They found the demographic factors had the strongest predictive value for Latinos in E/BD and LD. The academic block of factors "was differentially predictive for different categories of disability. It also differed in relative strength of prediction for different racial/ethnic groups, being stronger for African American and Asian/Pacific Islander students than for Latino or American Indian students" (p. 194). Overall, although the academic factors contributed significantly to two thirds of the models tested in the study, "the academic block of predictors was generally the weakest of the three blocks" (p. 194; see also Artiles, Aguirre-Muñoz, & Abedi, 1998, for an analysis of the discriminant value of academic achievement in Latino student special education placement).

An important consideration in special education placement is access to the general education curriculum and environments. Hence, a critical opportunity-to-learn question for Latino students is, to what extent are Latino students placed in more segregated special education programs compared to their White peers *with the same disability label*? Emerging evidence suggests Latinos are placed in more segregated settings than their peers with similar disability diagnoses (Fierros & Conroy, 2002).

Latino ELLs in Special Education The link between ethnicity and language proficiency status is complex in the case of Latinos. A major challenge for research that aims to understand the interplay between language status and ethnicity in disproportionality is the alarming lack of databases to examine this issue. For instance, some databases report data on ELL status and ethnic group status separately and do not allow cross tabulations of these variables. Thus, it is not possible, for example, to examine ELL special education placement by ethnic group (e.g., Latino ELL, Asian ELL, etc.). Nevertheless, some evidence is beginning to emerge. Rueda et al. (2002) reported a 283% increase in the identification of students in special education between 1993 and 1998 in California. Latino ELL placement in special education in these districts reflected a 345% increase even though the Latino ELL population grew only by 12% in the same time period. Latino ELLs were more likely to be overrepresented in secondary grades (Rueda et al., 2002). Others have reported that although Latinos were not overrepresented in a Southwestern state, ELLs were nearly three times as likely (2.74) to be identified as LD, and over twice as likely (2.20) as MR compared to their White peers (de Valenzuela et al., 2006). These authors also found these students were more likely to be subject to restrictive placements.

For many educators and school psychologists it is difficult to distinguish between poor achievement due to limited English proficiency and academic struggles due to disability. Language acquisition is often confused with learning problems (Artiles & Klingner, 2006). Moreover, home languages other than English can be undervalued in schools and linked to disability, rather than being perceived as strengths and assets to English acquisition and learning (Connor & Boskin, 2001). Disproportionality research suggests that Latino students are more likely to be overrepresented in special education where there are limited language supports available (Finn, 1982).

Many psychological examiners may fail to account for opportunities to learn, language proficiency, or the linguistic appropriateness of instruments used to assess cognitive and academic functioning when evaluating Latino students who are ELLs (Figueroa & Newsome, 2006). When English tests are used in the evaluation process, the validity of determinations can be confounded by the linguistic and cultural loading of the instruments (Abedi, 2006). Additionally, members of the child study and IEP teams can fail to consider language acquisition or opportunities to learn when making disability determinations (Harry & Klingner, 2006).

In summary, Latino placement in special education is a complex phenomenon that defies simplistic binary explanations (e.g., is it due to child poverty or do biased practices create the problem?). There are measurement problems as well as theoretical and contextual issues to consider. The available research suggests the need to analyze disproportionality at multiple levels (i.e., national, state, district, school) and consider simultaneously contextual factors. While national data suggest that disproportionality in special education is not an issue for Latinos, analyses at the state and district levels present a different portrait. In particular, these analyses highlight the need to examine variations in placement at the local level, as aggregated analyses can mask important disproportionate patterns.

Factors Influencing Latino Disproportionality: Complicating Static Markers in Future Research

In a recent review of overrepresentation research, Waitoller, Artiles, and Cheney (in press) found that studies have explained overrepresentation in three ways: A sociodemographic model that focused on characteristics of individuals and contexts, a framework that focused on the contributions of professional practices to the creation and maintenance of overrepresentation, and a sociohistorical lens that examined issues related to race and structural factors. A sizable literature has been produced on the sociodemographic characteristics of diverse students and their contexts, not only in relation to Latino student overrepresentation, but also with regard to minority student educational performance (Valencia, 1997). Most of these explanations stress variables that affect individuals' educational performance (e.g., poverty, school demographics, parental education). The latest NRC report provided an extensive research review on various kinds of threats to child development that ultimately increase the odds for disabilities. O'Connor and Fernandez (2006), however, took issue with the deficit assumptions of minority student disproportionality, particularly with regard to the role of poverty. They broadened the unit of analysis in the study of human development to understand it as embedded in dynamic contexts in which many minority children and their families actively use their agency to counter the effects of poverty (see also Artiles, Klingner, & Tate, 2006).

The second group of studies focused on professional practices that shape the special education identification process (e.g., assessments practices, eligibility decision-making practices, etc.), including mediators of these practices such as teacher beliefs and biases. This research constitutes the bulk of the disproportionality literature (Waitoller et al., in press). There is considerable evidence suggesting that many Latino students have not been receiving the educational services they need to succeed (Klingner et al., 2005). These students have long been subjected to inferior opportunities to learn, tend to receive poorer quality curricula, and are often taught by less qualified teachers (Nieto, 2004). In addition, these students also face lowered expectations that influence the behavior of both educators and students. In an analysis of twelve urban schools, Harry and Klingner (2006) found that numerous inequitable processes prior to special education placement contributed to the overrepresentation of Latino ELLs in special education. Examples included limited opportunities to learn prior to referral and flawed decision-making processes in the eligibility determination process.

Explanations that used a sociohistorical lens have received the least attention. Although these studies also included analysis of sociodemographic factors, they assumed that these factors were associated to structural forces such as power and racism that affects special education placement. For instance, school districts in the South that had a history of segregation practices had larger proportions of African American students in MMR classrooms (Eitle, 2002).

In addition, several aspects or factors that shape the educational attainment of Latinos and thus, might contribute to disproportionality, should be included in future research. These factors include length of residency in the United States, families' educational background and cultural capital, neighborhoods and school, legal residency status, seasonal work, late entry to American schools, and identification processes (Suárez-Orozco, Suárez-Orozco, & Doucet, 2004).

Hernandez and Charney (1998) found that the longer immigrant students lived in the United States, the more they engage in violent behavior or delinquent acts. Furthermore, foreign-born students reported to suffer more discrimination and had less English language skills than Latinos born in the United States. However, foreign-born Latino students were more academically successful than their American born counterparts. Thus, commitment to doing well in school, and academic achievement decreased with each successive generation of Latinos living in the United States (Portes & Rumbaut, 2001). In a study of ELLs in California in which the majority were Latinos, the greatest disproportionality patterns were observed in secondary grades and length of U.S. residency was not seemingly associated with disproportionality risk (Artiles et al., 2005).

A related consideration is that how Latino children and youth define themselves have implications for how they interact with institutions such as schools and for their aspirations for the future. Race and ethnicity play an important role in shaping identities. Latino students may be torn between parental culture and the mainstream American culture needed to fit in peer groups (Suárez-Orozco et al., 2004). Suárez-Orozco and Suárez-Orozco (2001) explained first generation immigrants use a *dual frame of reference* to interpret their experiences in the host society—i.e., they use the experiences, values, and frames of reference from their home countries to make sense of what happens to them in the new society. For instance, many undocumented working-class immigrants hold multiple minimum-wage jobs that strip them of labor rights such as basic benefits. They do it in part because their immigration status restricts the kinds of occupational options available to them. Nevertheless, it is ironic that the deplorable circumstances under which many of these people work still improve significantly their socioeconomic situation in comparison to the excruciating conditions under which they lived in their home country. In contrast, their children did not experience such oppressive situation in the nation of origin, and see all the other opportunities available in the host society that are not within their reach. This intergenerational gap creates tensions within families and can affect school engagement for second-generation children and youth. Suárez-Orozco and Suárez-Orozco (2001) also used the notion of *social mirroring* to understand immigrants' identity formation. Social mirroring implies looking oneself through the eyes of others. Children and youth from Latino families may be influenced by the negative reflections that others have of them, resulting in lower life expectations and self-defeating behaviors. Thus, Latino children and youth may enter the U. S. education system with positive attitudes, but these attitudes may change as a result of cultural hostility and socioemotional violence towards them (Suárez-Orozco et al., 2004). Links between identity formation processes across Latino generations, processes of stereotype threats, and their potential mediating effect on special education placement has not been studied at all.

These studies raise interesting questions about the dynamics of disproportionate representation of Latinos. How do adaptation processes to the dominant society shape the odds for immigrant Latinos to be placed in special education? Which subgroups of Latinos (e.g., first or second generation) have a greater probability of special education placement? What institutional and ideological processes mediate special education placement of these Latino subgroups? Does commitment to do well in school moderate special education placement odds and does it have a differential effect on various Latino subgroups (e.g., across generations)?

The Latino families' educational background is diverse, ranging from highly literate families to families with little schooling experience. The percentage of Latino children who live in families where the father or the mother had at least a bachelor's degree (11 and 10%, respectively) is the lowest among all racial categories (NCES, n.d.). In general, students coming from families with little schooling are in tremendous disadvantage because they do not posses the cultural capital that could support them to navigate successfully the school system. Artiles and his colleagues (1998) reported that Latino families that had children with LD had less structures and rules than Latino families that did not have children with LDs. We know little about the role of families in the processes that lead to Latino student special education placement. Does cultural capital make a difference in the way parents engage in these processes? Are Latino families with higher educational levels able to prevent disability misidentification?

Orfield and Yun (1999) reported that only 25% of Latinos attend majority White schools, and most Latinos are settling in highly segregated neighborhoods impacted by poverty, attending schools that that are also highly segregated. Schools whose enrolment is mostly comprised of students from minority backgrounds have a greater percentage of unqualified teachers, higher teacher turnover rates, and bigger class sizes (Donovan & Cross, 2002). Furthermore, these schools tend to emphasize the enforcement of discipline rules, while teaching tends to be neither culturally responsive nor academically engaging (Suárez Orozco, 1989). However, disproportionate representation patterns are ambiguously associated with school poverty and racial segregation levels. Disproportionality is clearly associated in some cases and not related at all in other studies. Future studies must do careful analyses of local practices to understand the unique configuration of factors that create these disparate patterns.

According to Suárez-Orozco et al. (2004), another factor impacting Latino's experiences in school is their legal status. Students who are undocumented often arrived to the United States under traumatic circumstances, and, once in the country, they continue to live under the fear of being deported. Even if they are able to graduate from high school, they find themselves unable to get a well-paid job or to get into college because they do not have a social security number or proof of their immigration status. Further, since national security measures implemented in the early 2000s as a consequence of the tragic events of September 11th, professionals providing social services are required to call the national security department when serving undocumented immigrants, and police officers in some states are now allowed to ask for documentation status when interrogating individuals. These new policies may increase the stress of undocumented families, impacting the academic performance of Latino students. How these experiences affect student chances for special education placement is unknown.

Legislation about undocumented students in schools has been controversial. In *Pyler v. Doe* in 1982, the Supreme Court ruled that it was unconstitutional to deny public education to undocumented immigrants. However, various laws and litigations have been sought to deny access to social services (including education) to undocumented immigrants and individuals whose language is other than English. For example, in Arizona, Proposition 106 sought to mandate that all state agencies and employees act in English. Proposition 106 was contested, and in 1998 the U.S Supreme Court declared it unconstitutional. In 1998, California voters passed Proposition 227, and voters in Arizona followed with Proposition 203 in 2000. These legislations required all public school instruction to be conducted in English. Although these propositions were framed as beneficial for bilingual students, they had equivocal effects on the improvement of bilingual students' academic outcomes (Parrish, Perez, Merickel, & Linquanti, 2006). Researchers have hardly begun to assess how these policies and the climates they created in schools and communities affected Latino student performance and their chances to be placed in special education.

Coming from a family whose members are seasonal workers and entering the school system at an older age may affect Latino students' participation in school. Children of seasonal work families tend to move around the country, which makes difficult for children to have any kind of continuity in school. Consequentially, Latino children whose family members are seasonal workers have higher drop out rates and lower grades. In addition, these students have work responsibilities that tend to isolate them from their peers (Walls, 2003). Moreover, Latino youth entering the school system may be in a greater disadvantage than their younger counter peers because they may not be awarded credits from their previous schooling, they may have knowledge gaps that set them far behind their classmates, they may have lower English skills, and they might face high-stakes exams that were not designed with them in mind (Suárez Orozco et al., 2004). Future Latino disproportionality research ought to assess how Latino students' unique needs (e.g., migrant workers) might exacerbate their chances for special education placement. Similarly, emerging evidence suggests Latino ELLs and ELLs in California's high schools have the greatest odds for special education placement (Artiles et al., 2005). The experiences of these students in the sending and receiving of educational contexts must be carefully examined to understand better special education placement patterns.

Conclusion

Although equity concerns about Latino student placement in special education has not been considered of national importance, changes in various arenas will likely change this situation. First, greater attention must be paid to the confluence of the major policies affecting Latino students in special education (general, special, and bilingual education) and their potential impact on Latino disproportionality. Careful attention must be given to potential unintended consequences of the confluence of these policies for Latino placement in special education. Furthermore, our review indicates the Latino population is immensely diverse and complex along ethnic, socioeconomic, language, nationality, and education lines. This source of diversity has been alarmingly ignored in the research on Latinos in special education. It is ironic that although this research has historically emphasized student factors, it has ignored within-group diversity, probably because the bulk of the work has stressed student deficits. Similarly, although the examination of institutional forces that create inequitable conditions for Latino students in special education has been somewhat examined, researchers have not taken into account the potential role of globalization and transborder influences that characterize the lives of immigrant Latino families in communities and schools. These are critical omissions in an area of research that requires attention to complexity.

The same criticism can be raised about the lack of attention to the ways in which the notion of culture is theorized in most studies. For the most part, culture is indexed in this literature with static demographic or background marker variables (e.g., ethnicity, income level). The rich interdisciplinary scholarship on culture and its role on learning and education have been virtually ignored in this literature (Artiles, 2003; Gutiérrez & Rogoff, 2003). This limitation has enormous consequences for the unit of analysis in research and constrains how the dynamic and historical nature of culture can be studied. Our review of the literature suggests it is time to refine the theoretical and methodological approaches to the study of Latinos in special education. This change in researchers' practices will have to occur concomitantly with changes in the refinement of information infrastructures, since our review also suggested an alarming lack of adequate databases to address the aforementioned issues. At a time when Latinos have become the largest minority group in the United States, it is critical to improve the kinds of equity questions raised in studies, how the questions are studied, and the implications of research findings for the education of this population.

Author's Note

The first author acknowledges the support of the Center for Advanced Study in the Behavioral Sciences at Stanford University and the National Center for Culturally Responsive Educational Systems (NCCRESt) under grant # H326E020003 awarded by the U.S. Department of Education, Office of Special Education Programs. Endorsement of the U.S. Department of Education of the ideas expressed in this special issue should not be inferred.

Notes

1. We consider Latinos a "minority group" because most of them occupy a "subordinate position in a multiethnic society, suffering from the disabilities of prejudice and discrimination, and maintaining a separate group identity. Even though individual members of the group may improve their social status, the group itself remains in a subordinate position in terms of its power to shape the dominant value system of the society or to share fully in its rewards" (Gibson, 1991, p. 358).
2. Students from other ethnic backgrounds can also be labeled language minority students and/or LEP or ELL.
3. There is an emerging research literature in special education for Latino students that address assessment and instructional issues. However, we focus this chapter on equity issues only due to the critical importance of these issues for policy, research, and practice. See Artiles et al. (2004) for a review of research on assessment and instruction for Latinos in special education.
4. We are using a relative risk ratio of 1.5 to determine overrepresentation and 0.5 for underrepresentation.
5. Sociodemographic factors included teacher-student ratio, per-pupil expenditures, percentage of student at-risk, percentage of non-White students, percentage of ELL, median housing value, median income for households, percentage of children in households below the poverty level, and percentage of adults in the community with a 12th-grade education or less (Coutinho et al., 2002).

References

Abedi, J. (2006). Psychometric issues in the ELL assessment and special education eligibility. *Teachers College Record, 108,* 2282–2303.

Artiles, A. J. (1998). The dilemma of difference: Enrich the disproportionality discourse with theory and context. *The Journal of Special Education, 32,* 32–36.

Artiles, A. J. (2003). Special education's changing identity: Paradoxes and dilemmas in views of culture and space. *Harvard Educational Review, 73,* 164–202.

Artiles, A. J., Aguirre-Muñoz, Z., & Abedi, J. (1998). Predicting placement in learning disabilities programs: Do predictors vary by ethnic group? *Exceptional Children, 64,* 543–559.

Artiles, A. J., & Klingner, J. K. (2006). Forging a knowledge base on English language learners with special needs. *Teachers College Record, 108,* 2187–2194.

Artiles, A. J., Klingner, J. K., & Tate, W. F. (2006). Representation of minority students in special education: Complicating traditional explanations. *Educational Researcher, 35*(6), 3–5.

Artiles, A., Rueda, R., Salazar, J. J., & Higareda, I. (2005). Within group diversity in minority disproportionate representation: English language learners in urban schools. *Exceptional Children, 71,* 283–300.

Artiles, A. J., & Trent, S. C. (1994). Overrepresentation of minority students in special education: A continuing debate. *Journal of Special Education, 27*(4), 410–437.

Artiles, A. J., Trent, S. C., & Palmer, J. (2004). Culturally diverse students in special education: Legacies and prospects. In J. A. Banks & C. M. Banks (Eds.), *Handbook of research on multicultural education* (2nd ed., pp. 716–735). San Francisco: Jossey Bass.

August, D., & Shanahan, T. (Eds.). (2006). *Developing literacy in second-language learners: Report of the National Literacy Panel on Language-Minority Children and Youth.* Mahwah, NJ: Erlbaum.

Bilingual Education Act, P.L. 90-247 (1968).

Bollmer, J., Bethel, J., Garrison-Mogren, & Brauen, M. (2007). Using the risk ration to assess racial/ethnic disproportionality in special education at the school-district level. *Journal of Special Education, 41*(3), 186–198.

Burdette, P. (2007, July). *States definition of significant disproportionality.* Brief Policy Analysis. Washington, DC: Project Forum at NASDSE.

Case, R. E., & Taylor, S. S. (2005). Language difference or learning disability? Answers from a linguistic perspective. *The Clearing House, 78*(3), 127–130.

Cashman, H. R. (2006). Who wins in research on bilingualism in an anti-bilingual state? *Journal of Multilingual and Multicultural Development, 27*(1), 42–60.

Casteñeda v. Pickard. 648 F. 2nd 289 (5th Cir. 1981).

Chinn, P. C., & Hughes, S. (1987). Representation of minority students in special education classes. *Remedial and Special Education, 8*(4), 41–46.

Civil Rights Act, P.L. 88-352 (1964).

Connor, M. C., & Boskin, J. (2001). Overrepresentation of bilingual and poor children in special education classes: A continuing problem. *Journal of Children & Poverty, 7*(1), 23–32.

Coutinho, M. J., & Oswald, D. P. (1998). Ethnicity and special education research: Identifying questions and methods. *Behavioral Disorders, 24,* 66–73.

Coutinho, M. J., Oswald, D. P., & Best, A. M. (2002). The influence of sociodemographics and gender to the disproportionate identification of minority students as having learning disabilities. *Remedial and Special Education, 23*(1), 45–59.

de Valenzuela, J, S., Copeland, S. R., Qi, C. H., & Park, M. (2006). Examining educational equity: Revisiting the disproportionate representation of minority students in special education. *Exceptional Children, 72,* 425–441.

Diana v. California State Board of Education. Civ. Act. No. C-70-37 (N.D. Cal., 1970, 1973).

Donovan, S., & Cross, C. (2002). *Minority students in special and gifted education.* Washington D C: National Academy Press.

Eitle, T. M. (2002). Special education or racial segregation: Understanding variation in the representation of Black students in educable mentally handicapped programs. *Sociological Quarterly, 43*(4), 575–605.

Equal Educational Opportunities Act of 1974, P.L. 93-380 (1974).

Ferguson, D. L., Kozleski, E. B., & Smith, A. (2003). Transforming general and special education in urban schools. In F. E. Obiakor, C. A. Utley, & A. F. Rotatori (Eds.), *Advances in special education, 15: Effective education for learners with exceptionalities* (pp. 104–116). Stamford, CT: JAI.

Fierros, E. G., & Conroy, J. W. (2002). Double jeopardy: An exploration of restrictiveness and race in special education. In D. J. Losen & G. Orfield (Eds.), *Racial inequity in special education* (pp. 39–70). Cambridge, MA: Harvard Education Press.

Figueroa, R. A., & Artiles, A. J. (1999). Disproportionate minority placement in special education programs: Old problem, new explanations. In A. Tashakkori & S. H. Ochoa (Eds.), *Education of Hispanics in the U.S.: Politics, policies, and outcomes* (pp. 93–117). New York: AMS.

Figueroa, R. A., & Newsome, P. (2006). The diagnosis or LD in English learners: Is it nondiscriminatory? *Journal of Learning Disabilities, 39,* 206–214.

Finn, J. D. (1982). Patterns in special education placement as revealed by the OCR surveys. In K. A. Heller, W. H. Holtzman, & S. Messick (Eds.), *Placing children in special education: A strategy for equity* (pp. 322–381). Washington, DC: National Academy Press.

Garcia, E. E. (2004). Educating Mexican American students: Past treatment and recent developments in theory, research, policy, and practice. In J. Banks & C. Banks (Eds.), *Handbook of research on multicultural education* (pp. 491–513). San Francisco: Jossey-Bass.

Garcia, E. E., & Cuellar, D. (2006). Who are these linguistically and culturally diverse students? *Teachers College Record, 108,* 2220–2246.

Garcia, E. E., & Wiese, A. (2002). Language, public policy, and schooling: A focus on Chicano English language learners. In R. R. Valencia (Ed.), *Chicano school failure and success: Past, present, and future* (2nd ed., pp. 149–169). New York: Routledge/Falmer.

Gibson, M. A. (1991). Minorities and schooling: Some implications. In M. A. Gibson & J. U. Ogbu (Eds.), *Minority status and schooling* (pp. 357–381). New York: Garland.

Guadalupe Organization, Inc. v. Tempe Elementary School District No. 3. No. 76-2029, 587 F.2nd 1022.

Gutiérrez, K. D., & Rogoff, B. (2003). Cultural ways of learning: Individual traits or repertoires of practice. *Educational Researcher, 32*(5), 19–25.

Harry, B., & Klingner, J. (2006). *Why are so many minority students in special education? Understanding race and disability in schools.* New York: Teachers College Press.

Hakuta, K., Butler, Y. G., & Witt, D. (2000). *How long does it take English learners to attain proficiency?* Los Angeles: University of California Linguistic Minority Research Institute.

Heller, K. A., Holtzman, W. H., & Messick, S. (Eds.). (1982). *Placing children in special education: A strategy for equity.* Washington, DC: National Academy Press.

Hernandez, D., & Charney, E. (Eds.). (1998). *From generation to generation: The health and well being of children of immigrant families.* Washington, DC: National Academy Press.

Hosp, J., & Reschly, D. (2004). Disproportionate representation of minority students in special education: Academic, demographic, & economic predictors. *Exceptional Children, 70,* 185–199.

Individuals with Disabilities Education Improvement Act (IDEA), P.L. 108-446, 20 U.S.C. 1400-87.

Johnson, E. (2005). Proposition 203: A critical metaphor analysis. *Bilingual Research Journal, 29,* 69–84.

Johnson, K. R., & Martinez, G. E. (2000). Discrimination by proxy: The case of Proposition 227 and the ban on bilingual education. *UC Davis Legal Review, 33,* 1227–1276.

Klingner, J. K., Artiles, A. J., Kozleski, E., Harry, B., Zion, S., Tate, W., et al. (2005). Addressing the disproportionate representation of culturally and linguistically diverse students in special education through culturally responsive educational systems. *Education Policy Analysis Archives, 13*(38). Retrieved December 14, 2005, http://epaa.asu.edu/epaa/v13n38

Kohler. A. D., & Lazarin, M. (2007). Hispanic education in the United States. *National Council of la Raza Statistical Brief, 8,* 1–16. Retrieved on April 10, 2008, from http://www.nclr.org/content/publications/download/43582

Larry P. v. Riles. 502 F.2nd 693 (9th Cir. 1984).

Lau v Nichols. 414 U.S. 563 (1973).

Losen, D. J., & Orfield, G. (Eds.). (2002). *Racial inequity in special education.* Cambridge, MA: Harvard Education Press.

Losen, D., & Welner, K. G. (2002). Contesting inappropriate and inadequate special education for minority children. In D. Losen & G. Orfield (Eds.), *Racial inequality in special education* (167–194). Cambridge, MA: Harvard Education Publishing Group.

MacAvoy, J. & Sidles, C. (1991). The effects of language preference and multitrial presentation upon the free recall of Navajo children. *Journal of American Indian Education, 30*(3), 33–43.

McLaughlin, M. J. (2008, April). *Evolving interpretations of special education: Standards-driven reform and new conceptions of equality of opportunity.* Paper presented at the Changing Conceptions of Special Education Conference: Past, Present, and Future. University of Delaware. Newark, DE.

Miller, P. J., & Goodnow, J. J. (1995). Cultural practices: Toward an integration of culture and development. In J. J. Goodnow, P. J. Miller, & F. Kessel (Eds.), *Cultural practices as contexts for development* (pp. 5–16). San Francisco: Jossey Bass.

Minow, M. (1990). *Making all the difference.* Ithaca, NY: Cornell University Press.

NCCRESt (2005). *Cultural considerations and challenges in Response to Intervention models: An NCCRESt position statement.* Denver, CO: Author.

NCES. (2006). *Public elementary and secondary students, staff, schools, and school districts: School year 2003–04.* Retrieved March 31, 2008, from http://nces.ed.gov/pubs2006/2006307.pdf

NCES. (n.d.a). *Public school student membership, by race/ethnicity and state or jurisdiction: School year 2005–06.* Retrieved November 25, 2007, http://nces.ed.gov/pubs2007/pesenroll06/tables/table_2.asp

NCES. (n.d.b). *Number and percentage of children ages 3 to 5 and 6 to 21 served under the Individuals with Disabilities Education Act (IDEA), by race/ethnicity and type of disability: 2004.* Retrieved November 25, 2007, from http://nces.ed.gov/pubs2007/minoritytrends/tables/table_8_1b.asp

NCES. (n.d.c). *Percentage of high school dropouts (status dropouts) among persons 16 through 24 years old, by sex and race/ethnicity: Selected years from 1960–2005* [table]. Retrieved on November 25, 2007, from http://nces.ed.gov/programs/digest/d06/tables/dt06_104.asp

NCES. (n.d.d). *Percentage of children ages 6 to 18 whose parents attained a bachelor's or graduate degree, by race/ethnicity: 2005* [table]. Retrieved on November 25, 2007, from http://nces.ed.gov/pubs2007/minoritytrends/ figures/ figure_5.asp

Nieto, S. (2004). *Affirming diversity: The sociopolitical context of multicultural education* (4th ed.). Boston, MA: Pearson.

No Child Left Behind Act of 2001 (NCLB). P.L. 107-110. 115 Stat. 1425.

O'Connor, C., & Fernandez, S .D. (2006). Race, class, and disproportionality. *Educational Researcher, 35*(6), 6–11.

Ochoa, S. H., Robles-Piña, E., Garcia, S. B., & Breunig, N. (1999). School psychologists' perspectives on referrals of language minority students. *Multiple Voices for Exceptional Learners, 3*(1), 1–14.

Orfield, G., & Yun, J. T. (1999). *Resegregation in American schools.* Cambridge, MA: Harvard University, Civil Rights Project.

Oswald, D. P., Coutinho, M. J., & Best, A. M. (2002). Community and social predictors of overrepresentation of minority children in special education. In D. J. Losen & G. Orfield (Eds.), *Racial inequity in special education* (p. 1–13). Cambridge, MA: Harvard Education Press.

Oswald, D. P., Coutinho, M. J., Best, A. M., & Singh, N. N. (1999). Ethnic representation in special education: The influence of school-related economic and demographic variables. *The Journal of Special Education, 32*(1), 194–206.

Ovando, C. J., Collier, V. P., & Combs, M. C. (2003). *Bilingual & ESL classrooms: Teaching in multicultural contexts.* New York: McGraw-Hill Higher Education.

Parrish, T. (2002). Racial disparities in the identification, funding, and provision of special education. In D. J. Losen & G. Orfield (Eds.), *Racial inequity in special education* (pp. 15–38). Cambridge, MA: Harvard Education Press.

Parrish, T. B., Perez, M., Merickel, A., & Linquanti, R. (2006). *The effects of the implementation of Proposition 227 on the education of English learners, K-12: Findings from a five-year evaluation.* Washington, D.C.: The American Institute for Research. (ERIC Document Reproduction Service No. ED491617)

PASE v. Hannon. 506 F. Supp. 831 (N.D. Ill. 1980).

Paul, D. (2004). The train has left: The No Child Left Behind Act leaves black and Latino literacy learners waiting at the station. *Journal of Adolescent and Adult Literacy, 47*(8), 648–656.

Portes, A., & Rumbaut, R. (2001). *Legacies: The story of the second generation.* Berkeley: University of California Press.

Rodriguez, R. (2007). Leaving most Latino children behind: No Child Left Behind legislation, testing and the misuse of data under George Bush administration. *Journal of Critical Statistics, 1,* 3–7.

Rolstad, K., Mahoney, K., & Glass, G. V. (2005). The big picture: A meta-analysis of program effectiveness research on English language learners. *Education Policy, 19*(4), 572–594.

Rueda, R., Artiles, A. J., Salazar, J., & Higareda, I. (2002). An analysis of special education as a response to the diminished academic achievement of Chicano/Latino students: An update. In R. R. Valencia (Ed.), *Chicano school failure and success* (2nd ed., pp. 310–332). New York: Routledge.

Skiba, R. J., Chung, C. G., Wu, T. C., Simmons, A. B., & St. John, E. P. (2000). *Minority overrepresentation in Indiana's special education programs.* Bloomington: Indiana Education Policy Center.

Skiba, R. J., Michael, R. S., Nardo, A. C., & Peterson, R. L. (2002). The color of discipline: Sources of racial and gender disproportionality in school punishment. *Urban Review, 34,* 317–342.

Skiba, R. J., Poloni-Staudinger, L., Simmons, A. B., Feggins-Azziz, R., & Chung, C. (2005). Unproven links: Can poverty explain ethnic disproportionality in special education? *Journal of Special Education, 39*(3), 130–144.

Skiba, R., Simmons, A., Ritter, S., Rausch, M. K., Feggins, L. R., Gallini, S., Edl, H., & Mukherjee, A. (2004). *Moving towards equity: Addressing disproportionality in special education in Indiana.* Bloomington, Indiana: Indiana Education Policy Center.

Suárez-Orozco, M. (1989). *Central American refugees and U.S high schools: A psychological study of motivation and achievement.* Stanford, CA: Stanford University Press.

Suárez-Orozco, M. M. (2001). Globalization, immigration and education: The research agenda. *Harvard Educational Review, 71,* 345–365.

Suárez-Orozco, M., Roos, P. M., & Suárez-Orozco, C. (2000). Culture, education, and legal perspective on immigration. In J. P. Heubert (Ed.), *Law and school reform: Six strategies for promoting educational equity* (pp. 160–204). New Haven, CT: Yale University Press.

Suárez-Orozco, M., & Suárez-Orozco, C. (2001). *Children of Immigration.* Cambridge: Harvard University Press.

Suárez-Orozco, C., Suárez-Orozco, M. M., & Doucet, F. (2004). The academic engagement and achievement of Latino youth. In J. Banks & C. Banks (Eds.), *Handbook of research on multicultural education* (2nd ed., pp. 420–437). San Francisco: Jossey-Bass.

Sullivan, A., Artiles, A. J., Caterino, L. C., & Moore, E. G. (under review). *Local complexities in minority representation in special education: Patterns across levels, disabilities, and structural factors.*

Sullivan, A., Kozleski, E., & Smith, A. (2008, March). *Understanding the current context of minority disproportionality in special education.* Paper presented at the annual meeting of the American Educational Research Association, New York, NY.

U.S. Census Bureau. (2004). *Foreign-born population by sex, age, and year of entry: 2004* [table]. Retrieved November 26, 2007, from http://www.census.gov/population/socdemo/foreign/ppl-176/tab02-1.pdf.

Valencia, R. (Ed.). (1997). *The evolution of deficit thinking.* London: Falmer.

Waitoller, F., Artiles, A. J., & Cheney, D. (in press). The miner's canary: A review of overrepresentation research and explanations. *The Journal of Special Education.*

Walls, C. (2003). *Providing highly mobile students with an effective education.* ERIC Clearing House on Urban Education. (ERIC Document Reproduction Service No. ED482918)

Westat. (2003). *Special populations study final report.* Rockville, MD: Author.

Wright, P., & Santa Cruz, R. (1983). Ethnic composition of special education programs in California. *Learning Disability Quarterly, 6,* 387–394.

26 Effective Practices that Matter for Latino Children

Teresa M. Huerta
California State University, Fresno

Carmina M. Brittain
University of California, San Diego

Introduction

Recent research suggests that teachers who work effectively with Latino students employ three non-traditional practices that are: (a) highly interactive, (b) student-centered, and (c) collaborative (Dalton, 1998; Moll, Amanita, Neff, & González, 1992; Padrón, Waxman, & Rivera, 2002). These contrast with traditional practices that tend to be teacher-directed, individualized, and competitive (Tharp & Gallimore, 1988). In addition, this research finds that successful teachers of Latino students tend to have a broader pedagogical perspective than others, one that extends beyond the traditional notion of content knowledge and instructional practices (Moll et al., 1992; Monzó & Rueda, 2001; Padrón et al., 2002).

Equally important, these studies find that effective teachers present academic content that has meaning and purpose for their students. Teachers gain this ability by becoming knowledgeable about their students' culture, language, and experiences through their relationships with students; in other words, they get to know their students and value their students' culture, values, and experiences. This knowledge guides them in selecting and tailoring instructional practices that facilitate learning. As a result, effective teachers interviewed for these studies state that their relationship with students is an essential part of their pedagogical practices (García, 1988; Huerta, 2002; Nieto & Rolón, 1997; Villegas & Lucas, 2002).

The following section provides an overview of empirical and conceptual literature on effective teaching practices for Latino students. This broad review begins with a brief discussion of the current workforce of teachers and those teachers most likely to be teaching Latino students. It is followed by a review of the literature on the specific attributes, beliefs, and teaching practices recognized as supporting Latino students. It then discusses humanizing pedagogy and culturally responsive teaching. The final section is on teacher-family partnerships, which provide a positive impact on the family's involvement in the children's education.

This chapter is grounded in the authors' experiences, research, and observations in culturally and linguistically diverse classrooms along with work with effective teachers. Furthermore, many of the teaching practices highlighted in this chapter are acknowledged as being useful in the general literature on effective teachers. The intent of this chapter is to focus on specific attributes, beliefs, and teaching practices that encompass the pedagogy of teachers who work towards enhancing Latino student learning and supporting them and their families. Further research is needed to assess whether the results of this research can also be applied to the teaching of other racial and ethnic groups of students, however, preliminary findings suggest that it is applicable to various U.S. immigrant and racial groups of students.

Demographics of Teachers and Latino Students

To understand the context of effective teachers of Latino students, it is important to examine the racial and ethnic makeup of the teaching workforce and the growing Latino student population.

Most teachers are predominantly non-Hispanic Caucasian. In 1999-2000, the national teaching workforce consisted of 84% non-Hispanic White, 8% Black, 5% Hispanic, 1% Asian/Pacific Islander, and 1% American Indian/Alaskan Native (U.S. Department of Education, 2003). In contract to non-Hispanic Caucasian teachers, there is an increase of racial and ethnic minority students. From 1972 to 2005, minority students increased as a percentage of total public school enrollments from 22% to 42% (U.S. Department of Education, 2007). Hispanic students had the largest increase, 6%, while Asian/Pacific Islander students increased by 1%, Black students and American Indian/Alaska Native students stayed at roughly the same percentage of enrollment during this time period (U.S. Department of Education, 2007).

This contrast is even greater in California, where racial and ethnic minority students are the majority. Furthermore, Hispanic children lead as the largest ethnic group at 48% and soon to be over half of California's K–12 public school students (California Dept. of Education, 2007a). Whereas, only 27% of California teachers are from minority groups and 15.6% are Hispanic (California Dept. of Education, 2007b).

Scholars (Sleeter, 2001; Gandará, Rumberger, Maxwell-Jolly, & Callahan, 2003; Villegas & Lucas, 2002) argue that it is crucial that educators recognize these demographics. Nationally, 39% of teachers have students with limited English proficiency in their classrooms, but only one quarter of those teachers have received training to work with them (U.S. Department of Education, 2007). Sleeter (2001) contends that the cultural gap between students and teachers is large and growing. Consequently, preparing culturally responsive teacher is a necessity.

Review of Effective Teachers Working with Latino Students

Attributes of Effective Teachers of Latino Students

Based on the literature reviewed, teachers who work effectively with Latino students share specific training, knowledge, life experiences, and beliefs. In the area of training, these teachers are fully credentialed, have an average of seven years of teaching experience, and are graduates of bilingual teacher training programs. For example, García's (1988) study on effective teachers of Latino students found that they had seven years of teaching experience as bilingual teachers and were fully credentialed. Huerta's qualitative study (2002) on four effective teachers of Latino students found that the teacher who exhibited the highest degree of student engagement also had the most training and teaching experience (over 20 years). Furthermore, this teacher was the only one of the group of four who had participated in a five-year teacher preparation program. This is noteworthy because a substantial body of research indicates that insufficient training and support contribute to teacher burnout and higher rates of attrition (Cohen & Himamauli, 1996; Darling-Hammond, 1999; Haberman, 1996).

Research on effective teachers working with Latino children (Dalton, 1998; García, 1994; Huerta, 2002; Moll et al., 1992; Monzó & Rueda, 2001; Nieto & Rolón, 1997; Ramirez, Yuen, Ramey, Pasta, & Billings, 1991; Tukunoff, 1985) finds that they have the following attributes in common:

- bilingual in English and Spanish,
- knowledgeable of subject matter and able to transform it into relevant lessons to promote student understanding,
- knowledgeable of the sociocultural aspects of their students' lives and the communities they serve,
- knowledgeable about the second-language acquisition process, particularly the theories on learning and culture,
- able to articulate their teaching philosophies to administrators, colleagues, and parents,

- able to draw parents and other community members into classroom and school activities and tap into the parents' knowledge and experiences to enhance classroom instruction, and
- continually upgrading their teaching skills by taking courses and attending workshops on techniques and approaches.

Pease-Alvarez, García, and Espinoza (1991) found that effective teachers of Latino students possessed the above attributes and in particular utilized the students' culture and linguistic resources. However, they also learned that these teachers used the culture and linguistic background of their students not only to link students' prior knowledge and cultural values to new concepts but also to enhances their students' self-esteem (in contrast to using the white, mainstream culture, values, and linguistic background). Essentially, these teachers felt that part of their job was to provide the cultural and linguistic validation that was missing from mainstream school experiences for Latino students.

In another study, Lucas, Henze, and Donato (1990) examined six high schools in California and Arizona recognized for providing quality education to Latino students and identified eight common features that coincide with the seven attributes listed above. They further highlighted the efforts of six school administrators that enhanced their faculty's teaching skills via special classes and seminars in second language acquisition, effective instructional approaches for teaching English language learners, and cooperative learning and cross-cultural counseling strategies. Teachers and other staff members also took Spanish language classes because they felt it enhanced their instructional practices.

Additional research acknowledges that effective teachers often develop sociocultural competencies based on their life experiences that parallel the social context of their Latino students' lives. In Huerta's (2002) qualitative study on elementary grade teachers, identified by focus groups of parents, students, and administrators as effective in working with Latino children, all four teachers shared several key life experiences with one another, and also with their Latino students. For example, English was a second language for three of the teachers and two had immigrated to the United States. One teacher was born in the United States, and his parents were working-class immigrants, whereas three of the teachers were Latino and one was Caucasian. However, the Caucasian teacher had worked for over 25 years in Latino communities in Mexico and the United States. In essence, all four had direct experience with Latinos and their culture. Furthermore, their life experiences seemed to strongly and positively influence their attitudes and beliefs about Latino students.

Nieto and Rolón (1997) suggest that effective teaching practices for Latino students center their curriculum development and school change on students' categories of identification and the social context of their lives. In other words, teachers create bicultural educational environments in which the exploration of the social and individual elements brings about the formation of identities and the social context of Latino children. Through this process, schools can further explore and affirm these elements. Huerta's study (2002) indicates that the pedagogical perspectives of effective teachers of Latino students incorporate their sociocultural knowledge to build relationships with their students and families, and to shape instructional practices to further link the curriculum to their students' culture, language, and interests.

Similarly, Lucas et al.'s (1990) research indicates that five of the six administrators from the six effective high schools examined were bilingual and bicultural. The study by Lucas et al. (1990) points out that due to the life experiences of these administrators, they could better understand what it is like to learn a second language and grow up between cultures, and this understanding influenced their administrative decisions. For example, the administrators moved toward replacing remedial classes to more rigorous courses over the objections of some staff members.

Beliefs of Effective Teachers of Latino Students

This section looks at the shared attitudes and beliefs of effective teachers working with Latino students. Based on the literature (García, 1994; Nieto & Rolón, 1997; Moll, Amanita, Neff, & González, 1992; Villegas & Lucas, 2002), effective teachers have developed well-articulated perspectives and teaching philosophies that underlie their instructional practices. Four views common among these teachers are (a) high expectations of students, (b) the need to incorporate students' linguistic and cultural resources into the curricula, (c) emphasis on strong literacy skills, and (d) valuing and incorporating parent involvement. Parent involvement will be discussed towards the end of this paper in order to provide a more in-depth discussion. It is important to recognize that the literature on effective teachers believes parent involvement is essential in supporting learning for Latino students.

Effective teachers believe that all students can be successful learners. This is communicated to students by holding high expectations and demanding that they work diligently to achieve excellence (Tikunoff, 1985, Villegas & Lucas, 2002). They do not have the *pobrecito* syndrome, in which some teachers imply, "He's just a poor little Latino child, so I won't push him academically" (García, 1994). Instead, they demand high academic performance from all students and persistently push students to try harder and do better, and accept no excuses from them for not doing their assigned work and doing it well. They are tough, demanding, and committed to helping all students achieve. They want them to achieve and believe they can do well in school.

Successful teachers of Latino children believe that ethnic-and language-minority students have greater academic success when instruction focuses on making meaning out of content (Moll, 1988). In other words, students are able to comprehend/understand the material based on their on knowledge and life experiences. One important method they use is to employ instructional practices that reflect their students' language and cultural resources to help them better comprehend and identify with their home cultures, which, in return, create pride in their culture thereby raising their self-esteem (Cummins, 1986; Tikunoff, 1985; García, 1994; Villegas, 1991). Tikunoff (1983) identified three ways that effective teachers incorporate home and community culture into the classroom: (a) by utilizing cultural referents, (b) by organizing instruction built on rules of discourse from the home and community cultures, and (c) by respecting the values and norms of students' home cultures even as the norms of the majority culture are taught.

Effective teachers of Latino students believe that comprehension, verbal, and written communications skills should be taught collaboratively with students by employing useful and meaningful language across the curricula. As a result, the most prominent characteristic of their classrooms is the ongoing creation of meaning, not the teaching of specific skills or subskills (Moll, 1988). Consequently, these teachers work towards creating literate environments in which many language experiences can take place and different types of literacy can be practiced, understood, and learned. These culturally rich literate environments are often child-centered and holistic.

Humanizing Pedagogy

The attributes and perspectives described under training, knowledge, life experience, and beliefs reflect what Freire (1987) describes as the humanizing pedagogy. Other educators (Bartolomé, 1994; Ladson-Billings, 1994; Nieto, 1996; Villegas & Lucas, 2002) also assert that there is too much emphasis on instructional practices and not enough on the attitudes and perspectives of teachers. These scholars indicate that the actual strength of each teaching practice depends primarily on the degree to which teachers embrace a humanizing pedagogy, which refers to the relationships forged by the teachers with their students. Freire termed this as "teaching in relationship with the other" (1987, p. 61), the other being the student. This type of pedagogy respects the human, inter-personal side of teaching, and emphasizes the richness of the teacher-student relationships. Teachers who practice this humanizing pedagogy incorporate the daily experience, history, and perspectives of their students and value their students' ideas, perspectives and experiences.

According to Freire (1987), education is by nature social, historical, and political, and all students learn in a political-social-historical context, whether teachers are aware of it or not. Hence, schools are not politically neutral; they reflect the political ideology, the power structures, and the attitudes and values of mainstream society, both positive and negative. Consequently, society's unequal power relations among various social and cultural groups are reproduced in the school and classroom. As a result, teachers do not play a universal, neutral role, nor are they immune from the biases (often unaware) from their social class, gender or race.

Teachers practicing a humanizing pedagogy recognize the socio, historical and political contexts of their lives and of their students' lives, which includes issues of power, racial and ethnic identities, and cultural values (Bartolomé, 1994; Nieto, 1996). Therefore, they have developed (or are striving to develop) a critical understanding of their purpose as educators and that of their students as unique individuals influenced by their culture, communities, and the larger society (Freire, 1987). Consequently, they believe that students differ in the way in which they learn, not in their ability to learn. Guided by this knowledge, teachers employ non-traditional practices in which students and teachers share knowledge and power (Bartolomé, 1994; Freire, 1987).

In contrast, teachers using traditional practices adopt an approach that ignores or downplays differences in the way students learn; they perceive that their main task is to impart knowledge to students (Cummins, 1989; Freire, 1987; Murrell, 2001). Consequently, their teaching practices tend to be a one-size fits all variety (Villegas, 1991). However, a teacher practicing a humanizing pedagogy invites students to recognize and critically explore their political-social-historical reality. This is accomplished through problem-posing investigation, both group and individual, and interaction with relevant content and with other students and teachers. Through this process, students reach their own understanding of issues and processes, and develop a more personal, well-rooted perspective of the world, which is often not the mainstream perspective.

Towards Culturally Responsive Teaching

Culture is central to learning in that it impacts the way in which groups and individuals communicate, receive information, and construct their thinking processes (Ladson-Billings, 1994). Reflecting a humanizing pedagogy and embraced by various scholars' research on effective instructional approaches of language-minority students is culturally responsive teaching. According to Gay (2000), culturally responsive teaching utilizes the cultural knowledge, experiences, frame of reference, and performance styles of diverse students to make learning more relevant and effective for students. Consequently, culturally responsive teaching acknowledges, responds to, and celebrates the various cultures represented in the classroom, and promotes full, equitable access to education for all students.

Advocating for culturally responsive teaching, Villegas and Lucas (2002) found that working effectively with culturally and linguistically diverse students, in particular, students who have been historically marginalized, involves more than just applying specialized teaching techniques. Similar to Freire (1987) and others (Bartolomé, 1994; Darder, 1991; Nieto, 1996), Villegas and Lucas assert the need for a new way of looking at teaching that is grounded in an understanding of the role of culture and language in learning. Furthermore, they have developed six salient qualities that can serve as a framework for professional development for teachers and school systems seeking to respond effectively to an increasingly diverse student population. It is also important to note that the six characteristics share similarities to the literature previous reviewed in this paper on effective teachers for Latino students.

Six Characteristics of Culturally Responsive Teachers

Villegas and Lucas (2002) provided six characteristics for culturally responsive teachers: (a) being socioculturally conscious, (b) using a constructivist approach to teaching, (c) being knowledgeable about students' culture, (d) having an affirming attitude, (e) using appropriate instructional strategies, and (f) advocating for all students. Each feature will be briefly discussed in the following pages.

Sociocultural consciousness is defined by Villegas and Lucas (2002) as an awareness that one's worldview is not universal but is profoundly shaped by one's life experiences and that these life experiences are influenced by a variety of factors including race and ethnicity, socioeconomic class, and gender.

Similar to Freire (1987) and Bartolomé (1994), Villegas and Lucas (2002) assert that teachers with a sociocultural awareness recognize the sociohistorical and political context of their lives and their students' lives, which includes issues of power, racial and ethnic identities, and contrasting cultural values. They can recognize the growing inequalities in U.S. society in which the middle class is disappearing, and a two-tiered society is emerging. The affluent class lives radically different lives than the mass majority. Included in these socioeconomic changes is the growing economic disparity between various racial, ethnic, social groups, and the language backgrounds of teachers and their students. Consequently, teachers who lack a sociocultural and political awareness unconsciously and inevitable rely on their cultural lenses, colored by racial, ethnic and socioeconomic-class experiences, to perceive students and their needs and perspectives. This, unfortunately, results in misinterpretations and disconnects on the teacher's part, which, in turn, hinder both the teaching and learning processes.

Therefore, culturally responsive teaching requires that teachers broaden their perceptions of the world if they are to learn to see life from the perspectives of their future students. This includes examining their own sociocultural identities in relationship to that of their students. They also need to understand that in all social systems, some positions are accorded greater status and economic rewards than others and such status differences result in differential access to power. As a result, they need to understand the intricate connection between school and society whereby traditionally organized schools help to reproduce existing social inequalities while giving the illusion that such inequalities are natural and fair and based on personal abilities and talents.

The constructivist approach to teaching involves viewing learning as a process whereby learners use their knowledge and beliefs to gain meaning from the new input (ideas, skills, and experiences) they encounter in school. The knowledge that children bring to school stems from their personal and cultural experiences. Consequently, teachers applying a constructivist approach find it important that they first recognize their children's personal and cultural perspectives and experiences as resources and then find ways to incorporate them into the classroom experience. In other words, these teachers support students' learning by helping them build bridges between what they already know about a topic and what they still need to learn about it (Villegas & Lucas, 2002).

Villegas and Lucas (2002) demonstrate ways in which teachers support a constructivist view of learning when working with students from culturally and linguistically diverse backgrounds. For example, they recommend that a topic such as "immigration" could be added to the social studies curriculum, and that students can incorporate their life experiences into the lesson, such as how their families' challenges with learning a new cultural system and language, finding work and building a social system in a new land has influenced them. To this end, Villegas and Lucas highlighted how a student who emigrated from the Dominican Republic learned more from her social studies unit on immigration when the teacher drew on her personal experiences as a newcomer to the United States (2002).

Knowledgeable about the students' culture refers to the need for teachers to learn about and seek to understand the lives and cultures of their students in order to support them in building bridges between their existing knowledge and experiences and the new material to be taught. Villegas and Lucas (2002) believe that for the curriculum and the teaching methodologies to have any real meaning or purpose for students, teachers must not only know their subject content well but also have knowledge about their individual students and family lives. This requires tapping into students' strengths, addressing their own bias, incorporating problem-solving activities that are relevant and meaningful to their students, explaining new concepts with illustrations or examples taken from their students' everyday lives, and providing opportunities for students to display what they know about the topic at hand.

To teach subject matter in meaningful ways requires that teachers learn about their students' experiences outside of school. For example, teachers need to learn about their families' backgrounds, immigration history, and languages spoken in the household, favorite activities, concerns and strengths. Villegas and Lucas (2002) argue that although it is possible for students to be successful learners without having relationships with their teachers, students who have been most marginalized from mainstream school practices are more likely to benefit from such relationships than students from dominant groups. According, they find that this is due to the fact that schools and institutions tend to devalue the way minority and language-minority students speak, interact, and think, sending a message to the children that they are not valued by society.

Effective strategies for learning about students' lives outside school include making home visits when appropriate, creating opportunities in the classroom for students to discuss their aspirations, posing culturally connected problems for students to solve and noting how each student solves them, and talking with parents and other community members about issues and concerns of students.

Various scholars (Cummins, 1986; Nieto, 1996; Villegas & Lucas, 2002) have found that effective teachers have an affirming attitude towards culturally and linguistically diverse students. An affirming attitude respects cultural differences and views children from non-dominant groups as capable learners even when they enter school with ways of thinking and behaving that differ from that of the dominant culture. In fact, they see these differences as resources for acquiring new learning. However, research (Nieto, 1996) indicates that many teachers perceive students in socially subordinated groups from a deficit perspective. Villegas and Lucas (2002) describe a deficit perspective in contrast to an affirming perspective within a continuum, where on one end is the deficit view and on the other end is the affirming view. All educators fall somewhere between these extremes.

Teachers who hold an affirming attitude recognize that White, middle-class perspectives and values are most valued in society; they understand that this status derives from the power of the White, middle-class group rather than from a superior quality (Villegas & Lucas, 2002). They therefore believe it is important to provide their students with knowledge of mainstream culture (e.g., standard English). Equally, they acknowledge the existence and validity the various perspectives, vernacular, behavior, and learning styles. Consequently, these teachers see all students, including children who are poor and of color, as learners who know a great deal and have valuable experiences, concepts, and language that can be built upon and expanded to help them learn even more. For example, the use of a student's native language is recognized as a tool (versus a hindrance) and is utilized to build on learning.

Villegas and Lucas (2002) defines culturally responsive teaching as creating instructional situations where teachers use teaching approaches and strategies that recognize, affirm, and build on culturally different ways of learning, behaving, and using language in the classroom. In this pursuit, teachers use their knowledge about students' lives to design instruction that builds on what they already know.

Villegas and Lucas (2002) have provided five broad culturally responsive teaching practices to help teachers make their classrooms more inclusive: (a) involve all students in the construction of knowledge, (b) build on students' personal and cultural strengths, (c) help students examine the curriculum from multiple perspectives, (d) use various assessment practices that promote learning, and (e) make the culture of the classroom inclusive of all students. Each practice is briefly reviewed below.

Contrary to having students memorize predigested information, culturally responsive teachers strive to support students in their construction of knowledge by actively involving them in learning tasks and challenging them with problems that promotes higher-order thought processes (i.e., hypothesizing, predicting, comparing, evaluating, integrating, and synthesizing). Activities that involve active roles include: inquiry projects, collaborative projects for small groups of mixed-ability students, authentic dialogues, and encouragement of students to assume increasing responsibility for their own learning.

Students feel alienated when they are unable to connect to the school's learning and social environment. For children from socially subordinated groups, this can often be the case, whereby the environment neither relates to their lives nor invites them to use their preexisting knowledge and skills.

The focus of these pedagogical practices is to build on students' knowledge while stretching their knowledge beyond that which is familiar to them. Practices consist of: helping students access their prior knowledge and beliefs, building on students' interests, developing students' linguistic resources, using examples and analogies from students' lives/culture, employing culturally appropriate instructional materials, tapping community resources that support Latino culture, and creating unique paths to learning using varied instructional activities.

Similar to the broader society, the school curriculum is socially constructed and value-laden based on the standards of the White, middle-class American culture. To assist students from subordinated groups to overcome the sense of alienation from school and to teach all students about social inequality and ways to counter it, rather than merely assimilating into inequitable social arrangements, culturally responsive teachers help students critically analyze the curriculum.

Analyzing the curriculum involves identifying and correcting inaccuracies, omissions, and distortions in the text and broadening it to include multiple perspectives. Other activities that support multiple perspectives in the classroom are asking students to: examine concepts, situations, and events from multiple perspectives using multicultural literature (e.g., historical narratives); examine content (e.g., social studies) to build on their personal and cultural knowledge relative to a topic; and interview family members or local community leaders from different cultural groups about issues or current events.

There are three areas of concern as to why Villegas and Lucas (2002) advocate the use of various assessments for culturally and diverse students. The first item is that historically standardized test scores have been used largely to sort students into different instructional tracks (Darling-Hammond, 1999; National Coalition of Educational Equity Advocates, 1994). Second, students enter school with culturally specific understandings of the appropriate means of displaying and conveying their knowledge. If the teacher and students do not share this understanding, the instructor could easily misjudge the pupils' competence unless he or she is sensitive to cultural differences. An example would be Native American children who are not familiar with responding to questions posed in a public setting to display knowledge (Au & Kawakami, 1994; Philips, 1983). Third, assessing students who speak native languages other than English can be challenging. For example, when informally assessed, bilingual students often appear to be competent in English and the teacher may assume that these students are competent enough to handle academic content without support for language comprehension. However, these students often later fail in mainstream classrooms and written text. The problem is that these students have a high degree of social English language skills but not enough academic language skills in a second language to succeed in the learning environment.

To assess students' progress, culturally responsive teachers use a variety of approaches. In addition, they use a learning-oriented assessment approach that asks students to construct their responses rather than select a right answer and to apply their knowledge to solving problems in the real world rather than using their skills in decontextualized ways. Furthermore, they are aware of the potential for cultural misunderstandings and thus interpret assessment results for students from diverse backgrounds cautiously, offering students a variety of ways to demonstrate what they know about the topic of instruction. This form of assessment is important because reliance on a single type of assessment creates a disadvantage for some children.

Make the culture of the classroom inclusive for all students is another appropriate instructional strategy for culturally responsive teaching. According to Villegas and Lucas (2002), most classroom cultures have some variation, but certain features have prevailed over time and persist today despite ongoing efforts to reform teaching and make classrooms more culturally inclusive. What prevails is the teacher-directed lesson, in which the teacher maintains complete control of students. The teacher determines the topics of discussion, selects who can speak or answer questions, and decides what qualifies as a correct response. In such settings, verbal participation is required for all students whether they are outgoing, introverted, or do not like speaking out loud in the classroom. Teaching and learning are equated with talking, and silence is interpreted as the absence of knowledge. Students are questioned in public and required to bid for the floor by raising their hands. For many children from nonmainstream backgrounds, their home culture clashes with many of the sociocultural demands of this type of practice.

Culturally responsive teachers understand that the classroom is not a neutral setting where all students can participate in instructional events equally and display what they know freely. In other words, they recognize that embedded in their teaching are implicit rules that govern what counts as knowledge, how questions are used, stories are told, access to the floor is gained, knowledge is displayed, space is organized, and time used (Villegas & Lucas, 2002). Some researchers further contend that many teachers believe that children need to learn not only the prescribed academic content but also to learn culturally appropriate ways of participating in learning events and of displaying what they know (Mehan, 1979; Villegas, 1991).

Based on this insight gained through such reflection, culturally responsive teachers create inclusive classroom communities in which all students understand the appropriate ways of participating in the various learning events by making explicit to children the sociocultural expectations built onto different learning activities, whenever needed. For instance, it can be culturally challenging for some students to participate in collaborative small group projects to devise solutions to problems if they have been accustom to learn through a different approach.

To enable these students to participate effectively in collaborative problem-solving projects, the culturally responsive teachers help them understand not only how to participate in this type of instructional event, but also why it is important for them to adopt ways of learning that are culturally unfamiliar, perhaps even clashing. Villegas and Lucas (2002) point out that their intent in the use of this pedagogical approach is not that teachers replace the cultural patterns of students but instead support them in adding on new patterns to their culture repertoire. This allows students to expand upon the way in which they participate in the world.

Advocating for all students is the final characteristic of culturally responsive teaching. Villegas and Lucas (2002) assert that current conditions for many nonmainstream groups puts them at a disadvantage by attending schools that are conducive to a culture of low expectations for students from low-status groups, inadequate facilities and multicultural learning materials, large class sizes, assignment of the least-experienced teachers to classes in which students need the most help, insensitivity toward cultural differences, questionable testing practices, and a curriculum that does not reflect diverse student perspectives. Culturally responsive teachers are aware of the need for educational and social change and have a desire to participate in bringing about such change.

In addition, such teachers see themselves as part of a community of educators working to make schools more equitable for all students. They believe that the profession of teaching is an ethical activity, and therefore see their jobs as an ethical obligation to help all students learn. To meet this obligation, teachers work as advocates for their students, especially those who have been traditionally marginalized in schools. They also believe that by actively promoting for greater equity in education, they can increase access to learning and to educational success and can challenge the prevailing perceptions that differences among students are problems rather than resources.

According to Villegas and Lucas (2002) teachers who see themselves as capable of making a difference in their students' learning—a sense of efficacy—are more likely to turn out academically successful students. When teachers accept the responsibility for teaching students, they view students' difficulties in learning as challenges to their ingenuity rather than as excuses for their ineffectiveness. Instead of blaming the students for academic problems, effective teachers find ways of restructuring learning activities to meet the children's needs.

Latino Parent Involvement

Part of accepting this responsibility to teach all students requires teachers to create meaningful partnerships with their students' families. If a truly culturally responsive pedagogy is to be achieved, teachers need to tap parents' vast fund of knowledge (Moll et al., 1992) and utilize parents as partners in providing the instructional strategies and learning environments that we have highlighted above. Therefore, it is crucial for effective teachers to prioritize Latino parental involvement in their teaching agendas. However, such efforts to increase Latino parental involvement should also be culturally responsive and respectful of the parents and their children (Villegas & Lucas, 2002). In fact, just as teachers of Latino students need to steer away from traditional practices that do not adequately address their students' learning needs and capabilities, teachers also need to steer way from traditional *definitions* of parental involvement, which may not be suitable for Latino parents. In fact, we propose that effective teachers redefine parental involvement for their Latino parents to establish a successful partnership with their students' families.

The discussion on the common practices of highly effective teachers who work with Latino student populations would be incomplete without discussing parental involvement. In fact, we consider that one of the main pieces of evidence of any effective teaching is positive and meaningful parental participation. Successful teachers believe that parent involvement is key to their children's educational success. Such teachers further believe that all parents want their children to succeed in school (Villegas & Lucas, 2002; Nieto & Rolón, 1997; Ladson-Billings, 1994). They also recognize that many of their students' parents have had minimal schooling. As a result, teachers understand that parents are limited in their ability to support their children's academic work and/or to navigate the educational system in the same way as middle-class families.

This does not stop teachers from conveying to parents the importance of their involvement in their child's education as they work to provide ways, either individually or through the support of school-wide parent programs, to support parent involvement (Villegas & Lucas, 2002; Nieto & Rolón, 1997; Ladson-Billings, 1994). However, we would also point out that effective teachers need to find non-traditional ways to involve Latino parents that respect their family configurations, beliefs, and working conditions. Effective teachers are able to have their student's parents become involved in their children's educational experiences inside and outside the classroom (Villegas & Lucas, 2007). That is why we would like to address the state of Latino parental involvement and the need to redefine what constitutes parental involvement to empower Latino parents and to enhance the educational opportunities of Latino students. In the traditional view of American schooling, parental involvement among Latino parents is not viewed as significant as compared to Anglo populations (Aparicio-Clark & Dickerson, 2006). When evaluated by using a battery of behaviors that traditionally have comprised parental involvement in the United States (e.g., going to PTA meetings, calling the teacher, providing a quiet study area at home), Latino parents do not seem to be involved (Olsen, 1997 Suarez-Orozco, 1995; Valenzuela, 1999; Portes & Rumbaut, 2001). However, cultural and language differences, as well as structural barriers in schools that are rooted in race and class have a significant impact on the ability of Latino parents to *be involved* in their children's schools, at least in the way that schools expect them to be involved (Valenzuela, 1999).

The current literature on the issue of Latino education points out that lack of parental involvement is one of the main contributors of the diminishing academic achievement of Latino populations (Tinkler, 2002). Such link is often made because of the vast amount of research that supports the notion that among mainstream populations there is a positive correlation between parental involvement and academic achievement (Tinkler, 2002). However, such simplistic view of Latino parental involvement may be misleading. First, research shows that Latino parents do value education (Delgado-Gaitan, 2001), but parents and schools have different views on their respective roles on the education of Latino students. There is a difference in the mentality of parents of Latino students in regards to whether they need to be involved in the school or in their children's education.

Gerardo Lopez suggests that in the case of Latino education, parental involvement is at home, not at school (2003). For many Latino parents, the way to support their children's teachers is by not interfering with school personnel's decisions and this may be misinterpreted as lack of parental involvement (Pollock, Coffman, & Lopez, 2002). Latino parents assume that teachers and other school personnel are better equipped, educated, and prepared to deal with their students' academic preparation than the parents (Brittain, 2001). In other words, lack of involvement as defined by the school does not necessarily mean lack of parental interest in their children's education (Tinkler, 2002). Further, in the case of immigrant parents, the chasm between parents and schools, often rooted in language and cultural differences, makes it very difficult for immigrant parents to meet the expectations of parental involvement of U.S. schools (Olsen, 1988).

The Barriers

Traditionally, language and cultural differences have been considered major barriers to Latino parental involvement (Tinkler, 2002). Parents who are not fluent in English or who do not understand the cultural norms of schools experience difficulty in their ability to participate in schools (Aparicio-Clark & Dickerson, 2006). We agree that English fluency and cultural competence among Latino parents are desirable skills to achieve. But we question whether such skills should be viewed as prerequisites for effective parental involvement. Valenzuela (1999) argues that such position only leads to resistance and lack of participation among parents and students to cooperate with schools. As the parents perceive that the school does not value them as effective parents, they feel as outsiders in the school environment. It has been documented that one of the major barriers to Latino parents to participate is the unfortunate unwillingness of teachers and school staff to adapt to the different cultural and language needs of Latino populations (Olsen, 1988). Many staff members view that it is the Latino parents, not the schools, who should acculturate into the school's culture. Such attitudes are limiting because they ignore the great role that the family culture plays in the education of Latino children. Rather than recognizing the funds of knowledge (Moll et al, 1992) that family life provides to these students, schools tend to support a blind assimilation perspective, or as Valenzuela labels it, *subtracting schooling* (1999). Lack of appreciation for the home culture along with the language barrier often promotes tensions between Latino parents and school personnel (Tinkler, 2002). An unwelcoming and intimidating school environment sends many parents away from schools and prevents collaboration with teachers (Tinkler, 2002). Further, just like school staff promotes subtracting *schooling* (Valenzuela, 1999) among students, we would argue that the same phenomenon happens in relation to the parents. When Latino parents feel that their culture is not validated by school staff, they feel that school is not a place for them and prefer not to interfere with teachers and other school officials' decisions regarding to their children (Sobel & Kugler, 2007). Some parents feel they cannot become a "partner" in their children's education at the same level with the teachers because they lack formal education, English proficiency, or technology skills (Brittain, 1998). Their rationale is that the school staff is more prepared to handle decisions and actions regarding their students. This is often viewed by school staff as lack of interest in their children education (Ascribe, 2003; Villegas & Lucas, 2007).

Another important barrier to Latino parental involvement is the definition of parental involvement. What U.S. schools construct as parental involvement (e.g., help with homework, reading at home, parental visits to school, quiet study area at home) are behaviors that need specific home and community structures that many Latino parents just cannot afford in terms of time or money.

As long as surveys and research continue to ask Latino parents to ascribe to these behaviors without assisting them in providing the infrastructure for such behaviors to take place, the research will continue to perpetuate the notion that Latino parents are not involved.

Some research indicates that the problem of lack of Latino parental involvement is not a matter of lack of interest, but lack of social capital on the *know-how* of parent participation in schools (Olsen, 1997; Delgado-Gaitan, 2001; Wadsworth & Remaley, 2007). While we agree with this notion, we would also like to argue that the problem also resides on the schools' limited ability to tap on the potential resources that their family and cultural lives are providing for Latino students on a daily basis. Specifically, we would like to recognize the great impact that some family values have on students' commitment to their own learning and doing well in school. Further, we would like to argue that the transnational lifestyle of many Latino students provides unique life experiences that teachers could draw from to make connections among students in their classrooms.

The relationship between family values for education and higher academic achievement has been clearly established in educational research (Gandará, 1995; Suarez-Orozco & Suarez-Orozco, 1995). Gandará (1995) established that among Latino students, family stories serve as great sources of cultural capital. As Latino students learn of the hard work and sacrifices their parents and even older relations have endured to ensure that younger generations in their families have a chance for success, these family stories provide some kind of motivation for the students to aspire to and achieve social mobility (Gandará, 1995). In Brittain's research with Mexican immigrant students (2001), students often spoke of learning responsibility from their parents by acknowledging how hard their parents worked and how their parents related to their bosses with respect and sense of duty. The students also spoke of how their parents viewed school as their children's job and their teachers as their bosses. The parents expected their children to behave responsibly at their *jobs*. While in many instances, these parents could not help their children with their homework, parents' behaviors within the household and in the workplace still provided positive role models that elicited positive attitudes toward school in the children.

Brittain (2001) also found that a significant way in which children feel motivated to do well in school was by recognizing how hard their parents have worked to make educational opportunities available for them, especially in the United States. Mexican children feel indebted to their parents for all the sacrifices they have made to make it possible for them to be in an American school—from the migration journey to the long hours their parents work. Also, for these Mexican children, the thought that they had access to an American education and many of their relatives left behind in Mexico did not, became a big motivator for them to try their best at school. Many Mexican children referred to their need to take advantage of the opportunity for an American education that they had and many of their cousins or siblings in Mexico did not.

Earlier we addressed the importance of family values in understanding Latino parental involvement. One aspect of the configuration of many Latino families is that their family unit is comprised of individuals who live in the United States but also in their countries of origin. Therefore, many of the Latino students in U.S. schools today are involved in a transnational family configuration (Brittain, 2001). That is, many Latino children are not only influenced by their families located in the United States, but also by those in their countries of origin. Sometimes those left behind are their own parents. Because of this, we deem important that a transnational perspective is used to understand Latino parental involvement and make a point of the richness in life experiences that transnational interactions can bring to Latino students.

The Transnational Perspective: A Hidden Source of Family Involvement and Partnership

While not all Latino populations are immigrant, the immigrant experience has been an important element in studying Latino education. Even second generation Latino populations often experience some kind of links to an immigrant community through their parents or their peers (Rumbaut & Portes, 2001). Research with Latino populations show that many Latinos live transnational lives (Menjivar, 2000; Brittain, 2001; Sanchez, 2004).

In our attempt to address how Latino parent involvement can be improved, we think it is necessary to frame it within a transnational perspective. We argue that in addition to the documented cultural and language differences between Latino parents and a school, a transnational perspective allows us to identify assets and barriers to Latino parental involvement. Some Latino children and their parents live transnational lives that physically cross borders between the United States and their countries of origin by living part of the time in their countries of origin (Sanchez, 2004). Some of this crossing takes place as the families visit their home countries, but also as part of family separation prior to the children migrating to the United States (Suarez-Orozco & Suarez-Orozco, 1995, 2001). However, for a person to become involved in a transnational interaction he or she does not necessarily need to experience an actual physical crossing of borders. Some families experience a more symbolic form of transnationalism where Latino parents and their children frame their experiences in the United States in relation to their countries of origin (Brittain, 2001). By communicating with family members in their country of origin via diverse media (e.g., computer, mail, video), a transnational social space is created as long as the actions of the people in one country affect the lives of other family members in another country (Brittain, 2001).

Transnational interactions within social spaces can also take more formal, institutionalized forms beyond a family unit. Some immigrant populations seem to be more organized and prepared to be involved in the community development of their towns in their countries of origin, rather than in the receiving community in the United States (Zhou et al, 2000). Through grass roots organizations such as Transnational Migrant Organizations; Menjivar 2000; Smith, 2001), many Latino communities have organized themselves and provide support to the educational systems of their countries of origin mainly by supporting the construction of local schools in their hometowns. Unfortunately, Zhou and her colleagues argue that immigrant groups that invest heavily in building their communities in the country of origin deplete their resources and have little left to provide for the building of the immigrant community in the United States (2000). Many of these transnational individuals possess greater understanding and social capital to socially and even politically participate in their countries of origin rather than in their receiving community in the United States. Therefore, they tend to allocate resources in those countries of origin, rather than in their communities in the United States, where they often feel alienated and disfranchised.

Another formal aspect of transnational parental involvement takes place in the form of government participation in U.S. education from their countries of origin. For example, the Mexican government, through their Mexican Communities Abroad program, has allocated resources to promote bilingual education, i.e., the use of Mexican textbooks in U.S. schools and transnational training for U.S. Teachers in Mexico (Figueroa-Aramoni, 1999). Unfortunately, such efforts are often not visible for parents and teachers in U.S. schools, therefore the scope of their effectiveness in promoting higher academic achievement among Latinos is not evidenced yet. Further, some argue that these government efforts often perpetuate inequalities among immigrant families because the benefits of such government initiatives seem to be allocated for the elites (Guarnizo, 1997).

Perhaps, the most important benefit of having transnational connections for Latino students is two-fold. First, the expansion beyond borders of the impact of family stories in their social mobility ought to be considered (Gandará, 1995). Children who have transnational connections not only see and hear of the sacrifices of their relatives in the United States, but also those in their countries of origin. The stories of the members of these transnational families who were left behind in their countries of origin serve as constant reminders for many students of their family responsibility to do well in school to make their families (here and there) proud. Second, the expansion of the family unit in a transnational configuration provides students with a unique opportunity to learn how to participate in two social spaces and two cultures (Sanchez, 2004). By participating in transnational social spaces, these children have the potential for learning two languages, learning new media and technological tools to keep in contact with their families, learning new cultural forms as they visit their countries of origin. All these life experiences and skills can very easily transfer into the classroom in the form of research, study, and communication skills.

Proposed Solutions—Beyond Limited Outcomes

The quest for the improvement of Latino parental involvement continues. Because of the strong belief among the education community in the link that increased parental involvement yields better academic performance, a number of programs have been implemented to increase Latino parental involvement (Pollock et al., 2002; Tinkler, 2002; Riggs & Medina; 2005; Ginsberg, 2007; Sobler & Kugler, 2007). Unfortunately, there is still an overwhelming emphasis in many of these efforts in imposing a subtracting attitude of *educating* the parents. For example, Generación Diez (Generation Ten), an after-school program in Pennsylvania that aims to increase parental involvement among Latino populations, based their efforts in mostly assimilation goals such as intensive English as a Second Language (ESL) and social skills classes (Riggs & Medina, 2005). The underlying attitudes in these programs are to try to *compensate* for what is assumed to be lacking in Latino parents. Implying that Latino parents need to learn English and acquire specific social skills before they can be involved in their children's education is not only disrespectful to the parents but also limiting in establishing any meaningful partnership in a configuration that does not value the Latino parents' current strengths and knowledge. It is imperative that schools place more importance on the funds of knowledge (Moll et al., 1992) that Latino families are already providing their children on a daily basis. Programs that emphasize culturally responsive home visits are a great resource to close the gaps between school and home cultures (Ginsberg, 2007).

Villegas and Lucas (2007) suggest that any outreach efforts that schools implement to improve parental involvement among Latino students must be culture-specific where personal relationships become a key. That is why it is important that school officials promote cultural affirmation in order not to alienate the parents. We suggest that communication between parents and school that is based on mutual respect and tolerance is key to establish meaningful partnerships. In fact, some successful parental involvement programs have been specifically designed on effective communication theories and practices (Pollack et al., 2002).

Pollack and colleagues (2002) concur that by using communication theory, schools can bridge the gaps between Latino parents and U.S. schools. By understanding how the elements that promote communication between parties (intention, environmental constraints, skills, attitudes, social norms, self-standards, emotion, and self-efficacy) are present in Latino parents, schools can establish a program that could promote better communication and therefore participation with Latino parents.

Pollack (2002) and her colleagues provide the following outline to promote better communication between Latino parents and schools:

1. Value the Latino parents' belief that education goes beyond academic preparation to include raising children with positive values and moral responsibility.
2. Recognize that Latino parents have environmental constraints and may lack the language and/or academic skills to implement the traditional expectations of parental involvement in their homes. We also add that schools should not emphasize that such constraints do not preclude Latino parents' from becoming active partners in their children's education.
3. Take steps to make school less intimidating for Latino parents. While Latino parents' attitudes may strongly support their children's education, negative experiences with school personnel may intimidate Latino parents and lead to negative attitudes toward becoming involved in school, but not in their children's education.
4. Latino parents tend to participate more in their children's schools if other people they trust (e.g., friends, colleagues) also participate. Incorporate welcoming programs where newcomer families sponsored by an established Latino family or school group can increase the participation rate of Latino parents (Varlas, 2002). This also includes utilizing existing personal relationships with key people in the community (Villegas & Lucas, 2007). School administrators can also identify community members who are respected by Latino parents and involve them in school affairs to create a sense of interest and trust in, and respect toward, the school among Latino parents.
5. While Latino parents may recognize their lack of English skills and academic training as an impediment to school involvement, they are also very proud of their capacity to provide moral values (education) to their children. Therefore, school administrators should develop projects that use Latino parents' knowledge and strengths. Classroom activities and home visits that emphasize the value of family and Latino culture can help Latino parents to feel more capable of providing educational guidance to their children (Ginsberg, 2007). We would also add that recognizing the transnational connections that many Latino families have is an important factor in promoting Latino parent involvement. These transnational connections provide at least two values in that they provide:
   - valuable learning experiences for students (e.g., family trips to countries of origin, the use of technology and communication skills to keep in touch with family members in multiple locales)
   - motivating factors for doing well in school (e.g., family stories that promote social mobility by eliciting loyalty to those family members left behind in their countries of origin). In this sense, school administrators could recognize that strong Latino parental involvement is already taking place.

By recognizing that Latino families—parents and children—participate in transnational social spaces, and the funds of knowledge available to them via this connection, can represent important assets that in turn can promote educational attainment. Teachers could tap into those funds of knowledge by implementing classroom activities that promote oral family histories, multiculturalism, cross-cultural experiences, and family life.

Conclusion

This vision of a culturally responsive teacher is derived from a large body of empirical and conceptual literature, researchers' observations in culturally and linguistically diverse classrooms, and their work with teachers and pre-service teachers. The literature clearly points out that culture and socio-political-cultural attitudes and perceptions are at the core of effective teaching. Effective teachers of Latino students embrace a cultural responsive pedagogy that is rooted in humanizing pedagogy (Bartolomé, 1994; Freire, 1987; Huerta, 2002). That is, effective teachers strive to look at their students as individuals, despite the ever-growing restraints and responsibilities imposed on the teaching profession such as standardized testing, overcrowded classrooms, and cultural and language gaps between home and school. This chapter outlines specific characteristics, attributes, beliefs, and instructional strategies that effective teachers of Latino students hold and utilize. Above all, recognizing students as individuals who have the right to learn and the ability to achieve is also common for effective teachers of Latino students. Effective teachers of Latino students also recognize that their students are as capable of learning as any other ethnic or racial group; it is up to teachers to capitalize on the vast sources of life experiences of their students and their families inside and outside the classroom. This recognition provides effective teachers with numerous instructional strategies that are culturally responsive and enriching for Latino students and their families.

References

Aparicio-Clark, A., & Dickerson, A. (2006). Promoting Latino parent involvement: Research-based techniques for middle school principals. *Middle Matters, 14*(3), 111–113.

Ascribe: The Public Interest Newswire. (2003). Parental involvement in migrant education is at home, not at school. Retrieved from http://www.ascribe.org/cgi-bin/spew4th.pl?ascribeid=20030203.074545&time=08%2031%20PST&year=2003

Au, K. H., & Kawakami, A. J. (1994). Cultural congruence in instruction. In E. R. Hollins, J. E. King, & W. C. Hayman (Eds.), *Teaching diverse populations* (pp. 5–24). Albany: State University of New York Press.

Bartolomé, I. L. (1994). Beyond the methods fetish: Toward a humanizing pedagogy. *Harvard Educational Review, 64,* 173–194.

Brittain, C. (1998). *Talking about school and learning: An analysis of learning goals training for Mexican immigrant children.* Unpublished Manuscript.

Brittain, C. (2001). *Transnational messages: Experiences of Mexican and Chinese immigrant children in American schools.* New York: LFB Scholarly.

California Department of Education, Educational Demographics Office. (2007a) *Students by Ethnicity, State of California, 2006–07.* Retrieved from http://www.ed-data.k12.ca.us

California Department of Education, Educational Demographics Office. (2007b). *Teachers by Ethnicity, State of California, 2006–07.* Retrieved from http://www.ed-data.k12.ca.us

Cohen, D., & Himamauli, D. (1996, July). The need for teachers in California. *Policy Analysis for California Education,* 1–49.

Cummins, J. (1986). Empowering minority students: A framework for intervention. *Harvard Education Review, 56,* 8–36.

Dalton, S. S. (1998). *Pedagogy matters: Standards for effective teaching practice* (Research Report 4). Santa Cruz, CA and Washington, DC: Center for Research on Education, Diversity & Excellence.

Darder, A. (1991). *Culture and power in the classroom.* Westport CT: Bergin & Harvey.

Darling-Hammond, L. (1999). *Professional development for teachers: Setting the stage for learning from teaching,* 3–20. Santa Cruz, CA: The Center for the Future of Teaching & Learning.

Delgado-Gaitan, C. (2001). *The power of community: Mobilizing for family and schooling.* Lanham, MD: Rowman and Littlefield

Freire, P. (1987). Letters to North-American teachers. In I Shor (Ed.), *Freire for the classroom* (pp. 211–214). Portsmouth, NH: Boynton & Cook.

Figueroa-Aramoni, R. (1999). A nation beyond its borders: The program for Mexican communities abroad [Electronic version]. *Journal of American History*. Retrieved from http://www.indiana.edu/~jah/mexico/rfigueroa.html

Gandará, P. (1995). *Over the ivy walls: The educational mobility of low-income Chicanos*. Albany: State University of New York Press.

Gandará, P., Rumberger, R., Maxwell-Jolly, J., & Callahan, R. (2003). English learners in California schools: Unequal resources, unequal Center for Research on Education, Diversity& Excellence outcomes [Electronic version]. *Education Policy Analysis Archives, 11*(36) Retrieved from http://olam.ed.asu.edu/epaa

García, E. (1988, August). Attributes of effective schools for language minority students. *Education and Urban Society, 20*(4), 387–398.

García, E. (1994). *Understanding and meeting the challenge of student cultural diversity*. Boston: Houghton Mifflin.

Gay, G. (2000). *Culturally responsive teaching: Theory, research, & practice*. New York: Teachers College Press.

Ginsberg, M. B. (2007, March). Lessons at the kitchen table. *Educational Leadership, 64*(6), 56–61.

Guarnizo, L. E. (1997). *The Mexican ethnic economy in Los Angeles: Capitalist accumulation, class restructuring, and the transnationalization of migration*. La Jolla: Center for U.S. Mexico Studies, University of California, San Diego.

Huerta, T. M. (2002). *Teachers matter: Humanizing pedagogy for Latino students*. Unpublished doctoral dissertation, Harvard University Graduate School of Education, Cambridge, MA.

Haberman, M. (1996). Selecting and preparing culturally competent teachers for urban schools. In J. Sikula J. (Ed.), *Handbook of Research on Teacher Education* (pp. 747–760). New York: Simon & Schuster Macmillan.

Ladson-Billings, G. (1994). *The dream keepers: Successful teachers of African-American children*. San Francisco: Jossey-Bass.

Lucas, T., Henze, R., & Donato, R. (1990). Promoting the success of Latino language minority students: An exploratory study of six high schools. *Harvard Educational Review, 60*, 315–334.

Mehan, H. (1979). *Learning lessons: Social organizations in the classroom*. Cambridge, MA: Harvard University Press.

Menjivar, C. (2000). *Fragmented Ties: Salvadoran Immigrant Networks in America*. Berkeley: University of California Press.

Moll, L. C. (1988). Some key issues in teaching Latino students. *Language Arts, 65*(5) 465–472.

Moll, L. C., Amanita, C., Neff, D., & González, N. (1992). Funds of knowledge for teaching: Using a qualitative approach to connect homes and classrooms. *Theory into Practice, 31*(2), 132–141.

Monzó D. L., & Rueda, S. R. (2001). *Sociocultural factors in social relationships: Examining Latino teachers' and para-educators' interactions with Latino students (Research Report 9)*. Santa Cruz, CA and Washington, DC: Center for Research on Education, Diversity & Excellence.

Murrell, P. C. (2001). *The community teacher: A new framework for effective urban teaching*. New York: Teachers College Press.

National Coalition of Educational Equity Advocates (1994). *Education America: A call for equity in school reform*. Retrieved from http://www.eric.ed.gov/ERICWebPortal/recordDetail?accno

Nieto, S. (1996). *Affirming diversity: The sociopolitical context of multicultural education*. New York: Longman.

Nieto, S., & Rolón, C. (1997). Preparation and professional development of teachers: A perspective from two Latinas. In J. J. Irvine (Ed.), *Critical knowledge of diverse teachers and learners* (pp. 89–123). Washington, DC: American Association of Colleges for Teacher Education.

Olsen, L. (1988). *Crossing the schoolhouse border: Immigrant students and the California public schools*. San Francisco: California Tomorrow.

Olsen, L. (1997). *Made in America: Immigrant students in our public schools*. New York: The New Press.

Padrón, N. Y., Waxman, C. H., & Rivera, H. H. (2002). Educating Hispanic students: Obstacles and avenues to improved academic achievement (Research Report 8). Santa Cruz, CA and Washington, DC: Center for Research on Education, Diversity & Excellence.

Pease-Alvarez, L., García, E., & Espinoza, P. (1991). Effective instruction for language minority students: An early childhood case study. *Early Childhood Research Quarterly, 6*, 347–363.

Philips, S. U. (1983). *The invisible culture: Communication in classroom and community on the Warm Springs Indian Reservation*. Prospect Heights, IL: Waveland. Retrieved from http:www.cal.org/resources/Digest/0313park.html

Pollock, A., Coffman, J., & Lopez, M. E. (2002). Using behavior change theory to communicate effectively: The case of Latino parent involvement [Electronic version]. *The Evaluation Exchange, 8*(3). Retrieved from http://www.gse.harvard.edu/hfrp/eval/issue20/theory.html

Ramirez, J. D., Yuen, S. D., Ramey, D J., Pasta, D. J., & Billings, D. K. (1991). *Longitudinal Study of Structured English Immersion Strategy, Early-Exit and Late-Exit Transitional Bilingual Education Programs for Language Minority Children*. Washington, DC: Office of Policy and Planning.

Riggs, N., & Medina, C. (2005). The "Generación Diez" after-school program and Latino parent involvement with schools. *The Journal of Primary Prevention, 26*(6). Retrieved from http://www.springerlink.com/content/prh3l25l15k0155m/

Rumbaut, R., & Portes, A. (Eds.). (2001). *Ethnicities: Children of immigrants in America*. Berkeley: University of California Press.

Sanchez, P. (2004). *At home in two places: Second-generation Mexicanas and their lives as engaged transnationals*. Unpublished doctoral dissertation. University of California, Berkeley.

Sleeter, C. E. (2001, March/April). Preparing teachers for culturally diverse schools: Research and the overwhelming presence of whiteness. *Journal of Teacher Education, 52*(2), 94–106.

Smith, R. C. (2001). Mexicans: Social, educational, economic, and political problems and prospects in New York. In N. Forner (Ed.), *New immigrants in New York* (pp. 275–300). New York: Columbia University Press.

Sobel, A., & Kugler, E. G. (2007, March). Building partnerships with immigrant parents. *Educational Leadership, 64*(6), 62–66.

Suarez-Orozco, M., & Suarez-Orozco, C. (1995). *Transformations*. Stanford, CA: Stanford University Press.

Suarez-Orozco, M., & Suarez-Orozco, C. (2001). *Children of immigration*. Cambridge, MA: Harvard University Press.

Tharp, R. G., & Gallimore, R. (1988). *Rousing minds to life: Teaching, learning, and schooling in social context*. New York: Cambridge University Press.

Tikunoff, W. (1985). *Applying significant bilingual instructional features in the classroom*. Rosslyn, VA: National Clearinghouse for Bilingual Education.

Tinkler, B. (2002). *A review of literature on Hispanic/Latino parent involvement in K-12 education. Assets for Colorado youth*. Retrieved from http://www.buildassets.org/products/latinoparentreport/latino-parentrept.htm

U.S. Department of Education. (2003). *Contexts of elementary and secondary education, 1999–2000*. Washington, DC: National Center for Education Statistics. Retrieved from http://nces.ed.gov/programs/coe/2003/setion4/tables/t29_1.asp

U.S. Department of Education. (2007). *The condition of education 2007*. Washington, DC: National Center for Education Statistics.

Varlas, L. (2002). Slowing the revolving door: Schools reach out to mobile families. *Education Update, 44*(7), 1–3.

Valenzuela, A. (1999). *Subtractive schooling: U.S.-Mexican youth and the politics of caring*. Albany: State University of New York Press.

Villegas, A. M. (1991). *Culturally responsive pedagogy for the 1990s and beyond*. Paper prepared for the Educational Testing Service, Princeton, NJ.

Villegas, A. M., & Lucas, T. (2002). *Educating culturally responsive teachers: A coherent approach*. Albany: State University of New York Press.

Villegas, A. M., & Lucas, T. (2007). The culturally responsive teacher. *Educational Leadership, 64*(6), 28–33.

Wadsworth, D., & Remaley, M. H. (2007, March). What families want. *Educational Leadership, 64*(6), 23–27.

Zhou, M., Adefuin, J., Chung, A., & Roach, E. (2000). *How community matters for immigrant children: Structural constraints and resources in Chinatown, Koreatown, and Pico-Union, Los Angeles (Final Report)*. Berkeley: California Policy Research Center.

27 Language, Culture, Policy, and the Law
Issues for Latino Students

Tom Stritikus and Bonnie English
University of Washington

Celia [teacher] holds up two books, one in Spanish and one in English. She tells the students, who are all sitting on the rug, that they are going to take a vote to decide which one they are going to read. As she holds up the Spanish book, Jesus calls out in an angry tone, "This is boring."
Luis, imitating Jesus' angry tone says, "I hate this."
Celia: What do you hate?
Jesus: Spanish.
Celia: (with a look of incredulity) ¿Què habla tu mama? [What does your mom speak?]
Jesus: (defiantly) Spanish.
Celia: Then you have to like it. You have to be proud of tu idioma [your language]. (Stritikus, 2002, p. 97)

The question of how to best educate Latino students frequently centers on issues of language of instruction: Should students be taught in the language they know best? Should Spanish be maintained and developed? Or, should students be *immersed* in English-only instructional contexts? While there are pedagogical aspects to these questions, the answers have frequently been shaped by legal decisions and policy directives. Understanding the political and legal context is crucial for understanding the educational opportunities for Latino students.

"Latino" refers to a broad group of people with diverse linguistic, cultural, and ethnic traditions. In this chapter we are specifically interested in exploring the interaction between race and language in educational policy. Over 80% of students identified as English language learners are Latino (National Center for Educational Statistics [NCES], 2005). This population of Latino students has been significantly affected by language policies as well as desegregation policies. Consequently, we will use the term *Latinos* in reference to the large number of Latino students who are bilingual.

As the opening exchange between Celia and the two students indicates, pedagogical contexts are deeply influenced by social, political, and cultural realities. Celia and her students had experienced the debate first hand about how best to educate Latino students through the sweeping and unprecedented reform known to its supporters as the English for the Children Initiative, Proposition 227 (California State Secretary Office, 1998). Celia taught in a school that had moved away from bilingual education. Despite widespread support for English-only approaches by the largely monolingual teaching staff at the school, Celia frequently sought opportunities to utilize the students' native language and culture. Her students' responses to her attempts show how quickly students can appropriate negative conceptions of their own language and culture and the educational costs of such reforms.

To more completely understand the instructional context of Latino education, we begin this chapter by tracing the evolution of language and educational rights of Latino students. In recent years, there has been a serious and prolonged attempt to undermine these rights through state-level anti-bilingual education initiatives. We examine how weak federal policy has created space for successful local anti-bilingual movements. We consider the impact of the current policy mix (local and federal) on the overall language rights and educational possibilities for Latino students. To conclude, we closely examine the research literature on current educational practices for Latino students to more fully understand how federal and state policy and legal decisions shape the education of Latino students.

Tracing the Evolution of Language and Educational Rights for Latino Students

The adoption of No Child Left Behind (2001) brought with it significant changes in educational policy for Latino students. No Child Left Behind was the most recent reauthorization of the Elementary and Secondary Education Act (ESEA). Title VII (The Bilingual Education Act) was merged into Title III (Language Instruction for Limited English Proficient and Immigrant Students) placing increased emphasis on English language development as a means for reaching state standards (Wright, 2005). Bilingualism and all references to bilingual education were completely removed from the Elementary and Secondary Education Act. In this section, we follow the historical progression of federal policy and legal precedents which set the stage for such a restrictive policy. By tracing the evolution of federal policy and court decisions, we situate the current educational policies that affect Latinos in the appropriate socio-historical context.

Nationally and locally, policies try to find balances between language paradoxes accepted in mainstream American ideology: promoting equal opportunity while celebrating diversity; finding a common purpose while encouraging variety; recognizing dignity of ethnicity while ensuring national stability (Baker, 2006). Educational policy for Latinos has been constructed through a negotiation of such controversial paradoxes. Policies have been influenced by segregation versus integration debates, local control versus federal protection arguments, and conflicting viewpoints of language as a problem, resource, or right.

The first tension shaping Latino educational policy is segregation versus integration. Arguments for the integration of diverse student populations draw attention to disparate educational opportunities available to White students and linguistically, culturally diverse students. Segregation persists in the modern American educational system, with minority students continuing to receive sub-standard educational services (Anyon, 1980; Darling-Hammond, 2004; Oakes, Joseph, & Muir, 2004). However, history has also revealed that integration is not an end in and of itself. Latinos integrated in English-dominant schools are often denied equitable educational opportunities through tracking or through lack of accommodation by mainstream teachers (Katz, 1999; Reeves, 2004; Walker, Shafer, & Iiams, 2004). Some research has shown that Latino students thrive in Latino-dominant schools with specially designed programs that draw upon and reflect the Latino culture and community (Cummins, 2000; Reyes, Scribner, & Scribner, 1999; Reyes & Halcon, 2001; Slavin & Calderon, 2001). The educational success of some community based Latino schools contradicts the notion of desegregation as an automatic and unproblematized equalizer. Desegregation alone does not guarantee the academic success of Latinos students (Orfield, 2001).

The second tension influencing policy for Latino students includes three opposing viewpoints present in language policy debates: *language as a problem, language as a right,* and *language as a resource* (Ruiz, 1984). Political views that see *language as a problem* position bilingualism as a threat to the nation, predicting numerous negative consequences, such as: lowering the GNP, increasing civil strife, fostering political and social unrest, and endangering US political and economic stability (Baker, 2006). In contrast, those who embrace the ideological stance of *language as a right* align themselves with the rights granted to all in the First Amendment. Language is an individual choice and the government should not intervene to determine the language preferences and uses of its citizens. As Ruiz (1984) points out, the language rights framework is complicated when it advocates for protection against group discrimination using an individual rights platform. A third viewpoint treats *language as a resource,* values bilingualism as an individual persona, as well as a community and regional resource. National educational policies have been strongly influenced by the *language as a problem* viewpoint. Resistance and changes have come about through arguments of *language as a right* or *language as a resource.*

The final tension underlying the policy and legal precedents for Latinos is local control versus federal protection. The federal government and the courts have been weary of interfering with local educational policy. Yet, to counter segregation and unequal educational practices, the courts have deemed it necessary to intervene to ensure equal protection under the law. In the following historical analysis, we explore the early court cases in which the courts intervened, enforcing integration as a right worthy of federal protection. Next, we follow the post-civil rights era in which federal bilingual policy was introduced at the same time the courts started favoring local control. Finally, we explore current tensions in federal policy.

Early Court Cases: 1930s–1960s

Segregation and unequal educational opportunities for Latinos have persisted throughout American history despite federal mandates and court decisions attempting to curtail them. In the early 1900s, school systems responded to increased Latino immigration by segregating Latinos into separate schools or separate classrooms. Data from the early 1900s reveal that over 85% of Mexican-American children in California and over 90% in Texas attended racially segregated schools (Valencia, Menchaca, & Donato, 2002). The first petition to challenge this segregation was in Texas. The judge in *Independent School District v. Salvatierra* (1931) ruled that segregating Mexican American students on the basis of *race* was illegal because they were considered members of the White race. This decision was overturned by the Texas Court of Civil Appeals on the basis that the school district did not intentionally segregate the Mexican American children by race; and, given that the children had special language needs, the school district had the authority to segregate students on educational grounds. The court took up the position of segregation as a legitimate means for schools to meet the specific linguistic needs of Latino students. By limiting their analysis of segregation to race, the state court ignored unequal resources and educational opportunities for Latinos in segregated schools.

Soon after *Salvatierra,* a similar case was introduced in California. *Alvarez v. Lemon Grove* (1931) was the first successful legal challenge to school segregation in the United States. Segregation of Mexican-American children was challenged through the argument that separate facilities for Mexican Americans were not conducive to Americanization or English language development. This decision reflected an assimilationist framework, which positioned *language as a problem.* Americanization and English language development as educational goals justified federal intervention for integration. The victory of *Alvarez* was significant, but it did not set any national or state-wide precedent.

Through the 1940s there were two more significant court cases on issues of educational equity for Latinos: *Mendez v. Westminister* (1946) in California and *Delgado et al. v. Bastrop Independent School District of Bastrop County, et al.* (1948) in Texas. *Mendez* was the first federal court decision to challenge de jure segregation in California. The court concluded that Mexican-American children had been segregated based on appearance and that such segregation had no legal or educational justification. The *Delgado* ruling mirrored the *Mendez* ruling except in one major area—the court ruled that separate classes on the same campus, in the first grade only, for "language-deficient" or "non-English-speaking students," as identified by language proficiency testing, was acceptable. Neither of these rulings was accompanied by any reinforcement or monitoring. Throughout the 1940s, Latinos continued to attend mostly segregated schools with inadequate opportunities to learn (Valencia et al., 2002). Judges in these early court cases intruded upon local control, attempting to open access for Latino students to mainstream American schools. Yet, the courts did not offer any guidance or structure for local districts to create integrated schools that would serve the needs of Latinos. Racial segregation was problematized, but segregating students for linguistic reason was justified through the *language as problem* discourse.

Brown v. Board of Education (1954) brought national attention to desegregation litigation. Donato (1997) documents how *Brown* and the subsequent Civil Rights Movement often overlooked the inequity of Latinos in American society. Segregation was commonly referred to as a Black vs. White issue. In fact, it wasn't until 1970 *Cisneros v. Corpus Christi Independent School District* (1977) that the courts recognized Latinos as a separate class that should benefit from the *Brown*'s desegregation policies. Prior to *Cisneros,* some districts were desegregating schools by pairing African American and Mexican American students under the pretext that Mexican Americans were White. The judge in *Cisneros* ruled that Mexican Americans were an ethnically identifiable minority group. The petitioners had argued that it was necessary for Mexicans to be identified as such to benefit from *Brown* (Valencia et al., 2002). *Cisneros* was followed by the U.S. Supreme Court case of *Keyes v. School District No. 1576* (1983). Focusing specifically on the segregation of Latinos, *Keyes* established that a school system could be labeled as segregated if any part of the system showed evidence of segregation. The expanded definition of segregation made a space for Latinos who had previously been excluded from *Brown*'s desegregation agenda. In these cases, the courts had willingly intervened in local policy to redress issues of educational inequity.

Lacking adequate legal, financial, and political support, these court decisions did not translate into increased integration or improved educational opportunities for Latinos. "The only period in which there was active positive support by both the courts and the executive branch of the government was the four years following the enactment of the 1964 Civil Rights Act" (Orfield, 2001, p.13). Without the joint effort of the three branches of government to promote desegregation, state-wide and local efforts often deteriorated. In the early 1970s, the Mexican American Education Study (MAES)[1] confirmed that little progress had been made on ending the segregation of Mexican American students (Valencia et al., 2002). While significant in their willingness to increase federal intervention for the integration of Latino students, these early court cases reinforced the prevailing *language as problem* orientation to the education of Latino students.

Introducing Federal Policy: 1960–1970s

The federal government of the United States turned its attention to the educational opportunities of Latino students in the late 1960s. Rather than taking up the desegregation agenda from the Supreme Court, Congress ventured down a different path, emphasizing bilingual education. In 1968 Lyndon B. Johnson signed Title VII: the Bilingual Education Act (BEA) into the Elementary and Secondary Education Act (ESEA). This marked the U.S. government's first commitment to addressing the specific needs of language minority students. Moran (1988) notes some significant limitations of the BEA: "Although community representatives optimistically claimed that the bill created a federal mandate for bilingual programs, the Act actually established only a modest grant-in-aid program to support experimental demonstration projects" (p. 1263). The BEA provided districts and schools minimal guidelines, leaving the creation and implementation of innovative programs up to local schools and districts. The first draft of Title VII included elements of the *language as a resource* rhetoric in that it encouraged primary language support and instruction. But, as a compensatory policy it invoked a *language as problem* orientation to the education of Latino students. Title VII funds were specified for students who were "both impoverished and educationally disadvantaged because of their inability to speak English" (Hakuta & Mostafapour, 1996, p. 41). Although the Title VII was born from a compensatory framework, from 1968 until 2002, Title VII provided funds for different types of programs for ELLs throughout the nation, including Transitional Bilingual Education (TBE) programs, two-way immersion programs, as well as English-only programs. It also provided funding for program evaluators and researchers investigating these different types of programs. There were 30 two-way immersion programs in 1987 which grew to 261 in 1999; most were supported by Title VII monies (Lindholm-Leary, 2001). Title VII embodied an internal conflict, with commitments to both *language as a resource* and *language as a problem* ideologies.

As the federal government increased their responsiveness to the rights of Latinos in the BEA, the courts lessened their commitment to desegregation. The U.S. Supreme Court issued a number of significant rulings in the early 1970s that had lasting effects, setting precedent for educating English language learners. *Lau v. Nichols* (1974) stated that schools must provide instructional supports for students who speak a language other than English. Congress responded to *Lau*, incorporating it into the Equal Education Opportunity Act: Section 1703(f). According to Section 1703(f), all schools must have programs for linguistically diverse students, regardless of whether they received funding from Title VII. *Lau* was the first precedent-setting court decision that identified the rights of students who speak a language other than English to have access to the mainstream curriculum. Lau extended previous civil rights litigation to incorporate discriminatory effect regardless of intent and thus greatly increased the range of civil rights protection (Moran, 2004). *Lau* toed the line between the *language as right* and *language as problem* frameworks, offering little guidance for how linguistically diverse students should be accommodated. It merely stated that it is a violation of students' linguistic rights to immerse them in English with no accommodations. Schools and districts had to negotiate this meaning of "accommodations" locally.

While celebrating the victories of *Lau*, advocates for Latino education were dealt a series of devastating blows throughout the 1970s. The potential gains of language rights envisioned in Lau came at the same time that students' rights to desegregated and equitable schools came under attack. A series of court cases in the 1970s weakened the effects of *Brown v. Board of Education*. *San Antonio Independent School District v. Rodriguez* (1973) set precedent for the funding and zoning of schools, allowing property taxes to serve as the primary source of revenue. The Supreme Court decided against equalizing finances among school districts (Petronicolos & New, 1999). In *Milliken v. Bradley* (1974) the Supreme Court rejected desegregation across city-suburban boundary lines, the result of which was segregation of schools that mirrored residential segregation. It set the background for future subtractive policies. In *Board of Education of Cincinnati v. Walter* (1979) the court deemed wealth based disparities in education as acceptable; stating that the state has no compelling interest in the equalizing educational opportunities across districts (Petronicolos & New, 1999). *Milliken v. Bradley II* (1977) encouraged magnet or choice schools as a means of desegregation. In *Dayton Board of Education v. Brinkman* (1977) federal judges stated that local control of schools was a national tradition that needed to be upheld and created the infrastructure to remove school desegregation. (Valencia et al., 2002). These decisions had lasting effects in the organization of school districts which allowed for the continued segregation of Latinos. The courts had shifted significantly towards a local control framework, decreasing federal intervention to protect the rights of underserved populations. Latino immigrants often encountered residential segregation, which in turn led to school segregation (Valencia et al., 2002). While Orfield (2001) acknowledges that there was never any significant enforcement of desegregation rights for Latinos, these court cases took a great deal of pressure off of schools to implement changes for equal educational opportunities. While we recognize that desegregation is not an end in and of itself, it is a beginning step to opening pathways and conversations to foster educational equity for Latino students. The movement away from integration set the course for future restrictive and subtractive policies against non-majority groups. "Since 1980 all states with significant Latino populations have seen increased segregation" (Orfield, 2001, p. 45).

Unsupported Guidelines: Policy and Court Decisions in the 1980s

In response to the ambiguities in *Lau* of what accommodations should be provided for linguistic minorities, in 1980 the U.S. Department of Education created guidelines in the *Notice of Proposed Rulemaking* (NPRM). The guidelines applied to all districts receiving federal monies, obligating them to: identify ELLs, assess their level of English proficiency, provide proper instructional services (usually with some native-language instruction) and determine criteria for exiting students from program. The NPMR was repealed within months in response to a strong backlash from districts across the nation. The justification for its repeal was the fact that the federal government should not intervene in prescribing practices for local school districts (Haas, 2005).

In 1981 the federal courts created vague guidelines for programs serving ELLs. In *Castañeda v. Pickard* (1981), the fifth Circuit established a science based test that required programs serving linguistic minorities to meet three standards. According to García (2005):

> After *Castañeda* it became legally possible to substantiate a violation of Section 1703(f), following from *Lau*, on three grounds: (1) The program providing special language services to eligible language-minority students is not based on sound educational theory; (2) the program is not being implemented in an effective way; (3) the program, after a period of 'reasonable implementation,' does not produce results that substantiate language barriers are being overcome so as to eliminate achievement gaps between bilingual and English-speaking student. (p. 80)

Castañeda's guidelines offered more structure than *Lau*, but they were still vague and ambiguous. Unfortunately, courts have interpreted *Castañeda* in ways that do not always serve the best interests of Latino students. One particular example of *Castañeda*'s ambiguities came in a plaintiff's challenge to Prop 227, the attempt to end bilingual education.

Courts placed a burden upon plaintiff ELLs to show that an English language assistance program was 'inappropriate' by demonstrating that a school district's language program was completely unsupported under all circumstances. Using the *Castañeda* test, the courts in *Teresa P. v. Berkeley Unified School District* and, most recently in *Valeria G. v. Wilson* held that one-year English immersion programs complied with Section 1703(f) though the educational theory upon which they are based was similar to that rejected by the court in *Lau* and which has been routinely criticized as unsound (Haas, 2005, p. 362).

Neither the federal government nor the Supreme Court wanted to assume the role of expert in educational theory or methods for linguistically diverse students. Concentration of decision-making power at the local-level made changes in districts that sought equitable treatment education for Latinos more difficult. The courts often relied on the opinions of district experts in determining the soundness of the educational theory upon which programs are based. The courts have tried to remain non-political by standing on the bylines of the debates among educational researchers about best programs and policies for ELLs. Haas (2005) suggests that by taking this course of action, the courts are violating pre-established guidelines for determining sound educational theory. Rather than accepting the "expert opinion" of district employees, Haas (2005) suggests that judges should use more rigorous scholarship, such as meta-analyses (e.g., Slavin & Cheung, 2005) to understand the current state of knowledge in the field of second language learning.

A more recent threat to the legacy of Lau has been laid out by the legal scholar Rachel Moran (2004) who has suggested that recent laws have limited the scope of Lau in multiple ways. In particular, she highlights that the Court has recently questioned the idea that racial discrimination includes impact as well as intentional wrongdoing. The Court has also concluded that "individuals can not bring a private right of action under Title VI to challenge policies that have adverse racial effects" (Moran, 2004, p. 3). The undoing of Lau limits the legal options for bilingual Latino students who are seeking redress from the courts.

Title VII (Bilingual Education Act) of the Elementary and Secondary Education Act was reauthorized twice in the 1980s (1984 & 1988). These reauthorizations reflected the shift in how immigrants were perceived by the U.S. government. The 1984 reauthorization required that students learn English to become productive members of society, which equivocates English proficiency with citizenship. But, the BEA also recognized that students brought with them linguistic resources. It emphasized the need for additional research and parent participation. The BEA finally ended some of the ambiguities about program models, only funding models that were: transitional bilingual programs, developmental bilingual programs, or programs which used English-only approaches (Wright, 2005). In 1988 the BEA was more strongly influenced by the *language as problem* ideology. There was a three year limit on students' participation in either transitional bilingual programs or special alternative instructional programs, which contradicts the findings of scientific research (Slavin & Cheung, 2005; Thomas & Collier, 2002).

In conclusion, in the 1980s there were a number of attempts to establish guidelines for instructional programming for English language learners. Yet, the federal government and the courts weakly enforced these guidelines. Local control of educational policy justified the lack of intervention on behalf of Latino students receiving inequitable educational opportunities. In a review of national statistics, Orfield (2001) found that from 1968 to 1984 the percentage of Latinos enrolled in predominantly White schools dropped by 36%. During those same years, the number of Latino students enrolled in 90 to 100% minority schools increased by 35%. Federal policy and legal cases side-stepped a number of issues regarding equitable education by exclusively focusing on language. Entering the 1990s, the education of Latino students was in a nebulous place. Nativism was on the rise, the courts were no longer behind school integration, and the federal policies for linguistic minorities leaned more heavily toward a *language as a problem* rhetoric.

Current Tensions: 1990s to Present

In 1994, the reauthorization Title VII in the Elementary and Secondary Education Act (ESEA) again refrained from taking any stance on offering guidance on programs and policies for linguistically diverse students. The BEA "recognized the complexity of educational responses to language-minority students and the necessity for locally designed and integrated programs" (García, 2002, p. 35). The lack of strong policy for Latinos and other culturally and linguistically diverse groups combined with the national trend towards re-segregation to perpetuate inequitable schooling

The current tensions in Latino education have been shaped through a historical process involving numerous court decisions and shifts in federal policy. While the courts at one time intervened in favor of integration, there is currently an emphasis on localized control. In 2001, the Elementary and Secondary Education act (ESEA) was reauthorized again. The Bilingual Education Act (Title VII), which included some *language as resource / language as right* viewpoints, had been dismantled. In its place, Title III emphasized standards and assessment using a *language as problem* framework (Wright, 2005). The educational equity for Latinos was minimally safeguarded by federal policy, which created a space for more restrictive and oppressive local policies.

Toward Extreme Language Restrictionism

The most blatant example of the language as problem orientation to federal and state policy making has been the proliferation of anti-bilingual education initiatives. Proposition 227 was the first such initiative. Passed in 1998, the initiative was an example of "people making law," written in response to apparent widespread discontent with the state's policies regarding the education of English-language learners in public schools. The passage of Proposition 227 marked a significant event in California's educational history. Never before had the voting public been asked to vote on a specific educational strategy. Curriculum and programmatic decisions for students have generally been the responsibility of the education community. Proposition 227 marked a reversal of this trend. Gándara et al. (2000) argue that because of this, the law was opposed by every major educational association in the state. Because each of the subsequent attempts to eliminate bilingual education have been modeled or predicated upon Proposition 227, we examine the development and implementation of the law in detail.

The intent of the Proposition was to end bilingual education. Specifically, the law required that "All children in California public schools shall be taught English by being taught in English" (California Education Code, Chapter 3, Article I. Section 305). The law represents the latest policy move in a long and often contentious debate surrounding bilingual education. California, one of the first states to enact a comprehensive bilingual education bill, has been at the center of that debate. Given that the over 80% of all English Learner students in California speak Spanish as a first language, the policy and practice implications of the bilingual debate are central to the education of Latino immigrants in California.

In the summer of 1997, when Ron Unz, a former Republican gubernatorial candidate and millionaire software developer, launched "English for the Children" the bilingual education debate occupied the center of public and political discourse. In the campaign against bilingual education, Unz leveraged a considerable amount of his personal fortune to attempt to persuade California voters to support his initiative. Much of his media efforts were directed at discrediting and demeaning the scholarly work regarding the effectiveness of bilingual education. Unz attempted to cast the restriction of native language instruction in terms of a benevolent pro-immigrant stance. Arguing that he represented the true will of immigrants across California, Unz maintained that he was merely assisting Latinos and other recent immigrants to free themselves from bilingual education (Gándara et al., 2000).

Although Unz attempted to maintain a "pro-immigrant" stance during the campaign, the campaign proved to be quite racially divisive. Inevitably, much of the public discourse supporting the passage of Proposition 227 took nativist and xenophobic positions (Kerper-Mora, 2000; Orellana, Ek, & Hernandez, 2000). California became the center of a national debate between "nativist" and "multiculturalist" visions of education. The nativist position represented by Proposition 227 assumed a benevolent view of Americanization and the role that rapid learning of English plays in the process (Kerper-Mora, 2000).

Because of Proposition 227, children entering California Public Schools with very little English must be "observed" for a period of 30 calendar days. Generally, this observation period occurs in an English-language classroom (Gándara et al., 2000). After 30 days, school personnel must decide if children have enough fluency in English to manage in a mainstream English classroom. If not, they are eligible to receive one year of "Sheltered English Immersion," also referred to as "Structured English Immersion." A program of English language instruction not described in detail in the law except for the requirement that instruction be "nearly all" in English (with the definition for the term *nearly all* is left up to the district's discretion).

After one year, children are normally expected to integrate into mainstream English classrooms, where instruction is required to be "overwhelmingly" in English. If parents or legal guardians find that district or school personnel, including classroom teachers, "willfully and repeatedly refuse" to provide English instruction as required, they have the right to sue for damages. Given the ambiguity of many of the law's provisions, the threat of legal sanction created a great sense of insecurity with many district and school personnel across the state (Stritikus & García, 2003).

The only legal alternative to Sheltered English Immersion and/or mainstream English classrooms is the parental waiver process. According to the new law, children who have special language needs, or whose parents specifically request it, can be placed in "Alternative Programs," most likely some form of bilingual program, which includes instruction in the child's primary language. In order for a child to be enrolled in an Alternative Program, the parent or guardian must visit the school annually and sign a waiver requesting the placement. However, the first year a child enters California schools she must go through 30 days of "observation," generally conducted in English language classrooms, even if she has a signed waiver. Once the 30 days is completed, the child can enroll in an Alternative Program.

Despite its attempt to prescribe a uniform solution for the education of linguistically and culturally diverse students across the state, the law's impact on educational services for language minority students has varied widely from district to district, school to school, and in some cases classroom to classroom. García and Curry-Rodriguez (2000) and Stritikus (2002) report that some districts across the state have used the waiver clause of the law to pursue district wide waivers, others have implemented the English Only provisions of the law, and a third group has left the primary decisions up to individual schools. Districts with longstanding histories of bilingual programs were more likely to pursue parental waivers in order to maintain their existing programs than were districts with weaker primary-language programs (Gándara et al., 2000; García & Curry-Rodriguez, 2000). The research by Eugene García and his colleagues examining implementation in over 40 districts throughout California showed that in the two years immediately following the passage of Proposition 227 that the overall number of students in bilingual programs in the districts did not dramatically change with the passage of Proposition 227.

The long-term impact of Proposition 227 on native language instruction has not been so positive. The move towards a restrictive language policy in California coincided with a move toward restrictive literacy policy. For example, the Gándara et al. study (2000) of the initial implementation of Proposition 227 in 22 schools in California found that the new law and the statewide emphasis on high-stakes assessment caused teachers to shift their focus from broader meaning-based literacy activities such as story telling and reading for meaning, to skill-based literacy activities to be tested on the statewide assessment. In classrooms observed in the study, literacy instruction became more reductive and narrow in scope. Language and literacy were rarely used as tools in overall academic development. Heavy emphasis was placed on decoding and oral development. In addition, schools and districts that might have considered taking the steps to maintain their bilingual program were often moved away from that direction by the high-stakes testing in English. In 2000–2001, California Department of Education data from the California Educational Data System indicated that only 10% of ELL students were still receiving substantial instruction in their first language.

While voter initiative propositions to eliminate bilingual education began in California, they did not stop there. Both Arizona and Massachusetts have passed state-wide initiatives severely limiting or eliminating bilingual education. For example, Arizona's Initiative 203 represents an even more restrictive policy environment for bilingual education. With the rise of nativist's sentiments during recent years, we can expect continued policy movements against bilingual education.

Views from the Classroom: The Impact of 'Language as Problem' Orientation on Bilingual Latino Student Learning

The combination of local anti-bilingual policies with weakened federal policies creates a political environment in which the unique strengths and needs of Latino students are unrecognized. The current mix of federal and local policies are grounded in *language as problem* rhetoric.

In this final section, we analyze classroom practice as the site of policy implementation and negotiation. First, we explore how the national standards movement has undermined learning opportunities for Latino students in both segregated and integrated settings. Second, we look at the consequences of federal and local policies that provide incentives for rapidly transitioning students into English. Finally, we examine the role of the teacher as policy maker and potential advocate for Latinos in this policy mix.

Integration + Standards = Sink or Swim   The weak federal policy environment, which never truly enforced equal access to education, can interact with local subtractive policies to reproduce sink-or-swim conditions. Gonzalez (2002) notes there is a growing distinction between best practices endorsed by research and those that are fundable by law. The alignment of standardized tests with content area standards has severely limited what can be taught and where a school will direct its resources. The narrowing of the curriculum is effectively silencing Latino students, limiting the choices they can make, and the resources they can draw on (Dixon, Green, Yeager, Baker, & Franquiz, 2000). As Orfield (2001) documents, Latinos attend highly segregated schools which are most susceptible to the sanctions and restrictions of No Child Left Behind. Gutierréz (2001) highlights how federal policy merges with local subtractive policies to provide unequal educational opportunities. She notes that the argument for standards and standardized curriculum is that all students will have access to the same materials. However, she found that schools with high test scores (i.e., segregated, White schools) are often exempt from the standardized curriculum. "In effect, poor schools, frequently those with the largest number of linguistically and culturally diverse students are the recipients of one-size-fits-all approaches that attempt to neutralize the effects of poverty, racism, high numbers of uncredentialed teachers, teachers with little experience teaching English language learners, and the presence of large numbers of linguistically diverse student populations" (Gutierréz, 2001, p. 565). Rather than creating more equitable schools, these policies are taken up at the local level in ways that exacerbate the differences between already segregated schools.

While segregation continues to be a significant problem, Latino students in integrated schools face a different set of challenges. Latino students who attend integrated schools are still receiving inequitable educational opportunities. DaSilva-Idding's (2005) qualitative study of students in an English immersion class documents strong instances of unequal participation, vague communication between teachers and ELLs, and the construction of a segregated community of practice of Latino students. The students in this study were officially integrated into a mainstream classroom, but effectively segregated because they lacked equal access to the learning community. Stritikus (2006) found that schools that adopted one-size-fits-all curriculum in the post-227 era created classroom cultures in which "making sense" was not valued. In these classrooms, studies reveal the unintended consequences of federal and state policy's attempts to remedy *language as a problem* through standardized instruction. Classroom implementation of subtractive policies can effectively deny Latino students meaningful learning opportunities. A cogent example of this is the work of Valenzuela (1999) who highlights how tracking and subtractive views of students works against Latino students' educational success.

Rapid English Acquisition   As states move away from bilingual education, schools with Latino populations fill that gap with English language development programs. In California, the Structured English Immersion component of Proposition 227 has exacerbated the unequal access to education for recent Latino immigrants. Kerper-Mora (2002) points out the irony of this policy "in many school districts, monolingual teachers with a minimum amount of training are expected to accomplish in one year what bilingual teachers with highly specialized training and skills in two languages were formally expected to accomplish in 3 to 5 years of instruction" (p. 39). This results in lost instructional time and a program that is transitory, inadequately funded, and uncoordinated with the rest of the school program (Rumburger & Gándara, 2000). 'Structured English Immersion segregates newcomers to accelerate their acquisition of English without acknowledging students' cultural and linguistic resources or their long-term academic trajectory (Rumberger & Gándara, 2000).

Once students exit the Structured English Immersion program, they enter into the mainstream with the label of Limited English Proficient. When the school decides (in accordance with local and federal policy) that the student no longer requires language support, he she is redesignated as Fluent English Proficient. Koyama (2004) reveals political pressure schools feel to rapidly transition students from LEP to FEP. Redesignation is equated with success in federal policy. This rapid transition into a fluent English category has negative long-term consequences for students. Once students are reclassified, they are denied access to services that support their linguistic development. FEP students are mainstreamed into English-only classrooms under the false assumption that linguistic competence erases all differences between them and their native English-speaking peers. In a quantitative analysis of EL reclassification rates in California, Grissom (2004) argues that students who are reclassified too early are at risk of academic failure. Students who are not reclassified before junior high or middle school run the risk of being placed in dead end tracks with unstimulating content. The short-sightedness of this policy omits all factors other than English language fluency. It ignores students' academic trajectories beyond reclassification. English linguistic ability is confused with academic ability (Meador, 2005; Harklau, 2003).

This overemphasis on English fluency distorts the academic and linguistic competences of Latino students. In Cuero and Dworin's (2007) study of a middle school student who had been exited in elementary school, they reveal the personal as well as academic consequences of this subtractive policy. Because the schools did not recognize or value her literacy in Spanish, the student overgeneralized standardized English test scores which portrayed her as a poor reader. The exclusive focus on English literacy influenced this student to opt out of taking honors courses. In the policy climate situated within a *language as problem* rhetoric, rapid English language fluency overshadows both the resources Latino students bring to school as well as the long-term academic success they achieve in school.

The Classroom Teacher   Teachers must negotiate the multiple demands of policy, curriculum, students, and time. The normative pressure from federal and state policies can discourage teachers from implementing what they know to be best practices for Latino students. Many districts and schools have adopted 'teacher proof' curriculum, constraining teacher's ability to address diverse students' needs (O'Day et al., 2004). In their survey of experienced third grade teachers in Arizona after Prop. 203, Wright and Choi (2005) found a pattern of decreasing effective ELL instructional strategies, coupled with increasing use of direct instruction, worksheets, and test preparation. Talented teachers are often prevented from adapting curriculum, creating innovative lesson plans, or tailoring their instruction (Gutiérrez, 2001). According to Wright (2002), teachers in a post-227 California school tried to tailor instruction to address individual needs of students and linguistic resources, but the emphasis on the standardized test scores made it "difficult to maintain their professional integrity" (p. 13).

Given the current one-size-fits-all climate, teachers with ELLs are facing tremendous pressure from both the district and state to abandon innovative practices in the name of raising test scores. A number of teachers in the Wright and Choi (2005) study were caught in an ideological bind because they were required to earn their English language development endorsements, yet there was little support or opportunity for implementing any innovative or personalized instruction. The existing policy mix serves to undermine the teachers and schools that have the capacity to effectively address the needs of Latino students. Wright and Choi (2005) examined how the policy mix serves to undermine teacher capacity. As one of the teachers in their study indicates: "I'm in the ESL [Endorsement] program right now and, like, all the strategies and everything they tell us to do, they teach us to do, we're really not allowed to do at our school. It's looked down upon, so, everything I'm learning are great strategies for ELLs, and I would love to do some of the things in my classroom, but I can't" (p. 45). This individual teacher's claim was supported by the recent quantitative analysis by Williams et al. (2007), which found that the presence of teachers with CLAD or BCLAD[2] did not have a significant relationship to the academic performance of English language learners (as measured by adequate yearly progress).

While teachers' pedagogical choices are constrained, we do not want to suggest that they are without agency. García, Stafford, and Arrias (2005) suggest that the type of certification a teacher holds has a strong effect on his or her attitude towards English language learners. Teachers within these restrictive policy environments react differently. Rumburger and Gándara (2000) found that teachers' post-227 dispositions depended on pre-227 skill experience, and beliefs. Many teachers expressed frustration at no longer being able to use the full range of skills they possessed to instruct ELLs. Stritikus (2002) compared two teachers' reactions to Proposition 227, finding one with a renewed commitment to bilingual education and the other who felt that it legitimized punitive, basic skills instruction. Teachers are always on the ground, ad-hoc policy makers. Teachers who are committed to *language as resource* or *language as right* frameworks can and do push back against policies that undermine the resources of their Latino students.

Conclusion

This chapter traced the evolution of language and educational rights for bilingual Latino students. Our analysis indicates that policy and legal decisions are closely connected to larger social and political tensions about race, language, and resources. Past and recent developments in legal and political history demonstrate the contradictory position of the United States toward Latino students and diversity. While we frequently celebrate our status as a nation of immigrants or as a land of equality, language policy in the United States has continually attempted to suppress and minimize linguistic diversity. Latino students in the United States have rarely seen their languages and cultures promoted at the federal and state levels. There have been glimmers of hope in legal and policy movements. In particular, the *Lau* and *Castañeda* rulings have established important constitutional guarantees for Latino students. Despite these important protections, these legal decisions are not, in and of themselves, enough to guarantee the educational rights of Latino students, and a widespread orientation of language as resource has yet to materialize as a guiding factor in Latino education. In addition, recent court rulings and laws passed by Congress have put *Lau* on shaky ground (Moran, 2004).

As the review of instructional practice indicates, legal and political decisions have real consequences in the manner in which Latino students are educated. Court decisions and policy have shaped educators' beliefs and practices in their interactions with and expectations for Latino students. The field of educational research has done important work in exposing the types of contexts which best capitalize on cultural and linguistic resources of Latino students. Unfortunately, local, state, and federal policy have not always aligned with the most appropriate educational approaches for Latino students.

While this examination can result in a prevailing sense of pessimism about the opportunities of Latino students, it is our hope that exposing the evolution of the current state of affairs will assist policy makers, researchers, and parents in their continued advocacy for Latino students. We believe that teachers, despite the constraints placed upon them, have a powerful role to play in the advocacy and promotion of equity and opportunity for Latino students. Researchers also play an enormous role, both through documenting the impact of policies and legal decisions and imagining what remains possible given current political and legal realities.

Notes

1. The Mexican American Education Study (MAES) was a five year study conducted by the U.S. Commission on Civil Rights. The study included schools across the southwestern part of the United States, where there was a large number of Mexican American students. The study concluded that Mexican American students were being denied equal educational opportunities in American schools.
2. CLAD: Crosscultural Language and Academic Development; BCLAD: Bilingual and Crosscultural Language and Academic Development. In California, CLAD is the equivalent of an English Language Development endorsement, and BCLAD is the equivalent of a bilingual teaching endorsement.

References

Alvarez v. Lemon Grove School District, Superior Court, San Diego County, No. 66625 (1931).

Anyon, J. (1980). Social class and the hidden curriculum of work. *Journal of Education, 162*(2), 67–92.

Baker, C. (2006). *Foundations of bilingual education and bilingualism.* Clevedon, England: Multilingual Matters.

Board of Education of Cincinnati v. Walter, 390 N.E.2d 813 (1979).

Brown v. Board of Education, 347 U.S. 483 (1954).

California Secretary of State's Office (1998). *California voter information: Proposition 227. Text of proposed law.* Sacramento: Secretary of State's Office.

Castenada v. Pickard, 648 F.2d 989 (5th Cir. 1981).

Cisneros v. Corpus Christi Independent School District 560 F.2d 190 (1977).

Cuero, K. K. & Dworin, J. E. (2007). Lessons from Jennifer: Addressing common assumptions regarding "former" English language learners. *Voices from the Middle, 14*(4), 15–25.

Cummins, J. (2000). "This place nurtures my spirit": Creating contexts of empowerment in linguistically-diverse schools. In R. Phillipson (Ed.), *Rights to language: Equity, power, and education* (pp. 249–258). Mahwah, NJ: Erlbaum.

Darling-Hammond, L. (2004). What happened to a dream deferred? The continuing quest for equal educational opportunities. In J. A. Banks & C. M. Banks (Eds.), *Handbook of research on multicultural education* (pp. 607–630). San Francisco: Jossey-Bass.

DaSilva-Idding, A. C. (2005). Linguistic access and participation: English language learners in an English-dominant community of practice. *Bilingual Research Journal, 29*(1), 165–183.

Dayton v. Brinkman, 433 U.S. 406 (1977).

Delgado v. Batrop Independent School District, Civ. No. 388 (W.D. Tex. June 15, 1948).

Dixon, C., Green, J., Yeager, B., Baker, D., & Franquiz, M. (2000). "I used to know that": What happens when reform gets through the classroom door. *Bilingual Research Journal, 24*(1&2), 1–14.

Donato, R. (1997). *The other struggle for equal schools: Mexican Americans during the Civil Rights era.* Albany: State University of New York Press.

Gándara, P., Maxwell-Jolly, J., García, E., Asato, J., Gutiérrez, K., Stritikus, T., et al. (2000). *The initial impact of Proposition 227 on the instruction of English learners.* Santa Barbara, CA: Linguistic Minority Research Institute. Retrieved from http://www.uclmrinet.ucsb.edu

García, A. G., Stafford, M. E., & Arias, B. (2005). Arizona elementary teachers' attitudes toward English language learners and the use of Spanish in classroom instruction. *Bilingual Research Journal, 29*(2), 295–317.

García, E. (2002). Bilingualism and schooling in the United States. *International Journal of the Sociology of Language, 155/156,* 1–92.

García, E. (2005). *Teaching and learning in two languages: Bilingualism and schooling in the United States.* New York: Teachers College Press.

García, E., & Curry-Rodriguez, J. (2000). The education of limited English proficient students in California schools: An assessment of the influence of Proposition 227 on selected districts and schools. *Bilingual Research Journal, 24*(1 & 2), 15–35.

Gonzalez, J. (2002). Bilingual education and the federal role, if any. Arizona State University Language

Policy Research Unit, Education Policy Studies Laboratory. Retrieved June 1, 2007, from http://www.language-policy.org/content/features/article1.htm

Grissom, J. B. (2004). Reclassification of English learners. *Education Policy Analysis Archives, 11*(36). Retrieved October 27, 2005, from http://epaa.asu.edu/epaa/v12n36/

Gutierréz, K.D. (2001). What's new in English language arts: Challenging policies and practices, y que? *Language Arts, 78*(6), 564–569.

Haas, E. (2005). The Equal Educational Opportunity Act 30 years later: Time to revisit "appropriate action" for assisting English language learners. *Journal of Law & Education, 34*(3), 361–387.

Hakuta, K. & Mostafapour, E. F. (1996). Perspectives from the history and politics of bilingualism and bilingual education in the United States. In I. Parasnis (Ed.), *Cultural and language diversity and the deaf experience* (pp. 38–50). Cambridge, England: Cambridge University Press.

Harklau, L. (2003). Representational practices and multi-modal communications in U.S. high schools: Implications for adolescent immigrants. In R. Bayley & S. Schecter (Eds.), *Language socialization in bilingual and multilingual societies* (pp. 83–97). New York: Multilingual Matters.

Independent School District v. Salvatierra, 33 S.W. 2d 790 (Tex. Civ. App., San Antonio 1930), cert denied sub nom Salvatierra v. Independent School District, 284 U.S. 50=80 (1931).

Katz, S.R. (1999). Teaching in tensions: Latino immigrant youth, their teachers, and the structures of schooling. *Teachers College Record, 100*(4), 809–840.

Kerper-Mora, J. (2000). Policy shifts in language-minority education: A mismatch between politics and pedagogy. *The Educational Forum, 64*, 204–214.

Kerper-Mora, J. (2002). Caught in a policy web: The impact of education reform on Latino students. *Journal of Latinos and Education, 1*(1), 29–44.

Keyes v. School District No. 1,576. Supp. 1503 (D. Colo. 1983).

Koyama, J. P. (2004). Appropriating policy: Constructing positions for English language learners. *Bilingual Research Journal, 28*(3), 401–425.

Lau v. Nichols, 414 U.S. 563 (1974).

Lindholm-Leary, K. J. (2001). *Dual language education. Bilingual education and bilingualism, 28.* Clevedon, England: Multilingual Matters.

Meador, E. (2005). The making of marginality: Schooling for Mexican immigrant girls in the rural southwest. *Anthropology and Education Quarterly, 36*(2), 149–164.

Mendez v. Westminster School District, et al., 64 F. Supp. 544 (S.D. Cal. 1946).

Milliken v. Bradley, 418 U.S. 717 (1974).

Milliken v. Bradley II, 433 US 267 (1977).

Moran, R. F. (1988). The politics of discretion: Federal intervention in bilingual education. *California Law Review, 76*, 1249–1365.

Moran, R. F. (2004). Undone by law: The uncertain legacy of Lau v. Nichols. *UCLMRI Newsletter, 13*(4). Retrieved June 12, 2006, from http://www.lmri.ucsb.edu/publications/newsletters/index.php

National Center for Educational Statistics (2005). *The condition of education 2005* (NCES 2005-094). Washington, DC: US Government Printing Office.

No Child Left Behind Act of 2001, 20 U.S.C. § 6319 (2001).

Notice of Proposed Rulemaking, 45 Fed. Reg. 52,052 (1980).

O'Day, J., Bitter, C., Kirst, M., Carnoy, M., Woody, E., Buttles, M., et al. (2004). Assessing California's accountability system: Successes, challenges, and opportunities for improvement. *Policy Brief 04-2.* Retrieved February 14, 2006, from http://pace.berkeley.edu/policy_brief.04-2.pdf

Oakes, J., Joseph, R., & Muir, K. (2004). Access to achievement in mathematics and science: Inequalities that endure and change. In J. A. Banks & C. A. M. Banks (Eds.), *Handbook of research on multicultural education* (2nd ed., pp. 69–90). San Francisco: Jossey-Bass.

Orellana, M. F., Ek, L., & Hernandez, A. (2000). Bilingual education in an immigrant community: Proposition 227 in California. In E. T. Trueba & L. I. Bartolome (Eds.), *Immigrant voices: In search of educational equity* (pp. 75–92). Lanham, MD: Rowman & Littlefield.

Orfield, G. (2001). *Schools more separate: Consequences of a decade of resegregation.* Cambridge, MA: The Civil Rights Project.

Petronicolos, L., & New, W. S. (1999). Anti-immigrant legislation, social justice, and the right to equal educational opportunity. *American Educational Research Journal, 36*(3), 373–408.

Reeves, J. (2004). "Like everybody else": Equalizing educational opportunity for English language learners. *TESOL Quarterly, 38*(1), 43–66.

Reyes, M., & Halcon, J. J. (Ed.). (2001). *The best for our children: Critical perspectives on literacy for Latino students.* New York: Teachers College Press.

Reyes, P., Scribner, J. D., & Scribner, A.P. (Eds.). (1999). *Lessons from high performing Hispanic schools: Creating learning communities.* New York: Teachers College Press.

Ruiz, R. (1984). Orientations in language planning. *NABE Journal, 8*(2), 15–34.

Rumberger, R. W., & Gándara, P. (2000). The schooling of English learners. *University of California Linguistic Minority Research Institute Policy Report.* Retrieved February 14, 2006 from http://lmri.ucsb.edu/publications/00_pace.pdf

San Antonio Independent School Dis. v. Rodriguez, 411 U.S. 1 (1973).

Slavin, R. E., & Calderon, M. (Eds.). (2001). *Effective programs for Latino students.* Mahwah, NJ: Erlbaum.

Slavin, R., & Cheung, A. (2005). A synthesis on language of reading instruction for English language learners. *Review of Educational Research, 75*(2), 247–284.

Stritikus, T. (2002). *Immigrant children and the politics of English-Only: Views from the classroom.* New York: LFB.

Stritikus, T. T. (2006). Making meaning matter: A look at instructional practice in additive and subtractive contexts. *Bilingual Research Journal, 30*(1), 219–227.

Stritikus, T. T., & García, E. (2003, August 6). The role of theory and policy in the educational treatment of language minority students: Competitive structures in California. *Education Policy Analysis Archives, 11*(26). Retrieved from http://epaa.asu.edu/epaa/v11n26/

Thomas, W., & Collier, V. (2002). *A national study of school effectiveness for language minority students' long-term academic achievement.* Santa Cruz, CA and Washington, DC: Center for Research on Education, Diversity & Excellence. Retrieved from http://www.crede.ucsc.edu/research/llaa/1.1_final.html

Valenzuela, A. (1999). Subtractive schooling: U.S.-Mexican youth and the politics of caring. New York: State University of New York Press.

Valencia, R. R., Menchaca, M., & Donato, R. (2002). Segregation, desegregation, and integration of Chicano students: Old and new realities. In R .R. Valencia (Ed.), *Chicano school failure and success: Past, present, and future* (2nd ed., pp. 70–111). New York: Routledge/Falmer.

Walker, A., Shafer, J., & Iiams, M. (2004). "Not in my classroom": Teacher attitudes towards English language learners in the mainstream classroom. *NABE Journal of Research and Practice, 2*(1), 130–160.

Williams, T., Perry, M., Oregon, I., Brazil, N., Hakuta, K., Haertel, E., Kirst, M., & Levin, J. (2007). *Similar English learner students, different results: Why do some schools do better? A follow up analysis based on a large-scale survey of California elementary schools serving low-income and EL students.* Mountain View, CA: EdSource.

Wright, W. E. (2002). The effects of high stakes testing in an inner-city elementary school: The curriculum, the teachers, and the English language learners. *Current Issues in Education, 5*(5). Retrieved February 22, 2007, from http://cie.ed.asu.edu/volume5/number5

Wright, W. E. (2005). *Evolution of federal policy and implications of No Child Left Behind for language minority students.* Tempe: Language Policy Research Unit, Education Policy Studies Laboratory, Arizona State University.

Wright, W. E., & Choi, D. (2005). *Voices from the classroom: A statewide survey of experienced third-grade English language learner teachers on the impact of language and high-stakes testing policies in Arizona.* Education Policy Studies Laboratory: EPSL-0512-104-LPRU. Retrieved February 14, 2006, from http://edpolicylab.org

Part IV

Teaching and Learning

Part Editors: Corinne Martínez and Esteban Díaz

28 Teaching and Learning

An Introduction

Corinne Martínez
California State University, Long Beach

Esteban Díaz
California State University, San Bernardino

Teaching and Learning: An Introduction

All across the country, schools are struggling with the same challenge: how to create schools and classrooms with teachers, staff, and administrators who ensure learning occurs for all students. We know that for many students, particularly Latina/o children of low income households, the economic possibilities and opportunity for social mobility offered by academic achievement is unparalleled by any other formal institution. Of equal importance is the socialization and development space that schools and communities offer Latina/o students and their families. While schools are considered the cornerstones of society, they are also the gatekeepers that help perpetuate an underclass of poorly educated youth with few skills and opportunities. Schools are institutions that are tailored for a particular mainstream, namely Euro-centric, middle class, and often male students. As such, students are required to perform within average scales that for Latina/o students often result in remediation and separation because of inherent cultural and economic biases. Latina/o students who drop out, or better yet, are "pushed out" of school, often experience learned helplessness as a result of repeated exposure to hostile and messages of hopelessness.

The issues of educational achievement and opportunity and its relationship to social responsibility are indeed complex. While there is no universal agreement or understanding as to the causes of low Latina/o student achievement, secondary school completion and their under representation on college campuses, there has been a charge to respond and identify ways to intervene. There are many areas for intervention to reduce the rate of school failure and improve Latina/o academic achievement.

In an effort to contribute to the ongoing discourse over what should be done to improve our nation's schools, this section addresses diverse K-12 teaching and learning related issues, from the deconstruction of theoretical models to explain low educational achievement to the emergence of interdisciplinary studies, to teaching and testing practices and further to professional practice within a linguistically and culturally diverse society. Moving beyond the simplistic explanations of low educational achievement of Latina/o students Rebeca Burciaga, Lindsay Perez Huber, and Daniel Solórzano examine the educational conditions that create such outcomes. Burciaga, Perez Huber, and Solórzano provide a comprehensive explanation of the "dismal education statistics of Latina/o students." Borrowing from the work of Shirley Malcom, these authors argue that in order to understand the reasons for the "mere trickle at the end of the …pipeline…we must go all the way back to the headwaters" to examine the unequal education structures, policies and practices that have severely limited Latina/os students overall access to quality education and resources that begin in preschool, continue through elementary school and secondary school.

Burciaga, Perez Huber, and Solórzano point out that Latina/o students have the lowest levels of attainment at every level of the educational pipeline when compared to their Native American,

African American, Asian American, and White peers. While there are substantial challenges Latina/o students face along the educational pipeline, none seems as detrimental to the overall success of Latina/os as the lack of adequate resources and educational opportunities students encounter at every level of education. Beginning with early childhood education, Burciaga, Perez Huber, and Solórzano argue that a lack of information about pre-school opportunities as well as a lack of affordable preschool programs position Latina/o children at a disadvantage. As students move into the elementary and secondary school environment, they are confronted with an additional set of challenges. Despite the rapid increase in the Latina/o school aged population, the K-12 teaching force remains overwhelmingly White.

Burciaga, Perez Huber, and Solórzano show that many Latina/o students find themselves in schools with limited resources, an unavailability of college preparatory courses, and tracked into remedial programs that undermine college preparedness and eligibility. This coupled with the experience of attending severely overcrowded, segregated, and under funded schools places students at a further disadvantage. For Latina/o migrant and undocumented students navigating the educational pipeline becomes especially difficult given language barriers and the constant moving in and out schools. To "change that meager outflow" at the end of pipeline, Burciaga, Perez Huber, and Solórzano propose a framework of hope that "focuses on the strengths and strategies Latina/o students utilize to persist despite the challenges they face along the educational pipeline."

The chapter by Pedro Portes, Margaret Gallego, and Spencer Salas frames the under-education of Latina/os as an ethical national phenomenon that carries potentially disastrous economic consequences. Employing a cultural historical theoretical approach, Portes, Gallego, and Salas begin by calling into question the political discourse of "scientific" research in education that buys into the notion that redressing decades of group based inequality can be achieved through rigorous "propagation of best practices implemented through a standardized curriculum by highly qualified teachers under a federalized program of reward and punishment." In advocating cultural historical understandings of education, Portes, Gallego, and Salas advance a multi-level, layered comprehensive strategy to improve educational opportunities for Latina/os students in diverse contexts at both the national and local level.

Portes, Gallego, and Salas advocate a policy framework grounded in an understanding of group based inequality as a cultural historical phenomenon perpetuated by the current system of education that continues to place Latina/o students at risk. At the macro-level, the authors push for policy actions aimed at dismantling the "distributed" mechanisms that shape the educational underdevelopment of many U.S. Latina/o students and implementing a locally-based system that consistently and seamlessly educates Latinos at grade level from preschool through college. Such an approach organizes policy action at four levels: better pre-school preparation for all Latina/o students, elementary school supports, a life-skills adolescent curriculum, and higher education transformation in preparing education all others. Portes, Gallego, and Salas further propose utilizing the same framework to examine policy implementation and address the relationships within schooling that impact teaching and learning as local situated practices in specific contexts. The authors conclude that a cultural historical approach can lay the foundation for policies and praxis that can radically reform the structures and thus the outcomes of the current education system that places too many Latina/os at risk.

The next chapter in this section provides a critical contribution to the efforts of scholars to understand and explain the role of ideology in shaping the school experiences of youth today, particularly in regard to the role of media in shaping ideology, and the behaviors of teachers, voters and the general public. Tara J. Yosso and David G. García analyze the social significance of racialized media portrayals to determine how exaggerated beliefs about Latino's intelligence, moral character, and cultural values shape public perception, legal and educational discourse and have historically validated the placement of Latinas/os in separate schools and classrooms, restricted access for Latinas/os beyond remedial or vocational tracks and lowered academic expectations for Latinas/os. Building on the notion of "societal curriculum," Yosso and García proceed to examine Hollywood's curriculum about Latinas/os in urban public high schools from 1955 to the present. Using specific films such as *Blackboard Jungle*, the authors provide a theoretical analysis of how the institutionalization of racism and racist ideology was used a means of asserting and maintaining power and control. Following in the tradition of *Blackboard Jungle*, the authors show how other films such as *The Principal, 187,* and *Dangerous Minds* bolster politically conservative agendas, blame victims of racialized inequalities, and deny institutional responsibility for the failures of public schools. Yosso and García end this chapter with a discussion of *Walkout*, as an example of a powerful component of the societal curriculum which leaves behind the one-dimensional, ahistorical, demeaning portrayals of Latina/o students and creates complex portrayals that attempt historical accuracy and disrupt Hollywood's urban school formula. To conclude, Yosso and Garcia reignite the possibilities of recovering historically complex narratives that transcend Hollywood distortions and deficit academic traditions.

Verónica E. Valdez and María E. Fránquiz report on early childhood education as the new frontier targeted by education reformers. This chapter serves to broaden the scope of this work as well as to discuss the implications of these new trends. The authors begin with an introductory overview of the issues and research that highlight current and emergent trends in early childhood education. The unparalleled focus on Latinas/os within this age group can be attributed to significant demographic shifts, increased participation of Latinas/os in early childhood programs, the reported educational achievement gaps among this population and the contentious debates surrounding the use of language and language support programs.

Highlighted in this discussion is research that expands the focus on individual child development by looking at the teaching and learning from a sociocultural perspective that focuses on the natural environments, in which children live, play, and learn. A second area of research discussed by Valdez and Fránquiz is the nature of language support programs provided within preschool settings for Latinas/os. This area of research is significant given that language input and support for literacy in the preschool years are early predictors of academic success.

Teachers play a key role in the achievement of Latina/o students. As such, Valdez and Fránquiz spend a significant amount of time discussing research that looks at the sociopolitical forces that challenge teachers' ability to provide culturally and linguistically appropriate teaching and learning as well as research that builds on the funds of knowledge tradition and provides innovative ways for teachers to build on what young Latina/o children and their families already know. Along these lines, Valdez and Fránquiz closely examine the ways in which Latina/o parents engage in teaching and learning with their young children. Valdez and Fránquiz emphasize the need to re-invent education that incorporates the needs and voices of young Latina/o children, their families, and the educators that serve them.

Up to this point, the chapters have focused on the academic achievement gap between Latinas/os and other ethnic groups in the United States, the patterns of social inequality that marginalize Latina/o students and limit their access to quality educational opportunities. The importance of this emphasis is evident, especially when we consider that more than 10.2 million school-aged children are Latina/o (U.S. Census Bureau, 2006). As pointed out in the previous chapters, educators and policy makers alike must challenge deficit explanations of Latina/o educational attainment and provide an alternative framework in the hope of continuing more critical conversations about Latina/o K-12 education. The next two chapters, which address the current practice and research in teaching and testing Latina/o students, present further discussions of the need to improve the way in which Latina/o students are treated. Josefina Villamil Tinajero, Judith Hope Munter, and Blanca Araujo and Zenaida Aguirre-Muñoz and Guillermo Solano-Flores discuss the education of Latina/o English Learners from somewhat overlapping but different perspectives. From Tinajero, Munter, and Araujo's discussion, the reader will better understand learning models underlying current teaching practices with Latina/o students. Aguirre-Muñoz and Solano-Flores focus on the educational challenges in the testing of Latina/o students focusing on English Language Learners.

First, Tinajero, Munter, and Araujo reiterate the "border crossing" experience of the Latino youth in the United States and suggest that a corollary of this phenomenon are the serious challenges these children are likely to encounter once in the U.S. educational system. The subtractive approaches to schooling, and the perception by educators that these children come to school cognitively handicapped, speaking a native language, and with cultural experiences that serve as barriers to learning has resulted in the persistent educational underachievement of Latino youth. Tinajero, Munter, and Araujo posit, that while there is no single formula for ensuring high achievement for the expanding and diverse population of Latinas/o students, a "central premise of 21st century policy and planning for all children in U.S. schools must be based on sound research and effective practice." These authors proceed to discuss research that illustrates the benefits of bilingualism and the role of schools in promoting native language literacy as a bridge to success in English. This chapter includes a discussion concerning the roles of native language, family involvement, and sociocultural and sociopolitical factors in planning for effective language and literacy development for English learners. This is followed by a review of selected research-based instructional methods that have helped to reverse subtractive approaches to schooling by focusing on the knowledge and experiences Latina/o students bring to the classroom: including *Sheltered Instruction, Two-Way Dual Language*. and the use of *Funds of Knowledge* as a culturally relevant framework of teaching and learning. This chapter closes with a discussion of the Family Book Project, a case study of best practices in action in which the role of native language, family involvement and sociocultural factors have been central to the educational planning for Latina/o students.

Next, Aguirre-Muñoz and Solano-Flores examine how effectively current testing practices address the tremendous linguistic and cultural diversity in the Latina/o school-aged population and propose new ways in which testing practices for Latinas/os learning English can be improved. Using a three-pronged approach, Aguirre-Muñoz and Solano-Flores examine assessment systems capacity to account for the cognitive, semantic, communicative and sociolinguistic factors involved in testing. Aguirre-Muñoz and Solano-Flores argue that Latinas/os constitute a tremendously diverse group, both culturally, and linguistically and thus, a testing model that foregrounds language and culture in testing design, interpretation, and reporting would generate more dependable evidence from which to make adequate reasoning about the academic achievement of English Learners. Additionally, an assessment system that systematically investigates the item construct validity informed by sociocultural and psycholinguistic theory would generate more equitable testing practices and yield more meaningful test scores.

This section concludes with a discussion of the centrality of teacher expertise in the academic achievement of Latina/o students in U.S. public schools. As the Latina/o K-12 student population continues to grow in number and diversity, so to must teachers' knowledge of best instructional practices. To that end, Liliana Minaya-Rowe and José Ortiz report on research-based strategies to train teachers on key aspects in their students' school success. Minaya-Rowe and Ortiz propose a theoretical framework for training and preparing all teachers, but particularly teachers of Latina/o English learners. While highlighting the importance of enacting standards for effective pedagogy, Minaya-Rowe and Ortiz argue that the professional development of teachers must "yield consistency in the instruction of Latina/o English learners, streamline the possibilities for instruction, and have the potential to give them the opportunity to obtain the language, literacy and the content necessary to succeed in schools." While there is consensus on what teachers need to teach and promote in their classroom, there are multiple training models in which teachers enact effective pedagogy to meet the linguistic and academic needs of their students. Minaya-Rowe and Ortiz describe professional development training models that feature the use of pedagogy standards and promote collegial working teams for professional growth and sustained improvement. According to Minaya-Rowe and Ortiz, such teacher training models must be teacher driven, focus on addressing the needs of teachers, and build teacher capacity in content knowledge and pedagogy. The professional training models discussed by Minaya-Rowe and Ortiz are very helpful to those working with pre-service and in-service teachers.

As shown, this section deals with diverse K-12 teaching and learning related issues, from the deconstruction of theoretical models to explain low educational achievement to the emergence of interdisciplinary studies, to teaching and testing practices and further to professional practice within a linguistically and culturally diverse society. The education of Latina/o students' plays a crucial role in the social and economic future of the United States. With the plurality of perspectives in mind, I strongly believe this section and the overall handbook will serve as a resource to those who are interested in the field of Latinos and Education.

References

U.S. Census Bureau. (2006). *Current population survey.* Retrieved February 10, 2009, from http:www.census.gov/population/www/socdemo/school/html

29 Going Back to the Headwaters

Examining Latina/o Educational Attainment and Achievement Through a Framework of Hope

Rebeca Burciaga
University of California, Santa Cruz

Lindsay Perez Huber and Daniel G. Solorzano
University of California, Los Angeles

> Indeed, to understand the reasons for the mere trickle at the end of the...pipeline and change that meager outflow, we must go all the way back to the headwaters.
>
> (Malcom, 1990, p. 249)

According to the U.S. Census Bureau (2004), the Latina/o[1] population in the United States is projected to increase from 14% of the overall population in 2004 to 18% in 2025—at which time Latina/o students will make up 25% of the nation's school-age population (President's Advisory Commission on Educational Excellence for Hispanic Americans, 2000). In the second largest school district in the nation, Los Angeles Unified School District (LAUSD), Latinas/os already comprise more than 70% of the student population. Despite this population growth, Latinas/os have the lowest levels of educational attainment than any other racial/ethnic group in the United States.[2] Within mainstream education literature, low educational attainment and achievement rates for Latina/o students have been falsely attributed to the students themselves, their families, and their communities (Valencia, 2002).

The epigraph above captures the need to look beyond such simplistic explanations of low educational attainment and achievement of Latina/o students to examine the educational conditions that create such outcomes. Shirley Malcom (1990) highlights the need to go back to the preschool, elementary, and secondary school "headwaters" to examine those educational conditions. This chapter presents research findings that, we believe, provide a more comprehensive and accurate understanding for the dismal education statistics of Latina/o students. We will demonstrate that low educational attainment and achievement is not a product of Latina/o students' lack of interest or their families' lack of caring. In fact, we present research findings that show Latina/o students have very high aspirations to pursue college. We argue that unequal education structures, policies, and practices have severely limited Latina/o students' opportunities to learn[3] that begin in preschool and continue throughout high school. To improve educational outcomes for these students, educational institutions must learn to draw from the strengths Latina/o students bring to schools, instead of focusing on false deficiencies.

We begin by presenting an overview of the educational attainment for Latinas/os in the United States in comparison to the four largest racial/ethnic groups in the country. Next, we explore the unequal educational opportunities for Latina/o students, beginning with early childhood education and continuing through the elementary and secondary levels of education. This chapter concludes with research that highlights the resilience and strengths that Latina/o students bring with them to educational settings as they strive to succeed despite the odds.

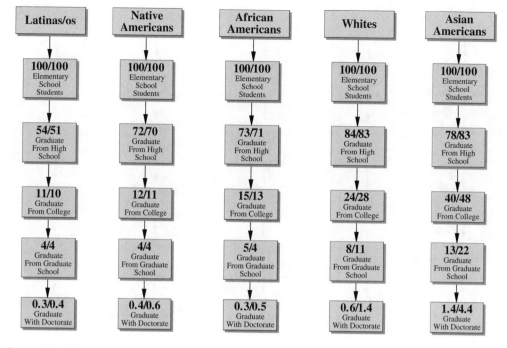

Figure 29.1 United Stated educational pipeline by race/ethnicity and gender. Note: The first number in each box represents females; the second, males. Source: United States Bureau of the Census (2004).

Educational Attainment of Latinas/os in the United States

Latina/o students have the lowest levels of attainment at every level of the educational pipeline, in comparison to their Native American, African American, Asian American, and White peers. Using 2000 U.S. Census data, Figure 29.1 provides a comparison of educational attainment among the five major U.S. racial/ethnic groups. Beginning with 100 Latina elementary school students, 54 Latinas graduate high school. Of the students who persist to college, 11 Latinas complete a baccalaureate degree. Only 4 Latinas receive a graduate degree and 0.3 Latinas attain a doctorate degree.

The Latina/o population is a diverse pan-ethnic group, each with a distinct history in the United States.[4] Figure 29.2 provides an overview of educational attainment by the five major Latina/o ethnic groups in the United States. Within the Latina/o population, Salvadorans and Chicanas/os have the lowest levels of educational attainment, while Cubans have substantially higher levels of attainment. Cubans' relative educational success is due, in part, to their higher socioeconomic status when compared to Salvadorans and other Latina/o groups (Boswell, 2002). Despite Cubans' higher levels of attainment, the fact remains that Latina/o students are not achieving educational milestones at the same rates as other racial/ethnic groups in the United States. The following sections explore the myriad challenges Latina/o students face along the educational pipeline.

Socio-Demographic Characteristics of the U.S. Latina/o Population

To better understand the Latina/o population and the low levels of educational attainment, we identify important background information on selected socio-demographic characteristics including size, age structure, and selected social and economic characteristics. This demographic sketch is taken primarily from the 2004 US Census Bureau, Current Population Survey (CPS).

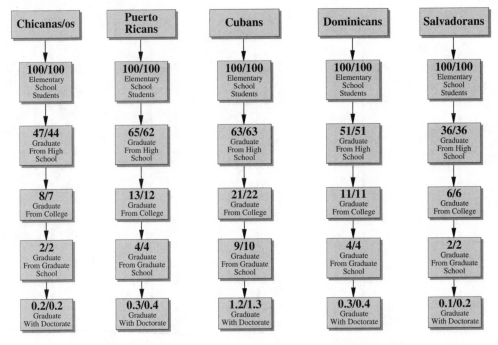

Figure 29.2 United States educational pipeline by Latina/o ethnicity and gender. Note: The first number in each box represents females; the second, males. Source: United States Bureau of the Census (2004).

Population Size

Latinos/as comprise 14% of the total U.S. population,[5] at 40 million inhabitants. Of the Latina/o population, the Chicana/o population is the largest (27 million) and represents 9% of the total U.S. population and 66% of the Latina/o population. Puerto Ricans comprise 9% of the overall Latina/o population, Cubans are 4%, Central Americans 8% and other Latinas/os are 13%. According to the 2000 Census, 77% of Latinas/os lived in seven states[6] and half (50%) lived in the states of California and Texas.

Average Age of Population

Latinos/as in the U.S. are younger than non-Latina/o Whites. In 2004, the median age of the Latina/o population was 26.8 years while the White population was 39.7 years —an average of 13 years difference between these two groups.[7] This data demonstrates that the Latina/o population is considerably younger than most other populations, which, along with their substantial immigration from Latin American countries, makes them the fastest growing population in the United States.

Foreign-Born Status[8]

In 2004, about 40% of Latinas/os were born outside of the United States while 4% of Whites were foreign-born. Among Latina/o subgroups, Central Americans are most likely to be born outside of the United States (67%), followed by Cubans (63%), Chicanas/os (40%), and finally Puerto Ricans (1%). Foreign-born status also includes "non-citizens." In 2004 there were 21 million non-citizens residing in the United States. Latinas/os comprise 58% (12.3 million) of the U.S. non-citizen population.

Poverty Rate

Despite comprising 14% of the total U.S. population, Latinas/os are 25% of those living below the poverty line. In comparison, Whites are 68% of the U.S. population but comprise only 44% of those living below the poverty line. Within the Latina/o subgroups, Chicanas/os are 9% of the U.S. population and 18% of those in poverty while Puerto Ricans are 1% of the population and 3% of those living below the poverty line. For young people under the age of 18, the poverty situation is even more dire. For instance, while Whites are 59% of the population under 18, they make up 33% of those in poverty. In comparison, African Americans are 16% of those under 18 and 30% of those in poverty, while Latinas/os are 19% of those under 18 and 32% of those in poverty. The data are clear; African American and Latina/o youth are much more likely to grow up in impoverished families than Whites. Most Latinas/os are among the working poor, holding occupations with little-to-no job security and low pay.[9]

It is in this sociodemographic context that we study Latina/o attainment along the educational pipeline. The underrepresentation and underachievement of Latina/o students at each point in the pipeline might be better explained by examining the educational conditions these students encounter at their preschool, elementary and secondary school "headwaters." Educators and policy makers must focus on these headwaters if we wish to see an increase in college eligibility and improvement in opportunities beyond schooling. Indeed, unequal opportunities have lasting, cumulative effects.

Unequal Opportunities for Latina/o Students

Latina/o students are likely to attend schools that are more racially segregated, overcrowded, underresourced, and underfunded (Donato, 1997; Ginorio & Huston, 2000; Moreno, 1999; President's Advisory Commission on Educational Excellence for Hispanic Americans, 2000; Valencia, 2002). This lack of access happens early in the educational pipeline. Such challenges also complicate resource allocation, often for the students who need them most. Research demonstrates that to secure the academic success of students, educational opportunities must be offered early and consistently. Unfortunately, Latina/o students are often denied early and consistent educational opportunities, contributing to their underachievement in comparison to their peers. We begin reviewing these unequal opportunities with a discussion of early childhood education.

Early Childhood Education

Despite the importance of preschool, Latina/o children do not receive equal early education opportunities. Children who attend preschool are less likely to be held back a grade and less likely to be placed in a special education program (Preschool California, 2004). Early childhood education also increases the likelihood of performing better on math and reading standardized tests and graduating from high school and continuing onto postsecondary education (National Association of State Boards of Education Study Group, 2006). The primary reason for Latina/o preschool under-enrollment is economic. Latina/o children are more likely to come from economically poor families with fewer resources and little-to-no access to information regarding early educational opportunities available to them (National Task Force on Early Childhood Education for Hispanics, 2007). According to Valencia, Pérez, Echeveste, and the Tomás Rivera Policy Institute (2006), despite Latina/o parents' belief in the importance of early childhood education, the two reasons cited most often for not enrolling their children in preschool programs were (a) the lack of information about pre-kindergarten options and (b) the in-affordability of pre-kindergarten programs.

The lack of preschool opportunities position Latina/o children at a disadvantage as they enter kindergarten steps behind their White peers. For example, a study commissioned by the National Task Force on Early Childhood Education for Hispanics found that Latina/o children do not perform as well as their White peers on reading skills at the beginning of the kindergarten academic year. Latina/o kindergarteners are less likely than their White peers to know the fundamentals of reading such as recognizing letters and understanding the beginning and ending sounds of words (National Task Force on Early Childhood Education for Hispanics, 2007). As many Latina/o children come from bilingual homes, early education initiatives also need to address the critical importance of linguistically and culturally sensitive education services for Latina/o and English language learner (ELL) children (National Council of La Raza, 2007; National Task Force on Early Childhood Education for Hispanics, 2007).

Elementary and Secondary Education

The inequalities at the preschool level become more evident in elementary and secondary education. In this section, we discuss the impact of under qualified teachers, some of the challenges migrant[10] and undocumented[11] students face, unequal access to academic enrichment programs such as Gifted and Talented Education (GATE), Advanced Placement (AP) courses, and finally, student retention.

Teachers

Research demonstrates a direct association between teacher qualifications and student test scores (Valencia, 2002). Unfortunately, Latinas/os and other non-White, low-income students rarely gain access to qualified teachers (Darling-Hammond & Berry, 1999; Valencia, 2002). Schools that educate predominantly Latina/o student populations tend to have fewer teachers with full teaching-credentials in comparison to schools with predominantly White student populations (Perez Huber, Huidor, Malagon, Sanchez, & Solorzano, 2006).

Despite the rapid population growth of Latina/o students in schools, the teaching force does not reflect this demographic shift as 90% of all teachers in the United States are White (National Collaborative in America's Teaching Force, 2004). This is especially problematic considering research that suggests most teachers do not have an adequate understanding of non-White student backgrounds and cultures (Dee, 2005; Perez Huber, Johnson, & Kohli, 2006; Valenzuela, 1999). For instance, in a report by the National Center for Education Statistics (NCES), about 70% of teachers surveyed admitted being moderately to not-at-all prepared to address the needs of culturally and linguistically diverse student populations (National Center for Education Statistics, 1999). As Latina/o students are often schooled in segregated, overcrowded, and underfunded schools, the presence of under-qualified teachers who do not feel prepared to address their needs sets them at a further disadvantage.

Latina/o Migrant Students

It is estimated that there are 800,000 migrant workers and families living in the United States who follow harvest seasons for produce that sustains the U.S. economy (Salinas & Fránquis, 2004). While the majority of Latina/o students attend schools in urban areas, Latina/o migrant students are more likely to attend rural schools where opportunities to learn are even more limited.[12] Migrant children frequently move throughout the country because they, and/or their parents, are migratory workers who move to obtain seasonal or temporary work in agriculture and fishing. The Latina/o educational pipeline is difficult to navigate in general, but is especially difficult for migrant families who are affected by poverty, substandard living conditions, and the constant moving in and out of schools.

Migrant students are faced with tremendous barriers in the educational pipeline beginning with discontinuity in school practices. Donna M. Johnson (1987) identifies three challenges schools have yet to address for migrant children. First, migrant students move frequently as their families travel to work, which often leads to falling behind academically. While some children return home to resume their education, others move to different schools or school districts with differing curricula, credit accrual systems, and testing requirements (Baca, 2004). Second, most migrant children are not fluent in English, making learning in English-only classrooms especially difficult. Third, academic achievement of migrant students, measured by standardized testing, is well below the average public school student. Language barriers and unfamiliarity with the public school system can hinder migrant parent participation in their child's schooling. Most schools do not engage in efforts to overcome such barriers and as a result, parents remain excluded from their child's education (Salinas & Reyes, 2004). Despite multiple factors that place Latina/o migrant students at risk for low educational attainment, studies have found migrant students to demonstrate tremendous resiliency to succeed in the educational pipeline (Gutiér-rez, 2008; Reyes, Garza, & Trueba, 2004; Salinas & Fránquis, 2004).

Undocumented Immigrant Students

While it remains a challenge to determine exactly how many students in the United States are undocumented, we know undocumented immigration has significantly increased during the past decade and is expected to continue. In 2005, there were an estimated 11.5 to 12 million undocumented people living in the United States. Moreover, the majority of undocumented immigrants are Latinas/os (Passel, 2006). The USC Center for Higher Education Policy Analysis (CHEPA) reports that every year there are an estimated 65,000 undocumented students graduating from high schools throughout the nation, with the majority residing in the state of California (Olivérez, Chavez, Soriano, & Tierney, 2006). However, considering undocumented immigration demographics, this number may be significantly underestimated. This data reveals an important fact that is often overlooked in Latina/o educational pipeline analyses. That is, there are a significant number of undocumented Latina/o students in schools throughout the country whose mere presence is often unacknowledged.

Similar to migrant students, undocumented immigrant students may also face challenges related to language barriers and unfamiliarity with U.S. school systems. Such challenges can be confounded by fear of deportation and family separation. Research has found that for some undocumented Latina/o students, challenges specific to their status do not arise until high school, when a social security number is needed for work, college and financial aid applications (Abrego, 2002; Perez Huber & Malagón, 2007). As such, many Latina/o undocumented immigrant students encounter most educational challenges in postsecondary education. Some of these challenges include lack of information about undocumented student's rights to campus resources and a hostile campus climate rooted in racist nativist[13] beliefs about Latina/o undocumented immigrant communities. The greatest barrier to postsecondary education for undocumented students is ineligibility for state and federal financial aid programs (Perez Huber & Malagón, 2007). Despite the obstacles that exist for Latina/o migrant and undocumented immigrant students during their educational trajectories, there are a wealth of lessons to learn from research that examine the ways students are resilient and resistant in the face of such adversity to become academically successful students.

Advanced Academic Programs and Courses

Latina/o students are less likely to be enrolled in college preparatory courses than their White and African American peers (President's Advisory Commission on Educational Excellence for Hispanic Americans, 2000). Ginorio and Huston (2000) highlight the extent of decreased opportunities to learn for Latina/o students by stating, "roughly 70% of Latina/o high school students are enrolled in classes that will not prepare them for college" (p. 4). English Language Learners (ELL) are even less likely to be enrolled in courses that would prepare them for college (González, Stoner, & Jovel, 2002). In addition, Latina/o students are underserved by academic enrichment courses, such as GATE and AP courses, throughout their schooling (Solorzano, Ledesma, Pérez, Burciaga, & Ornelas, 2001, 2003).

GATE programs are geared toward providing enriched and advanced instruction to students identified as gifted and talented learners. Programs may include special day classes (or groupings of gifted students), individualized learning plans, individual academic counseling, teacher and staff development courses, and supplementary services such as weekend seminars and extended day classes (California Department of Education, 2002). There are two principal phases to student identification for GATE, nomination and testing. Although students may be nominated by their peers, parents, or even themselves, they are most likely to be enrolled in GATE through nomination by teachers or administrators (Solorzano et al., 2002). However, research suggests that teacher racial and gender perceptions and expectations may have a direct impact on who is nominated for GATE programs (Castellano, 1998; Passow & Frasier, 1994; Plata & Masten, 1998; Plata, Masten, & Trusty, 1999; Siegle, 2001). In the testing phase, standardized tests often serve as the method of assessment. While poor scores on these exams result in denied access to advanced academic programs and courses, research has noted the cultural bias of standardized tests (Valencia, 2002).

Research by the Latina Equity in Education Project at the University of California, Los Angeles on participation in GATE programs in California reflects disparate inequalities across racial/ethnic lines (Solorzano et al. 2001, 2003).[14] These patterns of inequity are especially evident among Latina/o students. For example, in 2000–01, although Latinas were 43% of the female K-12 population enrolled in California public schools, they only represented 21% of the female students enrolled in California's GATE programs. Conversely, White females make up 36% of the female population enrolled in California public schools, while they represent more than half (52%) of all female students participating in California's GATE programs (Solorzano et al., 2003). At the state level, such unequal distribution of GATE enrollment is troubling. However, a closer inspection magnifies these inequities at the district level.

Table 29.1 demonstrates the unequal opportunities offered to Students of Color in comparison to their White peers in LAUSD, the second largest school district in the nation. According to the U.S. Department of Education (2002), despite comprising 72% of LAUSD's student enrollment during the 2002–2003 academic year, Latina/o students are almost five times less likely to be enrolled in GATE than their White peers. Whereas Latina/o students had a 1 in 24 chance

Table 29.1   Latina/o Students Are Least Likely to be Enrolled in GATE Despite Comprising the Majority of the Student Population in the Los Angeles Unified School District

Race/Ethnicity	GATE Enrollment	LAUSD Enrollment	Opportunity to Learn Ratio'
White	14,575	70,155	1 in 5
Latina/o	21,910	534,495	1 in 24
Black	4,145	90,260	1 in 22
Asian/Pacific Islander	9,340	46,680	1 in 5
Native American	200	2,245	1 in 11
All	50,165	743,840	1 in 15

Source: U.S. Department of Education, Office of Civil Rights Elementary and Secondary School Survey (2002)

of being identified for GATE, 1 in 5 White students were identified. This study also found that schools with higher Student of Color enrollments were more likely to not have GATE programs than predominately White schools.

Access to rigorous GATE programs provides Latinas/os with opportunities that are critical for educational advancement (Oakes, Rogers, McDonough, Solorzano, Mehan, & Noguera, 2000). Academic enrichment programs such as GATE provide early opportunities for students to access better colleges and universities (Bernal, 2002) as they provide gateways for entry into AP classes in high school (González, Stoner, & Jovel, 2002). Without access to enrichment programs early in their educational trajectories, Latina/o students are effectively "gated-out" from later placement in upper-level math, science, honors, and Advanced Placement courses, which are crucial for college eligibility (Solorzano et al., 2003).

Latina/o students are less likely to access AP programs in high school. Students who take certified AP courses are provided, by universities, one additional grade point for each grade. As a result, AP students tend to have higher grade point averages than students who do not have access to AP courses. According to the UCLA Admissions Office, students who were admitted to UCLA in the fall of 2007 took an average of 17 AP/Honors classes (UCLA Office of Admissions, 2007). Daniel Solorzano and Armida Ornelas (2002) found that schools offering more AP courses are most often available to suburban, affluent students. This study revealed that just over half (53%) of California's high schools offered between 0–4 AP classes, compromising students' opportunities too learn. Even with a significant increase of racial/ethnic minorities in the U.S. public school system, we fail to see their equitable representation in GATE and AP programs (Bernal, 2002; Ford, Harris, Tyson, & Trotman, 2002; Harmon, 2002; Morris, 2002; Passow & Frasier, 1994). With such patterns of unavailability of courses and under-enrollment, one is left to wonder if these numbers suggest that our schools do not believe Latina/o students are gifted, talented, or academically advanced.

Drop Out vs. Push Out

Many Latina/o students find themselves in schools with limited resources, poor schooling conditions, tracked into remedial programs and feel teachers do not care about their well-being, let alone their academic success (Valenzuela, 1999). As demonstrated in Figure 29.1, 46% of Latinas and 49% of Latinos were pushed out of school before graduating from high school, compared to just 16% of White women and 17% of White men in 2000. Given the challenges Latina/o students face, it is important to be critical of the language used to describe the effects of these educational inequalities. For example, the term "dropout" is most often used to describe students who are not enrolled in school and do not have a high school diploma or equivalent certificate (Valencia, 2002). The word dropout misplaces blame and responsibility on students instead of taking into account the unequal institutional structures such as segregated and overcrowded schools, underqualified teachers, and educational tracking that contribute to students' departures from schools. Instead, the term "push out" may be more appropriate. A student is pushed out of school when the school is ineffective in retaining the student until she has completed her full course of study (U.S. Commission on Civil Rights, 1971; Valencia, 2002). Thus, the burden of holding, or graduating, the student is placed on the school and administration. For Latinas/os, the decision to stay or leave school is facilitated by a process of disengagement and alienation experienced during their schooling, perpetuated by teachers, staff, and school administrators who have low academic expectations, withhold crucial information, and often reflect negative perceptions of Latinas/os and other Students of Color in their teaching and service practices (Valencia, 2002).

Many Latina/o students experience limited opportunities to learn at every level of the educational pipeline. The unequal access to educational opportunities for Latina/o students are cumulative, long lasting, and undermine college preparedness and eligibility. For instance, in

California in 2003, 6.2% of African Americans and 6.5% of Latina/o high school graduates were eligible for admission to the University of California while 16.2% of White graduates were eligible (California Postsecondary Education Commission, 2005). Yet despite these challenges and attainment trends, many Latina/o students aspire to beat the odds and pursue higher education. Taking a closer look at college aspirations of eighth grade students in the United States, we see the majority of Chicana and Chicano students aspiring to pursue a college education. These findings would support the concept of push out (versus dropout) because it challenges the erroneous belief that Latina/o students are *choosing* not to continue their education. Instead, research demonstrates that Latina/o student aspirations of attending college remain high even when controlling for socioeconomic status.

Aspiring for Higher Education

While some may falsely assume that Latina/o students do not care about their education, research demonstrates Latina/o students hold high educational aspirations, even when controlling for socioeconomic status (SES). Figure 29.3 compares the percent of U.S. eighth grade students aspiring to college by race/ethnicity, gender, and SES (see Solorzano, 1991, 1992a,b). When we examine college aspirations for Chicanas/os, African Americans, and Whites, we find the vast majority of all students aspire to attend college. Still, Chicanas and Chicanos have the lowest percentage of the three racial/ethnic groups. However, when we control for social class and examine low SES students, we see that African Americans have the highest percentage of students aspiring to college, followed by Chicanas/os and Whites. Considering most Chicana/o students live in low SES households, this table is a clear indication that most Chicana and Chicano students aspire to attend college. These high educational aspirations should be viewed as assets to be nurtured and built upon within education institutions to promote academic success.[15]

Education and *Educación*

For many Latinas/os, one of the earliest concepts of education is introduced to them by their parents. In the Latina/o culture, education, or schooling, is just as important as *educación*, or integrity. In Spanish, *educación* speaks to a comportment that includes integrity, respect, reciprocity, dignity, and humility.[16] The Spanish saying, *"la educación nace en la cuna"* (education begins in the cradle), celebrates and legitimizes the important roles community and culture play in developing *una persona educada* (a person of integrity) and a well-educated person. According to Angela Valenzuela (1999),

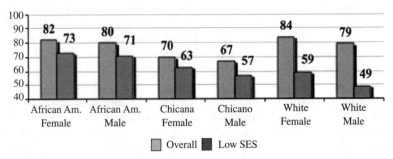

Figure 29.3 Chicanas and Chicanos aspire to attend college. Source: National Educational Longitudinal Survey (1988) as cited in Solorzano (1992a,b).

Educación [is a] foundational cultural construct that provides instructions on how one should live in the world. With its emphasis on respect, responsibility, and sociality, it provides a benchmark against which all humans are to be judged, formally educated or not. (p. 21)

Because *educación* is a cultural cornerstone for many Latinas/os, family and community members are respected and integral to one's upbringing. Valenzuela's book *Subtractive Schooling: U.S - Mexican Youth and the Politics of Caring* (1999) chronicles the experiences of high school students and how their culture is subtracted through schooling policies and practices,[17] and how this omission negatively impacts their schooling. Valenzuela's research reinforces the need for schools to incorporate and honor the bicultural understandings and approaches that students bring with them to educational settings. In the following section, we present some of the research-based frameworks of hope that focus on the strengths and strategies Latina/o students utilize to persist despite the challenges they face along the educational pipeline.

Researching Frameworks of Hope

Despite facing challenges in their preschool, elementary, and secondary schooling, some Latina/o students *are* succeeding and most *are* aspiring to higher education. Researchers concerned with the constant barrage of dismal Latina/o educational attainment have documented strategies of resistance and resilience within Latina/o communities (Burciaga, 2007; Ceja, 2004; Cuádraz, 1993; Gándara, 1995; Hayes-Bautista, 2004; Hurtado, 2003; Solorzano, 1986; Solorzano & Delgado Bernal, 2001; Stanton-Salazar, 2001; Talavera-Bustillos, 1998; The Latina Feminist Group, 2001; Valenzuela, 1999; Yosso, 2005). This asset- or strength-based research encourages an in-depth look at successful navigational strategies for Latinas/os whose families and communities have historically been denied equal access to educational opportunities in the United States. In this section, we discuss frameworks of hope by looking at three approaches to research that highlight Latina/o resilience at three distinct but interconnected levels—state, community, and family. We begin at the state level with David Hayes-Bautista's analysis of Latinas/os in California. Hayes-Bautista (2004) highlights the importance of educating Latina/o youth because of their promise as our future leaders. Next, we move to the community level with Tara Yosso's (2005) research on Community Cultural Wealth that provides an array of strategies for shifting our frames of reference to recognize strengths Students of Color bring to school settings. We conclude at the family level with Patricia Gándara's (1979, 1995) research on some of the family resources Chicana/o youth have called upon to navigate and persist in educational settings.

California's economy, one of the largest in the country, is supported by the largest Latina/o population in the United States. In his book, *La Nueva California: Latinos in the Golden State* (2004), David Hayes-Bautista addresses the future of California as it moves towards a Latina/o majority. While countering negative stereotypical portrayals of Latinas/os as gang members, welfare mothers and high school dropouts, Hayes-Bautista presents a historical look at how the Latina/o population in the United States has flourished since the 1940s and continues to grow at a rate faster than any other racial/ethnic group. Using U.S. Census Bureau data, health and behavioral data and primary source survey data, Hayes-Bautista demonstrates that from the 1940s to the year 2000, Latinas/os in the United States had higher rates of U.S. labor force participation, were the least likely to utilize the welfare system, were less prone to heart disease, cancer, and stokes, and have longer life expectancies than non-Latina/o Whites and African Americans in California.

Hayes-Bautista asserts that despite many Latinas/os living in the United States with limited access to economic and educational mobility, they are healthier, live longer, work more, and use fewer social services than the average American. These findings, contrary to Latina/o stereotypes, suggest that with greater access to equal educational opportunities and other opportunities for economic mobility, Latinas/os will contribute to a prosperous California future. For too long the low enrollment or absence of Students of Color in academic enrichment programs and college preparatory classes has been ignored, or falsely attributed to students' lack of interest or lack of hard work (Valencia, 2002). Yet Hayes-Bautista's research challenges these deficit beliefs and reinforces hope in addressing challenges facing Latinas/os in the United States.

Frustrated by the dominance of cultural deficit theories in educational and social science research that suggests Communities of Color possess a deficient culture, Tara Yosso (2005) presents a framework that draws upon the knowledges and resources that Students of Color bring to all settings. These knowledges, learned and nurtured by families and communities, are described as Community Cultural Wealth. Community Cultural Wealth is defined as the "cultural knowledge, skills, abilities, and contacts possessed by socially marginalized groups that often go unrecognized and unacknowledged" (Yosso, 2005, p. 69). Types of Community Cultural Wealth, described as forms of capital, included in Yosso's model include aspirational, familial, social, linguistic, resistant, and navigational. Aspirational capital is defined as the ability to maintain hope in the face of adversity. Next, familial capital includes the communal history, memory, and cultural intuition nurtured by families. Third, social capital is comprised of networks of people that provide access to community resources. Fourth, linguistic capital includes the ability to communicate in more than one language and/or style. Fifth, resistant capital includes the skills and knowledges one acquires by challenging unjust situations. Finally, navigational capital consists of the skills acquired from maneuvering social institutions. This Community Cultural Wealth and other forms of capital utilized within Communities of Color serves as a foundation for Latina/o resistance to inequality and resilience in the face of adversity. Building upon Freirean and Funds of Knowledge (Freire, 1970, 1973; González et al., 1995) frameworks, Community Cultural Wealth shifts the lens away from deficit models to examine the empowering potential of culture in Latina/o communities. Community Cultural Wealth provides a more complete picture of the ways communities accumulate and share cultural assets and resources to support youth.

Patricia Gándara's (1979, 1995) seminal research on the educational mobility of low-income Chicanas/os focuses on factors that contribute to academic success rather than failure. Her work highlights the individual family resources some Chicanas/os have relied upon to navigate and persist in educational settings. Gándara's research challenges stereotypes that Latina/o parents do not care about their children's educational advancement. Her analysis of family stories of migration to the United States demonstrates the power of the family narrative as a vehicle for social mobility through the transmission of beliefs, attitudes, aspirations and self-images. Gándara asserts that these stories, told mostly by parents, are like interventions in that they offer tangible evidence of previous family members who have become successful. Thus, hope is sustained through the telling of a family history that provides an example of social mobility. Positioning family stories as resources for social mobility challenges theories of social reproduction by disrupting the link between the parents' current occupational status and their children's future success (Gándara, 1995). Moreover, this research affirms that parents value education as a means for social mobility, contrary to stereotypes that assert the opposite (see Valencia & Black, 2002).

The aforementioned frameworks of hope are examples of research that reinforce the need to improve opportunities to learn by suggesting alternative approaches and possible remedies to these inequities at the state, community, and family levels. Despite the disheartening educational attainment trends of our Latina/o youth, Hayes-Bautista, Yosso, and Gándara provide examples of tangible frameworks to focus on the assets of Latina/o communities and build upon these strengths as solid foundations for educational success. In honoring what Latina/o students bring to educational settings, we may find new ways to encourage and support aspirations that have been cultivated by families and sustained by individuals, despite fewer opportunities to learn. These approaches help us focus on what is already present among Latina/o communities—namely hope.

Conclusion

In this chapter, we have presented data that confirms Latina/o students' lack of access to opportunities to learn throughout their educational trajectories. From a lack of access to preschool programs to a clear underrepresentation in GATE and AP courses, unequal opportunities are pervasive throughout the educational pipeline for Latina/o youth. In addition, we caution the use of certain language, such as dropout, that misplaces blame solely on students for academic underachievement. Indeed, school resources, teacher preparedness, and teacher expectations have proven to be powerful forces in shaping the academic performance of Students of Color—factors that are out of students' control.

We have shown that despite socioeconomic disadvantages, most Latina/o students maintain high aspirations to continue their education to earn a college degree. In addition, we offer several key studies on the strengths and assets of Latinas/os as frameworks of hope in an effort to challenge deficit explanations of Latina/o educational attainment. We believe these examples provide an alternative framework that challenges dominant beliefs and perceptions of low Latina/o educational attainment and achievement that blames the Latina/o culture for academic failure. These studies are presented in hopes of continuing more critical conversations about improving opportunities to learn for Latina/o students.

The future of the United States depends on investment in Latina/o communities and especially, the quality of education offered to Latina/o children. Without significant policy changes in the education system to better serve and reflect the needs of an increasing Latina/o student body, we risk a loss of talent among our future leaders. Latinas/os have shown their efforts for contributing towards a brighter educational future, now it is time for U.S. educational institutions to do the same. In particular, solutions must build upon the aspirations of our Latina/o youth to attend college. Our investment in the future of our country must consider the strengths these students bring with them to all settings, both in and beyond education. We hope that we may never have to look back and lament that perhaps Latina/o students were not failing our schools, but our schools were failing Latinas/os. Research demonstrates that our hope lies in recognizing Latina/o students' strengths that manifest in a variety of settings, nurturing early aspirations, and improving and increasing opportunities to learn. It is in this spirit that we call for an increased focus on improving and increasing opportunities to learn for Latina/o youth.

Notes

1. In this chapter, the terms Latina and Latino are defined as female and male persons of Latin American ancestry living in the United States. Data referring to specific Latina/o ethnic groups will be noted as such.
2. When compared to the largest racial/ethnic groups in the United States.
3. The opportunities to learn concept was introduced by the International Association for the Evaluation of Educational Achievement (IEA). The IEA recognized that curricular differences had to be considered when comparing students' achievements across national systems. While the concept of opportunities to learn began as a way of exploring the technical validity of IEAs findings, educators and policy makers have since used the term to explore overall educational quality including access to knowledge and the availability and use of resources (McDonnell, 1995; see also Guiton & Oakes, 1995).
4. For a more in-depth discussion of the sociohistorical schooling experiences of different Latina/o ethnic groups in the United States, see Spring, 2001.
5. The total U.S. population is 287 million.
6. These include the states of California, Texas, New York, Florida, Illinois, Arizona, and New Jersey.

7. Among the Latina/o subgroups the Chicana/o population is the youngest (25.4), followed by Puerto Ricans (27.4), then Central Americans (28.7), then Cubans (41.5).

8. According to the U.S. Census Bureau, those who are non-U.S. citizens are those respondents who indicated that they were not of U.S. citizenship at the time of the survey. Note: this non-citizen category includes those who are Lawful Permanent Residents, Temporary Migrants (e.g., foreign students), Humanitarian Migrants (e.g., refugees), or Unauthorized Migrants (e.g. people present in the United States without documentation). For a more in-depth discussion of Latina/o immigration to the U.S. see Gonzalez, 2000.

9. For a more in-depth discussion see Catanzarite, 2002, 2003.

10. Migrants are people who move from place to place to conduct seasonal work. Part C, section 1309 of the No Child Left Behind (NCLB) Act defines a migrant student as any child who is or whose parent is "a migratory agricultural worker, including a migratory dairy worker, or a migratory fisher, and who, in the preceding 36 months, in order to obtain, or accompany such parent or spouse, in order to obtain, temporary or seasonal employment in agricultural or fishing work a) has moved from one school district to another; b) in a State that is comprised of a single school district, has moved from one administrative area to another within such district; or c) resides in a school district of more than 15,000 square miles, and migrates a distance of 20 miles or more to a temporary residence to engage in a fishing activity."

11. The term "undocumented" is used to describe persons living in the United States who do not possess legal authorization to be in the country (see http://www.ed.gov/policy/elsec/leg/esea02/pg8.html).

12. According to Provasnik, KewalRamani, Coleman, Gilbertson, Herring, and Xie (2007), public schools in rural areas have the least percentage of racially and ethnically diverse teachers and experience difficulties filling vacancies in the field of English as a Second Language (ESL). In comparison to city schools, rural schools have less school counselors, social workers, school psychologists, and special education instruction aids than cities. Moreover, the percentage of public schools reporting student underenrollment in rural schools was greater (33%) than schools in cities, suburbs, and towns (12–18%).

13. Racist nativism describes the complex intersection of racism and nativism as forms of oppression that manifest within contemporary U.S. immigration discourse, which targets Latina/o undocumented immigrants and Mexican undocumented immigrants in particular (Perez Huber et al., 2008)

14. For a gendered analysis of a Southern California school district, see Solorzano et al. 2003.

15. This research also suggests the importance of controlling for gender and class in our racial analysis (see Solorzano, 1991, 1992a,b).

16. For a more in-depth discussion of *educación*, see Valenzuela, 1999; Burciaga, 2007.

17. One such practice that Valenzuela believes encourages assimilation is educational tracking, a practice that reinforces hierarchies between Latina/o students by situating English language learners along the lowest educational track thus discouraging bilingualism and biculturalism among students.

References

Abrego, L. (2002). *Beyond the direct impact of the law: Is assembly bill 540 benefiting undocumented students?* Unpublished manuscript.

Baca, L. (2004). Forward. In C. Salinas & M. Fránquis (Eds.), *Scholars in the field: The challenges of migrant education* (pp. ix–x). Charleston, WV: AEL.

Bernal, E. (2002). Three ways to achieve a more equitable representation of culturally and linguistically diverse students in GT Programs. *Roeper Review, 24*(2), 82–89.

Boswell, T. D. (2002). A demographic profile of Cuban Americans. Miami, FL: Cuban American National Council, Inc.

Burciaga, R. (2007). *Chicana Ph.D. students living nepantla: Educación and aspirations beyond the doctorate.* Unpublished doctoral dissertation, University of California, Los Angeles.

California Department of Education. (2002, September 18). *Gifted and talented education in California.* Retrieved November 15, 2002, from http://www.cde.ca.gov/cilbranch/gate/faq.html

California Postsecondary Education Commission. (2005, March). *Are they going? University enrollment and eligibility for African Americans and Latinos.* MS 05-03. Sacramento: California Postsecondary Education Commission.

Castellano, J. (1998). *Identifying and assessing gifted and talented bilingual Hispanic students.* ERIC Clearinghouse on rural education and small schools. (ERIC Document Reproduction Service No. EDO-RC-97-9)

Catanzarite, L. (2002). The dynamics of segregation and earnings in *brown-collar* occupations. *Work and Occupations, 29*(3), 300–345.

Catanzarite, L. (2003). *Wage penalties in brown-collar occupations* (No. 8). Los Angeles: UCLA Chicano Studies Research Center.

Ceja, M. (2004). Chicana college aspirations and the role of parents. *Journal of Hispanic Higher Education, 3*(4), 338–362.

Cuádraz, G. (1993). *Meritocracy (un)challenged: The making of a Chicano and Chicana professoriate and professional class.* Unpublished doctoral dissertation, University of California, Berkeley.

Darling-Hammond, L., & Berry, B. (1999). Recruiting teachers for the 21st century: The foundations of educational equity. *Journal of Negro Education, 68*(3), 254–279.

Dee, T. (2005). A teacher like me: Does race, ethnicity, or gender matter? *American Economic Review, 96*(2), 158–165.

Donato, R. (1997). *The other struggle for equal schools: Mexican Americans during the Civil Rights era.* Albany: State University of New York Press.

Ford, D., Harris, J., Tyson, C., & Trotman, M. (2002). Beyond deficit thinking: Providing access for gifted African American students. *Roeper Review, 20*(2), 52–58.

Freire, P. (1970). *Education for critical consciousness.* New York: Continuum.

Freire, P. (1973). *Pedagogy of the oppressed.* New York: Seabury Press.

Gándara, P. (1979). *Early environmental correlates of high academic attainment in Mexican Americans from low socio-economic backgrounds.* Unpublished doctoral dissertation, University of California, Los Angeles.

Gándara, P. (1995). *Over the ivy walls.* Albany: State University of New York Press.

Ginorio, A., & Huston, M. (2000). *¡Sí, se puede! Yes, we can: Latinas in school.* Washington, DC: American Association of University Women Educational Foundation.

Gonzalez, J. (2000). *Harvest of empire: A history of Latinos in America.* New York: Viking.

González, K., Stoner, C., & Jovel, J. (2002). Examining the role of social capital in access to college for Latinas: Toward a college opportunity framework. *Journal of Higher Education, 2*, 146–170.

González, N., Moll, L. C., Tenery, M. F., Rivera, M. F., Rendón, P., Gonzales, R., et al. (1995). Funds of knowledge for teaching in Latino households. *Urban Education, 29*(4), 443–470.

Guiton, G., & Oakes, J. (1995). Opportunity to learn and conceptions of educational equality. *Educational Evaluation and Policy Analysis, 17*(3), 323–336.

Gutiérrez, K. D. (2008). Developing a sociocritical literacy in the third space. *Reading Research Quarterly, 42*(2), 148–164.

Harmon, D. (2002). They won't teach me: The voices of gifted African American inner-city students. *Roeper Review, 24*(2), 68–75.

Hayes-Bautista, D. (2004). *La nueva California: Latinos in the golden state.* Berkeley: University of California Press.

Hurtado, A. (2003). *Voicing Chicana feminisms: Young women speak out on sexuality and identity.* New York: New York University Press.

Johnson, D. M. (1987, September). The organization of instruction in migrant instruction: Assistance for children and youth at risk. *Teachers of English to Speakers of Other Languages (TESOL) Quarterly, 21*(3), 437–459.

Malcom, S. (1990). Reclaiming our past. *Journal of Negro Education, 59*(3), 246–259.

McDonnell, L. M. (1995). Opportunity to learn as a research concept and a policy instrument. *Educational Evaluation and Policy Analysis, 17*(3), 305–322.

Moreno, J. (Ed.). (1999). *The elusive quest for equality: 150 years of Chicano/Chicana education.* Cambridge, MA: Harvard Educational Review.

Morris, J. (2002). African American students and gifted education: The politics of race and culture. *Roeper Review, 24*(2), 59–62.

National Association of State Boards of Education Study Group. (2006). *Fulfilling the promise of preschool.* Alexandria, VA: National Association of State Boards of Education.

National Center for Education Statistics. (1999). *The condition of education report.* Washington DC: U.S. Department of Education.

National Collaborative in America's Teaching Force. (2004). *Assessment of diversity in America's teaching force: A call to action.* Retrieved July 20, 2007, from http://www.nea.org/teacherquality/images/diversityreport.pdf

National Council of La Raza. (2007). *California: Preschool for all.* Retrieved July 10, 2007, from http://www.nclr.org/content/policy/detail/1508/

National Task Force on Early Childhood Education for Hispanics. (2007). *Para nuestros niños: Expanding and improving early education for Hispanics.* Tempe, AZ: Arizona State University, College of Education.

Oakes, J., Rogers, J., McDonough, P., Solorzano, D., Mehan, H., & Noguera, P. (2000). *Remedying unequal opportunities for successful participation in advanced placement courses in California high schools: A proposed action plan. An expert report submitted on behalf of the Defendants and the American Civil Liberties Union in the case of Daniel v. the State of California.* Unpublished paper prepared for the American Civil Liberties Union of Southern California.

Olivérez, P., M., Chavez, M. L., Soriano, M., & Tierney, W. G. (2006). The college and financial aid guide for AB 540 undocumented immigrant students. The AB 540 College Access Network. Los Angeles: University of Southern California (USC) Center for Higher Education Policy Analysis (CHEPA). Retrieved October 15, 2007, from http://www.usc.edu/dept/chepa/pdf/AB%20540%20final.pdf

Passel, J. S. (2006, March). *The size and characteristics of the unauthorized migrant population in the U.S.: Estimates based on the March 2005 current population survey.* Washington, DC: Pew Hispanic Center.

Passow, A., & Frasier, M. (1994). Toward improving identification of talent potential among minority and disadvantaged students. *Roeper Review, 18*(3), 198–202.

Perez Huber, L., Benavides Lopez, C., Malagón, M., Velez, V., Solorzano, D. (2008). Getting beyond the "symptom," acknowledging the "disease": Theorizing racist nativism. *Contemporary Justice Review, 11*(1), 39–51.

Perez Huber, L., Huidor, O., Malagón, M., Sanchez, G., & Solorzano, D. (2006). *Falling through the cracks: Critical transitions in the Latina/o educational pipeline.* Los Angeles: UCLA, Chicano Studies Research Center.

Perez Huber, L., Johnson, R., & Kohli, R. (2006). Naming racism: A conceptual look at internalized racism in U.S. schools. *UCLA Chicana/o-Latina/o Law Review, 26,* 183–206.

Perez Huber, L., & Malagón, M. (2007). Silenced struggles: The experiences of Latina and Latino undocumented college students in California. *Nevada Law Journal, 7*(3), 841–861.

Plata, M., & Masten, G. (1998). Teacher ratings of Hispanic and Anglo students on a behavior rating scale. *Roeper Review, 21*(2), 139–148.

Plata, M., Masten, G., & Trusty, J. (1999). Teachers' perception and nomination of fifth-grade Hispanic and Anglo students. *Journal of Research and Development in Education, 32*(2), 113–123.

Preschool California. (2004). *Kids can't wait to learn: Achieving voluntary preschool for all in California.* Oakland: Preschool California.

President's Advisory Commission on Educational Excellence for Hispanic Americans. (2000). *Creating the will: Hispanics achieving educational excellence.* Washington, DC: U.S. Government Printing Office.

Provasnik, S., KewalRamani, A., Coleman, M. M., Gilbertson, L., Herring, W., & Xie, Q. (2007). *Status of education in rural America* (NCES 2007-040). Washington, DC: National Center for Education Statistics, Institute of Education Sciences, U.S. Department of Education.

Reyes, P., Garza, E., & Trueba, E. (2004). *Resiliency and success: Migrant children in the U.S.* Herndon, VA: Paradigm.

Salinas, C., & Fránquis, M. (Eds.). (2004). *Scholars in the field: The challenges of migrant education.* Charleston, WV: AEL.

Salinas, C., & Reyes, R. (2004). Graduation enhancement and postsecondary opportunities for migrant students: Issues and approaches. In C. Salinas & M. Fránquis (Eds.), *Scholars in the field: The challenges of migrant education* (pp. 119–132). Charleston, WV: AEL.

Siegle, D. (2001, April). *Teacher bias in identifying gifted and talented students.* Paper presented at the Council for Exceptional Children Annual Convention, Kansas City, MO.

Solorzano, D. (1986). *A study of social mobility values: The determinants of Chicano parents' occupational expectations for their children.* Unpublished doctoral dissertation, Claremont Graduate University, Claremont, CA.

Solorzano, D. (1991). Mobility aspirations among racial minorities, controlling for SES. *Sociology and Social Research, 75,* 182–188.

Solorzano, D. (1992a). An exploratory analysis of the effect of race, class, and gender on student and parent mobility aspirations. *Journal of Negro Education, 61,* 30–44.

Solorzano, D. (1992b). Chicano mobility aspirations: A theoretical and empirical note. *Latino Studies Journal, 3,* 48–66.

Solorzano, D., Burciaga, R., Ledesma, M., Watford, T., Rivas, M., Sanchez, M., et al. (2002). *Unlocking GATE: A case study of Latina inequity in Los Angeles Unified School District's gifted and talented education program.* Los Angeles: University of California, Los Angeles, Graduate School of Education and Information Studies, Latina Equity in Education Project.

Solorzano, D., & Delgado Bernal, D. (2001). Examining transformational resistance through a critical race and LatCrit theory framework: Chicana and Chicano students in an urban context. *Urban Education, 36*(3), 308–342.

Solorzano, D., Ledesma, M., Pérez, J., Burciaga, R., & Ornelas, A. (2001). *Latina equity in education project.* Los Angeles: University of California at Los Angeles.

Solorzano, D., Ledesma, M., Pérez, J., Burciaga, R., & Ornelas, A. (2003). *Latina equity in education: Gaining access to academic enrichment programs* (Policy Brief No. 4). Los Angeles: UCLA Chicano Research Center.

Solorzano, D., & Ornelas, A. (2002). A critical race analysis of advanced placement classes: A case of educational inequality. *Journal of Latinos and Education, I*(4), 215–229.

Spring, J. (2001). *Deculturalization and the struggle for equality: A brief history of the education of dominated cultures in the United States.* Boston: McGraw Hill.

Stanton-Salazar, R. D. (2001). *Manufacturing hope and despair: The school and kin support networks of U.S.-Mexican youth.* New York: Teachers College Press.

Talavera-Bustillos, V. (1998). *Chicana college choice and resistance: An exploratory study of first-generation Chicana college students.* Unpublished doctoral dissertation, University of California, Los Angeles.

The Latina Feminist Group. (2001). *Telling to live: Latina feminist testimonios.* Durham, NC: Duke University Press.

UCLA Office of Admissions. (2007). *Fall 2007 daily extract file* (Preliminary). University of California, Los Angeles Office of Undergraduate Admissions.

United States Bureau of the Census. (2004). *Current population survey, 2004.* Retrieved November 3, 2007, from www.census.gov/population/www/socdemo/hispanic/cps2004.html

U.S. Commission on Civil Rights. (1971). *Mexican American education study, Report 2: The unfinished education. Outcomes for minorities in five southwestern states.* Washington, DC: U.S. Government Printing Office.

U.S. Department of Education, Office for Civil Rights. (2002). Office for civil rights elementary and secondary school survey: 2002. Retrieved October 20, 2007, from http://www.ed.gov/about/offices/list/ocr/data.html

U.S. Department of Education, Office of Elementary and Secondary Education (2002). No child left behind: A desktop reference. Retrieved October 10, 2007, from http://www.ed.gov/offices/OESE/reference.pdf

Valencia, R. (Ed.). (2002). *Chicano school failure and success: Past, present, and future* (2nd ed.). London: Routledge Falmer.

Valencia, R., & Black, M. (2002). "Mexican Americans don't value education!" — On the basis of the myth, mythmaking, and debunking. *Journal of Latinos and Education, 1*(2), 81–103.

Valencia, M., Pérez, P. Echeveste, J., & Tomás Rivera Policy Institute. (2006). *Latino public opinion survey of pre-kindergarten programs: Knowledge, preferences, and public support.* Los Angeles: Tomás Rivera Policy Institute.

Valenzuela, A. (1999). *Subtractive schooling: U.S. Mexican youth and the politics of caring.* Albany: State University of New York Press.

Yosso, T. (2005). Whose culture has capital? A critical race theory discussion of community cultural wealth. *Race Ethnicity and Education, 8*(1), 69–91.

30 Dismantling Group-Based Inequality in a NCLB Era, Effective Practices, and Latino Students Placed and Left at Risk

Pedro R. Portes
University of Georgia

Margaret A. Gallego
San Diego State University

Spencer Salas
University of North Carolina at Charlotte

With 2003 Census Bureau and National Center for Education Statistics data indicating that 43% of Latinos enter the workforce with less than a high school diploma (Chapa & De La Rosa, 2004), the emergence of a "rainbow underclass" (A. Portes & Rumbaut, 2001) threatens to desta-bilize America's competitiveness in a post-industrial global marketplace (Education Trust, 2003; [U.S.] President's Advisory Commission on Educational Excellence for Hispanic Americans, 1996, 2000, 2002). The National Council of La Raza (2007) reports that the 2.9 million Latinos enrolled in U.S. high schools are less likely than their non-Latino peers to complete a degree and recent immigrants are among the most likely to drop out of school. At the postsecondary level, Latinos, account for only 18% of the undergraduate college population. Among those age 25 and older, Latinos (12%) are less likely than African Americans (17.7%) or Whites (30.5%) to earn a bachelor's degree (cf., Chapa & De La Rosa, 2004; Fry, 2002, 2004, 2005).

The under-education of U.S. Latinos at the group level is a disquieting and ethical national phenomenon that not only presents immense developmental obstacles to Latinos themselves, but also carries potentially disastrous national economic consequences in a post-Fordist global marketplace. Latinos currently account for 1 in 4 children in the United States under the age of six, and recent projections have indicated that such numbers will triple by 2050 (Passel & Cohn, 2008). A pressing question, therefore, for policy makers is to what extent are they willing to ignore a de facto apartheid fueled by the very structure of the current educational system. As such, asking, "What can and needs to be done to curtail the longstanding and contemporary massive group based inequality K-16?" is not simply a rhetorical issue. Rather, we argue that the central concern of Group Based Inequality can be addressed through a cultural-developmental restructuring strategy with the dual goals of equity and excellence.

In this chapter, we employ a cultural historical theoretical approach (Cole, 1996; Kozulin, 1998; Vygotsky, 1978) to examine the orientation of a demographic revolution and under-edu-cation time bomb in advancing a multi-level, layered, comprehensive strategy to address the unsettled crisis of Latino Students Placed at Risk or "L-SPARS" and other vulnerable groups still left behind by U.S. public education. It is the manner in which the current under-education of the most vulnerable populations of U.S. students is being constructed that allows us to diagnose this complex, longstanding problem, and suggest means for reversing its outcomes structurally. Namely, here we attempt to broaden the discussion of often too narrowly conceptualized issues of L-SPARS by extending cultural historical theory across micro and macro planes of analysis in a dialogical manner.

To that end, we begin with a discussion of the phenomenon of Group Based Inequality (P. R. Portes, 2005), the ongoing Latino demographic revolution, and a critique of the current fragmented, neo-liberal policies that purportedly address group-based disparities of achievement. Subsequently, we examine the internal tensions that emerge from both subjective and objective dimensions of teachers' life worlds as they grapple with the discourse of "best or effective" practice in contexts that vary as activity settings for teaching and learning. Finally, employing cultural historical theory in its macro dimensions, we articulate a framework for *deterring* the current educational system from actively preserving a segmented policy approach and offer a set of practices to reform its very structure. The chapter concludes with an extended policy reflection on the masses of poverty-bound children who, as often is the case of English learners, struggle to learn in large part due to a lack of language support within a relentless high stakes environment.

Group-Based Inequality: A Cultural Historical Perspective

Nativist common sense would have it that the success of children of immigrants depends on their ability to shed their foreign ways for North American ones—quickly, permanently, and in a manner that ultimately serves to maintain the massive and longstanding group based inequalities in learning and teaching outcomes that, in turn, perpetuate U.S. economic and social caste (see, e.g., A. Portes & Rumbaut, 2001; Sanchez, 1997; Spring, 2004). Draped in the U.S. flag, such thinking has been used to dismantle bilingual K-12 education, prevent the cultivation of a bilingual mainstream population of college graduates and teachers, and has furthermore legitimized reductive models of learning and literacy in historic and new Latino communities amidst a frenzy of accountability (Gandara, Rumberger, Maxwell-Jolly, & Callahan, 2003; Gutiérrez, Asato, Santos, & Gotanda, 2002; Gutiérrez, Baquedano-Lopez, & Alvarez, 2000; Moll & Ruiz, 2002; Orfield & Chungmai, 2007; Valdés, 1996, 2001; Valencia & Suzuki, 2001; Valenzuela, 1999, 2000, 2004). Moreover, as championed by an ethnocentric media, the concept of the least restrictive environment is applied arbitrarily in a K-12 system that ignores empirical evidence such as that in favor of bilingual education while claiming to be guided by such (P. R. Portes & Salas, in press; Thomas & Collier, 1996). While the most advantaged students obtain quality and challenging education, the most in need are denied it. Meanwhile, the educational ring-masters invest millions of dollars for alternate strategies in funded studies while disregarding the findings from decades of bilingual education research.

No Child Left Behind and other reforms attempting to produce higher test scores rely mostly, if not completely, on a school-based analysis of the problem and a political discourse of "scientific" research in education. Latino children and their families, like those of any population category, vary in terms of the social capital they (do not) enjoy in mainstream, dominant, U.S. communities (see, A. Portes & Rumbaut, 2001). Common sense accepts that differences in educational outcomes exist across U.S. communities. What is remarkable, however, is that such differences have been routinely been singled out as the "problem" to be dealt with rather than a variable within larger and dynamic layers of K-12 activity. Consequently, current high-stakes reform plans do not target directly the massive between-group inequality in educational outcomes as a primary concern. Rather, such reform efforts presuppose that redressing decades of Group Based Inequality is possible through rigorous propagation and drills of "best practices" implemented through a standardized restructured curriculum by highly qualified teachers, assertive assessment programs of institutional annual yearly progress, and a federalized system of reward and punishment. On the way, the issue of equity in practices and resources as a means toward educational excellence takes a back seat to constant global comparisons of student performance against world-class standards. In the end, so-called comprehensive school reforms appear to be aimed at facilitating more of the same types of social stratification by educational designs requiring more content at faster rates that leave the least advantaged most surely behind the rest.

Decades after the promise of greater social opportunity by educational design, we find the contrary effect most pronounced in the fastest growing and largest minority population, U.S. Latinos—without deterrents for what have become legally sanctioned barriers to providing equity in learning and teaching opportunities. We advance the re-emergence of a not so old dialectic: increasing group based inequalities by (a reliable, segmented system of) under-education.

The Mind in Society

Differentials in social capital are one of the key variables for understanding how immigrants and children of immigrants interact with local, regional, and national educational policies and practices and the resulting trajectories they are afforded K-16. Another variable that we consider exceptionally critical, is the cultural history of these children's families in interaction with the social contexts and resources (not) deployed in the communities they live (see, P. R. Portes, 1996, 2005; P. R. Portes & Salas, in press). Massively disproportionate and long-standing measurable gaps in educational achievement, such as those we witness with L-SPARS, are developed interpsychologically over time in integrated or marginalized social contexts, relative to historical conditions found in societies.

Precisely, our understandings of Group-Based Inequality are shaped by the writings of Vygotsky (1978, 1986) and his contemporaries such as Luria (1976); Bakhtin (1981, 1986); and the subsequent writings of their American translators and scholars (Cole, 1996; Lave & Wenger, 1991; Leont'ev, 1978, 1981; Scribner & Cole, 1981; Van der Veer & Valsiner, 1994; Wertsch, 1985, 1998, 2002). While it is beyond the scope of this chapter to trace the evolution of contemporary cultural historical theoretical frameworks (for personal and historical accounts, see, e.g., Cole, 1996; Kozulin, 1984; Luria, 1979; Wertsch, 1985), as we have noted elsewhere, cultural historical theory represents a rich meta paradigm that unlike the other major forces in social science resists reductionism in its plasticity (P. R. Portes, 1996, 1999; P. R. Portes & Salas, in press).

For Vygotsky and the interdisciplinary psychology he helped inspire, human cognitive and emotional development is a fundamental transformation of interpersonal processes into intrapersonal through dialogical processing. Or, as Vygotsky (1978) explains, "All the higher functions originate as actual relations between human individuals" (p. 57). To be precise, children learn tools for thinking, the mediating devices their cultures provide, through social interactions with more skilled partners in what Vygotsky calls a *zone of proximal development* that in our analyses extend to groups having zones or affordances for development largely determined by the dominant community's agency.

Helping Means and the Distribution of Thinking

Embedded in the hypothesis of the social nature of human cognitive development is Vygotsky's particular emphasis on the use of material tools and symbolic artifacts to mediate cognition and emotion. Holland and Valsiner (1988) explain,

> He [Vygotsky] referred to these tools as "helping means" (in Russian vspomogatel'nye sredstva). These means (or activities, as Vygotsky with his emphasis on process might prefer) are psychological devices for mediating between one's mental states and processes and one's environment. (p. 248)

Illustrating "helping means" with the example of a woman tying a handkerchief into a knot around her arm to keep from forgetting, Vygotsky (1978) explains,

She is, in essence, constructing the process of memorizing by forcing an external object to remind her of something; she transforms remembering into an external activity.… The very essence of human memory consists in the fact that human beings actively remember with the help of signs. (p. 51)

Handkerchiefs are examples of mediating devices whereby an elementary memory connecting event A to event B is replaced in the following equation: "A to X and X to B, where X is an artificial psychological tool—a knot in a handkerchief, a written note, or a mnemonic scheme" (Kozulin, 1984, p. 106). As such, human thought is "distributed" (Salomon, 1993) across the material tools and social and cultural psychological devices that women and men have shaped over time and that have in turn shaped them (cf., P. R. Portes & Salas, in press).

The Contexts of Effective Practice

From a methodological point of view, researchers operating from cultural historical frameworks understand human development in conjunction with the social contexts in which individuals and groups either directly or peripherally participate (see, Lave & Wenger, 1991). Thinking Vygotsky, we consider the ways in which "effective practices" are currently conceived and defined as oversimplifications of the complexity of classroom life.

A federal emphasis on school accountability has led to increased federal, state, and district control over classroom instruction, just as the Brown decision (*Brown v. Board of Education of Topeka*, 347 U.S. 483 [1954]) impacted, to some extent, equity of resources in school learning environments. Through the installation of extensive academic content standards, standards-aligned, oftentimes scripted curricula, and high-stakes standardized tests, teachers—regardless of their training, background, or students—are commonly told what and how to teach (Achinstein & Ogawa, 2006). Schools with high concentrations of English learners are especially prone to being labeled as "underperforming" given their typical failure to meet narrowly prescribed state and/ or federal academic performance goals. Once labeled as such, schools can expect to undergo intense pressure to maintain fidelity to even more narrowly sanctioned "research based" teaching practices.

A "best practice" or, for that matter, any instructional strategy is realized in a dynamic relationship—one that necessarily responds to fluctuating needs and objectives of its participants. In effect, activities (e.g., effective practices) are social practices situated within communities invested with particular norms and values (Lewis, Enciso, & Moje, 2007). Adopting activities as a unit of analysis for examining life in classrooms begs the issue of what constitutes "context"—a complex and polysemic concept (Cole & Griffin, 1987).

Illustrating the complexity of activity, Engeström (1987, 1990) provides an expanded triangle characterizing human activity as a system comprised of subjects, (agents, viewpoints, or subjectivities); tools, (skills, equipment, ideas); the object (which provides motive); desired outcomes, (objects transformed into some end); rules (formal and informal, explicit or tacit ways of working with the object); a community (which shares the object with the subject, even if for different desired outcomes) and a division of labor (how actions are divided up in an activity).

We can apply this heuristic device to a hypothetical discussion of a class lesson as an activity. Let us position the teacher as the active subject. The teacher confronts a student or the students as the object of her work, to effect change in the children the "object."

The tools used might include a lesson plan, chalk and a blackboard, and past experiences. The students engage with the teacher and with one another. As the teacher acts toward the students/ object, she and others in the community who share the object (other students, others involved in the lesson plan, potentially including administrators concerned with what goes on in the classroom, or parents who hear about the child's day) are drawn together around the object but

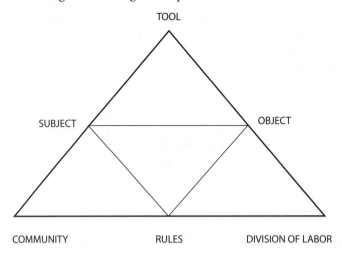

Figure 30.1 Engeström's expanded activity triangle.

hold variable orientations to it. Each participant is party to the work directed toward the object seeks to transform their own conception of the object into a desired outcome or end result, e.g., normatively, a successful lesson, a quiet student, a good speller, an efficient test taker, etc. Engeström's framework is a useful heuristic for analyzing the organization of educational activity and therefore the process of change at the micro level.

The Contexts of Interaction

Changes in practice are purposeful responses to features of context. That is to say, practices, even those deemed "best practices" are bound to their contexts and enjoy success or failure of impact accordingly. Therefore, the examination of such changes, be that at the level of classroom interaction, instruction, student achievement, etc., requires a broader unit of analysis that includes but is not limited to the implementation of a given instructional strategy or teaching technique (fidelity to practice) to examine impact i.e., practice effectiveness.

A cultural-historical framework requires consideration of the relationships between participants and the conditions (setting including but not limited to physical) of the practice in-use. From such a perspective, instructional strategies, in and of themselves, are benign (having no positive or ill effect). Rather, it is the conductions or context of their use that gives rise to success and/or failure of instruction/education. Accordingly, our emphasis is on understanding how as employed, instructional strategies in use (in-situ) influence teaching/learning.

Additional considerations include the variable positions and relationships to the instructional strategy held by teachers and researchers as part of the "practice." Often, researchers and teachers use different standards to deem a particular instructional approach "effective." Lessons are planned and prepared by a teacher whose explicit or implicit benchmarks gauge their success. Some of these criteria, though not all, are shared with more distant stakeholders represented by federal and district standards. The other participants in lessons, the students, also maintain both implicit and explicit definitions of success—definitions that may be quite distinct from those of teachers or policy makers.

On the one hand, the researcher who originated the innovation will likely document positive effects of its use. Teachers, on the other hand, may rightly consider the potential "effects" of its use within their particular classroom among their students. In the end, what one considers effective, for what purposes, and the degrees of effectiveness minimally required varies according to one's relative position. Nevertheless, the researcher may deem a strategy successful if 80% of the students experience 80% understanding 80% of the time. These results may be sufficient for significance that produces a publication.

Nonetheless, a teacher in practice is often ethically compelled to use additional instructional approaches in efforts to increase the degree of impact among all of his or her students. Rarely are these fundamental differences in goals and definition of "success" discussed among researchers. Despite the enormous ramifications for the implementation of an instructional practice and for student learning the different relative positions held by teachers and researchers is ignored. This critical oversight is particularly salient for students who experience school failure (Gandara et al., 2003).

In a functional way, the teaching practices that are deemed "effective" are those that have been systematically examined and whose significant results have been documented by sound research, what have currently come to be referred to as "research-based practices." Most academic journals publish studies that offer "solutions" or "what works." In this way, statements such as "if it is published/written it must be true" take on salience. Teachers' deference to researchers' knowledge engendered by the promotion of "research based practices" is a troubling trend within professional development.

In hopes of an increase in standardized test scores, teachers suppress their professional judgment when they elect the implementation of a strategy as described and prescribed by an often-unknown researcher. In effect, the "scripts" provided in the highly regulated implementation of effective practices may offer teachers a "language." Simultaneously, however, scripted instruction strips teachers of their professional "voices." From our view, an analysis of activity settings that reflects both objective and subjective aspects in communities of practice with personnel varying in not only scripts, but also beliefs and goals captures much of the value added by an evolving cultural theory focused on human development.

We do not diminish the potential of research-based practices for school reform. Yet, prescriptions for practice only have potential. What is needed to realize their effect are professionally grounded decisions made by competent teachers necessarily influenced by the great deal of diversity among what is thought to be "normative" classroom /school culture (Gallego & Cole, 2003).

Indeed, sociological research conducted in schools has consistently reported that the standard curriculum is rarely delivered nor received in a standard manner (cf., Anyon, 1980; Rist, 1970). Yet, educational research for "effective practice" often fails to document the varied ways that individual children experience a given teaching strategy/technique. Similarly, the myriad ways teachers interpret instructional strategies to better accommodate their classroom contexts are understudied. We believe that this time of teachers' fidelity to their students and to their profession is underappreciated.

We argue that teachers' practices be guided by a common sense range of fidelity to an instructional practice that takes into account the elements of each classroom life graphically represented by Engeström's (1987, 1990) expanded triangle. Indeed, this heuristic is a valuable tool to analyze the multiple directional tensions that researchers, teachers and policy makers navigate when considering instructional policy.

No Population Category Left Behind

As important as individual achievement is, especially for the individual whose achievement is being measured, we argue that even more than no child left behind, no population category should be left behind and propose a historical analysis of this persisting glitch in the system. Dismantling Group-Based Inequality, i.e., statistically disproportional disparity at the population level, must include a recognition and analysis of the histories of power relations among the groups and individuals of which schools are comprised and the specific and myriad contexts in which such power-inequalities have been historically established and sustained (Lewis et al., 2007; P. R. Portes, 1996; P. R. Portes & Salas, in press). It is therefore essential to underscore the importance of policy actions that aimed at dismantling the distributed mechanisms that shape or, in Vygotskian parlance, "mediate" the educational underdevelopment of many U.S. Latinos in a supposedly fair and equitable system of public education.

For this reason, policy makers perhaps need to think and function more like engineers, designing and implementing a system locally that consistently educates L-SPARs at grade level, from preschool preparation to college. Seamless approaches require support across districts and states for group differences to be systemically minimized. In other words, the learning that a preschool or the elementary grade(s) initiates must be sustained and sustainable as L-SPARS continue through K-16 and beyond.

A historical, mediated action approach would focus on altering various contexts through which incompatibility is constructed between L-SPARs' home and school life developmentally. It would help prevent and reverse many of the processes that currently place low SES students at-risk before they actually become risks. A lifespan-developmental model calls for a set of concerted actions in mediating the development of children from cultures placed at-risk.

P. R. Portes' (2005) macro framework for dismantling educational inequality advocates organizing policy action at four levels (better preschool preparation for all L-SPARs, elementary school supports, a life-skills adolescent curriculum, and higher education transformation in preparing educators and all others) in a seamless approach to sustain development of L-SPARs (see Figure 30.2).

- Young, poor, competent children having access to effective Head Start and other quality preschool programs are represented in the component at the top of Figure 30.1. For language learners, it is critical that their potential for bilingual development is assisted early in dual immersion, enriched learning environments. Once in elementary school, they would again encounter a new set of supports for mediated learning in and out of school with the primary goal of learning and performing at grade level each year. This restructuring calls for col-

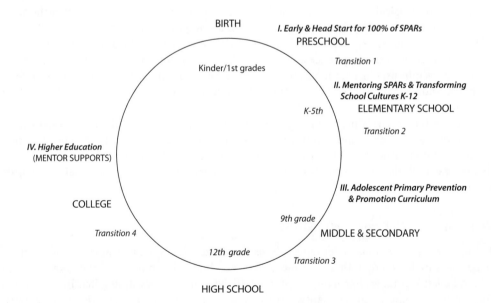

Figure 30.2 An intergenerational model—maximizing mediation, equity, and development means.

lege students and/or community personnel to participate in an additive plan by serving as mentors in after-school programs for L-SPARs. Again, support for literacy in two languages is critical in this model since the advantages of additive bilingualism are essential for this population (P. R. Portes & Salas, 2007).

- As adolescents, they would continue to have extra academic support to remain at grade level. In secondary schools, they would complete the cycle by participating in life-skills workshops focused on human and educational development to be structured within the educational system as a prevention/promotion strategy essential to those now under-represented. In addition to providing L-SPARs full coverage or support as they grow, direct academic supports in and out of school would be sustained to prevent the gap from emerging. What is most unique about this component is a two-step strategy that melds cognitive development with primary prevention. Adolescents often do not develop higher level, abstract thinking unless they interact with others, directly or peripherally in activities that promote critical thinking through a future orientation. The present system reserves the latter conditions for those already advantaged. Our model, instead, insists on fomenting life skills, both academic and socio-emotional, regardless of what NCLB tests. Empowering adolescents to act with formal operational thinking is a must for closing the achievement gap for it impacts indirectly on parent involvement and child development from an intergenerational perspective (P. R. Portes, 2005). Too often, the least advantaged students are the least likely to receive means to develop abstract life skills that can help future offspring obtain better parent involvement. Because the least advantaged children's parents are more often poor, this form of overcompensation in a culture free higher-order thinking might transfer toward the activation of the most illusive and important predictors of school success. Investing in future parents who are more likely to be involved in their family is a structural suggestion that aims to educate the whole child in life skills regarding child development, interpersonal skills, health and areas not dictated by today's mindless pursuit of bigger, better, and faster outcomes and school productivity.

- The political economy still today also dictates class sizes that are not in the best interests of those who would close the achievement gap. A strategy that links more helping means with better teachers in smaller groups almost year long would combine more academic learning time with strategic assisted development to improve learning (Kozulin, Gindis, Ageyev, & Miller, 2003; Ramey & Ramey, 2004).

- The last component requires transformations in the very professional preparation of educators and others in higher education. They need to be prepared with a more complete cultural knowledge base that can help drive the other components in reducing group based inequality which lies in the heart of the achievement gap. It is in this setting that future decision-makers are socialized and often insulated from understanding how a caste-like society is sustained each generation. In this dialectical framework, change must not be limited to just assisting under-represented groups but also educating the dominant groups through lived experiences in assisting others from our primary prevention lens. Primary prevention is defined by addressing the genesis of a disease or disorder (in human development) before symptoms emerge, at a time when it is most cost-effective to prevent the problem. The problem here is the imposition and organization of multiple risk factors in the lives of poor ethnic children in disproportional fashion on the basis of cultural history (that is not an option for most).

At the same time that we advocate aggressive and systemic change for dismantling group based inequality K-16, we recognize the possibility that even if all L-SPARs were at grade level, relative differences would remain that would still leave L-SPARs behind in many other (economic) areas. If poverty is likely to remain associated with ethnic membership, it need not be produced by a system and cause a disproportionate segment to perform below grade level.

Conclusions and Implications

At no time in history has the interaction among high proportions of poverty-bound, language learning children and high standards coalesced so extremely as to form a system that almost predictably leaves Latinos behind. One in four children under six are Latinos and of these many more need to be participating in quality preschools—institutional interventions associated with school success and lower drop out rates (Calderon, 2007). A bleak future awaits disproportionate numbers of children of immigrants in public institutions that consistently fail to provide language and cultural support required to keep students' performance at grade level (P. R. Portes & Salas, 2007).

Rather than synthesize the references we have complied in this chapter, we conclude by focusing one of the more neglected contradictions that must be addressed in Latino education today:

> How is it that one of the key and most empirically proven bases of knowledge, additive bilingualism that clearly suggests how language support can be best practice for a growing population left behind be ignored by policy and practices in education?

As research and policy continues to look for ways to help language learners placed at risk by poverty, additive bilingualism has been already shown to work (August & Hakuta, 1997; Chambers & Parrish, 1992; Thomas & Collier, 1996). Curiously, school districts continue to invest heavily in "pull out," sheltering or "push in" methods and practices—the default language support option offered to most poor Latino and other children of immigrants. Current pull-out/pull-in practices potentially have yet to be proven to given them any sustainable edge K-12. Likewise, sheltered instruction remains largely unproven as an alternative to current teacher preparation that might help English language learners catch up. Furthermore, although stories abound *a la* Horatio Alger about the survivors, the few L-SPARS who stand and deliver, more than four decades of multicultural teacher education has had little if no impact on the achievement gap at a national scale (see, P. R. Portes & Salas, 2007).

Despite its unique longitudinal research base, bilingual education is in Massachusetts, for example, outlawed. In other cases, bilingual education is simply ignored and/or under-applied. Precisely, the logic model we see operating by the dominant group's policy makers is to ignore the intellectual and economic benefits on having a more literate nation and to continue relying on the trickle of bilingual educators for very small groups of students without a systemic effort exists to prepare bilingual/bilingual content area teachers.

The bilingual educators that we do have in schools today are generally of three backgrounds: (a) non-Hispanic White background who are themselves Spanish learners; (b) native Spanish speakers who themselves have struggled to graduate from degree programs (we draw attention to the statistic that college bound seniors from Latino background score consistently lower in critical reading, math, and writing in the SAT; those who score lower are more likely become certified educators); and (c) foreign nationals on temporary visas (cf., P. R. Portes, Delgado-Romero, & Salas, in press).

All this is to say, the majority of Latino children will encounter disparities in learning and teaching each grade in school. Once the lack of language support tracks them into lower levels, the system logically produces or co-constructs group identity related discrepancies that last a lifetime and influence the next generation. We challenge the logic of a system of education for certain groups of children whose development is promoted less than others—possibly by design, certainly by law, and with no sign of a policy action change amidst compelling evidence for closing a learning gap it has structured

In light of overwhelming evidence about supporting development for English learners using the meaning-making literacy in the first language as English proficiency is being established, we conclude with the challenge and logic of ethics and the notion of an ethical K-16 system. A societal response to the conglomerated problem of under education, poor health and health care, and violence needs to be considered much as that of breaking the law to obtain a reliable cure for a dying relative when robbing a pharmacy.

If we already know that the underdevelopment of a population can be addressed by policies and practices that administer an effective treatment that is not only bilingual education but also an English plus approach, how ethical is it to take less "effective" approach or even no action at all. What are the repercussions of his course of (in) action, of this logic on the future of the emerging caste-like society in which we live? Do current think tanks consider the current language policy wise and in the best interest of a nation that leads a global economy? Aside from the benefits of reducing the achievement gap through evidenced-based changes in education, the developmental and cognitive advantages of additive bilingualism as social capital for the nation also deserves policy consideration.

We are mindful that our future readers will most likely still be dealing with the dialectic of diversity and hegemony for decades to come. As intellectuals, we extend the cultural historical framework toward ethics as we question what effective practice means and could mean. Confronted by the stark realities awaiting millions of capable children, we believe that promoting change to diminish the costly discrepancies instantiated daily at the group level is an ethical and moral imperative.

While various cultural historical perspectives have insisted on specificity of contexts, we resist at a policy level the potential myopia that an over-focus on testing and faux accountability might produce. Authentic efforts at confronting the internal tensions within the loose federation of what we deemed as a cultural historical paradigm are needed—now, more than ever. Namely, we underscore the need for concerted and systemic mediated praxis for radically reforming the structures and, by consequence, the outcomes of the current system that place too many Latinos at risk. A different, more cogent type of accountability is needed. Cultural historical approaches cannot only help us understand how entire populations have been left and are kept behind on the margins of dominant U.S. cultures, but also recognize the centrality of educational policy in mediating the development of our societies. Even more, cultural historical theory lays the foundation for policies and praxis for reshaping U.S. society in ways in which we might one day be prouder and for which we might one day be wiser.

References

Achinstein, B., & Ogawa, R. T. (2006). (In)Fidelity: What the resistance of new teachers reveals about professional principles and prescriptive educational policies. *Harvard Educational Review, 76*(1), 30–63.

Anyon, J. (1980). Social class and the hidden curriculum of work. *Journal of Education, 162*(1), 69–92.

August, D., & Hakuta, K. (1997). *Improving schooling for language-minority children: A research agenda.* Washington, DC: National Academy Press.

Bakhtin, M. M. (1981). *The dialogic imagination: Four essays* (M. Holquist & C. Emerson, Trans.). Austin: University of Texas Press.

Bakhtin, M. M. (1986). *Speech genres and other late essays* (M. Holquist & C. Emerson, Trans. 1st ed.). Austin: University of Texas Press.

Calderon, M. (2007). *Buenos principios: Latino children in the earliest years of life.* Washington DC: National Council of La Raza.

Chambers, J., & Parrish, T. (1992). *Meeting the challenge of diversity: An evaluation of programs for pupils with limited proficiency in English. Vol. IV, cost of programs and services for LEP students.* Berkeley, CA: BW Associates.

Chapa, J., & De La Rosa, B. (2004). Latino population growth, socioeconomic and demographic characteristics, and implications for educational attainment. *Education and Urban Society, 36*(2), 130–149.

Cole, M. (1996). *Cultural psychology: A once and future discipline.* Cambridge, MA: Belknap Press of Harvard University Press.

Cole, M., & Griffin, P. (1987). *Contextual factors in education.* Madison: Wisconsin Center for Education Research.

Education Trust. (2003). A new core curriculum for all: Aiming high for other people's children. *Thinking K-16, 7,* 1–29.

Engeström, Y. (1987). *Learning by expanding.* Helsinki, Finland: Orinta-Konsultit Oy.

Engeström, Y. (1990). *Learning, working, and imagining: Twelve studies in activity theory.* Helsinki, Finland: Orinta-Konsultit.

Fry, R. (2002). *Latinos in higher education: Many enroll, too few graduate.* Washington, DC: Pew Hispanic Center.

Fry, R. (2004). *Latino youth finishing college: The role of selective pathways.* Washington, DC: Pew Hispanic Center.

Fry, R. (2005). *Recent changes in the entry of Hispanic and White youth into college.* Washington, DC: Pew Hispanic Center.

Gallego, M. A., & Cole, M. (2003). Classroom culture and cultures in the classroom. In V. Richardson (Ed.), *The handbook of research on teaching* (pp. 951–997). Washington DC: American Educational Research Association.

Gandara, P., Rumberger, R., Maxwell-Jolly, J., & Callahan, R. (2003). English learners in California schools: Unequal resources, unequal outcomes. *Educational Policy Analysis Archives, 11*(36), 1–54.

Gutiérrez, K. D., Asato, J., Santos, M., & Gotanda, N. (2002). Backlash pedagogy: Language and culture and the politics of reform. *Review of Education, Pedagogy, & Cultural Studies, 24*(4), 335–351.

Gutiérrez, K. D., Baquedano-Lopez, P., & Alvarez, H. H. (2000). The crisis in Latino education: The norming of America. In C. Tejeda, C. Martinez & Z. Leonardo (Eds.), *Charting new terrains of Chicana(o)/Latina(o) Education* (pp. 213–232). Cresskill, NJ: Hampton Press.

Holland, D. C., & Valsiner, J. (1988). Cognition, symbols, and Vygotsky's developmental psychology. *Ethos, 16*(3), 247–272.

Kozulin, A. (1984). *Psychology in utopia: Toward a social history of Soviet psychology.* Cambridge, MA: MIT Press.

Kozulin, A. (1998). *Psychological tools: A sociocultural approach to education.* Cambridge, MA: Harvard University Press.

Kozulin, A., Gindis, B., Ageyev, V., & Miller, S. (Eds.). (2003). *Vygotsky's educational theory in cultural context.* New York: Cambridge University Press.

Lave, J., & Wenger, E. (1991). *Situated learning: Legitimate peripheral participation.* Cambridge, UK: Cambridge University Press.

Leont'ev, A. N. (1978). *Activity, consciousness and personality.* Englewood Cliffs, NJ: Prentice Hall.

Leont'ev, A. N. (1981). *Problems of the development of the mind.* Moscow: Progress Publishers.

Lewis, C., Encisco, P., & Moje, E. (2007). *Reframing sociocultural research on literacy.* Mahwah, NJ: Erlbaum.

Luria, A. R. (1976). *Cognitive development, its cultural and social foundations.* Cambridge, MA: Harvard University Press.

Luria, A. R. (1979). *The making of mind: A personal account of Soviet psychology* (M. Cole & S. Cole, Trans.). Cambridge, MA: Harvard University Press.

Moll, L. C., & Ruiz, R. (2002). The schooling of Latino children. In M. M. Suárez-Orozco & M. Páez (Eds.), *Latinos: Remaking America* (pp. 362–374). Berkley: University of California.

National Council of La Raza. (2007). *Hispanic education in the United States.* Washington DC: Author.

Orfield, G., & Chungmai, L. (2007). *Historic reversals, accelerating resegregation, and the need for new integration strategies.* Retrieved January 10, 2008, from http://www.civilrights.org/assets/pdfs/aug-2007-desegregation-report.pdf

Passel, J., & Cohn, D. (2008). *U.S. population projections: 2005–2050.* Washington, DC: Pew Research Center.

Portes, A., & Rumbaut, R. G. (2001). *Legacies: The story of the immigrant second generation.* Berkeley: University of California Press.

Portes, P. R. (1996). Ethnicity and culture in educational psychology. In D. Berliner & R. Calfee (Eds.), *The handbook of educational psychology* (pp. 331–357). New York: Macmillian.

Portes, P. R. (1999). Social and psychological factors in the academic achievement of children of immigrants: A cultural history puzzle. *American Educational Research Journal, 36*(3), 489–507.

Portes, P. R. (2005). *Dismantling educational inequality: A cultural-historical approach to closing the achievement gap.* New York: Peter Lang.

Portes, P. R., Delgado-Romero, E., & Salas, S. (in press). Latinos (not) in higher education and the continuum of group based inequality: A cultural historical perspective. In D. Sandhu, B. Hudson, & M. Taylor-Archer (Eds.), *A handbook of diversity in higher education.* New York: Nova Science Publishers.

Portes, P. R., & Salas, S. (2007). Dreams deferred: Why multicultural education has failed to close the achievement gap: A cultural historical analysis. *C & E-Cultura y Educacíon, 19*(4), 365–377.

Portes, P. R., & Salas, S. (in press). Poverty and its relation to development and literacy. In L. Morrow, R. Rueda & D. Lapp (Eds.), *Handbook of research on literacy instruction: Issues of diversity, policy, and equity.* New York: Guilford.

President's Advisory Commission on Educational Excellence for Hispanic Americans. (1996). *Our nation on the fault line: Hispanic American education.* Washington, DC: Author.

President's Advisory Commission on Educational Excellence for Hispanic Americans. (2000). *Creating the will: Hispanics achieving educational excellence. A report to the President of the United States, the Secretary of Education, and the nation.* Washington, DC: Author.

President's Advisory Commission on Educational Excellence for Hispanic Americans. (2002). *The road to a college diploma: The complex reality of raising educational achievement for Hispanics in the United States. An interim report.* Washington, DC: White House Initiative on Educational Excellence for Hispanic Americans.

Ramey, C., & Ramey, S. (2004). Early learning and school readiness: Can early intervention make a difference? *Merrill-Palmer Quarterly, 50*(4), 471–491.

Rist, R. C. (1970). Student social class and teacher expectations: The self-fulfilling prophecy. *Harvard Educational Review, 40*(3), 411–451.

Salomon, G. (1993). *Distributed cognitions: Psychological and educational considerations.* Cambridge, UK: Cambridge University Press.

Sanchez, G. J. (1997). Face the nation: Race, immigration, and the rise of nativism in late Twentieth Century America. *International Migration Review, 31*(4), 1009–1030.

Scribner, S., & Cole, M. (1981). *The psychology of literacy.* Cambridge, MA: Harvard University Press.

Spring, J. H. (2004). *Deculturalization and the struggle for equality: A brief history of the education of dominated cultures in the United States* (4th ed.). Boston: McGraw-Hill.

Thomas, W. P., & Collier, V. P. (1996). *Language Minority Student Achievement and Program Effectiveness.* Fairfax, VA: Center for Bilingual/Multicultural/ESL Education, George Mason University.

Valdés, G. (1996). *Con respeto: Bridging the distances between culturally diverse families and schools: An ethnographic portrait.* New York: Teachers College Press.

Valdés, G. (2001). *Learning and not learning English: Latino students in American schools.* New York: Teachers College Press.

Valencia, R. R., & Suzuki, L. A. (2001). *Intelligence testing and minority students : Foundations, performance factors, and assessment issues.* Thousand Oaks, CA: Sage.

Valenzuela, A. (1999). *Subtractive schooling: U.S.-Mexican youth and the politics of caring.* Albany: State University of New York Press.

Valenzuela, A. (2000). The significance of the TAAS test for Mexican immigrant and Mexican American adolescents: A case study. *Hispanic Journal of Behavioral Sciences, 22*(4), 524–539.

Valenzuela, A. (2004). *Leaving children behind: Why Texas-style accountability fails Latino youth.* Albany: State University of New York Press.

Van der Veer, R., & Valsiner, J. (Eds.). (1994). *The Vygostky reader.* Oxford, UK: Blackwell.

Vygotsky, L. S. (1978). *Mind in society: The development of higher psychological processes* (M. Cole, V. John-Steiner, S. Scribner, & E. Souberman, Trans.). Cambridge, MA: Harvard University Press.

Vygotsky, L.S. (1986), *Thought and language* (A. Kozulin, Trans., rev. ed.). Cambridge, MA: MIT Press.

Wertsch, J. V. (1985). *Vygotsky and the social formation of mind.* Cambridge, MA: Harvard University Press.

Wertsch, J. V. (1998). *Mind as action.* New York: Oxford University Press.

Wertsch, J. V. (2002). *Voices of collective remembering.* Cambridge, UK: Cambridge University Press.

31 "Who are These Kids, Rejects from Hell?"

Analyzing Hollywood Distortions of Latina/o High School Students

Tara J. Yosso and David G. García
University of California, Santa Barbara

Introduction

> I can't think of even one Chicano [on film] that played a part as a teacher or doctor or edu-
> cated person. (Antonio, quoted in Yosso, 2000, p. 101)[1]

Chicana/o students such as Antonio may not recall seeing themselves portrayed "as a teacher or doctor, or educated person" because too often, mainstream Hollywood filmmakers depict Latinas/os[2] using derogatory racial stereotypes. Film scholars have documented persistent patterns of Latina/o misrepresentation and critiqued the social psychological significance of these racialized and gendered media portrayals (Beltran, 2008; Keller, 1985, 1994; Pettit, 1980; Ramírez Berg, 2002; Rodriguez, 1997; Woll, 1977). Researchers have also examined how media-based beliefs about Latina/o intelligence, moral character, cultural values, and physical appearance influence Latina/o youth (e.g., Baez, 2008; Yosso, 2000, 2002) and shape public policy (e.g,. Bender, 2003; Delgado & Stefancic, 1992; Romero, 2001; Santa Ana, 2002). To expand on this scholarly literature, this chapter analyzes Hollywood film portrayals of urban high schools, focusing on their tendency to feature one-dimensional, negative images of Latina/o students. By presenting a distorted view of Latina/o youth, these cultural texts contribute to a history of institutional neglect of Latinas/os in U.S. public schools.

Historian Carlos Cortés (1992) explains, "so-called entertainment media...have a major impact in shaping beliefs, attitudes, values, perceptions, and 'knowledge' and influencing decisions and action. In short, movies teach" (p. 75). From 1955 to the present, Hollywood films have "taught" mass audiences about urban Latina/o high school students using a formulaic narrative. This formula tends to focus on an optimistic (White) novice teacher struggling to inspire urban (Black and Latina/o) youth. Often, in the introductory classroom scene students shoot spit wads and dance on the desks, fight with one another, ignore, or otherwise completely disrespect their new teacher. A student usually brutalizes and/or sexually threatens a female teacher in the first act. Having lost their belief in the sense of service or mission, deflated faculty work in misery to collect a paycheck and seek refuge from students in the teacher's lounge. The protagonist teacher distinguishes him/herself from these pessimists, determined to make a difference. Administrators perpetuate the system with cynical, authoritative, and often hostile management. Delinquent and remedial students eventually become inspired to learn academic basics, build up self-respect, and to pursue their education. The story of a male teacher/administrator protagonist often includes excessive violence and physical threats to force student achievement. The narrative of a female protagonist tends to focus on the process of establishing trust with students in a nurturing classroom, and usually features a scene where students show their teacher how to dance. The repetition of this cinematic formula contributes to publicly accepted myths about Latinas/os, endorsing politically conservative agendas that seek to rationalize a racially separate and unequal schooling system.

While the packaging of this formula has altered slightly from dramatic "uplifting" films to comedic parodies and action-thrillers, Hollywood's urban high school genre resurrects racialized allegations similar to those found in early 1900's biological determinist theories. Proponents of biological determinism claimed academic underachievement stemmed from inherent Latina/o and African American genetic deficiencies. For example, one of the main importers and translators of Alfred Binet's IQ test, Lewis Terman (1916), believed that Mexican and Black students "should be segregated into separate classes…They cannot master abstractions but they can often be made efficient workers" (pp. 91–92). Throughout the first half of the 20th century, such eugenicist views endorsed testing practices and policies that facilitated school segregation by race, emphasizing domestic skills and manual labor for Blacks and Latinas/os while regularly mislabeling Spanish-speaking students "Educable Mentally Retarded" (see Valencia & Solórzano, 1997). By the late 1960s, many social scientists shifted their blame of genetic makeup to focus primarily on cultural attributes seemingly responsible for disparate student achievement (see Solórzano & Yosso, 2002). They claimed dysfunctional cultural values, attitudes, and behaviors generate from problematic internal social structures within Latina/o families (e.g., large, disorganized households, Spanish or nonstandard English spoken in the home). Following this argument, since Latina/o parents fail to embrace the values of the dominant group, they hinder the social mobility of their children and reproduce a culture of poverty (Heller, 1966; Lewis, 1968). Ostensibly, Latina/o students display cultural values incongruent with schools, including a present time orientation (versus future), immediate gratification (instead of deferred), and an emphasis on cooperation (rather than competition). As a result of their socialization then, Latina/o students supposedly arrive at the classroom door with cultural "disadvantages" and a "distaste" for education that renders them almost "uneducable" (Banfield, 1970; Madsen, 1964; Sowell, 1981). To explain contemporary unequal educational outcomes, some social scientists continue to rely on the overtly racist arguments of the biological determinists, claiming Black and Chicana/o, Latina/o students show signs of diminished mental capacity in relation to Whites (e.g., Hernnstein & Murray, 1994), but more subtle cultural deficit arguments remain most prevalent. Schools continue to implement these deficit traditions by tracking Latina/o students toward remedial and vocational programs of study, promoting an "Americanized" cultural literacy curriculum (Hirsch, 1988, 1996; see Buras, 2008), and labeling Latina/o youth "at-risk."

In previous work, we challenged claims that the cultural knowledges, skills, abilities, and networks of People of Color hold very little, if any, value (Yosso & García, 2007). Such a historically inaccurate view of Latina/o communities creates myths about Latinas/os not valuing school and being somehow satisfied with underachievement (Baca Zinn, 1989; Garcia & Guerra, 2004; Valencia & Black, 2002). Blaming a supposedly faulty Latina/o value system for unequal social outcomes ignores the legacy of racism structuring these disparities. These claims also omit the history of Latina/o resistance to racism and the contributions of Mexican Americans in particular to struggles for educational equality. In social science theory and on film, racial mythmaking rationalizes the systematic discrimination of Latinas/os in schools. Because "movies help organize information and ideas about racial, ethnic, cultural, and national groups," they also "tend to reiterate and legitimize racial, ethnic, and social hierarchies" (Cortés, 1992, p. 82). Before examining the reiteration of these hierarchies in *Blackboard Jungle* (1955), *Dangerous Minds* (1995), and *187* (1997), we outline how films contribute to a "societal curriculum" steeped in racism and cultural deficit theory.

Historical Imperatives of Racial Stereotyping in an Era of Segregation

> Alongside school operates a parallel educational system, 'the societal curriculum'.... Within that societal curriculum, the media serve as pervasive, relentless, lifelong educators. (Cortés, 1992, p. 75)

> When I see movies and things that portray Chicanos in a bad way, I feel that they are putting us down. That's how other people feel about us...they see us and they see, 'Oh, that's how a Mexican is in school, that's why we're like that, that's why we don't progress or develop or grow as a people'. (Sara, quoted in Yosso, 2000, p. 140)[3]

Cortés' remark about the teaching function of media and Sara's observation about film portrayals informing larger social views about Chicana/o students challenge us to consider the "historical imperatives" served by cinematic lesson plans (Williams, 1985, p. 60). In analyzing how exaggerated racial beliefs inform imagery in entertainment media, we must not lose focus on the ideology that makes them possible—racism (Pierce, 1975, 1980). An ideology can be defined as a set of beliefs that explain or justify an actual or potential social arrangement. Ideologically, racism justifies White supremacy—the dominance of one race over others (Lorde, 1992; Marable, 1992). Just as racism intersects with other forms of subordination (e.g., gender, class, immigrant status, language), racial stereotypes also exhibit layers of gendered, classed, and nativist prejudice (Arriola, 1997; Valdes, 1998). Within a society founded on racism, stereotypes function as ideological tools that validate structures of systematic discrimination against those deemed racially inferior. Gordon Allport (1979) defined a stereotype as "an exaggerated belief associated with a category. Its function is to justify (rationalize) our conduct in relation to that category" (p. 191). Charles Ramírez Berg (1997) describes six basic film stereotypes of Latinas/os: the (a) *Bandido*, (b) Halfbreed Harlot, (c) Male Buffoon, (d) Female Clown, (e) Latin Lover, and (f) Dark Lady. Over the last century of filmmaking, he notes, "the core, defining characteristics [of Latina/o stereotypes] remain remarkably consistent" (Ramírez Berg, 1997, p. 113).

While we agree with Ramírez Berg, we also note these film stereotypes of Latinas/os, in their subtle and overt forms, have become so ubiquitous that both Latinas/os and Whites argue they are innocuous. Challenges to derogatory images of Latinas/os often elicit accusations of being too sensitive because "it's just a movie." This position dismisses the cultural and political implications of racist ideologies on film. Indeed, repeated imagery featuring irrational, violent, sexually promiscuous, unintelligent, and morally depraved Latinas/os upholds beliefs about White superiority and affirms the naturalness and necessity for Latina/o subordination (Almaguer, 1994; Flores, 1973). For our purposes here, we focus on the ways racial and cultural stereotypes of Latinas/os subtly shape public perception, electoral politics, and legal and educational discourse (Bender, 2003; Santa Ana, 2002; Solórzano, 1997).

Assessing such cinematic impact remains a complex task because films function as our society's main public narrative, created for mass distribution and replayed for generations (Cortés, 1995). Hollywood studios recognize and capitalize on the power of films to influence public perceptions and social policy. Filmmakers, just as other professionals, are aware of the impacts of their work. When it comes to images of Latina/o students, filmmakers have overtly sought to influence public perceptions about how to school these youth.

Hollywood reveals its consciousness about the power of film as a public text in World War II efforts to comply with President Franklin D. Roosevelt's 1940s Good Neighbor Policy. Nelson D. Rockefeller's Office for the Coordination of Inter-American Affairs recruited Walt Disney's assistance to court war alliances in Latin America (Woll, 1980). This collaboration resulted in two animated features wherein singing Latino birds celebrate the music and cultural wonders of Mexico and Brazil (*Saludos Amigos*, 1943; *The Three Caballeros*, 1945). With such direct propaganda films, The Rockefeller Committee sought to extend a symbolic "bouquet to every Latin

Country by telling and showing them what each country is contributing towards victory" (Woll, 1977, p. 56). Though Mexican advocacy groups had been mobilizing against racially derogatory portrayals on the silver screen for years, the transformation of greasers, *bandidos*, and spitfires into happy dancing, singing Latinas/os (e.g., Carmen Miranda) came only when the United States needed their Good Neighbors' resources for the war (Keller, 1985, 1994; Woll, 1977). Still, in creating these friendlier images, Hollywood tacitly admitted that films do hold power to impact social views and political relations. By the end of WWII, for the most part, Hollywood returned to the practice of portraying Latinas/os as stereotypical villains and promiscuous women.[4]

The subsequent 1950s blacklisting of films and filmmakers suspected of exhibiting communist sympathies further evidence Hollywood's concession that films project political ideologies and influence social views. For example, efforts to censure, shut down, and blacklist those involved in producing *Salt of the Earth* (1954), occurred in part because the film challenges cultural stereotypes. Based on an actual miner's strike in New Mexico, the film portrays a predominately Mexican American cast standing up against racism and economic exploitation by forming a workers' union. The filmmakers also depict Mexican American women displaying their agency by creating a ladies' auxiliary and taking over the picket line (see Baker, 2007). Benjamin Balthaser (2008) explains that *Salt of the Earth* challenges "central cultural and institutional doctrines of the postwar order: maintenance of the color line, the cold war cult of domesticity, and more than anything, the notion of labor-management 'peace' as key to the prosperity of working-class Americans" (p. 347).

That same year, the U.S. Supreme Court demonstrated acute awareness of the political ideologies their decisions presented to a mass audience. According to legal scholar Derrick Bell (1980, 1987), the 1954 *Brown v. Board of Education* (347 U.S. 483) decision to declare segregated schooling unconstitutional occurred in part as a public relations strategy, to uphold the moral standing of the United States as the champion of freedom and democracy. He argues that Whites in positions of leadership and power had begun to recognize that *de jure* racial segregation undermined the image of a colorblind U.S. society, and potentially threatened their ability to assert global power. Pressure to practice the democratic freedom the United States preached internationally and increasing domestic demand for an educated workforce in the newly industrialized South influenced the landmark 1954 ruling (see also Dudziak, 1988, 2000). In Bell's analysis then, the court's school desegregation decision evidenced the convergence of African American interests with the maintenance of the White power structure. In assessing civil rights gains since this time, he concludes, "the interest of blacks in achieving racial equality will be accommodated only when it converges with the interests of whites" (1980, p. 523).

Certainly, we remain concerned about this "interest-convergence" principle, especially in relation to the unrealized promise of *Brown* for Latina/o students (Perea, 2004; Valencia, Menchaca, & Donato, 2002).[5] To narrow our focus, we address the rarely acknowledged, yet conscious process of projecting ideological messages in the "societal curriculum." We are particularly interested in the timing of Hollywood's ideological messages about Latina/o students in relation to desegregation legislation and *de facto* segregation in California's public high schools. Our discussion of this evolution emphasizes the 1950s and the 1990s.

Ushering in an Era of Integration with the Urban High School Genre

> Whether situated in the past, present, or future, commercial motion pictures invariably resonate with the value crises of the times in which they appear. Thus, they are historical in the sense of being cultural artifacts and social-history evidence about the times in which they were made. But films are historical in another way as well: they reposition us for the future by reshaping our memories of the past. (Lipsitz, 1990, p. 164)

The 1955 film *Blackboard Jungle* inaugurated the narrative formula that became the urban high school genre featuring Youth of Color and including at least one identifiable Latino student. George Lipsitz (1990) suggests Hollywood films function as socio-cultural artifacts and lenses through which we reinterpret history. These cinematic texts reflect a very limited understanding of Latina/o students in particular.

Released one year after the *Brown v. Board of Education* desegregation case, *Blackboard Jungle* opens with scrolling text describing "producers'" concerns about increasing juvenile delinquency in urban schools. As the statement scrolls, the song "Rock around the Clock" blasts. Critics would later note how this editing established an enduring link between juvenile delinquency and rock-and-roll music. Written and directed by Richard Brooks, based on the novel by the same title, the film's plot recounts the story of a first year White male (former Navy serviceman) English teacher, Richard Dadier (Glenn Ford), at the all-boys North Manuel Trades High School. Set in New York City, the overcrowded, racially integrated school includes a large cast of ostensibly delinquent youth portrayed as predominately working-class Whites, and a handful of Blacks and Latinos. At the rally opening the school year, the only female teacher receives whistles and heckles from the mob of unruly, hormonally charged students. Early on in the school year, a White student attacks this teacher in the library. Just as she is about to be raped, Dadier fights off the assailant and saves his colleague. Violent and disrespectful students terrorize even the most optimistic of the all-White faculty. A particularly cynical veteran teacher explains to his novice colleagues, "This is the garbage can of the educational system. You take most of these kids and put them together and what do you get? One big, fat, overflowing garbage can."

The plot follows with scenes of Dadier seeking ways to engage his students, who appear disinterested in what "Daddy-oh" might have to teach. A young Sidney Poitier portrays Gregory Miller, the featured Black student in Dadier's rowdy English class, who initially appears to be the main agitator of the class' disrespectful antics and inattention. For example, while loud construction noises drone over his already rowdy class, a persistent Dadier instructs his students to take turns speaking into a voice recorder to learn techniques of public speech. Miller asks Dadier to choose the only Latino in the class, Pete Morales (Rafael Campos), asking, "You against Morales because he don't speak good English?" Hesitantly, Dadier invites Morales to give the first impromptu speech.

Morales: (to microphone) I got up at 7:30, go wash, but my stinkin' sister, she stayed in the bathroom, so I can't get in (class laughter).
Dadier: That's fine boy, just keep talking.
Morales: (to recorder and class) So then I go to stinkin' bathroom, I wash my stinkin' face and then I eat some stinkin' sausages (class laughter)
White student 1: Say it louder, come on.
White student 2: We can't hear you in the balcony!
Morales: (to class) So then I meet, I go down the stinkin' street, with my stinkin' books, and then I meet this stink face who lives near me. (class laughter) And he says, ah, 'you go to school Pete?' So I says, 'you stinkin' right bo.' (class laughter) So we walk to stinkin' L, and we wait for stinkin' train, and what do you think? The stinkin' train is late. So I gotta get into a stinkin' crowd. (laughs at self) And that's why I'm stinkin' late to school Teach. (class laughter) How was I, O, OK?

Even though the film is supposed to take place in a high school, Morales appears with an elementary-style alphabet banner behind his head, highlighting the ABC's across the screen and the American flag prominently placed to his left. These symbols, together with a brown-skinned youth using crude limited-English amidst class laughter, strongly suggest Morales' presence is not a natural fit in an "American" academic setting.

In other significant scenes, a number of youth depicted as Eastern European immigrants, threaten Dadier in a dimly lit alley outside of school. This attempted mugging occurs in apparent retaliation for Dadier's earlier act of chivalry on behalf of the female teacher. Later, to seek advice and encouragement, Dadier visits his former teacher at a private school, where he witnesses classes of well-behaved, intellectually engaged and respectful White students. Here, the camera pans the school's auditorium full of students singing "The Star Spangled Banner" in perfect harmony. With this scene, screenwriter/director Brooks hammers audience over the head with a view of good and bad schools, which idealizes "American" (White) students while issuing a warning about racially integrated urban youth.

Back at North Manual Trades, Dadier continues to struggle to overcome the cynicism and apathy of his faculty colleagues. He feels burdened with a sense of urgency to keep his job and continue believing in his students' potential. The stress of his job and threats from students lead his wife to go into preterm labor and push Dadier to his wits' end.

Dadier's persistence begins to win over the respect of most of his students, and he finds inspiration in a very unlikely source. Miller volunteers to help coordinate and to sing in the school's Christmas show. In the classroom, a climatic fight scene occurs, where two students try to stab Dadier, and the rest of the class, led by Miller, beat up the delinquents and support Dadier in bringing them to the principal's office for expulsion. Dadier decides that if Miller is not a lost cause, there may be hope for the troubled youth at North Manual Trades. The teacher and student make a pact: if Miller stays in school and graduates, Dadier will continue on as faculty.

Brooks, producer Pandro S. Berman, and MGM studios ostensibly believed *Blackboard Jungle* would function as a public service announcement, calling for "reform" in America's public schools while honoring the plight of public school teachers. Yet the movie poster tag line reads, "The most startling movie in years!" This marketing strategy suggests intent to scare audiences into theaters by capitalizing on fears about growing populations of uneducable, antisocial youth. Daniel Perlstein (2000) notes, "In portraying Dadier's campaign to control his delinquent students, *Blackboard Jungle* articulates Cold War liberalism's sophisticated strategy of social control" (p. 414). The film then can be read as a propaganda tool, contributing to Cold War policies of containment, vis á vis unruly youth. The solution given by the film establishes the lone heroic urban schoolteacher as the moral authority and enforcer of law and order, who must rid the classroom of delinquents or convert them.

MGM rushed to produce *Blackboard Jungle* even while the Ethan Hunt novel and basis for the script was still in press. Hunt apparently found inspiration for the book at Bronx Vocational High School, where he "spent seventeen days as a substitute teacher" (Perlstein, 2000, p. 417). New York City School Administrators denounced the film's misrepresentation of their students.[6] In observing the Bronx Vocational, they found "no evidence of chaos, pushing in the halls, vandalism, or inter-ethnic tension…but among themselves they shared many of the beliefs and anxieties portrayed in *Blackboard Jungle*" (Perlstein, 2000, p. 418). We argue that the timing of this sensationalized cinematic narrative confirmed such unfounded views, especially in relation to concerns about impending racial integration legislation.

Indeed, the release of *Blackboard Jungle* coincided with the Supreme Court's follow-up ruling to *Brown v. Board of Education*, commonly referred to as *Brown II* (349 U.S. 294). The 1955 ruling clarifies how states and districts might desegregate their schools, explaining that integration plans should occur "with all deliberate speed" (349 U.S. 294, 299). The Court had not specified a timeline for desegregation in their 1954 decision.[7] The filmmakers' insistence on launching a "public awareness" campaign at this precise historical moment provides further evidence that mainstream Hollywood considers itself to be a prominent shaper of public opinion and a significant influence on social policy. Public school districts across the country seemed to heed the concerns depicted in *Blackboard Jungle* as they began slow, methodical, careful desegregation plans.

Some progressive Whites eagerly participated in desegregation programs, while others protested integration loudly, refused to comply with even voluntary busing plans, or left the public school system altogether. School districts also varied in their compliance with the desegregation ruling. Some increased their offerings of academic enrichment-type courses (e.g., honors, college preparatory, magnet, and advanced placement). This curricular programming shift coincided in part with Russian's *Sputnik* missile launch in 1957 and President Dwight D. Eisenhower's urgent call for school reforming in order to prepare excellent students and ensure America's national security (Lansner, 1958; Cuban, 1990). In practice, these academic enrichment programs restricted enrollments to White students, and for all intents and purposes, maintained segregated schools within integrated schools (see Mickelson, 2005). The main burden of desegregation fell on African American students, who boarded busses to cross-town schools and districts, often enduring the shouts and threats of hostile anti-integration crowds before making their way onto historically White campuses (Bell, 2004). In California, school segregation had been ruled unconstitutional years earlier, in the 1946 *Mendez v Westminster School Board* case. However, *de facto* segregation remained and began to worsen for Chicana/o, Latina/o students (Orfield & Eaton, 1996; Valencia, in press). Richard Valencia, Martha Menchaca, and Ruben Donato (2002) explain,

> It has been well over five decades since *Méndez* and nearly five decades since *Brown*. There has been much deliberation, but very little speed in eliminating school segregation in our nation… Chicano/Latino segregation has intensified to such an extent that they are now the most segregated racial/ethnic minority group in the United States…the next generation of Chicano students will very likely experience more segregation than previous generations. (p. 105)

Such dismal educational outcomes have worsened incrementally in rhythm with conservative politics. Too often, social scientists and filmmakers fault Latina/o cultural attributes and attitudes as the source of academic underachievement (e.g., Bernstein, 1977; Chavez, 1992; Ogbu, 1990). Rather than acknowledge the ways under educating Latinas/os preserves the status quo, proponents of this deficit tradition blame victims of discrimination for conditions of racial inequality.

Blackboard Jungle avoided critique of racially separate and unequal schooling conditions to present a story of reforming delinquent urban youth. Some researchers believe the *Brown* decision sent a similar distorted message, positioning Black students as the source of the problem, as opposed to the racially unequal distribution of educational resources (Bell, 2004). W.E.B. DuBois (1935) had expressed this concern 19 years before the *Brown* decision, arguing, "A mixed school with poor and unsympathetic teachers with hostile public opinion, and no teaching of truth concerning black folk, is bad. A segregated school with ignorant placeholders, inadequate equipment, poor salaries, and wretched housing, is equally bad" (p. 335). Robert Carter (1980), co-author of an *amicus curiae* in the *Mendez* case and one of the lead architects of the NAACP legal strategy in the *Brown* case, echoed DuBois' concern that the legal arguments to remedy segregation should have focused on equal educational opportunity for Black students as opposed to mere integration with White students. "If I had to prepare for Brown today," Carter argues, "instead of looking principally to the social scientists to demonstrate the adverse consequences of segregation, I would seek to recruit educators to formulate a concrete definition of the meaning of equality in education" (p. 27). Indeed, the plaintiffs presented social science evidence in both the *Mendez* and *Brown* cases emphasizing the "tremendous burden and feelings of inadequacy and inferiority" Mexican American and Black students experience in racially isolated settings (see Clark & Clark, 1950, p. 350). This legal strategy successfully convinced the Court to rule for integrated schools. However, the integration rationale suggested Black and Mexican American students receive an inferior education because they sit next to inferior Black and Mexican American students (see Yosso, Parker, Solórzano, & Lynn, 2004). The Court's remedy to desegregate "with all deliberate speed" did not account for the layers of injustice evidenced in a racially segregated society. For example, the ruling did not address the ways residential segregation concentrates poverty in Black and Latina/o communities. This inability to recognize that segregated schools connect to racialized structures of inequality in housing, wages, wealth, the justice system, and health care. In the decades since *Brown*, lower courts and school districts often interpreted and implemented school desegregation plans based on the notion that African American and Chicana/o, Latina/o *students*—not unequal *schooling conditions*—are inferior.

Blackboard Jungle amplifies this distorted and incomplete view with a patronizing narrative characterizing Black and Latino delinquents dependent on the benevolence of a White teacher or administrator to help pull them out of a culture of poverty. Distracting audiences away from the complexities of structured educational inequality, Hollywood repeated this heroic-teacher/administrator-saves-helpless-students narrative at least nine times over the next 55 (e.g., *Up the Down Staircase*, 1967; *The Principal*, 1987; *Stand and Deliver*,[8] 1988; *Lean On Me*, 1989; *Dangerous Minds*, 1995; *The Substitute*, 1996; *High School High*, 1996; *187*, 1997; *Freedom Writers*, 2007).

Blackboard Jungle's Legacy in California Urban Schools

> In this latest era of films, inner-city public schools have become war zones....Metal detectors are de rigueur....Corridors are dark, dangerous, and depressing. Classrooms are not much better. Theme music has evolved from 'Rock Around the Clock' in *Blackboard Jungle* to loud, pulsating gangsta rap with violent lyrics and ominous tones. The students, who are increasingly African American and Latino instead of White, have become more angry and more severe. (Wells & Serman, 1998, p. 190)

As Amy Stuart Wells and Todd Serman (1998) observe, Hollywood resurrected the *Blackboard Jungle* formula and took the theme of "violent public schools enrolling dangerous and delinquent students...to new extremes" (pp. 189–190) with a barrage of films in the 1980s and 1990s. Building on their greaser, *bandido*, and spitfire counterparts from decades prior, films such as *The Principal, Lean On Me, Dangerous Minds, The Substitute, High School High*, and *187* transported *cholas/cholos* from the Chicana/o gang film genre (e.g., *Walk Proud*, 1979; *Boulevard Nights*, 1979; *Colors*, 1988; *American Me*, 1992, *Blood in Blood Out*, 1993; *Mi Vida Loca*, 1994) into the public school classroom. These images capitalized on White America's anxieties about growing populations of ostensibly uneducable and uncontrollable Black and Latina/o youth.

Depictions of violent, illiterate, and sexually promiscuous Latinas/os essentialized "racial (and gender) differences, creating a series of cultural oppositions, pitting the ethnic other against a mainstream white America," and suggesting "acculturation to white goals (education and hard work) as the preferred path out of the ghetto" (Denzin, 2002, p. 6). Ignoring all historical evidence to the contrary, these deficit cinematic narratives featured Latinas/os squandering educational opportunities instead of aspiring toward college and working hard to achieve academically. Gary Keller (1994) observes that within Hollywood's ideological lesson plan,

> Issues are reduced to good and evil, simple and clear-cut conflict, a them-and-us identification process where good equals us, the American (Anglo) values and social system. Them, the villains, are defined as those who reject and seek to destroy the proper set of American (Anglo) values. Conflict is typically resolved through the use of righteous force, with Anglo values winning out. (p. 115)

The Principal, *Lean On Me*, *The Substitute*, *High School High*, and *187* exemplify the use of brute force to beat down the juvenile delinquency problem, featuring the principal or teacher carrying a bat or gun at school, or engaging in some other incident of physical violence (see Lipsitz, 1998). *Dangerous Minds* and *Freedom Writers* present gentler versions of the same formula, because of the role given to the White female teacher. The righteously forceful dare-to-care philosophy of these White female English teachers convinces at-risk Youth of Color to become successful students. Following in the tradition of *Blackboard Jungle*, the Hollywood lesson plan for each film entails a teacher heroically convincing Latina/o and Black youth to embrace "the proper set of American (Anglo) values" (Keller, 1994, p. 115). Likewise, through drama, comedy, action, and psychological thriller, these films entertain a historical imperative. Bolstered by politically conservative agendas seeking to curtail even those minimal gains made by civil rights legislation, the films blame victims of racialized inequalities and deny institutional responsibility for the failures of public schools.

Similar to filmmakers, mainstream news media producers have historically framed stories in ways that associate Chicanas/os, Latinas/os with crime, drugs, welfare abuse, failing schools, disease, and unemployment (see Hayes-Bautista, 2004; Mirandé, 1987; Wilson & Gutierrez, 1995). Otto Santa Ana (2002) documents the use of metaphors in the *Los Angeles Times* endorsing fear-based imagery. Santa Ana uncovers a clear pattern of anti-Latina/o rhetoric warning of a *Brown Tide Rising* (Latinas/os) that would soon overpower White communities. He argues that the timing and intensity of these media messages influenced public perceptions in the early 1990s to such an extent that in 1994, California voters passed Proposition 187, a legislative initiative overtly informed by *racist nativism*[9] (see Garcia, 1995; Martin, 1996). Advocates of Proposition 187, such as California's then Governor Pete Wilson and actor Arnold Schwarzenegger, sought to deny social services including health care and public education to any person suspected of being an undocumented immigrant (Lopez, 1995).[10] We extend on Santa Ana's argument to note that Latina/o gang-themed films in the early 1990s, *American Me*, *Blood in Blood Out*, and *Mi Vida Loca* (all set in urban Los Angeles neighborhoods), reiterated distorted news narratives in the form of entertainment. Both new media and films fueled political fears of the White electorate in particular about organized racial violence exploding beyond urban neighborhoods and into their neighborhoods. In 1995, 40 years after *Blackboard Jungle*, Hollywood Pictures transported this one-dimensional narrative about urban Latina/o youth into a suburban school setting with the theatrical release of *Dangerous Minds*.

Dangerous Minds: A Lesson on Latina/o Integration in Northern California Schools

Written by Ronald Bass and directed by John N. Smith, *Dangerous Minds* recounts the story of a White female (former Marine) student teacher LouAnne Johnson (Michelle Pfeiffer) in her first full-time assignment, teaching high school English. Based on the book *My Posse Don't Do Homework*, by the real-life LouAnne Johnson, the film takes place in the Northern California Bay Area communities of Palo Alto and East Palo Alto. Mainstream news media accounts in the late 1980s and early 1990s identified alarming homicide rates in East Palo Alto, while reporting on Palo Alto's impressive SAT scores. Johnson's "at-risk" Latina/o and African American students take the bus from East Palo Alto's impoverished and drug-ridden neighborhoods to attend the upper-middle-class, predominately White Parkmont High School in Palo Alto. Smith's establishing shots include black-and white images of graffiti, street altars honoring the dead, and youth with backpacks, who board a school bus. The film does not become colorized until the bus reaches the suburbs and the school. Once on campus, the Latina/o and Black youth make their way to the Academy Program classroom.

On her first day, the conservatively dressed optimistic Johnson excitedly enters the classroom only to be greeted by a hostile mob of dancing, rapping youth who hurl insults at her. Across the hall, her friend and colleague, Hal Griffith (George Dzundza) is trying to teach history. When his quiet, studious White and Asian American students become distracted by the shouts from the Academy class, Griffith motions for them to stay focused, saying "Come on, come on, come on. You know what they're like!" A shaken Johnson collects her briefcase and flees the classroom only minutes after her arrival. Furious and humiliated, she questions Griffith in the hall, wondering why he did not warn her. She exclaims, "Who are these kids, rejects from hell?"

After finding no help from various classroom management books, Johnson changes her clothes and her attitude. "OK, you little bastards," she says, as she heads back into the classroom with a leather jacket and "dare to care" philosophy. She proceeds to throw out the old curriculum and focus on the poetry of Dylan Thomas and the music lyrics of Bob Dylan. She engages the would-be delinquents with bribes, including candy bars for right answers, a trip to an amusement park for completing class assignments, and dinner at a fancy restaurant for extra research.

Johnson's attempts to re-establish students' faith in themselves and the educational system revolves around her assertion, "There are no victims in this classroom!" She tells her students they have a choice—they can "choose" to work hard and graduate or they can "choose" to fail in school and in life. To support their efforts to choose education, Johnson intervenes in her students' personal, family, and social lives. Just as one very troubled student Emilio Ramirez (Wade Dominguez) begins to trust Johnson's advice to ask the principal for protection, the drug dealer he feared kills him. Apparently, the African American Principal, George Grandey (Courtney B. Vance), refused to even meet with Emilio because he did not knock before entering the office.

Johnson's more successful advocacy efforts include her convincing Callie Roberts (Bruklin Harris), a Black pregnant student to "choose" to graduate high school instead of dropping out to attend a teen mothers' program. She also supports Raul Sanchero (Renoly Santiago), a remedial reader suspended for fighting, by visiting his house and telling his parents he is one of her "favorites." Still, Johnson becomes disillusioned by the end of the school year, and hands in her letter of resignation. Though she has already packed up her things, the despondent students give her a candy bar and try to convince her to stay. Raul exclaims, "Ah, come on Ms. J. All those poems you taught us say you can't give in, you can't give up. Well, we ain't giving you up." Callie explains, "See 'cause we see you as being our light." Johnson "chooses" to continue teaching and the students enthusiastically show her how to dance.

The setting for *Dangerous Minds* mirrors the challenges Black and Latina/o students faced during an era of court-monitored integration. Just south of Palo Alto for example, the U.S. Appellate Court affirmed the lower court's decision to voluntarily desegregate schools in the City of San Jose. The 1988 case, *Diaz v. San Jose Unified School District*, was originally filed in 1974, when Mexican American parents challenged the ways persistent segregation restricted their children's educational opportunities. The plaintiffs complained about new schools being built to accommodate predominately White suburban students on the Southside, while the number of portable classrooms increased in the historically Mexican downtown, Northside areas. The district (defendant) responded that they could not control residential *de facto* segregation, but would initiate a strategy to desegregate schools. The Ninth Circuit judges decided that the district had not intentionally maintained segregated schools and the state could not mandate a specific form of desegregation, but that voluntary district plans should proceed. In March 1986, San Jose Unified began implementing a desegregation plan that included a combination of voluntary student assignment programs, including magnet, enrichment, and programs of "excellence."[11] Magnet high schools attracted students to engage in a particular area of study (e.g., performing arts, math/science) and enrichment programs enrolled students seeking an academically rigorous course of study that existed within a larger, comprehensive high school. The district established many of these programs in schools on the predominately White side of the city and granted local neighborhood students priority enrollment.

Differentiated tracks within magnet, enrichment, and comprehensive high schools, established with new requisites such as minimum test scores, teacher/counselor recommendations, and other restrictions, further hindered Latina/o access to academically rigorous, college preparatory courses of study (e.g., accelerated, honors, advanced placement). Chicanas/os residing on San Jose's Northside, who rode the bus to a predominately White school on the Southside would not necessarily gain admission to the same classes as the White students. This school-within-a-school model upheld the goals of integration on the surface, while racially maintaining segregated and unequal schooling opportunities (see Wells & Serna, 1996). Surrounding cities implemented similar integration plans. Johnson's Academy Class reflects one such voluntary desegregation program at a predominately White, upper-middle-class high school.

Henry Giroux (1997) explains that within an era of rising conservatism, *Dangerous Minds* functions as "part of a larger project for rearticulating 'whiteness' as a model of authority, rationality, and civilized behavior," reinforcing "the highly racialized, though reassuring, mainstream assumption that chaos reigns in inner-city public schools and that white teachers alone are capable of bringing order, decency, and hope to those on the margins of society" (p. 49). *Dangerous Minds* suggests Latinas/os and African Americans cannot achieve academically unless a White teacher bestows knowledge on them. The patronizing portrayal of these "at-risk" youth resonates with stereotypical, deficit assumptions about whose culture has capital in the classroom (Yosso, 2005). The real-life LouAnne Johnson explains, the filmmakers "were in love with the idea of Michelle [Pfeiffer] being white and the kids not...They have the notion that school is only a problem for poor minority kids" (Britt, 1995, B5). A *Washington Post* film reviewer notes, "In truth, a third of the Academy students were White" (Britt, 1995, B1).[12]

In the film, similar to Dadier, Johnson personifies the White missionary who "saves" the at-risk Youth of Color by imparting her superior cultural values to them. In her view, these "rejects from hell" do not bring any appropriate cultural knowledges or skills to school. The persistence of this cultural deficit perspective casts Latina/o students and their parents as problems to fix in schools, not resources who bring community cultural wealth to the classroom (Yosso, 2005). As Giroux (1997) observes, this "pedagogical blindness," assumes "whites can come into such schools and teach without acknowledging the histories and narratives that students bring to schools, and perform miracles in children's lives by mere acts of kindness" (p. 48). Taking a similar arrogant approach, Bay Area computer software creator Ron Unz, insisting that he could fix failing schools in California with a voter initiative mandating "English for the Children." The propaganda delivered by Unz's Proposition 227 avoided any discussion of the historical under-funding of bilingual education originating with President Johnson's administration and the documented success of appropriately resourced bilingual immersion programs. Long before Unz, conservatives banked on this historical amnesia, claiming that bilingual, multicultural programs threatened the "American" way of life. In an effort to jump-start his own political career, this monolingual English-speaking White millionaire with no background or training in public education initiated a manipulative campaign, which blamed Latina/o Spanish-speakers for statewide academic underperformance. While Latinas/os voted overwhelmingly against the proposition, the predominately White electorate passed Proposition 227 in 1998, and effectively eliminated bilingual education from California public schools.[13]

In real life, Johnson did draw on some of the cultural assets of her students. In particular, she recognized the students' familiarity with rap music and their ability to recount the realities of urban life through rhyme as an important skill and art form that can inform the English Language Arts classroom. While she utilized rap lyrics as part of her poetry lessons, the filmmakers chose to use Bob Dylan's lyrics. She acknowledges this likely occurred because the filmmakers "don't know anything about rap—they went to private schools. Most people in the movie industry, their perception of nonwhites is what they get from movies. They think they're breaking the stereotype, but they're creating another" (Britt, 1995, B5). This shift in the story's details also suggests that the film's producers, Don Simpson and Jerry Bruckheimer, sought to target a White liberal audience, who tend to devalue hip-hop and rap, while idolizing critical White voices of social protest.

Furthermore, contrary to the brief portrayal of disengaged Latina/o families in the film, research demonstrates that Latina/o parents foster their children's academic achievement, empowering them to take pride in their culture and to develop a sense of community responsibility (Villalpando, 1996). Indeed, when compared to other working-class families, Latina/o parents maintain higher educational aspirations for their children than do White parents (Espinosa, Fernández, & Dornbusch, 1977; Solórzano, 1992). Hollywood ignores this reality.

Sociologist Robert Bulman (2005) explains,

> Most of the urban public school films portray the individual attitude of the students as the *primary* obstacle to their academic achievement. These students don't have the right manners, the right behavior, or the right values to succeed in school… These are not students as middle-class Americans expect students to act. Their depiction as 'animals' suggests that the problems in these schools are rooted in student behavior and, furthermore, that their behavior is rooted in an inferior culture. (p. 51)

We expand on Bulman's arguments to reveal the racism embedded in this cinematic formula. According to Hollywood, Latina/o students lack not mere middle-class cultural capital, but White middle-class capital. Portraying Latinas/os as culturally inferior youth who behave savagely, infers their culturally superior counterparts (White students) deserve the educational privileges they have inherited in the system. Such a distortion omits the historical record of racism systematically restricting schooling access for Latinas/os, while bestowing Whites with educational opportunities.

In 1996, with the release of two additional urban high school films, *The Substitute* (Artisan Entertainment) and *High School High* (Tri-Star Pictures), Hollywood reproduced this racialized narrative about Latina/o youth failing to embrace "American" values and relying on a teacher-hero to facilitate their assimilation. Taken to its extreme, the heroic teacher becomes a martyr for his/her students. Filmmakers build up a sense of empathy for these educators, who hold onto hope for *barrio* youth and dare to teach in a broken schooling system. In the 1997 Warner Brothers film *187*, an African American substitute science teacher, and devout Catholic, literally sacrifices his life for his students. Unlike the uplifting storyline in *Dangerous Minds*, where Black and Latina/o students renew their teacher's spirits and instill a sense of hope for urban schools, *187* suggests Black youth cause their teacher to lose his faith and Latinas/os kill all hope for public education (see Fernández & Yosso, 1997).

187: A Hollywood Lesson on the Consequences of School Desegregation in Los Angeles

Written by Scott Yagemann and directed by Kevin Reynolds, *187* opens in New York, as the camera follows Trevor Garfield (Samuel L. Jackson), an African American science teacher working at an urban, predominately Black high school. A quick glimpse of a momentarily engaged science class is interrupted when Garfield discovers a vandalized textbook with the police homicide code "187" and his name on every page. The book belongs to an African American student and gang member, who is failing Garfield's course. The White, male Assistant Principal (Leonard Lee Thomas) minimizes Garfield's concern, stating, "You know what your problem is? On the one hand you think someone is trying to kill you. And on the other hand, you actually believe kids are paying attention in your classes." Within minutes, the student follows through with his threat, pushing Garfield up against the hallway lockers and stabbing him multiple times in the back.

Fifteen months later, the story is now located in Los Angeles, where Garfield (who now uses an inhaler) takes a long-term substitute position at John Quincy Adams High School. Here, the student body is predominately Chicana/o, Latina/o, with tattoos, body piercings, shaved heads, baggy pants, and oversized white T-shirts. Garfield's class features a number of menacing male *cholos*, who show no respect for life, let alone education. They smoke marijuana at lunchtime, sexually harass female students, and terrorize teachers and even their own mothers.

Garfield befriends and becomes romantically attracted to a White teacher, Ellen Henry (Kelly Rowan). She confides in him that one of the students, Benny Chacon (Lobo Sebastian), has been threatening her. This *cholo* happens to also be one of the problem students in Garfield's class. Not long after this conversation, Benny disappears. Later in the film, Henry accompanies Benny's mother to identify his body at the morgue. He apparently overdosed on drugs. Benny's homeboy Cesar Sanchez (Clifton González González)[14] becomes the new source of tension in Garfield's science class. Principal Garcia (Tony Plana) refuses to search Cesar when Garfield accuses him of stealing his watch. Within days, vandals destroy his entire classroom bungalow. When Garfield questions Cesar about the incident, he, of course, denies any knowledge of the culprits.

Garfield: You know, Garcia might not be able to prove anything, but you and I both know who's responsible, don't we?

Cesar: No, I'm serious man. I don't know what the fuck you talking about.

Garfield: (Notices marijuana symbol on Cesar's ring) The ring Cesar, give it to me.

Cesar: Better watch it man, that's my trigger finger.

Garfield: It's inappropriate attire!

Cesar: (points at Garfield, aiming to shoot) Pop!

Garfield: Are you finished?

Cesar: What? Am I finished? (Stands up to confront Garfield). Is that what you said? Don't try to get fuckin' crazy on me terón [derogatory slang for Black]. (Friends join Cesar and circle Garfield). 'Cause if you want to bring it on, let's go. (Pause as Garfield notices he is outnumbered). Wha'chu gonna do?

This dialogue demonstrates the cinematic evolution of the Latino student over the course of four decades—from the buffoonish Pete Morales in *Blackboard Jungle* recounting his reasons for being "stinkin' late to school" to the menacing *bandido/cholo* Cesar Sanchez in *187,* threatening violence while challenging the teacher's authority. As Garfield turns to walk away, the camera mimics his emotional distress, shaking with increasing intensity to the sound of a jet airplane taking off. Cesar and his jeering *cholo/chola* friends seem to have won this round. Later however, after Henry's dog is killed, Cesar is mysteriously attacked by someone shooting drug filled arrows. When he wakes up, Cesar realizes someone has cut off his "trigger finger." The finger arrives to the hospital in a small manila envelope. Apparently, whoever sliced off his finger also wrote on the phrase "R U Dun?" on it. The *cholos* begin to realize that Garfield has turned into a vigilante, and they want their own bloody revenge.

Inserted into the plot as a street-smart, academically remedial Chicana, Rita Martinez (Karina Arroyave) helps viewers empathize with Garfield. She lives in a trailer with no running water and engages in highly promiscuous sexual behavior, as a way of life. A White English teacher Dave Childress (John Heard) discovers her having sex with multiple *cholos* in a utility shed at lunchtime. Later, Childress reveals to Garfield he took his own turn with Rita. However, when Rita offers her body to "Mr. G.," in exchange for tutoring, he refuses her advances. "I wanted to thank you," she explains. Garfield replies, "I'm your teacher. You don't have to thank me." A bewildered Rita learns an embarrassing lesson about respecting herself.

In the climatic conclusion of *187*, students vandalize Garfield's home with the ominous police homicide code "187." He meditates under a large crucifix in his bedroom, in preparation for the arrival of his would-be assassins. Cesar and two other students wait in the car. Two ceremoniously shaved their heads and at sunset, they run toward Garfield's house, guns loaded. Inspired by the movie *Deer Hunter*, Cesar challenges Garfield to a game of Russian roulette. At gunpoint, Garfield complies three times while shouting, "I was a teacher! I wanted to help you! You can't kill me!" He convinces Cesar to participate in the game, berating him by saying, "Your whole way of life is bullshit. Macho is bullshit!" Cesar responds, "It's all I've got!" When Cesar hesitates to take another turn, Garfield takes it for him and shoots himself in the head. Shocked, the homeboys turn to leave, but Cesar feels ashamed that Garfield took his turn. To prove his worth, Cesar takes another turn and kills himself.

A montage of images play while Rita gives a speech at graduation. Garfield and Cesar's bodies lay side by side in the morgue, and Henry throws her teaching credential in the trash and leaves her classroom. In her teary-eyed speech, Rita attributes her achievement to Mr. G., and calls her accomplishment a Pyrrhic victory, "gained at too great a cost." As the ultimate savior, Garfield died to teach his students.

The setting for *187* reflects the challenges Chicana/o, Latina/o students endured in the wake of desegregation struggles throughout Southern California. Scholars such as John Rogers (2004a,b) also note that massive White flight from the Los Angeles Unified School District coincided with the desegregation lawsuit *Crawford v. Board of Education of the City of Los Angeles*, filed in 1963. By 1968, when the Mary Ellen Crawford's case was finally heard in court, LAUSD K-12 enrollments had already started decreasing, with 54% White students and 20% Latinas/os (see Haro, 1977). Local anti-integration groups such as BUSSTOP organized public protests against *Crawford*. In addition to White opposition to integration and hesitancy to support civil rights *en masse*, socioeconomic factors led to large-scale demographic shifts in major cities throughout the United States. In Los Angeles, shutting down and moving the steel, tire, and automobile factories to other countries wiped out thousands of high-wage, skilled union jobs (Sassen, 1988; Smith & Feagin, 1987). Reindustrialization occurred in the unskilled, service sector of the economy and coincided with a loosening of immigration restrictions, increasing the numbers of Latina/o and Southeast Asian immigrants in Los Angeles (Moore & Vigil, 1993; Sassen, 1992). Between 1970 and 1990, public school enrollments increased, reflecting these new demographics. During this same time period, per pupil expenditures dropped by 23% (see Silva & Sonstelie, 1995).

By the time of the 1981 *Crawford* settlement, the White student population in LAUSD had decreased to 25% (see Yosso, 2006). Disappearing financial resources coincided with White flight. For example, with the passage of Proposition 13 in 1978, California voters restricted homeowners' tax liability, which, in turn, limited the tax-based revenues available to school districts. This hindered promising efforts to equalize funding between districts (e.g., *Serrano v. Priest*, 557 P.2d 929 Cal. 1976).[15] Unequal distribution of funding and resources within districts also remained, further hindering the quality of the education available to an increasingly Chicana/o, Latina/o student population. Indeed, the 1992 consent decree stemming from the 1986 case *Rodriguez v. Los Angeles Unified School District* (C611 358) outlined a target date of the 1997–98 school year to remedy poor schooling conditions, which included lack of basic materials, under prepared teachers, and overcrowded deteriorating buildings.[16] *187* premiered in July 1997, at the onset of the school year, when the district's student population was 11% White and 69% Latina/o.[17] The depiction of a bungalow classroom with no air conditioning and lack of science materials suggests John Quincy Adams is an under resourced high school. However, the filmmakers fail to engage any genuine discussion of the socioeconomic and legislative factors shaping educational opportunities within this setting. Instead, they opt to simply blame the *cholos* for draining all hope from the public schooling system.

Similar to *Blackboard Jungle*, *187*'s production team and Warner Brothers' studios boasts a goal of contributing to safer schools with their film. While *Blackboard* opens with a disclaimer, *187* closes with the statement, "A teacher wrote this movie." Like Evan Hunt, whose novel became *Blackboard Jungle*, *187*'s White, male screenwriter Yagemann also worked as a *substitute* teacher. During his six-years substituting for LAUSD, Yagemann created the fictional story based on a newspaper headline he read about a teacher stabbed in New York City. Actor Samuel L. Jackson convinced director Reynolds and producers Bruce Davey and Stephen McEveety to cast him in this role written for a White teacher. Jackson believed this casting choice "would erase the whole race issue and put the focus on what this story is really about—authority" (Brennan, 1997, p. 1). In *187*, however, authority remains racialized because the filmmakers pit a Black teacher against Chicano students. With this story of righteous vigilante justice over the outlaws, "emphasis is shifted away from the exploitation and subordination of Chicanos…giving tacit approval and legitimation to police abuse [and vigilantism]. Such abuse is no longer viewed as abuse but rather as badly needed enforcement of the law" (Mirandé, 1987, p. 24). *187* shifts focus away from educational neglect of Chicana/o students and legitimizes abuse and violence against students by a teacher, claiming the screenwriter represents an authentic voice merely telling a race-neutral story about authority.

The film's portrait of lawlessness rampant among California's increasingly Latina/o youth population "must be addressed and understood within a broader set of policy debates about education and crime that often serve to legitimate policies that disempower poor and racially marginalized youth" (Giroux, 2002, p. 247). Though actual juvenile crime rates had been on a steady decline since the 1970s, California's investment in prison building significantly outpaced educational spending.[18] By 1996, researchers observed, California maintained "the most crowded classrooms in the country and the nation's highest juvenile incarceration rate" (see Connolly, Macallair, McDermid, & Schiraldi, 1996). Arrest statistics documented by a 1996 joint task force appointed by then-Governor Wilson and Riverside County District Attorney Grover Trask "belied the public's concern about juvenile crime because the juvenile crime rate had actually been going down."[19] The Center on Juvenile and Criminal Justice also reported, "The popular claim that the rising teenage population means more crime and violence is a myth… The current crime trends among youths indicates declining crime rates into the next century" (Macallair & Males, 2000). Ignoring these findings, Wilson and Trask became primary proponents of Proposition 21, a ballot measure advocating "wholesale revision of California's juvenile justice laws."[20]

Among conservatives, the "depictions of youth in *187* resonate powerfully with the growth of a highly visible criminal justice system whose get-tough policies fall disproportionately on poor black and brown youth" (Giroux, 2002, p. 246). Indeed, California voters passed Proposition 21 in the March 2000 election, extending the law to allow minors age fourteen and older to be tried and sentenced as adults. The initiative also enhanced "Juvenile Justice" by redefining a gang as three or more youth wearing similar clothing (as determined by police) and expanding the definition of a felony to cover a broader range of non-violent juvenile offenses, such as graffiti vandalism (see Martinez, 2000; Pintado-Vertner & Chang, 2000). Youth across the state campaigned against Proposition 21, raising awareness with "A Week of Rage," picketing major corporate supporters, and mobilizing online support for schools not jails.[21]

The Same Old Song and Dance about Latina/o Students

Under internal colonialism the dominant white society controls and maintains monopoly over the traditional means of cultural and ideological production—the schools, the media, and bureaucratic institutions. In this promulgation of stereotypes the media certainly play an important role. Stereotypes of the Chicano are used for at least two inter-related purposes: (1) to sell products and (2) to keep Chicanos in their place. (Flores, 1973, p. 206)

They always try to portray the Chicanos and Chicanas as being this lower class that is always the one making the trouble in society. They're always the troublemakers in society and they never succeed. They're always down below. (Monica, quoted in Yosso, 2000, p. 110)[22]

Like a broken record, mainstream Hollywood continues to produce the same self-righteous tune that rocked Americans with *Blackboard Jungle*, claiming that Black and Latina/o students, their families, and communities "choose" the street life over academics and thereby limit their own social mobility (see Bulman, 2002; Chennault, 2006; Giroux, 2002). Rather than holding schools responsible for retaining and graduating students, films portraying urban Latina/o students consistently claim these youth "need the cultural capital of white middle-class or upper-middle-class people" to succeed in school and life (Giroux, 1997, p. 49). Under the guise of entertainment, since 1955, films depicting Youth of Color in urban schools subtly rationalize institutional opposition to integration, justifying the consistent tracking of Latina/o students away from college-bound courses of study while validating White flight from the urban public school system. As Flores' 1973 observation demonstrates, the practice of capitalizing on anti-Latina/o sentiment for political gain is not new. Indeed, stereotypes in media and schooling practices continue to function to maintain the status quo, keeping Chicanas/os "in their place" at the margins of society, or as Monica (quoted in Yosso, 2000) explains, "always down below."

The distortions in *187* and *Dangerous Minds* also coincide with California's multi-year electoral assault against working-class Communities of Color. Influencing conservative voters to usurp the legislature, these propositions cast immigrants, English Language Learners, and urban Youth of Color as "suspects" who burden and menace mainstream society. Throughout the 1990s, politicians and filmmakers sent similar, repetitive messages, suggesting moral depravity and cultural poverty emanate from Latina/o and African American parents and communities. The propositions utilized duplicitous language, such as *Save our State* (Prop 187), *English for the Children* (Prop 227), and *Juvenile Justice* (Prop 21) in an attempt to disguise the cultural deficit narratives and racial stereotypes they evoked. Similarly, Hollywood producers' appropriation of an urban youth aesthetic (e.g., hip-hop clothing, rap music) criminalized Latina/o and Black youth insidiously. Contributing to one-dimensional, negative portraits of Communities of Color, the three films we examine offer individual remedies for the social problems besetting these communities and by default they relieve institutions (and audiences) from responsibility to change structures of inequality.

How have teachers' perceptions of Latinas/os been shaped by these films (see Glenn Paul, 2001; Rist, 1970)?[23] How do Latina/o students internalize the barrage of negative messages sent by Hollywood filmmakers? As 18-year-old Marco[24] observes, "[On film,] I never see a Chicano/Chicana valedictorian with honors and all that, basically it's always a juvenile delinquent" (Yosso, 2000, p. 101). Indeed, how do Latina/o students respond to and resist distorted cinematic versions of themselves (see Cortés, 2000; Solórzano, 1989; Yosso, 2002)? Latinas/os comprise approximately 49% of the K-12 California public school population.[25] These students attend racially segregated, overcrowded schools in dilapidated buildings with an insufficient number of textbooks, desks, fully credentialed teachers, or functioning bathrooms (see Californians for Justice, 2003; Darling-Hammond, 1988; Harris, 2002; Oakes & Lipton, 2004). Within these schools, Latinas/os continue to be tracked toward remedial and vocational courses of study as opposed to academically rigorous, college-preparatory curricula. The historical continuity of such institutional neglect contributes to a 47% dropout (putout) rate for Latina/o high school students nationally (Burking, Perez Huber, & Solórzano, this volume). Within these contexts, there remains an urgent need for critical media literacy research and action.

Discussion: Walking Out on Hollywood's Formula

> I do take comfort in the knowledge that truth and justice are ultimately on the side of the oppressed and only the oppressor finds it necessary to distort history so that it will conform to and justify the socially created order. (Mirandé, 1987, p. x)

We draw on Miranda's sentiments above to recognize that as a powerful component of the societal curriculum, films need not present one-dimensional, historical, demeaning portrayals of Latina/o students. Filmmakers can create complex portrayals that attempt historical accuracy and disrupt Hollywood's urban school formula (e.g., *Lone Star*, 1996; *Walkout*, 2006). We close this chapter with a brief analysis of HBO's *Walkout* (Yosso & García, 2008). Written by Marcus Deleon, Ernie Contreras, and Timothy J. Sexton, this film recovers the collective history and community memory of Chicana/o students and their parents as they challenge a savagely unequal educational system (see Yosso, 2006).

Told from the perspective of a Chicana student, *Walkout* presents the real-life story of the March 1968 East Los Angeles High School Blowouts. Directed by Edward James Olemos and produced by Montezuma Esparza, the film follows the experiences of Paula Crisostomo (Alexa Vega), a college-bound senior at Lincoln High School. She becomes one of the student leaders who mobilize a walkout of over ten thousand students from at least five schools—Lincoln, Garfield, Roosevelt, Belmont, and Wilson. These youth boycott their schools in protest of unequal conditions, poor treatment, and lack of culturally relevant curriculum (Delgado Bernal, 1998; Haney López, 2003; Ruiz, 1998). Her history teacher, Sal Castro (Michael Peña) is one of the only Mexican American faculty at Lincoln.[26] Inspired by his revisionist historical pedagogy, Paula and her peers begin to exercise their critical voice and question school policies that humiliate students and restrict their progress (e.g., locked bathrooms, corporal punishment for speaking Spanish, omission from history textbooks). Under threat of expulsion and in defiance of her father, Paula works alongside her peers to mobilize a walkout of all five Eastside High Schools. Bolstered by support from their teacher, parents, and community allies, the students sustain their protest until the School Board of Los Angeles agrees to hear their demands for equal educational access and opportunity (e.g., removal of racist teachers, an end to vocational tracking, upgraded libraries, recruitment of Mexican American teachers, bilingual education).

The filmmakers acknowledge the important role of Castro without reverting to the teacher-as-hero formula or the singular solution of individuals making better moral choices. Castro fosters student leadership by encouraging critical thinking, not dependence on the teacher. His students do not wait to be saved. They take personal risks on behalf of their community.

The film's message about creating institutional change shifts the formulaic "blame the individual" and "hope for a hero" approach evidenced in *Blackboard Jungle*, *Dangerous Minds*, and *187*. In the face of seemingly insurmountable odds, the students in *Walkout* demonstrate self-determination that projects a sense of collective responsibility to carry on their struggle. Their massive social protest does not relieve institutions or audiences of responsibility. The film affirms the urgent need for educators, legislators, and filmmakers to listen to and acknowledge the voices of those most marginalized in society.

Walkout reignites our hopes about the possibilities of recovering historically complex narratives that transcend Hollywood distortions and deficit academic traditions. Indeed, "Once minority representations are seen and understood for what they are, the invisible architecture of the dominant-dominated 'arrangement' is exposed and there is a chance for a structural 'rearrangement'" (Ramírez Berg, 1997, p. 116). Building on these hopes, we recommit ourselves to the work of preparing another generation of students who will identify and critique Hollywood's formula and those structures of domination that demonize them as *Dangerous Minds*.

Acknowledgments

Thank you to Juan Gómez-Quiñones, George Lipsitz, Marcos Pizarro, and Rebeca Burciaga for their insightful comments and editing suggestions. We dedicate this chapter to those Chicana/o, Latina/o, and African American students who are too often demeaned by Hollywood films.

Notes

1. Pseudonym for self-identified Mexican American male, 31 years old, who participated in a multi-method critical media literacy study at a community college in the greater Los Angeles area during 1998–99 school year.

2. Latinas/os refers to women and men of Latin American origin or descent (e.g., Salvadoran, Guatemalan, Puerto Rican), residing in the United States, regardless of immigrant status. When data refers to Hispanics, we replace that term with Latina/o. Demographically, students of Mexican origin or descent (Chicanas/os) comprise the numerical majority of the Latina/o population in and out of schools (see Acuña, 1988; Chapa & Valencia, 1993; Cortés, 1985). We also use the term Mexican American when referring to a specific time period, such as the 1940s. We recognize that the history of U.S. colonization across the Americas can potentially conflate the diverse experiences of Chicanas/os, which includes recent Mexican immigrants along with Mexicans who have resided for generations in the areas of what became the United States. Additionally, we note that some Latinas/os identify as Chicanas/os to acknowledge their shared political consciousness as a marginalized U.S. group.

3. Pseudonym for self-identified Chicana, 19 years old (see note 1).

4. This resurrection of derogatory depictions coincides with "Operation Wetback," wherein Attorney General Brownwell appointed a military commissioner to head up the Immigration and Naturalization Services and increased deportations of Mexicans (both U.S. and Mexico born) to over one million in 1954 (see Mirandé, 1987).

5. An in-depth examination of how "interest-convergence" applies to Latina/o struggles for educational equity is beyond the scope of this chapter.

6. In Daniel Perlstein's (2000) critique of the film, he documents New York City administrator concerns that they "had never seen students 'remotely resembling'" those portrayed in *Blackboard Jungle*," and the then-Assistant Superintendent estimated that perhaps only one percent of students in NYC high schools could be identified as "actually or potentially delinquent" (p. 417).

7. Concerns about massive protests against desegregation may have influenced the wording of the Brown II. In his initial draft of the ruling, Chief Justice Warren wrote, "Decrees in conformity with this decree shall be prepared and issued forthwith by the lower courts," but after conferencing with the other Justices, he changed the text to read "all deliberate speed" (349 U.S. 294, 299).

8. *Stand and Deliver* maintains many aspects of the Hollywood formula, but perhaps because it was written and directed as an independent film and later received Hollywood distribution (Warner Brothers), it contains narrative elements that contradict the urban high school genre (e.g., protagonist Latino teacher, no on-screen violence, no unplanned pregnancies or gratuitous sex scenes, intelligent Chicana/o students struggling against institutionalized discrimination).

9. For a full discussion of racist nativism in contemporary contexts, see Perez Huber, Benavides Lopez, Malagon, Velez, & Solórzano, 2008.

10. California's Supreme Court found Proposition 187 unconstitutional in 1998. Still, the damage had been done in revealing strong resentment against immigrant communities in general and Latina/o students in particular. This resentment continues to reverberate throughout California and the nation. See, for example, Daniel Hernandez. "Backers of prop. 187 push for new initiative: Proposed measure to deny services to illegal immigrants raises fears of divisive racial politics." *Los Angeles Times*, December 20, 2003, A1.

11. The court affirmed this voluntary desegregation plan in 1988, see *Diaz v. San Jose Unified School District* 861 F.2d 591; 1988 U.S. App.

12. James Ryan, then-head of Carlmont's Academy Program, confirmed this demographic estimate in a phone interview with Yosso (personal communication, March 15, 1996).

13. Researchers have recently confirmed that the English-only route has not led to positive outcomes for California's public school students. In a five-year study, the American Institutes for Research (AIR) found persistent high drop out rates for English Language Learners and widening achievement gaps pointing to a larger structural problem only exacerbated by Proposition 227. See Sarah Jane Tribble, "Study averts teaching debate: Learning English, no answers given." *San Jose Mercury News*, local edition, February 22, 2006. See also press release and report by AIR and WestEd, http://www.air.org/news/documents/Release200602prop227.htm (Retrieved May 25, 2008).

14. Grandson to actor Pedro González González, in subsequent films, Clifton dropped his Spanish surnames and now goes by Clifton Collins, Jr.

15. The Serrano plaintiffs initially attempted to level state funding allocated to California schools, arguing that Equal Protection under the U.S. Constitution's 14th Amendment required the state to equalize funding to all school districts (*Serrano v. Priest*, 487 P.2d 1241, Cal. 1971). The 1976 follow up decision required all districts to equalize per pupil spending within $100 of each other. Researchers such as William A. Fischel (1988, 1996, 2004) find strong evidence indicating that voters in California voted for Proposition 13 hoping to circumvent perceived effects of *Serrano v. Priest II*.

16. By the 1997–98 school year, LAUSD agreed to: (1) equalize basic norm resources, (2) equalize access to experienced teachers, (3) build new schools to alleviate overcrowding, (4) reorganize large schools into more educationally sound structures, and (5) bring decision making to the local level. A decade later, at this writing, dismal schooling conditions remain all-too-prevalent throughout LAUSD, and indeed, across California's public schools. Jeannie Oakes and Martin Lipton (2004) discuss the *Williams v. State of California* case, initially filed in 2000 and settled in August 2004 (Case No. 312236 Superior Court of the State of California for the County of San Francisco). Plaintiffs sought to ensure minimal standards in public education, including well-maintained school facilities that meet the capacity of the number of students, trained teachers, and sufficient numbers of updated textbooks.

17. See http://data1.cde.ca.gov/dataquest/

18. Kathleen Connolly, Daniel Macallair, Lea McDermid, and Vincent Schiraldi (1996) describe, "The cost to maintain a ward in the California Youth Authority is about $31,000 per year, while spending per K-12 student in the public schools is about $4,500.37." For full archived report, see "From classrooms to cellblocks," http://www.cjcj.org/pubs/higher/highercal.html (Retrieved May 24, 2008).

19. see March 2, 2000 press release of report "Dispelling the myth" by Daniel Macallair and Michael Males http://www.cjcj.org/pubs/myth/mythpr.html (Retrieved May 24, 2008).

20. Ibid.

21. see also http://www.brothermalcolm.net/archivedsites/schools_not_jails.htm (Retrieved May 13, 2008).

22. Pseudonym for self-identified Chicana, 18 years old (see note 1; see also Yosso, 2002).

23. While Latinas/os comprise almost half of the students in California public schools, at least 72% of California teachers and 69% of administrators are White, see http://data1.cde.ca.gov/dataquest/

24. Pseudonym for self identified Chicano (see note 1; see also Yosso, 2006).

25. See state-wide enrollment by ethnicity, academic year 2007–08, http://data1.cde.ca.gov/dataquest/

26. In academic year 2006–07, Latinas/os comprised 29% of administrators in LAUSD and 17% in California. That same year, Latinas/os made up 30% of teachers in LAUSD and 16% in statewide. Numbers for LAUSD and California Latina/o teachers and administrators have increased in the last decade. In 1997-98, Latinas/os comprised 21% of teachers in LAUSD and 12% statewide. Similarly, Latinas/os made up 20% of administrators in LAUSD administrators and 12% statewide. See http://data1.cde.ca.gov/dataquest/

References

Acuña, R. (1988). *Occupied America: A history of Chicanos* (3rd ed.). New York: Harper Collins.

Allport, G. (1979). *The nature of prejudice* (25th anniversary ed.). Reading, MA: Addison-Wesley.

Almaguer, T. (1994). *Racial fault lines: The historical origins of White supremacy in California*. London: University of California Press.

Arriola, E. R. (1997). LatCrit theory, international human rights, popular culture, and the faces of despair in ins raids. *Inter-American Law Review, 28*(2), 245–262.

Baca Zinn, M. (1989). Family, race, and poverty in the eighties *Signs: Journal of Woman in Culture and Society, 14,* 856–874.

Baker, E. (2007). *On strike and on film: Mexican American families and blacklisted filmmakers in cold war America.* The University of North Carolina Press.

Balthaser, B. (2008). Cold war revisions: Representation and resistance in the unseen *Salt of the Earth. American Quarterly, 60*(2), 347–371.

Banfield, E. C. (1970). *Schooling versus education. The unheavenly city: The nature and future of our urban crisis* (pp. 132–157). Boston: MA: Little Brown.

Bell, D. A. (1980). *Brown v. board of education* and the interest-convergence dilemma. *Harvard Law Review, 93*(3), 518–533.

Bell, D. A. (1987). *And we will not be saved: The elusive quest for racial justice.* New York: Basic Books.

Bell, D. A. (2004). *Silent covenants:* Brown v. Board of Education *and the unfulfilled hopes for racial reform.* New York: Oxford University Press.

Beltran, M. (2008). When Dolores Del Rio became Latina: Latina/o stardom in Hollywood's transition to sound. In A. N. Valdivia (Ed.), *Latina/o communication studiest today* (pp. 118–131). New York: Peter Lang.

Bender, S. W. (2003). *Greasers and gringos: Latinos, law, and the American imagination.* New York University Press.

Bernstein, B. (1977). *Class, codes, and control: Vol. 3 towards a theory of educational transmission.* London: Routledge and Kegan Paul.

Brennan, J. (1997, February 17). Reynolds resurfaces: "Waterworld" director is once again swirling in controversy. *Los Angeles Times,* Calendar, p. 1.

Britt, D. (1995). *Washington Post.*

Brooks, R. (Director). (1955). *Blackboard jungle* [Motion picture]. USA: MGM.

Brown v. Board of Education, 347 U.S. 483 (1954).

Brown v. Board of Education, 349 U.S. 294 (1955).

Bulman, R. C. (2002). Teachers in the 'hood: Hollywood's middle class fantasy. *The Urban Review, 34*(3), 251–276.

Bulman, R. C. (2005). *Hollywood goes to high school: Cinema, schools, and American culture.* New York: Worth.

Buras, K. L. (2008). *Rightist multiculturalism: Core lessons on neoconservative school reform.* New York: Routledge.

Californians for Justice Education Fund. (2003, May 17). *First things first: Why we must stop punishing students and fix California's schools: A report on school inequality and the impact of the California High School Exit Exam.* Oakland, CA: Author.

Chapa, J., & Valencia, R. R. (1993). Latino population growth, demographic characteristics, and educational stagnation. *Hispanic Journal of Behavioral Sciences, 15,* 165–187.

Chavez, L. (1992). *Out of the barrio: Toward a new politics of Hispanic assimilation.* New York: Basic Books.

Chennault, R. E. (2006). *Hollywood films about schools: Where race, politics, and education intersect.* New York: Palgrave MacMillan.

Clark, K. B., & Clark, M. P. (1950). Emotional factors in racial identification and preference in Negro children. *Journal of Negro Education, 19*(3), 341–350.

Connolly, K., Macallair, D., McDermid, L., & Schiraldi, V. (1996). *From classrooms to cellblocks: How prison building affects higher education and African American enrollment in California.* San Francisco: Center on Juvenile and Criminal Justice.

Cortés, C. E. (1985). Chicanas in film: History of an image. In G. D. Keller (Ed.), *Chicano cinema: Research, reviews, and resources* (pp. 94–108). Binghamton, NY: Bilingual Press/Editorial Bilingüe.

Cortés, C. E. (1992). Who is Maria? Who is Juan? Dilemmas of analyzing the Chicano image in U.S. feature films. In C. Noriega (Ed.), *Chicanos and film: Representation and resistance* (pp. 74–93). Minneapolis: University of Minnesota Press.

Cortés, C. E. (1995). Knowledge construction and popular culture: The media as multicultural educator. In J. A. Banks & C. A. Banks (Eds.), *Handbook of research on multicultural education* (pp. 169–183). New York: Macmillan.

Cortés, C. E. (2000). *The children are watching: How the media teach about diversity*. New York: Teachers College Press.

Crawford v. Board of Education of the City of Los Angeles, 17 Cal. 3d 280 (1976).

Crawford v. Board of Education of the City of Los Angeles, 458 U.S. 527 (1982).

Cuban, L. (1990). Reform again, and again, and again. *Educational Researcher, 19*, 3–13.

Darling-Hammond, L. (1988). *Teacher quality and equality*. Manuscript presented at the Colloquium on Access to Knowledge, Educational Equity Project, College Board, Oakland, CA.

Delgado, R., & Stefancic, J. (1992). "Images of the Outsider in American law and culture: Can free expression remedy systemic social ills?" *Cornell Law Review, 77*, 1258–1297.

Delgado Bernal, D. (1998). Grassroots leadership reconceptualized: Chicana oral histories and the 1968 east Los Angeles school blowouts. *Frontiers: A Journal of Women Studies 19*, 113–142.

Denzin, N. K. (2002). *Reading race: Hollywood and the cinema of racial violence*. London: Sage.

Diaz v. San Jose Unified School District, 412 F. Supp. 310 (N.D. Cal. 1976).

Diaz v. San Jose Unified School District, 733 F.2d 660 (9th Cir. 1984).

DuBois, W. E. B. (1935). Does the Negro need separate schools? *Journal of Negro Education, 4*, 328–335.

Dudziak, M. L. (1988). Desegregation as a cold war imperative. *Stanford Law Review, 41*(1), 61–120.

Dudziak, M. L. (2000). *Cold war civil rights: Race and the image of American democracy*. Princeton, NJ: Princeton University Press.

Espinosa, R. W., Fernández, C., & Dornbusch, S. M. (1977). Chicano perceptions of high school and Chicano performance. *Aztlan: A Journal of Chicano Studies, 8*, 133–155.

Fernández, J., & Yosso, T. J. (1997, August 18). "187" Demonizes Latino, African American Students. *Los Angeles Times*, F3.

Fischel, W. A. (1988). Did *Serrano* really cause proposition 13? *National Tax Journal, 42*(4), 465–473.

Fischel, W. A. (1996). How *Serrano* caused proposition 13. *Journal of Law and Politics, 12*, 607.

Fischel, W. A. (2004). Did John Serrano vote for proposition 13? A reply to Stark and Zasloff, 'tiebout and tax revolts: Did *Serrano* really cause proposition 13? *UCLA Law Review, 51*(4), 887–932.

Flores, G. V. (1973). Race and culture in the internal colony: Keeping the Chicano in his place. In F. Bonilla & R. Girling (Eds.), *Structures of Dependency* (pp. 189–223). Oakland, CA: Prensa Sembradora.

Garcia, R. J. (1995). Critical race theory and proposition 187: The racial politics of immigration law. *Chicano-Latino Law Review, 17*, 118–148.

García, S. B., & Guerra, P. L. (2004). Deconstructing deficit thinking: Working with educators to create more equitable learning environments. *Education and Urban Society, 36*(2), 150–168.

Giroux, H. (1997). Race, pedagogy, and whiteness in *Dangerous minds. Cineaste, 22*(4), 46–49.

Giroux, H. (2002). *Breaking in to the movies: Film and the culture of politics*. Malden, MA: Blackwell.

Glenn P., D. (2001). The blackboard jungle: Critically interrogating Hollywood's vision of the urban classroom. *Multicultural Review, 10*(1), 20–27, 58–60.

Haro, C. M. (1977). *Mexicano/Chicano concerns and school desegregation in Los Angeles. Monograph no. 9*. Chicano Studies Center Publications. University of California, Los Angeles.

Harris, L. (2002). *A survey of the status of equality in public education in California: A survey of a cross-section of public school teachers*. San Francisco: Public Advocates, Inc.

Haney López, I. F. (2003). *Racism on trial: The Chicano fight for justice*. Cambridge, MA: The Belknap Press of Harvard University Press.

Hayes-Bautista, D. E. (2004). *La nueva California: Latinos in the golden state*. Berkeley: University of California Press.

Heller, C. (1966). *Mexican American youth: Forgotten youth at the crossroads*. New York: Random House.

Herrnstein, R., & C. Murray. (1994). *The bell curve: Intelligence and class structure in American life*. New York: Free Press.

Hirsch, E. D., Jr. (1988). *Cultural literacy: What every American needs to know*. New York: Vintage Books.

Hirsch, E. D., Jr. (1996). *The schools we need and why we don't have them*. New York: Doubleday.

Keller, G. D. (Ed.). (1985). *Chicano cinema: Research, reviews, and resources*. Binghamton, NY: Bilingual Press/Editorial Bilingüe.

Keller, G. D. (1994). *Hispanics and United States film: An overview and handbook*. Tempe, AZ: Bilingual Press/Editorial Bilingüe.

Keller, G. D. (1997). *A biographical handbook of Hispanics and United States film.* Tempe, AZ: Bilingual Press/Editorial Bilingüe.

Kozol, J. (1991). *Savage inequalities: Children in America's schools.* New York: Crown.

Lansner, K. (1958). *Second-rate brains.* New York: Doubleday.

Lewis, O. (1968). The culture of poverty. In D. Moynihan (Ed.), *On understanding poverty: Perspectives from the social sciences* (pp. 187–200). New York: Basic Books.

Lipsitz, G. (1990). *Time passages: Collective memory and American popular culture.* Minneapolis: Minnesota University Press.

Lipsitz, G. (1998). *The possessive investment in whiteness: How White people profit from identity politics.* Philadelphia: Temple University Press.

Macallair, D., & Males, M. (2000). *Dispelling the myth: An analysis of youth and adult crime patterns in California over the past 20 years.* San Francisco: Center on Juvenile and Criminal Justice.

Madsen, W. (1964). *Mexican-Americans of South Texas.* New York: Holt, Rinehart and Winston.

Martin, P. (1996). Proposition 187 in California. In, D. Hamamoto & R. Torres (Eds.), *New American destinies: A reader in contemporary Asian and Latino immigration* (pp. 325–332). New York: Routledge.

Martinez, E. (2000). The new youth movement in California: It looks like one, it moves like one, it sounds like one, it just may be one. *Z Magazine,* March 1.

Mendez v. Westminster, 64 F. Supp. 544 (S.D. Cal. 1946).

Mendez v. Westminster, 161 F. 2d 744 (9th Cir. 1947).

Mickelson, R. A. (2005). How tracking undermines race equity in desegregated schools. In J. Petrovich & A. S. Wells (Eds.), *Bringing equity back: Research for a new era in American educational policy.* New York: Teachers College Press.

Mirandé, A. (1987). *Gringo justice.* University of Notre Dame Press.

Moore, J., & Vigil, J. D. (1993). Barrios in transition. In J. Moore & R. Pinderhughes (Eds.), *In the barrios: Latinos and the underclass debate* (pp. 27–49). New York: Russell Sage.

Oakes, J., & Lipton, M. (2004). "Schools that shock the conscience": *Williams v. California* and the struggle for education on equal terms fifty years after *Brown. La Raza Law Journal, 15,* 25–48.

Ogbu, J. (1990). Minority education in comparative perspective. *Journal of Negro education, 59,* 45–57.

Orfield, G., & Eaton, S. E. (1996). *Dismantling desegregation: The quiet reversal of Brown v. Board of Education.* New York: New Press.

Perez Huber, L., Benavides Lopez, C., Malagon, M., Velez, V., & Solórzano, D. (2008). Getting beyond the "symptom," acknowledging the "disease": Theorizing racist nativism. *Contemporary Justice Review, 11*(1), 39–51.

Perlstein, D. (2000). Imagined authority: *Blackboard Jungle* and the project of educational liberalism. *Paedagogica Historica, 36*(1), 407–424.

Pettit, A. G. (1980). *Images of the Mexican American in fiction and film.* College Station: Texas A&M University Press.

Pierce, C. M. (1975). Poverty and racism as they affect children. In I. N. Berlin. (Ed.), *Advocacy for child mental health* (pp. 92–109). New York: Brunner/Mazel.

Pierce, C. M. (1980). Social trace contaminants: Subtle indicator of racism in tv. In S. B. Withey & R. P. Abeles (Eds.), *Television and social behavior: Beyond violence and children. A report of the committee on television and social behavior social science research council* (pp. 249–257). Hillsdale, NJ: Erlbaum.

Pintado-Vertner, R., & Chang, J. (2000, Winter). The war on youth. *Colorlines,* 9–15.

Ramírez Berg, C. (1997). Stereotyping in films in general and of the Hispanic in particular. In C. Rodríguez (Ed.), *Latin looks: Images of Latinas and Latinos in the U.S. media* (pp. 104–120). Boulder, CO: Westview Press.

Ramírez Berg, C. (2002). *Latino images in film: Stereotypes, subversion, and resistance.* Austin: University of Texas Press.

Reynolds, K. (Director). (1997). *187* [Motion picture]. USA: Icon Entertainment.

Rist, R. (1970). Student social class and teacher expectations: The self-fulfilling prophesy in ghetto education. *Harvard Educational Review, 40*(3), 411–451.

Rogers, J. (2004a, March 14). *School segregation and educational opportunity in Los Angeles.* Paper presented at C. Haro & N. Bermudez (chairs) Symposium: *Mendez v. Westminster School District*: Paving the Path for School Desegregation and *Brown v. Board of Education.* University of California, Los Angeles Chicano Studies Research Center.

Rogers, J. (2004b, March 27). Shining a light on the journey to educational justice. In S. Cooper & M. Welsing (Eds.), *On equal terms: Advancing educational justice in Los Angeles* (pp. 8–9). Los Angeles: The Southern California Library for Social Studies and Research.

Rodríguez, C. (Ed.). (1997). *Latin looks: Images of Latinas and Latinos in the U.S. media.* Boulder, CO: Westview Press.

Romero, M. (2001). State violence and the social and legal construction of Latino criminality: From el bandido to gang member. *Denver University Law Review, 78*(4), 1081–1118.

Ruiz, V. L. (1998). *From out of the shadows: Mexican women in twentieth-century America.* New York: Oxford University Press.

Santa Ana, O. (2002). *Brown tide rising: Metaphors of Latinos in the contemporary American public discourse.* Austin: University of Texas Press.

Sassen, S. (1988). *The mobility of labor and capital: A study in international investment and labor flow.* New York: Cambridge University Press.

Sassen, S. (1992, July). Why immigration? *Report on the Americas, 26*(1), 14–19.

Silva, F., & Sonstelie, J. C. (1995). Did *Serrano* cause a decline in school spending? *National Tax Journal, 48*(2), 199–215.

Smith, J. W. (Director). (1995). *Dangerous minds* [Motion picture]. USA: Hollywood Pictures.

Smith, M. P., & Feagin, J. R. (1987). (Eds.). *Capitalist city: Global restructuring and community politics.* New York: Basil Blackwell.

Solórzano, D. G. (1989). Teaching and social change: Reflections on a Freirean approach in a college classroom. *Teaching Sociology, 17,* 218–225.

Solórzano, D. G. (1992). Chicano mobility aspirations: A theoretical and empirical note. *Latino Studies Journal, 3,* 48–66.

Solórzano, D. G. (1997). Images and words that wound: Critical race theory, racial stereotyping, and teacher education. *Teacher Education Quarterly, 24*(3), 5–19.

Solórzano, D. G., & T. J. Yosso. (2002). Critical race methodology: Counter-storytelling as an analytical framework for educational research. *Qualitative Inquiry, 8*(1), 23–44.

Sowell, T. (1981). *Ethnic America: A history.* New York: Basic Books.

Terman, L. M. (1916). *The measurement of intelligence: An explanation of and a complete guide for the use of the standard revision and extension of the Binet-Simon intelligence scale.* Boston: Houghton Mifflin.

Valdes, F. (1998). Under construction: LatCrit consciousness, community and theory. *La Raza Law Journal, 10*(1), 1–56.

Valencia, R. R. (Ed.). (2002). *Chicano school failure and success: Past, present, and future* (2nd ed.). New York: Routledge/Falmer.

Valencia, R. R. (in press). *Chicano students and the courts: The Mexican American legal struggle for educational equality.* New York University Press.

Valencia, R. R., & Black, M. S. (2002). "Mexicans don't value education!": On the basis of the myth, mythmaking, and debunking. *Journal of Latinos and Education, 2*(2), 81–103.

Valencia, R. R., Menchaca, M., & Donato, R. (2002). Segregation, desegregation, and integration of Chicano students: Old and new realities. In R. R. Valencia (Ed.), *Chicano school failure and success: Past, present, and future* (2nd ed., pp. 70–113). London: Routledge.

Valencia, R. R., & Solórzano, D. G. (1997). Contemporary deficit thinking. In R. R. Valencia (Ed.), *The evolution of deficit thinking in educational thought and practice* (pp. 160–210). Washington, DC: Falmer Press.

Valenzuela, A. (1999). *Subtractive schooling: U.S.-Mexican youth and the politics of caring.* Albany: State University of New York Press.

Wells, A. S., & Serman, T. W. (1998). Education against all odds: What films teach us about schools. In G. Maeroff (Ed.), *Imaging education: The media and schools in America* (pp. 181–194). New York: Teachers College Press.

Wells, A. S., & Serna, I. (1996). The politics of culture: Understanding local political resistance to detracking racially mixed schools. *Harvard Educational Review, 66*(1), 93–118.

Williams, L. (1985). Type and stereotype: Chicano images in film. In G. D. Keller (Ed.), *Chicano cinema: Research, reviews, and resources* (pp. 59–63). Binghamton, NY: Bilingual Press/Editorial Bilingüe.

Wilson, C. C., II, & F. Gutierrez. (1995). *Race, multiculturalism, and the media: From mass to class communication*. Second Edition. Thousand Oaks, CA: Sage.

Woll, A. L. (1977). *The Latin image in American film*. Los Angeles: UCLA Latin American Center Publications.

Woll, A. L. (1980). Bandits and lovers: Hispanic images in American film. In R. M. Miller (Ed.), *The kaleidoscopic lens: How Hollywood views ethnic groups* (pp. 54–72). New York: Jerome S. Ozer.

Yosso, T. J. (2000). *A critical race and LatCrit approach to media literacy: Chicana/o resistance to visual microaggressions*. Unpublished doctoral dissertation, University of California, Los Angeles.

Yosso, T. J. (2002). Critical race media literacy: Challenging deficit discourse about Chicanas/os. *Journal of Popular Film and Television, 30*(1), 52–62.

Yosso, T. J. (2005). Whose culture has capital? A critical race theory discussion of community cultural wealth. *Race, Ethnicity, and Education, 8*(1), 71–93.

Yosso, T. J. (2006). *Critical race counterstories along the Chicana/Chicano educational pipeline*. New York: Routledge.

Yosso, T. J., & García, D. G. (2007). "This is no slum!": A critical race theory analysis of community cultural wealth in Culture Clash's Chavez Ravine. *Aztlan: A Journal of Chicano Studies, 32*(1), 145–179.

Yosso, T. J., & García, D. G. (2008). "Cause It's Not Just Me": Walkout's history lessons challenge Hollywood's urban high school formula. *Radical History Review, 102,* 171–184.

Yosso, T. J., Parker, L. Solórzano, D. G., & Lynn, M. (2004). From Jim Crow to affirmative action and back again: A critical race discussion of racialized rationales and access to higher education. *Review of Research in Education, 28,* 1–25.

32 Latin@s in Early Childhood Education
Issues, Practices, and Future Directions

Verónica E. Valdez
The University of Utah

María E. Fránquiz
The University of Texas at Austin

Latin@s[1] are the fastest growing and youngest segment of the U.S. population. The experiences of Latin@ children as they enter the early years of care and schooling have significant implications for their future academic success. In response, the field of early childhood is not only undergoing growth but fundamental change. Research in early childhood education[2] has also broadened in scope as it seeks to understand the implications of these new trends and how best to serve young Latin@ children and their families. The last decade in particular has witnessed some dramatic impacts from social and political forces on early childhood programs. The advent of testing of 4-year-olds[3] and standardized preschool curriculums is morphing early childhood education into an extension of K-12 education with the corresponding pressures of accountability. These trends and forces impact the policy, programmatic, and research decisions we make. Thus, it is imperative that we not underestimate the potential impact of these decisions made on behalf of young Latin@ children.

In this chapter, we provide an introductory overview of issues and research that highlight the implications of these trends for Latin@s in early childhood education. We do this to entice the reader to explore these issues further and use this knowledge to help inform and broaden their own ideas and practices related to Latin@s in early childhood education. Specifically, in this chapter, we discuss (a) current and emerging early childhood issues and trends impacting young Latin@s and the early childhood programs that serve them, (b) key research areas related to teaching and learning practices in early childhood education for Latin@s, and (c) what this means for the future directions of research on Latin@s in early childhood education.

Early Childhood Issues and Trends

Early childhood education has surfaced as the new target of education reformers. The human brain develops more rapidly between birth and age five than during any other period of life. Recent research on brain research and cognitive development has shown that the early years of a child's life are important for children's learning throughout life because of the significant social-emotional and cognitive gains made during this time span (Bowman, Donovan, & Burns, 2001; Magnuson, Meyers, Ruhm, & Waldfogel, 2003; Shonkoff & Phillips, 2000). This has raised interest in the potential benefits early childhood education offers young children.

Early childhood education, depicted as a time of "learning through play," is undergoing changes. Its focus is being shifted to more traditional academic oriented teaching and learning. As a first grade teacher who has been in the teaching field for over 30 years recently commented, "Preschool has become the new first grade." Her point was that the academic work and standards that her preschool colleagues were expected to implement were the same as those she used 10 years ago as a first grade teacher. In fact, over 10 years ago, Goals 2000: Educate America Act (1994) was signed into law. It emphasized accountability and improved academic achievement for K-12 education, and stated that its goal was that all children enter school "ready to learn."

Since then the academic learning provisions specified in the law have filtered down to the preschool level and have been codified through specific policy initiatives such as the Good Start, Grow Smart Early Learning Initiative (2002), an extension of No Child Left Behind's (2002) educational reform efforts. As a result, preschools are becoming increasingly standardized with scripted teaching viewed as more practical in light of a preschool workforce that is unevenly trained (Fuller, Bridges, & Pai, 2007).

The result is government regimenting what very young children learn and how they are taught in ways that are often inconsistent with local family and community practices. One-size-fits-all early education has thus extended public schooling downward below kindergarten and created an expectation that preschoolers, whatever their home languages and language abilities, should master early literacy skills in English by the time they start kindergarten. What has led to these changes and the focus on Latin@s? There are several factors that have converged to change the way early childhood is viewed and utilized on behalf of Latin@s: demographic shifts, Latino participation rates in early childhood programs, reported educational achievement gaps among this population, and the language debates. These factors have led to early childhood education being seen as a wise investment that would increase the odds of Latin@s closing the achievement gap later on in their public school career—a noble cause that in the last decade has resulted in unparalleled focus on this age group and an increased focus on Latin@s in particular.

Latin@ Shifting Demographics

Latin@s are becoming an increasing presence across the country (U.S. Census Bureau, 2004). Currently, Latin@s make up one in five children under the age of five (Calderón, González, & Lazarin, 2004). It is estimated that by 2050, the number of Latin@ children under five will increase by 146 %. Many of these children are from Spanish-speaking homes, have limited English proficiency (LEP), and are considered by schools to be English language learners (ELLs).[4] Of the ELLs enrolled in U.S. schools, Latin@ Spanish-speaking children make up 70 % of the total (NCELA, 2002). Overall, Spanish-speaking children who are learning English as a second language during the early childhood years are the most likely of all children to live in poverty and have a mother without a high school education (Espinosa, Laffey, & Whittaker, 2005). Historically, Latin@s have concentrated in nine states (CA, TX, NY, FL, IL, AZ, NJ, CO, and NM); however, they are now a presence in every state in the United States (Hernández, 2006). The result of this demographic trend for early childhood educators is that nationwide more Latin@ students are entering programs earlier.

Latino Early Childhood Participation Rates

While attending some form of preschool prior to formal schooling has now become normative in the United States (Takanishi, 2004), Latin@ children, particularly children of immigrant parents, have the lowest preschool participation rates (Brandon, 2004). In 1999, the White House released a report, *Latinos in America*, which found Latin@s under the age of five were less likely to be enrolled in early childhood programs than other groups: 20% as compared to 42% of non-Latin@ Whites. The reasons for these reduced participation rates have not been found to be due to any negative attitudes by Latin@ families toward preschool education. A survey of 1,000 Latin@ families across the country found that 75% considered it "very important" that children attend prekindergarten, and 95% believed that attending prekindergarten was an advantage for school success (Pérez & Zarate, 2006). Although parental education, income, employment, family size/structure, and the region where they lived were determined to significantly influence Latin@ participation in early childhood programs, the overriding explanation was inadequate access

(Barnett & Yarosz, 2007). Thus, as focus has shifted to Latin@s in early childhood education, more is being done to address the disparity in preschool participation rates among Latin@s.

Latin@ Educational Achievement Trends and the Role of Early Childhood Education

Although many Latin@ children enter school with the needed skills and knowledge, a considerable number enter school at a disadvantage. When Latino children start kindergarten, their reading and mathematics skills are well behind those of their non-Latino peers (Jacobson, 2007). On average, Latin@s achieve at lower levels from kindergarten forward than non-Latino whites (García & Jensen, 2006). Bridges Fuller, Rumberger, and Tran (2004) looked at preschools in California and found that Latin@ kindergarteners with minimal English proficiency performed below Whites in pre-reading and numeracy skills. Further, these researchers found that these gaps in early cognitive development persisted through fourth grade. Indeed, Latin@s consistently perform below the national average in the National Assessment of Educational Progress (NAEP). In 2003, 30% of all Latin@s had not completed high school by age 24, compared to 7% of Whites. Among first generation Latin@s, 43% left school without a diploma. (Hochschild & Scouronick, 2005). Limited English proficiency, low parent education, and low socioeconomic status contribute to relatively lower academic outcomes among Latin@ students (Lee & Burkam, 2002; Schneider, Martínez, & Owens, 2006). According to a 2007 report, despite some progress, Latin@ children's academic achievement remains low (NTFECEH, 2007).

Using data from the Early Childhood Longitudinal Survey-Kindergarten Cohort, Magnuson, Lahaie, and Waldfogel (2006) examined the link between preschool attendance and school readiness among children of immigrants compared to those of native born parents. They found that preschool attendance raised reading and math scores for both groups of children. In addition, attendance for children of immigrants also served to raise their English language proficiency. Latin@ children with limited English proficiency achieved twice the gains in language and pre-reading skills compared with non-Latino white children. Additionally, research has indicated that quality early childhood education can decrease academic delays, grade retentions, and the rates of entrance into remedial or special education services (Barnett & Camilli, 2002). These findings reinforce prior research that has suggested positive effects for children enrolled in pre-school programs (Brandon, 2004; Hernández, 2004; Hernández & Charney, 1998). Quality early childhood model studies such as High/Scope Perry, the Abecedarian, and Chicago Child-Parent Centers have demonstrated that Latin@ children participating in a high-quality early education program showed dramatic gains in cognitive and language skills, areas that predict strong kindergarten readiness (Barnett & Hustedt, 2003). As educational reformers noted that educational gaps get more difficult and costly to address as children advance through the grades, their reform efforts in K-12 education expanded to include preschool education. The early childhood impact studies described above convinced reformers to increase preschool education funding as a means to better prepare children for school and help close the achievement gaps. However, the question of language of instruction remains a contested area for reformers.

The Language Debates

In the United States, the issue of language has been a contentious one aligned with themes of patriotism and what it means to be an American (Olsen, 1997). The K-12 education system has often found itself in the middle of this controversy as powerful lobby groups such as the English-only movement have focused on establishing the United States as an English-only society (Wong-Fillmore, 1996). In light of the current English-only, anti-immigration political and social climate in the United States (Macedo, 1997), these groups have successfully passed English-only policies in schools in California, Arizona, and Massachusetts (Wiese & García, 2006).[5] As the education of young children has been pushed to younger ages, these language debates have surfaced in early childhood programs. In fact, recent educational policies (i.e., Good Start, Grow Smart Early Learning Initiative [2002]) have instituted accountability-based testing that measure progress toward English proficiency beginning in preschool populations. As early childhood settings work to increase children's rates of progress toward English within their programs, the unintended consequence of these policies can be more preschool programs offering earlier and a more rapid transition to English instruction for young ELLs, a circumstance that may lead to only short term benefits at the cost of long term academic achievement (Rumberger & Anguiano, 2004). These types of educational policies advance an educational system that promotes subtractive bilingualism (Lambert, 1975) a phenomenon that focuses on English acquisition at the expense of the native language rather than as an addition to it (MacGregor-Mendoza, 2000; Portes & Hao, 1998; Wong-Fillmore, 2000).

Sociopolitical forces which support the exclusive use of English perpetuate themselves not only within institutions such as schools but also within the individual internalizations of the negative mainstream society views of Spanish (Souto-Manning, 2007; Tse, 2001). As Souto-Manning (2007) found in the case study she conducted with an immigrant mother from Mexico, there remain widespread misconceptions about the impact of bilingualism and the learning of two languages on children's cognitive development; the perception being that learning two languages somehow diminishes a child's capacity to learn other things. In addition, there remain misconceptions among educators and policymakers that the achievement gap cannot be narrowed without pushing children toward English fluency more aggressively and earlier in their young childhoods (Fuller et. al., 2007). There is also a strong belief that young children acquire languages easily, even second languages, and ELLs often spend too much time in native-language instruction (Gersten, 1999). Thus, strong forces remain pushing early childhood programs toward English-only instruction despite evidence on the benefits of continued support of the native language (Barnett, Yarosz, Thomas, Jung, & Blanco, 2007; Cummins, 1981; Genishi, 2002; Rodríguez, Díaz, Duran, & Espinoza, 1995; Soto, 1993; Winsler, Diaz, Espinose, & Rodriguez, 1999) and the resourcefulness of becoming an emergent bilingual (García, Kleifgen, & Falchi, 2008).

Taken collectively, the issues and trends described have led to the promotion of early childhood education as holding the most promising opportunities for raising Latin@ achievement. In response, we have seen steady increases across the country in the support for and the provision of early childhood education programs for young children. The largest wave of early childhood education activity has been the federally funded preschool Head Start program. In addition, over 38 states have provided funding for at least half-day pre-kindergarten (pre-k) producing a 40% increase in enrollment over the last 5 years (Barnett, Hustedt, Hawkinson, & Robin, 2006). Programs such as Head Start and state-funded pre-k produce broad positive effects for most children. Although there have been benefits, they have been more limited for children in Head Start from primarily Spanish-speaking homes (U.S. Health and Human Services, 2005). Based on these findings, researchers have been working to identify what works with this population of students and what other factors may be contributing to the less positive impacts of early childhood programs seen among young Latin@ children. In the next section we highlight research themes on Latin@s in early childhood education: culture and language considerations, teachers of young Latin@ children, and Latino family engagement.

Highlights of Research on Latin@s in Early Childhood Education

Early childhood education is a relatively young field. It wasn't until the late 1950s to early 60s that a research base began to develop. As the government's War on Poverty in the 1960s began directing money to the development of early childhood programs, it also directed funding to research efforts to develop and determine the effectiveness of various curriculum interventions for children living in poverty. Over the years the field has broadened to include not just studies that focus on individual child development but that are looking at teaching and learning from a sociocultural perspective. This perspective has introduced research that looks at the influence of the broader social context (communities, teachers, peers, etc.) on children and has taken researchers into the natural environments in which children live, play, and learn. Early childhood policy initiatives introduced as part of educational reforms have produced a research agenda to raise academic achievement that has focused on identifying evidence-based practices based on research that meets the rigors of scientific inquiry. Accompanying this focus have been significant increases in federal research funding opportunities made available to study issues related to this research agenda, including research on the education of young Latinos. As a result, there is a growing body of research on Latin@s in early childhood education. One important perspective in the research literature is a cultural perspective.

Cultural Perspectives on Teaching and Learning

Society is increasingly diverse and thus reflective of competing ideologies about language and the nature of culture (Martínez-Roldan & Malavé, 2004). For the teacher of English language learners (ELLs), the role of language and the issue of culture—what it is and how it directly and indirectly influences academic learning—are particularly important. First attempts to respond to children's cultural backgrounds centered on bringing cultural content into the curriculum in ways that allowed children to learn about themselves and others (Day, 2006). These then evolved into better understanding how culture affects learning. Recent efforts have incorporated the children's histories, language, early experiences, and values in the classroom activities in an effort to improve academic learning (Au, 1993; Fránquiz & Reyes, 1998). Culture has often been looked at as a fixed set of traits assigned to a particular group of people. Recently, researchers such as Gutiérrez and Rogoff (2003) have cautioned against this approach because it leads to instructional adjustments based on group categorization. Rather, culture should be viewed as dynamic and individual members of a culture embedded to different degrees within their cultural group (Day, 2006). Thus, rather than teaching to preconceived traits, emphasis is placed on helping children navigate through both the familiar and the unfamiliar ways of doing things to which they are exposed in school. For young children, language development and learning about one's own culture are closely linked and essential to children's cultural and linguistic identities (Genesee, Paradis, & Crago., 2004). With early childhood being viewed as a time where the foundation for future learning is established, analyzing how language(s) express themselves in the classrooms of young Latin@ children has become a focus in recent research.

Language Considerations in Teaching and Learning

Children learn about language in the same way they learn about other experiences—by imitating, exploring, trying out new ideas, and participating in their cultures. It is the foundation on which children's teaching, learning, identity formation, and socialization is based (García, 1991). We also know that language input and support for literacy in the preschool years are predictive of later success in school (Tabors & Snow, 2001). With many young children coming from Latin@ communities exposed to two languages within the context of their daily lives, research has focused on better understanding how the presence of two languages impacts teaching, learning, and academic outcomes for young Latin@ children.

When looking at the types of language supports that are provided within preschool settings for Latin@ ELLs, Tabors (1997) explained there are basically three types in which preschool

Latin@ ELLs will find themselves: an English language classroom, a bilingual classroom, or a Spanish-language classroom. Unlike public school settings that have particular legal requirements of specific language support services they must make available to children classified as limited English proficient upon entering, these non-public school early childhood settings are determining how they will support Spanish in the classroom based on accountability requirements regarding progress toward English and/or the language skills of the personnel they have available in their local context. If these decisions are grounded in research, significant Spanish language supports would be provided to young Latin@ children. Research has shown that a strong base in the home language not only facilitates acquisition of English, but continued and parallel gains in the home language and in their academic achievement (Cummins, 1981; Rodríguez et al., 1995; Soto, 1993; Winsler et al., 1999). In particular, Thomas & Collier (1997, 2002) found that children allowed to develop their home language to high levels of proficiency as they acquired English, until at least 6th grade, matched the level of academic success of native English speakers after 4 to 7 years of schooling. In contrast, children who had been forced to only learn in English at an early age by being placed in all-English classrooms in kindergarten took 7 to 10 years to achieve the 50th percentile on standardized achievement tests given in English. Thomas and Collier's research along with that of others suggests that failing to continue to develop the home language of the child at an early age has negative long term impact on their academic achievement and leads to Spanish language loss (Barnet et. al, 2007; Rumberger & Anguiano, 2004). Thus, instructional approaches designed for Latin@ ELLs must effectively address their language needs and their academic development (Cummins, 1993).

Research in the area of bilingualism has looked at how languages develop when young Latin@s are exposed to two languages either simultaneously from birth or sequentially after entering early care and education settings (Bialystok, 2001; García, 2004; Tabors, 1997). Reyes (2006) provides case studies of 4-year-old Latin@ children showcasing their dual language development and its connections to their emerging biliteracy. She, along with other researchers, has also been able to document young Latin@ children's learning and development of their own theories and "embryonic ideologies" about language (Martínez-Roldan & Malavé, 2004; Pastor, 2008).

Bilingualism and biliteracy are interrelated language processes that develop in a parallel fashion with one enriching the other (Grosjean, 1982; Moll & Dworin, 1996; Pérez & Torres-Guzmán, 1996; Reyes, 2006). Moll and Dworin (1996) looked at case studies of elementary Latin@ students' development of biliteracy. Their findings suggest that there are multiple paths to biliteracy impacted by student's histories, the social contexts they have for learning, and their opportunities to use each language in language and literacy events. The research on biliteracy suggests that literacy development for someone who is exposed to two languages rather than one presents itself in some unique ways and must be studied from a bilingual perspective (Berzins & López, 2001; De La Luz Reyes, 2001; Dworin, 2003; Gort, 2006; Hornberger, 2003; Martínez-Roldan & Sayer, 2006; Moll & Dworin, 1996; Moll Saéz, & Dorwin, 2001; Reyes, 2006). As a result, recent studies have sought to document this uniqueness. Among the characteristics documented have been: (a) the use of *strategic codeswitching* where the alternating of languages is used purposefully for instructional purposes (Gort, 2006); (b) the practice of *codeswitching* and using a dialect such as Spanglish as a routine language practice (Martínez-Roldan & Sayer, 2006; Reyes, 2006); (c) the phenomenon of *spontaneous biliteracy* where the development of literacy in one language occurs despite not receiving literacy instruction in both languages (De La Luz Reyes, 2001; Gort, 2006); (d) the occurrence of *interliteracy* where in the process of developing a two language system, linguistic elements of one language are used in the other language (Gort, 2006); and (e) the *bidirectional* nature of bilingualism and biliteracy development between parents and their children and children with their peers (Reyes, 2006). In many of the cases documented in the research on biliteracy, there were key factors that facilitated the presence of these phenomena in the classrooms of Latin@ ELLs. For example, De La Luz Reyes (2001) found that as she followed the four Latina girls from K-2nd grade, it was the teacher's ability to set up an environment that respected and allowed the use of both languages without any negative stigma that allowed the development of both languages to flourish.

Teachers of Young Latin@ Children

Teachers play a key role in the achievement of Latin@ students (Fránquiz, 2002; Fránquiz & Salazar, 2004; Nieto, 2004). However, teachers are often disempowered within schools. They are often isolated in their own classrooms with their autonomy eroded as teaching becomes more legislated from outside the classroom. Professional development opportunities are often limited and/or are determined by administration rather than by the expressed needs of the teachers. Moreover, teachers are often discouraged from taking an active role in program decision-making. Yet, teachers play key roles in the creation of classroom environments that are conducive to learning. Michelle Fine (1991) reported research findings that teacher empowerment correlates highly with the attitudes teachers express toward their students. The more powerless teachers feel the more negative they are toward their students. In addition, Nieto (2003) found that in order to foster teacher's positive view of teaching, schools need to develop themselves as professional communities of practice that allow teachers to take more responsibility for their own learning on the role of language and the issue of culture when working with young Latin@ ELLs.

Language serves a critical function in the classroom because it is the medium in which teachers teach, learn, mediate, and construct meaning with children. Teachers of Latin@ ELLs must deliberately adapt the ways they use language to accommodate the needs of these students. There is growing evidence that teachers are underprepared to meet the needs of Latin@ ELLs; 67% of teachers from urban fringe/large town, 58% of teachers from central cities, and 82% of teachers from rural areas report never having participated in professional development regarding ELLs (Lewis et al., 1999). Although 41% of teachers report teaching ELLs, less than 13% of these received eight or more hours of training focused on their needs (National Center for Education Statistics, 2002). Among preschool teachers, 70% asserted that they were not fully prepared to teach students with limited English proficiency or from diverse cultural backgrounds.

There is growing consensus that teachers of Latin@ ELLs require additional pedagogical preparation, including an understanding of "basic constructs of bilingualism and second language development, the nature of language proficiency, [and] the role of the first language and culture in learning" (Clair & Adger, 1999; NAEYC, 1996). These teachers must develop the skills to (a) make content comprehensible, (b) integrate language with content instruction, (c) respect and incorporate first languages, and (d) recognize how culture and language impact children's classroom participation (Antúnez, 2002; NTFECE, 2007). While available strategies provide valuable benefits, the need to improve the quality and quantity of teacher training remains.

New research looks at innovative ways for educators to build on what young Latin@ children and their families already know by building on the funds of knowledge research tradition that has documented the various forms of capital and knowledge that households possess (Moll, Amanti, Neff, & González, 1992; Vélez-Ibáñez & Greenberg, 1992). This research looks at how to tap into the knowledge of the homes for classroom teaching and learning. As an example, Riojas-Cortez (2001) looked at what happened when preschool teachers structured dramatic play around episodes or events at home or involving family members. She found that Latin@ preschoolers tapped into the moral lessons and values of their parents and used them in their theatrical performances. In this way, the children raised their cognitive development and also addressed their social-emotional development needs. Sometimes, teachers of Latin@ ELLs are faced with socio-political forces that challenge their ability to provide culturally and linguistically appropriate teaching and learning in the classroom. For example, in a 2-year ethnographic study conducted by Manyak (2006), the efforts of two teachers of Latin@ ELLs were documented as they worked to teach in ways that supported the cultural and linguistic needs of their students despite being in an English-only mandated environment as established by California's Proposition 227. Although difficult, the teachers were successful because they were guided by their knowledge base regarding the importance of Spanish as a teaching tool for young children and persisted in their commitment to additive instructional approaches for the Latin@ students in their classrooms. What this research demonstrates is that teachers can make a difference in the lives of their students. As Manyak goes on to recommend, in order to successfully continue additive instructional practices in the face of outside challenges, it is necessary for teachers to form coalitions with other teachers, parents, and community members.

Latin@ Family Engagement

Research underscores the importance of parent participation, including the finding that the more intensively parents are involved, the greater are the cognitive and non-cognitive benefits to their children (Bronfenbrenner 1974; Irvine 1982). Thus, parents have been encouraged to reinforce the curriculum at home through various educational activities, such as reading with their children and helping them with homework. The problem is that much of the parent involvement activities encouraged by schools focus on school-directed family involvement that allow families' input but only centered on the issues important to the school and conducted in ways structured by the school. New scholarship has begun to document the vibrant family values and social capital that support child socialization in many Latin@ families.

Latin@ parents recognize the importance of academic schooling. However, they also view the lessons provided at home as an essential element of their children's overall education—what many Latin@ parents refer to as *una educación*. *Una educación* is a broader conception of education that refers to both formal schooling and the way in which a person should live morally in the world with others (Delgado-Gaitán, 2004; Valdés, 1996; Villenas & Moreno, 2001). However, although Latin@ parents value education, they often face barriers to meaningful school involvement as their culturally preferred ways of supporting their children's achievement through practices such as *consejos*, *dichos*, and promoting the value of "hard work" may not be supported within traditional educational settings (Delgado-Gaitán, 2004; Espinosa-Herold, 2007; López, 2001).

In efforts to better serve the linguistic and cultural needs of Latin@ families and those of their children, researchers are examining more closely the ways in which Latin@ parents engage in teaching and learning with their young children. For example, Eisenberg (2002) found that Mexican American mothers asked a greater quantity of questions with preschool-like activities (i.e., block building), and more complex concepts and language were used in home-like activities (i.e., baking). Although much of the literature focuses on mothers, in recent years researchers have provided evidence that Latino fathers also value early literacy for themselves and their families. For example, Ortiz (2004) documented how Latino fathers contributed to their children's early literacy development by participating in literacy activities at home such as sharing religious materials with their children, reading brochures and pamphlets from work related to shared interests, reading story books and board games instructions, among others. One of the more interesting studies examined how Latin@ immigrant families incorporated school-dictated literacy activities into their existing practices (Perry, Kay, & Brown, 2008). What Perry et al. found was that they only used the school-based literacy practices when they believed it was best for their children's academic success. Otherwise, literacy activities were modified to reflect their existing cultural beliefs and practices.

The findings highlighted by these studies showcase the richness of language and literacy practices used by Latin@ parents when interacting with their children through familiar routines (as compared to their language use in an assigned, and non-routine task), on topics and activities that engage their interest, and which fit with their cultural practices. This line of research changes the way we think about early learning across diverse families. As Fuller et al. (2007), stated, "It has strong implications for how we…define what 'effectiveness' means when early education is formally organized within a particular community" (p. 236). It is important to note that as a heterogeneous group, there are differences among Latin@ families, particularly among dominant English-speaking, bilingual, and Spanish-speaking parents (Zentella, 2005). Sáenz and Felix (2007), for example, surveyed the literacy practices of 45 English-speaking Latin@s and found their literacy practices (i.e., number of books, visits to library, shared book reading) to be comparable to those of the general U.S. population rather than to those of Spanish-speaking Latin@s. Thus, research on Latin@s is becoming more nuanced as these distinctions are incorporated.

Future Directions

Our examination of the issues and trends impacting young Latin@s and the early childhood programs that serve them makes evident that many factors converged to affect the way early childhood is viewed, funded, and utilized, particularly for Latin@ communities. As we look toward the future, it is important for us to highlight areas that require our attention if we are to maximize Latin@ children's educational opportunities. For example, the potential many Latin@ children have for dual language development is often ignored. In doing so, schools diminish Latin@ children's cognitive and linguistic potentials. Additive instructional approaches that build on Latin@ children's and their families' strengths are crucial in producing the kinds of outcomes that policymakers, educators, and families seek. Research can lead the way in continuing to develop and evaluate new educational approaches while also allowing room for the documentation of successful early childhood practices that are uniquely responding to particular community characteristics and nuanced within-group differences related to country of origin, language, immigration and generational status. With clear evidence of the long-term benefits of dual language development, setting dual language goals and incorporating dual language planning into the curriculum need to be a central part of early childhood education. This means that more longitudinal research is needed on: dual language use in the classroom with Latin@ children in different instructional environments; the continuity of those practices within and across early childhood programs including the public school; the role of English and Spanish popular media on young Latin@ children's language and literacy development; and children's own role and values toward dual language development.

There is no doubt that early childhood education is the new frontier into which K-12 education is expanding. The sociopolitical forces are conspiring to make it so. The first such attempt to expand public school education led to the addition of kindergarten. That effort was heralded as the solution to public education's inadequacies with underachieving populations. Current efforts to standardize teaching and learning in early childhood diminish local input and control, place heavy emphasis on accountability as determined by standardized tests, and underscore a lack of understanding of current theories and research concerning language development and diversity. They also undercut the strengths of Latin@ families and communities and disempower Latin@ parents in the raising of their children (Fuller et al., 2007). Thus, as educational researchers and advocates for Latin@s, it is important for us to be vigilant of current educational reform efforts in early childhood to assure that they are not just a pushing down of public school education but rather a re-invention that incorporates the needs and voices of young Latin@ children, their families, and the teachers that serve them.

Notes

1. Latin@ is utilized throughout this document as a gender neutral substitute for the terms Latino/
   Latina.

2. Early childhood education has traditionally been defined as the care and education received by children from birth to eight years of age (Bredekamp & Copple, 1997). For purposes of this chapter, we have chosen to focus our attention on young Latin@ children preschool through kindergarten (age 3 to 6) because this group is experiencing the most significant programmatic changes as a result of policy initiatives geared to this age group. There has also been increasing attention and expansion of services to infants and toddlers. However, this age group remains a relatively small population in early childhood programs. For those interested in learning more about research on issues related to Latin@ infants, we refer you to M. L. Lopez, S. Barrueco, & J. Miles (2006), *Latino Infants & Their Families: A National Perspective of Protective & Risk Factors for Development* (Report). Washington, DC: National Task Force on Early Childhood Education for Hispanics. Retrieved March 1, 2008, from http://www.ecehispanic.org/work/Latino_Infants.pdf. This report provides characteristics and early indicators of Latino infant development utilizing a large, nationally-representative sample of 9-month-old infants and their families. Research conducted on children in the early primary grades has informed the research conducted on younger children. Thus, aspects of the body of research related to the early primary grades will be incorporated into our discussions.

3. It is important to note that the testing of young Latin@ children for accountability purposes has raised significant validity and reliability concerns. For further reading on assessment issues related to English language learners see Rueda and Yaden (2006).

4. English Language Learners (ELLs) are students whose first language is not English and who are at some stage of learning English. Limited English proficient (LEP) is the term used by the federal government, most states and local school districts to classify those students who have insufficient English to succeed in English-only classrooms and thus require language support services. The term ELL is a broader term that includes children classified as LEP.

5. For a more thorough discussion of educational policy issues related to bilinguals in early childhood education see Wiese and García, 2006.

References

Antúnez, B. (2002). *The preparation and professional development of teachers of English language learners.* Washington, DC: ERIC Clearinghouse on Teaching and Teacher Education. (ERIC Document Reproduction Service No. ED 477724). Retrieved January 15, 2006, from ERIC Online Database.

Au, K. H. (1993). *Literacy instruction in multicultural settings.* New York: Harcourt Brace.

Barnett, S., Hustedt, J. T., Hawkinson, L. E., & Robin, K. B. (2006). *The state of preschool 2006: State preschool yearbook.* New Brunswick, NJ: The National Institute for Early Education Research.

Barnett, W. S., & Camilli, G. (2002). Compensatory preschool education, cognitive development, and "race." In J. M. Fish (Ed.), *Race and intelligence: Separating science from myth* (pp. 369–406). Mahwah, NJ: Erlbaum.

Barnett, W. S., & Hustedt, J. T. (2003). Preschool: The most important grade. *Educational Leadership* [Online], *60*(7), 54–57.

Barnett, W. S., & Yarosz, D. J. (2007).Who goes to preschool and why does it matter? (Revised). *Preschool Policy Brief 15.* New Brunswick, NJ: National Institute for Early Education Research.

Barnett, W. S., Yarosz, D. J., Thomas, J., Jung, K., & Blanco, D. (2007). Two-way and monolingual English immersion in preschool education: An experimental comparison. *Early Childhood Research Quarterly, 22*(3), 277–293.

Bialystok, E. (2001). *Bilingualism in development: Language, literacy, and cognition.* Cambridge, UK: Cambridge University Press.

Berzins, M. E., & López, A. E. (2001). Starting off right: Planting the seeds for biliteracy. In J. J. Halcón & M. L. Reyes (Eds.), *The best for our children: Critical perspectives on literacy for Latino students* (pp. 81–95). New York: Teachers College Press.

Bowman, B. T., Donovan, M. S., & Burns, M. (Eds.). (2001). *Eager to Learn: Educating our preschoolers.* Washington, DC: National Reading Council.

Brandon, P. (2004). The child care arrangements of preschool age children in immigrant families in the United States. *International Migration Review 42*(1), 65–88.

Bredekamp, V. S., & Copple, C. (Eds.). (1997). *Developmentally appropriate practice in early childhood programs revised edition.* Washington, DC: National Association for the Education of Young Children.

Bridges, M., Fuller, B, Rumberger, R., & Tran, L. (2004). *Preschool for California's children: Promising benefits, unequal access* (Working Paper Series 05-I). Berkeley: Policy Analysis for California Education.

Bronfenbrenner, U. (1974). *Is early intervention effective? A report on longitudinal evaluations of preschool programs*. Washington, D C: Office of Child Development, Dept. of Health, Education, and Welfare.

Calderón, M., González, R., & Lazarin, M. (2004). *State of Hispanic America 2004: Latino perspectives on the American agenda*. Washington, DC: National Council of La Raza.

Clair, N., & Adger, C. T. (1999). *Professional development for teachers in culturally diverse schools*. Washington, DC: ERIC Clearinghouse on Languages and Linguistics. (ERIC Document Reproduction Service No. ED435185)

Cummins, J. (1981). The role of primary language development in promoting educational success for language minority students. In California State Department of Education (Ed.), *Schooling and language minority students: A theoretical rationale* (pp. 3–49). Los Angeles: California State University.

Cummins, J. (1993). Empowering minority students: A framework for intervention. In L. Weis & M. Fine (Eds.), *Beyond Silenced Voices* (pp. 101–118). Albany: State University of New York.

Day, C. B. (2006). Leveraging diversity to benefit children's social-emotional development and school readiness. In B. Bowman & E. K. Moore (Eds.), *School readiness and social-emotional development: Perspectives on cultural diversity* (pp. 23–32). Washington, DC: National Black Child Development Institute, Inc.

De La Luz Reyes, M. (2001). Unleashing possibilities: Biliteracy in the primary grades. In M. De La Luz Reyes & J. J. Halcón (Eds.), *The best for our children: Critical perspectives on literacy for Latino students* (pp. 96–121). New York: Teachers College Press.

Delgado-Gaitán, C. (2004). *Involving Latino families in schools: Raising student achievement through home-school partnerships*. Thousand Oaks, CA: Corwin Press.

Dworin, J. E. (2003). Insights into biliteracy development: Theory of bilingual pedagogy. *Journal of Hispanic Higher Education, 2*(2), 171–186.

Good Start Grow Smart Early Learning Initiative (2002). Washington, DC: Executive Office of the President, Washington, DC.

Eisenberg, A. (2002). Maternal teaching talk within families of Mexican descent: Influence of task and socioeconomic status. *Hispanic Journal of Behavioral Sciences, 24*, 206–224.

Espinosa, L., Laffey, J., & Whittaker, T. (2005). *Language minority children analysis: Focus on technology use*. Washington, DC: CREST/NCES.

Espinosa-Herold, M. (2007). Stepping beyond sí se puede: Dichos as a cultural resource in mother-daughter interaction in a Latino family. *Anthropology & Education Quarterly, 38*(3), 260–277.

Fine, M. (1991). *Framing dropouts: Notes on the politics of an urban high school*. Albany: State University of New York Press.

Fránquiz, M. E. (2002). Caring literacy and identity struggles: The transformation of a Chicano student. In L. Soto (Ed.), *Making a difference in the lives of bilingual/bicultural children* (pp. 185–194). New York: Peter Lang.

Fránquiz, M., & Reyes, M. (1998). Creating inclusive learning communities through English-language arts: From chanclas to canicas. *Language Arts, 75*(3), 211–220.

Fránquiz, M. E., & Salazar, M. (2004). The transformative potential of humanizing pedagogy: Addressing the diverse needs of Chicano/Mexicano students. *The High School Journal, 87*(4), 36–53.

Fuller, B., Bridges, M., Pai, S. (2007). *Standardized childhood: The political and cultural struggle over early education*. Stanford, CA: Stanford University Press.

García, E. E. (1991). Caring for infants in a bilingual child care setting. *Journal of Educational Issues of Language Minority Students, 9*, 1–10.

García, E. E. (2004). Bilingualism is not the arithmetic sum of two languages. In O. N. Saracho & B. Spodek (Eds.), *Contemporary perspectives on language policy and literacy instruction in early childhood education* (pp. 243–258). Greenwich, CT: Information Age.

García, E. E., & Jensen, B. (2006). Advancing school readiness for young Hispanic children through universal prekindergarten. *Harvard Journal of Hispanic Policy, 19*, 25–37.

García, O., Kleifgen, J., & Falchi, L. (2008). *Equity in the education of Emergent Bilinguals: The case of English language learners*. Research Review Series Monograph, Campaign for Educational Equity, Teachers College, Columbia University.

Genesee, F., Paradis, J., & Crago, M. (2004). *Dual language development & disorders: A handbook on bilingualism and second language learning.* Baltimore: Paul H. Brookes.

Genishi, C. (2002). Young English language learners: Resourceful in the classroom. *Young Children, 57*(4), 66–72.

Gersten, R. (1999). The changing face of bilingual education. *Educational Leadership, 56*(7), 41–45.

Goals 2000: Educate America Act. Pub. L. No. 103-227 (1994).

Gort, M. (2006). Strategic codeswitching, interliteracy, and other phenomena of emergent bilingual writing: Lessons from first grade dual language classrooms. *Journal of Early Childhood Literacy, 6*(3), 323–354.

Grosjean, F. (1982). *Life with two languages.* Cambridge, MA: Harvard University Press.

Gutiérrez, K. D., & Rogoff, B. (2003). Cultural ways of learning: Individual traits or repertoires of practice. *Educational Researcher, 32*(5), 19–25.

Hernández, D. (2004). Demographic change and the life circumstances of immigrant families. *The Future of the Children Journal, 14*(2), 17–47. Retrieved from http://www.futureofchildren.org/usr_doc/hernandez.pdf

Hernández, D. (2006). *Young Hispanic children in the U.S.: A demographic portrait based on Census 2000.* Report to the National Task Force on Early Childhood Education for Hispanics. Tempe: Arizona State University.

Hernández, D. J. & Charney, E. (Eds.). (1998). *The health and well-being of children in immigrant families.* Washington, DC: National Academy Press.

Hochschild, J., & Scouronick, N. (2005). Demographic change and democratic education. In S. Fuhrman & M. Lazerson (Eds.), *The public schools: Institutions of democratic society.* New York: Oxford University Press.

Hornberger, N. H. (Ed.). (2003). *Continua of biliteracy: An ecological framework for educational policy, research, and practice in multilingual settings.* Clevedon, UK: Multilingual Matters.

Irvine, D. J. (1982). *Evaluation of the New York state experimental prekindergarten program.* Albany: New York State Department of Education.

Jacobson, L. (2007). Early-childhood programs urged for Hispanic population. *Education Week, 26*(27), 11.

Lambert, W. E. (1975). Culture and language as factors in learning and education. In A. Wolfgang (Ed.), *Education of immigrant students.* Toronto: O.I.S.E.

Lee, V., & Burkam, D. (2002). *Inequality at the starting gate.* Washington, DC: Economic Policy Institute.

Lewis, L., Parsad, B., Carey, N., Bartfai, N., Farris, E., Smerdon, B., & Green, B. (1999). *Teacher quality: A report on the preparation of public school teachers.* (NCES 1999-080). Washington, DC: National Center for Education Statistics. Retrieved January 15, 2006, from http://nces.ed.gov/pubs99/1999080.pdf

López, G. R. (2001). The value of hard work: Lessons on parent involvement from an (im)migrant household. *Harvard Educational Review, 71*, 416–437.

Macedo, D. (1997). English-only: The tongue-tying of America. In A. Darder, R. D. Torres, & H. Gutiérrez (Eds.), *Latinos and education: A critical reader* (pp. 269–278). New York: Routledge.

MacGregor-Mendoza, P. (2000). Aquí no se habla español: Stories of linguistic repression in Southwest schools. *Bilingual Research Journal, 24*(4), 355–368.

Magnuson, K., Lahaie, C., & Waldfogel, J. (2006). Preschool and school readiness of children of immigrants. *Social Science Quarterly, 87*(5), 1241–1262.

Magnuson, K., Meyers, M., Ruhm, C., & Waldfogel, J. (2003). *Inequality in preschool education and school readiness.* New York: Columbia University.

Manyak, P. C. (2006). Fostering biliteracy in a monolingual milieu: Reflections on two counter-hegemonic English immersion classes. *Journal of Early Childhood Literacy, 6*(3), 241–266.

Martínez-Roldan, C. M., & Malavé, G. (2004). Language ideologies mediating literacy and identity in bilingual contexts. *Journal of Early Childhood Literacy, 4*(2), 155–180.

Martínez-Roldan, C. M., & Sayer, P. (2006). Reading through linguistic borderlands: Latino students' transactions with narrative texts. *Journal of Early Childhood Literacy, 6*(3), 293–322.

Moll, L. C., Amanti, C., Neff, D., & González, N. (1992). Funds of knowledge for teaching: Using a qualitative approach to connect homes and classrooms. *Theory into Practice, 31*, 132–141.

Moll, L. C., & Dworin, J. (1996). Biliteracy in classrooms: Social dynamics and cultural possibilities. In D. Hicks (Ed.), *Child discourse and social learning* (pp. 221–246). New York: Cambridge University Press.

Moll, L. C., Sáez, R., & Dworin, J. (2001). Exploring biliteracy: Two student case examples of writing as a social practice. *Elementary School Journal, 101*, 435–449.

National Center for Education Statistics (2002). *Schools and staffing survey: 1999–2000.* Retrieved January 15, 2006, from http://nces.ed.gov/pubs2002/2002313.pdf

Nieto, S. (2003). *What keeps teachers going?* New York: Teachers College Press.

Nieto, S. (2004). *Affirming diversity: The sociopolitical context of multicultural education.* Boston: Pearson Education.

National Association for the Education of Young Children (NAEYC). (1996). NAEYC position statement: Responding to linguistic and cultural diversity-recommendations for effective early childhood education. *Young Children,* 4–12.

National Clearinghouse for English Language Acquisition (NCELA). (2002). *What are the most common language groups for ELL students?* Washington, DC: National Clearinghouse for English Language Acquisition and Language Instruction Educational Programs. Retrieved January 2, 2007, from http://www.ncela.gwu.edu/expert/faq/05toplangs.html

National Task Force on Early Childhood Education for Hispanics (NTFECEH). (2007). *Para nuestros niños: Expanding and improving early education for Hispanics main report.* Tempe, AZ: National Task Force on Early Childhood Education for Hispanics. Retrieved December 5, 2007, at http://www.ecehispanic.org/work/expand_MainReport.pdf

No Child Left Behind (NCLB) Act of 2001, Pub. L. No. 107-110, § 115, Stat. 1425 (2002).

Olsen, L. (1997). *Made in America: Immigrant students in our public schools.* New York: The New Press.

Ortiz, R. W. (2004). Hispanic/Latino fathers and children's literacy development: Examining involvement practices from a sociocultural context. *Journal of Latinos and Education, 3*(3), 165–180.

Pastor, A. M. R. (2008). Competing language ideologies in a bilingual/bicultural after-school program in southern California. *Journal of Latinos and Education, 7*(1), 4–24.

Pérez, B., & Torres-Guzmán, M. (1996). *Learning in two worlds* (2nd ed.). New York: Longman.

Pérez, P., & Zarate, M. E. (2006). *Latino public opinion survey of pre-kindergarten programs: knowledge, preferences, and public support.* Los Angeles: Tomás Rivera Public Policy Institute, University of Southern California.

Perry, N. J., Kay, S. M., & Brown, A. (2008). Continuity and change in home literacy practices of Hispanic families with preschool children. *Early Child Development & Care, 178*(1), 99–113.

Portes, A., & Hao, L. (1998). E pluribus unum: Bilingualism and loss of language in the second generation. *Sociology of Education, 71*, 269–294.

Reyes, I. (2006). Exploring connections between emergent biliteracy and bilingualism. *Journal of Early Childhood Literacy, 6*, 267–292.

Riojas-Cortez, M. (2001). Preschoolers' funds of knowledge displayed through sociodramatic play episodes in a bilingual classroom. *Early Childhood Education Journal, 29*, 35–40.

Rodríguez, J. L., Díaz, R. M., Duran, D., & Espinoza, L. (1995). The impact of bilingual preschool education on the language development of Spanish-speaking children. *Early Childhood Research Quarterly, 10*, 475–490.

Rueda, R., Yaden, Jr., D. B. (2006). The literacy education of linguistically and culturally diverse young children: An overview of outcomes, assessment, and large-scale interventions. In B. Spodek & O. N. Saracho (Eds.), *Handbook of research on the education of young children* (2nd ed., pp. 167–186). Mahwah, NJ: Erlbaum.

Rumberger, R., & Anguiano, A. (2004). *Understanding and addressing the California Latino achievement gap in early elementary school.* Working paper 2004-01. Santa Barbara: University of California.

Sáenz, T. I., & Felix, D. M. (2007). English-speaking Latino parents' literacy practices in southern California. *Communication Disorders Quarterly, 28*(2), 93–106.

Schneider, B., Martínez, S., & Owens, A. (2006). Barriers to educational opportunities for Hispanics in the United States. In M. Tienda & F. Mitchell (Eds.), *Hispanics and the future of America* (pp. 179–221). National Research Council, Panel on Hispanics in the United States and Committee on Population, Division of Behavioral and Social Sciences and Education. Washington, DC: The National Academies Press.

Shonkoff, J. P., & Philips, D. A. (Eds.). (2000). *From neurons to neighborhoods: The science of early child development.* National Research Council, Institute of Medicine. Washington, DC: National Academy Press.

Soto, L. D. (1993). Native language for school success. *Bilingual Research Journal, 17*, 83–97.

Souto-Manning, M. (2007). Immigrant families and children (re)develop identities in a new context. *Early Childhood Education Journal, 34*(6), 399–405.

Tabors, P. (1997). *One child, two languages.* Baltimore: Paul H. Brookes.

Tabors, P., & Snow, C. (2001). Young bilingual children and early literacy development. In S. Neumann & D. Dickinson (Eds.), *Handbook of early literacy research* (pp 159–178). New York: Guilford.

Takanishi, R., (2004). Leveling the playing field: Supporting immigrant children from birth to eight. *Future of Children, 14*(2), 61–80.

Thomas, W., & Collier, V. (2002). *A national study of school effectiveness for language minority students' long-term academic achievement.* Santa Cruz, CA and Washington, DC: Center for Research on Education, Diversity, & Excellence. Retrieved from http://www.crede.ucsc.edu/research//llaa/1.1_final.html

Thomas, W., & Collier, V. (1997). *School effectiveness for language minority students NCBE (Resource Collection Series No. 9).* Washington, DC: National Clearinghouse of Bilingual Education.

Tse, L. (2001). Heritage language literacy: A study of U.S. biliterates. *Language, Culture, and Curriculum, 14*(3), 256–268.

U.S. Census Bureau (2004). Hispanic and Asian Americans increasing faster than overall population. *United States Dept of Commerce News* [Online]. Retrieved June 14, 2004, from http://www.census.gov/PressRelease/www/releases/archives/race/001839.html

U.S. Department of Health and Human Services, Administration for Children and Families. (2005, May). *Head Start Impact Study: First Year Findings.* Washington, DC: U.S. Government Printing Office.

Valdés, G. (1996). *Con respeto: Bridging the distance between culturally diverse families and schools.* New York: Teachers College Press.

Vélez-Ibáñez, C., & Greenberg, J. (1992). Formation and transformation of funds of knowledge among U.S. Mexican households. *Anthropology and Education Quarterly, 23*, 313–335.

Villenas, S., & Moreno, M. (2001). To valerse por si misma between race, capitalism, and patriarchy: Latina mother-daughter pedagogies in North Carolina. *International Journal of Qualitative Studies in Education, 14*(5), 671–687.

White House Initiative on Educational Excellence for Hispanic Americans (1999). *Latinos in education: Early childhood, elementary, secondary, undergraduate, graduate.* Washington, DC: ED 440 817. Retrieved from http://www.ericdigests.org/2001-3/facts.htm

Wiese, A., García, E. E. (2006). Educational policy in the United States regarding bilinguals in early childhood education. In B. Spodek & O. N. Saracho (Eds.), *Handbook of research on the education of young children* (2nd ed., pp. 361–374). Mahwah, NJ: Erlbaum.

Winsler, A., Díaz, R. M., Espinosa, L., & Rodríguez, J. L. (1999). When learning a second language does not mean losing the first: Bilingual language development in low-income, Spanish-speaking children attending bilingual preschool. *Childhood Development, 70*, 349–362.

Wong-Fillmore, L. (1996). What happens when languages are lost? An essay on language assimilation and cultural identity. In D. I. Slobin, J. Gerhardt, A. Kyratzis, & J. Guo (Eds.), *Social interaction, social context, and language* (pp. 435–446). Mahwah, NJ: Erlbaum.

Wong-Fillmore, L. (2000). Loss of family languages: Should educators be concerned? *Theory into Practice, 39*(4), 203–210.

Zentella, A. C. (Ed.). (2005). *Building on strength: Language and literacy in Latino families and communities.* New York: Teachers College Press.

33 Best Practices for Teaching Latino English Learners in U.S. Schools

Josefina Villamil Tinajero, Judith Hope Munter, and Blanca Araujo

University of Texas at El Paso

Overview

The increase in the number of students who speak a native language other than English in U.S. schools has been dramatic and is expected to remain so. Spanish-speaking children in grades K-12 constitute the largest subgroup within this growing segment of the school population. Educators serving these children must keep in mind that English learners (ELs) are a diverse group, with varying educational experiences, primary language skills, and levels of English proficiency. The No Child Left Behind (NCLB) legislation requires schools to identify and serve both ELs and immigrant students and makes them strictly accountable for ensuring that these children make rapid progress in learning English while monitoring concomitant advances in their reading, math, and science skills. At the same time, there is much ambiguity about how schools can best help students to bridge the gap between languages and cultures, with all that entails. This chapter will present an overview of research on best practices for teaching English learners, focusing on specific applications for Latino ELs and highlighting the roles of native language and culturally relevant contexts for language and literacy development. The chapter concludes with an overview and examples of best practices for Latino ELs in U.S. schools.

Best Practices for Teaching Latino English Learners in U.S. Schools

As the pace of immigration to the United States accelerates, providing high quality educational opportunities for first- and second-generation immigrant children is a pressing concern for educational researchers, practitioners, and policy makers. Discourse on this issue ranges from concerns about equity and access to growing pressures in relation to standards-based achievement for all students in public schools. English learners (ELs) are the most rapidly growing population in U.S. schools. Between 1994 and 2004, the number of ELs in grades K-12 increased by more than 56% while the overall student population increased by only 12% in the same period (Kohler & Lazarin, 2007). Some states (e.g., Alabama, Arkansas, Colorado, Indiana, and North Carolina) have experienced even more dramatic EL student growth rates—as high as 200% or more.

Current federal law under the No Child Left Behind (NCLB) Act defines linguistically diverse students according to Title IX general provisions as "limited English proficient" (LEP), interpreted as "persons from ages 3 to 21, enrolled in elementary or secondary education, often born outside the United States or speaking a language other than English in their homes, and not having sufficient mastery of English to meet state standards and excel in an English-language classroom" (US Department of Education, 2002). In this chapter, the authors refer to these students as English learners (ELs), precluding the official terminology that characterizes these children in relation to limitations or deficiencies.

While the overall number of school-aged English learners attending U.S. schools has risen rapidly over the past decade; the growth in numbers of Spanish-speakers has outpaced all other linguistic groups. In 2000, the population of all ELs in the United States spoke over 400 native languages; 79% of that group identified Spanish as their native language and Hispanic/Latino as their ethnicity. Projections indicate that these demographic trends will continue in coming years and decades (Kohler & Lazarin, 2007; Morse, 2005).

English learners tend to be immigrants or the children of immigrants (first- second-, and, in some instances, third-generation). Thus, the "border crossing" experience of the large and growing population of Latino youth in the United States (Anzaldúa, 1999; Ewing, 1998; Giroux, 2005) refers not only to the geographical distances traversed from their native homes to the United States; the borders these young people have crossed are also physical, emotional, and psychological. A corollary of this phenomenon is that children and families from non- English-speaking backgrounds are likely to encounter serious problems within the U.S. educational system. One of the first realities confronted by many is the clash between their primary language(s) and the norms of U.S. schools. In a nation in which relatively few educational policy makers or practitioners can speak or write a language other than English, skills and knowledge in Spanish are often proscribed by mainstream educators who have adopted subtractive approaches to schooling, characterizing diverse learners' native languages and cultures as "barriers" to learning, rather than assets (Nieto, 2002; Valenzuela, 1999). As a result, Latino ELs (and other children) from diverse cultural/linguistic backgrounds frequently start off on an uneven playing field in U.S. schools in which diversity is viewed as a liability rather than an intellectual accomplishment and a national treasure.

This chapter will discuss these and other important issues concerning schooling for ELs in the US. First, the authors present an overview of research on best practices in teaching English learners, focusing on the roles of native language and culturally relevant contexts for language and literacy development, followed by an overview and examples of best practices for Latino English learners in U.S. schools.

Learning in Two Languages: A Paradigm Shift

In the first half of the 20th century, most people in the United States generally believed that second language learning early in life resulted in confused learning, interfering with children's ability to develop normal cognitive functions. A landmark study by Peal and Lambert (1962), demonstrating the superiority of bilingual learners over monolingual learners in a wide range of intelligence tests shifted the focus of research on bilingual education (to some degree) to examination of the benefits of learning in two languages; yet the knowledge base about best practices for teaching ELs in U.S. public schools merits continuous attention from the educational research community. Recent studies have been more balanced, using mixed methods and longitudinal designs (e.g., Genesee, Lindholm-Leary, Saunders, & Christian, 2005; Kenner, 2000; Peregoy & Boyle, 2000) to identify and illustrate the benefits of bilingualism on children's overall cognitive development. This line of research indicates an important role for schools in promoting native language literacy as a means for these children to develop language proficiency and cognitive skills in English (the second language). As they develop skills and knowledge using bilingual/biliterate modalities, ELs become adept in the school language and reap the most positive benefit from their educational experience.

Thoughtful analysis of data collected over the last 50 years clearly indicates that bilingual children are not cognitively handicapped. In fact, studies indicate that bilingualism is a positive force that enhances young children's cognitive and linguistic development, improving access to literacy; this outcome is even more pronounced when the two writing systems correspond (e.g., Rolstad, Mahoney, & Glass, 2005; Slavin & Cheung, 2005). For example, Bialystok & Shapero (2005) examined four groups of children in first grade to compare their development on early literacy tasks. Children in three of the groups were bilingual, each group representing a different combination of language and writing system, and children in the fourth group were monolingual speakers of English. All the bilingual children used both languages daily while learning to read in both languages. The children solved decoding and phonological awareness tasks, and the bilinguals completed all tasks in both languages. Initial differences between the groups in factors that contribute to early literacy were controlled in an analysis of covariance. While the results showed a general increment in reading ability for all the bilingual children, a larger advantage resulted for youngsters learning two alphabetic systems. Similarly, bilingual children transferred literacy skills across languages when both languages were written in the same system. These studies indicate that the extent of bilingual facilitation for early reading corresponds to the relationship between the two languages and writing systems.

The effects of bilingualism also extend to children's linguistic and educational development. When children continue to develop their skills and abilities in two or more languages throughout their primary school years, they gain a deeper understanding of language and how to use it effectively. They have more practice in processing language, especially when they develop literacy in both, and are able to compare and contrast the ways in which the two language systems organize reality. The research suggests that reading instruction in the home language may serve as a bridge to success in English because decoding and comprehension strategies transfer between languages, particularly those that use similar orthographies (see Dressler & Kamil, 2006; Francis, Lesaux, & August, 2006).

Additionally, recent studies indicate that the positive benefits of bilingualism reach beyond impacts on developmental stages during the early years of one's life, and may help to delay the development of dementia in later years. Examining the diagnostic records of 184 patients, researchers with the Rotman Research Institute at the Baycrest Research Centre for Aging and the Brain found evidence that bilingualism enhances attention and cognitive control in both young children and older adults. Their studies found that the age of onset of impairment of cognitive functioning (determined by interviewing the patients' neurologists during the first clinic visit) was on average four years earlier in monolingual patients than in the bilingual group. Results were consistent even after other influencers, including formal education, cultural differences and gender, were controlled (Bialystock, Craik, & Freedman, 2007).

However, in spite of the evidence indicating the positive impacts of bilingualism, most of the research on Latino youth in U.S. schools today points to their persistent educational underachievement (Brice, 2002; Garcia, 2001; Scribner, 1999; Short & Fitzsimmons, 2007). Many Latino students read English two or more grade levels below grade placement, and comparatively few score at advanced levels on standardized tests. Among all groups in the United States, Latino students have been found to have the lowest rate of participation in early childhood development programs (Fry, 2002) and over one third (35%) are retained at least once while in school. Except for Native Americans, Latinos are also more likely than other minority groups in the United States to be retained one, two, or more grades and to drop out before completing high school (Armas, 2003; ERIC Clearinghouse on Urban Education, 2001; Hernandez, 1997; Olson 2003). These statistics are unacceptable.

The dilemma facing schools serving these children demands knowledge, will and determination from policy makers and practitioners. NCLB requires schools to leave no child behind, identifying and serving ELs and immigrants with the best educational resources possible, but makes them strictly accountable for ensuring that these populations make rapid progress in learning English, as well as in all content areas of the curriculum (reading, math, science, social studies). To date, many school districts throughout the United States have been reluctant to adopt changes in policy; few have committed resources to further research about second language learners. In relation to Hispanic youth, the results of the disconnect between school policies and EL student success have been detrimental, producing alarming statistics, such as: (a) a steady decline in high school completion rates, (b) a rise in the dropout rate at younger ages and lower grade levels, (c) large numbers of students who are two or more years behind grade level, and (d) the achievement gap (Fix & Batalova, 2005; Fry, 2002; Ruiz de Velasco, Fix, & Clewell, 2001).

It is our position that a central premise of 21st century educational policy/planning for all children in U.S. schools must be based on sound research and effective practice; ELs merit the attention of researchers and policy makers, particularly at this juncture when a substantial body of research-based evidence clearly points to the devastating outcomes of English-only and similar narrow linguistic policies. Empirical studies indicate that the more literate one becomes in the native or first language (L1), the better the progress in a second language (e.g., Genesee, Christian, Saunders, & Lindholm-Leary, 2006; Rolstad, Mahoney, & Glass, 2005; Slavin & Cheung, 2005). The research on second language acquisition has demonstrated that students with limited English proficiency who acquire strong literacy skills in their primary language apply these skills to the acquisition of English literacy (e.g., August & Shanahan, 2006; Cummins, 2000; Genesee et al., 2005; Ramírez, Yuen, Ramey, & Pasta, 1991). Skills and knowledge attained in the primary language facilitate the acquisition of English literacy. The opposite is equally true; students who do not receive primary language support are challenged in acquiring both literacy and academic knowledge in English (or their native language) at grade level.

Several states with large EL populations (e.g., California, Arizona, and Massachusetts) have implemented policies that require students to receive an English-only curriculum after just one year of receiving language support, leading to renewal of policies based on old paradigms, and an increased focus on language learners' limitations (e.g., LEP as a title) rather than highlighting the assets of Latino students. Several other states are following suit, moving towards the implementation of English-only policies, in spite of evidence indicating that English-only is not the best policy for serving our schools' rapidly increasing numbers of ELs.

The sections that follow discuss key points concerning the roles of native language, family involvement and diverse contexts in planning for effective language and literacy development for English learners, followed by an overview of best practices for Latino children in U.S. schools. Two research-based instructional methods, *Sheltered Instruction* and *One-Way/Two-Way Dual Language*, are highlighted. *Funds of Knowledge* as a culturally relevant framework for teaching and learning is briefly described as well. The section closes with an example of best practices in action (the *Family Book Project*) and concluding statements about the need for further research and action.

Native Language and Literacy Development

Literacy skills are developed most effectively as a natural outgrowth of the lived experience that students bring with them from their diverse home and community environments to school. Landmark studies from the 1980s and 1990s (e.g., Heath, 1996) revealed that each community has its own rules for socializing children through language and that ways of making meaning through print differ across communities. Optimal literacy instruction for culturally and linguistically diverse students builds on children's previous learning, enabling them to derive meaning from their own reservoir of background experiences.

Research has also shown a key to successful teaching and learning is creating personal connections with students' lives and prior experiences inside and outside of school. In relation to language development, this view is derived from the concept of emergent literacy, emphasizing that learning literacy cannot be reduced to a set of mechanical techniques (Berninger et al., 2006; Clay, 2001; Flood, Lapp, Tinajero, & Hurley, 1997; Ormrod, 1999; Peregoy & Boyle, 2000). Each learner's background knowledge, experience, attitudes, and perspectives determine the ways that information is perceived, understood, valued, and stored (Flood, Lapp, & Fisher, 2003). In schools that fail to take into account the contexts in which teaching and learning take place, children from culturally and/or linguistically diverse backgrounds are frequently deprived from opportunities for establishing the connections that form early on in the development of cognitive abilities, impeding their later ability to think critically about higher order, complex concepts.

Studies on optimal literacy development for young children (e.g., Gay, 2000; Igoa, 1995; Snow, 1990; Valenzuela, 1999) underscore the need for schools to show sensitivity and appreciation for the language and cultural norms that Latino students bring to the classroom. The evidence points to the need for high quality teachers not only to introduce new skills and knowledge, but also to establish continuity between the home and the school while validating the cultural values and linguistic knowledge of these students. By so doing, schools can maximize the self-esteem of students, enhance caring relationships between teachers and learners, and provide the foundation for successful pedagogical activity (Noddings, 2005).

Moreover, using the language of the home as a tool for instruction is one of the most natural elements of cultivating each learner's sense of worth and fully developing the intellectual potential that is often stripped away from groups of children who are designated as limited (LEP) learners when they enter the culture of the monolingual U.S. public school. The importance of this vital component of the Latino child's classroom experience is affirmed by the research of numerous scholars who contend that positive self-identification is intrinsically linked to educational success (e.g., Jimenez, 2000; Lindholm-Leary & Borsato, 2002; Nieto, 2002; Portes & Zady, 1999).

Authentic and effective literacy learning involves building intricate networks of concept relations, structuring and restructuring understandings, connecting them to previous knowledge, and practicing multiple complex skills in diverse environments. When ELs explore print in their mother tongue, they are learning about the lexical, grammatical, and semantic possibilities of a linguistic system that they already are able to use to "interpret and reinterpret their experiences" (Perez & Torres-Guzman, 2002, p. 29). At this early stage in their development, these beginning readers have acquired a sociolinguistic perspective on how to explain, orient, argue, negate, and express emotions; furthermore, they are able to predict others' responses (i.e., the ways in which individuals in their speech community will think, feel, behave, or react) to their utterances (Laliberty & Berzins, 2000). These reactions, interpretations and interactions enable these children, at early stages in their personal/social/cognitive development, to learn to affirm their own sense of self identity and moral agency in the world.

Given the multifaceted nature of the reading process, when EL youngsters attain a level of reading proficiency in their native language that enables them to discover the meanings, ideas and messages that can come from books and print, they have learned a great deal at a deep level about language and the social nature of linguistic communication (Chomsky, 1968, 1986; Strickland, Snow, Griffin, Burns, & McNamara, 2002). These beginning readers are taking significant steps towards gaining an analytical knowledge of the symbolic potential of language. Thus, providing children with well-designed literacy instruction in their native language prepares them for literacy development by furnishing them with strong foundations for understanding multiple, expressive possibilities in the second language—English.

Research indicates that as long as students have well-developed skills in key native language (L1) domains, they can draw on L1 language and metacognitive responses to strengthen their second language (i.e., English) literacy development (e.g., Cummins et al., 2005; Francis et al., 2006; Genesee et al., 2005; Reese, Garnier, Gallimore, & Goldenberg, 2000). The linguistic interdependence principle (Cummins, 1979), a description of the transfer of language knowledge from an individual's L1 to his/her L2, is useful in explaining the processes involved that enable young native Spanish speakers to perform well in English when they have previously attained literacy proficiency in their mother tongue (Cloud, Genesee, & Hamayan, 2000; Cummins, 2003). When these children learn about the intricacies of print relationships through materials that highlight their own language and social reality, the linguistic interdependence principle predicts that they will be able to extend their repertoire of literacy expertise to a range of language and social contexts in their L2, connecting the known world of the home language to the unknown foreign world of the second language (Krashen & Biber, 1998). While a large and growing number of studies confirm the assertion that there is a positive correlation between the development of L1 skills and L2 literacy (e.g., Kenner, 2000; Lindholm & Zierlein, 1991; Snow, 1990; Snow, Burns, & Griffin, 1998; Thomas & Collier, 1997/1998), further research is needed on this timely and important topic, exploring implications for educational programming and policy development.

Sociocultural and Sociopolitical Contexts for Learning

Students of all backgrounds tend to learn best when the classroom affirms their culture, language, and lived experience. This tenet is as true of English learners as it is of their peers and classmates in U.S. schools today (Nieto, 2002). Sociocultural factors influence behaviors, values, beliefs, cognitive processes, and assumptions and each one of these has direct and indirect influences on learning. Goldenberg, Rueda, and August (2006) define sociocultural influences as "factors that make up the broad social context in which children and youth live and go to school" (p. 250). For English learners to fully benefit from U.S. schools' educational opportunities, classroom curricula need to acknowledge and value the children's home cultures. Homes, communities, families, and cultural knowledge must be integrated into the curriculum. Goldenberg et al. (2006) state that "minimizing differences between home and school literacy/academic interactions can help to promote high levels of achievement" (p. 255).

Research studies examining the impacts of effective home-school communication affirm these findings. Bartolomé and Trueba (2000), for example, conducted a study of successful teachers of ELs and found that key characteristics of effective teaching included rejection of a deficit and assimilationist view; promotion of L1 instruction in the classroom; and conscious, explicit valuing of the socio-cultural strengths of students, and including each student's native language and lived experiences.

Montecel and Cortez' (2002) study of exemplary bilingual education programs in ten schools found that each of the schools had 25 common characteristics and criteria that contributed to their students' high academic achievement. One of these characteristics was that curricula reflected and valued the students' culture. Their research also found that in these schools, the students engaged in active learning, working cooperatively in heterogeneous groups and hands-on activities. Teachers provided bilingual books of all types and genres, and writing assignments tended to reflect the cultural background of the students. Assignments included discussions of a wide variety of topics and promotion of higher order thinking skills (e.g., application, analysis and synthesis). For example, in one of these cases, a student began a discussion about an uncle who had achieved a significant goal in his life. This led to further discussion about other students and their family members, resulting in group stories written by the students as the teacher modeled the writing process (Montecel & Cortez, 2002).

Implications for Best Practices in K-12 Classrooms

Latino students frequently confront many of the challenges that other minority students do in relation to academic achievement in public schools—inadequate preparation for higher education and limited resources available to support educational goals. Professional educators know very well, however, that individual characteristics (such as language, socioeconomic status, culture, and ethnicity) do not in and of themselves impair learning or preclude success for all (Stritikus & Garcia, 2003). English learners in U.S. schools, however, frequently face additional barriers in K-12 school systems because of narrow linguistic policies that devalue students' native language and background knowledge, in spite of substantial evidence that bilingual proficiency and biliteracy are positively related to academic achievement (e.g., Genesee et al., 2005; Lindholm-Leary, 2001; Slavin & Cheung, 2005).

Following here, we review selected best practices in K-12 classrooms that have helped to reverse deficit thinking and underachievement by focusing on Latino students' strengths and assets in U.S. schools: Sheltered Instruction, One- and Two-Way Dual Language (OWDL/TWDL), and Funds of Knowledge; a model program—the Family Book Project—is described to illustrate best practices in action.

Sheltered English Instruction

Echevarria, Short, and Powers (2006) developed an effective strategy for teaching content to English learners, the Sheltered Instruction Observation Protocol (SIOP). The model consists of lesson planning and delivery in English with instructional strategies grouped into eight components to help ELs succeed in school. The SIOP method is built on best practices research from mainstream classrooms (e.g., Honigsfeld & Cohan, 2008; Tharp et al., 2003), adding strategies that focus on developing English language skills. The model is based on the principle that language acquisition is enhanced within social and cultural contexts through meaningful application and interaction (Minaya-Rowe, 2004). The eight components of SIOP are: preparation, building background, comprehensible input, strategies, interaction, practice/application, lesson delivery, and review/assessment (Short & Echevarria, 2005).

A key feature of SIOP is activating and strengthening background knowledge or linking to students' personal experiences and knowledge. In a social studies classroom, for example, students who have not studied the U.S. Civil War in their native countries but have studied (or experienced) other instances of civil unrest firsthand can talk about these experiences to help set the context for studying U.S. history and the U.S. Civil War (Abadiano & Turner, 2002). Echevarria, Short, and Powers (2006) tested the SIOP model for its effects on student achievement and academic literacy development, discovering positive outcomes for ELs, including significant gains in writing performance, specifically in expository writing (Echevarria et al., 2006). A single-group study to examine impacts of the SIOP model on teacher attitudes was conducted at the University of Connecticut in a course with a group of 15 graduate student/teachers. The objective of the course was to enhance or to improve the adult learners' Spanish proficiency. The SIOP model was used for content selection and lesson preparation. Spanish lessons integrated the eight components of SIOP. At the completion of the semester, participants' self-assessments indicated that they had made progress in learning content knowledge as well as enhancing and improving their Spanish. They also expressed positive attitudes and overall satisfaction in relation to the use of SIOP strategies in their own classrooms (Minaya-Rowe, 2004).

One- and Two-Way Dual Language Education

While dual language programs share many characteristics that contribute to student achievement, two distinct variations on the model have been developed and tested, two-way and one-way dual language (TWDL and OWDL) education programs. The primary distinction between the two is in the student populations the programs serve. Two-way programs include both language minority and language majority children, whereas one-way developmental programs focus on serving the language minority population. Emerging results of studies of one-and two-way bilingual programs tell us of their effectiveness in educating non-English speaking students, of expanding and enriching our nation's language resources by conserving the native language of English learners, and of developing second language skills in English speaking students. Two-way dual language education also enhances cross-cultural communication and appreciation.

In both OWDL and TWDL education, students develop bilingualism and attain academic achievement. Developing proficiency in the first language has many advantages for language minority students (e.g., Cummins, 2000; Genesee et al., 2005). First, students develop cognitive and academic concepts, and then learn corresponding labels in English. The native language facilitates the development of both the basic and advanced literacy. It helps students increase their knowledge of the world in all subject areas and use the native language to make English more comprehensible. Furthermore, students in one- and two-way programs benefit greatly from an additive bilingual environment in which students see their language as valuable and positive. In monolingual (and even some bilingual) classrooms, the native language of ELs is treated as a problem or a deficiency, resulting in students feeling uncomfortable and even embarrassed about their proficiency in the native language. In two-way programs, *all* students are second language learners.

Additionally, it is important for English-speaking students to have the opportunity to learn a second language. While educators in many nations of the world have long recognized that bilingual/multilingual education equips all students to be more prepared to live and work in a world that is interconnected, interdependent and international, US education policy has yet to fully acknowledge that dual language education provides immense benefits for monolingual English speakers, as well as for EL students.

In OWDL/TWDL programs, both the language minority and the monolingual English-speaking students are challenged to solve problems expressing clearly what they know in two languages, and they both have opportunities to share and display competence in L1 and L2. While social prestige markers may still favor English in U.S. schools, the experiences of learning together about each other and in each other's language often help students see diverse others as human beings developing cognitively, socially, and linguistically, understanding commonalities and interconnectedness in new ways. Thus, OWDL/TWDL programs protect minority cultures and promote cultural and linguistic diversity among all students.

Culturally relevant instruction is a critical feature of effective dual language programs. Within this context, the following are important: (a) inclusion of original works from the worlds of the language minority groups so that the children see the authors as intellectual role models; and (b) acknowledgment of what students bring into the classroom, including experiences, cultural ways, and family history—as legitimate knowledge upon which to build.

Numerous scholars (e.g., Cummins, 2000; Lindholm & Zierlein, 1991) add that acquiring improved higher order thinking skills in the native language allows ELs to acquire higher order thinking skills in English as well. Taylor and Whittaker (2003) affirm that bilingualism, bidialectalism, and biculturalism must be viewed as strengths; using the child's native language does not impede the acquisition of English, rather it offers many advantages in relation to linguistic, cognitive and social development. Bilingual language instruction is most effective when schools integrate programs like TWDL or OWDL that define bilingualism and cultural pluralism as resources of great value. Furthermore, the communication of ELs and English proficient students in two-way dual language classrooms helps to promote change by creating bonds among students as they work on common goals.

For ELs, the burden of unidirectionality is lifted when they participate in one- and two-way dual language programs. Bilingualism is transformed from a deficit to a socially desirable commodity. The goal is to develop individuals who are fully competent in two languages in a variety of domains. An important parallel goal is biliteracy, the ability to decode and encode print that conveys messages in a variety of contexts using two linguistic and cultural systems (Pérez & Torres-Guzman, 2002). As research suggests, a strong foundation in the first language of the child transfers to the second language, and literacy is deemed critical to all academic tasks.

The dual language approach highlights the ways in which bilingual education, at its best, can integrate English native speakers with speakers of another language in the common pursuit of L2 acquisition, while continuing to develop each learner's native language. Research has shown that dual language programs emphasize full bilingual proficiency for native and nonnative speakers, promote positive attitudes towards language learning, and result in optimal outcomes for Latino children. Yet, because these programs are connected to the language rights of minority groups and the struggle to maintain native languages, some U.S. educators have continued to politicize and challenge their validity in the policy arena (Christian, Howard, & Loeb, 2000; Perez & Torres-Guzman, 2002; Tinajero & Pardo, 2000).

Funds of Knowledge

Background knowledge about a wide variety of topics (such as mediating household communication with outside institutions, caring for younger siblings, or repairing appliances) is a valuable asset that students and family members bring to schools and is factored into instructional planning in the most effective classroom for ELs. This construct, "funds of knowledge" (Gonzalez, Moll, & Amanti, 2005; Moll, Amanti, Neff, & Gonzalez, 1992), constitutes knowledge that is learned at home and has been successfully used in promoting effective teaching/learning in schools and stronger sense of community, especially in localities with large numbers of Latino students, parents, and community members.

Moll et al. (1992) provided examples of effective dialogues and interviews, during which teachers learned how to listen to immigrant children's and families' stories, enabling a deeper understanding of the cultural knowledge that these students possess. Through home visits, teachers were able to deconstruct previously held stereotypes about households by learning about students' cultural backgrounds and family histories. These teacher/researchers moved from theory to practice, taking what was learned from the research and using the new understandings (i.e., funds of knowledge) in the classroom. These teachers shifted their own deficit views by bridging the world of the students at home to the school environment and using the children's lived experiences as topics and resources for teaching.

Following here, the authors present an example of an effective teaching/learning project in which educators have promoted high achievement for ELs and helped to develop stronger community life. These interactions have profoundly influenced goals and activities developed by teachers, schools, and college students. Furthermore, the community's voice has energized efforts to develop projects and activities that create new and more inclusive opportunities for all.

The Family Book Project: A Case Study of Best Practices in Action

In many language minority homes, the primary storehouses of knowledge are the extended family members, and significant bodies of knowledge and information are transmitted orally from generation to generation. One technique used on the U.S./Mexico border in El Paso's urban schools to provide support for culturally/linguistically diverse children as they learn to integrate the two worlds of home and school has consisted of encouraging children and parents to write books together, featuring themselves and other family members as the main protagonists.

There is not a "one-size-fits-all" formula or format for the creation of the family books. However, we list below a set of general guidelines that schools can follow to set the stage for enabling teachers to work with Latino children and families as authors and creative designers of their own unique book projects.

1. A primary goal of the Family Book Project (FBP) is, in large part, to create a new tool for opening up channels for communication through which parents can view themselves as co-equals and vital components of a collaborative educational team.

Immigrant parents frequently experience uncertainty about the roles they can play in U.S. public schools. Some low-income Latino parents view the school system as a bureaucracy governed by authorities whom they have no right to question. Hesitation and uncertainty about their own capability to carry out educational activities of value (such as helping with homework, reading with their children, and establishing routines) may impede parents from undertaking home-based teaching/learning activities. Communication problems about roles and respon-sibilities are often compounded when parents sense that the school personnel are accentuat-ing the distance between them by using unfamiliar words and phrases (i.e., technical jargon) in their messages with the home. The FBP, particularly when implemented in a dual language context, enables teachers to learn how to communicate with parents concerning values, and teaching/learning objectives of the classroom, providing appropriate examples when needed. Parents' native language and cultural knowledge is valued in every component of the project, often resulting in bonds of trust and authentic partnerships between teachers and parents with mutual recognition of the vital role that each play in supporting children's learning.

2. The project aims to involve parents and children as co-equals in the process, engaged in open conversation with each other about significant events in their lives. Family photographs and/or other artifacts may be useful in generating these dialogues.

Writing a book together allows parents and children to learn to appreciate each other's worlds. The creative process provides an opportunity for children to develop a greater sense of their own identity through conversations about their hopes, fears, insights, and dreams with their parents. The co-authoring experience also provides excellent opportunities for parents to share their unique family histories, background knowledge and childhood experiences with their own children. Opportunities for mutual understanding and personal growth often occur through the process of co-authoring a book which parents and children might not otherwise experience. Teachers frequently discover unique opportunities to build on the parents' skills to help students progress and practice new skills in language, mathematics, social studies, science, etc. For example, a parent with expertise in gardening/agriculture could share that knowledge, while teachers engage students in reading comprehension activities, writing exercises, math-ematics and/or science lessons based on the topics introduced by the parent. The SIOP model lends itself well to these school-home interactions.

3. There are many possible formats for both the product and the process of book creation.

Family members are encouraged to share their creative skills and knowledge with one another by designing a book that reflects their unique history and experience. Educators who work with immigrant parents and families recognize that the logistical barriers that these families face in their everyday lives create enormous obstacles that make it very difficult for them to participate in urban U.S. schools. These barriers include concerns about: *time*—parents often work, and in the case of immigrant/migrant families, the work site may be a considerable distance from school; *resources*—parents who work very hard to provide the bare essentials for their families may find that (over the short term) their children's schooling reduces daily income, actually compounding the problem of the family's extreme poverty level; *safety*—migrant/immigrant families often feel that they have much to fear, recognizing that they are not always welcome in the communities on whose behalf they labor; and *child care*—making arrangements becomes more difficult for migrant families and recent immigrants when they no longer have extended family members nearby to support them by providing free, trusted daycare services for young children.

Furthermore, the schools themselves may unknowingly create additional barriers for fami-lies when, for example, their programs and curricula are segmented; different programs target-ing distinct groups can make it difficult to facilitate family-wide learning. For example, in some urban school districts the young child's pre-K class may be on one campus, while the mother's English as a Second Language (ESL) classes are housed in another location, often far away. In light of these precautions and recommendations, the flexibility and creative planning generated by the Family Book Project can help establish greater trust and confidence between teachers and families, schools and homes. Families can meet at times and locations of their own choosing.

Teachers may or may not be involved in these sessions, yet should always be available to assist. The Funds of Knowledge approach ensures that parents understand that they are key players in the education of their children, enhancing authentic partnerships between the school and home.

4. Educational teams are engaged as reflective practitioners throughout the project. Teachers' and administrators' understanding and knowledge of local families will be deepened through this process, empowering them to work more effectively with the diverse children in the school.

Some of the reflective questions that K-12 teachers involved in the project have posed include: What have I learned about parents' life experiences and knowledge that enhance their role as contributors to their children's social, emotional and intellectual development? How can I use this knowledge to more effectively partner with parents in educating their children? How can I tap into the skills and talents of parents to engage them in the school in creative ways? The process of book authorship offers unique opportunities for teachers to fully benefit from their own and others' creative energies, fostering authentic learning communities and dynamic community participation. Educators committed to recognizing the human potential of each individual can use the Funds of Knowledge framework to learn to be open to new possibilities for integrating equity and social justice into the classroom. The Family Book Project provides unique opportunities for learning and practicing democratic skills through collaborative teamwork, dialogue, and reflection.

5. Parents are viewed as lifelong learners and are equally engaged in reflection on the project and its implications for the family's role in supporting the literacy development of their own children.

The migratory experience, for many, magnifies the individual's sense of insignificance. Immigrants have been the focus of harsh press in the United States relative to the expense of education, health care, and other public and social welfare services. These families may view school personnel with suspicion and ambivalence if teachers pressure them to conform to the dominant culture and/or to reject the values and beliefs of their own cultures. U.S. schools traditionally have made few efforts to help new immigrants adjust to their new homes in the United States and become involved in the educational processes. The processes of collaborative planning, implementation, and celebration of the Family Book Project must be respectful and participatory; in fact, the creative processes are as important as the final product itself.

6. Projects finalize with a celebration during which families come together to share and reflect on their work.

The final product that is created has great significance in and of itself. It is a concrete demonstration of the accomplishment of overall project goals; caring relationships throughout the generations in the child's family are now visible evidence of the child's linkages to the world with which he/she is learning to identify. Learning to appreciate the family members' achievements over time through the native language and expressions of relatives and ancestors can help to bring families, schools, and community members together. For many participants, celebration of the completion of this activity creates a renewed understanding of the family as a vital link in the education of their children, empowering them as they gain a real sense of history and of purpose.

Bilingual Learners and Academic Achievement

The authors conclude this chapter with a note on outcomes to date on the U.S.-Mexico border community, where many of best practices for teaching Latino English learners have been implemented and evaluated for more than a decade. Notable progress has been made in schools with large numbers of ELs in El Paso, Texas, during the last decade, including a decrease in the number of low-performing schools and an increase in the number of El Paso schools recognized for their gains in student achievement by the Texas Education Agency (Cawelti & Protheroe, 2001; Tinajero & Spencer, 2002). While a number of critical elements have contributed to successful reform in El Paso's urban school districts, best practices in instruction for Latino ELs, based on the SIOP model, OWDL/TWDL education, and Funds of Knowledge perspectives (e.g., effective native language literacy instruction embedded within programs that integrate parents, inclusion of schools and community members in educational planning, and cooperative learning) have been central and vital components. However, the need for further research on this important and timely topic cannot be overstated.

Conclusion

While there are variations in pedagogical approach, the role of native language, family involvement and diverse contexts in effective educational planning for Latino students are critical. As a whole, native Spanish-speaking children learn to perform better in English in an environment that respects their native language and provides continued growth in that language. The education of English-speaking children is enriched as well by participating in bilingual/multilingual learning environments. Research also tells us that children develop cognitive/social/intellectual skills best when they learn and are engaged in real life situations that are meaningful, purposeful, and safe for taking risks (Cummins, 2000).

This nation has arrived at a critical crossroads with regard to providing evidence of high quality education for Latino students who are English learners. On one hand, expectations have been raised for these students and our systems of accountability strive to ensure that they reap all the benefits of standards-based reform. Yet on the other hand, most educators are not well informed about exactly what English learners know as they enter and move through the U.S. educational system, and there is a paucity of research on best practices for English learners, such as SIOP, OWDL/TWDL education programs, Funds of Knowledge frameworks, and family involvement in schools' instructional strategies. While there is no single formula for ensuring high achievement for the large and diverse population of Latino students in today's K-12 schools, attention and resources must be focused on additional research on best practices and school improvement.

Latino English learners are one of the fastest-growing student populations in U.S. schools today and improving education outcomes for these children is one of our nation's most significant challenges. Now is the time for researchers, policy makers, and practitioners to work collaboratively, channeling resources to develop a deeper understanding of the great potential that these children present, and focus new resources on the tremendous opportunities for present and future success.

References

Abadiano, H., & Turner, J. (2002). Sheltered instruction: An empowerment framework for English-language learners. *The NERA Journal, 38*(3), 50–55.

Advisory Commission on Educational Excellence for Hispanic Americans. (2003). *From risk to opportunity: Fulfilling the educational needs of Hispanic Americans in the 21st century. Final report of the president's advisory commission on educational excellence for Hispanic Americans.* Washington, DC: White House Initiative on Educational Excellence for Hispanic Americans. (ERIC Document ED475876).

Anzaldúa, G. (1999). *Borderlands: La frontera.* San Francisco: Aunt Lute Books.

Armas, G. (2003, June 13). Hispanic dropout rate more complex than high. *Chicago Sun Times.* Retrieved June 8, 2003, from http://www.suntimes.com/output/education/cst-nws-hisp13.html

August, D., & Shanahan, T. (2006). *Developing literacy in second-language learners: Report of the national literacy panel on language-minority children and youth.* Mahwah, NJ: Erlbaum.

Bartolomé, L., & Trueba, E. (2000). Beyond the politics of schools and the rhetoric of fashionable pedagogies: The significance of teacher ideology. In E. Trueba & L. Bartolomé (Eds.), *Immigrant voices in search of educational equity* (pp. 277–292). Lanham, MD: Rowman & Littlefield.

Berninger, V., Abbott, R., Jones, J., Wolf, B., Gould, L., Anderson-Youngstrom, et al. (2006). Early development of language by hand: Composing, reading, listening, & speaking connections: Three letter-writing modes; and fast mapping in spelling. *Developmental Neuropsychology, 29*(1), 61–92.

Bialystok, E., Craik, F., & Freedman, M. (2007). Bilingualism as a protection against the onset of symptoms of dementia. *Neuropsychologia, 45*(2), 459–464.

Bialystok, E., & Shapero, D. (2005). Ambiguous benefits: The effect of bilingualism on reversing ambiguous figures. *Developmental Science, 8,* 595–604.

Brice, A. (2002). *The Hispanic child: Speech, language, culture and education.* Boston: Allyn & Bacon.

Cawelti, G., & Protheroe, N. (2001). High student achievement: How six school districts changed into high-performance districts. Arlington, VA: Educational Research Service.

Chomsky, N. (1968). *Language and mind.* New York: Harcourt Brace Jovanovich.

Chomsky, N. (1986). *Knowledge of language.* Westport, CT: Praeger.

Christian, D., Howard, E., & Loeb, M. (2000). Bilingualism for all: Two-way immersion education in the United States. *Theory into Practice, 39*(4), 258–266.

Clay, M. (2001). *Change over time in children's literacy development.* Portsmouth, NH: Heinemann.

Cloud, N., Genesee, F., & Hamayan, E. (2000). *Dual language instruction: A handbook for enriched education.* Boston: Heinle & Heinle.

Cummins, J. (1979). Linguistic interdependence and the educational development of bilingual children. *Review of Educational Research, 49*(2), 222–251.

Cummins, J. (2000). *Language, power, and pedagogy: Bilingual children in the crossfire.* Clevedon, UK: Multilingual Matters.

Cummins, J. (2003). Reading and the bilingual student: Fact and fiction. In G. G. Garcia (Ed.), *English learners: Reaching the highest level of English literacy* (pp. 2–33). Upper Saddle River, NJ: Pearson.

Cummins, J., Bismilla, V., Chow, P., Cohen, S., Giampapa, F., Leoni, L., et al. (2005). Affirming identity in multilingual classrooms. *Educational Leadership, 63*(1), 38–43.

Dressler, C., & Kamil, M. (2006). First- and second-language literacy. In D. August & T. Shanahan (Eds.), *Developing literacy in second-language learners* (pp. 197–238). Mahwah, NJ: Erlbaum.

Echevarria, J., Short, D., & Powers, K. (2006). School reform and standards-based education: A model for English-language learners. *The Journal of Educational Research, 99*(4), 195–210.

ERIC Clearinghouse on Urban Education (2001). *Latinos in school: Some facts and findings.* ERIC Digest #162. New York: Columbia University, Institute for Urban & Minority Education. (ERIC Doc Reproduction Service No. ED449288)

Ewing, K. (1998). Crossing borders and transgressing boundaries: Metaphors for negotiating multiple identities. *Ethos, 26*(2), 262–267.

Fix, M., & Batalova, J. (2005). *English language learner adolescents: Demographics and literacy achievements.* Washington, DC: Migration Policy Institute.

Flood, J., Lapp, D., & Fisher, D. (2003). Reading comprehension instruction. In J. Flood, D. Lapp, J. Squire, & J. Jensen (Eds.), *Handbook of research on teaching the English language arts* (2nd ed., pp. 857–867). Mahwah, NJ: Erlbaum.

Flood, J., Lapp, D., Tinajero, J., & Hurley, S. (1997). Literacy instruction for students acquiring English: Moving beyond the immersion debate. *The Reading Teacher, 50*(4), 356–358.

Francis, D., Lesaux, N., & August, D. (2006). Language of instruction. In D. August & T. Shanahan, (Eds.), *Developing literacy in second-language learners* (pp. 365–413). Mahwah, NJ: Erlbaum.

Fry, R. (2002, September). *Latinos in higher education: Many enroll, too few graduate.* Washington, DC: Pew Hispanic Center.

Garcia, E. (2001). *Hispanic education in the United States: Raices y alas.* Lanham, MA: Rowman & Littlefield.

Gay, G. (2000). *Culturally responsive teaching: Theory, research and practice.* New York: Teachers College Press.

Genesee, F., Christian, D., Saunders, W., & Lindholm-Leary, K. (2006). *Educating English language learners: A synthesis of research evidence.* New York: Cambridge University Press.

Genesee, F., Lindholm-Leary, K., Saunders, W., & Christian, D. (2005). English language learners in U.S. schools: An overview of research. *Journal of Education for Students Placed at Risk, 10*(4), 363–385.

Giroux, H. (2005). *Border crossing, second edition: Cultural workers and the politics of education.* New York: Taylor & Francis.

Goldenberg, C., Rueda, R., & August, D. (2006), Synthesis: Sociocultural contexts and literacy development. In D. August & T. Shanahan (Eds.), *Developing literacy in second-language learners* (pp. 249–268). Mahwah, NJ: Erlbaum.

Gonzalez, N., Moll, L., & Amanti, C., (2005). *Funds of knowledge: Theorizing practice in households, communities and classrooms.* Mahwah, NJ: Erlbaum.

Heath, S. (1996). *Ways with words: Language, life, and work in communities and classrooms.* New York: Cambridge University Press. (Original work published 1983)

Hernandez, H. (1997). *Teaching in multilingual classrooms: A teacher's guide to context, process, and content.* Upper Saddle River, NJ: Prentice-Hall.

Honigsfeld, A. & Cohan, A. (2008). The power of two: Lesson study and SIOP help teachers instruct ELLs. *Journal of Staff Development, 29*(1), 24–26, 28.

Igoa, C. (1995). *The inner world of the immigrant child.* New York: St. Martin's Press.

Jimenez, R. (2000). Literacy and the identity development of Latina/o students. *American Educational Research Journal, 37* (4), 971–1000.

Kenner, C. (2000). Biliteracy in a monolingual schools system? English and Gujarati in South London. *Language, Culture and Curriculum, 13*(1), 13–20.

Kohler, A. & Lazarin, M. (2007). *Hispanic education in the United States* (Statistical Brief No. 8). Retrieved March 10, 2008, from National Council of La Raza website http://www.nclr.org

Krashen, S., & Biber, D. (1998). *On course: Bilingual education's success in California.* Sacramento: California Association for Bilingual Education.

Laliberty, E., & Berzins, M. (2000). Creating opportunities for emerging iliteracy. *Primary Voices K-6, 8*(4), 11–17.

Lindholm, K., & Zierlein, A. (1991). Bilingual proficiency as a bridge to academic achievement: Results from bilingual/immersion programs. *Journal of Education, 173*(2), 99–113.

Lindholm-Leary, K. (2001). *Dual language education.* Avon, UK: Multilingual Matters.

Lindholm-Leary, K., & Borsato, G. (2002). *Impact of two-way immersion on students' attitudes toward school and college.* ERIC Digest. Washington, DC: ERIC Clearinghouse on Languages and Linguistics. (ERIC Document Reproduction Service No. ED 464514)

Minaya-Rowe, L. (2004). Training teachers of English language learners using their students' first language. *Journal of Latinos and Education, 3*(1), 3–24.

Montecel, M., & Cortez, J. (2002). Successful bilingual education programs: Development and the dissemination of criteria to identify promising and exemplary practices in bilingual education at the national level. *Bilingual Research Journal, 26*(1), 1–21.

Moll, L., Amanti, C., Neff, D., & Gonzalez, N. (1992). Funds of knowledge for teaching: Using a qualitative approach to connect homes and classrooms. *Theory Into Practice, 31*(2), 132–141.

Morse, A. (2005). *A look at immigrant youth: Prospects and promising practices.* National Conference of State Legislatures. Children's Policy Initiative. http://www.ncsl.org/print/health/CPIimmigrantyouth.pdf

Nieto, S. (2002). *Language, culture and teaching: Critical perspectives for a new century.* Mahwah, NJ: Erlbaum.

Noddings, N. (2005). Caring in education. *The encyclopedia of informal education.* Retrieved May 12, 2003 from www.infed.org/biblio/noddings_caring_in_education.htm

Olson, L. (2003, April 16). Panel asks for action on Hispanic achievement gap. *Education Week on the Web.* Retrieved May 22, 2003, from http://www.edweek.org/ew/ewstory.cfm?slug=31hispanic.h22

Ormrod, J. (1999). *Human learning, 3rd ed.* Upper Saddle River, NJ: Merrill.

Peal, E., & Lambert, W. (1962). The relation of bilingualism to intelligence. *Psychological Monographs, 76,* 1–23.

Peregoy, S., & Boyle, O. (2000). English learners reading English: What we know, what we need to know. *Theory into Practice, 39*(9), 237–247.

Pérez, B., & Torres-Guzman, M. (2002). *Learning in two worlds: An integrated Spanish/English biliteracy approach* (3rd ed.). Boston: Allyn & Bacon.

Portes, P., & Zady, M. (1999). *Children of immigrants' self-esteem in early adolescence: The role of ethnicity, context, language and family on cultural adaptation.* Chicago: Spencer Foundation, National Science Foundation. (ERIC Document Reproduction Service No. ED457253)

Ramírez, J., Yuen, S., Ramey, D., & Pasta, D. (1991). *Final Report: Longitudinal study of structured English immersion strategy, early exit and late-exit bilingual education programs for language minority children.* (Prepared for U.S. Department of Education). San Mateo, CA: Aguirre International. No. 300-87-0156.

Reese, L., Garnier, H., Gallimore, R., & Goldenberg, C. (2000). Longitudinal analysis of the antecedents of emergent Spanish literacy and middle-school English reading achievement of Spanish-speaking students. *American Educational Research Journal, 37*(3), 633–662.

Rolstad, K., Mahoney, K., & Glass, G. (2005). The big picture: A meta-analysis of program effectiveness research on English language learners. *Educational Policy, 19*(4), 572–594.

Ruiz de Velasco, J., Fix, M., & Clewell, B. (2001). *Overlooked and underserved: Immigrant students in U.S. secondary schools.* Washington, DC: The Urban Institute

Scribner, A. (1999). High-performing Hispanic schools: An introduction. In P. Reyes, J. Scribner, & A. Scribner (Eds.), *Lessons from high-performing Hispanic schools: Creating learning communities.* (pp. 1–18). New York: Teachers College Press.

Short, D., & Echevarria, J. (2005). Teacher skills to support English-language learners. *Educational Leadership,* 8–13.

Short, D., & Fitzsimmons, S. (2007). *Double the work: Challenges and solutions to acquiring language and academic literacy for adolescent English language learners – A report to Carnegie Corporation of New York.* Washington, DC: Alliance for Excellent Education.

Slavin, R., & Cheung, A. (2005). A synthesis of research on language of reading instruction for English language learners. *Review of Educational Research, 75*(2), 247–284.

Snow, C. E. (1990). Rationales for native language instruction. In A. Padilla, H. Fairchild, & C. Valdez (Eds.), *Bilingual education: Issues and strategies* (pp. 60–74). Newbury Park, CA: Sage.

Snow, C., Burns, M., & Griffin, P. (Eds.). (1998). *Preventing reading difficulties in young children.* Washington, DC: National Academy Press.

Strickland, D., Snow, C., Griffin, P., Burns, M., & McNamara, P. (2002). *Preparing our teachers: Opportunities for better reading instruction.* Washington, DC: Joseph Henry Press, National Academy of Sciences.

Stritikus, T., & Garcia, E. (2003, August 6). The role of theory and policy in the educational treatment of language minority students: Competitive structures in California. *Education Policy Analysis Archives, 11*(26). Retrieved August 9, 2003, from http://epaa.asu.edu/epaa/v11n26/

Taylor, L., & Whittaker, C. (2003). *Bridging multiple worlds: Case studies of diverse educational communities.* Boston: Allyn & Bacon.

Tharp, R., Doherty, R., Echevarria, J., Estrada, P., Goldenberg, C., Hilberg, R., et al. (2003). *Research evidence: Five standards for effective pedagogy and student outcomes.* Technical Report No. G1. Center for Research on Education, Diversity & Excellence. Retrieved March 25, 2008, from http://crede.berkeley.edu/research/crede/products/print/occreports/g1.html

Thomas, W., & Collier, V. (1997/98). Two languages are better than one. *Educational Leadership, 55*(4), 23–26.

Tinajero, J., & Pardo, E. (2000). Literacy instruction through Spanish: Linguistic, cultural, and pedagogical considerations. In J. Tinajero & R. DeVillar (Eds.), *The power of two languages 2000: Effective dual-language use across the curriculum* (pp. 42–53). New York: McGraw-Hill.

Tinajero, J., & Spencer, D. (2002). Models of bilingual teacher preparation: What has worked at the University of Texas at El Paso. In L. Minaya-Rowe (Ed.), *Teacher training and effective pedagogy in the context of student diversity: Research in bilingual education.* Greenwich, CT: Information Age. (ERIC Document Reproduction Service No. 467579)

U.S. Department of Education. (2002). *Elementary and Secondary Education Act. Title IX General Provisions.* Retrieved March 10, 2008, from http://www.ed.gov/policy/elsec/leg/esea02/pg107.html#sec9101

Valenzuela, A. (1999). *Subtractive schooling: U.S.-Mexican youth and the politics of caring.* Albany: State University of New York Press.

34 Accountability and Educational Assessment for Latino English Language Learning Students

Improving Practices through Multidisciplinary Approaches

Zenaida Aguirre-Muñoz
Texas Tech University

Guillermo Solano-Flores
University of Colorado at Boulder

Introduction

[T]he testing of bilingual individuals has developed from the practice of testing monolinguals without the necessary examination of the assumptions underlying the measurement of monolingual abilities and applicability of these assumptions and theories to the measurement of the same abilities in persons who function in two language systems... (Valdes & Figueroa, 1994, p. 2)

Although the opening quote was written well over a decade ago, current testing practices for students who are not proficient in the language in which they are tested have not changed substantially. The identification of language as a major construct-irrelevant factor in testing (AERA, APA, & NCME, 1999) has not been accompanied by improved practice in the testing of English language learners (ELLs). Reasonings from the language sciences and knowledge on the nature of bilingualism and its crucial relevance to the testing of these students have been available for years. Amazingly, these reasonings and knowledge do not guide standard practice intended to minimize language as a source of error in the testing of ELLs.

In this chapter, we examine the limitations of current testing practices that are relevant to the testing of Latino ELLs in an era of accountability. One of the most serious challenges in this field is the lack of multidisciplinary approaches that allow development of testing models that are compatible with current knowledge on language development, bilingualism, and cultural anthropology (Solano-Flores & Trumbull, 2003). A theory that addresses the complex relations among language, culture, cognition, test taking, and test development is yet to be developed. In addition, a critical body of knowledge on the characteristics of multiple linguistic groups relevant to testing is lacking. While there is a considerable body of research on ELL testing, linguistic groups are not properly defined, and information about the linguistic backgrounds of ELLs and their proficiency in both their first language (L1) and their second language (L2) is fragmented or inaccurate (Solano-Flores, 2008). As a consequence, it is not possible to identify the set of factors that are specific to the testing of ELLs from a given ethnic or linguistic group. Thus, rather than attempting to identify testing issues that are specific to Latino ELLs, we discuss the challenges of fairly and validly testing any ELL population that is as numerous, complex, and diverse as the Latino population of ELLs in the United States. By examining the limitations of current testing practices in their effectiveness to address linguistic diversity, we hope to be able to show the limitations and challenges of testing Latino ELLs.

The academic achievement gap between Latinos and other ethnic groups in the United States, the patterns of social inequality that marginalize Latino students and limit their access to high quality education and their opportunities to advanced courses are issues beyond the scope of this chapter. Rather, we focus on examining how effectively current testing practices address the tremendous linguistic and cultural diversity in the Latino population and proposing ways in which testing practices for ELL Latinos (as well as any other linguistic and cultural groups) can be improved. We argue that valid test score interpretation rests on the extent to which language and culture are addressed throughout the entire process of testing.

Our conceptual framework for examining assessment practices for Latino, ELLs is an adaptation of the conceptual framework proposed by the National Research Council's report, *Knowing What Students Know* (NRC, 2001). According to this report, three components are critical to properly assessing student knowledge: (a) a model of how students represent and learn subject matter, (b) a set of tasks that elicit the desired performance observation, and (c) a method for drawing inferences from performance evidence. These components have been proven to be useful in examining the limitations of assessment systems (Solano-Flores, in press).

Figure 34.1 presents the triangle used in NRC's report to show how the three components are interconnected. Since NRC's triangle is silent about language and culture, we have added the shaded circle seen in its center. Language and culture are moved to the foreground to highlight the need for approaches that take into account the cognitive, semantic, communicative, and sociolinguistic factors involved in testing (August & Hakuta, 1997; Solano-Flores, 2003).

Our chapter is organized in four sections according to the circle and triangle in Figure 34.1. Section II addresses the circle, language, and culture. It examines Latino ELLs as a tremendously linguistically and culturally diverse group and discusses empirical evidence which shows that the performance of ELLs is extremely sensitive to dialect variation and that failure of testing models to consider the characteristics of populations of ELLs within a given broad linguistic group such as "Latino, native Spanish speakers" ultimately affects the validity of interpretations of test scores for that broad linguistic group.

Section III addresses cognition and the need for comprehensive approaches in assessment which recognize the importance of language in the process of test development. NCR establishes that the test development process begin with a clear conceptualization of a model of learning. We contend that language should be incorporated in the learning model as a critical component that shapes the cognitive processes involved in test taking.

Section IV addresses observation and discusses why, since ELLs are included in large-scale testing, language should be part of the factors guiding item development actions. While all states offer accommodations for ELLs, those accommodations are not usually designed with the

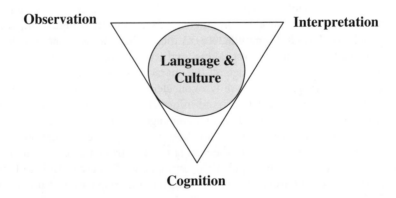

Figure 34.1 Assessment model for Latino ELLs.

same level of attention and detail with which assessment tasks are selected or developed. The development of test items should include a set of specifications regarding accommodations to ensure that they will elicit responses from ELLs in a manner that is consistent with the learning model that supports a test.

Section V addresses interpretation and discusses why the collection of construct validity evidence is critical to the validation process in the testing of ELLs. Since assessment results are based on *estimates* of understanding and skills which are inherently imperfect, valid interpretations of test scores are possible only when test items are sensitive to the knowledge and skills targeted.

We end this chapter with a short summary and a discussion of the implications for future development in ELL assessment.

Current Practice Concerning the Definition and Treatment of ELL Populations

From the perspective of testing, the population of ELL Latinos poses two important and complex sets of technical challenges. First, ELL Latinos comprise 80% of the population of ELLs in America's public schools (Kindler, 2002; Zehler et al., 2003). Second, Latinos constitute a tremendously diverse group, both culturally and linguistically.

The population of Latinos in the United States increased by 50% between 1990 and 2000 (U.S. Census Bureau, 2000), has dispersed to 22 states that have not previously experienced large numbers of Latino populations (U.S. Census Bureau, 2003), and is more likely to live in poverty than non-Latinos. A vast majority of Latinos who are of employment age, have low-skill, low-paying jobs (U.S. Bureau of Labor Statistics, 2006, as cited in Martinez-Aleman, 2006).

Although school-aged Latino children are predominately of Mexican descent, the number of students from Central and South American descent is increasing rapidly (U.S. Census Bureau, 2002). Latino children are more likely to: be retained in grade, particularly as they get older (Martinez-Aleman, 2006); attend large and disadvantaged public high schools (Fry, 2005); are twice as likely than African Americans and four times more likely than Whites to drop out of school (National Center for Education Statistics, 1997); and are more likely to attend highly segregated schools (U.S. Census Bureau, 2002).

Latino ELLs face additional challenges as they learn English, negotiate the U.S. culture, and learn the academic content of the curriculum in all subject areas (Abedi & Gándara, 2006). Not surprisingly, ELLs have historically lagged behind their non-ELLs counterparts, especially in subjects with high linguistic demands (Abedi, 2002; Butler, Lord, Stevens, Borrego, & Bailey, 2004). A tremendously increasing diversity of the dialects of Spanish and the dialects of English spoken by Latinos results from their increasing growth and dispersion in the country, their multiple cultural heritages and countries of origin, and the fact that the great majority of ELL student populations are U.S. native born—children of immigrants (Capps, Fix, Murray, Ost, Passel, & Herwantoro, 2005). Compared to other linguistic and cultural groups in the United States, the tremendous heterogeneity resulting from the combination of these factors places Latino students in a precarious educational context—a context which poses a unique set of technical challenges and ethical issues in testing practices (Abedi & Gándara, 2006).

Critical to examining the effectiveness of current practice and research in ELL testing is understanding how ELL populations are defined and viewed. Research, practice, and state policies concerning ELL testing are mainly based on classifying students according to a small number of levels of proficiency in English (e.g., "limited English proficient," "English proficient") or according to a small number of categories intended to describe histories of language development (e.g., "monolingual," "native English speaker"). Even state mandated English development assessments, which may evaluate students' listening, speaking, reading, and writing proficiency in English, are used with the purpose of making broad classifications of students' L2 proficiency.

Research, practice, and state policies concerning ELL testing also are mainly based on assigning students to treatment conditions. Individuals are assigned to different testing conditions such as the language used in a test (e.g., English, Spanish), the language mode in which the test is given to students (e.g., orally, in printed form), or the language mode in which students provide their responses to that test (e.g., verbal responses, written responses). A testing condition also may be produced by modifying the linguistic properties of a test with the intent to reduce its linguistic demands (e.g., simplifying the wording of items, including glossaries with word-to-word translations) or from modifying properties of the test that are not related to language but which are thought to be relevant for cognitively processing language (e.g., administering a test with no completion time limit).

A body of research on the use of testing accommodations for ELLs has explored a wide variety of testing conditions intended to reduce the linguistic demands of mathematics and science test items (see the reviews by Abedi, Hofstetter, & Lord, 2004; and Sireci, Li, & Scarpati, 2003). One issue investigated is the extent to which the use of a given testing accommodation reduces the score gap between ELL and non-ELLs. ELLs who receive and who do not receive a form of accommodation are compared to non-ELLs as to their test scores. If the accommodation is effective, then its impact should be reflected in a decrease of score differences between ELL and non-ELLs; also, the test scores should be higher for ELLs who received the accommodation than the scores for ELLs who did not receive the accommodation.

This kind of research also has examined the extent to which an accommodation benefits only ELLs. To examine this effect, non-ELLs who receive the accommodation are compared with non-ELLs who do not receive the accommodation (e.g., Abedi, 2002; Abedi & Hejri, 2004). If the accommodation truly operates on the linguistic demands of tests, then the scores obtained by non-ELLs with and without the accommodation should not differ substantially.

Issues and Limitations of Current Practice Concerning the Definition and Treatment of ELL Populations

Current research and state policies concerning the definition of ELL populations can be characterized as guided almost exclusively by a predominant view of language as a factor—an attribute which can adopt two or more conditions. As with any construct-irrelevant factor (see Messick, 1989), language is treated as something to be controlled or accounted for if valid measures of academic achievement or valid research results are to be obtained.

While, from the methodological perspective, the treatment of language as a factor is necessary in research, scientific soundness in educational research is not guaranteed with good research designs without a solid theoretical support (see Johnson, Kirkhart, Madison, Noley, & Solano-Flores, 2008). Serious limitations in current testing practice stem from the kinds of assumptions made about the nature of language and the accuracy of English proficiency measures.

Regarding the assumptions on the nature of language, it should be taken into account that language can be viewed not only as a factor, but also as a system (Solano-Flores, 2007). A view of language as a system recognizes that different forms of language are governed by rules and conventions, and that language is dynamic, rather than static. As a consequence, in addition to referring to different languages or different levels of proficiency in a given language, linguistic diversity is addressed as referring to different dialects of a given language (e.g., Standard English, African American Vernacular English), different forms of a language (e.g., informal language, formal language, academic language), the condition of being bilingual, the order of development of the languages of a bilingual individual (i.e., L1, L2), different language modes (listening, speaking, reading, and writing), and the fact that the proficiency of a given individual may vary considerably across language modes. A view of language as a system also allows examination of language as a social phenomenon, not simply as a condition of an individual. From this perspective, the condition of being bilingual is not only viewed as a matter of proficiency but also as a matter of social behavior that is shaped by context (Mackey, 1962).

While it could be used in combination with approaches in which language is treated as a factor, this view of language as a system is not reflected in current approaches to defining and treating ELL populations. As a consequence, these approaches are not sensitive to the enormous linguistic variation among Latino ELLs discussed at the beginning of this section. Rather, they are based on assuming that linguistic groups are homogeneous.

Current approaches to defining ELLs fail to recognize three important notions. First, language proficiency is shaped by context—a person can be proficient in L2 for some contexts, not others (e.g., De Avila, 1988; Grosjean, 1985; MacSwan, 2000). Second, different language proficiency tests emphasize different aspects of language (e.g., García, McKoon, & August, 2006). In addition, the fact that categories such as ELL and English proficient have different meanings across states (National Clearinghouse for English Language Acquisition and Language Instruction Educational Programs, 2006) poses a serious limit to the comparability and equivalence of measures of language proficiency. Third, due to multiple differences in migration histories and formal education background, bilingual individuals may have very different patterns of language dominance across language modes (see Baker, 2001; Bialystok, 2001; Durán, 1989; Solano-Flores & Trumbull, 2008). As a consequence, a single measure of language proficiency may provide inaccurate information about an individual's actual competences in English.

Given these serious limitations in the ways in which ELLs are defined, we question the extent to which serious testing decisions about students should be based on categories of language proficiency. An overreliance on single measures of language proficiency may contribute to erroneous classifications of students as either proficient or limited proficient in English and compromises the validity of measures of academic achievement.

Improving Practice Concerning the Definition and Treatment of ELL Populations

From our perspective, there are three kinds of actions that need to be taken if we are serious about improving the ways in which ELL populations are defined and treated. First, legal definitions of ELLs should be revised to ensure that they make sense according to current knowledge in the field of language development and bilingualism. For example, while the definition of ELL in current legislation (No Child Left Behind Act of 2001) acknowledges the multi-faceted nature of language (i.e., the ability to speak, read, write, and comprehend English) and the consequences of not being proficient in English (e.g., not benefiting from instruction), it also includes socio-demographic attributes such as age, place of birth, and being an immigrant—attributes which are associated with but not determinant of the condition of being an ELL. As a consequence of this vagueness, this definition of ELL is likely to be interpreted in multiple ways, operationalized, based on proxy variables that are not directly related to English proficiency, and likely to produce multiple erroneous student classifications.

Second, assessment systems should use a wider variety of measures of English proficiency which are sensitive to the language needs of students in the school context, focus on academic language, and address different language modes. An overreliance of single measures of English proficiency aggravates the problem of misclassification.

Finally, assessment systems should develop testing models which are consistent with the notion of linguistic variation and which incorporate randomness as critical to defining ELL populations. Consistent with this notion, we (Solano-Flores & Li, 2006) have proposed the use of generalizability (G) theory—a psychometric theory of measurement error (Cronbach, Gleser, Nanda, & Rajaratnam, 1972; Shavelson & Webb, 1991)—as an approach for examining measurement error due to language. With this approach, ELLs are tested with the same set of items in two languages (or two dialects of the same language). The purpose is not to give students bilingual tests, but to determine the number of items that are needed to obtain dependable measures of academic achievement when students are tested in each language or in each dialect (Solano-Flores & Trumbull, 2008). Our approach has shown that ELLs tend to perform well on some items in one language (or dialect) but less well for other items on the other language (or dialect). This interaction is due to the fact that ELLs have different sets of weaknesses and strengths in each language and items pose different sets of linguistic challenges in each language—a finding that is consistent with the notion that each ELL has a unique set of strengths and weaknesses in L1 and in L2 (Solano-Flores & Li, 2006).

As the results show, the elusive nature of ELL populations can be better characterized by developing probabilistic models that are sensitive to randomness and uncertainty, rather than forcing students into narrow, conceptually-weak categories of English proficiency.

Current Practice on Cognition, Development, and Adaptation of Tests

This section examines the way in which linguistic and cultural variation is addressed in the process of testing as it relates to the underlying theory of cognition inherent in testing models. Current thinking about testing practices dictates that the test development process begin with a clear conceptualization of a model of learning which, in turn, is reflected in the kinds of assessment data sought and in the types of interpretations that are made based on the evidence elicited from test items (NRC, 2001). From this conceptualization, targets of inference are identified and should guide the design of the assessment.

If assessments are going to yield more dependable and meaningful information about what Latino students know, language and culture must be directly addressed by the learning theory that drives the design of an assessment to yield adequate "reasoning from evidence" (NRC, 2001 p. 178) regarding the academic achievement of Latino ELLs. Although the practice of inclusion of ELLs in accountability systems is a step forward in equitable testing, the use of learning models that do not attend to linguistic and cultural factors undermines the potential for achieving equity. A focus on linguistic and cultural factors impacting how ELLs represent, organize, and process learned knowledge would address some of the linguistic issues current testing models tend to ignore. We do not mean to suggest that the basic architecture of the mind (e.g., working memory, long-term memory, etc.) and its corresponding cognitive processes (e.g., processes involved in schema development such as subsumption) are different for different linguistic and cultural groups. Rather, we maintain that if cognition is mediated by culturally-specific activities (e.g., Vygotsky, 1978; Wertsch, 1985), testing approaches informed by a sociocultural view of cognition will yield more equitable testing practices for ELLs. However, such a model would need to be supported by both general theories of language use (e.g., Halliday, 1975; 1978) and those that address how language is used to develop understanding in communities of learning (e.g., Mercer, 2004; Gee, 2005).

The primary strategy used by states to include ELLs in state-mandated assessments is to provide accommodations (Rivera & Collum, 2006). Rivera and Collum (2006) define accommodations as "changes to a test or testing situation [that] are used widely for the assessment of students who, because of limited proficiency in English or physical or cognitive disabilities, are deemed unable to participate meaningfully in state assessments without adjustments to the language or administration of the test" (p. 1). To be effective, these accommodations should address the unique needs of ELLs to allow them to overcome the linguistic and sociocultural barriers that may prohibit them from accessing the content of the test (Rivera & Collum, 2006). That is, accommodations are intended to eliminate construct-irrelevant variance and produce more meaningful test scores for ELLs. However, accommodations can be problematic if they give an unfair advantage to students who receive them over students who do not because validity is compromised (Aguirre-Muñoz & Baker, 1999; Elliot, Kratochwill, & Schultz, 1998).

Rivera and Collum (2006) report that in the 2000–2001 school year 47 states allowed accommodations to ELLs. Of the 75 accommodations available to ELLs across these states, 44 (39%) provide direct or indirect linguistic support. One of the most common accommodation strategies is translation of all or part of tests originally developed in English. During this time period, states also reported 11 native language accommodations available to ELLs that can be classified into four categories: (a) written translation, (b) scripted oral translation, (c) sight translation, and (d) student response in the native language (Rivera & Collum, 2006). Written and sight translations were the two most commonly used accommodations across states (19 and 29, respectively).

Issues and Limitations of Current Practice on the Development and Adaptation of Tests

Ignoring momentarily the fact that the provision of accommodations fails to address the need for fundamental changes to the learning models underlying current testing practices, Rivera and Collum (2006) found policies governing the use of accommodations for ELLs problematic in at least two ways. First, these researchers found inconsistencies across states in test accommodation policies and many of these practices did not target the unique needs of ELLs. That is, ELLs tend to be grouped with students with disabilities as students with "special needs," "at-risk students," or "special populations." Second, the great majority of accommodation strategies involve the test administration process and not the language of the test. Rivera and Collum point out that the variation in state's policies "suggest a lack of consistent focus on the needs of ELL" (p. 29). Consistent with earlier research (e.g., Ferrara, Macmillan, & Nathan, 2004), many states used an accommodation classification system originally developed for students with disabilities. Furthermore, the list of accommodations in about 40% of the states that identified accommodation did not target the specific needs of ELLs and often included strategies irrelevant to the ELL, such as use of Braille and assistive devices. To this list, we add an additional concern that Rivera and Collum alluded to but did not explicitly address in their investigation: States also do not make it explicit which accommodations are appropriate for ELLs with low, intermediate, or early advanced English proficiency. That is, with the exception of policies that exempt ELLs from testing in English in their first or second year in U.S. public schools, assignment of students to accommodations is conducted by broad linguistic status categories (i.e., ELL or non-ELL). In other words, there appears to be no effort on the part of states to guide districts and school site personnel in the selection of accommodations that are appropriate for particular levels of English proficiency or profiles of ELLs.

Thus, test accommodations policies do not appear to provide ELLs with equitable opportunities to participate in accountability systems. Although some have found a positive impact of appropriate assignment of accommodations on ELL test performance (e.g., Kopriva, Emick, Hipolito-Delgado, & Cameron, 2007), we question whether test accommodations can achieve optimal levels of equity if their design and development are not based on what is known from cognitive science and on addressing linguistic and cultural factors impacting performance.

Regrettably, there is a general lack of systematic approaches to test development in general (see Baxter, Shavelson, Goldman, & Pine, 1992), which amounts to a failure to address language and culture even when attempts are made to account for language proficiency (Solano-Flores & Trumbull, 2003). Although sociocultural theories informed by the work of Vygotsky recognize the significant role of language in the development of understanding, much of this work is descriptive in nature; it does not offer ways to bridge to and enhance the acquisition and assessment of one or more forms of school-based language (Gee, 2005). Sociocultural approaches have demonstrated the importance of social context in the learning process (Rogoff, 1990; Saxe, 1991);

however current sociocultural frameworks do not offer strategies for reviewing items designed to reveal the ways in which language and culture interact in how students make sense of individual test items (Solano-Flores & Trumbull, 2003).

A related issue is the lack of research on the cognitive effects of different types of bilingualism. While there is general consensus that the L1 and L2 constitute a single language system in bilingual individuals and that there are some cognitive advantages of being bilingual (Bialystok, 2001, 2002), little research has been done to examine the cognitive activity of bilinguals in relation to academic tasks and test taking.

The degree of such interaction may vary according to the level of competence in the L1 and L2 achieved by the student, which in turn is influenced by the quality of the educational programming the student receives (Cummins, 1979). The process of problem solving and knowledge construction is optimized when bilingual students are allowed to use the totality of their linguistic resources—both their L1 and L2 (Moschkovich, 2000)—which sets them apart from monolinguals of both languages. Escamilla (2000) demonstrates that current assessment practices underestimate students' literacy knowledge because they do not take into account ELLs' distinct linguistic repertoires such as the frequent and systematic use of both languages to respond to a reading assessment. Unfortunately, current testing practices do not address the simultaneous use of both languages to make sense of content concepts, and in many instances regard the use of both languages as indicating a deficit in their knowledge system (see Escamilla, 2000). Literacy knowledge is not only underestimated; also, inaccurate conclusions about bilingual students' capabilities are ascribed when they use both languages to support their understanding.

The lack of attention to the relationship between language and thought and, more specifically, how ELLs' developing knowledge in both languages impacts how they approach test items is evident in test specifications. Test specifications typically do not include sufficient guidance on linguistic or cultural factors that can increase the accessibility of individual items for ELLs. Despite findings from studies that reveal linguistic complexity of assessments as a major factor contributing to the performance gap between ELLs and non-ELLs (Abedi, 2006; Abedi et al., 2004), item writing procedures are not sensitive to linguistic and cultural variation. Indeed, when verbal protocols have been used to examine the cognitive validity of test items, the samples of participant students have not included ELLs.

A great deal of the process of developing tests for any population consists of refining the wording of test items or tasks to ensure that students understand what they are asked to do and can communicate their responses effectively (Solano-Flores & Shavelson, 1997). Unfortunately, efforts to address the linguistic needs of ELL populations do not go much far beyond wording. In addition, alignment of the intended and observed response processes is not the goal of such refinement. In this way, tests are developed based on mainstream students (Valdes & Figueroa, 1994) which can threaten construct validity and hinder equitable outcomes of an accountability system. However, such analysis examines directly when and how ELLs interpret items differently, which in turn can provide information pertaining to the kinds of claims that can be made about the inferences that can be drawn from test scores. Unfortunately, the notion of ELL inclusion in large-scale testing has not permeated the process of test development. Rarely, if ever, have test developers reported including ELLs among their samples of pilot students, in spite of the fact that ELLs are also tested in English.

Improving Practice on the Development and Adaptation of Tests

Undoubtedly, testing that reflects what is known from cognitive science will improve current testing practice. The test, as an observational tool, should be based on a model of how students represent knowledge and develop competence in the domain of interest (NRC, 2001). Further, the model should be contextualized within a theory of how expertise is developed in that domain (Lohman & Nichols, 2006). As Lohman and Nichols (2006) point out, a model focused on student cognition specifies what students know and can do at different levels of understanding as well as the conceptual understandings and procedural strategies that exemplify different levels of development. Although there has been an increase in the application of cognitive psychology in test development frameworks and psychometrics (Gorin, 2006), this work has been dominated by a cognitive information-processing perspective, particularly for summative assessments which does not examine how English proficiency mitigates known development patterns in content areas.

This perspective assumes that language and culture operate independently despite the fact that knowledge is learned and assessed through language—a cultural manifestation. Hence, there is a need to turn to sociocultural views of cognition and psycholinguistics to inform the entire process of test development and adaptation. Evidence is accumulating showing that an important source of validity evidence can be collected from the cognitive activity of students when they take tests. Solano-Flores and his colleagues (Solano-Flores & Li, 2006; Solano-Flores & Trumbull, 2003; Solano-Flores et al., 2007) argue that the manner in which a student approaches an item is influenced by their schemas for approaching said item, which in turn, is shaped by their cultural and linguistic background. For this reason, they maintain that if cognition is viewed as independent of culture and language, the processes by which culture and language influence student performance on individual items will not be adequately accounted for when determining the technical quality of the test, in particular with respect to its impact on cognitive validity evidence (Solano-Flores & Nelson-Barber, 2001).

In light of this evidence, Solano-Flores and his colleagues have developed a model for integrating both cognitive and sociolinguistic factors in item reviews (Solano-Flores & Trumbull, 2003). In the test review process, items undergo item microanalysis which is defined as "the set of reasonings used to examine how the properties of items and students' linguistic, cultural, socioeconomic backgrounds operate in combination to shape the ways in which students make sense of test items" (p. 4). Unlike the focus of traditional item analysis mentioned above, targets of analysis, as proposed by Solano-Flores et al., include: the language used in the items, how the student interprets the item, as well as how their interpretations are shaped by the interplay between their linguistic and cultural background and the language of the item. This analysis, an enhanced version of the methodology employed to obtain information about an item's *cognitive validity* (described in more detail in the "Observation and the Administration of Tests" section below), is conducted utilizing think-aloud protocols and interviews with students in addition to examining the linguistic properties of the item.

Such analysis is important to identify and understand the source of differences in response processes across different linguistic and cultural groups. For example, Solano-Flores and Trumball (2003) found that a mathematics item involving a context that involved figuring out "the number of $1.00 bills [...needed...] to buy lunch for 5 days" was interpreted differentially by students from different socioeconomic and cultural groups because of the wording of the item coupled with the student's background experiences. Low income students were more likely to interpret the problem as only having $1 and not having enough money, whereas none of the upper income, White students interpreted this item in this way. Thus, this kind of analysis revealed interpretation patterns that were influenced by students' lived experiences.

Figure 34.2, adapted from Kathleen Graves (2000), illustrates more vividly how the language and background impacts how a stimulus is interpreted.

$$\boxed{\text{IGH} \quad \text{ROP}}$$

Figure 34.2 Text message requiring knowledge of language and context.

Most would not be able to decipher the message contained in the text presented in Figure 34.2 initially or from a quick glance taken out of context. If, however, one knew that this was taken from a sign printed on the front door of a popular video rental building, many with sufficient knowledge of English would be able to then discern the message as "Night Drop," provided they also have experience with renting videos and their script for such an event included being able to drop them off through a slot in the door whenever the store is not open. Without this background knowledge (or schema), in addition to an understanding of the English language (vocabulary, spelling patterns, and idiomatic expressions), it would be very difficult to interpret the message. While this might be an extreme case, similar processes occur during testing situations involving tests constructed in a language the test taker has not mastered. The language effect is compounded when the context on which the item is based is not part of the examinee's schema or conceptual frame (MacSwan, Rolstand, & Glass, 2002).

The information that is gained from this analysis informs both the design of items and adaptations that yield more accurate information about ELL understanding and skills. Improving practice in the item development process would entail incorporating microanalysis in both the development of items as well as in the pilot testing phase. While it is useful for a panel of experts to review items prior to field testing to examine the language of the item and potential interpretations, more direct evidence of possible differences in interpretation is gleaned from verbal protocols and cognitive interviews of students who have attempted to respond to the items. Incorporating such practices coupled with more appropriate sample sizes and composition of ELLs in pilot testing would provide more meaningful information about how well the items elicited the intended cognitive processes, and thus minimize construct-irrelevant variance; two requisite criteria for equitable and fair testing practices.

Another form of improved practice in test development consists of involving teachers in the process of adapting the linguistic features of test items according to the characteristics of the language use in their own school settings (Solano-Flores et al., 2007). Unlike linguistic simplification, in this approach, called *item localization*, it is the teachers who teach the students tested (rather than a team of specialists who do not interact with students on a daily basis) who decide how the wording of the items should be modified according to the usage of language in their communities. Available evidence indicates that the technical properties of localized items are similar to those of linguistically simplified items. This evidence also indicates that the technical properties of items in their original version do not change when they are localized. The results also show that item localization and linguistic simplification are sensitive to different aspects of linguistic complexity, which indicates that the two methods should be used in combination. From a broader perspective, the results also indicate that empowering teachers to participate more directly in the characteristics of the items given to their students based on their knowledge of the language used in their communities, is an effective approach to minimizing measurement error in the testing of ELLs.

Current Practice on Observation and the Administration of Tests

As stated earlier, state policies regarding the inclusion of ELLs in accountability systems are based on broad classifications of students into linguistic groups, such as ELL or non-ELL (Solano-Flores, 2006). Such practices imply that states continue to regard this population as homogeneous, which is not surprising since much of the available research utilizes designs that compare ELLs with mainstream non-ELLs. That is, the published research on accommodations has been focused on either examining the effect of accommodations on ELL performance (e.g., CRESST studies such as Abedi et. al., 2004) or on the comparability of data over time (e.g., ETS studies such as Kopriva et al., 2007). These studies compared the performance of ELLs who received accommodations with ELLs who did not receive them.

The kinds of items selected for an assessment, including the allowable test accommodations, must be designed to reflect the learning model underlying the assessment as well as support the kinds of inferences and decisions that will be based on the test performance (NRC, 2001). This model should be specified in the construct definition which serves as the framework for all test development activities (Gorin, 2006). The development of individual test items then includes a set of task specifications that will elicit responses from students in a manner that is consistent with the learning model within a given domain. As all states offer a set of accommodations for ELLs, it is imperative that the specifications for the accommodations are also consistent with the learning model and elicit the kinds of responses that are consistent with the learning model. The lack of guidance to schools by states in this regard may be due to the general lack of research addressing this issue directly.

Available evidence indicates cultural background and experience shape the effectiveness of testing accommodations for ELLs (Aguirre-Muñoz, 2000). Yet, accommodations are assumed to have intrinsic properties that are universal; if evidence exists that a certain kind of accommodation is beneficial for one linguistic group, it is assumed that it is equally beneficial for any linguistic group. If language is known to contribute to construct-irrelevant variance, for example, it is reasonable to argue that dialect (language variations across groups of users) and register (language variations across different situations or contexts) also act in the same way. Further, considering dialect and register addresses the known variation in L1 and L2 dominance found within individual students as well as the in their linguistic proficiencies across language modes (e.g., written and oral) and content areas (see Stevens, Butler, & Castellon-Wellington, 2000).

Issues and Limitations of Current Practice on Observation and the Administration of Tests

Item reviews are generally not linked to construct definitions that are based on learning theory and when they are, the theory does not reflect linguistic and cultural factors that impact the learning process. Instead, they target language or culture superficially and occur separately from content reviews. In California, for example, all items for each state assessment involved in the Standardized Testing and Reporting System (STAR) first undergo a formal content review conducted by the Content Review Panel, followed by a review from the State Panel Assessment Review targeting item bias. The latter is focused on evaluating items for potential gender and cultural stereotyping and the former on ensuring the integrity of the content targeted by the item.

The mathematics item described in the previous section and the video store sign example demonstrate the need to incorporate sociolinguistic theory into psychometrics. Against common sense (which holds that the linguistic load in mathematics is less severe than in other subjects such and science and social studies) language background has been found to impact understanding in mathematics and performance in mathematics tests (see Abedi & Lord, 2001). For example, the findings of Campbell, Adams, and Davis (2007) on the aspects of mathematics problems that increase the cognitive demands for ELLs are consistent with the results obtained by Solano-Flores and his colleagues, described above. In a mathematics problem involving the use of the pythagorean theorem to determine the distance that a catcher needed to throw the ball in order to throw the runner out at second base, an ELL was not able to solve the problem because she did not know where the catcher stood. The ELLs' unfamiliarity with the context of the problem precluded her from constructing the appropriate problem situation even though she had sufficient content knowledge to solve this kind of problem. Like the lunch money example, this example shows how assumptions about prior experiences or the failure to attend to cultural and linguistic factors in the construction and review of items can increase the cognitive demands for ELLs, thereby impacting the cognitive validity of test scores.

Cognitive validity refers to the degree of correspondence between intended task demands and the cognitive activity elicited by the task as well as the correspondence between the quality of the cognitive activity and the performance score (Baxter & Glaser, 1998). If the language or assumptions about the background knowledge needed to correctly respond to items are not directly addressed in the construction and review of items/tasks, a disconnect between intended and observed cognitive activity is likely to occur for ELLs. Yet item reviews are not conducted in a manner that would reveal such discrepancies.

Furthermore, testing and testing accommodation decisions are based on inconsistent criteria of language proficiency and fragmented information on the linguistic proficiency of ELLs in both the L1 and English (Abedi, 2002; Mahoney & MacSwan, 2005). Many states, for example, use academic achievement tests to identify ELLs. Although there may be some overlap between language knowledge and general school-based knowledge, many educational linguists point out that the two are distinct constructs and therefore should be measured separately (see Mahoney & MacSwan, 2005). Also contributing to the complexity of adequately identifying the ELL population is the design flaws of many tasks in commonly used language proficiency assessments, as is the case of story retelling used as an oral language component in language assessments. MacSwan et al. (2002) found that most of ELLs who were classified as "limited" speakers of their own language by the proficiency measure (Pre-LAS Español) scored very well on most of the test and 20% of these students did not respond to the story retell at all. These researchers concluded that the test inappropriately assessed students' familiarity and readiness to engage in a retelling task, rather than their proficiency in their native language. Similar technical issues were observed with tasks that require students to respond in complete sentences (Idea Proficiency Test-IPT). These issues are relevant to reclassifying and monitoring ELLs, given that assessments used for these purposes employ the same item types.

At the implementation level, states allow certain practices that can introduce additional construct-irrelevant variance even if cognitive validity is adequately addressed. Accommodations such as site translations, for example, raise questions regarding the fidelity of implementation. For example, one test proctor may translate directions very differently than another and may confuse rather than assist the ELL to understand what they are to do (Rivera & Collum, 2006; Valdes & Figueroa, 1994).

Improving Practice on Observation and the Administration of Tests

Recently, there has been considerable attention given to *item construct validity*. This notion is based on the premise that if valid inferences are to be drawn from test scores, then test items must first be designed to validly assess what is intended because they are the building blocks for test scores and thus form the basis of inferences from those scores (Ferrara et al., 2003). Test items are construct-valid when they minimize the likelihood for an examinee to use construct-irrelevant knowledge to respond successfully to them. Some measurement experts disagree with the notion of item construct validity and argue that inferences drawn from tests can only be based on test scores. However, since language of a test has been shown to be the primary construct-irrelevant factor for ELLs, investigating item construct validity is relevant and necessary for the development of equitable and fair testing practices (Solano-Flores, 2006).

Although there have been considerable gains in the methodology for examining item construct validity, this methodology generally does not consider dialect, register, or other contextual factors as part of the cognitive and linguistic resources that an examinee uses in test taking. The studies discussed thus far illustrate the need for developing methodologies that can account for contextual factors mediating response processes. Figure 34.3 represents the linguistic and contextual factors that are particularly relevant for Latino ELLs.

A promising approach for improved practice in observation and the administration of tests

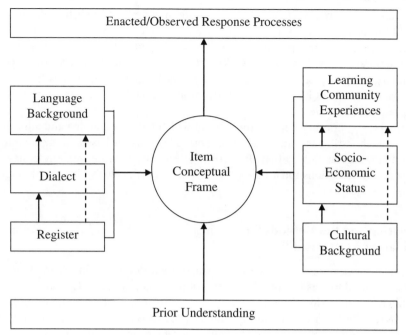

Figure 34.3 Linguistic and contextual factors mediating item response process impacting item construct validity for Latino ELLs.

consist of addressing the correspondence between the kind of accommodations provided to ELLs and the cultural and personal experiences. In a quasi-experimental study, Aguirre-Muñoz (2000) investigated the appropriateness of different accommodations for students with vary-ing degrees of Spanish and English proficiency. Students were provided with three types of accommodations on a complex history performance assessment: (a) Spanish translation only, (b) simplified text, and (c) English and Spanish side by side. Aguirre-Muñoz found a signifi-cant interaction between language background and type of accommodation. While students with higher Spanish proficiency scored higher on the Spanish version of the assessment, this finding varied by topic. Smaller differences in means between English and Spanish versions of the assessments were found on topics for which students had some previous exposure in their home country (e.g., Aztec civilization). As Muñoz's findings confirm the notion that blanket approaches to ELL testing are limited in their effectiveness to address language issues in test-ing, and that cultural background and personal experiences are powerful factors that need to be properly considered if effective testing accommodations are to be developed.

Another promising approach to observation and test administration to address score varia-tion due to linguistic factors (dialect and register) is the use of generalizability (G) theory, which can distinguish between two kinds of sources of score variation: variation due to the student and variation due to various facets or sources of measurement error (Allen & Yen, 1997; Shavel-son & Webb, 1991). Solano-Flores (2006) investigated the contribution of language to measure-ment error and found the greatest score variation was found in the student by item by language interaction, indicating that ELLs have different sets of strengths and weaknesses in English and their L1 and thus test items can pose different sets of linguistic challenges depending on stu-dents' linguistic background. Similar results were found for dialect (Solano-Flores & Li, 2006), which suggests that the dialect of the language in which they were tested can significantly shape ELLs' performance. These results indicates the possibility of developing testing models intended to address the linguistic needs of ELLs based on the dependability of measures of academic achievement rather than gross (and seldom accurate) measures of English proficiency. Administering ELLs tests in L1 or L2 is not an absolute matter (Solano-Flores & Trumbull, 2008) given the fact, discussed before, that performance on tests is shaped by the interaction of the linguistic features of items and the strengths and weaknesses of ELLs in each language. The dependability of scores for a given group of ELLs may be higher in one language than in the other for a specific topic; the pattern may not be the same for the same group of students on another topic of for another group of ELL students.

In summary, any improvement on the ways in which tests are adapted and administered or the ways in which testing accommodations are provided must be based on taking into account culture and language as factors that shape their effectiveness. Moreover, any policy concerning testing accommodations must take into consideration the elusive nature of language and culture.

Interpretation and the Methods for Scoring and Validating Assessment Results

The interpretation component of the assessment triangle presented in Figure 34.1 represents all the methods used to reason from the observations which, as the NRC report clearly pointed out, are inherently imperfect. That is, assessment results represent *estimates* of understanding and skills (NRC, 2001). In accountability contexts, the reasoning from evidence involves a set of statistical tools needed to determine student achievement levels and increasingly also include qualitative tools to determine the degree of correspondence between an item-specific cognitive model and what is observed (see Gorin, 2006). Central to the validation process is the collection of construct validity evidence which involves whether or not the processes measured by the items and tests are those that were intended by the test developer (Ferrara et al., 2004). When the intended and observed processes are aligned, valid interpretations are supported.

Current approaches to interpretation and scoring in ELL testing are mainly based on item response theory (IRT), a psychometric theory of scaling (see, for example, Hambleton, Swaminathan, & Rogers, 1991). Efforts are oriented to detecting bias due to language or culture by examining score differences between linguistic groups (e.g., Camilli & Shephard, 1994) and differential item functioning (DIF; Solano-Flores, 2006). DIF analysis determines the extent to which ELLs and non-ELLs have "different probabilities of responding correctly to an item despite having comparable levels of performance on the underlying measured attribute" (Solano-Flores, 2006, p. 2359). Thus the analysis compares group performance for each of the items on the test.

Issues and Limitations of Current Practice on Interpretation and the Methods for Scoring and Validating Assessment Results

Validation utilizing IRT focuses on group differences at the item level by comparing ELLs to mainstream students and thus does not directly examine language as a source of measurement error. While IRT is important for determining how well items on a test are functioning with respect to various groups, the information gleaned from this analysis provides little information that can be used to build more equitable models for ELLs. Model development necessitates collection of information about the sources of errors for specific task types and items and the degree to which items produce the intended cognitive processes.

Consistent with this notion, the G studies described above suggest that testing ELLs based on broad linguistic categories "may not address important linguistic differences among students from the broad linguistic group and may affect the dependability of their achievement scores" (Solano-Flores & Li, 2006, p. 19).

Improving Current Practice on the Interpretation and the Methods for Scoring and Validating Assessment Results

A strong case has been made for the use of G theory to develop testing models that minimize construct-irrelevant variance related to language and culture. For two groups of ELLs, code (language and dialect) has been found to be a significant source of measurement error (Solano-Flores & Li, 2006, 2006). These results suggest that a minimum number of items necessary to obtain dependable scores from ELLs may vary depending on the dialect of the language in which they are tested. This finding complements the research in linguistics, described above, that demonstrates that rarely language development of bilingual children is symmetrical (Bialystok, 2001). Many factors influence the degree of proficiency that a student poses in either their native language or English and dominance often varies depending on the context and subject matter.

Recall that over half of the ELL population in the United States is native born. This change in demographics suggests that many ELLs are coming into the educational system with some familiarity with the English language and the U.S. culture and/or they may not be exposed to their native language to the same degree that a child coming from their native country would. Therefore, previous assumptions about their knowledge of their home language and culture as well as English need to be reexamined. As previously noted, bilingual children rely on both language knowledge systems to approach academic tasks even when they have not received instruction in English (Escamilla, 2000). Drawing on findings from that literature, it is reasonable to assume that native-born ELLs have several years of contact with English before entering the educational system that they bring to bear in the school context in ways that may not be valued or utilized as sources of support for school-based learning. For many of these students, the most equitable test may be one that is developed in the dialect they speak. Incorporating dialect alone, however, will not lead to more equitable accountability inclusion for Latino students. Better identification and monitoring of their progress in both L1 and English development also needs to occur in order to make informed decisions about what kind of tests will lead to the most accurate inferences about what they know and can do. As their English proficiency develops, changes in the way ELLs are assessed should also be considered as needed.

Whenever test results are used to make important decisions about students it is imperative to conduct continuous investigations of validity (AERA, APA, & NCME, 1999). These investigations should include both gaps in performance between groups of students as well as examinations of score dependability. Expanding the practice of the collection of validity evidence that incorporates social-cultural dimensions is also necessary. To accomplish this goal, qualitative methods, such as think-alouds and the cognitive interview described earlier should be incorporated to determine the extent to which items elicit the intended processes of the test developer. These investigations however, need to explicitly examine the complex nature of language and its interrelationship with culture (Solano-Flores & Trumbull, 2003). As previously described and presented in Figure 34.3, students' language background, language of the item (including dialect and register), cultural background, prior understanding of the targeted subject matter, and experiences in the classroom, all shape their interpretation (conceptual frame) of test items. The student's conceptual frame, in turn influences the response processes used to respond to test items. Therefore, microanalysis of test items targeting these contextual factors need to be incorporated into validity investigations given the evidence that demonstrates the way a student interprets the testing event is relevant in making accurate interpretations of performance (Solano-Flores & Trumbull, 2003). Unfortunately, the growing body of literature on cognitive validity (e.g., Ayala, Shavelson, Yin, & Schultz, 2002; Baxter, Elder, & Glaser, 1996; Hamilton, Nussbaum, & Snow, 1997; Ruiz-Primo, Shavelson, Li, & Schultz, 2001) does not focus on cultural or linguistic diversity. How culture shapes cognition in test taking is a promising area in testing yet to be systematically investigated.

Consequently, traditional testing paradigms attempt to eliminate the effects of language and culture as evident in efforts to develop culture-free tests. Tests are cultural artifacts and therefore attempts to develop culture-free tests would be unproductive in our view. The research summarized here suggests that effectively addressing the linguistic diversity requires that language and culture be "incorporated as part of the reasoning that guides the entire assessment process" (Solano-Flores & Trumbull, 2003, p. 9). Adequately addressing the validity of test score interpretations for Latino ELLs involves multidisciplinary approaches to test development and test review in addition to test use and test score interpretation.

Adequately addressing the validity of test score interpretations for ELLs also may require properly interpreting the context in which ELLs are tested. Consistent with this notion, we have taken a step forward in the use of G theory as an approach for interpreting ELL scores from a systemic perspective. We have submitted that the systematic analysis of sources of measurement error can address not only language and dialect but also the actions taken by assessment systems in the testing of ELLs (Solano-Flores. 2008, in press). From this perspective, actions such as the kind of testing accommodation used with ELLs or the forms in which these accommodations are implemented can be viewed as facets in G studies. An approach like this has the potential of allowing systematic analysis and improvement of assessment systems for ELLs.

Whereas it is yet to be refined and implemented, this approach supports the notion that, in the context of accountability, proper interpretations of academic achievement measures for ELLs cannot occur without examining the effectiveness of a given assessment system in addressing language issues. As can be seen, improved practices in ELL testing cannot take place unless test validity and the evaluation of assessment systems are properly linked.

Summary and Implications for Future Developments

The quotation at the beginning of the chapter suggests that there is a lack of commitment from the testing community in general to critically examine both its practices and underlying assumptions regarding the testing of ELLs. Solano-Flores (2008) has recently echoed this concern and outlined how views about language in the entire process of testing have contributed to the testing communities' inability to create equitable testing practices. Although the practice of inclusion of ELLs in accountability systems is a step forward in equitable testing, the use of learning models that do not attend to linguistic and cultural factors undermines the potential for achieving equity. A focus on linguistic and cultural factors impacting how ELLs represent, organize, and process learned knowledge would address some of the linguistic issues current testing models tend to ignore.

Systematically addressing the contextual factors impacting the test performance of Latino ELLs requires that test developers and users move beyond the provision of accommodations that do not serve well ELLs specific cultural and linguistic needs. A testing model that foregrounds language and culture and systematically investigates the item construct validity informed by socio-cultural and psycholinguistic theory would both generate more equitable testing practices and yield more meaningful test scores. Such a system is more likely to lead to more appropriate educational programming for Latino ELLs. We recognize, however, that testing alone will not result in equitable outcomes associated with accountability systems. Adequately addressing the achievement gap also requires equal attention to improving ELLs' opportunity to learn (OTL) the content of the tests used in accountability systems and access to the full curriculum implied by the content standards that form the basis of tests used in accountability systems (Aguirre-Muñoz & Boscardin, 2008). Otherwise, assessments that are developed utilizing the multidisciplinary approach described here will only serve to highlight the resource and instructional disparities that yield differences in achievement outcomes.

In light of these technical difficulties in assessing Latino ELLs, there is a critical need for a testing approach that integrates appropriately language and cultural diversity in test design, interpretation, and reporting, particularly given the changing demographics of Latinos in the United States. The model presented here incorporates knowledge gained from the language sciences and the nature of bilingualism pertaining to testing situations that we believe would generate more dependable evidence from which to make adequate reasoning about the academic achievement of ELLs.

Acknowledgments

Some of the research reported here was funded by National Science Foundation Grants REC-9909729, REC-0126344, REC-0336744, and SGER-0450090 awarded to the second author. Other research was funded by the Educational Research and Development Centers Program, PR/Award Number R305B960002, as administered by the Institute of Education Sciences, U.S. Department of Education as well as the University of California, Language Minority Research Institute. The opinions expressed here are not necessarily those of these funding agencies or our colleagues.

References

Abedi, J., (2002). Standardized achievement tests and English language learners: Psychometric Issues. *Educational Assessment, 8*(3), 231– 257.

Abedi, J., (2006) Language issue in item-development. In S. M. Downing & T. M. Haladyna (Eds.), *Handbook of test development* (pp. 377–398). Mahwah, NJ: Erlbaum.

Abedi, J., & Gándara, P. (2006). Performance of English language learners as a subgroup in large-scale assessment: Interaction of research and policy. *Educational Measurement: Issues and Practice*, 36–46.

Abedi, J., & Hejri, F. (2004). Accommodations for students with limited English proficiency in the National Assessment of Educational Progress. *Applied Measurement in Education, 17*(4), 371–392.

Abedi, J., Hofstetter, C., & Lord, C. (2004). Assessment accommodations for English language learners: Implications for policy-based empirical research. *Review of Educational Research, 74*(1), 1–28.

Abedi, J., & Lord, C. (2001). The language factor in mathematics tests. *Applied Measurement in Education, 14*(3), 219–234.

Aguirre-Muñoz, Z. (2000). The impact of language proficiency on complex performance assessments: Examining linguistic accommodation strategies for English language learners. *Dissertation Abstracts International* (UMI No. 9973171).

Aguirre-Muñoz, Z., & Baker, E. L. (1999). Improving the equity and validity of assessment-based information systems. In M. Nettles (Ed.), *Measuring up: Challenges minorities face in educational assessment* (pp. 121–136). Norwell, MA: Kluwer.

Aguirre-Muñoz, Z., & Boscardin, C. K. (2008). Opportunity to Learn and English Learner Achievement: Is Increased Content Exposure Beneficial? *Journal of Latinos and Education, 7*(3), 185–210.

Allen, M. J., & Yen, W. M. (1997). *Introduction to measurement theory*. Monterey, CA: Brooks/Cole.

American Educational Research Association, American Psychological Association, National Council on Measurement in Education. (1999). *Standards for Educational and Psychological Testing*. Washington, DC: American Educational Research Association.

August, D., & Hakuta, K. (1997). *Improving schooling for language-minority children: A research agenda*. National Research Council Committee on Developing a Research Agenda on the Education of Limited-English-Proficient and Bilingual Students. Washington, DC: National Academy Press.

August, D., & Shanahan, T. (2006). *Developing literacy in second-language learners: Report of the National Literacy Panel on Language-Minority Children and Youth*. Mahwah, NJ: Erlbaum.

Ayala, C.C., Shavelson, R., Yin, Y., & Schultz, S.E., (2002). Reasoning dimensions underlying achievement: The case of performance assessment, *Educational Assessment, 8*(2), 101–121.

Baker, C. (2001). The development of bilingualism. In C. Baker (Ed.), *Foundations of bilingual education and bilingualism, Fourth edition* (pp. 95–141). Clevedon, UK: Multilingual Matters.

Baxter, G. P., Elder, A. D., & Glaser, R. (1996). Knowledge-based cognition and performance assessment in the science classroom. *Educational Psychologist, 31*(2), 133–140.

Baxter G. P., & Glaser, R. (1998). Investigating the complexity of science assessments. *Educational Measurement: Issues and Practice, 17*(3), 37–45.

Baxter, G. P., Shavelson, R. J., Goldman S. R., & Pine, J. (1992). Evaluation of procedure-based scoring for hands-on science assessments. *Journal of Educational Measurement, 29*(1), 1–17.

Bialystok, E. (2001) *Bilingualism in development: Language literacy and cognition.* Cambridge, UK: Cambridge University Press.

Bialystok, E. (2002). Cognitive processes of L2 users. In V. Cook (Ed.), *Portrait of the L2 user* (pp. 147-165). New York: Multilingual Matters.

Butler, F. A., Lord, C., Stevens, R., Borrego, M., & Bailey, A. L. (2004). *An approach to operationalizing academic language for language test development purposes: Evidence from fifth-grade science and math* (CSE Tech. Rep. No. 626). Los Angeles: University of California, National Center for Research on Evaluation, Standards, and Student Testing (CRESST).

Camilli, G., & Shephard, L. A. (1994). *Methods for identifying biased test items.* Thousand Oaks, CA: Sage.

Campbell, A. E., Adams, V. M., & Davis, G. E. (2007). Cognitive demands and second-language learners: A framework for analyzing mathematical instructional contexts. *Mathematical Thinking and Learning, 9*(1), 3–30.

Capps, R., Fix, M., Murray, J., Ost, J., Passel, J., & Herwantoro, S. (2005). *The new demography of American schools: Immigration and the No Child Left Behind Act.* Washington DC: The Urban Institute.

Cronbach, L. J., Gleser, G. C., Nanda, H., & Rajaratnam, N. (1972). *The dependability of behavioral measurements.* New York: Wiley.

Cummins, J. (1979). Linguistic Interdependence and the educational development of bilingual children. *Review of Education Research, 49*(2), 222–251.

De Avila, E. A. (1988). Bilingualism, cognitive function, and language minority group membership. In R. R. Cocking & J. P. Mestre (Eds.), *Linguistic and cultural influences on learning mathematics* (pp. 101–121). Hillsdale, NJ: Erlbaum.

Durán, R. P. (1989). Testing of linguistic minorities. In R. L. Linn (Ed.), *Educational measurement, third edition.* New York: American Council on Education-Macmillan.

Elliott, S. N., Kratochwill, T. R., & Schultz, A. G. (1998). The assessment accommodation checklist: Who, what, where, when, why, and how? *Council for Exceptional Children,* 10-14.

Escamilla, K. (2000). *Bilingual means two: Assessment issues, early literacy and Spanish-speaking children. Proceedings from a research symposium on High Standards in Reading for Students From Diverse Language Groups: Research, Practice & Policy.* Washington DC: U.S. Department of Education, Office of Bilingual Education and Minority Language Affairs.

Ferrara, S., Duncan, T., Perie, M., Freed, R., McGiven, J., & Chilukuri, R. (2003). *Item construct validity: Early results from a study of the relationship between intended and actual cognitive demands in a middle school science assessment.* Paper presented at the annual meeting of the American Educational Research Association, Chicago.

Ferrara, S., Macmillan, J., & Nathan, A. (2004). *Enhanced database on inclusion and accommodations: Variables and measures* (NAEP State Analysis Project Report to the National Center for Education Statistics). Washington, DC: NCES.

Fry, R. (2005). *The high schools Hispanics attend: Size and other key characteristics.* Washington, DC: Pew Hispanic Center.

García, G. E., McKoon, G., & August, D. (2006). Language and literacy assessment of language-minority students. In D. August & T. Shanahan (Eds.), *Developing literacy in second-language learners: Report of the National Literacy Panel on Language-Minority Children and Youth* (pp. 597–626). Mahwah, NJ: Erlbaum.

Gee, J. P. (2005). Language in the science classroom: Academic social language as the heart of school-based literacy. In R. K. Yerrick & W. Roth (Eds.), *Establishing scientific classroom discourse communities: Multiple voices of teaching and learning research* (pp. 131–147). Mahwah, NJ: Erlbaum.

Gorin, J. S. (2006). Test design with cognition in mind. *Educational Measurement: Issues and Practice,* 21–35.

Graves, K. (2000). *Designing language courses: A guide for teachers.* Boston: Heinle & Heinle.

Grosjean, F. (1985). The bilingual as a competent but specific speaker-hearer. *Journal of Multilingual and Multicultural Development, 6*, 467–477.

Halliday, M. A. K. (1975). *Learning how to mean: Explorations in the development of language.* London: Edward Arnold.

Halliday, M. A. K. (1978). *Language as a social semiotic: The social interpretation of language and meaning.* London: Edward Arnold.

Hambleton, R. K., Swaminathan, H., & Rogers, H. J. (1991). *Fundamentals of item response theory.* Newbury Park, CA: Sage.

Hamilton, L. S., Nussbaum, E. M., & Snow, R. E. (1997). Interview procedures for validating science assessments. *Applied Measurement in Education, 10*, 181–200.

Johnson, E. C., Kirkhart, K. E., Madison, A. M., Noley, G. B., & Solano-Flores, G. (2008). The impact of narrow views of scientific rigor on evaluation practices for underrepresented groups. In N. L. Smith & P. R. Brandon (Eds.), *Fundamental issues in evaluation* (pp. 197–218). New York: Guilford.

Kindler, A. (2002). *Survey of the states' limited English proficient students and available educational programs and services 2000–2001, summary report.* Washington, DC: Prepared for Office of English Language Acquisition by the National Clearinghouse for English Language Acquisition & Language Instruction Educational Programs. Retrieved from http://www.ncela.gwu.edu/policy/states/reports/seareports/0001/sea0001.pdf

Kopriva, R. J., Emick, J. E., Hipolito-Delgado, C. P., & Cameron, C. A. (2007). Do proper accommodation assignments make a difference?: Examining the impact of improved decision making on scores for English language learners. *Educational Measurement: Issues and Practice*, 11–20.

Lohman, D. F., & Nichols, P. (2006). Meeting the NRC Panel's recommendations: Commentary on the papers by Mslevy and Haertel, Gorin, and Abedi and Gándara. *Educational Measurement: Issues and Practice*, 58–64.

Mackey, W. F. (1962). The description of bilingualism. *Canadian Journal of Bilingualism, 7*, 51–85.

MacSwan, J. (2000). The threshold hypothesis, semilingualism, and other contributions to a deficit view of linguistic minorities. *Hispanic Journal of Behavioral Sciences, 22* (1), 3–45.

MacSwan, J., Rolstad, K., & Glass, G. V. (2002). Do some school-age children have no language? Some problems of construct validity in the Pre-LAS. Español. *Bilingual Research Journal, 26*(2), 213–238.

Mahoney, K. S., & MacSwan, J. (2005) Reexamining Identification and Reclassification of English language learners: A critical discussion of select state practices. *Bilingual Research Journal, 29*, 31–42.

Martinez-Aleman, A. M. (2006). Latino demographics, democratic individuality, and educational accountability: A pragmatist's view. *Educational Researcher, 35*(7), 25–31.

Mercer, N. (2004). *Words and minds: How we use language to think together.* New York, Routledge.

Messick, S. (1989). Validity. In R. L. Linn (Ed.), *Educational measurement* (3rd ed., pp. 13–103). Washington, DC: American Council on Education.

Moschkovich, J. N. (2000) Learning mathematics in two language: Moving from obstacles to resources. In W. Secada (Ed.), *Changing the faces of mathematics: Perspective on multicultural and gender equity* (pp. 85–93). Reston, VA: NCTM.

National Clearinghouse for English Language Acquisition and Language Instruction Educational Programs. (2006). NCELA frequently asked questions, revised October 2006. Retrieved February 25, 2007, from http://www.ncela.gwu.edu/expert/faq/25_tests.htm

National Center for Educational Statistics. (1997). *Status trends in the education of Hispanics.* Washington DC: U.S. Department of Education.

National Research Council. (2001). *Knowing what students know.* Committee on the Foundations of Assessment. J. Pelligrino, N. Chudowsk, & R. Glaser (Eds.), Board on Testing and Assessment, Center for Education. Division of Behavioral & Social Sciences and Education. Washington, DC: National Academy Press.

No Child Left Behind Act of 2001. (2001). Pub. L. No. 107-110, 115 stat. 1961 (2002). Retrieved February 25, 2007, from http://www.ed.gov/policy/elsec/leg/esea02/107-110.pdf

Rivera, C., & Collum, E. (Eds.). (2006). *State assessment Policy and practice for English language learners: A national perspective.* Mahwah, NJ: Erlbaum.

Rogoff, B. (1990). *Apprenticeship in thinking.* New York: Oxford University Press.

Ruiz-Primo, M. A., Shavelson, R. J., Li, M., & Schultz, S. E. (2001). On the validity of cognitive interpretations of score from alternative concept-mapping techniques. *Educational Assessment, 7*(2), 99–141.

Saxe, G. B. (1991). *Culture and cognitive development: Studies in mathematical understanding.* Hillsdale, NJ: Erlbaum.

Shavelson, R. J., & Webb, N. M. (1991). *Generalizability theory: A primer.* Newbury Park: Sage.

Sireci, S. G., Li, S., & Scarpati, S. (2003). *The effects of tests accommodations on test performance: A review of the literature.* Commissioned paper by the National Academy of Sciences/National Research Council's Board on Testing and Assessment. Washington, DC: National Research Council.

Solano-Flores, G. (2006). Language, Dialect, and Register: Sociolinguistics and the Estimation of Measurement Error in the Testing of English Language Learners. *Teachers College Record, 108*(11), 2354–2379.

Solano-Flores, G. (2007). *Function and form in the research on language and mathematics education.* White paper for the Spencer Foundation.

Solano-Flores G. (2008). Who is given tests in what language by whom, when, and where? The need for probabilistic views of language in the testing of English language learners. *Educational Researcher, 37*(4), 189–199.

Solano-Flores, G. (in press). The testing of English language learners as a stochastic process: Population misspecification, measurement error, and overgeneralization. In K. Ercikan & W. M. Roth (Eds.), *Generalizing from educational research.*

Solano-Flores, G., & Li, M. (2006). The use of generalizability (G) theory in the testing of linguistic minorities. *Educational Measurement: Issues and Practice, 25*(1), 13–22.

Solano-Flores, G., Li, M., Speroni, C., Rodriguez, J., Basterra, M., & Dovholuk, G. (2007). *Comparing the properties of teacher-adapted and linguistically-simplified test items for English language learners.* Paper presented at the annual meeting of the American Educational Research Association. Chicago, IL. April 9–13.

Solano-Flores, G., & Nelson-Barber, S. (2001). On the cultural validity of science assessments. *Journal of Research in Science Teaching, 38*(5), 553–573.

Solano-Flores G. & Shavelson, R. J. (1997). Development of performance assessments in science: Conceptual, practical, and logistical issues. *Educational Measurement: Issue and Practice, 16*(3), 16–24.

Solano-Flores, G., & Trumbull, E. (2003). Examining language in context: The need for new research and practice paradigms in the testing of English-language learners. *Educational Researcher, 32*(2), 3–13.

Solano-Flores, G., & Trumbull, E. (2008). In what language should English language learners be tested? In R. J. Kopriva (Ed.), *Improving testing for English language learners: A comprehensive approach to designing, building, implementing and interpreting better academic assessmeets* (pp. 213–227). New York: Routledge.

Stevens, R. A., Butler, R. A., & Castellon-Wellington, M. (2000). *Academic language and content assessment: Measuring the progress of English Language Learners* (ELLs) (CSE Tech. Rep. NO. 552). Los Angeles: University of California: National Center for Research on Evaluation, Standards, and Student Testing.

U.S. Bureau of Labor Statistics. (2006). *Overview of BLS statistics on employment and unemployment.* Washington, DC: U.S. Department of Labor. Retrieved June 12, 2007, from http://www.bls.gove/bls.gov/employment.htm

U.S. Census Bureau. (2000). *We the people: Hispanics in the United States* (Census 2000 Special Report): Retrieved June 12, 2007, from http://www.census.gov/prod/2004pubs/censr-18pdf

U.S. Census Bureau. (2002). *Hispanic population in the United States: March 2002.* Retrieved June 12, 2007, from http://www.census.gov/2003pubs/p.20-545.pdf

U.S. Census Bureau. (2003). *American factfinder.* Retrieved June 12, 2007, from http://www.census.gove/population/www/pop-profile/hispop.html

Valdes, G., & Figueroa, R. A. (1994). *Bilingualism and testing: A special case of bias.* Norwood, NJ: Ablex.

Vygotsky, L. S. (1978). *Mind in society: The development of higher psychological processes.* Cambridge, MA: Harvard University Press.

Wertsch, J. V. (1985). *Vygotsky and the social formation of mind.* Cambridge, MA: Harvard University Press.

Zelher, A., Fleischmann, H., Hopstock, P., Stephenson, T., Pendzick, M., & Sapru, S. (2003). *Descriptive study of services to limited English proficient students.* Washington, DC: Development Associates.

35 Boosting the Professional Development of Teachers of Latino English Learners

Liliana Minaya-Rowe

Johns Hopkins University

José A. Ortiz

New Haven Public Schools

Overview

This chapter addresses the centrality of teacher expertise in the academic achievement of middle and high school Latino English learners (ELs) and focuses on ways to boost the knowledge and skills of their teachers using standards or principles for effective pedagogy. The standards are used as pedagogical content knowledge and for training; teachers learn about the standards by enacting them during their training. The chapter compares the standards with English as a second language and content area standards and presents professional development samples. It also examines ways to promote collegial working teams for professional growth via team products and co-teaching formats. The chapter concludes with steps to maintain quality teaching of Latino students.

Introduction

Recent reports reveal the national challenge to improve academic achievement and point to 89% of secondary school Latino students reading below grade level (NCES, 2005). Additionally, only 4% of eighth-grade ELs and 20% of students classified as "formerly ELs" scored at the proficient or advanced levels on the reading portion of the 2005 National Assessment of Educational Progress (Short & Fitzsimmons, 2006). By 2030, Latino students are predicted to account for over 40% of the school-age population. Since the numbers of Latino students will continue to rise steadily, schools require instructional programs to prepare them to learn English and the content areas.

As the country grows and diversifies so must the teacher knowledge of best instructional practices to accelerate the academic achievement of all students. No longer do teachers in our public schools face a homogeneous class of learners who are at the appropriate level of English mastery for their age and grade. Now the general education teacher needs to teach both content and language to ELs (Darling-Hammond & Bransford, 2005; Snow, Griffin, & Burns, 2005). Thus, the issue confronting schools and districts at present is teacher quality and ways to offer *all* teachers the professional development they need to help Latino ELs succeed in a school reform context that affects learning positively in all classrooms.

The opportunities for Latino students to succeed academically depend upon teachers' knowledge and enactment of effective pedagogy to address their linguistic and academic needs. Recent reports also focus on research-based strategies to train content teachers on key aspects of literacy when teaching adolescent Latino to integrate academic vocabulary, reading comprehension and writing with the content areas. Content teachers are not expected to become reading and writing teachers, but rather that they need to emphasize the reading and writing practices that are specific to their subjects (Biancarosa & Snow, 2004; Graham & Perin, 2007). For example, teachers need the tools to differentiate instruction and to accommodate to the literacy levels and academic English proficiency needs of ELs in their math labs and classes. Teachers can help their students develop the proficiency to comprehend math concepts, for example, and to explain orally and in writing the steps they followed to solve a problem.

This chapter is based on the authors' experiences working as teachers, teacher trainers, and administrators in three school districts with large numbers of Latino students. We address the centrality of teacher expertise in their students' school success and propose learning about and enacting the Five Standards for Effective Pedagogy (henceforth the Standards) in professional development. We also illustrate ways for teachers to work together within a collegial interdisciplinary team setting in which language and content teachers collaborate towards a common goal. Whether they are in bilingual, ESL, or content teachers, they ensure that Latino ELs have access to rigorous content knowledge and language essential for their academic success.

We present what teachers want to better teach Latino students. Then we describe the professional development contents using the Standards. We also illustrate ways of teacher cooperation where collegial interdisciplinary working teams plan, co-teach, and reflect on their craft and how the school administration supports their professional learning communities. Finally, we conclude with teacher-driven professional development steps to support quality teaching to Latino students and to facilitate teacher instructional expertise, classroom use and comfort levels in instruction.

What do Teachers of Latino ELs Want?

When surveyed on what they needed to improve their practice, new and experienced teachers responded that they wanted meaningful and relevant training aligned to expected student outcomes. They wanted professional development with the following characteristics: (a) *contextualized* within the overall school mission and vision and related to their classroom needs and practices; (b) *total school commitment* that includes classroom, content area, bilingual, ESL, special education teachers, paraprofessionals, aides, tutors, and literacy and numeracy teachers/coaches with common planning time and grade level meetings within the school day to plan, implement, and collaborate; (c) *sustained and ongoing* with follow-up meetings to evaluate what is being implemented and put into practice within the schools; (d) *practical,* based on classroom, school, or district specific needs and that relate to ongoing programs or interventions already in place; (e) *research-based* strategies and techniques with ample opportunities to practice them; (f) *differentiated support* to new teachers to align their instruction to school and district goals; and (g) *administrative involvement* and support for team planning, and co teaching through the implementation of professional learning communities. Based on these data, we were able to customize professional development sessions that were responsive to teachers' needs.

The Five Standards for Effective Pedagogy

The Standards are principles considered critical for improving learning outcomes for all students and especially those at risk of academic failure due to cultural, linguistic, or economic factors (Tharp & Gallimore, 1988; Tharp, Estrada, Dalton, & Yamauchi, 2000; Tharp, Dalton, & Hilberg, 2002). The Standards yield consistency in the instruction of Latino ELs, streamline the possibilities for instruction, and have the potential to give them the opportunity to obtain the language, literacy, and the content necessary to succeed in school (Genesee, Lindholm-Leary, Saunders, & Christian, 2006). They have been designed to generate activity patterns of collaboration, reflection, and activity involvement of teachers and students during classroom instruction. They are interrelated and aim to address the academic needs of Latino ELs: (a) *Joint Productive Activity* allows teacher and students to produce and learn together, (b) *Language and Literacy Development across the Curriculum* is fostered through meaningful use and purposeful

Table 35.1   Indicators and Examples for the Five Standards for Effective Pedagogy

1. *Joint Productive Activity.* Student collaboration, seating to match individual and group needs, teacher as part of the team, group variability, smooth transitions, within the time frame, access to technology and materials, and positive monitoring. For example: A lab experiment in science; creating a time-line in social studies.
2. *Language and Literacy Development.* Listen and respond to student talk, assist through modeling, restating, and clarifying, interact with students, connect academic vocabulary, reading and writing to content literacy, and uses English and EL's first language. For example, editing drafts for response to writing in English language arts; several ways of signaling a math function like *add* could also be *plus, combine, sum, increased.*
3. *Contextualization.* Student's background knowledge, meaningful activities, students, parents, and community involvement, relevant and application to student's life, community-based learning, parents' participation in the classroom, student's learning preferences. For example, identifying "cognates*" as instant connectors to the concept objective in the lesson in math: estimate/estimar, symmetry/simetría, intersect/intersectar.
4. *Challenging Activity toward Cognitive Complexity.* Whole to parts, high expectations, moving to the complex level, real life experiences, gives clear and direct feedback. For example, lab reports in science; research reports in social studies, question formulation using Bloom's Taxonomy by teachers to draw background knowledge, to debrief, to develop metacognitive and metalinguistic skills, and by students to use in peer study and cooperative learning activities.
5. *Instructional Conversation.* Classroom arrangement, clear academic goal, higher rate of student talk, student's views and ideas, according to student's preferences, levels of understanding, and questioning, restating. For example: A purposeful dialog connected to any content area lesson including open-ended questions.

Source: Based on Tharp et al., 2000.

conversation, (c) *Making Meaning* allows the teacher to find connections between the students' reality and the curriculum, (d) *Complex Thinking* promotes challenging activities that allow for higher-order thinking, and (e) *Instructional Conversation* promotes dialogue to engage students in the learning process. The Standards promote learning as opportunity to intercalate social experience with academic content in an atmosphere that provides assisted learning (Tharp & Gallimore, 1988; Vygotsky, 1986). They are combined to provide effective instruction (Saunders & Goldenberg, 1999). Table 35.1 presents the indicators that must be present in each of the Standards.

Comparing the Standards with Language and Content Area Standards

The Standards do not encompass all teaching, all content area knowledge or pedagogical and content knowledge; they are guiding principles for instruction that need to be adapted to meet specific student needs (Tharp et al., 2000). The Standards can go hand in hand with other well-known teaching strategies, like cooperative learning, thematic instruction or sheltered content instruction, and other effective teaching strategies. Doherty, Hilberg, Pinal, and Tharp (2003) have found that teachers who use the Standards in their teaching are more likely to use them in conjunction with other teaching strategies.

The Standards compare well with content area standards and with the second language acquisition standards set forth by the Teaching English to Speakers of Other Languages organization (TESOL, 2006). The professional development uses the TESOL English language proficiency standards across grade levels, the four language domains (listening, speaking, reading, and writing), descriptive language proficiency levels, and anchors in and aligns with academic content standards. In this way, the TESOL Standards add to the district's models for academic English instruction. In terms of pedagogical knowledge, the how-to-teach components, we find more commonalities than differences in all standards as they focus on similar goals: collaboration, communication, contextualization, cognitive demand, and dialogic thinking (Ortiz, 2000; Robles-Rivas, 2001).

Focus on Collaboration   The Standards call for Joint Productive Activity where students and their teacher work together to develop a common product and where students assist one another. Similarly, the National Science Education Standards (NSES, 1996), the National Council of Teachers of Mathematics (NCTM, 2003), the National Council for the Social Studies (NCSS, 2000), the National Council of Teachers of English (NCTE, 2006), and TESOL call for teaching that groups students to analyze, create; synthesize ideas and projects in meaningful activities.

Focus on Communication   The Standards call for oral and written language development activities where students develop their second language through questioning, restating, and modeling. The content area and TESOL standards also call for teaching students to communicate, represent, inquire, interpret, translate representations, and explain content phenomena orally and in writing.

Focus on Contextualization   The Standards call for use of the students' knowledge as a foundation for new knowledge and to connect school to students' lives. The content area and the TESOL standards also call for teaching students to draw on prior experiences, to process skills in context using various representations and multiple process skills like manipulation, cognitive and procedural. They also place emphasis on the interplay of cultural, linguistic, social, and cognitive processes in language and academic development.

Focus on Cognitive Demand   The Standards call for instruction that is cognitively challenging with a focus on thinking and analysis of appropriate levels of tasks. Similarly, the TESOL and content area standards call for teaching students to investigate—observe, infer, and experiment—over extended periods of time to develop understanding ability, to create and interpret models of more complex phenomena from various content area perspectives, and to use scaffolding to move students to more complex and challenging activities.

Focus on Dialogic Thinking   The Standards call for the use of the Instructional Conversation where teachers and students dialogue, question, and share ideas and knowledge through assistance dialogue to develop thinking and problem solving skills. By the same token, the TESOL and content area standards call for teaching that promotes dialogic thinking so that students share and explain ideas about specific content-area problems with learner-generated questions and solutions, investigation, hypotheses and models, and at the same time promotes their active participation, regardless of their level of second language proficiency, and dialogue among them.

   In summary, all there is consensus among the standards on what teachers need to teach and promote in their classrooms. The Standards and the NCES, NCTM, NCSS, and NCTE standards all focus on similar goals in the context of collaboration, communication, contextualization, cognitive demand, and dialogic thinking. The professional development uses strategies to meet these standards.

Professional Development

Participants are cohorts of teachers from middle and high schools who teach ESL, English, science, math, and social studies and have Latino ELs in their classrooms. Most of these students are newly arrived to the United States with limited or no formal schooling. Participants' performance is defined as their ability to identify the elements of the Standards and to implement them in their classroom (Hammerness, Darling-Hammond, & Bransford, 2005; Marzano, 2007). In addition to their teaching experience, educators already bring to the professional development training their content area expertise, a foundation of factual and theoretical knowledge within a conceptual framework usually acquired during their pre-service teacher education program. The added Standards can facilitate retrieval of that knowledge and put it into effective action when teaching ELs. There is a great possibility that instruction will tend to produce knowledge and skills in students that will continue active and vibrant as they leave the classroom and enter the real world (Tharp et al., 2000, 2002).

The training topic and the medium for training are the Standards. The professional development plan is designed to train teachers on how to use the Standards in their classrooms by using them in the professional development sessions. In other words, teachers learn about using the Standards with their students by enacting them during their training (Minaya-Rowe, 2002, 2004; Rueda, 1998; Téllez & Waxman, 2006). Teachers also learn about and enact the Standards as they work with peers or teams in their professional learning communities, developing lessons, or planning thematic units.

The professional development sessions are based on the sequence with four conditions proposed by Joyce and Showers (2002):

1. *Knowledge—exploration of theory or rationale* through discussions, readings, and lectures of the Standards; teachers need to understand the concepts behind each of the Standards, when and how to use them. A sound knowledge of the Standards facilitates skill acquisition, understanding of the enactment of each, a mental image of how they work, and attainment and control of the Standards.
2. *Demonstrations or modeling* of skills to facilitate learning of each Standard. These are demonstrated during the professional development. Demonstrations can be mediated through videos and scenarios of how each Standard works. Demonstrations facilitate the understanding of underlying socioconstructivist theory behind the Standards.
3. *Practice of skills under simulated conditions*; teachers get closer to the classroom setting by enacting the Standards. Peer teaching sessions are also encouraged when teachers practice with other teachers how to conduct an Instructional Conversations and other Standards.
4. *Peer coaching during Standards classroom implementation.* Teachers collaborate to strengthen their teaching skills, to plan lessons, and to solve problems.
5. *Effective implementation of the Standards* with continuous coaching, classroom observations, debriefings and follow-up training sessions during the school year.

Training consists of two-week summer institutes and five full-day follow-up sessions. The first week of the summer institute focuses on training. During the second week, teachers work in teams to review the mandated curriculum, develop lesson templates, and prepare thematic units. The content of the first week training includes the Standards, practical applications and demonstrations designed to meet the ELs' immediate needs. It focuses on training teachers to develop students' language and academic skills across the content areas. It provides extensive modeling of research-based instructional strategies and techniques, peer practice sessions, and feedback from trainers and peers. Training delivery also includes activities for the development of professional learning communities. Trainers also give teachers models of lessons and a teacher's guide with theory and effective practices. Through guided questions and templates, the teachers work in teams and groups to develop their own lesson templates and write their own lessons integrating what they have learned with the existing curriculum, textbooks, and materials they currently use with their students.

The professional development is also based on the needs of teachers to become more active participants in the process of change and collective problem solving. It focuses on the process by which they acquire the knowledge, skills and attitudes necessary to be effective. Teachers exercise professional judgment on the training contents about what works, with whom, and why. Rather than give teachers quick-fix solutions and recipes for what to do in the classroom to differentiate instruction, the educators are helped to develop a conceptual understanding of why the Standards are being proposed and advocated and how they can be useful in their teaching.

Training Phases

Apprenticeship is the underlying principle of the interactions taking place in the professional development sessions. This socioconstructivist concept focuses on a system of interpersonal involvement and arrangements in which participants engage in organized activities that promote a shared responsibility of learning between novice and expert (Rogoff, 1995). The five-day, full week training is presented in the follows phases:

Phase 1. Foundation: Learning about the Standards (One and one-half days)

Focus: Awareness building, introduction of the Standards for Effective Pedagogy, reflection on practice, understanding the elements of the Instructional Conversation, the settings of Joint Productive Activities, means for Contextualization, the conditions for Language and Literacy Development, the format for Challenging Activity toward Cognitive Complexity, modeling and scaffolding, practice with feedback, debriefing and reflection, and professional learning communities.

Phase 2. Construction: Integrating the Five Standards with the Content and Language Standards (One and one-half days)

Focus: Awareness building, in depth study of one Standard, modeling and scaffolding, enacting chosen Standard, reflection on practice, comparing elements of Standards, moving towards implementation, how the Standards can be integrated with content area standards, how language and content goals are used in lesson planning and teaching, consensus building, meeting the state-mandated curriculum, debriefing and reflection, and professional learning communities.

One of the benefits of the implementation of professional learning communities at schools is that teachers work together, share teaching strategies, and practice using the Standards embedded contents and teaching in their curriculum in a harmonious way. For example, the instructional units are developed by all grade-level teachers together; the social studies teacher refers to what students have been taught in the science class around the theme of the unit. Bilingual, ESL and content area teachers work together to prepare and teach culturally and linguistically diverse Latino students, and to reflect on their teaching. In this way, teachers co-teach or team-teach the same students they would be teaching separately. This is one way of illustrating the contributions of both ranks of teachers. ESL and bilingual teachers who are trained on second language development stages, and language acquisition and teaching strategies are extremely useful to content area teachers in the planning and delivery of content lessons.

Phase 3. Implementation: Preparing Standards-Based Lessons and Units (two days)

Focus: Awareness building, using the Instructional Conversation to integrate all standards (JPAs, contextualization, language and literacy and challenging activities toward cognitive complexity), modeling and scaffolding, enacting the Standards within an IC, reflection on practice, moving toward implementation in the classroom, review of standards-based curriculum, review of lessons samples with the Standards, thematic units, lesson preparation, vocabulary building, debriefing and reflection, and professional learning communities.

Embedded in these activities are related practices that include: brainstorming, background information, video, quick write, small group share, popcorn share with whole group, review information, read about the Standards, revisit video, reflective write, small group share, create a visual, consensus building, debriefing, among others. All lessons address the Standards; they include complex thinking, English language and literacy development, contextualization, collaboration and instructional conversations. All lessons include English language and specific content objectives to address linguistic and academic needs of Latino students. The Standards are so intertwined in the lessons and curriculum units that it is difficult to separate them.

Teachers Planning Together within their Professional Learning Communities

The Standards are implemented in the context of the professional learning community as the infrastructure for school improvement to achieve sustainability. We have found that these communities are empowering; they encourage teacher pedagogical content knowledge and promote opportunities for collegial collaboration, learning together, in-depth analysis, inquiry, development, evaluation, and create change.

Grade-level content teachers (mathematics, science, social studies, language arts) plan their lessons and thematic units together with the ESL teacher, bilingual teacher, and the special education teacher and co-teach classrooms with Latino students. Teachers have the opportunity to work together towards a common goal to improve their teaching and can accomplish a number of activities together. For example, they examine: (a) student strengths and needs, their levels of English language development; their progress in language development and the content areas— toward meeting the curriculum standards; (b) curriculum implementation, alignment with state, district standards and grade level materials; and (c) their own teaching, areas of success, areas for improvement, beliefs and biases about students, and ways to improve their teaching. Moreover, teachers support each other to improve their co-teaching by coaching and providing feedback to each other, modeling and demonstrating teaching strategies for each other, and conferring, doing problem solving, and sharing.

Integrated Approach to Co-Teaching

Two teachers co-teach using their own lesson template and selecting the strategies and activities to cover the content. Both decide their roles before the class but focus on the lesson template as a whole. They both teach students English and the content area through building background, debriefing, vocabulary presentation and application, and cognitive organizers. They teach vocabulary (word, concepts, cognates, polysemous or multiple meanings); they also promote classroom interactions, through JPAs cooperative learning strategies (like Think-Pair-Share/ Square, Round Table, Jigsaw Problem Solving, Numbered Heads Together, Write Around, Turn to your Partner, Three-Step Interview), reading fluency and comprehension, question formulations using Bloom's taxonomy question stems and instructional conversations. Their focus is to construct and provide subject matter in spoken and written forms. Furthermore, their teaching connects school to their students' lives, home, and community.

Bilingual or ESL teachers teach students to use English to communicate content knowledge. Teachers possess knowledge of and can use a variety of second language teaching strategies to teach technical specialized vocabulary, joint productive activities, and instructional conversations. Furthermore, most are bilingual and can use Spanish to instruct them when needed. Monolingual content teachers also relate to the students' first language when teaching specific content knowledge. For example, what is the cognate for *democracy* in Spanish? Students may respond *democracia*. Even though some ELs may not be proficient enough in their first language, orally or in writing, and thus are not always able to use word knowledge transfer as a resource for word meaning; the relationship to a cognate may produce an affective connection with the words, hence producing a sense of word ownership.

Using the integrated approach, teachers select and unify thematic units across the curriculum (e.g., Ancient Greece). Strategies implemented in thematic units focus on the integration of language and literacy development objectives as well as content area objectives and how they can be combined to develop an effective lesson to ensure students' academic success. Throughout the team meetings for common preparation of lessons, teachers have opportunities to revise testing data from the state mastery test, and identify strands—critical strands—that students have the most difficulty to learn and that are state-mandated. Utilizing formative assessment data, teachers develop thematic units that are aligned to these strands and help all students to increase content vocabulary, improve reading comprehension and fluency skills, and increase critical thinking skill development and content area knowledge. For example, in the preparation of an interdisciplinary thematic unit for reading, social studies, language arts, science, and math with the theme of "Ancient Greece," teachers co-plan to teach the state mastery testing strands which are critical stance, fractions and decimals, and character education with a main title of "Trust and Responsibility".

Thematic units and a coordinated effort for an instructional pace are important products of their collegial work. The benefit is two-fold for the teachers involved. First, they contribute to the development of thematic units that ensure students' academic and language development, and second, teachers who are at higher grade levels are well informed of what their peers' practices are and how it impacts the students they will be receiving in future years (Zwiers, 2008).

Professional Development Cycle

The model depicted in Figure 35.1 reflects the professional development cycle created with this training experience. The process can be repeated to meet the needs of teachers or their professional learning community. We have been able to identify seven steps on a full-year cycle when professional development is ongoing and sustained:

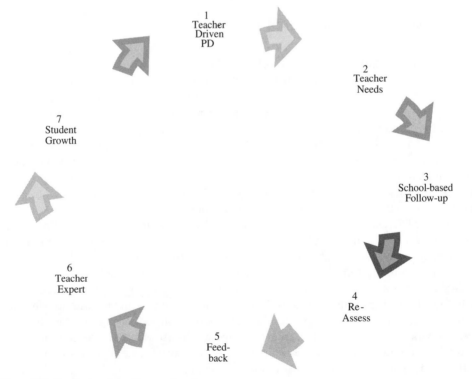

Figure 35.1 Professional development cycle.

Teacher driven (Step 1), based on *teacher needs* (Step 2) when the present status of teacher knowledge and skills is determined before the training. *School-based follow-ups* (Step 3) and learning communities during the school year are scheduled for refresher training, classroom observations, modeling, and peer feedback. The next step (Step 4) is to *re-assess teacher knowledge and skills* (e.g., how much of the training on the Standards is part of the teacher's repertoire; how the Standards are being implemented in the classroom).

Follow-up training (Step 5) to provide feedback to the teacher and to highlight what has been successful in the classroom and what needs to be strengthened with peer feedback. In this way, *teacher instructional expertise* (Step 6) increases when using the Standards. In addition, as teachers become more comfortable using them, they develop ownership. This effort can result in *Latino ELs' academic growth* (Step 7).

Summary

We have proposed ways to boost the professional development of teachers of Latino ELs using the Five Standards for Effective Pedagogy to meet their linguistic and academic needs. During the training, teachers not only learn about the Standards but also enact them. We have also examined and compared the Standards to language and content area standards proposed by national organizations and found common goals. The chapter has addressed what language and content teachers need and want. It has included samples of training using the Standards and examined ways to promote collegial working teams for professional growth through examples from the field. We pose a seven-step cycle to strengthen teacher expertise and to support quality teaching of Latino students. This professional development is teacher driven, addresses training needs, and builds on teacher knowledge and teacher skills. Follow-up school-based training strengthens teacher knowledge and skills and facilitates teacher instructional expertise, classroom use, and comfort levels in instruction, which, in turn, promote student academic growth.

References

Biancarosa, G., & Snow, C. E. (2004). *Reading next. A vision for action and research in middle and high school literacy: A report from Carnegie Corporation of New York.* Washington, DC: Alliance for Excellent Education.

Darling-Hammond, L., & Bransford, J. (Eds.). (2005). *Preparing teachers for a changing world: What teachers should learn and be able to do.* San Francisco: Jossey-Bass.

Doherty, R. B., Hilberg, R. S., Pinal, A., & Tharp, R. G. (2003). Five standards and student achievement. *NABE Journal of Research and Practice, 1*(1), 1-24.

Genesee, F., Lindholm-Leary, K., Saunders, W. M., & Christian, D. (2006). *Educating English language learners. A synthesis of research evidence.* New York: Cambridge University Press.

Graham, S., & Perin, D. (2007). *Writing Next. Effective strategies to improve writing of adolescents in middle and high schools.* New York: Carnegie Corporation of New York.

Joyce, B., & Showers, B. (2002). *Student achievement through staff development* (3rd ed.). Alexandria, VA: Association for Supervision and Curriculum Development.

Marzano, R. J. (2007). *The art and science of teaching. A comprehensive framework for effective instruction.* Alexandria, VA: Association for Supervision and Curriculum Development.

Minaya-Rowe, L. (2004). Training teachers of English language learners using their students' first language. *Journal of Latinos and Education, 3*(1), 3-24.

Minaya-Rowe, L. (Ed.). (2002). *Teacher training and effective pedagogy in the context of student diversity.* Greenwich, CT: Information Age.

National Center for Education Statistics (NCES). (2005). The NAEP Reading Achievement Levels by grade. Retrieved May 1, 2007, from http//www.nces.ed.gov/nationsreportcard

National Council for the Social Studies (NCSS). (2000). National standards for social studies teachers. Retrieved August 2, 2007, from http://www.socialstudies.org/teacherstandards/

National Council of Teachers of English (NCTE). (2006). Guidelines for the preparation of teachers of English language arts. Retrieved August 2, 2007, from http://www.ncte.org/groups/cee/links/126867.htm

National Council of Teachers of Mathematics (NCTM). (2003). NCATE/NCTM program standards programs for initial preparation of mathematics teachers: Standards for secondary mathematics teachers. Retrieved August 2, 2007, from http://www.ncate.org/ProgramStandards/NCTM/NCTMSECON-Standards.pdf

National Research Council (NRC). (1996). National science education standards. Retrieved August 2, 2007, from http://www.nap.edu/readingroom/books/nses/

Ortiz, J. A. (2000). *English language learners developing academic language through sheltered instruction.* Unpublished doctoral dissertation, University of Connecticut, Storrs.

Robles-Rivas, E. (2001). *An examination of standards for effective pedagogy in a high school bilingual setting.* Unpublished doctoral dissertation, University of Connecticut, Storrs.

Rogoff, B. (1995). Observing sociocultural activity on three planes: Participatory appropriation, guided participation, and apprenticeship. In J. V. Wertsch, P. Del Rio, & A. Alvarez (Eds.), *Sociocultural studies of mind* (pp. 139–164). New York: Cambridge University Press.

Rueda, R. (1998). *Standards for professional development: A sociocultural perspective.* Santa Cruz, CA: Center for Research in Education, Diversity, and Excellence.

Saunders, W., & Goldenberg, C. (1999). Effects of instructional conversations and literature logs on limited and fluent English proficient students' story comprehension and thematic understanding. *Elementary School Journal, 99*(4), 277-301.

Short, D., & Fitzsimmons, S. (2006). *Double the work: Challenges and solutions to acquiring language and academic literacy for adolescent English language learners.* Washington, DC: Alliance for Excellent Education.

Snow, C.E., Griffin, P., & Burns, S. (2005). *Knowledge to support the teaching of reading: Preparing teachers for a changing world.* San Francisco: Jossey-Bass.

Teachers of English to Speakers of Other Languages. (2006). *ESL standards for pre-K-12 students.* Alexandria, VA: Author.

Téllez, K., & Waxman, H. C. (Eds.). (2006). *Preparing quality educators for English language learners. Research, policies, and practices.* Mahwah, NJ: Erlbaum.

Tharp, R, Dalton, S., & Hilberg, S. (2002). *Teaching Alive for the 21st Century in Secondary Settings* (CD-ROM). Santa Cruz, CA: Center for Research on Education, Diversity & Excellence.

Tharp, R. G., Estrada, P., Dalton, S. S., & Yamauchi, L. A. (2000). *Teaching transformed: Achieving excellence, fairness, inclusion, and harmony.* Boulder, CO: Westview Press.

Tharp, R. G., & Gallimore, R. (1988). *Rousing minds to life: Teaching, learning, and schooling in social context.* New York: Cambridge University Press.

Vygotsky, L. S. (1986). *Thought and language.* Cambridge, MA: MIT Press.

Zwiers, J. (2008). *Building academic language. Essential practices for content classrooms.* San Francisco: Jossey-Bass.

Part V

Resources and Information

Part Editor: Margarita Machado-Casas

36 Resources and Information

An Introduction

Margarita Machado-Casas
University of Texas at San Antonio

The purpose of this handbook is to provide the most significant and influential work in the field of Latinos and education and to serve as a guide that traces and documents the most important aspects of Latino education in the United States along with resources and the most up-to-date information available on research relating to this topic.

The primary goal of this "Resources and Information" section is to provide significant supplementary material regarding Latino education. Second, the goal is to create a national database and disseminate it both via the handbook and a Web site that can also be updated on a continuing basis. For this reason the handbook editorial staff created the National Latino Education Network (NLEN), whose Web site serves as the "live" information database parallel to this "Resources and Information" section. The NLEN is a member-based electronic community currently sponsored by the *Journal of Latinos and Education*, and it is made up of researchers, teaching professionals and educators, academics, scholars, administrators, independent writers and artists, policy and program specialists, students, parents, families, civic leaders, activists, and advocates. The Web site (www.nlen.csusb.edu/) provides online features, one of which is a "Resource Guide/Clearing-house" that allows members to browse for resources, opportunities, and activities in the Latino educational community. An online and e-mail newsletter also allows members to access the latest information, news, and research on Latinos and education. We have an e-mail list serve informing members of breaking news that requires immediate attention and action, as well as programs and news broadcasts via video and audio broadband through our partner, the Latino Scholastic Achievement Corporation, a 501(c)3 organization. This Web site is available 24 hours a day, 7 days a week. In this way the resources and information provided in this handbook are not "static" but like the innovations in our field constantly undergoing change.

This concluding section of the handbook serves as an extended appendix for the entire volume, and is divided into 12 subject areas: (1) Adult/Continuing Education; (2) Commercial Products; (3) Demographics/Statistics and Government; (4) Events; (5) Groups; (6) Higher Education; (7) Internet Tools/Technology; (8) Libraries/Galleries/Museums; (9) Nonprint Media; (10) Parents and Teachers; (11) Periodicals; and (12) Publications. Although we are aware that it is impossible for this section to include *all* resources available, we feel that it covers the most pertinent resources available for the education of Latinos in the United States and serves as a base for information in this area. But also, because this section has a live component that will continue to be updated daily via the NLEN Web site, we see this compilation as the beginning of an ever-expanding database of resources about Latino education in the United States.

In the "Adult/Continuing Education" section, Carlos Martín Vélez provides a synthesis of academic and nonacademic resources available regarding adult/continuing education. Dr. Velez covers ESL, civics education, vocational training, extended studies, career training, literacy, and funding opportunities available in this field.

In the "Commercial Products" section, Minda López has compiled a brief picture of the most important commercial resources, including subcategories such as software, audio/video tapes, DVDs, teaching supplies, and overall education aid.

In the "Demographics/Statistics and Government" section, Norma A. Guzmán provides us with the most trusted sites available for obtaining census, demographics, and statistical information about Latinos in education. In addition, she provides a list of policies and legislation that have had a direct impact in the fields of bilingual education, special education, bilingual special education, and the most relevant and important cases and regulations that in general affect the education of Latinos in the United States.

In the "Events" section, Victor A. Castillo and Sonia N. Sánchez present a list of annual conferences and conventions on Latinos in education. Furthermore, they provide a list of educational and cultural organizations as well as legal, medical, and political organizations. In addition, they provide a list of innovative research centers, directories, and other online resources.

In the "Groups" section, Silvia Cristina Bettez gives an overview of the most significant organizations, agencies, community projects, associations, and professional societies that serve the needs of Latinos in education.

In the "Higher Education" section, Belinda Treviño Schouten and Katherine Graves-Talati have compiled a list that includes colleges, universities, institutes, centers, degrees, and programs that focus on Latino education in the United States. Furthermore, they provide information about funding opportunities, academic competitions, awards, mentorship, internships, and training available for those working with and researching in this area.

In the "Internet Tools and Technology" section Victor H. Pérez presents a list of relevant Web sites, Webliographies, clearinghouses, portals, digital/virtual libraries, and directories that collect information in this area.

In the "Libraries/Galleries/Museums" section, Belinda Treviño Schouten compiles a list and information that provides an overview of collections, archives, permanent exhibitions, museums, and more that relates to Latino history and life in the United States.

In the "Nonprint Media" section, Grisel Y. Acosta compiles a list of television programming, recordings, motion pictures, radio programming, and more that touch on Latinos in education. This information can be useful for educators or those who need to use the media to discuss the subject.

In the "Parents and Teachers" section, Esther Garza and Keren Zuniga-McDowell provide parents and teachers working with pre-K/early childhood and K-12 Latino students with a list of resources. They have compiled a list of academic journals that publish the most recent research about Latino students in the United States. There is a list of important articles and books, and also Web sites for organizations that provide funding opportunities and resources.

In the "Periodicals" section, Evelyn M. Gordon and Daniella Ann Cook compiled a list of the most influential print media, such as magazines, newsletters, newspapers, and more that cover the subject area.

Finally, in the "Publications" section, Norma A. Guzmán, Janet López, and Mary Ruth Fernández have compiled a list of some of the most influential research conducted on Latinos in education. This section includes articles, special journal issues, book/media reviews, conference proceedings/presentations, reference works, encyclopedias, bibliographies, dictionaries, books, book chapters, literature, technical papers/research reports, and other ERIC documents that present current and past academic research.

To conclude, the editors and contributors aim at providing the most current and influential academic research and resources for the education of Latinos in the United States. Again, we are aware that this does not cover all resources available on this subject but hope that it will serve as a guide that traces and documents the most important sources.

37 Adult/Continuing Education

Carlos Martín Vélez

Brescia University

ESL/CIVICS INSTRUCTION, GED, VOCATIONAL TRAINING, EXTENDED STUDIES, COMMUNITY COLLEGES, CAREER TRAINING, LITERACY, FUNDING OPPORTUNITIES, AND MORE.[1]

ESL/Civics Instruction—Literacy

CAELA—The Center for Adult English Language Acquisition
www.cal.org/caela/about_caela

CAELA was created to help states build their capacity to promote English language learning and academic achievement of adults learning English. This Web site provides access to ESL resources, research findings, and a newsletter targeted to professionals teaching adults learning English in the United States.

English Literacy and Civics Education (EL/Civics)
www.cde.state.co.us/cdeadult/ELCivics.htm

This Colorado Department of Education Web site provides information resources, instructional resources, EL/Civics programs, and current Colorado EL/Civics State Leadership Projects.

EL/Civics Online Integrating EL/Civics into Adult ESL Classes
www.elcivicsonline.org/what-is-elcol

EL/Civics Online (English Literacy and Civics Education) is a four-part series of online courses to prepare ESL instructors and volunteers to integrate U.S. history, U.S. government, civic engagement, and the naturalization process into adult ESL classes. Teachers who complete these courses will learn strategies to further their students' knowledge about the United States along with increased English language acquisition.

Bureau of Adult Basic and Literacy Education
www.able.state.pa.us/able/site/default.asp

This Pennsylvania Department of Education Web site provides a full range of instructional services and access services such as English learning and civics that address the basic educational needs of immigrant adults and families and other populations with limited English speaking skills.

CAAL—Council for Advancement of Adult Literacy
www.caalusa.org/publications.html

The Council for Advancement of Adult Literacy (CAAL) is a national nonprofit public charity. Its broad mission is to help advance adult education and literacy in the United States. The Web site provides recent research on ESL topics to non-English speaking immigrants.

Centro Latino for Literacy
www.centrolatinoliteracy.org

The Centro Latino's mission is to teach literacy and provide educational opportunities to those who have not had the benefit of an education, especially Latino immigrants. Spanish language information on programs and services is available periodically.

Hispanic Family Learning Institute

www.famlit.org

> The Hispanic Family Learning Institute (HFLI), a division of the National Center for Family Literacy, is dedicated to providing important resources and information to aid in creating an educational community for Hispanic families across the country. They seek to provide programs and resources to professionals who work with adult English language learners (ELL) so that they may better understand and educate their Hispanic students and families.

Low Educated Second Language and Literacy Acquisition (LESLLA)

www.leslla.org/default.htm

> Low Educated Second Language and Literacy Acquisition (LESLLA) for Adults is an international forum of researchers who share an interest in research on the development of second language skills by adult immigrants with little or no schooling prior to entering a country. This international forum should be joined by researchers interested in adult Latino immigrants learning English in ESL centers in the United States.

National Coalition for Literacy

www.national-coalition-literacy.org/about.html

> The National Coalition for Literacy (NCL) aims to advance adult education, family literacy, and English language acquisition in the United States by increasing public awareness for the need to increase funding and programs; affecting public policy to increase funding; and serving as an authoritative resource for the field on national adult education issues.

National Institute for Literacy

www.nifl.gov

> The National Institute for Literacy, a federal agency, provides leadership on literacy issues, including the improvement of reading instruction for children, youth, and adults. In consultation with the U.S. departments of Education, Labor, and Health and Human Services, the Institute serves as a national resource on current, comprehensive literacy research, practice, and policy.

The Latino Family Literacy Project

www.latinoliteracy.com

> The Latino Family Literacy Project offers training workshops for teachers who work with Latino parents and their children in building a regular family reading routine and developing strong English-language skills.

The Penn State University Institute for Adult Literacy

www.ed.psu.edu/isal/links.htm

> This university-based institute provides recent accessible online publications on adult learning/teaching strategies and English language learning among adult non-English-language learners, as well as other relevant information on adult literacy.

GED

General Educational Development (or GED) tests are a battery of five tests which, when passed, certify that the taker has American or Canadian high school-level academic skills. To pass the GED tests and earn a GED credential, test takers must score higher than 40% of graduating high school seniors nationwide. Some jurisdictions require that students pass additional tests, such as an English proficiency exam or civics test. There are free GED preparation Web sites such as www.gedforfree.com/.

Obtaining Your GED with English as Your Second Language
www.malt.cmich.edu/eslcorr_hlresc.htm
> This Central Michigan University Web site provides a variety of Hispanic/Latino American cultural resources such as Chicano: History of the Mexican American Civil Rights Movement and Building Chicana/o Latina/o Communities Through Networking and other links such as ESL resources to build up knowledge skills to pass GED tests.

High School Diploma or GED?
www.online-education.net/highschool/high-school-ged_2.html
> Accredited online high schools are becoming more popular, and the GED is no longer the only option for those who didn't finish high school. This Web site offers links to online high schools that offer flexible and supportive environments to get a high school diploma.

GED Resources for Students (in Spanish language as well)
www.sanjacinto.episd.org/sjtech/ged.html
> The San Jacinto Adult Learning Center located in El Paso, Texas offers a variety of GED resources (in Spanish language as well) such as test preparation resources and the different sections of the GED exam.

Links to GED Research, Information, and Instructional Resources
www.cde.state.co.us/cdeadult/GEDlinks.htm#instr
> This Colorado Department of Education Web site offers links to GED research, information, and instructional resources as well as to publishers of GED preparation and study materials for adults.

Community Colleges

American Association of Community Colleges
www.aacc.nche.edu
> This Web site provides general and specific information on U.S. community colleges. Community colleges are centers of educational opportunity. They are an American invention that put publicly funded higher education at close-to-home facilities, beginning nearly 100 years ago with Joliet Junior College. Since then, they have been inclusive institutions that welcome all who desire to learn, regardless of wealth, heritage, or previous academic experience.

National Community College Hispanic Council
www.ncchc.com/
> The National Community College Hispanic Council was established over 20 years ago to prepare Hispanic leaders for America's community and technical colleges. NCCHC is committed to delivering a quality leadership development experience that provides Hispanics in community colleges with an opportunity to continue their personal and professional growth.

Latino/a Transfer Students in Postsecondary Institutions in California
www.chicano.ucla.edu/press/briefs/documents
> This UCLA Chicano Studies Research Latino policy brief offers an examination of Latino transfer students in California Postsecondary institutions in 2002–2003.

Career Training/Vocational Training/Extended Studies

Career training is focused education designed to prepare you for a specific job once you have finished. For many people, a career training school can offer many benefits that a 4-year school can't and is often a more logical choice. Career colleges offer some or all of these advantages:

practical classes, career programs, job placement, wide variety of courses, personalized degree tracks and practical schedules. See more general information at www.careerexplorer.net/

ASPIRA

www.aspira.org/about.html

The ASPIRA Association, Inc. is the only national nonprofit organization devoted solely to the education and leadership development of Puerto Rican and other Latino youth. ASPIRA takes its name from the Spanish verb aspirar, "aspire."

Hispanic Alliance for Career Enhancement (HACE)

www.hace-usa.org/overview.htm

HACE is dedicated to nurturing Latinos at all stages of the career continuum, from high school to college and on to the professional years, as the organization seeks to develop increasing numbers of successful Latino professionals and leaders.

Hispanic Association on Corporate Responsibility (HACR)

www.hacr.org/

HACR is one of the most influential advocacy organizations in the nation representing 13 national Hispanic organizations in the United States and Puerto Rico. Our mission is to advance the inclusion of Hispanics in corporate America at a level commensurate with our economic contributions. To that end, HACR focuses on four areas of corporate responsibility and community reciprocity: employment, procurement, philanthropy, and governance.

Hispanic Association of Colleges and Universities

www.hacu.net/hacu

HACU is committed to Hispanic success in education, from kindergarten through graduate school and into the work force of tomorrow. Everyone has a stake in HACU's crucial goals: to promote the development of member colleges and universities; to improve access to and the quality of postsecondary educational opportunities for Hispanic students; and to meet the needs of business, industry, and government through the development and sharing of resources, information, and expertise.

U.S. Department of Labor—Employment and Training Administration

www.doleta.gov/etainfo/

The Employment and Training Administration (ETA) administers federal government job training and worker dislocation programs, federal grants to states for public employment service programs, and unemployment insurance benefits. These services are primarily provided through state and local workforce development systems.

Vocational Training

Vocational education—or Vocational Education and Training (VET), also called Career and Technical Education (CTE) prepares learners for careers that are based in manual or practical activities, traditionally nonacademic and totally related to a specific trade, occupation, or vocation, hence the term, in which the learner participates. It is sometimes referred to as *technical education*, as the learner directly develops expertise in a particular group of techniques.

EnterWeb

www.enterweb.org/edutrain.htm

This Web site lists and rates electronic resources related to education and training with a particular focus on technical and vocational education.

The Hispanic Center, Inc.

www.pghhispaniccenter.org/about-us.html

This Web site provides information on how to recruit, train, provide employment, referrals, and services to, and retain individuals in Southwestern Pennsylvania (SWPA), by promoting skill enrichment, career opportunities, and personal development of Hispanic individuals and their families.

The Hispanic/Latino Initiative

www.chs-urc.org

In 2007, the nonprofit organization University Research Co. (URC) and the Center for Human Services (CHR) launched the new Hispanic–Latino Initiative to address these complex immigration issues. This initiative is designed to (1) provide Hispanic–Latino communities with access to critical services focusing on behavior change, education, and skill development; (2) raise community awareness and participation; and (3) focus attention on policies needed to both motivate positive actions and ensure the sustainability of the changes that occur.

White House Initiative on Educational Excellence for Hispanic Americans

www.yesican.gov

This government initiative created in 2001 aims to examine the underlying causes of the existing education achievement gap between Hispanic-American students and their peers.

Recent funding has been allocated under American Competitive Initiative to encourage students to take more challenging courses in high school and to pursue college majors in high demand in the global economy, such as science, mathematics, technology, engineering, and critical foreign languages.

Extended Studies

www.unco.edu/extendedstudies/homelinks/about-us.html

Various U.S. universities have an Office of Extended Studies (OES). These provide continuing education and other outreach activities. For example the University of Northern Colorado (above) has a Web site with the information on their OES. The services to the Hispanic–Latino community are embedded within each university's outreach goals.

The University of Texas at San Antonio, Office of Extended Studies

www.utsa.edu/VPEE/index.htm

The Office of Extended Education provides continuing education offerings to a national audience, along with continuing to offer South Central Texas and the San Antonio communities with top quality programs and workshops. As you look through our Web site, you will find a variety of quality workshops and programs in professional and career development, computer training, test preparation, and certification programs.

Scholarships/Funding Opportunities

Adelante U.S. Scholarship Fund

www.adelantefund.org/adelante

The ¡Adelante! Fund is a national nonprofit based in San Antonio, Texas. The organization uses a holistic approach to prepare college students for leadership roles upon entry into the workforce. Since its designation as a 501(c)3 ten years ago, ¡Adelante! Fund has awarded nearly $1 million in scholarships to undergraduate students across the nation.

Hispanic College Fund

www.site.hispanicfund.org

In 1994 the Hispanic College Fund awarded $30,000 in scholarships to 14 Hispanic students on the business career track. Since then the HCF Scholars program has expanded to awarding over $2 million every year to over 600 students who demonstrate financial need and are pursuing degrees in business, science, engineering, technology, and math.

Hispanic Scholarship Fund

www.hsf.net

The Web site provides information on the scholarship programs of the Hispanic Scholarship Fund, the nation's largest provider of college financial aid for Latinos.

Hispanic Scholarship Fund State Farm Insurance

www.statefarm.com/about/part_spos/grants/hispanic.asp

State Farm Companies Foundation has assisted Hispanic college students through its relationship with the Hispanic Scholarship Fund since 1990. Each year, $2,500 scholarships are provided to 20 Hispanic college students who are pursuing a teaching career.

Hispanic-Serving Institutions Education Grants Program

www.csrees.usda.gov/fo/hispanicservinginstitutionseducationhep.cfm

This competitive grants program is intended to promote and strengthen the ability of Hispanic-Serving Institutions to carry out higher education programs in the food and agricultural sciences.

Latino Issues Forum (LIF) Summer Fellowship Program

www.lif.org

Over the past 19 years, LIF has had the distinction of developing outstanding leaders through its summer fellowship program. The LIF Summer Fellowship is a 3-month, full-time program where students gain valuable, hands-on experience shaping public policy, conducting research, organizing advocacy campaigns, and working with the media. The program is open to undergraduate and graduate students as well as recently graduated professionals.

Scholarships for Hispanics

www.scholarshipsforhispanics.org

The National Association of Hispanic Publications (NAHP) Hispanic Higher Education Initiative provides access to a scholarship directory targeted to Hispanic students in their pursuit to higher education.

Scholarships for Hispanic BLOG

www.scholarshipsforhispanics.blogspot.com/

This blog is designed to further encourage young Hispanic students to pursue higher education by connecting them to mentors, advisors, and professionals with up-to-the- minute dialogues relating to financial aid, high school preparation, college savings advice, and professional insight.

The Congressional Hispanic Caucus Institute Education Center Fellowship and Scholarship

www.chci.org/chciyouth/scholarship/scholarship.htm

The Congressional Hispanic Caucus Institute (CHCI), the nation's premier Hispanic educational and youth leadership development organization, today launched a national campaign to recruit Hispanic students—undergraduate and graduate—for its nationally recognized youth development leadership programs.

The Gates Millennium Scholars (GMS)

www.gmsp.org

The goal of GMS is to promote academic excellence and to provide an opportunity for outstanding minority students with significant financial need to reach their highest potential by reducing financial barriers for African-American, Hispanic-American, American-Indian/ Alaska Native, and Asian Pacific Islander-American students with high academic and leadership promise who have a significant financial need.

The Lagrant Foundation

www.lagrantfoundation.org

The Lagrant Foundation is a nonprofit 501(c)(3) organization whose mission is to increase the number of ethnic minorities in the fields of advertising, marketing, and public relations by providing scholarships, career development workshops, professional development, mentors, and internships to African-American, American-Indian/Native American, Asian Pacific-American, and Hispanic/Latino undergraduate and graduate students.

Note

1. The author(s) and editor(s) do not necessarily endorse the entries in this chapter; they are listed for informational purposes only. Most descriptions have been gathered by conducting extensive electronic searches with key words related to these topics and are taken directly from these online sites in order to provide clear descriptions. In order to honor the words chosen to describe themselves and others, each overview incorporates the terms and language utilized (such as Latino/a, Hispanic, Chicano, etc.) on the individual sites.

38 Commercial Products

Minda López

Texas State University at San Marcos

COMMERCIAL PRODUCTS: SOFTWARE, AUDIO/VIDEO TAPES, DVDS, TEACHING SUPPLIES/AIDS, AND MORE.[1]

Software

Inspiration Software Products

www.inspiration.com/edresources/index.cfm

This software provides students and teachers with ways to create visual maps and organizers of their thinking processes, of content area material, and of curriculum. There are multiple versions for different purposes, ages, and grade levels.

Word Problem Square Off

www.gamco.com/index.php?cPath=21_24_30

This learning game engages students in solving a wide variety of word problems, thanks to a special mystery phrase game. Students solve word problems to earn points which they use to select or buy letters. Point values are randomly generated to give all students an equal chance to win. Mystery phrases are divided into several cross-curricular categories, including language arts and social studies.

Visual Thesaurus

www.visualthesaurus.com/

The Visual Thesaurus from Thinkmap is an interactive dictionary and thesaurus which creates word maps that appear with connected meanings and synonyms as well as antonyms. It is a great tool for students and educators of all levels working on writing. Both an online and desktop version is available.

Animoto

animoto.com/

Animoto is software available free to educators through the Web site. The software is for presentations and digital storytelling and can be used to combine music, video, still photos, and text into dynamic and customized videos.

Capzles

capzles.com/

Capzles is free software educators can use to create interactive timelines, which incorporate video, photos, sound, and other media and can be displayed in a variety of formats.

Dipity

www.dipity.com/

Dipity is free software that can be used to create interactive timelines and to post topics. The timeline can incorporate a vast array of multimedia files.

Audio/CDs

Jose Luis Orozco

www.joseluisorozco.com/frameset_index.htm

CDs include:

Lirica Infantil—Latin American Children's Songs, Games and Rhymes, multiple volumes

Orozco's music is fun, playful, and authentic. He incorporates traditional songs, games, and rhymes along with his own new creations. Some examples include: De San Francisco Vengo, El chocolate, Las vocales, Sana, sana, Nochebuena, Aserrín, aserran, Guantanamera, De Colores, Buenos Dias, El buque de papel, etc.

He also has CDs of corridos Mexicanos and Chicanos, including songs such as: Los oprimidos, Don Miguel Hidalgo, Cinco de Mayo, Joaquin Murrieta, Emiliano Zapata, Cesar Chavez, Dolores Huerta, etc.

The Taco Shop Poets

www.tacoshoppoets.org/about.html

The Taco Shop Poetry and Spoken Word collective began in 1994 in San Diego and has grown to over 30 performance artists. They are devoted to creating community empowerment through the performing arts.

Tish Hinojosa

www.theconnextion.com/index.cfm?ArtistID=324&NoFrame=Yes

Hinojosa's CD for children is called *Cada Nino: Every Child* and includes original bilingual songs written by the singer songwriter. Songs include "Siempre abuelita," "The Barnyard Dance," "Nina Violina," "Quien/Who," "Las Fronterizas The Frontier Women," "Señora Santa Ana," etc.

Video/DVDs

Films and Documentaries

Fear and Learning at Hoover Elementary. Laura Simon (1997 Release)

Info@transitmedia.net; www.transitmedia.net; www.andersongoldfilms.com

Laura Simon, a fourth grade teacher/filmmaker and immigrant from Mexico made a film about the impact of Proposition 187 on her school and the surrounding community. Located in Pico Union, Hoover Elementary school had over 2,700 students speaking 32 languages. The ballot initiative was meant to deny education and health care to immigrants in California. This film won the 1997 Sundance Freedom of Expression Award. (Available from: Transit Media, 190 Route 17M, P.O. Box 1084, Harriman, NY 10926)

My American Girls. Aaron Matthews (2001 release)

www.pbs.org/pov/pov2001/myamericangirls/wherearetheynow.html

This film is about the lives of the Ortiz family, first generation immigrants from the Dominican Republic. The family lives in Brooklyn and consists of the mother and father Sandra and Bautista, and three daughters, Mayra, Aida, and Monica. The accompanying Web site updates viewers on where members of the Ortiz family are now and their struggles pursuing the American dream. (Available from: Filmmakers Library, 124 E. 40th Street, Suite 901, New York, NY 10016; e-mail: info@filmakers.com; Web site: www.filmakers.com)

Our House in Havana. Stephen Olsson (2000 release)

www.globalinsightmedia.com

This film captures the complex journey of Silvia Morini as she returns to her childhood home in Cuba. She is forced to confront her nostalgia for pre-Castro Cuba with modern reality and discovers an evolving Cuba. (Available from: Cultural and Educational Media, Industrial Center Bldg., Suite 250, 480 Gate 5 Rd., Sausalito, CA 94965)

The New Americans. Steve James, Gordon Quinn, Gita Saedi, Indu Krishnan, Susana Aiken, Carlos Aparicio, Renee Tajima-Peña, Jerry Blumenthal, Evangeline Griego, Fenell Dorimus, and David E. Simpson.

www.pbs.org/independentlens/newamericans/newamericans.html

This series of videos explores the complex stories of immigrants from Nigeria, Palestine, the Dominican Republic, Mexico, and India. There is a corresponding Web site with educational materials, a blog and opportunities for "talking back" about issues in the film. (For VHS copies of The New Americans series, contact justine@kartemquin.com; individual stories from The New Americans with accompanying study guides are also available: www.activevoice. net; to order The New Americans companion book published by The New Press, call 800-233-4830)

Accordion Dreams. Hector Galan (2001 release)

This is the story of Conjunto Music. It begins with the music genre's roots in South Texas in the early 19th century and presents the pioneers and innovators through archival footage and photos. (Available from: http://www.galaninc.com)

The Borinqueneers. Noemi Figueroa Soulet (2007 release)

This documentary tells the story of the Puerto Rican 65th Infantry Regiment. The only all-Latino unit in the history of the U.S. Army was created in 1899 and soldiers from the unit served in both World Wars and the Korean War. A comprehensive story guide is also available. (Available from www.thecinemaguild.com)

The Fight in the Fields: César Chávez and the Farmworkers' Struggle. Ray Telles and Rick Tejada (1996 release)

This documentary follows the life of César Chávez and the farmworkers' movement. A study guide is available. (Available from: www.thecinemaguild.com)

Educational DVDs

Literate Days: Reading and Writing with Preschool and Primary Children. Gretchen Owocki, Saginaw Valley State University; ISBN 978-0-325-00873-8/0-325-00873-6/ 8/31/2007/368pp /Teacher's Guide + 3 Lesson Books + DVD

Literate Days: Reading and Writing with Preschool and Primary Children is a multimedia curriculum resource for preschool, kindergarten, and first-grade teachers looking to enrich and broaden their literacy-related instructional practices. Framed by research notes and kidwatching forms, lessons present ideas for enhancing existing teaching practices (such as whole-group read-aloud and circle time) and for extending the quality of students' literacy experiences in times that are not typically considered "instructional" (such as independent reading and play). Ample research evidence shows that when teachers accomplish the types of teaching described in this resource, children's achievement soars—and their lives as literate individuals flourish.

Components   A jump-in-and-get-started Teacher's Guide outlines the thinking behind *Literate Days.*

33 lessons are organized into three lesson books.
  • Book 1: *Grounding Children in Routines and Procedures for Meaningful Learning*
  • Book 2: *Building, Energizing, and Re-Envisioning the Literacy*
  • Book 3: *Deepening the Scholarship in the Classroom Community*

Framed by research notes and kidwatching forms, lessons provide that provide detailed plans, teaching tools, and reproducibles for children.

The *Lessons from Literate Days* DVD models effective literacy instruction with two hours of live-from-the-classroom video footage. (Available from Heinemann: www.books.heinemann.com/products/E00873.aspx)

What Every Teacher Should Know About Reading Comprehension Instruction (DVD) P. David Pearson, Stephanie Harvey, and Anne Goudvis. P. David Pearson, University of California, Berkeley, interviewed by Stephanie Harvey and Anne Goudvis; ISBN 978-0-325-00881-3/0-325-00881-7/2005/DVD

In *What Every Teacher Should Know About Reading Comprehension Instruction*, Stephanie Harvey and Anne Goudvis give teachers, administrators, and literacy specialists the chance to listen in as they interview renowned reading researcher and comprehension theorist P. David Pearson to get the inside scoop on the research behind high-quality comprehension instruction.

Both a professional conversation and a meeting of some of the most influential thinkers about comprehension, this DVD presents theories and studies about teaching comprehension as well as practical classroom applications. Pearson fields nine key questions from Harvey and Goudvis, speaking to important issues regarding reading comprehension and provides lucid, easy-to-understand explanations of why strategy-based instruction works. There is an accompanying user's guide.

Big Lessons from Small Writers: Teaching Primary Writing. Lucy Calkins.

Featuring Lucy Calkins, Teachers College Reading and Writing Project, Columbia University; ISBN 978-0-325-00748-9 / 0-325-00748-9 /2005/ DVD

Drawing on 22 instructional video clips, this comprehensive, easy-to-navigate DVD vividly conveys the inner workings of writing workshops in a variety of elementary classrooms. The 2 hours of live-from-the-classroom video clips are supported and enhanced by an optional voice-over coaching commentary from Lucy Calkins that explains the teaching moves and strategies. Most conferences are also supported and enhanced by an optional voice-over coaching commentary from Lucy Calkins.

Navigating Informational Texts: Easy and Explicit Strategies, K-5. Featuring Linda Hoyt; ISBN 978-0-325-00586-7/0-325-00586-9/2003/30 minutes each /3 Videos + Viewing Guide *Top of Form Bottom of Form*

Linda Hoyt discussed nonfiction in her practical, classroom-friendly guides *Make It Real* and *Exploring Informational Texts*. Now, in this three-video set, Hoyt and several colleagues demonstrate a wide array of ways to navigate this genre. They show you how to infuse informational texts into read alouds, guided reading, and guided writing. They also offer strategies to help make informational texts inviting, teach reading skills across content areas, and attend to the needs of English language learners.

Learning to Love Informational Texts Follow teachers as they weave nonfiction into every content area, model strategies that help improve reading comprehension and fluency, and make nonfiction more accessible to all learners.

Guiding Readers and Writers with Informational Texts Observe guided reading lessons with informational texts, content-area studies infused with interactive writing, and guided writing blended into writing workshops and guided reading.

Information Circles and Reciprocal Teaching Learn the specifics for conducting literature circles and reciprocal groups with nonfiction through various group-interaction and discussion strategies, including student-led teaching and teacher-modeled discussion.

Each video runs approximately 30 minutes. The set comes with a viewing guide to assist staff developers to train teachers, K-5.

Michelle Fine et al., Echoes of Brown: Youth Documenting and Performing the Legacy of Brown v. Board of Education (2004). Featuring Michelle Fine, Rosemarie A. Roberts, Maria Elena Torre, Janice Bloom, April Burns, Lori Chajet, Monique Guishard, and Yasser Payne; 96

pages; Paper with abridged 55-minute DVD: ISBN: 0807745162; cloth with full length DVD that includes videos, teaching resources, and complete interviews: ISBN: 0807744972

This DVD showcases participatory action research. Whether you're studying the history of *Brown* or discussing issues of diversity and racial equality, this multimedia resource is a valuable teaching tool that integrates a book and DVD. *Echoes of Brown* features a performance by a diverse ensemble of youth from suburban and urban schools who speak back to the victories and continuing struggles for justice and democracy in public schools. *Echoes* weaves youth, spoken word, and dance with rich video interviews with "elders" in the community and explores America's long history of yearning, betrayal, victory, and search for social justice. (Available from: Teacher's College Press)
www.store.tcpress.com/0807745162.shtml)

Guidelines for Setting Up a Service Program. Phyllis Tashlik and Cathy Tomaszewski (Release 2006). Teacher to Teacher Publications; 48 pages; *Paperback and DVD;* ISBN: 0807746886

This resource offers the basics to help you set up and maintain a successful service-learning program in your school. The book answers questions that teachers and administrators might have about initiating a service learning program and includes an array of ideas for school-wide discussions and activities that focus on the importance of serving the community. The DVD follows students as they attend a series of diverse sites in New York City, including a pre-K classroom, a museum, a kitchen in a homeless shelter, and an activist group that recycles bicycles for shipment to Third World countries. (Copublished by the Center for Inquiry in Teaching and Learning. Ann Cook, Series Editor, Cochair, New York Performance Standards Consortium)

Teaching Supplies/Aids

Necessary Conversations about English Language Learners: Templates for Success. Helene Grossman (Available from: Delta Systems)
www.delta-systems.com/proddetail.cfm?cat=1&toc=19&stoc=0&pronum=3689

This book supports school administrators and teachers in the effort to communicate effectively about issues related to educating English language learners. In workbook format, the reader will unpack the most challenging issues and will be offered an opportunity to plan how to communicate with success.

The book is intended for administrators, ELL/ESL Program Coordinators, ELL/ESL Teachers, Welcome Center Staff, preservice teacher instructors, and community agency staff. The scenarios address elementary, secondary, and adult education levels. This book connects to educators with little or no experience as well as those who have worked with English language learners and their families over time. Everyone needs to build their skill at communicating with newcomers. The book will supplement courses addressing speaking, listening, school administration and program management. New teachers and those new to ESL will also find it helpful.

Note

1. The author(s) and editor(s) do not necessarily endorse the reference entries in this chapter; they are listed for informational purposes only. Most descriptions have been gathered conducting extensive electronic searches with key words related to these topics and are taken directly from these online sites in order to provide true and clearer descriptions. In order to honor the words chosen to describe themselves and others, each overview incorporates the terms and language utilized (such as Latino/a, Hispanic, Chicano, etc.) on the individual sites.

39 Demographics/Statistics and Government

Norma A. Guzmán

University of Texas at San Antonio

CENSUS AND STATISTICS AGENCIES, LEGISLATION, POLICY, LEADERSHIP, POLITICS, AND MORE.[1]

General Web Sites

U.S. Census Bureau

www.census.gov

> The U.S. Census Bureau serves as the leading source for U.S. data in terms of the population and the economy. The U.S. Census is part of the U.S. Department of Commerce. The first U.S. Census was in 1790. The U.S. Census provides access to information on Latinos/Hispanics using the "Minority" link on their Web site. This area provides information on Latino educational attainment based on data collected by the U.S. Census.

U.S. Department of Education

www.ed.gov

> The U.S. Department of Education (DOE) was established to oversee all U.S. educational programs. The DOE is charged with establishing, monitoring, and allocating funding for U.S. education. The DOE collects data on the status of U.S. educational programs and practices. Research, based on data collected, is also disseminated to assist with policy planning and programming. The DOE is also charged with ensuring that all students have equal access to education. The DOE assists state and local education agencies in improving public education. Statistics are available at the national, state, and district level from the DOE, through the National Center for Education Statistics (NCES).

National Center for Education Statistics

www.nces.ed.gov

> The National Center for Education Statistics (NCES) is located within the U.S. Department of Education. The center is charged with the collection, analysis, and dissemination of data related to U.S. public education. The NCES was established by a congressional mandate to collect, collate, analyze, and report full and complete statistics on the condition of U.S. education. The NCES also publishes reports to assist federal, state, and local education agencies with their statistical activities. The NCES can be accessed through the DOE. All publications by NECS are provided free of charge to the public. Some documents are available in Spanish.

National Clearinghouse for English Language Acquisition

www.ncela.gwu.edu/

> A part of the Office of English Language Acquisition (OELA), the National Clearinghouse for English Language Acquisition collects, analyzes, synthesizes, and disseminates information about language instruction educational programs for English language learners (ELLs).

School Data Direct
www.schooldatadirect.org

 School Data Direct is an online service for the State Education Data Center (SEDC), which can be accessed from the DOE Web site. School Data Direct aims to serve as national advocacy leader for quality education collection. It will also aim to provide a user friendly Web site in which the public is able to access state education data, free of charge.

Government: Legislation, Policy, Leadership, Politics, and More

Federal U.S. policies for education are interconnected with civil rights, language rights, and human rights, as well as the sociopolitical context of the time. For Latinos in education, each of these areas has been affected by federal policies enacted since the 1960s. Legal requirements have established minimal standards for practice by educators.

 The passage of the Elementary and Secondary Education Act (1965) was followed by an amendment to ESEA in 1968 that included the implementation of the Bilingual Education Act (Title VII). In 1975, the Education for All Handicapped Children's Act (94-142) was passed, which provided free and appropriate public education for students with disabilities. An amendment to each of these policies has affected Latino students in the United States. A brief description of bilingual education, special education, and education policies is provided, followed by a brief summary of legislation that has affected Latino students in terms of bilingual education and special education in the United States.

Legislation

Bilingual Education   The Office of English Language Acquisition (OELA), a part of the U.S. Department of Education, is charged with identifying issues related to English language learners and to assist federal, state, and local education agencies.
www.ed.gov/about/offices/list/oela/index.html

 Bilingual education programs were developed in the 1960s out of a need for a system of education where language minority students would receive equal access to education. Bilingual education, a program established based on research in the areas of linguistics and psycholinguistics, advocated for the teaching of literacy to Spanish-speaking children in their mother tongue (Flores, 2005, p. 85), in addition to providing a setting in which the student's native language and culture would be valued (Lindhom, 1990).

 In the United States, the goal of bilingual education is to transition to English as soon as possible. Since the passage of the Bilingual Education Act (BEA) of 1968, bilingual education has consistently been criticized as a method of instruction for linguistic minorities. According to Padilla (1990), the key issue has been whether bilingual education has provided a benefit to students or "whether federal monies could be better spent on other educational programs" (p. 15).

 The passing of the BEA was seen by many as a victory for linguistic human rights as well as a research based program. Yet the BEA has been positioned as an educational program that threatens national unity, which makes the practice of bilingual education controversial and political. In addition, BEA did not define or mandate the specific type of bilingual program to be created, but districts were provided with federal funds to develop bilingual programs for students considered limited English proficient (LEP). The current term for this group of students is *English language learner* (ELL).

Special Education   www.ed.gov/about/offices/list/oela/index.html The Education for All Handicapped Children Act (PL 94-142), passed in 1975, is a landmark piece of legislation which, for the first time, "guaranteed that all handicapped children in the U.S. had a right to a free appropriate public education, an individualized education program (IEP), education in the least restrictive environment, nonbiased assessment procedures, and a series of due process protections" (Ruiz, Figueroa, Rueda, & Beaumont, 1992, pp. 350–351). Prior to PL-94-142, Section 504 of the Rehabilitation Act of 1973 established that:

> No otherwise qualified handicapped individual in the United States as defined in Section 7(6) shall, solely by reason of his handicap, be excluded from the participation in, be denied benefits of, or be subjected to discrimination under any program or activity receiving federal financial assistance. (Fernandez, 1992, p. 121)

Fernandez (1992) states that the Section 504 regulations of 1990 were similar to the nondiscrimination requirement under Title VI and Equal Educational Opportunity Act (EEOA) of 1974, which pertains to all students, including those with disabilities.

The Education of all Handicapped Children Act (Public Law 94-142) guaranteed that all handicapped children in the U.S. have a right to a free appropriate public education, an individualized education program (IEP), education in the least restrictive environment, nonbiased assessment procedures, and a series of due process protections (Ruiz et al., 1992). The processes for receiving special education services were delineated in terms of referral, assessment, and placement. The mandated federal policies are interpreted and appropriated in a variety of ways by state, district, and campus educators. Public Law 94-142 also established guidelines that included parents as an integral part of the educational program (Fernandez, 1992).

In 1990, the Education of all Handicapped Children's Act was renamed the Individuals with Disabilities Education Act (IDEA). The amendments to the law for the first time addressed the needs of students who are ELL/LEP and disabled. IDEA regulations for students who are ELL/LEP and disabled indicate that students should be afforded bilingual education, special education, and related services to meet their needs, including their linguistic needs. The language in the *Lau* decision (1974) also included students who are ELL/LEP and disabled, in terms of their right to specialized language appropriate services (cited in Fernandez, 1992). The *Lau* remedies were codified by the passing of the Equal Educational Opportunity Act of 1974 (EEOA).

The Office of Special Education Programs (OSEP), in the U.S. Department of Education, is dedicated to meeting the needs of students with disabilities from birth to age 21. The Individuals with Disability Education Act serves approximately 6.8 million children and students with disabilities.

Bilingual Special Education Bilingual special education is defined as the use of the home language and the home culture along with English in an individually designed program of special instruction for the student in an inclusive environment (Baca & De Valenzuela, 1998). Fernandez (1992) defines bilingual special education as special instruction and related services individually designed to meet the educational needs of students who are considered LEP/ELL and also have disabilities.

The development of bilingual special education can be viewed as an extension of the equal educational opportunity movement in the 1960s and 70s. According to Baca (1998), there are currently no laws formulated to deal specifically with bilingual special education as an entity.

Cases and Regulations Court cases and regulations related to students who are ELL/LEP and students with disabilities can be traced to the Civil Rights Act of 1964 (Title VI). The Civil Rights Act has been seen as the legal base for bilingual education and language appropriate related services for ELL/LEP students with disabilities. This section outlines some of the key legislation that has impacted Latino students with disabilities.

Diana v. California State Board of Education (1970): The Diana v. SBOE case was the first case to challenge the testing and practice of placement of Hispanic students in special education, specifically in classes for students with mental retardation (Valdés & Figueroa, 1994). This case set the precedent for the Larry P. v. Wilson Riley (1971/1979) case which had an impact on decreasing the use of intelligence testing with African-American students in California for program placement in classes for students with MR (Lambert, 1981). In 1975, the California State Board of Education imposed a moratorium on the use of intelligence tests as a result of the civil rights suit based on the overrepresentation of minority children in special education under the MR category (Lambert, 1981). This case was one of the first to address the disproportionate representation of bilingual, Spanish-surnamed students being placed in special education. The consent decree for this case mandated that students be assessed in their native language or with tests that do not require knowledge of the English language (Rhodes, Ochoa, & Ortiz, 2005).

Guadalupe v. Tempe (1972): The Guadalupe v. Tempe case required school districts to provide non-English speaking Hispanic and Yaqui Indian students with bilingual–bicultural education. This case also required that students be assessed in their native language or through the use of nonverbal measures (Rhodes, Ochoa, & Ortiz, 2005).

Lau v. Nichols (1974): The Lau v. Nichols (1974) case established the need for schools to teach students in a language they can understand. The Lau case moved beyond equality to look at the equity in education that language minority students were receiving or entitled to under the BEA of 1968.

Jose P v. Ambach (1979): Jose P was a class action suit which merged three cases in which the rights of students with disabilities living in New York City were being violated. Jose P. was a class action suit on behalf of CLD students, (1) who claimed they were denied an appropriate education due to failure to properly evaluate and place students into special programs; (2) an individual with central nervous system impairment; and (3) Hispanic students who were not receiving needed bilingual special education (Fernandez, 1992). Based on Jose P., the court ordered the state of New York to: (1) provide data on all the students who were ELL/LEP and disabled; (2) provide a plan that described the programs available to ELL/LEP and disabled students; (3) establish an outreach office for dissemination of information regarding special education; and (4) establish procedures for the provision of competent interpreters (Fernandez, 1992). This case set the precedent for ELL/LEP and disabled students in terms of providing appropriate educational services within the all educational programs available to students based on the notion of a free and appropriate public education (FAPE). The results of the Jose P. case also included the training and use of competent interpreters within the referral to placement process.

In addition to cases that address bilingual and special education students, Latino education has been directly affected by court cases that address inequitable schooling conditions. Desegregation cases Alvarez v. Lemon Grove (1931/1932); Mendez et al. v. Westminster (1946) set the foundation for the Brown v. Board of Education (1954). Mexican Americans had been successful in eliminating segregation in their communities primarily by setting Mexican Americans as a separate group from Black, Indian, or Asian.

Note

1. The author(s) and editor(s) do not necessarily endorse the reference entries in this chapter; they are listed for informational purposes only. Most descriptions have been gathered conducting extensive electronic searches with key words related to these topics and are taken directly from these online sites in order to provide true and clearer descriptions. In order to honor the words chosen to describe themselves and others, each overview incorporates the terms and language utilized (such as Latino/a, Hispanic, Chicano, etc.) on the individual sites.

Sources

Baca, L., & Cervantez, H. (1998). *The bilingual special education interface* (3rd ed.). Columbus, OH: Prentice-Hall.

Baca, L., & De Valenzuela, J. S. (1998). Background and rationale for bilingual special education. In L. Baca & H. Cervantez (Eds.), *The bilingual special education interface* (3rd ed., pp. 98–118). Upper Saddle River, NJ: Prentice Hall.

Fernandez, A. (1992). Legal support for bilingual education and language appropriate related services for limited English proficient students with disabilities. *Bilingual Research Journal, 16*(3 & 4), 117–140.

Flores, B. M. (2005). The intellectual presence of the deficit view of Spanish-speaking children in the educational literature during the 20th century. In P. Pedraza & M. Rivera (Eds.), *Latino education: An agenda for community action research* (pp. 75–98). Mahwah, NJ: Erlbaum.

Lambert, N. M. (1981). Psychological evidence in Larry P. v. Wilson Riles: An evaluation by a witness for the defense. *American Psychologist, 36*(9), 937–952.

Lindhom, K. J. (1990). Bilingual immersion education: Criteria for program development. In A. M. Padilla, H. H. Fairchild, & C. M. Valadez (Eds.), *Bilingual education: Issues and strategies* (pp. 91–105). Newbury Park, CA: Sage.

Padilla, A. M. (1990). Bilingual education: Issues and strategies. In A. M. Padilla, H. H. Fairchild, & C. M. Valadez (Eds.), *Bilingual education: Issues and perspectives* (pp. 15–26). Newbury Park, CA: Sage.

Rhodes, R. L., Ochoa, S. H., & Ortiz, S. O. (2005). *Assessing culturally and linguistically diverse students: A practical guide.* New York: Guilford Press.

Ruiz, N. T., Figueroa, R. A., Rueda, R., & Beaumont, C. (1992). History and status of bilingual special education for Hispanic handicapped students. In R. V. Padilla & A. H. Benavides (Eds.), *Critical perspectives on bilingual education research* (pp. 349–380). Tempe, AZ: Bilingual Press.

Valdés, G., & Figueroa, R. A. (1994). *Bilingualism and testing: A special case of bias.* Norwood, NJ: Ablex.

40 Events

Victor A. Castillo and Sonia N. Sánchez
University of Texas at San Antonio

EVENTS: CONFERENCES, SOCIETY MEETINGS, WORKSHOPS/ SEMINARS, CELEBRATIONS/FESTIVALS, AND MORE.[1]

Annual Organizational Conferences and Conventions

Fall Conferences

Alabama Association of Foreign Language Teachers Annual Conference
www.uab.edu/aaflt/Conference.html

AAFLT provides a united action in promoting in the state of Alabama the effective teaching, study, and appreciation of foreign languages and cultures through our annual conference and other activities, while advocating for the advancement of the study of languages, their literatures and cultures at all levels of instruction.

Annual Black, Brown and College Bound Summit
www.hccfl.edu/bbcb.aspx

The Annual Black, Brown and College Bound Summit focuses on preparing and empowering African-American and Latino males for success in a global society. Participants are challenged to become change agents and empowered to overcome barriers to success. The professional thematic tracks examine the influence of race, language and ethnic identity factors on cultural understanding.

Annual Latino/a Educational Achievement Project Education Conference
www.leapwa.org

In an effort to address the significant challenges, LEAP, along with its Advisory Board, each year establishes educational priorities aimed at improving academic achievements of Latino students. LEAP policies are presented to state legislature, governors, U.S. Congress, state boards of education, higher education coordinating boards, state boards for community and technical colleges, boards of trustees and regents, and local school boards.

Annual Meeting of the Linguistic Society of America
www.lsadc.org/info/meet-annual.cfm

The Linguistic Society of America is the major professional society in the United States that is exclusively dedicated to the advancement of the scientific study of language. As such, the LSA plays a critical role in supporting and disseminating linguistic scholarship, as well as facilitating the application of current research to scientific, educational, and social issues concerning language.

Annual TRPI National Education Conference
www.trpi.org

Tomas Rivera Policy Institute is a nonprofit, freestanding research organization that advances critical, insightful thinking on key issues affecting Latino communities through objective, policy-relevant research and its implications for the betterment of the nation.

Conference of the Puerto Rican Studies Association

www.puertorican-studies.org/

> PRSA was founded to help promote scholarship in the field and offer a place for scholars to come together. The Association meets every other year (in even-numbered years) in a different location.

Executive Leadership Training & Mujer Awards Conference

National Hispana Leadership Institute

www.nhli.org

> The Institute's goals include: Ensuring that Hispanic women are in leadership positions and have the access and power to influence public policy and shape an equitable and humane society; enhancing and developing leadership abilities among Hispanic women whose commitment, contribution, and dedication will help ensure a vibrant and sustainable future for the United States; providing visible role models and mentors for Hispanic women leaders; and improving services provided to the Hispanic community by local, state, and national organizations.

International Mexican Association of Teachers of English Annual Convention

www.mextesol.org

> MEXTESOL is a professional academic association which seeks to develop in its members, as well as in nonmembers, the highest standards for teaching English to speakers of other languages so that their students can communicate effectively in all the diverse situations in which they may find themselves.

Latin American Studies Annual Conference

www.conferences.dce.ufl.edu/LAS/

> This multidisciplinary conference aims to gather scholars and professionals dedicated to improving the quality of life in urban Latin America. This forum will provide participants with an opportunity to share their research and experiences, and to engage in dialogue to generate ideas and identify solutions to advance social inclusion in Latin American cities: University of Florida.

National Association for Multicultural Education Conference

www.nameorg.org

> NAME's membership encompasses the spectrum of professional educators and specialists, including early childhood, classroom and higher education faculty, administrators, psychologists, social workers, counselors, curriculum specialists, librarians, scholars, and researchers. Persons affiliated with teacher education, ethnic studies, ESL and bilingual education, social science, anthropology, liberal and fine arts programs, and other departments, colleges, and schools with an emphasis on multiculturalism are also encouraged to become members.

National Latina/o Psychological Association National Conference

www.nlpa.ws/

> The National Latina/o Psychological Association (formerly the National Hispanic Psychological Association) was established in 1979 by a group of Latino psychologists and colleagues, primarily affiliated with the American Psychological Association. The mission of the National Latina/o Psychological Association is to generate and advance psychological knowledge and foster its effective application for the benefit of the Hispanic/Latino population.

National Society of Hispanic MBA Annual Conference and Career Expo

www.nshmba.org/conferencesites.asp

> NSHMBA fosters Hispanic leadership through graduate management education and professional development while working to prepare Hispanics for leadership positions throughout the United States, so that they can provide the cultural awareness and sensitivity vital in the management of the nation's diverse workforce.

New Mexico Association of Bilingual Education Annual Conference

www.nmabe.net/

The mission of NMABE, a diverse, dedicated community of education stakeholders, is to foster, encourage, and promote bilingualism for all children in an environment that nurtures the rich cultural and linguistic diversity of the state through advocacy, professional development, networking, and current research application and dissemination.

Postgraduates in Latin American Studies Annual Conference

www.pilas.slas.org.uk/annualConference.htm

PILAS aims to foster interaction among postgraduates working in the field of Latin American Studies at institutions of higher education throughout the United Kingdom, as well as those in Europe and the Americas: Cambridge, UK.

Spanish in the U.S. Annual Conference

Spanish in the United States & Spanish in Contact with Other Languages

www.aatsp.org/images/pdf/2009_spanish_conf_us.pdf

Founded in 1980, the Spanish in the US Conference brings together researchers from various disciplines—such as linguistics, sociology, anthropology, education, and legal studies to investigate a wide range of topics related to Spanish and Spanish-speaking communities in the United States.

Latino Leaders Summit

www.llsummit.com

Latino Leaders magazine's mission is to promote, through example, the image of the Latino leader and to help create future leaders in the most vibrant and fastest growing minority community in America. The Latino Leaders Summit is a forum created to celebrate, reflect, and recognize such tremendous examples of leadership and success.

Society of Hispanic Professional Engineers National Conference

www.shpe.org/shpe2008

Each year, the SHPE Conference attracts nearly 5,000 engineering professionals, students, and corporate representatives. The conference is an opportunity for engineering companies and corporations to recruit top talent from SHPE membership. It also provides educational, technical, and career opportunities for professional and student engineers.

Linguistic Association of the Southwest Annual Conference

www.clas.cudenver.edu/lasso/

LASSO is a regional linguistics association in the United States whose purpose is the advancement of the scientific study of language, particularly in the geographical region covering the states of Arizona, Arkansas, California, Colorado, Louisiana, New Mexico, Oklahoma, and Texas. While LASSO is primarily interested in languages of these southwestern states, it draws its membership from any region in the world.

Inter University Program for Latino Research Conference

www.nd.edu/~iuplr/

IUPLR is a national consortium of university-based centers dedicated to the advancement of the Latino intellectual presence in the United States. IUPLR works to expand the pool of Latino scholars and leaders and increase the availability of policy-relevant Latino-focused research.

The Julian Samora Research Institute Annual Conference

www.jsri.msu.edu/whatsnew/index.html

The Julian Samora Research Institute is committed to the generation, transmission, and application of knowledge to serve the needs of Latino communities in the Midwest.

Spring Conferences

American Association of Hispanics in Higher Education National Conference
www.aahhe.org

AAHHE is an agent of change for improving education, thus enabling Hispanic students to fully participate in a diverse society, while working collaboratively with all sectors of education, business, industry, as well as community and professional organizations to enhance the educational aspirations and to meet the needs of a significantly increasing Hispanic population.

Annual Business Association of Latin American Studies Conference
www.balas.org/annual.php

BALAS is an international organization dedicated to bringing together scholars, professional managers, and decision makers to facilitate the exchange of information and ideas and to provide leadership in the areas of Latin American business and economic research and practice. BALAS provides a leadership role in sponsoring forums for exchanges of ideas, information dissemination, and research collaboration and education activities of the highest professional quality.

Annual Bilingual Educators Emphasizing and Mastering Standards Conference
www.academics.utep.edu

The BEEMS conference offers a very unique opportunity for administrators, teachers, and parents. Administrators will receive updates on policy and the English Language Proficiency Standards; educators will enhance their teaching skills and cultural awareness; and parents will learn more about ways to get involved in their children's education and success.

Annual Conference of the Rocky Mountain Council for Latin American Studies
http://www.rmclas.org/

The Rocky Mountain Council for Latin American Studies (RMCLAS) is the oldest Latin American academic organization in the world. Formation of the organization began in 1953 at the University of New Mexico (UNM) and the first annual meeting was held in 1954.

Annual New England Latino Leadership Conference
www.latinoleadershipconference.org/index.php

The purpose of the New England Latino Student Leadership Conference is to initiate and encourage connections between Latino student college leaders within the New England region.

Annual Pennsylvania National Association of Multicultural Education Conference
www.juniata.edu/services/diversity/PA%20NAME%202009.html

PA-NAME seeks to create an environment of acceptance, understanding, and community building by featuring numerous pedagogical experts, workshops, and performances from which we can all learn.

Annual International Bilingual/Multicultural Education Conference
www.NABE.org

The National Association for Bilingual Education's (NABE) mission is to advocate for our nations bilingual and English language learners and families and to cultivate a multilingual and multicultural society by supporting and promoting policy, programs, pedagogy, research, and professional development that yield academic success, value native language, lead to English proficiency, and respect cultural and linguistic diversity.

Annual National Network of Latin American Medical Students National Conference
www.nhmamd.org/

The mission of the organization is to improve the health of Hispanics and other underserved populations. As a rapidly growing national resource based in the nation's capital,

NHMA provides policymakers and health care providers with expert information and support in strengthening health service delivery to Hispanic communities across the nation.

Hispanic Association of Colleges and Universities Annual Conference

www.hacu.net/hacu/Sponsorship_Opportunities9_EN.asp

Each spring, advocates for the higher education success of the nation's youngest and largest population group gather in Washington, DC to shape and promote an agenda for Congress and the country at the annual HACU Capitol Forum. Leaders of HACU member and partner colleges and universities join public policymakers, key federal agency leaders, allied organizations, corporate, community, and philanthropic representatives at what has become a powerful national platform for winning public- and private-sector support for Hispanic higher education.

Colorado Congress of Foreign Language Teachers Annual Spring Conference

www.ccflt.org/conferences/ccflt_conferences.htm

CCFLT was incorporated for the purpose of providing foreign language teachers a forum for mutual support, a means for sharpening their pedagogical skills, and a vehicle for keeping culturally and linguistically current.

Teachers of English to Speakers of Other Language Annual Convention and Exhibit

www.tesol.org

TESOL works with diverse cultural backgrounds in a wide variety of settings, and is uniquely positioned to give a coordinated, knowledgeable response at the global, national, and local levels to issues affecting institutions that foster the development of effective human communications.

NAAAS Joint National Conventions: National Association of African-American Studies; National Association of Hispanic and Latino Studies; National Association of Native-American Studies; International Association of Asian Studies

www.naaas.org

Supports and hosts a national convention each year that provides students and scholars with an opportunity to present research in an open forum, while serving as a resource for scholars in the field who desire information and support for research related to the African and African-American, Hispanic and Latino, Native-American, or Asian experience.

Texas Association of Chicanos in Higher Education National Conference

www.tache.org/

TACHE provides state, regional, and local forums for the discussion of issues related to Chicanos/Latinos in higher education and enables individuals to collaborate with institutions of higher learning to create workable solutions for these issues.

Latina Leadership Network of the California Community Colleges Annual Conference

www.latina-leadership-network.org

The Latina Leadership Network is a mutual support and advocacy organization committed to providing effective opportunities to develop innovative approaches to increase the participation of Latinas in leadership roles and to promote and maintain "la cultural Latina" and nonsexist familial values.

The Center for Women's and Gender Studies Program: Annual Graduate Student Conference

www.utexas.edu/cola/centers/cwgs/

The central mission of CWGS is to further knowledge and understanding of the role of gender and the experience of women in our society. Every year the Center for Women's and Gender Studies brings together scholars and researchers trained in different methodologies and disciplinary traditions around a common theme.

Institute of Latin American Studies Student Association Annual Conference
www.latinomediastudies.wordpress.com/2008/10/07/call-for-papers-xxix-annual-ilassa-
student-conference/

The Student Conference on Latin America, organized by the Institute of Latin American Studies Student Association (ILASSA) at the University of Texas at Austin, is an interdisciplinary forum for students involved in Latin American research topics. The conference provides students with the opportunity to present research activities, develop presentational skills, exchange ideas and information, and meet other scholars from around the world.

The Lozano Long Conference
www.utexas.edu/cola/insts/llilas/conferences/contested_modernities/index/

The Teresa Lozano Long Institute of Latin American Studies (LLILAS) seeks to improve knowledge and understanding of Latin America through education, research, and exchange. LLILAS programs serve University of Texas (UT) students enrolled in related courses; UT faculty members specializing in Latin America; UT academic support units with major involvement in the region; civic, nonprofit, and business associations with activities in Latin America; academic leaders and institutions from Latin America with collaborative agreements with LLILAS; governmental and multilateral agencies dedicated to social and economic betterment in Latin America; and the general public in Texas and the United States whose world outlook includes Latin America.

Cuban Research Institute Conference on Cuban and Cuban American Studies
www.lacc.fiu.edu/centers_institutes/?body=centers_cri_conference&rightbody=centers_cri

In collaboration with its affiliates, other academic institutions, and public and private organizations, LACC regularly holds conferences, lecture series, workshops, and other events related to Latin America and the Caribbean. In addition to frequent lectures and roundtables, major annual events include the Journalists and Editors Workshop, Teacher Training Workshops, and the Miami Security Roundtable, a joint project with the University of Miami's North-South Center and the U.S. Southern Command to encourage dialogue with policy makers and hemispheric security officials.

National Latino Congreso
The Politics and Policy Convention of the Latino Community
www.wcvi.org/index.html

The purpose of WCVI is to: conduct research aimed at improving the level of political and economic participation in Latino and other underrepresented communities; to provide information to Latino leaders relevant to the needs of their constituents; to inform the Latino leadership and public about the impact of public policies on Latinos; to inform the Latino leadership and public about political opinions and behavior of Latinos.

Summer Conferences

Annual Immigration/Emigration Summit
www.conferences.unl.edu/immigration/

The Summit is designed to engage educators, community leaders, senior political and university leaders, students, researchers, health professionals, educational administrators, policy makers, and others toward a dialogue on immigration and emigration. By uniting speakers and participants from diverse backgrounds, the summit is intended to strengthen collaboration among academics, communities, and leaders.

Annual American Association of Teachers of Spanish and Portuguese Conference
www.aatsp.org/menu.php?gotoPage=Conference

AATSP promotes the study and teaching of Hispanic, Luso-Brazilian, and other related languages, literatures, and cultures at all educational levels. Through an exchange of pedagogical and scholarly information, the AATSP encourages heritage and second-language study and supports projects to that end.

Annual League of United Latin American Citizens (LULAC) National Convention and Exposition

www.lulac.org/events/convention09.html

LULAC is the largest and oldest Hispanic Organization in the United States. LULAC advances the economic condition, educational attainment, political influence, health and civil rights of Hispanic Americans through community-based programs operating at more than 700 LULAC councils nationwide. The organization involves and serves all Hispanic nationality groups.

International Congress of the Latin American Studies Association

www.lasa.international.pitt.edu/eng/congress/index.asp

The Latin American Studies Association (LASA) is the largest professional Association in the world for individuals and institutions engaged in the study of Latin America. With over 5,000 members, 25% of whom reside outside the United States, LASA is the one Association that brings together experts on Latin America from all disciplines and diverse occupational endeavors, across the globe.

National Council of La Raza (NCLR) Annual Conference

www.nclr.org

NCLR is the largest national Hispanic civil rights and advocacy organization in the United States, and works to improve opportunities for Hispanic Americans. To achieve its mission, NCLR conducts applied research, policy analysis, and advocacy, providing a Latino perspective in five key areas: assets/investments; civil rights/immigration; education; employment and economic status; and health. In addition, it provides capacity-building assistance to its affiliates who work at the state and local level to advance opportunities for individuals and families.

National Association of Latino Elected and Appointed Officials (NALEO) Annual Conference

www.naleo.org

The NALEO is the nation's leading membership organization that promotes the advancement and policymaking success of Latino elected and appointed officials. NALEO has been serving its members since 1976, and with more than 6,000 Latino elected and appointed officials across the country, you will join the largest national network of Latino public officers and civic leaders committed to shaping and improving American society.

Texas Association of Mexican American Chamber of Commerce (TAMACC) State Convention

www.tamacc.org

TAMACC was founded by a small group of Hispanic businesspersons interested in increasing business opportunities for themselves and other similar business owners. The association, with headquarters in Austin, Texas acts as the organizational umbrella providing advocacy, technical support, programs, and services to the network of local Hispanic chambers.

Educational and Cultural Organizations

ASPIRA Association

www.aspira.org/

Founded in 1961, ASPIRA promotes empowerment among Puerto Rican and Latino youth by cultivating leadership skills and cultural awareness to better serve the Latino community. ASPIRA provides leadership training, career and college counseling, financial aid, scholarship assistance, educational advocacy, cultural activities, and continuing opportunities to implement community action projects.

American Association of Teachers of Spanish and Portuguese

www.aatsp.org/

Established in 1917, the American Association of Teachers of Spanish and Portuguese encourages the study of heritage and second languages through its support of ventures that challenge issues facing teachers and learners in the Spanish and Portuguese communities. AATSP is one of the oldest, largest, and most comprehensive language-specific professional associations in the United States.

Association of Hispanic Arts

www.latinoarts.org/index.html

The Association of Hispanic Arts is a not-for-profit organization committed to the development of the Latino arts in order to promote their importance in the national culture.

Engaging Latino Communities for Education

www.enlacenm.org/index.html

Engaging Latino Communities for Education is a community organization that strives to eliminate domestic violence and advance immigrants' rights through counseling, legal services, community education, leadership development, and organizing to impact system change.

League of United Latin American Citizens

www.lulac.org/about.html

Established in 1929, the League of United Latin American Citizens is the largest and oldest Hispanic Organization in the United States. LULAC advances the economic condition, educational attainment, political influence, health and civil rights of Hispanic Americans through community-based programs, scholarship opportunities, voter registration drives, and youth leadership training programs.

National Association for Chicana and Chicano Studies

www.naccs.org/naccs/Default_EN.asp

Formed during the height of the Chicano Movement, the National Association for Chicana and Chicano Studies fosters an environment where Chicana/o students can develop intellectually and culturally in the realm of higher education.

National Hispanic Scholarship Fund

www.hsf.net/

Established in 1975, the National Hispanic Scholarship Fund is dedicated to raising the rates of Hispanics earning college degrees. NHSF promotes higher education for Hispanics by providing scholarships and outreach support.

National Latino Education Institute

www.scj-usa.org/aboutscjhistory.html

The National Latino Education Institute, formerly known as the Spanish Coalition for Jobs, began as a social advocate to a successful job-training agency. Through training, programs, and leadership development the National Latino Education Institute has advanced the cause for equal opportunity among Latinos.

National Migrant and Seasonal Head Start Association

www.nmshsa.org/

Established in 1969, the National Migrant and Seasonal Head Start Association has been a leader in providing services in the most rural areas in the United States. MSHS meets the needs of the children of migrant farm workers by providing services and programs that help migrant families.

Legal Organizations

Illinois Latino Law Student Association
www.illsa.org/

Dedicated to increasing diversity in law schools throughout Illinois, the Illinois Latino Law Student Association aims to promote the benefits of an education and career in law with a focus on minority students from high school to college.

National Latino/a Law Student Association
www.nllsa.org/

The National Latino/a Law Student Association is a not-for-profit organization focused on advancing Latino academic success and commitment to the community through resources, dialogue, and action. It aims to provide a positive experience in law for Latino students.

Northwestern Latino Law Student Association
www.law.northwestern.edu/llsa/

Comprised of both Spanish and non-Spanish speakers, the Northwestern Latino Law Student Association aims to provide members with various academic and social resources. Members can take advantage of exam-writing and outlining workshops, access a shared outline bank, receive information about scholarships and job opportunities, and attend various networking functions with alumni.

University of Wisconsin Law School Latina/o Law Student Association
www.uwllsa.com/index.shtml

The University of Wisconsin Law School Latina/o Law Student Association promotes and encourages the participation of former alumni in the academic and social involvement of present Latino law students and the Latino community at large. It aims to increase the number of Latinos at the university.

Medical Organizations

California Latino Medical Association
www.calma.org/

Founded in 1998, it is one of the largest Latino physician associations in California advocating for health benefits of the Latino community. Members are qualified community leaders in the health profession who aim to improve quality and coverage of healthcare to Latinos both in the state and in the nation.

Latin American and Native American Medical Association
www.umich.edu/~lanama/

Based out of the University of Michigan Medical School, this student organization seeks to provide a nurturing atmosphere for the cooperation of both Latino and Native communities in the public health care sector.

Latino Medical Student Association
www.lmsa.net/

Comprised of alumni, students and health professionals, the Latino Medical Student Association's mission is to support the development of Latino students through volunteer and networking opportunities in addition to community service within the Latino population.

Political Organizations

Cuban American National Foundation

www.canf.org/

The Cuban American National Foundation is a nonprofit organization dedicated to the advancement of freedom and democracy in Cuba. CANF is the largest Cuban organization in exile outwardly claiming anti-Castro sentiments.

Hispanas Organized for Political Equality

www.latinas.org/site/c.qwL6KiNYLtH/b.2247283/k.BE35/Home.htm

A nonprofit organization, HOPE is dedicated to promoting political and economic equality for Latinas through the development of leadership skills and education that serve to benefit the community and the status of women.

La Nueva Raza

www.larazaunida.com/index.php?option=com_frontpage&Itemid=47

La Nueva Raza addresses all aspects of Chicano and Latino affairs through the development of community programs, symposiums, publications, and investigative reporting.

National Council of La Raza

www.nclr.org/

Founded in 1968, the National Council of La Raza is the largest national Latino civil rights and advocacy organization in the United States. NCLR conducts applied research, policy analysis, and advocacy, providing a Latino perspective in five key areas: assets/investments; civil rights/immigration; education; employment and economic status; and health.

National Latino Children's Institute

www.nlci.org/common/index2.htm

Founded in 1997, the National Latino Children's Institute is the only national Latino organization focused on Latino children. The mission of NLCI is to focus the nation's attention on Latino children and empower communities for the full and healthy development of young Latinos in a culturally relevant environment.

United Farm Workers of America AFL-CIO

www.ufw.org/

Founded in 1962 by César Chávez, the United Farm Workers of America represents American farm workers through a vision that promotes five key pillars: integrity; si se puede attitude; innovation; empowerment; and nonviolence.

Research Centers

Center for Latino Policy Research, University of California at Berkeley

www.clpr.berkeley.edu/

The Center for Latino Policy Research focuses research on any policy that directly impacts the Latino/Chicano population in the United States with a strong emphasis on higher education access, migration, and political/civic participation.

Center for Latino Research, DePaul University

www.condor.depaul.edu/~dialogo/center_for_latino_research.htm

Founded in 1985, the Center for Latino Research enhances the Latino experience by supporting the relationship between DePaul University and the Latino communities in Chicago through qualitative and quantitative research, publications, and organizations. Since its establishment, the Center has generated and produced publications focusing on Latino communities in Chicago and the United States and organized collaborative research projects involving students and faculty.

Center for Mexican American Studies, University of Texas at Austin
www.utexas.edu/depts/cmas/

Formed in 1970, the Center's mission is to serve Texas and the nation as a leader in the intellectual development of Mexican-American studies. CMAS promotes the presence and experience of Mexican Americans and Latinos in the United States through teaching, research, and publications that are recognized at a national level.

Center for Multilingual, Multicultural Research, University of Southern California
www.usc.edu/dept/education/CMMR/home.html

The Center for Multilingual, Multicultural Research facilitates the research, collaboration, dissemination, and professional development activities of faculty, students, and others across university and outside organizational lines. CMMR strives to promote research, publications, training, and public service through research and program collaborative projects.

Cuban Research Institute
www.lacc.fiu.edu/cri/

Established in 1991, the Cuban Research Institute has become one of the leading institutes for research and academic programs on Cuban and Cuban-American issues. CRI's mission is to create and disseminate knowledge on Cuba and Cuban-Americans through research and public programs.

Hispanic Reading Room, Library of Congress
www.loc.gov/rr/hispanic/

The Hispanic Reading Room serves as the primary access point for research relating to those parts of the world encompassing the geographical areas of the Caribbean, Latin America, and Iberia; the indigenous cultures of those areas; and peoples throughout the world historically influenced by Luso-Hispanic heritage, including Latinos in the United States and peoples of Portuguese or Spanish heritage in Africa, Asia, and Oceania.

Latino Intersections Research Center, Dartmouth College
www.journals.dartmouth.edu/latinox/resource_center/index.shtml

The Latino Intersections Research Center is affiliated with the Department of Spanish and Portuguese, and the Latin American, Latino, and Caribbean Studies Program at Dartmouth College, Hanover, New Hampshire. The Center's mission is to create a gateway that facilitates access to information regarding the Latino community in the United States. Resources include teaching tools, Latino media and books, politics and Latino policy, and professional development.

Latino Research Center, University of Nevada, Reno
www.unr.edu/latinocenter/

The Latino Research Center is committed to the research, advocacy, educational efforts, and outreach on issues related to the Latino community in Nevada and the United States. The Center contributes to the positive exchange of ideas by providing opportunities for discussion and by giving the Latino community the opportunity to express their ideas and concerns.

Pew Hispanic Center
www.pewhispanic.org/

Founded in 2001, the Pew Hispanic Center is a nonpartisan research organization that seeks to improve understanding of the U.S. Hispanic population. The Center conducts and commissions studies on a wide range of topics that only provides information and does not take position on policy issues. The Center also regularly conducts public opinion surveys that aim to illuminate Latino views on a range of social matters and public policy issues.

Smithsonian Latino Center

www.latino.si.edu/

> Established to promote and celebrate Latino culture, spirit, and achievement in America, the Smithsonian Latino Center facilitates the development of exhibitions, research, collections, and educational programs.

The National Institute for Latino Policy

www.latinopolicy.org/

> Established in 1982, The National Institute for Latino Policy is a nonpartisan, nonprofit policy center using an action research model to address Latino issues. NILP focuses on policy analysis and advocacy, civic participation, and policy networking to promote Latino empowerment.

The Tomás Rivera Policy Institute

www.trpi.org/

> Founded in 1985, the Tomás Rivera Policy Institute promotes critical thinking on key issues affecting Latino communities through objective, policy-relevant research.

Directories

Beginning Library Research on Chicano/Latino Studies

www.library.stanford.edu/depts/ssrg/adams/shortcu/chic.html

> The Stanford University Libraries provide a collection of handbooks, encyclopedias, bibliographies, periodical indexes, databases, and statistical information for the research of Chicanos/Latinos.

Center for Multilingual, Multicultural Research: Latino/Hispanic Resources

www.bcf.usc.edu/~cmmr/Latino.html

> This Web site provides a list of publications and sites addressing Latino/Hispanic issues.

English Language Latino/Hispanic News

www.lasculturas.com/lib/libEngNews.htm

> This site provides links to English language news from Latin America or focused on Latinos.

Latin American Network Information Center

www1.lanic.utexas.edu/

> The Latin American Network Information Center is affiliated with the Lozano Long Institute of Latin American Studies at the University of Texas at Austin. LANIC's mission is to facilitate access to Internet-based information about Latin America. LANIC's directories contain over 12,000 unique URLs, one of the largest guides for Latin American content on the Internet.

Latino Resources

www.latinoresources.com/

> This site provides links to all things Latino including educational, legal, medical, political, and historical information.

Latino Resources on the Net

www.estrellita.com/latino.html

> This site provides links to resources related to Latinos.

The Latino Directory: Research Centers and Institutes

www.journals.dartmouth.edu/latinox/resource_center/academics2.shtml

> The Latino Directory is a comprehensive directory of Latino associations, institutions, and organizations with an Internet presence, which focus on academic, cultural, and professional activities in the United States.

Zona Latina

www.zonalatina.com/

This site provides links to all types of Latino media including magazines, newspapers, radio, photographs, and television.

Other Online Resources

Azteca

www.azteca.net/aztec/

This site provides information gathered about Latinos, Chicanos, and Mexican Americans to better understand their history, language, and current issues affecting this population.

Chicano/Latino Net

www.latino.sscnet.ucla.edu/

The Chicano/Latino Net is a digital library on Chicanos/Latinos in the United States. It promotes the building of Latino communities through networking.

Hispanic Online

www.hisp.com/

Besides covering the biggest stories of the day impacting Hispanics, the site includes: political news, plus opinion columns written from a Hispanic perspective, coverage of Latinos in arts and entertainment, information for anyone interested in moving ahead in the workplace, in business, or on Wall Street, and entire channels dedicated to the critical fields of technology and education.

Note

1. The author(s) and editor(s) do not necessarily endorse the reference entries in this chapter; they are listed for informational purposes only. Most descriptions have been gathered conducting extensive electronic searches with key words related to these topics and are taken directly from these online sites in order to provide true and clearer descriptions. In order to honor the words chosen to describe themselves and others, each overview incorporates the terms and language utilized (such as Latino/a, Hispanic, Chicano, etc.) on the individual sites.

41 Groups

Silvia Cristina Bettez
University of North Carolina at Greensboro

GROUPS: ORGANIZATIONS, AGENCIES, COMMUNITY PROJECTS, ASSOCIATIONS, PROFESSIONAL SOCIETIES, AND MORE.[1]

Educational and Cultural Associations

American Association of Teachers of Spanish and Portuguese
www.aatsp.org

> AATSP, founded in 1917, "has promoted the study and teaching of Hispanic, Luso-Brazilian, and other related languages, literatures, and cultures at all levels." AATSP encourages not only the study of language, but also an understanding of Hispanic cultures and heritages. They offer pedagogical and scholarly information about Hispanic language and culture through an academic journal, two newsletters, and various publications. Of particular interest for educators of Latino students may be the *Handbook for Teachers K-16 on Spanish for Native Speakers*.

The APRENDES Foundation, Inc.
www.aprendesnyc.org

> The APRENDES Foundation is a Community-Based Public Foundation that seeks to improve public education for Latinos in New York City. APRENDES recognizes that through advocacy, activism and social action Latinos can transform the "deplorable circumstances" of the public education system into a system that fosters a positive educational environment and a healthy learning community. As a grant making institution, APRENDES funds nonprofit organizations led by Latinos. The foundation seeks to improve the quality of education for Latino students in New York City public schools through acting as a volunteer clearinghouse, creating opportunities for organized Latino philanthropy, and assisting in organizational capacity-building through research grants.

ASPIRA Association
www.aspira.org/

> ASPIRA is a national nonprofit Hispanic organization that works to develop the educational and leadership capacity of Hispanic youth. The ASPIRA Association is comprised of various statewide organizations that serve Latino youth and their families by providing programs that improve the educational achievement of youth, particularly Hispanics, and advance youth leadership capabilities. ASPIRA has offices in seven states and Puerto Rico and hundreds of national partners that deliver programs originated by ASPIRA. The organization utilizes an intervention model, the "ASPIRA Process," to teach young people to understand and analyze barriers to their success, take action to create change in their lives and their community, and maintain pride in their cultural background.

Association of Hispanic Arts (AHA)
www.latinoarts.org/

AHA is a nonprofit organization that assists Latino artists and arts administrators in career development, financial independence, and networking opportunities. AHA is a partner in the Urban Arts Initiative which awards fellowship grants to visual, literary, media, and performing artists.

Center for Latino Studies in the Americas (CELASA)
www.usfca.edu/celasa/

The Center for Latino Studies in the Americas is a University of San Francisco based organization that utilizes Jesuit networks to connect USF and the San Francisco Bay Area community to Latin America. Based in the academic community, it supports research opportunities for USF student and faculty scholars to study abroad and engage in international exchanges. There is a visiting scholars program that may be of interest.

Hispanic Association of Colleges and Universities (HACU)
www.hacu.net

The HACU is a national association representing the accredited colleges and universities in the United States where Hispanic students constitute at least 25% of the total student enrollment. HACU's goal is to bring together colleges and universities, schools, corporations, governmental agencies, and individuals to establish partnerships for: promoting the development of Hispanic-serving colleges and universities; improving access to and the quality of postsecondary educational opportunities for Hispanic students; and meeting the needs of business, industry, and government through the development and sharing of resources, information, and expertise. The Web site provides a list of Hispanic-serving institutions for those who may be interested in attending an HSI.

Hispanic Educational Technology Services (HETS)
www.hets.org/

Formerly known as the Hispanic Educational Telecommunications System, HETS is a bilingual technology-oriented consortium that seeks to enhance the success of Hispanic students in higher education through facilitating the effective use of technology by promoting alliances among HETS members, promoting collaborative funding opportunities, and identifying expert technology support. Consortium members include colleges and universities, corporations, nonprofit organizations, and individuals.

Hispanic Genealogy Center
www.hispanicgenealogy.com/

Based in New York, the Hispanic Genealogy Center assists Hispanics in researching their roots, heritage, and family history in order to foster cultural pride. The organization provides assistance in genealogical research and lobbies for Hispanic collections in libraries.

Hispanic Scholarship Fund
www.hsf.net/

Founded in 1975, The Hispanic Scholarship fund is a nonprofit organization that strives to increase the rate of Hispanics earning college degrees. The Fund provides college scholarships and educates students and their families about other resources available for paying for college. They provide financial aid to graduating high-school senior, community college students who wish to transfer to 4-year universities, continuing students seeking to complete their degrees and graduate and professional students. HSF also provides outreach programs designed to provide students and families with the information, support, and encouragement they need to apply for college financial aid and make it through the admissions process.

Latin American Studies Association (LASA)
www.lasa.international.pitt.edu

> The Latin American Studies Association (LASA) is a professional member organization that brings together individuals and institutions across the globe who are engaged in the study of Latin America. LASA strives to "foster intellectual discussion, research, and teaching on Latin America, the Caribbean, and its people throughout the Americas." Every 18 months, LASA holds an International Congress that features over 900 sessions that include expert discussions on Latin America and the Caribbean.

Latinos in Higher Education.com
www.latinosinhighered.com/

> LatinosinHigherEd.com is a Latino professional employment Web site that helps employers connect with Latino professionals in higher education in the United States, Puerto Rico, and internationally. Employers and candidates for employment can subscribe to join the network.

League of United Latin American Citizens (LULAC)
www.lulac.org/

> LULAC works to advance the economics, education, health, political influence, and civil rights of the United States Hispanic population. LULAC operates more than 700 councils nationwide. Through member councils, LULAC provides scholarships to Hispanic students, develops low income housing units, conducts citizenship and voter registration drives, and provides youth leadership training programs.

Mexican-American Legal Defense and Education Fund (MALDEF)
www.maldef.org

> MALDEF, a nonprofit institution founded in 1968 in San Antonio, Texas, provides litigation, advocacy, and educational outreach to empower and promote the civil rights of Latinos living in the United States. They provide leadership programs to aid Latinos in serving on boards that make policy and offer law school scholarships to Latino students. Through parent leadership programs MALDEF provides parents with the knowledge needed to advocate for their children to receive a quality education. They have offices in Los Angeles, Atlanta, San Antonio, Chicago, Washington, DC, Sacramento, and Houston.

NAHP Foundation: Scholarships for Hispanics
www.scholarshipsforhispanics.org

> NAHP provides a comprehensive Hispanic Scholarship Directory. Their Web page also provides high school students with time management tips, test-taking tips, questions to ask a school counselor, college prep action plans for each year of high school, and a financial aid calendar.

National Association for Chicana and Chicano Studies (NACCS)
www.naccs.org

> The National Association for Chicana and Chicano Studies is an "academic organization that serves academic programs, departments, and research centers that focus on issues pertaining to Mexican Americans, Chicana/os, and Latina/os." NACCS holds an annual meeting at which people can present scholarly papers related to Chicana/o Studies. They publish a directory of Chicana/o, Latina/o, and Latin American Studies Program, Research and Policy Centers.

National Association of Latino Arts and Culture (NALAC)
www.nalac.org/

> NALAC provides programs related to Latino arts and culture that include funding support, leadership trainings, research, and convening regional and national events. NALAC is "committed to the continuing struggle for the elimination of racism, sexism, ageism and

discrimination against gay, lesbian and physically challenged populations." They award direct funding to Latino artists as well as Latino arts and culture organizations across the country.

REFORMA

www.latino.sscnet.ucla.edu/library/reforma.html

REFORMA is a national association that promotes library services for Spanish-speaking and Hispanic people in the United States. They hold an annual scholarship drive that awards scholarships to students in library schools who express interest in working with Hispanics.

Political and Labor Associations

Congressional Hispanic Caucus Institute (CHCI)

www.chci.org

CHCI is a nonprofit and nonpartisan organization established in 1978 that creates opportunities for Hispanics to participate in and impact United States policy. They offer educational and leadership development programs including a congressional internship program and a public policy fellowship program. In addition they provide scholarships with no GPA or major requirement to Latino students who "have a history of performing public service-oriented activities in their communities and who plan to continue contributing in the future." Their Web site offers publications related to college preparation and financial aid and scholarship applications.

Congressional Hispanic Caucus (CHC)

www.house.gov/baca/meetjoe/cau_hisp.htm

The CHC "is an informal group of 21 Members of Congress of Hispanic descent. The Caucus is dedicated to voicing and advancing issues affecting Hispanic Americans in the United States and the insular areas."

The Cuban American National Foundation (CANF)

www.canf.org/

The Cuban American National Foundation (CANF) is a nonprofit organization, established in Florida in 1981, that is "dedicated to advancing freedom and democracy in Cuba." CANF members represent a cross-section of the Cuban exile community from around the world. The organization provides information about the political, economic, and social status of Cuban people.

Hispanas Organized for Political Equity (HOPE)

www.latinas.org

HOPE is a nonprofit, nonpartisan organization promoting equity for Latinas. HOPE provides Latina leadership programs for adults and youth; engages in policy work related to health care, education, economic empowerment and civic participation for Latinas; and promotes and develops education programs and publications to empower Latinas.

Hispanic Association on Corporate Responsibility (HARC)

www.hacr.org/

Founded in 1986, HARC strives to increase the inclusion of Hispanics in "Corporate America." HARC provides a Hispanic Corporate Research Institute, a Leadership Program for Hispanic leaders, and a Corporate Index that ranks Hispanic inclusion practices of U.S. corporations.

Labor Council for Latin American Advancement (LCLAA)

www.lclaa.org

LCLAA is a national nonprofit, nonpartisan organization based in Washington, DC that represents the interests of Latino/a trade unionists throughout the United States and Puerto Rico. LCLAA strives to empower and provide a voice for working Latino families.

Partido Nacional La Raza Unida (PNLRU)

www.members.tripod.com/larazaunida/program/index.htm

PNLRU's mission is to support "a revolutionary alternative that will change current power structures, realize economic democracy and foster spiritual and cultural growth." They utilize the Internet to provide information about regarding "Raza liberation."

Latino Issues Forum

www.lif.org/

Latino Issues Forum (LIF) is a nonprofit public policy and advocacy institute for California Latinos. In 1987, Latino social justice leaders founded LIF to address issues through research and advocacy not addressed by other Latino organizations.

National Association of Latino Elected and Appointed Officials (NALEO)

www.naleo.org/

NALEO is a nonprofit, nonpartisan, membership organization that provides information on Latino political participation in the United States. NALEO holds an annual conference that provides an opportunity for elected officials from all levels of government and their supporters to meet.

National Congress for Puerto Rican Rights (NCPRR)

www.columbia.edu/~rmg36/NCPRR.html

NCPRR is a volunteer, grassroots organization with chapters in New York City, Boston, Philadelphia, and San Francisco. It works to end discrimination against Puerto Ricans and promote equity. Every 2 years NCPRR publishes a "Status Report on Puerto Ricans in the U.S."

National Council of La Raza (NCLR)

www.nclr.org

NCLR is a nonprofit, nonpartisan organization that works to improve opportunities for Hispanic people through applied research, policy analysis, and advocacy. They strive to provide a Latino perspective in five key areas: assets/investments; civil rights/immigration; education; employment and economic status; and health. NCLR provides capacity building assistance to its network of almost 300 affiliated community-based organizations (CBO). Their Web site provides links to all their CBO affiliates and thus serves as a useful tool for finding Latino service organizations across the United States.

United Farm Workers of America (UFW)

www.ufw.org

The United Farm Workers of America was founded in 1962 by César Chávez. It was the nation's first successful farm workers union and is active in 10 states. The UFW operates with five core values to provide farm workers with tools and inspiration to thrive in society: integrity, a "si se puede" attitude, nonviolence, empowerment, and innovation.

United States Hispanic Chamber of Commerce (USHCC)

www.ushcc.com/

USHCC, founded in 1979, is an Hispanic business network. USHCC holds an Annual National Convention and Business Expo to establish opportunities for business partnerships as well as information and training that impact the Hispanic entrepreneur. They also hold an Annual Legislative Convention that provides corporate executives opportunities to discuss legislative policy issues that impact the small business community. These events provide opportunities for people within education to partner with Hispanic-owned businesses.

Other Professional Associations and Organizations

CCNMA: Latino Journalists of California
www.ccnma.org/

CCNMA is a nonprofit, professional member organization that strives to foster an accurate and fair portrayal of Latinos in the news media and promote news media diversity. CCNMA offers scholarships to Latino students pursuing careers in journalism and holds a Journalism Opportunities Conference, the largest job fair for journalists of color on the West Coast. CCNMA is affiliated with the University of Southern California School of Journalism and has seven chapters in California.

Latino Social Workers Organization
www.lswo.org/

The LSWO is a progressive social work organization that specializes in recruitment and retention strategies for Latino social workers. They hold an annual Latino Social Workers conference.

The National Coalition of Hispanic Health and Human Services Organizations (COSSMHO)
www.clnet.ucla.edu/community/cossmho.html

COSSMHO is a nonprofit membership organization, founded in 1974, that is "dedicated to improving the health and psychosocial well-being of the nation's Hispanic population." COSSMHO pursues its mission by coordinating research and publishing studies, developing prevention programs, and serving as a source of technical assistance and information through training and conferences.

State and Local Organizations

There are too many state and local organizations to list them all here. Below is a limited selection of state and local organizations that have education programs or scholarships. There are also two national organizations listed (Latinos in Higher Ed.com and National Council on La Raza) which provide lists of state and local Latino/a organizations.

El Pueblo
www.elpueblo.org

El Pueblo works to strengthen the Latino community in North Carolina through advocacy and public policy. They spearhead a comprehensive family literacy program—¡Leamos Juntos!—that addresses the needs of low income, first generation, limited-English-proficiency Latino families with children aged from birth to 5 years. They also have a Higher Education Program which informs Latino students about the benefits of pursuing higher education and assists students with applying for college scholarships.

Latino Education Alliance (LEA)
www.latinoeducationalliance.org

An Illinois group, they strive to support and promote education for Latino students with a goal of improving graduation rates of Latinos in Illinois. Their programs focus on first-year high school students.

Latinos in Higher Ed.com
www.latinosinhighered.com/index.php?page=partners

See this Web site for a list of state (and national) organizations that offer professional development, research grants, fellowships, scholarships, conferences, political call for action, and other issues impacting Latinos in higher education.

National Council on La Raza (NCLR)
www.nclr.org/section/network/
> To find a fairly comprehensive list of Latino local and state organizations, check the NCLR community-based organization affiliates.

New Mexico Alliance for Hispanic Education
www.nmalliance.org/index2.html
> The New Mexico Alliance for Hispanic Education provides fundraising for undergraduate and graduate scholarships given to Hispanic students attending colleges and universities in New Mexico. The regional review procedures of the Hispanic Scholarship fund are utilized to select scholarship recipients.

Note

1. The author(s) and editor(s) do not necessarily endorse the reference entries in this chapter; they are listed for informational purposes only. Most descriptions have been gathered conducting extensive electronic searches with key words related to these topics and are taken directly from these online sites in order to provide true and clearer descriptions. In order to honor the words chosen to describe themselves and others, each overview incorporates the terms and language utilized (such as Latino/a, Hispanic, Chicano, etc.) on the individual sites.

42 Higher Education

Belinda Treviño Schouten
Our Lady of the Lake University

Katherine Graves-Talati
University of Texas at San Antonio

HIGHER EDUCATION: COLLEGES, UNIVERSITIES, INSTITUTES, CENTERS, DEGREES, PROGRAMS, CONCENTRATIONS, FUNDING OPPORTUNITIES, ACADEMIC COMPETITIONS, AWARDS, MENTORSHIP, INTERNSHIPS, TRAINING, AND MORE.[1]

Colleges, Universities, Institutes, Centers, Degrees, Programs, Concentrations

Colleges and Universities

Central Arizona College, Coolidge, Arizona
www.centralaz.edu

Central Arizona College is a dynamic and multifaceted institution of higher education featuring nine campuses and centers strategically located throughout Pinal County for the purpose of educating the diverse population of the region. From students of Hispanic and Native-American descent to participants in Central Arizona's Lifelong Learners program, the institution's diverse college community values the power of innovation, continuous quality improvement, and the contribution of the individual.

Bakersfield College, Bakersfield, California
www.bakersfieldcollege.edu

The mission of Bakersfield College is to provide quality instruction and services for their diverse community needs in order for individuals to achieve personal, academic, and occupational success.

Pueblo Community College, Pueblo, Colorado
www.pueblocc.edu

Pueblo Community College is one of the most dynamic and progressive community colleges in Colorado. They strive to provide modern facilities, state-of-the-art equipment, and comprehensive technical and transfer programs that prepare students to enter the job market or transfer to a 4-year school. Our faculty and staff are committed to student success, offering quality classroom instruction and academic support. The U.S. Department of Education has designated PCC as a Hispanic-Serving Institution based on the college's commitment to serve Hispanic and low-income students, and two Title V grants are helping PCC meet this commitment.

Harry S. Truman College, Chicago, Illinois
www.trumancollege.edu

Truman is the largest of the City Colleges of Chicago with a yearly enrollment of over 23,000 students, and has the largest English as a second language and GED program in Illinois with more than 12,000 students annually. Truman students come from approximately 140 countries and speak approximately 180 languages. Nearly half are Hispanic. They live all over Chicago, but most come from communities close to the college. Truman College has the oldest and most successful 2-year nursing program in Illinois, as well as the state's only 2-year biotechnology program.

Eugenio Maria de Hostos Community College, Bronx, New York

www.hostos.cuny.edu

Hostos Community College takes pride in its historical role in educating students from diverse ethnic, racial, cultural, and linguistic backgrounds, particularly Hispanics and African Americans. An integral part of fulfilling its mission is to provide transitional language instruction for all learners of English as a second language along with Spanish/English bilingual education offerings to foster a multicultural environment for all students. Hostos Community College, in addition to offering degree programs, is determined to be a resource to the South Bronx and other communities served by the College by providing continuing education, cultural events, and expertise for the further development of the communities it serves.

Palo Alto College, San Antonio, Texas

www.accd.edu/pac

The emphasis of Palo Alto College always has been its students. Enrollment reached a peak in fall 2005 with 8,100 students reported. Historically, Hispanics comprise more than half of Palo Alto's enrollment, and females generally outnumber males. Palo Alto's education outreach extends well beyond its campus and into "the heart of the community," the college slogan adopted in 1993.

National Hispanic University, San José, California

www.nhu.edu

National Hispanic University was established 25 years ago. It is a model university for providing accessible and affordable quality education for underserved students. Through innovation, engagement, and student-centered learning, the National Hispanic University, a fully accredited 4-year private university, is fostering successful academic and economic futures for its students.

Woodbury University, Burbank, California

www.woodbury.edu

Woodbury University is a Hispanic serving institution with a broadly diverse student body. Woodbury graduates have played an important role in shaping the economic history of Los Angeles for 124 years and Woodbury looks forward to extending this historical role.

Colorado State University, Pueblo, Colorado

www.colostate-pueblo.edu

Colorado State University-Pueblo is committed to excellence, setting the standard for regional comprehensive universities in teaching, research, and service by providing leadership and access for its region while maintaining its commitment to diversity. CSU-Pueblo strives to produce the environment to enhance positive, challenging, inclusive leaders with a global understanding of multiculturalism, who are accountable to our society.

University of Miami, Coral Gables, Florida

www.miami.edu

The University of Miami's mission is to educate and nurture students, to create knowledge, and to provide service to our community and beyond. Committed to excellence and proud of the diversity of our university family, the institution strives to develop future leaders of our nation and the world.

Northeastern Illinois University, Chicago, Illinois

www.neiu.edu

Founded in 1867, Northeastern Illinois University continues to meet the demand for quality, affordable education, serving 12,000 students at the 67-acre main campus on Chicago's North Side and three additional campuses in the metropolitan area. NEIU is the most diverse university in the Midwest (according to *U.S. News and World Report*) and a federally designated Hispanic Serving Institution.

New Jersey City University, Jersey City, New Jersey

www.njcu.edu

The mission of New Jersey City University is to provide a diverse population with an excellent university education. The University is committed to the improvement of the educational, intellectual, cultural, socioeconomic, and physical environment of the surrounding urban region and beyond. The vision of New Jersey City University is to become a nationally recognized leader in urban public higher education.

University of Texas at San Antonio, San Antonio, Texas

www.utsa.edu

The University of Texas at San Antonio serves the San Antonio metropolitan area and the broader region of South Texas. The university's three campuses provide access and opportunity for large numbers of historically underserved students. More than 56% of UTSA's students come from groups underrepresented in higher education. Many students are the first in their families to attend a college or university.

Texas A&M University, Kingsville, Texas

www.tamuk.edu

The mission of Texas A&M University-Kingsville is to develop well-rounded leaders and critical thinkers who can solve problems in an increasingly complex, dynamic and global society. Located in South Texas, the university is a teaching, research, and service institution that provides access to higher education in an ethnically and culturally diverse region of the nation. Ethnically, the campus reflects the demographics of the area, with 62% of the students Hispanic.

Heritage University, Toppenish, Washington

www.heritage.edu

Heritage University is a nonprofit, independent, nondenominational accredited institution of higher education offering undergraduate and graduate education. Its mission is to provide quality, accessible higher education to multicultural populations which have been educationally isolated. Within its liberal arts curriculum, Heritage offers strong professional and career-oriented programs designed to enrich the quality of life for students and their communities.

Institutes and Centers

Hispanic Institute for Research and Development, Paramus, New Jersey

www.hird.org/

The mission of the Institute is to enhance the social, economic, and educational status of the Hispanic community by empowering its members, through education and orientation, to seek and obtain better career opportunities.

Hispanic Association on Corporate Responsibility

www.hacr.org/research/

The HACR Research Institute (The Institute) is the research arm of the Hispanic Association on Corporate Responsibility. The Institute is devoted to objective research, analysis, and publication of Hispanic-related issues in corporate America. The Institute focuses its research in the areas of corporate governance, workforce, employment, corporate philanthropy, procurement, Hispanic economics and national demographics. The goal of the Institute is to assess current Hispanic affairs and stimulate discussion on Hispanic inclusion in corporate America.

The Latin American and Latino Studies Institute at Fordham, New York

www.fordham.edu/Academics/Programs_at_Fordham_/Latin_American_and_L/

The Latin American and Latino Studies Institute (LALSI) is home to an interdisciplinary program that brings together faculty members from nine different departments. Originally founded as the Puerto Rican Studies Institute, the program expanded in the early 1990s and changed its name. Today, LALSI faculty work on all major areas of Latin America, including the Caribbean, and on U.S. Latino issues. Fordham has, from its inception, educated students from Latin America and today's students also include members of Spanish-speaking immigrant communities in New York City. Fordham led the way as one of the first institutions in New York City to recognize the importance of Latino Studies. One of the great strengths of the LALS program is its embrace of a comparative approach that brings together scholars on U.S. Latinos, Latin America, and the Iberian Peninsula.

Chicano Resource Center, San Jose, California

www.sjlibrary.org/research/special/chc/chicano_hist.htm

The Chicano Resource Center (a collaboration of San Jose Public Libraries and San Jose State University Library) arose out of planning efforts in 1979 and early 1980, which involved faculty from the Mexican American Studies Department, the College of Social Work, the bilingual program in the College of Education, and the University Library. Dedicated in 1982, the Chicano Resource Center has provided a single focus for books, periodicals, reference tools, pamphlets, and clippings relating to Mexican-American history, culture, and community.

Center for the Study of Latino Health and Culture, Los Angeles, California

www.cesla.med.ucla.edu/

Since 1992, CESLAC has provided cutting-edge research, education, and public information about Latinos, their health, and their role in California. The Center for the Study of Latino Health and Culture at UCLA has been the lead institution in: exploding myths and stereotypes about Latinos in California society; providing reliable data on Latino health; emphasizing the positive contributions of Latinos to the state's economy and society; and informing the public about the important emerging Latino medical market.

Hispanic Research Center at Arizona State University

www.asu.edu/clas/hrc/

The Hispanic Research Center (HRC) at ASU is an interdisciplinary unit dedicated to research and creative activities that is university wide but administered through the College of Liberal Arts and Sciences. The HRC performs basic and applied research on a broad range of topics related to Hispanic populations, disseminates research findings to the academic community and the public, engages in creative activities and makes them available generally, and provides public service in areas of importance to Hispanics.

La Casa Cultural Latina at the University of Illinois

www.studentaffairs.illinois.edu/diversity/lacasa/

Since its founding in 1974, La Casa Cultural Latina has demonstrated an unwavering commitment to Latina/o students and the campus community, as well as local and global communities. La Casa reflects the diversity of Latina/o cultures and exemplifies el éxito Latino that shapes the Americas in our contemporary world.

Midwest Latino Health Research, Training and Policy Center at the University of Illinois at Chicago

www.uic.edu/jaddams/mlhrc/mlhrc.html

The Midwest Latino Health Research, Training and Policy Center (MLHRC) was founded in 1993 under the leadership of Aida L. Giachello, PhD in partnership with the UIC College of Medicine's Hispanic Center of Excellence and the School of Public Health. The mission of MLHRC is to work to improve the health, well-being, and quality of health services delivered to Latinos and other underserved populations in Chicago and throughout the Midwest.

Degrees, Programs, Concentrations

Latino Studies Program at Columbia University
www.columbia.edu/cu/latino/mags/index2.htm

The Latino Studies Program was established to survey and study the history, culture, and social fabric of the Latino populations of the United States. Courses in the program offer students an interdisciplinary perspective on the various Latino communities in the country. The curriculum includes courses placing the Latino experience in the context of U.S., Caribbean, and Latin American history, discussing the key socioeconomic and political issues facing Latinos in the United States, and presenting the Latino expression in literature, music, and art. Students can pursue an undergraduate major or a concentration in Latino Studies. The program also sponsors research projects and academic conferences.

Chicano Education Program at Eastern Washington University
www.ewu.edu/x2393.xml

The Chicano Education Program originated in the spring of 1977 when a group of Chicano and Chicana students and Chicano Art Professor Ruben Trejo proposed the formation of a program. Under the administration of President George Fredrickson, the program was founded to recruit Chicano/a students and begin a search for a program director. In the fall of 1977 an acting director was appointed, Santos Hernandez, assistant professor in Social Work. He continued for two years. In 1981 two classes were being offered, Chicano Culture Experience and Chicano History. In the 1990s, Survey of Chicano Literature and Chicano-Latino Politics were added. In the 2000 decade, a minor was approved and several courses added.

Latino Studies Program at Indiana University, Bloomington
www.indiana.edu/~latino/index.php?page=home

Latino Studies at Indiana University is expanding to meet the growing student demand for courses about Latinos. Their mission is to empower individuals with skills and concepts to better understand Latino communities; to advance innovative research and scholarship on Latino cultures, histories, and social conditions; and to engage students, scholars, and the larger community in collaborative projects, civic programs, and service learning.

The César E. Chávez Center for Interdisciplinary Instruction in Chicana/o Studies, University of California, Los Angeles
www.sscnet.ucla.edu/chavez/

The mission of the César E. Chávez Department of Chicana and Chicano Studies is to study, analyze, and research the historical and contemporary experiences of people of Mexican origin within the United States, as well as of other Latino/a and indigenous populations in the Americas.

Department of Ethnic Studies, University of California, Riverside
www.chicanobbstudies.ucr.edu/about_us/index.html

The Chicano Bilingual/Bicultural Studies minor at the University of California, Riverside provides students with a basic understanding of the Spanish language and introduces students to the social, cultural, and linguistic diversity of the Chicano population in California and the southwestern United States. The minor prepares students to examine the educational condition of the Chicano population and the educational needs of language-minority populations. The Chicano Bilingual/Bicultural minor is administered by the Department of Ethnic Studies. The advisory committee for the minor consists of faculty members from various academic disciplines, including Chicano Studies, Education, Sociology, and Spanish and Portuguese. The interdisciplinary character of the advisory committee enhances the multidisciplinary focus of the minor. The Chicano Bilingual/Bicultural minor is especially advantageous to students interested in teaching careers focused on Chicano and language minority students.

Mexican American Studies Department at San José State University

www.info.sjsu.edu/web-dbgen/catalog/departments/MAS.html

The Mission of the Mexican American Studies Department is to serve SJSU students and diverse communities through an interdisciplinary Chicana/o Studies Program that is based on principles of social justice. The program prepares students to critically examine and address intellectual traditions and contemporary issues resulting from race, ethnicity, class, and gender intersections in Chicana/o-Latina/o and other communities. The overall goal of the MAS Department is to prepare students to critically assess the conceptualization of race and ethnicity, as it relates to and is challenged by Chicana/o communities. Students develop critical thinking skills and a comparative analysis between Chicana/o and other communities. In the end, students integrate major issues and theories from MAS courses and apply them to current problems as they plan for postgraduate work.

Division of Bicultural Bilingual Studies at The University of Texas at San Antonio

www.bbl.utsa.edu/

The Department of Bicultural-Bilingual Studies offers a bachelor of arts (BA) degree in Mexican-American Studies and a bachelor of applied arts and sciences (BAAS) degree in Mexican-American Studies as well as minors in Bicultural Studies and English as a Second Language. The BA in Mexican-American Studies prepares students to enter graduate school or pursue a career as an educator, researcher, community leader, or community advocate. The department also offers courses that may be used to fulfill the core curriculum requirements or that may be taken as support courses for programs within the University or as electives. Courses in bicultural–bilingual studies offer students the opportunity to prepare for bilingual or second language teaching and give insights into bilingual and multicultural functions in society. Courses in teaching English as a second language (ESL) offer students the opportunity to learn appropriate methods and strategies for teaching at the elementary, secondary, and adult levels. Courses are designed for students who plan to teach second languages, but are also designed for those who intend to teach in other areas or to enter fields that rely heavily on an understanding of language learning and bilingualism. In addition, the department offers advanced courses in English for international students that are appropriate for both graduate and undergraduate students. The Department of Bicultural–Bilingual Studies offers coursework required for teacher certification in the area of bilingual education and ESL. Students seeking certification in this area should complete requirements for either the Early Childhood–Grade 4 Bilingual Generalist Certificate, the Grades 4–8 Bilingual Generalist Certificate, or the Grades 4–8 ESL Certificate.

Chicano/a Studies Department at Loyola Marymount University, Los Angeles, CA

www.bellarmine.lmu.edu/page29626.aspx

The academic field of Chicana/o Studies developed at LMU over 30 years ago. It examines and investigates the lives, histories, and cultures of Mexican-origin people living in the United States. Chicana/o Studies developed in the context of the Civil Rights movements of the late 1960s and has become an area of study recognized both nationally and internationally. The department's academic strengths lie in history, anthropology, political science, and literature, as well as in feminist, cultural, and media studies. Students majoring or minoring in Chicana/o Studies will be prepared to participate in a diversifying society, one in need of expertise about racial, ethnic, economic, political, and social differences. Our graduates are committed to the mission of the university, including the promotion of justice.

Scholarships and Funding Opportunities

¡Adelante! U.S. Education Leadership Fund: HOPE Scholarships
www.adelantefund.org
> HOPE scholarships are available only in Texas to applicants who attend an accredited college or university in San Antonio, Texas. Community service involvement is required.

¡Adelante! U.S. Education Leadership Fund: Hispano Scholarship
www.adelantefund.org
> This scholarship is open to any incoming freshman or college student at a 4-year university and is open to any major.

¡Adelante! U.S. Education Leadership Fund: MillerCoors
www.adelantefund.org
> This scholarship is available to eligible junior and senior status students at a partnering college or university. Applicant must be pursuing a degree in one of the following areas: international business, general business, economics, finance, accounting, marketing, public relations, or sales.

¡Adelante! U.S. Education Leadership Fund: MillerCoors Chicago
www.adelantefund.org
> The MillerCoors Chicago Scholarship is available to Chicago Metro area students who meet eligibility criteria.

¡Adelante! U.S. Education Leadership Fund: MillerCoors Texas
www.adelantefund.org
> The MillerCoors Texas Scholarship is available to Texas students who are attending a college or university in Dallas, Houston, or El Paso.

ALPFA Annual Scholarship Program
www.alpfa.org/index.cfm?fuseaction=Page.viewPage&pageId=354
> The Association of Latino Professionals in Finance and Accounting (ALPFA) offers scholarships to students, in the United States or Puerto Rico, who are pursuing studies in accounting, finance, or business related fields. The purpose of these scholarships is to encourage those students who have demonstrated academic excellence to continue pursuing their professional careers.

American Architectural Foundation Minority/Disadvantage Scholarship
www.archfoundation.org/aaf/aaf/Programs.Fellowships.htm
> The American Architectural Foundation offers the Minority/Disadvantaged Scholarships in order to encourage diversity and equity in the architectural profession. These scholarships are open to high school seniors and college freshmen who plan to study architecture at a NAAB-accredited program.

American Association of Law Libraries (AALL) & Thomson West-George A. Strait Minority Scholarship Endowment
www.aallnet.org/services/sch_strait.asp
> The George A. Strait Minority Scholarship is awarded to college graduates with law library experience who are members of a minority group as defined by current U.S. government guidelines and are degree candidates in accredited library or law schools and who intend to have a career in law librarianship.

American Chemistry Society Scholars Program
www.portal.acs.org/portal/acs/corg/content?_nfpb=true&_pageLabel=PP_TRANSITIONMAIN&node_id=1234&use_sec=false&sec_url_var=region1&__uuid=534dece2-50f4-44ed-9e6f-b7231bc7ce6a
> American Chemical Society awards renewable scholarships to underrepresented minority students who want to enter the fields of chemistry or chemistry-related fields. Awards are

given to qualified applicants based on academic standing, financial need, career objective, leadership skills, and involvement in school activities and community service.

ASCO Numatics Industrial Automation Engineering College Scholarships
www.asconumatics.com/LiteratureRequest/ASCO-Numatics-Scholarship.aspx

ASCO Numatics, a division of Emerson, is the world's leading manufacturer of comprehensive fluid automation solutions, flow control, and pneumatics. The engineering college scholarship program is aimed at rewarding exceptional undergraduate and graduate students pursuing a career in manufacturing and processing engineering. The scholarships are merit-based and will be awarded on the candidate's potential for leadership and for making a significant contribution to the engineering, instrumentation, systems, and automation professions, particularly as they relate to the application of fluid control and fluid power technologies. Scholarship recipients may be eligible for an ASCO Numatics internship.

The BECA Foundation—A Nonprofit Latino Scholarship Organization
www.becafoundation.org/scholarship.htm

The BECA Foundation, Inc. a non-profit corporation was formed to provide scholarship funds to promising students of Hispanic descent living in San Diego County. The BECA Foundation's purpose is to seek out these promising students and provide them with the necessary financial assistance, moral support, and guidance to complete their education, thereby promoting higher educational and leadership standards within the Hispanic community.

BOCES Geneseo Migrant Center Scholarship Funds
www.migrant.net/migrant/scholarships.htm

The Geneseo Migrant Center, Inc. provides financial assistance to students across the country with a recent or ongoing history of movement to obtain work in agriculture since the inception of its first scholarship fund in 1974. These scholarships encourage and support deserving migrant students in the pursuit of their educational goals.

Coca-Cola Scholars Foundation
www.coca-colascholars.org/cokeWeb/index.jsp?navigation=1

The Coca-Cola Scholars Foundation awards scholarships to students who exemplify the potential to become the leaders of tomorrow. Scholarships are awarded based on character, personal merit, and commitment. Merit is demonstrated through leadership in school, civic, and extracurricular activities, academic achievement, and motivation to serve and succeed.

College Assistance Migrant Program (CAMP)
www.migrantstudents.org/campapplicants.html

The College Assistance Migrant Program (CAMP) is a unique federally funded educational support and scholarship program that helps more than 2,000 students annually from migrant and seasonal farm working backgrounds to reach and succeed in college. Participants receive financial support during their freshman year of college and ongoing academic support until their graduation.

Congressional Hispanic Caucus Institute (CHCI) Alumni Association Dream Scholarship
www.chci.org/scholarships/page/chci-alumni-association-dream-scholarship

The CHCI Alumni Association Dream Scholarship is funded by contributions from the Alumni Association and its sponsors. The scholarship is awarded to first-generation (first generation to go to college) immigrant students (not born in the U.S.) who have a history of involvement in public service-oriented activities in their communities and who demonstrate a desire to continue their civic engagement in the future. There is no GPA or major requirement. Students with leadership potential are encouraged to apply.

Congressional Hispanic Caucus Institute (CHCI) Scholarship
www.chci.org/scholarships/page/chci-scholarship-program

Scholarships are awarded to Latino students who have a history of performing public service-oriented activities in their communities and who demonstrate a desire to continue their civic engagement in the future. There is no GPA or major requirement. Students with excellent leadership potential are encouraged to apply.

The Gates Millennium Scholars

www.gmsp.org/

Funded by a grant from the Bill & Melinda Gates Foundation, it was established in 1999 to provide outstanding African-American, American-Indian/Alaska Native, Asian Pacific Islander American, and Hispanic-American students with an opportunity to complete an undergraduate college education in all discipline areas and a graduate education for those students pursuing studies in mathematics, science, engineering, education, public health or library science. The goal of GMS is to promote academic excellence and to provide an opportunity for thousands of outstanding students with significant financial need to reach their fullest potential.

The Gates Millennium Scholars program is available to graduating high school seniors. It provides substantial scholarship awards to exceptional high school seniors for study at the college of their choice. Eligible applicants must have a minimum grade point average (GPA) of 3.3 on a 4.0 scale, demonstrated leadership skills, and significant financial need.

Harry S. Truman Scholarship Foundation

www.truman.gov/index.htm

The Truman Scholarship Foundation awards merit-based grants of $30,000 to undergraduate students who wish financial support to attend a graduate or professional school in preparation for careers in government. The Foundation seeks candidates who have extensive records of public and community service, are committed to careers in government or elsewhere in public service, and have an outstanding leadership potential and communication skills.

Hispanic Association of Colleges & Universities (HACU): DaimlerChrysler Scholarship Award

www.scholarships.hacu.net/applications/applicants/

Full-time undergraduate students attending 2- or 4-year institutions. All majors welcome to apply.

Hispanic Association of Colleges & Universities (HACU): GAP, Inc. Scholarship Award

www.scholarships.hacu.net/applications/applicants/

Full-time or part-time undergraduate and graduate students attending 4-year institutions with declared majors in merchandise management, retail management, fashion design or related fields.

Hispanic Association of Colleges & Universities (HACU): General Motors Engineering Excellence Award

www.scholarships.hacu.net/applications/applicants/

Full-time undergraduate students at 4-year institutions with declared majors in an engineering degree program may apply. Scholarship is renewable based on availability of funds and student's continuing eligibility.

Hispanic Association of Colleges & Universities (HACU): Lockheed Martin Scholarship Award

www.scholarships.hacu.net/applications/applicants/

Full-time undergraduate students at 4-year institutions with declared majors in Electrical Engineering, Computer Engineering or Computer Science. Student must be interested in Lockheed Martin employment opportunities.

Hispanic Association of Colleges & Universities (HACU): NASCAR/Wendell Scott Award

www.scholarships.hacu.net/applications/applicants/

Undergraduates and graduate students in a 2- or 4-year institution with a declared major in: Business, Engineering, Public Relations, Mass Media, Technology, Marketing and Sports Marketing/Management.

Hispanic Association of Colleges & Universities (HACU): Office Depot Scholarship
www.scholarships.hacu.net/applications/applicants/
Undergraduate students attending 4-year institutions in any of the following majors: business, international business, marketing, merchandising, or information technology.

Hispanic Association of Colleges & Universities (HACU): Wachovia Scholarship Award
www.scholarships.hacu.net/applications/applicants/
Full-time undergraduate students attending 2- or 4-year institutions in any of the following majors: finance, accounting, or business administration; student must be within Wachovia's retail markets.

Hispanic Association of Colleges & Universities (HACU): Wal-Mart Achievers Scholarship
www.scholarships.hacu.net/applications/applicants/
Full-time undergraduate students attending 2- or 4-year institutions in any of the following majors: business administration, general management, retail management or food merchandising. Students must possess an interest in retail and preferably be working while attending school.

Hispanic College Fund: Ford Blue Oval 2 Program
www.scholarships.hispanicfund.org/applications/subsectionID.1,pageID.122/default.asp
The HCF Ford Blue Oval 2 program supports Hispanic undergraduate students studying any discipline nationwide.

Hispanic College Fund: Google Scholarship Program
www.scholarships.hispanicfund.org/applications/subsectionID.1,pageID.123/default.asp
The Google Scholarship Program offers funds to students studying computer science or computer engineering who are juniors or seniors in college or pursing a master's or doctorate.

Hispanic College Fund: Kaiser Permanente College to Caring Program
www.scholarships.hispanicfund.org/applications/subsectionID.1,pageID.151/default.asp
Kaiser Permanente College to Caring Program offers funds to students who are juniors or seniors in college pursuing a bachelor's degree in nursing.

Hispanic College Fund: Manuel Candamo Memorial Scholarship Program
www.scholarships.hispanicfund.org/applications/subsectionID.1,pageID.165/default.asp
The Manuel Candamo Memorial Scholarship program is for students who are Puerto Rican or of Puerto Rican descent. Applicants must be enrolled full time at an accredited university in the United States or Puerto Rico.

Hispanic College Fund: Marriott Scholars Program
www.scholarships.hispanicfund.org/applications/subsectionID.1,pageID.156/default.asp
The Marriott Scholars Program offers financial support of up to 4 years coupled with opportunities for ongoing career guidance and mentoring by Marriott hotel managers and corporate executives.

Hispanic College Fund: Pharmacy Scholars Program
www.scholarships.hispanicfund.org/applications/subsectionID.1,pageID.150/default.asp
Pharmacy Scholars Program offers funds to students who are pursuing a degree in pharmacy and who have completed one year of pharmacy school or are in their second year of their pharmacy education.

Hispanic College Fund: Sallie Mae First in My Family Scholarship Program
www.scholarships.hispanicfund.org/applications/subsectionID.1,pageID.113/default.asp
The Sallie Mae Scholarship program is dedicated to assisting students who are the first person in their family to attend college and who are Hispanic.

Hispanic College Fund Scholars Program
www.scholarships.hispanicfund.org/applications/subsectionID.1,pageID.114/default.asp
The HCF Scholars program is available to Hispanics who are enrolled full time as an undergraduate student at an accredited university in the U.S. or Puerto Rico.

Hispanic College Fund: United Health Foundation Latino Health Scholars Program
www.scholarships.hispanicfund.org/applications/subsectionID.1,pageID.200/default.asp
> The United Health Foundation Latino Health Scholars program is available for students wanting to pursue or currently pursuing a degree that will lead to a career in the health field. Applicants must demonstrate a commitment to working in underserved communities, including community health centers.

Hispanic College Fund: Verizon Scholarship Program
www.scholarships.hispanicfund.org/applications/subsectionID.1,pageID.193/default.asp
> The Verizon Scholarship program offers funds to students pursuing a degree in business administration, finance, accounting, computer science, computer engineering, or information technology.

Hispanic Scholarship Fund: Atrisco Heritage Foundation Scholarship Program
www.hsf.net/atrisco.aspx
> The Hispanic Scholarship Fund (HSF) and Atrisco Heritage Foundation have partnered to provide scholarship awards to assist outstanding Latinos who are heirs of the Atrisco Land Grant of New Mexico. Applicants may reside nationwide and be graduating high school seniors, undergraduate students, or graduate students.

Hispanic Scholarship Fund: BB&T Charitable Scholarship
www.hsf.net/BBT.aspx
> This scholarship is designed to provide financial resources to outstanding Latino and African-American undergraduate students at a 4-year university. Scholarships are available on a competitive basis with a potential internship opportunity at BB&T.

Hispanic Scholarship Fund: Cien Años Scholarship
www.hsf.net/cien.aspx
> The Hispanic Scholarship Fund and Cien Años have partnered to provide financial resources to assist outstanding Latino undergraduate students who reside and attend school in Arizona or Southern California. Applicants must be 21 years of age at the time of the application. Preference is given to students who demonstrate a high level of community involvement.

Hispanic Scholarship Fund: Citi Fellows Program
www.hsf.net/scholarships.aspx?id=462
> This scholarship is designed for students pursuing a degree in business administration, economics, or finance. Applicants must currently be a sophomore enrolled full time at an accredited 4-year institution and live in a select geographical location.

Hispanic Scholarship Fund: Ford Motor Company Scholarship
www.hsf.net/scholarships.aspx?id=482
> The Ford Motor Company Scholarship is designed to help graduating seniors of Hispanic heritage nationwide obtain a bachelor's degree. Applicants must be of Hispanic heritage, legal U.S. citizens or legal permanent residents, have a minimum GPA of 3.0 on a 4.0 scale, and plan to enroll full-time at a 2- or 4-year U.S. accredited institution.

Hispanic Scholarship Fund: General College Scholarships
www.hsf.net/Scholarships.aspx?id=460
> General College Scholarships are designed to assist students of Hispanic heritage obtain a college degree. Scholarships are available on a competitive basis to: graduating high school seniors, community college students and transfer students, undergraduate students, and graduate students. Applicants must be of Hispanic heritage, legal U.S. citizens or legal permanent residents, have a minimum GPA of 3.0 on a 4.0 scale, and plan to enroll full-time at a 2- or 4-year U.S. accredited institution.

Hispanic Scholarship Fund: General Motors Scholarship

www.hsf.net/scholarships.aspx?id=314

The Hispanic Scholarship Fund and General Motors have partnered to provide financial resources to assist outstanding Latino students pursuing degrees in engineering and business. Applicants may be graduating high school seniors or current undergraduates (freshman, sophomore, and junior). Applicants must be of Hispanic heritage, legal U.S. citizens or legal permanent residents, have a minimum GPA of 3.0 on a 4.0 scale, and plan to enroll full-time at a 2- or 4-year U.S. accredited institution. Applicants must also be majoring in engineering (electrical, industrial, manufacturing and mechanical) or Business (accounting, business administration, economics, and finance) or human resources.

Hispanic Scholarship Fund: GMAC SmartEdge Book Scholarship

www.hsf.net/gmac.aspx

The Hispanic Scholarship Fund and GMAC Financial services have partnered to provide book scholarships to assist outstanding Latino students in their purchase of college textbooks. This scholarship is open to undergraduate students in selected geographic locations pursuing degrees in business, education, or urban planning.

Hispanic Scholarship Fund: HSBC-North America Scholarship

www.hsf.net/Scholarships.aspx?id=856

The HSBC-North America Scholarship Program is available on a competitive basis to outstanding Latino undergraduate students.

Hispanic Scholarship Fund: HP Scholars Program

www.hp.com/scholars/

This program is designed to provide scholarships and productivity packages to African-American, Latino, or American-Indian students. Applicants must pursue a degree in computer engineering, computer science, or electrical engineering at partnering universities (UCLA, University of Washington, San Jose State, Morgan State, or North Carolina A&T).

Hispanic Scholarship Fund: IDT Hope High School Scholarship

www.hsf.net/scholarships.aspx?id=480

This scholarship program is designed to assist graduating high school seniors of Hispanic heritage obtain a bachelor's degree. Applicants must be a dependent of an IDT employee and reside in the U.S. or Puerto Rico or reside in Maryland, Virginia, Washington DC, or metropolitan areas of New York City or Newark.

Hispanic Scholarship Fund: Macy's College Scholarship

www.hsf.net/macys.aspx

This scholarship provides financial resources to assist outstanding Latino undergraduate students. This scholarship is open to students attending selected universities.

Hispanic Scholarship Fund: Marathon Oil Corporation College Scholarship Program

www.hsf.net/Scholarships.aspx?id=464

The Marathon Oil Corporation Scholarship is for students who will be a sophomores majoring in chemical engineering, civil engineering, electrical engineering, mechanical engineering, petroleum engineering, geology, geophysics, accounting, marketing, global procurement or supply chain management, environmental health & safety, energy management or petroleum land management, transportation & logistics or geotechnical engineering, or a senior planning to enroll in a master's degree program in geology or geophysics.

Hispanic Scholarship Fund: Margoes Foundation Scholarship

www.hsf.net/scholarships.aspx?id=478

The Morgues Foundation in partnership with the Hispanic Scholarship Fund provide scholarship awards to assist outstanding Latino high school seniors from San Francisco, California, who are active participants of the College Connect Program.

Hispanic Scholarship Fund: MassMutual Multicultural College Scholarship
www.hsf.net/massmutual.aspx

Through the Hispanic Scholarship Fund, the MassMutual Financial Group is offering scholarships to assist outstanding undergraduate minority students in selected geographic locations in selected majors.

Hispanic Scholarship Fund: McNamara Family Creative Arts Grant Project
www.hsf.net/scholarships.aspx?id=466

This grant is designed to provide financial resources to outstanding Latino undergraduate and graduate students enrolled in a creative arts related field: media, film, performing arts, communication, writing, etc.

Hispanic Scholarship Fund: Peierls Rising Star Scholarship
www.hsf.net/peierls.aspx

This scholarship is available to current high school seniors from Colorado and Texas who participate in selected local precollegiate programs.

Hispanic Scholarship Fund: Proctor & Gamble Company Scholarship
www.hsf.net/PG.aspx

The Hispanic Scholarship Fund and Procter & Gamble Company have partnered to provide financial resources to assist outstanding Latino undergraduates pursuing degrees in the STEM field (science, technology, engineering, and mathematics).

Hispanic Scholarship Fund: Toyota Motor Sales, U.S.A., Inc. Scholarship
www.hsf.net/Scholarships.aspx?id=2644

This scholarship provides financial resources to assist outstanding Latino undergraduate students who reside and attend school in the Greater Los Angeles, Houston, and San Antonio areas. Scholarships are available on a competitive basis.

Hispanic Scholarship Fund: TU@UT Austin Scholarship
www.hsf.net/Scholarships.aspx?id=438

This scholarship is available to high school seniors who plan to enroll at the University of Texas at Austin. Students must graduate from one of the following high schools in Texas: Harlingen, Harlingen South, Rio Hondo, San Benito, Los Fresnos, Gladys Porter, Simon Rivera, James Pace, Homer Hanna, Lopez, John H. Reagan, Sidney Lanier, William B. Travis. Applicants for this scholarship must demonstrate financial need with priority given to students who are Pell grant eligible.

Hispanic Scholarship Fund: University of Georgia University Alliance Scholarship
www.hsf.net/Scholarships.aspx?id=436

This scholarship is available to high school seniors classified as Georgia residents for tuition purposes and planning to enroll at the University of Georgia.

Hispanic Scholarship Fund: Valley Alliance of Mentors for Opportunities and Scholarships (VAMOS) Scholarship Program
www.hsf.net/vamos.aspx

The Hispanic Scholarship Fund/VAMOS Scholarship Program is designed to assist high school seniors of Hispanic heritage from Hidalgo County in Texas obtain a bachelor's degree.

Hispanic Scholarship Fund: Wal-Mart Stores, Inc. High School Scholarship
www.hsf.net/Scholarships.aspx?id=1872

The Wal-Mart Stores, Inc. High School Scholarship Program is available on a competitive basis to graduating high school seniors of Hispanic heritage from selected geographical locations.

Hispanic Scholarship Fund: Wells Fargo Scholarship

www.hsf.net/scholarships.aspx?id=468

This scholarship is designed for Latino undergraduate students who are interested in the financial and banking institution based careers. This program aims at making a positive impact on students' education through scholarship support and career preparedness via internship opportunities.

Hispanic Scholarship Fund: Western Governors University Scholarship

www.hsf.net/Scholarships.aspx?id=318

This scholarship is available to students enrolled full time at Western Governors University.

LULAC: GE Scholarship

www.lnesc.org/index.asp?Type=B_BASIC&SEC={3AEDB506-F425-4E58-B9F6-44867E2FD943}

This program is run solely through the LNESC national office. Qualified applicants are chosen through a very rigorous selection process by members of LNESC's scholarship committee. Only those preparing to enter their sophomore year at an accredited institution and having declared majors in business or engineering are eligible.

LULAC: GM Scholarship

www.lnesc.org/index.asp?Type=B_BASIC&SEC={3AEDB506-F425-4E58-B9F6-44867E2FD943}

This program is also run solely through the LNESC national office and candidates are selected by members of the scholarship committee. This scholarship is only for students currently enrolled in an accredited institution, seeking a degree in Engineering.

LULAC: Pepsi Escribe tu Futuro Scholarship

www.lnesc.org/index.asp?Type=B_BASIC&SEC={3AEDB506-F425-4E58-B9F6-44867E2FD943}

This scholarship may be utilized for educational expenses during college or postsecondary vocational school that leads to an associate's degree.

LULAC National Scholarship Fund

www.lnesc.org/index.asp?Type=B_BASIC&SEC=%7BA9E53D4E-6ADF-431B-A59A-E92DEDD44793%7D

LULAC Councils will award scholarships to qualified Hispanic students who are enrolled or are planning to enroll in accredited colleges or universities in the United States.

The MALDEF Law School Scholarship Program

www.maldef.org/leadership/scholarships/law_school_scholarship_program/

The Mexican American Legal Defense & Educational Fund (MALDEF) Law School Scholarship Program awards scholarships every year to Latino law school students based upon three primary factors: demonstrated involvement in and commitment to serve the Latino community through the legal profession; academic and professional achievement; and financial need. Through its scholarship program, MALDEF seeks to increase the number of Latinos in the legal profession.

Mexican American Engineers & Scientists (MAES) Scholarship Program

www.maes-natl.org/index.php?module=ContentExpress&func=display&ceid=392&meid=241

The purpose of the MAES Scholarship Program is to increase the number of Hispanic students completing their higher education goals. Student Excellence Scholarships are available on a competitive basis to MAES student members in the fields of science, technology, engineering, and mathematics. The scholarship applicants are selected on the basis of academic achievement, financial need, leadership, community service, personal qualities, and completeness of application.

Microsoft Underrepresented Minority Scholarship

www.microsoft.com/college/ss_overview.mspx

> This scholarship encourages student populations currently underrepresented in the field of computer science to pursue technical degrees.

Motivating Undergraduates in Science and Technology (MUST) Project

www.nasa.gov/offices/education/programs/descriptions/Motivating_Undergraduates_Science_Technology.html

> The MUST project, funded by NASA, is a joint partnership between the Hispanic College Fund, the United Negro College Fund Special Programs, and the Society for Hispanic Professional Engineers. MUST awards scholarships and internships to undergraduates who are pursuing degrees in science, technology, engineering, and mathematics (STEM fields). The MUST project is open to all students and is particularly focused on engaging students from underserved and underrepresented groups to enter STEM fields.

National Association of Hispanic Journalists (NAHJ) Ruben Salazar Scholarship Fund

www.nahj.org/educationalprograms/nahjscholarships.shtml

> The National Association of Hispanic Journalists (NAHJ) offers several scholarships through our Rubén Salazar Scholarship Fund program. These scholarships are designed to encourage and assist Latino students pursue careers in journalism. Hispanics remain woefully underrepresented in mainstream U.S. newsrooms. One of NAHJ's goals is to help more qualified Hispanic students to move from the classroom to the newsroom. NAHJ offers scholarships to college undergraduates and graduate students pursuing careers as print, photo, broadcast or online journalism.

Questbridge

www.questbridge.org/index.html

> QuestBridge is a nonprofit program that links bright, motivated low-income students with educational and scholarship opportunities at some of the nation's best colleges.

Sodexo STOP Hunger Scholarship Program

www.scholarships.hispanicfund.org/applications/subsectionID.1,pageID.119/default.asp

> The Sodexo Foundation is committed to being a driving and creative force that contributes to a hunger-free nation. The scholarship program is available to students who are committed to alleviating hunger and poverty in the United States.

Xerox Technical Minority Scholarship Progam

www.xerox.com/go/xrx/template/009.jsp?Xcntry=USA&Xlang=en_US&ed_name=Careers_Technical_Scholarship&view=Feature&metrics=notrack

> The Xerox Technical Minority Scholarship Program provides scholarships for full-time undergraduate and graduate minority students in the following fields: chemistry, information management, computing & software systems, material science, printing management science, laser optics, physics and engineering (chemical, computer, electrical, imaging, manufacturing, mechanical, optical or software engineering).

Note

1. The author(s) and editor(s) do not necessarily endorse the reference entries in this chapter; they are listed for informational purposes only. Most descriptions have been gathered conducting extensive electronic searches with key words related to these topics and are taken directly from these online sites in order to provide true and clearer descriptions. In order to honor the words chosen to describe themselves and others, each overview incorporates the terms and language utilized (such as Latino/a, Hispanic, Chicano, etc.) on the individual sites.

43 Internet Tools/Technology

Victor H. Pérez

University of Illinois at Urbana-Champaign

INTERNET TOOLS/TECHNOLOGY: SITES, WEBLIOGRAPHIES, CLEARINGHOUSES, PORTALS, DIGITAL/VIRTUAL LIBRARIES, DIRECTORIES, AND MORE.[1]

Research Centers and Institutes

Center for Chicano Studies, University of California, Santa Barbara
www.chicst.ucsb.edu/center/
> The Center for Chicano Studies is an organized research unit founded in 1969 to develop and support research on the history and contemporary sociocultural, political, artistic, and economic conditions of Chicanos/as, Mexicanos/as, and Latinos/as.

Center for Latino Policy Research, University of California at Berkeley
www.clpr.berkeley.edu/
> The Center for Latino Policy Research (CLPR) was founded in 1989 in response to the research and policy challenges of limited educational and economic opportunities facing the Latino/Chicano population. CLPR is committed to sponsoring research efforts that have a direct policy impact on the Latino/Chicano population in the United States.

Center for Mexican American Studies, University of Texas at Austin
www.utexas.edu/depts/cmas/
> The Center for Mexican-American Studies (CMAS) focuses on Mexican-American scholarship and educational programs on the University of Texas campus, and is a national leader in teaching, research, and publications. Since its creation in 1970, CMAS has worked to enhance our understanding of the Mexican and Mexican-American experience, as well as the broader Latino experience, and to strengthen the presence of Mexican Americans and other Latinos in the intellectual terrain, both within and beyond U.S. borders.

Center for Multilingual, Multicultural Research (CMMR), University of Southern California
www.usc.edu/dept/education/CMMR/
> Faculty in the Rossier School of Education developed the USC Center for Multilingual, Multicultural Research (CMMR) in the Spring of 1983, as a result of deliberations of the Dean's Task Force for Bilingual Cross-Cultural Education. The Center provides a base for those interested in multilingual education, English as a second language, and foreign language instruction, multicultural education, and related areas; and the opportunity to come together for research and program collaboration.

Center for Research on Latinos in a Global Society, University of California at Irvine
www.repositories.cdlib.org/crlgs/
> Interdisciplinary research in Chicano/Latino Studies is conducted under the auspices of the Center for Research on Latinos in a Global Society (CRLGS). Its multifold goals are: (1) to examine the emerging role of Latinos as actors in global economic, political, and cultural events; (2) to promote Latino scholarship; (3) to enhance the quality of research in Latino

studies; (4) to provide a forum for intellectual exchange and the dissemination of research findings; and (5) to promote the participation of undergraduate and graduate students in research on Latino issues.

Center for the Study of Latino Health and Culture, University of California at Los Angeles
www.cesla.med.ucla.edu/

Since 1992, CESLAC has provided cutting-edge research, education and public information about Latinos, their health, and their role in California.

Centro de Estudios Puertorriqueños at Hunter College, City University of New York
www.centropr.org/

The Centro is a research center dedicated to the study and interpretation of the Puerto Rican experience in the United States. The Centro is committed to making this research available and useful to those in community organizations, public policy, and academia. The Centro is also the world's only repository of archival and library materials dedicated exclusively to the Puerto Rican diaspora.

César Chávez Institute, San Francisco State University
www.cci.sfsu.edu/

Inspired by César Chávez's commitment to social justice, the César E. Chávez Institute (CCI) is dedicated to studying and documenting the impact of social oppression on the health, education, and well-being of disenfranchised communities in the United States.

Chicano / Latino Research Center, University of California at Santa Cruz
www.clrc.ucsc.edu/

The Chicano/Latino Research Center (CLRC) is an internationally recognized site for the support of scholarship on Chicano and Latino issues. Promoting cross-border perspectives linking the Americas and the study of U.S. changing demographic and cultural panorama, the Center focuses on globalization and transculturation, processes that are redefining cultural, social, and political identities in the Americas.

Chicano Studies Research Center, UCLA
www.chicano.ucla.edu/

The UCLA Chicano Studies Research Center (CSRC) was founded in 1969 with a commitment to foster multidisciplinary research efforts as part of the land grant mission of the University of California. That mission states that University of California research needs to be in the service of the state and that it must maintain a presence in the local community.

Congressional Hispanic Caucus Institute (CHCI)
www.chci.org/

The Congressional Hispanic Caucus Institute (CHCI) is one of the leading Hispanic non-profit and nonpartisan 501(c)3 organizations in the country. CHCI was established in 1978 by Congressman Edward Roybal, Congressman E. "Kika" de la Garza, and Congressman Baltasar Corrada to help increase opportunities for Hispanics to participate in and contribute to the American policy making process.

Cuban American Institute
www.lacc.fiu.edu/

The Cuban Research Institute (CRI) is the nation's leading institute for research and academic programs on Cuban and Cuban-American issues. Since its founding in 1991, a blend of scholarship and the singular resources of the Greater Miami community has enabled the CRI to produce an exceptional level of research and public programs in the field.

CUNY Dominican Studies Institute (CUNY-DIS)
www.ccny.cuny.edu/dsi/

The CUNY Dominican Studies Institute (CUNY DSI) is an interdisciplinary research unit of the City University of New York devoted to the study of Dominicans in the United States and other parts of the world, as well as in the Dominican Republic.

David Rockefeller Center for Latin American Studies, Harvard University

www.drclas.harvard.edu/

The David Rockefeller Center for Latin American Studies works to increase knowledge of the cultures, histories, environments, and contemporary affairs of Latin America; to foster cooperation and understanding among the people of the Americas; and to contribute to democracy, social progress, and sustainable development throughout the hemisphere.

Ernesto Galarza Applied Research Center, University of California at Riverside

www.clnet.sscnet.ucla.edu/EGARC/

The Ernesto Galarza Applied Research Center has been established to develop applied research, training, and practicing projects and programs that contribute to the intellectual growth and social well-being of the Mexican/Latino populations.

Excelencia in Education

www.edexcelencia.org/default.asp

Excelencia in Education aims to accelerate higher education success for Latino students. Launched in 2004, Excelencia links research, policy, and practice to serve Latino students and the institutions and programs where they participate.

Hispanic Heritage Foundation

www.hispanicheritage.org/

The Hispanic Heritage Foundation (HHF) identifies, inspires, promotes, and prepares Latino role models through national leadership, cultural, educational, and workforce programs.

Hispanic Research Center (HRC), Arizona State University

www.asu.edu/clas/hrc/

The Hispanic Research Center (HRC) at ASU is an interdisciplinary unit dedicated to research and creative activities that is university wide but administered through the College of Liberal Arts and Sciences. The HRC performs basic and applied research on a broad range of topics related to Hispanic populations, disseminates research findings to the academic community and the public, engages in creative activities and makes them available generally, and provides public service in areas of importance to Hispanics.

Inter-University Program for Latino Research (IUPLR)

www.nd.edu/~iuplr/

IUPLR is a national consortium of university-based centers dedicated to the advancement of the Latino intellectual presence in the United States. IUPLR works to expand the pool of Latino scholars and leaders and increase the availability of policy-relevant Latino-focused research.

Julian Samora Research Institute (JSRI), Michigan State University

www.jsri.msu.edu/

The Julian Samora Research Institute is committed to the generation, transmission, and application of knowledge to serve the needs of Latino communities in the Midwest. To this end, it has organized a number of publication initiatives to facilitate the timely dissemination of current research and information relevant to Latinos.

Latino Issues Forum, a Public Policy and Advocacy Institute

www.lif.org/

Latino Issues Forum (LIF) is a nonprofit public policy and advocacy institute dedicated to advancing new and innovative public policy solutions for a better, more equitable, and prosperous society. Established in 1987, LIF's primary focus is on the broader issues of education, health care, the environment, telecommunications, and civic participation.

Latino Policy Coalition

www.latinopolicycoalition.org/

The Latino Policy Coalition is a national nonpartisan nonprofit consortium of the country's leading Latino research organizations and scholars.

League of United Latin American Citizens (LULAC)
www.lulac.org/
> With approximately 115,000 members throughout the United States and Puerto Rico, LULAC is the largest and oldest Hispanic Organization in the United States. LULAC advances the economic condition, educational attainment, political influence, health and civil rights of Hispanic Americans through community-based programs operating at more than 700 LULAC councils nationwide.

Mexican American Legal Defense and Education Fund (MALDEF)
www.maldef.org/
> Founded in 1968 in San Antonio, Texas, the Mexican American Legal Defense and Educational Fund (MALDEF) is the leading nonprofit Latino litigation, advocacy, and educational outreach institution in the United States. MALDEF's mission is to foster sound public policies, laws and programs to safeguard the civil rights of the 45 million Latinos living in the United States and to empower the Latino community to fully participate in our society.

Mexican American Studies & Research Center
masrc.arizona.edu/
> The Mexican American Studies & Research Center is committed to contemporary applied public policy research on Mexican Americans. As the leading public policy research center addressing issues of concern to this minority group in Arizona, the MASRC works collaboratively with key community agencies in promoting leadership and empowerment of Mexican Americans within the state and the nation.

National Association of Latino Elected Officials Educational Fund
www.naleo.org/naleoeducationalfund.html
> The National Association of Latino Elected Officials is the nation's leading organization that promotes the full participation of Latinos in the American political process, from citizenship to public service.

National Community for Latino Leadership, Inc.
www.latinoleadership.org/
> The National Community for Latino Leadership, Inc. was established to develop leaders who are (1) committed to the ethical, responsible, and accountable actions on behalf of the U.S. Latino population and the broader community; and (2) dedicated to promoting the social, cultural, and economic advancement of the Latino community.

National Council of La Raza
www.nclr.org/
> The largest national Latino civil rights and advocacy organization in the United States, NCLR works to improve opportunities for Hispanic Americans.

National Hispana Leadership Institute (NHLI)
www.nhli.org/about.htm
> The National Hispana Leadership Institute was established to develop Hispanas as ethical leaders through training, professional development, relationship building and community, and world activism.

Pew Hispanic Center
www.pewhispanic.org/
> Founded in 2001, the Pew Hispanic Center is a nonpartisan research organization supported by The Pew Charitable Trusts. Its mission is to improve understanding of the U.S. Hispanic population and to chronicle Latinos' growing impact on the entire nation.

Smithsonian Latino Center
www.latino.si.edu/
> The Smithsonian Latino Center promotes the cultural, educational, and scientific advancement of America's fastest growing population. The Center helps ensure that young Latinos become the nation's future scientists, historians, curators, and artists.

Southwest Hispanic Research Institute, UNM

www.unm.edu/~shri/

> SHRI's mission is to promote scholarly discourse, conduct teaching and research, and disseminate information concerning historical, contemporary, and emerging issues that impact Hispano people and communities.

The Caribbean Research Center, the City University of New York

www.caribbeanrescenter.org/

> The Caribbean Research Center is an integral academic component of Medgar Evers College, the City University of New York. Since its establishment in 1985, it has been funded by annual appropriations from the New York State legislature, to address the concerns, problems, and needs of the rapidly growing Caribbean segment of the metropolitan New York State population.

The Center for Mexican American Studies (CMAS), University of Texas at Austin

www.utexas.edu/depts/cmas/

> The Center for Mexican-American Studies (CMAS) focuses on Mexican-American scholarship and educational programs on the University of Texas campus, and is a national leader in teaching, research, and publications.

The Institute for Latino Studies, University of Notre Dame

www.nd.edu/~latino/

> The Institute for Latino Studies, in keeping with the distinctive mission, values, and traditions of the University of Notre Dame, promotes understanding and appreciation of the social, cultural, and religious life of U.S. Latinos through advancing research, expanding knowledge, and strengthening community.

The Latino Institute

www.thelatinoinstitute.org/The_Latino_Institute_home.html

> The Institute for Latino Studies, Research & Development, Inc. is a nonprofit entity, recognized by the federal government as a 501(c)3 organization. The Institute's main undertaking is to empower Latinos in New Jersey through access to information, advocacy, and implementation of programs that have a positive impact on the local communities.

The Mauricio Gastón Institute for Latino Community Development and Public Policy

www.gaston.umb.edu/

> The Mauricio Gastón Institute for Latino Community Development and Public Policy was established at the University of Massachusetts Boston through the initiative of Latino community activists and academicians in response to a need for improved understanding of Latino experiences and living conditions in Massachusetts. The task of the institute is to inform policy makers about issues vital to the Commonwealth's growing Latino community and to provide this community with information and analysis necessary for effective participation in public policy development.

The National Institute for Latino Policy

www.latinopolicy.org/

> The National Institute for Latino Policy (formerly the Institute for Puerto Rican Policy) was established in 1982 in New York City as a private independent nonpartisan and nonprofit policy center to address Latino issues.

The National Latino Research Center (NLRC), California State University San Marcos

www.csusm.edu/nlrc/

> The National Latino Research Center (NLRC) at California State University San Marcos specializes in applied research, training, technical assistance, and research-based services that contribute to the knowledge and understanding of the rapidly growing U.S. Latino population.

The Tomás Rivera Policy Institute (TRPI)

www.trpi.org/

Founded in 1985, the Tomás Rivera Policy Institute (TRPI) advances informed policy on key issues affecting Latino communities through objective and timely research contributing to the betterment of the nation.

William C. Velasquez Institute

www.wcvi.org/index.html

The William C. Velásquez Institute (WCVI) is a tax-exempt, nonprofit, nonpartisan public policy analysis organization chartered in 1985. The purpose of WCVI is to: conduct research aimed at improving the level of political and economic participation in Latino and other underrepresented communities; to provide information to Latino leaders relevant to the needs of their constituents; to inform the Latino leadership and public about the impact of public policies on Latinos; to inform the Latino leadership and public about political opinions and behavior of Latinos.

Webliographies/Clearinghouses

Annotated Bibliography of Children's Literature

www.clnet.sscnet.ucla.edu/Latino_Bibliography.html

This is a briefly annotated bibliography of children's literature that focuses on Latino people, history, and culture.

Celebrate Hispanic Heritage Month

www.educationworld.com/a_lesson/lesson023.shtml

Here you will find different activities and ideas to use in the classroom, such as finding geographic names derived from Hispanic origins and creating books using Spanish vocabulary. This site includes a ready-to-use worksheet of Hispanic Americans in History.

Clearinghouse on Early Education and Parenting

www.ceep.crc.uiuc.edu/index.html

The Clearinghouse on Early Education and Parenting (CEEP) is part of the Early Childhood and Parenting (ECAP) Collaborative at the University of Illinois at Urbana-Champaign. CEEP provides publications and information to the worldwide early childhood and parenting communities.

Culture Quest

www.geocities.com/Athens/Oracle/6676/quests.html

Culture Quest guides students through Hispanic culture on the Internet. Students search the Internet for information in order to complete their quest. Teachers will find suggestions, directions, and formal lesson plans to use with these "quests."

¡del Corazón! Latino Voices in American Art

www.delcorazon.si.edu/

Powerful, provocative, and contemplative, the Latino artists featured here speak through their artworks. Each work expresses the rich and varied experience of being Latino in the United States. ¡del Corazón! Latino Voices in American Art goes behind-the-scenes and uses photographs, videos, and other resources to reveal the artists and their works.

Latin American Network Information Center

www.lanic.utexas.edu

LANIC, a site sponsored by the University of Texas, provides information about the countries, economy, society and culture of Latin America. LANIC has reviewed over 12,000 sites on Latin America and provides searchable access to these.

Learn Spanish

www.studyspanish.com

Learn Spanish online. This free site provides tutorials, verb drills, and vocabulary practice. Teachers can also register to monitor student progress of tutorials.

National Register of Historic Places: Hispanic Heritage Month

www.cr.nps.gov/nr/feature/hispanic

Provides links to lesson plans that feature historic locations related to Hispanic heritage. Included are many images with accompanying questions to stimulate student interest in Hispanic heritage.

Resources for Teaching about the Americas

www.ladb.unm.edu/retanet

Sponsored by the Department of Education and compiled by the University of New Mexico with the help of secondary teachers, educational specialists, and scholars, this site provides over 65 lesson plans dealing with Latin America, the Caribbean, and culture studies.

Andanzas al Web Latino

www.lib.nmsu.edu/subject/bord/latino.html

This is an extensive list of briefly annotated links to Hispanic-related sites. Included are links to entertainment, news, culture, and political sites.

National Clearinghouse for English Language Acquisition and Language Instruction Education Programs

www.ncela.gwu.edu/

OELA's (Office of English Language Acquisition) National Clearinghouse for English Language Acquisition & Language Instruction Educational Programs (NCELA) collects, analyzes, synthesizes, and disseminates information about language instruction educational programs for English language learners and related programs.

National Clearinghouse for Paraeducator Resources

www.usc.edu/dept/education/CMMR/Clearinghouse.html

The NCPR clearinghouse is committed to the charge of providing a comprehensive repository of information, as well as a forum to further discussion, for achieving the goal of bringing talented paraeducators into the ranks of our nation's teaching force.

National Clearinghouse for Professions in Special Education

www.special-ed-careers.org/index.html

The National Clearinghouse for Professions in Special Education (NCPSE) is committed to enhancing the nation's capacity to recruit, prepare, and retain well-qualified diverse educators and related service personnel for children with disabilities.

Recommended U.S. Latino Web sites by Susan A. Vega García

www.public.iastate.edu/~savega/us_latin.htm

This Web site includes Chicano/Mexican-American, Puerto Rican, and Cuban-American Web resources, as well as sites that pertain to Salvadorans, Dominicans, Colombians, Guatemalans, and other Latinos residing in the United States.

SearchLatino.com

www.searchlatino.com

This Web site provides links to various educational resources for the Latino community.

The New York Latino Research Clearinghouse

www.tc.columbia.edu/latinoresearch/

The New York Latino Research Clearinghouse has been created to disseminate research on Latinos in New York State and elsewhere. It gathers and organizes the most recent research reports, academic papers, and policy news relating to the Latino populations of the United States.

Other Web Resources

Abya Yala Net
www.abyayala.nativeweb.org/
> This site presents information on Indigenous peoples in Mexico, Central, and South America.

Brooklyn Expedition
www.brooklynexpedition.org/latin/
> The Brooklyn Expedition Web site is a collaborative project of the Brooklyn Children's Museum, the Brooklyn Museum of Art, and the Brooklyn Public Library. The site introduces users to three "themes." These are Latin America, Structures, and Brooklyn. Latin America focuses on the arts, cultures, and natural worlds of Mexico and South America from pre-Columbian times to today. Structures explores the shared characteristics among animal skeletons and homes, architecture, art forms, and information cataloguing systems. Brooklyn celebrates the history and culture of this unique borough. Africa is scheduled to launch at a later date and will use art to introduce the diverse cultures of the continent.

Hispanic Scholarship Fund
www.hsf.net/
> HSF has had an impact on the undereducation of the Hispanic community by providing clear solutions. HSF provides financial support for Latinos going to college and educates students and families about the resources available for paying for college outside of HSF.

Library of Congress Handbook of Latin American Studies
www.lcweb2.loc.gov/hlas/
> The *Handbook* is a bibliography on Latin America consisting of works selected and annotated by scholars. Edited by the Hispanic Division of the Library of Congress, the multidisciplinary *Handbook* alternates annually between the social sciences and the humanities. Each year, more than 130 academics from around the world choose over 5,000 works for inclusion in the *Handbook*. Continuously published since 1936, the *Handbook* offers Latin Americanists an essential guide to available resources.

Library of Congress Hispanic Reading Room
www.loc.gov/rr/hispanic/
> In 1927, Archer M. Huntington, founder of the Hispanic Society of America, established an endowment fund in his name, the first of several important donations for Hispanic studies at the Library of Congress. The second "area studies division" to be founded by the Library, in 1939 the Hispanic Division was established to acquire Luso-Hispanic materials in a systematic fashion. In that same year, the division's reading room, the "Hispanic Society Reading Room," named after the New York Hispanic Society of America, was inaugurated to service the Library's growing Luso-Hispanic collections.

Scholarships for Hispanics
www.scholarshipsforhispanics.org/
> The Scholarships for Hispanics was designed to build a stronger American community, particularly among those of Hispanic origin, by promoting professionalism in the publications industry; by enhancing the skills of all those involved in the industry, particularly publishers, advertising, and marketing professionals, graphic designers, photographers, Web masters, layout and circulation management, and journalists.

The Borderlands Encyclopedia, the University of Texas at El Paso
www.utep.edu/border/
> This Web site is a digital educational resource on contemporary United States–México border issues.

VivirLatino

www.vivirlatino.com/

VivirLatino is a daily publication developed by Blogs Media, featuring all the latest in Latino style, products, entertainment, culture, and politics created for the diverse and influential Latino and Latina community in the United States.

Zona Latina

www.zonalatina.com/

This Web site provides links to various media resources from across Latin America.

Note

1. The author(s) and editor(s) do not necessarily endorse the reference entries in this chapter; they are listed for informational purposes only. Most descriptions have been gathered conducting extensive electronic searches with key words related to these topics and are taken directly from these online sites in order to provide true and clearer descriptions. In order to honor the words chosen to describe themselves and others, each overview incorporates the terms and language utilized (such as Latino/a, Hispanic, Chicano, etc.) on the individual sites.

44 Libraries/Museums/Galleries

Belinda Treviño Schouten
Our Lady of the Lake University

**Libraries/ Museums/Galleries: Collections, Archives,
Permanent Exhibitions, and more.**[1]

Libraries

Bancroft Library: Latin Americana Collection, University of California, Berkeley
www.bancroft.berkeley.edu/collections/latinamericana.html
   The Bancroft Collection of Latin American manuscripts, imprints, newspapers, broadsides, and pamphlets has grown into one of the world's great repositories for historical and contemporary research on México and Central America. As a specialized area collection, the collection contains all forms of primary and secondary sources, including all forms of printed material, microfilm of related records from other repositories, bibliographical and reference sources, and critical editions of major historical texts.

Benson Latin American Collection, University of Texas at Austin
www.lib.utexas.edu/benson/
   The Nettie Lee Benson Latin American Collection, a unit of the University of Texas Libraries, is a specialized research library focusing on materials from and about Latin America, and on materials relating to Latinos in the United States. The Benson Collection contains over 970,000 books, periodicals, pamphlets, and microforms; 4,000 linear feet of manuscripts; 19,000 maps; 11,500 broadsides; 93,500 photographs; and 50,000 items in a variety of other media (sound recordings, drawings, videotapes and cassettes, slides, transparencies, posters, memorabilia, and electronic media). Periodical titles are estimated at over 40,000 with 8,000 currently received titles and over 3,000 newspaper titles. Initially endowed with a superb collection of rare books and manuscripts relating to Mexico, the Benson Collection now maintains important holdings for all countries of Latin America with special concentrations on the countries of the Río de la Plata, Brazil, Chile, Peru, and Central America. The Mexican American Library Program, a department of the collection established in 1974, has gathered extensive research materials in all subject areas related to the U.S. Southwest and Latino culture in the United States. In sum, the book collection of the Benson Collection represents approximately 10% of all of the volumes in the University of Texas Libraries, the fifth largest academic library in the United States. While the purchase of private libraries laid the foundation for the Benson Collection, the acquisition of current publications is now the major factor in its growth. Researchers from the United States and abroad have been attracted to this remarkable resource through the last eight decades, coming to consult materials accumulated from all parts of the world, in many languages, dating from the 15th century to the present.

Boeckmann Center for Iberian and Latin American Studies, University of Southern California

www.usc.edu/libraries/archives/arc/libraries/boeckmann/index.html

Unique on the West Coast, the Boeckmann Center for Iberian and Latin American Studies was established in 1985. The Boeckmann Center serves as a link between the library's collections and services and the scholarly activities of faculty and students in the areas of Iberian, Latin American, and Chicano/Latino studies. The Center's materials include an 80,000 volume and several distinguished but smaller book collections, such as the L. A. Murillo Cervantes Collection, the Radell Cuban Collection, the Lorente Cuban Exiles Studies Collection, South American books and pamphlets, archival materials of the Central American Research Institute (CARIN) Collection, and the Cuban California Archive. The Collection achieves its distinction by virtue of the geographical focus, the historical and chronological coverage, and the interdisciplinary and multilingual nature of its holding.

Center for Southwest Research and Special Collections, University of New Mexico

www.elibrary.unm.edu/cswr/

The Center specializes in subjects relating to New Mexico, the Southwestern United States, Mexico, and Latin America, as well as rare books from around the world, the holdings are made up of the following collections: architectural archives, books and periodicals, pictorial collections, manuscripts, music archives, and University archives.

César E. Chávez Collection, Michigan State University

www.lib.msu.edu/coll/main/chavez/

The César E. Chávez Collection is an interdisciplinary browsing collection consisting of titles in a variety of formats, research levels, and locations on Chicano and Boricua Studies. The collection is representative of César's life. It reflects his commitment to unions and labor, nonviolence, truth, respect, and an appreciation of diversity, education, and his cultura.

Chicano Research Collection, Arizona State University

www.asu.edu/lib/archives/chicano.htm

The Chicano Research Collection is part of the Department of Archives and Manuscripts, which includes the Arizona Collection, the University Archives, the Benedict Visual Literacy Collection, and the Labriola National American Indian Data Center. The collection seeks to acquire and strengthen holding of primary resources relevant to Mexican Americans in the Southwest in general, and in Arizona in particular, and to continue to make the material available to scholars, researchers, and students nationwide. The Chicano Research Collection still collects, houses, and maintains a solid representation of Mexican-American or Chicano thought, expression, and research on Arizona's largest ethnic group, the Mexican American.

Chicano Studies Research Center Library, University of California, Los Angeles

www.chicano.ucla.edu/library/default.asp

The Chicano Studies Research Center Library was established in 1969 to support the development of scholarship, teaching, and research in Chicano Studies at UCLA. The library serves the field worldwide through a variety of information resources: print materials, digital resources, and archival holdings, as well as through reference assistance and bibliographic instruction. It also has an extensive archive of Mexican-American music.

Cuban Heritage Collection, University of Miami

www.library.miami.edu/search/special/special_collections.html

The Cuban Heritage Collection (CHC) collects and preserves primary and secondary source materials pertaining to the history of Cuba from its discovery to the present. The CHC is also a repository of materials on Cuban exiles and Cuban Americans and their impact on the growth and development of many parts of the United States, including the state of Florida and Miami-Dade County. Holdings include many formats such as books, periodicals, maps, posters, and photographs.

Donald C. Davidson: Department of Special Collections, University of California, Santa Barbara

www.library.ucsb.edu/speccoll/collections/cema/index.html

The California Ethnic and Multicultural Archive, also known as CEMA, is a division of the Special Collections Department of the University Libraries at the University of California, Santa Barbara. CEMA is a permanent program that advances scholarship in ethnic studies through its varied collections of primary research materials. These unique collections document the lives and activities of African Americans, Asian/Pacific Americans, Chicanos/Latinos, and Native Americans in California. The collections represent the cultural, artistic, ethnic, and racial diversity that characterizes the state's population. Its materials are widely used not only by scholars, but also in K-12 classrooms and museum exhibitions. Organizations and individuals have committed to establishing personal papers and archival materials for preservation and to be made accessible for research and study.

Duke University—University of North Carolina at Chapel Hill Libraries

www.library.duke.edu/research/subject/guides/lastudies/dukeunclibrariescollections.html

Current Duke holdings on Latin America and the Caribbean total approximately 300,000 volumes, 3,700 serials, 400 currently received journals, and 10 newspapers. Duke subscribes to six databases focused exclusively on Latin America and the Caribbean. These include strong, complementary collections in social sciences and literature which emphasize political and institutional history, labor history, political economy, political humor, sociology, women's studies, demography, anthropology and archeology, and international and inter-American relations. In literature there is a broad representation of the belles-lettres of all the Latin American countries. Other significant collections include national and international statistics, philosophy, folklore, cultural studies, maps, film, sustainable development, and rare books and manuscripts.

George A. Smathers Libraries, University of Florida

www.hrc.utexas.edu/collections/guide/latin/

University of Florida's Latin American Collection contains approximately 450,000 volumes, 1,100 current/active serial titles, some 50,000 microforms, and a growing amount of computer-based information and access. The Latin American Collection itself is one of a small number in the United States that is housed separately and that maintains its own reading room and reference services. These quarters have been upgraded by the University of Florida with state and private money, and these improvements have resulted in greatly enhanced service capabilities for Latin American researchers.

Harry Ransom, University of Texas at Austin

www.hrc.utexas.edu/collections/guide/latin/

The Ransom Center offers a rich variety of materials in the field of Latin American studies. Collections include manuscripts, rare books, artifacts, artwork, and photography from noted Latin American artists, authors, and cultural figures.

Hillman Library, University of Pittsburgh

www.library.pitt.edu/libraries/latam/latam.html

The Eduardo Lozano Latin American Collection contains extensive files, including catalogs and addresses, of publishers and vendors of Latin American materials. One of the sources for the collecting of Latin American materials has been the vast exchange program. The library maintains exchange agreements with other libraries, research centers, universities, and governmental institutions all over the world.

Hispanic Heritage Resources, Indiana University, Bloomington
www.libraries.iub.edu/index.php?pageId=3524

Indiana University documents the cultures and peoples of North America, South America, Central America, and the Caribbean with a deep and varied collection of informational resources. The library also has an extensive resource list for the Caribbean, Cuba, Mexican Americans, Puerto Rico, and South America which supports Latin American and Caribbean Studies, Chicano-Riqueno Studies and Religious Studies.

Hispanic Reading Room, Library of Congress
www.loc.gov/rr/hispanic/hispdiv.html

The Hispanic Society Reading Room, named after the New York Hispanic Society of America, was inaugurated to service the Library's growing Luso-Hispanic collections. Although primary emphasis has always been the acquisition of current materials and government documents the Hispanic Division has also acquired a rich collection of rare items. The Division was instrumental in acquiring significant gifts of manuscripts, music scores, and posters, photographs, and films. It made efforts to develop special groups of materials such as collecting folk music from San Antonio, Texas, and pioneering the recording of Hispanic poets. Through the generosity of countless donors, the Library of Congress has amassed the world's finest collection on the history and culture of Latin America, Iberia, and the Caribbean.

Howard-Tilton Memorial Library: Latin American Library, Tulane University, New Orleans
www.lal.tulane.edu/

The Latin American Library is among the world's foremost collections in Latin American archaeology, anthropology, history, literature, literary criticism, cultural studies, linguistics, art, architecture, film, women's studies, economics, and many other subject areas. The collection is comprised of more than 420,000 volumes, including over 500 current periodical subscriptions, and is one of the most comprehensive of its kind, including materials from the contact period to the present. It is one of only three stand-alone Latin American research collections in U.S. universities.

Ibero-Amerikanisches Institut, Preussischer Kulturbesitz
www.iai.spk-berlin.de/en/home.html

The Ibero-American Institute (IAI) is an interdisciplinary center for academic and cultural exchange between Germany and Latin America, the Caribbean, Spain, and Portugal. It is home to the largest specialist library in Europe for the Ibero-American region. It is also a place of knowledge production, exchange, and cultural translation. Combining an information center, a research center, and a cultural center, the IAI is both a platform for cooperation and a catalyst for intercultural and transcultural dialog. The IAI was founded in 1930 and is today located in the Berlin Kulturforum complex on Potsdamer Strasse. It has been part of the Stiftung Preussischer Kulturbesitz (Prussian Cultural Heritage Foundation) since 1962.

John Carter Brown Library, Brown University
www.brown.edu/Facilities/John_Carter_Brown_Library/index.html

The John Carter Brown Library is an independently administered and funded center for advanced research in history and the humanities, founded in 1846 and located at Brown University since 1901. Housed within the Library's walls is an internationally renowned, constantly growing collection of primary historical sources pertaining to the Americas, both North and South, before ca. 1825. For 150 years the Library has served scholars from all over the United States and abroad.

Latin American Collection, Yale University
www.library.yale.edu/humanities/latinamerican/collection.html

The Latin American Collection at Yale University is one of the foremost collections in the United States, containing a wealth of research material and offering a variety of research opportunities for Latin American studies. The collecting policy is to acquire the important editorial production in the fields of the humanities and social sciences published in South America, Mexico, Central America, and the Caribbean. Within this policy of developing a general, area wide collection, special strengths have resulted from the acquisition of important collections during the past 100 years.

Latin American and Iberian Studies, Columbia University

www.columbia.edu/cu/lweb/indiv/latam/about.html

The Latin American collection contains over 300,000 volumes and 1,500 serial titles, along with manuscripts, oral histories, maps, prints, microform materials, and a variety of electronic resources. The Library collects materials published in or about Latin America across many disciplines. The collection is strong in coverage of Mexico, Brazil, and the countries of the Southern Cone. Subject strengths include architecture, economic development, history, languages and literature, political science, sociology, and anthropology. Materials are acquired in English, Spanish, and Portuguese, and in other European and indigenous Latin American languages.

New Mexico State University Library—Andanzas al Web Latino

www.lib.nmsu.edu/subject/bord/latino.html

Andanzas al Web Latino offers many resources and Web links to sites that assist students and the community in finding information on Latinos.

San Antonio Public Library—Latino Collection

www.sat.lib.tx.us/Latino/latinoinfo.htm

The Latino Collection is a cultural and educational resource that chronicles and celebrates the literature, heritage, and contemporary life of Latinos in the United States. The majority of these works deal with the Mexican-American or Chicano experience, but materials about Puerto Rican, Cuban-American, and other Latin American heritages are also included in the collection. The collection was established in 1996 and currently includes more than 5,000 volumes.

San Jose Library: Chicano Resource Center, San Jose State University Library, and San Jose Public Libraries

www.sjlibrary.org/research/special/chc/chicano_index.htm

The Chicano Resource provide a single focus for books, periodicals, reference tools, pamphlets, and clippings relating to Mexican American history, culture, and community. The Center also has a Chicano Oral History Project, a Chicano History of San Jose, and other programs related to Chicano communities and scholarship.

Stanford University Library

www-sul.stanford.edu/depts/hasrg/latinam/index.html

Green Library's main holdings exceed 350,000 volumes on Latin America and several thousand periodicals principally in the humanities and social sciences. The historical strength of the collection at Stanford has been on 19th and 20th century Mexico and Brazil. In recent years acquisition of the Fernando Alegría and other collections have given Stanford unique holdings on Chilean Literature and Culture.

Sutro Library: Mexicana Collection, University of California, Berkeley

www.bancroft.berkeley.edu/collections/latinamericana.html

The Sutro Mexican Collection was acquired by Adolph Sutro through the purchase of the entire stock of the Librería Abadiano in Mexico City in 1889. The oldest bookshop in Mexico at the time, the Abadiano stock had accumulated since 1753. The entire Sutro Library was donated to the California State Library by his heirs in 1913. The Mexicana Collection includes material in the following formats and subject areas: pamphlets, periodicals, official decrees and broadsides, circulars and annual reports, laws and decrees, the church and religion, manuscripts, history, biography, and travel, the Tlatelolco Library, graphic arts, lithography, calendars, photographs, maps, and atlases.

Widener Library, Harvard University

www.hcl.harvard.edu/libraries/widener/collections/latinam_sp_port.html

The collection includes materials from Latin America and the Caribbean, Spain, Portugal, and Macau in the humanities and social sciences. While most of these materials are in Spanish or Portuguese, our acquisitions include publications in English, French, and Dutch (from the Caribbean), various indigenous languages, and regional languages and dialects of Spain such as Catalan, Galician, and Basque.

Museums

Art Museum of the Americas

www.museum.oas.org/index.html

With its unique regional focus, the Art Museum of the Americas serves as an important repository for information on art from Latin America and the Caribbean. Dedicated to the arts, the museum preserves, studies, and exhibits works by outstanding artists and carries out other activities of an educational nature which increase understanding and appreciation of these cultures. The museum's permanent collection of 20th century Latin American and Caribbean art is one of the most important collections of its kind in the United States. The museum also maintains a regular schedule of special Latin American art exhibits and related educational programs.

Arte Latino, Smithsonian American Art Museum

www.americanart.si.edu/collections/exhibits/t2go/1la/

Arte Latino celebrates the vitality of Latino art traditions and innovations from the 18th through the 20th century. The art is based on a series of eight exhibitions from the Smithsonian American Art Museum which toured the nation commemorating Treasures to Go.

El Museo del Barrio

www.elmuseo.org/

The mission of El Museo del Barrio is to present and preserve the art and culture of Puerto Ricans and all Latin Americans in the United States. Through its extensive collections, varied exhibitions and publications, bilingual public programs, educational activities, festivals, and special events, El Museo educates its diverse public in the richness of Caribbean and Latin American arts and cultural history. By introducing young people to its cultural heritage El Museo is creating the next generation of museum-goers, while satisfying the growing interest in Caribbean and Latin American art of a broad nation and international audience.

El Museo Latino

www.elmuseolatino.org/

The first Latino Art and History Museum, as well as Cultural Center in the Midwest, this museum provides many opportunities for the local communities. In conjunction to the exhibits, El Museo Latino develops educational programs that include lectures, slide presentations, films, art classes, workshops, demonstrations, art history classes, gallery talks, guided visits, and dance classes.

Hispanic Society of America Museum and Library

www.hispanicsociety.org/

The Society has a free museum and reference library that provide materials for the study of the arts and cultures of Spain, Portugal, and Latin America.

Jack S. Blanton Museum, University of Texas at Austin

www.blantonmuseum.org/works_of_art/collections/latin_american/index.cfm

The Blanton Museum collections of Latin American art features over 2,000 works and reflects the enormous diversity of artistic tradition in the region, with particular strengths in Mexican graphics of the early 20th century, and post-1970s paintings and drawings from South

America. More than 600 artists from Mexico, South and Central America, and the Caribbean are represented in the collection. The collection is one of the oldest, largest, and most comprehensive collections of Latin American art in the country.

Latino Art Museum

www.lamoa.net/

The Latino Art Museum is a nonprofit organization created to promote the works of talented Latin American contemporary artists living in the United States and instill a sense of appreciation for Latino art in the minds and hearts of children and adults. The museum hosts an array of Latin American Art through its permanent collection, exhibitions, special events, art auction, and art education/open studio.

Latino Museum of History, Art, and Culture

www.thelatinomuseum.com/

The Latino Museum is committed to building a broader understanding of the rich history of Latino art and to increasing public awareness of outstanding works of contemporary Latino artists. Through their various outreach programs and educational services, they strive to encourage young people to develop their sensitivity to art in its many forms and to pursue their creative aspirations. The museum holds a unique collection of work from emerging and established contemporary Mexican, Latino and Chicano artists working and living in the United States as well as throughout Central and South America.

Mexican Museum

www.mexicanmuseum.org/

The Mexican Museum holds a unique collection of over 12,000 spectacular objects representing thousands of years of Mexican art and culture within the Americas. The Museum's permanent collection includes five areas: Pre-Conquest, Colonial, Popular, Modern and Contemporary Mexican and Latino, and Chicano Art. The Museum also has an impressive number of rare books and a growing collection of Latin American art.

Mexic-Arte Museum

www.mexic-artemuseum.org/

Mexic-Arte Museum is dedicated to enriching the community through outreach education programs and exhibitions about traditional and contemporary Mexican, Latino, and Latin American art and culture. Since its founding in 1984, Mexic-Arte Museum has been designated as the Official Mexican and Mexican American Fine Art Museum of Texas by the 78th Legislature of the State of Texas.

Michael C. Carlos Museum, Emory University

www.carlos.emory.edu/ancient-american-art/

The Carlos Museum's collection of art of the ancient Americas is substantial, consisting of more than 2,300 pieces. The Museum is fortunate in the breadth and depth of the collection as a whole. All three principal cultural centers of the Americas are represented: Mesoamerica, Central America, and the Andes. Most of the important art-producing cultures—from the Maya and Aztec to the Chavin to the Inca—can be appreciated during a visit to the permanent collection galleries. The Carlos Museum's collections are unusually strong in ancient Costa Rica, featuring over 600 works from all periods.

Museum of Latin American Art (MOLAA)

www.molaa.org/

MOLAA's mission is to educate the public about contemporary Latin American fine art (by artists who have lived and worked in Latin America since World War II) through the presentation of a significant permanent collection, dynamic exhibitions, and related cultural and educational programs.

Museum of Latin International Folk Art, New Mexico Department of Cultural Affairs

www.internationalfolkart.org/

The Museum has a collection of more than 135,000 artifacts which form the basis for exhibitions in four distinct wings: Bartlett, Girard, Hispanic Heritage, and Neutrogena. The Hispanic Heritage Wing of the Museum of Latin International Folk Art is one of the few museum wings in the United States which is devoted to the art and heritage of Hispanic/ Latino cultures.

Nelson A. Rockefeller Center for Latin American Art, San Antonio Museum of Art

www.samuseum.org/collections/collection.php

The San Antonio Museum of Art has one of the most comprehensive collections of Latin American art in the United States. Housed in the Nelson A. Rockefeller center for Latin American Art, which opened to the public in 1988, the Center offers an overview of over 3,000 years of artistic expression from Mexico, Central and South America, and many countries in the Caribbean.

Smithsonian Latino Center

www.latino.si.edu/

The Smithsonian Latino Center promotes the cultural, educational, and scientific advancement of America's fastest growing population. The Center helps to ensure that young Latinos become the nation's future scientists, historians, curators, and artists.

Galleries

Avenue 50 Studio, Inc.

www.avenue50studio.com/index.shtml

Avenue 50 Studio, Inc. is an arts presentation organization grounded in Latino/Chicano culture. Their monthly shows principally exhibit artists of color who display a high quality of work, and who have not been represented in mainstream galleries. They seek to build bridges of cultural understanding through artistic expressions. Using content-driven art to educate and to stimulate intercultural understanding, they build relationships and collaborations with artists and communities.

Casa de la Cultura, Center for Latino Arts

www.avenue50studio.com/index.shtml

The Gallery at Casa de la Cultura is dedicated exclusively to promoting local, national, and international Latino artists. From installations of photography and sculpture to painting, they present established and upcoming artists, diverse points of view and aesthetics.

Centro Cultural De La Raza

www.sananto.org/

The Centro's mission is to create, preserve, promote and educate about Chicano, Mexicano, Latino, and Indigenous art and culture. The Centro's permanent collection features a variety of media including oil, acrylic, watercolors, prints, poster art, photography, and 3-dimensional work.

Chicano Humanities & Arts Council (CHAC)

www.chacweb.org/page/28

The Chicano Humanities & Arts Council (CHAC) was founded in 1978 by a group of visual and performing artists. The organization was established as a place where Chicano/Latino artists were provided with a venue to explore visual and performance art and promote and preserve the Chicano/Latino culture through the expression of the arts.

Galería de la Raza

www.galeriadelaraza.org/

The mission of the Galería de la Raza is to foster public awareness and appreciation of Chicano/Latino art and culture. It is an interdisciplinary space for art, thought, and activism. The Galería organizes art exhibitions, multimedia presentations, performances and spoken word events, screenings, computer-generated murals, and educational activities.

Grady Alexis Gallery, El Taller Latino Americano/The Latin American Workshop

www.tallerlatino.org/Gallery.html

El Taller Latino Americano (The Latin American Workshop) is a nonprofit arts and education organization that was founded in New York City in 1979 to bridge the distance between Latin Americans and North Americans through the language of art and the art of language. Their Art Gallery features works of well-known established artists, as well as emerging artists who are exhibiting for the first time.

Hispanic Research Center Art Gallery, Arizona State University

www.asu.edu/clas/hrc/art/ArtGal.html

The purpose of the Hispanic Research Center Art Gallery is to provide for a worldwide audience a pictorial panorama of the varied dimensions of Hispanic Art. The art viewer can appreciate a variety of styles highlighting symbols, images, and color. Such styles include campesina, folkloric, traditional, contemporary Chicano/Latino, and magic realism.

La Peña Media Gallery

www.lapena.org/index.php?s=19

La Peña provides opportunities for artists to share diverse cultural traditions, to create and perform their work, and to support and interface with diverse social movements. The Media Gallery is part of a vibrant community cultural center that promotes peace, social justice, and cultural understanding through the arts, education, and social action.

Latina/o Art Community

www.latinoartcommunity.org/community/LAC.html

A worldwide Web site for Latina/o art.

Latino Arts Inc. Gallery

www.latinoartsinc.org/display/router.asp?docid=115

Latino Arts, Inc. Gallery is dedicated to showcasing the work of Hispanic and Latin American artists, ranging from indigenous craftspeople to contemporary masters of the avant garde.

Latino Legends in Sports Multimedia Gallery

www.latinosportslegends.com/multimedia_gallery.htm

A sports media company created to pay tribute to and honor superstar and legendary Latino athletes. Their goal is to educate and inform people of all cultures about the great achievements many Latin Americans have made in the world of sports. With articles written in English and Spanish this site provides a valuable learning tool for English-speaking Americans and Spanish speakers worldwide.

Latino Virtual Gallery, Smithsonian Center for Latino Initiatives

www.latino.si.edu/virtualgallery/LVGhome.html

The Virtual Gallery is an electronic virtual environment. It invites the viewer to explore and discover. It provides a dynamic interactive space for both the creators of the exhibitions and the Internet visitor. The intent of the Gallery is to provide unique experiences, transmit emotions, and provoke reflection.

Sister Karen Boccalero's Gallerias Otra Vez, Self Help Graphics and Art

www.selfhelpgraphics.com/gallery.php

Self Help Graphics is a nationally recognized center for Latino arts that develops and nurtures artists in printmaking. It seeks to advance Latino art broadly through programming, exhibitions, and outreach to diverse audiences and to engage young and emerging artists.

The Gallerias consist of the Brooklyn Avenue Gallery, the East Side Project Gallery, Estudio Regeneracion, and the Print Room Gallery.

Social and Public Art Resource Center (SPARC)

www.sparcmurals.org/sparcone/index.php?option=com_frontpage&Itemid=1

SPARC is an arts center that produces, preserves, and conducts educational programs about community based public art works. The Center has three main areas of activity: production, education, and preservation. It is particularly committed to producing and promoting work that reflects the lives and concerns of America's ethnically and economically diverse populations: including women, the working poor, youth, the elderly and newly arrived immigrant communities.

Other Online Resources

Chicano, Hispano, Latino Program (CHIPOTLE), University of New Mexico

www.repository.unm.edu/dspace/handle/1928/2502

The Chicano, Hispano, Latino Program (CHIPOTLE) of the University Libraries at the University of New Mexico, created in 2005, serves the information, collections, and knowledge discovery needs of UNM programs, students, faculty, and the community at large. CHIPOTLE provides singular assistance to learn how to use the library and acquire research skills. They are especially committed to promoting those proficiencies required for successful academic pursuits and preparation for being well-informed citizens, leaders, and lifelong learners. The collections in their community document the work of faculty research and outreach activities.

Corridos Sin Fronteras, Smithsonian Institution of Traveling Exhibition Service

www.corridos.org/

A traveling exhibition and educational Web site celebrating the style of narrative song known as corridos.

¡Del Corazon! Latino Voices in American Art, Smithsonian American Art Museum

www.americanart.si.edu/education/corazon/index.cfm

This Web site is dedicated to expressing the rich and varied experience of being Latino in the United States through the use of art. Powerful, provocative, and contemplative, the Latino artists featured speak through their artworks.

Guadalupe Cultural Arts Center

www.guadalupeculturalarts.org/

The Guadalupe Cultural Arts Center is the largest community based multidisciplinary organization in the United States. The mission of the Center is to preserve, promote, and develop the arts and culture of the Chicano/Latino/Native American peoples for all ages and background through public and educational programming in six disciplines: dance, literature, media arts, theatre arts, visual arts, and Xicano music.

Hispano Music and Culture of the Northern Rio Grande: The Juan B. Rael Collection, The American Folklife Center, Library of Congress

www.memory.loc.gov/ammem/rghtml/rghome.html

The Library of Congress presents these documents as part of the record of the past in online presentation of a multiformat ethnographic field collection documenting religious and secular music of Spanish-speaking residents of rural Northern New Mexico and Southern Colorado. In 1940, Juan Bautista Rael of Stanford University, a native of Arroyo Hondo, New Mexico, used disc recording equipment supplied by the Archive of American Folk Song (now the Archive of Folk Culture, American Folklife Center) to document *alabados* (hymns), folk drama, wedding songs, and dance tunes. The recordings included in the Archive of Folk Culture collection were made in Alamosa, Manassa, and Antonito, Colorado, and in Cerro and Arroyo Hondo, New Mexico. In addition to these recordings, the collection includes manuscript materials and publications authored by Rael which provide insight into the rich musical heritage and cultural traditions of this region.

San Anto Cultural Arts

www.sananto.org/

It is the mission of the San Anto Cultural Arts to utilize arts as a vehicle to foster human and community development.

U.S. Latino and Latino World War II Oral History Project, the University of Texas at Austin

www.lib.utexas.edu/ww2latinos/

The purpose of this site is to foster a greater awareness of contributions made by Latinos and Latinas during World War II. On the site there are thousands of stories, thousands of photos, and oral history training videos. World War II was a turning point for the United States, and the war had an impact on U.S. Latinos just as much as other groups. It has been estimated that anywhere from 250,000 to as many as 750,000 Latinos and Latinas served in the armed forced during World War II.

Note

1. The author(s) and editor(s) do not necessarily endorse the reference entries in this chapter; they are listed for informational purposes only. Most descriptions have been gathered conducting extensive electronic searches with key words related to these topics and are taken directly from these online sites in order to provide true and clearer descriptions. In order to honor the words chosen to describe themselves and others, each overview incorporates the terms and language utilized (such as Latino/a, Hispanic, Chicano, etc.) on the individual sites.

45 Nonprint Media

Grisel Y. Acosta

University of Texas at San Antonio

Nonprint Media: Television Programming, Recordings, Motion Pictures, Radio Programming, and more.[1]

Web sites

AfroCubaWeb, 1997–2008
www.afrocubaweb.com/
   Countless articles, links to conferences, literature, and film.
Carrillo, Karen Juanita, and Lisa J. Scott, Afropresencia, 2008
www.afropresencia.com/index.html
   The Web site is meant to cover issues in "the Black Americas." Articles can be found on Blacks in the U.S., South American and the Caribbean.
      There are also good links.
Centro de Estudios Puertorriqueños, Hunter College/The City University of New York, 2007
www.centropr.org/home.html

Links to Grants, Articles, and Research Tools

"Education Index," *National Geographic*, **1996–2008**
www.nationalgeographic.com/siteindex/education.html
   International resources are found at the lesson plan links.
Facets Multimedia, 2008
www.facets.org/asticat
   One of the most comprehensive libraries of international film can be found here. The Chicago-based entity regularly stocks films that were shown at the Chicago International Latino Film Festival and will rent to members all over the world.
Fernandez, Eugenio, Revista Quilombo, 2005–2008
www.revistaquilombo.com.ar/
   Named after the Afro-Brazilian film, this Spanish-language Web site is an online version of the print magazine. It has articles on music, political figures, and cultural artifacts.
Grassian, Esther, "Thinking Critically about World Wide Web Resources"
UCLA College Library, June 2006
www.library.ucla.edu/college/help/critical/
   This is a good tool to use when choosing which Web sites are the most reliable.
Infomine: Scholarly Internet Resource Collections, 1994–2008
www.infomine.ucr.edu/
   This search engine can provide good statistics on Latino health, housing, and income.

Hispanic Online, 2008

www.hol.hispaniconline.com/

> Even though the Web site is mostly Cuban-centered, it still has some good links to articles on issues that affect all Latinos.

"Hispanic Population of the United States," U.S. Census Bureau, February 12, 2008

www.census.gov/population/www/socdemo/hispanic/hispanic.htm

Links to Current and Past Statistics

"Hispanic Reading Room," The Library of Congress, February 20, 2008

www.loc.gov/rr/hispanic/

Hispanic Scholarship Fund, 2007

www.hsf.net/

> Includes donor information and successes of fellows.

Las Culturas, 2004–2008

www.lasculturas.com

> A rich library of Latino leaders and articles about Latino issues. Historical figures can be accessed through a hard to get to link found here: www.lasculturas.com/lib/libFamosos.php

"Latino page" Independent Lens, 2008

www.pbs.org/independentlens/latino.html

> Several documentaries on relevant Latino issues.

Latino Public Broadcasting, 2003–2008

www.lpbp.org/index.html

> Press releases about new documentaries and national events are found here.

"Latino Video page" Media Resources Center, UCLA-Berkeley, April 21, 2008

www.lib.berkeley.edu/MRC/LatinoVid.html

> Comprehensive listings of Latino film and links.

Pew Hispanic Center, 2008

www.pewhispanic.org/

> Many other pages have a link to this page. Unparalleled statistics and reports on Latinos in the United States.

"Researching Multicultural Resources on the World Wide Web," RIT Libraries, The Rochester Institute of Technology, 2003

www.wally.rit.edu/depts/ref/research/multi.html

> This Web site has some of the most important Latino links that can be found on the Web, including the Hispanic American Chamber of Commerce, the National Council of La Raza, and the Pew Hispanic Center, among others. It also has multicultural links and a list of search engines that allow better keyword searches.

Robinson, Lori, Vida Afro-Latina, 2008

www.vidaafrolatina.com/Home_Page.html

> This Web site has many articles, national events, and other Afro-Latino resources.

"Smithsonian Latino Center," Smithsonian Institute, 2006

www.latino.si.edu/

> Lesson plans and a wealth of information on Latino culture and people.

The Congressional Hispanic Caucus Institute, 2008

www.chci.org/

> This Web site has scholarships, educational publications, and educational resources.

The National Hispanic Media Coalition, 2008
www.nhmc.org/
   Links to cultural programs throughout the U.S. can be found on this Web site.
Vega-García, Susan A., "Recommended U.S. Latino Web sites, Diversity and Ethnic Studies,"
Iowa State University, June 3, 2005
www.public.iastate.edu/~savega/us_latin.htm
   Tons of sites and updates on sites that have moved.
Virtual Boricua, 2008
www.virtualboricua.org/
   A large directory of Puerto Rican/Boricua performers, activists and writers. Poetry and news
   articles are updated frequently.

Motion Pictures/Documentaries

A Day Without a Mexican, Dir. Sergio Arau. Xenon, 2004
   The feature film supposes what Los Angeles would be like if all Mexican and Mexican-
   American workers disappeared.
A Language of Passion; Un Lenguage de Pasión, Dir. Patricia Cunliffe, Joie de Vivre Produc-
tions, 2004
   Latino artists in California are interviewed.
Americanos: Latino Life in the United States, Dir. Susan Todd and Andrew Young, Prod. Edward
James Olmos, BAK Productions, 2000
   Guillermo Gómez Peña, Robert "El Vez" López, Tito Puente, and Crissy Guerrero are among
   those featured.
Beyond the Screams/Mas Alla De Los Gritos, Dir. Martin Sorrondeguy, Lengua Armada Video
Data Bank, 1999
   A documentary on the Los Angeles Latino punk scene from 1976 to 1990. Bands like the
   Plugz and Los Crudos are included.
Botín de Guerra/Spoils of War, Dir. David Blaustein, Luis Alberto Asurey, and Luisa Irene
Ickowicz, Zafra Difusión, S.A., 2000
   Winner of several international film festivals, the film covers the Desaparecidos in Argentina
   during the years 1976 to 1983. Some of the reunions between the missing children and their
   relatives are shown in the film.
Bronx Burning, Dir. Edwin Pagan, Pagan-Images, 2008
   "Fire-for-hire" insurance fraud crime nearly destroys the South Bronx and displaces its resi-
   dents, but they reclaim it.
Chalino Sanchez: Una Vida de Peligros, Dir. Henry Zakka, Uno Productions, 2004
   The life and death of the Mexican singer who is credited with creating the "narcocorrido."
*Cuando Nueva York se Vistió de Guatemala/The Day New York Put On the Guatemalan Man-
tle,* Maya Media, 2006
   St. Patrick's Cathedral in New York celebrates the mass of the Black Christ and this docu-
   mentary records why this was important to the Guatemalan population in New York City.
Cuban Roots/Bronx Stories, Dir. Pam Sporn. Latino Public Broadcasting/Latin American
Video Archives, 2000
   Interview with a Black Cuban family which moved to the Bronx in 1962.
De Nadie/No One, Dir. Tin Dirdamal, Writers Lizzette Arguello and Iliana Martinez, Produc-
ciones Tranvía, 2005
   This documentary interviews Central American folks who have attempted to enter the United
   States.

En el Hoyo/In the Pit, Dir. Juan Carlos Rulfo, La Media Luna Producciones S.A. de C.V., 2006
  Homage is paid to the largely ignored workers who built a freeway overpass in Mexico City.

El Coronel No Tiene Quien Le Escriba, Dir. Arturo Ripstein, Feat, Fernando Luján, Salma Hayek, Maverick Latino, 2003
  This feature film is based on one of the most highly acclaimed Gabriel García Marquez short stories.

Fidel: The Untold Story, Dir. Estela Bravo, Feat. Harry Belafonte, Alice Walker, Angela Davis, First Run Features, 2001

Folklorico: Music and Dance Traditions, Dir. Joseph Tovares and Felicia Kongable, Chip Taylor Communications, 2004
  Southwest dance traditions. Recommended ages for viewing include 7th grade and up.

Hispanics and the Medal of Honor, Dir. Arthur Drooker, Narr. Hector Elizondo, A&E Television Networks/New Video, 2002
  The overlooked role of Latinos in the armed forces is brought to light in this documentary.

Images from the Spanish-Speaking World, Heinle & Heinle, 2000
  Spanish-speaking people offer their views on their worlds. Intended for students.

In Our Voices: Latino Students on Higher Education, Intercultural Development Research Association, 2002
  Through interviews and songs, students convey their difficulties and triumphs within the higher education system.

Jesse Treviño: A Spirit Against All Odds, Dir. Skip Cilley, Narr. Martin Sheen,. Busch Creative Series Corp., 2000
  The artist, who learned to paint with his left hand when he lost his right in war, shows his paintings.

La Raza Unida, Dir. Jesús Salvador Treviño, Cinema Guild, 2002
  The documentary visits El Paso, Texas in 1972, to cover the first national convention and the formation of La Raza Unida political party.

Latino Artists: Pushing Artistic Boundaries, Films for the Humanities and Sciences, 1995
  Linda Cuellar, Roy Flores and Charles Vaughn cover the performance group ASCO and visit the Nuyorican Poets Café in New York City.

Latino Parents as Partners in Education, KLRN San Antonio and Alamo Public Communications Council, Films for the Humanities and Sciences, 2003
  Linda Cuellar and Charles Vaughn produce a segment depicting the successful collaboration between parents and educators.

Lost in Translation: Latinos, Schools and Society, Dir. Sonia Slutsky. PBS Home Video, 1998
  This documentary documents the high Latino dropout rate in the 1990s and makes connections to language issues and California's Proposition 227.

Nuestra Comunidad: Latinos in North Carolina, Dir. Joanne Hershfield and Penny Simpson,New South Productions, 2001
  Students and families are interviewed regarding the Latino population explosion in North Carolina. Successes and difficulties are addressed.

Piñero, Dir. Leon Ichaso, Feat. Benjamin Bratt and Giancarlo Esposito, Buena Vista Home Entertainment, 2002
  Miguel Piñero, one of the first Nuyorican poets and the first Latino writer to be nominated for a Tony award, is highlighted in this feature film. The strongest sequences are when Bratt recites Piñero's poetry.

Portrait of Artists as Latino Immigrants, Dir. Facundo Lujan and Taina Weisberg, Amazon Unbox/Custom Fix, 2007
  The lives of four California Latino immigrants who are artists are followed in this documentary short.

Resistencia: Hip-Hop in Colombia, Dir. Tom Feiling. Faction Films, 2002
Colombia's finest rappers, DJs and break dancers are featured here.

Saudade do Futuro, Dir. César Paes. Laterit, 2000
The illiterate "Nordestinos" come to Brazil for a better life, but long for what they once had. Poverty and lack of options is depicted. Portuguese with English subtitles.

Soy Cuba/I am Cuba, Dir. Mikhail Kalatozov, Milestone Film and Video, 2007
The new release of the classic film on DVD includes a documentary on how it was made and both English, Spanish, and Russian voice-overs. Depicts prerevolutionary Cuba through the eyes of the Russian director and Enrique Pineda Barnet, the Cuban poet who cowrote the screenplay.

The Borinqueneers, Dir. Noemi Figueroa Soulet and Raquel Ortiz, Narr. Hector Elizondo, Various production companies, 2007
The story of the Puerto Rican 65th Infantry, the only all-Latino unit in U.S. Army history, is followed through World War I & II and the Korean War.

The Bronze Screen: 100 Years of the Latino Image in American Cinema, Dir. Nancy De Los Santos, Alberto Domínguez and Susan Racho, Questar, 2003
Features archive and original footage from many Latino stars like Dolores Del Rio, Rita Moreno, and John Leguizamo.

The College Track: America's Sorting Machine, Dir. Alice Markowitz, Films for the Humanities and Sciences, 2004
The three videodiscs, which include a planning guide and an educator's guide, provide a critical look at the barriers to higher education.

The Cuban Hip Hop All-Stars, Dir. Joshua Bee Alafia, Raptivism, 2004
Spanish and English interviews with various Cuban rappers and activists DVD bonus features include a New York City concert.

The Latino Family, Films for the Humanities and Sciences, 1993
Linda Cuellar and Roy Flores follow the migration patterns of a Mexican-American family for three generations.

The Motorcycle Diaries/Diarios de Motocicleta, Dir. Walter Salles, Feat. Gael Garía Bernal and Rodrigo de la Serna, Universal Films, 2005
The feature film, based on the diaries of Ernesto Ché Guevara, shows Guevara and his friend traveling through South America and discovering the inequities in Latin America.

Women of Hope/Latinas Abriendo Camino: 12 Groundbreaking Latina Women, Dir. Maria Peralta and Moe Foner, Films for the Humanities, 1996
Interviews with Sandra Cisneros, Julia Alvarez and Miriam Colón, among others.

Yo Soy Boricua, Pa' Que Tu Lo Sepas, Dir. Liz Garbus and Rosie Pérez, Independent Film Channel, 2006
A comprehensive history of Puerto Ricans and Nuyoricans is outlined in this documentary through interactions with Pérez's family and interviews with significant activists.

Television Programming

Accordion Dreams, Latino Public Broadcasting, Dir. Hector Galán, Galán Productions, 2001
This made-for-TV documentary was also shown in various film festivals. It depicts the history of Tejano accordion music.

American Latino TV, My Network,. Dir. Renzo Devia, Maximas Productions, 2004
The show airs on Sundays at 4:00 p.m. and highlights Latino culture in the United States.

Compañeras, Independent Lens, Dir. Elizabeth Massie and Matthew Buzzell, PBS. April 1, 2008
The first U.S. all-female mariachi band, Mariachi Reyna.

Conversations with Ilan Stavans: Achy Obejas, Dir. Bob Comisky, WGBH Educational Foundation, 2001
> The acclaimed cultural analyst interviews the Cuban poet and journalist.

Every Child is Born a Poet: The Life and Work of Piri Thomas, Dir. Jonathan Robinson, Latino Public Broadcasting. PBS, April 6, 2004
> Documentary of the life of the first Latino (Cuban and Puerto Rican) to be published in the United States.

Interview with Lena Guerrero, CSPAN, June 15, 1991, National Cable Satellite Corp., 2006
> The first Latina to be named chair of the Railroad Commission of Texas and former Texas House of Representatives member is interviewed.

La Lupe, Independent Lens, Dir. Ela Troyano, PBS, March 2, 2007
> Archive footage and interviews about the eccentric Black Cuban performer who was embraced by New York Latinos.

LatiNation, Various stations and affiliates, 2007
www.aimtvgroup.com/ln/
> LatiNation and American Latino Television are AIM TV Group productions and they are syndicated newsmagazines that focus on national and international Latino interests. More information about them can be found on the Web site.

Latinos Now: A National Conversation, NOW with Bill Moyers, PBS, May 12, 2006
> The special episode features interviews with Henry Cisneros and Maria Hinojosa.

Los Braceros: Strong Arms to Aid the U.S.A, Viewfinder, Episode 312, KVIE Public Television, 2006
> The episode, which shows how Mexicans and Mexican Americans offered a much needed workforce during World War II, can be found on video disk.

Pancho Gonzalez: The Latino Legend of Tennis, Narr. Benjamin Bratt and Pancho Gonzalez, Dir. Nick Athas and Danny Haro, Various U.S. stations and affiliates, September 16, 2005
> The documentary covers the life of an awarded but unknown Latino (Mexican American) athlete.

The Chavez Ravine, Independent Lens, Dir. Jordan Mechner, Don Normark, Andrew Andersen, and Mark Moran, Narr. Cheech Marin, PBS, June 7, 2005
> How Mexican Americans were displaced to build Dodger Stadium in Los Angeles.

The Life and Times of Frida Kahlo, Dir. Amy Stechler, Daylight Films Production Company, PBS, March 23, 2005

The Official Story/La Historia Official, Dir. Luis Puenzo, Koch Lorber Films, 1985, DVD, 2004
> This feature films tells the story of the missing children in Argentina through the life of the wife of a government official.

Voces, Series. Latino Public Broadcasting, Dir. Mario Anaya, PBS, Original start date, September 2, 2006
> This series airs on PBS regularly and is usually scheduled on Wednesday mornings. Check local listings.

Visiones: Latino Art and Culture, Dir. Hector Galán, Galán Productions, Inc., Latino Public Broadcasting and PBS, September 6, 2004
> The six 30-minute episodes aired on PBS and featured famous visual artists, dancers, theater artists and musicians.

Writ Writer, Dir. Susanne Mason, Writer, Dagoberto Gilb, Narr. Jesse Borrego, Passage Productions and the Independent Television Service, June 3, 2008
> Fred Cruz, a man with less than an eighth-grade education, taught himself law and exposed the unjust Texas legal system. This documentary covers his story.

Radio Programming

All Shows Page, The WBAI Archives, November 17, 2007
www.archive.wbai.org/allshows.php?sort=nameaz
  Includes archives of Louis Reyes Rivera's *Perspectives* show.
Bienvenidos a América, Hispanic Communications Network, 2006
www.hcnmedia.com/radio_bienvenidos.html
  Listen to archived shows or a live show focusing on immigration issues. Spanish language.
Epicentro Político, Epicentro Político, 2006
www.epicentroradio.com
  This digital radio show has archives and weekly streams on international politics. Spanish language.
Latin American Radio, Zona Latina, May 14, 1997
www.zonalatina.com/Radio.htm
  This comprehensive Web site has links to nearly every Latin American radio station on the planet, including Central and South America, the U.S. and Canada, and even some European countries.
Latino USA, NPR, Various affiliates
  María Hinojosa interviews Latino leaders and legends. Archives can be heard at www.latinousa.org/program/index.html
Radio, Sí, Spain, 20 Jan. 2007
www.sispain.org/english/media/radio.html#radio
  This has a list of Spanish Web radio stations and links.
Radio Arte, WRTE 90.5 FM in Chicago
www.wrte.org/
  Shows in English and in Spanish include *Sin Papeles, Cruzando Culturas,* and *Polyforum.* The only "Latino-owned, youth driven station in the country," a which according to its Web site encourages social activism.
Radio Bilingue, Various affiliates
  La Hora Mixteca, a bilingual show in Spanish and indigenous Mixteco, is one of the most original shows by Radio Bilingue. Others include *Your Legal Rights* and *Radionovelas,* which presents old time radio soap operas. Local affiliates can be found at www.radiobilingue.org/affiliates.htm

Audio Recordings

Barchas, Sarah, *The Giant and the Rabbit: Six Bilingual Folktales from Hispanic Culture,* High Haven Music, 1996
  The audio recording comes with a guidebook for educators or readers.
Bachata Roja: Acoustic Bachata from the Cabaret Era, IASO, 2007
Beltrán, Brent, *Raza Spoken Here,* Calaca Press [sound recording], 1999
  Various Mexican American poets recite their work on this CD.
Carbó Ronderos, Guillermo, *Tambora: Baile cantado en Colombia,* Tambora-YAI Records, 2003
  The CD comes with a 23-page booklet in English, Spanish, and French.
Chapinlandia, *Marimba Music of Guatemala,* Smithsonian Folkways, 2007
Colombia: The Golden Age of Discos Fuentes, Soundway, 2007
  The various artists on this CD cover the history of one of Colombia's major labels.

Culture, Clash, *Feat,* Lisa Peterson, Zilah Mendoza, Richard Montoya, Ricardo Salinas, Herbert Siguenza, John Avila, Randy Rodarte, Scott Rodarte, and Susan Albert Lowenberg, L.A. Theaterworks, 2005
  The comedy troupe records a series of live performances that reflect the community that was displaced when Dodgers Stadium was built.

Espada, Martín, *Now the Dead Will Dance Mambo: The Poems of Martín Espada,* Leapfrog Press [sound recording], 2004

Los de Azuero, *Traditional Music from Panama,* Nimbus Records, 1999

Los Gaiteros de San Jacinto from Colombia, *Un Fuego de Sangre Pura,* Smithsonian Folkways, 2006
  Cumbias are only the beginning on this CD.

Martinez, Aurelio. *Garifuna Soul.* Stonetree Records, 2006
  Songs combine African, indigenous and Spanish roots.

Music of New Mexico: Native American Traditions, Smithsonian Folkways, 1992

Nati Cano's Los Mariachis Camperos. Viva el Mariachi!, Smithsonian Folkways, 2002

Panama: Latin, Calypso and Funk on the Isthmus 1965-75, Soundway, 2006

Paz, Suni, Bandera Mía: Songs of Argentina, Smithsonian Folkways, 2006

Poetry on Record: 98 Poets Read their Works, 1888–2006, Shout Factory, 2006
  Poets like Pedro Pietri and Luis Rodriguez can be heard on this recording.

Poets Around the River: Fifteen San Antonio Poets, Mesilla Press [sound recording], 1991
  Ray Gonzalez, Jesús Cardona, and a rare recording of Angela de Hoyos.

Rolas de Aztlán: Songs of the Chicano Movement, Smithsonian Folkways, 2005
  Sánchez, Elba Rosario, and Olga Angelina García Echevarría.

When Skin Peels, Calaca Press [sound recording], 1999
  Mexican-American original poetry in both English and Spanish.

Si, Para Usted: The Funky Beats of Revolutionary Cuba, Part 1, Waxing Deep, 2006
  This covers the music of the 1960s and 1970s that flourished under the revolutionary regime. Much of it is soul and psychedelic-oriented.

Si, Soy Llanero: Joropo Music from the Orinoco Plains, Smithsonian Folkways, 2004
  Traditional and improvised Colombian music using guitars and male and female singers.

Smithsonian Folkways World Music Collection, Smithsonian Folkways, 1997
  South American and Caribbean tracks are included.

Taco Shop Poets. Chorizo Tonguefire, Calaca Press [sound recording], 1999
  The Roots of Chicha: Psychedelic Cumbias from Peru. Barbes, 2007.

Wild Poppies: A Poetry Jam across Prison Walls; Poets and Musicians Honor Poet and Political Prisoner Marilyn Buck, Freedom Archives, 2004
  Maria Poblet, Presente!, Carlos Quiles and Piri Thomas are among the contributors.

Note

1. The author(s) and editor(s) do not necessarily endorse the reference entries in this chapter; they are listed for informational purposes only. Most descriptions have been gathered by conducting extensive electronic searches with key words related to these topics and are taken directly from these online sites in order to provide true and clearer descriptions. In order to honor the words chosen to describe themselves and others, each overview incorporates the terms and language utilized (such as Latino/a, Hispanic, Chicano, etc.) on the individual sites.

46 Parents and Teachers

Esther Garza
University of Texas at San Antonio

Keren Zuniga McDowell
Suffolk University

PARENTS AND TEACHERS: PRE-K/EARLY CHILDHOOD, K-12, FUNDING OPPORTUNITIES, AND MORE.[1]

Journals

Bilingual Research Journal
www.brj.asu.edu/

The BRJ welcomes manuscripts dealing with bilingual education, bilingualism, and language policies in education (e.g., language assessment, policy analysis, instructional research, language politics, biliteracy, language planning, second language learning and teaching, action research, and sociolinguistics). As the official organ of the National Association for Bilingual Education, the journal has a strong interest in matters related to the education of language minority children and youth in the United States, grades K-12, but articles focusing on other countries are often included.

The Hispanic Journal of Behavioral Sciences (HJBS)
www.hjb.sagepub.com/
www.sagepub.com/journalsProdDesc.nav?prodId=Journal200809

For nearly 30 years, researchers, educators, mental health professionals, sociologists, and policy makers have turned to the Hispanic Journal of Behavioral Sciences for the latest research and analyses on Hispanic issues. Each quarterly issue of HJBS brings you the latest theoretical work, research studies, and analyses you need to stay on top of this dynamic field. Distinguished experts from diverse fields of study present scholarly articles that keep you up-to-date with the latest behavioral research on a wide variety of Hispanic concerns, including cultural assimilation, communication barriers, intergroup relations, employment discrimination, substance abuse, AIDS prevention, family dynamics, and minority poverty.

The Hispanic Research Journal (Maney Publishing)
www.maney.co.uk/search?fwaction=show&fwid=166

Hispanic Research Journal promotes and disseminates research into the cultures of the Iberian Peninsula and Latin America, from the Middle Ages to the present day. The fields covered include literature and literary theory, cultural history and cultural studies, language and linguistics, and film and theater studies. *Hispanic Research Journal* publishes articles in four languages: Spanish, Portuguese, Catalan, and English and encourages, especially through its features section, debate and interaction between researchers all over the world who are working in these fields.

International Journal of Bilingualism and Bilingual Education
www.informaworld.com/smpp/title~db=all~content=t794297780~tab=summary

From the beginning, the *International Journal of Bilingual Education and Bilingualism* has contained a rich stream of United States papers in two senses. First, almost every number contains one or more articles on languages in contact in the United States. These papers range from historical analyses of bilingual education in United States to the effects of the No Child Left Behind (2001) legislation. Particular themes include the language education of immigrant children, the achievement of bilingual children, and the changing nature of bilingual education in the United States. This particular stream is an important contribution that United States scholars make to an understanding of bilingualism and bilingual education in the United States for two audiences: internal United States readers and those outside the United States who want to understand this fast-changing political and educational context.

Second, many scholars writing on global issues, and on bilingualism and bilingual education in different countries around the world have an important role in informing and contributing to the scene in the USA. They are increasingly choosing this journal to share their research with their colleagues in the USA and beyond. Thus, the *International Journal of Bilingual Education and Bilingualism* has become a major journal for scholars who wish to contribute both to the national agenda and to themes of international importance.

Journal of Latino-Latin American Studies (JOLLAS)
www.unomaha.edu/jollas/

This peer-reviewed journal was formerly known as the *Latino Studies Journal* and represents another mode for the dissemination of research and analysis in the evolving realm of transnational Latino and Latin American political, social, and economic issues.

The Journal of Latinos and Education (JLE)
www.jle.csusb.edu/

The *Journal of Latinos and Education* (JLE) provides a cross-, multi-, and interdisciplinary forum for scholars and writers from diverse disciplines who share a common interest in the analysis, discussion, critique, and dissemination of educational issues that impact Latinos. There are four broad arenas which encompass most issues of relevance: (1) Policy, (2) Research, (3) Practice, and (4) Creative and Literary works. The broad spectrum of researchers, teaching professionals and educators, academics, scholars, administrators, independent writers and artists, policy and program specialists, students, parents, families, civic leaders, activists, and advocates. In short, the journal is addressed to individuals, groups, agencies, organizations, and institutions sharing a common interest in educational issues that impact Latinos.

The Latino Journal Blog
www.thelatinojournal.blogspot.com/2008/11/latinos-differ-on-predicting.html

The *Latino Journal Blog* is a Web space that provides discussion about public policy and government from a Latino perspective.

Nabe News
www.nabe.org/

Nabe News provides researchers, educators, and parents the opportunity to keep up with important events and spotlights new research or other topics in bilingual education.

Articles

Ada, A. & Zubizarreta, R. (2001). Parent narratives: The cultural bridge between Latino parents and their children. In M. Reyes & J. Halcon (Eds.), *The best for our children: Critical perspectives on literacy for latino students* (pp. 234–240). New York: Teachers College Press.

Amstutz, D. (2000). Family literacy: Implications for public school practice. *Education and Urban Society*, 2, 207–220.

Aulls, M., & Sollars, V. (2003). The differential influence of the home environment on the reading ability of children entering grade one. *Reading Improvement*, 4, 164–178.

Behnke, A., Piercy, K., & Diversi, M. (2004). Educational and occupational aspirations of Latino youth and their parents. *Hispanic Journal of Behavioral Sciences*, 1, 16–35.

Cassidy, J., Garcia, R., Tejeda-Delgado, C., Garrett, S., Martinez-Garcia, C., & Hinojosa, R. (2004) A learner-centered family literacy project for Latino parents and caregivers. *Journal of Adolescent & Adult Literacy, 6,* 478–488.

Chapa, J., & De la Rosa, B. (2004). Latino population growth, socioeconomic and demographic characteristics, and implications for educational attainment. *Education and Urban Society, 36,* 130–149.

Darling, S., & Lee, J. (2004). Linking parents to reading instruction. *The Reading Teacher, 57*(4), 382–384.

DeBord, K., & Ferrer, M. (2000, July). Working with Latino parents/families. Retrieved November 8, from www.cyfernet.org/parent/latinofam.html

Delgado-Gaitan, C. (2004). *Involving Latino families in schools: Raising student achievement through home-school partnerships.* Thousand Oaks, CA: Sage.

Delgado-Gaitan, C. (2005). Family narratives in multiple literacies. *Anthropology & Education Quarterly, 36,* 265–272.

Ek, L. D.(2008). Language and literacy in the Pentecostal Church and the public high school: A case study of a Mexican ESL student. *The High School Journal, 92,* 1–13.

Gillanders, C., & Jimenez, R. (2004). Reaching for success: A close up of Mexican immigrant parents in the USA who foster literacy success for their kindergarten children. *Journal of Early Childhood Literacy, 4,* 243–269.

Gilliam, B., Gerhna, J., & Wright, G. (2004). Providing minority parents with relevant literacy activities for their children. *Reading Improvement, 4,* 226–234.

Green, S. (2003). Involving fathers in family literacy: Outcomes and insights from the fathers reading every day program. *Family Literacy Forum and Literacy Harvest, 10,* 34–38.

Haggard, G. (2004). Making a difference: Stamping out illiteracy. *The Delta Kappa Gamma Bulletin, 2,* 26–28.

Menard-Warwick, J. (2007). Biliteracy and schooling in an extended-family Nicaraguan immigrant household: The sociohistorical construction of parental involvement. *Anthropology & Education Quarterly, 38,* 119–137.

Nieto, S. (2004). *Affirming diversity: The sociopolitical context of multicultural education* (4th ed.). Boston: Pearson.

Ortiz, R. W., & Ordonez-Jasis, R. (2005). Leyendo juntos (Reading Together): New Directions for Latino Parents' Early Literacy Involvement. *The Reading Teacher, 59,* 110–121.

Perez, B. (Eds.). (2004). *Sociocultural contexts of language and literacy* (2nd ed.). Mahwah, NJ: Erlbaum.

Perez, B., & Torres-Guzman, M. (2002*). Learning in two worlds: An integrated Spanish/English biliteracy approach* (3rd ed.). Boston: Pearson.

Reese, L., & Gallimore, R. (2000). Immigrant Latinos' cultural model of literacy development: An evolving perspective on home-school discontinuities. *American Journal of Education, 108.* 103–134

Riojas-Cortez, M., Bustos, B., Smith, H., Clark, E., & Smith, K. (2003). Cuentame un cuento [Tell me a story]: Bridging family literacy traditions with school literacy. *Language Arts, 81,* 62.

Roldan, C., & Malave, G. (2004). Language ideologies mediating literacy and identity in bilingual contexts. *Journal of Early Childhood Literacy, 4,* 155–180.

Shanahan, T., Mulhern, M. M., & Rodríguez-Brown, F. V. (1995). Project FLAME: Lessons learned from a family literacy program for linguistic minority families (Family Literacy: Aprendiendo, Mejorando, Educando [Learning, Bettering, Educating] in Chicago). *The Reading Teacher, 48,* 586–593.

Smetana, L. (2005). Collaborative storybook reading: Bring parents and at-risk kindergarten students together. *Reading Horizons, 4,* 283–320.

Smythe, S. & Isserlis, J. (2003). The good mother: Exploring mothering discourses in family literacy texts. *Family Literacy Forum & Literacy Harvest, 2,* 25–31.

Vasquez, L. (2000a). *Programs for Hispanic fathers: Perspectives from research. Hispanic fathers and family literacy: Strengthening achievement in Hispanic communities.* www.fatherhood.hhs.gov/hispanic01/research.htm

Vasquez, L. (2000b). Examining Latino paraeducators' interactions with Latino Students. Center for Research on Education, Diversity & Excellence. *CAL Digest.* Retrieved from Center for Research on Education, Diversity & Excellence. Occasional Reports. Paper eric_00_12_latino. http://repositories.cdlib.org/crede/occrpts/eric_00_12_latino

Vasquez, L. (2005). Convivencia to empowerment: Latino parent organizing at la familia. *The High School Journal, 2*, 32–42.

Parents and Families

Alba, R. D., Massey, D. S., & Rumbaut, R. G. (1999). *The immigration experience for families and children: Congressional Seminar, June 4, 1998.* Washington, DC: American Sociological Association.

Alva, S. A. (1991). Academic invulnerability among Mexican-American students: The importance of protective and resources and appraisals. *Hispanic Journal of Behavioral Sciences, 13*(1), 18–34.

Anguiano, R. P. V. (2004). Families and schools: The effect of parental involvement on high school completion. *Journal of Family Issues, 25*, 61–85.

Battle, J. J. (1997). Academic achievement among Hispanic students from one- versus dual-parent households. *Hispanic Journal of Behavioral Sciences, 19*, 156–170.

Board on Children and Families. (1995). Immigrant children and their families: Issues for research and policy. *Future of Children, 5*, 72–89.

Bulcroft, R. A., Carmody, D. C., & Bulcroft, K. A. (1998). Family structure and patterns of independence giving to adolescents: Variations by age, race, and gender of child. *Journal of Family Issues, 19*, 404–435.

Dishion, T. J., Patterson, M., Stoolmiller, M., & Skinner, M. L. (1991). Family, school, and behavioral antecedents to early adolescent involvement with antisocial peers. *Developmental Psychology, 27*, 172–180.

Fuligni, A. J. (1997). The academic achievement of adolescents from immigrant families: The roles of family background, attitudes and behavior. *Child Development, 68*, 351–363.

Henderson, P. (1997). Educational and occupational aspirations and expectations among parents of middle school students of Mexican descent: Family resources for academic development and mathematics learning. In R. D. Taylor & M. C. Wang (Eds.), *Social and emotional adjustment and family relations in ethnic minority families* (pp. 99–132). Mahwah, NJ: Erlbaum.

Hernandez, A., Vargas-Law, L., & Martinez, C. L. (1994). Intergenerational Academic Aspirations of Mexican-American females: An examination of mother, daughter, and grandmother triads. *Hispanic Journal of Behavioral Sciences, 16*, 195–204.

McClelland, J., & Chen Chen, J. (1997). Standing up for a son at school: Experiences of a Mexican immigrant mother. *Hispanic Journal of Behavioral Sciences, 19*(3), 281–300.

Pérez-Granados, D. R., & Callanan, M. A. (1997). Parents and siblings as early resources for young children's learning in Mexican-descent families. *Hispanic Journal of Behavioral Sciences, 19*, 3–33.

Ramirez, A. Y. F. (2003). Dismay and disappointment: Parental involvement of Latino immigrant parents. *The Urban Review, 35*, 93–110.

Rodriguez, J. L. (2002). Family environment and achievement among three generations of Mexican American high school students. *Applied Developmental Science, 6*, 88–94.

Latino/a School Achievement and Success

Bankston, C. L., III, & Zhou, M. (1994). Being well vs. doing well: Self-esteem and school performance among immigrant and nonimmigrant racial and ethnic groups. *International Migration Review, 36*, 389–415.

Barajas, H. L., & Pierce, J. L. (2001). The significance of race and gender in school success among Latinas and Latinos in college. *Gender & Society, 15*, 859–-878.

Bernal, M., Saenz, D., & Knight, G. (1991). Ethnic identity and adaptation of Mexican American youth in school settings. *Hispanic Journal of Behavioral Sciences, 13*, 135–154.

Dunn, R., & Griggs, S. (1996). *Hispanic-American students and learning styles.* ERIC Digest, Report Number EDO-PS-96-4. Urbana, IL: ERIC Clearinghouse on Elementary and Early Childhood Education.

Gandara, P. (1995). *Over the ivy walls: The educational achievement of low-income Chicanos.* Albany, NY: State University of New York Press.

Gonzalez, R., & Padilla, A. M. (1997). The academic resilience of Mexican American high school students. *Hispanic Journal of Behavioral Sciences, 19*(3), 301–317.

Grant, L., & Rong, X. L. (1999). Gender, immigrant generation, ethnicity and schooling progress of youth. *Journal of Research and Development in Education, 33,* 15–26.

Hampton, S., Ekboir, J. M., & Rochin, R. I. (1995). The performance of Latinos in rural public schools: A comparative analysis of test scores in Grades 3, 6, and 12. *Hispanic Journal of Behavioral Sciences, 17*(4), 480–498.

Harker, K. (2001). Immigrant generation, assimilation, and adolescent psychological well-being. *Social Forces, 79,* 969–1004.

Henriksen, J. A. S. (1995). *The influence of race and ethnicity on access to postsecondary educations and the college experience.* (ERIC Document Reproduction Service No. EDO-JC-95-05)

Hurtado, M. T., & Gauvain, M. (1997). Acculturation and planning for college among youth of Mexican descent. *Hispanic Journal of Behavioral Sciences, 19,* 506–516.

Hyams, M. S. (2000). "Pay attention in class… [and] don't get pregnant": A discourse of academic success among adolescent Latinas. *Environment and Planning A, 32,* 635–654.

Johnson, M. K., Crosnoe, R., & Elder, G. H., Jr. (2001). Students' attachment and academic engagement: The role of race and ethnicity. *Sociology of Education, 74,* 318–340.

Jordan, W. J., Lara, J. & McPartland, J. M. (1996). Exploring the causes of early dropout among race-ethnic and gender groups. *Youth & Society, 28,* 62–94.

Kitano, M. K. (1998). Gifted Latina women. *Journal of the Education of the Gifted, 20,* 131–159.

Lopez, N. (2002). Rewriting race and gender high school lesson: Second-generation Dominicans in New York City. *Teachers College Record, 104,* 1187–1203.

Lopez, N. (2003). *Hopeful girls, troubled boys, race and gender disparity in urban education.* New York: Routledge.

Macgregor-Mendoza, P. (1999). *Spanish and academic achievement among Midwest Mexican youth: The myth of the barrier.* New York: Routledge

Okagaki, L., Frensch, P. A., & Gordon, E. W. (1995). Encouraging school achievement in Mexican American children. *Hispanic Journal of Behavioral Sciences, 17,* 160–179.

Rumbaut, R. G. (1995). The new Californians: Cooperative research findings on the educational progress of immigrant children. In R. G. Rumbaut & W. A. Cornelius (Eds.), *California's immigrant children: Theory, research, and implications for educational policy* (pp. 17–70). San Diego: University of California.

Rumbaut, R. G. (2000). Profiles in resilience: Educational achievement and ambition among children of immigrants in Southern California. In R. D. Taylor & M. C. Wang, (Eds.), *Resilience across contexts: Family, work, culture and community* (pp. 257–294). Hillsdale, NJ: Erlbaum.

Smith, R. C. (2002). Gender, ethnicity, and race in school and work outcomes of second-generation Mexican Americans. In M. M. Suerez-Orozco & M. M. Paez (Eds.), *Latinos: Remaking America* (pp. 110–125). Los Angeles: University of California Press.

Suárez-Orozco, C., & Suárez-Orozco, M. M. (1995). The Cultural patterning of achievement motivation: A Comparison of Mexican, Mexican immigrant, Mexican American, and non-Latino White American students. In R.G. Rumbaut & W. A. Cornelius (Eds.), *California's Immigrant Chidren: Theory, Research, and Implications for Educational Policy* (pp. 161–190). San Diego: University of California.

Waxman, H. C., Huang, S. L., & Padron, Y. N. (1997) Motivation and learning environment differences between resilient and nonresilient Latino middle school students. *Hispanic Journal of Behavioral Sciences, 19,* 137–155.

Books

Bridging Cultures between Home and School: A Guide for Teachers, Trumbull, E., Rothstein-Fish, C., Greenfield, P. M., & Quiroz, B. (2001)

Bridging Cultures is intended to stimulate broad thinking about how to meet the challenges of education in a pluralistic society. It is a powerful resource for in-service and preservice multicultural education and professional development. The Guide presents a framework for understanding differences and conflicts that arise in situations where school culture is more individualistic than the value system of the home. It shares what researchers and teachers of the Bridging Cultures Project have learned from the experimentation of teacher-researchers in their own classrooms of largely immigrant Latino students and explores other research on promoting improved home-school relationships across cultures. The framework leads to specific suggestions for supporting teachers to cross-cultural communication; organization parent-teacher conferences that work; use strategies that increase parent involvement in schooling; increase their skills as researchers; and employ ethnographic techniques to learn about home cultures. Although the research underlying the Bridging Cultures Project and this Guide focuses on immigrant Latino families, since this is the primary population with which the framework was originally used, it is a potent tool for learning about other cultures as well because many face similar discrepancies between their own more collectivistic approaches to childrearing and schooling and the more individualistic approach of the dominant culture.

Building Culturally Responsive Classrooms, Delgado-Gaitan, C. (2006)

Teachers today are faced with the enormous responsibility of respecting students' various cultures while creating learning settings that challenge them academically. Concha Delgado Gaitan shows how teachers honoring real culture can transform the context and content within their classroom and become culturally responsive to all their students. This invaluable resource covers the topics of classroom discipline, classroom arrangement, and parent and community involvement in order to create a culturally inclusive learning setting. In addition, Gaitan explains how teachers can use instructional strategies that are culturally responsive to teach literacy, mathematics, science, and more.

Building on Strength, Zentella, A. C. (Ed.) (2005)

This book offers an exciting new perspective on language socialization in Latino families. Tackling mainstream views of childhood and the role and nature of language socialization, leading researchers and teacher trainers provide a historical, political, and cultural context for the language attitudes and socialization practices that help determine what and how Latino children speak, read, and write. Representing a radical departure from the ways in which most educators have been taught to think about first language acquisition and second language learning, this timely volume: Introduces the theories and methods of language socialization with memorable case studies of children and their families; highlights the diversity of Latino communities, covering children and caretakers of Mexican, Caribbean, and Central American origin living in Chicago, San Antonio, the San Francisco Bay Area, Los Angeles, San Diego, Miami, Tucson, and New York City. Offers important insights into the ways in which children learn to speak and read by negotiating overlapping or conflicting cultural models. Suggests universal practices to facilitate language socialization in multilingual communities, including applications for teachers.

Con Respeto, Valdes, G. (1996)

This book presents a study of 10 Mexican immigrant families, describing how such families go about the business of surviving and learning to succeed in a new world. Guadalupe Valdés examines what appears to be a disinterest in education by Mexican parents and shows, through extensive quotations from interview data, that these struggling families are both rich and strong in family values and bring with them clear views of what constitutes success and failure. The study's conclusion questions the merit of typical family intervention programs designed to promote school success and suggests that these interventions–because they do not genuinely respect the values of diverse families–may have long-term negative consequences for children.

Funds of Knowledge: Theorizing Practices in Households and Classrooms, Gonzalez, N., Moll, L., & Amanti, C. (Eds.) (2005)

The concept of "funds of knowledge" is based on a simple premise: people are competent and have knowledge, and their life experiences have given them that knowledge. The claim in this book is that first-hand research experiences with families allow one to document this competence and knowledge, and that such engagement provides many possibilities for positive pedagogical actions. Drawing from both Vygotskian and neo-sociocultural perspectives in designing a methodology that views the everyday practices of language and action as constructing knowledge, the funds of knowledge approach facilitates a systematic and powerful way to represent communities in terms of the resources they possess and how to harness them for classroom teaching.

This book accomplishes three objectives: It gives readers the basic methodology and techniques followed in the contributors' funds of knowledge research; it extends the boundaries of what these researchers have done; and it explores the applications to classroom practice that can result from teachers knowing the communities in which they work. In a time when national educational discourses focus on system reform and wholesale replicability across school sites, this book offers a counterperspective stating that instruction must be linked to students' lives, and that details of effective pedagogy should be linked to local histories and community contexts. This approach should not be confused with parent participation programs, although that is often a fortuitous consequence of the work described. It is also not an attempt to teach parents "how to do school" although that could certainly be an outcome if the parents so desired. Instead, the funds of knowledge approach attempts to accomplish something that may be even more challenging: to alter the perceptions of working-class or poor communities by viewing their households primarily in terms of their strengths and resources, their defining pedagogical characteristics.

Involving Latino Families in Schools: Raising Student Achievement through Home–School Partnerships, Delgado-Gaitan, C. (2004)
Involving Latino Families in Schools provides tools and strategies for including Latino parents in developing sustained academic improvement. Sharing numerous first person success stories, author Concha Delgado Gaitan stresses three conditions of increased parental participation: connecting to families, sharing information with parents, and supporting continued parental involvement. Offering easily applied techniques for cultivating communication, this practical handbook examines Latino families and their educational aspirations for their children, the communication systems needed between schools and Latino families, how Latino families can assist their children at home, techniques to foster Latino parent involvement, and how to organize schoolwide parent involvement programs. Through suggested activities, case examples, and vignettes, the author provides insights and instruction for planning, designing, and implementing parental participation programs that enhance the classroom curriculum and effectively engage Latino students. Designed primarily for elementary and secondary school principals and teachers, this innovative text is also an indispensable resource for district-level administrators.

Parents' and Teachers' Guide to Bilingualism (parents' and teachers' guides), Baker, C. (2007)
Written in a very reader-friendly style, the book is a practical introduction for parents and teachers to bilingualism. Straightforward and realistic answers are given to a comprehensive set of frequently asked questions about bilingualism and bilingual education. Areas covered include family, language, culture, identity, reading, writing, schooling and issues.

The Power of Community: Mobilizing for Family and Schooling (Immigration and the Transnational Experience), Delgado-Gaitan, C. (2001)
Fifteen years ago, Concha Delgado-Gaitan began literacy research in Carpinteria, California. At that time, Mexican immigrants who labored in nurseries, factories, and housekeeping, had almost no voice in how their children were educated. Committed to participative research, Delgado-Gaitan collaborated with the community to connect family, school, and

community. Regular community gatherings gave birth to the Comité de Padres Latinos. Refusing the role of the victim, the Comité paticipants organized to reach out to everyone in the community, not just other Latino families. Bound by their language, cultural history, hard work, respect, pain, and hope, they created possibilities that supported the learning of Latino students, who until then had too often dropped out or shown scant interest in school. In a society that accentuates individualism and independence, these men and women look to their community for leadership, support, and resources for children. *The Power of Community* is a critical work that shows how communities that pull together and offer caring ears, eyes, and hands, can ensure that their children thrive—academically, socially, and personally. It offers a fresh approach and workable solution to the problems that face schools today.

Websites

California Association for Bilingual Education
www.bilingualeducation.org/about_cabe.php

> The California Association for Bilingual Education (CABE) is a nonprofit organization incorporated in 1976 to promote bilingual education and quality educational experiences for all students in California. CABE has 5,000 members with over 60 chapters/affiliates, all working to promote equity and student achievement for students with diverse cultural, racial, and linguistic backgrounds. CABE recognizes and honors the fact that we live in a rich multicultural, global society and that respect for diversity makes us a stronger state and nation.

The Congressional Hispanic Leadership Institute (CHLI)
www.chli.org/

> The Congressional Hispanic Leadership Institute (CHLI) is the premier national nonprofit, nonpartisan organization dedicated to advancing the Hispanic community's diversity of thought.

Hispanic Association of Colleges and Universities (HACU)
www.hacu.net/hacu/Default_EN.asp

> HACU represents more than 450 colleges and universities committed to Hispanic higher education success in the U.S., Puerto Rico, Latin America, Spain and Portugal. Although our member institutions in the U. S. represent less than 10% of all higher education institutions nationwide, together they are home to more than two-thirds of all Hispanic college students. HACU is the only national educational association that represents Hispanic-Serving Institutions (HSIs).

Immigrant Rights of Network of Iowa and Nebraska
www.irnin.org/

> The mission of the IRNIN is to facilitate full immigrant participation in decision-making processes, promote respect for immigrant contributions, and build inclusive communities. We support immigrants regardless of their immigration status.

Latinos for Education
www.latinos4education.org/Grants-New.html

> Our mission is to promote the educational advancement of the Latino and Native American Communities in order to attain economic and political advancement within the United States.

Mexican American Legal Defense Fund (MALDEF)
www.maldef.org/

> Founded in 1968 in San Antonio, Texas, the Mexican American Legal Defense and Educational Fund (MALDEF) is the leading nonprofit Latino litigation, advocacy and educational outreach institution in the United States.

National Association for Billingual Education (NABE)

www.nabe.org/

NABE's mission is to advocate for our nations Bilingual and English Language Learners and families and to cultivate a multilingual multicultural society by supporting and promoting policy, programs, pedagogy, research, and professional development that yield academic success, value native language, lead to English proficiency, and respect cultural and linguistic diversity. As tireless advocates that work to influence and create policies, programs, research, pedagogy and professional development, we know that we are investing in our children's education, our nation's leadership, and our world's well-being. By using native and second languages in everyday life, we not only develop intercultural understanding, but we also show by example that we respect and can effectively cross cultural and linguistic borders.

The Office of Latino/Latin American Studies of the Great Plains

www.unomaha.edu/ollas/

The Office of Latino/Latin American Studies of the Great Plains—OLLAS (pronounced "oy yas")—at the University of Nebraska at Omaha (UNO) was established in the summer of 2003 as the result of ongoing efforts made by the faculty, staff, and students of the UNO Chicano/Latino Studies (CLS) Program, a federal appropriation made possible by the U.S. Department of Education and the support of the Greater Omaha community. OLLAS helps fill a void in the Nebraska and Great Plains region's academic infrastructure by being dedicated to the productive incorporation of the new and growing Latino population into the political, economic, and social life of the region.

Pre-K and Latinos: The Foundation for America's Future

www.preknow.org/documents/Pre-KandLatinos_July2006.pdf

Based upon the extensive body of research on early childhood development, bilingualism, socio-economics, and the value of high quality pre-k-for-all programs, this report explores the policies and practices that Pre-K Now believes will best serve our nation's growing Latino population.

Preschool Technical Assistance Network

www.ptan.seresc.net/informationresources.html

PTAN is a statewide technical assistance and support network that promotes quality, developmentally appropriate and culturally competent early care and education/special education programs. It is a project of the Southeastern Regional Education Service Center (SERESC), a nonprofit education collaborative in Bedford, NH.

Technical Assistance Center on Social Emotional Intervention for Young Children (TACSEI)

www.challengingbehavior.org/explore/camtasia/tacsei_overview/tacsei_overview_smith.html

The Technical Assistance Center on Social Emotional Intervention for Young Children (TACSEI), is a 5-year grant made possible by the U.S. Department of Education, Office of Special Education Programs. TACSEI takes the research that shows which practices improve the social-emotional outcomes for young children with, or at risk for, delays or disabilities and creates **FREE** products and resources to help decision makers, caregivers, and service providers apply these best practices in the work they do every day. Most of these free products are available right here on our website for you to view, download and use. Watch an overview of TACSEI for more detailed information about who we are and what we do.

Texas Association for Bilingual Education (TABE)

www.tabe.org

Through a balanced program of research, professional development, and public education, TABE pursues the implementation of educational policies and effective bilingual-bicultural programs that promote equal educational opportunity and academic excellence for Bilingual/ESL students. TABE firmly believes that only enrichment (additive) forms of bilingual education ensure that Bilingual/ESL students are successful academically and develop age-appropriate English proficiency. To this end, TABE fully endorses and promotes the implementation of research-based One Way/Two Way dual language programs and maintenance (late-exit) bilingual programs.·

Texas Association of Chicanos in Higher Education (TACHE)

www.tache.org/

TACHE collaborates with you, the Texas Higher Education Coordinating Board, the Texas legislature, and other organizations to push for increased participation and success rates for Latinos. Thanks to TACHE's educational, corporate, and other partners for support as TACHE strives for healthy, financially stable, well-educated Latino local, state, and national communities.

Events

National Conferences and Society Meetings

American Association of Hispanics in Higher Education (AAHHE)–National Conference

www.aahhe.org

This annual conference is held each Spring and focuses on issues related to Latino/a education among other factors influencing Latino/a participation in Higher Education at the student, faculty, and administrative level. The highlight of the National Conference is the Tomas Rivera Lecture program and the Latino/a Graduate Fellows program.

American Educational Research Association (AERA), Annual Meeting

www.aera.net

The American Educational Research Association Annual Meeting is held each Spring convening educational researchers from across the country.

American Educational Studies Association (ASA), Annual Conference

www.educationalstudies.org

The American Educational Studies Association Annual Conference is held each Fall convening educational researchers from across the country.

Ford Support of College Scholarships and Funding

www.ford.com/our-values/education/education-america/scholarship-support/college-scholarships-482p

We continue to support a number of college scholarship programs designed to reward students who shine. In 2007, we'll fund college scholarships for more than 200 young people across the country through our major scholarship partner organizations and programs.

Heartland Hispanic Education Conference-Annual Conference

www.casb.org/Conferences/HeartlandHispanicConference.aspx

The Heartland Hispanic Education Conference is centered around disseminating applicable innovative strategies and programs that have been proven to improve Latino/a student education.

Hispanic Association of Colleges and Universities (HACU)–National Conference

www.hacu.net

The Hispanic Association of Colleges and Universities convenes its member institutions at its annual Fall conference to share information about the best practices in Latino/a education with a special emphasis on Hispanic Serving Institutions of Higher Education.

Hispanic Scholarship Fund

www.HispanicFund.org

The mission of HSF is to develop the next generation of Hispanic professionals. We accomplish our mission by providing Hispanic high school and college students with the vision, resources, and mentorship needed to become community leaders and achieve successful careers in business, science, technology, engineering and math.

Latino/a Education Summit
www.chicano.ucla.edu/center/events/LatinoEducationSummit2008.htm

Sponsored by the UCLA Chicano Studies Research Center and the Graduate School of Education and Information Studies, the Latino/a Education Summit brings together researchers, students, community leaders and policy makers to discuss factors influencing Latino/a Education. The Summit focuses on factors influencing Latino/a educational attainment at each step in the education pipeline, as well as policy initiatives for increasing the number of Latino/a students who earn college degrees.

League of United Latin American Citizens (LULAC), National Convention and Exposition
www.lulac.org/events.html

Mexican American Legal Defense and Education Fund (MALDEF)
www.maldef.org/

National Association of Chicana and Chicano Studies (NACCS)
www.naccs.org/naccs/Default_EN.asp

National Association of Latino Elected and Appointed Officials (NALEO) Education Leadership Initiative–National Summit on the State of Latino Education
www.naleo.org

Sponsored by the NALEO Education Leadership Initiative (NELI), the National Summit on the State of Latino Education is a unique Fall event that brings together elected officials to learn from national leading Latino/a Education policy experts. Elected officials and policy makers will learn about the latest trends, research, best practices, and policy recommendations for improving the state of Latino/a preschool to graduate studies (P-20) education.

National Council for Community and Education Partnerships (NCCEP) and GEAR UP-Annual Conference
www.edpartnerships.org/Content/NavigationMenu/Events/2008_NCCEP_Annual_Conference/2008_NCCEP_Conference_Main_Page.htm

The NCCEP is the founding partner of the Hispanic Education Initiative.

Summit on Education Reform and Hispanic Education Attainment
www.yesican.gov/news/events.html

The Summit on Education Reform and Hispanic Education Attainment is hosted by the White House Initiative on Educational Excellence for Hispanic Americans. The summit focuses on the best and promising practices being used by White House Initiative partners to improve Latino/a educational outcomes.

Tomas Rivera Policy Institute (TRPI)–Education Conference
www.trpi.org

The Tomas Rivera Policy Institute hosts its annual Education Conference each fall. The conference highlights national presentations on research and programs that increase Latino/a college application, enrollment, and graduation rates.

United States Hispanic Leadership Institute (USHLI)–Annual Conference and Regional Student Leadership Conferences
www.trpi.org

The USHLI Annual Conference brings together a national cross-section of Latino leaders. Among attendees are Latino/a high school and college students. The conference focuses on growing future Latino/a leaders by promoting education and unity, and providing attendees with professional and leadership skills development.

Throughout the year USHLI sponsors regional Student Leadership Conferences in the Northeast, Midwest, Central States, and Northwest. Please visit their website for more details.

Note

1. The author(s) and editor(s) do not necessarily endorse the reference entries in this chapter; they are listed for informational purposes only. Most descriptions have been gathered conducting extensive electronic searches with key words related to these topics and are taken directly from these online sites in order to provide true and clearer descriptions. In order to honor the words chosen to describe themselves and others, each overview incorporates the terms and language utilized (such as Latino/a, Hispanic, Chicano, etc.) on the individual sites.

47 Periodicals

Evelyn M. Gordon
University of North Carolina at Chapel Hill

Daniella Ann Cook
Duke University

Periodicals: Journals, Magazines, Newsletters, Newspapers, and more.[1]

Journal of Latinos in Education (JLE)
This peer-reviewed journal is published 4 times per year. Described as a multi-, cross-, and interdisciplinary forum for scholars and writers focusing on educational issues that impact Latinos; its contents generally address four broad areas including (1) Policy (2) Research (3) Practice and (4) Creative and Literary Works.

Journal of Hispanic Higher Education (JHHE)
This quarterly international journal focuses on the advancement of knowledge and understanding of issues at Hispanic-serving institutions. JHHE publishes both quantitative and qualitative articles that specifically relate to issues of interest at Hispanic-serving institutions of higher learning.

Hispanic American Periodicals Index (HAPI)
This database provides over 275,000 journal article citations about Central America, South America, the Caribbean, Mexico, Brazil, and Hispanics/Latinos in the United States. HAPI makes available over 60,000 links to the full text of articles appearing in more than 600 key social science and humanities journals published throughout the world.

Midwest (Illinois, Iowa, Indiana, Kansas, Michigan, Minnesota, Missouri, Nebraska, North Dakota, Ohio, South Dakota, Wisconsin)

El Día USA News (Cicero/Chicago, IL), weekly
    www.eldianews.com
Hoy (Chicago, IL), daily
    www.hoyinternet.com
Lawndale News (Chicago, IL), twice weekly
    www.lawndalenews.com
El Puente (South Bend, IN), every 2 weeks
    www.webelpuente.com
Lazo Cultural (Grand Rapids, MI), weekly
    www.lazocultural.com
El Vocero Hispano (Grand Rapids, MI), weekly
    www.elvocerous.com
Latino Midwest News (Robbinsdale, MN), monthly
    www.latinomidwestnews.com
Dos Mundos (bilingual; Kansas City, MO), weekly
    www.dosmundos.com
Spanish Journal (Milwaukee, WI), monthly
    www.spanishjournal.com

South (Alabama, Arkansas, Kentucky, Louisiana, Mississippi, Oklahoma, Tennessee, West Virginia)

Mundo Hispano (Knoxville, TN), twice monthly
    www.mundohispanotn.com
La Prensa Latina (Memphis, TN), weekly
    www.laprensalatina.com

Southeast (Florida, Georgia, North Carolina, South Carolina, Virginia)

Las Américas Newspapers (Annadale, VA), weekly
    www.lasamericasnews.com
El Colombiano (Fort Lauderdale, FL), weekly
    www.elcolombiano.net
Calle Ocho News (Miami-Dade, FL), twice monthly
    www.calle8news.com
Diario Las Americas (Miami, FL), daily
    www.diariolasamericas.com
El Heraldo (Miami, FL), monthly
    www.elheraldo.com
Diario Sur (Miami, FL), weekly
    www.diariosurdigital.com
La Nación Cubana (Miami, FL), approximately weekly
    www.lanacioncubana.com
La Gaceta (Tampa, FL), 3 times weekly
    www.lagacetanewspaper.com
Nuevo Siglo (Tampa, FL), weekly
    www.nuevosiglotampa.com
El Popular (Miami, FL), twice monthly
    www.elpopular.com
El Sol de la Florida (Miami, FL), monthly
    www.elsoldelaflorida.com
El Venezoano (Miami, FL), weekly
    www.el-venezolano.net
Venezuela Al Día (Miami, FL), every 2 weeks
    www.venezuelaaldia.com
La Prensa (Orlando, FL), weekly
    www.impre.com/laprensafl/home.php
El Sentinel (Orlando, FL), weekly
    www.orlando.elsentinel.com
El Sentinel (South Florida, FL), weekly
    www.southflorida.elsentinel.com
Siete Días (Tampa, FL), twice weekly
    www.7dias.us
Atlanta Latino (Atlanta, GA), weekly
    www.atlantalatino.com
Mundo Hispánico (Atlanta, GA), weekly
    www.mundohispanico.com
La Visión (Georgia), weekly
    www.lavisionnewspaper.com/online

La Noticia (Charlotte, NC), weekly
www.lanoticia.com
La Conexión (Raleigh, NC), weekly
www.laconexionusa.com

Pacific States (Alaska, California, Hawaii, Oregon, Washington)

El Latino (Chula Vista, CA), weekly
www.ellatinoonline.com
La Opinión (Los Angeles, CA), daily
www.impre.com/laopinion/home.php
Crónicas (Napa, CA), twice monthly
www.cronicasnewspaper.com
Diario San Diego (San Diego, CA), twice weekly
www.diariosandiego.com
La Prensa (San Diego CA), weekly
www.laprensa-sandiego.org
Brazilian Pacific Times (San Francisco, CA), monthly
www.brazilianpacifictimes.com
El Observador (San José, CA), weekly
www.el-observador.com
La Oferta Review (San José, CA), weekly
www.laoferta.com

Southwest (Arkansas, Arizona, California, Colorado, Louisiana, Nevada, New Mexico, Oklahoma, Texas, Utah)

Bajo El Sol (San Luis, AZ), weekly
www.bajoelsol.com
El Imparcial (Tucson, AZ)
www.elimparcial.com
Prensa Hispana (Phoenix, AZ), weekly
www.prensahispanaaz.com
La Voz (Phoenix, AZ), weekly
www.azcentral.com/lavoz
Hispania News (Colorado Springs, CO), weekly
www.hispanianews.com
Ahora (Reno, NV), weekly
www.ahoranews.com
Hispano de Tulsa (Tulsa, OK), weekly
www.hispanodetulsa.com
La Semana del Sur (Tulsa, OK), weekly
www.lasemanadelsur.com
El Día (Houston, TX), daily
www.eldianet.com
La Estrella (Dallas/Fort Worth, TX), weekly
www.diariolaestrella.com
El Heraldo News (Dallas, TX), weekly
www.elheraldonews.com
El Hispano News (Dallas, TX), weekly
www.elhispanonews.com

Novedades News (Dallas, TX), weekly
  www.novedadesnews.com
La Prensa (San Antonio, TX), 3 times weekly
  www.laprensasa.com

New England (Connecticut, Maine, Massachusetts, New Hampshire, Rhode Island, Vermont)

El Canillita (CT), weekly
  www.elcanillita.com
El Mundo Boston (Boston, MA), weekly
  www.elmundoboston.com
El Planeta (Boston, MA), weekly
  www.tuboston.com
Providence en Español (Providence, RI), weekly
  www.providenceenespanol.com

MidAtlantic (Delaware, District of Columbia, Maryland, New Jersey, New York, Pennsylvania)

El Aguila (Hudson Valley, NY), every 2 weeks
  www.elaguilanews.com
Brazilian Voice Newspaper (Newark, NJ), weekly
  www.brazilianvoice.com
Noticias Del Mundo (Long Island City, NY), daily
  www.noticiasdelmundo.com
El Diario/La Prensa (New York City), daily
  www.impre.com/eldiariony
Al Día (Philadelphia, PA), weekly
  www.pontealdia.com
El Tiempo Latino (Washington, DC), weekly
  www.eltiempolatino.com
Washington Hispanic (Washington, DC), weekly
  www.washingtonhispanic.com

Note

1. The author(s) and editor(s) do not necessarily endorse the reference entries in this chapter; they are listed for informational purposes only. Most descriptions have been gathered conducting extensive electronic searches with key words related to these topics and are taken directly from these online sites in order to provide true and clearer descriptions. In order to honor the words chosen to describe themselves and others, each overview incorporates the terms and language utilized (such as Latino/a, Hispanic, Chicano, etc.) on the individual sites. The newspapers had to meet the following criteria: print circulation, presence online, more than just a Spanish translation of English newspaper (e.g., *El Nuevo Herald* is the *Miami Herald* in Spanish and not included in this list), and content that included news and not solely entertainment, health, and lifestyle information. Newspapers are listed by region of the country they serve and alphabetically within each region.

References

Echo Media. (2008). Hispanic newspapers. Retrieved August 5, 2008 from www.echo-media.com/target-cat.asp?TargetType=HispanicNP

Zona Latina. (2008). Latin American newspapers: USA. Retrieved August 5, 2008 from http://www.zona-latina.com/Zlpapers.htm#USA

48 Publications

Norma A. Guzmán
University of Texas at San Antonio

Janet López
University of Colorado-Denver

Mary Ruth Fernández
Our Lady of the Lake University

Publications: Articles, Special Issues of Journals, Book/Media Reviews, Conference Proceedings/Presentations, Reference Works, Encyclopedias, Bibliographies, Dictionaries, Books, Book Chapters, Literature, Monographs, Technical Papers/Research Reports, Dissertations/Theses/Scholarly Projects, ERIC Documents, and more.[1]

Journal Articles

Altwerger, B., Edelsky, C., & Flores, B. (1987). Whole language: What's new? *Reading Teacher, 41*(2), 144–154.

Altwerger, B., & Flores, B. (1989). Abandoning the basal: Some aspects of the change process. *Theory into Practice, 28*(4), 288–294.

Auerbach, S. (2002). "Why do they give the good classes to some and not to others?" Latino parent narratives of struggle in a college access program. *Teachers College Record, 104*(7), 1369–1392.

Contreras, F. (2005). Access, achievement, and social capital: Standardizing exams and the Latino college-bound population. *Journal of Hispanic Higher Education, 4*(3), 197–214.

Chapa, J., & De La Rosa, B. (2006). The problematic pipeline: Demographic trends and Latino participation in graduate science, technology, engineering, and mathematics programs. *Journal of Hispanic Higher Education, 5*(3), 203.

Edelsky, C., Hudelson, S., Flores, B., Barkin, F., Altwerger, B., & Gilbert, K. (1983). Semilingualism and language deficit. *Applied Linguistics, 4*(1), 1–22.

Ek, L. D. (2008). Language and literacy in the Pentecostal Church and the public high school: A case study of a Mexican ESL student. *The High School Journal, 92*(2), 1–13.

Ek, L.D. (2009). "Allá en Guatemala": Transnationalism, language, and identity of a Pentecostal Guatemalan-American young woman. *The High School Journal, 92*(4), 67–81.

Elenes, C. A, Gonzalez, F., Delgado Bernal, D., & Villenas, S. (2001). Introduction—Chicana/Mexicana feminist pedagogies: Consejos, respeto, y educación in everyday life. *International Journal of Qualitative Studies in Education, 14*(5), 595–602.

Flores, B. (1981). Bilingual reading instructional practices: The three views of the reading process as they relate to the concept of language interference. *California Journal of Teacher Education, 8*(3), 98–122.

Flores, B., Cousin, P. Tefft, & Diaz, E. (1991).Transforming deficit myths about learning, language, and culture. *Language Arts, 68*(5), 369–379.

Flores, B., & Garcia, E. (1984). A collaborative learning and teaching experience using journal writing. *Journal of the National Association for Bilingual Education, 8*(2), 67–83.

Flores, B., & Hernandez, E. (1988). A kindergartner's sociopsychogenesis of literacy and biliteracy. *Dialogue, 5*(3), 2–3.

Flores, S. Y. & Murillo Jr., E. G. (2001). Power, language, and ideology: Historical and contemporary notes on the dismantling of bilingual education. [Special issue] Under cultural assault: Navigating through california's proposition 227. *Urban Review, 33*(3).

Flores, B., Rueda, R., & Hidalgo, G. (1988). Everyone belongs when using dialogue journals: A story about literacy development. *Dialogue, 5*(3), 6–7.

Foley, D. E. (1976). Legalistic and personalistic adaptations in a south Texas school. *Journal of Research and Development in Education, 9*(4).

Foley, D. E. (1977). Anthropological studies of schooling in developing countries: Some recent findings and trends. *Comparative Education Review, 21*(2–3).

Foley, D. E., with W. Elwood Smith. (1978). Mexicano resistance to schooling in a south Texas colony. *Education and Urban Society, 10*(2).

Foley, D. E. (1988). The legacy of the Raza Unida in south Texas: A class analysis. *Journal of Ethnic Affairs, 3*, 1–24.

Foley, D. E. (1989). Does the working class have a culture in the anthropological sense? *Cultural Anthropology, 14*, 35–52.

Foley, D. E. (1991a). Reconsidering anthropological explanations of ethnic school failure. *Anthropology and Education Quarterly, 22*(1), 60–85.

Foley, D. E. (1991b). Rethinking school ethnographies of colonial settings: A performance theory of cultural reproduction and resistance. *Comparative Education Review, 35*(3), 532–551.

Foley, D. E. (1993). Mesquaki adolescent rites of passage and sports. *Journal of Ritual Studies, 12*(3), 24–34.

Foley, D. E. (1999). The fox project: A reappraisal. *Current Anthropology, 40*(2), 171–191.

Foley, D. E. (2000, Spring). Studying the politics of Raza Unida politics: Reflections of a White anthropologist. *Reflexiones: New Directions in Mexican American Studies, 3*, 51–81.

Foley, D. E. (2002). Critical ethnography: The reflexive turn. *International Journal of Qualitative Studies in Education, 15*(4), 469–490.

Foley, D. E. (2004). Ogbu's theory of academic disengagement: Its evolution and its critics. *Intercultural Education, 15*(4), 385–397.

Foley, D. E. (2005a). Enrique Trueba: A Latino critical ethnographer for the ages. *Anthropology and Education Quarterly, 36*, 354–366.

Foley, D. E. (2005b). The heartland chronicles revisited: The casino's impact on settlement life. *Qualitative Inquiry, 11*(2).

Foley, D. E., Hurtig, J., & Levinson, B. (2001). Anthropology goes inside: The new ethnography of ethnicity and gender. In W. Secada (Ed.), *Review of research in education* (pp. 37–98). Washington, DC: American Educational Research Association.

Foley, D. E., Valencia, R., Valenzuela, A., & Sloan, K. (2001, December). Let's treat the causes, not the symptoms: Equity and accountability in Texas revisited. *Phi Delta Kappan,*

Fox, J. (2006). Reframing Mexican migration as a multi-ethnic process. *Latino Studies, 4*, 39–61.

Fránquiz, M. E., & Brochin-Ceballos, C. (2006). Cultural citizenship and visual literacy: U.S.–Mexican children constructing cultural identities along the US/Mexico border. *Multicultural Perspectives, 8*(1), 5–12.

Fránquiz, M. E., & Salazar, M. (2007). Ni de aquí, ni de allá: Latin@ youth crossing linguistic and cultural borders. *The Journal of Border Educational Research, 6*(1), 101–117.

Gallegos, B. (1998). Remember the Alamo: Imperialism, memory, and postcolonial educational studies. *Educational Studies, 29*, 232–247.

García, E. (2002). Bilingualism and schooling in the United States. *International Journal of the Sociology of Language, 134*(1), 1–123. (Monograph).

Garcia, L., & Bayer, A. (2005). Variations between Latino Groups in U.S. post-secondary educational attainment. *Research in Higher Education, 46*(5), 511.

Gonzalez, K. (2002). Campus culture and the experiences of Chicano students in a predominantly White university. *Urban Education, 37*(2), 193.

Gonzalez, K., Marin, P., Figueroa, M., et al. (2001). Inside doctoral education in America: Voices of Latinas/os in pursuit of a PhD. *Journal of College Student Development, 42*(6), 540–579.

Gonzalez, K., Stoner, C., & Jovel, J. (2003). Examining the role of social capital in access to college for Latinas: Toward a college opportunity framework. *Journal of Hispanic Higher Education, 2*(1), 146–170.

González, N., Moll, L. C., Floyd Tenery M., Rivera A., Rendon P., Gonzales R., et al. (1995). Funds of knowledge for teaching in Latino households. *Urban Education, 29*(4), 443–470.

Hammer, C. S., Detwiler, J. S., Detwiler, J., Blood, G. W., & Qualls, C. D. (2004). Speech–language pathologist's training and confidence in serving Spanish–English bilingual children. *Journal of Communication Disorders, 37*(2), 91–108.

The purpose of the investigation was to determine the level of training and confidence of speech–language pathologists in serving Spanish–English bilingual children. Surveys were completed by 213 speech–language pathologists working in the public schools. Comparisons were made among responses from nondiverse rural, nondiverse urban, and diverse urban areas. Results revealed that approximately one-third of the sample did not receive training in multicultural/multilingual issues as undergraduates or graduate students. Approximately, one-fifth of the sample could not recall whether or not they had received training in this area. Eighteen to 25% of the respondents in the three groups received information through lectures in one or more courses. A larger percentage of speech–language pathologists from nondiverse urban areas received training on specific topics related to multicultural/multilingual topics and participated in a larger number of continuing education activities than speech–language pathologists from diverse urban and nondiverse rural areas. No differences were found among the three groups with regard to their confidence in serving bilingual children. Although speech–language pathologists had some confidence when assessing bilingual children whose primary language was English, and when working with bilingual parents and interpreters, respondents lacked confidence when assessing bilingual children whose primary language was Spanish and when working with parents who do not speak English. Implications for the profession are discussed.

Hamann, E. T., Wortham, S., & Murillo Jr., E. G. (2004). Education in the new Latino Diaspora: A reflection on polyvocality. *Journal of Thought, 39*(1), 83–102.

Hurtado, S., & Ponjuan, L. (2005). Latino educational outcomes and the campus climate. *Journal of Hispanic Higher Education, 4*(3), 235.

Machado-Casas, M. (2004). Arts in the classroom: "La Llave" (The key) to awareness, community relations, and parental involvement. *The Journal of Thought.*

Machado-Casas, M. (2008). Multilingualism and the new global transnational citizen. *NABE News.* 31.

Machado-Casas, M. (2009, April/May). The politics of organic phylogeny: The art of parenting and surviving as transnational multilingual Latino indigenous immigrants in the U,S. *High School Journal, 92*(4), 82–99.

Massey, D. S. (1999). International migration at the dawn of the twenty-first century: The role of the state. *Population and Development Review, 25,* 303–323.

Massey, D. S., & Zenteno R. (1999). The dynamics of mass migration. *Proceedings of the National Academy of Sciences, 96*(8), 5328–5335.

McLaren, P., Muñoz, J., Tejeda, C., & Leonardo, Z. (1996). La Lucha continua in Gringolandia. *The International Journal of Educational Reform.*

Mehan, H. (1994). *Tracking untracking: The consequences of placing low track students in high track classes.* Santa Cruz, CA: National Center for Research on Cultural Diversity and Second Language Learning.

Miller, L. (2005). Exploring high academic performance: The case of Latinos in higher education. *Journal of Hispanic Higher Education, 4*(3), 252.

Moll, L. C., Armanti, C., Neff, D., & Gonzalez, N. (1992). Funds of knowledge for teaching: Using a qualitative approach to connect homes and classrooms. *Theory into Practice, 31*(2), 132–141.

Muñoz, J. (2002a) (Dis)integrating technology with multiculturalism. *Multicultural Education, 8*(4), 19–23.

Muñoz, J. (2002b). [En]Gauging opportunity: Examining equity, access and appropriateness of computer mediated learning. *American Association of Social and Behavioral Sciences, 5*(2), 65–69.

Muñoz, J. (2003). Community resource mapping- an exciting tool for decision making in the social studies classroom. The *Social Studies, 94*(1), 20–23.

Muñoz, J. (2005). The social construction of alternative education: Re-examining the margins of public education for at-risk Chicano/a student. *The High School Journal, 88*(2), 3–22.

Muñoz, J., Jasis-Ordonez, R., Young, P., & McLaren, P. (2004). The hidden curriculum of domestication. *Urban Review, 36*(3), 169–187.

Murillo Jr., E. G. (1997). Pedagogy of a Latin American festival. *The Urban Review, 29*(4), 263–281.

Murillo Jr., E. G. (1999). Mojado crossings along neoliberal borderlands. *Educational Foundations, 13*(1), 7–30.

Murillo Jr., E. G. (2003). Indigenous inscriptions: Reflective notes on educational ethnographic writing from a multicentric postchicano positionality. *Educational Studies, 34*(2), 169–181.

Murillo Jr., E. G., & Flores, S. Y. (2002). Reform by shame: Managing the stigma of labels in high stakes testing. *Educational Foundations, 16*(2), 93–108.

Murillo Jr., E. G., Flores, S. Y., & Martinez, C. (2002). From the editor's desk. *Journal of Latinos and Education, 1*(1), 1–5.

Olivas, M. (2004). IRIRA, the DREAM act and undocumented college student residency. *30 J.C.U.L. 435*, 435 –464.

Oliverez, P., Chavez, M., Soriano, M., & Tierney, W. (2006). *The college and financial aid guide for AB 540 undocumented immigrant students*. Los Angeles: Center for Higher Education Policy Analysis, University of Southern California.

Since the passage of California Assembly Bill 540 in 2001, authored by the late Assemblyman Marco Antonio Firebaugh, more than 5,000 undocumented students in California have had improved financial access to higher education. AB 540 has become a pinnacle in the lives of students, who because of their immigration status have historically been denied access to financial aid to fund their college education, despite demonstrated academic excellence. Even since the passage of AB 540 in 2001, many undocumented students remain unaware of the law as well as the rights and opportunities available to them in the United States. Through this resource guide the authors hope to inform not only those undocumented students who can benefit from AB 540 but also the counselors, teachers, and other advocates who support them. This guide is the result of a collaborative effort by individuals who work and advocate for students' postsecondary access. It provides a comprehensive resource detailing the law, history of relevant legislation, immigration definitions and resources, important information about applying for college, tips on succeeding in college including funding their education, and providing the motivation and examples of students like them who have succeeded. The following are appended: (1) AB 540 Affidavit; (2) California's Four Systems of Higher Education; (3) AB 540 Student College Preparation Timeline; and (4) College Knowledge Glossary. (Contains 1 table and 12 footnotes.) This resource guide was produced by the AB 540 College Access Network, a collaboration between the Center for Higher Education Policy Analysis (CHEPA) at the University of Southern California, the Salvadoran American Leadership and Educational Fund (SALEF), and Maria Lucia Chavez.

Orellana, M. F., Ek, L. D., & Hernández, A. (2000). Bilingual education in an immigrant community: Proposition 227 in California. In E. Trueba & L. Bartolome (Eds.), *Immigrant voices: In search of educational equity* (pp. 75–92). Lanham, MD: Rowman & Littlefield. (Original work published 1999)

Peña, E., Quinn, R., & Yglesias, A. (1992). The application of dynamic methods of language assessment: A non-biased procedure. *The Journal of Special Education, 26*(3), 269–280.

Dynamic methods are discussed as interactive and process oriented procedures for nonbiased assessment of communicative competence and language learning potential. Specifically, this study demonstrates the application of mediated learning experience to language assessment. Significant results of the study supported the hypothesis that a task matching young children's socialization better differentiates between nondisabled and language disordered children than a static standardized measure. Dynamic methods were most effective in differentiating nondisabled children from those with possible language disorders.

Low socioeconomic status (SES) Latino-American and African-American children enrolled in Head Start programs are often described as educationally at risk. This label is frequently ascribed to this population of children as being a function of the poor academic achievement of most members of these populations. One area in which these children often perform below the national average is on standardized tests. Frequently, these children are described as having poor vocabulary, a word-finding deficit, or a vocabulary (language) delay. Many of these tests, however, are based on labeling tasks, and one-word labeling of objects is not emphasized in the same manner or frequency across all cultural/linguistic groups.

Perna, L. (2000). Differences in the decision to attend college among African Americans, Hispanics and Whites. *The Journal of Higher Education, 71*(2), 117–134.

Perna, L., & Titus, M. (2005). The relationship between parental involvement as social capital and college enrollment: An examination of racial/ethnic group differences. *The Journal of Higher Education, 76*(5), 485–517.

Richardson, T., & Villenas, S. (2000). Other encounters: Dances with whiteness in multicultural education. *Educational Theory, 50*(2), 255–273.

Rosado, L. A., & Aaron, E. B. (1991). Parental involvement: Addressing the educational needs of Hispanic inner-city parents. *Journal of Educational Issues of Language Minority Students, 8*, 23–29.

Sánchez, P. (2007a). Urban immigrant students: How transnationalism shapes their world learning. *The Urban Review, 39*(5), 489–517.

Sánchez, P. (2007b). Cultural authenticity and transnational Latina youth: Constructing a metanarrative across borders. *Linguistics and Education, 18*(3–4), 258–282.

Sánchez, P. (2008). Coming of age across borders: Family, gender, and place in the lives of second-generation transnational Mexicanas. In R. Márquez & H. Romo (Eds), *Transformations of la familia on the U.S.-México border* (pp. 185–208). Notre Dame, IN: Notre Dame Press.

Sánchez, P. (2009, April/May). Even beyond the local community: Transnational funds of knowledge and return trips to Mexico. *High School Journal 92*(4), 49–66.

Sánchez, P., & Ek, L. D. (2008). Escuchando a las maestras/os: Immigration politics and Latina/o preservice educators. *Bilingual Research Journal, 31*(1), 1–24.

Sánchez, P., & Machado-Casas, M. (2009, April/May). Introduction: At the intersection of transnationalism, Latino youth, and education. *High School Journal, 92*(4), 3–15.

Segura, D. (1989). Chicana and Mexican immigrant women at work; The impact of class, race, and gender on occupational mobility. In *Gender and Society* (pp. 37–52.)

Segura D. (1994). Inside the work world of Chicana and Mexican immigrant women. In M. Baca-Zinn & B. Dill (Eds.), *Women of color in U.S. Society* (pp. 95–111). Philadelphia: Temple University Press.

San Miguel, G. Jr., & Valencia, R. R. (1998). From the Treaty of Guadalupe Hidalgo to Hopwood: The educational plight and struggle of Mexican Americans in the Southwest. *Harvard Educational Review, 68*, 353–412.

Solórzano, D., Villapando, O., & Oseguera, L. (2005). Educational inequities and Latina/o undergraduate students in the United States: A critical race analysis of their educational progress. *Journal of Hispanic Higher Education, 4*(3), 272–304.

Solórzano, D., & Yosso, T. (2001). Critical race and LatCrit theory and method: Counter-storytelling: Chicana and Chicano graduate school experiences. *Qualitative Studies in Education, 14*(4), 471–495.

Trinidad Galván, R. (2001). Portraits of mujeres desjuiciadas: Womanist pedagogies of the everyday, the mundane and the ordinary. *International Journal of Qualitative Studies in Education, 14*(5), 603–621.

Trinidad Galván, R. (2005). Transnational communities en la lucha: Campesinas and grassroots organizations globalizing from below. *Journal of Latinos and Education, 4*(1), 3–20.

Trinidad Galván, R. (2008). Global restructuring, transmigration and Mexican rural women who stay behind: Accommodating, contesting and transcending ideologies. *Globalizations, 5*(4), 523–540.

Trueba, H. T. (1998). Culturally-based explanations of minority students' academic achievement. *Anthropology and Education Quarterly, 19*(3), 270–287.

Urrieta, L., Jr. (2003). *Las identidades también lloran*/Identities also cry: exploring the human side of Latina/o indigenous identities. *Educational Studies, 34*(2).

Urrieta, L. Jr. (2004a). Dis-connections in "American" citizenship and the post/neo-colonial: People of Mexican descent and whitestream pedagogy and curriculum. *Theory and Research in Social Education, 32*(4), 433–458.

Urrieta, L., Jr. (2004b).Chicana/o activism and education: An introduction to the special issue. *The High School Journal, 87*(4).

Urrieta, L. Jr. (2006). Community identity discourse and the Heritage Academy: Colorblind educational policy and white supremacy. *International Journal of Qualitative Studies in Education, 19*(4).

Urrieta, L. Jr. (2007a). Identity production in figured worlds: How some Mexican Americans become Chicana/o activist educators. *The Urban Review, 39*(2).

Urrieta, L. Jr. (2007b). Figured worlds and education: An introduction to the special issue. *The Urban Review, 392*.

Villapando, O. (2003). Self-segregation or self-preservation? A critical race theory and Latina/o critical theory analysis of a study of Chicana/o college students. *International Journal of Qualitative Studies in Education, 16*(5), 619–646.

Villenas, S. (1996). The colonizer/colonized Chicana ethnographer: Identity, marginalization, and co-optation in the field. *Harvard Educational Review, 66*(4), 711–731.

Villenas, S. (2000). This ethnography called my back: Writings of the exotic gaze, "othering" Latina, and recuperating Xicanisma. In E. St. Pierre & W. Pillow (Eds.), *Working the ruins: Poststructural feminist theory and methods in education* (pp. 74–95). New York: Routledge.

Villenas, S. (2001). Latina mothers and small-town racisms: Creating narratives of dignity and moral education in North Carolina. *Anthropology and Education Quarterly, 32*(1), 3–28.

Villenas, S. (2002). Reinventing education in new Lation communities: Pedagogies of change and continuity in North Carolina. In S. Wortham, E., Murillo Jr., & E. Hamann (Eds.), *Education in the new Latino diaspora: Policy and the politics of identity* (pp. 17–35). Westport, CT: Ablex.

Villenas, S. (2005a). Latina literacies in convivencia: Communal spaces of teaching and learning. *Anthropology and Education Quarterly, 36*(3), 273–277.

Villenas, S. (2005b). Between the telling and the told: Latina mothers negotiating education in new borderlands. In J. Phillion, M. F. He, & M. Connelly (Eds.), *Narrative and experience in multicultural education* (pp. 71–91). Thousand Oaks, CA: Sage.

Villenas, S. (2006). Latina feminist postcolonialities: Perspectives on un/tracking educational actors' interventions. *The International Journal of Qualitative Studies in Education, 19*(5), 659–672.

Villenas, S. (2007). Diaspora and the anthropology of Latino education: Challenges, affinities, and intersections. *Anthropology and Education Quarterly, 38*(4), 419–425.

Villenas, S. (2009). Knowing and unknowing transnational Latina/o lives in teacher education: At the intersection of educational research and the Latino humanities. *The High School Journal, 92*(4), 129–136.

Villenas, S., & Deyhle, D. (1999). Critical race theory and ethnographies challenging the stereotypes: Latino families, schooling, resilience and resistance. *Curriculum Inquiry, 29*(4), 413–445.

Villenas, S., & Foley, D. (2002). Chicano/Latino critical ethnography of education: Cultural productions from la frontera. In R. Valencia (Ed.), *Chicano school failure and success: Past, present and future* (2nd ed., pp. 195–226). New York and London: Routledge Falmer.

Villenas, S., & Moreno, M. (2001). To valerse por si misma between race, capitalism, and patriarchy: Latina mother/daughter pedagogies in North Carolina. *International Journal of Qualitative Studies in Education, 14*(5), 595–602.

Zarate, M., & Gallimore, R. (2005). Gender differences in factors leading to college enrollment: A longitudinal analysis of Latina and Latino students. *Harvard Educational Review, 75*(4), 383.

Zúniga-Hill, C., & Yopp, R. H. (1996). Practices of exemplary elementary school teachers of second language learners. *Teacher Education Quarterly, 23*(1), 83–97.

Journals: Special Issues

Artiles, A. J., & Klingner, J. K. (2006). Forging a knowledge base on English language learners with special needs: Theoretical, population, and technical issues [Special issue]. *Teachers College Record, 108*(11), 2187–2194.

This special issue of *Teachers College Record* includes contributions commissioned by the National Center for Culturally Responsive Educational Systems (NCCRESt) for a national conference on English language learners (ELLs) with special needs. NCCRESt pursued this initiative as part of its mandate to address the disproportionate representation of minority students in special education. At the heart of this problem are ability and competence ideologies that structure opportunities to learn for minority students. This 37-year-old literature shows African American and Native American students are most affected in the so-called high incidence disabilities (mental retardation, learning disabilities, and emotional/behavioral disorders; Donovan & Cross, 2002). Attention to this problem has increased in recent years in the policy and research communities. Thus, federal legislation now requires states to gather evidence on, monitor, and address this problem.

Artiles, A. J., Klingner, J., & Tate, W. F . (2006). Theme issue: Representation of minority students in special education: Complicating traditional explanations [Special issue]. *Educational Researcher, 35*(6), 3–5.

This theme issue focuses on a problem that was officially acknowledged 37 years ago but has been largely ignored by researchers and practitioners in general education, namely, the disproportionate representation of minority students in special education (Donovan & Cross, 2002). The articles in this theme issue focus on the fundamental questions that researchers grapple with in terms of responding to this issue as well as how to respond to cultural differences in education of culturally and linguistically diverse students.

The contributions in this theme issue broaden the way that disproportionate placement of minority students in special education is theorized. The authors' hope is that the theme issue will inform future research and practice efforts that aim to enhance learning opportunities for historically marginalized students.

Foley, D. E. (2005). Elusive prey: John Ogbu and the search for a grand theory of academic disengagement [Special Issue]. *International Journal of Qualitative Studies in Education, 18*(5).

Moreno, J. F. (Ed.). The elusive quest for equality: 150 years of Chicano/Chicana education [Special issue]. *Harvard Educational Review.*

Multicultural Perspectives. Mahwah, NJ: Erlbaum.

www.nameorg.org/publications.html

Multicultural Perspectives is the official journal of the National Association for Multicultural Education (NAME). This publication promotes the philosophy of social justice, equity, and inclusion. It celebrates cultural and ethnic diversity as a national strength that enriches the fabric of society. The journal encourages a range of material from academic to personal perspectives: poetry and art; articles of an academic nature illuminating the discussion of cultural pluralism and inclusion; articles and position papers reflecting a variety of disciplines; and reviews of film, art, and music that address or embody multicultural forms.

Murillo Jr., E. G. (Guest Eds.). (2001, September). Under cultural assault: Navigating through California's Proposition 227 [Special issue]. *Urban Review, 33*(3).

Sánchez, P., & Machado-Casas, M. (Guest Eds.). (2009, April/May). At the intersection of transnationalism, Latino youth, and education. [Special issue]. *High School Journal, 92*(4).

Urrieta, L. Jr. (Guest Ed.). (2004). Chicana/o activist educators: theories and pedagogies of trans/formation. [Special issue]. *The High School Journal, 87*(4).

Urrieta, L. Jr. (Guest Ed.). (2007). Figured worlds and education [Special issue]. *TheUrban Review, 39*(2).

Journals

Bilingual Research Journal

www.nabe.org

The *Bilingual Research Journal* is the official journal of the National Association of Bilingual Education (NABE). The Bilingual Research Journal is peer reviewed. NABE is a national professional organization devoted to representing bilingual learners and bilingual education professionals. NABE's mission is to advocate for our nation's bilingual and English language learners and families and to cultivate a multilingual, multicultural society by supporting and promoting policy, programs, pedagogy, research, and professional development that yield academic success, value native language, lead to English proficiency, and respect cultural and linguistic diversity.

The *Bilingual Research Journal* covers a wide range of topics related to bilingual education, bilingualism in society, and language policy in education. Submissions are encouraged from scholars and practitioners in a wide range of areas: language assessment, policy analysis, instructional research, language politics, all forms of bilingual education, bilingualism and biliteracy, language planning, critical theory as applied to language issues, action research, sociolinguistics, second language teaching and learning, etc.

International Journal of Bilingual Education and Bilingualism. Clevendon, UK: Multilingual Matters.

This journal aims to spread international developments, initiatives, ideas, and research on bilingualism and bilingual education, and to ensure collaboration between different continents, allowing rapid access to up-to-date information in an easily digestible form. In recent decades, few topics have become so internationally important as bilingualism, multilingualism, bilingual education, and the acquisition of new languages. In the first century of the new millennium, as international communications increase, technological changes facilitate international relationships, and traveling between countries and across oceans becomes more common, the international importance of bilingual education and bilingualism is expected to rise steeply. At the same time, there is increasing concern and interest about language minorities and the survival of indigenous and immigrant languages. Just as there has been interest in preserving the wonderful variety among flora and fauna, the preservation of linguistic and cultural diversity has become internationally important so as to maintain the colorful diversity of human existence.

Journal of Latinos and Education. Philadelphia, PA: Taylor & Francis.

www.jle.csusb.edu/

The *Journal of Latinos and Education* (JLE) provides a cross-, multi-, and interdisciplinary forum for scholars and writers from diverse disciplines who share a common interest in the analysis, discussion, critique, and dissemination of educational issues that impact Latinos. There are four broad arenas which encompass most issues of relevance: (1) Policy, (2) Research, (3) Practice, and (4) Creative & Literary Works.

The journal encourages novel ways of thinking about the ongoing and emerging questions around the unifying thread of Latinos and education. The journal supports dialogical exchange—for researchers, practitioners, authors, and other stakeholders who are working to advance understanding at all levels and aspects—be it theoretical, conceptual, empirical, clinical, historical, methodological, or other in scope. A range of formats for articles is encouraged, including research articles, essay reviews and interviews, practitioner and community perspectives, book and media reviews, and other forms of creative critical writing.

Latino Studies. Houndmills, UK: Palgrave Macmillan.

www.palgrave-journals.com/lst/index.html

Latino Studies is an international, peer-reviewed journal. The principal aim of the journal is to advance interdisciplinary scholarship about the lived experience and struggles of Latinas and Latinos for equity, representation, and social justice. Sustaining the tradition of activist scholarship of the founders of Chicana and Chicano Studies and Puerto Rican Studies, the journal engages critically the study of the local, national, transnational, and hemispheric realities that continue to influence the Latina and Latino presence in the United States. The journal is committed to developing a new transnational research agenda that bridges the academic and nonacademic worlds and fosters mutual learning and collaboration among all the Latino national groups.

Dictionaries

Mattes, L.J. (1993). *Bilingual language, speech and hearing dictionary* (3rd ed.). Oceanside, CA: Academic Communication Associates.

A resource of Spanish-English terminology that can be used with parents, other professionals, clients, students, patients during the evaluation, treatment, and consultation in spoken or written forms of communication.

Books

Acuña, R. (1981). *Occupied America: A history of Chicanos* (2nd ed.). New York: Harper & Row.

Artiles, A. J. & Ortiz, A. A. (2002). *English language learners with special education needs: Identification, asessment, and instruction*. McHenry, IL: Delta Systems.

The book describes the challenges involved in identifying, placing, teaching, and assessing English language learners with special education needs. It describes model programs and approaches, including early intervention programs, assessment methods, parent/school collaboration, and native and dual language instruction. All students deserve an education that meets their individual needs and capitalizes on their strengths. This book takes us a long way toward achieving that goal.

Basch, L., Schiller, N., & Szanton Blanc, C. (1994). *Nations unbound: Transnational projects, postcolonial predicaments and deterritorialized nation-states*. Amsterdam: Gordon & Breach.

Carter, P. (2005). *Keepin' it real: School success beyond black and white*. New York: Oxford University Press.

Chavez, L. R. (1992). *Shadowed lives. Undocumented immigrants in American Society.* Fort Worth, TX: Harcourt Brace Jovanovich.

Chicano Coordinating Council on Higher Education. (1970). *El Plan de Santa Barbara. A Chicano plan for higher education; Analyses and positions by Chicano Coordinating Council on Higher Education.* La Causa Publications.

Conchas, G. (2006). *The color of success: Race and high-achieving urban youth.* New York: Teachers College Press.

Cummins, N. L., & Miramontes, O. B. (2005). *Linguistic diversity and teaching: Reflective teaching and the social conditions of schooling a series for prospective and practicing teachers.* Mahwah, NJ: Erlbaum.

This book raises questions and provides a context for reflection regarding the complex issues surrounding new English learners in schools. These issues exist within a highly charged political climate and involve not only language, but also culture, class, ethnicity, and the persistent inequities that characterize our educational system. The text addresses these issues through conversations among experts, practitioners, and readers that are informed by representative case studies and by a range of theoretical approaches.

Darder, A. (1991). *Culture and power in the classroom: A critical foundation for biculture education.* New York: Bergin & Garvey.

This book examines the viability of critical pedagogy as an effective educational approach for bicultural students in the United States and lays the foundation for a theory of critical bicultural education. Darder first looks at the deep-rooted contradictions inherent in the current educational theory and practice and then considers the relationship between culture and power and the need for an emancipatory political construct. She brings together the theoretical principles within the context of classroom practice by describing liberatory classroom structures, circular materials, student participatory research projects, and other critical educational practices.

Darder, A., Torres, R. D., & Gutiérrez, H. (Eds.). (1997). *Latinos and education: A critical reader.* New York: Routledge.

This reader on Latinos and education establishes a clear link between educational practice and the structural dimensions which shape institutional life, and calls for the development of a new language that moves beyond disciplinary and racialized categories of difference and structural inequality. The essays discuss themes such as political economy, historical views of Latinos and schooling, identity, the politics of language, cultural democracy in the classroom, community involvement, and Latinos in higher education. Puerto Rican, Cuban, Central and South American, Mexican, and Chicano viewpoints are all included and the volume reflects the educational experiences of students in urban centers like New York and Chicago, as well as the South, Southwest, and West.

Delgado Bernal, D., Elenes, C. A., Godinez, F. E., & Villenas, S. (Eds.). (2006). *Chicana/Latina education in everyday life: Feminista perspectives on pedagogy and epistemology.* Albany, NY: SUNY Press.

Delgado-Gaitan, C. (1990). *Literacy for empowerment: The role of parents in children's education.* London: Falmer Press.

Delgado-Gaitan, C. (2004). *Involving Latino families in schools: Raising student achievement through home-school partnerships.* Thousand Oaks CA: Corwin Press.

Concha Delgado-Gaitan's book, *Involving Latino Families in Schools* provides tools and strategies for including Latino parents in developing sustained academic improvement. In sharing numerous first person success stories, Delgado-Gaitan stresses three conditions for increased parental participation: connecting to families, sharing information with parents, and supporting continued parental involvement. The book offers easily applied techniques for cultivating communication, in which this practical handbook examines: Latino families and their educational aspirations for their children; the communication systems needed between schools and Latino families; how Latino families can assist their children at home; techniques to foster Latino parent involvement; and how to organize schoolwide parent involvement programs. Delgado-Gaitan provides insight and instruction for planning, designing, and implementing parental participation programs that enhance the classroom curriculum and effectively engage Latino students. This book is designed primarily for elementary and secondary school principals and teachers, but this innovative text is also an indispensable resource for district-level administrators.

Delgado-Gaitan, C., & Trueba, H. (1991). *Crossing cultural borders: Education for immigrant families in America*. London: Falmer Press.

Diaz Soto, L. (Ed.). (2007). *The Praeger handbook of Latino education in the U.S.* Westport, CT: Praeger.

Donato, R. (1997). *The other struggle for equal schools: Mexican Americans during the civil rights era*. Albany, NY: SUNY Press.

Flores-Gonzalez, N. (2002). *School kids/street kids: Identity development in Latino students*. New York: Teachers College Press.

Flores-Gonzalez describes the sociopsychological dimensions of student identity development and the effect that school practices have on them. It also offers recommendations on how schools can facilitate the development of school–student identities among Latinos and discusses how school reform can lead to their school success.

Foley, D. E. (1990). (Series on Contemporary Ethnography). *Learning capitalist culture: Deep in the heart of Tejas*. Philadelphia: University of Pennsylvania Press.

Frederickson, J., & Flor Ada, A. (Eds.). (1995). *Reclaiming our voices: Bilingual education critical pedagogy & praxis*. Ontario, CA: California Association for Bilingual Education.

Individuals who believe that fulfillment of the American dream is incomplete but still possible, will find inspiration in the words of the educators and students in this book. You are invited to enter into their dialogue as they dare to dream of a saner, more caring world and struggle to understand and transform this wounded one.

Freire, P. (1985). *The politics of education: Culture, power and liberation*. New York: Bergin & Garvey.

The Politics of Education contributes to a radical formulation of pedagogy through its revitalization of language, utopianism, and revolutionary message....Freire not only heightens our awareness but invites us to engage in the emancipatory process brought about by critique. His politics puts history back into our hands. Beyond the power of the alphabet is the power of knowledge and social action. This book enlarges our vision with each reading, until the meanings become our own."

Freire, P. (1999). *Pedagogy of the oppressed*. New York: Continuum. (Original work published 1970)

In the course of Freire's work and travels in the Third World, and as a result of his studies in the philosophy of education, he evolved a theory for the education of people who are illiterate, especially adults, based on the conviction that every human being, no matter how "ignorant" or submerged in the "culture of silence," is capable of looking critically at the world in a dialogical encounter with others. Provided with the proper tools for such an encounter, the individual can gradually perceive his or her personal and social reality, and deal critically with it. This book represents a fresh expression of a work that will continue to stimulate the thought of educators and good citizens everywhere .

Freire, P., & Macedo, D. (1987). *Literacy: Reading the word and the world*. New York: Bergin & Garvey.

"The Brazilian educator Paulo Freire and his co-author Donald Macedo would redefine literacy to include an understanding of the reality denoted by language as well as of language itself. Consciousness of this connection, they contend in Literacy, is essential to the transformation of education systems and, ultimately, of social structure."

Foley, D. E. (1990). *Learning capitalist culture: Deep in the heart of Tejas*. Philadelphia: University of Pennsylvania Press.

Foley, D. E. (2003). *The heartland chronicles*. Philadelphia: University of Pennsylvania Press.

Foley, D. E., Levinson, B., & Holland D. (1996). *The cultural production of the educated person: Critical ethnographies of schooling practices*. Buffalo, NY: SUNY Press.

Fox, J., & Rivera-Salgado G., (Eds.). (2004). *Indigenous Mexican migrants in the United States*. La Jolla, CA: University of California, San Diego, Center for Comparative Immigration Studies and Center for US–Mexican Studies.

Fry, R. (2002). *Latinos in higher education: Many to enroll, few to graduate*. Washington, DC: Pew Hispanic Center.

Fry, R. (2004). *Latino youth finishing college: The role of selective pathways*. Washington, DC: Pew Hispanic Center.

Gándara, P. (1995). *Over the ivy walls: The educational mobility of low-income Chicanos*. Albany, NY: SUNY Press.

Unique in the literature on minority and Chicano academic achievement, *Over the Ivy Walls* focuses on factors that create academic successes rather that examining school failure. It weaves existing research on academic achievement into an analysis of the lives of 50 low income Chicanos for whom schooling "worked" and became an important vehicle for social mobility. Gándara examines their early home lives, school experiences, and peer relations in search of the clues to what "went right."

Garcia, E. (2001). *Hispanic education in the United States: Raices y alas.* Lanham, MD: Rowan & Littlefield.

García, E. (2005). *Teaching and learning in two languages: Bilingualism and schooling in the United States.* New York: Teachers College Press.

Gibson, M., Gándara, P., & Koyama, J. (2004). *School connections: U.S. Mexican youth, peers, and school achievement.* New York: Teachers College Press.

González, N. (2001). *I am my language: Discourses of women and children in the borderlands.* Tucson: University of Arizona Press.

Gonzalez, N. (2002). *School kids/street kids. Identity development in Latino students.* New York: Teachers College Press.

González, N., Moll, L., & Amanti, C. (2005). *Funds of knowledge: Theorizing practices in households and classrooms.* Mahwah, NJ: Erlbaum.

The concept of "funds of knowledge" is based on a simple premise: people are competent and have knowledge, and their life experiences have given them that knowledge. The claim in this book is that first-hand research experiences with families allow one to document this competence and knowledge, and that such engagement provides many possibilities for positive pedagogical actions. Drawing from both Vygotskian and neosociocultural perspectives in designing a methodology that views the everyday practices of language and action as constructing knowledge, the funds of knowledge approach facilitates a systematic and powerful way to represent communities in terms of the resources they possess and how to harness them for classroom teaching.

This book accomplishes three objectives: It gives readers the basic methodology and techniques followed in the contributors' funds of knowledge research; it extends the boundaries of what these researchers have done; and it explores the applications to classroom practice that can result from teachers knowing the communities in which they work.

In a time when national educational discourses focus on system reform and wholesale replicability across school sites, this book offers a counterperspective stating that instruction must be linked to students' lives, and that details of effective pedagogy should be linked to local histories and community contexts. This approach should not be confused with parent participation programs, although that is often a fortuitous consequence of the work described. It is also not an attempt to teach parents "how to do school" although that could certainly be an outcome if the parents so desired. Instead, the funds of knowledge approach attempts to accomplish something that may be even more challenging: to alter the perceptions of working-class or poor communities by viewing their households primarily in terms of their strengths and resources, their defining pedagogical characteristics.

Guerra, J. C. (1998). *Close to home: Oral and literate practices in a transnational Mexicano community.* New York: Teachers College Press.

Levitt, P. (2001). *The transnational villagers.* Berkeley: University of California Press.

Levitt, P., & Waters, M. (2002). *The changing face of home: The transnational lives of the second generation.* New York: Russell Sage Foundation.

Lopez, N. (2003). *Hopeful girls, troubled boys. Race and gender disparity in urban education.* New York and London: Routledge.

MacDonald, V. M. (Ed.). (2004). *Latino education in the United States: A narrated history from 1513–2000.* New York: Palgrave Macmillan.

Massey, D., Alarcon, R., Durand, J., & Gonzalez, H. (1987). *Return to Aztlan. The social process of international migration from western Mexico.* Berkeley: University of California Press.

Nieto, S. (1999). *The light in their eyes: Creating multicultural learning communities.* New York: Teachers College Press.

Nieto, S. (2000). *Affirming diversity: The sociopolitical context of multicultural education* (3rd ed.). New York: Longman,

Noguera, P. (2003). *City schools and the American dream: Reclaiming the promise of public education.* New York: Columbia University Press.

Pedro Noguera provides a compelling vision of the problems plaguing urban schools and how to address them. City schools and the American dream are replete with insights from a scholar and former activist who makes great use of both personal professional experiences.

Olsen, L. (1997). *Made in America, immigrant students in our public schools*. New York: New Press New York.

Orellana, M. F., Ek, L. D., & Hernández, A. (2000). Bilingual education in an immigrant community: Proposition 227 in California. In E. Trueba & L. Bartolome (Eds.), *Immigrant voices: In search of educational equity* (pp. 75–92). Lanham, MD: Rowman & Littlefield.

Parker, L., Deyhle, D., & Villenas, S. (Eds.). (1999). *Race is...race isn't: Critical race theory and qualitative studies in education*. Boulder, CO: Westview Press.

Pedraza, P., & Rivera, M. (Eds.). (2005). *Latino education: An agenda for community action research*. Mahwah, NJ: Erlbaum.

This landmark volume represents the work of the National Latino/a Education Research Agenda Project (NLERAP), an initiative focused on school reform and educational research with and for Latino communities. NLERAP's goal is to bring together various constituencies concerned with public education within the broad Latino community to articulate a Latino perspective on research-based school reform. In addition they want to use research as a guide to improving the public school systems that serve Latino students and to maximizing their opportunities to participate fully and equally in all social, economic, and political contexts of society.

Latino Education: An Agenda for Community Action Research conceptualizes and illustrates the theoretical framework for the NLERAP agenda and its projects. This framework is grounded in three overlapping areas of scholarship and activism, which are reflected within the chapters in this volume: critical studies, illuminating and analyzing the status of people of color in the United States; Latino/a educational research, capturing the sociohistorical, cultural, and political schooling experiences of U.S. Latino/a communities; and participatory action research, exemplifying a liberation-oriented methodology for truly transformative education. The volume includes both descriptive educational research and critical analyses of previous research and educational agendas related to Latino/a communities in the United States.

According to current U.S. Census data, Latinos now comprise the largest minority group in the total U.S. population. Historically, reflecting larger sociohistorical and economic inequalities in U.S. society, the Latino community has not been well served by U.S. public school systems. More attention to Latino students' educational issues is needed to redress this problem, especially given the tremendous population increase and projected growth of Latino communities in the United States. *Latino Education: An Agenda for Community Action Research* is a major contribution toward this goal.

Pérez, B. (Ed.). (2004). *Becoming biliterate: A study of two-way bilingual immersion education*. Mahwah, NJ: Erlbaum.

Pérez (2004) describes the development process and dynamics of change in the course of implementing a two-way bilingual immersion education program in two school communities. The focus is on the language and literacy learning of Latino elementary school students and on how it is influenced by parents, teachers, and policymakers. The book provides highly detailed descriptions, both quantitative and qualitative, of the change process at the two schools involved, including student language and achievement data for 5 years of program implementation that were used to test the basic two-way bilingual theory, the specific school interventions, and the particular classroom instructional practices. The book seeks to offer a comprehensive description of contextual and instructional factors that might help or hinder the attainment of successful literacy and student outcomes in both languages.

Portes, A., & Bach, R. (1985). *Latin journey: Cuban and Mexican immigrants in the United States*. Berkeley: University of California Press.

Portes, A., & Rumbaut, R. G. (2001). *Legacies: The store of the immigrant second generation*. New York: Russell Sage Foundation.

Reyes, P. Scribner, J. D., & Paredes Scribner, A. (Eds.) (1999). *Lessons from high-performing Hispanic schools: Creating learning communities*. New York: Teachers College Press.

This practical volume provides school administrators and teachers with the tools they need to transform ordinary schools into high-performing schools: It provides a framework for creating successful learning communities; shows teachers specific classroom practices that academically motivate minority children; outlines strategies for involving parents in their children's education; describes specific assessment practices.

Rhodes, R. L., Ochoa, S. H., & Ortiz, S. O. (2005). *Assessing culturally and linguistically diverse students: A practical guide.* New York: Guilford Press.

This book provides educators with needed background information and strategies when faced with needing to assess culturally and linguistically diverse students in U.S. schools. The process of assessment and evaluation is complex and requires educators to have knowledge and training to assist them in this process.

This is the first book to present a practical, problem-solving approach and hands-on tools and techniques for assessing English-language learners and culturally diverse students in K-12 settings. It meets a crucial need among practitioners and special educators working in today's schools. Provided are research-based, step-by-step procedures for conducting effective interviews with students, parents, and teachers; making the best use of interpreters; addressing special issues in the prereferral process; and conducting accurate, unbiased assessments of academic achievement, intellectual functioning, language proficiency, and acculturation. Among the book's special features are reproducible worksheets, questionnaires, and checklists—including several in both English and Spanish—in a ready-to-use, large-size format.

Romo, H. D., & Falbo, T. (1996). *Latino high school graduation: Defying the odds.* Austin: University of Texas Press.

Salinas, C., & Fránquiz, M. E. (Eds.). (2004). *Scholars in the field: The challenges of migrant education.* Charleston, WV: ERIC Clearinghouse on Rural Education and Small Schools .

San Miguel, G., Jr.. "Let Them All Take Heed" Mexican Americans and the Campaign for Educational Equality in Texas, 1910-1981. Austin: University of Texas Press, 1987.

Santa Ana, O. (2002). *Brown tide rising: Metaphors of Latinos in contemporary American public discourse.* Austin: University of Texas Press.

Santiago, D. (2004). *Federal policy and Latinos in higher education.* Washington, DC: Pew Hispanic Center.

Stanton-Salazar, R. D. (2001). *Manufacturing hope and despair: The school and kin support networks of U.S.–Mexican youth.* New York: Teachers College Press.

Stephen, L. (2007). *Transborder lives: Indigenous Oaxacans in Mexico, California, and Oregon.* Durham, NC: Duke University Press.

Suárez-Orozco, C., & Suárez-Orozco, M. (1995).*Transformations: Migration, family life, and achievement motivation among Latino adolescents.* Stanford, CA: Stanford University Press,

Suárez-Orozco, M., & Páez, M. (Eds.). (2002). *Latinos: Remaking America.* Berkeley: University of California Press.

Latinos are the fastest growing ethnic group in the United States and will comprise a quarter of the country's population by midcentury. The process of Latinization, the result of globalization, and the biggest migration flow in the history of the Americas, is indeed reshaping the character of the United States. This landmark book brings together some of the leading scholars now studying the social, cultural, racial, economic, and political changes wrought by the experiences, travails, and fortunes of the Latino population. It is the most definitive and comprehensive snapshot available of Latinos in the United States today.

How are Latinos and Latinas changing the face of the Americas? What is new and different about this current wave of migration? In this pathbreaking book, social scientists, humanities scholars, and policy experts examine what every citizen and every student needs to know about Latinos in the United States, covering issues from historical continuities and changes to immigration, race, labor, health, language, education, and politics. This book recognizes the diversity and challenges facing Latinos in the United States, and addresses what it means to define the community as such and how to move forward on a variety of political and cultural fronts. All of the contributions to *Latinos* are original pieces written especially for this volume.

Swail, W.S., Cabrera, A., Lee, C., & Williams, A. (2005). *Pathways to the bachelor's degree for Latino students.* Washington, DC: Educational Policy Institute.

Tejeda, C., Martinez, C., & Leonardo, Z. (2000). *Charting new terrains of Chicana(o)/Latina(o) education.* Cresskill, NJ: Hampton Press.

Tejeda et al., contribute to a fuller understanding of the education of the Chicano/Latino population by exploring a range of themes and issues that in the United States surround the relationships between educational realities and socioeconomic, sociocultural, and sociopolitical contexts. They employ a range of theoretical and methodological frameworks toward an analysis and interpretation of various dimensions of this population's educational experience.

Trueba, H. T. (1999). *Latinos Unidos: From cultural diversity to the politics of solidarity.* New York: Rowman & Littlefield.

Trueba, H. T., & Bartolomé, L. (Eds.). (2000). *Immigrant voices: In search of educational equity.* New York: Rowman & Littlefield,

Urrieta, L. Jr. (2009). *Fighting from within! Chicana and Chicano educators in U.S. schools.* Tucson: University of Arizona Press

Valdés, G. (1996). *Con Respeto: Bridging the distances between culturally diverse families and schools.* New York: Teachers College Press.

Valdés, G. (2003). *Expanding definitions of giftedness: The case of young interpreters from immigrant countries.* Mahwah, NJ: Erlbaum.

Valdés volume examines bilingual young people who have been selected by their families to carry out the work of interpreting and translating to mediate communication between themselves and the outside world, examining their experiences and the skills they develop in order to fulfill this role. This is a major study on extending the current definitions of "gifted" and "talented" by examining these young bilingual youngsters' experiences.

Valdés, G., & Figueroa, R. A. (1994). *Bilingualism and testing: A special case of bias.* Norwood, NJ: Ablex.

This book is directly concerned with the reasons underlying bilingual children's poor performance on standardized tests. It is the authors' contention that without an understanding of the nature of bilingualism itself, the problems encountered by bilingual individuals on such tests will continue. The volume's primary purpose is to contribute to the development of a research, knowledge, and theoretical base which can support the testing of bilingual individuals. By reviewing and discussing both the nature of bilingualism and the nature of standardized testing and by presenting a detailed agenda of the questions that must be answered the authors hope to influence existing and future policies which govern the use of tests and test results. This area is of increasing importance to American education and the policy implications are evident.

Valencia, R. R. (Ed.). (1997). *The evolution of deficit thinking: educational thought and practice.* London. Falmer Press,

Valencia, R. R. (Ed.). (2002). *Chicano school failure and success: Past, present, and future.* New York: Routledge Falmer.

The 2nd edition has been updated and expanded to provide state-of-the-art coverage of the Chicano school experience. The contributors include experts in the fields of anthropology, psychology, testing, educational history and policy, bilingual and special education, and child and family studies, reflecting the wide and complex range of issues affecting Chicano students.

Valenzuela, A. (1999). *Subtractive schooling, U.S. –Mexican youth and the politics of caring.* Albany, NY: SUNY Press.

Vélez-Ibañez, C. G., Sampaio, A., & González-Estay, M. (2002). *Transnational Latina/o communities: Politics, processes, and cultures.* Lanham, MD: Rowman & Littlefield.

Winn Tutwiler, S. J. (2005). *Teachers as collaborative partners: Working with diverse families and communities.* Mahwah, NJ: Erlbaum**.**

This book is aligned with standards and field experiences that are a part of preservice teacher education programs. The content and exercises are equally helpful for in-service teachers wanting to document skills and knowledge in this area as required for National Board Certification. The goals of the text are supported by pedagogical tools that provide opportunities for readers to make connections between information in each chapter and realistic family-community-school situations.

Wolfram, W., & Schilling-Estes, N. (1998). *American English: Dialects and variation* (2nd ed.). MA: Blackwell.

This book provides a very readable and up-to-date description of language variation in American English, covering regional, ethnic, and gender-based differences. The authors include situations ranging from historically isolated, rural dialects to developing, urban ethnic varieties as they consider the descriptive, theoretical, and applied ramifications of dialects in American society. The second edition of *American English* includes new chapters on social and ethnic dialects, including more comprehensive discussions of Latino, Native-American, Cajun English, and other varieties, samples from a wider array of U.S. regions, and a separate chapter on African-American English. Updated chapters and exercises as well as features such as a phonetic symbols key, and a section on the notion of speech community, combine to make the new edition a valuable resource for students and specialists alike.

Wortham, S., Hamann, E., & Murillo Jr., E. G. (Eds.). (2001). *Education in the new Latino Diaspora: Policy and the politics of identity.* Westport, CT: Ablex.

Zentella, A. C. (1997). *Growing up bilingual: Puerto Rican children in New York.* Malden, MA: Blackwell.

Zentella, A. C. (Ed.). (2005). *Building on strength: Language and literacy in Latino families and communities.* New York: Teachers College Press.

This edited volume provides a sociolinguistic perspective on different aspects of Latino families and communities as it relates to the complexities of language maintenance and literacy development. It examines the language and literacy beliefs and practices of Latinos through the lens of the historical, economic, and political contexts that shape them. Contributors to this collection reveal the intergroup and intragroup diversity of Latino communities and the efforts that families make to cross cultural and linguistic frontiers.

Book Chapters

Cabrera, A. F., & La Nasa, S. M. (2002). Hispanics in higher education. In J. F. Forest & K. Kinser (Eds.), *Higher education in the United States: An encyclopedia.* Santa Barbara, CA: ABC-CLIO.

Deyhle, D., Swisher, K., Stevens, T., & Trinidad Galván, R. (2007). Indigenous resistance and renewal: From colonialist practices to self-determination. In F. M. Connelly (Ed), *Sage handbook of curriculum and instruction* (pp. 329–348). Thousand Oaks, CA: Sage.

Ek, L. D. (2005). Staying on God's path: Socializing Latino/a immigrant youth to a Christian Pentecostal identity in Los Angeles. In A. C. Zentella (Ed.), *Building on strength: Language and literacy in Latino families and communities* (pp. 77–92). New York: Teachers College Press and California Association for Bilingual Education.

Foley, D. E. (1997). Deficit thinking models based on culture: The anthropological protest. In R. R. Valencia (Ed.), *The evolution of deficit thinking* (pp. 113-131). Washington, DC: The Falmer Press.

Foley, D. E. (2000). Reconceptualizing ethnicity and school achievement. In N. K. Shimahara (Ed.), *Ethnicity and schooling in the era of globalization.* Mahwah, NJ: Erlbaum.

Foley, D. E. (2002). Critical ethnography in the postcritical moment. In E. Trueba & Y. Zou (Eds.), *Ethnography and education: Qualitative approaches in the study of education* (pp. 139–170). Lanham, MD: Rowman & Littlefield.

Foley, D. E. (2004). Performance theory and critical ethnography: Studying Chicano and Mesquaki youth. In G. Anderson, B. Alexander, & B. Gallegos (Eds.), *Performing education: Teaching, reform, and social identities as performances.* Mahwah, NJ: Erlbaun.

Foley, D. E., & Meadowcroft, J. (1977). Life in a changing multi-ethnic school: Anglo teachers and their views of Mexicano children. In H. La Fontaine (Ed.), *Bilingual Education.* Wayne, NJ: Avery.

Foley, D. E., & Moss, K. (2000). Theories of cultural diversity in America. In I. Susser & T. Patterson, (Eds.). *Teaching cultural diversity.* Malden, MA: Blackwell/American Anthropological Association.

Foley, D. E., & Valenzuela, A. (2005). Critical ethnography: The politics of collaboration. In N. Denzin & Y. Lincoln (Eds.), *The handbook for ethnographic research* (3rd ed., pp. 217–234). Beverly Hills, CA: Sage.

Foley, D. E., & Villenas, S. (2002). Chicano/Latino critical ethnography of education: Borderlands cultural productions from la Frontera. In R. R. Valencia (Ed.), *Chicano school failure and success: Past, present, and future.* London: Routledge Falmer.

Foley, D. E., & White, R. (1981). Revitalizing the bilingual education movement through community-based approaches. In H. T. Trueba (Ed.), *Bilingual education: A search for theoretical foundations.* Boston: Newbury.

García, E. (2002). Addressing linguistic and cultural diversity in early childhood: From equity to excellence, from "raíces" to "alas." In O. N. Saracho & B. Spodek (Eds.), *Contemporary perspectives on early childhood curriculum.* Greenwich, CT: Information Age.

García, E. (2003). K-12 public education: Bedrock or barrier? In D. López & A. Jiménez (Eds.), *Latinos and public policy in California: An agenda for opportunity*. Berkeley: Regents of the University of California.

García, E. (2004). Education of Mexican American students, past treatment and recent developments in theory, research, policy, and practice. In J. A. Banks & C. A. McGee Banks (Eds.), *Handbook of research on multicultural education* (pp. 491–514). San Francisco: Jossey-Bass.

García, E., Hurtado, A., Vega, L. A., & Gonzalez, R. (2003). Beyond stigma: Social identities and the educational achievement of Chicanos. In D. J. León (Ed.), *Diversity in higher education: Latinos in higher education*.

Genesee, F., & Cenoz, J. (2001). First words. In J. Cenoz & F. Genesee (Eds.), *Trends in bilingual acquisition* (pp. 1–9). Philadelphia: John Benjamins.

This text is the first in a series to be published by the International Association for the Study of Child Language. The book contains nine chapters that present a variety of research topics ranging along the time of bilingual language acquisition from infant language differentiation through discourse and communication repair strategies. Each chapter provides a comprehensive summary of literature, research design, results, and discussion. The content provides insights into the typical development of bilingualism in children. This work has a variety of applications including the discernment of language use in the classroom from early childhood, consulting with parents, and discernment in making referrals to special education.

Goldstein, B. A. (2004). Bilingual language development and disorders: Introduction and overview. In B. A. Goldstein (Ed.), *Bilingual language development and disorders in Spanish-English speakers* (pp. 3–19). Baltimore, MD: Paul H. Brookes.

This text reviews research on bilingual and monolingual children from birth to 7 years of age. It provides a basis for the examination of bilingual language development across types of bilingual children, across domains of language, and across language modalities. The contributions include contemporary academic responses to first language bilingualism; simultaneous and sequential bilingualism in the context of the contributions of Wei, Romaine, and Fishman regarding aspects of bilingualism; and categorization of bilingualism and the context for bilingualism found in the community. A common thread running through the chapters is the interactive model of language development in bilingualism. The contributors provides current finding for practice in assessment and treatment of the domains of language (phonology, morphology, syntax, semantics, pragmatics, discourse, and reading) that will inform educators preparing to make referrals for services and speech-language pathologists preparing the serve the bilingual populations.

González, N., & Amanti, C. (1997). Teaching anthropological methods to teachers: The transformation of knowledge. In C. Kottak, J. White, R. Furlow, & P. Rice (Eds.), *The teaching of anthropology: Problems, issues, and decisions*. Mountain View, CA: Mayfield.

González, N., Amanti, C., & Moll, L. C. About culture: Using students' lived experiences to build curriculum. In A. Rosebery & B. Warren (Eds.), *Teaching science to English language learners*. Washington, DC: National Science Foundation.

McLaren, P., & Muñoz, J. (2000). Contesting whiteness: Critical perspectives on the struggle for social justice. In *The politics of multiculturalism and bilingual education: Students and teachers caught in the cross fire*. Boston: McGraw-Hill.

McLaren, P., & Muñoz, J. (2005). Dis-investing whiteness: Toward a common struggle for social justice. In *Red seminars: Radical excursions into educational theory, cultural politics, and pedagogy*. Cresskill, NJ: Hampton Press.

Moll, L. C., & González, N. (2004). Engaging life: A funds of knowledge approach to multicultural education. In J. & C. McGee Banks (Eds.). *Handbook of research on multicultural education* (pp. 699–715). San Francisco: Jossey-Bass.

Mora, J. K. (2001). Effective instructional practices and assessment for literacy and biliteracy development. In S. R. Hurley & J. V. Tinajero (Eds.), *Literacy assessment of second language learners* (pp. 149–166). Boston: Allyn & Bacon.

Murillo Jr., E. G. (2001). How does it feel to be a problem?: "Disciplining" the transnational subject in the American South. In S. Wortham, E. Hamann, & E. G. Murillo Jr. (Eds.), *Education in the new Latino diaspora: Policy and the politics of identity* (pp. 215-240). Westport, CT: Ablex.

Murillo Jr., E. G. (2004). Mojado ethnography: Making meaning of the alliances-reversals-paradoxes-positionalities along the neoliberal borderlands. In G. W Noblit, E. G. Murillo, Jr., & S. Y. Flores (Eds.), *Postcritical ethnography in education*. Cresskill, NJ: Hampton Press.

Olivas, M. (2005). The story of *Plyler v DOE*: The education of undocumented children, and the polity. In D. Martin & P. Schuck (Eds.), *Immigration stories* (pp. 197–220). New York: Foundation Press.

Orellana, M. F., Ek, L., & Hernández, A. (2000). Bilingual education in an immigrant community: Proposition 227 in California. In H. Trueba & L. I. Bartolome (Eds.), *Immigrant voices: In search of educational equity* (pp. 75–92). Lanham, MD: Rowman & Littlefield. (Original work published 1999)

Ortiz, A. A. (2002). Prevention of school failure and early intervention for English language learners. In A. J. Artiles & A. A. Ortiz (Eds.), *English language learners with special education needs: Identification, assessment and instruction* (pp. 31–48). McHenry, IL; Delta.

This chapter describes three types of students at risk for failure in three categories. Type I students are those who struggle in classrooms where the "teaching–learning environment" (p. 31) is not conducive to student learning; for example, students who require bilingual education but are attending schools that do not provide this program. Type II students are those who experience academic difficulties that cannot be explained by a language, learning, or other disability. These students are having difficulties for a variety of reasons such as not having enough time to master the curriculum content before advanced curriculum is presented. Type III includes students who have genuine disabilities such as mental retardation and language learning disabilities. Models for prevention, early intervention, and the referral process to special education are presented that are designed to assist professionals to differentiate students who are Type III from Types I and II. This chapter provides practical information related to practice in serving bilingual bicultural students in the public schools. Ortiz's work provides a theoretical basis for difficulty students may present in learning and provides a professional discourse that addresses differences, disorders, and learning problems which cannot be accounted for by either.

Trinidad Galván, R. (2006). Campesina pedagogies of the spirit: Examining women's sobrevivencia. In D. Delgado Bernal, A. Elenes, F. Gonzalez, & S. Villenas (Eds.), *Chicana/Latina education in everyday life: Feminista perspectives on pedagogy and epistemology* (pp. 161–179). Albany, NY: SUNY Press..

Trinidad, R., & Villenas, S. (1999). Teachers attitudes toward ESL students and programs. In S. Wade (Ed.), *Preparing teachers for inclusive education: Case pedagogies and curricula for teacher educators* (pp. 139–148). Mahwah, NJ: Erlbaum..

Vigil, D., & Muñoz, J. (2004). Community contexts and Chicano/a methods of inquiry: Grounded research and informed praxis. In J. Mora & D. Diaz (Eds., *Research in action: A participatory model for advancing Latino social policy*. New York: Haworth Press.

Villenas, S. (2000). This ethnography called my back: Writings of the exotic gaze, "mothering" Latina, and recuperating Xicanisma. In E. St. Pierre & W. Pillow (Eds.), *Working the ruins: Poststructural feminist theory and methods in education* (pp. 74–95). New York: Routledge.

Villenas, S. (2002). Reinventing educación in new Latino communities: Pedagogies of change and continuity in North Carolina. In S. Wortham, E. Murillo Jr., & E. Hamann (Eds.), *Education in the new Latino diaspora: Policy and the politics of identity* (pp. 17–35). Westport, CT: Ablex.

Villenas, S. (2005). Between the telling and the told: Latina mothers negotiating education in new borderlands. In J. Phillion, M. F. He, & M. Connelly (Eds.), *Narrative and experience in multicultural education* (pp. 71–91). Thousand Oaks, CA: Sage.

Villenas, S. (2006). Pedagogical moments in the borderlands: Latina mothers and daughters teaching and learning. In D. Delgado Bernal, C. A. Elenes, F. Godinez, & S. Villenas (Eds.), *Chicana/Latina education in everyday life: Feminista perspectives on pedagogy and epistemology* (pp.147–159). Albany, NY: SUNY Press.

Villenas, S. (forthcoming). Thinking Latino education with and from Chicana/Latina feminist cultural studies: Emerging pathways, decolonial possibilities. In Z. Leonardo (Ed.), *Handbook of cultural politics in education*. Sense Publishers.

Villenas, S., & Foley, D. (2002). Chicano/Latino critical ethnography of education: Cultural productions from la frontera. In R. Valencia (Ed.), *Chicano school failure and success: Past, present and future* (2nd ed., pp. 195–226). New York and London: Routledge Falmer.

Villenas S., Delgado Bernal, D., Elenes, C. A., & Godinez, F. (2006). Chicanas/Latinas building bridges: Education and Chicana/Latina feminista perspectives. In D. Delgado Bernal, C. A. Elenes, F. Godinez,

& S. Villenas (Eds.), *Chicana/Latina education in everyday life: Feminista perspectives on pedagogy and epistemology* (pp. 1–9). Albany, NY: SUNY Press.

Villenas, S., Deyhle, D., & Parker, L. (1999). Critical race theory and praxis: Chicana(o)/Latino(a) and Navajo struggles for dignity, educational equity and social justice. In L. Parker, D. Deyhle, & S. Villenas (Eds.), *Race is…race isn't: Critical race theory and qualitative studies in education* (pp. 31–52). Boulder, CO: Westview Press.

Literature

Day, F. A. (2003). *Latina and Latino voices in literature*. Westport, CT: Greenwood Press.

Gándara, P. (1995). *Over the ivy walls: The educational mobility of low-income Chicanos*. Albany, NY: SUNY (Social context of education series).

Gándara, P. (2006). *Fragile futures: Risk and vulnerability among Latino high achievers*. Princeton, NJ: Educational Testing Services.

Santa Ana, O. (2004). *Tongue tied: The lives of multilingual children in public education*. Lanham, MD: Rowman & Littlefield.

> *Tongue Tied* is an anthology that gives voice to millions of people who, on a daily basis, are denied the opportunity to speak in their own language. First-person accounts by Amy Tan, Sherman Alexie, bell hooks, Richard Rodriguez, Maxine Hong Kingston, and many other authors open windows onto the lives of linguistic minority students and their experience in coping in school and beyond. Selections from these writers are presented along with accessible, abridged scholarly articles that assess the impact of language policies on the experiences and life opportunities of minority-language students. Vivid and unforgettable, the readings in *Tongue Tied* are ideal for teaching and learning about American education and for spurring informed debate about the many factors that affect students and their lives.

Technical Papers/Research Reports/Special Collections

Artiles, A. & Harry, B. (2004). *Addressing culturally and linguistically diverse student overrepresentation in special education: Guidelines for parents*. Boulder, CO: The National Center for Culturally Responsive Educational Systems.

> This brief work helps parents understand if bias or inappropriate practice play a role in the placement of culturally and linguistically diverse students in special education in their children's schools. It addresses issues such as: (1) How can parents tell if there is overrepresentation in a special education program? (2) Why is it a problem and what are its causes? (3) Actions parents can take. and (4) Resources. This work as well as other publications and information can be accessed through the NCCRESt Web site: www.nccrest.org.

August, D., & Hakuta, K. (Eds.). (1997). *Improving schooling for language-minority children: A research agenda*. Washington, DC: National Academy Press.

> In *Improving Schooling for Language-Minority Children*, a committee of experts focuses on the central question of, "How do we effectively teach children from homes in which a language other than English is spoken?" The committee strives toward the construction of a strong and credible knowledge base to inform the activities of those who educate children as well as those who fund and conduct research. The book reviews a broad range of studies—from basic ones on language, literacy, and learning to others in educational settings. The committee proposes a research agenda that responds to issues of policy and practice yet maintains scientific integrity.
>
> This comprehensive volume provides a perspective on the history of bilingual education in the United States; summarizes relevant research on development of a second language, literacy, and content knowledge; reviews past evaluation studies; explores what we know about effective schools and classrooms for these children; examines research on the education of teachers of culturally and linguistically diverse students; critically reviews the system for the collection of education statistics as it relates to this student population; and recommends changes in the infrastructure that supports research on these students.

Donovan, M. S., & Cross, C. T. (Eds.). (2002). *Minority students in special and gifted education.* Washington, DC: National Academy Press.

Special education and gifted and talented programs were designed for children whose educational needs are not well met in regular classrooms. From their inception, special education programs have had disproportionate representation of racial and ethnic minority students. What causes this disproportion? Is it a problem? *Minority Students in Special and Gifted Education* considers possible contributors to that disparity, including early biological and environmental influences and inequities in opportunities for preschool and K-12 education, as well as the possibilities of bias in the referral and assessment system that lead to placement in special programs. It examines the data on early childhood experience, on differences in educational opportunity, and on referral and placement. The book also considers whether disproportionate representation should be considered a problem. Do special education programs provide valuable educational services, or do they set students off on a path of lower educational expectations? Would students not now placed in gifted and talented programs benefit from raised expectations, more rigorous classes, and the gifted label, or would they suffer failure in classes for which they are unprepared?

By examining this important problem in U.S. education and making recommendations for early intervention and general education, as well as for changes in referral and assessment processes, *Minority Students in Special and Gifted Education* will be an indispensable resource to educators throughout the nation, as well as to policy makers at all levels, from schools and school districts to the state and federal governments.

Gándara, P., Maxwell-Jolly, J., García, E., Asato, J., Gutiérrez, K., Stritikus, T., et al. (2000). *The initial impact of Proposition 227 on the instruction of English learners.* Davis, CA: University of California Linguistic Minority Research Center,

Hagedorn, L., Chi, W., Cepeda, R., & McLain, M. (2007). An investigation of critical mass: The role of Latino representation in the success of urban community college students. *Research in Higher Education, 48*(1), 73.

Latinos in School: Some Facts and Findings. ERIC Digest Number 162. (1999). Based on *Latinos in education: Early childhood, elementary, secondary, undergraduate, graduate.* Washington, DC: The White House Initiative on Educational Excellence for Hispanic Americans. (see ED 440 817)

Sánchez, G. I. George I. Sánchez Papers. Benson Latin American Collection, University of Texas at Austin.

Swail, W. S., Cabrera, A., & Lee, C. (2004). *Latino youth and the pathway to college.* Washington, DC: Pew Hispanic Center.

Thomas, W. P., & Collier, V. (1997). *School effectiveness for language minority students.* (NCBE Resource Collection Series, No. 9). Washington, DC: National Clearinghouse for Bilingual Education. www.ncbe.gwu.edu/ncbepubs/resource/effectiveness/

Encyclopedias

Encyclopedia Britannica Hispanic Heritage. Encyclopaedia Britannica Online (2007).

The Oxford Encyclopedia of Latinos and Latinas in the U.S. S. Oboler & D. J. Gonzalez (Eds.). New York: Oxford University Press (2005).

Encyclopedia Latina,. Ilan Stavans (Ed.). Amherst, MA: Grolier (2005).

Note

1. The author(s) and editor(s) do not necessarily endorse the reference entries in this chapter; they are listed for informational purposes only.

List of Contributors

Grisel Y. Acosta, University of Texas at San Antonio

Jennifer Adair, Arizona State University

Zenaida Aguirre-Muñoz, Texas Tech University

Blanca Araujo, University of Texas at El Paso

Gabino Arredondo, University of California, Berkeley

Alfredo J. Artiles, Arzona State University

Angela E. Arzubiaga, Arizona State University

Dolores Delgado Bernal, University of Utah

Patricia Baquedano-Lopéz, University of California, Berkeley

Silvia Cristina Bettez, University of North Carolina, Greensboro

Carmina M. Brittain, University of California, San Diego

Rebeca Burciaga, University of California, Santa Cruz

Juan F. Carrillo, University of Texas at Austin

Victor A. Castillo, University of Texas at San Antonio

Karina Cervantez, University of California, Santa Cruz

Rudolfo Chávez Chávez, New Mexico State University

Gilberto Q. Conchas, University of California, Irvine

Frances E. Contreras, University of Washington

Daniella Ann Cook, Duke University

Esteban Díaz, California State University, San Bernardino

Rubén Donato, University of Colorado at Boulder

Jeffrey M. R. Duncan-Andrade, San Francisco State University

Michael Eccleston, University of California, Santa Cruz

C. Alejandra Elenes, Arizona State University

Bonnie English, University of Washington

Edward Fergus, New York University

Mary Ruth Fernández, Our Lady of the Lake University

Stella M. Flores, Vanderbilt University

Douglas E. Foley, University of Texas at Austin

María E. Fránquiz, University of Texas at Austin

Margaret A. Gallego, San Diego State University

Ruth Trinidad Galván, University of New Mexico

David G. García, University of California, Santa Barbara

Eugene García, Arizona State University at Tempe

Ofelia García, The City University of New York

Esther Garza, University of Texas at San Antonio

Norma González, University of Arizona

Virginia González, University of Cincinnati

Evelyn M. Gordon, University of North Carolina at Chapel Hill

Katherine Graves-Talati, University of Texas at San Antonio

Norma A. Guzmán, University of Texas at San Antonio

Linda Harklau, University of Georgia

José Salvador Hernández, California State University, San Bernardino

Nicole D. Hidalgo, University of California, Santa Cruz

Edmund T. Hamann, University of Nebraska-Lincoln

Lindsay Perez Huber, University of California, Los Angeles

Teresa M. Huerta, California State University, Fresno

Aída Hurtado, University of California, Santa Cruz

Jason G. Irizarry, University of Connecticut

Janet López, University of Colorado at Denver

Minda López, Texas State University at San Marcos

Victoria-María MacDonald, University of Maryland, College Park

Jeff MacSwan, Arizona State University

Margarita Machado-Casas, University of Texas at San Antonio

Margary Martin, New York University

Corinne Martínez, California State University, Long Beach

Keren Zuniga McDowell, Suffolk University

Carmen I. Mercado, Hunter College, CUNY

Celoni Espínola Mesa, University of Massachusetts, Boston

Liliana Minaya-Rowe, Johns Hopkins University

Martha Montero-Sieburth, University of Amsterdam

Juan Sánchez Muñoz, Texas Tech University, Lubbock

Judith Hope Munter, University of Texas at El Paso

Enrique G. Murillo, Jr., California State University, San Bernardino

Rebecca A. Neal, Arizona State University

Sonia Nieto, University of Massachusetts, Amherst

Pedro Noguera, New York University

José A. Ortiz, New Haven Public Schools

Lidia Cabrera Pérez, University of La Laguna, Canary Islands, Spain

Victor H. Pérez, University of Illinois, Urbana-Champaign

Pedro R. Portes, University of Georgia

Luis O. Reyes, Hunter College, CUNY

Flora V. Rodríguez-Brown, University of Illinois at Chicago

Kellie Rolstad, Arizona State University

Spencer Salas, University of North Carolina at Charlotte

Sonia N. Sánchez, University of Texas at San Antonio

Guadalupe San Miguel, Jr., University of Houston

Belinda Treviño Schouten, Our Lady of the Lake University

Guillermo Solano-Flores, University of Colorado at Boulder

Jorge Solís, University of California, Santa Cruz

Daniel G. Solorzano, University of California, Los Angeles

Tom Stritikus, University of Washington

Amanda L. Sullivan, Arizona State University

Josefina Villamil Tinajero, University of Texas at El Paso

Rosario Torres-Guevara, Borough of Manhattan Community College, CUNY

Luis Urrieta, Jr., University of Texas at Austin

Verónica E. Valdez, The University of Utah

Carlos Martín Vélez, Brescia University

Octavio Villalpando, University of Utah

Sofia A. Villenas, Cornell University, Ithaca

Federico R. Waitoller, Arizona State University

Tara J. Yosso, University of California, Santa Barbara

María Estela Zarate, University of California, Irvine

Index

Enroll Online: http://nlen.csusb.edu/

Who are we: The broad spectrum of researchers, teaching professionals and educators, academics, scholars, administrators, independent writers and artists, policy and program specialists, students, parents, families, civic leaders, activists, and advocates. In short, those sharing a common interest and commitment to the educational issues that impact Latinos.

NLEN has been in existence since 2003.

Online Features and Benefits include:

An **Archive/Directory** that allows members to search and network with other registered members (individuals, institutions, businesses, agencies and groups).

A **Resource Guide/Clearinghouse** that allows members to search and browse for resources, opportunities and activities in the Latino Educational community.

An online and email **Newsletter** that allows members to access the latest information, news, stories and research on Latinos and Education.

E-Mail Listserve informing members of **Breaking News** that require immediate attention and action.

Programs and **News** broadcasted via video and audio broadband.

Plans for a **National Conference on Latinos and Education**.

* We welcome your forwarding this web address on to others that you feel might benefit from membership. Our goal is to facilitate a larger network to disseminate useful information and news with respect to Latinos and Education.

All members of our list remain secure and will not be distributed or sold to other organizations.

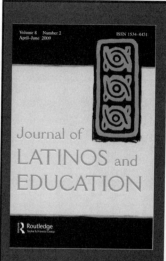

Volume 8 Number 2
April–June 2009

ISSN 1534-8431

Journal of
LATINOS and
EDUCATION

Routledge
Taylor & Francis Group

Journal of Latinos and Education

The *Journal of Latinos and Education* (*JLE*) provides a cross-, multi-, and interdisciplinary forum for scholars and writers from diverse disciplines who share a common interest in the analysis, discussion, critique, and dissemination of educational issues that impact Latinos. There are four broad arenas which encompass most issues of relevance:

(1) Policy

(2) Research

(3) Practice

(4) Creative & Literary Works.

JLE encourages novel ways of thinking about the ongoing and emerging questions around the unifying thread of Latinos and education. The journal supports dialogical exchange--for researchers, practitioners, authors, and other stakeholders who are working to advance understanding at all levels and aspects--be it theoretical, conceptual, empirical, clinical, historical, methodological, and/or other in scope. A range of formats for articles is encouraged, including research articles, essay reviews and interviews, practitioner and community perspectives, book and media reviews, and other forms of creative critical writing.

To view an Online Sample, visit
www.tandf.co.uk/journals/HJLE

Recent Contents

Editor
Enrique G. Murillo, Jr.
California State University, San Bernardino
Email: emurillo@csusb.edu

Journal of Latinos and Education
Volume 9, 2010
4 issues per year
ISSN Print 1534-8431
ISSN Online 1532-771X

Visit the Routledge Education Arena

The **Routledge Education Arena** provides information about the Routledge publishing program as well as a gateway to the online journals, book, and eBooks. In addition, there are useful resources for researchers, teachers, and students.

www.educationarena.com

Routledge
Taylor & Francis Group

Online Services

Alerting services from informaworld™
This free email contents alerting service is designed to deliver tables of contents in advance of the printed edition. To receive the table of contents for *Journal of Latinos and Education,* visit the journal homepage at: *www.tandf.co.uk/journals/HJLE*

To sign up for other table of contents, new publication and citation alerting services from informaworld™ visit: *www.informaworld.com/alerting*

Online Sample Copies
A full searchable sample copy of this journal is available by visiting:
www.tandf.co.uk/journals/HJLE

eUpdates
Register your email address at *www.informaworld.com/eupdates* to receive information on books, journals and other news within your areas of interest